Money the Financial System and the Economy

R. Glenn Hubbard
Columbia University

Addison-Wesley Publishing Company

Reading, Massachusetts • Menlo Park, California • New York
Don Mills, Ontario • Wokingham, England • Amsterdam • Bonn • Sydney
Singapore • Tokyo • Madrid • San Juan • Milan • Paris

Editor-in-Chief	Barbara Rifkind
Senior Sponsoring Editor	Marjorie Williams
Development Editor	Stephanie Botvin
Executive Managing Editor	Bette Aaronson
Managing Editor	Kazia Navas
Senior Production Supervisor	David Dwyer
Production Technology Supervisor	Laurie Petrycki
Electronic Production Specialist	John F. Webber
Electronic Production Administrator	Sally Simpson
Prepress Services Manager	Sarah McCracken
Publishing Technology Consultant	Edwin Zeitz
Senior Art Development Editor	Meredith Nightingale
Technical Art Supervisor	Joseph Vetere
Technical Art Consultant	Loretta Bailey
Cover Designer	Peter M. Blaiwas
Senior Manufacturing Manager	Roy Logan
Senior Marketing Manager	Dave Theisen
Advertising Manager	Eileen Spingler
Development Assistant	Susan D. Howard
Text Design	Sametz Blackstone
Proofreader	Phyllis Coyne
Illustrator	American Composition & Graphics, Inc.
Film Output Source	Pre-Press Co., Inc.

Many of the designations used by manufacturers and sellers to distinguish their products are claimed as trademarks. Where those designations appear in this book, and Addison-Wesley was aware of a trademark claim, the designations have been printed in initial caps or all caps.

Library of Congress Cataloging-in-Publication Data
Hubbard, R. Glenn
    Money, the financial system, and the economy
        p. cm.
    Includes index
    ISBN 0-201-54708-2
    1. Finance.   2. Money.   3. Banks and banking.

93–74172
CIP

Reprinted with corrections, June 1994.

2 3 4 5 6 7 8 9–VH–97969594

For Constance and Raph

About the Author

Professor of economics and finance at the Graduate School of Business at Columbia University, Glenn Hubbard received his B.A. and B.S. from the University of Central Florida and a Ph.D. in economics from Harvard University, where he was honored with both National Science Foundation and Alfred P. Sloan Foundation fellowships.

Hubbard began his teaching career at Northwestern University in 1983, moving to Columbia University in 1988. He has been teaching money and banking courses for over ten years to both undergraduate and graduate students, and he has been awarded several teaching commendations.

Hubbard served as deputy assistant secretary of the U.S. Treasury Department in Washington D.C. during the Bush administration.

Hubbard has published numerous articles in financial economics, public finance, macroeconomics, industrial organization, energy economics, and public policy. He has been a research consultant for the Federal Reserve Board, the Federal Reserve Bank of New York, the Internal Revenue Service, the Social Security Administration, the U.S. Department of the Treasury, the U.S. International Trade Commission, the National Science Foundation, and the World Bank.

He also served as a visiting professor at Harvard's John F. Kennedy School of Government and a John M. Olin Fellow at the National Bureau of Economic Research, where he remains a research associate.

Hubbard has also been honored with research grants from the National Bureau of Economic Research, the National Science Foundation, the U.S. Department of Energy, the Bradley Foundation, and the Institute for Fiscal Studies.

Hubbard, his wife Constance, and son Raph live in New York City.

Thinking about the Book

When I took money and banking as an undergraduate in 1979, the course emphasized real-world topics: Why is inflation high (as it was in those days), and where does it come from, anyway? Why does a boom in the stock or bond market excite news commentators, and how are prices of stocks and bonds determined in the first place? What do banks do with my money? Like me, students often come to this course expecting to learn simple answers to questions such as these. The answers were not simple in 1979, and they are more complex in the mid-1990s. Today's students are faced with an even greater challenge: trying to memorize the organization of U.S. financial markets and institutions and the Federal Reserve System in the face of domestic and global change.

Having taught money and banking courses to undergraduate and graduate students for ten years, I was frustrated that existing books simply stressed the current organization of the financial system and failed to give students a coherent framework for understanding new regulations and events. Adding to my dissatisfaction was the fact that texts addressed new developments by increasing the number of topics to be covered during an already crowded term. Even with all this material, students still lacked the tools they needed to predict the effects of changes to the financial system.

A Better Approach

My goal in writing this text is to teach students underlying economic explanations for why the financial system is organized as it is and to show them how the financial system and the economy are interconnected. With this approach, the student learns a paradigm for interpreting events, not a laundry list of facts that quickly becomes outdated. I wanted to go beyond the traditional approach and teach students how to apply the theory that they learn in the classroom to the practice of the real world. To achieve this goal, I have built three advantages into this text: (1) a framework for understanding, evaluating, and predicting, (2) a contemporary economic approach, and (3) integration of international material throughout the book.

Framework of the Text: Understand, Evaluate, Predict. The framework underlying all discussion in this text has three levels: First, the student is shown how to *understand* economic analysis. "Understanding" refers to the development of economic intuition for organizing concepts and facts. Second, economic analysis is used to *evaluate* current developments and the financial news. This requires the ability to use financial data and to think critically about interpretations of current events. Finally, the student is taught how to use economic tools and principles to *predict* future events. "Predicting" means applying economic analysis to anticipate the effects of changes in the economy and the financial system.

This approach offers students a way to think critically about developments in financial markets and institutions and in monetary institutions and policy. Current events can then be interpreted as the logical outcome of principles that students understand. For example, in Parts II and III, which examine the roles of financial markets and institutions in the economy, I repeatedly use the concepts of risk-sharing, liquidity, and information services to explain such topics as how different financial arrangements bring together borrowers and savers (Ch. 3), why particular financial markets and institutions have developed (Ch. 13), how they respond to changes in regulation (Ch. 15), why they differ in different countries (Ch. 16), and how their functioning affects the macroeconomy (Ch. 27).

A Contemporary Approach. Throughout this text, I incorporate recent research in a way that is accessible to students. Current research on monetary policy, financial institutions, and inflation is used to develop a general model for how monetary policy affects the economy (Ch. 26). The examination of "credit crunches" (Ch. 27) integrates the economic role of financial institutions in a simple macro model. Efficient markets are covered early (Ch. 10) to lay a groundwork for the discussion of information problems in financial markets (Ch. 11).

Integration of International Topics. Students today are keenly interested in the workings of the international financial system and in differences in financial systems across countries. Therefore, international applications have been integrated throughout the text. For example, international comparisons of financial systems and international constraints on central bank decision making are discussed concurrently with events in the United States (Ch. 22). Separate, optional chapters on exchange rates (Ch. 8), international banking (Ch. 16), and the international monetary and financial system (Ch. 22) appear where they fall naturally. Instructors who wish to omit this material or use it later in the course can do so.

Putting the Book to Work: Chapter Pedagogy

The features of this text are intended to help the student learn to view the financial system and the economy as an economist does. As much as possible, I have tried to place the student in the role of decision maker. In addition, I use real-world situations throughout the text so that students see the relevance of the material.

Chapter Openers and Margin Q&As. The dramatic episode beginning each chapter is intended to show students the real-world relevance and application of the material. The anecdote is followed by an overview of the topics to be studied in the chapter and a series of key questions to guide students' reading. The answers to these questions appear in the margin at appropriate places within the chapter to aid students in reviewing the material.

Checkpoints. These features test students' understanding by applying the chapter's economic approach to real-world situations. They address such issues as why some firms in cyclical industries don't rely on debt (p. 257) and how one can discern the Fed's goals from its actions (p. 510). These study aids help prepare students to answer the end-of-chapter exercises.

Consider This. These topical illustrations of the chapter's economic approach have been drawn from current events or research. Included are discussions of the ups and downs of the junk bond market (p. 154), whether U.S. banks are big enough (p. 352), the possiblitity of a deposit insurance crisis in Japan (p. 382), and the effect of the Gulf War on the U.S. economy.

Other Times, Other Places. These features extend the chapter's economic approach to historical events or to developments in other countries. Examples include learning about money from Moscow cab drivers (p. 23), similarities in the development of money market mutual funds in the United States and Japan (p. 371), and differences in monetary policy tools across countries (p. 512).

Using the News. This feature presents data from *The Wall Street Journal* or other sources. Students learn not only how to read and interpret such information but also how to use it for predicting changes within the financial system and the economy.

Moving from Theory to Practice. In my experience, students are especially interested in applying the economic tools they acquire to analyze events and policy developments in the news. To help students learn how to read news about the financial system and the economy critically, I have included an application feature at the end of each chapter. It consists of an actual news article (usually from *The Wall Street Journal*), followed by a section that uses the chapter's economic principles to evaluate the argument of the article. Articles deal with both domestic and international situations, including the effects of German reunification on U.S. interest rates (p. 120), the debate over whether the U.S. Treasury should issue 30-year bonds (p. 164), and the question of whether the actions of the Fed exacerbated the 1990–1991 recession (p. 690).

Summary Tables. These pedagogical aids present easy-to-understand explanations of the causes and effects of changes within the financial system and the economy. They utilize small analytical diagrams to reinforce relationships visually.

Process Diagrams. Because many students learn visually, the text has many process diagrams that illustrate the underlying economic forces that shape events, institutions, and markets. For example, I introduce a basic diagram in Chapter 3 (p. 41) showing that savers and borrowers value risk-sharing, liquidity, and information services. The basic diagram, shown here, is modified and repeated so that students internalize the model and can begin to make predictions based on it.

Analytical Graphs. To aid students in seeing the principles and factors underlying events in the financial system and the economy, I use color functionally in analytical graphs. For example, on p. 146, the initial conditions are consistently indicated by blue curves, and the final state by red curves. A blue-to-red shift arrow highlights the curves' movement, and yellow "shock" boxes explain the events that are causing the curves to shift. The shock boxes are numbered, allowing students to follow the sequence of events easily by referring to the numbers in the captions that accompany the graphs. These captions explain the economic factors fully so that students do not have to search for explanations within the text.

End-of-Chapter Summary. An aid for exam review, this feature presents the key terms and concepts and summarizes the main points of the chapter.

End-of-Chapter Exercises. Each chapter concludes with three types of exercises: *Review Questions* test students' recall of concepts and events. *Analytical Problems* give students a chance to apply the chapter's economic approach to specific cases and events. *Data Questions* ask students to collect data from specific sources in the library and use them to evaluate an economic argument. Numerous questions have been provided to give the instructor flexibility in making assignments.

Content and Organization

The text's consistent theoretical approach and thorough coverage of contemporary events, institutions, and data offer students a well-balanced picture of the interactions among money, the financial system, and the economy. Although related economic models are used throughout the book, individual parts and chapters of the book can be used independently. It is not necessary to cover the chapters in sequence.

Part I: Introduction (Chapters 1–3). This introduction to the text includes the reasons for using an economic approach to studying money, financial markets and institutions, and the economy (Ch. 1); the role of money within the financial system (Ch. 2); and an overview of the role played by different elements of the financial system in matching savers and borrowers and providing risk-sharing, liquidity, and information services (Ch. 3).

Part II: The Financial System and Interest Rate Determination (Chapters 4–10). These chapters develop a unified approach to studying how interest rates and asset returns are determined. After different measures of interest rates and the concept of present value are discussed (Ch. 4), an economic model of interest rate determination based on saving and investment decisions in the domestic economy and abroad is introduced (Ch. 5). Chapter 6 applies the concepts of risk sharing, liquidity, and information to portfolio allocation. The risk and term structures of interest rates are examined and applied to forecasting problems in Chapter 7. An optional chapter, Chapter 8, introduces exchange rate determination and explores the connection between exchange rates and interest rates. For instructors desiring a finance orientation, Chapter 9 introduces the role of derivative markets for financial futures and options. Chapter 10 caps off Part II by applying the concepts of risk sharing, liquidity, and information to an analysis of financial market efficiency.

Part III: Financial Markets and Institutions (Chapters 11–16). Part III continues to use the concepts of risk sharing, liquidity, and information to explain why and how financial institutions and instruments evolve. Chapter 11 explores the impact of transactions and information costs on financial structures and introduces adverse selection and moral hazard problems. Chapter 12 explains how the provision of risk-sharing, liquidity, and information services results in the development of different financial institutions. Chapter 13 examines the activities of banking firms and concludes with an analysis of how banks have exploited transactions and information cost advantages to enter new lines of business. Chapter 14 analyzes the development and current organization of the U.S. banking industry (and banking industries in other countries) and summarizes economic arguments for and against regulation. Chapter 15 examines financial regulation using a model of crisis, regulation, financial innovation, and regulatory response. This chapter also offers an up-to-date description of the regulatory debate in the aftermath of the Treasury Department's bank reform proposals of 1991 and the passage of the Federal Deposit Insurance Corporation Improvement Act of 1991. Chapter 16 focuses on banks' provision of risk-sharing, liquidity, and information services in international transactions and introduces students to Euromarkets and global trends.

Part IV: The Money Supply Process and Monetary Policy (Chapters 17–22). This part opens the discussion of the links between the financial system and the macroeconomy. It begins with the money supply process, focusing on the role of the Fed, banks, and the nonbank public in determining the monetary base and the money multiplier (Ch. 17). Next is an optional chapter on the determinants of changes in the monetary base (Ch. 18). Chapter 19 analyzes the organization of the Fed and offers comparisons with the central banks of other countries. Chapter 20 introduces the tools of monetary policy and offers a simple graphical analysis of the reserves market so that students can apply their understanding. The conduct of monetary policy and contemporary developments in Fed procedures are explored in Chapter 21. Chapter 22, an optional chapter, examines constraints on the conduct of monetary policy in an open economy using the model of exchange rate determination introduced in Chapter 8.

Part V: The Financial System and the Macroeconomy (Chapters 23–28). The final part studies the impact of monetary policy on the macroeconomy. Chapter 23 explains the demand for money based on the determinants of portfolio allocation and discusses the measurement of money. For those instructors wishing to use the *IS-LM* model, Chapter 24 presents a modern development of the model using the full-employment output line and a synthesis of the models of savings and investment, portfolio allocation, and money demand developed earlier in the book. For those instructors wishing to use the aggregate demand–aggregate supply model, Chapter 25 intuitively derives the *AD* curve and presents a modern development of aggregate supply in the short run and the long run. Chapter 26 provides a concise treatment of short-run economic impacts of monetary policy, with analysis of competing approaches and empirical evidence. Chapter 27 expands the analysis of the role of financial institutions in macroeconomic models, including the debate over the extent to which a "credit crunch" worsened the 1990–1991 recession. Chapter 28 uses the *AD–AS* framework to analyze determinants of inflation in the short run and the long run.

Flexibility

To illustrate the great flexibility that this text allows, several sample course sequences have been outlined below. A more detailed discussion of alternate paths through the text is included in the *Instructors' Manual.*

General Money and Banking Course: Chapters 1–7, 10–15, 17, 19, 22, 27

General Course with International Topics: Chapters 1–8, 10–17, 19–23, 27

Financial Markets and Institutions: Chapters 1–15, 8 (optional), 16

Monetary Institutions and Policy: Chapters 1–3, 13, 14, 17–21, 22 (optional)

Monetary Economics: Chapters 13–15, 17-21, 22 (optional), 23–28

Supplements

Study Guide. Written by Christopher Erickson and Elliott Willman of New Mexico State University, the *Study Guide* gives students a review of each chapter, along with a variety of questions and problems with answers and helpful study hints.

Instructors' Manual and Test Bank. Prepared by Anthony Patrick O'Brien of Lehigh University, this supplement includes overviews for every chapter, along with tips for enhancing students' interest and understanding, answers to end-of-chapter exercises a listing of additional readings, and additional essay and discussion questions. The testing portion for each chapter includes multiple choice, essay, and discussion questions.

Computerized Testing. This supplement provides test items on IBM-PC disks, so that instructors can edit them and create their own problem sets and examinations. It is available free to adopters.

MacNeil-Lehrer Business Reports Video Library. Noted reporter Paul Solman presents high-interest news stories about the economy and the financial system.

Readings in Money, the Financial System, and the Economy. Prepared by Charles Calomiris of the University of Illinois at Champaign-Urbana, this customizable reader offers articles in 18 units. Introductions to each unit integrate the articles, link them to themes in the text, and pose questions for building critical thinking skills.

Acknowledgments

In the years during which I developed the material for this book, I learned much from the reactions of my students at Northwestern and Columbia. Throughout the project, Robert Defina of Villanova University and Dean Croushore of the Federal Reserve Bank of Philadelphia provided critical, substantive suggestions. The book has been improved greatly by their advice and by suggestions from Charles Calomiris of the University of Illinois, Steven Cunningham of the University of Connecticut, Anil Kashyap of the University of Chicago, V. T. Mathews of Seton Hall University, and Douglas McMillin of Louisiana State University. I would also like to thank the following reviewers and focus group participants:

Edward Day	University of Central Florida
John Lapp	North Carolina State University
Tom Havrilesky	Duke University
Rowena Pecchenino	Michigan State University
Mary English	DePaul University
Owen Gregory	University of Illinois at Chicago
Don Dutkowsky	Syracuse University
Dean Popp	San Diego State University
Karen Johnson	Baylor University
Steve Miller	University of Connecticut at Storrs
Anthony O'Brien	Lehigh University

Bassam Harik	Western Michigan University
Ehsan Ahmed	James Madison University
Frank Steindl	Oklahoma State University
Michael Marlow	California Polytechnic State University
Richard Schiming	Mankato State University
Magda Kandil	University of Wisconsin at Milwaukee
Willie Belton	Georgia Institute of Technology
Ben Bernanke	Princeton University
Maureen Burton	California Polytechnic State University
Charles Leathers	University of Alabama
Ron McNamara	Bentley College
Chung Pham	University of New Mexico
Hal McClure	Villanova University
Nancy Jianakoplos	Colorado State University
Michael Redfearn	University of North Texas
Sung Lee	St. John's University
Ira Saltz	Florida Atlantic University
Fred Joutz	George Washington University
John Wassom	Western Kentucky University
Robert Herren	North Dakota State University
Hugh Courtney	George Washington University
Thomas Kopp	Siena College
Fred Thum	University of Texas at Austin
Doug Cho	Wichita State University
Harry Greenbaum	South Dakota State University
Walter Rogers	Middle Tennessee State University
Christine Amsler	Michigan State University
Doug Copeland	Johnson County Community College
Richard MacDonald	Saint Cloud State University
Owen Gregory	University of Illinois

I am also fortunate to have worked with the individuals who prepared the supplements that accompany the text: Christopher Erickson, Elliott Willman, Anthony O'Brien, and Charles Calomiris.

The publication of the book is a team effort in the truest sense, and I have been gratified to work with so many talented professionals at Addison-Wesley. Editor-in-chief Barbara Rifkind, sponsoring editor Marjorie Williams, and developmental editor Stephanie Botvin contributed challenging and valuable input at every stage; the book has been greatly improved by their efforts. I would also like to thank the art development editors, Dick Morton and Meredith Nightingale, the production supervisor, David Dwyer, and the marketing manager, Dave Theisen, for all of their hard work and enthusiasm about the book. I also thank Cindy Johnson, who managed the supplements, and Kari Heen and Kim Kramer, who helped her coordinate that material.

It is traditional to conclude acknowledgments by thanking one's family for their support. I cannot begin to thank my wife Constance for her emotional support, patience, ideas, and countless hours of assistance in preparing the manuscript. She often reminded me that my reason for writing this book was to synthesize ideas from my research and teaching that I believed would further the development of the course. Our son Raph has taken it all in stride. I can only hope that this book will please them.

New York, New York   R.G.H.

Brief Table of Contents

4 Interest Rates and Rates of Return 69

18 Changes in the Monetary Base 457

19 Organization of the Federal Reserve System 478

part I

Introduction

The Roles of Money and the Financial System

Investors around the world—from small savers to wealthy financiers, from local entrepreneurs and owners of small businesses to the leadership of Exxon and Nissan— were nervous about how financial markets would react. The 1992 presidential campaign in the United States had fueled speculation about which candidate, George Bush or Bill Clinton, would affect the economy more. As Clinton's lead solidified prior to his election as president, investors, business managers, and policymakers awaited the responses of the stock market, the bond market, and the foreign-exchange markets throughout the world for signals of what might lie ahead. The financial media were full of suggestions for reform of the country's beleaguered banks. Editorial writers and pundits regularly discussed what the Federal Reserve System, the U.S. central bank, should do about the nation's money supply and what the president and Congress should (and could) do about annual budget deficits and the national debt.

The extensive media coverage of financial-system events— prices of stocks and bonds, the health of the banks, what the Federal Reserve chairman did or didn't say—reflects the importance of money and the financial system to the U.S. economy and other economies around the world. Simply stated, money and the financial system are essential components in trade and in bringing together savers and borrowers. In this book we identify and discuss the roles that money and the financial system play in the economy. Understanding the workings of financial markets and financial institutions within the financial system will help you interpret current events, predict future developments, and make better informed decisions as a consumer, saver, borrower, or business manager.

You also will learn how to use some economic ideas, principles, and models to make sense of complex and, at times, confusing news accounts, reports, and statistics.

Throughout this chapter we will focus on the following question. **Q:** What roles do money and the financial system play in the economy?

Getting Started

In this chapter, we introduce five main topics important to economists, businesspeople, policymakers, and individuals making their own financial decisions. First, we describe briefly how the financial system and the economy are connected in the United States and around the world. Second, we examine the role played in the financial system by **financial markets,** which are markets for buying and selling bonds, stocks, foreign exchange, and other financial instruments. Third, we consider the functions of **financial institutions**, such as banks or insurance companies, which are the go-betweens for savers and borrowers. Next, we identify ways in which money influences economic variables that affect our daily lives, such as economic activity, prices, and interest rates. Finally, we develop an economic approach that offers more than a roadmap for interpreting today's information and decisions; it can help you predict future events and the effects those events can have on your own decisions. We focus on tools for analyzing information and making decisions rather than on just describing the mechanics of money, the financial system, and the economy. In particular, we help you develop the tools necessary for answering questions such as the following and applying the answers in making your own decisions.

- Why should you care about money? Are changes in the money supply responsible for booms and busts in the economy?
- What does the financial system do?
- Why do banks and other financial institutions exist? How do they affect your financial decisions?
- Should financial markets and institutions be regulated? Who wins and who loses from financial regulation?
- How are interest rates determined?
- What causes inflation?
- Living in a global economy, what do you need to know as a saver and borrower about financial developments outside the United States?

The Financial System and the Economy

The massive changes in Eastern Europe and the former Soviet Union in the late 1980s and early 1990s startled even the geopolitical experts. The sudden collapse of a system in which the government made the basic decisions about saving, investment, production, wages, and prices left a vacuum in those economies. For example, how would individuals invest their savings? How would consumers borrow to buy new cars and homes? Who would decide which business enterprises should be funded and for how much?

Those Eastern European countries are engaged in a struggle to create a **financial system,** which is a network of markets and institutions to bring savers and borrowers together. In the U.S. economy and those of many other industrialized countries, the financial system already brings savers and borrowers together. At some time in your life, you will want to save some of your income for future purchases: to buy a car, finance your retirement, or pay for your children's education. At other times, you may want to spend more than you currently have on hand: To do so you must borrow.

The three groups of potential savers and borrowers in an economy are households, businesses, and governments. The financial system transfers savers' funds to borrowers and provides savers with payments for the use of their funds. The financial system accomplishes this transfer by creating IOUs known as **financial instruments**, which are assets for savers and liabilities for (claims on) borrowers. An example of a financial instrument is a car loan, which is a liability for you—you owe the bank money—and an asset for the bank—it owns the right to receive future payments from you.

As an individual saver, you could seek out potential borrowers yourself, but that would be cumbersome and costly. Instead, the financial system acts as your go-between. Funds can be transferred between savers and borrowers in several ways. One option is for the government to allocate funds among the sectors of the economy. The recent experiences of Eastern Europe and the former Soviet Union demonstrated the folly of this approach. In the U.S. economy and other industrial economies, private networks in the financial system generally bring savers and borrowers together.

The reason that savers and borrowers use the financial system is that each gets something in return: Borrowers can use savers' funds productively until the savers themselves need the funds, and borrowers are willing to pay savers for that privilege. Moreover, the financial system provides three key **financial services:** risk sharing, liquidity, and information.

Risk refers to the degree of uncertainty of an asset's return. Most of us do not gamble with our savings, seeking a relatively steady return on our assets as a whole. When we borrow we also want the cost of borrowing to be predictable. The financial system provides **risk sharing** by giving savers and borrowers ways to reduce the uncertainty to which they are exposed.

Second, most people care about how easily they can exchange their assets for cash, a feature known as **liquidity.** For example, if you used all your savings to buy a plot of land in Arizona, you might find it difficult to sell it quickly if you need money to fix your car or pay your tuition. The financial system enables people to hold assets in liquid form, such as checking accounts, stocks, or bonds.

Finally, the financial system plays an important role in gathering and communicating **information** about borrowers' circumstances, so that individual savers do not have to search out prospective borrowers. The financial system provides this information to make sure that funds are allocated efficiently.

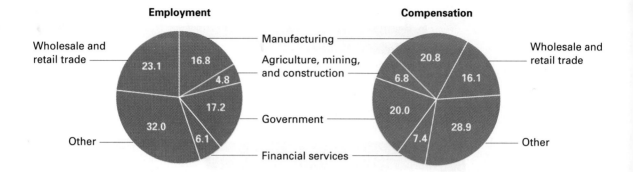

Employment

Compensation

**The Financial System's Place
in the Economy, 1991**
The financial system is an important source of high-paying jobs
in the United States.
*Source: U.S. Department of the
Commerce Survey of Current Business,
various issues.*

An understanding of these three key services helps explain how the financial system has developed and how it will likely change in the future. Changes in the financial system may well affect your opportunities to save or borrow, or even your career choices.

The financial system matches savers and borrowers and provides risk-sharing, liquidity, and information services through two channels: financial markets and financial institutions. In this chapter we merely sketch the features of these two channels. We present a more complete picture of the financial system throughout the rest of this book.

The financial system is a relatively small but important source of jobs and income for the U.S. economy. As Fig. 1.1 shows, the financial system accounts for about 6% of all private employment in the United States and more than 7% of total employee compensation. In addition, jobs in the financial services sector pay relatively well. At 122% of the national average, the pay is better than the average in wholesale and retail trade, manufacturing, agriculture, mining, construction, and government.

Financial Markets

Actual events in the world of high finance in mid-September 1992 resembled a thriller novel. Confusion seemed to dominate international financial markets. The British pound and the Italian lira sank in foreign-exchange markets, while the U.S. dollar and German mark rose. Stock prices fluctuated around the world, and interest rates on bonds rose and fell as traders, bankers, and finance ministers tried to maintain stability. Also, the 1980s and early 1990s were volatile times in financial markets in the United States. Interest rates on bonds, stock prices, and the value of the U.S. dollar relative to other currencies fluctuated significantly. To understand the rollercoaster behavior of domestic and global financial markets, you need to understand the role that financial markets play in the economy and what movements in financial markets tell savers and borrowers.

Financial markets such as the stock or bond markets are one way in which savers' surpluses are transferred to borrowers. Moreover, financial markets extend beyond any single country's borders. Indeed, as indicated in

Consider this...

BOX 1.1

Is the Financial System Truly Global?

Although an international capital market for certain types of lending has existed for centuries, analysts point to the 1980s and early 1990s as a time when the greatest number of boundaries separating national financial markets in the United States, Europe, Japan, and emerging economies dissolved. These changes mean that the money in your savings account might go to help finance a new factory in Germany. They also mean that your job prospects may depend as much on movements in the Japanese stock market or actions of the German central bank as on events in the United States. Three trends toward globalization are of interest.

First, business is global: At the beginning of the 1990s, the global investment in the stock of some 35,000 multinational corporations was $1.7 trillion. Second, financial markets are global: During the 1980s, the volume of worldwide cross-border transactions in stocks and bonds grew at an annual rate of 28%. Finally, lending is global: During the 1980s, international bank lending grew twentyfold. Throughout this book, you will encounter reasons for those developments and what they mean for households, businesses, and governments and for U.S. banks and financial markets.

Box 1.1, the **international capital market,** that is, the market for lending and borrowing across national boundaries, grew rapidly during the past twenty years. In addition to helping businesses and governments around the world raise funds, financial markets communicate important information through the prices of financial assets. In Part II, we show that changes in interest rates, stock prices, and exchange rates can influence decisions about whether to save more or spend more (Should you save to buy a new home or buy a sports car?) and about how to invest savings (Should you buy a U.S. Treasury bond or invest in a new business?).

Financial Institutions

Every day, people lend money to a large number of borrowers, including the U.S. government, IBM, the local hardware store, or their neighbors, without even knowing it. They don't approach these borrowers directly through financial markets, but indirectly through financial institutions acting as intermediaries. **Financial intermediaries** are institutions such as commercial banks, credit unions, savings and loan associations, mutual savings banks, mutual funds, finance companies, insurance companies, and pension funds that borrow funds from savers and lend them to borrowers. When you deposit money in a savings account, the bank can lend it to a local business. Similarly, when you contribute to a pension plan, the fund managers invest your retirement savings in shares of Mitsubishi, U.S. Treasury bonds, or other financial instruments.

Problems in financial institutions have been big news in the United States recently, particularly the deposit insurance crisis in the 1980s and early 1990s. The eventual cost to taxpayers for this crisis is estimated to be as high

> FIGURE 1.2

Sources of Funds for Nonfinancial Businesses: Markets versus Institutions
Most external funds raised by nonfinancial businesses are loans from financial institutions (mainly banks), with far less reliance on funds raised through bond and stock issues in financial markets. Data are averaged for 1970–1985.

Source: Adapted from Colin Mayer, "Financial Systems, Corporate Finance, and Economic Development," in R. Glenn Hubbard, ed., *Asymmetric Information, Finance, and Investment* (Chicago: U of Chicago Press, 1990, p312). Reprinted with permission.

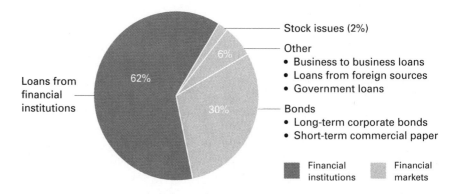

Stock issues (2%)

Other
• Business to business loans
• Loans from foreign sources
• Government loans

Bonds
• Long-term corporate bonds
• Short-term commercial paper

Loans from financial institutions

Financial institutions   Financial markets

as $200 billion. This crisis led to bank regulatory reforms, the effects of which are the subject of vigorous political debate. Another controversy has arisen over whether other financial institutions, especially pension funds, insurance companies, and mutual funds, may also be heading for financial crises that would require even more tax funds to resolve.

Why should you study the role of financial institutions as intermediaries between savers and borrowers? After all, you hear and read much more about the bond market and the stock market daily. Despite their visibility, the bond and stock markets are not the most important means for businesses to raise money. Figure 1.2 shows that, during the 1970s and 1980s, new stock issues accounted for only about 2% of funds raised externally by firms (that is, over and above their own profits). Bonds account for more of the funds raised externally, but still account for less than 30%. The majority of funds raised—nearly two-thirds—comes from loans from banks and other financial institutions. Households also raise most of the funds they borrow through financial institutions. This role for financial institutions as go-betweens for savers and borrowers is true not only in the United States but in most industrialized countries.

As you study financial institutions in Part III, you will learn why they play such a major role in the financial system. In this book we emphasize the activities of banks for two reasons: (1) they are the largest financial intermediaries; and (2) they lend to many sectors of the economy, including households and small and medium-sized businesses. In particular, we describe the business of banking, how and why banks are regulated by the government, and why the banking industry went through a crisis and transformation in the 1980s and early 1990s. Our economic analysis explains how banks and other financial institutions provide risk-sharing, liquidity, and information services to savers and borrowers. As the Other times, other places box indicates, our analysis also addresses how and why banks and other financial institutions compete with one another and the consequences of that competition for the financial system, savers and borrowers, and the economy.

Other times, other places...

The Only Thing Constant in the Financial System Is Change

The pace of change in the activities of financial intermediaries accelerated in the 1980s and early 1990s. When I was an undergraduate money and banking student in 1979, small savers (as I definitely was) could invest in a checking account (which paid no interest) and passbook savings accounts (which paid a low rate of interest limited by regulation). Higher yielding Treasury bonds and corporate bonds were available only in large denominations to wealthy savers. By contrast, in the mid 1990s, financial intermediaries offer a broad array of products with market yields for small savers, including money market mutual funds and interest-bearing checking accounts. These new products are the result of financial innovation by and competition among banks and other financial intermediaries.

In 1979, government tightly regulated the lines of business of banks and other financial intermediaries. However, the pace of competitive innovation by financial intermediaries has led to calls for major changes in regulation.

Understanding the risk-sharing, liquidity, and information services provided by intermediaries helps in understanding the types of regulation needed and to predict how those intermediaries will respond to new regulation. Because the pace of change in the financial system is so rapid, that understanding provides a way to assess developments in financial intermediaries in order to analyze new financial products, to get a job in the financial services industry, or to be informed about investment opportunities.

Money

As analysts were trying to figure out who was to blame for the crises in the nation's financial institutions, economists, businesspeople, and government officials were talking about the money supply. Before reviewing those conversations, let's define money: **Money** represents anything that people are willing to accept in payment for goods and services or to pay off debts. The **Federal Reserve System** (often called *the Fed*) is the central bank in the United States. It collects data on various measures of the **money supply,** that is, the quantity of money in the economy.

So, what was all the talk about money? In 1991 and 1992, the Bush administration blamed the economy's woes—slow growth and too many people out of work—on the Federal Reserve's decisions about the money supply. Many economists warned that the money supply was growing too slowly. Others praised the Fed's decisions for helping to hold interest rates and inflation at their lowest levels in many years. Talk about money is prominent in the news media, where reports of changes in the money supply are reported with fanfare. The reason is that such changes are associated with current and future changes in economic variables, including the economy's output of goods and services. These changes have an impact on your daily life, affect the prices you pay for goods and services, and determine the interest rates you earn on savings or pay on borrowed funds.

Because money supply movements are associated with movements in many economic variables, many private analysts focus their attention on predicting changes in the money supply. They are not the only ones: Government policymakers and the Fed actively try to manage the quantity of money. **Monetary policy** refers to the management of the money supply and its links to prices, interest rates, and other economic variables. In Part IV, we show that the Federal Reserve System, banks, businesses, and consumers together are responsible for determining the money supply. Nonetheless, the Fed is the most influential of those responsible. We give you the basic tools of Fed watching so that you can predict changes in the money supply and their effects on variables that concern you as an investor, businessperson, or interested student of current events.

In Part V, we focus on **monetary theory,** which explores the relationships linking changes in the money supply to changes in economic activity and prices. In discussing monetary theory in this book, we also examine the ways in which changes in the health of financial intermediaries, especially banks, affect economic activity. Many analysts believe, for example, that a collapse in bank lending worsened the U.S. economic downturn in the early 1990s.

The Role of Economic Analysis

A course in money, the financial system, and the economy covers many topics. To give you a way to organize your thoughts and to see the relationships among these topics, we stress economic analysis as a tool. Economic analysis allows you to (1) *explain* current developments or events, and (2) *predict* future developments or events.

Developing an Economic Approach

To show how economic analysis helps you develop a framework for explaining and predicting, let's begin with an example. Suppose that you want to work out a theory of why graduates of your college or university choose a particular mix of careers, that is, the percent of students entering law, medicine, business, engineering, teaching, and so on. In order to develop a simple model, you need to focus on a few key factors. You could start, for example, by assuming that graduates choose the careers that offer the greatest incomes; that is, if lawyers' incomes rise relative to incomes in other fields, a greater proportion of your school's graduates will enter law.

You know that income is not the only factor explaining career choice. Some individuals choose a career based on its time requirements, opportunities for self-fulfillment, or other nonmonetary aspects. Even though real-world decisions involve many elements, a simple model based on key assumptions is useful. You can determine how appropriate your assumption that income motivates career choice is by *testing* it, that is, by comparing its predictions to actual data.

Q: What roles do money and the financial system play in the economy?

A: Money is anything that people are willing to accept in payment for goods and services or to settle debts. Changes in the quantity of money affect other economic variables, such as the nation's output, prices, and interest rates. The financial system matches savers and borrowers and provides risk-sharing, liquidity, and information services.

Let's see how this method works. Suppose that you collect data from your college alumni office on the proportion of graduates entering different careers along with information on average income by career. You can compare your theory's prediction—that the careers with the highest incomes in a given year should draw the greatest percentage of students—to the actual data. This comparison will indicate whether your theory is reasonable.

If the data confirm your theory, you have a way of *explaining* current career choices and *predicting* how those choices will evolve as relative incomes of different careers change. If the data from the alumni office indicate no relationship between career choice and income prospects, you have to find a new theory. One possibility is that prospective income is an important variable influencing career choice but that it cannot explain more than, say, half the actual mix of career choices. In that case, you must decide whether to make additional assumptions, leading to a more complicated theory, or to settle for simplicity.

How useful is the theory on which you settle? Three criteria can help you assess its usefulness: (1) Are your assumptions reasonable? (2) Does the theory generate predictions that you can verify with actual data? (3) Are the predictions actually corroborated by the data? For a successful theory, the answer to all three questions is yes. Does that mean that there can be only one successful theory for any problem? No. You and other analysts might differ regarding whether the assumptions are reasonable or how well your theory stood up to testing. In this course you will discover that economists sometimes differ in their views of the best theory to explain a particular problem or predict a particular event.

Applying an Economic Approach

Developing theories and testing them form the basis of the economic analysis of money, financial markets, and financial institutions presented in this book. Economic analysis does not have to mean pages of mathematical formulas; it can mean simply organizing a study by setting out what you want to explain (the problem), how you believe it can be explained (the theory), and what actual information, events, and data say about your interpretation (the test). Let's consider three examples of applying an economic approach that are developed later in this book.

1. One reason to study the bond market in a course on money, financial markets, and financial institutions is to understand how interest rates are determined. In Part II, the economic analysis of interest rate determination focuses on decisions made by savers and borrowers in the bond market. The theory identifies factors that determine saving and borrowing in order to explain interest rates. We then analyze information about those factors to explain, for example, why interest rates were higher in the early 1980s than the early 1990s. Or why the interest rate on a 30-year

General Motors bond is greater than on a thirty-year U.S. Treasury bond. The analysis also allows prediction, for example, of the likely effects on U.S. interest rates from a Japanese decision to spend tens of billions of dollars to rebuild its highways, bridges, and schools.

2. Earlier in this chapter we noted that the financial system consists of financial markets and institutions that bring savers and borrowers together and provide financial services. In Chapter 3 and in more detail in Part III, we develop a theory that explains the activities of financial markets and institutions. The theory combines two features: (1) savers' and borrowers' desire for risk-sharing, liquidity, and information services and (2) differences in the cost of providing those services in different markets and institutions. We confirm the theory with observations about the activities of actual financial markets and institutions. This use of economic analysis helps predict how financial markets and institutions adapt to changing conditions in the United States. It also helps to explain why financial systems are organized differently in different countries.

3. We noted that movements in the growth rate of the money supply often are associated with movements in the growth rate of the economy's output, inflation, and interest rates. In Part V, we evaluate simple theories of these relationships to see whether their prediction is consistent with actual economic events in the United States and other countries. With a reasonable theory in hand, what information should you look for to forecast changes in the money supply, the economy's output, inflation, and interest rates?

These are only some of the ways in which we apply the economic approach of theory, testing, and evaluation in this book. Because one of the most important applications of the economic approach to your own economic and financial decisions is to think critically, the book offers four regular features in each chapter.

An Other times, other places exhibit applies the chapter's economic approach to historical events or to developments in other countries.

Consider this boxes provide topical applications of the chapter's economic approach.

Checkpoints throughout the chapter encourage you to apply the chapter's economic approach to a particular question.

At the end of each chapter, a Moving from theory to practice exhibit analyzes an article from a newspaper or magazine, using the chapter's economic approach to evaluate the author's points.

Taken together, these features are designed to make the economic approach a lively and useful way to organize your thoughts

Key Terms and Concepts

Financial institutions

Financial intermediaries

Financial markets

Financial services
  Information
  Liquidity
  Risk sharing

Financial system

Financial instruments

International capital market

Monetary theory

Money
  Federal Reserve System
  Money supply
  Monetary policy

Summary

1. The financial system brings together savers and borrowers: It channels funds from savers to borrowers while giving savers claims on borrowers' future income. The financial system also provides three key services for the benefit of savers and borrowers: risk sharing, liquidity, and information.

2. Financial markets match savers and borrowers, and prices of financial assets in those markets affect the wealth and spending decisions of individuals, spending decisions by businesses, and the efficiency of the U.S. and global economies.

3. Financial intermediaries are institutions that borrow funds from savers and lend them to borrowers, providing risk-sharing, liquidity, and information services in the process. The principal types of financial intermediaries are commercial banks, credit unions,

savings and loan associations, mutual savings banks, mutual funds, finance companies, insurance companies, and pension funds. Competitive innovation by banks and other intermediaries has changed the way these institutions do business.

4. Money represents anything that someone is willing to accept in payment for goods and services or to pay off debts. In the United States, measures of the money supply are calculated and published by the Federal Reserve. Households, businesses, and governments are interested in movements in the money supply, because those movements are associated with changes in important economic variables, including the economy's output, the price level, inflation, and interest rates.

Review Questions

1. Could a central planning agency allocate funds between savers and borrowers more efficiently than many different financial institutions? Explain.

2. What are the three main services offered by financial institutions? Describe each briefly.

3. Who determines the money supply? Who deter-

mines monetary policy?

4. Why is monetary theory important? Why should policymakers at the Federal Reserve System understand monetary theory? Why should you understand monetary theory?

Analytical Problems

5. Why might you lend money to individuals and businesses in your city through a local bank rather than directly?

6. Suppose that the government prohibited banks from paying interest on checking account deposits. What would you do with the funds in your checking account? What might your bank try to do?

7. Suppose that monetary policy induces a recession (economic downturn) in the United States. How might the economies of Germany or France be affected?

8. What do you think would happen to the economy if new regulations prevented banks from making as many loans to businesses as they previously did? What would the firms try to do in response?

Data Question

9. Look in The Wall Street Journal and find today's interest rate on three-month Treasury bills. What do you think the interest rate is likely to be in one year? In five years? Now look in the latest *Economic Report of the President* and find a table listing interest rates on three-month Treasury bills for the past several decades. Note how high the interest rate is in some years and how low it is in other years. Do you feel comfortable with your forecast now?

2

Money and the Payments System

Imagine how complicated and costly

trade in the United States would be if each state had its own money. Worse yet, what if no one could agree on what to use as money? Now imagine how much easier traveling from England to France to Germany to Italy—countries that now use different currencies would be if each country used the same currency. In the early 1990s, European countries debated moving toward such a monetary union. Businesspeople and economists have pointed out that economic gains from such a union could be significant, reducing costs incurred in converting currencies in cross-border trade and helping to unify the European market.

In this chapter, we define the role that money has played in the development of economic trade and the role of money in modern economies. We will see that money refers to anything that is generally accepted as payment for goods and services and that it is also an asset. Money figures prominently in virtually all economies. We will also see that money allows the economy to operate more efficiently and improves the standard of living. In particular, studying money and the payments system lays the groundwork for understanding how the financial system has evolved to make trade more efficient. All that information will be useful when you turn to the study of banking and monetary policy.

This chapter focuses on three main questions. **Q:** How does money meet the needs of trade? **Q:** What serves as money? **Q:** How is money measured?

Meeting the Needs of Trade with Money

Mention the word *money* and several things immediately come to mind: cash stacked floor to ceiling in a bank vault, coins cascading from a slot machine, or a $1 million check presented to a lottery winner, to name a few. Money is all that—and more. But before we get into specifics, we need a better definition although there is no one, perfect definition of money.

Money refers to anything that is generally accepted as payment for goods and services or in the settlement of debts, also called the **medium of exchange**. For example, *currency*, such as bills and coins, is one type of money. The amount of food you can buy at Burger King or Pizza Hut is usually limited by the amount of cash you have in your pocket. For many purchases, however, currency is too narrow a definition of acceptable money. You probably can buy books at your local bookstore by writing a check, for example.

Money also exemplifies what economists call an **asset**, or a thing of value that can be owned. We often say that individuals in *Forbes* magazine's list of richest Americans have a lot of money. By that, we don't really mean that they have a lot of currency in their pockets (or hidden away in their mansions or yachts) but that they own valuable assets, such as stocks, bonds, or houses. Money, like other assets, is a component of **wealth**, which is the sum of the value of assets. However, only if an asset serves as a medium of exchange can it be called money.

Although *wealth* and *income* (the flow of earnings over a period of time) are important concepts, we do not use these terms interchangeably with *money* in this book. That is, the amount of money an individual has is represented by the *stock* of currency and currency substitutes (such as checking account deposits or traveler's checks) owned, not by wealth or a monthly or yearly salary.

Money has become an integral part of virtually all economies. Why? A partial answer is that money allows the economy to operate more efficiently and hence improves the standard of living. But to fully understand how money improves efficiency, imagine first a world without money.

In economies in early stages of development, individuals are likely to be relatively self-sufficient. In farming societies, for example, extended family units grow food to feed themselves, build their own homes, and make their own clothes and tools. Such an arrangement does not allow a society to prosper greatly because in doing everything an individual would do some tasks well (say, building furniture) and do others poorly (say, growing wheat).

More developed economies rely on specialization. With **specialization**, each individual produces the goods or services for which he or she has relatively the best ability. Individuals then *trade*, or exchange the goods or services they produce for those they need. If an artisan who makes furniture and an artisan who makes boats trade with each other, more and better boats and furniture would be produced than if each produced both with no trade. Moreover, by encouraging production and higher quality—and thus income—an economy's allowance for specialization and trade increases its citizens' standard of living. To reap the benefits of specialization, an economy must develop ways for individuals to trade goods with one another. In this way, each person can obtain all the goods he or she needs, or wants, to consume. We next examine three options that society has developed to meet the needs of trade: barter, government allocation, and the use of money.

Barter

One way to obtain the benefits of specialization is to **barter**, whereby each individual trades output directly with another. For example, the furnituremaker could trade chairs for a bushel of wheat. The furnituremaker and farmer could agree that the price of eight chairs is three bushels of wheat. In a barter system, each such potential trade requires a price to be set in terms of the two goods.

The effort spent searching for trading partners to barter with is a type of **transactions cost**, that is, the cost of trade or exchange. An important problem in a barter system is that any two individuals wanting to trade must have exactly the goods each other wants. If a furnituremaker wants to buy books, that person must find a book seller who wants to buy chairs. Economists refer to this problem as a *double coincidence of wants*.

A barter system imposes significant costs on all but the smallest economies. First, as all trade is one good for another, many prices for each good must be maintained—a separate price for trade with each other good. This problem is akin to reading a recipe in which the amounts of some ingredients are in ounces, others in pounds, others in grams, others in liters, and so on. Baking a loaf of bread would take a week! Another cost of the barter system is the inconsistency in prices: One bookstore might quote the price of one type of notebook as five pens, another as six eggs, and still another as half a movie ticket. Needless to say, you would have to carry around a personal computer to make informed decisions about which is the best buy! A barter economy with only 100 goods would have 4950 prices, while one with 10,000 goods would have 49,995,000 prices.[†]

A third complication arises from lack of standardization: A chair and a container of wheat can vary substantially in quality and size. Fourth is the problem of finding two people who each want what the other produces. What if the boatmaker wants to buy wine from a winemaker who does not want a boat? Will trade take place? The winemaker could accept the boat for a lower

---

[†] These calculations are based on the formula for telling us how many prices we need with N goods, that is, the number of prices when there are N items: Number of Prices = $N(N-1)/2$.

value relative to that offered by the boatmaker and try to trade it to someone else. The winemaker's willingness to do so will depend on whether other traders would be willing to accept boats in payment for their goods. Finally, imagine the difficulty of storing value when goods are perishable. Tomatoes are valuable in exchange only when they are fresh, for example.

Government Allocation

Another option for allocating goods and services in a specialized economy is to sidestep voluntary trade and use **government allocation**. In this system, a central authority collects the specialized output of each individual producer and distributes it to others according to some plan. Although such a system may seem simpler than barter, it is not likely to prove useful in a changing economy (even if the authority could make everyone happy initially). Shifts in the costs of producing individual goods and services or in the value that consumers place on different goods and services will not be reflected in the trade accomplished by allocation. Ignoring market forces reduces incentives to produce and leaves consumers unhappy with the goods and services they receive. The collapse of economic systems based on government allocation in Eastern Europe and the former Soviet Union during the late 1980s and early 1990s demonstrated that this approach to trade and exchange is not the most successful one.

Money

How can people benefit from specialization without incurring the high trading costs of barter or the misallocations associated with government allocation? They can use money. The use of money eliminates the need for people to have a double coincidence of wants. Money has four key features that make it the most efficient means of trade: (1) It acts as a medium of exchange, (2) it is a unit of account, (3) it is a store of value, and (4) it offers a standard of deferred payment. As Fig. 2.1 shows, these features of money make it easier for people to trade with one another.

Medium of Exchange. As a medium of exchange, money is a generally accepted means of payment for settlement of trade in goods and services. To go back to our earlier example, the furnituremaker would not have to want wheat, and the farmer would not have to want a chair. Suppose that a boatmaker values gold because other traders do not want to trade their goods for boats. The boatmaker probably would give a furnituremaker a better deal on a boat if the furnituremaker paid in gold instead of chairs. In the same way, if a single good, such as gold, were accepted by many individuals with specialized goods to sell, all would get a better deal in trade. Thus society achieves greater prosperity when a single good is recognized as a medium of exchange.

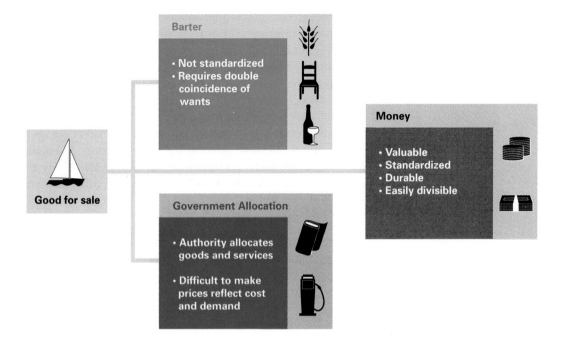

Methods of Trade
Society has developed three methods to gain the efficiency benefits of specialization: barter, government allocation, and the use of money. Money facilitates trade best by being accepted as a medium of exchange, by serving as a unit of account, and by acting as a store of value and standard of deferred payment.

Unit of Account. Using a good as a medium of exchange confers another benefit: It reduces the need to quote so many different prices in trade. Instead of having to quote the price of a single good in terms of many other goods, a single price can be quoted in terms of the medium of exchange. This function of money gives traders a **unit of account**, or a way of measuring value in the economy in terms of money. When an economy uses a commodity such as gold, then wheat, chairs, and other goods each has a price in terms of gold.

Store of Value. Money allows value to be stored easily, resulting in a **store of value**: If you do not use all your accumulated dollars to buy goods and services today, you can hold the rest for future use. In fact, a fisherman and a farmer would be better off maintaining their wealth in money rather than in inventories of their perishable goods. The acceptability of money in future transactions may be greater, and their goods may not retain their value over time.

Money is not the only store of value. Any asset—shares of General Motors stock, Treasury bonds, real estate, or Renoir paintings, for example—represents a store of value. Indeed, financial assets offer an important benefit relative to holding money, because they generally pay a higher rate of interest or offer the prospect of gains in value. Other assets (such as a house) also have advantages relative to money, as they provide services (such as a place to sleep).

Why, then, would you bother to hold any money? The answer goes back to one of the financial services introduced in Chapter 1: *liquidity*, or the ease with which a given asset can be converted into the medium of exchange. When money is the medium of exchange, it is the most liquid asset. You incur transactions costs when exchanging other assets for money. When you sell bonds or shares of stock to buy a car, for example, you pay a commission to your broker. If you have to sell your house on short notice to finance an unexpected major medical expense, you pay a commission to a real estate agent and probably have to accept a lower price in order to exchange the house for money quickly. To avoid such transactions costs, people are willing to hold some of their wealth in the form of money, even though other assets offer a greater return as a store of value.

Standard of Deferred Payment. Money also is useful because of its ability to serve as a **standard of deferred payment** in credit transactions. Money can facilitate trade and exchange *at a given point in time* by providing a medium of exchange and unit of account. It can facilitate trade and exchange *over time* by providing a store of value and standard of deferred payment. Hence a furnituremaker may be willing to sell the boatmaker a chair now in exchange for money in the future.

How important is it that money be a reliable store of value and standard of deferred payment? People care about how much their dollars will buy in food, clothing, and other goods and services. The value of money depends on its **purchasing power,** or the ability of money to be used to acquire goods and services. A decline in the purchasing power of money is known as **inflation**, a condition in which rising prices cause a given amount of money to purchase fewer goods and services. The opposite condition, in which the value of money increases, indicating falling prices, is called **deflation**.

You must have heard relatives or friends exclaim, "A dollar doesn't buy what it used to!" They really mean that the purchasing power of a dollar has fallen, that a given amount of money will buy a smaller quantity of the same goods and services in the economy than previously.

Just how much has the dollar shrunk? Consider the quantity of real goods and services that $1.00 would buy at the beginning of the 1990s. To buy the same quantity would have cost 68¢ in 1980, 33¢ in 1970, 24¢ in 1960, 19¢ in 1950, and 10¢ in 1940. A dime earned in 1940 would buy $1.00 worth of goods and services today! Obviously, the U.S. economy has experienced significant inflation since 1940.

Changes in the purchasing power of money affect money's usefulness as a store of value and standard of deferred payment and, in turn, individuals' willingness to hold money. For example, in 1989 newly elected Argentine President Carlos Menem faced an inflation rate of 12,000% per year. With such rapid inflation (inflation rates in excess of 50% per month are referred to as *hyperinflation*), households and firms refused to hold official money. Instead they resorted to barter and the use of U.S. dollars. This example underscores

Consider this...

Did the CIA Damage Iraq's Currency?

For a government-issued currency to be useful as money, it must be able to function as a medium of exchange. Although inflation reduces the purchasing power of a country's currency, a still greater problem is created by *counterfeiting*, or forging official money. If a currency is easily counterfeited, official currency becomes less useful in exchange.

In the spring of 1992, rumors surfaced that the U.S. Central Intelligence Agency (CIA) was shipping large volumes of counterfeit Iraqi dinars into Iraq in order to make trade and exchange more costly in that country. As a result, many merchants stopped accepting large-denomination bills, and many merchants in cities purchased expensive machines to

detect fake dinars. In short, the reported counterfeiting efforts reduced the usefulness of Iraq's currency in exchange and raised the cost of trade in the economy. The Iraqi government did not take the situation lightly: It imposed the death sentence on counterfeiters. Nonetheless, the threat of counterfeiting raised questions about the value of Iraq's currency throughout 1992.

our analysis of what serves as money: for money to be acceptable as a medium of exchange, households and firms must believe that it has value and will be acceptable. In Argentina, rapid erosion of money's purchasing power undermined this belief. As indicated in Box 2.1, policymakers have significant concerns about maintaining the purchasing power of official money.

How are changes in the value of money measured so that adjustments can be made for changes in purchasing power? Because value reflects the ability of money to purchase a quantity of goods and services, a price index can be useful. A **price index** is a summary statistic that incorporates changes in the price of a group of goods and services relative to the price in a base year. Some commonly used price indexes are summarized in the Appendix to this chapter.

Now that we understand *what* money is, we'll examine *how* money is used to settle transactions in the economy.

What Can Serve as Money?

As the preceding discussion showed, having a medium of exchange helps make transactions easier and thus allows the economy to work more smoothly. The next logical question is, What can serve as money? That is, which assets should be used as the medium of exchange? You learned earlier that an asset must, at a minimum, be generally accepted as payment in order to serve as money. In practical terms, however, it must be even more.

Criteria for Money

What determines the best good to use as a medium of exchange? There are five criteria. First, the good must be *acceptable* to (that is, usable by) most traders. Second, it should be of *standardized quality*, so that any two units are identical. Third, it should be *durable*, so that value is not lost by product spoilage. Fourth, it should be *valuable relative to its weight*, so that amounts large enough to be useful in trade can be easily transported. Finally, because different goods are valued differently, the medium of exchange should be *divisible*. Dollar bills meet all these criteria.

What determines the acceptability of dollar bills as a medium of exchange? Basically it is through self-fulfilling expectations: You value something as money only if you believe that others will accept it from you as payment. Our society's agreement that green paper notes issued by the Federal Reserve System are money makes them an acceptable medium of exchange. This property is not unique to money: Your personal computer has the same keyboard organization of letters as other computer keyboards because manufacturers agreed on a standard layout. You learned to speak English because that's the language most people around you speak.

The Payments System

Money facilitates transactions in the economy. The mechanism for conducting such transactions is known as a **payments system**. The payments system has evolved over time from precious metals to currency and checks to electronic funds transfer services. **Definitive money** is money that does not have to be converted into a more basic medium of exchange, such as gold or silver. The use of definitive money for trading goods and services at a point in time or over time, through credit, is the simplest type of payments system.

Commodity Money. Traders used precious metals such as gold and silver as mediums of exchange in earlier times. These physical goods were the dominant means by which trade was accomplished and were known as **commodity money**. Commodity money meets the criteria for a medium of exchange, but it has a significant problem: Among other factors, its value is related to its purity. Therefore someone who wanted to cheat could mix impure metals with a precious metal to create more wealth. Hence, unless traders trusted each other completely, they needed to check the weight and purity of the metal at each trade. Respected merchants (predecessors of bankers) solved this problem by assessing metals and stamping them with a mark certifying weight and purity, earning a commission in the process. Unstamped (uncertified) commodity money was acceptable only at a discount. It wasn't long before rulers became interested in this process. If a profit was to be made from the minting of commodity money of certified purity and weight, why shouldn't the sovereign claim it? Kings and dukes with wars and palaces to finance found this opportunity difficult to resist.

Fiat Money. An economy's reliance on precious metals alone makes for a cumbersome payments system. What if you had to transport gold bullion to settle your transactions? Not only would doing so be difficult and costly,

Q: How does money meet the needs of trade?

A: Money facilitates exchange among households and firms. It serves four functions: as a medium of exchange (accepted means of payment), as a unit of account (way to measure value), as a store of value (means of storing purchasing power), and as a standard of deferred payment (in credit transactions).

but the risk of being robbed would be great. To get around this problem, private institutions or governments began to store the definitive money and issue paper certificates representing it. In modern economies, paper currency generally is issued by a **central bank**, which is a special governmental or quasi-governmental institution in the financial system that regulates the medium of exchange. (We discuss the activities of central banks in Part IV.) If you look at a U.S. dollar bill, you will see that it is actually a Federal Reserve Note, issued by the Federal Reserve System (the Fed), which is the central bank in the United States. Federal Reserve currency is **legal tender** in the United States; that is, the federal government mandates its acceptance in transactions and requires that dollars be used in payment of taxes. Nonetheless, without everyone's acceptance, dollar bills would not be a good medium of exchange and could not serve as money (see the Other times, other places box).

The modern U.S. system is a **fiat money** system. In such a system, money authorized by a central bank is the definitive money and does not have to be exchanged by the central bank for gold or some other commodity money. What this means is that the Federal Reserve System is not required to give you gold or silver (or even aluminum cans) for your dollar bills. You, along with everyone else, agree to accept Federal Reserve currency as money. In the United States, the Federal Reserve System issues dollar bills and holds deposits of banks and the federal government. Banks can use these deposits to settle transactions with one another. In the United States, the Fed has a monopoly on the right to issue currency. Although checks drawn on accounts at private banks are a substitute for Federal Reserve Notes in paying for goods and services, private banks cannot issue their own bank notes.

Other times, other places...
What's Money? Ask a Taxi Driver!

A few years ago, I learned a great lesson about money in a cab. In August 1989, along with a group of American economists, I traveled to Moscow and Leningrad (now St. Petersburg) to discuss with Soviet economists some economic problems faced by both countries.

Taking taxis in Moscow to and from meetings and dinners proved to be an ordeal. Our hosts had given us rubles (Soviet currency at the time), but payments in rubles were discouraged. A bewildering array of fares were always quoted in terms of U.S. dollars or German marks or Japanese yen. And the fares varied inconsistently from cab to cab.

When I relayed this frustration to my wife at our hotel one evening, she told me that she had encountered no such difficulty. She used Marlboro cigarettes! When I experimented with her Marlboros the next day (no other brand worked as well), I found my exchange problems vastly simpli-fied. The cigarettes served as a medium of exchange, as well as a unit of account, as all the taxi drivers could convert easily all major currencies to Marlboro equivalents.

Official money (rubles) had been displaced by Marlboros as a medium of exchange. Marlboros are of standardized quality, are easily recognized, and retain their value when unused: a logical money indeed.

At the beginning of 1993, outstanding Federal Reserve Notes totaled $294 billion. What stops the Fed from issuing as many dollars as it wants? In principle, nothing! We discuss this important issue in Part IV. For now, however, let's assume that the Fed issues the "right" amount of dollars.

Q: What serves as money?

A: Precious metals, currency, bank checks, and electronic funds transfer services have been used as money in the payments system. The payments system consists of mechanisms for conducting monetary transactions in the economy. An efficient payments system makes commercial and financial transactions cheaper to complete.

Checks.   Paper money also can be expensive to transport for settling large commercial or financial transactions. Imagine going to buy a car with a suitcase full of dollar bills! Another major innovation in the payments system came from the use of a substitute for definitive money, checks. **Checks** are promises to pay definitive money on demand and are drawn on money deposited with a financial institution.[1] They can be written for any amount and are more difficult to use fraudulently than currency or precious metals. As a result, they are a convenient way to settle transactions. Another benefit of using checks is that[2] traders avoid paying the cost of shipping currency back and forth, as many payments among parties cancel each other. Traveler's checks serve a similar purpose; purchased from a financial institution, they are pieces of paper that can be used to settle transactions.

Settling transactions with checks requires more steps than settling transactions with currency. Suppose that your roommate owes you $50. If she gives you $50 in cash, nothing further is needed to settle the transaction. Suppose, however, that she writes you a check for $50. You first take the check to your bank. Your banker, in turn, must present the check for payment to your roommate's bank, which then must collect the money from her account. This process generally takes several business days. Processing the enormous flow of checks in the United States costs the economy several billion dollars each year.

The use of checks and other substitutes for definitive money has associated problems of liquidity and information. Again, liquidity refers to the cost with which an asset can be converted to definitive money. The cost of converting checks affects the seller's willingness to accept them in a transaction instead of definitive money. If you had to pay $10 to cash each check you received, undoubtedly you would prefer to receive cash. Another cost relates to information in terms of the time and effort required for the seller to verify whether the checkwriter (the buyer) has a sufficient amount of definitive money on deposit to cover the amount of the check. Accepting checks requires more trust on the part of the seller than accepting dollar bills.

Electronic Funds.   Electronic telecommunication breakthroughs have improved the efficiency of the payments system, reducing the time needed for clearing checks and the costs of paper flow for making payments. Settling and clearing transactions can now be done with computers in **electronic funds transfer systems**, computerized payment clearing devices. Important examples include *debit cards* for point-of-sale transfers and *automated teller machines* (ATMs). Debit cards can be used like checks: Cash registers in stores are linked to bank computers, so that when a customer uses the debit card to buy groceries, the customer's bank instantly credits the store's account with the amount and deducts it from the customer's account. Such a system eliminates the problem of trust between the buyer and seller that is associated with checks because the bank computer authorizes the transaction. Lest you think such electronic transactions are just futuristic glimpses of the 21st century, more than 80% of the dollar value of transactions among financial institutions are conducted electronically.

Twenty years ago, you had to stand in line at a bank teller's window during working hours to make deposits, withdrawals, and payments. Today, ATM machines allow you to perform the same transactions at your bank whenever it is most convenient for you. Moreover, ATMs are connected to networks (such as Cirrus), so that you can make withdrawals of cash away from your home bank. At the beginning of the 1990s, there were about 75,000 ATMs in the United States, at which about 400 million transactions were conducted each month. Some ATM networks are even international, so that you can withdraw money in Paris to buy a fabulous box of chocolates!

Through the years, the payments system has continually evolved as laws have been changed and technology has advanced. The forms of money have evolved with it. The use of gold and silver has given way to fiat money and checking accounts, which in turn have yielded to accounts holding funds that can be electronically transferred. In recent years, credit cards have become an important means of payment, as discussed in Box 2.2.

Consider this...   **BOX 2.2**

Are Credit Cards Part of the Payments System?

When you buy books or records or clothes, you probably use your VISA® or MasterCard® as credit to settle the transaction. These credit cards involve payments over time.

Credit can be *personal*, based on a long-term relationship between the buyer and seller, or *impersonal*, based on an isolated transaction or set of transactions. Examples of personal credit include informal credit arrangements between individual customers and stores, such as when the owner of a small store allows some long-term customers to maintain a charge account. Larger stores can conduct impersonal credit transactions by delaying the time until definitive money is required in payment, by maintaining a staff to evaluate the creditworthiness of customers, and by issuing store credit cards. Store credit cards are useful for large retailers such as Sears, but smaller stores would find such payment arrangements too costly.

To resolve this problem, small stores and businesses join a network of financial institutions that resolve commercial transactions through the use of credit networks such as VISA® and MasterCard®. The bank assesses creditworthiness and receives a fee from the retailer. The store sends the credit charge slip to the bank that issued the customer's credit card, which then pays the store immediately and bills the customer later. Upon receipt of the bill, the customer can pay it immediately or pay it later with an additional finance charge.

The proliferation of credit cards in recent years has made them an important part of the payments system.

The *efficiency* of the payments system, which increases as the cost of settling transactions decreases, is important for the economy. Suppose that the banking system broke down and all transactions—commercial and financial—had to be carried out in cash. You would have to carry large amounts of cash to finance all your purchases and would incur additional costs for protecting your cash. No bank credit would be possible, severely harming the financial system's role in matching savers and borrowers. Thus disruptions in the payments system increase the cost of trade and credit. Many economists, for example, blame the collapse of the banking system for the severity of the Great Depression of the 1930s. The importance of an efficiently functioning payments system for the economy is a significant public policy concern. Governments typically regulate the medium of exchange and establish safeguards to protect the payments system.

▶ C H E C K P O I N T *Do you think that one day cash and checks will become obsolete and all payments will be made electronically? What benefits do you see from such an arrangement? What might prevent such an arrangement from being fully realized?* By the early 1990s, analysts speculated that debit cards would be used for a significant fraction of consumers' purchases by the end of the decade. These electronic transactions are less costly than checks and more convenient for consumers than cash. A cashless society is not likely, however. Cash would still be used for small purchases. In addition, certain legal issues have not been resolved, such as whether you would be liable if someone discovered your secret account access code and illegally transferred funds from your account. Finally, some individuals value the anonymity afforded by using currency. Individuals engaging in illegal transactions (drug deals or tax evasion schemes, for example) would be unlikely debit card users. ◀

Measuring Money

Households, firms, and policymakers are all interested in measuring money because, as we noted in Chapter 1, changes in the quantity of money are associated with changes in prices and economic activity. How can money be measured? The definition of money (a medium of exchange for goods and services and the settlement of debts) depends on beliefs about whether the medium will be used by others in trade now and in the future. This definition offers guidance for measuring money in an economy. Interpreted literally, this definition says that money should include only those assets that function obviously as a medium of exchange: currency, checking account deposits, and traveler's checks. These assets can easily be used to buy goods and services and thus act as a medium of exchange.

This strict interpretation is too narrow in the real world, though. Many other types of assets can be used as mediums of exchange, but they are not as liquid as a checking account deposit or cash. For example, you can convert your savings account at a bank to cash without paying a large transactions cost. Likewise, if you have an account at a brokerage firm, you can write checks against the value of securities the firm holds for you. Although there are restrictions in these alternatives and some transactions costs, these assets are plausibly part of the medium of exchange.

Money can be measured using many different definitions. A definition can range from narrow to broad, according to how closely substitutable various assets are for definitive money. Substitutability refers to the ease with which an asset can be converted to definitive money with no loss in value. Thus the most narrow money measure is definitive money itself. A broad measure would include other assets that could be easily converted to cash— your checking account or savings account, for example. In the United States, the Fed has defined certain measures of money as part of its effort to estimate the effects of the money supply on prices and economic activity.

The Fed has conducted several studies of the appropriate definition of money. This job has become more difficult during the past two decades as innovation in financial markets and institutions has created new substitutes for the traditional measures of the medium of exchange. During the 1980s, the Fed adapted its definitions of money in response to financial innovation.

Measuring Monetary Aggregates

Charged with regulating the quantity of money in the United States, the Fed defines **monetary aggregates** as measures of money broader than currency. Let's see how the current set of definitions works (see also the Using the news exhibit).

M1 Aggregate.   The narrowest measure of money is *M1*. As Fig. 2.2 shows, *M1* measures money as the traditional medium of exchange, including currency, traveler's checks, and checking account deposits. Through the early 1980s, checking accounts were deposits that paid no interest and thus were close substitutes for definitive money. Since then, financial innovation in the banking industry and government deregulation in the 1970s and 1980s increased the types of bank accounts accepted as close substitutes for checking deposits. These new accounts include checking accounts at savings institutions and credit unions, as well as interest-bearing checking accounts at commercial banks. We present the origin of such innovations in Chapter 15. Measures of *M1* now include these other deposits against which checks may be written, along with noninterest-bearing checking account deposits, traveler's checks, and currency.

M2 Aggregate.   The next broader aggregate, *M2*, shown in the third tier in Fig. 2.2, includes *M1* and short-term investment accounts. These accounts can be converted to definitive money but not as easily as the components of *M1*. Originally, *M2* consisted predominantly of small-denomination time deposits and savings accounts. Now it also includes some assets with

Using the news...

Finding Up-to-Date Information on Money

To get an indication of how rapidly the money supply is growing, consult the "Money and Investing" section of *The Wall Street Journal*. On Fridays, the *Journal* publishes data on *M1*, *M2*, and *M3*. The example shown here summarizes information available on January 28, 1993. The *sa* entries have been seasonally adjusted. This adjustment removes seasonal fluctuations in the money supply (such as the increase in money holdings during the summer vacation season or the Christmas shopping season) from the data.

For the week ending January 18, 1993, *M1* averaged $1042.8 billion. Is this an exact count of all components of *M1*? No. It is based on initial estimates by the Fed.

MONETARY AGGREGATES (daily average in billions)		
	One week ended:	
	Jan. 18	Jan. 11
Money supply (M1) sa	1031.6	1034.4
Money supply (M1) nsa	1042.8	1062.9
Money supply (M2) sa	3493.8	3500.6
Money supply (M2) nsa	3506.8	3533.4
Money supply (M3) sa	4160.5	4153.4
Money supply (M3) nsa	4170.6	4179.7
	Four weeks ended:	
	Jan. 18	Dec. 21
Money supply (M1) sa	1031.0	1021.0
Money supply (M1) nsa	1056.8	1037.9
Money supply (M2) sa	3497.7	3504.5
Money supply (M2) nsa	3520.2	3518.2
Money supply (M3) sa	4156.0	4185.5
Money supply (M3) nsa	4175.6	4196.7
	Month	
	Dec.	Nov.
Money supply (M1) sa	1024.3	1019.0
Money supply (M2) sa	3503.4	3507.3
Money supply (M3) sa	4176.9	4192.2
nsa-Not seasonally adjusted. sa-Seasonally adjusted.		

Source: From *The Wall Street Journal*, January 29, 1993. Reprinted by permission of *The Wall Street Journal*, © 1993 Dow Jones & Co., Inc. All Rights Reserved Worldwide.

Revisions to money stock estimates can be significant, so initial estimates may not be a reliable guide to short-term movements in the money supply. Forecasters have found, however, that over longer periods, such as a year, the initial and revised money supply series produce similar longer-term growth rates.

check-writing features, such as money market deposit accounts at banks, money market mutual fund shares, and certain liquid assets of firms, including overnight repurchase agreements and overnight Eurodollars.

M3 Aggregate.   Broader still is **M3**, which includes *M2* and some less liquid assets, including large-denomination time deposits, institutional money market mutual fund balances, term repurchase agreements, and Eurodollars.

L Aggregate.   The broadest Fed measure, **L**, is designed more as a measure of total liquid assets that could be converted to cash at low cost than of money as a medium of exchange. The aggregate, *L*, include *M3* plus short-term Treasury securities, commercial paper, savings bonds, and bankers' acceptances. We explore the differences among these assets in Chapter 3 and in Part IV.

Selecting Monetary Aggregates

Which is the correct measure of money? The answer depends on the purpose of the measurement. Until the 1980s, *M1* was accepted as the

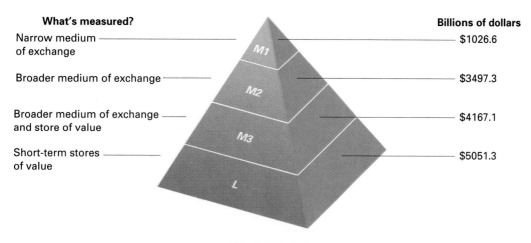

What's measured?

Narrow medium of exchange ———————————————— $1026.6

Broader medium of exchange ———————————— $3497.3

Broader medium of exchange and store of value ——— $4167.1

Short-term stores of value ——————— $5051.3

Billions of dollars

M1

M2

M3

L

What's included?

M1	M2	M3	L
Currency in circulation + • Traveler's checks • Demand deposits • Other checkable deposits	M1 + • Small denomination time deposits • Savings deposits • Money market deposit accounts • Noninstitutional money market fund shares • Overnight repurchase agreements • Overnight Eurodollars	M2 + • Large denomination time deposits • Institutional money market fund balances • Term repurchase agreements • Term Eurodollars	M3 + Nonbank holdings (net of money market fund holdings) of: • Short-term U.S. Treasury securities • Commercial paper • Savings bonds • Bankers' acceptances

FIGURE 2.2

Measuring Monetary Aggregates, January 1993
Monetary aggregates offer measures of different definitions of money. Each measure includes the content of the level above plus other assets.
Source: Federal Reserve Bulletin.

measure of money. In the 1980s, *M1*'s role as a measure was challenged as the new substitutes for simple checking accounts were included in *M2*. In the 1980s and early 1990s economists and policymakers generally have considered *M2* the measure for the medium of exchange, though developments in the financial system during that period made defining money difficult. The Fed also has experimented with hybrid measures of money using portions of components of the monetary aggregates. For example, if money market mutual fund shares are held for both transactions and investment purposes, they could be allocated in part to an *M1*-type measure and in part to an *M2*-type measure.

Because the Fed's monetary aggregates are attempts to measure some underlying true stock of money, economists and policymakers want to know whether the aggregates move together. If, for example, *M1, M2,* and *M3* tend to rise or fall together, the Fed could use any one of them to try to influence the economy's output, prices, or interest rates. If these measures of money do not move together, they may tell different stories about what is

MOVING FROM THEORY TO PRACTICE...

THE WALL STREET JOURNAL   JANUARY 31, 1992

Ukraine Falters Over Creating Currency

In its first month of modern nationhood, Ukraine, the second most important of the former Soviet republics, hoisted its own flag, started using its own language in government matters and moved to create its own currency.

But this hat trick of independence—carried out on a wave of national pride—went haywire when it came to the Ukrainian money. Soaring prices in Russia, the preeminent former Soviet republic, combined with round-the-clock printing of rubles there, forced Kiev to quickly raise its own prices and issue a temporary currency sooner than it wanted to.

If it hadn't raised prices in line with Russia, market forces would have sucked Ukraine dry of food and consumer goods as Russians sought cheaper goods than they could get at home. But for Ukraine, the result is monetary mayhem: Transactions now are for dollars, rubles and hastily printed "coupons"—the stopgap Monopoly money the National Bank of Ukraine hired a French printer to churn out.

Amid this bonfire of currencies, Ukrainians await the *grivna,* pronounced HRIV-na, that's meant to be the permanent national currency, due this summer [1992]...

"To have your own currency is to have your own country," declares Volodymir Pylypchuk, head of Ukraine's commission on economic reform and management.

Creating currencies is the most treacherous job of economic independence. A worthless, hyperinflationary money attacks the entire economy: Foreign investors steer clear, panicky consumers hoard, producers sit on goods, and gangsters feed on the confusion...

The cheap-looking notes offer an opportunity for criminals: An official at the National Bank of Ukraine shows a visitor a handful of coupons produced by a laser copier, almost indistinguishable from the real ones. He says that he didn't run them off himself as an experiment but, without providing details, says he "found" them, presumably in circulation somewhere...

Ukraine's new government isn't really crazy, just woefully inexperienced when it comes to money matters. The National Bank of Ukraine has just become a central bank rather than an outpost of Moscow's Gosbank. At the moment, the bank employs only one economist and no supervisory officials. It has never tried to measure money supply; but that doesn't matter much, because the central bank isn't in charge of the supply of coupons right now. The politicians are.

"This system will destroy itself in a couple of months," says Oleksander Savchenko, deputy governor of the National Bank of Ukraine. "The grivna is my last hope. But if we are to introduce the grivna in five or six months, we must establish a real central bank, we must take control of all hard-currency circulation, we must calculate the balance of payments and calculate our gross national product." The Ukrainian government is paying Canadian Bank Note Co. $30 million to print up the first supply of grivnas.

The West is mustering help. The International Monetary Fund and the Bank of England have put on crash courses on the basics of central banking and monetary management. The government plans to set up a school of public administration to create a better class of bureaucrats.

ANALYZING THE NEWS...

The breakup of the former Soviet Union created new, independent countries with a desire to avoid many of the problems of government rationing of goods and services, some with a desire for independent official currencies. For an official money to be accepted as a medium of exchange, citizens must have confidence in its purchasing power.

(a) In Russia, the rapid growth of the money supply reduced the value of the ruble, forcing Russian merchants to raise prices. If Ukrainian merchants did not raise prices, eager Russians would buy up the Ukraine's goods with low-valued rubles. As a result, Ukrainian authorities increased the Ukraine's money supply, reducing the value of its money.

Confusion over what money is raises costs of carrying out transactions in the economy. Bartering, hoarding, and crime lower the standard of living for citizens. For the grivna to be successful, it will have to provide a more acceptable means of trading than bartering or relying on foreign currencies.

(b) Rapidly rising prices with an inflation rate of hundreds or thousands of percent each year is known as *hyperinflation*. As of early 1992, the National Bank of Ukraine, the new central bank, had no means of measuring money, or economic activity for that matter. This made it difficult to ascertain the quantity of the medium of exchange in the economy.

(c) The importing of economists and statisticians from the West will help the new central bank to measure money and assess its purchasing power in the Ukraine. Unless the central bank assumes more control over the growth of the Ukraine's money supply, the resulting rapid money growth and inflation will destroy money's usefulness in making it easier for Ukrainian citizens to trade with each other.

For further thought...

Suppose that Ukrainians lose confidence in the grivna as a medium of exchange. Can you suggest a way in which private banks and small businesses could create a new money in its place?

Source: Excerpted from Tim Carrington, "Ukraine Falters Over Creating Currency," January 31, 1992. Reprinted by permission of *The Wall Street Journal,* ©1992 Dow Jones & Co., Inc. All Rights Reserved Worldwide.

Growth Rates of *M1*, *M2*, and *M3*, 1960–1992
Monetary aggregates move together broadly over long periods of time. However, their growth rates diverge during some periods.
Source: Federal Reserve Bulletin

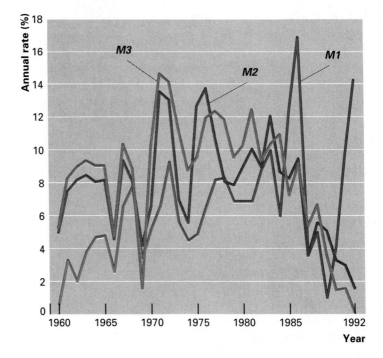

happening to money. As a result, policymakers would have difficulty deciding on an appropriate monetary policy.

As shown in Fig. 2.3, it turns out that monetary aggregates move broadly together over long periods of time. However, some significant differences in monetary aggregate movements have occurred during certain periods of time. For example, while the growth rate of *M1* rose during the 1970s and mid-1980s, the growth rates of the broader *M2* and *M3* aggregates actually decreased. Hence the different monetary aggregates give a different picture of movements in the money supply over time. We will explore these differences in more detail in Chapter 23.

How then do the Fed and private forecasters decide which measures to use? As we noted earlier, the Fed continues to experiment with hybrid measures of money in which different assets have different degrees of liquidity. In addition, Federal Reserve economists, academic economists, and private forecasters conduct research on which monetary aggregates are most closely tied to movements in economic variables, such as the economy's total output, the price level, and interest rates. In Part V, we examine these empirical approaches more carefully.

Key Terms and Concepts

Asset	Monetary aggregates (*M1, M2, M3, L*)
Central bank	Payments system
Definitive money	Checks
Facilitating exchange	Commodity money
Barter	Electronic funds transfer systems
Government allocation	Fiat money
Money	Specialization
Functions of money	Transactions cost
Medium of exchange	Deflation
Standard of deferred payment	Inflation
Store of value	Price index
Unit of account	Purchasing power
Legal tender	Wealth

Summary

1. Specialization enhances economic efficiency: Individuals produce things they are good at producing. Because of such specialization, people create surpluses and need ways to trade the things they produce. The three possible trading mechanisms are: barter, government allocation, and money. The problem with barter is that it cannot easily match the highly specific needs of buyers and sellers. Government allocation often fails because it misallocates resources. Money works well in facilitating trade, allocating resources efficiently, and avoiding the need for matching each buyer and seller.

2. In its role as a medium of exchange, money is a generally accepted means of payment. A particular item becomes a medium of exchange because people believe that it will be mutually acceptable.

3. Money provides a unit of account, so that all prices can be quoted in monetary terms. Money also reduces the costs of trading over time. As a store of value, money allows people to hold it today and buy things with it in the future. As a standard of deferred payment, money makes credit transactions possible.

4. Definitive money is money that does not have to be converted into a more basic legal medium of exchange. In commodity money systems, commodities (such as gold) are definitive money. In fiat monetary systems, paper currency and coin issued by the government or central bank are definitive money.

5. The payments system consists of ways of conducting transactions in the economy. Over time, payments systems have changed from simple (paper currency as the main method of payment) to complex (automatic clearing of payments by computer).

6. Financial assets are grouped into different monetary aggregates, depending on their liquidity, or how easily they can be traded for definitive money.

The Federal Reserve System, the central bank of the United States, defines monetary aggregates and collects data on them. These aggregates include measures designed to reflect money's role as a medium of exchange (*M1* and *M2*) and those designed to capture its role as a short-term store of value (*M3* and *L*).

Review Questions

1. What makes a dollar bill money? What makes a personal check money? What factors, if changed, would affect your willingness to accept a dollar bill or a check as money?

2. How does specialization improve an economy's standard of living?

3. What are the costs of a barter system?

4. What are the four main functions of money? What do they mean?

5. What is commodity money? How does it differ from fiat money?

6. How does a monetary system affect the development of a credit system? If legal money is not broadly accepted as a medium of exchange, are credit contracts likely to be expressed in monetary terms? Why or why not?

7. What is a payments system? What would be some costs to the economy of a decrease in the efficiency of the payments system?

8. What are the effects of high and accelerating inflation on the value of money? On the usefulness of such money as a medium of exchange?

9. Is the store-of-value function unique to money? Give some other examples of stores of value. Must money be a store of value to serve its function as a medium of exchange? Why or why not?

10. Which roles of money are adversely affected by inflation?

Analytical Problems

11. Why would someone keep currency in her pocket when money in the bank pays interest?

12. Suppose that your bank lowers its minimum balance requirement on a NOW account (a checking account that pays interest). You take $500 out of your NOW account and put it in a passbook savings account (a type of savings deposit) that pays a slightly higher interest rate. What is the overall effect on *M1* and *M2*?

13. If your income increases 10% in a year, are you better off? Why or why not?

14. Suppose that a primitive economy uses a particular type of rare stone as its money. Suppose also that the number of stones declines as stones are accidentally destroyed or used as weapons. What happens to the value of the stones over time? What would be the consequence if someone discovered a large amount of new stones?

15. Consider the country of Friedmania where the money is gold "crowns" that each contain one gram of gold. The Royal Mint in Friedmania freely makes crowns out of raw gold. Then one day a new king orders the mint to put only 0.9 grams of gold

in all new crowns and orders that the new crowns trade one-for-one with the old crowns. What do you think happens to the use of crowns as a medium of exchange? If you lived in Friedmania and had some old crowns and some new crowns, which would you spend first?

16. During the 1980s, broad price indexes in Germany rose less than those in Italy. What should happen to the value of money in Germany relative to the value of money in Italy? Suppose that Germany and Italy trade freely. Predict what would happen to the purchasing power of Germans in buying Italian goods. Of Italians buying German goods.

17. Define *liquidity*. Rank the following assets in terms of liquidity, from most to least liquid: money market mutual fund, passbook savings account, corporate stock, dollar bill, house, gold, checking account.

18. Match each of the following items with the smallest monetary aggregate (*M1*, *M2*, *M3*, or *L*) it is part of: money market deposit account, term repurchase agreement, commercial paper, traveler's check, overnight repurchase agreement, U.S. savings bond, currency, large time deposit, small time deposit, short-term Treasury bond, checking account.

Questions 19 and 20 pertain to the Appendix.

19. The consumer price index (CPI) had the value 311.1 for 1984, with 1967 as the base year (that is, the CPI in 1967 is taken as 100). Now suppose that 1984 becomes the base year (that is, the new CPI in 1984 is taken as 100). What is the new CPI for 1967?

20. If the price index was 100 for 1980 and 120 for 1990, and nominal gross domestic product (GDP) was $720 billion for 1980 and $960 for 1990, what is the value of 1990 real GDP in terms of 1980 dollars?

Data Questions

Questions 21 through 23 pertain to the Appendix.

21. In the latest copy of the *Economic Report of the President*, (a) look up the value of nominal GDP, (the value of all final goods and services produced in the economy during the course of a year) for 1980 and 1990; (b) find the value of the GDP implicit price deflator in 1980 and 1990; (c) calculate real GDP for both years; and (d) find the percentage change in real GDP over the decade.

22. Find the consumer price index in the latest copy of the *Economic Report of the President*. Find the value of the index in the years 1950, 1960, 1970, 1980, and 1990. Calculate the inflation rates for the decades of the 1950s, 1960s, 1970s, and 1980s.

23. Repeat Problem 22 for the GDP implicit price deflator and the producer price index. How do the inflation rates compare?

24. In the latest issue of the *Federal Reserve Bulletin*, find the current figures for *M1*, *M2*, *M3*, and *L*. Now look in the *Economic Report of the President* to find the latest data on the population of the United States. Divide the money aggregate numbers by the population to get average money holdings per person. Do the numbers look reasonable to you? Explain why the numbers are so large.

Appendix: Calculating Price Indexes

A price index is calculated by dividing the price of selected goods making up a marketbasket P in some year t by the price of the marketbasket in a base year 0 (and multiplying by 100 to convert to percentage terms):

$$(\text{Price index})_t = \frac{P_t}{P_0} \times 100.$$

If, for example, prices increased by 20% between the year 0 and year t, the index would be $1.20 \times 100 = 120$.

The most commonly watched price indexes in the United States are:

GDP deflator: the index of prices of all goods and services included in the gross domestic product (the final value of all goods and services produced in the economy).

Producer price index (PPI): the index of prices that firms pay in wholesale markets for crude materials, intermediate goods, and finished goods.

Consumer price index (CPI): the index of prices of the marketbasket of goods purchased by urban consumers (used as a measure of the cost of living).

CHAPTER 3

Overview of the Financial System

Throughout 1991 and during the course of the presidential campaign in 1992, segments of the business community complained that the financial system was simply not working. Small and medium-sized businesses, important sources of jobs for the recovering economy, sent lobbyists to Washington to let the Treasury Department and the Federal Reserve Board know that businesses could not get the credit they needed to expand. Politicians and economists began to take a hard look at how well the American financial system brought together borrowers with good ideas and savers with money to lend.

Although you may not march to Washington to express your concerns about the financial system, the health of financial services nonetheless affects you significantly. For example, what do you do if you want to save money for retirement? To borrow money to buy a house? Or to build a plant to produce your great invention? At some time you are likely to experience the need to save or to borrow.

The financial system makes such transactions possible. It encompasses all the ways for savers to channel funds to borrowers and for borrowers to pay them back. An efficient financial system increases the health of the economy by making rapid economic growth possible: Borrowers can obtain funds for consumption and investment, and savers can obtain extra funds they might otherwise not have.

What does the financial system do? How does it accomplish its objectives? We address these questions in Parts II and III by examining financial markets and institutions in detail. Before we do so, however, we need to discuss broadly five questions about the financial system. **Q:** What is the purpose of the financial system? **Q:** What are the key services provided by the financial system? **Q:** How does the financial system bring participants together? **Q:** How can we explain changes in the financial system? **Q:** What are the goals of financial regulation?

What Is the Purpose of the Financial System?

What do you have in common with a farmer, an inventor, and the federal government? All of you at one time or another may need more funds than you have on hand. For example, you may want to go to graduate school and delay your entry into the job market. A farmer may need money to meet planting expenses. An inventor may want to finance the start of a new high-technology company. The federal government may run a budget deficit, spending more than it collects in taxes. Those finding themselves with a mismatch between income and spending needs may be willing to pay for obtaining the funds they need.

At the same time, others prefer to spend less than their incomes allow. For example, your parents may be saving for their retirement or to pay for your education. A business may receive a big payment on a government contract and decide not to spend all the money at once. Even governments sometimes have more money on hand than they need immediately. Those having surplus funds may be willing to let someone else use their savings if they receive compensation for doing so.

The mismatch of income and spending needs for individuals and businesses creates an opportunity to trade. The money being saved by your parents for the future could be used by the inventor to start a business now. The inventor would be better off by earning a profit from investing funds in a new venture. Your parents would be better off by receiving the return that the inventor pays them for "renting" their funds. They would not have earned this extra income if they had kept their savings in a shoebox in a closet.

Not all financial transactions involve investing in a new project or business venture. Suppose that you have a good job and decide to buy a house. There's only one problem: Although you earn $30,000 per year, the house you want to buy costs $80,000. You could rent an apartment and save your money slowly until you accumulate enough to buy the house. That would probably take many years, though, and you and your family may want to enjoy owning a home sooner. As an alternative, someone could lend you the money to buy the house now. Just as you would be better off by being able to enjoy the benefits of homeownership sooner, the person who loaned you the money would be better off, too. The interest that you pay the lender would be extra income—income that the lender would not have received without making the loan.

Now you can begin to see why the financial system provides valuable functions for the economy. Its primary purpose is to move funds from those who want to spend less than they have available to those with productive investment opportunities. This matching process increases the economy's ability to produce goods and services. In addition, it makes consumers better off by allowing them to time purchases according to their needs and desires. A smoothly functioning financial system thus improves the economy's efficiency and people's economic welfare.

The **financial system** provides mechanisms to transfer funds from individuals and groups who have saved money to individuals and groups who want to borrow money. **Savers** are suppliers of funds, providing funds to borrowers in return for promises of repayment of even more funds in the future. **Borrowers** are demanders of funds for consumer durables, houses, or business plant and equipment, promising to repay borrowed funds based on their expectation of having higher incomes in the future. These promises are financial **liabilities** for the borrower, that is, both a source of funds and a claim against the borrower's future income. Conversely, the promises, or IOUs, are financial **assets** for savers, that is, both a use of funds and a claim on the borrower's future income. For example, your car loan is an asset (use of funds) for the bank and a liability (source of funds) for you. If you buy a house, the mortgage is your liability and your lender's asset. If your uncle buys Treasury bonds for his retirement account, the bonds are assets for him and liabilities for the U.S. government.

Figure 3.1 shows that the financial system channels funds from savers to borrowers and channels returns back to savers, both directly and indirectly. Savers and borrowers can be households, businesses, or governments, both domestic and foreign. **Financial markets,** such as the stock market or the bond market, issue claims on individual borrowers directly to savers. **Financial institutions** or **intermediaries,** such as banks, mutual funds, and insurance companies, act as go-betweens by holding a portfolio of

▼ FIGURE 3.1

Moving Funds Through the Financial System
The financial system transfers funds from savers to borrowers. Borrowers transfer returns back to savers through the financial system. Savers and borrowers include domestic and foreign households, businesses, and governments.

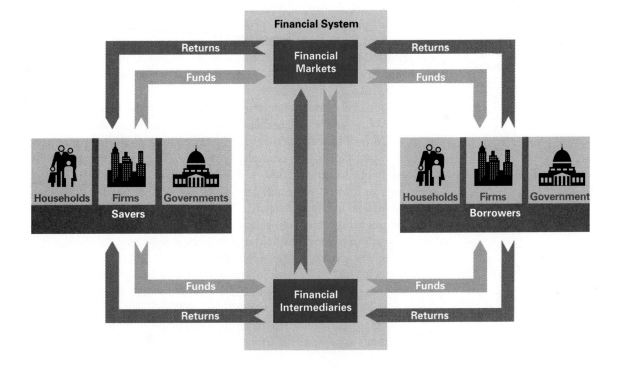

assets and issuing claims based on that portfolio to savers. We discuss the participants in these activities and their roles later in this chapter. First, however, let's consider the financial services that motivate savers and borrowers to use the financial system.

▶ **C H E C K P O I N T** *As a saver, what sort of claims might you hold?* You can hold claims on a variety of borrowers. Your checking account is a claim on your bank. If you have savings bonds, you own a claim on the U.S. government. Money market accounts with Fidelity, Merrill Lynch, or any of their competitors are claims on a portfolio of assets held by the brokerage firm. If your aunt left you a Disney bond, you own a claim against that firm. ◀

Q: What is the purpose of the financial system?

A: Because the incomes of households, firms, and governments do not always match their spending, the financial system transfers funds from savers to borrowers. In the process, it creates financial assets, or savers' claims on borrowers' future income.

Key Services Provided by the Financial System

The financial system provides three key services to savers and borrowers: *risk sharing, liquidity,* and *information,* as illustrated in Fig. 3.2. Savers and borrowers value these services in part because the financial system provides them in different ways to meet varying individual needs. Availability of these services helps explain many of the financial actions of households and businesses.

Risk Sharing

Your brother-in-law asks you to invest all your savings in shares of stock in his new company. You know that it's a risky proposition. If the economy booms, sales of the product—glow-in-the-dark earrings—might make you rich. But if the economy sours, those earrings might not be such a great product. You would like to invest in the business, but you're not convinced that you should tie up all your savings in such an investment. Are you being too cautious?

No. One of the greatest advantages of using the financial system to match individual savers and borrowers is that it allows the sharing of risks. *Risk* refers to the chance that the value of financial assets will rise or fall relative to what you expect. For example, if you buy a bond of Okayco for $1000, that bond might be worth $900 or $1100 in one year's time, depending on fluctuations in interest rates and Okayco's prospects. Most individual savers are not gamblers and seek a steady return on their assets rather than erratic swings between high and low earnings. The financial system provides **risk sharing** by allowing savers to hold many assets. A collection of assets is called a **portfolio.** For example, you might hold some U.S. savings bonds, some shares of stock, and some shares in a mutual fund. Although one asset or set of assets may perform well and another not so well, overall the returns tend to average out. This splitting of wealth into many assets is known as **diversification.** As long as the individual returns do not vary in the same way, the risk of severe fluctuations in a portfolio's value will be reduced.

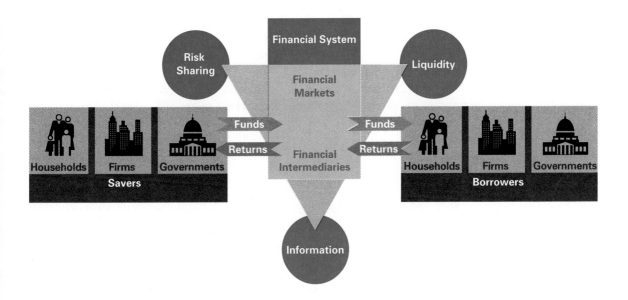

Key Services Provided by the Financial System
The financial system provides risk-sharing, liquidity, and information services. These services are valued by savers and borrowers.

We describe the advantages of diversification in Chapter 6, along with ways that the financial system enables individuals to *transfer risk*. Financial markets can create instruments to transfer risk from savers or borrowers who do not like uncertainty in returns or payments to savers or investors who are willing to bear risk. For example, you might be willing to accept a lower return on your investment in your brother-in-law's business if he or one of his other investors guaranteed you that return.

The ability of the financial system to provide risk sharing makes savers more willing to buy borrowers' IOUs. This willingness, in turn, increases borrowers' ability to raise funds in the financial system.

Liquidity

The second service the financial system offers savers and borrowers is **liquidity,** which refers to the ease with which an asset can be exchanged for other assets or for goods and services. Savers care about liquidity of financial assets. When they need their assets for their own consumption or investment, they want to be able to exchange them easily. In general, the more liquid an asset, the easier it is to exchange the asset for something else. For example, if you have a dollar bill in your pocket, you can easily exchange it for a hamburger. Thus, a dollar bill is highly liquid. You could also cash a check within a short period of time to buy clothes. Selling your car, however, takes more time because personal property is not very liquid. By holding financial claims (such as stock or bonds) on a factory, individual investors have more liquid savings than they would if they owned the machines in the factory. The reason is that the investor can more easily sell the claim than a specialized machine in order to buy other assets or goods. Liquidity means that an individual or firm can respond quickly to new opportunities or unexpected events. Financial assets, such as stocks, bonds, or checking accounts, are more liquid than cars, machinery, or real estate.

No asset is totally liquid. However, financial markets and intermediaries provide trading systems for making assets more liquid. The type of assets considered to be liquid changes as a financial system develops. In the United States, for instance, investors can readily sell their holdings in government securities and stocks and bonds of large corporations, making those assets very liquid. During the past two decades, the financial system has made many other assets liquid. Twenty years ago, for example, financial intermediaries had to hold mortgage loans and loans made to businesses until the loans were paid off. Now, those institutions can sell the loans to other investors and buy loans made by other institutions. As a result, mortgages and other loans have become more desirable assets for savers to hold. Savers are willing to accept a lower return, reducing the costs of borrowing obligations for less well-known firms. One measure of the efficiency of the financial system is the extent to which it can transform illiquid assets into the liquid claims that savers want.

Information

The third service the financial system provides to savers and borrowers is to gather and communicate **information,** or facts about borrowers and expectations about returns on financial assets. The first informational role the financial system plays is to *gather* information. That involves finding out about prospective borrowers and what they will do with borrowed funds. Obtaining such information would be costly and time-consuming for savers, who of course want all the facts before lending their money. For example, if your neighbor comes to you for a loan, you may not have any information about whether he or she can repay it. When borrowers possess information about their opportunities or activities that they don't disclose to lenders or creditors, a condition of **asymmetric information** exists. Sometimes financial arrangements have to be structured so that borrowers do not take advantage of asymmetric information at the expense of lenders. For example, if you borrow $10,000 to start a business, the lender will try to make sure that you don't use the funds to take a trip around the world. Parts of the financial system specialize in information gathering and monitoring, and specialized arrangements exist for solving asymmetric information problems.

The second informational role the financial system plays involves *communication* of information. If you read a newspaper headline announcing that a pharmaceutical company has found a cure for cancer, how would you determine the effect of this discovery on the company's financial position? Financial markets do that job by incorporating information into the prices of stocks and bonds and other financial assets. In this example the expectation of higher future profits would boost the prices of the pharmaceutical company's outstanding stocks and bonds.

Savers and borrowers receive the benefits of information from the financial system by looking at asset returns. As long as financial market participants are informed, the information works its way into asset returns and prices. Information is communicated to borrowers as well as to savers. For example, if the price of the pharmaceutical company's stock goes up, the company may decide to sell more shares and invest the proceeds in new research projects. The incorporation of available information in asset returns is the distinguishing feature of well-functioning financial markets.

Q: What are the key services provided by the financial system?

A: The financial system provides three key services: risk sharing, liquidity, and information. These services make financial assets more attractive to savers and lower costs for borrowers.

Financial Markets in the Financial System

Financial markets bring savers and borrowers together directly. When you buy a new share of Boomco stock for $100, you are investing the $100 directly in Boomco to finance its growth. In this form of finance, known as **direct finance,** an individual saver holds financial claims issued directly by an individual borrower. These direct finance arrangements take place through financial markets, markets in which investors lend their savings directly to borrowers. To analyze the structure of financial markets, we focus on the two principal tasks of the financial system: matching savers and borrowers, and providing risk-sharing, liquidity, and information services.

Matching Savers and Borrowers: Debt and Equity

Primary markets. markets in which newly issued claims are sold to initial buyers by the borrower, are used by businesses to raise funds for new ventures and by governments to finance budget deficits. Borrowers can raise funds in a primary financial market in two ways, which result in different types of claims on the borrower's future income. The first and most commonly used claim is **debt,** which requires the borrower to repay the amount borrowed, the **principal,** plus a rental fee, or **interest.**[†] The other type of claim is **equity,** which is a claim to a share in the profits and assets of a firm. Let's explore the main differences between these two ways of raising funds.

Debt instruments are promises to repay the principal and interest, all at once or in periodic payments over a fixed period of time. The length of the period of time before the debt instrument expires is its **maturity,** or term. The maturity can be a short period of time (30 days or even overnight) or a

---

[†] The formula for computing how much interest is paid can be either an agreed-upon percentage, as is used for your bank account or student loan, or an indexed percentage, tied to some economic indicator such as the inflation rate or some published interest rate. Many business loans made by banks—especially in international lending—fall into the second category.

long period of time (30 years or more). **Short-term debt** instruments have a maturity of less than one year. **Intermediate-term debt** instruments have a maturity of between one year and 10 years. **Long-term debt** instruments have a maturity of 10 years or more. Debt instruments include student loans, government bonds, corporate bonds, and loans by financial institutions.

Suppose that you take out a student loan to study business, and when you graduate, you land a Wall Street position paying $50,000 a year. The fact that you got such a good job does not mean that you have to pay back more than the agreed-upon loan amount. In general, in a debt contract, a lender does not get more than the amount promised if the borrower does exceptionally well. The lender, however, may get less than the amount promised: If, for example, you cannot find a job and consequently can't pay back your loan, the lender gets less than the full amount of the loan. Lenders face the risk that borrowers will **default,** or not be able to repay all or part of their obligations.

The second means of raising funds—equity—allows for variable payments from the borrower to the lender. A good example is common stock, which entitles stockholders in a business to get their share of the firm's profits after all expenses, including payments of principal and interest to debtholders, have been settled. For example, if you own 100 shares of Bigco, which has 1 million shares outstanding, you own the right to 1/10,000 (100/1 million) of the firm's profits and assets. Equity owners generally receive periodic payments (usually once each quarter) from the firm, known as **dividends.** If the business does exceptionally well, equity owners receive more, while the debtholders still get only their promised payment. However, if the business's profits are weak, there may be nothing left after payments to debtholders are made. If you buy shares in Oopsco and it loses money, do you have to pay the firm's losses? No. Shareholders in corporations can lose only the amount of funds they invest in the venture. In Chapter 11, we examine the relative merits of using debt or equity to finance businesses, and we use economic intuition to explain major developments in the use of debt or equity.

Although you hear about the stock market's fluctuations each night on the evening news, debt instruments actually account for more of the funds raised in the financial system. At the beginning of 1993, the value of debt instruments was about $11.5 trillion versus $5.1 trillion for equities.

Providing Risk-Sharing, Liquidity, and Information Services

Risk-sharing, liquidity, and information services are provided in **secondary markets,** markets in which claims that have already been issued are sold by one investor to another. Suppose, for example, that you start a software company, Hitechco, which after a few years is growing rapidly but is in need of new capital for expansion. If you sell shares in Hitechco, you are turning to a primary market for new funds. Once Hitechco shares are issued, investors trade the shares in the secondary market. Note that as an owner of Hitechco, you do not receive any new funds when your company's shares are traded in secondary markets.

Most of the news about events in financial markets is about secondary markets rather than primary ones. Most primary market transactions involve sales of new debt or equity instruments to initial buyers and are conducted behind closed doors. The most widely reported secondary markets are those for already issued equities, such as the New York, American, and Tokyo Stock Exchanges. Even larger volumes of secondary market transactions take place in the bond market, where U.S. government and corporate debt instruments are traded. Secondary markets also are important for global foreign-exchange transactions. Regardless of the type of instrument being traded, the buyer of the instrument in a secondary market pays money to the seller. The *initial* seller of the instrument—a corporation or government agency, for example—does *not* receive the proceeds. The initial issuer receives only the proceeds from the sale of the instrument in the primary market.

If the initial seller of a financial instrument raises funds from a lender only in the primary market, why are secondary markets so important? The reasons relate to risk sharing, liquidity, and information. Smoothly functioning secondary markets make it easier for investors to reduce their exposure to risk by holding a diversified portfolio of stocks, bonds, and other assets. Secondary markets also promote liquidity for stocks, bonds, foreign exchange, and other financial instruments, so that it is easier for investors to sell the instruments for cash. This liquidity makes investors more willing to hold financial instruments, thereby making it easier for the issuing firm or government agency to sell the securities in the first place. Finally, secondary markets convey information to both savers and borrowers by determining the price of financial instruments. When the price of your shares of Hitechco rises, you are richer, which tells you that you can spend more if you want to. Likewise, the managers of Hitechco can get information on how well the market thinks they are doing from secondary market prices. For example, a major increase in Hitechco's stock price conveys the market's good feelings about the firm's investment possibilities and management skills, and the firm may decide to issue new debt or equity and expand. Hence secondary market prices are valuable sources of information for corporations thinking about issuing new debt or equity. As a result, we will focus mainly on secondary markets in our discussion.

Three aspects of secondary markets will figure in our analysis of financial markets in Part II: (1) maturity of the claim, (2) how trading takes place, and (3) when settlement takes place.

Maturity: Money and Capital Markets. Debt instruments with a maturity of greater than one year are traded in **capital markets**. Equities, which have no fixed maturity, also are traded in capital markets. Short-term instruments, with a maturity of less than one year, are traded in **money markets.** Funds raised by issuing long-term instruments in capital markets are generally used for long-term investments in housing or business plant and equipment. Money market instruments are generally issued by well-known corporations or the government to finance inventories or to meet short-term needs for funds. (The principal money and capital market instruments are described in the Appendix.)

The three primary differences for investors in money market and capital market instruments relate to risk, liquidity, and information. First, short-term instruments have relatively small increases or decreases in price, so they are less risky as investments than long-term instruments are. As a result, financial institutions and corporations typically invest short-term surplus funds in money markets. Some financial institutions, such as pension funds and insurance companies, are willing to hold assets for a long time and risk price fluctuations in capital markets. Second, money market instruments are generally more liquid than capital market instruments because their trading volume is greater. Thus households and businesses can invest their funds for a short period of time relatively cheaply. Finally, information costs are lower for money market instruments because the borrowers are well known and the length of time for which funds are loaned is relatively short.

Trading Places: Auction and Over-the-Counter Markets. Secondary financial markets also can be categorized according to how assets are traded between buyers and sellers. The first is **auction markets,** in which prices are set by competitive bidding by a large number of traders acting on behalf of individual buyers or sellers. The most common auction markets are **exchanges,** or central locations at which buyers and sellers trade. These include the New York and American Stock Exchanges, the Tokyo Stock Exchange, the London Stock Exchange, and others.

Secondary markets also can be organized as **over-the-counter (OTC) markets,** in which there is no centralized place for auction trading. Over-the-counter dealers buy and sell stocks and bonds through computerized trading to anyone willing to accept their posted prices. Close electronic contact keeps the over-the-counter market competitive. You are unlikely to pay a much higher price for a share of stock in Newco at one dealer than at another.

The equities of the largest corporations are traded on exchanges, as are the bonds of the most well-known corporations. The shares of smaller, less well-known firms are generally traded in over-the-counter markets, as are U.S. government bonds. The market for these bonds has the largest trading volume of any debt or equity market. Other major OTC markets include those for foreign exchange, federal funds, and negotiable certificates of deposit.

Settlement: Cash or Derivative Markets. Finally, financial markets can be categorized by whether the claims traded are direct or derivative. **Cash markets** refer to those markets in which actual claims are bought and sold with immediate settlement: The buyer pays money to the seller in exchange for the asset. Examples include the stock and bond markets. Alternatively, in **derivative markets,** trades are made now, but settlement is made at a later date. For example, an investor could agree to buy a Treasury bond from a bond dealer one year from now at a prespecified price. Why would anyone want to do this? The reason is that households and businesses use derivative markets to reduce their exposure to the risk of price fluctuations in cash markets (and sometimes even to bet on future price fluctuations).

Derivative claims, whose value is determined by (derived from) underlying assets (such as stocks, bonds, or foreign exchange), include financial futures and options. **Financial futures** imply settlement of a purchase of a financial instrument at a specified future date, with the price determined at the outset. **Options** on financial contracts, as the name suggests, confer on the trader the right (or option) to buy or sell a particular asset (shares of stock, bonds, or units of foreign currency, for example) within a specified time at a specified price.

▶ **C H E C K P O I N T** *Using the components of the structure of financial markets, characterize a transaction in which you buy 100 shares of Growthco from someone through a dealer. Debt or equity:* Shares of stock are equities. *Primary or secondary market:* The stock is already outstanding, so the transaction takes place in a secondary market. *Money or capital market:* The equities have no fixed maturity and so are traded in the capital market. *Auction or over-the-counter market:* The transaction takes place through a dealer rather than through an exchange, so it is conducted in an over-the-counter market. *Cash or derivative market:* You pay money to the dealer and receive the stock now, so the transaction takes place in a cash market. ◀

Financial Intermediaries in the Financial System

The financial system also channels funds from savers to borrowers indirectly through intermediaries. These are institutions that facilitate financial trade by raising funds from savers and investing in the debt or equity claims of borrowers. This indirect form of finance is known as **financial intermediation.** Like financial markets, financial intermediaries have two tasks: matching savers and borrowers, and providing risk-sharing, liquidity, and information services.

Matching Savers and Borrowers

When you deposit funds in your checking account, the bank may then lend the money (together with the funds of other savers) to Jane's Sub Shop to open a new store. In this intermediated transaction, your checking account is an asset for you and a liability for the bank. The loan becomes Jane's liability and the bank's asset. Rather than your holding a loan to Jane's

Sub Shop as an asset directly, the bank is a go-between for you and Jane. Financial intermediaries, such as banks, insurance companies, pension funds, and mutual funds, also make investments in stocks and bonds on behalf of savers. We analyze the services provided by and the regulation of financial intermediaries in Part III.

Intermediaries pool the funds of many small savers to lend to many individual borrowers. They pay interest to savers in exchange for the use of savers' funds and earn a profit by lending money to borrowers and charging borrowers interest on the loans. For example, a bank might pay you as a depositor a rate of interest of 5%, while lending the money to a local business at an interest rate of 8%.

Providing Risk-Sharing, Liquidity, and Information Services

Q: How does the financial system bring participants together?

A: The financial system brings savers and borrowers together via markets and intermediaries. In direct finance through financial markets, individual savers hold the claims issued by individual borrowers. Alternatively, savers can hold claims against intermediaries, and intermediaries hold claims against borrowers.

Intermediation adds an extra layer of complexity and cost to financial trade. Why don't savers just deal directly with borrowers, bypassing the costs of financial intermediation? Again, the three main reasons are risk sharing, liquidity, and information. First, as a saver, you want to share risk. If you had $5000 in cash, you could loan it to your neighbor. But how do you know that your neighbor will pay you back? If you deposit your $5000 in the bank, it puts your money to work by making various loans and investments. Because banks have a large quantity of deposits and access to numerous borrowers and investments, they can provide risk-sharing services to you at a lower cost than you could obtain on your own. Second, bank deposits and other intermediary claims are liquid. Thus, if your car breaks down, you can easily withdraw funds from your bank account to pay for repairs. (Your neighbor likely would not be able to pay you back early or appreciate having to do so.) Finally, financial intermediaries also provide information services that are important to savers who may not have the time or resources to research investments on their own. You can easily get information about the likely return on a U.S. Treasury bond or a bond issued by a major corporation such as Exxon. More difficult, however, is obtaining information about the likely financial prospects of individuals or small and medium-sized businesses.

Your local bank is an information warehouse. It collects information on borrowers by monitoring their income and spending as reflected in their checking account transactions. Borrowers fill out detailed loan applications, and the bank's loan officers determine how well each borrower is doing financially. Because the bank collects and processes information on behalf of you and other depositors, its costs for information gathering are lower than yours would be if you tried to gather information on a pool of borrowers. The intermediary's profits from lending compensate it for investing in information.

Financial intermediaries are the largest group in the financial system. They move more funds between savers and borrowers than financial markets in the United States and in most other countries (see Box 3.1). Many

Consider this...

Where Do Households Put Their Savings?

The Federal Reserve System publishes quarterly and annual data on assets and liabilities of sectors of the U.S. economy. Clues about trends in direct and intermediary finance are provided by examining the Fed's data on household holdings of financial assets.

The table reports holdings of assets in financial markets and of assets supplied by financial intermediaries. These data show the importance of financial intermediation for savers. About one-half of household financial assets are held through financial intermediaries. Note particularly the increasing importance of mutual funds and pension funds, which helped increase the percentage of financial assets in intermediaries from 46.3% in 1978 to 55.8% in 1992. We describe the changing pattern of intermediation in Part III.

Household Holdings of Financial Assets (Billions of Dollars, Various Years)

Financial Assets in Financial Markets

	1978	1985	1992
U.S. government securities	148.6	447.5	687.6
State and local government securities	94.0	305.0	578.1
Corporate bonds	57.0	18.9	154.7
Mortgages	76.0	127.4	253.3
Commercial paper	31.4	128.7	163.4
Corporate equities	663.9	1700.0	2268.8
Equity in unincorporated businesses	1398.9	2040.6	2370.1
Miscellaneous assets	68.0	132.5	288.5
Subtotal	**2537.8**	**4900.6**	**6764.5**
% in direct finance	*53.7%*	*50.8%*	*44.2%*

Financial Assets in Financial Intermediaries

	1978	1985	1992
Bank deposits	1280.1	2306.7	2885.3
Money market mutual fund shares	9.4	211.1	474.3
Mutual fund shares	41.1	206.9	797.6
Life insurance reserves	196.0	256.7	413.4
Pension fund reserves	661.5	1794.5	3962.7
Subtotal	**2188.1**	**4775.9**	**8533.3**
% in indirect finance	*46.3%*	*49.2%*	*55.8%*
Total Financial Assets	**$4,725.9**	**$9,676.5**	**$15,297.8**

These data come from the Fed's publication entitled *Flow of Funds Accounts, Financial Assets and Liabilities,* which you can find in the library.

economists believe that intermediaries' advantage in reducing information costs accounts for this pattern globally as well as nationally. Even in the United States, where financial markets are the most highly developed, businesses raise about twice as much of their external funds from intermediaries as they do directly from financial markets.

▶ C H E C K P O I N T *Why might you be willing to buy a bond issued by IBM, but prefer to lend to the local computer store through a bank?* This preference reflects differences in *information costs.* Information about IBM is readily available, but you would have to incur significant costs to investigate the creditworthiness of the computer store. A bank can collect information on behalf of many small savers, reducing the cost of lending to the computer store and reducing the chance that you will invest your savings in a losing proposition.◀

Competition and Change in the Financial System

Let's say that you've sold your car and have decided not to buy a new one. What will you do with the proceeds from the sale? Your choices are many: Depending on how much you have to invest, you could place your funds in one of the instruments discussed in the preceding section or in a financial institution. As in other industries, financial markets and financial intermediaries compete for your funds and more generally for market share in the financial system. Their tools for competition are the risk-sharing, liquidity, and information services they offer to savers and borrowers.

Mutual funds and banking institutions, for example, offer savers the chance to hold a diversified portfolio of assets at a lower cost than savers could arrange individually (a risk-sharing service). Mutual funds offer assets that are money market or capital market instruments, whereas a bank's assets are the loans originated and monitored by the bank. The existence of these two options results in competition for savers' funds. Borrowers also can choose from an array of financial arrangements. A firm could seek short-term finance through money markets or from an intermediary such as a bank. A firm could raise long-term funds through capital markets or from an intermediary such as a life insurance company.

Financial Innovation

With all the competition among financial markets and institutions, how do savers and borrowers choose among them? They base decisions on the risk-sharing, liquidity, and information characteristics that are best suited for their needs. If you value a low degree of risk, for example, you might turn to financial markets that match savers with low-risk borrowers, such as the U.S. government or well-known corporations. If you want a diversified portfolio without doing your own research, you might turn to intermediaries such as banks, which specialize in reducing information costs and have an accumulated stock of information about borrowers. However, the types of services offered by markets and intermediaries change over time.

Changes in costs of providing risk-sharing, liquidity, or information services or changes in demand for these services lead to alterations in the operation of financial markets and institutions. These changes in the financial system are called **financial innovation.** Financial innovation can benefit everyone, as Box 3.2 illustrates. Indeed, financial markets and institutions that have survived and thrived are those that combine low cost of operation with high demand (meeting households' and firms' preferences for risk-sharing, liquidity, and information services). Shifts in the cost of and demand for financial services also can alter the competitive balance among markets and institutions in the financial system.

Consider this...

BOX 3.2

Will Financial Innovation Help You Buy Your Home?

For most of us, the largest transaction we ever make is financing the purchase of a home. Luckily, you might have an easier time finding and paying for financing than your parents did. Why? Increased efficiency in housing finance has lowered the cost of mortgages. A generation ago, home mortgage loans generally were made and held by local savings and loan institutions and mortgage bankers. As a result, housing finance tended to be a regional business, making diversification of mortgage loans into different geographical areas difficult for lenders.

In the early 1980s, the situation changed. The federal government's credit agencies developed secondary markets to increase the liquidity of home mortgages in order to increase their desirability for investors. Through the Federal National Mortgage Association ("Fannie Mae"), Government National Mortgage Association ("Ginnie Mae"), and Federal Home Loan Mortgage Corporation ("Freddie Mac"), the government made possible the development of mortgage pools. These pools could package mortgages from different original lenders and sell claims on the package to savers. This process is known as "securitization." The claims are traded in secondary markets.

As trading of home mortgages claims became easier, savers gained access to improved means of investing in mortgages, and mortgage financing costs decreased. That's why you may be able to obtain funds from a lender to purchase a house at a lower cost than your parents could obtain 20 years ago.

Changes in Financial Integration and Globalization

Financial systems in the United States and around the world become linked more closely every day. The funds in your checking account can help finance a car loan in your hometown, a new drill press in Chicago, a new steel mill in Seoul, or a loan to the government of Brazil. Bringing together savers and borrowers from around the country and around the world helps the global economy.

Integration. One measure of the system's efficiency is its degree of **financial integration,** or the way in which financial markets are tied together geographically. Early nineteenth-century U.S. financial markets were fragmented geographically. Because of the high costs of gathering and communicating information, eastern capital to a large extent was used in the East; western or southern capital was used in the West or South. Hence interest rates charged to borrowers tended to be different in different parts of the country, making financing a high-quality investment project more costly in the West than in the East. As a result, savers sank too much capital in mansions and silver tea sets in Boston, while potentially profitable mining and industrial ventures in California lacked funds.

The increasing ease of communicating information has enabled U.S. financial markets to become much more integrated. Now borrowers who raise funds through securities have access to national markets.

Globalization. A major development during recent decades has been the global integration of financial markets. Just as capital became more mobile among regions in the United States, moving capital between countries became increasingly important in the 1970s, 1980s, and 1990s. New York's Citibank can raise funds in London as well as it can in Brooklyn, and it can lend money to finance an industrial development project in Queensland, Australia, as easily as it can in Queens, New York. The globalization of financial markets improves the ability of the financial system to channel savers' funds to the highest-value borrowers, wherever they may be.

Over most of the period following World War II, U.S. financial markets dominated financial markets elsewhere. This dominance eroded substantially during the 1980s and early 1990s for two reasons. First, rapid postwar economic growth in Japan and Europe increased the pool of savings brought to foreign financial markets. Second, during the past decade, many countries lifted regulations that kept their citizens from exporting their savings or foreigners from importing it, thereby enabling savers to transfer their funds to borrowers around the world. In the early 1990s, capital market funds crossed national borders at a rate of several trillion dollars per year. The foreign-exchange market now has a volume of trading of more than $1 trillion per day.

The globalization of financial markets has had two effects. First, the easy flow of capital across national boundaries helps countries with productive opportunities grow, even if their current resources are insufficient. For instance, the U.S. economy grew rapidly in the 1980s, but domestic saving was insufficient to fund the demand for investment. Foreign funds filled the gap between U.S. investment and U.S. saving. Second, increasing financial integration around the world reduces the cost of allocating savers' funds to the highest-valued uses wherever they may be. And that is what the financial system is supposed to do (see the Other times, other places box).

Q: How can we explain changes in the financial system?

A: Differences in the demand for and cost of providing key services of risk sharing, liquidity, and information can explain changes in the financial system over time, as well as international differences.

▶ C H E C K P O I N T *Why do you think many experts have encouraged emerging market economies in Eastern Europe to develop financial intermediaries before relying on financial markets?* Financial intermediaries can reduce the information costs of lending in these countries, while offering risk-sharing and liquidity services to savers. After information about companies becomes better known to savers, financial markets will become more important. ◀

Financial Regulation

Financial markets and institutions around the world are regulated by their countries' governments. Over time, regulations imposed by governments change, causing the services and instruments offered by markets or

Other times, other places...
The Growth of International Bond and Stock Markets

Prior to the 1960s, the term "international bond market" referred to *foreign bonds,* or bonds sold in another country and denominated in that country's currency. Since the 1960s, a new form of finance known as a *Eurobond* has grown rapidly. Unlike foreign bonds, Eurobonds are denominated in a currency other than that of the country where they are sold, usually in U.S. dollars. Currently, about 85% of new issues in the international bond market are Eurobonds, and the value of new issues in the Eurobond market exceeds the value of new issues of the U.S. corporate bond market. Historically the center of foreign borrowing, London has retained its dominance as a center for Eurolending, but competition from other European nations and Japan is expected in the 1990s.

In the mid-1980s, another new market developed, this time in *Euroequities,* or new equity issues sold to investors abroad. This market has grown rapidly relative to domestic equity issues. Cross-border equity trading is now substantial. The tremendous increase in cross-border equity trading has improved the ability of the financial system to match savers' funds with the highest-value users. But it exposes savers to risks unfamiliar a generation ago. For example, a stock market crash in Japan could affect the ability of a Japanese bank to pay its creditors around the world.

Global stock and bond transactions are likely to become even more important in the 1990s. In the 1980s, sales and purchases of bonds and stocks involving a U.S. resident and a nonresident were about 9% of gross domestic product (GDP). By the beginning of the 1990s, they were 93%. In Japan, the corresponding figures are 7% and 119%; in Germany, 8% and 58%. The internationally integrated financial markets in New York, London, Tokyo, and other cities are making the financial system truly global.

institutions to change. Three reasons account for most financial regulation: (1) provision of information, (2) maintenance of financial stability, and (3) advancement of other policy objectives.

Provision of Information

The quality of many of the things people buy—from fish in the supermarket to clothing in a department store—is relatively easy to assess. The quality of other goods and services—from cars to legal services—is harder to judge. Even more difficult to evaluate are debt instruments traded in financial markets. A small investor cannot easily judge whether shares or bonds issued by a business are safe investments. The investor could pay a financial analyst or an accounting firm to evaluate corporations issuing stocks and bonds, but the cost of gathering this information is likely to be prohibitive. Because of the demand for this type of service, private firms organized to collect information on the quality of financial instruments. (Moody's Investor Service and Standard and Poor's Corporation are leading examples.) These firms earn profits by selling the information to individual investors.

However, private firms are not always able to collect truthful information. As a result, the federal government has intervened in financial markets to require issuers of financial instruments to disclose information about their financial condition and to impose penalties on issuers that do not comply. The leading federal regulatory body for financial markets in the United States is the Securities and Exchange Commission (SEC). It was established by the Securities Act of 1933 in response to investors' concerns over the stock market crash of 1929 and fraud by securities dealers during the 1920s. The SEC mandates that corporations issuing bonds or stocks disclose information about earnings, sales, assets, and liabilities. It also limits trading by managers owning large amounts of a firm's stock or others having privileged information (often called *insider trading*). These regulations ensure that securities dealers communicate information and that investors are protected from fraud. The SEC prosecuted two leading financiers of the 1980s, Ivan Boesky and Michael Milken, for violating information disclosure and insider trading rules. In derivative markets, the Commodities Futures Trading Commission (CFTC) guards against fraud in futures trading.

Maintenance of Financial Stability

Most regulation of the financial system is concerned with its stability, meaning the ability of financial markets and intermediaries to provide the three key services (risk sharing, liquidity, and information) in the face of economic disturbances. For example, if the stock market were to cease functioning efficiently, stock liquidity would be reduced, and individuals' willingness to hold stocks would diminish. Companies' ability to raise capital for investment and job creation would therefore be hindered. Reductions in the ability of the financial system to provide the three key services raise the cost of moving funds from savers to borrowers. For instance, many economists link the severity of the Great Depression of the 1930s to the breakdown in the banking system's ability to provide financial services. A sudden collapse of a segment of the financial system can lead to sharp reductions in economic activity. Such dramatic instances can lead to new government regulation. Indeed, the length and depth of the Great Depression were responsible for the development of many elements of U.S. financial regulation.

Because most financial assets are held by intermediaries such as banks or insurance companies, policymakers are concerned about the financial soundness of those intermediaries. The federal government has implemented four types of regulations that address such concerns: disclosure of information, prevention of fraud, limitations on competition, and safety of investors' funds. We analyze these regulations in Part III.

Advancement of Other Policy Objectives

Financial regulation also may be used to further public policy objectives unrelated to the efficiency of the financial system. These objectives include controlling the money supply and encouraging particular activities, such as homeownership.

▼ TABLE 3.1   REGULATION OF FINANCIAL INSTITUTIONS AND MARKETS IN THE UNITED STATES

Effect on Key Services of the Financial System

Regulatory body	Risk sharing	Liquidity	Information
Securities and Exchange Commission (SEC)	—	Supervises trading in organized exchanges and financial markets	Mandates information disclosure
Commodities Futures Trading Commission (CFTC)	—	Sets rules for trading in futures markets	—
Office of the Comptroller of the Currency (OCC)	Restricts assets held by federally chartered commercial institutions	—	Charters and examines federally chartered banks
Federal Deposit Insurance Corporation (FDIC)	Provides insurance to depositors	Promotes liquidity of bank deposits	Examines insured banks
Federal Reserve System	Restricts assets of participating financial institutions	Promotes liquidity of bank deposits	Examines commercial banks in Federal Reserve System
State banking and insurance commissions	Impose restrictions on assets held Impose restrictions on bank branching	—	Charter and examine state-chartered banks and insurance companies
Office of Thrift Supervision (OTS)	Restricts assets held by savings and loan associations	—	Examines savings and loan associations
National Credit Union Administration	Restricts assets held by credit unions	—	Charters and examines federally chartered credit unions

Controlling the Money Supply. Because banks affect movements in the money supply, which in turn influence the economic variables that affect people's daily lives, policymakers have implemented rules to facilitate control of the quantity of money. For example, the Federal Reserve System requires banks to hold a specified fraction of their deposits in cash or in accounts with the Fed, giving the Fed some control over the money supply.

Encouraging Particular Activities. Several regulations are designed to promote homeownership, a politically popular objective. One way in which the federal government fosters homeownership is by allowing the deduction

MOVING FROM THEORY TO PRACTICE...

THE ECONOMIST MARCH 14, 1992

Taiwan: Sitting On Its Billions

In only one year during the past 20 has Taiwan not saved more than it invested. Since 1982 the excess has been no less than 5% of GDP; in 1986 it reached 20%. Like other countries in this position (Japan, for instance), Taiwan has inevitably run current-account surpluses. Unlike Japan, Taiwan has also usually seen net inflows of capital. The result has been one of the world's biggest accumulations of financial assets.

At the end of January, deposits in Taiwan's legal banking system were NT$7.5 [NT$ = New Taiwan dollars] trillion ($300 billion)—roughly $15,000 for each person on the island. Deposits outside the legal system, together with private hoards of gold, might add nearly as much again to liquid savings…

These may sound like enviable problems—and they are no problem at all for the western private bankers who are discreetly flocking to the island to pick over the world's biggest idle concentration of personal wealth. But they point to a serious flaw in Taiwan's economic management. The Taiwanese economy grew during the four decades to 1990 at an annual real rate of 9% and is still expected to grow by 7% a year as far as the eye can see. It can lay claim to being one of the world's most successful economies. Yet hyperconservative financial policies are squandering its potential…

A large chunk of savings is not recycled into productive investment. At the end of 1991 the postal savings system—whose assets are second only to those of the government-run banks—had loans equal to a little more than 0.1% of its assets; 83% of postal savings were idly on deposit with the central bank. Credit and farmers' co-operatives did better than that, with 50–60% of their assets out in loans. But overall some 30–40% of the money legally deposited in Taiwan is immobilised in the central bank, or in institutions under its control. It is no wonder that surveys in the mid-1980s found that 45% of all lending was done through private "credit clubs," with 20 or so mainly middle-class members, or on the black market. The equity market offers little alternative. New issues are designed to raise cash for the owners of a company, rather than for the company itself. The secondary market is closer to a casino than to an organised first-world stock exchange. Nor is foreign competition likely to change things much…

Incredibly, the central bank said last year that, because of heavy financing demands arising in the next few years, it was important to keep money inside the country. Such mercantilism is costly. The government is paying 8–9% to borrow at home when it could be tapping world markets at several percentage points less…

It would make far more sense this time to start removing the restraints that dam Taiwan's vast flow of savings away from where it can do the most good.

ANALYZING THE NEWS...

The financial system plays a crucial role in economic development and growth: It brings together savers and borrowers. That is, active financial markets and/or institutions provide the link between savers' funds and able borrowers.

The problems of Taiwan's financial system are often faced in the process of economic development. The Japanese financial system, for example, modernized very slowly in the 1960s and 1970s, with rapid change occurring only since the early 1980s.

(a) Taiwan's financial system has not performed its role of matching savers and borrowers. Households wanting to buy new cars or homes are forced to save up the full amount of the purchase price, and businesses are forced to save up their profits to finance spending on new plants and equipment. While the Taiwanese seem rich (measured by bank deposits per capita), the nation is hindering its ability to grow by not providing ways for borrowers to tap the large pool of savings.

(b) The current problems in matching savers and borrowers create opportunities for clever entrepreneurs. Already, individuals have organized private credit clubs that, instead of banks, are providing most investment funds by direct matching of savers and borrowers.

The experience of other newly industrialized economies suggests that banks will eventually increase their role in commercial lending.

(c) The Taiwanese stock market is perceived to be an ineffective means for firms to raise funds. This ineffectiveness imposes costs on Taiwan's economy. When financial markets are poorly developed, savers cannot make informed decisions about investments. Financial institutions can step in to gather and monitor information to allocate savers' funds. These institutions are efficient at obtaining information about a business in its early stages. However, obtaining information on mature businesses from financial markets is less costly for investors. Thus it is in Taiwan's economic interest to develop liquid financial markets.

For further thought...

Using Taiwan's experience as a model, what advice would you give to emerging economies in Eastern Europe regarding their newborn financial systems?

Source: Excerpted from "Taiwan: Sitting on Its Billions," March 14, 1992. ©1992 The Economist Newspaper Group, Inc. Reprinted with permission.

of interest paid on a home mortgage from income subject to federal income taxes, something the taxpayer no longer can do for interest on a car loan or credit card debt. In addition, Congress created large government-sponsored financial intermediaries to make home mortgages accessible to many borrowers and, before 1980, restricted savings and loan associations and mutual savings banks to mortgage loans. This restriction was intended to make more funds available for mortgage lending; in fact, it made these institutions vulnerable to certain types of risks. Regulators weakened these limitations in the 1980s. Many economists and policymakers question whether regulations designed to direct savings to finance home mortgages improved the efficiency of the financial system.

The federal government has also intervened in credit markets to subsidize lending for agriculture, college tuition, and other activities that it regards as beneficial to the economy. In each case, the interventions created specialized intermediaries and provided guarantees for certain types of loans.

Q: What are the goals of financial regulation?

A: Regulation generally seeks to (1) guarantee provision of information, (2) improve financial stability, or (3) advance other policy objectives.

Effects of Regulation

Regulation affects the ability of financial markets and institutions to provide risk-sharing, liquidity, and information services. Restrictions on the types of instruments that can be traded in markets affect liquidity. Regulations limiting the ability of financial institutions to hold certain types of assets or to operate in various geographic locations affect risk sharing and the potential for diversification. Policymakers should consider the effects of regulation on the financial system's ability to provide risk-sharing opportunities, liquidity, and information. Stringent limits placed on these activities in domestic markets create opportunities for international competition. Table 3.1 presents a summary of current regulation of U.S. financial institutions and markets and its effects on their key services.

Key Terms and Concepts

Assets
Asymmetric information
Auction markets
Borrowers
Capital markets
Cash markets
Debt
   Default
   Interest
   Intermediate-term debt
   Long-term debt

Maturity
Principal
   Short-term debt
Derivative markets
Diversification
Dividends
Equity
Exchanges
Financial futures
Financial innovation
Financial institutions

Financial integration

Financial intermediation

Financial markets

Financial system

Intermediaries

Key financial system services
    Information
    Liquidity
    Risk sharing

Liabilities

Money markets

Options

Over-the-counter (OTC) markets

Portfolio

Primary markets

Savers

Secondary markets

Summary

1. The basic motivation for financial trade, and hence for the development of a financial system, is that individuals, businesses, and governments sometimes need to save and at other times need to borrow. The financial system channels funds from savers to borrowers, giving savers claims on borrowers' future income.

2. The financial system provides three key services: risk sharing, liquidity, and information. These services make financial claims attractive to savers and can lower the cost of finance for borrowers. Differences in the demand for and the cost of providing these services partially explain changes in the U.S. financial system over time, as well as differences among financial systems internationally.

3. The financial system brings together savers and borrowers in two ways. In direct finance through financial markets, individual savers hold the claims issued by individual borrowers. In indirect finance through financial intermediaries, claims held by savers are claims against intermediaries that are backed by their portfolios of assets, which are claims on the borrowers.

4. Financial assets may be categorized in five ways: (a) whether they are debt or equity; (b) whether the claims are newly issued (primary market) or already outstanding (secondary market); (c) whether the claims mature in less than one year (money market) or more than one year (capital market); (d) whether

claims are traded by auction or over-the-counter; and (e) whether the claims are traded in cash or derivative markets.

5. Financial intermediaries act as go-betweens for savers and borrowers. These institutions acquire funds from savers and then make loans to or purchase financial instruments issued by borrowers. In the process, financial intermediaries provide risk-sharing, liquidity, and information services that especially benefit small savers and borrowers.

6. Changes in the financial system are called financial innovations. Shifts in the demand for and cost of providing risk-sharing, liquidity, and information services lead to changes in the operation of financial markets and institutions.

7. An important measure of the financial system's efficiency is its degree of integration, or the way in which markets are tied together geographically. Financial markets have become much more integrated over many years in the United States and are now becoming integrated globally.

8. Another cause of differences and changes in financial systems is variation in regulation. Three basic motivations for regulatory intervention are: (a) to guarantee provision of information, (b) to maintain the stability of the financial system, and (c) to advance other policy objectives.

Review Questions

1. Why do households save? Why do businesses borrow? Why are the financial services of risk sharing, liquidity, and information valued by savers and borrowers?

2. Under what circumstances does financial regulation improve the efficiency of the financial system?

3. What is meant by *integration* of financial markets? What effect would increased integration of financial markets, domestically and internationally, have on returns for savers? On costs to borrowers?

4. What are the benefits to savers and borrowers if financial markets communicate all available information about financial instruments via their prices?

   In Questions 5–10, categorize the transactions described according to whether they: (a) rely on financial markets or intermediaries; (b) occur in the primary or secondary market; or (c) are carried out in the money or capital market.

5. A bank makes a 30-year mortgage loan to a household.

6. The bank sells a mortgage loan to a government sponsored financial intermediary.

7. ABC corporation opens for business by selling shares of stock to 10 private investors.

8. Joan Robinson sells her shares of ABC stock to someone else.

9. The DEF money market mutual fund buys $100,000 of three-month Treasury bills in the government's weekly auction.

10. DEF buys $100,000 of three-month Treasury bills from First Bank.

Analytical Problems

11. An important attribute of financial assets that is sometimes forgotten is their tax treatment. Suppose that you are an investor with a choice between three assets that are identical in every way except in their rate of return and taxability. Which asset yields the highest after-tax return?

    A: interest rate 10%, interest taxed at a 40% rate.
    B: interest rate 8%, interest taxed at a 25% rate.
    C: interest rate 6.5%, no tax on interest.

12. Suppose that asset A in Question 1 paid 11%. Would your answer change?

13. Why do people want to share risk? After all, the only way to get rich is to take risks.

14. Do banks and other financial intermediaries like high interest rates? Why or why not?

15. Traditionally, financial markets in Germany and Japan have played a small role in financing businesses relative to markets in the United States and Great Britain, while financial institutions play a larger role in corporate finance. What factors determine whether an economy relies more heavily on one mechanism or the other?

16. You have not yet studied the effects of financial regulation on incentives for borrowers and savers. Do you think that insuring savers against fluctuations in the value of claims on financial institutions necessarily makes the financial system more efficient? Why or why not?

Data Question

17. Look in a current issue of *The Wall Street Journal*. Try to find assets that are examples of each of the financial markets discussed in this chapter (primary and secondary, money and capital, auction and over-the-counter, direct and derivative). Compare the yields on these different assets. Can you explain the different yields?

Appendix: Financial Instruments

Financial instruments are the tools by which financial markets channel funds from savers to borrowers and provide returns to savers. We will first consider the differences among the major instruments, or securities, traded in the financial system. For convenience, we analyze money market and capital market instruments separately. (Recall that money market claims mature in less than a year and capital market claims mature in more than a year.) Both money market and capital market assets are actively traded in U.S. financial markets. We introduce the most widely used instruments here and discuss them in more detail in Parts II and III.

Money Market Instruments

The short maturity of money market assets doesn't allow much time for their prices to vary. Thus these instruments are safe investments for short-term surpluses of households and firms. However, in making investment decisions, savers must still consider the possibility of default—the chance that the borrower will be unable to repay all the amount borrowed plus interest at maturity.

U.S. Treasury Bills. United States Treasury securities are short-term debt obligations of the U.S. government. They also are the most liquid money market instrument because they have the largest trading volume. The federal government has the option of raising taxes and/or issuing currency in order to repay the amount borrowed, so there is virtually no risk of default.[†] Treasury securities with maturities of less than one year are called Treasury

[†] Technically, in the United States, the Federal Reserve issues currency.

bills (T-bills). Although individuals can hold them, the largest holders of T-bills are commercial banks, followed by other financial intermediaries, businesses, and foreign investors.

Commercial Paper. Commercial paper issues provide a liquid, short-term investment for savers and a source of funds for corporations. High-quality, well-known firms and financial institutions use commercial paper to raise funds. Because these borrowers generally are the most credit-worthy, the default risk is small, but the interest rate is higher than that on Treasury bills. The growth in the commercial paper market during the past two decades is part of a shift by many corporations toward direct finance (and away from bank loans).

Bankers' Acceptances. Designed to facilitate international trade, bankers' acceptances are instruments that establish credit between parties who do not know each other. A bankers' acceptance is a checklike promise that the bank will pay the amount of funds indicated to the recipient. It is issued by a firm (usually an importer) and is payable on a date indicated. The bank that marks the draft "accepted" guarantees the payment to the recipient (usually an exporter or its representing bank). The issuing firm is required to deposit funds in the bank sufficient to cover the draft; if it does not do so, the bank is still obligated to make good on the draft. The bank's good name is likely to enable an importer to buy goods from an overseas exporter that lacks knowledge about whether the importer will be able to pay. In recent years, acceptances generally have been resold in secondary markets and held by other banks, households, and businesses.

Repurchase Agreements. Repurchase agreements, also known as repos or RPs, are used for cash management by large corporations. They are very short-term loans, typically with maturities of less than two weeks. In many cases a firm loans a bank money overnight. For example, if a large firm such as IBM has idle cash, it purchases T-bills from a bank that agrees to buy them back the next morning at a higher price, reflecting the accumulated interest. The T-bills serve as collateral; that is, if the borrower defaults, the lender receives the T-bills. Since their inception in 1969, repurchase agreements have become a significant source of funds for banks.

Federal (Fed) Funds. Federal funds instruments represent overnight loans between banks of their deposits with the Federal Reserve System (the U.S. central bank). Banking regulations require that banks deposit a percentage of their deposits as reserves with the Fed. If a bank is temporarily low on reserves, it can borrow funds from another bank that has reserves greater than the required level. The federal funds market reflects the credit needs of commercial banks, so the *federal funds rate* (the interest rate charged on these overnight loans) is closely watched by money market analysts. When it is high, banks need additional funds; when it is low, banks have low credit needs.

Eurodollars. Eurodollars are U.S. dollars deposited in foreign branches of U.S. banks or in foreign banks outside the United States (not necessarily in Europe). Rather than being converted into the currency of the foreign country, the deposits remain denominated in dollars. U.S. banks can then borrow these funds. Eurodollar funds raised abroad have become an important source of funds for American banks.

Negotiable Bank Certificates of Deposit. A certificate of deposit (CD) is a fixed-maturity instrument sold by a bank to depositors; it pays principal and interest at maturity. You might, for example, take the $1000 you earned over vacation and put it in a CD for six months at 5% interest (an annual rate). After six months, your investment would be worth $1025. Before 1961, CDs were illiquid because they were nonnegotiable; that is, they could not be sold by the depositors to someone else prior to redemption. In 1961, Citibank created the *negotiable certificate of deposit*—a CD in a large denomination (over $100,000, and today typically over $1,000,000), which could be sold again in a secondary market. Negotiable CDs are an important source of funds for banks today and are held principally by mutual funds and nonfinancial corporations.

Concluding Remarks. Figure A3.1 shows the amounts of the principal money market instruments outstanding in 1970, 1980, and 1992.

▼ FIGURE A3.1

Money Market Instruments in the United States
U.S. Treasury bills, commercial paper, and negotiable CDs are the leading money market instruments. Since 1980, commercial paper issues have grown relative to negotiable CD issues.

Sources: Federal Reserve Flow of Funds Accounts; Council of Economic Advisers, Economic Report of the President; Federal Reserve Bulletin.

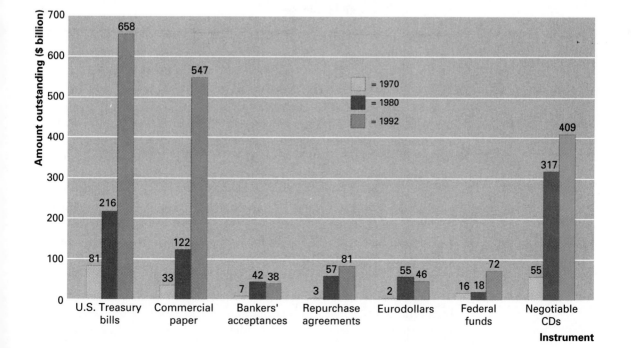

Information on interest rates for these instruments appears each business day in the Money Rates column of *The Wall Street Journal.* Note the especially rapid growth in commercial paper, repurchase agreements, Eurodollars, and negotiable certificates of deposit. In Part III, we show that this growth reflects important changes in the business of banking during the past two decades.

Capital Market Instruments

Because capital market instruments have longer maturities than money market instruments, they are subject to greater price fluctuations. For this reason, borrowers who seek to use funds for a long period of time and savers with long investment horizons invest in them. With the exception of U.S. government obligations, all capital market instruments contain some risk of default.

U.S. Treasury Securities. Intermediate-term and long-term U.S. Treasury securities are bonds issued by the federal government to finance budget deficits. They are widely traded and hence are liquid. These government securities are held by domestic banks and households, foreigners, and the Federal Reserve System.

U.S. Government Agency Securities. United States government agency securities are intermediate-term or long-term bonds issued by the federal government or government-sponsored agencies. For example, the Farm Credit System issues bonds to raise money to finance agricultural activities, and the Government National Mortgage Association (GNMA) issues bonds to finance home mortgages. Many such securities are officially guaranteed by the government (with a pledge of the government's "full faith and credit"); others are implicitly guaranteed, so that the default risk is still low.

State and Local Government Bonds. State and local government bonds (often called municipal bonds) are intermediate- or long-term bonds issued by municipalities and state governments. These governmental units use the funds borrowed to build schools, roads, and other large capital projects. The bonds are exempt from federal income taxation (and typically also income taxation by the issuing state). These bonds often are held by high-tax-bracket households, commercial banks, and life insurance companies. Although generally considered safe, these instruments do have some default risk. In the early 1930s, for example, many state and local governments defaulted on their bonds.

Stocks. Stocks are issued as equity claims by corporations and represent the largest single category of capital market assets. However, new stock issues are not a major source of funding for nonfinancial businesses in the

United States and many other countries. From the end of World War II through 1980, new share issues accounted for about 5% of total funds raised. During the late 1980s, new share issues were substantially *negative* (–30% of funds raised in 1988, for example), as U.S. corporations used funds raised with debt to buy back shares. That trend reversed in the early 1990s.

Corporate Bonds. Corporate bonds are intermediate- and long-term obligations issued by large, high-quality corporations to finance plant and equipment spending. Typically, corporate bonds pay interest twice a year and repay the principal amount borrowed at maturity. There are many variations, however. *Convertible bonds,* for example, allow the holder to convert the debt into equity (for a specified number of shares). By using such variations, firms sometimes can lower their borrowing costs by giving bond buyers an extra return if the firm does exceptionally well. Corporate bonds are not as liquid as government securities because they are less widely traded. Corporate bonds have greater default risk than government bonds, but they generally fluctuate less in price than corporate equities.

Although the corporate bond market is smaller than the stock market in the United States, it is more important for raising funds because corporations issue new shares infrequently. Most funds raised through financial markets take the form of corporate bonds. Investors in corporate bonds are a diverse group, including households, life insurance companies, and pension funds.

Mortgages. Mortgages are loans (usually long term) to households or businesses to purchase buildings or land, with the underlying asset (house, plant, or piece of land) serving as collateral. In the United States, the mortgage market is the largest debt market. Residential mortgages, the largest component, are issued by savings institutions and commercial banks. Mortgage loans for industrial and agricultural borrowers are made by life insurance companies and commercial banks. Since World War II, the growth of the mortgage market has been spurred by federal government interventions to encourage homeownership by creating a liquid secondary national mortgage market. Three government agencies—Federal National Mortgage Association (FNMA), Government National Mortgage Association (GNMA), and the Federal Home Loan Mortgage Corporation (FHLMC)—borrow in bond markets to provide funds for mortgage financing.

Commercial Bank Loans. Commercial bank loans include loans to businesses and consumers made by banks and finance companies. Secondary markets for commercial bank loans are not as well developed as for other capital market instruments, so loans are less liquid than mortgages. In Chapter 13, we show how recent developments in banking and financial markets are improving the liquidity of these loans.

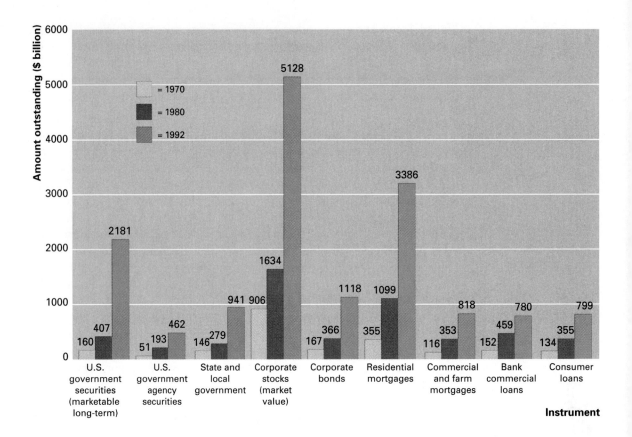

Capital Market Instruments in the United States

The leading capital market instruments are corporate stocks, residential mortgages, and U.S. government securities. Since 1970, the share of outstanding capital market instruments represented by U.S. government securities has doubled.

Sources: Federal Reserve Flow of Funds Accounts; Federal Reserve Bulletin.

Concluding Remarks. Figure A3.2 summarizes the amounts of principal capital market instruments outstanding in 1970, 1980, and 1992. Note the enormous growth in U.S. government and government agency securities. This growth reflects the borrowing necessitated by large federal budget deficits in the 1980s and early 1990s and the increasing prominence of federal credit agencies in the capital market.

part II

The Financial System and Interest Rate Determination

CHAPTER 4

Interest Rates and Rates of Return

The news media discuss interest rates every day—and with good reason. Interest rates affect individuals' decisions about whether to spend more or save to buy a house or for retirement. They also affect decisions by businesspeople about whether to invest in new plants and equipment or buy Treasury bonds. In 1992, interest rates on bank deposits and money market funds declined to about 3%, which was bad news for investors who had obtained double-digit (10% or greater) rates only a few years earlier. As a result, many individual savers sought higher interest rates from investments, such as long-term Treasury securities and corporate bonds. Investment decisions are complex, however, because thousands of financial instruments are available.

Before continuing with the study of the financial system, you need to become more familiar with the term *interest rates*. In this chapter, we describe how interest rates and rates of return are measured and how to compare rates of return for different financial instruments. These tools are important for understanding the meaning of interest rates, and we apply them when explaining how interest rates are determined and how savers allocate their wealth (in Chapters 5–8).

Three questions shape the discussion in this chapter. **Q:** How can returns on alternative investments with different interest rates be compared? **Q:** How are the interest rate and the price of a financial asset related? **Q:** What is the relevant interest rate for saving and investment decisions?

Categorizing Interest Rates

When you place your savings in a financial market or institution, the financial system channels those funds to borrowers. The funds are assets to you (the saver) and liabilities, or claims on future income, to the borrowers. If you save through a bank, the bank pays you interest, and borrowers pay the bank interest for the indirect use of your funds. Likewise, if you buy a Treasury bond, the U.S. government pays you interest for the use of your money.

Debt instruments (also known as credit market instruments) are essentially IOUs, or promises by a borrower to repay principal plus interest to a lender. Because individual savers and borrowers have different needs, the IOUs sold by borrowers to savers in the financial system take different forms and result in various patterns of repayment. For convenience, we group credit market instruments into a few simple categories, in order to explain what different interest rates actually mean for savers and borrowers.

Credit Market Instruments

In Chapter 3, we introduced the major **credit market instruments** in the financial system. We can classify these instruments as simple loans, discount bonds, coupon bonds, and fixed payment loans. The first two involve a single payment of principal and interest, whereas the last two involve multiple payments of interest and/or principal.

Simple Loan. With a **simple loan,** the borrower receives from the lender an amount of funds called the *principal* and agrees to repay the lender the principal plus an additional amount called *interest* (as a fee for using the funds) at a given date (maturity). For example, suppose that Sunbank makes a one-year simple loan of $10,000 at 10% interest to Nelson's Nurseries. We can illustrate this transaction on a time line to show the return to the lender (saver), or payment of interest and principal by the borrower. After one year, Nelson's would repay the principal plus interest: $10,000 + (0.10) ($10,000), or $11,000. On a time line, the lender views the transaction as[†]

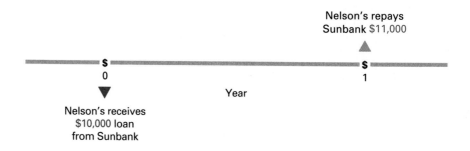

† While we illustrate the payments from the saver's perspective, the interest rate concepts we develop in the chapter are important for both savers' and borrowers' decisions.

We can generalize this transaction by using an expression for computing the total payment to a lender of principal P and interest at the interest rate i for a simple loan:

$$\text{Total payment to lender} = \underbrace{P}_{\text{Principal}} + \underbrace{iP}_{\text{Interest}} = P(1 + i).$$

The most common type of simple loan is a short-term commercial loan from a bank.

Discount Bond. The second type of credit market instrument, a **discount bond**, also is repaid by the borrower in a single payment. In this case, however, the borrower pays the lender the amount of the loan, called the *face value* (or par value), at maturity but receives less than the face value initially. For example, if Nelson's Nurseries issued a one-year discount bond with a face value of $10,000 and an implicit interest rate of 10%, it would receive approximately $9091 ($10,000/1.10) and repay $10,000 after one year. Hence the time line for Nelson's Nurseries discount bond would be

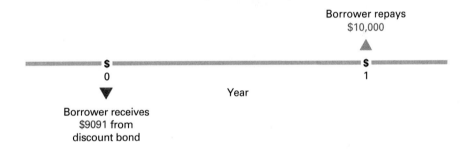

The lender receives interest of $10,000 − $9091 = $909 for the year. The most common types of discount obligations are U.S. savings bonds, U.S. Treasury bills, and zero-coupon bonds.

Coupon Bond. The third category of credit market instrument, the **coupon bond**, requires multiple payments of interest on a regular basis, such as semiannually or annually, and a payment of the face value at maturity. A coupon bond specifies the maturity date, face value, issuer (a governmental unit or private corporation), and coupon rate. The *coupon rate* equals the yearly coupon payment divided by the face value. For example, if Pond Industries issued a $10,000, 20-year bond, promising a coupon rate of 10%, it would pay $1000 per year for the 20 years and a final payment of $10,000 at the end of 20 years (the face value). The time line of payments on the Pond Industries' coupon bond would be

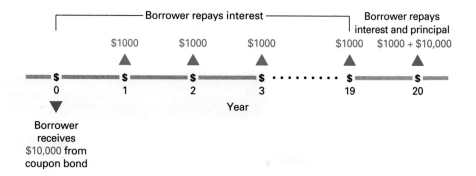

Long-term U.S. Treasury bonds and notes and long-term corporate bonds of relatively well-known firms are the most prominent examples of coupon bonds.

Fixed Payment Loan. The fourth category of credit market instrument, a **fixed payment loan**, requires the borrower to make a regular periodic payment (monthly, quarterly, or annually) to the lender. The payments include both interest and principal; thus at maturity there is no lump sum payment of principal. Commonly used fixed payment loans include home mortgages, student loans, and various installment loans (such as automobile loans). For example, repaying a $10,000, 10-year student loan with a 9% interest rate means a monthly payment of approximately $127. The time line of payments from the lender's perspective would be

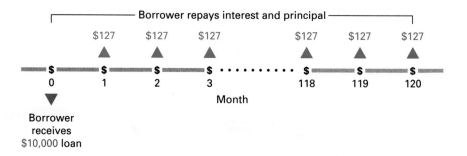

Although we can group most credit market instruments according to the four categories just discussed, the changing needs of savers and borrowers lead to development of new instruments having characteristics of more than one category (see Box 4.1).

Comparing Instruments. We can now turn to the important task of comparing the returns from simple loans, discount bonds, coupon bonds, and fixed payment loans. This comparison is not easy because the four types of

Consider this...

BOX 4.1

Can They STRIP? Creating New Financial Instruments

In the late 1970s and early 1980s, the U.S. Treasury issued only two types of instruments: Treasury bills, which are discount bonds, and long-term Treasury bonds, which are coupon bonds. However, interest rates began fluctuating significantly, and investors could not predict whether they would rise or fall from their current level. Investors were concerned that if interest rates fell over the life of a coupon bond, they would have to reinvest their coupon payments at an interest rate lower than the original coupon rate. Therefore, investors demanded longer-term discount bonds, on which they would know the exact return if they held the instruments to maturity.

With the hope of earning a profit, financial markets responded to investors' demands. In 1982, Merrill Lynch created a new instrument called a TIGR (Treasury Investment Growth Receipt), which works like Treasury bills (discount bonds). Merrill Lynch buys $1 million of 20-year Treasury bonds with a coupon rate of say 9%. It is then entitled to receive $90,000 each year for 20 years from the Treasury, plus the $1 million face value after 20 years. Merrill Lynch, however, does not hold the bonds. Instead it sells $90,000 of one-year TIGR bills, which are fully backed by the underlying $1 million of 20-year bonds, to investors. The rights to these individual interest payments received by investors are known as Treasury "Strips."

The Treasury soon realized the potential profits of offering longer-term bills and, in 1984, introduced its own version of Merrill Lynch's innovation. Called STRIPS (Separate Trading of Registered Interest and Principal of Securities), the new instrument allowed investors to register and trade ownership for each interest payment and the face value. Hence, individuals could effectively obtain long-term discount bonds or coupon bonds from the government, increasing their options for investment.

instruments make payments to lenders (savers) in different amounts at different times. The solution to this problem is the concept of **present value**, a measure that provides a way to compare interest rates on different instruments.

Present Value

Comparing interest and principal payments on different credit market instruments can be difficult. Is a 30-year, $10,000 Treasury bond with an annual coupon payment of $800 a better investment than a six-month Treasury bill which gives you $10,000 for an investment of $9,500? Would you be better off financing your new home with a 15-year mortgage at 9% or by borrowing for five years at 8% and refinancing thereafter? To decide, you need to consider several factors: How often do you want to receive or make payments? What is the interest rate? What is the time until maturity? Recall, though, that payments are made at different times under alternative types of promises—periodically in coupon bonds and fixed payment loans and all at once in simple loans and discount bonds. How then can you decide which instrument offers the highest return?

The problem is this: Dollars paid in different periods are not in the same units. Suppose, for example, that a friend offers you a dollar and says that you can either have it today or a year from today. Which would you pick? Most people would take the dollar today. A dollar received in the future is worth less to them than a dollar received today. Because credit market instruments pay different amounts in different periods, we need to devise a way to compare amounts paid at different times.

To understand the difficulty of comparing credit market instruments, consider the difficulty of comparing three items weighing 1 pound, 8 ounces, and ¼ ton. How can you total the weights? Because they all are in different units, you cannot add them directly. However, if you convert them to a common unit, say, pounds, you can then add them. That is, 1 lb. + ½ lb. + 500 lbs. = 501½ lbs. Just as you cannot add weights in different units, you cannot add measures of money paid in different periods. The reason is that money paid at different times has different values. What we need to do is find the present value of each payment by putting all payments in *today's dollars* so that we can add them.

Let's see how present value works. Suppose that you have just won $6500 in a contest. You would like to save the winnings so that eventually you can buy a car. You take the money to your bank, which offers you 5% interest each year. After one year, you have a total of $6825, or your original $6500 plus interest of $325. The time line is

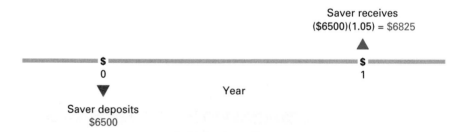

What if you want and can afford to save the money for longer than one year? If the interest rate remained constant at 5% and you reinvested, or rolled over, your principal and accumulated interest, you would earn 5% interest on your accumulated savings each period. This process of earning interest on the interest (as well as on the principal) is known as **compounding.** At the end of two years, you would have ($6825)(1.05) = $7166. At the end of three years, you would have ($7166)(1.05) = $7525. At the end of n years, you would have $(\$6500)(1.05)^n$, as shown on the time line at the top of the next page.

Looking at the payments of interest using a time line helps explain the value that savers and borrowers put on credit market instruments. The next step is to formalize the preceding discussion by developing a measure to use in comparing different credit market instruments.

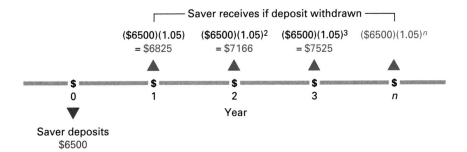

How do savers and borrowers evaluate credit market instruments? They do so by placing each payment in present value terms. Let's return to the example of saving for a car, where you put aside $6500 today. At an interest rate of 5%, you could buy an $8300 car five years from now. If 5% is the prevailing interest rate for savers, $6500 today and $8300 in five years have the same present value. That is, at a 5% annual interest rate, you would be indifferent about receiving $6500 today or $8300 in five years.

Now let's generalize this concept. What is the present value of $1 received n years in the future? If we assume that the interest rate is constant at rate i over the n years,

$$\text{Present value of future } \$1 = \frac{\$1}{(1+i)^n} \; . \qquad (4.1)$$

Equation (4.1) shows that a future dollar is worth less than a current dollar because the denominator is greater than 1. In other words, you can invest a dollar today and earn interest at rate i.

The concept of present value helps to sort out the difference between the sum of payments made over time and the value of those payments today. Suppose that Mary Lucky wins $2 million in the state lottery, to be paid in $100,000 installments each year for 20 years. If the interest rate is currently 10% and expected to remain at 10% for the next 20 years, Ms. Lucky is not as rich as she thought. The $100,000 she receives this year has a present value of $100,000, but next year's payment is worth only $100,000/1.10, or $90,909 in today's dollars. Hence, the sum of the payments over 20 years has a present value of $936,492, or less than half of the stated value of the prize (although we would likely shed no tears for Ms. Lucky).

We use the concept of present value as a measure in evaluating savers' returns from different credit market instruments that have different time patterns for payments. The concept of present value reveals that payments received at different times effectively are in different units. Therefore, savers cannot simply compare total payments to determine which instrument is the best investment. They can compare the returns on different instruments by finding the present value of payments in each year and adding them: The sum of these payments equals the present value of the instrument.

For example, suppose that the interest rate is 10%, and you are offered either a discount bond paying you $1000 in five years or a fixed payment loan paying you $150 per year for five years for a price of $600. Which (if either) should you buy? To answer the question, you need to calculate the present value of the payments from the two financial instruments. The present value of the discount bond's payments is

$$\frac{\text{Present value}}{\text{(discount bond)}} = \frac{\$1000}{1.10^5} = \$620.92,$$

whereas the present value of the payments from the fixed payment loan is

$$\frac{\text{Present value}}{\text{(fixed payment loan)}} = \frac{\$150}{1.10} + \frac{\$150}{1.10^2} + \frac{\$150}{1.10^3} + \frac{\$150}{1.10^4} + \frac{\$150}{1.10^5} = \$568.62.$$

As the present value of the payments from the discount bond is greater than $600 and that of the payments on the fixed payment loan is less than $600, you would be willing to buy the discount bond at the $600 offering price.

Figure 4.1 summarizes repayment methods for the four main categories of credit market instruments—simple loan, discount bond, coupon bond, and fixed payment loan—from the lender's perspective. Each has the same present value: $1000 for a five-year loan at an interest rate of 10%. Note that, although the four instruments have the same present value, the time patterns of the payments differ significantly. In the case of a simple loan or discount bond, for example, no payment is received until year 5. For the coupon bond and the fixed payment loan, however, the lender receives payments each year. Thus, the saver can compare the present values of returns on different credit market instruments, even though the returns in any given period need not be comparable. The comparisons we study here are much easier than some required historically, as you can see in the Other times, other places box.

▶ **C H E C K P O I N T** *Suppose that you are offered a deal from Sports Illustrated magazine: a two-year subscription for $50 or a subscription this year for $30 and another next year for an additional $30. Which deal should you choose?* To make the two methods of payment comparable, you must put them in present value terms. At an interest rate of 5%, the present value of the two one-year subscriptions is $30 + ($30/1.05) = $58.57. Because the present value of the two-year subscription is $50, it is the better deal. ◀

FIGURE 4.1

Time Lines for Credit Market Instrument Repayment
The four main categories of credit market instruments (shown from the lender's perspective) have the same present value, but different time patterns of repayment.

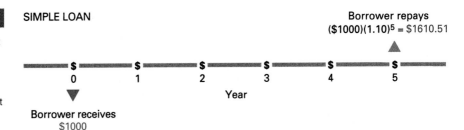

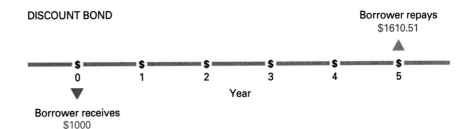

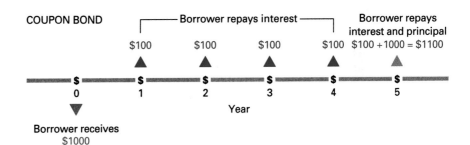

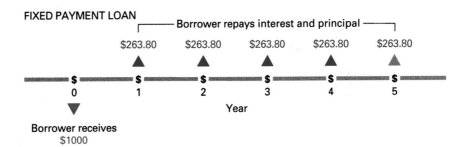

Using Yield to Maturity as a Yardstick

Let's now consider a way to compare the interest rates for different instruments. Savers often confront alternative investment opportunities. For example, which is a better investment to buy: a $10,000 coupon bond for $10,220 with a coupon rate of 8% or a six-month, $10,000 Treasury bill for $9600? How can the saver evaluate which is the best deal in the financial

Other times, other places...

An Interest in Interest

If you think it is hard to compare the interest returns on the many simple loans, discount bonds, coupon bonds, and fixed payment loans available from financial markets and institutions today, imagine comparing rice, pigs, and reindeer! In barter economies, loans are often made "in kind," that is, with payments made in the same kind of goods in which the loan is made. As a result, interest payments are difficult to compute and compare.

Sidney Homer, a distinguished financial economist, once illustrated these complications in describing "interest" arrangements in developing economies. Homer notes that in-kind loans entailed different notions of interest than those we encounter in the high-tech financial marketplace of today. The Ifugao tribes in the Philippines used in-kind loans in this century. In *simple loans,* where the borrower received rice and pigs, the principal was repaid with 100% interest—two pigs for one, for example. The Ifugaos even had a *discount bond* (called a *patang*) whereby interest on the loan of an animal was paid in advance. That is, the borrower received one pig for a two-pig loan, repaying the lender with two pigs. In Northern Siberia earlier in this century, the Kirghez tribes made loans in reindeer, horses, and sheep. The usual interest rate was 100%.

These examples show how the development of a financial system enhances economic development. By substituting financial claims for physical goods, loans can be structured to allow more varied repayment schedules and opportunities.

Source: Sidney Homer and Richard Sylla, *A History of Interest Rates,* 3rd ed., New Brunswick, NJ: Rutgers University Press, 1991, pp. 22–23.

marketplace? The solution is to use a present value calculation but in a way that allows comparison of interest rates. Instead of asking "At the going interest rate, what payment today puts me in the same financial position as some set of payments in the future?" ask "If I pay a price P today for a set of future payments, what is the interest rate at which I could invest P and get the same set of future payments?" Thus, for example, instead of calculating the present value of the payments to be received on a 30-year Treasury bond, we calculate the interest rate at which the money paid for the bond could be invested for 30 years to get the same present value.

That is, we need to find the interest rate at which the present value of the asset's returns is equal to its value today, a measure called the **yield to maturity**. The yield to maturity comes from the economically sensible concept of present value and is the interest rate measure used most often in financial markets. Calculating yields to maturity for alternative investments allows comparison of investments in any of the four categories of credit market instruments. For example, you can compare the yield to maturity on a 30-year Treasury bond and a 20-year fixed payment loan to determine which investment gives you the greatest return. Let's examine the yield to maturity for each of the four types of credit market instruments.

Simple Loans.   The calculation of yield to maturity for a simple loan is straightforward. We seek the interest rate that would make the lender indifferent about having the amount of the loan today or the final payment at maturity. Let's return to the earlier example of a $10,000 loan to Nelson's Nurseries. If the value today of a one-year simple loan to Nelson's is $10,000 at 10% interest, the loan requires payment of the $10,000 plus $1000 in interest one year from now. We calculate the yield to maturity as follows:

$$\text{Value today} = \text{Present value of future payment}$$

$$10,000 = \frac{10,000 + 1000}{1 + i},$$

from which we solve for i:

$$i = \frac{11,000 - 10,000}{10,000} = 0.10, \text{ or } 10\%.$$

Note that the yield to maturity, 10%, is the same as the simple interest rate. From this example, we can generalize that, for simple loans, the yield to maturity and the specified interest rate are equivalent.

Discount Bonds. Calculating the yield to maturity of a discount bond is similar to finding that of a simple loan. For a one-period (quarter, year) discount bond, the yield to maturity is the interest rate that equates the current purchase price with the present value of the future payment. Consider a one-year, $10,000 discount bond of Nelson's Nurseries. We use the same strategy as we did in the case of a simple loan, beginning with the expression for present value. If Nelson's Nurseries receives $9200 today, we calculate the yield to maturity by setting the present value of the future payment equal to the value today, or $9200 = $10,000/(1 + i)$. Solving for i gives

$$i = \frac{10,000 - 9200}{9200} = 0.087, \text{ or } 8.7\%.$$

Generalizing from this example, we note that, for a one-period discount bond at price D with face value F, the yield to maturity i is

$$i = \frac{F - D}{D}. \tag{4.2}$$

Coupon Bonds. Coupon bonds have many payment periods. Because the yield to maturity equates the present value of all the bond's payments with its price today, we write an expression for the present value of each payment, calculate each amount, and add them. For example, suppose that Growthco issued a 10-year, $10,000 coupon bond with an annual coupon payment of $1000. What is the present value of the $1000 received next year? If i is the yield to maturity,

$$\text{Present value of \$1000 payment in one year} = \frac{\$1000}{1+i}.$$

Similarly, the present value of the second year's coupon payment would be

$$\text{Present value of \$1000 payment in two years} = \frac{\$1000/(1+i)}{1+i} = \frac{\$1000}{(1+i)^2}.$$

The last year's payment includes a coupon payment of $1000 plus the face value of $10,000, for a present value of $\$11{,}000/(1+i)^{10}$. So, the present value of the coupon bond is the sum of all 10 future coupon payments plus the payment of the face value at the end.

$$\text{Present value of coupon bond payments} = \frac{\$1000}{1+i} + \frac{\$1000}{(1+i)^2} + \cdots + \frac{\$1000}{(1+i)^{10}} + \frac{\$10{,}000}{(1+i)^{10}}.$$

To calculate the yield to maturity, we find the interest rate that equates this present value to the price of the bond. Typically, this calculation is complex, requiring either a published present value table or a programmable calculator to find the yield to maturity.[†] In general, for a coupon bond with coupon payment C, face value F, and maturity after n periods,[††]

$$\text{Price of coupon bond} = \frac{C}{1+i} + \frac{C}{(1+i)^2} + \cdots + \frac{C}{(1+i)^n} + \frac{F}{(1+i)^n}. \quad (4.3)$$

[†] Using algebraic manipulation, we can simplify the required expression to

$$\text{Price of coupon bond} = \frac{C}{1+i}\left[\frac{(1+i)^{-n}-1}{(1+i)^{-1}-1}\right] + \frac{F}{(1+i)^n}$$
$$= \frac{C}{i}\left[1-(1+i)^{-n}\right] + \frac{F}{(1+i)^n}.$$

Using published present value tables or most programmable calculators, you can calculate the yield to maturity i if you know C, F, n, and the current price.

[††] The case of a coupon bond with infinite maturity—a perpetual, or *consol*, bond— generates a simpler expression. Note that, as n increases toward infinity, the present value of the final (face value) payment approaches zero; it is received too far in the future to have any value today. For example, if $i = 10\%$ and $n = 100$ years, today's value of a $1000 payment 100 years from now equals $\$1000/(1+i)^{100}$, or less than a penny. Hence the price of the bond comes from the present value of the coupon payments:

Present value of payments = Price of consol = C/i.

In Eq. (4.3), we can solve for the yield to maturity i because the coupon payment C, face value F, and number of periods n are known variables. For example, what is the yield to maturity on a 10-year, $1000 bond with a coupon rate of 10% currently selling for $955? Using a programmable calculator or published bond tables, you can calculate the yield to maturity to be about 10.75%. Note that, if the bond were selling for $1000, the yield to maturity would be the same as the coupon rate, 10%. To summarize, if i is the yield to maturity of a coupon bond, the price of the coupon bond today equals the present value of the coupon bond payments discounted at rate i.

Fixed Payment Loans. The calculation of the yield to maturity for a fixed payment loan closely resembles that for a coupon bond. Recall that fixed payment loans require periodic payments of interest and principal but no face value payment at maturity. Consider the example of a 20-year commercial mortgage with annual payments of $12,731. If the loan's value today is $100,000, the yield to maturity can be calculated as the interest rate that solves the equation

$$\text{Value today} = \text{Present value of payments}$$

$$\$100,000 = \frac{\$12,731}{1+i} + \frac{\$12,731}{(1+i)^2} + \cdots + \frac{\$12,731}{(1+i)^{20}}.$$

Using a calculator to solve this equation for i, we find that $i = 11.2\%$. In general,[†] for a fixed payment loan with fixed payments FP, interest rate i, and maturity at period n,

$$\text{Loan value} = \frac{FP}{1+i} + \frac{FP}{(1+i)^2} + \cdots + \frac{FP}{(1+i)^n}. \tag{4.4}$$

Bankers use programmable calculators or published tables to calculate alternative mortgage payments for loan applicants at different interest rates and numbers of periods until maturity. To summarize, if i is the yield to maturity of a fixed payment loan, the amount of the loan today equals the present value of the loan payments discounted at rate i.

Concluding Remarks. The concept of present value provides a way of explaining why a dollar received today is more valuable than a dollar received in the future. A dollar today can be invested to earn interest; a dollar received n years from now has a value of $\$1/(1+i)^n$ or less than $1 today. To

---

[†] This expression can be simplified to

$$\text{Value} = \frac{FP}{i}\left[1 - (1+i)^{-n}\right].$$

obtain the present value of payments for a debt instrument, we calculate the present value of each future payment and then add them. Thus investors can compare returns on alternative financial instruments using the yield to maturity, or the interest rate that equates the value of the instrument today with the total present value of future payments.

▶ C H E C K P O I N T *To make sure that you are comfortable with calculations of present discounted value, write the expression to solve for the yield to maturity: (a) for a simple loan for $500,000 that requires a payment of $700,000 in four years; (b) for a discount bond for which $9000 is initially received by the borrower, who must pay the lender $10,000 in one year; (c) for a corporate bond with a face value of $10,000 and a coupon payment of $1000 with five years until maturity; (d) for a student loan of $2500 to finance tuition for which $315 per year must be paid for 25 years, starting two years after graduation this year.*

Answers:

(a) $500,000 = $700,000/(1 + i)^4$

(b) $i = (\$10,000 - \$9000)/\$9000$

(c) $\$10,000 = 1000/(1 + i) + \$1000/(1 + i)^2 + \$1000/(1 + i)^3 + \$1000/(1 + i)^4 + \$11,000/(1 + i)^5$

(d) $\$2500 = \$315/(1 + i)^2 + \$315/(1 + i)^3 + ... + \$315/(1 + i)^{26}$ ◀

Q: How can returns on alternative investments with different interest rates be compared?

A: We calculate an interest rate measure known as the yield to maturity. The yield to maturity is the interest rate that equates the current value of the obligation with the present value of its payments.

Bond Yields and Prices

The yield to maturity is an important concept because it enables investors to compare returns on credit market instruments that have different maturities and payment patterns. Another application of the concept of yield to maturity is explaining changes in the price of an individual financial instrument over time. Suppose that you are holding a 20-year bond of Bigco with a coupon rate of 9%, and market interest rates rise to 12% for several years. What happens to the price of your bond? Suppose that you expect interest rates to fall during the next several years. Is it a good time to buy 30-year Treasury bonds or three-month Treasury bills? In this section, we demonstrate that the yield to maturity and the price of a credit market instrument are linked. We also show that current and expected future changes in yields lead to changes in the prices of financial instruments, affecting, for example, the value of savings or the cost of a mortgage. We discuss the relation between prices and yields using coupon bonds, but the points made apply generally to all instruments.

To understand how bond yields and prices are linked, let's begin by asking why a bond's price might change. Then we can get more precise about the relationship between yields and prices.

Why Can Price and Face Value Differ?

Suppose that you buy a bond for a face value of $1000 with a yield to maturity of 5%. Now suppose that market interest rates rise to 10%. How much is your bond worth? Nobody would pay $1000 for your bond because doing so results in a 5% yield, which is no longer competitive. To be competitive with the now higher market interest rates, you must lower the asking price for your bond. Only if someone pays a lower price for your bond's future stream of payments will the investor's rate of return rise above 5%. Indeed, you will have to keep lowering the price of your bond until its return rises to 10% and is competitive with the market. Thus, as interest rates fluctuate, so will the market price of your bond, and it may no longer equal the face value.[†]

We can make this relationship between yield to maturity and price more precise by answering the following question: How does the yield to maturity reflect both the initial interest rate and a change in the price of the bond? To begin, we express the yield to maturity for a coupon bond or a fixed payment loan as the sum of two components. The first is the **current yield**, which equals the coupon payment C divided by the current price of the bond P:

$$\text{Current yield} = \frac{C}{P}. \tag{4.5}$$

For example, suppose that a $1000 coupon bond has an annual coupon payment of $100 and is selling for $750. Although the coupon rate is $100/$1000, or 10%, the current yield is

$$\frac{C}{P} = \frac{\$100}{\$750}, \quad \text{or} \quad 13.3\%.$$

Should you compare the 13.3% current yield on this bond with current yields on other bonds to determine how you should invest your savings? To look ahead for a moment, the answer is *no*. Recall that the interest rate used to compare returns on financial instruments is the yield to maturity. The current yield is one component of the yield to maturity, but a second component reflects the future cash flows you would have if you hold the bond to maturity. For example, if you hold the bond to maturity, you expect to receive $1000, realizing a capital *gain* of $250 because you bought the bond for $750. (However, if the price of the bond were greater than $1000, you would still expect to receive only $1000 at maturity, realizing a capital *loss*.)

This analysis leads to three observations:

1. If the current price of the bond P equals the face value F, there is no capital gain or loss from holding the bond until maturity. Hence, the yield to maturity i equals the current yield C/P which is equal to the coupon rate C/F.

[†] As we show in Chapter 7, the price of a bond also may change in response to a change in the borrower's ability to repay the loan. Here we focus only on price changes due to interest rate movements.

2. If the current price is less than the face value, $P < F$, an investor receives a capital gain by holding the bond until maturity. Hence, the yield to maturity i is greater than the current yield C/P, which in turn is greater than the coupon rate C/F.
3. If the current price is greater than the face value, $P > F$, an investor receives a capital loss by holding the bond until maturity. Hence, the yield to maturity i is less than the current yield C/P, which in turn is less than the coupon rate C/F.

These observations hold for any coupon bond and follow directly from our definition of *yield to maturity*. If a 10-year bond with a face value of $1000 and a 10% coupon rate sells for $1000, you receive an interest rate of 10% if you hold the bond for 10 years. This yield to maturity is equal to the current yield and the coupon rate, which also are 10%. If that same bond sold for $900, you would realize a capital gain at maturity, so that the yield to maturity (which is 11.75%) is greater than the current yield ($100/$900 = 11.1%) and the coupon rate ($100/$1000 = 10%). Finally, if the same bond sold for $1100, you would realize a capital loss at maturity, so that the yield to maturity (which, calculated on a programmable calculator, is 8.48%) is less than the current yield ($100/$1100 = 9.09%) and the coupon rate ($100/$1000 = 10%).

The three observations illustrate how the yield to maturity relates to the current yield or coupon rate, depending on whether the bond price is greater than, less than, or equal to its face value. We can use these observations to ask how bond yields and prices are related.

Q: How are the interest rate and the price of a financial asset related?

A: The yield to maturity and the price of a credit market instrument are inversely related. An increase in the yield to maturity leads to a decrease in the instrument's price; a decrease in the yield to maturity leads to an increase in the instrument's price.

How Are Bond Yields and Prices Related?

The preceding discussion shows that a bond's price and the yield to maturity are inversely related. Thus, as the price falls, the yield to maturity rises because the buyer is paying less for the same future stream of income. Conversely, as the price rises, the yield to maturity will fall. This inverse relationship between the yield to maturity and the current price of the instrument is important, and the reason for it can be explained in this way: Discounting future payments at a higher rate necessarily reduces the present value of the payments and hence the value or price of the bond. A lower yield to maturity raises the present value of the future payments and hence the price of the bond.

Moreover, the longer the time until a bond matures, the greater is the price change associated with a specific change in the yield to maturity. Let's examine why this is so. Suppose that the initial yield to maturity and current yield on a $10,000 bond are 10%. Because of a boom in investment opportunities and a higher demand for funds, the yield to maturity for this bond is expected to rise to 15% a year from now. What happens to the price of the bond? The price can fall dramatically in response to the increase in yield. As Fig. 4.2 shows, for a bond that matures one year from now, the price

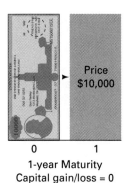

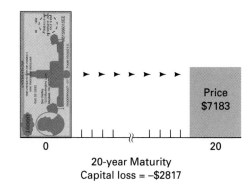

0   **1**
1-year Maturity
Capital gain/loss = 0

0   **5**
5-year Maturity
Capital loss = –$1298

0   **20**
20-year Maturity
Capital loss = –$2817

▲ **FIGURE 4.2**

Sensitivity of Bond Prices to Changes in Interest Rates
The price of a bond and the yield to maturity are negatively related. Suppose that the yield to maturity for a bond is expected to rise from 10% to 15% one year from now. What happens to the price of the bond? A change in the yield to maturity affects the prices of long-term bonds more than the prices of those closer to maturity.

is unaffected because the current price equals the face value. For a bond that matures five years from now, we use Eq. (4.3) to calculate that the price of the bond *falls* by $1298 because the future interest payments are worth less. Even more striking is the capital loss for a bond that matures 20 years from now because the bond's payments occur well into the future: Using Eq. (4.3), we calculate that the bond's price falls by $2817.

Thus, when yields to maturity change, investors face the risk of a change in bond price. For example, even though U.S. Treasury obligations carry no risk of default on either the principal or interest, these obligations still are risky in that changes in the yield to maturity can affect the value of the instruments.

Thus, credit market instruments display differing price sensitivities to fluctuations in the yield to maturity, depending on their maturity. The present value expressions derived earlier show that the present value of short-term instruments is relatively unaffected by an increase or decrease in the interest rate. As time to maturity increases, prices become more sensitive to changes in the yield to maturity (see Box 4.2).

We can illustrate this relationship by using a coupon bond, for which Eq. (4.3) links the price of the bond P and the yield to maturity i. An increase or decrease in i decreases or increases P more as the number of periods until maturity n increases. This results because additional future payments have to be discounted more heavily.

To summarize, the longer the maturity of a bond, the larger will be the price change in response to a change in the yield to maturity. The only case for which the bond price does not react to a change in the yield to maturity is when the holding period is the same as the number of periods until maturity.

In the Using the news box, we show how to apply what you have learned about relationships among bond yields and between bond yields and bond prices. The information presented appears daily in *The Wall Street Journal.*

Consider this...

Who Will Buy Those Fabulous Fifties?

In a new offering in April 1992, the Tennessee Valley Authority (TVA), a quasi-governmental agency and utility, sold $1 billion of 50-year bonds. Priced to yield 8.5%, the bonds' interest rate was about 0.5% above the yield on the Treasury's 30-year bonds. Institutional investors such as pension funds and insurance companies that seek long-term investments in order to pay their long-term liabilities found the TVA's bond so attractive that the demand for the bonds exceeded the supply.

This phenomenon is known as *over-subscription*. Why would investors buy these "fabulous fifties"?

Our analysis predicted correctly that longer-maturity assets have a greater price sensitivity to interest rate changes than do shorter-maturity assets. Investing in 50-year coupon bonds is not for the faint of heart, because the potential to incur capital losses is great. For example, a two-percentage-point *increase* in the yield to maturity would *reduce* the bond's price by about 19%, whereas a two-

percentage-point *decrease* in the yield to maturity would *raise* the bond's price by about 26%. In the case of the TVA's 50-year bonds (which would pay no interest for 20 years, then pay interest for the next 30 years), a $1000 bond sold for $160, with an initial yield to maturity of 8.5%. Thus, a two-percentage-point increase in the yield to maturity would reduce the bond price by about 47%, whereas a two-percentage-point decrease in the yield to maturity would raise the bond price by 78%!

Comparing Interest Rates with Total Rates of Return

So far we have discussed the use of the yield to maturity in comparing returns for financial instruments. Also, we have described the inverse relationship between the yield to maturity and the current price of an instrument. The yield to maturity is the interest rate that equates the present value of future payments to the current price. Over any given holding period, however, an investor may receive a different rate of capital gain or loss than expected originally. As a result, the **total rate of return**, which is the sum of current yield and the *actual* capital gain or loss, can differ from the yield to maturity.

Suppose that Swifty Rich buys a $1000 face value bond in Goodnewsco, which has a coupon rate of 8%, for $1000. After one year, he sells the bond for $1100. How well did Swifty do on his investment? The total rate of return R is

$$R = \frac{\$80}{\$1000} + \frac{\$1100 - \$1000}{\$1000}, \quad \text{or} \quad 18\%.$$

The first term reflects Swifty's interest return: His $1000 investment brought him $80 in interest, or an 8% interest return. The second term reflects Swifty's capital gain. Swifty made a profit of $100 on the Goodnewsco bond, or a 10% additional return on his investment of $1000. Hence, his total rate of return is 8% + 10% = 18%.

Swifty's brother Never B. Rich bought a $1000 face value bond in Badnewsco at the same time; the bond had a coupon rate of 8% and sold for $1000. In one year, he sells the bond for $900. In this case, the total rate of return actually is negative:

$$R = \frac{\$80}{\$1000} + \frac{\$900 - \$1000}{\$1000}, \quad \text{or} \quad -2\%.$$

While Never B. earned the same interest return as Swifty, his capital loss of $100 represented an additional return of −10%. Never B. lost money on his investment.

We can generalize from these examples for coupon bonds. The total rate of return R from holding a coupon bond over the period from t to $t + 1$ is equal to the current yield plus the actual capital gain or loss. To find the initial current yield, divide the coupon payment C by the price at time t, or P_t. Thus, the initial current yield equals C/P_t. To find the percentage change in price, subtract P_t from P_{t+1}, and divide by P_t. Thus, the percentage change in price, or **rate of capital gains** equals $(P_{t+1} - P_t)/P_t$. If the value of this expression is positive, the investor has a capital gain; if it is negative, the investor has a capital loss. The total rate of return is

Total rate of return = Initial current yield + Rate of capital gains

$$R \qquad = \qquad \frac{C}{P_t} \qquad + \qquad \frac{P_{t+1} - P_t}{P_t} \qquad (4.7)$$

This yield can vary significantly from the yield to maturity, as Fig. 4.2 shows. Indeed, a large enough capital loss on a bond results in a negative total rate of return, even if the current yield is positive, as Never B. Rich found to his consternation. Hence investors are concerned with the total rate of return over a holding period and not just the current yield.

To understand why capital gains or losses from interest rate changes can be larger than the interest return, you need to recall that a rise in a bond's yield leads to a fall in its price (and a capital loss), and a fall in a bond's yield leads to an increase in its price (and a capital gain). Hence, if you own long-term bonds and you read about a large increase in yields, don't get excited about receiving a greater interest return. You may well have lost your investment.

Real versus Nominal Interest Rates

Our discussion of interest rates and rates of return has centered on ways to measure **nominal interest rates** and rates of return, that is, rates unadjusted for changes in purchasing power. For example, suppose that you

Using the news...

Keeping Up with Bond Prices and Yields

Each day, the *Credit Market Instruments* page of *The Wall Street Journal* lists information on bond prices and yields. We use several examples to show you how to extract the information you need to compare yields. The categories illustrated are Treasury notes and bonds, Treasury bills, and New York Stock Exchange Corporation bonds.

TREASURY BONDS, NOTES & BILLS

Tuesday, January 12, 1993

Representative Over-the-counter quotations based on transactions of $1 million or more.

Treasury bond, note and bill quotes are as of mid-afternoon.

Source: Federal Reserve Bank of New York.

Panel 1: Treasury Bonds and Notes

GOVT. BONDS & NOTES

	Rate	Maturity Mo/Yr	Bid	Asked	Chg.	Ask Yld.
	$5\frac{3}{8}$	Apr 94n	101:25	101:27	....	3.90
	$4\frac{1}{8}$	May 93-94	100:17	101:01	+ 1	1.02
	7	May 94n	103:27	103:29	....	3.97
	$9\frac{1}{2}$	May 94n	107:01	107:03	− 1	3.99
Bond B	$13\frac{1}{8}$	May 94n	111:25	111:27	....	3.93
	$5\frac{1}{8}$	May 94n	101:15	101:17	....	3.97
	5	Jun 94n	101:10	101:12	....	4.02
	$8\frac{1}{2}$	Jun 94n	106:06	106:08	− 1	4.05
	$8\frac{5}{8}$	Jan 95n	107:26	107:28	− 1	4.47
	3	Feb 95	98:15	99:15	− 1	3.27
	$5\frac{1}{2}$	Feb 95n	101:27	101:29	− 1	4.53
	$7\frac{3}{4}$	Feb 95n	106:08	106:10	− 2	4.55
Bond A	$10\frac{1}{2}$	Feb 95	111:24	111:26	− 1	4.51
	$11\frac{1}{4}$	Feb 95n	113:05	113:07	− 1	4.54
	$8\frac{3}{8}$	Apr 95n	108:01	108:03	− 1	4.55
	$11\frac{7}{8}$	Nov 03	137:19	137:23	− 4	6.88
	$12\frac{3}{8}$	May 04	142:14	142:18	− 6	6.90
	$13\frac{3}{4}$	Aug 04	153:29	154:01	− 6	6.90
	$11\frac{5}{8}$	Nov 04	136:20	136:24	+ 3	7.01
Bond C	$8\frac{1}{4}$	May 00-05	107:24	107:28	+ 4	6.87
	12	May 05	140:12	140:16	− 2	7.03
	$10\frac{3}{4}$	Aug 05	130:09	130:13	+ 2	7.06
	$9\frac{3}{8}$	Feb 06	119:12	119:16	− 4	7.07
	$7\frac{5}{8}$	Feb 02-07	103:26	103:30	− 2	7.03
	12	Aug 08-13	143:00	143:04	− 2	7.32
	$13\frac{1}{4}$	May 09-14	155:23	155:27	− 2	7.33
	$12\frac{1}{2}$	Aug 09-14	148:27	148:31	− 7	7.35
	$11\frac{3}{4}$	Nov 09-14	141:31	142:03	− 4	7.35
	$11\frac{1}{4}$	Feb 15	140:00	140:02	− 7	7.51
	$10\frac{5}{8}$	Aug 15	133:15	133:17	− 6	7.52
	$9\frac{7}{8}$	Nov 15	125:12	125:14	− 6	7.53
	$9\frac{1}{4}$	Feb 16	118:15	118:17	− 7	7.54

Panel 2: Treasury Bills

TREASURY BILLS

Maturity Rate Mo/Yr	Mat.	Bid	Asked	Chg.	Ask Yld.
Jan 14 '93	0	3.07	2.97	+0.01	0.00
Jan 21 '93	7	2.98	2.88	−0.02	2.92
Jan 28 '93	14	2.74	2.64	....	2.68
Feb 04 '93	21	2.87	2.77	−0.03	2.81
Feb 11 '93	28	2.93	2.83	−0.03	2.88
Feb 18 '93	35	2.91	2.87	−0.04	2.92
Feb 25 '93	42	2.90	2.86	−0.04	2.91

Panel 3: New York Stock Exchange Bonds

CORPORATION BONDS

Volume, $26,510,000

	Bonds	Cur Yld	Vol	Close	Net Chg.
	PacTT 8.65s05	8.4	9	$102\frac{5}{8}$ +	$\frac{1}{8}$
	PacTT $8\frac{3}{4}$06	8.5	45	$102\frac{7}{8}$ +	$\frac{1}{8}$
	PacTT 7.8s07	7.8	5	$100\frac{1}{2}$ −	$\frac{1}{4}$
	PacTT $7\frac{5}{8}$09	7.6	30	$100\frac{3}{4}$ +	$\frac{1}{4}$
Bond D	PacTT $9\frac{1}{2}$11	9.0	20	$105\frac{1}{8}$ −	$\frac{3}{8}$
	PacTT $8\frac{7}{8}$15	8.5	30	$104\frac{1}{2}$	.....
	PacTT $8\frac{3}{8}$17	8.2	27	$101\frac{5}{8}$	.....
	PacTT 9s18	8.6	4	$104\frac{3}{4}$	.....

Source: From *The Wall Street Journal*, January 13, 1993. Reprinted by permission of *The Wall Street Journal*,

Panel 1

Panel 1 refers to U.S. Treasury bonds and notes. These obligations are coupon bonds with different maturities. Treasury notes have a maturity of less than 10 years from their date of issue; Treasury bonds have a maturity of more than 10 years from their date of issue.

The first two columns tell you the coupon rate and maturity date, respectively. Bond A, for example, has a coupon rate of 10.5%, so it pays $105 each year on a $1000 face value bond; its maturity date is February 1995. Some bonds, Bond C, for example, have two maturity dates. In this case, the Treasury has the option of paying off the face value any time between May 2000 and May 2005. Such callable bonds offer more flexible financing for the U.S. Treasury. They present a risk to investors however, because, if market rates should fall below the coupon rate, the Treasury might redeem the bond early.

The next three columns refer to the bond's price. All prices are reported per $100 of face value; numbers following the colon refer to thirty-seconds of a dollar. For Bond A, the first price listed, 111:24, means "111 and $\frac{24}{32}$," or an actual price of $1117.50 for a $1000 face value bond. The *bid* price is the price you will receive from a government securities dealer if you sell the bond; the *asked* price is the price you must pay the dealer for the bond. The difference between the asked price and the bid price (known as the *bid-asked spread*) is the profit margin for dealers. Bid-asked spreads are low in the government

Using the news...

Continued...

securities markets, indicating low transactions costs and a liquid and competitive market. The "Chg." column tells you by how much the bid price increased or decreased from the preceding trading day. For Bond A, the bid price fell by ½ point from the previous day. The final column refers to the yield to maturity calculated using the method we discussed for coupon bonds and the asked price. The asked price is used because readers are interested in the yield from the buyer's—investor's—perspective. Hence you can construct three interest rates from the information contained in the table: the yield to maturity just described, the coupon rate, and the current yield (equal to the coupon rate divided by the price, or 10.50/111.81, or 9.39% for Bond A).

Note that the current yield of Bond B is a poor substitute for the yield to maturity. The current yield, 13.125/111.84, or 11.7%, is significantly greater than the yield to maturity of 3.93%. This illustrates that the current yield is not a good substitute for the yield to maturity for instruments with a short time to maturity, because it ignores the effect of expected capital gains or losses on the yield to maturity.

The Wall Street Journal also lists prices and yields for securities issued by U.S. government agencies, such as the Government National Mortgage Association (GNMA), which borrows funds to acquire mortgages, state and local governments, and international

credit agencies. Prices and yields for federal agency bonds, state and local government bonds, and bonds of international agencies are reported in the same way as those for Treasury bonds.

Panel 2

Information about U.S. Treasury bill yields is presented in Panel 2. Recall that Treasury bills are discount bonds, unlike Treasury bonds and notes, which are coupon bonds. Accordingly, they are identified only by their maturity date (first column). The second column gives the number of days to maturity. In the Treasury bill market, yields are quoted on a discount basis.[†] The bid yield is the discount yield for investors who want to sell the bill to dealers; the asked yield is the discount yield for investors who want to buy the bill from dealers. The dealers' profit margin is the difference between the asked yield and the bid yield. The last column shows the yield to maturity (based on the asked price).

Note that the yield to maturity on short-term Treasury bills is less than that on long-term Treasury bonds. Should you invest all your money in long-term bonds to get the higher yield? Probably not. Remember, an increase in interest rates would drive down the price of the bonds in the secondary (resale) markets. In that case, if you wanted to sell the bond before maturity, you would lose part of the principal. Of course, if interest rates fell, the price of your bonds would increase.

You might decide to invest some of your savings in short-term Treasury bills and the balance in longer-term bonds, depending on your guess about whether interest rates will rise or fall.

Panel 3

Panel 3, gives quotations for corporate bonds listed on the New York Stock Exchange (corporate bonds traded on the American Stock Exchange are reported similarly). The first column tells you the name of the corporation issuing the bond—in this case, Pacific Telephone and Telegraph (PacTT), a large telecommunications company. The next column gives you the current yield, 9.0%, for Bond D. The third column reports trading volume; in this case, 20 bonds were traded on the day reported. The last traded price (per $100 of face value) is presented in the "Close" column, 105.125 for Bond D. The last column tells you how much the closing price changed from the preceding trading day: Bond D's price rose by 37.5¢ per $100 of value. The yield to maturity is not reported, though you can calculate it using a programmable calculator or published tables. Note that yields on long-term corporate bonds are higher than those on long-term U.S. Treasury bonds.

[†] The yield on a discount basis for a bond with face value F and a purchase price D is $(F-D)/F \times (360/\text{number of days to maturity})$. Data Question 24 at the end of this chapter compares the yield on a discount basis with the yield to maturity.

buy a $1000 bond that pays you $50 in interest each year for 20 years. If the purchasing power of the dollars you receive declines over time, you are losing part of your interest income to inflation.

Recognizing that inflation reduces the purchasing power of interest income, savers and borrowers base their investment decisions on interest rates and rates of returns adjusted for changes in purchasing power. Such adjusted rates are known as **real interest rates**. Because savers and borrowers don't know what the *actual* real interest rate will be at the maturity of their investment, they must make saving or investment decisions based on the real interest rate they *expect* at that time. Savers and borrowers know the nominal interest rate in advance; they estimate the expected real interest rate by guessing about inflation. The **expected real interest rate** r equals the nominal interest rate i minus the expected rate of inflation π^e, or

$$r = i - \pi^e. \tag{4.8}$$

Does a change in expected inflation affect the real interest rate and saving and investment decisions in the economy? Generally, it doesn't. Suppose, for example, that Tristate Automotive Services Company borrows $10 million for one year from Amalgamated Financial Services at the prevailing *real* interest rate of 5%. Now suppose that borrowers like Tristate and lenders like Amalgamated expect that over the next year, the prices of goods and services in the economy will rise 5%; that is, the expected rate of inflation is 5%. As a return on the loan, Amalgamated expects to earn ($10,000,000)(0.05) = $500,000. However, because expected inflation is 5%, the purchasing power of the $10 million principal is expected to decline by $500,000. Therefore Tristate will benefit because the money it received from the loan is worth more than the amount it expects to repay, adjusted for changes in purchasing power. Amalgamated's loss in purchasing power is Tristate's gain. Tristate and Amalgamated can secure an expected real interest rate of 5% by agreeing to a nominal interest rate of 10%, which would provide the extra return needed to compensate for the expected decline in the value of the principal.

A noted economist, Irving Fisher, generalized this relationship many years ago. The **Fisher hypothesis** states that the nominal interest rate rises or falls point-for-point with expected inflation. Do actual data corroborate the Fisher hypothesis? Nominal interest rates *do* increase when expected inflation increases, but empirical estimates do not generally support a one-for-one movement. Some reasons for this difference include the facts that the basic Fisher hypothesis omits taxes and that quantifying expectations of inflation is difficult. Nonetheless, the likelihood that nominal interest rates reflect changes in expected inflation is not disputed.

The Fisher hypothesis does not imply that the actual real interest rate (the nominal rate less actual inflation) is unaffected by changes in the actual inflation rate. In the preceding example, if the rate of inflation were 10% rather than 5%, the purchasing power of the $10 million principal declines by $1 million, not $500,000. Tristate (the borrower) would gain at

Q: What is the relevant interest rate for saving and investment decisions?

A: The expected real interest rate—the nominal interest rate minus the expected rate of inflation—is the interest rate that savers and borrowers use in making decisions. The expected real rate of return is the nominal rate of return minus the expected rate of inflation.

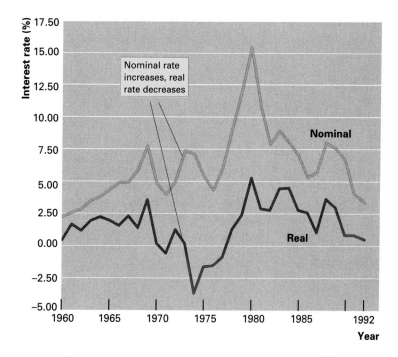

FIGURE 4.3

Real and Nominal Interest Rates, Three-Month Treasury Bills, 1960–1992
Nominal interest rates are higher than real interest rates as long as expected inflation is positive. Real and nominal rates do not always move together.
Source: U.S. Department of the Treasury, Office of Economic Policy.

Amalgamated's (the lender's) expense relative to the agreement, with an expected real return of 5%. If actual inflation were less than 5%, this transfer or redistribution reverses: The lender gains and the borrower loses.

Nominal interest rates are not always a good indicator of real interest rates.[†] For example, how do you know whether a nominal interest rate of 10% is high or low? If expected inflation were 2%, the expected real interest rate, 10% − 2% = 8%, would be high by U.S. standards (real interest rates are normally about 2–3%). If expected inflation were 10%, however, the expected real interest rate, 10% − 10% = 0%, would be low by U.S. standards. Figure 4.3 shows that, although nominal interest rates on three-month

---

[†] For taxable investments, the relevant interest rate is the real after-tax interest rate. If t is the investor's marginal tax rate, ti is tax paid, and expected inflation is π^e, then a nominal yield i corresponds to a real after-tax interest rate of

Nominal Yield − Tax Paid − Expected Inflation

$$i - ti - \pi^e = (1 - t)i - \pi^e.$$

Real after-tax interest rates can be quite low, even negative. In 1981, the nominal (annualized) yield on six-month certificates of deposit averaged 15.8% versus 6.5% in 1986. But the real after-tax yield (ATY) for a high-income investor in 1981, using actual inflation π, was

$$ATY = (1 - t)i - \pi = (1 - 0.59)(15.8\%) - 8.9\%, \text{ or } -2.4\%,$$

whereas in 1986, it was

$$ATY = (1 - 0.45)(6.5\%) - 1.1\%, \text{ or } +2.5\%.$$

MOVING FROM THEORY TO PRACTICE...

THE NEW YORK TIMES   FEBRUARY 13, 1993

The Rush to Refinance Home Mortgages

American homeowners, who last year pared billions of dollars in interest payments off personal balance sheets by refinancing their mortgages, are at it again.

Fueled by a rally in the bond market that has pushed long-term mortgage interest rates to 20-year lows, the latest surge in refinancing activity began right around Christmas, mortgage bankers said, and has intensified in the last few weeks...

Interest rates on 30-year Treasury bonds, which influence mortgage rates, fell to 7.12 percent yesterday, a seven-year low.

At the moment it is not clear which mortgage products homeowners are favoring as they refinance. Last year, for example, many chose to move out of 30-year mortgages and into 15-year loans. Although monthly payments are higher on shorter-term loans, homeowners can pay down debt faster...

Yesterday the Federal Home Loan Mortgage Corporation, or Freddie Mac, which buys pools of mortgages from lenders, reported that the average interest rate for a 30-year fixed-rate mortgage fell for the eighth week in a row, to 7.75 percent, from 7.80 percent a week ago. The 7.75 percent is the lowest average rate since June 15, 1973, when the rate was 7.73 percent.

At 7.75 percent, the monthly principal and interest payment is $707.23 on a 30-year loan of $100,000. That compares with $834 a month for a similar loan at 9.5 percent...

In 1991 and 1992, years when the Federal Reserve Board steadily pushed down short-term interest rates to help stimulate the economy, nearly half a trillion dollars in mortgages were refinanced, according to estimates by the mortgage bankers group.

Those refinancings, in turn, pushed down debt service costs by nearly $10 billion, the [Mortgage Bankers Association] estimated.

Nevertheless, bankers said the pool of mortgage loans that have not yet been refinanaced remained huge.

Mr. Leareah [chief economist at the Mortgage Bankers Association] said that in August he identified $2.4 trillion worth of mortgages that were candidates for refinancing. "There is a very large pool of mortgage holders out there paying anywhere from 9.5 percent to 10 percent that still have not refinanced," he said. "It may take two or three refinanacing booms in a row before these people wake up."

ANALYZING THE NEWS...

Buying a house is a major investment, the biggest one most people will make. Standard fixed-rate home mortgages are an example of long-term fixed payment loans. Over the life of a mortgage loan, most of the value of the total payments represents interest. For a 30-year, $100,000 mortgage at 9.5% interest, for example, about $200,000 in interest is paid over the life of the mortgage.

(a) When market interest rates drop, the present value of the payments on a fixed-rate mortgage increases. As a result, when interest rates drop—as they did in the early 1990s—many homeowners rush to refinance their home mortgages, to obtain a lower interest rate.

To understand why so many homeowners are eager to refinance, let's return to the concept of present value. When market interest rates fall, as they did in early 1993, the present value of a fixed-rate mortgage rises. This is good news for the lender, but bad news for you if you are a borrower: You're paying more than you would have to at current interest rates.

Would you be willing to pay a bank to let you refinance? Your savings could be substantial. For a 30-year, $100,000 mortgage, if the interest rate fell from 9.5% to 7.75%, total interest paid over the life of the mortgage would fall by $45,630 to $154,610. Moreover, lower interest rates offer a homeowner the chance to convert from a 30-year mortgage to a 15-year mortgage with only a small increase in the monthly payment.

(b) A reason homeowners have not yet refinanced is the cost which includes appraisals, inspections, mortgage servicing, and so on. How much would you be willing to pay to refinance? Suppose that your banker tells you that the cost of refinancing is $5000. You would compare this cost with the present value of the savings in mortgage payments (which you can determine using a published table or programmable calculator). If the savings exceed this cost, it pays to refinance. Most experts agree that it makes sense to refinance if you can cut your mortgage interest rate by 1.5 percentage points or more and plan to remain in your home for more than a few years.

For further thought...

Falling interest rates offer a valuable opportunity for homeowners to refinance their mortgages. Are all participants in the financial system better off as a result? Why or why not?

Source: Excerpted from Kenneth N. Gilpin, "Another Surge of Refinancing Sweeps Over Mortgage Lenders," February 13, 1993. Copyright ©1993 by The New York Times Company. Reprinted with permission.

Treasury bills were higher in the 1970s than in the 1960s, real rates were lower (sometimes quite negative). Thus, while nominal interest rates were indicating a high return to savers and a high cost of funds to borrowers, real interest rates were indicating a low return to savers and a low cost of funds to borrowers. Because savers and borrowers use the expected real interest rate in determining how to allocate their wealth to alternative assets, the low real interest rates spurred spending by businesses and households.

The *real rate of return* reflects the amount of additional goods and services an investor can buy from earnings on a financial instrument. Suppose that your total rate of return (including capital gains) from holding a Treasury bond over the last five years was 40%. However, if inflation had been 22% over the same period, your real rate of return, taking account of the decline in your purchasing power, would have been 40% − 22% = 18%. Just as the real interest rate is the interest rate adjusted for purchasing power of goods and services, the real rate of return equals the nominal rate of return adjusted for expected inflation.

▶   C H E C K P O I N T   *In the late 1960s and early 1970s, savings and loan institutions traditionally made long-term (20- or 30-year) home mortgage loans at fixed nominal interest rates, when expected inflation and nominal interest rates were low. Most experts believe that an important cause of the savings and loan crisis of the late 1980s was unexpected inflation in the late 1970s and early 1980s. Why might unexpected inflation be costly for mortgage lenders?* The unexpected burst of inflation later in the 1970s reduced the real value of the mortgage loans to savings and loan institutions. As a result, for many institutions, the present value of the long-term mortgages they held (their assets) fell below the present value of their short-term liabilities to savers, making the institutions insolvent. ◀

Key Terms and Concepts

Compounding

Credit market instruments
   Coupon bond
   Discount bond
   Fixed payment loan
   Simple loan

Current yield

Expected real interest rate

Fisher hypothesis

Nominal interest rates

Present value

Rate of capital gains

Real interest rates

Total rate of return

Yield to maturity

Summary

1. The time pattern of interest payments from borrowers to lenders varies widely among credit market instruments. To facilitate comparison, we can group those instruments into four main categories: simple loans, discount bonds, coupon bonds, and fixed payment loans. The first two categories involve a single payment of principal and interest; the last two involve multiple payments of interest and/or principal.

2. To compare returns on assets that have different maturities requires calculating the present value of each asset's payments. The concept of present value also allows calculation of an interest rate for comparing returns—the yield to maturity. This measure is the interest rate that equates the current value of the asset with the present value of its payments.

3. Fluctuations in prices of bonds or loans are associated with fluctuations in yields to maturity. If the yield to maturity increases, the price of a bond or loan falls; if the yield to maturity decreases, the price of a bond or loan increases. The longer the maturity of an instrument, the larger is the price change in response to a change in the yield to maturity.

4. The total rate of return from holding a financial instrument over a period is the sum of the current yield and the rate of capital gain (or loss). The current yield understates the total rate of return when there is a capital gain and overstates the total rate of return when there is a capital loss.

5. The interest rate relevant for saving and investment decisions is the expected real interest rate. The expected real interest rate is the nominal interest rate minus the expected rate of inflation. Accordingly, for any expected real rate of interest, an increase in the expected rate of inflation raises the nominal interest rate (the Fisher hypothesis). A decrease in the expected rate of inflation decreases the nominal interest rate. Unexpected inflation or deflation leads to a redistribution of resources between borrowers and lenders.

Review Questions

1. How does a discount bond differ from a simple loan?

2. What is the main difference between a coupon bond and a fixed payment loan?

3. What is the yield to maturity of an asset? How can it be derived?

4. What is the current yield on a bond paying $1000 this year with an initial interest rate of 5% and a current price of $18,000?

5. What is the total rate of return on an asset? How can it be calculated?

6. How is the expected real interest rate defined? How does it compare to the actual real interest rate?

7. What is the Fisher hypothesis? Is it valid? Explain.

8. Discuss some factors affecting yields on credit market instruments in general and factors affecting yields on particular instruments or groups of instruments. Would you expect yields to vary more among U.S. Treasury obligations or among private corporate bonds? Why?

Analytical Problems

9. What is the present value of a bond that pays $340 one year from now and $5340 two years from now at a constant interest rate of 6.8%?

10. If the interest rate is 8%, what is the present value of $1000 payable two years from now?

11. Would you prefer to receive (a) $75 one year from now, (b) $85 two years from now, or (c) $90 three years from now, if the interest rate is 10%?

12. What would be your answer to Problem 11 if the interest rate is 20%?

13. Suppose that you have just bought a four-year, $10,000 coupon bond with a coupon rate of 7% when the market interest rate is 7%. Immediately after you buy the bond, the market interest rate falls to 5%. What happens to the value of your bond?

14. Suppose that you are considering subscribing to *Economic Analysis Today* magazine. You are offered a one-year subscription for $60 or a two-year subscription for $115. You plan to keep getting the magazine for at least two years, and the advertisement says that the two-year subscription saves you $5 compared to two successive one-year subscriptions. If the interest rate is 10%, should you subscribe for one or two years?

15. The British government sells consols that pay interest forever. Suppose that you want to buy a consol that pays 100 pounds sterling every year, and the current interest rate is 5%. How much would you be willing to pay for the consol? Suppose that you buy the consol, and the interest rate rises suddenly and unexpectedly to 10%. What is the consol worth now?

16. Suppose that you bought 100 shares of stock in Cruella, Inc., on December 31, 1992 for $55 a share. It paid $2 a share in dividends during 1993,

and on December 31, 1993, its price was $60 per share. What total return did you receive in 1993?

17. Suppose that you are considering the purchase of a coupon bond that has the following future payments: $600 in one year; $600 in two years; $600 in three years; and $600 + $10,000 in four years.

   a. What is the bond worth today if the market interest rate is 6%? What is the bond's current yield?

   b. Suppose that you have just purchased the bond, and suddenly the market interest rate falls to 5% for the foreseeable future. What is the bond worth now? What is its current yield now?

   c. Suppose that one year has elapsed, you have received the first coupon payment of $600, and the market interest rate is still 5%. How much would another investor be willing to pay for the bond? What was your total return on the bond? If another investor had bought the bond a year ago for the amount you calculated in (b), what would that investor's total return have been?

   d. Suppose that two years have elapsed since you bought the bond, and you have received the first two coupon payments of $600 each. Now suppose that the market interest rate suddenly jumps to 10%. How much would another investor be willing to pay for your bond? What will the bond's current yield be over the next year? Suppose that another investor had bought the bond at the price you calculated in (c). What would that investor's total return have been over the past year?

18. From an investor's point of view, the stock market drop in the mid-1970s actually was *worse* than the stock market crash of 1929, even though stock prices fell by a greater percentage in 1929. How is this result possible?

19. Suppose that you bought an asset that pays a 7% nominal interest rate, you expect the inflation rate

to be 3%, and actual inflation is 5%. Calculate the expected real interest rate and the actual real interest rate.

20. Your brother-in-law tells you at a family picnic that investors in the Wild Fund, the bond fund he manages, have been lucky; they now have a current yield on their portfolio of 20%. At the same time, the current yield on the Safe Fund, a competitor, is 10%. Should you join the ranks of Wild Fund investors? Why or why not?

21. In the city of Midborough, two financial institutions have borrowed funds from community residents through notes with a maturity of three months. The first institution invests the proceeds in short-term corporate credit market instruments. The second makes 30-year fixed-rate mortgage loans to local homeowners. Describe the likely effects on the net worth (value of assets less value of liabilities) of the two institutions if the general level of interest rates increases substantially.

Data Questions

22. If your library or your professor has the yearbook *Stocks, Bonds, Bills, and Inflation* by Ibbotson Associates, you can look up total returns on different assets. Try to find data on the total returns of common stocks, short-term Treasury bills, and long-term Treasury bonds over the past 30 years. What asset pays the highest return? The lowest? What attributes of the assets do you think caused this pattern?

23. In the yearbook *Stocks, Bonds, Bills, and Inflation* by Ibbotson Associates, look up the total returns on different assets (Treasury bills, Treasury bonds, and stocks) during each of the 12 months last year. If you could switch your portfolio between these different assets each month, how would you do so? What would your total return be from switching, compared to keeping the same asset throughout the year? Suppose that each time you switched, you paid 0.5% of your assets in transactions costs. Would you want to switch as often? What would your total return be if you subtracted transactions costs?

24. As a carryover from the days before computerization, dealers in U.S. Treasury bills often quote a yield measure called "yield on a discount basis." It differs in two ways from the yield to maturity. First, the return is divided by the face value rather than by the purchase price. Second, the number of days in a year (used for annualizing returns on bills with a maturity of less than one year) is set at 360, rather than 365. That is, the yield on a discount basis for a bond with face value F and purchase price D is

$$\left(\frac{F-D}{F}\right)\left(\frac{360}{\text{Number of days to maturity}}\right).$$

The yield for a discount bond in this chapter is

$$\left(\frac{F-D}{D}\right)\left(\frac{365}{\text{Number of days to maturity}}\right).$$

Find a copy of *The Wall Street Journal* and select a Treasury bill with about 90 days to maturity. Calculate the yield on a discount basis and the yield to maturity. Is the yield on a discount basis less than or greater than the yield to maturity? Why? Would you expect the two yield measures to move together? Explain.

5

Saving, Investment, and Interest Rate Determination

The interest rate on Treasury bills

more than doubled in the three years prior to 1981, reaching 15% in that year. Businesses complained that they could not invest to expand and would have to lay off workers. Households were nervous about the health of the country's financial institutions. In Washington, frustrated policymakers pointed fingers at the Federal Reserve System, foreign central banks, and the alarming U.S. budget deficits and national debt.

What accounts for such upsurges in interest rates? How are interest rates on financial assets determined in the first place? In this chapter, we describe how households' and businesses' decisions about saving and investment produce a supply of and demand for funds in the financial system. We show how such decisions affect interest rate determination. We also demonstrate that the market clearing "price" of these funds is, in fact, the interest rate. As in other markets you studied in your first economics course, the equilibrium price (here the interest rate) depends on supply and demand considerations.

Building on the tools developed in Chapter 4, we address three main questions in this chapter. **Q:** What are the determinants of saving and investment by savers and borrowers in the economy? **Q:** How do the determinants of saving and investment affect interest rates in the economy? **Q:** How do international borrowing and lending affect interest rate determination in the economy?

Saving and Investment

When you begin working full-time, how much of your paycheck should you put aside or save? How much money should firms such as Xerox invest next year? Our analysis of interest rate determination must begin with consideration of the factors influencing saving (the supply of loanable funds) and investment (the demand for loanable funds). In this section, we first discuss determinants of saving by individual households and of investment by individual firms. We then extend that discussion to describe determinants of total saving by households in the economy and total investment by firms. We identify the role played by saving and investment decisions of the government and of foreign firms and households later in the chapter. Studying saving and investment decisions provides a basic supply-and-demand framework for analyzing how interest rates are determined. As you will see, the equilibrium interest rate is determined by all the saving and investment decisions made in our economy—and even elsewhere in the world.

Saving Decisions by Households

If you save about 5% of your take-home pay, you are just about average for an American (though you would be a spendthrift by Japanese standards). Although you don't calculate how much to save each time you receive a paycheck, from time to time you may set saving goals and decide how to achieve them. By following this thought process, we can explain not only how much you as an individual might save in a year, but also how much households collectively are likely to save in a year. This information can help predict interest rates in the economy.

What determines households' tendency to save? Let's examine four factors: life-cycle considerations, precautionary saving, saving for bequests, and the expected real interest rate.

Life-Cycle Considerations. As you might expect, students and retirees usually are not able to save much. Rather, most individuals save during the middle years of their lives. The most substantial amount of saving occurs during a person's forties and fifties when income is typically highest. The pattern of income, or earnings profile, over a lifetime typically is "arched" or "humped" during an individual's middle years. The reason is that income usually is low when a person begins a career, is likely to rise during the individual's working lifetime, and probably will fall when the person retires. (Pension benefits, Social Security benefits, and interest income are likely to be less than peak earnings during the working years.)

This lifetime pattern of income would pose no problem if individuals' spending patterns followed the same path, that is, if people had low consumption needs at the beginning and end of their lives and high consumption

▶ **FIGURE 5.1**

The Life-Cycle Model of Consumption and Saving
In the life-cycle model, consumption is smoother than income over time (here consumption is depicted as constant). Income typically rises during a person's working life, peaking before retirement. Saving is the difference between income and consumption. It is negative during the individual's early years (consumption exceeds income), positive during middle age (as debts are paid and savings for retirement are built), and negative again during retirement (as households dissave, drawing down to finance consumption).

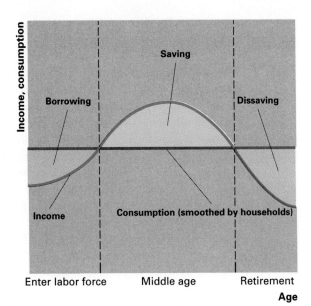

needs during their peak earning years. However, matching spending to the earnings profile is not very appealing. Instead, individuals prefer to spend at a steadier rate over their lifetimes. For example, you might save gradually to finance your children's education, rather than eating soup and crackers the entire time they are in college. The financial system allows you to solve the problem of matching your consumption needs to your income. You can borrow money when young and broke, pay back debts and save for retirement when middle-aged and better-off financially, and live on pensions and savings after retirement. This pattern of using the financial system to match saving with consumption needs is known as the **life-cycle model of consumption and saving.**[†] Figure 5.1 illustrates the pattern.

For simplicity, let's assume that households want to smooth completely the rate of spending (consumption) over their lifetimes (depicted as the straight line in Fig. 5.1). But the typical earnings profile is humped. As a result, in their first few years in the labor force, individuals may be borrowers because they expect to earn more money in the future and want to smooth their spending over time.[††] In their peak earning years, households build assets and pay off debts. Finally, when people retire, they *dissave*, or spend their savings.

[†] Franco Modigliani of M.I.T., a Nobel laureate in economics, first explained the life cycle of wealth accumulation for a saver following ground-breaking research during the 1950s on household consumption and saving.

[††] In reality, most people cannot borrow very much against their future income when they are just beginning their careers. (Try asking a banker for a loan against your income 10 years hence.) That is, *actual* borrowing may be much less than *desired* borrowing.

We can use the typical earnings profile and the desire for steady spending during the life cycle to make four observations:

1. In order to maintain your spending in old age, you will need to put money aside while you are working. Financing spending in retirement is an important motivation for saving.

2. If you had access to sources of income in old age other than your own funds, you would not need to save as much for retirement. Government programs that provide income support for retirees, such as Social Security, can lead to lower household saving.

3. Your greatest saving occurs in your peak (typically middle-aged) earnings years. The larger the fraction of the population that is in peak earning years, the greater is the country's tendency to save. Demographics are key to understanding saving trends over time and in different countries.

4. You base your spending decisions not only on your current income, but also on your expected future income and your wealth. When you get new information about your future income (say, that you are promoted), you will change your spending now and in the future. Unexpected changes in current and future income and wealth will be reflected in spending throughout people's lifetimes.

Let's explore this last observation further and consider the effects of changes in current income, expected future income, and wealth on consumer spending. Suppose that you win $10,000 in the state lottery. The life-cycle model suggests that you should not spend all of it now but that you should put some of the winnings aside to finance future consumption. Similarly, if you bet your paycheck on the outcome of the World Series and lose, you probably will not reduce your spending immediately by the amount of the loss; you will use money from your savings, which, in effect, spreads the burden over time. We apply this reasoning in a broader way to households collectively. For the household sector as a whole, an increase in current income or wealth, holding future resources constant, increases current saving. A decrease in current income or wealth decreases current saving.

Suppose that you are in your third year of law school and have accepted a job with a prestigious law firm. The life-cycle model suggests that you will accept the credit card invitations you are receiving and borrow against your expectation of future income. Suppose, however, that you are working at a plant that will close in 18 months. You will want to cut your spending of current income, thereby increasing your saving now to prepare for losing your job. Again, this behavior is exhibited by households collectively. For the household sector as a whole, an increase in expected future income or wealth, holding current resources constant, decreases current saving. A decrease in expected future income or wealth increases current saving.

Precautionary Saving.   Another important determinant of aggregate saving by households is the need to be prepared for emergencies, such as sudden health care needs or car repairs. Such saving is called **precautionary saving.** Because no one can predict when such emergencies might arise, many people put aside some funds as a precautionary measure. Some economists believe that this motivation for saving is almost as important as life-cycle saving in explaining total household saving. In addition, different needs for precautionary saving help to explain saving differences in various countries. For example, in countries that have unemployment insurance, such as in the United States, workers need to save less than do workers in countries without such programs. As another example, Canada has a national system guaranteeing health care for all, whereas the United States has primarily privately funded health care. Hence people in the United States are likely to save more than Canadians as a precaution against health emergencies.

Saving for Bequests.   Saving for bequests is another component of total private savings. Not all individuals save exclusively to finance their own future spending. Many who can afford to do so save in order to leave money to their children and other heirs through *bequests,* or instructions written in a will. Recipients of a bequest inherit savings of the deceased and use the funds to finance their own future spending. In addition, many individuals transfer savings to their children or other relatives before death (to assist with a down payment on a home, for example).

Expected Real Interest Rate.   Suppose that, during the course of the year, the real interest rate paid on your savings rises. You might make either of two possible decisions based on this information. On the one hand, a higher interest rate means that you will earn more on your savings, making future consumption cheaper (relative to current consumption), which may encourage you to save more. This decision reflects the *substitution effect.* On the other hand, a higher real interest rate could make you want to save less. If you want to accumulate a fixed amount of money to buy a house five years from now, a higher return on your savings means that you can save less today and still meet your goal. This offsetting effect is called the *income effect.* Economists studying household saving generally have found that the substitution effect dominates; that is, a higher interest rate raises the overall amount of saving. This result is especially true in terms of *net saving,* that is, total saving less borrowing. Household borrowing decisions are sensitive to the interest rate because a change in the rate has only a substitution effect (and no income effect). Hence for the household sector as a whole, an increase in the expected real interest rate tends to raise saving.

The Saving Curve

We can now show graphically what we just presented about the determinants of aggregate saving. Specifically, we develop the **saving curve,** which illustrates the relationship between aggregate saving and the real rate of interest. As Fig. 5.2 shows, the saving curve S slopes upward: Holding households' current and expected future income constant, an increase in the expected real rate of interest leads households to save more of their current income. Thus, holding other determinants of saving constant, when interest rates are high, households will put aside more of their earnings—in a savings account, mutual fund, bonds, or stocks. The increase in the expected real interest rate from r_0 to r_1 in Fig. 5.2 results in an increase in aggregate saving from S_0 to S_1. However, a decrease in the expected real interest rate leads households to save less of their current income. The decrease in the expected real interest rate from r_0 to r_2 in Fig. 5.2 results in a decrease in aggregate saving from S_0 to S_2.

What determines the position of the saving curve in the graph? The other determinants of aggregate saving—demographics and growth, current income, expected future income and wealth, precautionary saving, and bequest saving—shift the saving curve to the right or left. Let's examine the impact of each determinant on aggregate saving while assuming that the other determinants are constant.

Demographics and Growth. The first factor that affects levels of aggregate saving is demographics, in particular the age profile of a population. An increase in the number of people in their peak-earning, middle-aged years relative to the number of young or old individuals will increase the level of saving at any expected real interest rate, shifting the saving curve to the right. Conversely, a relative decrease in the number of middle-aged savers will decrease the level of saving at any expected real rate of interest, shifting the saving curve to the left. Now consider what might happen if the fraction of the population that is retired increases: Total saving likely will decrease. The aging of the population could explain part of the decline in U.S. saving in recent decades.

▶ **FIGURE 5.2**

The Saving Curve
The saving curve S shows a positive relationship between saving and the expected real interest rate: An increase in the expected real interest rate from r_0 to r_1 increases the level of saving from S_0 to S_1; a decrease in the expected real interest rate from r_0 to r_2 decreases the level of saving from S_0 to S_2.

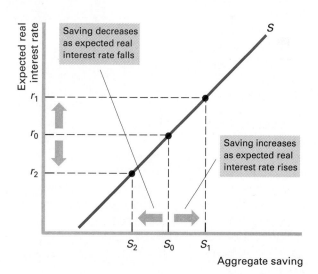

Economic growth also is important in this respect. In a growing economy, younger and middle-aged people have more income and hence are able to save more than the elderly dissave. This results in an increase in aggregate household saving. An increase in the rate of economic growth will increase the level of saving at any expected real interest rate, shifting the saving curve to the right. The high saving rates in rapidly growing economies, such as Taiwan and South Korea, illustrate this effect. (See Box 5.1 for an explanation of cross-country differences in saving patterns.)

Current Income.   A second factor that can affect the level of saving is the amount of current income in an economy. When current income increases (as in economic boom times), the level of saving at any expected real

---

Consider this...

BOX 5.1

Why Are Saving Rates Different among Countries?

The accompanying bar graph shows that household saving rates in 1990 varied widely among countries. We can apply the life-cycle approach to explain the variation in saving among industrialized countries, taking into account such additional factors as attitudes toward risk and how well-developed financial markets are.

The life-cycle model indicates that a significant factor in determining saving is the age structure of the population. Consider the United States, Great Britain, and Japan. The United States and Britain, with significantly greater fractions of their populations retired than in Japan, have lower saving rates. In addition, Japan's rapid economic growth should increase its saving rate according to the life-cycle model, because its population is younger than the U.S. or British population.

The life-cycle model also suggests that countries with different levels of social insurance or different stages of development of

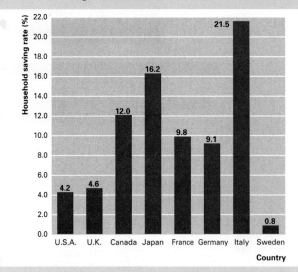

financial markets will have different saving patterns. Japan, with less generous social insurance programs and less well-developed credit markets for consumer borrowing than the United States, has a higher saving rate for precautionary considerations. Sweden has very generous social insurance programs and well-developed credit markets and thus low household saving rates.

Other factors that can influence cross-country differences in household saving rates include differences in the taxation of returns on assets and shifts in household wealth. An example of the latter, some economists argue, is that the increase in wealth in the early and mid 1980s from the stock market and real estate boom made households richer and decreased their saving from current income.

interest rate increases because households spread their spending of the higher income over a long period of time. Hence the saving curve shifts to the right. A decrease in current income decreases the level of saving at any expected real interest rate, shifting the saving curve to the left. Thus aggregate saving from current income generally falls during a recession.

Expected Future Income and Wealth. Expectations of future income and wealth are a third factor in determining the level of saving in an economy. An increase in expected future income and wealth decreases the level of saving from current income, as households increase current spending in anticipation of higher income and greater wealth. As a result, the saving curve shifts to the left. A decrease in expected future income and wealth increases the level of saving at any expected real interest rate, shifting the saving curve to the right. For example, a belief that future productivity and incomes will be higher than they are today should decrease saving, whereas an expectation that productivity and incomes will fall in the future will increase saving from current income.

Precautionary Saving. An increase in households' demand for precautionary saving increases the level of saving at any expected real interest rate, shifting the saving curve to the right. A decrease in households' demand for precautionary saving decreases the level of saving at any expected real interest rate, shifting the saving curve to the left. For example, the introduction of a government-financed national health insurance system should decrease precautionary saving for medical expenses.

Bequest Saving. An increase in households' saving for bequests increases the level of saving at any expected real interest rate, shifting the saving curve to the right. A decrease in households' saving for bequests decreases the level of saving at any interest rate, shifting the saving curve to the left.

Concluding Remarks. Table 5.1 summarizes the factors that account for shifts in the saving curve. The saving curve represents possible combinations of saving and the expected real interest rate. In order to determine which of the possible combinations will actually occur, we need to know both the amount of savings supplied and demanded at each interest rate.

▶ C H E C K P O I N T *Why might household saving fall in response to forecasts of higher income growth in the future?* This good news raises consumers' expected future resources, increasing current consumption and decreasing the need for current saving. The saving curve shifts to the left (represented by row 3 in Table 5.1). ◀

Investment and Borrowing Decisions by Firms

The three potential customers for funds saved by households are (1) domestic businesses (which may want to invest more than their current

TABLE 5.1   FACTORS THAT SHIFT THE SAVING CURVE

An increase in ...	Causes saving to ...	Because ...	Graph of effect ...
middle-aged individuals relative to younger or older individuals in the population	increase	most saving is done by individuals when they are middle-aged	*graph: $S_0 \to S_1$*
current income	increase	individuals try to smooth their spending over time, so current saving rises	*graph: $S_0 \to S_1$*
expected future income and wealth	decrease	individuals increase current spending in anticipation of future wealth, so current saving falls	*graph: $S_1 \leftarrow S_0$*
precautionary saving	increase	individuals save more in response to uncertain income in order to finance emergencies	*graph: $S_0 \to S_1$*
saving for bequests	increase	individuals save more to finance spending by their heirs	*graph: $S_0 \to S_1$*

profits), (2) domestic governments (which may want to spend more than their current tax revenues), and (3) foreign households, firms, and governments. Let's focus first on domestic firms. Later in the chapter we consider domestic governments and the foreign sector.

Businesses borrow from households through the financial system to finance short-term and long-term expenses. Firms seek short-term loans when they lack sufficient resources to pay their workers and suppliers before receiving sales revenue or to pay expenses incurred in the production of goods and services. Firms seek long-term loans when they want to invest in new plants and equipment at a rate faster than their profits are expanding.

Firms may be savers just as households are, but saving by individual firms does not imply saving for the business sector as a whole. In a growing economy, firms will be making new investments, and the business sector will be a net borrower of funds. In a shrinking economy, few growth opportunities will exist, investment will be low, and the business sector will be a net saver of funds. Current profits from old investments will exceed new credit needs.

What factors determine desired total investment by firms? Businesses invest in new capital goods in order to achieve the greatest possible profits. The amount of profit that firms can earn on their investments must be weighed against the returns they could earn by a different use of their funds. Hence businesses compare potential profit with the expected interest rate they could earn by investing their funds in financial assets, such as Treasury bonds. Thus the two basic determinants of desired total investment by firms are (1) the expected profitability of invested capital and (2) the expected real interest rate.

Expected Profitability of Capital. The first factor that influences business investment is the expectation of the profitability of capital invested. Most capital goods acquired by firms last for at least several years. Thus, when businesses consider investment decisions they are concerned about both *current* and *future* profitability. Factors such as innovation, the development of new technologies, and anticipated future demand strongly influence expectations about future profitability. For example, when deciding whether to invest in the development of a new drug, a pharmaceutical company will consider the likely future demand for the drug.

Corporate taxes also affect expectations about future profitability because businesses are concerned only about the profits they retain after taxes. As a result, special tax breaks for investment increase the profitability of investment and increase firms' investment demand (see Box 5.2). Conversely, higher tax burdens on the profits earned by new investment reduce firms' investment demand. An increase in the expected profitability of capital (after taxes) increases investment; a decrease in the expected profitability of capital (after taxes) decreases investment.

Expected Real Interest Rate. The second factor influencing investment demand is the expected real interest rate, which affects investment just as it does saving. We showed that, holding other factors constant, an increase in the real interest rate increases the volume of saving in the economy. Similarly, a decrease in the real interest rate decreases the volume of saving in the economy. An increase in the expected real interest rate decreases the level of business investment. A decrease in the expected real interest rate increases

Consider this...

BOX 5.2

U.S. Investment: Too Many Houses and Too Few Machines?

Many economists believe that the composition of U.S. investment—the mix between residential housing and business plant and equipment investment—has been badly distorted by the tax system. We can look for some confirmation of this contention by analyzing how these different types of investment are taxed.

Currently, investment in owner-occupied housing is more lightly taxed than business investment in the United States. The imputed income that homeowners receive from dwelling in their homes is not taxed, whereas returns on business investment are taxed. In addition, housing is generally financed with substantial debt through home mortgages, and home mortgage interest is a deductible expense for taxpayers. Businesses generally rely on equity financing for investment funds, and payments to shareholders are not a deductible business expense. The differences in taxation on housing and business investment suggest that the government may be promoting housing investment at the expense of business investment. Indeed, Edwin Mills of Northwestern University found that tax considerations raised housing's share of the total capital stock in the early 1980s by about one-third.[†] Our analysis indicates that taxation of returns on investment shifts the investment curve to the left because the after-tax return from investing is lower. Less taxation of returns on investment shifts the investment curve to the right because the after-tax return from investing is higher.

[†] See Edwin Mills, "Has the U.S. Overinvested in Housing?" Federal Reserve Bank of Philadelphia *Business Review*, March/April 1987, pp. 13–23.

the level of business investment. Suppose, for example, that Midstate Iron Works is thinking about buying a new machine that will reduce its labor costs, producing a gross rate of return of 15%. If the real cost of funds is 8%, should the company buy the machine? Yes, Midstate should buy the new machine because 15% is greater than 8%. Indeed, in so doing, it will enjoy a net rate of return of 7%. Midstate could pursue many other potential projects, each of which has a gross profit associated with it. The company will continue to take on projects so long as its gross rate of profit exceeds the cost of funds. The company will want to borrow to finance new projects until the rate of return on the last project equals the cost of funds.

Even if firms can use their own funds and do not have to borrow to finance investment, they must still consider the opportunity cost of those funds, that is, the amount they could earn if they invested funds in assets outside the firm. The opportunity cost in this case is the expected real interest rate, because that is the return firms could expect to receive from outside investments. Hence a high expected real interest rate reduces desired investment even for firms that do not have to borrow. In general, the higher the expected real interest rate is, the lower the net expected profitability of new investment will be. The lower the net profitability of new investment is, the lower the firms' demand for investment funds will be.

Q: What are the determinants of saving and investment by savers and borrowers in the economy?

A: The determinants of desired saving by the household sector are demographics, current income and wealth, expected future income, precautionary saving, bequest saving, and the expected real interest rate. The determinants of desired investment by firms are the expected future profitability of capital (after taxes) and the expected real interest rate.

The Investment Curve

As we did for aggregate saving, we can illustrate graphically the relationship between the expected real interest rate and aggregate investment. The **investment curve**, I, shows the relationship between investment and the expected real interest rate. Figure 5.3 shows the inverse relationship between the expected real interest rate and investment: An increase in the expected real interest rate decreases firms' investment. Hence an increase in the expected real interest rate from r_0 to r_1 in Fig. 5.3 decreases investment demand from I_0 to I_1. Conversely, a decrease in the expected real interest rate increases firms' investment. A decline in the expected real interest rate from r_0 to r_2 in Fig. 5.3 increases investment demand from I_0 to I_2.

What determines the position of the investment curve in Fig. 5.3? Essentially, it is the other determinant of investment: the expected profitability of capital. As summarized in Table 5.2, the investment curve shifts to the right when the expected profitability of capital increases but shifts to the left when it decreases. Note that the tax rate and tax subsidies for investment can affect the profitability of capital and thus must be factored in as part of expected profitability.

Determining the Real Interest Rate

The saving and investment curves describe the relationships between the expected real interest rate and desired saving and investment, respectively. To determine the equilibrium real interest rate and volume of loanable funds, we need to combine the two curves. Figure 5.4, the **saving-**

The Investment Curve
The investment curve I shows the negative relationship between investment and the expected real interest rate: An increase in the expected real interest rate from r_0 to r_1 decreases the level of investment from I_0 to I_1; a decrease in the expected real interest rate from r_0 to r_2 increases the level of investment from I_0 to I_2.

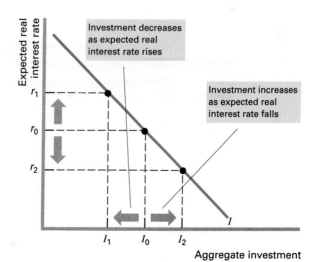

Investment decreases as expected real interest rate rises

Investment increases as expected real interest rate falls

FIGURE 5.4

The Saving-Investment Diagram

The equilibrium real interest rate (r^*) is determined by the intersection of the saving curve S and the investment curve I. At a real interest rate r_1, there is an excess supply of savings (1a), and the real interest rate falls (1b). At a real interest rate r_2, there is an excess demand for savings (2a), and the real interest rate rises (2b).

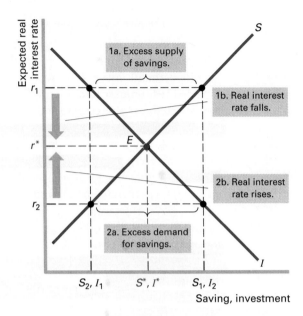

Equilibrium in Lending and Borrowing

investment diagram, does so. As we demonstrated earlier, the saving curve, S, slopes upward and to the right, and the investment curve, I, slopes downward and to the left. Where the two curves intersect determines the expected real interest rate. For convenience, let's assume that actual inflation equals expected inflation and, for now, refer to the expected real interest rate as the real interest rate.

Equilibrium in Lending and Borrowing

Which real interest rate prevails? The **equilibrium real interest rate** r^* is determined by the intersection of the saving curve, S, and the investment curve, I, which is at point E in Fig. 5.4. What do we mean by *equilibrium*? Essentially, in equilibrium, the real interest rate and the amounts of saving and investment tend to remain the same. In the financial system, this condition means that neither savers nor borrowers have a financial incentive to alter the existing situation.

Let's explore what happens when the real interest rate is not at equilibrium. Suppose that the real interest rate shown in Fig. 5.4 is r_1 which is higher than r^*. In this case (1a), desired saving, S_1, is greater than desired investment, I_1, creating an excess supply of savings. Borrowers are happy because they are getting all the funds they want at the going interest rate. But some people who want to save cannot find borrowers for their funds. Thus they have an incentive to reduce their interest rate demands (1b) so that firms will borrow from them. As the interest rate falls, two things happen. First, some people who did not want to borrow before do so, as the cost of funds has declined. Second, some people who wanted to lend before are no longer inter-

TABLE 5.2 FACTORS THAT SHIFT THE INVESTMENT CURVE			
An increase in ...	Causes investment to ...	Because ...	Graph of effect ...
expected profitability of capital	increase	businesses invest to maximize profits	
corporate taxes on profits	decrease	taxes reduce the profitability of investment	
tax subsidies for investment	increase	subsidies lower the cost of investment, thereby increasing the profitability of investing	

ested in doing so, as their expected return is lower. The real interest rate continues to fall until the excess supply of savings is eliminated and equilibrium is reached. The financial system makes this return to equilibrium possible.

Suppose, however, that the real interest rate in Fig. 5.4 is r_2 which is lower than r^*. In this case (2a), desired investment, I_2, is greater than desired saving, S_2, creating an excess demand for savings. Now savers are happy because they can find borrowers willing to take all their funds at the going interest rate. But some people who want to borrow cannot obtain funds. Thus they have an incentive to raise the real interest rate they are willing to pay (2b) so that savers will lend to them. As the interest rate rises, some people who did not want to save before do so because the return on savings has increased; some who wanted to borrow before are no longer interested in doing so because the cost of funds is higher. The real interest rate continues to rise until the excess demand for savings is eliminated. Equilibrium is restored at a real interest rate of r^*, to point E, where desired saving and investment are equal.

What factors change the equilibrium real interest rate? Essentially, shifts in the saving and investment curves will change the equilibrium real interest rate. Factors that increase total desired saving for any value of the real interest rate shift the S curve to the right, raising equilibrium saving, S^*, and investment, I^*, and reducing the equilibrium real interest rate r^*. Factors that decrease desired total saving for any value of the real interest rate shift the S curve to the left, lowering S^* and I^* and increasing r^*. Factors that increase desired total investment for any value of the real interest rate shift the I curve to the right, raising S^* and I^* and increasing r^*. Factors that decrease desired total investment for any value of the real interest rate shift the I curve to the left, lowering S^* and I^* and reducing r^*. Table 5.3 summarizes the factors affecting the equilibrium real interest rate. An application of this activity is discussed in Box 5.3.

Government Saving and the Real Interest Rate

So far we have emphasized the influence on the real interest rate of saving and investment decisions by domestic households and firms and ignored the role played by domestic governments and the foreign sector. Saving decisions by domestic governments and the foreign sector can affect

---

Consider this...

BOX 5.3

Why Do Real Interest Rates Fall During Recessions?

We have shown that movements in the real interest rate reflect shifts in desired saving or investment in the economy. In practice, both the saving and investment curves may shift. An important example is the movement of the real interest rate over *business cycles*, or periodic fluctuations in economic activity. At the beginning of a downturn, households and firms expect that economic activity and incomes will be lower than usual for a period of time. As the accompanying diagram shows, the decline in current income relative to expected future income reduces desired current saving (as households dissave to maintain consumption), shifting the S curve to the left from S_0 to S_1. At the same time, firms expect profitability of capital to be low for a period of time, so the I curve shifts to the left from I_0 to I_1. The equi-

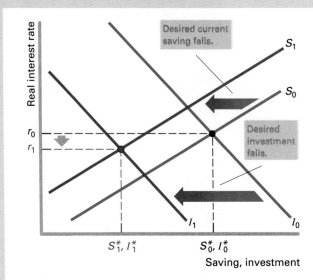

librium quantities of desired total saving and desired investment decline from S_0^*, I_0^* to S_1^*, I_1^*. The leftward shift of the S curve raises the real interest rate, whereas the leftward shift of the I curve lowers the real interest rate. Evidence

from U.S. data indicates that real interest rates rise during economic upturns and fall during economic downturns, suggesting that the investment shift dominates, as shown.

▼ TABLE 5.3	CHANGES IN THE EQUILIBRIUM REAL INTEREST RATE		
An increase in . . .	**Causes the real interest rate to . . .**	**Because . . .**	**Graph of effect . . .**
the number of savers in the population	fall	desired saving increases	
current income	fall	desired saving increases	
expected future income and wealth	rise	desired saving decreases	
precautionary saving	fall	desired saving increases	
bequest saving	fall	desired saving increases	
expected profitability of capital (after taxes)	rise	desired investment increases	

Other times, other places...

Do Real Interest Rates Rise During Wartime?

In wartime, governments often become temporary borrowers, as purchases of military hardware and expenditures for soldiers' compensation, accommodations, and transport increase. These increased expenditures are temporary, and governments generally do not increase current taxes sufficiently to pay for the war. Instead, they typically borrow during wars, financing them in part by future taxes.

What are the effects of wars on investment and the real interest rate? In the saving-investment diagram, we note that a temporary increase in government purchases (holding taxes constant) should decrease total investment by firms and increase the real interest rate. Thus, our analysis of the saving-investment process predicts that a military buildup raises the real interest rate, thereby crowding out

(reducing) some private investment.

Because the British fought several major and minor wars during the period from 1730 to 1913, British data are particularly useful for analyzing the effects of wars on the saving-investment process and the real interest rate. Robert Barro of Harvard University analyzed movements in real interest rates during wars using British data for that period of time.[†] He found that inflation was essentially nonexistent over most of this period, making movements in nominal interest rates a good approximation of movements in the real interest rate. Averaging about 3.5% over the period, long-term nominal interest rates in Britain rose to 5.5% during the American Revolution (late 1770s and early 1780s) and 6% during the Napoleonic Wars (early 1800s).

Barro's analysis suggests that real interest rates rise during wars. Applying Barro's findings to U.S. wartime experiences is more difficult because, unlike the historical British experience, the U.S. government imposed price controls and direct controls on interest rates. However, during major conflicts such as the Korean War and especially World War II, private investment significantly declined relative to GNP while government purchases relative to GNP rose significantly. The decline of private investment during wartime suggests that interest rates do rise during wars. This result is consistent with the graph in Fig. 5.5.

[†] Robert J. Barro, "The Neoclassical Approach to Fiscal Policy." In Robert J. Barro (Ed.), *Modern Business Cycle Theory.* Cambridge, Mass.: Harvard University Press, 1989.

real interest rates in the economy. Many economists believe, for example, that the large U.S. government budget deficits during the 1980s and early 1990s caused the real interest rate to be higher than it otherwise would have been. We introduce such saving decisions here and explore them more fully when we examine the interrelationships between the financial system and the macroeconomy in Part V.

What is the domestic government sector? It includes not only the federal government, but also state and local governments. Like households and firms, the government sector can be a net saver or dissaver. In some periods, income from tax receipts exceeds current expenditures, so that the government sector has a surplus and is a net saver of funds. At other times, the government sector runs a deficit, with expenditures greater than tax receipts, and is a net borrower of funds. In either case, governments, like households, must consider their income and spending over time. Cumulatively over the

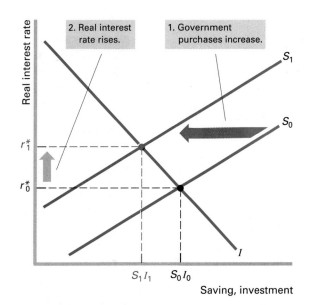

FIGURE 5.5

Effect of Increased Government Purchases on the Real Interest Rate
Assuming that household saving does not increase sufficiently to offset the government's dissaving, an increase in government purchases (without raising current taxes) shifts the saving curve from S_0 to S_1, raising the real interest rate from r_0^* to r_1^* and lowering total saving and investment in the economy from S_0, I_0 to S_1, I_1.

long run, the government sector cannot spend more than it collects in taxes, although it can have a surplus or deficit in any given year.

From 1970 through 1992, the domestic government sector was a net borrower. The federal budget deficit for fiscal year 1993 was $333 billion, which far more than offset the collective state and local government budget surpluses of about $20 billion. How does government saving and borrowing affect the economy's real interest rate (which, in turn, affects private saving and investment decisions)? Let's assume that the government's saving decisions are determined by public policies about taxes and expenditures and are not sensitive to changes in the real interest rate. We can then add saving or dissaving by the government to the saving curve.

Suppose that the federal government increases its purchases of military equipment and doesn't increase taxes; that is, the government is borrowing to finance the new purchases. If households do not change their saving in response to the increased dissaving by the government, the saving curve shifts to the left, as shown in Fig. 5.5, reducing total saving and investment and increasing the expected real interest rate (see the Other times, other places box). Households could increase their saving when the government borrows in order to pay the future taxes required to pay off the government's debt. However, empirical studies by economists suggest that households do not increase their current saving by the full amount of the government's dissaving. Hence, if nothing else changes, a fall in government saving reduces total saving and investment and increases the expected real interest rate. A rise in government saving increases total saving and investment and decreases the expected real interest rate.

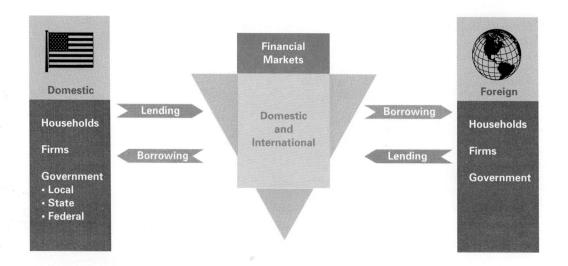

▲ FIGURE 5.6·

Flow of Funds in an Open Economy
In an open economy, domestic savers can lend to domestic or foreign borrowers, as can foreign savers.

The International Capital Market and the Real Interest Rate

The foreign sector also influences total savings available for investment in the economy. So far, we have analyzed saving and investment decisions for a **closed economy,** that is, an economy that neither borrows from nor lends to foreign countries. However, this scenario is unrealistic in today's global economy. Figure 5.6 illustrates the flows of international borrowing and lending.[†] Foreign households, businesses, and governments may want to lend funds for investment in the United States if the expected real returns from saving are higher there than in other countries. Similarly, if opportunities for investment are more promising outside the United States, savings will be drawn away from U.S. markets to fund investment abroad. In the 1980s and early 1990s, the United States generally was a net borrower of foreign funds, receiving a net inflow of savings from abroad to finance investment by firms and dissaving by the U.S. government.

In an **open economy,** capital is mobile internationally. Borrowing and lending take place in the international capital market, the capital market in which households, firms, and governments borrow and lend across national borders. The **world real interest rate** r_w is the real interest rate determined in the international capital market. Desired total saving in an open economy equals desired domestic investment plus the amount of its savings that the country lends abroad. Saving and investment decisions in small open economies, such as The Netherlands or Belgium, do not have much effect on the world real interest rate. However, shifts in domestic saving and invest-

---

[†] Countries record statistics on borrowing and lending by households, firms, and governments in *flow of funds accounts.* These accounts trace the sources and uses of funds for the household, business, government, and foreign sectors of the economy. Combining gross inflows and outflows of funds for a sector produces net flows. In the United States, the flow of funds accounts are maintained by the Federal Reserve.

ment in large open economies, such as Germany or the United States, do affect the world real interest rate. Let's consider real interest rate determination for each case.

Q: How do the determinants of saving and investment affect interest rates in the economy?

A: Factors that increase desired saving lower the real interest rate, whereas factors that decrease desired saving raise the real interest rate. Factors that increase desired investment raise the real interest rate, whereas factors that decrease desired investment lower the real interest rate.

Small Open Economy. For a closed economy, the equilibrium real interest rate is the rate at which desired saving and investment are equal; it is determined by the intersection of the saving curve and the investment curve. In a **small open economy,** total saving is too small to affect the world real interest rate, and the economy takes the world interest rate as a given. If the principality of Monaco pursued tax policies to increase domestic saving, for example, any increased saving would have only a trivial effect on worldwide saving and the world interest rate.

For a small open economy, the domestic real interest rate must equal the world real interest rate r_w; otherwise, domestic savers would invest their money outside the country. Suppose that the world real interest rate is 4% and that the domestic real interest rate in Monaco is 3%. A saver in Monaco would not accept a real interest rate of less than r_w = 4% in the domestic capital market because foreign investment options are available. But if Monaco's real interest rate is 5%, domestic borrowers would be unwilling to pay a real interest rate greater than r_w = 4%, as they have access to the international capital market.[†]

Because a small open economy takes the world real interest rate as a given, we can determine its level of domestic desired saving and investment and level of international borrowing or lending from the saving-investment diagram. Figure 5.7 shows the saving and investment curves for a small open economy. If the world real interest rate is 3%, domestic desired saving and investment are equal (point E); that is, the country neither borrows nor lends funds in the international capital market.

Suppose instead that the world real interest rate is 5%. In this case, desired saving at home, S_1, exceeds desired borrowing for domestic investment, I_1, as shown in Fig. 5.7. Because it is small, however, this economy can lend as much as it wants in the international capital market at the going rate of 5%. Hence it brings the savings that cannot be lent at home, $S_1 - I_1$, to the international capital market where there are willing borrowers.

But suppose that the world real interest rate is 1%. Desired borrowing for domestic investment now exceeds desired domestic saving, S_2, as Fig. 5.7 depicts. As a small open economy, the country can borrow as much as it wants in the international capital market at the going rate of 1%. Hence it borrows the savings, $I_2 - S_2$, from the international capital market, where foreign savers are willing to lend. The real interest rate in a small open economy is the real interest rate in the international capital market. If domestic desired saving exceeds domestic desired investment at that interest rate, the country

---

[†] Here we assume that the country imposes no barriers to international lending or borrowing. In Chapter 22, we discuss such barriers.

FIGURE 5.7

Determining the Real Interest Rate in a Small Open Economy
The domestic real interest in a small open economy is the world real interest rate r_w.

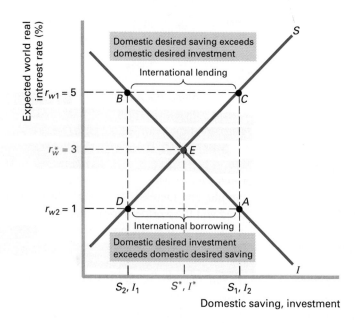

Q: How do international borrowing and lending affect interest rate determination in the economy?

A: The equilibrium world real interest rate equates desired international lending and desired international borrowing. A small open economy takes the world real interest rate as a given. Saving and investment shifts in a large open economy can affect the world real interest rate.

invests some of its savings abroad. If domestic desired investment exceeds domestic desired saving at that interest rate, the country finances some of its domestic investment with savings from abroad.

Large Open Economy. Shifts of domestic saving and investment do not affect the world real interest rate in many countries. However, the economies of some countries—such as the United States, Japan, and Germany—are sufficiently large that their domestic saving and investment shifts *do* affect the real interest rate in the international capital market. Such a financially powerful country is an example of a **large open economy,** or an economy large enough to affect the world real interest rate.

In the case of a large open economy, we can no longer assume that the domestic real interest rate is the real interest rate in the international capital market. Recall that in a closed economy, the equilibrium real interest rate equated desired saving by savers with desired borrowing by investors. By extension, if we think of the world as two large open economies—the United States and the rest of the world—the real interest rate in the international capital market equates desired international lending by the United States with desired international borrowing by the rest of the world.

Figure 5.8 illustrates the process of interest rate determination for a large open economy. Saving-investment diagrams for two economies are presented in the figure, labeled *United States* and *Rest of the world.* If the world real interest rate prevailing in the international capital market is 3%, desired saving S^* and investment I^* are equal in the United States. However, at that real interest rate, desired investment, I_1, exceeds desired saving, S_1, in the rest of the world by $100 billion; that is, foreign borrowers want to borrow $100

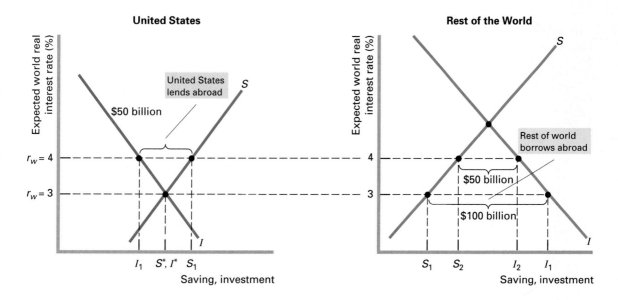

Determining the Real Interest Rate in a Large Open Economy

Saving and investment shifts in a large open economy can affect the world real interest rate. The world real interest rate r_w adjusts to equalize desired international borrowing and desired international lending. At a world real interest rate of 4%, desired international lending by the domestic economy equals desired international borrowing by the rest of the world.

FIGURE 5.8

billion from the international capital market. If they can obtain a higher real interest rate, domestic savers will lend funds to foreign borrowers. So long as savings may be invested at home or abroad, foreign borrowers will agree to pay savers in the United States a real interest rate greater than 3%.

Figure 5.8 shows that the demand for funds by the rest of the world would push up the real interest rate in the international capital market to 4%. At a real interest rate of 4%, desired saving, S_1, in the United States exceeds desired investment, I_1, by $50 billion. Similarly, at a real interest rate of 4%, desired investment, I_2, in the rest of the world exceeds desired saving, S_2, by $50 billion. At a 4% real interest rate, then, desired international lending by the United States equals desired international borrowing by the rest of the world. As a result, the international capital market is in equilibrium. The equilibrium world real interest rate equates international lending by one large open economy with international borrowing by others. Factors that increase desired international borrowing relative to desired international lending raise the world real interest rate. Factors that increase international lending relative to international borrowing lower the world real interest rate.

▶ **CHECKPOINT** *You may have read in newspaper that a recent economic study concludes that Japanese households are likely to save much less of their current income in the 1990s than they did in the 1970s and 1980s. What, if anything, does this finding imply for real interest rates on home mortgage loans and business loans in the United States?* Japan and the United States are large open economies, so shifts in their domestic saving and investment patterns affect the world real interest rate. The predicted decline in Japanese saving reduces desired international lending, putting upward pressure on the world real interest rate. A higher world real interest rate increases the cost of funds for home mortgages and business loans. ◀

MOVING FROM THEORY TO PRACTICE ...

THE NEW YORK TIMES   MARCH 26, 1991

Will a Worldwide Savings Shortage Raise Interest Rates?

The growing appetite for long-term investment funds may make interest rates higher than they might otherwise have been in coming years as countries in the Middle East and Eastern Europe seek huge sums to rebuild their battered economies.

A new study by Morgan Stanley & Company said the total demand for capital by Eastern Europe, Latin America and the Middle East would exceed the Western world's supply by more than $200 billion a year in the next few years.

Such a shortage and the resulting rise in interest rates would send ripples throughout the world economy. It would hurt corporate borrowers worldwide and home buyers in Europe and the United States, and make it more difficult for debtor nations in Africa and Latin America to attract development loans—and repay them. Higher interest rates would also raise the cost of financing Washing-ton's growing debt load.

David Hale, the chief economist with Kemper Financial Services in Chicago, said Eastern European developments had already pushed up interest rates. He said Bonn's decision to spend $85.5 billion to revive eastern Germany had caused the German central bank to raise interest rates to keep the economy from overheating. Mr. Hale said the move had pushed up interest rates worldwide by at least 50 basis points, or one-half of a percentage point. A basis point is one-hundredth of a percentage point.

"If the Soviet flag were still flying over East Berlin," Mr. Hale said, speaking figuratively, "American mortgage rates might be 50 or 75 points less."

Still, in the eyes of many economists, there can never, strictly speaking, be a capital shortage: If the demand for capital suddenly exceeded the supply of savings, then interest rates would rise, bringing the demand for capital into equilibrium with the supply of savings...

Many economists stress the importance of reducing Washington's budget deficit, which would translate into an increase in savings. This would in theory stimulate long-term growth by lowering interest rates and allowing more money to be spent on growth-producing investment, rather than on current consumption.

Officials in developing nations often complain that by borrowing so much from abroad to finance its deficit, Washington is using savings that could—and they say should—be used to modernize factories in Poland or explore for oil in Mexico.

"The United States may be a place where people can make good investments, but you wouldn't think that we should use the rest of the world's savings," Mr. Bryant said.

ⓐ

ⓑ

ANALYZING THE NEWS...

The article argues that shifts in domestic saving and investment can affect the real interest rates in international financial markets.

a Using this reasoning, the collapse of socialist regimes in Eastern Europe in the early 1990s and the ensuing rise of market economies should increase the demand for capital in the 1990s. Hale's comment about mortgage interest rates reveals that U.S. financial markets could be directly affected by Germany's decision to raise interest rates. Consider the accompanying saving-investment diagrams of the United States and Germany, both of which are large open economies. Before the reunification of Germany, West Germany was a significant lender in the international capital market, and the United States was a borrower. The equilibrium world interest rate is r_{w0}. In this equilibrium, Germany lends $B - A$ through the international capital market, while the United States borrows $F - E$.

Because of the increase in the expected profitability of investment in the former East Germany after reunification, German investment shifts from I_0 to I_1. The increase in German government dissaving from the $85.5 billion in spending shifts the German saving curve from S_0 to S_1. To balance international borrowing and lending, the world real interest rate rises to r_{w1}. In the new equilibrium, Germany lends $C - D$, and the United States borrows less, $G - H$. Hence Hale is correct to predict that a surge in German investment demand will raise interest rates, including mortgage interest rates in the United States.

b Shifts in saving and investment schedules in the United States and abroad do not generate capital shortages or capital surpluses. The international capital market balances desired international lending and desired international borrowing to determine the world real interest rate. Note that at the initial world real interest rate r_{w0}, Germany's increased demand for funds leads to an excess demand for world savings. Suppose that, as shown, saving and investment shifts reduce Germany's net lending at the initial world real interest rate. This shift means that a previously large supply of funds is no longer available, creating a shortage of capital at the going world real interest rate. The world real interest rate rises to a higher equilibrium for all economies, including the United States.

For further thought...

Suppose that U.S. households doubled their saving rate from current income for a long period of time. What would be the effect on the real interest rate on (1) bank loans in the United States, (2) bonds in Japan, and (3) bonds in Brazil? Why?

Source: Excerpted from Steven Greenhouse, "World's Finances Facing Strains as Troubled Areas Try to Rebuild," March 26, 1991. Copyright © 1991/1992 by The New York Times Company. Reprinted with permission.

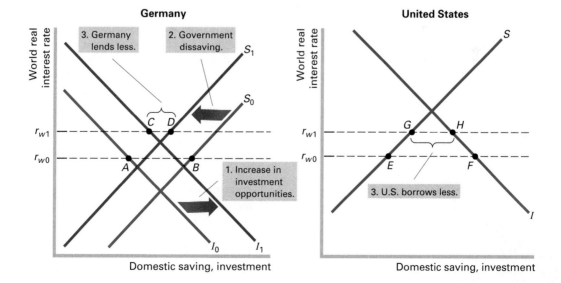

Key Terms and Concepts

Closed economy

Equilibrium real interest rate

Life-cycle model of consumption and saving

Open economy
 Large open economy
 Small open economy

Opportunity cost

Precautionary saving

Saving-investment diagram
 Investment curve
 Saving curve

World real interest rate

Summary

1. Households try to smooth their spending over time. Because income and spending patterns do not match precisely, households generally will save or dissave (draw down accumulated assets or borrow) during any given period of time. In a life-cycle pattern, individuals typically spend more than they earn when young, save and accumulate assets through their working years, and dissave in retirement. In addition, people save to finance the purchase of durable goods, as a precaution against an emergency, or to leave bequests. In an economy with a growing population and income, households collectively are net savers. The dissaving of older households is exceeded by the saving of younger households.

2. Like households, businesses both save and dissave. Business dissaving (using internal funds or borrowing) finances new investment opportunities. Business saving is used to retire outstanding debt or accumulate internal funds to finance future investment opportunities. In a growing economy, businesses collectively are net dissavers as expansion and borrowing by growing firms exceed saving by mature firms.

3. The saving curve presents the level of desired saving in the economy at any expected real interest rate. The saving curve slopes upward: A higher real interest rate increases the returns from saving by households, increasing household saving. Factors that shift the saving curve include demographics,

economic growth, current income, expected future income and wealth, precautionary saving, and bequest saving.

4. The investment curve shows the level of desired investment in the economy at any expected real interest rate. The investment curve slopes downward: A higher real interest rate raises the financing cost of investment, lowering its profitability and reducing business investment. Factors that shift the investment curve include the before-tax expected profitability of capital and taxes on business profits and investment.

5. If savings are not internationally mobile, the equilibrium real interest rate lies at the intersection of the saving and investment curves of a country. Any factor that raises desired saving at any real interest rate shifts the saving curve to the right, decreasing the equilibrium real interest rate. Any factor that lowers desired saving at any real interest rate shifts the saving curve to the left, increasing the equilibrium real interest rate. Any factor that raises desired investment at any real interest rate shifts the investment curve to the right, increasing the equilibrium real interest rate. Any factor that lowers desired investment at any real interest rate shifts the investment curve to the left, decreasing the equilibrium real interest rate.

6. If capital is mobile internationally (an open economy), in equilibrium, desired saving equals the

sum of desired domestic investment and the amount the domestic economy lends abroad. A small open economy takes the real interest rate of the international capital market as a given because the amount of its saving or borrowing is not substantial enough to influence the international capital market. Shifts in desired saving or desired investment in a large open economy can affect the real interest rate in the international capital market (the world real interest rate). Factors increasing desired saving or decreasing desired investment lower the world real interest rate; factors decreasing desired saving or increasing desired investment raise the world real interest rate.

Review Questions

1. Give a reason why each of the following actions might occur.

   a. The saving curve shifts left.

   b. The saving curve shifts right.

   c. The investment curve shifts left.

   d. The investment curve shifts right.

2. Why does the saving curve slope up and the investment curve slope down in the saving-investment diagram?

3. In what types of economies can saving not equal investment at equilibrium? How can this occur?

4. How would you describe the life-cycle pattern of income and consumption for most people? What does this pattern imply about saving and dissaving over a person's lifetime?

5. How does a small open economy differ from a large open economy?

Analytical Problems

6. When expected inflation rises, many changes in desired investment, desired saving, and the equilibrium real interest rate are possible. This happens because the tax system distorts saving and investment decisions, as do certain aspects of the financial structure (such as the criteria used by banks to justify loans). The result is that the saving and investment curves could shift to the left or right in response to a change in expected inflation. Draw a saving-investment diagram to illustrate each of the following scenarios.

   a. In a closed economy, the saving and investment curves both shift to the left, leaving the real interest rate unchanged.

   b. In a closed economy, the saving curve shifts to the left, and the equilibrium real interest rate declines.

   c. In a closed economy, the saving curve doesn't shift, the investment curve shifts to the left, and the equilibrium quantity of investment is unchanged.

   d. In a small open economy that initially neither borrows nor lends abroad, the saving curve shifts to the left, and the investment curve shifts to the right. Does the economy now borrow or lend abroad?

   e. In a small open economy that initially neither borrows nor lends abroad, the saving and investment curves both shift to the left so that the economy still neither borrows nor lends.

   f. In a small open economy that initially lends abroad, investment is unchanged, and the saving curve shifts to the left so that the economy no longer lends abroad.

7. When an economy initially comes out of a recession, people receive higher incomes, so they increase their saving, and businesses invest more as they anticipate higher profits. With both the saving and investment curves shifting to the right in the saving-investment diagram, the effect on the real interest rate is ambiguous. But data suggest that the real interest rate usually rises as the United States comes out of a recession. Draw saving-investment diagrams that show this condition for both a closed economy and a large open economy. Is this result possible for a small open economy? Why or why not?

8. In a closed economy, how would each of the following events affect the real interest rate and the quantity of investment?

   a. A natural disaster destroys bridges and roads in California, leading to increased investment spending to rebuild.

   b. Future taxes of businesses are expected to be increased.

   c. A popular TV miniseries runs every night for a month, causing people to stay home to watch it and spend much less than usual.

   d. The government proposes a new tax on savings, based on people's balances on December 31 each year.

9. Repeat Question 8 for a small open economy.

10. Repeat Question 8 for a large open economy.

11. Suppose that a system of national health care is instituted in the United States, with all health care costs for people to be paid by the government. How might this change affect aggregate saving and the real interest rate in equilibrium? Why? (Assume a closed economy.)

12. How would the following events affect aggregate saving in the United States?

   a. Oil reserves 10 times as large as those in the Middle East are discovered in Montana.

   b. The economy grows twice as fast as expected, owing to higher productivity growth, so unemployment falls substantially.

   c. Reconstruction projects in Eastern Europe require $1 trillion, causing an increase in the world real interest rate.

13. How would the following events affect U.S. investment?

   a. U.S. cities nationwide, overburdened with payments for social problems, increase business taxes.

   b. Increased computerization in corporations allows them to decrease substantially inventories and their associated costs.

   c. The tax deduction for home mortgage interest payments is eliminated.

14. Suppose that the government plans to undertake one of two possible spending projects: Project A involves spending $10 billion to build more military aircraft; project B involves spending the same amount to improve local bridges and water systems. In each case the saving curve shifts to the left as the project is financed. Project A has no effect on investment, but project B improves the profitability of businesses by lowering their costs for transportation and water. Show how this difference leads to a different real interest rate, depending on which project is chosen and assuming a closed economy. Do you think this result is true generally? In which case is the economy better off?

15. Suppose that a large open economy initially has saving equal to investment. Then a change in business taxes discourages investment. Show how this change affects the quantities of investment and saving and the world real interest rate. Does this economy now borrow or lend internationally?

16. Two countries alike in all other respects differ markedly in their provision of social insurance. One country provides old-age retirement pensions, unemployment insurance, and catastrophic illness insurance; the other country provides no social insurance. What is your prediction about the difference in household saving rates between the two countries? Why?

17. Throughout the 1980s, the U.S. government had budget deficits (spending greater than current tax receipts), necessitating large amounts of government borrowing. Using the saving-investment diagram, illustrate the effects of government dissaving on the expected real interest rate and business investment. What would happen if households believed that deficits will be financed by higher taxes in the near future and increased their saving in anticipation of those higher taxes?

18. Most economists argue that a boom in the stock market is a sign that profitable business opportunities are expected for the future. Describe the likely effects on business investment and the expected real interest rate of such a boom. What assumptions did you make?

19. Suppose that two countries have completely separate financial systems; that is, savings do not flow between them to finance investment. One country is just beginning to develop, with only limited saving and a small amount of accumulated savings. The other country is mature, with few new investment opportunities but a large amount of saving. Using a saving-investment diagram, describe the difference in the expected real interest rates in the two countries. What would happen to the return on savings in the two countries if savings could flow without restriction between them? Would more profitable investment projects be financed and undertaken? Why or why not?

20. During some years in the 1970s, the real rate of interest on many debt securities in the United States was negative; that is, actual inflation exceeded the nominal interest rate. Were lenders willing to accept a negative real return during those years? Why or why not?

Data Question

21. To get some idea of the size of international borrowing and lending by the United States, obtain a copy of the latest *Economic Report of the President* at the library. Look up the table of U.S. international transactions and find the balance on current account. Except for a few differences, and a fairly large statistical discrepancy, this balance should equal the difference between U.S. investment and saving. What happened to the current account balance in the mid-1980s? What do you think might explain this event?

6

The Theory of Portfolio Allocation

In October 1987, investors suddenly shifted their money from stocks into U.S. Treasury bonds and other financial instruments, causing one of the largest single-day drops in stock market history. What accounts for this shift in preference for one type of asset over another? More generally, how do people decide among the many possible ways to hold their wealth—stocks, bonds, houses, paintings, and so on?

Recall that people may be motivated to save for several reasons: to smooth spending over time, to purchase durable goods, to accumulate precautionary (or emergency) funds for retirement, and to leave bequests. In meeting these needs, savers are concerned about the expected real return on their savings. They also care about how easily their savings can be converted into a secure and steady source of income to finance future spending.

In this chapter we explore portfolio allocation in order to understand how savers decide to allocate their wealth among alternative assets. The theory of portfolio allocation helps predict key determinants of asset demand and choices of assets. We also explain why people should put their savings in several different assets, that is, diversify. Our subsequent analysis of interest rate determination, the behavior of financial institutions, and innovation in financial markets and institutions builds on the concepts presented in this chapter.

We focus on two important questions. **Q:** What are the principal determinants of how people allocate their savings among alternative assets? **Q:** What benefits can people obtain from holding many assets (a portfolio) rather than holding all their savings in one asset?

Determinants of Portfolio Allocation

The financial system encompasses trading in a wide array of assets. A saver regularly makes decisions about which assets to include in his or her **portfolio**, or collection of assets, and how to allocate savings among these assets. For example, if you earn $1000 during your school vacation, you may choose to invest it in stocks, bonds, a money market fund, commodities, property, machines, gold, paintings, or hold your earnings as cash. Such assets represent a store of value; that is, they can be sold to finance spending on goods and services.

The **theory of portfolio allocation** predicts how savers distribute their assets across alternative investments. It indicates that when deciding what investments to make, savers consider five key factors, or **determinants of asset demand:** the saver's *wealth*, or the total stock of savings to be allocated; the saver's *expected return* on the asset relative to the expected return on other assets; the *degree of risk* associated with the asset's return relative to that of other assets; the *liquidity* of the asset relative to other assets; and the *cost of acquiring information* about the asset relative to information costs associated with other assets.

As we discuss each factor in turn, think about how these determinants shape your own financial decisions. As we discuss in Part III, the same factors affect the portfolio allocation decisions of businesses and financial intermediaries.

Wealth: Size of Portfolio

As their wealth increases, people have more savings to allocate among assets and so may demand a greater quantity of individual assets. However, as people grow richer, they do not increase proportionately the quantities of all assets demanded. Rather, they decrease their relative holdings of some assets and increase their relative holdings of other assets. For example, cash is an asset in which you might choose to decrease your relative holdings. If your total wealth were $1000, you might hold 10%, or $100, in cash. If your total wealth were $1 million, however, you probably would not hold $100,000 in cash. Cash holdings would make up a smaller percentage of your wealth, and you would increase your relative holdings in other assets, such as stocks. Although holding many shares of different high-quality stocks with wealth of only $1000 is difficult, you might well own a variety of stocks with $1 million.

The **wealth elasticity of demand** describes how responsive the percentage change in the quantity of an asset demanded is to a percentage change in wealth. Like the elasticity concepts you learned in your principles of economics course, the wealth elasticity of demand does not depend on the actual dollar value of your wealth. Rather, it equals the percentage increase in the quantity of an asset you demand divided by the percentage increase in your total wealth; that is,

$$\text{Wealth elasticity of demand for an asset} = \frac{\% \text{ change in quantity demanded of the asset}}{\% \text{ change in wealth}}$$

To understand the implications of this concept, let's return to the preceding example. We imagined that you would hold 10%, or $100, of your wealth as cash if your total wealth were $1000 but would hold less of your wealth (proportionately) in cash as you grew richer. Let's say that when your wealth reaches $1 million, you hold 0.1%, or $1000, in cash. Thus your wealth elasticity of demand for cash is .01, which is less than 1. This means that an increase in wealth generates a decrease in percentage terms of cash held. However, your wealth elasticity of demand for stocks and other assets is greater than 1. This means that an increase in wealth generates an increase in percentage terms of stocks and other assets held.

A *necessity* asset is one for which the wealth elasticity of demand is less than 1. Savers demand necessity assets, such as cash or checking accounts, in order to conduct regular transactions. A *luxury* asset, however, is one for which the wealth elasticity of demand exceeds 1. What makes some assets luxuries? They are those assets, such as stocks, held for investment rather than for facilitating transactions. Savers also must consider the high fixed cost of owning a luxury asset, such as real estate taxes and insurance costs for a $1 million house, or the high transactions costs of acquiring the asset, such as stockbroker or dealer fees for stocks. For savers with less wealth, these costs make up a larger percentage of their investment than for savers with more wealth. Thus acquiring some assets, such as buying a famous painting, is feasible only for wealthy individuals.

As wealth increases, the quantity demanded for most assets increases, with quantity demanded for necessities increasing proportionately less and quantity demanded for luxuries increasing proportionately more.

Expected Returns on Assets

What factors determine how savers, whether wealthy or poor, choose to allocate their wealth among assets? One determinant of asset demand is the expected returns on various assets. Given the choice between two otherwise similar assets, a saver will pick the one with the higher expected return. Recall from Chapter 4 that the correct measure of expected return is the *real* rate of return. That is, savers deciding whether to invest in stocks or bonds will compare the expected real returns on each. Because savers care about expected returns for financing current and future spending, they focus on the amount that they can keep after taxes; that is, they compare expected real after-tax returns.

Taxation of returns on savings varies significantly in the United States. Interest on private corporate bonds, bank deposits, and dividends from holdings of corporate stock are taxed at the federal, state, and local levels. Interest received from U.S. Treasury securities is subject to federal income taxation, but not to state and local income taxation. The obligations of state and local governments (called municipal bonds) generally are exempt from all taxation and often are called *tax-exempt bonds*. All such differences affect savers' portfolio decisions.

When assets are similar—that is, holding all other factors constant—an increase in the expected return on one asset relative to other assets leads to an increase in the quantity of that asset demanded. The remaining three determinants of asset demand—risk, liquidity, and information—are attributes that we use to assess whether two assets are similar.

▶ **C H E C K P O I N T** *The interest received from municipal bonds is tax-exempt in the United States. Should you switch your savings from taxable assets to municipal bonds to take advantage of their favorable tax treatment?* Not necessarily. Investors compare expected *after-tax* returns when making their investment decisions. Suppose that a taxable bond pays an interest rate of 10%. If investors have a marginal tax rate of 30%, this after-tax return is equivalent to the return on the tax-exempt bond of 10% − 0.3(10%) = 7%. If the tax-exempt rate were higher (say, 8%), the expected return on the tax-exempt bond would exceed that on the taxable bond. Investors would increase their demand for tax-exempt bonds, bidding up their price and reducing their yield. (Bond prices and yields are inversely related.) At a marginal tax rate of 15%, investors would prefer to invest in the taxable bond because they could receive an expected after-tax return of 10% − 0.15(10%) = 8.5%. This is greater than the 7% expected rate of return on the tax-exempt bond. Investors subject to high tax rates are more likely to invest in tax-exempt bonds than are investors subject to low tax rates. ◀

Risk Associated with Asset Returns

Savers care not only about the expected return on their savings, but also about the variability (fluctuations up and down) of that return as well. Because households use their assets largely to smooth their spending over time, they want to avoid having assets fall in value just when they need funds.

For example, suppose that you have $1000 to invest in stocks and are comparing the shares of Solid Enterprises and Rollercoaster Industries. Solid Enterprises' shares yield a return of 10% all the time (with certainty), whereas Rollercoaster Industries' shares yield a return of 20% half the time and 0% half the time. We calculate the expected return on Rollercoaster's shares by using a weighted average of its possible returns:

$$\left(\frac{1}{2}\right)(0.20) + \left(\frac{1}{2}\right)(0) = 0.10, \ \ \text{or } 10\%.$$

Solid's expected return, 10%, is the same. How do you choose between them?

Consider this...
How Much Risk Should You Tolerate in Your Portfolio?

BOX 6.1

As you develop your own asset allocation plan, you probably will find that your attitude toward risk depends on how far in the future your saving goal extends. For most people, an important saving goal is retirement, and thus retirement savings comprises a significant component of their wealth. Financial planners generally argue that if your retirement is many years away, you should focus on expected long-term real returns, without much concern for short-term variability in returns. Then, as you approach retirement, you

should adopt a more conservative strategy, sacrificing some expected return in order to reduce the risk of losing a substantial por-

tion of your savings. Financial planners often define portfolios for these two cases.

Young Saver

Description:
Below age fifty and wishes to build his or her net worth over a relatively long time.

Goal:
Accumulate funds by earning high long-term return.

Portfolio plan:
Select porfolio based on maximizing expected real return with only limited concern for variability.

Older Saver

Close to retirement age with a portfolio at or near the amount needed to retire.

Conserve existing funds to earn a return slightly above the inflation rate.

Reduce risk, by selecting safe assets to earn an expected real return of about zero.

The answer lies in the degree of risk associated with the two investments. Most people are **risk-averse savers**. They seek to minimize variability in the return on their savings and prefer security in their investments. A risk-averse saver would even accept a lower return from Solid Enterprises because of this desire for stability. **Risk-neutral savers** judge assets only on their expected returns; variability of returns is not a concern. A few individuals are **risk-loving savers**, who actually prefer to gamble by holding a risky asset with the possibility of maximizing returns.

Empirical evidence on expected returns from financial markets confirms the risk-averse behavior of most investors. For example, annual real rates of return (adjusted for inflation) on U.S. common stocks averaged 7.2% from 1926 to 1992, while annual real rates of return on long-term government bonds averaged only 1.7%.[†] Why do investors accept such low returns on government bonds when they could earn more by investing in stocks? The principal reason is that government bonds involve less risk. Stocks offer higher potential returns to compensate savers for taking the higher risk associated with equity investment (see Box 6.1).

[†] These data are based on the calculations by economists Roger Ibbotson and Rex Sinquefield and cover data from 1926 through 1992, as reported in Lynn Asimov, "Double-Digit Returns May Be Tougher to Find," *The Wall Street Journal*, July 27, 1992.

Because savers are generally risk-averse, an increase in the risk of one asset relative to other assets leads to a decline in the quantity of that asset demanded.

Liquidity of Assets

Greater liquidity helps savers to smooth spending over time or to draw down funds for emergencies. For example, if you maintain some savings in financial assets in order to meet unanticipated medical expenses, you want to be able to sell those assets quickly if you need the money for an operation.

Obviously, cash is the most liquid asset. Many marketable securities, such as U.S. government bonds or shares of IBM, are very liquid assets because finding a buyer for them with minimal transactions costs is easy. Real estate, coins, and fine paintings are relatively illiquid assets because substantial transactions costs are involved in their sale. For example, a saver who wants to sell a house may need to wait months or even years before finding a buyer willing to pay the full asking price.

Holding all other factors constant, an increase in the liquidity of an asset relative to other assets leads to an increase in the quantity of that asset demanded.

▶ **C H E C K P O I N T** *Certificates of deposit (CDs) offered by banks have a penalty for early withdrawal. For example, if you invest $1000 in a one-year CD paying 7% interest, you receive less interest if you withdraw your savings before the end of a year. Why are investors willing to accept a lower interest rate (say, 5¼%) on savings accounts without a penalty for early withdrawal?* Savers are generally willing to sacrifice some portion of expected return in order to be able to convert an asset to cash quickly to finance planned or emergency spending. ◀

Information Costs

Savers seek to lower the risk associated with an asset but want to do so without devoting time or resources to assessing the creditworthiness of the issuer or monitoring the borrower's actions. For some assets, such as cash or government securities, information is readily available to the public at low cost. For example, if you want to buy a government bond, you can easily find prices and returns in *The Wall Street Journal*. Similarly, savers can gather information about the stocks and bonds of large corporations inexpensively because financial analysts widely publicize information about these assets.

If a new company issues financial claims, however, investors must spend time and resources to collect and analyze information about the company before deciding to invest. Therefore savers prefer to hold assets with low information costs. An increase in the information cost for an asset raises the required rate of return on the asset; a decrease in information costs reduces the required rate of return (see the Other times, other places box). Specialists in the financial

Other times, other places...
Information Costs and International Portfolio Investment

Investors tend to invest a disproportionately large share of their savings in financial assets in their own country. The reason for this is the cost of acquiring information about foreign investments. Most countries have a set of accounting rules for disclosing information to investors. In the United States, for example, the Securities and Exchange Commission (a federal regulatory agency) makes rules for disclosing information to shareholders and bondholders in financial markets; the Financial Accounting Standards Board (a private organization) issues guidelines for reporting information by firms about their financial condition. Finding out where and how this information on companies is disclosed in other countries can

take time and money.

Comparing expected returns on stocks in various countries can be difficult. A popular measure used in the United States is the ratio of the stock price to the earnings per share: the *price-earnings (P-E) ratio*. A high P-E ratio means that investors believe that earnings will grow rapidly and so are willing to pay a high price for the firm's shares today. In February 1992, the P-E ratio for U.S. stocks was 25.6 versus 36.7 in Japan and 15.9 in Germany. Does that mean that as an investor you should expect greater earnings growth in Japan than in the United States or Germany?

Not necessarily. Smithers and Company,[†] a London-based research organization, found that

Japanese earnings tend to be understated: Japanese companies do not consolidate the earnings of subsidiaries in which they have an interest of less than 20%. They also found that German earnings are misleadingly small by U.S. standards: German firms write off the cost of investment faster than U.S. firms do. After making various technical adjustments to standardize definitions, Smithers found that Japan's P-E ratio should be 22.1, or lower than the ratio of 25.6 calculated for the United States and only slightly higher than the ratio of 19.1 calculated for Germany. Investors benefit from obtaining such information, but acquiring it can be costly.

[†] See "All the World's a Ratio," *The Economist*, February 22, 1992.

system acquire and analyze such information and make it available for a fee. Holding other factors constant, a higher cost of information for an asset relative to other assets leads to a decrease in the quantity of that asset demanded.

Table 6.1 summarizes the principal determinants of asset demands. The underlying assumption is that all other factors remain constant.

Advantages of Diversification

The theory of portfolio allocation indicates that people compare assets when determining how to allocate their savings. The theory seems to suggest that savers can calculate a "best" asset in which to invest their wealth. That is not the case in the real world, which is full of uncertainty. To compensate for this inability to find a perfect asset, individuals typically hold various types of assets, including financial instruments, property, and durable goods. Even within categories of financial assets (stocks, for example), investors usually hold many individual issues. Allocating savings among many different assets is known as **diversification**.

▼ TABLE 6.1	DETERMINANTS OF ASSET DEMAND	
An increase in...	**Causes the quantity of the asset demanded to ...**	**Because ...**
wealth	rise	savers have greater stock of savings to allocate
expected return on asset relative to expected returns on other assets	rise	savers gain more from holding asset
risk (variability of returns)	fall	savers are generally risk-averse
liquidity (ease with which asset can be converted to cash	rise	asset can be cheaply converted to cash to finance consumption
information costs	fall	savers must spend more resources acquiring and analyzing data on the asset and its returns

Q: What are the principal determinants of how people allocate their savings among alternative assets?

A: Wealth, the expected return on the asset relative to expected returns on other assets, and risk, liquidity, and information costs of assets are the principal determinants.

In the real world, returns on assets do not move together perfectly because their risks are imperfectly correlated. Thus the return on a diversified portfolio is more stable than the returns on the individual assets comprising the portfolio. Diversification effectively allows the investor to divide risk into smaller and thus less potentially harmful pieces. Research on the benefits of diversification led to three Nobel prizes in economics, to James Tobin of Yale University, Harry Markowitz of Baruch College, and William Sharpe of Stanford University.

How does diversification reduce portfolio risk? Let's use an example to answer this question. Suppose that you want to invest $1000 in stocks and are choosing between two investments—shares in Boomco, Inc., and shares in Bustco, Inc.—whose returns vary with the economy's performance in different ways. Suppose that Boomco does well half the time and not so well the other half. When the economy does well, Boomco prospers. Its shares have a return of 20%, and you earn $200. But in a weak economy, sales of Boomco's products are poor. Then the stock's return is 0%, and you have nothing. Boomco's expected return is

$$\left(\frac{1}{2}\right)(\$200) + \left(\frac{1}{2}\right)(\$0) = \$100.$$

If you invest only in Boomco, you can expect a rate of return of 10%.

Suppose that Bustco's returns follow an opposite pattern. The return on Bustco shares is high (20%) when the economy is weak, and you earn $200. When the economy does well, you earn nothing (0%). Like

Boomco shares, Bustco shares have an expected return of

$$\left(\frac{1}{2}\right)(\$0) + \left(\frac{1}{2}\right)(\$200) = \$100.$$

If you invest only in Bustco, you can expect a rate of return of 10%. Of course, if you invest only in Boomco shares or only in Bustco shares, you incur risk because the returns vary with the economy's performance.

Now consider what happens if you invest equal amounts in Boomco and Bustco shares. In good times, Boomco's return is 20%, and Bustco's return is 0%. Therefore your total return in good times is

$$\left(\frac{1}{2}\right)(\text{Boomco return}) + \left(\frac{1}{2}\right)(\text{Bustco return}) = 10\%,$$

or

$$(\$500)(0.20) + (\$500)(0) = \$100.$$

Similarly, in bad times, you earn

$$\left(\frac{1}{2}\right)(\text{Boomco return}) + \left(\frac{1}{2}\right)(\text{Bustco return}) = 10\%,$$

or

$$(\$500)(0) + (\$500)(0.20) = \$100.$$

By this strategy, you earn the same expected return (10%) as you would earn from buying the shares of only one of the companies. However, you lessened the risk affecting your portfolio's returns by limiting the influence of one source of variability: the economy. The strategy of dividing risk by holding multiple assets ensures steadier income (see Box 6.2).

Investors cannot eliminate risk entirely because assets share some common risk called **market** (or **systematic**) **risk**. For example, general fluctuations in economic conditions can increase or decrease returns on stocks collectively. Assets also carry their own unique risk called **idiosyncratic** (or **unsystematic**) **risk**. For example, the price of an individual stock may be influenced by factors such as discoveries, strikes, or lawsuits that influence the profitability of the firm and its share value. Diversification can eliminate idiosyncratic risk but not market risk.[†]

Figure 6.1 illustrates the results of an empirical study that attempted to determine how much risk can be eliminated through diversifi-

---

[†] Indeed, even if asset returns are independent (completely uncorrelated), increasing the number of assets held in a portfolio reduces overall risk.

> **FIGURE 6.1**

Reducing Risk through Stock Portfolio Diversification
Increasing the number of New York Stock Exchange–listed stocks held in a portfolio decreases the variability of the portfolio's return. While diversification can reduce individual risk, there is a certain amount of risk that cannot be reduced.

Source: Based on calculations presented in Meir Statman, "How Many Stocks Make a Diversified Portfolio?" *Journal of Financial and Quantitative Analysis,* 22:353–364, 1980.

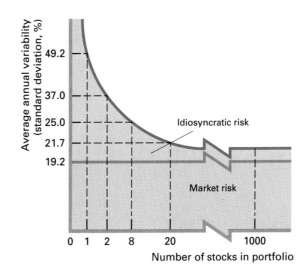

Q: What benefits can people obtain from holding many assets (a portfolio) rather than holding all their savings in one asset?

A: Diversification reduces the riskiness of the return on savers' portfolios. It benefits risk-averse savers, who are concerned not only about the expected return on their savings, but also about the variability of that return.

cation in a portfolio of stocks traded on the New York Stock Exchange. It illustrates the relationship between the average annual variability on equally weighted portfolios and the different numbers of stocks (selected randomly) in the portfolios. Although a single security had an average annual variability (measured by the standard deviation) of about 49%, holding two stocks reduced the variability by about one-quarter, to just over 37%.[†] Holding eight stocks cut the average annual variability in half, to just less than 25%. Increasing the number of assets to 20 cut the average annual variability further to about 21.7%. Holding the entire portfolio of stocks listed on the New York Stock Exchange reduced the average annual variability to 19.2%. This remaining variability is traceable to market risk and cannot be eliminated by holding additional stocks, that is, the risk is nondiversifiable. In the (unlikely) event that returns are perfectly and positively correlated, adding additional assets does not reduce the variability of the portfolio.

Diversification reduces the riskiness of the return on a portfolio unless assets' returns move together perfectly. The less the returns on assets move together, the greater the benefit savers reap from diversification in reducing portfolio risk. As savers generally are risk-averse, portfolios typically contain an array of different assets. Savers' ability to diversify is limited by the cost of acquiring information about alternative assets and the transactions costs of buying and selling individual assets. Another potential limit to diversi-

---

[†] The variance of a portfolio return is the squared deviation from the expected return. The standard deviation is the square root of the variance.

MOVING FROM THEORY TO PRACTICE...

THE NEW YORK TIMES   FEBRUARY 28, 1992

In Search of Higher Returns

Mutual fund investors appear to have pulled back slightly from the hectic pace of early 1992, when money was being put into long-term funds at the most rapid rate in five years. Fund managers said yesterday that both bond and stock funds continued to pull in huge amounts of money in February, although not at January's rate.

"We are running at about half the pace of last month, but it is still a good month," said Jane White, a spokeswoman for the T. Rowe Price group of funds. At the Vanguard Group, Brian Mattes said that cash flow was down substantially from January, but that February was still the third best month in the company's history.

a These initial reports on February's activity came as the Investment Company Institute, a trade group, reported that the net cash flow into long-term stock and bond funds in January totaled $14.6 billion, up from $11.6 billion in December. January's total was the largest for any month since January 1987, when a rapidly rising stock market combined with a solid bond market to bring in a record $18.7 billion.

By contrast, in all of 1989 the funds took in only $8.9 billion...

The prosperity is even making some managers nervous. Asked what was selling well, Richard S. Strong, the chairman of Strong Group of Milwaukee, replied, "Everything." Then he added, **b** "The worrisome thing about all this is you have people taking money from savings accounts and investing the money in equities. They are taking a lot more risk, and greed is starting to prevail."

But as a group, the fund managers seem even more bullish than their customers. In January, funds invested a net $7.8 billion in common stocks. Combined with rising stock prices, that left stock funds with just 7.9 percent of their assets in cash, the lowest percentage since 7.8 percent in December 1983.

Fund managers said some buyers seemed to be trying to minimize risk, while others were actively courting it. On the low-risk side, several fund groups said adjustable-rate mortgage funds were big sellers. Those funds, now yielding about 6.4 percent, are set up to have only small fluctuations in the net asset value of their shares and are being sold as alternatives to money market funds, whose yields are substantially lower.

c On the other side are the junk bond funds, which have rapidly been gaining cash from investors seeking to maintain high yields in the face of declining interest rates. "Junk bonds and the adjustable-rate fund, together, account for all of the net inflows into our bond funds" Mrs. White of T. Rowe Price said.

ANALYZING THE NEWS...

In late 1991 and early 1992, short-term interest rates declined significantly, with smaller declines in long-term interest rates. Many economists noted that the decline in interest rates was good news for the economy as a whole, a tonic that would accelerate the economic recovery. At the same time, however, the decline in short-term interest rates led to a smaller return for savers.

(a) In early 1992, savers switched from bank deposits into stock and bond mutual funds. As short-term interest rates declined, the expected rate of return on stocks and long-term bonds became more attractive, leading investors to increase their demand for those assets. Because mutual funds offer investors more diversified portfolios at a low transactions cost, much of the greater demand for stocks and bonds materialized as an increase in the demand for mutual fund shares.

(b) A decline in the expected rate of return on short-term assets should increase investors' desire to allocate more of their savings to other assets, but differences in risk must be considered. Because the variability of the rate of return on bank deposits is much less than the variability of the rate of return on stocks and bonds, the assets are not perfect substitutes. An investor who exchanges bank deposits for growth stocks assumes additional risk.

(c) Different investors are willing to bear different amounts of risk. As this article shows, some savers invested in mortgage funds that were structured to provide a higher rate of return than bank deposits or money market funds but without much additional risk. Others were willing to switch their savings into mutual funds invested in junk bonds (very risky debt obligations of corporations). Investing in alternative assets that yield different rates of return is rational. The higher rates of return on junk bond mutual funds compensate investors for the risk that they might lose part of their investment.

For further thought...

Venture capital firms are firms that have a portfolio of investments in start-up companies. Why does the average return on venture capital investments generally exceed the return for the stock market as a whole? (Focus on the risk, liquidity, and information costs of venture capital investments relative to those of stocks as a group.)

Source: Excerpted from "Funds Are Still Surging, But Pace Slows Slightly," by Floyd Norris, February 28, 1992. Copyright 1991/1992 by The New York Times Company. Reprinted by permission.

Consider this...
How Can Small Savers Diversify?

One barrier to diversification is the cost of buying and selling financial assets. Such transactions costs can be high for small savers. Financial institutions responded to this barrier by creating the mutual fund. Investors in a mutual fund buy shares in diversified portfolios of assets from financial markets. Because a mutual fund has a great quantity of money to invest (the collective funds of the individual savers), it can easily afford the transactions and information costs of many assets. Thus mutual funds

can offer diversified portfolios of stocks, government or private bonds, and money market instruments such as Treasury bills and commercial paper.

Assets in U.S. mutual funds grew from $240 billion in 1982 to about $1.4 trillion at the beginning of 1993. One American household in four now has an investment in a mutual fund. New mutual funds are even being created to permit investors to own stakes in credit card receivables.

Mutual funds are a valuable

method of diversification for several reasons: They offer a way for savers to pool risk; they allow maintenance of liquidity through low transactions costs and, in many cases, check-writing features, and they provide information to investors about the portfolio of assets. The funds earn a profit for the fund managers, as investors are willing to sacrifice some of the expected return on investments to obtain these benefits.

fication comes from legal restrictions on the assets that can be held by individual savers or by certain financial intermediaries on their behalf. In Part III, we apply the same logic to explain why diversification is valuable for the portfolios held for savers by financial intermediaries.

Key Terms and Concepts

Determinants of asset demand

Diversification

Idiosyncratic (unsystematic) risk

Market (systematic) risk

Risk-averse savers

Risk-loving savers

Risk-neutral savers

Theory of portfolio allocation

Wealth elasticity of demand

Summary

1. The theory of portfolio allocation helps predict how savers select assets to hold as investment. The demand for a particular asset is influenced by five

determinants: (1) wealth (with greater responsiveness for luxury assets than for necessity assets); (2) expected return on the asset relative to expected returns on other assets; (3) risk of the return on the asset relative to other assets; (4) liquidity of the asset relative to other assets; and (5) cost of gathering information about the asset relative to information costs associated with other assets.

2. Diversification (holding more than one asset) reduces the risk of the return on a portfolio unless the returns on the individual assets move together perfectly. The less the returns on assets move together, the greater is the reduction in risk provided by diversification. This reduction in risk is valued by risk-averse savers, who are concerned not only about the expected return on their savings (portfolio of assets), but also about the variability of that return.

Review Questions

1. What are the five key determinants of demand for a particular asset?

2. What is the difference between a necessity asset and a luxury asset? Give some examples of each.

3. What are the differences in being *risk-averse, risk-neutral*, and *risk-loving*? Which type of saver is likely to own only stocks and stock options? Which type of saver is likely to hold more bonds and cash than stocks?

4. U.S. citizens invest mostly in the U.S. stock market; Japanese citizens invest mostly in the Japanese stock market. Why do they do so if there are gains to diversification?

5. The saying "You shouldn't put all your eggs in one basket" is an example of what principle in investing? What does it mean?

6. What is the difference between market risk and idiosyncratic risk? Which type of risk can be reduced by diversification?

7. Why don't all risk-averse investors hold a fully diversified portfolio?

8. Would you expect the variability of returns on individual stocks traded on the New York Stock Exchange to be greater or less than the variability of the return on a portfolio consisting of all stocks traded on the exchange? Why or why not?

Analytical Problems

9. Suppose that your wealth elasticity of demand for IBM stock is 2, you own 1000 shares of IBM stock, and your total wealth is $1 million. You earn a $100,000 bonus at work. How much more IBM stock will you buy?

10. Suppose that you are an investor with a choice of three assets that are identical in every way except in their rate of return and taxability. Which asset yields the highest after-tax return?

Asset 1: interest rate 10%, interest taxed at a 40% rate

Asset 2: interest rate 8%, interest taxed at a 25% rate

Asset 3: interest rate 6.5%, no tax on interest

11. Suppose that Asset 1 in Problem 10 had a return of 11%. Would your answer change? If so, in what way?

12. U.S. government bonds with 30-year maturities used to be sold with a call provision: After 25 years, the government could call the bonds and make a final interest payment plus principal repayment. When the government eliminated the call provision in 1985, it found that it could offer a different interest rate on the bonds than it could before. Was the interest rate higher or lower? Why? When was the government likely to call the outstanding callable bonds?

13. In the mid-1980s, a new technique was developed that divides payments on government coupon bonds into two parts: One part consists of the coupon payments on the bonds, and the other part consists of the principal repayment on the bonds. Sold separately, the two parts are worth more to investors than the entire bond. Why?

14. Suppose that you are investing money in a portfolio of stocks and are choosing from among Badrisk Company, which returns 30% in good years and loses 50% in bad years; Worserisk Company, which returns 30% in good years and loses 75% in bad years; Norisk Company, which returns 10% all the time; and Lowrisk Company, which returns 20% in good years and loses 5% in bad years.

    a. If you were completely risk-averse and your only goal was to minimize your risk, which stock(s) would you buy?

    b. If you were risk-neutral, and good years and bad years each occurred half the time, which stock(s) would you buy?

    c. If you were somewhat risk-averse, would you ever have both Badrisk and Worserisk in your portfolio? Why or why not?

    d. If you decided on a portfolio consisting of one-third Badrisk, one-third Norisk, and one-third Lowrisk, what would be your rate of return in good years? In bad years? What would be your average rate of return over all years if good years and bad years each occurred half the time? If good years occurred 80% of the time and bad years 20% of the time?

15. Suppose that you want to hold a stock portfolio for just one year. You have $1000 to invest in stocks, and you can choose to invest in Topgunner, Inc., which has returns of 20% in good years and −10% in bad years, or in Lowrunner, Inc., which has returns of 35% in good years and −15% in bad years.

    a. What is your return in a good year if you buy just Topgunner? In a bad year? What is your return in a good year if you buy just Lowrunner? In a bad year? What is your return in a good year if you put half your money in Topgunner and half in Lowrunner? In a bad year?

    b. Now suppose that, for every stock you buy, you must pay transactions costs equal to $50. Repeat (a) with your return reduced by these transactions costs. What happens to your portfolio choice?

16. You are a member of an investment club that owns shares in a firm that manufactures men's clothing. Explain the arguments for and against buying:

    a. shares in a company that manufactures women's clothing; and

    b. shares in a chemical manufacturing concern.

    Which investment is more likely to decrease the overall risk of your club's portfolio? Why?

17. Using the theory of portfolio allocation, state why you would be more willing or less willing to buy a share of IBM stock if you:

    a. win $1 million in the state lottery;

    b. expect that stock prices will become more volatile;

    c. expect the price of IBM shares to increase over the next year; and

    d. read about new developments increasing the liquidity of the bond market.

18. Using the theory of portfolio allocation, state why you would be more willing or less willing to buy corporate bonds if you:

    a. expect interest rates on bonds to rise;

    b. expect a large capital loss next month on the sale of your house;

    c. learn that the transactions costs of selling bonds will increase; and

    d. expect inflation to increase significantly in the future.

Data Questions

19. You can find information about mutual funds through advertisements in *The Wall Street Journal*. Such ads invite you to write to the fund manager to obtain a copy of the *prospectus* which contains information about the fund's portfolio, management strategy, and fees. Write for a prospectus (or locate one in your library) for a fund specializing in equities, and examine the list of stocks held. Is the fund well diversified? How can you tell?

20. The Federal Reserve periodically publishes a summary of assets and liabilities of U.S. households and businesses. Locate a copy of *Balance Sheets for the U.S. Economy, 1949–1990* in your library. Calculate for 1990 the ratio of foreign corporate equities held (page 6, line 10) to total corporate equities held (page 6, line 23). Using the theory of portfolio allocation, explain why such a small fraction of equity holdings of U.S. residents are in non–U.S. stocks.

CHAPTER 7

Risk and Term Structure of Interest Rates

In December 1991, the Federal Reserve Board announced a dramatic 1-percentage-point cut from 4.5% to 3.5% in the rate it charged on loans to banks. This action immediately affected the yields of other assets: Yields on short-term Treasury bills and money market funds fell to about 3.5%, their lowest levels in 20 years. At the same time, the yield on 30-year Treasury bonds was almost 8%, and yields on many corporate bonds were more than 10%. Why are there so many rates for savers to choose among? What do these different rates tell savers?

In Chapter 5, we discussed interest rates as if there were only one rate. In reality, there are many interest rates: For example, the rate earned on your savings account or money market mutual fund is different from the one on your car loan or credit card account. When you peruse the financial pages of your local daily newspaper or *The Wall Street Journal*, you find hundreds of different interest rates and yields quoted on many different types of financial instruments. As a saver, you need to understand why there are differences among the many rates. Understanding the reasons for these differences will improve the portfolio allocation decisions you make with your savings.

In this chapter, we develop simple ways of characterizing variation in yields among financial instruments. In particular, we focus on three questions. **Q:** For instruments with the same maturity, what factors determine differences in yields? **Q:** If two instruments have equal risk, liquidity, information, and taxation characteristics, how do differences in maturity result in differences in yields? **Q:** How can savers use reported interest rates to forecast conditions in financial markets and the economy?

Risk Structure of Interest Rates

Interest rates and yields on credit market instruments of the same maturity vary because of differences in default risk, liquidity, information costs, and taxation. These determinants are known collectively as the **risk structure of interest rates.** Understanding such differences helps explain the variation in rates reported in the media and provides important information for forecasting.

Default Risk

One characteristic of a credit market instrument that influences its interest rate is its **default risk,** or *credit risk*, which is the probability that a borrower will not pay in full the promised interest, principal, or both. For example, a loan to O.K. Used Cars may have a high probability of not being repaid. Some private firms may be thought incapable of repaying their obligations in full and thus must offer high yields to compensate savers for risk. We analyze default risk in two steps: First, we examine how default risk affects the required return on a financial instrument. Then we determine how changes in default risk affect the return.

Risk Premium. To analyze the effect of default risk on yields, we need for comparison an instrument that has no default risk. U.S. Treasury securities provide a basis for comparing different credit instruments of the same maturity because they are **default-risk-free instruments.** In other words, the U.S. government guarantees that all the principal and interest will be repaid in nominal terms; if necessary, it can issue money to settle debts. Nonetheless, the prices of Treasury securities can fluctuate as market interest rates increase or decrease. For example, an increase in market interest rates raises yields on Treasury securities, reducing their prices.

The **risk premium** on a financial instrument is the difference between its yield and the yield on a default-risk-free instrument of comparable maturity. In other words, it measures the additional yield a saver requires for holding a risky instrument. For example, if the yield on Treasury bonds were 8%, you would demand a higher interest rate, say 12%, on a corporate bond by Worry Free Company, which has a middling credit history. The risk premium on the Worry Free bond is 12% − 8% = 4% (see the Using the news box).

The risk premium consists of two components. First, for the risk-neutral savers who care only about expected returns and not about the variability of those returns, the interest rate for an instrument that carries risk must be greater than that for a default-risk-free instrument. The higher rate compensates savers for losses in the event of default on interest and/or principal. The risk premium makes the expected return on the investment with default risk equal to the certain return from the default-risk-free instrument.

Using the news...
Using Bond Yields to Assess Risk

As you learned in Chapter 4, *The Wall Street Journal* reports daily the prices of corporate bonds traded on major exchanges. Note that yields on corporate bonds vary substantially: The ATT bond due in 2026 with an 8.625% coupon rate has a current yield of 8.3%, whereas the Chrysler bond due in 2015 with a 12% coupon rate has a current yield of 11.0%. (Since both are very long-maturity bonds, the current yield is approximately equal to the yield to maturity.) On the same day, the yield to maturity on a Treasury bond due in 2015 was about 7.5%. Hence the risk premium on the ATT bond is 8.3% − 7.5% = 0.8%, and the risk premium on the Chrysler bond is 11.0% − 7.5% = 3.5%. Since both bonds have similar tax, liquidity, and information

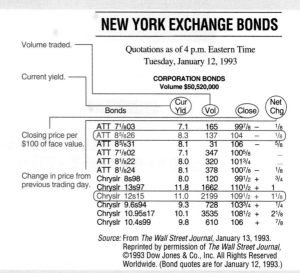

characteristics and both have a long maturity, this difference in risk premiums reflects investors' belief that Chrysler is more likely than ATT to default on interest or principal payments. Investors use these quotes as a guide to bond market participants' assessment of the risk of different bonds.

Second, because savers in general are risk-averse and care about the variability of returns as well as about expected returns, yields incorporate an extra premium for bearing risk.

To determine the size of the default-risk premium to assign to a bond or loan agreement, lenders try to assess the creditworthiness (the ability to repay) of borrowers. The cost of acquiring information about a borrower's creditworthiness can be high. Accordingly, investors often pay professional analysts to gather and monitor such information. For corporate debt instruments, private firms such as Standard and Poor's Corporation (S&P) and Moody's Investors Service assign ratings that are published and updated periodically (see Table 7.1). A **bond rating** is a single statistic summarizing the assessment of the firm's net worth, cash flow, and prospects—in short, of its likely ability to meet its debt obligations. Because they are less risky, instruments with high ratings, such as AAA by S&P, have lower yields than risky instruments with low ratings, such as C by S&P. Both borrowers and lenders are concerned about ratings. For borrowers, the rating affects their risk premium and hence their cost of funds. Savers look to the rating as a source of information about default risk.

	Moody's	S&P's	Meaning

TABLE 7.1 READING THE RATINGS PROVIDED BY MOODY'S AND STANDARD AND POOR'S

	Moody's	S&P's	Meaning
Investment-grade bonds	Aaa	AAA	Bonds of the best quality, offering the smallest degree of investment risk. Issuers are exceptionally stable and dependable.
	Aa	AA	Bonds of high quality by all standards. Slightly higher degree of long-term investment risk.
	A	A	Bonds with many favorable investment attributes.
	Baa	BBB	Bonds of medium-grade quality. Security appears adequate at present but may become unreliable.
Non-investment-grade bonds	Ba	BB	Bonds with speculative element. Moderate security of payments; not well safeguarded.
	B	B	Cannot be considered a desirable investment. Small long-term assurance of payments.
	Caa	CCC	Bonds of poor standing. Issuers may be in default or in danger of default.
	Ca	CC	Bonds of highly speculative quality; often in default.
	C	C	Lowest rated class of bonds. Very poor prospects of ever attaining investment standing.
	—	D	In default.
Commercial paper	P1	A1	Issues of the highest quality, offering the smallest degree of investment risk.
	P2	A2	Lower quality commercial paper.
	P3	A3	Lowest investment-grade quality commercial paper.
	Unrated		

Source: The description of bond ratings is excerpted from Richard Saul Wurman, Alan Siegel, and Kenneth M. Morris, *The Wall Street Journal Guide to Understanding Money and Markets,* New York: Access Press, 1989, p. 52.

Changes in Default Risk and the Risk Premium. In Chapter 4, we noted that the overall level of interest rates rises and falls over time. How does a change in default risk affect the interest rate on a particular financial instrument, such as, General Electric bonds? The default-risk premium can fluctuate as new information about the creditworthiness of a borrower becomes available to investors. In other words, shifts in the market's perception of default risk can lead to a change in yield.

For two assets with the same maturity, the expected inflation component of their nominal yields is the same. Hence we focus on the determination of the expected real interest rate. We can examine the determination of

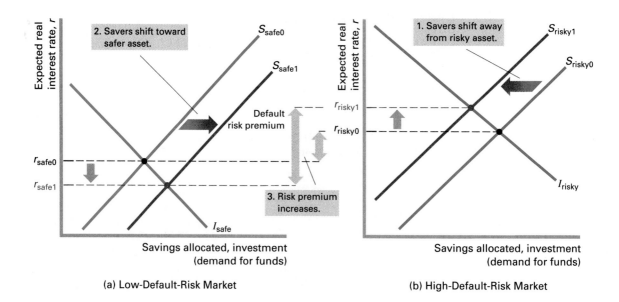

(a) Low-Default-Risk Market

(b) High-Default-Risk Market

FIGURE 7.1

Determining Default-Risk Premiums in Yields

The expected real rate on a riskier asset, r_{risky}, exceeds that on a safer asset, r_{safe}, to compensate savers for bearing risk.

1. The initial default-risk premium, then, is, $r_{risky0} - r_{safe0}$. As savers revise upward the expected default risk in the high-default-risk market, the saving curve shifts to the left (from S_{risky0} to S_{risky1}) in that market.

2. The rise of default risk in the high-risk market causes investors to shift their funds to less risky markets causing the S curve to shift to the right (from S_{safe0} to S_{safe1}) in the low-default-risk market.

3. The premium between the high-default-risk and low-default-risk market increases to $r_{risky1} - r_{safe1}$.

the expected real interest rate for high-default-risk and low-default-risk instruments with the saving-investment diagram developed in Chapter 5. Figure 7.1(a) illustrates determination of the market yield for a low-risk asset, and Fig. 7.1(b) illustrates determination of the market yield for a high-risk asset. In both diagrams, desired investment by borrowers in those markets decreases as the expected real interest rate rises. The saving curves represent the funds that savers are willing to supply to those markets, based on returns available in other markets. Those curves slope upward because savers are willing to supply more funds as the expected real interest rate rises.

Let's assume that savers compare the expected real rate of return in one market (the low-risk or the high-risk market) with expected real rates of return in other markets and that they take into consideration default risk, liquidity, information costs, and taxation differences. If these other factors do not change, the yield on a risky security should be greater than that on a safe security. Such is the case in Fig. 7.1: The initial expected real rate on the riskier security, r_{risky0}, exceeds that on the safer security, r_{safe0}. The risk premium, $r_{risky0} - r_{safe0}$, compensates savers for the default risk on the riskier security.

Now suppose that market participants believe that the likelihood of default on the riskier instrument has increased, owing to bad news about the profits of high-risk firms. Accordingly, savers require a higher real interest rate on the riskier security to compensate them for bearing additional default risk. The saving curve in Fig. 7.1(b) shifts to the left, reducing the volume of funds channeled for investment to that market and increasing the expected real interest rate.

When savers perceive an increase in the default risk on risky instruments, they tend to shift their funds to low-risk instruments. This is called a *flight to quality*. Note in Fig. 7.1(a) that the saving curve in the safer market shifts to the right because the return on the risky security now has greater default risk. The theory of portfolio allocation indicates that the increase in the risk of return relative to that on the safer investment increases the supply of funds to the safer market for any real interest rate. As Fig. 7.1 shows, the risk premium widens from $r_{risky0} - r_{safe0}$ to $r_{risky1} - r_{safe1}$. The two instruments have the same maturity (and expected inflation is the same for both), so the risk premium for the nominal interest rates rises by the same amount. The yield on a bond with default risk carries a risk premium. An increase in expected default risk reduces the supply of funds to the now riskier markets, shifting funds to safer markets.

In practice, how do changes in default risk work to cause investors to shift funds from one asset to another? Figure 7.2 highlights two actual episodes of such shifts in U.S. financial markets. It shows that, although long-term interest rates generally move together (as do short-term rates), episodes do occur in which risk premiums fluctuate. In the early 1980s, when a recession caused concern about corporations' ability to repay, investors reallocated funds away from long-term risky corporate debt to safe government debt. Note the

> **FIGURE 7.2**

Long-Term and Short-Term Yields in the United States, 1960–1992
In periods when investors are concerned about the ability of corporations to repay, investors reallocate funds from corporate debt to safe government debt, seen here in 1974–1975 and again in the early 1980s.

Source: Council of Economic Advisers, *Economic Report of the President*, various issues.

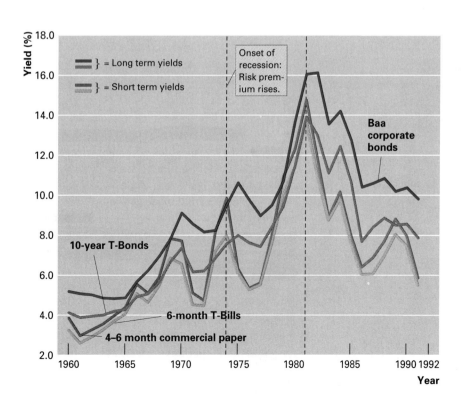

dramatic increase in the yield on medium-quality (Baa) bonds relative to the yield on long-term Treasury securities in the early 1980s. The 1974–1975 recession raised investors' concern about default risk in the short-term market. Note the significant increase in the commercial paper rate relative to the Treasury bill rate. These episodes reflect market perceptions of an increase in default risk, raising the required yield on alternatives to default-risk-free instruments.

Another striking example of a flight to quality occurred from 1929 to 1931. As expectations of the downturn worsened during the Great Depression, savers shifted their funds away from risky corporate securities. They shifted their savings to government securities, actually pushing yields close to zero. The spread between Baa and long-term government bond rates increased significantly—from 2 percentage points in 1929 to 6 percentage points in 1931. Other changes in default-risk premiums occurred in the early 1970s in the commercial paper market. The default of the Penn Central Railroad in 1970 raised the perceived risk on corporate commercial paper. In the municipal bond market in the early 1980s, the default of the Washington State Public Power System bonds increased the perceived risk of investments in the municipal bond market.

▶ **C H E C K P O I N T** *Hitechco, a relatively young technology company, has $10 million in bonds outstanding. You notice in* The Wall Street Journal *that the firm has been awarded a $30 million settlement in a patent dispute with an electronics conglomerate. What would you predict to be the effect of the settlement on the price of Hitechco's bonds?* The news of the settlement reduces the default risk on any Hitechco debt. The risk premium on Hitechco bonds should then fall, and the decline in the yield should increase the bonds' value. ◀

Liquidity

The second factor that affects the risk premium of a bond or loan is *liquidity.* The way in which a financial instrument is traded affects its liquidity, which is a key determinant of asset demand. Because investors care about the cost required to convert a financial instrument into cash, an increase in liquidity can make an instrument more desirable to investors, who will then accept a lower rate of return. Thus a less liquid asset, also called an *illiquid* asset, must pay a higher yield in order to compensate savers for their sacrifice of liquidity. This *liquidity premium* is commonly combined with default risk as part of the risk premium.

As with default risk, U.S. Treasury securities provide a basis for comparing liquidity among different financial instruments. Markets for Treasury securities are extremely liquid because, relative to these securities, matching buyers and sellers of corporate bonds is more difficult. Therefore corporate bond markets are much less liquid, and so investors require an additional premium in their yields. How does a change in the liquidity of a financial instrument affect its yield? The theory of portfolio allocation indicates that for any yield, investors prefer to hold more liquid instruments (such as government bonds) than illiquid ones. Therefore, if the market for corporate bonds becomes less liquid, the spread between yields on less liquid and more liquid instruments increases.

Figure 7.3 illustrates the effect of a change in liquidity on the liquidity component of the risk premium. Figure 7.3(a) shows the determination of the expected real interest rate in a more liquid market (such as that for U.S. Treasury bonds). Figure 7.3(b) shows the determination of the expected real interest rate in a less liquid market (such as that for corporate bonds). Because we want to focus on consequences of a change in liquidity for the risk premium, for simplicity we assume that the initial expected real interest rates in the two markets are equal, or $r_{illiq0} = r_{liq0}$.

Suppose that the less liquid instrument becomes even more illiquid. Savers then will require a higher expected return to compensate them for the loss of liquidity; that is, the saving curve shifts to the left from S_{illiq0} to S_{illiq1} in Fig. 7.3(b). As savers reallocate their funds toward the more liquid market, the saving curve in Fig. 7.3(a) shifts to the right from S_{liq0} to S_{liq1}. The risk premium now equals $r_{illiq1} - r_{liq1}$. Savers require a higher return on the less liquid instrument, and borrowers using that instrument to raise funds will have a higher cost of funds. An increase in the liquidity of an asset reduces its required return; a decrease in liquidity raises the required return.

Information Costs

The third factor determining the risk structure of interest rates is the *cost of acquiring information*. Gathering information requires resources and

FIGURE 7.3

Effect on the Risk Premium of a Decrease in Liquidity
Liquidity is valued by savers. Thus an instrument traded in a more liquid market will have a greater expected real return than an instrument traded in a less liquid market.

1. A decrease in liquidity causes savers to decrease their demand for that asset, shifting the saving curve from S_{illiq0} to S_{illiq1}.

2. Savers reallocate their funds from the less liquid market to more liquid markets, shifting the saving curve from S_{liq0} to S_{liq1}.

3. The liquidity premium—the difference in the yield on the less liquid and more liquid instruments—equals $r_{illiq1} - r_{liq1}$.

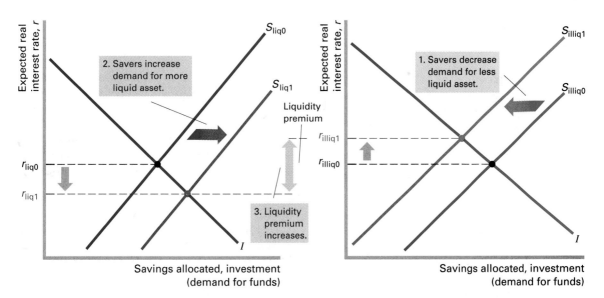

(a) More Liquid Market

(b) Less Liquid Market

reduces the expected return on a financial asset. The cost of using those resources thus is reflected in the borrowing cost charged by the lender, just as the cost of labor is reflected in the price of a sweater. When all other factors are equal, investors prefer to hold assets with low information costs.

Government obligations, such as Treasury bills and bonds, have the lowest information costs because all savers know with certainty that the principal and interest will be repaid (in nominal terms). Rating agencies reduce information costs associated with gathering data on and monitoring well-known borrowers, but such costs are higher for loans made to less well-known borrowers. For example, if you want to start a business of selling customized T-shirts and go to your local bank for a loan, the bank will have to assess your ability to repay based on your income and the chances that your business will succeed. The cost of collecting this information leads to higher costs either directly (in terms of a higher interest rate on your loan) or indirectly (through restrictions on your activities that the bank will write into your loan contract).

Financial instruments with high interest rates due to higher information costs also tend to be relatively illiquid. The reason is that, without readily available information, trading these instruments in financial markets is difficult. Figure 7.4 illustrates the effect of an increase in information costs on the risk premium for a financial instrument. Figure 7.4(a) shows the determination of the expected real interest rate on low-information-cost instruments. Figure 7.4(b) shows the determination of the expected real interest rate on high-information-cost instruments. Again, for simplicity, let's assume that

FIGURE 7.4

Effect on Risk Premium of an Increase in Information Costs
An increase in information costs in a high-information-cost market causes the difference in the expected real interest rate on high-information-cost lending and low-information-cost lending to rise.

1. An increase in information costs in the initially high-information-cost market causes savers to decrease the demand for that asset, shifting the saving curve from S_{high0} to S_{high1}.

2. Savers reallocate their funds toward the low-information-cost market, shifting the saving curve from S_{low0} to S_{low1}.

3. The information premium rises to ($r_{high1} - r_{low1}$).

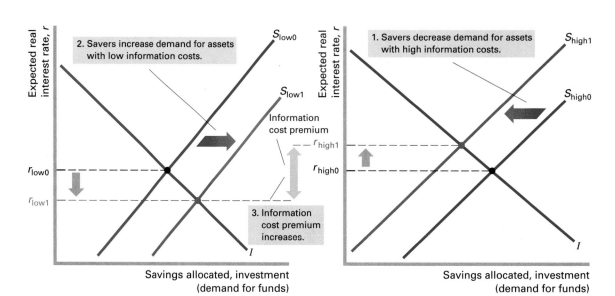

(a) Low-Information-Cost Market   (b) High-Information-Cost Market

yields on two instruments are initially equal, or $r_{high0} = r_{low0}$.[†] When information costs rise for the high-information-cost market, savers are less willing to invest their funds in the market for that instrument at the going interest rate, shifting the saving curve to the left in Fig. 7.4(b). As the funds are reallocated to the low-information-cost market, the saving curve shifts to the right in the market for that instrument, as shown in Fig. 7.4(a). As a result, the expected real interest rate falls in the low-information-cost market and rises in the high-information-cost market. The information-cost component of the risk premium rises to $r_{high1} - r_{low1}$. An increase in information costs increases the required return on a financial instrument. A decrease in information costs decreases the required return on a financial instrument.

Taxation

Another reason for differences in yields across credit market instruments is *taxation*. If returns on all instruments were taxed identically, the relative comparisons of default risk, liquidity, and information costs we have been making would be unchanged. However, three important differences in the taxation of returns create differences in yields among credit market instruments, assuming that risk, liquidity, and information costs don't change.

The first taxation issue that savers consider is whether interest payments are taxable. For example, interest received on **municipal bonds,** which are obligations of state and local governments, is exempt from federal, state, and local income taxes. Owing to this exemption, savers accept a lower interest rate on municipal bonds than on comparable instruments (including some with lower default risk) because the after-tax yield of municipal bonds is greater. For example, suppose that you are comparing the returns on a $1000 Treasury bond with a 9% coupon rate and a $1000 municipal bond paying 7.5% interest. The before-tax yield on the Treasury bond (9%) is greater than that on the municipal bond (7.5%). If your marginal income tax rate is 30%, 30¢ of each additional dollar of interest income goes to the government through taxes. An annual coupon payment of $90 on the $1000 taxable Treasury bond provides you with $(90)(1 - 0.3) = \$63$ in after-tax interest income. Alternatively, a $1000 municipal bond with a $75 coupon payment and no taxes provides you with $75 in after-tax interest income. Thus you might be willing to hold the municipal bond.

Figure 7.5 depicts the effect of a tax exemption for municipal bond interest on the yields of a U.S. government bond and a municipal bond. For simplicity suppose that, with no difference in tax treatment, the expected real interest rate on the two instruments is the same. If yields on municipal bonds become tax-exempt, U.S. government bonds are less attractive to savers

---

[†] In practice, of course, $r_{high0} > r_{low0}$. This difference reflects the difference in costs that savers incur to gather information on the two instruments.

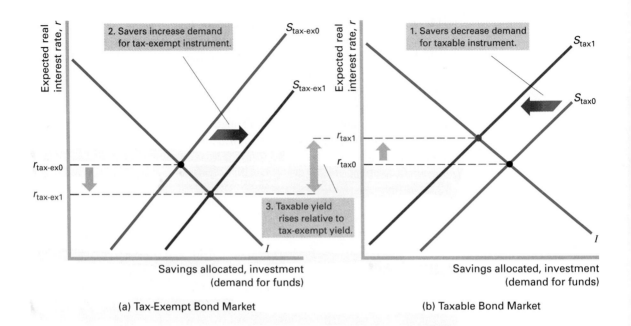

(a) Tax-Exempt Bond Market

(b) Taxable Bond Market

Effect of Differences in Tax Treatment on Yields

If nothing else changes, a decrease in a bond's tax liability decreases its yield.

1. If municipal bonds become tax-exempt, savers decrease their holdings of taxable U.S. government bonds so that the saving curve shifts from S_{tax0} to S_{tax1} in (b).

2. Savers increase their demand for tax-exempt bonds, so that the saving curve shifts from $S_{tax-ex0}$ to $S_{tax-ex1}$ in (a).

3. If municipal bonds become tax-exempt, the premium on taxable bonds increases to $r_{tax1} - r_{tax-ex1}$ and makes the marginal investor indifferent between a taxable bond or a tax-exempt bond.

because their yields are taxable. Hence the saving curve shifts to the left in Fig. 7.5(b). At the same time, savers will increase their demand for municipal bonds, shifting the saving curve to the right in Fig. 7.5(a). At equilibrium, the tax premium equals the difference in the taxable and tax-exempt rates, $r_{tax1} - r_{tax-ex1}$. In other words, savers then would be indifferent between holding the taxable U.S. government bond and holding the tax-exempt municipal bond.[†]

A second taxation issue that savers consider is that, under U.S. law, interest and capital gains (or losses) on a credit market instrument are taxed differently. Interest income is taxed at the same rate as wage and salary income. However, capital gains carry a lower effective tax rate, as they are taxed when they are *realized* (when the asset is sold) and not as they accrue; that is, the taxes are deferred. For example, if you hold shares of Boomco for 20 years before you sell them and realize a capital gain, you will not be taxed until you sell the shares. The benefit of a deferred tax obligation is that the *present value* of the tax paid on the gain when it is realized is lower than the present value of the tax payments if you paid the tax incrementally as the gain accrued. Prior to 1986, capital gains were subject to a lower explicit tax rate as well as the implicit tax benefit of deferral.

Finally, the exemption of interest returns on U.S. government securities from state and local taxation provides these obligations with favorable tax treatment relative to taxable corporate securities. For example, part of the

[†] In reality, income taxes are levied on nominal, rather than real, returns on financial assets.

risk premium between commercial paper and Treasury bill yields reflects this difference in tax treatment. Holding constant the attributes of default risk, liquidity, and information costs, shifts in the tax treatment of returns on certain obligations will affect before-tax yields. Investors, however, will compare after-tax expected returns in making their portfolio allocation decisions.

The example in Box 7.1 illustrates the effects of changes in default risk, liquidity, and information costs on the yield of a financial instrument. Table 7.2 summarizes the determinants of the risk structure of interest rates.

Q: For instruments with the same maturity, what factors determine differences in yields?

A: The risk structure of interest rates characterizes variation in yields, holding maturity constant. Principal sources of variation include differences in default risk, liquidity, information costs, and taxation.

▶ **C H E C K P O I N T** *Suppose that Congress enacted and the president signed a tax increase to reduce the federal budget deficit by increasing marginal income tax rates. What should happen to the difference in the yield on tax-exempt municipal bonds and that on taxable bonds?* The increase in income taxes raises the value of tax exemption associated with municipal bonds, causing their yield to fall relative to that on taxable bonds. Although higher tax rates might be bad news for savers, holders of outstanding municipal bonds would receive some good news: As yields fall on their bonds, they receive a capital gain from the increase in the bonds' value. ◀

Using the Risk Structure for Forecasting

Many business and government analysts use financial data for forecasting, or predicting, changes in economic variables such as total output of the economy or prices. Businesspeople use forecasts in making investment, production, and employment decisions. Government officials use forecasts to predict future tax revenues and expenditures and to guide policy decisions.

Many commercial forecasting models make use of the risk structure of interest rates to predict future changes in economic activity. When you think about it, this application is sensible: Risk premiums reflect the differ-

TABLE 7.2   THE RISK STRUCTURE OF YIELDS

An increase in an asset's...	Causes its yield to...	Because...
default risk	rise	savers must be compensated for bearing additional risk
liquidity	fall	savers incur lower costs of exchanging the asset for cash
information costs	rise	savers must spend more resources to evaluate an asset
tax liability	rise	savers care about after-tax returns and must be compensated for the tax liability

Consider this...

BOX 7.1

Why Did the Junk Bond Market Go Bust in the Late 1980s?

In the early 1980s, improved liquidity and lower perceived default risk gave a big push to the junk bond market. Between 1982 and 1986, new issues of junk bonds expanded at about an 85% annual rate. In 1986, the bubble burst. In a heavily publicized case, LTV, a firm highly indebted with junk bonds, defaulted on its bonds, shaking the junk bond market badly. In the same year, the courts indicted financier Ivan Boesky for violations of securities laws forbidding trading on inside information. The indictment reduced the confidence of investors in the stock market in general. The market perceived these events as increasing default risk and began requiring a higher return on junk bonds relative to

higher-quality bonds.

The stock market crash in October 1987 further dampened the pace of corporate mergers, acquisitions, and leveraged buyouts, which had been key elements in fueling the junk bond market. Financier Robert Campeau's troubles in meeting interest payments on debt in his retailing empire raised the specter that companies with a heavy reliance on junk bonds had too much debt. Even New York real estate developer Donald Trump struggled to make interest payments, and the value of his outstanding junk bonds declined significantly. The liquidity of the junk bond market declined sharply in the wake of the bankruptcy of

Drexel Burnham Lambert, a securities firm that had been a key provider of information in the high-yield debt finance market. New issues of junk bonds grew at a slower rate through 1988 and declined significantly in 1989 and 1990.

Although in transition in the early 1990s, a streamlined junk bond market no doubt will remain as a source of funds for many borrowers. Many healthy, growing firms have raised funds for expansion of investment and operations through public offerings of risky debt. Nonetheless, in the early 1990s, experts' prediction of a shift back toward more equity financing was borne out.

ence between the yields of a corporate instrument and a Treasury instrument of similar maturity. They also include assessments of the underlying risk-structure considerations of default risk, liquidity, information costs, and taxation. The *Other times, other places* box discusses the development of a risk structure for Japan.

For example, increases in risk premiums may reflect market participants' anticipation of periods of difficulty in servicing debt obligations because of, say, lower expected future profits. Analysts have successfully used increases in the risk premium of certain broad classes of securities, such as the Baa bond and Treasury bond yield differential or the commercial paper and Treasury bill yield differential, to forecast business recessions (in which the likelihood of default increases). The National Bureau of Economic Research, an independent research organization responsible for determining the onset of recessions in the United States, uses risk premiums in formulating its *leading indicators* of future economic activity and for forecasting when a recession is to begin or end. Private forecasters widely use these measures to advise financial and business clients.

Other times, other places...

Creating a Risk Structure for Japan?

A well-functioning corporate bond market gives investors information about risk premiums on corporate debt instruments. Before 1991, the long-term bond market in Japan was poorly developed relative to that in the United States. As a result, investors were reluctant to trade Japanese corporate bonds because determining what they were worth was difficult. Japanese firms relied much more heavily on bank loans and new equity issues than on external bonds as sources of funds for investment.

In the late 1980s, John Wadsworth, president of the Japanese office of the investment firm Morgan Stanley, aggressively urged development of a liquid secondary market for Japanese corporate bonds. In December 1991, Morgan Stanley introduced U.S.-style risk-structure pricing for the ¥50 billion ($390 million at the time) bond issue for Nippon Telegraph and Telephone Company (NTT). That issue was priced at a fixed spread over the benchmark Japanese government bond. The risk premium reflected the default-risk and liquidity premiums for the issue. To reduce the liquidity premium component of the risk premium, Morgan Stanley and Nomura Securities, a Japanese financial services company, agreed to maintain a secondary market in NTT's new bonds. As the Ministry of Finance discouraged new equity issues in the early 1990s and Japanese banks cut back on lending, Japanese corporations eagerly supported the experiment.

Some observers have noted that a well-functioning risk structure of corporate bond yields in Japan is still several years away. A significant problem is the relative absence of bond-rating agencies to reduce information costs for investors. Moody's Investors Service and Standard & Poor's Corporation, the leading U.S. rating agencies, have rated few Japanese nonfinancial companies, and the reports of Japanese rating agencies are not widely respected.

Term Structure of Interest Rates

Let's now turn our attention to variations in yields among instruments with common default risk, liquidity, information cost, and taxation characteristics but with different maturities. The variation in yield for related instruments differing in maturity is known as the **term structure of interest rates.** Because the risk-structure factors can be held constant most easily for U.S. government obligations, term structure usually is defined with respect to yields on those securities.

In order to obtain information about investors' expectations of credit market conditions, market analysts often study the yields to maturity on different default-risk-free instruments as a function of maturity. The graph of this relationship is known as a **yield curve.** In principle, yield curves can be upward sloping, flat, or downward sloping. An upward-sloping yield curve indicates that long-term yields are higher than short-term yields. A flat yield curve indicates that yields on short-term and long-term obligations are the same. A downward-sloping yield curve indicates that short-term yields are higher than long-term yields. The yield curve in *The Wall*

Using the news...

How to Read the Yield Curve

Each day in its Credit Markets section, *The Wall Street Journal* plots the yield curve for U.S. Treasury securities. The numbers on the horizontal axis indicate the maturity, ranging from three months (Treasury bills) to 30 years (Treasury bonds). The numbers on the vertical axis indicate yields to maturity at the end of the previous trading day. Since the current and four-weeks-ago yield curves are close together, the overall level of yields on Treasury securities did not change much over the month. Nevertheless, there is considerable variation in yields by maturity. The yield curve rises slightly over the range from three months to one year, then rises steeply thereafter.

Should you invest in long-term Treasury bonds because their yield is higher than that of short-term Treasury bills? We answer this question when we discuss the term structure.

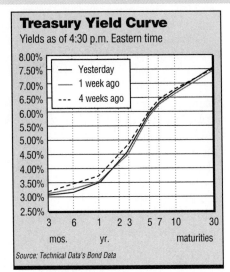

Treasury Yield Curve
Yields as of 4:30 p.m. Eastern time

Source: Technical Data's Bond Data

Source: From *The Wall Street Journal*, January 13, 1993. Reprinted by permission of *The Wall Street Journal*, ©1993 Dow Jones & Co., Inc. All Rights Reserved Worldwide. (Quotes are from January 12, 1993.)

Street Journal contains valuable information for savers and borrowers (see the Using the news box).

Since World War II, yield curves for U.S. Treasury securities have exhibited two interesting patterns. First, as is the case for the yield curve shown in Using the news, term structure usually slopes upward, so that long-term yields are generally higher than short-term yields. Second, yields on default-risk-free instruments with different maturities typically move together, increasing or decreasing collectively. Hence the yield curve typically shifts up or down rather than twisting. Understanding these patterns can help you use yield curves to forecast economic variables such as interest rates and inflation rates.

Economists have advanced three theories as explanations of patterns in the yield curve: the segmented markets theory, the expectations theory, and the preferred habitat theory. How can we judge these theories? One useful method is logical consistency: *Does the theory offer an internally consistent model of financial markets that explains real-world events?*

A second method addresses predictive power: *How well does the theory explain the two patterns in the data for yield curves?*

Segmented Markets Theory

The **segmented markets theory** holds that the yield on each instrument, from three-month T-bills to two-year notes to 30-year bonds, is determined in a separate market, with separate market-specific demand and supply considerations. This general approach is based on the assumption that borrowers have particular periods for which they want to borrow and that lenders have particular holding periods in mind. For example, individuals may want to match maturities and holding periods because they are saving for retirement or their children's education. By doing so, they know exactly what their nominal return is. Or, borrowers may have a particular period in mind because they know that a business investment project will pay off over 20 years, and the business wants to match its debt repayments with its expected revenues. Under the segmented markets theory, borrowers and lenders are unwilling to move from one market to another, and therefore obligations with different maturities have no substitutability.

According to the segmented markets theory, the yield in each market reflects only demand and supply in that market. Hence the slope of the yield curve represents many smaller demand and supply decisions. An upward-sloping yield curve implies that the demand for short-term bonds is high relative to that for long-term bonds. As we showed in Chapter 4, this demand exerts upward pressure on the price and downward pressure on the yield for short-term bonds. A flat yield curve implies that demand and supply conditions are similar in the various markets. A downward-sloping yield curve implies a higher demand for long-term bonds relative to that for short-term bonds. Does this theory pass the first test of explaining observable conditions? Because upward-sloping yield curves are most prevalent in post–World War II data for the United States, the segmented markets theory suggests that investors generally prefer to hold short-term rather than long-term bonds. Therefore the theory can explain upward-sloping yield curves as long as investors prefer short-term instruments.

Does this theory pass the second test of explaining the two patterns in the data for yield curves? As we just noted, under the segmented markets theory, demand for a bond typically falls as the bond's maturity increases. In equilibrium, the yields on longer-maturity bonds exceed those on shorter-maturity bonds. The yield curve then slopes upward. Of course, preferences for bonds of different maturities shift on occasion. At times, investors become more willing to hold longer-term bonds. When they do, the equilibrium yields on those bonds fall, causing the yield curve to flatten or slope downward.

However, the segmented markets theory cannot explain the observation that yields on different instruments tend to move together. Because the theory claims that only market-specific demand and supply determine yields,

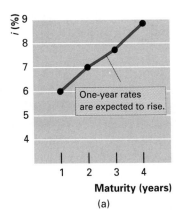

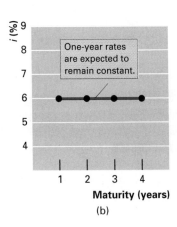

Maturity (years)

(a)   (b)   (c)

**Using the Yield Curve to
Predict Interest Rates: The
Expectations Theory**
Under the expectations theory,
the slope of the yield curve
shows future short-term interest
rates are expected (a) to rise, (b)
to remain the same, or (c) to fall
relative to current levels.

the curves could move together only by coincidence.[†] Thus the theory does not explain why an investor would turn down potentially higher returns in other markets in order to meet a particular holding-period preference.

Expectations Theory

In contrast to the segmented markets theory, the **expectations theory** states that investors view assets of all maturities as perfect substitutes at the same levels of default risk, liquidity, information costs, and taxation. This view implies that a long-term bond rate equals the average of short-term rates covering the same investment period. In addition, it suggests that the yield curve shape depends on the expected pattern of short-term rates.

Let's begin with an example of how you can infer expectations of future short-term rates from current long-term rates. Suppose that the interest rate on a one-year bond is 6%, the interest rate on a two-year bond is 7%, the interest rate on a three-year bond is 8%, and the interest rate on a four-year bond is 9%. Figure 7.6(a) shows this upward-sloping yield curve. The simple description of the expectations theory tells you how to infer the (unobservable) expectations of future short-term interest rates from this yield curve. The two-year rate (7%) is an average of the current one-year rate (6%) and the expected future one-year rate, or

$$\frac{6\% + \text{Expected future one-year rate one year ahead}}{2} = 7\%.$$

The expected future one-year rate then is 8%.

Similarly, you can infer the expected future one-year rate two periods from now by looking at the three-year bond rate. That rate should be the average

---

[†] Technically, the segmented markets theory can explain the up and down movements in the yield curve if there are movements into and out of the bond market *at all maturities*. This occurrence certainly would be coincidental.

of the current one-year bond rate (6%), the expected one-year rate one year ahead (just calculated to be 8%), and the expected one-year rate two years ahead, or

$$\frac{6\% + 8\% + \text{Expected one-year rate two years ahead}}{3} = 8\%.$$

The expected one-year rate two years ahead is 10%. Finally, you can infer the expected one-year rate three years ahead, which is 12%.[†] Under the expectations theory, when short-term rates are expected to rise, the yield curve slopes up.

Figure 7.6(b) shows a flat yield curve, in which the yields on one-year, two-year, three-year, and four-year bonds all are 6%. Thus, under the expectations theory, you can infer that one-year rates will remain unchanged at 6% for the next three years. Under the expectations theory, when short-term rates are expected to remain unchanged, the yield curve is flat.

Figure 7.6(c) shows a downward-sloping yield curve in which the yields are: 6% for the one-year bond, 5.5% for the two-year bond, 5% for the three-year bond, and 4.5% for the four-year bond. What would you expect future one-year rates to be one, two, or three years from now? The two-year bond rate is an average of the current one-year rate (6%) and the expected future one-year rate, or

$$\frac{6\% + \text{Expected future one-year rate one-year ahead}}{2} = 5.5\%.$$

The expected one-year rate one year from now is 5%. The expected one-year rate two years from now can be found from

$$\text{Rate on three-year bonds} \ = \ \frac{6\% + 5\% + \text{Expected one-year rate two years ahead}}{3} = 5\%.$$

The one-year rate that you can infer for two years from now is 4%. Using the same approach, you can find the expected one-year rate three years from now:

$$\text{Rate on four-year bonds} = \frac{6\% + 5\% + 4\% + \text{Expected one-year rate three years ahead}}{3} = 4.5\%.$$

The one-year rate that you can infer for three years from now is 3%. Under the expectations theory, when short-term rates are expected to fall, the yield curve slopes down.

[†] Here

$$\frac{6\% + 8\% + 10\% + \text{Expected one-year rate three years ahead}}{4} = 9\%,$$

so that the expected one-year rate three years ahead is 12%.

We can generalize from these examples. The perfect substitutability assumption of the expectations theory implies that expected returns for a holding period must be the same for bonds of different maturities. Otherwise, investors would change their relative demand for instruments with different maturities to take advantage of differences in yields. In addition, the perfect substitutability assumption implies that the yield on a long-term bond will equal an average of expected short-term yields over the life of the bonds. Why? Take an investment horizon of, say, 10 years. If all instruments are perfect substitutes, investors should get the same expected return from holding a 10-year bond, a sequence of five two-year notes, a sequence of 40 three-month bills, and so on. Under this theory, if the long-term yield is higher than the short-term yield, investors should expect short-term rates to increase over the 10-year period.

Let's further clarify the prediction of the expectations theory about relationships among yields on bonds with different maturities. Suppose that you are considering two strategies for a two-year investment, where i is the interest rate of the bond:

Buy-and-hold strategy

Buy a two-year bond and hold it until maturity. The interest rate today is i_{2t}, where t represents the time period.

Roll-over strategy

Buy a one-year bond today and hold it until maturity. The interest rate today is i_{1t}. After the one-year bond matures $(t + 1)$, buy another one-year bond and hold it until maturity. The precise interest rate on that bond is unknown. As of today, we expect that it will be $i^e_{1,t+1}$, where e represents expectation.

What are the expected returns on a $1 investment after two years for each strategy? If you buy and hold, your $1 is worth $\$(1 + i_{2t})$ after the first year and $\$(1 + i_{2t})(1 + i_{2t})$ after two years. Under the roll-over strategy, your $1 is worth $\$(1 + i_{1t})$ after the first year and, as you expect to earn $i^e_{1,t+1}$ on a one-year bond in the second year, your initial $1 will be worth: $\$(1 + i_{1t})(1 + i^e_{1,t+1})$.

Under the expectations theory, the two instruments are perfect substitutes. Therefore their expected net returns over the two-year holding period must be equal:

$$(1 + i_{2t})(1 + i_{2t}) - 1 \quad = \quad (1 + i_{1t})(1 + i^e_{1,t+1}) - 1.$$

Simplifying, we get

$$2i_{2t} + i^2_{2t} = i_{1t} + i^e_{1,t+1} + i_{1t}(i^e_{1,t+1}).$$

Simplifying further, we make use of the fact that the product of two interest rates is small. [Note, for example, that if $i = 0.08$, then $i^2 = 0.0064$, and the i_{2t}^2 and i_{1t} ($i_{1,t+1}^e$) terms can be ignored.] With that approximation, the yield on the two-year bond is an average of the expected yields on the two one-year bonds:

$$i_{2t} = \frac{i_{1t} + i_{1,t+1}^e}{2}. \tag{7.1}$$

More generally, for an n-period bond, a more precise statement of the expectations theory is

$$i_{n,t} = \frac{i_{1t} + i_{1,t+1}^e + \cdots + i_{1i,t+n-1}^e}{n}.$$

The n-period bond yield is an average of the expected short-term yields over the life of the bond.

Unlike the segmented markets theory, the expectations theory suggests that the slope of the yield curve reflects market expectations, based on the assumption that instruments with different maturities are perfect substitutes. A flat yield curve implies that market participants expect future short-term rates to be the same as current short-term rates, making current short-term rates and long-term rates (the average of expected future short-term rates) equal. A downward-sloping yield curve indicates that investors believe that short-term rates will decline in the future relative to current levels. Finally, an upward-sloping yield curve reflects expectations that short-term rates will be higher in the future, thereby increasing long-term rates today.

How successful is this theory at explaining actual patterns in yield curves? In contrast to the segmented markets theory, the expectations theory offers a logically consistent explanation of movement together by interest rates on bonds of different maturities. For the post–World War II period, movements in U.S. interest rates have been persistent; that is, increases (or decreases) in short-term rates tend to continue for many periods. An increase in short-term rates today increases expected future short-term rates and current long-term rates. Hence the expectations theory can explain movement together by short-term and long-term interest rates.

The expectations theory, however, does not explain well the general pattern of an upward-sloping yield curve. If we strictly interpret the theory, an upward-sloping yield curve would mean that short-term interest rates are expected to rise always. This is a pattern inconsistent enough with actual experience to warrant skepticism. Nonetheless, the theory offers a logically consistent foundation for explaining investor decisions and interest rate co-movements.

► C H E C K P O I N T   *Use the expectations theory to answer the following question. Studying* The Wall Street Journal, *you notice that the yield curve slopes upward: Yields on 30-year Treasury bonds are greater than those on seven-year notes, which are in turn greater than those on six-month bills. As all Treasury securities have the same default risk, liquidity, information costs, and tax treatment, should you invest all your money in the 30-year bonds?* No. Under the expectations theory, the long-term bond rate is just the average of the expected future short-term rates. You would not earn a higher *expected* return by holding long-term as opposed to intermediate-term or short-term Treasury instruments. ◄

Preferred Habitat Theory

Neither the segmented markets theory nor the expectations theory provides a complete explanation of the yield curve. Essentially, their shortcomings arise from the extreme position each takes. Under the segmented markets theory, investors view maturities as completely unsubstitutable; under the expectations theory, investors view maturities as perfect substitutes. A third theory, the preferred habitat theory, seeks a middle ground and thus is able to explain the important attributes of the yield curve.

The **preferred habitat theory** holds that investors care about both expected returns and maturity: They view instruments having different maturities as substitutes—but not perfect substitutes. Specifically, investors prefer shorter to longer maturities, as in the segmented markets theory. (This preference accounts for "habitats," or natural environment, at different maturities.) As a result, they will not buy a long-term bond if it offers the same yield as a sequence of short-term bonds. Instead, investors require something extra, a **term premium,** to compensate them for investing in a less preferred maturity. An example helps to make the point.

Suppose that one-year bonds currently yield 6% but are expected to yield 8% next year. Would investors be just as happy buying a two-year bond yielding 7%? The two-year bond offers the same yield as the average of two one-year bonds. But as investors *prefer* to buy one-year bonds, they must be given an even higher yield, say, 7.5%, to lure them into the less desirable 2-year maturity. If they are offered only 7%, they will choose the one-year bonds. The additional 0.5% needed to make the two-year bonds competitive is the term premium.

Let's generalize this example to compare the predictions of the expectations theory and the preferred habitat theory. Let i represent yields as before, n the number of periods until maturity, and h (habitat) the term premium for the particular maturity. Under the preferred habitat theory, the interest rate on an n-period bond (approximately) equals the average of expected future one-period yields over the life of the bond plus a term premium for that maturity. In general, then, the preferred habitat theory predicts that the yield on an n-period bond is

$$i_{n,t} = \frac{i_{1t} + i^e_{1,t+1} + \cdots + i^e_{1,t+n-1}}{n} + h_{n,t}. \tag{7.2}$$

Q: If two instruments have equal risk, liquidity, information, and taxation characteristics, how do differences in maturity result in differences in yields?

A: The term structure of interest rates underlies variations in yield for different maturities, holding constant characteristics of default risk, liquidity, information costs, and taxation. The segmented markets, expectations, and preferred habitat theories explain this variation.

▼ TABLE 7.3	THEORIES OF THE TERM STRUCTURE		
Theory	**Assumes...**	**Predicts...**	**Evaluation...**
Segmented markets	Maturities are not substitutable. Shorter maturities preferred to longer maturities	Yields on different maturities are determined in separate markets	Explains shapes of the yield curve but not why short-term and long-term rates move together
Expectations	Maturities are perfect substitutes	Yield on an n-period bond equals the average of yields on one-period bonds over next n periods	Explains why short-term and long-term rates move together but not the usual upward slope of the yield curve
Preferred habitat	Maturities are substitutable but not perfectly	Yield on an n-period bond equals the average of yields on one-period bonds over next n periods plus a term premium	Explains both the shapes of the yield curve and why short-term and long-term rates move together

Under the expectations theory, assets are perfect substitutes; there are no habitats, and h is always zero. The term premium $h_{n,t}$ is not a constant under the preferred habitat theory. Data for post–World War II U.S. financial markets reveal, on average, a positive term premium for longer-term securities. Because shorter maturities are preferred to longer maturities, $h_{n,t}$ increases as a bond's maturity increases. Thus, the preferred habitat theory predicts a built-in upward slope in the yield curve, regardless of the expected path of short-term rates—an important correction of the strictly interpreted expectations theory. Thus the shape of the yield curve depends on both the expected pattern of short-term rates *and* the size of the term premium at each maturity.

Under the preferred habitat theory, then, a flat yield curve reflects an expectation of slightly falling future short-term rates, because of the built-in upward tilt in the yield curve. An upward-sloping yield curve reflects a smaller expected increase in future short-term rates than under the expectations theory. A downward-sloping yield curve reflects a more significant expected decline in future short-term rates than the expectations theory predicts. As with the expectations theory, the slope of the yield curve under the preferred habitat theory provides information on market expectations about future short-term rates. The preferred habitat theory is logically consistent and explains both the usual pattern of an upward-sloping yield curve and the movement together by yields on bonds having different maturities.

Concluding Remarks

Recall that the term structure usually is defined in relation to yields by maturity. Three theories are used to explain patterns in yield curves: the segmented markets theory, the expectations theory, and the preferred habitat theory. Table 7.3 summarizes these theories.

MOVING FROM THEORY TO PRACTICE...

THE WALL STREET JOURNAL   JANUARY 6, 1992

Should the 30-Year Treasury Bond Be Extinct?

Can the government really save taxpayers money and at the same time stimulate business activity by curbing sales of 30-year Treasury bonds?

In Washington and on Wall Street, government officials, economists and bond dealers are hotly debating the pros and cons of a move to eliminate—or at least sharply reduce—sales of long-term Treasury bonds...

Since the Treasury began selling 30-year bonds in the early 1960s, the Treasury's long-term bond has become the most-actively traded security in the world. It's considered the bellwether security for the entire bond market; its yield is used as a benchmark from which yields on other long-term securities are determined by the market. Because the long bond, as it is known on Wall Street, is far more volatile than other fixed-income securities—its price moves further up or down with swings in interest rates—it is a favorite for speculators who like to make big bets on interest rate changes.

But economists and the Bush Administration are frustrated at how slowly yields on 30-year Treasury bonds have fallen, even though the Federal Reserve has been aggressively pushing down short-term interest rates. In the past 12 months, for example, the Fed has driven down the federal funds rate, which banks charge each other for overnight loans, to 4% from 7%. In response, yields on three-month Treasury bills have fallen 2.7 percentage points to just under 4%.

But yields on the 30-year Treasury bond have fallen just three-quarters of a percentage point to about 7.5%. In fact, the gap between yields on short-term and long-term securities is now the widest it has ever been. Part of the problem is that long-term bonds reflect investors' inflation expectations. Long-term rates in turn directly influence mortgage rates and corporate borrowing costs.

Proponents of paring back sales of 30-year bonds argue that reducing the supply of long-term bonds would give them a scarcity value, causing their yield to decline and their price to rise.

Burton Malkiel, a Princeton University economist and a student of markets and interest rates, suggests that a substantial move by the Treasury to curb its sale of 30-year bonds could reduce long-term interest rates by as much as one-half a percentage point...

But opponents of the idea of eliminating 30-year bonds doubt that the Treasury would achieve its objectives. In a 15-page research report, Mr. Robert Giordano of Goldman Sachs said that a shift away from long-term bonds is "unlikely to lower long-term interest rates appreciably, save the government much, if any, money or help the private sector." Goldman is one of the biggest government bond dealers on Wall Street. Many dealers oppose a curb on 30-year bonds, which they say would increase uncertainty about the Treasury's borrowing plans and, perhaps, reduce dealers' profits.

ANALYZING THE NEWS...

In late 1991 and early 1992, there were discussions within and outside the U.S. Treasury Department about whether the Treasury should change the maturity of the public debt (a strategy later attempted in 1993). Specifically, some economists and financial market participants argued that the Treasury should reduce its sales of 30-year bonds, replacing them with a larger volume of short-term issues. The concern was that, while the Federal Reserve had reduced short-term interest rates by 3% during the year, yields on long-term Treasury bonds fell only slightly. Since yields on long-term private debt, which follow those on long-term Treasury debt with an additional risk premium, are important determinants of household and business spending, the failure of the long-term yields to fall substantially did not go unnoticed.

(a) How would you advise the Treasury as to which maturity structure would minimize the government's borrowing costs? You would first need an economic model of how term structure is determined. What about the recommendation by Malkiel to sell more Treasury bills and fewer long-term bonds? The article reflects the *preferred habitat* theory of the term structure. In that approach, the interaction of investor preferences and the supply of Treasury debt at different maturities determine a term premium for longer-term maturities. Holding investor preferences constant, a reduction in the quantity of 30-year bonds supplied would raise their price and reduce their yield. If yields on long-term Treasury bonds fell, interest rates on corporate debt also would decline (assuming no change in the risk premium).

(b) The opponents of Malkiel's view adopt the *expectations theory* of the term structure. Under this view, suggested in Giordano's comments in the article, short-term and long-term Treasury obligations are perfect substitutes. As a result, a relatively high long-term bond rate reflects market participants' expectations of higher short-term interest rates in the future. Some analysts were concerned about the effects of anticipated future government budget deficits on future interest rates. Previous Treasury experiments at debt management to reduce long-term Treasury bond rates were not viewed as successful by many economists.

For further thought...

The 30-year Treasury bond is the only long-term default-risk-free instrument in the United States, and it serves as a benchmark for pricing long-term obligations with default risk. What if certain investors, such as life insurance companies and pension funds, actually *prefer* to hold long-term bonds? How might you explain the fact that long-term rates were much higher than short-term rates in late 1991 and early 1992?

Source: Excerpted from Constance Mitchell and David Wessel, "Will 30-Year T-Bond Become Extinct Species?," January 6,1992. Reprinted by permission of *The Wall Street Journal*, © 1992 Dow Jones & Co., Inc. All Rights Reserved Worldwide.

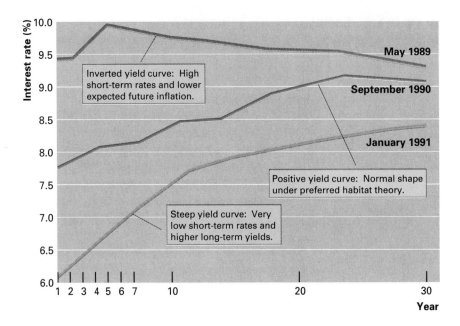

> ►FIGURE 7.7
>
> **Interpreting the Yield Curve**
> Models of term structure, such as the preferred habitat theory, help analysts use data from *The Wall Street Journal* as a forecasting tool. Understanding the shape of the yield curve makes reading *The Wall Street Journal* data more meaningful.

Q: How can savers use reported interest rates to forecast conditions in financial markets and the economy?

A: Because risk premiums incorporate expectations about default risk, they are good predictors of future levels of economic activity and the ability of firms to meet debt obligations. The term structure reveals expectations of future short-term rates in the values of current long-term rates.

Using the Term Structure for Forecasting

Investors, businesspeople, and policymakers also use information contained in the term structure of interest rates for forecasting. Under the expectations and preferred habitat theories, the slope of the yield curve provides information about market participants' expectations about future short-term nominal interest rates. In addition, if fluctuations in expected real interest rates are small, the yield curve provides information about expectations of future inflation rates. Suppose that you want the financial markets' best guess about the rate of inflation in five years. If the real interest rate is expected to remain constant, you can interpret an upward-sloping yield curve to mean that inflation is expected to rise. Indeed, the Fed and many financial market participants use the yield curve to forecast future inflation.

Figure 7.7 presents three yield curves: one that slopes downward, one that slopes upward slightly, and one that slopes upward steeply. If we apply the preferred habitat theory, these three yield curves—representing three points in time between 1989 and 1991—tell a story about financial markets' expectations and the economy.

The top yield curve characterizes the term structure in the spring of 1989. The belief that the Fed would pursue a policy to reduce inflation led market participants to expect that future short-term rates would be lower than current short-term rates. The preferred habitat theory of the term structure suggests that long-term rates should fall relative to short-term rates. In this case, the yield curve actually is *inverted* from the normal upward-sloping case.

The upward slope shown in the middle curve is characteristic of a normal yield curve under the preferred habitat theory. It characterizes the term structure in the fall of 1990, when the economy was experiencing a recession. However, investors expected that, as economic activity increased in the future, the demand for credit would increase, causing interest rates to increase. In other words, investors expected future short-term rates to rise above current levels.

The bottom yield curve represents the term structure in early 1991, when the Fed continued to reduce short-term rates. However, concerns about inflation and government budget deficits kept expected future short-term rates—and hence current long-term rates—high. The inflation fears added to the normal upward slope of the yield curve predicted by the preferred habitat theory.

Key Terms and Concepts

Risk structure of interest rates
    Bond rating
    Default risk
    Default-risk-free instruments
    Municipal bonds
    Risk premium

Term structure of interest rates
    Expectations theory
    Preferred habitat theory
    Segmented markets theory
    Term premium
    Yield curve

Summary

1. There are two ways to categorize the differences in interest rates on different bonds. The risk structure of interest rates refers to variation in yields among financial instruments having the same time to maturity but differences in default risk, liquidity, information costs, and taxation. The term structure of interest rates refers to variation in yields between instruments with the same risk, liquidity, information costs, and taxation but different maturities.

2. The risk premium is the amount of additional yield that a saver requires to hold a risky instrument rather than a default-risk-free instrument with the same maturity. Although the major component of the risk premium reflects default risk, differences in liquidity, information costs, and taxation also are important. U.S. government securities serve as a benchmark against which to calculate risk premiums because they are default-risk-free, are traded in liquid markets, and have low information costs.

Differential taxation of returns on credit market instruments affect their risk premiums.

3. Because government securities are instruments for which default risk, liquidity, information costs, and taxation can be held constant most easily, the term structure usually refers to the yields. A graph of the yields to maturity on default-risk-free instruments as a function of maturity is known as a yield curve.

4. Two features of historical yield curves are important. First, the graph of term structure usually slopes upward, so long-term yields generally are higher than short-term yields. Second, yields on default-risk-free instruments with different maturities often move together.

5. Economists use three theories to explain the two yield curve features. The theories differ in the relative emphasis placed on expected return or matu-

rity. Under the segmented markets theory, borrowers and lenders want only a particular maturity. This theory can explain upward-sloping yield curves so long as investors have a preference for short-term instruments, holding other factors constant. It cannot explain the observation that interest rates tend to move together. Under the expectations theory, borrowers and lenders care only about getting the highest expected return; instruments with different maturities are perfect substitutes. The expectations theory implies that the interest rate on a long-term bond is an average of expected future short-term rates. This approach can explain movement together of interest rates so long as increases (or decreases) in short-term rates continue for many periods. An upward-sloping yield curve, however, predicts ever-increasing short-term rates, casting doubt on the theory in its simplest form. The third approach is a hybrid of the first two theories and is based on the assumption that investors care about both maturity and expected returns. Known as the preferred habitat theory, it describes the interest rate on a long-term bond as an average of expected future short-term rates over the life of the bond plus a term premium. The term premium is affected by demand and supply considerations for the specific maturity. With an investor preference for short-term instruments (all other factors equal), the yield curve slopes upward even if short-term rates are not expected to rise.

6. The risk and term structures of interest rates contain important information about expectations of future economic variables and, for that reason, are useful for forecasting. Because risk premiums reflect expectations about default risk, they are good predictors of future levels of economic activity and the ability of firms to meet debt obligations. Under the expectations theory and preferred habitat theory the term structure includes expectations of future short-term rates in current long-term rates. If real interest rates are expected to be constant over the long run, the term structure may contain information about expected future rates of inflation.

Review Questions

1. A yield curve shows the relationship between the market interest rates on bonds that are identical except in what aspect?

2. What is the term structure of interest rates?

3. According to the expectations theory of the term structure of interest rates, what happens to long-term interest rates when short-term interest rates are expected to fall in the future?

4. When does the yield curve slope upward, according to the expectations theory? According to the segmented markets theory? According to the preferred habitat theory?

5. Why does the yield curve often slope slightly upward, according to the preferred habitat theory?

6. What theory is being used by analysts who examine the demand and supply of funds at different maturity levels in order to predict the term structure of interest rates?

7. Why is the interest rate on a U.S. Treasury bond usually less than that on a corporate bond?

8. What factors affect the interest rate paid on a bond?

9. Does a taxable bond or a tax-free bond pay a higher before-tax interest rate?

10. If the risk premium on a corporate bond increases, does its interest rate necessarily rise? In answering this question, be sure to define risk premium.

11. At the start of the recession in 1990, interest rates on lower-rated corporate bonds rose relative to that

on Treasury bonds. Why did this happen? What is this phenomenon called?

12. Would you expect the yield on a six-month Treasury bill to be higher or lower than that on commercial paper of comparable maturity? Why?

13. Describe factors affecting the difference between a 10-year General Motors bond and a 10-year U.S. Treasury bond. What additional factors would you consider in explaining the difference between a 10-year junk bond and a 10-year U.S. Treasury bond?

14. Suppose that the risk premiums on new issues of corporate bonds and commercial paper increase. Explain how the shifts would affect your guess about the likelihood of an economic downturn in the near future.

15. Why are credit market instruments with high information costs often illiquid?

Analytical Problems

16. Suppose that interest rates for one-year bonds are expected to follow this pattern: 3% today, 5% one year from now, and 7% two years from now. What are the current interest rates on two-year and three-year bonds, according to the expectations theory?

17. Suppose that an investor wants to invest for three years to get the highest possible return. The investor has three options: (a) roll over three one-year bonds, which pay interest rates of 8% in the first year, 11% in the second year, and 7% in the third year; (b) buy a two-year bond paying 10% today, then roll over the amount received when that bond matures into a one-year bond paying 7%; or (c) buy a three-year bond today paying 8.5%. Assuming annual compounding and no transactions costs, which option should the investor choose?

18. Suppose that you have $1000 to invest in the bond market on January 1, 1995. You could buy a one-year bond paying 4%, a two-year bond paying 5%, a three-year bond paying 5.5%, or a four-year bond paying 6%. You expect interest rates on one-year bonds in the future to be 6.5% on January 1, 1996, 7% on January 1, 1997, and 9% on January 1, 1998. You want to hold your investment until January 1, 1999. Which of the fol-

lowing investment alternatives gives you the highest expected return by 1999: (a) buy a four-year bond today; (b) buy a three-year bond today and a one-year bond in 1998; (c) buy a two-year bond today, a one-year bond in 1997, and another one-year bond in 1998; or (d) buy a one-year bond today and then additional one-year bonds in 1996, 1997, and 1998?

19. Answer Problem 18 if a $10 transactions cost is added for every bond you purchase. In other words, if you have $1000 now, you can buy a bond for only $990, as $10 goes for the transactions cost. Which set of bonds should you buy now?

20. In June 1981, the yield curve sloped downward, and in June 1984, the yield curve sloped upward. Interpret these slopes according to the expectations theory.

21. Suppose that short-term interest rates fall during recessions and rise during expansions. What would you expect the slope of the yield curve to be (according to the expectations theory) when: (a) the economy is at a peak and a recession is beginning; (b) the economy is midway between a peak and a trough; (c) the economy is in a trough, and an expansion is beginning; and (d) the economy is midway between a trough and a peak?

22. Suppose that your marginal federal income tax rate is 40%. What is your after-tax rate of return from holding to maturity a one-year municipal bond with an 8% yield? What is your return from holding to maturity a one-year corporate bond with a 10% yield? If both securities had the same default risk and liquidity, which would you prefer to own?

23. If you looked at the data on interest rates, you would see less difference between rates on U.S. government bonds and municipal bonds in the 1980s than earlier. Why do you think this happened?

24. What happens to the yields on junk bonds as the level of economic activity rises and falls?

25. You are considering investing in Fred's Fine Fur Factory. It is an expanding firm with fine prospects whose future looks fabulous. Based on solid information, your analysis of Fred's finances shows that the company is sound. You decide that the risk of such an investment is small relative to other investments and that the return looks better than average. What other factor might be important to your decision about investing in Fred's?

26. Some aspects of an asset's taxability may cause the yield to maturity to be an inaccurate measure of return. Suppose that Bob's bond was issued some years ago and has one year left to maturity; it has a yield to maturity of 7%, with a current yield of 3% and an expected capital gain of 4%. Suppose that Betty's bond is newly issued and matures in a year, with a yield to maturity equal to the current yield of 8%. If you are an investor with a 33% marginal tax rate on interest income but a 0% tax rate on capital gains, whose bond would you prefer to own? Why?

27. The Federal Reserve System holds many U.S. government bonds, which it acquires when it issues money. When the yield curve slopes upward sharply, the Fed could earn a higher return by buying long-term bonds instead of short-term bonds. Should it do so?

28. Under what conditions can you infer expectations about future rates of inflation from the yield curve (according to the expectations theory of the term structure)? Are these conditions more likely to hold for short or long time periods?

29. Using the expectations theory, explain why a firm borrowing for two years is unlikely to save money (over the two years) by borrowing short-term (and refinancing) instead of borrowing long-term when the current short-term rate is lower than the long-term rate.

Data Question

30. Look at *The Wall Street Journal* today or sometime this week and find a plot of the yield curve. (It is a regular feature in Section C.) Compare this plot with the yield curve on the same date one, two, and three years ago. How do the yield curves compare? Can you use the theories of the term structure of interest rates to explain why the yield curve has changed over time?

Exchange Rates and Interest Rates

In mid-September 1992, the global financial system trembled. A disagreement between Germany and other European countries over whether German interest rates were too high led to a "currency crisis," in which financial markets were jolted by fluctuations in the values of European currencies and interest rates. The tremors were felt across the Atlantic in the United States: Consumers were frustrated because the dollar was suddenly worth less abroad, making foreign travel and purchases of imports more expensive. Homebuilders worried that interest rates might rise, discouraging people from buying new homes. A beleaguered President Bush worried that the crisis might weaken the federal government's ability to stimulate the slowly recovering U.S. economy.

Understanding exchange rate movements is important in evaluating differences among interest rates in the international capital market. This information is significant not only to the currency trader or manager of a multinational corporation; knowledge of exchange rate movements helps individuals decide the best time to go to France or anticipate whether interest rates on their money market funds or adjustable-rate home mortgages are likely to rise or fall. For the global economy, the expected real interest rate in the international capital market is determined by desired international lending and borrowing. Comparing expected rates of return for international financial instruments requires considering different currencies, such as the Japanese yen, German mark, or British pound. How does a 5% expected rate of return in dollars on a bank deposit in Chicago compare with a 7% expected rate of return in yen on a bank deposit in Tokyo? In this chapter, we examine how exchange rates influence expected rates of return on international investments and how exchange rates are determined.

We address four main questions in this chapter. **Q:** What are nominal and real exchange rates? **Q:** What factors determine exchange rates in the long run? **Q:** What factors determine exchange rates in the short run? **Q:** How do savers use information about current and expected future exchange rates to compare expected rates of return on assets from different countries?

Why Exchange Rates Are Important

In the 1990s, markets for goods and finance are global. When individuals, businesses, and governments in one country want to trade, borrow, or lend in another country, they have to conduct their transactions in different currencies. The **exchange rate** is the price of one country's currency in terms of another's: Japanese yen per U.S. dollar or French francs per British pound, for example. Exchange rate fluctuations affect the prices of goods bought from other countries and the prices of goods sold there. Those fluctuations affect businesses' profits and returns on financial assets for investors. To understand differences in interest rates in international financial markets requires a grasp of how exchange rates are determined and why they change.

Although the United States uses the dollar as its currency, the dollar is neither a unit of account nor a medium of exchange in Japan, which uses the yen; in Switzerland, which uses the Swiss franc; or in Germany, which uses the mark. Nearly every country has its own currency. Hence, in order to buy goods and assets in other countries, people usually must exchange currencies first. When a U.S. business buys foreign goods, dollars are exchanged for foreign currency to buy the goods. A similar transaction takes place when a U.S. investor purchases a foreign asset: U.S. dollars from dollar-denominated bank deposits are converted to bank deposits in the foreign currency. Most currency transactions are done for the purpose of buying and selling assets in the international capital market, instead of buying and selling goods.

How do currency transactions affect the buying and selling of goods and services overseas? The dollar price of a foreign good, service, or asset, which U.S. consumers and investors care about, actually has two parts: (1) the foreign-currency price, and (2) the number of dollars needed to obtain the desired amount of foreign currency. For example, when a U.S. citizen buys a German bond or camera, two factors determine the dollar price: the price of the bond or camera in German marks, and the exchange rate between the dollar and the mark. This exchange rate changes over time. We call it **appreciation** when a currency increases in value against another currency and **depreciation** when a currency decreases in value against another currency.

Suppose that a German camera sells for 500 marks. If the mark is worth $0.50, the dollar price of the camera is $250. Now suppose that three months later the value of the mark has appreciated to $0.60. The dollar price of the camera will have risen from $250 to $300. The mark's appreciation makes German goods more expensive relative to comparable non-German goods. At the same time, non-German goods become cheaper in Germany. The opposite happens if the mark *depreciates* relative to the dollar. If the value of the mark falls from $0.50 to $0.40, the dollar price of the German camera will fall from $250 to $200. German goods are now more attractive in foreign markets, and the rising dollar makes American goods less attractive in Germany. When a currency appreciates, the price of that country's goods abroad increases and the price of foreign goods sold in that country decreases.

When a currency's exchange rate falls, prices of that country's goods abroad decrease and prices of foreign goods sold in that country increase.

These relationships explain why domestic manufacturers and their workers are so concerned about the foreign-exchange value of the dollar. When the dollar appreciates significantly, U.S. goods become more expensive abroad and U.S. exports decline, hurting U.S. industries. At the same time, U.S. consumers benefit from the appreciating dollar because foreign consumer products sold in the United States become more affordable.

Nominal Exchange Rate

Strictly speaking, our discussion of exchange rates thus far has focused on the **nominal exchange rate,** or the value of one currency in terms of another currency. This rate changes daily. When you go abroad, you must convert U.S. dollars into Japanese yen, German marks, French francs, or British pounds, depending on the country you visit. If the dollar rises in value, you can buy more of other currencies during your travels, enabling you to savor a fine meal or bring back more souvenirs. Figure 8.1 shows that, during the early 1980s, the

▼ FIGURE 8.1

Nominal Exchange Rate: U.S. Dollar versus Other Major Currencies
The U.S. dollar exchange rate rose in the first half of the 1980s and generally declined through the early 1990s.

Source: Council of Economic Advisers, *Economic Report of the President,* various issues.

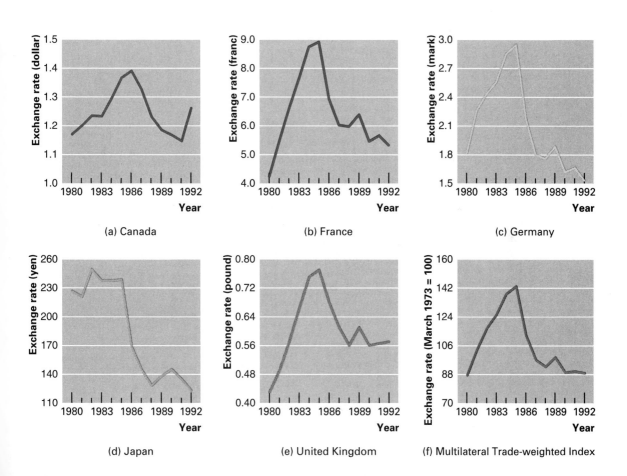

(a) Canada

(b) France

(c) Germany

(d) Japan

(e) United Kingdom

(f) Multilateral Trade-weighted Index

value of the dollar generally increased substantially relative to other major currencies. The strong dollar was a boon to American tourists, who flocked across the Atlantic to travel in Europe. But in the late 1980s, the dollar's value lost ground to other leading currencies, and large numbers of tourists from other countries descended on the United States. In order to understand why these fluctuations in nominal exchange rates occurred, we first need to focus on the way exchange rates are determined in the market for international currencies.

Foreign-Exchange Markets

International currencies are traded in **foreign-exchange markets** around the world. Foreign-exchange markets are over-the-counter markets; that is, there is no single physical location at which traders gather to exchange currencies, as there is for many domestic stocks and bonds. Computer networks link traders in commercial banks in many countries. Most foreign-exchange trading takes place in London, New York, and Tokyo, with secondary centers in Hong Kong, Singapore, and Zurich. Just as transactions in domestic-debt markets determine domestic interest rates, transactions in foreign-exchange markets determine the rates at which international currencies are exchanged. Those exchange rates affect costs of acquiring foreign financial assets or foreign goods and services.

With daily turnover approaching $1 trillion, the worldwide foreign-exchange market is one of the largest financial markets in the world. Major market participants are importers and exporters, banks, investment portfolio managers, and central banks. They trade currencies such as the U.S. dollar ($), British pound (£), German mark (DM), Japanese yen (¥), and French franc (FF) around the clock. The busiest trading time is in the morning (U.S. Eastern Standard Time) when the London and New York markets are open for trading, but trading is always taking place somewhere. A trader in New York might be awakened in the middle of the night to adjust foreign-exchange positions in response to events overseas.

Two types of currency transactions are conducted in foreign-exchange markets. In **spot market transactions,** currencies or bank deposits are exchanged immediately (subject to a two-day settlement period). In **forward transactions,** currencies or bank deposits are to be exchanged at a set date in the future. In the Using the news box, we show how to read and use newspaper reports of spot and forward exchange rates.

Real Exchange Rates

Nominal exchange rates set the value of a currency in terms of other currencies. They do *not*, however, reflect the *purchasing power*, or **real exchange rate,** of the currency. For example, suppose that $1.00 can be exchanged for 1230 Italian lira (L). Although L1230 may seem like a large number, in Rome, a hamburger costs L4100 and an espresso at a chic outdoor café costs L4500. In other words, the purchasing power of the lira is substantially less than the purchasing power of a dollar.

Using the news...

Reading Exchange Rates

Current spot and forward exchange rates for all major currencies are reported each day in *The Wall Street Journal*. The first entry for a country is the spot exchange rate. For Germany, on January 12, 1993, DM1.00 could be exchanged for $0.6131, or (equivalently) $1.00 = DM1.631. However, the 180-day forward exchange rate is $0.5995 per mark, so that $1.00 = DM1.668. The difference between the forward and spot rates reflects the fact that investors expect the foreign-exchange value of the dollar to rise relative to the mark by about 2.3%, or from DM1.631 to DM1.668. In general, when the forward rate is greater than the spot rate, investors expect the domestic currency to appreciate. When the forward rate is less than the spot rate, investors expect the domestic currency to depreciate. At its peak in 1985, $1.00 could be exchanged for DM2.942; that is, the foreign-exchange value of the dollar fell by about 45% between 1985 and January 1993.

CURRENCY TRADING

EXCHANGE RATES

Tuesday, January 12, 1993

The New York foreign exchange selling rates below apply to trading among banks in amounts of $1 million and more, as quoted at 3 p.m. Eastern time by Bankers Trust Co., Telerate and other sources. Retail transactions provide fewer units of foreign currency per dollar.

		U.S. $ equiv.		Currency per U.S. $	
Country		Tues.	Mon.	Tues.	Mon.
Argentina (Peso)	....	1.01	1.01	.99	.99
Australia (Dollar)	....	.6730	.6735	1.4859	1.4848
Austria (Schilling)	....	.08715	.08709	11.47	11.48
Bahrain (Dinar)	....	2.6522	2.6522	.3771	.3771
Belgium (Franc)	....	.02978	.02977	33.58	33.59
Brazil (Cruzeiro)	....	.0000776	.0000693	12880.01	14435.01
Britain (Pound)	....	1.5430	1.5555	.6481	.6429
30-Day Forward	......	1.5370	1.5495	.6506	.6454
90-Day Forward	......	1.5286	1.5409	.6542	.6490
180-Day Forward	......	1.5173	1.5298	.6591	.6537
Canada (Dollar)	....	.7834	.7828	1.2765	1.2775
30-Day Forward	......	.7809	.7803	1.2806	1.2816
90-Day Forward	......	.7767	.7761	1.2875	1.2885
180-Day Forward	.....	.7709	.7703	1.2972	1.2982
Czechoslovakia (Koruna)					
Commercial rate	......	.0350754	.0349650	28.5100	28.600
Chile (Peso)	....	.002679	.002688	373.29	372.08
China (Renminbi)	....	.171233	.171233	5.8400	5.8400
Colombia (Peso)	....	.001607	.001607	622.20	622.20
Denmark (Krone)	....	.1587	.1586	6.3006	6.3054
Ecuador (Sucre)					
Floating rate	....	.000552	.000552	1812.02	1812.02
Finland (Markka)	....	.18425	.18399	5.4273	5.4352
France (Franc)	....	.18051	.18041	5.5400	5.5430
30-Day Forward	......	.17901	.17892	5.5862	5.5892
90-Day Forward	......	.17677	.17667	5.6572	5.6602
180-Day Forward	......	.17426	.17417	5.7385	5.7415
Germany (Mark)	....	.6131	.6130	1.6310	1.6312
30-Day Forward	......	.6100	.6099	1.6395	1.6397
90-Day Forward	......	.6055	.6054	1.6516	1.6518
180-Day Forward	......	.5995	.5994	1.6681	1.6683
Greece (Drachma)	....	.004588	.004579	217.95	218.40
Hong Kong (Dollar)	....	.12921	.12919	7.7395	7.7406
Hungary (Forint)	....	.0120846	.0120351	82.7500	83.0900

Name of Country and unit of account. → Country (first column)

Price as of last trading day. → Canada (Dollar)

Spot exchange rate. → Germany (Mark)

Forward exchange rate. → 180-Day Forward

Source: From *The Wall Street Journal*, January 13, 1993. Reprinted by permission of *The Wall Street Journal*, ©1993 Dow Jones & Co., Inc. All Rights Reserved Worldwide. (Quotes are from January 12, 1993.)

Let's find out why. Real and nominal exchange rates are different concepts, but we can compare them in a simple relationship. Suppose that a Big Mac® costs $2.20 in Columbus, Ohio and L4100 in Rome. If $1.00 buys L1230 on foreign-exchange markets, we find the real exchange rate, or relative purchasing power, by comparing the costs of the hamburgers in dollar terms. Let:

EX = nominal exchange rate in foreign currency per dollar (lira per dollar in our example);

P_f = foreign-currency price of goods in the foreign country (lira price of a hamburger in Rome);

P = domestic-currency price of domestic goods (dollar price of a hamburger in Columbus, Ohio); and

EX_r = real exchange rate (number of comparable goods that domestic consumers can get by trading a unit of domestic goods).

The real exchange rate EX_r is given by the equation

$$EX_r = \frac{EX \times P}{P_f}. \tag{8.1}$$

To find the cost of the hamburger in dollar terms, we substitute and solve Eq. (8.1):

$$EX_r = \frac{(\text{L}1230\,/\,\$)\ (\$2.20/\text{American Big Mac})}{\text{L}4100/\text{Italian Big Mac}}$$

$$= 0.66 \text{ Italian Big Mac per American Big Mac.}$$

Hence, at the nominal exchange rate used in the example, \$2.20 buys one hamburger in the United States, but only 0.66 hamburger in Italy. The purchasing power of a hamburger—the real exchange rate—is 0.66 Italian Big Mac per American Big Mac.

In reality, of course, different countries produce many different goods, so that the real exchange rate usually isn't defined good by good. Instead, it is computed from *price indexes*, which compare the price of a group of goods in one country with the price of a similar group of goods in another country. The consumer price index and the price deflator for the gross domestic product are two examples of price indexes. Just as we did for nominal exchange rates, we can apply the concepts of appreciation and depreciation to real exchange rates.[†] When a currency's real exchange rate rises (it appreciates), the country can trade its goods for more units of foreign goods. When a currency's exchange rate falls (it depreciates), the country obtains a smaller volume of foreign goods per unit of domestic goods.

Relating Changes in Nominal and Real Exchange Rates

Let's consider how changes in nominal and real exchange rates are related. We know that the real exchange rate EX_r is given by Eq. (8.1). We can calculate the *percentage change* in the real exchange rate $\Delta EX_r / EX_r$ as the

---

[†] In using the terms *appreciation* and *depreciation*, we are treating exchange rates as *flexible*, or determined purely by market forces. In Chapter 22, we discuss attempts by governments and central banks to fix exchange rates.

percentage change in the numerator of Eq. (8.1) minus the percentage change in the denominator:

$$\begin{array}{c}\text{\% change in} \\ \text{real exchange rate}\end{array} = \begin{array}{c}\text{\% change in nominal} \\ \text{exchange rate}\end{array} + \begin{array}{c}\text{\% change in} \\ \text{domestic prices}\end{array} - \begin{array}{c}\text{\% change in} \\ \text{foreign prices}\end{array}$$

or

$$\frac{\Delta EX_r}{EX_r} = \frac{\Delta EX}{EX} + \frac{\Delta P}{P} - \frac{\Delta P_f}{P_f}. \tag{8.2}$$

The *percentage change* in domestic prices $\Delta P/P$ is the domestic rate of inflation π. Similarly, the percentage change in foreign prices is the foreign rate of inflation π_f. Accordingly, we rewrite Eq. (8.2):

$$\frac{\Delta EX}{EX} = \frac{\Delta EX_r}{EX_r} + (\pi_f - \pi). \tag{8.3}$$

Q: What are nominal and real exchange rates?

A: The nominal exchange rate is the price of one currency relative to another. The real exchange rate is the price of a group of goods in one country relative to that in another. Changes in the nominal exchange rate reflect changes in the real exchange rate, domestic inflation, and foreign inflation.

Equation (8.3) shows that the percentage change in the nominal exchange rate has two parts: the percentage change in the real exchange rate, and the difference between the foreign and domestic inflation rates. Considering these parts separately reveals two explanations for a rising nominal exchange rate: a rising real exchange rate and/or a high foreign inflation rate relative to the domestic inflation rate. Similarly, a falling nominal exchange rate reflects some combination of a falling real exchange rate and a high domestic inflation rate relative to the foreign inflation rate.

▶ **C H E C K P O I N T** *Bicca and Montblanca are companies in two countries whose currencies are the crown and the royal. Bicca manufacturers ballpoint pens that are sold for 2 crowns each. Montblanca manufactures high-quality fountain pens that are sold for 10 royals each. The real exchange rate between Bicca and Montblanca is 10 ballpoint pens per fountain pen. What is the nominal exchange rate? The real exchange rate is 10 ballpoint pens per fountain pen, so 20 crowns (the cost of 10 ballpoint pens) equal 10 royals (the cost of one fountain pen), or 1 royal = 2 crowns.* ◀

Determining Long-Run Exchange Rates

Having examined the distinctions between real and nominal exchange rates, we are now ready to analyze how exchange rates are determined. First, we examine how they are determined in the long run and then we apply that understanding to their determination in the short run.

The Law of One Price

The simplest way to understand how long-run exchange rates are determined is by examining the **law of one price.** This law states that if two countries produce an identical good, profit opportunities should ensure that its price is the same around the world, no matter which country produces the good.[†] Suppose that a yard of cloth produced in the United States sells for $10 and that the same type of cloth produced by a French manufacturer costs 50 French francs (FF) per yard. The law of one price says that the exchange rate between the U.S. dollar and the French franc must be FF50/$10, or FF5 per $1. Why? If, at going exchange rates, U.S. cloth is cheaper than French cloth, the demand for dollars to buy the U.S. cloth would rise, pushing up the value of the dollar. But if, at going exchange rates, French cloth is cheaper than U.S. cloth, the demand for francs to buy French cloth would rise, pushing up the value of the franc.

Let's consider an example of the profit opportunities that make this process work. If the exchange rate were FF4 per $1, U.S. cloth would be cheaper than French cloth. In France, U.S. cloth would sell for ($10)(4) = FF40, which is cheaper than the FF50 charged by French manufacturers. In the United States, French cloth would sell for FF50/4 = $12.50 per yard, which is more expensive than U.S.-produced cloth (at $10 per yard). As a result, there would be no demand for French cloth. However, if the exchange rate were FF6 per $1, French cloth would be cheaper in both the United States and France, eliminating the demand for U.S. cloth. As long as the dollar price of U.S. cloth and the franc price of French cloth remain constant, the exchange rate must settle at FF5 per $1.

The Purchasing Power Parity Theory

When we compare the international prices for an identical good, the law of one price holds. When we generalize the concept and apply it to a group of goods, it becomes the purchasing power parity theory of exchange rate determination. The **purchasing power parity (PPP) theory** is based on the assumption that real exchange rates are constant. It states that changes in the nominal exchange rate between two currencies are accounted for by differences in the inflation rates of the two countries. Rearranging terms in Eq. (8.1) gives the nominal exchange rate:

$$EX = EX_r \left(\frac{P_f}{P} \right).$$

[†] There is an important qualification, however: The good should be tradeable, and price differences are allowed to the extent that they reflect transportation costs. In the Big Mac example earlier, trading Big Macs between Rome and Columbus would be difficult.

Because the law of one price holds that EX_r is constant, increases or decreases in EX reflect changes in relative price levels between the two countries.

In the U.S. and French cloth example, a 5% expected increase in the French price level relative to the U.S. price level should cause the dollar to appreciate by 5% because EX_r is constant:

$$\frac{\Delta EX}{EX} = \frac{\Delta EX_r}{EX_r} + (\pi_f - \pi) = 0 + 0.05, \quad \text{or} \quad 5\%.$$

When French expected inflation exceeds U.S. expected inflation and the real exchange rate doesn't change, the dollar rises in value. Under the PPP theory, the dollar's purchasing power has risen relative to that of the franc.

In general, the PPP theory of exchange rate determination suggests that whenever a country's price level is expected to rise relative to another country's price level, its currency should depreciate relative to the other country's currency. In the preceding example the French franc depreciated by 5% relative to the dollar. Conversely, whenever a country's price level is expected to fall relative to another country's price level, its currency should appreciate, as the U.S. currency did in the example.

Does the Theory Match Reality?

Despite the logical clarity of the PPP theory, empirical researchers have found that actual exchange rate movements do not simply reflect differences in price levels. That is, movements in exchange rates are not completely consistent with the PPP theory, especially in the short run. Part of this failure is traceable to the fact that commodities (oil, steel, and wheat, for example) are pretty much the same regardless of where they are produced but that most other goods are *differentiated*, or not identical. For example, Kodak and Nikon both manufacture cameras, but their products' characteristics are different and so the prices may differ. For differentiated products, the law of one price doesn't hold.

Another measurement problem with the PPP theory is that not all goods and services are traded in international markets. The fact that health club dues may be cheaper in Paris than in New York probably would not entice many New Yorkers to join health clubs in Paris. Similarly, services such as child care and haircuts or goods such as meals in restaurants and houses are not tradeable internationally. Thus significant differences in prices in various countries do not affect exchange rates.

Finally, the PPP theory's underlying assumption that the real exchange rate is constant is incorrect, even in the long run. Three factors are important in explaining changes in real exchange rates: (1) shifts in preferences for domestic or foreign goods, (2) differences in productivity, and (3) trade barriers. If inflation rates do not change, these factors also can explain shifts in nominal exchange rates.

Preferences for Domestic or Foreign Goods. If U.S. consumers demand Japanese-made goods (cars, cameras, televisions, and so on), they are willing to pay more dollars per yen, and the dollar depreciates. Conversely, if Japanese consumers demand U.S. goods (clothes, compact discs, and so on), they are willing to pay more yen per dollar, and the dollar appreciates. Thus the real exchange rate changes in response to a shift in households' and firms' preferences for domestic or foreign goods. Unless inflation rates change, nominal exchange rates also change. Let's hold everything else constant and generalize this connection. A country's currency appreciates in the long run in response to an increase in demand for its exports. A decrease in the demand for imports causes the currency to depreciate in the long run.

Differences in Productivity. Productivity growth measures the increase in a country's output *relative to* the increase in its inputs. When a country has a high rate of productivity growth relative to other countries, its firms can produce goods more cheaply than its foreign competitors can. As a result, that country's domestic goods can be supplied at prices lower than comparable foreign goods, thereby increasing the demand for domestic goods and the domestic currency. But if a country's productivity growth is low relative to other countries, the goods it sells become more expensive, and all else being equal, its currency will depreciate. An increase in a country's productivity relative to that of other countries causes its real and nominal exchange rate to appreciate.

Trade Barriers. Countries do not always allow goods to be traded freely with no market intervention. One common trade barrier is **quotas,** or limits on the volume of foreign goods that can be brought into a country. Another trade barrier is **tariffs,** or taxes on goods purchased from other countries. Suppose, for example, that the United States places a tariff on German cameras. American consumers then find German-made cameras more expensive than U.S.-made cameras. As a result, the trade barrier increases cost-conscious American consumers' demand for U.S.-made cameras. As a result, the demand for dollars (to buy U.S.-made cameras) is higher than if there were no tariff. Hence, all else being equal, with trade barriers, the quantity of U.S.-made cameras sold will remain high even when the dollar's value on foreign exchange markets is high. Trade barriers lead to a higher nominal exchange rate in the long run for the country imposing the barriers.

Q: What factors determine exchange rates in the long run?

A: In the long run, changes in the nominal exchange rate between two countries reflect changes in: (1) relative price levels, (2) preferences for domestic or foreign goods, (3) relative productivity, and (4) trade barriers.

▶ C H E C K P O I N T *Suppose that U.S. consumers follow a* Buy American *strategy in their purchases for a long period of time. Predict the consequences for the nominal exchange rate.* Holding constant other determinants of the nominal exchange rate, an increased preference for domestic goods over imports will raise the nominal exchange rate. The domestic currency will appreciate. ◀

Determining Short-Run Exchange Rates

The theory of exchange rate determination in the long run helps in predicting trends in rates over several years, but we need a way to analyze exchange rate movements over shorter periods of time. Currency fluctuations over a few months or even weeks can affect interest rates in the United States and abroad, the profitability of businesses' investments overseas, and the agendas of policymakers. These fluctuations can be quite large—as much as several percentage points during a single day. Hence our next step is to develop a theory to explain how short-run exchange rates are determined.

We begin by building on a basic assumption: In the short run, exchange rates represent prices of financial assets in one currency relative to prices of similar financial assets in another currency. In particular, the nominal exchange rate represents the price of domestic financial assets (bank deposits or Treasury bills) denominated in domestic currency in terms of foreign financial assets (foreign bank deposits or government bonds) denominated in foreign currency. For example, if the United States and Japan have an exchange rate of ¥105/$1, a $100 U.S. bank deposit costs ¥10,500. By treating the exchange rate as the price of one asset relative to another, we can use the determinants of asset demand (introduced in Chapter 6) to show how exchange rates are determined in the short run.

The Exchange Rate–Interest Rate Connection

Let's begin with an example of how exchange rate movements affect your comparison of interest rates on financial instruments in different countries. Suppose that you want to invest $1000 for one year. You narrow your choices to a U.S. Treasury bill or a Japanese government bond. The U.S. instrument pays interest and principal in dollars with a nominal interest rate of 5% per year. The Japanese instrument pays interest and principal in yen and carries a nominal interest rate of 5% per year.

If the risk, liquidity, and information characteristics of the two instruments are comparable,[†] which one should you buy? The theory of portfolio allocation (Chapter 6) tells you that if both instruments are denominated in the same currency, you should invest in the one with the higher yield. However, as the two assets are denominated in different currencies, you also have to consider whether the exchange rate between the U.S. dollar and the Japanese yen will change during the year.

How can you allow for a change in exchange rates in making an investment decision? You need to measure the return on the two instruments,

---

[†] Recall that the theory of portfolio allocation implies that investors should compare expected returns on assets with similar risk, liquidity, and information characteristics. Comparing the expected return on a U.S. Treasury bond with that on a debt security for a high-risk Japanese firm, for example, would not be appropriate.

using dollars as a common yardstick. To do so, convert expected returns on both securities into dollars. If you invest $1000 in the U.S. Treasury bill, you will receive an interest return of $50, so your investment will be worth $1050 after one year.

For the Japanese bond, you first must convert your $1000 into yen; a year from now, you must convert your principal and interest from yen back into dollars in order to compare the return with that from the U.S. bond. Suppose that the current nominal exchange rate is ¥100/$1 and that you expect the exchange rate to appreciate by 5% during the coming year. The expected future exchange rate EX^e, then, is (¥100)(1.05)/$1 = ¥105/$1. When you convert $1000 into yen at the current exchange rate, you have ¥100,000 for investment. After receiving a 5% interest return, your investment is worth ¥105,000 after a year. You expect the exchange rate at that time to be ¥105/$1, so the expected dollar value of your investment will be ¥105,000/105 = $1000. Hence, even though the Japanese bond pays the same stated rate of interest as the U.S. Treasury bill, it carries a lower expected return: $0 instead of $50.[†]

We can generalize from the example to compare total returns from investing $1 in a domestic or a foreign asset. Let i and i_f represent the interest rate for the domestic and the foreign security, respectively. Investing $1 in the domestic security yields $(1 + i)$ after a year. Now let EX represent foreign currency units per dollar; that is, $1 will buy EX of the foreign security. At the end of a year, the amount invested yields a total of $EX(1 + i_f)$ in the foreign-currency units. Converting back to dollars, the total expected value of the investment after a year will be $EX(1 + i_f)/EX^e$, where EX^e is the expected future exchange rate.

Returning to the example of the one-year Japanese government bond,

$$\text{Value of \$1 investment after one year} = \frac{EX(1 + i_f)}{EX^e} = \frac{(¥100/1)(1.05)}{¥105/\$1} = 1.00,$$

or $1000 for an investment of $1000, as we calculated previously.

For simplicity, we can approximate this expression with one that divides the return into two parts: interest and expected exchange rate change.

$$\text{Value of \$1 investment after one year} = 1 + \underbrace{i_f}_{\text{Interest}} - \underbrace{\frac{\Delta EX^e}{EX}}_{\substack{\text{Expected exchange} \\ \text{rate change}}}$$

where $\Delta EX^e/EX$ represents the expected percentage change in the exchange rate for the year. In our example, $\Delta EX^e/EX = 5\%$, so

Value of \$1 invested in a Japanese bond for 1 year $= 1 + 0.05 - (0.05) = \$1.00$,

or the same zero return calculated before. When deciding between domestic and foreign investments, investors consider *both* the interest return and the expected change in the exchange rate during the investment time horizon. The decision-making process is guided by the reasoning: For each \$1 you invest in a U.S. Treasury bill, you get back \$1 plus 5¢ in interest, or

$$\$1 \xrightarrow[\text{Interest}]{\text{Earns}} i \xrightarrow{\text{Yielding}} (1+i).$$

Investing \$1 in a Japanese bond requires more steps. First, you exchange your \$1 for ¥100. That ¥100 earns interest of 5% for the year. At the end of the year, you must convert the principal and interest back to dollars at the exchange rate at that time (which you expect to be \$1 = ¥105). Thus

$$\$1 \xrightarrow[]{\substack{\text{Exchanged for} \\ \text{foreign currency}}} EX \xrightarrow[\text{Interest}]{\text{Earns}} i_f \xrightarrow{\text{Yielding}} EX(1+i_f).$$

When you exchange $EX(1 + i_f)$ for domestic currency at the expected future exchange rate,

$$EX(1+i_f) \xrightarrow{\text{Converts to}} \frac{EX(1+i_f)}{EX^e} \xrightarrow[\text{approximately}]{\substack{\text{Yielding}}} 1 + i_f - \frac{\Delta EX^e}{EX}.$$

Now, you can compare these two investments in terms of dollars.

Proceeds from Domestic Asset	Proceeds from Foreign Asset
$1 + i$	$1 + i_f - \dfrac{\Delta EX^e}{EX}$

As was the case in the example, you would prefer to invest in U.S. Treasury bills if your return, i, is greater than the return you would get from investing in Japanese bonds, $i_f - \Delta EX^e/EX$. However, you would prefer to invest in Japanese bonds if your return, $i_f - \Delta EX^e/EX$, is greater than the return, i, you would get from investing in U.S. Treasury bills. If the returns on the U.S. and Japanese financial instruments were equal—that is, if $i = i_f - \Delta EX^e/EX$—you would be indifferent between investing in either. This result is analogous to the comparisons investors make between short-term and

Q: What factors
determine
exchange rates in
the short run?

A: In the short
run, nominal
exchange rates are
determined in
financial markets
as savers compare
expected rates of
return on domestic
and foreign assets.

long-term debt instruments in the domestic market. When buying a long-term bond, investors consider both the current stated interest rates and the expected future interest rates.

International Capital Mobility

Today's global economy requires significant **international capital mobility,** that is, the ability of investors to move funds among international markets easily. Hence investors can buy financial assets (with similar risk, liquidity, and information characteristics) denominated in many different currencies at many places around the world as shown in Fig. 8.1.

Would a situation in which investors could earn a higher expected rate of return from buying Japanese rather than U.S. assets persist for a long period of time? To anticipate a bit, the answer is *no.* Let's assume that the U.S. and Japanese assets have identical risk, liquidity, and information characteristics. The determinants of asset demand suggest that investors should be indifferent between Japanese and U.S. assets. In other words, the expected returns on the two assets should be the same.

In reality, the opportunity to make a profit ensures this result. If the Japanese asset has a higher expected rate of return than the U.S. asset, investors around the world recognize a chance to make a profit by selling U.S. Treasury bills to buy Japanese bonds. (As the two assets are similar, investors have no reason not to do so.) Now, what effect do these buying and selling transactions have on the expected returns? As investors sell dollar-denominated assets (Treasury bills) and buy yen-denominated assets (Japanese bonds), they increase the demand for yen. This higher demand for yen pushes up the yen's value relative to the dollar to the point where investors are indifferent between holding U.S. or Japanese assets.

Foreign-Exchange Market Equilibrium

What does international capital mobility imply about the relationship of expected returns from different international investment strategies? Let's look at how market forces equalize expected returns on domestic and foreign assets. We use a graphical analysis to illustrate the process for the U.S. versus Japanese investment example and short-run exchange rate determination in general.

Figure 8.2 shows our basic exchange rate model. The y-axis is the current exchange rate, or the number of yen per dollar. The x-axis is the expected rate of return, in dollar terms, from investing in a U.S. or Japanese asset. For U.S. assets, the expected rate of return R equals the U.S. interest rate i. The expected rate of return on foreign assets in dollar terms R_f equals $i_f - \Delta EX^e/EX$. Hence, for Japanese assets, the expected rate of return R_f equals the Japanese interest rate i_f less the expected appreciation of the dollar.

A graph of R against the current yen/dollar exchange rate is simply a vertical line because the return on a U.S. asset in dollar terms is the same

> FIGURE 8.2

Determining the Exchange Rate in Financial Markets
In the short run, financial markets determine the exchange rate. At the equilibrium exchange rate EX^*_{100}, investors' expected rate of return on domestic assets, R, equals the expected rate of return on foreign assets, R_f.

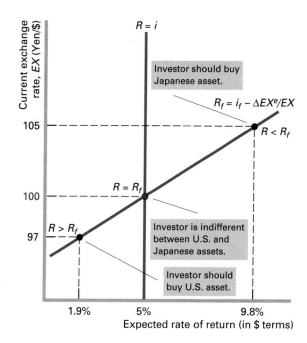

regardless of the exchange rate. (It is paid in dollars.) The diagram is based on a U.S. interest rate of 5%.

To graph R_f against the exchange rate, we must first specify the expected future yen/dollar exchange rate. This assumption allows us to calculate the dollar's expected rate of appreciation, a key component of R_f. Whenever the current yen/dollar exchange rate exceeds that expected future level, investors will believe that the dollar is unusually strong and that it eventually will command fewer yen. That is, they will expect the dollar to depreciate. Thus, for an expected level of the exchange rate, a graph of R_f against the current exchange rate slopes upward: As the yen/dollar exchange rate rises, the dollar's expected rate of appreciation falls, pushing up R_f.

For example, suppose that the future yen/dollar exchange rate is expected to be 100, and that Japanese interest rates are 5%. If the current exchange rate also is 100, no appreciation is expected, and R_f equals the 5% Japanese interest rate. If the current exchange rate rises to ¥105/$1, the dollar is expected to depreciate. In this case, investors predict that a dollar will bring only ¥100 in the future, not ¥105 as it does now. This expected 4.8% depreciation of the dollar (from ¥105/$1 to ¥100/$1) increases R_f to 9.8% (5% interest rate minus −4.8% expected appreciation). Alternatively, if the yen/dollar exchange rate falls to 97, the dollar is expected to appreciate 3.1% (from ¥97/$1 to ¥100/$1), and R_f falls to 1.9% (the 5% interest rate minus 3.1% expected appreciation). Placing these points on the graph and connecting the three combinations of exchange rate and expected rate of return yields the upward-sloping R_f line in Fig. 8.2.

Using the news...

Interest Rates on International Bonds

Yields on government bonds in selected countries are reported each day in *The Wall Street Journal*. The top tabulation shows that yields in local currency terms vary significantly between countries. The Japanese bond maturing in the year 2000 has a yield of 4.47% in yen terms, whereas the British bond maturing in 2002 has a yield of 8.45% in pound terms. If international investors are indifferent between Japanese or British bonds, they must expect that the yen will appreciate against the pound. Using Eq. (8.4) we obtain:

4.47% = 8.45% minus Expected appreciation of yen,

or

Expected appreciation of the £/¥ exchange rate = 8.45% − 4.47% = 3.98%.

The bottom tabulation shows that local currency and dollar total rates of return from international bonds over a time period differ substantially. Look at the "12 mos" column, which presents total rates of return in local currency terms and dollar terms. Note, for

INTERNATIONAL GOVERNMENT BONDS

Prices in local currencies, provided by Salomon Brothers Inc.

	COUPON	MATURITY (Mo./ yr.)	PRICE	CHANGE	YIELD*
JAPAN (3 p.m. Tokyo)					
#89	5.10%	6/96	104.055	+ 0.157	3.83%
#108	4.80	6/98	102.665	+ 0.225	4.25
#129	6.40	3/00	111.787	+ 0.336	4.47
#15	6.70	3/11	111.456	+ 0.304	5.68
#73	6.80	6/95	107.282	+ 0.083	3.65
UNITED KINGDOM (5 p.m. London)					
	9.00%	10/08	101.375	− 0.219	8.83%
	9.75	8/02	108.375	− 0.062	8.45
	10.00	6/94	104.375	− 0.031	6.68
	9.00	3/00	106.000	− 0.062	7.88
	8.75	9/97	105.500	− 0.031	7.32

*Equivalent to semi-annual compounded yields to maturity

Total Rates of Return on International Bonds

In percent, based on Salomon Brothers' world government benchmark bond indexes

— LOCAL CURRENCY TERMS —	
	12 MOS
Japan +	9.54
Britain +	14.91
Germany +	10.91
— U.S. DOLLAR TERMS —	
Japan +	11.02
Britain −	1.48
Germany +	7.14

Source: From *The Wall Street Journal*, January 13, 1993. Reprinted by permission of *The Wall Street Journal*, ©1993 Dow Jones & Co., Inc. All Rights Reserved Worldwide. (Quotes are from January 12, 1993.)

example, that the total rate of return in terms of marks from holding German bonds over the preceding 12 months was 10.91%, and the corresponding total rate of return in dollar terms was 7.14%.

This difference indicates that payments in marks bought fewer dollars at the end of the 12 months than at the beginning, meaning that the dollar appreciated against the mark.

Which exchange rate represents equilibrium? It is the rate that equates R and R_f. The intersection of R and R_f occurs at ¥100/$1, at which both R and R_f equal 5%. At any other current exchange rate, the expected appreciation or depreciation of the dollar causes R_f to differ from R.

What guarantees that the equilibrium current exchange rate is ¥100/$1? Suppose, for example, that the current yen/dollar exchange rate is 97. Hence the dollar is expected to appreciate by 3.1%. The expected rate of return on Japanese assets in dollar terms is 1.9% (the 5% interest rate minus 3.1% expected appreciation). Investors then will sell Japanese assets and buy American assets because the U.S. interest rate is 5%. The increase in the demand for dollars puts upward pressure on the current yen/dollar exchange rate. Only when the current yen/dollar exchange rate rises to 100 will investors again be indifferent between Japanese and U.S. assets.

Now, suppose that the current yen/dollar exchange rate is ¥105/$1. Hence the dollar is expected to depreciate by 4.8% (from ¥105 to ¥100). The expected rate of return on Japanese assets in dollar terms is 9.8% (the 5% interest rate minus −4.8% expected appreciation). In this case, investors will sell American assets and buy Japanese assets because the U.S. interest rate is 5%. The increase in the demand for yen puts downward pressure on the current yen/dollar exchange rate. Only when the current yen/dollar exchange rate falls to 100 will investors again be indifferent between holding U.S. and Japanese assets. (For another application, see the Using the news box)

Interest Rate Parity

The market equilibrium condition is called the **nominal interest rate parity condition**: When domestic and foreign assets have identical risk, liquidity, and information characteristics, their nominal returns (measured in the same currency) also must be identical. Thus any difference between the nominal interest rates on U.S. and those on Japanese assets reflects expected currency appreciation or depreciation. When the domestic interest rate is higher than the foreign interest rate, the domestic currency is expected to depreciate. When the domestic interest rate is lower than the foreign interest rate, the domestic currency is expected to appreciate. Using the expressions for domestic and foreign expected returns, we have

Expected return on domestic asset = Expected return on foreign asset, or

$$i = i_f - \frac{\Delta EX^e}{EX}. \tag{8.4}$$

The nominal interest rate parity condition does *not* imply that nominal interest rates are the same around the world. Rather, it says that expected nominal returns on comparable domestic and foreign assets are the same. If domestic and foreign assets are perfect substitutes, international investors are willing to hold outstanding domestic and foreign assets only when the expected returns on those assets are equivalent. Again, if we let R represent the expected rate of return on the domestic asset in dollar terms (equal to i) and R_f represent the expected rate of return on the foreign asset in dollar terms (equal to $i_f - \Delta EX^e/EX$), the nominal interest rate parity condition implies that

$$R = R_f. \tag{8.5}$$

For an application of portfolio allocation, see Box 8.1. We can also express interest rate parity in terms of the expected real interest rates in the domestic country, r, and that in the foreign country, r_f, and the current and

Consider this...

BOX 8.1

Should You Bank on International Investments?

In 1991 and 1992, falling interest rates in the United States sent many individual investors scurrying to international markets for higher yields. Nominal interest rates on bank deposits in some other countries, such as Germany and England, were higher than those in the United States. If this situation repeats itself, should you move your money into foreign-currency bank accounts in overseas branches of U.S. banks?

Not necessarily. The interest rate parity condition tells you that you need to consider changes in exchange rates when comparing expected rates of return for bank deposits denominated in different currencies. As the accompanying table shows, the interest offered on three-month, pound-denominated certificates of deposit issued in England by Citibank for the period ending May

Three-Month Bank Deposits	British Pound	Canadian Dollar	German Mark	U.S. Dollar
Interest (for three months)	2.8%	2.1%	1.9%	1.5%
Foreign-Exchange Gain or Loss	−12.0	0.0	−14.0	0.0
Total Rate of Return	−9.2	2.1	−12.1	1.5

31, 1991 was greater than the comparable U.S. interest rate. However, exchange rate changes (in this case, appreciation of the dollar) can reverse the advantage. Forecasting firms and banks can help you predict whether the dollar will appreciate.

Consider what happened to investors with money in the currencies shown in the table. For British assets, appreciation of the dollar against the pound led to a net loss in dollar terms. Because the exchange rate between U.S. and Canadian dollars did not change, the U.S. dollar rate of return equaled the Canadian dollar

rate of return. For German bank deposits, appreciation of the dollar against the mark led to a loss in dollar terms. Finally, U.S. deposits offered a 1.5% three-month dollar return. To summarize, if you are thinking of putting some of your savings in assets denominated in a foreign currency, be sure to consider the consequences of exchange rate changes.

Source: The bank deposits are three-month certificates of deposit offered by Citibank for the period ending May 31, 1991. Calculations are from Georgette Jasen, "The Dollar Rally: Hit on Profits May Drag Down Stock Market and Cut Foreign CD Returns," *The Wall Street Journal,* July 8, 1991, p. C1.

expected values of the real exchange rate, EX_r and EX_r^e, respectively. The **real interest rate parity condition** states that expected real rates of interest measured in terms of the same group of goods are equal, or

$$\frac{\text{Expected gross real return}}{\text{on domestic investment}} = \frac{\text{Expected gross real return}}{\text{on foreign investment}}, \text{ or}$$

$$1 + r = (1 + r_f)\left(\frac{EX_r}{EX_r^e}\right). \tag{8.6}$$

The domestic real interest rate r and the foreign real interest rate r_f do not have to be equal to be consistent with real interest rate parity. Equation (8.6) requires that the two real interest rates be equal when measured in the same group of goods.[†]

▶ **C H E C K P O I N T** *Suppose that the current mark/dollar exchange rate is 1.6 and that investors expect the dollar to appreciate to DM1.7/$1 during the next year. If the current U.S. nominal interest rate is 7% per year, what should be the interest rate on a German financial instrument with similar risk, liquidity, and information characteristics to maintain nominal interest rate parity?* The nominal interest rate parity condition indicates that the U.S. interest rate minus the expected appreciation of the mark equals the German interest rate. The mark is expected to depreciate (1.7 − 1.6)/1.6, or 6.25%. With the U.S. interest rate at 7%, the German interest rate would be 7% − (−6.25%), or 13.25%. ◀

Exchange Rate Fluctuations

Fluctuations in exchange rates are of great concern to households, businesses, and policymakers. For businesses, changes in exchange rates affect rates of return on international investments. In addition, major exchange rate movements can affect the competitiveness of U.S. businesses. For example, the soaring value of the dollar in the early 1980s reduced the demand for U.S. exports, affecting American firms and workers. Policymakers (especially politicians) are concerned with keeping U.S. businesses profitable and workers employed. Our graphical analysis of exchange rate determination allows us to examine what happens when exchange rates change in response to shifts in the determinants of domestic interest rates and foreign interest rates.

Changes in Domestic Real Interest Rates

The expected return on domestic bonds depends on the interest rate i on those instruments. That interest rate is the sum of the expected real rate of interest (determined in the saving-investment process) and the expected rate of inflation. As Fig. 8.3(a) shows, holding expected inflation constant, an increase in the domestic rate interest rate increases the expected rate of return on domestic assets, shifting the R curve to the right from R_0 to R_1. Because of the higher return on domestic assets, investors increase their demand for dollars to buy domestic assets, resulting in an increase in the exchange rate from EX_0 to EX_1. But, as Fig. 8.3(b) shows, a decrease in the domestic real interest rate causes the expected real rate of return to shift to the left from R_0 to R_1. The lower return on domestic assets increases investors' demand for foreign assets and thus for foreign currency. The higher demand for foreign currency

---

[†]If there were only one good, $EX_r = EX_r^e = 1$ and $r = r_f$. This corresponds to the world real interest rate discussed in the analysis of saving, investment, and interest rate determination in Chapter 5.

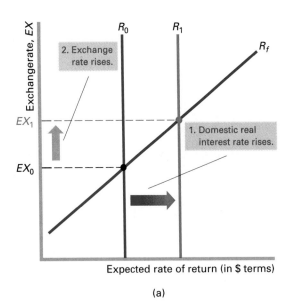

(a)

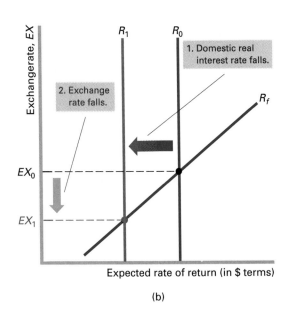

(b)

Effect of a Change in the Domestic Real Interest Rate on the Exchange Rate

The (a) portion of this graph shows:

1. An increase in the domestic real interest rate shifts R to the right from R_0 to R_1.

2. The domestic currency appreciates from EX_0 to EX_1; the exchange rate rises.

The (b) portion of this graph shows:

1. A decrease in the domestic real interest rate shifts R to the left from R_0 to R_1.

2. The domestic currency depreciates from EX_0 to EX_1; the exchange rate falls.

exerts downward pressure on the current exchange rate, which falls from EX_0 to EX_1. To summarize, if nothing else changes, an increase in the domestic real interest rate causes the domestic currency to appreciate. A decrease in the domestic real interest rate causes the domestic currency to depreciate. This link between the domestic real interest rate and the exchange rate is illustrated in the Other times, other places box.

Changes in Domestic Expected Inflation

A change in the domestic nominal interest rate also can be caused by a change in expected inflation for any real rate of interest. In making our graphical analysis of the effect of changes in the domestic real interest rate on the current exchange rate, we assumed that the foreign expected rate of return, R_f, does not shift. However, when domestic expected inflation changes, the expected change in the exchange rate likely is affected. Why? An increase in domestic expected inflation erodes the currency's purchasing power, causing it to depreciate, or lose value against other currencies. Conversely, a decrease in domestic expected inflation raises the domestic currency's purchasing power, causing the domestic currency to appreciate.

Figure 8.4 shows that two effects are at work when the domestic interest rate increases because of an increase in expected inflation. First, the higher domestic nominal interest rate shifts the expected rate of return to the right from R_0 to R_1. Since returns on U.S. assets become more attractive relative to returns on foreign assets, investors increase their demand for dollars, and the current exchange rate rises. Second, because expected appreciation of the domestic currency falls, the expected foreign rate of return shifts to the

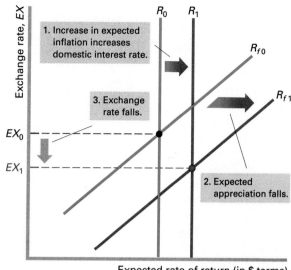

> **FIGURE 8.4**

Effect of an Increase in Domestic Expected Inflation on the Exchange Rate

1. For a constant domestic real interest rate, an increase in expected inflation raises the domestic nominal interest rate from R_0 to R_1.

2. At the same time, the higher domestic expected inflation reduces the expected appreciation of the domestic currency. The R_f curve shifts to the right from R_{f0} to R_{f1}.

3. Most empirical studies show that the second effect dominates the first, so that the current exchange rate falls from EX_0 to EX_1.

right from R_{f0} to R_{f1}, and foreign assets become more attractive for investors. Hence the demand for dollars decreases, and the current exchange rate falls. These two effects pull the current exchange rate in opposite directions.

Which effect dominates? Most analyses indicate that the decline in the anticipated appreciation of the domestic currency is greater than the increase in the domestic interest rate from the increase in expected inflation. Hence, for any current exchange rate, the expected return on domestic assets rises by less than the expected return on foreign assets.[†] As shown in Fig. 8.4, the shift from R_0 to the right to R_1 is smaller than the shift from R_{f0} to R_{f1}, causing the exchange rate to decline from EX_0 to EX_1. To summarize, an increase in the domestic interest rate in response to an increase in domestic expected inflation leads to depreciation of the domestic currency. A decrease in the domestic interest rate in response to a decrease in domestic expected inflation leads to appreciation of the domestic currency.

Changes in Foreign Interest Rates

In mid-1992, when German short-term real interest rates rose relative to U.S. short-term real interest rates, domestic tourist industry groups expected that the dollar's value overseas would fall, raising the cost of foreign vacations. Indeed, the dollar's exchange value against the mark did drop. How could the tourist industry anticipate that this would happen?

[†] This effect is a feature of models of exchange rate determination in asset markets. See, for example, Rudiger Dornbusch, "Expectations and Exchange Rate Dynamics," *Journal of Political Economy*, 84:1061–1076, 1976.

Other times, other places...

Real Interest and Exchange Rates in the 1980s

Our analysis of the relationship between exchange rates and interest rates suggests that shifts in the real interest rate in the United States, relative to other countries, can affect nominal and real exchange rates. The figure in this feature shows the real interest rate and the effective real exchange rate index, which is a trade-weighted real exchange rate calculated by the Fed. As you can see in the figure, the real interest rate and the real exchange rate both increased during the early 1980s. Both peaked in 1985 and fell for the next three years, again rising somewhat in 1989.

What events caused these fluctuations? We know that changes in the real interest rate reflect shifts in the underlying determinants of saving and investment. The rise in the real interest rate reflects shifts in desired saving, desired investment, and international lending and borrowing. In the early 1980s, a rising stock market, probusiness policies of the Reagan administration, and a cut in taxes on investment made the United States an attractive place in which to invest. In addition, many international investors were concerned that less developed countries (LDCs) had borrowed too much from the international capital market in the 1970s, and they wanted to shift funds from those countries. At the same time, large U.S. budget deficits reduced

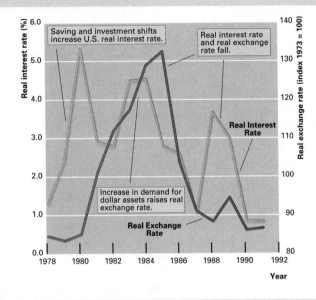

national saving. This combination of events increased the real interest rate and demand for U.S. assets, raising the real exchange rate. Thus the U.S. real interest rate exceeded foreign real interest rates in the early 1980s. The real interest rate parity condition, Eq. (8.6), implies the dollar would appreciate. This did indeed happen.

In the second half of the 1980s, real interest rates in the United States were generally lower than in the first half, and were not significantly greater than those in other industrial countries (in part because of an increase in investment demand abroad). With this change of events, the demand for dollar-denominated assets declined relative to assets denomi-

nated in other currencies. Using the real interest rate parity condition, we would predict a decline in the real exchange rate, which subsequently materialized.

These events in the international capital market teach us two lessons. First, understanding shifts in the underlying determinants of saving and investment (and thereby, desired international lending and borrowing) is important for explaining changes in real interest rates around the world. Second, movements in interest rates and exchange rates are related and should be examined together.

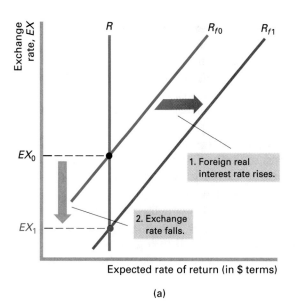

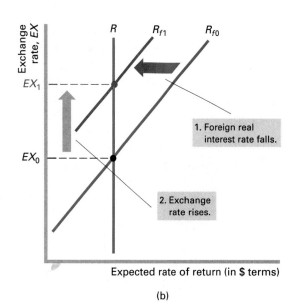

(a)   (b)

Effect of a Change in the Foreign Interest Rate on the Exchange Rate

The (a) portion of this graph shows:

1. An increase in the foreign real interest rate shifts R_f to the right from R_{f0} to R_{f1}.

2. The exchange rate falls; the domestic currency depreciates.

The (b) portion of this graph shows:

1. A decrease in the foreign real interest rate shifts R_f to the left from R_{f0} to R_{f1}.

2. The exchange rate rises; the domestic currency appreciates.

To answer that question, let's explore the general case. The expected rate of return for foreign assets depends on both the foreign interest rate and the expected change in the exchange rate. Figure 8.5(a) shows that an increase in the foreign real interest rate shifts the foreign expected rate of return R_{f0} to the right to R_{f1} because, at any exchange rate, the foreign rate of return increases. As a result, the current exchange rate falls. Because the rate of return on foreign assets has gone up, investors buy more foreign currency to buy foreign assets. The availability of a higher expected rate of return on foreign assets increases the demand for those assets relative to domestic assets, increasing the demand for foreign currency and decreasing the demand for domestic currency. As a result, the domestic currency depreciates.

If the foreign real interest rate declines instead, as Fig. 8.5(b) shows, the expected rate of return on foreign assets declines. That shifts the expected rate of return R_{f0} to the left to R_{f1} and increases the exchange rate leading to an appreciation of the domestic currency. Investors now buy more domestic currency to buy domestic assets because the rate of return on domestic assets has gone up.

To summarize, a rise in the foreign real interest rate causes the domestic currency to depreciate. A fall in the foreign interest rate causes the domestic currency to appreciate.

Changes in the Expected Future Exchange Rate

As our analysis of the interest rate parity condition showed, the expected appreciation or depreciation of the domestic currency also affects the expected rate of return on foreign assets. Changes in the current exchange rate account for movements in the foreign rate of return, R_f. Changes in the expected future exchange rate can account for shifts in R_f. Let's examine how this process works through market forces. As Fig. 8.6(a) shows, if the expected future exchange rate increases, expected appreciation of the domestic currency rises. Hence the expected rate of return on foreign assets falls, thereby shifting the expected rate of return from R_{f0} to the left to R_{f1} and increasing the exchange rate.

If instead the expected future exchange rate decreases, as Fig. 8.6(b) shows, expected dollar appreciation declines, shifting the expected rate of return from R_{f0} to the right to R_{f1}. Investors now expect a higher return from investing in foreign assets, because they will be able to exchange foreign currency for more units of domestic currency. As foreign assets now have a higher expected rate of return, R_f shifts to the right in Fig. 8.6(b), and the exchange rate falls. In September 1992, for example, international investors' belief that the foreign exchange value of the British pound would soon fall pushed the current exchange rate down. The British government was forced to abandon its efforts to stabilize the pound's value in foreign-exchange markets.

An increase or decrease in the expected future exchange rate reflects shifts in one or more of the underlying determinants of the exchange rate—differences in price levels, shifts in preferences for domestic or foreign goods, differences in productivity growth, and differences in trade barriers—as well as changes in expected future interest rates.

Factors that increase the expected future exchange rate shift the foreign expected rate of return to the left and cause the domestic currency to appreciate. Factors that decrease the expected future exchange rate shift the foreign expected rate of return to the right and cause the domestic currency to depreciate.

▼ FIGURE 8.6

Effect of Changes in Exchange Rate Expectations on the Exchange Rate

The (a) portion of this graph shows:

1. An increase in the expected future exchange rate decreases the expected return on foreign assets, causing R_f to shift to the left from R_{f0} to R_{f1}.

2. The current exchange rate rises.

The (b) portion of this graph shows:

1. A decrease in the expected future exchange rate increases the expected return on foreign assets, causing R_f to shift to the right from R_{f0} to R_{f1}.

2. The current exchange rate falls.

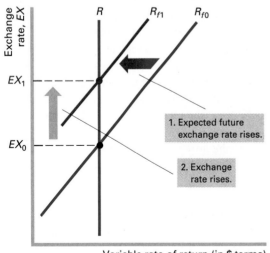

(a)

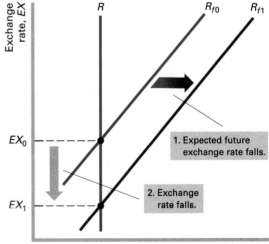

(b)

Q: How do savers use information about current and expected future exchange rates to compare expected rates of return on assets from different countries?

A: The theory of portfolio allocation suggests that the expected rates of return on domestic and foreign assets with similar risk, liquidity, and information characteristics should be the same. The nominal interest parity condition states that the domestic nominal interest rate equals the foreign nominal interest rate minus the expected appreciation of the domestic currency. Hence any factor that shifts domestic or foreign interest rates causes the exchange rate to change.

Currency Premiums in Foreign Exchange Markets

The nominal interest rate parity condition in Eq. (8.4) is based on the assumption that domestic and foreign investments are perfect substitutes. This assumption is similar to the concept in the expectations theory of the term structure of interest rates (Chapter 7): If we hold default risk, liquidity, information costs, and taxation constant, assets of different maturities have perfect substitutability. That is, you should be indifferent between holding a 30-year Treasury bond and holding a sequence of three-month Treasury bills, one after the other. When we discussed the term structure, we pointed out that the preferred habitat theory allowed for imperfect substitutability of assets so that differences in yield partially reflect a term premium. For example, investors might require a higher rate of return to induce them to hold long-term bonds.

We can modify the nominal interest rate parity condition by incorporating into it imperfect substitutability between domestic and foreign currency assets. We do this by using a currency premium. The **currency premium** is a number that indicates investors' collective preference for financial instruments denominated in one currency relative to those denominated in another. That is,

$$i = i_f - \frac{\Delta EX^e}{EX} - h_{f,d}, \tag{8.7}$$

where $h_{f,d}$ is the currency premium.

For example, suppose that the one-year Treasury bill rate in the United States is 8% and the one-year government bond rate in Germany is 5%. Suppose also that investors expect the dollar to depreciate against the mark by 4% over the coming year. Using Eq. (8.7), we find that the one-year mark/dollar currency premium is

$$8\% = 5\% - (-4\%) - h_{f,d}, \quad \text{or} \quad h_{f,d} = 1\%.$$

That is, investors require a 1% higher expected rate of return on the German bond relative to the U.S. Treasury bond to make the two financial instruments equally attractive.

If $h_{f,d}$ is positive, the modified nominal interest rate parity condition, Eq. (8.7), implies that investors prefer the domestic-currency asset, assuming that nothing else changes. In other words, investors will not buy a foreign bond if the expected rate of return just equals that of a domestic bond. The foreign bond is less preferable, so investors must receive something extra—a currency premium—to offset their hesitancy. The size of the currency premium depends on investors' aversion to currency risks, differences in liquidity in markets, a lack of information about foreign investment opportu-

MOVING FROM THEORY TO PRACTICE...

THE ECONOMIST MAY 2, 1992

Using Interest Parity: Can Europe's Currencies Come Together?

The European exchange-rate mechanism (ERM) has been dominated by the D-mark almost since its birth in 1979. Decades of sound money in West Germany made its currency the ideal anchor for the system. No longer. With inflation, government borrowing and strikes on the rise, united Germany is hardly the iron man of Europe...

Many countries saw pegging their money to the D-mark—in effect, handing monetary control to the Bundesbank, Europe's most independent central bank—as the best route to low inflation. But Germany no longer has the lowest inflation in the ERM: in seven of the other ten member countries prices are rising at less than Germany's 12-month rate of 4.8%. And the German government has abandoned sound finance: its huge budget deficit, equal to around 6% of GDP, has forced the Bundesbank to push interest rates to their highest level since 1945...

The markets still believe the D-mark is the best anchor, and back the Bundesbank to beat inflation. This is shown by the fact that Germany's long-term government-bond yields remain the lowest in the ERM; they have actually fallen over the past 18 months, and are now only half a percentage point higher than just before the collapse of the Berlin Wall, in November 1989...

Interest-rate differentials between Germany and other countries have narrowed over the past three years. In 1989 France's short-term interest rates were three percentage points above Germany's; today they are only a quarter of a point higher. But German short rates—now 9.8%—nonetheless set a floor for those in the rest of the ERM. Other countries must stick to higher real interest rate than their sluggish economies need.

The gap between two countries' interest rates reflects the expected future movement in their exchange rates. Take France as an example: the markets have traditionally kept French interest rates above Germany's, to make up for the greater risk that the franc might be devalued. As French inflation has dwindled, so has that risk, and with it the devaluation premium included in French interest rates. But French rates cannot actually fall below Germany's for long, unless investors expect the D-mark to be devalued against the French franc. Alone among the ERM's eight original currencies, the D-mark has never been devalued against another currency. This looks unlikely to change. The best way to lower European interest rates would be for Germany to cut its budget deficit, so letting the Bundesbank ease monetary policy. This is unrealistic at present. An alternative is to revalue the D-mark against all other ERM currencies.

ANALYZING THE NEWS...

Since 1979, European countries have agreed to stabilize the values of their currencies among themselves, thereby reducing fluctuations in their nominal exchange rates. The nominal interest rate parity condition implies that interest rates, then, should not vary significantly among countries. Further, if expected real interest rates are approximately equivalent, expected inflation rates also should not vary much.

(a) Germany has been the anchor of Europe's exchange rate agreement since its inception because of its traditionally low and stable nominal interest rate and expected rate of inflation. What do Germany's low long-term interest rates reveal about expectations of inflation in Germany? According to the preferred habitat theory of the term structure of interest rates, Germany's low long-term government bond rates indicate that investors expect short-term interest rates in Germany to remain low. For constant expected real interest rates, low expected nominal interest rates indicate that market participants expect a low rate of inflation.

(b) The article notes that French interest rates traditionally have been higher than German interest rates to compensate investors for the risk that the value of the French franc might fall. Using the nominal interest rate parity condition (assuming that French and German bonds are perfect substitutes), we have

$$i_G = i_F - \left(\frac{\Delta EX^e_{FF/DM}}{EX_{FF/DM}} \right).$$

If investors believe that the franc will be devalued, then

$$\left(\frac{\Delta EX^e_{FF/DM}}{EX_{FF/DM}} \right) > 0 \ \text{ and } i_F > i_G.$$

If investors believe that Germany will not raise the franc/mark exchange rate within the European agreement, i_F is unlikely to be less than i_G.

(c) The article argues that cutting Germany's budget deficit would lower European interest rates. Why? An increase in government saving (reduction in the government budget deficit) will increase Germany's domestic saving and desired international lending. As a result, if nothing else changes, the lower deficit will lower the expected real rate of interest because Germany is a large open economy. If expected inflation does not change, the German nominal interest rate also will decline. If investors do not expect any change in exchange rates among European currencies, the nominal interest rate parity condition predicts that European interest rates should fall as the German interest rate falls.

For further thought...

Suppose that purchasing power parity relationships indicate that the mark is overvalued relative to other European currencies. How would that affect the expected rate of return that you would require to invest in German long-term government bonds?

Source: Excerpted from "Currencies on the Verge of a Nervous Breakdown," May 2, 1992. © 1992 The Economist Newspaper Group, Inc. Reprinted with permission.

nities, and investors' belief that one country is more stable or safer than another. These three factors contribute to currency risk and make investors prefer to hold domestic assets rather than foreign assets.

Recent Developments in Europe and Exchange Rate Fluctuations

Among the exchange rates that investors watch most closely are European currencies, including the German mark, French franc, Swiss franc, and British pound. By the late 1990s, they may no longer need to watch so many, because the nations of the European Community are considering conversion of national currencies to a common currency, the **European Currency Unit** (ecu). In principle, national currencies would disappear, and exchange rates with leading non-European currencies would be defined in relation to the ecu.

Created in 1979 as a weighted combination of the values of the 12 currencies of the European Community, the ecu is not yet a legal currency. However, markets in ecu-denominated bonds, commercial paper, and bank loans have emerged and are growing. (In January 1993, the ecu was worth about $1.20.) Meeting in Maastricht, The Netherlands, in December 1991, European Community leaders devised a plan for a single currency for Europe, a plan that is experiencing ups and downs in the mid-1990s.

A key problem with converting the 12 currencies to a single currency is the disparity among interest and inflation rates in Europe. Adopting a single currency is equivalent to fixing nominal exchange rates irrevocably, just as North Carolina and Texas have a fixed nominal exchange rate, since both states use the U.S. dollar as their currency. The nominal interest rate parity condition suggests that if exchange rates do not change, interest rates will have to come together. European Community leaders understand the need to go slowly; the European Commission, the multilateral governing body in Brussels, Belgium will decide at the end of 1996 whether interest rates and inflation are close enough to move to the ecu. Few analysts expect an immediate transition even at that point. The Maastricht agreement says only that the conversion to a single currency be "rapid," but offers no specific timetable. If the many political problems surrounding the agreement are solved (a big "if"), Europe might have a single currency, thereby eliminating exchange rate fluctuations among European currencies.

Key Terms and Concepts

Appreciation

Currency premium

Depreciation

European currency unit

Exchange rate
    Nominal exchange rate

Real exchange rate

Foreign-exchange markets

    Forward transactions

    Spot market transactions

International capital mobility

Law of one price

Nominal interest rate parity condition

Purchasing power parity theory

Quotas

Real interest rate parity condition

Tariffs

Summary

1. The nominal exchange rate is the price of one currency in terms of another currency. The real exchange rate is the price of a group of goods in one country relative to the price of the same group of goods in another country. Changes in the nominal exchange rate reflect changes in the real exchange rate, domestic inflation, and foreign inflation.

2. In the long run, changes in the real exchange rate between two countries reflect changes in preferences for domestic or foreign goods, relative productivity levels, and trade barriers.

3. In the short run, financial markets determine nominal exchange rates as investors compare expected rates of return on domestic and foreign assets.

4. The theory of portfolio allocation suggests that the expected rates of return on domestic and foreign assets with similar default risk, liquidity, and information costs should be the same. The nominal interest rate parity condition states that the domestic nominal interest rate equals the foreign nominal interest rate minus the expected appreciation of the domestic currency. Hence any factor shifting domestic or foreign interest rates will cause the exchange rate to change. When domestic and foreign assets are not perfect substitutes, the domestic expected rate of return equals the foreign expected rate of return minus a currency premium reflecting risk, liquidity, and information costs.

Review Questions

1. What is the idea that domestic nominal interest rates should equal foreign nominal interest rates minus the anticipated rate of change of the exchange rate known as?

2. What is the difference between the nominal exchange rate and the real exchange rate?

3. If the dollar appreciates against the French franc and the British pound, but depreciates against the Japanese yen and the German mark, do the following exchange rates rise or fall? (a) franc/dollar;

(b) dollar/pound; (c) yen/dollar; (d) dollar/mark.

4. Suppose that the price in the United States of German BMWs rises from $31,000 to $33,000; the price of Japanese Nikon cameras falls from $110 to $105; the price of Swiss Lanco watches falls from $205 to $180; and the price of French truffles rises from $35 to $40 per box. Which currencies have appreciated against the dollar and which have depreciated?

5. The inflation rate is 3% in Germany, 1% in Japan,

and 5% in the United States. The mark/dollar real exchange rate is rising at a 2% rate, and the yen/dollar real exchange rate is falling at a 3% rate. Find the percentage change in the dollar's nominal exchange rate relative to the mark and the yen.

6. If a cow costs $500 in the United States, ¥150,000 in Japan, and FF3000 in France, and if the law of one price holds, what are the franc/dollar and yen/dollar exchange rates?

7. If inflation is 3% in both Germany and the United States, what does the purchasing power parity theory imply about whether the dollar will appreciate or depreciate against the mark? What assumption is vital to this theory?

8. American goods have always been popular in Eastern Europe, but because of trade barriers, few imports of such goods were allowed. With the opening of Eastern European economies, what should happen to the value of the dollar?

9. France has focused public policies on investment and efficient production during the past decade. If the French program is successful (relative to other countries), what should happen to the French franc exchange rate?

10. Suppose that real returns on investments in the United States rise relative to returns in other countries. What would you expect to happen to the value of the dollar?

11. Suppose that, owing to political uncertainty, the market places a currency premium on assets in the country of Panama. Now suppose that constitutional reform provides political stability. What should happen to the difference between U.S. and Panamanian interest rates?

Analytical Problems

12. Suppose that the pound/yen exchange rate rises while the dollar/yen exchange rate falls. What should happen to the prices of imports into Japan from Britain and the United States?

13. If the dollar/pound exchange rate rises and the yen/dollar exchange rate falls, which of the two foreign currencies (if either) appreciates relative to the dollar? Which (if either) depreciates?

14. If $2 buy £1 and FF10 buy £1, how many French francs are required to buy $1?

15. Where would you invest (at home or abroad) if the domestic interest rate is 6%, the foreign interest rate is 4%, and the expected depreciation of the domestic currency is 1%?

16. If the expected real return on U.S. assets rises while real returns on foreign investments remain unchanged, what should happen to the exchange rate?

17. Suppose that the real interest rate in the United States is substantially higher than the real interest rate in Japan and exchange rates are fixed so as to avoid expected appreciation or depreciation of either currency. What should happen to investment flows into and out of each country?

18. If $1 buys FF10, £1 buys FF15, and £1 buys $2, can you trade these currencies to make a profit? If so, how much money can you make if the exchange rates remain fixed at these levels?

19. If a compact disc (CD) costs $16 in the United States, £6 in Britain, and ¥3500 in Japan—and the exchange rates are $2/£1 and ¥200/$1—what are the real exchange rates in terms of CDs?

20. Suppose that you are a U.S. investor considering investment opportunities in the United States, Canada, and Mexico. You can earn nominal returns

of 7% in the United States, 8% in Canada, and 15% in Mexico. Should you invest in Mexico? Why or why not?

21. Suppose that the current exchange rate is ¥250/$1 and that the interest rate is 6% in Japan and 7% in the United States. According to the nominal interest rate parity condition, what is the expected future exchange rate?

22. If the current exchange rate is FF3/£1 and it is expected to fall to FF2.7/£1 next year, and if the current nominal interest rate in Britain is 12%, what should be the interest rate in France (assume no differences in risk, liquidity, and information characteristics), according to the nominal interest rate parity condition?

23. Compare the assumptions underlying the expectations theory of the term structure of interest rates with the assumptions underlying the nominal interest rate parity condition. Then compare the

assumptions underlying the preferred habitat theory of the term structure with assumptions underlying currency premiums in foreign-exchange markets. Is a segmented markets model of foreign-exchange markets consistent with international capital mobility? Why or why not?

24. Most economists believe that the attractiveness of investment in the United States increased relative to the attractiveness of investment in other countries during the early 1980s. Using a saving-investment diagram, explain the consequences for the real rate of interest in the United States. Using the interest rate parity condition, predict what would happen to the effective real exchange rate index.

25. Suppose that German bonds pay a lower nominal rate of interest than British bonds do but that both bonds have similar default risk, liquidity, and information costs. Describe circumstances under which portfolio investors would prefer to invest in German bonds.

Data Question

26. Locate the table of foreign exchange rates in a recent issue of the *Federal Reserve Bulletin* in your library. You should find average exchange rates for many foreign currencies relative to the U.S. dollar for the past few years. Against how many of the currencies listed did the dollar appreciate? Against

how many did it depreciate? You should also find an index of the value of the dollar against a weighted average of 10 industrial countries' currencies. Did the dollar rise or fall according to this index during the past two years?

Understanding Derivative Markets

The markets for financial futures

and options had a turbulent year in 1987. Early in the year, economists and market analysts praised these rapidly growing markets for providing valuable tools for savers and borrowers to manage risk in the face of increasingly volatile interest and exchange rates. Later in the year, however, a chorus of market analysts and policymakers blamed these same markets for the dramatic stock market crash on October 19, 1987. What should an investor believe? Do futures and options markets provide investors with ways to gamble with their funds or do they provide important risk-sharing, liquidity, and information services for savers and borrowers?

Futures and options contracts usually are discussed together because they share some common characteristics. First, they are both derivative instruments: Their economic value comes from (derives from) an underlying asset, such as bonds or shares of stock. Second, their trading mechanisms generate liquidity and information: Both types of contracts are traded on organized exchanges with common arrangements for clearing and settling transactions. However, futures and options contracts have some important economic differences, which we will describe and analyze.

In this chapter, we search for an answer to one significant question. **Q:** How do derivative markets provide risk-sharing, liquidity, and information services to savers and borrowers?

The Need for Derivative Markets

So far, we have concentrated on ways that financial markets bring savers and borrowers together through financial instruments. An increasingly significant amount of activity in financial markets does not take place through actual instruments for borrowing and lending. Rather, it occurs in **derivative markets,** in which assets that derive their economic value from underlying assets are traded. These assets, known as **derivative instruments,** are principally futures and options contracts, which offer benefits to traders.

Characteristics of Forward Transactions

Savers and borrowers often would like to negotiate today the rates of return or costs of funds for finance trades to be executed in the future. For example, a business might want to agree now to its cost of funds on future loans. In contrast to **spot transactions,** in which settlement is immediate, **forward transactions** provide savers and borrowers with the ability to conduct a transaction now and settle it in the future. Historically, forward transactions originated in agricultural and other commodity markets to solve price fluctuation problems. Such fluctuations imposed significant risks on sellers, for whom the revenue was their sole source of income. For example, if a farmer planted wheat and expected to earn $1000 for the crop and then the price dropped, leaving only $750, the farmer would lose $250 on the crop relative to what was expected. Buyers, whose costs of production fluctuate with input prices, also would suffer from this uncertainty. However, by agreeing on the price in advance, buyers and sellers use forward transactions to reduce risks associated with price fluctuations. But what happens if prices change between the time of the agreement and the time of settlement? Fluctuations in prices over the life of the forward transaction confer capital gains and losses on the contracting parties, much as movements in market interest rates affect the values of savers' assets and borrowers' obligations over time.

Characteristics of Derivative Market Instruments

Although forward transactions provide risk sharing, they do have problems related to liquidity and information. Because forward contracts generally contain terms specific to the particular buyer and seller involved, convincing other traders to take over the contract and accept the same terms may be difficult. Thus the contracts are likely to be illiquid. In addition, forward contracts are subject to default risk, or the possibility that the buyer or seller may be unable or unwilling to fulfill the contractual obligation. As a result, buyers and sellers will incur information costs when analyzing the creditworthiness of potential trading partners. Derivative markets evolved to reduce both liquidity and information problems. To show how they do so, we first trace the development of two categories of derivative market instruments: futures and options.

Futures Contracts. Futures contracts evolved in markets for agricultural and mineral commodities to maintain the risk-sharing features of forward transactions, while increasing liquidity and lowering information costs. A **futures contract** is an agreement that specifies the delivery of a commodity or financial instrument at an agreed-upon future date at a currently agreed-upon price. For example, you might buy a futures contract requiring you to buy a Treasury bill six months from now at a price you agree to today. We focus on *financial* futures because the traditional business of trading futures contracts on agricultural and mineral commodities declined from 70% of total transactions in 1981 to about 35% in 1992. The principal financial futures contracts traded in the United States include those for interest rates (Eurodollar rates; Treasury bills, notes, and bonds; and the municipal bond index), stock indexes (S&P 500, NYSE Composite, and Value Line indexes), and currencies (U.S. dollars, Japanese yen, German marks, Canadian dollars, British pounds, Swiss francs, and Australian dollars).

Futures trading traditionally has been dominated by markets in Chicago (the Chicago Board of Trade and the Chicago Mercantile Exchange), although strong competition is coming from markets in New York, London, Paris, Tokyo, Sydney, and Singapore. Significant computer and telecommunications improvements have strengthened trading links among exchanges. The Chicago Mercantile Exchange (along with the London-based Reuters News Service) is creating a system called Globex for round-the-clock trading throughout the world.

Options Contracts. A second category of derivative instruments is the **options contract,** which confers the rights to buy or sell an asset at a predetermined price by a predetermined time. For example, you might purchase the option to buy 100 shares of Boomco for $50 per share sometime during the next six months. Options on individual stock issues have been traded in over-the-counter markets and exchanges for decades. Since the 1970s, traders have reduced the risk of fluctuations in security returns by using contracts traded on the Chicago Board Options Exchange, the New York Stock Exchange, and the American Stock Exchange. In addition, the popularity of options on futures such as Treasury or Eurodollar interest rate futures or foreign currency futures has grown. The principal options contracts traded in the United States include options on individual stocks, stock index options (S&P 500 or NYSE Composite indexes), options on stock index futures contracts (S&P 500 or NYSE Composite indexes), interest rate options on futures (Eurodollar rates, U.S. Treasury notes and bonds, and the Municipal Bond index) and currency options and currency futures options (Japanese yen, German marks, Swiss francs, Canadian dollars, and British pounds).

Rights and Obligations of Buyers and Sellers

Before discussing the risk-sharing, liquidity, and information services provided by their markets, we discuss briefly how futures and options contracts work in practice. In particular, we emphasize the rights and obligations of buyers and sellers of futures and options contracts.

Futures Contracts. Futures contracts specify both rights and obligations regarding the underlying asset. In particular, buyers and sellers have symmetric rights. The *buyer* of a futures contract assumes the **long position,** or the right and obligation to receive the underlying financial instrument (say, Treasury bonds) at the specified future date. The *seller* assumes the **short position,** or the right and obligation to deliver the instrument at that time. The price at which the transfer takes place is decided upon when the contract is sold to the "long" by the "short" through a futures exchange. We explain shortly *how* the futures price is determined.

Options Contracts. In an options contract, the buyer and seller have asymmetric rights. The seller has obligations and the buyer has rights, in contrast to symmetric rights and losses under futures contracts. Options represent the right to buy or sell an underlying asset—shares of a stock or a basket of stocks, for example. If an investor buys a **call option,** he or she acquires the *right to buy* the underlying asset. Sellers of call options have the *obligation to sell* the asset. Sellers also may purchase a **put option,** or the *right to sell* the underlying asset. Sellers of put options have the *obligation to buy* the asset. The price at which the asset is bought or sold is called the **strike price,** or **exercise price.** The period over which a call or put option exists is determined by its **expiration date.** Essentially, a person providing call or put options is giving rights to another person. Those rights (to buy or sell at a specified price) are potentially valuable and so are not simply given away. Instead, the writer of the option charges a fee, called the **option premium.**[†]

Pricing of Futures and Options

Let's now turn to an analysis of how demand and supply considerations determine prices in derivative markets. We will then examine who uses these markets and why.

Futures Pricing. Unlike other characteristics, such as amount or time and location for delivery, the **futures price** is not specified in the contract but is determined by demand and supply. The buying and selling activities of traders take place in futures markets. In the steel futures market, for example, a car manufacturer might buy a futures contract because of concern about future increases in the price of steel. Or an investor might believe that the price of steel will fall substantially and thus want to capitalize on the difference between this expectation and the market's expectation as reflected in

---

[†] Throughout this discussion, we describe *American options,* which may be exercised at any time until the expiration date. *European options* may be exercised only on the expiration date.

the price. The futures price reflects traders' expectations of the **spot price,** or the price on the date of delivery. On the date of delivery for futures contracts, the futures price and the spot price equalize. Why? The reason is that traders search for profitable investment opportunities and have an incentive to buy and sell futures to make this condition happen.

For example, suppose that you buy a $1 million futures contract in three-month U.S. Treasury bills (T-bills) to be delivered in June. Recall from Chapter 4 that T-bills are discount obligations. Hence the futures price say, $980,000, which represents today's futures price for T-bills to be delivered in June, is less than the face amount.

The futures price of $980,000 implies an expected future three-month interest rate of just over 2%, or an annualized rate of 8.42%. If the current annual interest rate on T-bills is 10.4%, the *current spot price* of $1 million in T-bills (that is, for immediate delivery) will be $975,610. Of course, you don't know what the actual spot price of the three-month T-bills will be in June; it will depend on the market interest rate at that time. If that interest rate turns out to be 10.4% as well, you will have lost money on your long position and the seller will have gained on his or her short position.

In the futures market on any particular day, either the buyer or the seller may gain with respect to their initial positions. Because buyer and seller trade with each other anonymously through an exchange, the exchange requires collateral from traders by mandating that gains and losses be settled each day.[†] This daily settlement of positions is called **marking to market** the accounts of the buyer and seller, whose values are set at that day's market value. If the price of your $1 million, three-month T-bill contract rises from $975,610 to $985,610, the value of your long position has increased by $10,000, and the holder of the short position correspondingly loses. In this case, the exchange would collect $10,000 from the holder of the short position and transfer it to your account.

Options Pricing.   Determination of the option premium is different from that of the futures price owing to the asymmetry of rights and obligations for options contracts. The size of the option premium reflects the chances that the option will be exercised, in the same way that a car insurance premium reflects the risk of an accident. Just as a driver with a history of car accidents pays higher insurance rates, anything that increases the chance of the option's being exercised increases the size of the option premium.

Four factors influence the size of the option premium for put and call options. First, the more distant the expiration date, the higher the premium will be, because of the additional time allowed for the option to be

---

[†] In a forward contract, movements in current and expected future prices do not require transfers among buyers and sellers. The transaction is settled at the agreed-upon date at the agreed-upon price.

exercised. Second, greater volatility in the share price increases the premium because the share price is more likely to rise above the strike price, increasing the value of the options contract.

Third, as the option nears its expiration date, the size of the premium approaches its intrinsic value. The **intrinsic value,** or the amount the option actually is worth if immediately exercised, is the current price of the asset less the price of the underlying asset. Suppose, for example, that you are considering investing in a call option to buy stock in Consolidated Instruments at $60 per share in June; the share price is 62⅛, and the option premium is 4½. A portion of that premium (2⅛ of the 4½) reflects the fact that the option, if exercised, would bring an immediate profit of 2⅛ per share (that is, from buying a share for 60 and selling it for 62⅛). That portion is said to be *in the money.* A put option is in the money when the market price of the underlying asset is less than the strike price.

Fourth, the fact that buyers of call options in effect are buying the underlying asset on credit also helps determine the option premium. You pay the option premium today but do not pay the strike price until you exercise the option. A longer time until expiration increases the value of the right conferred by the call option and hence increases the option premium. For put options as well, the further from expiration, the higher is the option premium.

Each day *The Wall Street Journal* prints financial futures and options quotations. Some samples are presented in the Using the news box (page 210).

Role of Futures and Options in Risk Sharing

We are now ready to examine how derivative instruments offer risk-sharing services to investors. By gaining the right to buy or sell an asset (say, a Treasury bond) at a known price at a specified future date, buyers or sellers can reduce their exposure to risk, which is called **hedging.** People who go after profits by anticipating changes in price are referred to as *speculators.* The role of speculators in futures or options markets is important: By betting on anticipated price movements, they provide liquidity in markets for hedgers.

Hedgers taking either long or short positions in financial futures include lenders, borrowers, suppliers, or customers concerned about the risk of fluctuations in interest rates and firms and financial services companies exposed to fluctuations in the value of foreign currencies. Hedgers receive three key benefits by participating in financial futures markets: (1) the ability to spread the risk of price fluctuations, (2) the promotion of liquidity, and (3) the reduction of information costs by the introduction of organized exchanges. At the same time, derivative markets offer buyers and sellers opportunities to profit from disagreements among traders about future prices of a commodity or financial instrument by **speculation,** or anticipating changes in prices (see Box 9.1).

The Timing of Futures Trading: Twenty Minutes or Three Seconds?

Traditionally, trading in futures has taken place in frenzied floor action. Chicago, home of the Chicago Mercantile Exchange and the Chicago Board of Trade, built its status as the leader in futures exchange when it was a hub of agricultural trading. Today, these exchanges are pioneers in modern-day financial futures, including popular contracts based on Eurodollars and Treasury securities. The forces of global competition have reduced the U.S. share of the worldwide futures business to about 50% by late 1992, down from more than 90% in 1985.

The Chicago exchanges made a multiyear, multimillion dollar investment in a 24-hour electronic trading system known as Globex for futures and options contracts. Several major exchanges around the world have signed up to use this system. Its advantage is gains in efficiency: Prices are set by computer, matching incoming orders with sales in only three seconds. By contrast, the old system of phoning in, haggling over, and recording trades in the pits took more than 20 minutes to match buyers and sellers.

Many experts believe that electronic matching will make futures and options more efficient, as well as make detecting fraud easier. Other experts are skeptical, noting that slightly sluggish and inefficient human hands and minds might add stability during a crisis.

Hedging and Risk Sharing

Fluctuations in market interest rates can change the value of fixed-rate financial instruments having long maturities. As interest rates became more volatile in the 1980s, savers and borrowers seeking to hedge their investments dramatically expanded derivative markets. That growth has continued unabated in the 1990s.

How does hedging actually work? Suppose that Bigtime Financial Services wants to extend a $10 million, two-year loan to Smokestack Industries. After analyzing the creditworthiness of the company, Bigtime charges an interest rate of 10% per year for each of the two years. Bigtime can raise funds for the first year at a cost of 8%, but it will have to go to the market to raise the funds for the second year. Borrowing at an interest rate differential of two percentage points offers a comfortable margin for the first year. However, Bigtime is worried that market interest rates might rise for the second year, increasing its cost of funds and reducing (or even eliminating) the profitability of the loan.

One way for Bigtime to hedge the loss from possible interest rate increases in the second year is to sell Treasury bill futures contracts. Specifically, it could agree to *sell* 10 contracts for one-year, $1 million T-bills when the second year begins. The price that Bigtime charges for the T-bills at that time will reflect the interest rate expected to prevail during the second year.

To examine this strategy, let's suppose that the market expects the rate on one-year, $1 million T-bills to be 8% when the second year begins. The futures price of a $1 million contract will then be $926,000 (rounding to the nearest $1000). That is, Bigtime will pay $926,000 and receive $1 million, or a one-year yield to maturity of 8%. Thus Bigtime will promise to sell 10 contracts at $926,000 each at the start of the second year.

Who would buy such a contract? Perhaps a speculator who feels strongly that T-bill prices will rise, say, to $930,000. Such a person would want to lock in Bigtime's price of $926,000 per T-bill because the speculator expects to resell the T-bills immediately for $930,000. Hence speculators' self-interest adds liquidity to the market, allowing lenders to hedge their interest rate risk.

Suppose now that interest rates rise to 12%, or four percentage points above the expected 8% and two percentage points above the rate that Bigtime charged Smokestack Industries. On the one hand, Bigtime is harmed, as it loses money on its loan to Smokestack in the second year. The $10 million loan brings in 10%, or $1 million, but the cost of funds is now 12%, or $1,200,000. Thus, instead of earning a $200,000 *profit* ($1,000,000 – $800,000 expected cost of funds), Bigtime incurs a second-year loss of $200,000. Overall, then, the higher interest rate reduces Bigtime's earnings by $400,000.

On the other hand, Bigtime is helped by the unexpected interest rate increase, which lowers the cost of T-bills. At a one-year interest rate of 12%, the market price of a $1 million T-bill is $1,000,000/1.12 or $893,000 (rounding to the nearest $1000). Thus, to fulfill its futures contract, Bigtime will buy $10 million worth of T-bills for $8,930,000 (10 × $893,000 each) and sell them to the speculator for the agreed-upon futures price of $9,260,000 (10 × $926,000). Bigtime thus receives a profit of $330,000.[†]

On balance, if the interest rate rises to 12%, Bigtime loses $400,000 on its loan and gains $330,000 on its futures contract—a net loss of –$400,000 + $330,000 = –$70,000. Of course, if Bigtime had not sold futures, its loss would have been the full $400,000. The futures markets thus allowed Bigtime to reduce its potential loss.

Of course, the hedging strategy allowed by financial futures cut both ways. Had interest rates fallen, Bigtime would have gained on the loan because the cost of funds would have fallen but would have lost on the futures contract because the price of T-bills would have risen. By limiting potential gains and losses, then, futures markets allow investors to limit the risks from unexpected interest rate changes.

Futures markets do not provide this risk-sharing service free: Buyers and sellers pay transactions costs on futures contracts. Such costs aren't likely to be significant, particularly for very large transactions. Two other, more problematic concerns are anticipated price movements and basis risk.

Anticipated Price Movements. The futures hedge in the Bigtime example was successful because the movement in the T-bill yield was *unanticipated*. If market participants had *anticipated* the interest rate movement, the higher expected future rate likely would have been incorporated into the ini-

---

[†] The speculator, much to his chagrin, lost money. He must buy the T-bills for $926,000 each while the market price is $893,000.

Using the news...
Reading Financial Futures and Options Listings

Futures

The format shown here for futures contracts reports quotations for interest rate futures on U.S. Treasury securities. The uppermost set of quotations refers to Treasury bond futures traded on the Chicago Board of Trade (CBT). The heading shows that the size of a contract is $100,000; individual quotations report percentage points plus thirty-seconds of a percentage point per $100 of face value.

The leftmost column states the contract month for delivery (from March 1993 to September 1994). The next four columns present price information from the previous trading day: the opening (Open) price, the high and low for the day, and the closing (Settle) price. The Chg column reports the change in the price of the futures contract from the previous day's closing price. The March 1993 contract closed at 103 21/32, down 7/32 from the previous day, so each contract's value fell by (7/32)($1000) = $218.75. The Yield Settle column reflects the settlement price calculation of a yield to maturity based on an 8% coupon, 15-year Treasury bond. Note that the price of the March 1993 contract, 103 21/32, is higher than the face value of 100. Therefore (as you learned in Chapter 4), the yield to maturity should be less than the coupon rate of 8%, which indeed is the case; the yield to maturity is 7.640%. The Yield Chg column tells you that the yield rose by

FUTURES PRICES

INTEREST RATE

Yield to maturity — Closing price.

TREASURY BONDS (CBT) $100,000; pts. 32nds of 100%

	Open	High	Low	Settle	Chg	Yield Settle	Yield Chg	Open Interest
Mar	104-01	104-06	103-17	103-21	— 7	7.640	+ .021	282,495
June	102-24	102-30	102-10	102-13	— 7	7.761	+ .021	16,19
Sept	101-19	101-23	101-07	101-08	— 6	7.875	+ .019	3,713
Dec	....	....	....	100-05	— 5	7.984	+ .016	2,324
Mr94	....	....	....	99-04	— 5	8.089	+ .016	1,203
June	98-15	98-15	98-06	98-06	— 7	8.186	+ .023	126
Sept	....	....	....	97-11	— 8	8.274	+ .026	72

Est vol 260,000; vol Mon 200,822; op int 306,200, – 3,274.
TREASURY BONDS (MCE) – $50,000; pts. 32nds of 100%

Mar	104-02	104-06	103-17	103-24	— 5	7.631	+ .015	9,905

Est vol 4,100; vol Mon 3,137; open int 9,938, – 425.

FUTURES OPTIONS PRICES

INTEREST RATE

T-BONDS (CBT)
$100,000; points and 64ths of 100%

Entries under dates are the option price, or premium.

Strike Price	Calls – Settle Feb	Mar	Jun	Puts – Settle Feb	Mar	Jun
100	......	3-51	3-35	0-01	0-10	1-10
102	1-48	2-11	2-22	0-06	0-34	1-59
104	0-27	0-63	1-28	0-49	1-22	2-63
106	0-02	0-20	0-52	2-24	2-41	4-21
108	0-01	0-05	0-27	......	4-26	5-60
110	......	0-01	0-14	......	6-22	7-46

Est. vol. 55,000;
Mon vol. 30,672 calls; 40,050 puts
Op. int. Mon 237,823 calls; 220,721 puts

T-NOTES (CBT)
$100,000; points and 64ths of 100%

Strike Price	Calls – Settle Feb	Mar	Jun	Puts – Settle Feb	Mar	Jun
105	......	2-19	2-02	0-02	0-17	1-22
106	1-11	1-35	1-32	0-09	0-33	1-52
107	0-31	0-60	1-05	0-30	0-59	2-24
108	0-09	0-33	0-49	1-07	1-30	......
109	0-02	0-16	0-33	......	2-13	3-51
110	0-01	0-07	0-22	......	3-04	......

Est. vol. 15,000;
Mon vol. 2,050 calls; 8,029 puts
Op. int. Mon 54,467 calls; 82,698 puts

Source: From *The Wall Street Journal*, January 13, 1993. Reprinted by permission of *The Wall Street Journal*, ©1993 Dow Jones & Co., Inc. All Rights Reserved Worldwide. (Quotes are for January 12, 1993.)

0.021% from the previous day. The last column, Open Interest, reports the volume of contracts outstanding: 282,495 for the March 1993 contract.

You can get free information from these quotes. The interest rate futures contracts tell you market participants' expectations of future interest rates. Note that

futures prices are falling and yields are rising for March 1993 to September 1994, telling you that futures market investors expect long-term Treasury interest rates to rise.

Although not shown, you can also find interest rate futures quotations for Treasury notes and bills and foreign currencies. The finan-

Using the news...
Continued...

cial futures page also gives you quotes on stock index futures, such as contracts on Standard and Poor's 500 stocks (known as the S&P 500). Investors use stock index futures to anticipate broad stock market movements.

Options

The format for options contracts contains many of the same features as that for futures listings. However, there are some differences for individual options, according to whether the underlying asset is a direct claim (for example, a bond or shares of stock) or a futures contract (for example, a stock index futures contract).

The quotations shown here for options contracts are for options on Treasury bond and note futures (such as those discussed earlier) traded on the Chicago Board of Trade. Again, the size of the underlying futures contract is $100,000, but the prices are given in percentage points plus sixty-fourths of a percentage point per

$100 of face value.

Open interest in Treasury bond calls is 237,823 contracts, with a trading volume the previous day of 30,672 contracts. Open interest in the Treasury bond puts is 220,721 contracts, with a trading volume of 40,050 contracts. Because calls and puts are different types of options, the open interest for the two types of options need not be the same.

The first column conveys the strike price, which ranges from 100 in the first line to 110 in the last line. The second, third, and fourth columns list the closing (Settle) prices for call options expiring in February, March, and June, respectively. The 102 calls with a February expiration date have a closing price of 1 48/64. Each percentage point of the $100,000 Treasury bond contract is worth $1000, so these calls cost 1 48/64 ($1000) = $1,750.00. For some contracts (for example, the 100 calls with a February expiration date), no price is given

because the contract did not trade that day. The last three columns give the closing price for put options with expiration dates of February, March, and June, respectively.

As with futures price quotations, options price quotations tell you about expectations. Note that the price of 100 calls is lower in the June contract than the March contract, indicating that investors expect the option to buy the Treasury bond futures at 100 to be worth less in June. Thus investors expect the bond price to fall and the yield to rise. The closing prices for the 108 and 110 calls are low, indicating that investors believe that Treasury bond prices are unlikely to be so high or yields so low.

Although not shown, quotations for options on individual stocks contain information on the closing price of the option (the premium) and the closing price of the individual stock. Volume statistics (such as trading volume or open interest) usually are not reported.

tial T-bill futures price. That price per contract would have been $893,000 ($1,000,000/1.12), rather than $926,000 ($1,000,000/1.08). The futures hedge is most valuable for protecting against unanticipated changes in the price of the underlying asset.

Basis Risk. In the Bigtime example, the spread between the rate on the hedged instrument (cost of funds) and the rate on the instrument actually traded in the futures market (T-bills) remained constant. We assumed that both rose by four percentage points. However, correlation between the changes in the two rates isn't necessarily one to one. This imperfect correlation is known as **basis risk.** If the cost of funds moves imperfectly (that is, in a more than or less than one-to-one manner) with the yield on T-bills, Bigtime will experience a significant net loss on the combination of its lending and futures positions. For instance, suppose that the T-bill rate rose only two percentage points, to 10%. The market price would be $909,000 (rounded to the nearest $1000), or $9,090,000 for $10 million of T-bills. Bigtime would buy the T-bills and sell them at the contract price of $9,260,000 for a gain of $170,000. However, when the $400,000 loss on the loan in the second year is subtracted, Bigtime's profit will fall by $230,000. That loss is considerably more than the $70,000 lost when T-bill rates changed point for point with Bigtime's cost of funds.

▶ C H E C K P O I N T   *What would happen to Bigtime's profits if interest rates fell to 6% during the second year?* Instead of earning $200,000 on the loan, Bigtime would net $400,000 ($1,000,000 income minus $600,000 funding costs). However, Bigtime would lose money on the futures contract. At 6%, the market price of a one-year, $1 million T-bill is about $943,000 ($1,000,000/1.06). Thus Bigtime would have to spend $9,430,000 to obtain $10 million in T-bills but could only sell them for $9,260,000, losing $170,000. On balance, Bigtime gains $30,000 ($200,000 gain on the loan minus $170,000 lost in the futures contract). Had it not sold the futures contract, it would have gained the full $200,000. ◀

Choosing Between Futures and Options

As with futures, hedgers can use options to reduce the risk of adverse fluctuations in commodity or stock prices, interest rates, and foreign currency exchange rates. The extent to which an options hedge is satisfactory depends on basis risk, that is, how closely movements in the value of the asset underlying the option mirror those of the hedged asset. Unlike futures contracts, options allow hedgers to keep profits on their positions in the presence of favorable shifts in the price of the underlying asset.

An options contract is more like insurance (hence the use of the term *premium*) than is a futures contract. In a futures hedge, a hedger can *sell* Treasury futures at any time, reducing potential net losses should market interest rates increase. If rates decrease, however, the hedger cannot earn an additional net profit. With options, a hedger can *buy* Treasury puts to protect against an increase in rates while still earning an extra return if market rates fall. The benefit to the options buyer must be measured against the cost of the option premium, however. If the option premium is high, the transactions costs of using options may well exceed those for futures. Hence the choice between futures and options reflects a trade-off between the generally higher cost of using options and the extra insurance benefit that options provide. As an option buyer, you assume less risk than with a futures contract because the maximum loss is the option premium. The option seller bears the risk of unfavorable price movements in the underlying asset.[†]

[†] In the conventional *covered option*, the seller owns the underlying asset. In a *naked option*, the seller does not have an interest in the underlying asset.

Effect of Derivative Markets on the Financial System

Liquid derivative markets in futures and options generate important risk-sharing benefits for hedgers, and information about expectations of future prices for all market participants. These markets also provide a means for speculation. As a group, speculators play important roles in derivative markets because their presence facilitates risk sharing with hedgers. Active market participation by speculators generates liquidity, thereby improving market efficiency and the information content of futures and options prices. This increased efficiency benefits not only the derivative markets, but also the markets for underlying assets (Treasury instruments, stocks, foreign exchange, and so on), which benefit from the information generated by prices in derivative markets. Hence, derivative markets contribute positively to the three key services of risk sharing, liquidity, and information provided by the financial system. Nonetheless, some observers are critical of the role played by derivative markets in the financial system (see the Other times, other places box).

We noted previously that hedgers use futures and options markets to transfer risks to speculators willing to bear them. Let's now turn to ways that derivative markets provide liquidity and reduce information costs to make such risk sharing possible.

Other times, other places...

Futures Trading, Index Arbitrage, and the Stock Market Crash of 1987

Some market analysts blame a form of trading known as *index arbitrage* for the stock market crash of October 19, 1987. Index arbitrage involves simultaneous trading in stock index futures and the underlying stocks in order to exploit price differences. Such price differences would arise if an investor could buy a portfolio of the stocks used in the S&P 500 index at a price slightly lower or higher (net of transactions costs) than the price of the index futures. Suppose, for example, that the futures index for delivery one year from now sells for $1.1 million, while the stocks are selling for $1 million and the interest rate on a one-year Treasury instrument is 8½%. Let's say that you buy the stocks now, and sell the index futures at the same time. At the end of the futures contract, you sell the stocks in order to close your futures position. You have received $1.1 million for the stocks, so you earned $100,000, or 10%, on your $1 million investment, irrespective of stock price fluctuations in the interim. That return is greater than the return on the default-risk-free Treasury instrument (8½%). Index arbitrage is facilitated by computer monitoring of price margins.

This activity can contribute to market efficiency by eliminating price differentials among markets. Why, then, the controversy? The reason is that large trading volume can be generated by index arbitrage, particularly on days on which index futures contracts expire. On October 19, 1987, large sell orders on the New York Stock Exchange were placed as a result of S&P 500 index arbitrage, which some claimed worsened stock price fluctuations. However, there is little formal evidence to support the claim. Indeed, the presidential commission appointed to assess the origins of the stock market crash did not place much blame on index arbitrage.

MOVING FROM THEORY TO PRACTICE...

THE NEW YORK TIMES JULY 17, 1991

Clearing the Air: Futures for the Future?

Ever searching for new ways to make markets and money, commodity exchanges have broadened their horizons from familiar products like soybeans and wheat to concepts like Eurodollar futures contracts that only a business school graduate could love. Now the nation's largest commodity mart has gone a step further, approving trading in Government permits to pollute.

The Chicago Board of Trade voted to create a private market for rights to emit sulfur dioxide. The rights are to be issued to electric utilities by the Environmental Protection Agency as part of Washington's strategy to reduce acid rain.

Besides providing a service to the electric power industry, such a market would allow trading by individuals, letting them stake investment money on a rise or fall in the value of pollution rights, much as they now speculate on stocks and bonds...

Under the plan, the exchange will begin trading "cash forward" contracts in 1993—simple agreements to deliver allowances after they are issued in 1995. It will also ask the Commodity Futures Trading Commission for permission to establish a continuing "futures" market, permitting anyone to gamble on emissions rights in standardized 25-ton allotments up to three years in advance.

A utility might, for example, buy 100 contracts due in 1997, thereby nailing down the right to spew an extra 2,500 tons of sulfur dioxide that year. The seller might be another utility that is planning to close down an old coal plant in 1997. Or it might be a mutual fund run by a brokerage house, whose manager thinks the price of allowances will fall, and is prepared to risk clients' money on the bet...

Not everyone is convinced that the plan will work smoothly. John Palmisano, the president of Aer-X, a Washington firm that is a pioneer in the private trading of local pollution allowances for smog-creating chemicals says he thinks the market will be hard to establish. Most of the exchanges in sulfur allowances, he suspects, will be made directly between utilities in large blocks. He worries, moreover, that some state regulators will balk at allowing utilities to participate in a national market for pollution rights.

The volume of trading may be light by the standards of the Board of Trade, acknowledges Mr. Richard Sandor, who drafted the proposal along with Philip Senechal, chief executive of the Bellefonte Lime Corporation in Bellefonte, Pa...

But computerized trading could be used to match buyers and sellers at low cost. And in any case, notes Jim Thompson,... "the Board of Trade has social benefits as well as members' profits in mind."

Those benefits could spill into market-based approaches to environmental regulation that are just now reaching the public agenda. Southern California regulators are pondering the wisdom of creating a computerized market for business permits to emit volatile organic chemicals...

Mr. Sandor said the Board of Trade's venture might prove invaluable both in designing these local markets for emissions permits and gaining legitimacy for the concept with local regulators.

ANALYZING THE NEWS...

Futures contracts evolve to match savers and borrowers and/or to provide risk-sharing, liquidity, and information services in the financial system. As part of a market-oriented approach to reducing air pollution, the Clean Air Act of 1990 gave polluters the right to buy and sell rights to emit sulfur dioxide. The price established in such a market will send important signals for investment: A higher price for pollution rights will make firms more willing to invest in pollution abatement equipment or new technologies to control emissions. Liquidity for a market in pollution rights will be provided by speculators.

(a) Electric utilities would like to write forward contracts in order to lock in a price for emissions—a hedging motive—whereas some investors would like to speculate on the future value of pollution rights. The article notes an interest in forward contracts. Forward contracts improve liquidity by standardizing emission allotments and contract terms. Futures exchanges could provide for anonymous trading by reducing information costs required of buyers and sellers in forward contracts.

(b) How would the viability of a futures market in emissions be affected if most of the trading of pollution rights were among utilities? If most of the trading were among utilities, liquidity and information problems normally associated with forward contracts probably would be less severe. Because setting up a futures market can be expensive, the benefits (relative to forward contracts) may not outweigh the costs.

(c) The creation of a market for trading chemical emission permits encourages the development of low-cost technologies for reducing pollution. A futures market aids planning by providing information on the expected future value of the permits. The liquidity provided by the futures market improves the information content of the permit prices.

For further thought...

Suppose that the United States, in concert with other countries, passed laws restricting emissions of carbon dioxide (affecting thousands of businesses) rather than restricting sulfur dioxide (emitted by only a relatively small number of utilities). What value might a futures market have as a signal for investment decisions? Do you think a futures market would be more viable in this case? Why or why not?

Source: Excerpted from "A New Commodity to Be Traded: Government Permits for Pollution," by Peter Passell, July 17, 1991. Copyright 1991/1992 by The New York Times Company. Reprinted by permission.

Standardization and Liquidity

In order for financial markets in derivative instruments to be liquid, futures and options contracts must apply to standardized products. Here, **standardization** means that contracts contain exact specifications—for example, the weight, quality, and grade of a commodity. The enhanced liquidity of a standard contract produces increased trading volume for the market as a whole, because traders do not have to spend time and money to determine the exact specifications of the financial instrument or good being traded. The terms of a futures contract specify the type of financial instrument or commodity, the amount or value of the financial instrument or commodity, and the location and time of delivery.

The specifications of financial assets—particularly government debt, foreign exchange, and groups of stocks—can be standardized easily. In the case of financial futures, the assets underlying the contracts are specific instruments, such as Treasury bills or bonds, or the cash value of the S&P 500 stocks. Sponsoring exchanges specify the terms of futures contracts, and trading practices in the United States are regulated by the Commodities Futures Trading Commission (CFTC). The National Futures Association (NFA) also exercises self-regulation.

Standardization also is important for options. An options contract is defined with respect to an underlying asset, traditionally 100 shares of a particular stock. For index options, the underlying asset is a group of equities represented by the index, say, the S&P 500. For options on futures contracts, the underlying obligations are futures; the buyer receives a T-bill futures contract rather than the underlying T-bill itself.

Rules for standardizing options contracts are developed by the exchange on which they are traded. An options contract specifies different strike prices and expiration dates, as determined by the exchange. As with futures contracts, the intent of standardization is to interest the greatest possible number of potential traders in order to provide liquidity.

Anonymous Trading and Information

Derivative markets also promote risk sharing by reducing information costs for hedgers and speculators. Exchanges permit buyers and sellers of futures contracts to trade at arm's length through an exchange, instead of trading with each other personally. This approach overcomes certain information problems: The clearinghouse function of the exchange, whose capital is provided by its members, guarantees that contracts will be honored. Thus trade can be *anonymous;* that is, buyers and sellers do not have to search for each other and do not have to assess the creditworthiness of trading partners. Organized exchanges match buyers and sellers as part of the exchange mechanism, through which prices are determined in an auction market by demand and supply. In the United States, only a commodity broker can trade futures

Q: How do derivative markets provide risk-sharing, liquidity, and information services to savers and borrowers?

A: Derivative markets provide risk-sharing services by bringing together hedgers and speculators. Speculation in derivative markets is beneficial for the financial system because it increases liquidity and facilitates the incorporation of information into financial market prices.

on exchanges. Options contracts also are traded anonymously through exchanges by any broker registered to trade stocks.[†]

► **C H E C K P O I N T** *Some futures and options contracts have failed after their introduction because there was insufficient demand for them. What factors do you think determine whether a particular futures or options contract will be demanded by hedgers or speculators?* The underlying asset or commodity should exhibit significant price fluctuations in order to create a demand for hedging and speculation. In addition, the underlying asset should be standardized so that it can be easily traded on organized exchanges. ◄

Figure 9.1 summarizes the value added by financial futures and options in providing risk-sharing, liquidity, and information services in the financial system.

FIGURE 9.1

Derivative Markets Add Value in the Financial System
Derivative markets for financial futures and options provide valuable risk-sharing, liquidity, and information services for savers and borrowers.

[†] Some options contracts are traded over the counter, but most are listed on an exchange (though, in the case of stocks options, not necessarily on the same exchange as the underlying stocks). Just as exchanges do not set futures prices, exchanges do not contractually specify or regulate the prices of options contracts.

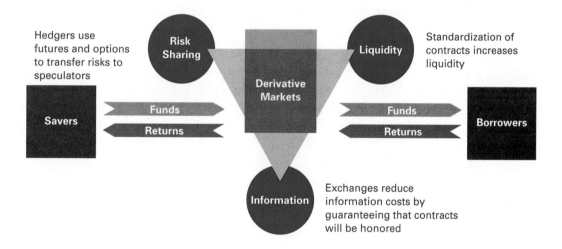

Key Terms and Concepts

Derivative instruments

Derivative markets

Forward transactions

Futures contract
 Basis risk
 Futures price
 Hedging
 Long position
 Marking to market
 Short position
 Speculation
 Spot price

Options contract
 Call option
 Exercise price
 Expiration date
 Intrinsic value
 Option premium
 Put option
 Strike price

Spot transactions

Standardization

Summary

1. An increasingly significant amount of activity in financial markets takes place not in actual instruments for borrowing and lending, but in derivative instruments. A derivative instrument's economic value comes from the value of some underlying asset. Futures and options contracts, the two most widely used derivative instruments, facilitate risk sharing by bringing together individuals who want to reduce their exposure to fluctuations in the price of the underlying asset (hedgers) and individuals who hope to profit from anticipated fluctuations in the price of the underlying asset (speculators).

2. Derivative instruments specify rights and obligations regarding the underlying asset. The buyer of a futures contract, who assumes the long position, has both the right and obligation to receive the underlying asset (say Treasury bonds) at the agreed-upon future date. The seller, who assumes the short position, has the obligation to deliver the asset at that time. With an options contract, the seller has obligations, and the buyer has rights. Buyers of call options have the right to buy the underlying asset. Buyers of put options have the right to sell the underlying asset. Because of the asymmetry of rights and obligations between the buyer and seller, the buyer of a call or put option pays an option premium to the seller. The buyer of the option has the right to pay an agreed-upon price (called the strike, or exercise, price) by a certain time (expiration date).

3. Costs of using futures contracts include transactions costs and basis risk (movements in the spread between the price of the hedged instrument and the instrument actually traded in the futures market). In addition, the hedging strategy cuts two ways. The hedger's potential losses are reduced by holding an offsetting futures position, but so are the gains if there is a favorable price movement in the underlying asset. With an options contract, a hedger is protected against adverse movements in the price of the underlying asset while benefiting from favorable price movements.

4. Speculation in derivative markets is beneficial for the financial system because it increases liquidity and helps incorporate information into market prices. This increased efficiency benefits not only the derivative markets, but also the markets for underlying financial claims, which gain from the integration of price information.

Review Questions

1. What is the difference between a spot transaction and a forward transaction? What advantages does a futures contract have over a forward transaction?

2. What is an options contract? What are the rights and obligations of buyer and seller? How does a call option differ from a put option?

3. What is the difference between using options to hedge and using options to speculate?

4. What are the main costs of using futures as a hedge?

5. What type of financial contract can be used like insurance to protect the value of other assets? How does the insurance aspect of this approach work?

6. Why is standardization important in futures and options markets?

7. What is important about anonymity in the trading of futures and options?

8. Why do the futures exchanges require marking to market every day?

9. Consider options on Bigmove Corporation stock. Suppose that there are call options with a strike price of $75 and put options with a strike price of $65. Which, if any, of the options are in the money if the current price of Bigmove's stock is: (a) $60, (b) $70, and (c) $80?

10. Why are option premiums generally greater than intrinsic value, prior to the expiration date?

11. Suppose that a presidential candidate planned to include in her platform a plan to abolish options and futures markets, arguing that they are simply a "casino for the rich." As her economic advisor, would you agree with her position or try to change her mind?

12. Explain *index arbitrage* (see Other times, other places box). By using it, how can you obtain a greater risk-free return than by buying Treasury bills?

Analytical Problems

13. Suppose that a court decision will have a major impact on a firm's profits. If the court decision is favorable, you estimate that the firm's stock will be worth $100 per share. If the court ruling is unfavorable, you estimate that the stock will be worth only $60 per share. Currently, the price is $80 per share, as half the market participants are betting on each possibility. Is there any way to use options contracts to profit from this situation?

14. Suppose that a U.S. firm signs a contract to buy factory equipment from a Japanese firm at a cost of ¥250 million. The equipment is to be delivered to the United States and paid for in one year. The current exchange rate is ¥250/$1. The current interest rate is 6% in the United States and 4% in Japan.

   a. If the U.S. firm trades dollars for yen today and invests the yen in Japan for one year, how many dollars does it need today?

   b. If the U.S. firm enters a futures contract, agreeing to buy ¥250 million in one year at an exchange rate of ¥245/$1, how many dollars does it need today to invest at the U.S. interest rate of 6%?

c. If the U.S. firm invests in the United States at 6% today, without entering into any other type of contract, does the firm know how many dollars it needs today to fulfill its equipment contract in one year?

d. Which of the methods described in parts (a)–(c) provide(s) a hedge against exchange rate risk? Which do(es) not? Which method is the U.S. firm likely to prefer?

e. *Bonus:* What does the futures contract exchange rate have to be in part (b) for the results in (a) and (b) to be equivalent?

15. Suppose that you own Treasury bonds with a face value of $1 million. You believe that the economy is growing strongly and that interest rates are about to rise. You want to protect the value of your assets without incurring the transactions costs of selling them. How could you use options to protect their value?

16. Suppose that you believe the fundamental value of Wal-Grey stock is about to rise from $50 to $100 because of its new management team. You have $20,000 that you can risk in the market, and you can think of four possible ways to profit: (a) use your $20,000 to buy shares of Wal-Grey; (b) borrow (at a 6% interest rate) an additional $20,000 on margin to buy a total of $40,000 worth of Wal-Grey stock; (c) enter into a futures contract to buy 400 shares of Wal-Grey in one year for $21,200 (you can invest safely for a year at a 6% interest rate); and (d) buy a call option (for every $1000 you spend on call options, you have the right to buy 100 shares of Wal-Grey at the current price of $50 per share). Calculate how much you earn or lose by each method if

(i) Wal-Grey stock rises to $100 per share in one year.

(ii) Wal-Grey stock stays at $50.

17. Suppose that you manage a bank that has made many loans to people at a fixed interest rate. You are worried because you believe that inflation might rise and that your bank will suffer a capital loss on its loans. How might you use options to protect your bank's portfolio, which includes many Treasury securities?

Data Questions

18. In the library, look in the latest *Economic Report of the President* for annual data on the rise in the consumer price index (CPI). Suppose that options exist on the CPI. Call options on the CPI pay off whenever the CPI rises by 5% or more during the year. Put options pay off whenever the CPI rises by 2% or less during the year. In what years would CPI call options pay off? In what years would CPI put options pay off? How could a bank or other financial intermediary use these types of options to protect its portfolio? How expensive do you think these options were in the early 1960s? In the 1970s?

CHAPTER 10

Information and Financial Market Efficiency

It happened again on March 17, 1992.

The Japanese stock market plummeted, with shares losing 3% of their value in a single trading day. Rumors spread that the Japanese government would intervene to avert panic in financial markets. Economists expressed concern that the falling stock market would erode confidence in the Japanese economy and that households and firms would reduce their spending. This concern illustrates the expectation that savers and borrowers base investment decisions on information contained in prices observed in financial markets.

What if the price of a U.S. Treasury bond failed to reflect expected future changes in interest rates? What if risky bonds had lower interest rates than safe bonds? What if the prices of stocks were divorced from analysts' beliefs about companies' growth possibilities? If these situations seem strange to you, the reason is that investors look to shifts in stock and bond prices, exchange rates, the risk structure of yields, and the term structure of yields for *information* about investment opportunities and expectations of future returns. In turn, returns on and prices of financial assets provide important signals for saving, investment, and portfolio allocation. When prices of financial instruments summarize available information, financial markets provide a valuable service. Such communication of information is a hallmark of well-functioning financial markets.

In this chapter, we focus on one key question. **Q:** How do prices of financial instruments communicate information to savers and borrowers?

The Message of Market Prices

If the financial system is performing well its tasks of matching savers and borrowers while providing risk-sharing, liquidity, and information services, prices of financial instruments give valuable signals for saving and investment decisions and portfolio allocation. You probably encountered this concept in your principles of economics course. For example, an increase in the price of wheat indicates to farmers that extra profits can be earned by planting more wheat; similarly, a fall in the price of machines relative to workers' wages tells business managers to further mechanize their factories. In such cases buyers and sellers look to *market prices* for information to use in making spending or production decisions. Indeed, the information content of prices of goods and services is a major benefit of a market economy.

In the markets for bonds, stocks, foreign exchange, and other financial instruments, asset prices communicate information in three ways. First, they represent expectations of future value. Second, the expectations and preferred habitat theories of the term structure say that long-term bond yields provide information about expected future short-term yields. Finally, differences in interest rates in various countries reveal information about expected changes in exchange rates.

Role of Expectations

Expectations affect decisions of individuals, firms, and institutions in the financial system. Recall from our previous discussion (Chapter 5) that expectations of future income affect household saving. (If you get a promotion and a raise, you will increase your current spending.) And expected future profits influence business investment. (If you expect to make a lot of money from your new computer invention, you will want to invest in a factory to produce the equipment.) In addition, expectations of future inflation affect nominal interest rates and exchange rates. Finally, expected rates of return on alternative assets provide information for portfolio allocation decisions.

To understand how expectations influence prices in financial markets, consider the following cases. If Middleroad, Inc. bonds yield 10% while U.S. Treasury bonds of the same maturity yield 7%, financial markets have set the risk premium on Middleroad's bonds at 10% − 7% = 3%. Or, if the dollar is expected to appreciate against the Japanese yen during the next 60 days, the 60-day forward yen/dollar exchange rate should be higher than the current exchange rate. Finally, if Newfangleco discovers a cure for the common cold, the price of its shares should rise dramatically. In each case, the current values today of Middleroad's bonds, the yen/dollar exchange rate, and Newfangleco stock reflect the present value of expected future returns. When the market price of the financial instrument equals that present value, savers and borrowers can be sure that the price communicates information about market participants' expectations of value.

For example, if financial market participants expect that Slipperyslope Company may default on its bonds at some point during the next five years, the interest rate that lenders will charge to Slipperyslope on new debt will rise, and the price of its outstanding bonds will fall. This incorporation of new information into the price of the bonds tells savers to require a higher expected rate of return on loans to Slipperyslope. It also tells the managers of Slipperyslope that the cost of funds has gone up to reflect the investment risk associated with the firm.

For now, our assessment of the role that expectations play in determining market prices is based on the assumption that the same information potentially is available to all parties (borrowers, savers, and traders).[†] However, an individual investor might find that gathering all available information is too costly or time-consuming. By summarizing information in market prices, financial markets provide signals for saving and investment.

Efficient Financial Markets

In an **efficient financial market,** all information available to market participants is reflected in market prices. The efficient market model holds that participants use all information available to them, an assumption known as **rational expectations.** The information they use includes not only past experiences, but also their expectations and predictions for the future. Therefore, in an efficient market, the market price of an asset equals the present value of expected future returns, or is the asset's **fundamental value.**

For any asset, the expectation of the asset's price, P^e, equals the price forecast, P^f; if the market uses all available information, that is $P^e = P^f$. For example, recall that the value of a bond today equals the present value of future interest and principal payments. If the price is greater than the value of the expected future returns, investors will sell the asset, forcing the price down to the current value. But if the assets price is less than the present value of its expected future returns, investors will buy the asset, putting upward pressure on the price until it equals the current value.

How does this mechanism actually work? Suppose that you are considering buying a share of stock in Consolidated Instruments. Using all the information available today (time t) regarding the prospects of the company, the industry, and the economy, you determine that Consolidated Instruments' shares are mispriced. Although the stock is priced at $20 per share, your forecast of the present value of future returns suggests that the stock price should be $30 per share. This information prompts you (and other investors) to buy shares in order to realize the higher expected rate of return. In reaction to this surge of interest, the stock price will rise until it reaches the higher price of

---

[†] In Chapter 11, we identify problems arising from *asymmetric information*—when, for example, a borrower has information about prospects or risks not shared by other market participants.

$30. By trading on the basis of your forecast, you profit from the ensuing increase in the price of shares in Consolidated Industries. Rational expectations provide the incentive to profit from mispricing, which in turn contributes to market efficiency. In this way, the self-interested actions of major, informed traders cause available information to be incorporated in market prices.

We can generalize from this example. Using all available information, you arrive at your forecast price for tomorrow (time $t + 1$). Let P_{t+1} represent the actual price of a share tomorrow and P_{t+1}^e equal the expected price based on the information available at time t. Let's assume that market participants have rational expectations. While no one can predict exactly an asset's future price, the deviation of the expected price from the actual future value is not predictable. Therefore, even if you use the same information that market participants use in formulating their expectations, you can't predict their mistakes. In an efficient market with rational expectations, the actual price equals the expected price plus a random (unforecastable) error:[†]

$$P_{t+1} = P_{t+1}^e + \text{Error}_{t+1}. \tag{10.1}$$

The Efficient Markets Hypothesis

So long as the transactions costs of buying and selling financial instruments are low, the activities of traders will eliminate deviations from the price that available information predicts. Individual investors may profit from mispricing, and those who invest in gathering new information may also earn a profit from forecasting mispricing. However, over a reasonable length of time an efficient market should allow no unexploited profit opportunities. In other words, in an efficient market, everyone can look to the market price as the best available signal of value. As Fig. 10.1 shows, the information provided in an efficient market provides signals for saving, investment, and portfolio allocation decisions.

The **efficient markets hypothesis** applies rational expectations to the pricing of assets. It says that when traders and investors use all available information in forming expectations of future rates of return and when the cost of trading is low, the equilibrium price of the asset equals the optimal forecast of fundamental value based on the available information.

[†] An implication of market efficiency is that prices of financial assets should approximately follow a *random walk*, meaning that the change in price from one trading period to the next is not predictable. The reason is that, since the current market price in an efficient market incorporates all available information, any change in market price from one period to the next reflects new information.

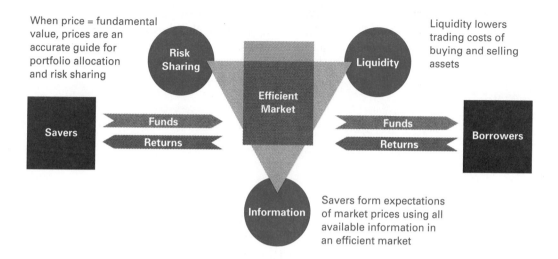

When price = fundamental value, prices are an accurate guide for portfolio allocation and risk sharing

Liquidity lowers trading costs of buying and selling assets

Savers form expectations of market prices using all available information in an efficient market

Characteristics of an Efficient Market
Efficient markets benefit both savers and borrowers. Since prices reflect all available information, they guide decisions about saving, investment, and portfolio allocation.

▶ C H E C K P O I N T *In the former Eastern Bloc countries of Europe, stock markets were nonexistent until 1990–1991. Can you imagine some likely problems in setting up stock markets there?* The value of financial markets in channeling funds from savers to borrowers and in providing risk sharing for savers depends on market liquidity and the information content of market prices. Initially, new stock markets are likely to lack liquidity and efficient trading mechanisms for savers. Even more important, as little information about enterprises is available to market participants, market prices may not provide meaningful signals for saving and investment decisions. (And even if more information were available, individual savers might not know what to do with it.) ◀

Theoretical Efficiency in Financial Markets

We know from the analysis of interest rate determination and the theory of portfolio allocation that the current market value of a financial instrument depends on its returns relative to returns on other investments with similar risk, liquidity, and information characteristics. Think of the income from a bond or shares of stock in two parts—a current return and the value of expected future returns. For a bond, your income comes from the coupon payments you receive while you hold the bond plus your expected future capital gain (or loss) when you redeem the bond. For shares of stock, your income comes from the dividends you receive while you hold the shares plus your expected future capital gain (or loss) when you sell the shares. Thus

P_t, the price of an asset at time t, equals the sum of the expected return on the asset, D^e, over the next period, $t + 1$, plus the expected price of the asset at $t + 1$. In order to account for the asset's risk, the price must be discounted by 1 plus the risk-adjusted interest rate so that the asset's current price equals the present value of future returns from holding it, or

$$P_t = \frac{D^e_{t+1} + P^e_{t+1}}{1 + i} \tag{10.2}$$

where

P_t = price of a financial asset at time t;

D^e_{t+1} = expected periodic return on the asset (coupon payment for a bond or a dividend for a share of stock) for time $t + 1$;

i = interest rate, adjusted for asset's risk; and

P^e_{t+1} = expected price of; financial instrument at time $t + 1$.

We can use Eq. (10.2) to determine whether a financial asset has a high price or a low price in an efficient market. A financial asset will have a high price today if (1) it is expected to have high returns (high D^e); (2) it is not very risky (low i); or (3) it is expected to rise in value in the future (an expected capital gain, or high P^e).

In an efficient bond market, bonds with higher default risk have a lower price than default-risk-free bonds with the same returns. In an efficient stock market, a stock's price reflects the present value of expected future dividends. Investors are better off when financial asset prices are determined in an efficient market because funds will flow from savers to borrowers offering the most profitable investment opportunities.

Price Fluctuations

The fact that the efficient markets hypothesis says that the price of a financial instrument is based on all available information does not imply that prices of financial assets such as stocks and bonds are unchanging. Because their prices reflect information about fundamental value, they constantly change to reflect news about changes in fundamental value. The expression for the price of a financial instrument in Eq. (10.2) suggests that prices change in reaction to changes in expected future returns or in risk, liquidity, or information costs associated with the instrument. This reaction occurs whether the instrument is a bond, shares of stock, a foreign-exchange contract, a futures contract, an options contract, or any other financial instrument.

One source of price fluctuations in an efficient market is shifts in market interest rates. An increase in market interest rates reduces the present value of future interest and principal payments from a long-term bond. As a result, the price of a bond falls when yields rise. Similarly, an increase in expected future interest rates raises long-term yields relative to short-term yields. Exchange rates fluctuate too in response to movements in interest rates at home and abroad. Finally, an increase in default risk increases a bond's risk premium and lowers its price.

Most of the news about price fluctuations reported by the media concerns the stock market. One reason is that price fluctuations for individual stocks can be large. For example, in a single day, a share of stock might rise in price from $10 to $12, a 20% gain, or fall from $10 to $8, a 20% loss. Can such large fluctuations be consistent with an efficient financial market? The answer is *yes*. To find out why, let's examine a change in the price of a stock. Suppose that, using all currently available information, shareholders forecast dividends per share of Consolidated Industries (CI) stock to be $2.00 this year, $2.08 next year, and $2.16 two years from now. Based on their assessment of prospects, market participants expect dividends to increase steadily at a rate of 4% per year. The value of a share today is the present value of future dividends. Thus, if i is the risk-adjusted interest rate appropriate to CI, the present value (PV) of expected future dividends is

$$\text{Present value} = 2.00 \quad + \quad \frac{2.08}{1+i} \quad + \quad \frac{2.16}{(1+i)^2} \quad + \quad \ldots$$

| Current dividend | PV of year 1 dividend | PV of year 2 dividend |

The efficient markets hypothesis holds that, if the CI share price is greater than this value, traders will sell shares, forcing the price down. Conversely, if the CI shares are undervalued, traders will buy shares, forcing the price to rise until the current value and the market price are equal.

Changes in expected dividends for just one period are unlikely to have much effect on share price, which represents the present value of all expected future dividends. Therefore, in principle, the efficient markets hypothesis allows for large movements in share prices. Let's find out why. Using our assumption that the CI dividend per share is expected to grow forever at a constant rate g (4% in this example), we can express the present value as

$$PV = (\$2.00) \left(\frac{1+i}{i-g} \right).$$

This equation restates the fundamental value, or price, of the share as the product of the current dividend per share (the first term on the right) and an expression involving the risk-adjusted interest rate and the expected growth rate of dividends (the second term on the right). In other words, the equation says that a higher expected dividend growth rate increases value, whereas a higher risk-adjusted interest rate decreases the value of expected dividend returns.

If we expect a constant growth rate of $g = 0.04$ and a risk-adjusted interest rate $i = 0.10$, the fundamental value of Consolidated Industries shares (and price per share under the efficient markets hypothesis) is

$$PV = (\$2.00) \left(\frac{1.10}{0.10 - 0.04} \right) = \$36.67.$$

Suppose that bad news about the long-term growth prospects of CI's industry causes the expected growth rate of dividends g to fall to 2%. Then the share price falls to

$$PV = \$2.00 \left(\frac{1.10}{0.10 - 0.02} \right) = \$27.50$$

a decline in value of 25%. Hence, although news about short-term fluctuations in prospects affects prices only slightly under the efficient markets hypothesis, large swings in prices are possible in response to good or bad news about long-term prospects.

Investment Strategies

When prices of financial instruments summarize all information available to market participants, savers and borrowers obtain the information necessary to make decisions at low cost, as Table 10.1 shows. For example,

TABLE 10.1	SIGNALS FOR SAVERS AND BORROWERS IN AN EFFICIENT MARKET	
An increase in...	**Signals...**	**Because...**
stock prices	businesses should invest more	greater investment opportunities
bond prices	savers should lower their required rate of return and borrowers should increase investment	lower default risk or lower overall level of interest rates
risk premiums	savers should increase their required rate of return and borrowers should decrease investment	greater default risk, lower liquidity, or higher information costs
upward slope of the term structure	savers should require higher yields on long-term instruments relative to short-term instruments	higher expected future inflation or real interest rates
difference between domestic and foreign real interest rates	savers should adjust their lending to domestic and foreign borrowers and exchange rates will shift	shifts in desired international lending and borrowing

higher stock prices tell businesses that investors expect profits to rise in the future and that the businesses should increase their spending on new plants and equipment. Higher bond prices indicate that market interest rates or risk premiums are falling, reducing returns to savers and the cost of funds for borrowers. Recall that an upward-sloping yield curve informs borrowers of likely higher future real interest rates, or inflation. Widening differences between domestic and foreign real interest rates reveal shifts in desired international borrowing and lending and likely changes in exchange rates.

Understanding the efficient markets hypothesis allows you to formulate strategies for portfolio allocation, trading, assessing the value of financial analysis, and predicting changes in market prices of stocks, bonds, and other financial assets.

Q: How do prices of financial instruments communicate information to savers and borrowers?

A: Market prices of financial assets represent market participants' expectations of fundamental value. In an efficient market, all information available to market participants is reflected in market prices. Prices fluctuate in an efficient market—guiding saving and investment decisions—as fundamental value increases or decreases.

Portfolio Allocation. So long as all market participants have the same information, the efficient markets hypothesis predicts that all above-normal profit opportunities will be exploited in the trading process. Hence you should not risk your savings in only one asset without information superior to that generally available (known as *inside information*) about a company's prospects. That is, investors should follow a strategy of holding a diversified portfolio.

Many individuals diversify their investments by means of mutual funds, some of which invest in broad market portfolios or index funds, such as S&P 500 stocks. Hiring an investment firm to manage your funds actively would cost many times more than simply placing all your money in a mutual fund that holds a broad market portfolio. Large institutional investors are also placing larger portions of their equity investments in these index funds even though evidence shows that actively managed funds often provide lower rates of return than broad market portfolio funds over most time horizons.

Trading. Similarly, if prices reflect available information, buying and selling individual assets regularly is not a profitable strategy. Lacking superior information, an investor is ill-advised to constantly move funds from one asset to another, or *churn* a portfolio. Thus you should buy and hold a market portfolio over a long time horizon.

Financial Analysis and Hot Tips. The efficient markets hypothesis suggests that predicting an individual asset's price by focusing simply on past price data doesn't give the best possible forecast. Why? The reason is that these historical data do not reflect all available information. "Tips" published in leading commercial or financial publications are equally unlikely to lead you to profitable trades. The news already will be reflected in the market price by informed traders who have learned about it before its publication. By chance, some analysts may appear to outperform broad-based market rates of return over an extended period of time. However, you should not expect to "beat the market" through forecasting gimmicks.

Consider this...

Stock Analysts: Can They Pick Straight?

Being a Wall Street analyst can be lucrative—for newly minted M.B.A.s and for seasoned stars (who can earn as much as $1,000,000 each year). Much of the day-to-day work of analysts involves forecasting earnings of individual firms, and the consensus forecasts of analysts provide valuable information for investors.

How well can analysts forecast earnings? Essentially, not so well. One study noted that, for 1992, only 12% of corporate earnings reported came in at the consensus of analysts' positions; 38% came in worse than expected, while 50% came in better than expected. What's more, another study found a steady decline in analysts' accuracy in predicting firms' earnings over the period from 1973 to 1990. Even the top analysts in *Institutional Investor* magazine's "All America Research Team" made big mistakes predicting earnings swings. One reason for the decline in accuracy is that research takes time, and analysts have little of that. In addition, the number of U.S. analysts fell by about one-third between 1987 and 1991 (rebounding in 1992), while the average number of companies they follow rose significantly over the same period.

So, are the big salaries too high? Possibly, but firms keep financial analysts busy in a never-ending search for new information in hopes of beating the rest of the market to a bargain.

Source: Susan Antilla, "Analysts: The Gang That Couldn't Pick Straight?" *The New York Times*, August 10, 1992.

Does this conclusion mean that financial analysis is worthless? Not necessarily. The efficient markets hypothesis states that all *available* information is incorporated into the market price of a financial asset. If you can uncover new information that can change market prices, you may be able to profit (see Box 10.1).

Predicting Price Changes.   Under the efficient markets hypothesis, today's price of an asset reflects all the information available today. But a price increase or decrease between today and tomorrow is unforecastable. Why? Today's price is based on currently available information, and the only reason for a price change is tomorrow's "news."

Suppose that IBM announces that its earnings this year are 5% lower than last year's. Will the price of a share of IBM fall? Not necessarily. Analysts following IBM may have anticipated the decrease in earnings and incorporated that decrease into the share price. Only if the information of experts had differed from IBM's announcement would the price change. For example, if analysts studying IBM had forecast a decrease in earnings of 15%, that pessimistic expectation would have been incorporated previously into the price of IBM stock. Hence an earnings decrease of only 5% represents good news, and the share price may rise. Although the link between announcements and price movements may seem complex, the efficient markets hypothesis provides some simple guidance. Only the unexpected component of announcements (the true news) will affect the price.

▶ C H E C K P O I N T *Your sister-in-law has told you that her specialized stock market fund has outperformed the total market for the last three years by constantly churning funds from one investment to another. Should you invest all your savings in her fund?* No. The efficient markets hypothesis tells you that, unless your sister-in-law has superior information relative to other market participants, you should invest in a broad market portfolio instead. ◀

Actual Efficiency in Financial Markets

In theory, financial asset prices determined in an efficient market provide valuable information for saving, investment, and portfolio allocation decisions. We now consider the question of whether markets for stocks, bonds, and other financial instruments are efficient in practice.

Many analysts believe that highly liquid markets in which information costs are low (such as those for U.S. Treasury securities, foreign-exchange contracts, financial futures and options, some low-risk corporate bonds, mortgages, and commercial paper) are efficient. Prices and returns determined in these markets appear to reflect available information about fundamental values.

Other analysts are more skeptical about whether the stock market is efficient. They have expressed concerns about three factors that may impair the efficiency of the stock market: (1) pricing anomalies in above-normal profit opportunities, (2) price changes that are predictable using available information, and (3) excess volatility, or fluctuations in stock prices that appear to be larger than fluctuations in fundamental values.

Pricing Anomalies

The efficient markets hypothesis predicts that an investor will not be able to earn above-normal profits over an extended period of time from buying and selling individual stocks or groups of stocks. However, analysts have found strategies by which stock trading can result in above-normal returns. From the perspective of the efficient markets hypothesis, these trading opportunities are *anomalies*. Two such anomalies are the *small-firm effect* and the *January effect*.

Small-Firm Effect. Evidence from data collected since the mid-1920s indicates that savers could have earned above-normal profits by investing in the stocks of small firms—even after taking into account the greater risk associated with returns from those firms. Although the small-firm effect was less pronounced during the 1980s, its long existence is inconsistent with the efficient markets hypothesis. Some economists believe, however, that the relatively low liquidity of markets for stocks of small firms and the relatively large information costs incurred by investors in evaluating those firms could explain why returns appear to be high.

January Effect.   For a long period of time, rates of return on stocks were abnormally high each January. Market participants often argue that the January effect is tax-motivated: Investors sell stocks on which they have lost money at the end of the year in order to deduct the losses against capital gains realized on other assets during the year. In January of the new year, buying pressures emerge as investors rebalance their portfolios. Although this explanation seems logical, it is not consistent with the efficient markets hypothesis because institutional investors (such as private pension funds) are the largest market participants. These investors do not pay capital gains taxes and so should buy stock rather than sell stock in December if prices are abnormally low. In the 1980s, economists found that the January effect diminished in importance except for shares of small firms.

Mean Reversion

Another aspect of the efficient markets hypothesis is that changes in asset prices, and thus returns, should not be predictable from currently available information—that only news can change prices and returns. The efficient markets hypothesis therefore is inconsistent with what is known as *mean reversion.* This is the tendency for stocks with high returns today to experience low returns in the future and for stocks with low returns today to experience high returns in the future. Some economists have found evidence consistent with mean reversion and against the efficient markets hypothesis. Other economists have noted that results supporting mean reversion are strongest for small-firm stocks and for data from the period prior to World War II. These observations suggest that lower liquidity and higher information costs could be responsible for the apparent inefficiency.

Excessive Volatility

The efficient markets hypothesis implies that the price of an asset equals the market's best estimate of its fundamental value. Fluctuations in the actual market price therefore should be no greater than the fluctuations in the fundamental value. Robert Shiller of Yale University used actual data on dividends over a long period of time to calculate the fundamental value of the S&P 500 stocks.[†] He found that the actual market price fluctuated much more than his estimate of fluctuations in fundamental value, a rejection of the efficient markets hypothesis. Other economists are critical of Shiller's tests on a technical level, but those tests do cast some doubt on the validity of the efficient markets hypothesis as it applies to the stock market.

Statistical evidence from studies of financial markets generally confirms that stock prices reflect available information. However, examination of pricing anomalies, mean reversion, and excessive fluctuations in stock prices

---

[†] Robert J. Shiller, "Do Stock Prices Move Too Much To Be Justified by Subsequent Changes in Dividends?," *American Economic Review*, 81: 463-486.

has generated controversy over whether the observed price fluctuations reflect only changes in fundamental value. Much of this debate centers on explanations for the tremendous volatility of stock prices in the late 1980s, particularly that surrounding the stock market crash of October 19, 1987.

Application: The Crash of 1987

On Monday, October 19, 1987, the stock market crashed. The Dow Jones Industrial Average, the most often quoted stock index fell by 508 points, losing nearly 23% of its value in a single day! Trading volume was a record 600 million shares. The decline in the market value of equities was significantly greater than occurred in the famous crash of October 28, 1929, when the Dow Jones Industrial Average fell by about 13%.

The 1980s had been a period of significant stock price increases—an unprecedentedly strong bull market. Soaring above 2500 in October 1987, the Dow Jones Industrial Average had been at 1500 as recently as 1985 and at only 1000 in 1982. Although stock prices had declined the week before the crash, the downturn on "Black Monday" was breathtaking.

This highly visible episode caused many economists and financial analysts to question the efficient markets hypothesis. There was no clearly identifiable bad news that day or during the previous weekend to suggest such a dramatic downward revaluation of the long-run profitability of U.S. business. Attempts to isolate particular bits of bad news—including congressional legislation thought harmful to equity markets and statements by policymakers in the United States and abroad—were unsuccessful. Economists then began trying to explain the crash on the basis of new approaches to asset pricing that did not rely on the efficient markets hypothesis.

Noise Traders and Fads. One explanation for the 1987 crash points to relatively uninformed traders called **noise traders,** who pursue trading strategies with no superior information. Noise traders often pursue **fads,** that is, overreaction to good or bad news about an issue or a class of assets (say, stocks or bonds in general). For example, noise traders may aggressively sell shares of stock or bonds of a company whose outlook is described unfavorably in a leading business publication. Of course, the efficient markets hypothesis holds that information available to market participants will have been reflected in the price long before the noise trader even removes the business publication from the mailbox! Nonetheless, the selling pressure from noise traders can force the share price down by more than the decrease suggested by the change in fundamental value.

Can't better informed traders simply profit at the expense of noise traders? Not always. Albert Kyle of the University of California, Berkeley has shown that the presence of a significant fringe of noise traders creates additional risk in the market. An investor who believes in the efficient markets hypothesis has no assurance that price will return to fundamental value after noise traders overreact.

Other times, other places...

What Goes Up...

Plunging stock prices in Japan in the early 1990s caused many market analysts and economists to believe that a bubble in Japanese equities was bursting. As of April 1992, the Japanese Nikkei stock index had fallen by 53% from its all-time high at the end of 1989. If indeed the collapse in Japanese stock prices was a bubble bursting, historical episodes of bubbles suggest that the decline could reach 80% or more.

Bubbles are nothing new, as the accompanying table shows. The "tulipmania" in Holland in the seventeenth century is considered the father of bubbles, followed by a bubble in the price of shares in a firm developing French holdings in what is now the United States. Even Sir Isaac Newton discovered gravity in the bubble when he invested in the shares of South Sea Company in the early eighteenth century. In the twentieth century, U.S. markets experienced bubbles in stocks in the Roaring Twenties and in silver in the early

Booms and Busts				
	% rise bull phase	Length of bull phase (months)	% decline peak to trough	Length of bear phase (months)
Tulips Holland (1634–37)	+5900%	36	–93%	10
Mississippi shares France (1719–21)	+6200%	13	–99%	13
South Sea shares Britain (1719–20)	+1000%	18	–84%	6
American stocks US (1921–32)	+497%	95	–87%	33
Mexican stocks Mexico (1978–81)	+785%	30	–73%	18
Silver US (1979–82)	+710%	12	–88%	24
Hong Kong stocks Hong Kong (1970–74)	+1200%	28	–92%	20
Taiwan stocks Taiwan (1986–90)	+1168%	40	–80%	12
Japanese stocks Japan (1965–?)	+3720%	288	*	*

*–53% over 27 months to date

1980s. Stock markets in Mexico, Hong Kong, and Taiwan all suffered through the bursting of bubbles in recent years. The fear that Japanese stock prices had a bubble led many investors to sell their Japanese shares at a loss in the early 1990s.

Source: "When Bears Run Wild," April 4, 1992. © 1992 The Economist Newspaper Group, Inc. Reprinted with permission.

Bubbles. Another explanation for the 1987 crash focuses on speculative episodes in the mid 1980s. When the price of an asset is more than its fundamental value, the price is said to contain a **bubble.** In those years of frantic stock market activity, some investors bought assets not to hold them but to resell them quickly at a profit, even though they knew that prices were greater than fundamental values.

With a bubble, the "greater fool" theory comes into play: An investor is not a fool to buy the asset as long as there is a greater fool to buy it later for a still higher price. In other words, some investors might buy at inflated prices if they believe that they can sell to someone else for substantially more money. For example, suppose that you strongly suspect that the shares of Biogenetics, Inc., selling for $10, will never pay a dividend; that is, they have no fundamental value. However, knowing that the industry is "hot," you might still expect to find someone who will pay $12 a share next year. The stock would be a profitable investment for you as a buy-and-sell trader, so long as the risk-adjusted interest rate is less than 20%.

So long as the bubble grows at a slower pace than the economy as a whole, informed investors can profit by buying and selling the asset at prices greater than fundamental value. However, if the bubble grows at a faster rate than the economy as a whole, it eventually will absorb all the wealth in the market. Hence, at some point, the bubble must burst! Some observers believe that the prices in the U.S. stock market in the mid-1980s, the Japanese stock market in the late 1980s, and in certain U.S. urban real estate markets in the late 1980s contained bubbles. The Other times, other places box discusses some of the historically famous bubbles that have been documented.

Trading Mechanisms. Rather than disputing the efficient market hypothesis, some economists instead have examined the role of trading mechanisms in fueling the downturn during the 1987 crash. Commissioned by President Reagan, this research was done by a group chaired by Nicholas Brady, later Secretary of the Treasury. The Brady Task Force identified several weak links in the market mechanism as explanations for the crash, rather than irrationality of market participants or fundamental imbalances in the economy as a whole.

First, the Task Force identified the way that trades are executed on the New York Stock Exchange (NYSE) as one of the weak links. The large volume of sell orders early on October 19, 1987 overwhelmed the market makers known as *specialists*, who match buy and sell orders in individual stocks. In addition, as their capital eroded during the day, the specialists' financial stability began to be questioned. If specialists are unable to function, the liquidity of stocks is reduced, and the ability of market prices to communicate information is curtailed. In response to the Commission's findings, the NYSE increased the minimum equity capital required of specialists and the minimum level of inventory of shares they would be required to maintain. Even with these changes, the specialists may not be able to cope much better today during such events.

Second, the Task Force suggested ways to avoid failure of the market trading mechanism. It recommended **circuit breakers,** or interventions designed to restore orderly markets. When prices or order volumes reach certain levels, trading will be halted. Staff economists argued that halts based on large price movements might unnecessarily block the flow of information contained in market prices to participants. They did, however, endorse trading halts based on large order imbalances. One proposal suggested that, during a trading halt specialists would open their order books to take nonbinding orders and announce what they believe to be the market-clearing price. After a few rounds of such open-order periods, the market could be reopened. The incentive to participate could be provided by executing first the orders of those traders who participated in the open-order period.

Following the publication of the Task Force report, the Working Group on Financial Markets (composed of officials from the Treasury Department, the Federal Reserve, the Commodity Futures Trading Commission, and the Securities and Exchange Commission) recommended trading halts after major declines in stock market indexes. The Working Group composed a report recommending open-order periods during a trading halt. These recommendations were adopted, and the circuit breakers are still in place.

The effectiveness of these proposals was tested almost exactly two years after the 1987 crash, when the Dow Jones Industrial Average dropped 190 points on October 13, 1989. Trading was not halted on the New York Stock Exchange, but price-based circuit breakers were in place in futures and options markets. Problems in the trading mechanism between the markets was a cause for concern, suggesting that, to be most effective, the use of circuit breakers should be coordinated among the markets.

A third market mechanism identified by some observers as a reason for the 1987 crash is computer-based, or program, trading. In **program trading,** computer-generated orders to buy or sell many stocks at the same time cause rapid adjustments of institutional portfolios. The large volume of sell orders generated by program trading during the crash met with NYSE disapproval. However, no solid evidence links program trading to stock price volatility.

Costs of Inefficiency in Financial Markets

We need to examine two potential costs to the economy from financial market inefficiency: (1) those arising from excessive fluctuations in asset prices, and (2) those arising from inefficiency caused by high information costs.

Costs of Excessive Price Fluctuations

When changes in prices of financial assets, such as stocks and bonds, do not reflect shifts in fundamental value, the information content of market prices is limited. As a result, financial markets fail to send the appropriate signals for saving and investment decisions. In addition, if prices are more volatile than fundamental values, the risk-sharing service provided by stock and bond markets is hindered. At the same time that financial assets become less useful for risk sharing, trading volume may decline, making financial assets less liquid. Although these costs are possible, there is no reliable way to measure them.

A recent concern of financial analysts and policymakers is the possibility that excessive fluctuations in the stock market could cause excessively volatile economic activity. They focus on the links between the financial system and the economy through saving and investment decisions (see Box 10.2). For example, would household consumption and business investment

Consider this...

BOX 10.2

Should the Federal Government Try to Reduce Stock Price Volatility?

Despite the lack of evidence linking volatility in the stock market with fluctuations in economic activity, some policymakers have proposed regulatory interventions. In addition to the circuit breakers suggested by the Brady Task Force, transaction taxes and changes in margin requirements have been considered.

Transaction Taxes. If conducting transactions costs very little, bubbles might stimulate too much trading, contributing to excessive volatility. One proposal for preventing this situation is to charge a transaction tax for each market transaction. This tax would effectively raise the cost of trading and decrease trading activity. The tax has appeal, but it also has two

significant costs. First, decreasing trading volume can reduce liquidity in the stock market. Second, if the tax raises trading costs in the United States, stock trading activities along with revenue and jobs in the securities industry might move overseas. Such concerns have prompted the reduction or elimination of transaction taxes in Germany, Great Britain, The Netherlands, and Sweden.

Margin Requirements. In the United States, the Federal Reserve Board sets a *margin requirement*, which is the minimum proportion of the purchase price of shares that an investor must supply from nonborrowed funds. Only the amount of the purchase price above the margin requirement may

be borrowed from brokers. Some analysts claim that buying shares on credit encourages speculation and generates greater swings in gains and losses. One proposal for reform is to raise margin requirements in order to discourage speculation. There is no clear evidence, however, that stock price volatility declines when margin requirements are increased, or vice versa. Moreover, as with transaction taxes, an additional cost of raising margin requirements to reduce trading is that it might reduce liquidity.

To summarize, arguments for government intervention to reduce stock price volatility outside of periods of market crisis are weak.

increase and decrease as stock prices fluctuate, even if those price movements were the result of a fad or bubble? Evidence from the U.S. economy after the stock market crash of 1987 suggests that consumption and investment didn't decline immediately, although segments of the securities industry were hit hard with sharply reduced profits and layoffs. Rather, research indicates that consumers and businesses pay more attention to long-run movements than to short-term shifts in asset prices.

Information Costs

A second potential cost of market inefficiency relates to information costs for savers and borrowers. If information is not readily available to participants, market prices may not represent fundamental value—even if the prices reflect all *publicly available information*. In order to obtain the missing information, savers and borrowers must incur research and monitoring costs. Such expenses are unnecessary for individual savers and borrowers when market prices represent the best estimate of fundamental value.

One cost to the economy of inefficiency due to high information costs is a weakened role for financial markets in matching savers and borrowers in the saving-investment process. Recall that businesses raise most of

MOVING FROM THEORY TO PRACTICE...

THE NEW YORK TIMES MARCH 17, 1992

What Should We Make of a Plunge in Japanese Stock Prices?

Anxieties over the faltering Japanese economy intensified sharply, as the stock market plunged to its lowest point since 1987, closing below the psychologically important 20,000 level on the Nikkei index.

The closely watched index lost 618.90 points, or 3 percent, to close at 19,837.16 in extremely thin trading—200 million shares. The last time the index closed below 20,000 was on Feb. 23, 1987, when it plunged 139.89 points to close at 19,940.50...

Although the 20,000 threshold for the Nikkei index means nothing in itself, it has been regarded for years as a make-or-break point, a plank in the stock market's emotional foundations. The market is now in the third year of a deep depression, having given up almost half its value since reaching a peak of 38,915.87 on the last day of trading in 1989, Dec. 29. But it only once slid toward 20,000 on Oct. 1, 1990.

As the indicator flirted with the mark that day—it hit 19,782.70 before rallying to close at 20,221.86— hints from the finance minister that action would be taken sent the market soaring 13.2 percent the next day, for one of the sharpest one-day rises in history. Officially, there have not been any indicators this time of what, if anything, the government might do to prop up prices and confidence. But at the least some expect a reduction in interest rates.

Dan O'Keefe, an analyst here with Merrill Lynch Japan Ltd., said expectations were growing for some sort of government bailout and that much of Monday's losses appeared to reflect disappointment over a rumor that the Bank of Japan would lower the discount rate by a half-point, to 4 percent.

"We're at the point now where a half-point cut would not be good news," said Yuichi Matsushita, a market strategist at Nikko Securities Ltd. "People are hoping for at least three-fourths of a point."

The tumbling stock market has raised many concerns. One is that corporations will find it increasingly difficult, and expensive, to raise the capital they need to invest and grow.

Corporate profits are already falling rapidly, and companies are slashing their budgets for new plants and equipment. That is rippling through the economy, as orders for new plants and technology fall, for instance, and consumer demand slackens. In fact, the amount of new capital being raised on the stock market has been plunging over the last three years.

The weak stock market is also causing growing problems for Japanese banks. Nearly half of the capital of many large banks is in the form of stock holdings. As the value of those portfolios fall, the banks' ability to expand their lending and fuel economic growth also declines.

ANALYZING THE NEWS...

Between December 1989 and March 1992, the Japanese stock market (price movements are recorded in the Nikkei index) lost about one-half of its value. As the article notes, investors and policymakers were worried about implications for the financial system and the economy.

(a) Why would the expectation that the Japanese Finance Ministry and the central bank would lower interest rates in response to market fears cause the stock market to rally? If market participants expect interest rates to fall, the rate at which future equity returns are discounted will fall, and the present value of those returns will rise. The efficient markets hypothesis states that, if there is liquidity in the Japanese stock market and investors use all available information in forming expectations of returns, stock prices equal the present value of expected future returns. Hence, by raising the present value of expected returns, a fall in interest rates would boost stock prices.

(b) In an efficient market, expected movements already are reflected in the prices of financial assets. Only *unexpected* interest rate movements affect bond and stock prices. Hence, unless the Bank of Japan lowered the interest rate it charged on loans by more than the one-half percentage point expected by the market, stock and bond prices would not change.

(c) Why would investment demand fall as stock market values drop? A decline in stock prices indicates lower expected profitability of capital, sending a signal that firms should cut back on plant and equipment investment and that households should reduce their investment in consumer durable goods. Investment demand did indeed decline in Japan in early 1992.

For further thought...

The article suggests that the weak stock market is causing problems for Japanese banks as investors. It goes on to suggest that resulting cutbacks in bank lending might adversely affect economic growth. If banks and financial markets offered the same risk-sharing, liquidity, and information services to savers and borrowers at the same cost, could a cutback in bank lending affect the economy? Why or why not?

Source: "5-Year Low for Stocks in Tokyo," by James Sterngold, March 17,1992. Copyright 1991/1992 by The New York Times Company. Reprinted by permission.

►FIGURE 10.2

**Sources of Finance for
Business Firms**
Business firms rely more heavily
on financial intermediaries than
on financial markets to raise
external funds.

Source: U.S. data were averaged for the
period 1946–1991 and are from Board of
Governors of the Federal Reserve
System, *Flow of Funds Accounts,* various
issues. Data for other countries were
averaged for the period 1970–1985 and
are adapted from Colin Mayer,
"Financial Systems, Corporate Finance,
and Economic Development," in R. Glenn
Hubbard, ed., *Asymmetric Information,
Finance, and Investment.* Chicago:
University of Chicago Press, 1990, p. 312.
Reprinted with permission.

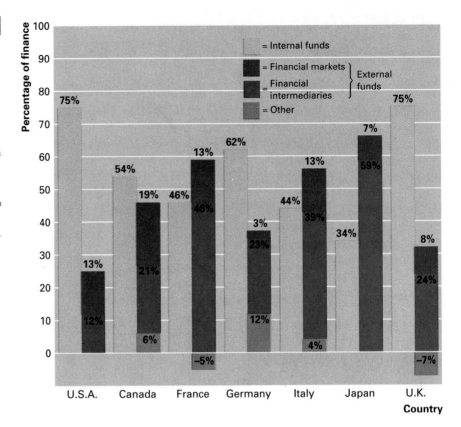

their funds from current and accumulated profits, not from financial markets.
As Fig. 10.2 shows, since World War II, nonfinancial corporations in the
United States raised more than two-thirds of the funds they needed internally.
A similar pattern holds for most other industrialized countries. Figure 10.2
also shows that in none of the other industrialized countries listed do firms
raise a substantial fraction of their financing from stock and bond markets.
Most external funds needed are raised through financial intermediaries such
as banks. There is mounting evidence that financial market prices do not provide the signals for investment that the efficient markets hypothesis predicts.
In fact, several studies show that businesses use their internally generated
funds for investment spending regardless of the signals being given by financial markets regarding the firms' share and bond prices.

Savers and borrowers reduce actual information costs by channeling
funds through intermediaries (particularly banks, but also mutual funds, pension funds, and insurance companies) instead of through markets. In fact, the
largest participants in markets for bonds, stocks, and other financial instruments in the United States and other industrialized countries are not individual savers and borrowers, but financial intermediaries (Chapter 3). As a
result, policymakers in many countries are more concerned about the stability
of financial intermediaries than about volatility in financial markets.

Key Terms and Concepts

Bubble

Circuit breakers

Efficient financial market
    Fundamental value
    Rational expectations

Efficient markets hypothesis

Fads

Noise traders

Program trading

Summary

1. Market prices for financial instruments contain important information for saving, investment, and portfolio allocation. An efficient financial market is one in which all information available to market participants is reflected in market prices. The efficient markets hypothesis states that, when traders and investors use all available information in forming their expectations of future returns, the equilibrium price of a financial instrument is equal to the optimal forecast of fundamental value.

2. Under the efficient markets hypothesis, changes in the price of a financial instrument reflect news about changes in fundamental value and are not forecastable. Price fluctuates in an efficient market as fundamental value increases or decreases.

3. Although statistical evidence suggests that prices of liquid assets traded in financial markets reflect available information about fundamental value, stock prices appear to be more volatile than the efficient markets hypothesis suggests. For example, no apparent "fundamental" can explain the precipitous drop in stock prices during the stock market crash of October 19, 1987.

4. Potential costs to the economy from inefficient financial markets arise from excessive fluctuations of asset prices relative to fundamental values and from high information costs. Most economists believe that information costs resulting from the lack of substantial amounts of information are especially severe. These costs help explain the relative unimportance of financial markets in raising funds for businesses.

Review Questions

1. Is there a connection between market liquidity and market efficiency? Why or why not?

2. Give a concise definition of the efficient markets hypothesis. What assumptions does it require about liquidity and information?

3. Suppose that the price of a stock rises only because people believe that it will rise, not because the corporation is likely to earn higher profits. What is this situation called? What is likely to happen to the price sometime in the future? Has it ever happened to an entire market?

4. Suppose that you believe that General Motors' earnings will rise by 20% this year, compared to only 10% last year. Should you buy GM stock?

5. If you are an informed trader, would you be happy to see numerous noise traders in the market?

6. State whether each of the following statements is true or false and under the efficient markets hypothesis, briefly explain why.

    a. Stock prices do not change.

b. Stock prices go up with published good news and down with published bad news.

c. Stock prices reflect true underlying (fundamental) value.

Analytical Problems

8. "They make money the old-fashioned way. They churn it." Why might someone who believes in market efficiency make this statement?

9. Suppose that in looking at data on stock market returns, you find that returns are higher than average in January but below average during the rest of the year. Is this consistent with market efficiency? Why or why not? What could an investor do to take advantage of this situation?

10. Suppose you find that, after accounting for differences in risk, liquidity, and information costs, some stocks are overpriced ($P_{t+1} = 1.1P_{t+1}^e + Error_{t+1}$) and others are underpriced ($P_{t+1} = 0.9P_{t+1}^e + Error_{t+1}$). Are the markets efficient? What should you do to make expected profits?

11. According to the efficient markets hypothesis, would you be better off paying someone 5% of your savings to pick stocks for you *or* picking your own stocks by throwing darts at the stock pages of the newspaper? Why?

12. Suppose that you are shopping and find a wonderful new product that you think will be a big

7. Why are fads inconsistent with the predictions of the efficient markets hypothesis?

seller. It should increase tremendously the profits of the company that sells it. Should you buy shares in that company? Why or why not?

13. Suppose that Bigbucks Company pays a dividend this year of $7 per share. You expect the dividend to grow by 2% per year, so you discount Bigbucks's dividends at 4%. What is the most you would be willing to pay for a share of stock in Bigbucks? Suppose instead that you discount Bigbucks's dividends at 3%. Now how much would you be willing to pay per share? If Bigbucks's dividends grow only 1% per year instead of 2% (using 4% as the discount rate again), how much would you be willing to pay per share?

14. What do you think caused the stock market crash of October 19, 1987? Why? What do you think is wrong, if anything, with the other explanations presented in the text?

15. Suppose that people generally overreact to news. That is, when good news arrives, the prices of a company's stocks and bonds increase too much, and, after bad news arrives, the prices decline too much. How can you profit from this knowledge?

Data Question

16. Find the most recent *Economic Report of the President* in your library. Table B-91 in the back of the report lists common stock prices and yields. The next-to-last column of the table reports the "dividend-price ratio," which is defined as the average ratio of dividends to price for the S&P 500 stocks. An increase in the dividend-price ratio over time implies that

dividends are growing more rapidly than market prices. A decrease in the dividend-price ratio over time implies that dividends are growing more slowly than market prices. What happened to the dividend-price ratio over the decade of the 1980s? If you believe that the stock market is efficient, how would you explain this pattern?

part III

Financial Markets and Institutions

CHAPTER 11

Information Costs and Financial Structure

The collapse of communist governments

in Eastern Europe and the former Soviet Union led to much rejoicing and hope for the emergence of individual freedom, political democracy, and market economies. As attention turned to getting private businesses started, financial analysts foresaw a daunting task. Savers seemed unwilling to lend their funds to local borrowers, preferring to invest in government bonds or foreign exchange. Borrowers found financial markets too poorly developed to be of much use. One prominent economist noted wearily that "hundreds of billions of dollars were being left on the table" because eager entrepreneurs were unable to fund new businesses while savers were unable to earn returns on their savings. Most financial experts suggested that efforts should focus on organizing financial intermediaries.

Why place so much emphasis on intermediaries rather than markets? The efficient markets hypothesis holds that, if information costs are low, financial markets communicate information to savers and borrowers. In fact, however, information costs often are significant in financial markets, reducing the markets' efficiency in channeling funds from savers to borrowers. As we describe in this chapter, when costs to savers for gathering and monitoring information about borrowers are high, opportunities are created to develop and profit from new arrangements that match savers and borrowers. Financial intermediaries are one such arrangement.

Two questions shape our analysis in this chapter. **Q.:** How do high information costs affect financial markets? **Q.:** How does the financial system respond to reduce information costs for savers and borrowers?

Financial Structure

Financial structure refers to the mix of finance between equity and debt and to the source of funds—through financial markets or through financial intermediaries. In Chapter 10, we noted that borrowers use debt more often than they use equity to raise funds externally. We noted also that, when borrowers raise funds through debt, they are more likely to turn to financial intermediaries than to financial markets. In this chapter, we examine why savers and borrowers prefer particular types of financial structures. We also use this economic analysis to explain why actual financial contracts between savers and borrowers are more complicated than our earlier, simple description of bonds and stocks suggests.

Two factors explain the structures of financial systems in the United States and around the world. The first factor is **transactions costs,** or the costs of buying or selling a financial instrument, such as a bond or a share of stock. The second and more significant factor is **information costs,** or the costs that savers incur to determine the creditworthiness of borrowers and to monitor how borrowers use the funds acquired.

The presence of transactions costs and information costs increases the cost of funds that borrowers must pay and lowers the expected returns to savers, reducing the efficiency of the financial system. This inefficiency creates profit opportunities for individuals and institutions that can reduce transactions and information costs. We look at how these costs affect financial structure and, in particular, how they explain the development and influence of financial intermediaries in channeling funds from savers to borrowers.

Transactions Costs and Financial Structure

Suppose that you saved $3000 from working part-time and that you want to invest it. Should you invest the money in stocks? A stockbroker will tell you that the commissions you must pay will be large relative to the size of your purchases because you are investing a small amount of money. This cost is particularly high if you are attempting to diversify by buying a few shares each of different stocks. Should you turn instead to the bond market to buy, say, a Treasury bill? Your broker will tell you, sorry, but the minimum face value is $10,000.

Undaunted, you decide to bypass the financial system. Conveniently, your roommate's brother-in-law needs $3000 to develop a potentially successful new computer program. Unfortunately, your lawyer tells you that to draw up the contract describing the terms of your investment will cost $1500, or half the amount you have to invest. Hence you give up on the investment. The cost that you face and your decision not to invest also hurt the computer program designer. He will have the same difficulty raising funds from other individual investors.

These problems—the brokerage commission, the minimum investment requirement, and the lawyer's fee—are examples of transactions costs. The existence of such transactions costs creates a profit opportunity for someone who can bring together small savers and match them with small borrowers. Financial intermediaries emerged as part of the financial system to take advantage of this opportunity and to ensure that small savers have a way to invest their savings and that small borrowers can raise funds—both without incurring large transactions costs. The economy also benefits from the growth generated by financial intermediaries, while the intermediaries earn a profit by charging savers and borrowers fees for reducing transactions costs.

Financial intermediaries reduce transactions costs by bringing many different investors together. Mutual funds, for example, sell shares to many individual savers and, in turn, invest in a diversified portfolio of bonds or stocks. By doing so, intermediaries exploit **economies of scale,** that is, transactions costs per dollar of investment decline as the size of transactions increases. For example, the transactions cost of buying $1,000,000 of Treasury bonds is not much greater than that of buying $10,000 of bonds. In such cases, individual investors can reduce transactions costs by combining their purchases through an intermediary. Thus 100 investors with $10,000 each to invest face lower costs per dollar if together they buy $1,000,000 of bonds.

Another area in which economies of scale offer an advantage is in the costs of writing legal contracts. Financial intermediaries spread these costs among many individual savers so that each saver who wants to invest in an invention, the corner drugstore, or an IBM bond doesn't have to seek costly, customized legal advice. Financial intermediaries also take advantage of economies of scale to purchase sophisticated computer systems that provide financial services, such as automatic teller machines.

In Chapters 12 and 13, we examine in more detail how mutual funds, banks, and other financial intermediaries reduce transactions costs for savers and borrowers. For the remainder of this chapter, we focus on another cost that savers and borrowers encounter in the financial system: information costs. Here, too, financial intermediaries help lower costs of lending and borrowing for individuals and businesses.

Information Costs and Financial Structure

In Chapter 10, we pointed out that an efficient financial system channels funds from savers to borrowers so that the highest-value uses of funds are financed. Thus savers benefit from high returns, and borrowers benefit from the successful operation of sound projects. When all the information about the borrower is made available to the saver, financial markets can do their job most effectively. How does the financial market know which borrowers are good risks and which are not? As a saver and investor, how do you know that the financial system will ensure that Greatidea, Inc. gets your money, and not Loseabuck Industries? Once they have invested in a firm, how do savers know whether the firm's managers are using invested funds profitably?

In the remainder of this chapter, we focus on ways that financial markets handle such information problems. We stress the role that information costs play in determining financial structure to explain why particular financial structures emerge. Recall that savers weigh the cost of acquiring information when making portfolio allocation decisions (Chapter 6). For example, suppose that you are trying to decide whether to invest $1000 in bonds of Wellknown, Inc. or those of Newcomer, Inc. If the bonds have the same expected rate of return, but you will have to spend considerable time and money to assess Newcomer's creditworthiness, you should invest in Wellknown. Financial markets usually uncover such information initially through firms' financial disclosures, which government regulations require. Also, private firms, such as rating agencies, investigate the creditworthiness of borrowers and distribute their findings to financial market participants.

So far we have assumed that savers and borrowers have the same information, or *symmetric information*. This assumption does not mean that the parties will have *perfect* information; conditions may unfold differently from their initial expectations. In the real world, borrowers may have private information, called **asymmetric information,** that is better than the information that lenders have about borrowers' prospects and uses of funds. Two types of problems related to asymmetric information arise: (1) adverse selection, or finding out the true risk of the borrower before the loan is made; and (2) moral hazard, or making sure, after the loan is made, that the borrower uses the funds as promised.

Adverse Selection.   Suppose that you would like to lend your $3000 of savings in order to earn a return. Your aunt runs a dry cleaning business and says that she will pay you 8% interest if you lend her $3000 for one year. Your next-door neighbor also asks to borrow your money to manufacture hula-hoops in Bulgaria, promising you a 150% return in one year.

Which investment should you choose? Your neighbor's return sounds great, but his venture is very risky and may not pay anything. Hence you would be better off lending to your aunt. So far this situation matches our analysis of default risk in lending (Chapter 7). Let's move a step further. What if borrowers other than your aunt and your neighbor were seeking your funds? You wouldn't know anything about their ability to pay you back. Indeed, if you knew nothing about them, you probably wouldn't lend to any of them, opting instead to invest in Treasury bonds yielding 4%. In that case, you get a relatively low return, and the potential borrowers don't get loans.

This problem, known as **adverse selection,** is one of distinguishing good-risk borrowers from bad-risk borrowers before making a loan. Adverse selection in the saving-investment process occurs when borrowers who are bad risks are more likely than borrowers who are good risks to accept a loan. If lenders knew who the bad risks were, they could set up contracts charging them a higher interest rate. Without such knowledge, lenders have to set the terms of all loans to reflect the likelihood that they are financing bad risks, with the possible result that good-risk borrowers may not obtain loans.

Moral Hazard. Asymmetric information also may give rise to problems after a loan is made. Suppose that your roommate's sister asks you for a $3000 loan to buy a used car for use in a delivery business. However, after she cashes your check, she buys lottery tickets with the money, hoping to win the $1 million Superlotto prize, repay your $3000, and keep the rest. You would not knowingly lend money to her for this purpose, but it is costly (probably even impossible) for you to monitor her activities. Because you don't know whether she will use your funds wisely, you may decide not to lend the money to her—or to anyone else.

This problem, known as **moral hazard,** reflects savers' difficulties in monitoring borrowers after making the loan. Suppliers of funds cannot easily observe what borrowers are doing with the funds they receive. Although verifying whether a firm makes physical investments in, say, buildings or machines may be easy, it is more difficult to find out how research and development funds are allocated, how well facilities are maintained, or how efficiently a firm is run.

Concluding Remarks. Problems of asymmetric information— adverse selection and moral hazard—impede the efficiency of financial markets in channeling funds from savers to borrowers. In other words, the costs of gathering information about a borrower's prospects before the loan is made and the borrower's activities after the loan is made may be high enough to stop all lending except to government or other well-known borrowers. Next we analyze these problems of asymmetric information in greater detail and examine ways in which financial markets attempt to reduce their costs.

Q: How do high information costs affect financial markets?

A: High information costs reduce the efficiency of financial markets in the saving-investment process. Adverse selection problems arise from the difficulty in distinguishing the true prospects of the borrower before the loan is made. Moral hazard problems stem from the need to monitor the borrower's use of funds after the loan is made.

Adverse Selection: Telling Who's Who

The used car market provides a good example of the problems that adverse selection can pose for buyers and sellers in a market. Suppose that your parents are trying to sell their used 1992 Chevrolet Caprice. Among all the 1992 Chevrolet Caprices in the newspaper ads, some are good cars and others are "lemons" (constantly in the repair shop). Sellers, such as your parents, know fairly well the quality of their cars, but uninformed readers of newspaper ads do not. Because these potential buyers can't distinguish good cars from lemons, they will apply the price of an *average quality* Caprice to all used 1992 Caprices. This frustrates your parents, who consider their good Caprice to be *undervalued*. The pricing delights the Sunkists down the street who own a lemon. Their Caprice is *overvalued* at the average price, and the Sunkists can hardly wait to unload it. As a result of this pricing process, owners of good Caprices may decide not to sell their cars. Hence individual buyers and sellers find trading used cars among themselves costly. The "lemons problem," first articulated by George Akerlof of the University of California, Berkeley, is an illustration of the adverse selection problem.[†]

In the used car market, dealers act as intermediaries between buyers and sellers to reduce adverse selection costs. Dealers desire to maintain their reputations with buyers, which limits their willingness to take advantage of their private information about the quality of the used cars that they are selling. As a result, dealers sell both lemons and good cars for their true values. In addition, government regulations require that certain types of information be communicated to consumers. Just as in the used car market, lemons problems make lending in financial markets more costly, and financial information disclosure regulations again come to the rescue.

"Lemons Problems" in Financial Markets

How do adverse selection problems affect the stock and bond markets' ability to channel funds from savers to borrowers. First, let's look at the stock market. Suppose that Hitechco is a new maker of computer chips. If the firm obtains capital, it will be able to finance an exciting new technological development in chip making. If Hitechco issues new shares of stock, it can pursue the chip-making project. If it doesn't, it loses the opportunity.

At the same time, Lemonco is seeking funds to develop a product similar to Hitechco's but, unknown to the market, Lemonco's product is inferior. In fact, based on available information, investors can't distinguish the quality of the firms' scientific expertise and their productive capabilities. When Hitechco tries to sell stock, then, the market will assign the same value to it and Lemonco's stock, and Hitechco's shares will be undervalued. Hitechco's cost of funds is higher than they would be if potential shareholders had all the information the firm possessed.

This adverse selection problem is present in the bond market as well. Suppose that Hitechco and Lemonco know more about the risk involved in their projects than do investors in the bond market. If an increase in interest rates on default-risk-free Treasury bonds makes them a more attractive investment than Hitechco or Lemonco bonds, savers raise the interest rate required for them to hold Hitechco and Lemonco bonds. In this situation, as savers generally raise their required returns on bonds, adverse selection occurs. The reason is that, at high interest rates, only very risky borrowers, such as Lemonco, will be likely to borrow funds. If their projects are successful, both lenders and borrowers win big; if (as is more likely) they

---

[†] George A. Akerlof, "The Market for 'Lemons': Quality Uncertainty and the Market Mechanism," *Quarterly Journal of Economics*, 84: 488–500, 1970.

aren't, the lenders suffer. Lenders are aware of this problem and may restrict the availability of credit rather than raise rates to the level at which the quantity of funds demanded and supplied are equal. This restricting of credit is known as **credit rationing**. When lenders ration credit, borrowed funds become more costly for unknown firms—both good and bad.

Adverse selection problems are potentially costly for the economy. When good firms have difficulty communicating information to financial markets, their external finance costs rise. This situation forces firms to grow primarily through investment of internal funds, or investment by firm insiders and accumulated profits.[†] Because the firms that are most affected usually are in dynamic, emerging sectors of the economy, opportunities for growth of physical capital, employment, and production are likely to be restricted.

Reducing Information Costs

The costs to savers and borrowers of adverse selection problems reduce the ability of good borrowers to raise money in financial markets and lower the returns obtained by savers. A profit opportunity is created because savers are willing to pay for information about the quality of potential borrowers. Similarly, good borrowers are willing to pay to communicate information about their prospects. Financial intermediaries step into this profit opportunity, using their information-gathering skills to obtain information and then disclose it directly to savers. In doing so, they lower adverse selection costs in financial markets.

Direct Disclosure of Information. One solution to adverse selection problems is for private firms to collect information on individual borrowers and sell the information to savers. So long as the information-gathering firm does a good job, savers purchasing the information will be better able to judge the quality of borrowers, improving the efficiency of lending. Although savers must pay for the information, they can benefit from the information by earning higher returns. A number of companies specializing in information—including Moody's Investor Service, Standard & Poor's Corporation, Value Line, and Dun and Bradstreet—collect information from businesses' income statements, balance sheets, and investment decisions and sell it to subscribers. Buyers include individual investors, libraries, and financial intermediaries. You can find some of these publications in your college library or the local public library. Private information-gathering firms cannot eliminate adverse selection problems, but they can help to minimize them.

Although only subscribers actually pay for the information collected, others can benefit without paying for it. Known as the **free-rider problem**, this situation generally arises when individuals obtain and use infor-

[†] If entrepreneurs have to avoid high information costs associated with external finance by investing most of their savings in their businesses, they lose risk-sharing benefits of diversification.

mation paid for by others. Suppose that you subscribe to Infoperfect, a service that gives you the best possible information on the stocks and bonds of many companies. You are willing to pay a fee to subscribe to Infoperfect because it enables you to profit by buying undervalued stocks and bonds (using information that is better than other investors have). While you are reminding yourself of your cleverness and foresight, Freeda Frieryde and her colleagues decide to buy and sell particular stocks and bonds whenever you do. Because Freeda broadcasts your every move, others are sharing in your profits. As a result, you are willing to pay less to Infoperfect, as are other investors. Deprived of the additional revenue, Infoperfect is less willing to collect as much information to sell to savers.

In most industrialized countries, government agencies set requirements for information disclosure for firms desiring to sell securities in financial markets. In the United States, government regulations require standardized accounting methods and disclosure to investors of available information on income statements and balance sheets. Such disclosure reduces the information costs of adverse selection, but it doesn't eliminate them for two reasons. First, some good firms may be too young to have much information for potential investors to evaluate. Second, lemon firms will try to present the required information in the best possible light so that investors will overvalue their securities.

Roles of Collateral and Net Worth.   When borrowers invest little of their own money in their business, their loss is small if they default on their loans. To prevent this type of adverse selection problem, lenders often require borrowers to pledge some of their own assets as **collateral,** which the lender claims if the borrower defaults. Suppose that Eleanor Riche wants to borrow $10,000 to start a clothing store called Newvo Riche. If she has a home worth $250,000, a lender might not hesitate to lend her the money. In the event that Eleanor defaults, the bank could claim the house or other assets that she might have pledged as collateral. Collateral reduces the likelihood of adverse selection and is widely used in debt contracts for individuals and businesses.

We can generalize the concept of collateral by considering a firm's **net worth,** which is the difference between its assets and its liabilities. Lenders can make a claim against the firm's net worth if it defaults on its loans, which makes the firm cautious about making risky investments. When a firm's net worth is high, the chance that it will default is low: Debtholders (bondholders) must be paid off (from the firm's net worth, if necessary) before funds can be distributed to equityholders (shareholders). As a result, adverse selection problems are less likely in lending to borrowers with high net worth.

Financial Intermediaries and Information.   Banks, in particular, specialize in gathering information about the default risk of many borrowers. These intermediaries raise funds from depositors and, using their superior information, lend them to borrowers that represent good risks. Because banks are better able than individual savers to distinguish good from lemon borrowers, banks earn a profit by charging a higher rate on their loans than the interest rate they pay to depositors.

Banks generally avoid the free-rider problem faced by individual savers by holding the loans they make. Thus investors can't observe banks' activities and profit by mimicking them. By mainly holding loans that are not traded in financial markets, banks earn a profit on information collection.

Banks are the leading source of external finance (funds raised by the business in addition to internally generated profits) for businesses in most countries. Banks' information advantage in reducing adverse selection problems accounts for this dominance. Their specialization in handling adverse selection problems also explains why largely unknown, small and medium-size businesses depend on banks when they need a loan, whereas large, mature corporations have access to stock and bond markets.

Concluding Remarks. Adverse selection problems increase the information costs of channeling funds from savers to borrowers in financial markets. Increased information costs in turn increase the demand for financing arrangements in which information about borrowers can be collected at a lower cost (see Box 11.1). These arrangements include direct information disclosure, collateral and net worth requirements, and reliance on financial intermediaries.

Consider this...

BOX 11.1

Are Stock Market Signals Affected by Adverse Selection?

In an efficient capital market, the stock market valuation of a firm provides the best signal to managers about the profitability of new investments. Market valuations increase in response to good news, suggesting that more capital should be allocated to the firm's lines of business. Similarly, a decline in market valuation of the firm's assets should reflect news about market pessimism regarding the firm's prospects.

How do problems due to asymmetric information affect these relationships? In the case of an adverse selection, or lemons, problem for the stock market, the market's valuation of a good firm can be too low, sending inaccurate signals about prospects. In such a situation, management knows that the firm's prospects are better than the market price signals and will not turn to the market. Instead, the firm might choose to avoid the market altogether and use internal funds to finance future growth.

A study of some 300 manufacturing firms during the 1970s and 1980s found that firms that rely heavily on internal funds tend to be younger, more rapidly growing firms. Moreover, the capital spending of these firms is closely tied to their internal funds. In contrast, capital spending by more mature firms capable of raising funds in financial markets is not. Hence adverse selection problems affect financing and investment decisions for many U.S. firms.

Source: Steven M. Fazzari, R. Glenn Hubbard, and Bruce C. Petersen, "Financing Constraints and Corporate Investment," *Brookings Papers on Economic Activity,* 1: 143–195, 1988.

► C H E C K P O I N T *Why might the founder of a young firm in the growing biotechnology industry not raise funds by selling new shares in the firm, even to finance a very profitable investment opportunity?* Information costs associated with adverse selection problems are most significant for firms in emerging, growing industries. Faced with the high information costs of distinguishing between good and lemon firms, savers investing in financial markets require a higher return on investments in all firms in these industries to compensate them for the risk of investing in lemons. As a result, shares of good firms will be undervalued, and entrepreneurial firms will prefer to grow by using internal funds or loans from banks, which specialize in reducing problems of adverse selection. ◄

Moral Hazard: Monitoring the Borrower

Lending money to a firm sets the scene for moral hazard problems. Such problems arise when the borrower has incentives to conceal information and to act in a way that may not reflect the lender's interests. For example, say that you lend money to Bigdream, Inc. How do you know whether the firm is investing the funds in its research and development laboratory or in wood paneling for the new executive dining room? The investment in R&D is likely to increase Bigdream's profits and your returns; the wood paneling is not. To find out whether the firm is using funds in a way that will benefit you, you need to spend time and money monitoring its activities. Monitoring costs can complicate financing arrangements for even the largest corporations, limiting the attractiveness of using financial markets to obtain finance and influencing the choice between equity and debt.

Equity Finance: The Principal-Agent Problem

Monitoring problems increase the information costs of raising funds through equity finance. When Bigdream's managers tell you that your $1000 investment earned no returns, how do you know whether the claims are true? Having raised external equity finance, the firm has an incentive to understate profits and reduce payments to the lender. To police such underreporting, outside suppliers of funds must conduct costly audits of the firm's finances every time an earnings report is issued.

The federal government and the business community itself regulate reporting by firms to reduce the chance of fraud. In particular, the Securities and Exchange Commission (SEC)—a government agency—and the Financial Accounting Standards Board—a private agency—have set standardized accounting principles for firms to use in reporting their earnings and overall financial condition. These accounting principles are designed to help investors understand the financial condition of the firms in which they have invested. In addition, federal laws have made misreporting or stealing profits belonging to shareholders a federal offense, punishable by large fines and/or prison terms.

Another moral hazard problem involves a firm's principals and agents. The shareholders, who *own* the firm's net worth, are **principals**, and the managers, who *control* the firm's assets, are **agents**. Called the **principal-agent problem**, this type of moral hazard problem may arise when managers do not own much of the firm's equity and thus do not have the same incentive to maximize the firm's value as the owners do. Because a firm's shareholders have a residual claim on its earnings, improvements in profitability accrue to them and not to the managers charged with controlling the firm's assets. In the United States, for example, the majority of private economic activity occurs in large public corporations, whose managers do not own a significant part of the firm. Indeed, the stake of top management in a firm's ownership usually is less than 5%.

In one study, data on large firms from the early 1980s showed that firms' performance was greater (defined as higher market value of the firm's shares) when management ownership was between 5% and 20% of shares outstanding than when its stake was less than 5%. Performance doesn't increase uniformly when management stakes rise above 20%, because managers may then maximize perquisites of ownership other than the firm's value.[†] Because management's stake in large U.S. corporations is typically less than 5%, an increase in management ownership might benefit their shareholders.

Let's explore the principal-agent problem in equity finance. Suppose that your neighbor, Reed Moore, asks you to join him in his new business venture, a bookstore. He needs $50,000 to open the bookstore, but he only has $2500. He read in the newspaper that you won the lottery and knows you could invest $47,500. After you make the investment, you own 95% of the bookstore, and Reed owns the other 5%. You're pleased with the investment: If Reed provides savvy tips on the best books and chats with the customers over coffee, the bookstore could make $50,000 each year after paying his salary. Your share would be $47,500, a 100% return; Reed's share would be $2500 (in addition to his salary). But maybe not. Reed might decide to buy mahogany bookcases and oriental rugs and chat with customers over champagne, leaving no profit. Although Reed would forgo the $2500 in profits, he would still receive a salary—and enjoy working in plush surroundings.

The principal-agent problem is a general one in equity contracts. Many uses of funds by corporate managers are highly visible (such as large-scale investment projects), but many are hidden from view (such as expenses for research, maintenance, management, and organizational efficiency). Although not fraudulent, expenses such as corporate art collections, mahogany desks, limousines, and jets do not directly benefit shareholders. Managers often run firms to satisfy their personal goals, including accruing

[†] *Source:* Randall Mørck, Andrei Shleifer, and Robert Vishny, "Management Ownership and Market Valuation, " *Journal of Financial Economics*, 20: 293-315.

prestige and power. If managers aren't motivated to maximize a firm's value, nonmanagement shareholders may get shortchanged.

The shareholders own the firm, so why can't they just fire bad managers? To determine whether management is using corporate funds efficiently requires detailed and costly audits. No individual small shareholder has an incentive to pay these monitoring costs. Even if some individual shareholder offered to do so, others might not contribute, preferring to wait and see what the individual learns. This situation is another example of the free-rider problem.

Reducing Costs of Principal-Agent Problems

The financial system develops ways to reduce the information costs of principal-agent problems. As we have noted, regulation of accounting methods and antifraud laws reduce the opportunities for agents to take advantage of equity-owning principals. Principal-agent problems can be reduced further through financial intermediaries and by using debt finance.

Financial Intermediaries. Principal-agent problems raise information costs for small shareholders because of the free-rider problem. However, other investors, such as financial intermediaries, can address the problem by holding large blocks of shares. These large investors have an incentive to monitor closely how their funds are being used. Some **venture capital firms**, which raise equity capital from investors and invest in emerging or growing entrepreneurial business ventures, use this method successfully. Venture capital firms insist on holding large equity stakes and sitting on the firm's board of directors in order to monitor management's activities closely. In addition, when a venture capital firm acquires equity in a new firm, the shares are not marketable to other investors. As a result, the venture capital firm avoids the free-rider problem: Other investors are unable to take advantage of its monitoring efforts. The venture capital firm is then able to earn a profit from its monitoring activities, reducing the information costs of moral hazard problems and improving the allocation of funds from savers to borrowers.

Not all efforts by intermediaries to reduce the costs of principal-agent problems focus on young firms. **Corporate restructuring firms** raise equity capital to acquire large blocks of the equity in mature firms to reduce free-rider problems (see the Appendix at the end of this chapter). The leaders of many such firms (including Ivan Boesky, Carl Icahn, T. Boone Pickens, and Henry Kravis) became rich and famous (or notorious) in the 1980s (see the Other times, other places box).

Debt Finance. Another way to decrease the information costs of moral hazard problems is to use debt rather than equity finance. For example, rather than investing $47,500 in equity in Reed Moore's bookstore and receiving 95% of the bookstore's profits, you could lend Reed $47,500 and require him to pay you a fixed interest rate of 10%. In this case, you would get

Other times, other places...
Corporate Control Then and Now

The idea that gains can be realized from concentrated equity ownership and close monitoring of managers by corporate restructuring firms was well understood by J. P. Morgan, a prominent financier of the late nineteenth and early twentieth centuries. Morgan's many financial accomplishments include the creation in 1901 of the U.S. Steel Corporation. Morgan banking interests often held debt and equity securities of firms, and Morgan partners served on the boards of directors of controlled companies. They monitored managers and even engineered changes in top management, activities not allowed for commercial banks in the United States in the 1980s and early 1990s. Skeptical analysts of the period also note that, although Morgan helped give birth to the modern corporation, much of Morgan's merger activity was undertaken to form profitable monopolies.

Michael Milken can be considered the J. P. Morgan of the 1980s. In fact, his employer (now-bankrupt Drexel Burnham Lambert) originally was Drexel Morgan, a Morgan partnership founded in 1871. As Morgan did before him, Milken made large pools of capital available to finance acquisition of corporate equity. He created liquid markets in junk bonds and provided information to potential investors. Like Morgan, he profited handsomely, receiving more than $1 billion in compensation between 1983 and 1987.

Toward the end of their eras, both men became targets of investigations. Morgan was grilled in congressional hearings in 1912 and 1913 but later entered genteel retirement. His fate was better than Milken's, who was indicted for violation of securities laws in March 1989. Following his conviction, he was sentenced to 10 years in a federal prison, a sentence later shortened.

$4750 each year. As the debt promises a fixed payment, you (or your accountant) don't need to conduct costly audits of Reed's operation of the bookstore unless he fails to meet the interest and principal payments and defaults on the loan. So long as Reed keeps making debt payments to you, you aren't concerned with whether the bookstore reports earnings of $10,000 or $100,000 each year. The lower costs of monitoring make debt attractive relative to equity in many cases.[†]

▶ **C H E C K P O I N T** *Firms in cyclical industries—those whose profits rise and fall with economywide booms and busts—tend to borrow less than firms in noncyclical industries. If monitoring costs are lower for debt finance than equity finance, why don't all firms rely on debt?* The strategy of using debt finance to reduce moral hazard problems is based on the assumption that fluctuations in the borrowing firm's profits reflect the efforts of its managers. If most of the profit swings reflect movements in economywide profitability, too much debt could cause a firm to go bankrupt when its profits slump and it cannot repay debtholders. As a result, the use of debt is concentrated in firms whose profitability depends less on economic movements. ◀

[†] Many analysts believe that the dramatic increase in corporate borrowing and the decrease in the use of equity finance by corporations in the 1980s reflected an attempt to reduce the costs of principal-agent problems. In the Appendix to this chapter, we examine the shifts in corporate financial structure in the 1980s, focusing on "winners" and "losers" and what our analysis of information costs predicts for future developments in corporate finance.

Moral Hazard in Debt Finance

Even though debt finance can reduce moral hazard problems relative to equity finance in many cases, it does not eliminate moral hazard. Because a debt contract allows the borrower to keep any profits that exceed the fixed amount of the debt payment, borrowers have an incentive to assume greater risk to earn these profits than is in the interest of the lender. Let's return to the example of Reed Moore's bookstore. Suppose that you think you are lending money to Reed to finance the purchase of bookcases and a computer system. However, once the money is in Reed's hands, he decides to invest the money in a machine that sends subliminal messages to shoppers, telling them to buy expensive books. If the machine works, the bookstore—and Reed—will make a fortune. In the more likely case that it doesn't work, he won't be able to repay you. Even with a debt contract, the risk of moral hazard is present. The financial system uses two basic tools to combat moral hazard in debt finance: restrictive covenants and financial intermediaries. Let's explore each in turn.

Restrictive Covenants. The basic moral hazard problem you encountered in making a loan to Reed was that he might use the proceeds for risky purposes. Even if he does not have $25,000 of net worth to commit to the venture, you may be able to reduce the likelihood of moral hazard by placing restrictions, known as **restrictive covenants**, on Reed's management activities in the debt contract. The most typical restrictive covenant in business lending is a limit on the borrower's risk taking. For example, the lender can restrict the borrower to buying only particular goods or prohibit the borrower from buying other businesses.

A second type of restrictive covenant requires that the borrower maintain a certain minimum level of net worth. For example, if you apply for a mortgage loan to buy a house, the bank may ask you to take out sufficient life insurance to pay off the loan in the event that you die before the mortgage is repaid. Businesses may be required to maintain a certain level of net worth, particularly in liquid assets, to reduce incentives to take on too much risk.

Financial markets often address moral hazard in debt contracts by insisting that entrepreneurs or managers of firms place their own funds at risk. In that case, taking on risky projects increases the chance that insiders like Reed Moore will lose their own money if they make bad decisions, thereby reducing the incentive to use outside investors' funds in risky ways. Suppose that Reed invested $25,000, rather than $2500 of his own net worth (his assets less his liabilities) in the bookstore. He is likely to be much more cautious in making management decisions. Thus, in general, the greater the net worth (equity capital) contributed by a firm's managers, the less likely is a moral hazard problem to occur. Thus the greater is the firm's ability to borrow. At quite low levels of invested net worth, moral hazard problems may prevent borrowing altogether (see Box 11.2).

Q: How does the financial system respond to reduce information costs for savers and borrowers?

A: The financial system reduces information costs by developing low-information-cost financing arrangements, especially through financial intermediaries. These intermediaries specialize in gathering and monitoring information about borrowers on savers' behalf.

Consider this...

Can Falling Prices Raise Information Costs?

High levels of borrower net worth reduce information costs associated with adverse selection and moral hazard problems. However, sudden reductions in borrower net worth can increase information costs of lending, sometimes to levels that sharply reduce borrowers' ability to raise funds for new plant and equipment and job creation. The classic example of this link among net worth, finance, and the economy is *debt deflation*. In debt deflation, falling prices raise the real value of firms' outstanding debt, reducing their net worth. As a result, savers know that the likelihood of

adverse selection and moral hazard problems increases, and they reduce their willingness to lend to all but the safest borrowers (for example, the government). Faced with severe credit declines, firms significantly cut their spending, reducing economic activity.

The best known example of debt deflation came during the Great Depression of the early 1930s. Declining prices increased the real debt burdens of borrowers by nearly 40% between 1929 and 1933. The combined effect of declining output and deflation sharply reduced bor-

rowers' net worth, constraining borrowers' ability to obtain credit and leading to a collapse in lending, investment, and employment. More recent episodes of debt deflation in particular sectors include the collapse in farmland values in the early 1980s, the fall in oil prices in the mid-1980s, and the sharp decline in commercial real estate prices in the late 1980s and early 1990s. In each case, the collapse in borrower net worth initiated by debt deflation raised the cost of funds to borrowers because of the increased severity of adverse selection and moral hazard problems.

A third type of restrictive covenant, common in consumer lending, requires the borrower to maintain the value of any collateral offered to the lender. For example, if you take out a loan to buy a new car, you will have to carry a minimum amount of insurance against theft and collision, and you can't sell the car to a friend if you haven't paid off the loan. If you take out a mortgage loan to buy a house, you will have to carry insurance on the home, and you can't sell your house without first repaying your mortgage loan.

However, restrictive covenants complicate debt contracts and reduce their marketability for savers. The cost of monitoring whether firms actually are complying with restrictive covenants further hampers marketability and liquidity. Finally, restrictive covenants cannot protect a lender against every possible risky activity in which the borrower might engage.

Financial Intermediaries. Marketability and liquidity problems arising from restrictive covenants are exacerbated by free-rider problems associated with the cost of monitoring whether or not firms are abiding by restrictive covenants. Whenever monitoring is costly, free-rider problems may occur. As an individual saver, you would find monitoring the activities of Reed Moore or General Motors (if you bought a GM bond) to be very expensive. Thus you and others like you are likely to try to seek a free ride on the moni-

MOVING FROM THEORY TO PRACTICE...

THE ECONOMIST   MARCH 13, 1993

On the Cutting Edge of Corporate Control in Eastern Europe

Some time after April 1st, Eastern Europe's boldest experiment in privatisation begins. Investors will start trading shares in almost 1,500 companies once owned by the Czechoslovak state and distributed to its people through vouchers. At one stroke this is supposed to inaugurate a stockmarket, create a class of citizen-capitalists, and give sound management to firms that have never known market discipline. If countries could hold their breath, the Czech and Slovak republics, heirs of ex-Czechoslovakia, would do so.

a Questions abound. Will the share prices of these newly-privatised companies crash as soon as trading starts? Will investment funds, as new to capitalism as the companies they own, provide effective corporate governance? Will banks, which control most big investment managers, abuse their powers? Will the share registry and exchanges cope with the strain of trading? At this stage, there are only guesses.

The scheme has set one fear to rest: that ownership would be spread too thinly for shareholders to exercise control over the managers of privatised firms. If anything, economic power may prove excessively concentrated. Promising to redeem privatisation vouchers at 10–50 times their cost, the 437 investment funds scooped up almost three-quarters of the coupons that entitled Czech and Slovak citizens to bid for state companies. The dozen biggest funds snared 40% of the vouchers distributed for the first wave of voucher privatisation...

b If all Czech and Slovak fund managers were Pierpont Morgans, the countries' companies would be effectively, if brutally, restructured. But few, if any, have Morgan's expertise, and none has his money. Fund groups that buy stakes in 100 companies or more may have trouble providing guidance to all of them. Prvni Investicni, the second-biggest group, invested in 266 firms.

Many funds are strapped for cash, moreover. Until share-trading starts, they cannot easily raise money to pay their expenses. Most big fund companies can rely on rich banking parents for support... Smaller ones are desperate to liquidate part of their holdings.

That is why some investors fear that share prices will plunge as soon as trading begins. Karl Hauptmann, chief of Europa Capital Management, a Prague-based asset manager, reckons that, taken together, funds may have to sell a fifth of their shares immediately to raise cash. Many will start with their most promising holdings because buyers for the others may prove scarce.

c The longer funds must wait to trade, the more desperate they become. Banks say that trading may not start until June, since the computerised share registry is not yet working properly. Small funds detect in this a plot by the banks to drive them out of business. Some observers believe that up to half of the funds will disappear within a year.

ANALYZING THE NEWS...

A major goal in shifting the economies of Eastern Europe from socialism to capitalism is privatization of state-owned enterprises. Citizens of the Czech and Slovak republics were given the right to purchase vouchers to be used in bidding on previously state-owned enterprises. Once shares were distributed, owners were free to sell them to anyone else. Our analysis of information problems in financial markets predicts that diffuse ownership is not likely to be successful. The article considers the problems experienced in the Czech and Slovak republics.

(a) Because individual entrepreneurs generally own, finance, and manage their own small businesses, privatization of these businesses can proceed relatively smoothly. However, larger enterprises requiring external finance present important information problems. Because of the previous lack of private financial markets and institutions, investors will have a difficult time distinguishing good from bad firms. Moreover, for corporate control, new shareholders will incur significant monitoring costs. Numerous small shareholders will thus face significant adverse selection and moral hazard problems in the emerging financial market. Without new developments to reduce the information costs associated with these problems, the reconstituted enterprises will face high financing costs. The article suggests that investment funds, which pool the resources of individual shareholders, may be able to act as large shareholders, reducing problems of corporate control.

(b) When privatization was first initiated, officials did not anticipate the concentration of shares in investment funds. However, the absence of disclosure rules (such as those enforced by the SEC) reduces the likelihood that all relevant information will be available to investors and traders. Where there are information problems, financial markets respond because profits are to be made from developing new financing arrangements that benefit savers and borrowers. Investment funds propose to hold large blocks of stock in a few firms in order to reduce moral hazard problems; savers would then hold shares in the mutual fund, rather than shares in the individual companies. This approach provides information benefits to savers, but it doesn't address savers' risk-sharing and liquidity needs.

(c) Market efficiency requires well functioning secondary markets with low information and transactions costs. If liquid markets for the underlying shares do not develop, then as savers withdraw their investment fund balances, as they will to finance consumption, investment funds might have to liquidate their holdings at a loss.

For further thought...

Can you suggest a way that the Czech government might reduce the likelihood of the liquidity problem discussed in (c)? In other words, if mutual funds held relatively illiquid claims on borrowers while holding liquid claims to savers, how might the government avoid mass liquidation of underlying Czech shares if mutual fund shareholders withdraw their funds?

Source: Excerpted from "Eastern European Privatisation: Making It Work," March 13, 1993. ©1993 The Economist Newspaper Group, Inc. Reprinted with permission.

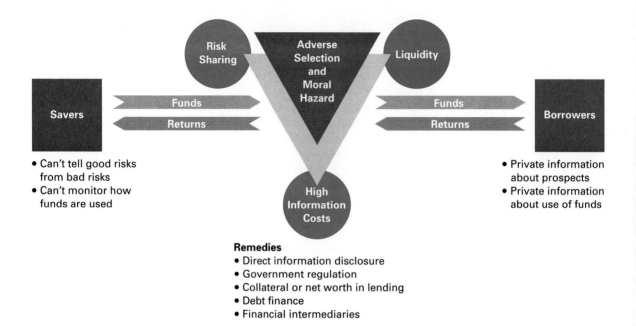

Savers
- Can't tell good risks from bad risks
- Can't monitor how funds are used

Funds →
← Returns

Risk Sharing

Adverse Selection and Moral Hazard

Liquidity

High Information Costs

Funds →
← Returns

Borrowers
- Private information about prospects
- Private information about use of funds

Remedies
- Direct information disclosure
- Government regulation
- Collateral or net worth in lending
- Debt finance
- Financial intermediaries

▲ FIGURE 11.1

Remedies for Problems of Adverse Selection and Moral Hazard

When borrowers and savers have private information about their prospects or use of funds, information costs to savers arise. With adverse selection, savers can't tell good risks from bad risks; with moral hazard, savers can't monitor how funds are used. These problems impede the flow of funds to borrowers and returns to savers.

toring efforts of others. Borrowers may be tempted to violate restrictive covenants if they believe that lenders will not pay the costs of monitoring.

Financial intermediaries, particularly banks, reduce this problem and earn a profit by acting as *delegated monitors* for many individual savers, who deposit their funds with the intermediary. (We examine this role for banks in Chapter 13.) When an intermediary such as a bank holds the loans it makes, other investors are unable to gain a free ride on the intermediary's monitoring efforts. As delegated monitors, financial intermediaries reduce the information costs of moral hazard and improve the channeling of funds from savers to borrowers. This result is a major reason that most lending takes place through financial intermediaries rather than through the direct issuance of marketable securities.

Figure 11.1 summarizes the remedies used to fight problems of moral hazard and adverse selection.

Key Terms and Concepts

Asymmetric information
    Adverse selection
    Moral hazard

Collateral

Corporate restructuring firms

Credit rationing

Economies of scale

Financial structure

Free-rider problem

Summary

1. Financial markets do not efficiently match savers and borrowers when the transactions and information costs of lending are high. As a result, most lending takes place through financial intermediaries rather than in financial markets.

2. Transactions costs make investing in debt and equity instruments in financial markets costly for small savers. Financial intermediaries take advantage of economies of scale by pooling savers' funds to lower transactions costs. As a result, individual savers are able to earn a higher return on their savings, and borrowers realize a lower cost of funds.

3. Information costs result from problems of asymmetric information: adverse selection (difficulty in knowing the true prospects of the borrower before the transaction) and moral hazard (need to monitor the borrower's use of funds after the transaction). Information costs arising from adverse selection and moral hazard reduce returns for savers and increase the cost of funds for borrowers. In general, the financial system reduces costs of asymmetric

information by developing low-information-cost financing arrangements in financial markets and relying on financial intermediaries that specialize in gathering and monitoring information about borrowers.

4. Strategies to reduce adverse selection problems include direct disclosure of information, financial intermediation, and use of collateral and net worth provisions in financial contracts.

5. The principal-agent problem, in which managers (agents) do not have the same incentive to maximize profits that shareholders (principals) have, illustrates moral hazard in equity finance. Solutions to the principal-agent problem include regulation of information disclosure, financial intermediation, and use of debt instead of equity finance.

6. Moral hazard problems in debt finance are reduced by net worth requirements, use of restrictive covenants, and financial intermediation.

Review Questions

1. Distinguish symmetric information from asymmetric information, and state why the distinction is important for the financial system.

2. What is the difference between moral hazard and adverse selection? How does each contribute to making information asymmetric?

3. Why might the number of loans that aren't repaid to banks rise as interest rates rise? What might be a better strategy for banks than raising interest rates?

4. Suppose that a bank makes a loan to a business and that the loan contract specifies that the business is not to engage in certain lines of business. What is this type of provision called? Why would the bank make such a provision?

5. What is the name of the main problem associated with the separation of ownership from management? What do managers do that owners don't like? What types of solutions are available?

6. Is a large firm with thousands of shareholders more or less likely to suffer a principal-agent problem than a small firm with just a few shareholders? Explain.

7. Describe opportunities for specialized investors or financial institutions in mitigating financing problems associated with adverse selection and moral hazard.

Questions 8–11 Pertain to the Appendix

8. Why does free cash flow contribute to principal-agent problems?

9. What is the difference between a takeover and a restructuring?

10. How does a management buyout (MBO) increase the efficiency of a firm? What happens in a leveraged buyout (LBO) in general?

11. What are the consequences for the economy if U.S. firms have too much debt?

Analytical Problems

12. At a used car lot, a nearly new car with only 2000 miles on the odometer is selling for half the car's original price. The salesperson tells you that the car was "driven by a little old lady from Pasadena" who had it for two months and then decided that she "didn't like the color." The salesperson assures you that the car is in great shape and has had no major problems. What type of asymmetric information problem is present here? How can you get around this problem?

13. Why don't insurance companies sell income insurance? That is, if a person loses his or her job or doesn't get as big a raise as anticipated, that person would be compensated under his or her insurance coverage.

14. In which of the following situations is moral hazard likely to be less of a problem? Explain.

    a. A manager is paid a flat salary of $150,000.

    b. A manager is paid a salary of $75,000 plus 10% of the firm's profits.

15. A banker is thinking of making a loan to a small business. The owner of the business also owns a home and has a $40,000 investment in stocks and bonds. What kind of loan contract should the banker write to minimize moral hazard problems?

16. Describe some of the information problems in financial markets that lead firms to rely more heavily on internal funds than external funds for investment. Do these problems necessarily imply that, as a result, too little good investment is being made? Why or why not?

17. Do you think that lemons problems are likely to be important in emerging stock and bond markets in Eastern Europe? Why or why not?

Questions 18–21 Pertain to the Appendix

18. Suppose that you own some corporate bonds issued by the Buyusout Company. Would you be happy if the company underwent a leveraged buyout? Why or why not? Would you be happy if the company

were taken over by a much larger firm, reducing its default risk? Why or why not?

19. As a shareholder in a large corporation that has a large free cash flow and few new investment opportunities, what should you try to get the firm to do? How can you accomplish this?

20. How might corporate takeovers lead managers to focus on the short run rather than the long run?

21. On average, Japanese nonfinancial corporations have greater leverage than U.S. corporations. Does that imply that Japanese firms are more "financially fragile" than U.S. firms? Why or why not?

Data Question

22. Suppose you believe that adverse selection problems are important in the stock market. If a firm announces that it will issue new shares, what pattern would you look for in data on the price of the firm's outstanding shares following the announcement? Explain.

Appendix: Information Costs and Corporate Restructuring

Efforts to reduce information costs associated with moral hazard led to large shifts in financial structure in the 1980s and early 1990s. In particular, corporate restructuring firms acquired controlling interest in the equity of many large corporations and increased corporations' use of debt. Both steps are consistent with our analysis of ways that the financial system responds to information costs of moral hazard. Here we examine (1) how corporate restructuring firms predicted where principal-agent problems were most severe (and hence where potential profits were greatest), and (2) why corporations significantly increased their relative reliance on debt.

Predicting Principal-Agent Problems

Let's use the understanding of moral hazard developed in the chapter to predict some cases in which principal-agent problems are likely to be important.

Engaging in risky investments always is easier with someone else's money than with your own. Thus managers have an incentive to maximize the quantity of funds over which they have discretion and control. These funds are known as **free cash flow**, or the difference between the firm's cash receipts and cash disbursements, including payments to equityholders and debtholders. The incentive to maximize free cash flow is not conducive to an efficient capital market. Rather, in an efficient market, if a firm has excess cash but no new opportunities, the money should be distributed to the firm's owners so that they can invest it in more profitable, higher-value projects. Because managers may be concerned with personal goals, such as the size of the organization they control, they may use the firm's free cash flow to expand, even if new operations are not profitable for owners. Michael Jensen of Harvard University has stressed the importance of free cash flow in explaining the behavior of corporate managers.

Evidence of Principal-Agent Problems.   The existence of serious principal-agent problems has been confirmed by solid evidence. Various large U.S. industries had matured by the late 1970s and early 1980s, in the sense that they generated large amounts of free cash flow. Leading examples include the oil industry, flush with profits from the oil shocks of the 1970s but with limited new investment opportunities; the tobacco industry, where profits were high, but declining numbers of smokers made new investment unattractive; and the food and beverage products industry, in which established brand names produced significant cash flow with investment limited to advertising and image maintenance. These industries offered prominent examples of principal-agent struggles in corporate finance.

Avoiding Principal-Agent Problems.   Avoiding principal-agent problems is not easy. Institutional restrictions make relating managerial compensation directly to performance somewhat difficult. Indeed, studies show that increases in the market value of their firms do not substantially enhance the long-term compensation of chief executive officers and other high-ranking managers. Nor do boards of directors generally provide effective control mechanisms. In some cases, boards are virtually controlled by management; in other cases, even strong-willed directors often have less complete information than top management does.

The principal-agent struggles in corporate finance in the late 1970s and early 1980s involved billions of dollars. With such large amounts of money at stake, the solution to moral hazard problems is to align the principals and agents so that each group has the same incentive to maximize the firms' value. Finding the solution is the key to millions—even billions—of dollars in profits.

Shifts in Financial Structure in the 1980s and 1990s

In the 1980s and early 1990s, U.S. corporations shifted their relative reliance on debt and equity finance. Let's examine the reasons for this shift and identify the winners and losers.

The Struggle for Corporate Control.   High information costs increase the likelihood of inefficient behavior by managers. However, such behavior can be averted if the organizational structure is arranged so as to prevent moral hazard problems. Strategies include (1) replacing many individual shareholders with a smaller, more coordinated group of shareholders, and (2) using alternatives to equity finance that increase the control over managers by outside shareholders. Financial markets used these strategies in a wave of corporate takeovers and restructurings in the 1980s.

Corporate control is a contest for ownership and control of the firm. It pits shareholders against managers in an effort to direct the firm's resources to their highest valued use. This contest may involve a **takeover,** in which a group of current or new shareholders buys a controlling interest in the firm, reshapes the board of directors, and even replaces managers. Alternatively, a **restructuring** rearranges the financial structure of the firm to shift control over the resources of the firm and to provide incentives for managers to maximize the firm's value. Both strategies can involve the assumption of substantial amounts of debt, raising the question of whether corporations incur "too much" debt in the process.

A corporate takeover replaces inefficient management with new managers committed to the goal of raising the firm's value. It is based on the premise that a new, more efficient management team will maximize the firm's value instead of spending free cash flow. If it does so, the result will be an increase in the market value of the firm's assets. Hence an outside group of investors, called corporate raiders, can bid for corporate control of the firm in the market at a price higher than current market price and still earn a profit from more efficient operation by new management. Contests for corporate control, pitting corporate raiders against incumbent managers, figured prominently in the business news of the 1980s. In some cases, even the *threat* of a corporate takeover can affect the behavior of managers. As the takeover wave continued during the 1980s, the threat of a takeover frequently led management to cut costs or to distribute free cash flow to shareholders. Such distributions involved increasing dividends or repurchasing shares, thereby raising share prices and creating capital gains for shareholders.

Restructuring provides another way to combat principal-agent problems. One difficulty with equity finance is that managers get to decide on the level of distributions to shareholders. Suppose that a now mature Hitechco finds that its annual earnings have grown dramatically. The firm has an annual free cash flow of $50 million, and research opportunities in its basic businesses are not promising. Hitechco's initial external finance has come from equity issues, now held by many individual shareholders. Hitechco isn't legally required to increase its payout as its free cash flow increases, creating the potential for corporate control and takeover battles.

Suppose that Hitechco's management borrows money from financial markets or institutions to buy back the shares of the other owners. Now, the free cash flow is associated with a debt claim, not an equity claim. Thus management acquires both ownership and control, increasing its incentive to maximize the firm's value. The debt claim on the free cash flow provides more discipline because promised payments to debtholders are legally enforceable. When a firm's managers acquire a greater stake in the firm by buying back shares from other shareholders, this form of restructuring is known as a **management buyout** (MBO). By eliminating incentive problems, the new structure permits more efficient operation of the firm, raising the firm's value. This increase in value now accrues to the managers as owners of the firm. Other shareholders also benefit from higher prices as their shares are repurchased.

Restructurings that substitute debt for equity do not have to be voluntary, as with an MBO. In fact, management buyouts are but one type of restructuring generally known as the **leveraged buyout** (LBO), in which external equity is replaced by debt. The holders of the firm's equity can be outside investors or corporate raiders instead of or in addition to the managers. A common driving force in LBOs is the desire to reduce the costs of moral hazard by increasing the use of debt relative to equity, thereby raising the market value of the firm.

Throughout the 1980s, nonfinancial corporations continued to rely heavily on internal funds. However, they sharply increased reliance on debt; net new issues of equity were actually negative in the late 1980s. Later, we will explore the economic implications of this shift in financial structure.

Factors Affecting Gains to Agents.   Most studies of changes in corporate control during the 1980s (from takeovers and restructurings) concluded that, on average, efficiency improved substantially because of rising productivity, declining costs, and increasing profitability. However, gains to shareholders probably reflect both efficiency gains and redistribution of resources from other parties, including the government, debtholders, employees, customers, and suppliers.

Favorable tax treatment by government explains some of the increased share values during takeovers and restructurings. The U.S. tax code favors debt finance over equity finance because interest payments to debtholders are tax-deductible at the corporate level, but dividend payments to equityholders are not. Hence tax revenue is likely to decline when debt replaces equity in the capital structure.[†] Firms' ability to use the tax subsidy for debt increased during the 1980s, as liquid markets for junk bonds made selling risky debt easier. Studies of management buyouts show that a significant part of the gain to prebuyout shareholders results from tax savings.

[†] The argument actually is more subtle. Traditionally, equity has been favored in tax-code provisions affecting the individual's income tax, so the net subsidy to debt finance (taking into account both corporate and personal income taxes) is, in principle, ambiguous. Most economists argue that, on balance, debt is still favored by the U.S. tax code.

One potential cost of takeovers and restructurings is that of discouraging managers from taking a long-term view. Some critics of the wave of corporate takeovers and restructurings in the 1980s expressed concern that corporations would be less likely to make long-term investments in research and development, physical capital, and employee training (human capital). Their argument was that, faced with high current debt-service burdens, managers would cut back on long-term investment.

This claim is hard to assess. Some studies show that takeovers per se do not seem to generate large cuts in research and development (R&D) spending but that highly leveraged takeovers or buyouts apparently depress investment spending for both R&D and physical capital. Nonetheless, the effect of takeovers and restructurings on investment spending probably is not large. Recall that restructuring involving greater use of debt is most likely in mature industries, where opportunities for new investment are relatively limited anyway.

Is There "Too Much" Corporate Debt?   Many economists worry that the shifts in financial structure during the 1980s that were designed to reduce information costs left the economy with too much debt. Their concern is that firms relying only on high debt levels to control moral hazard problems will become financially fragile. In other words, even if a firm has promising investment opportunities, its debt burden may keep it from attracting the funds it needs to invest, employ workers, and increase production.

An important effect of the shift to debt finance in the 1980s was a substantial rise in bankruptcies and defaults. Interest payments per dollar of corporate earnings (before interest and taxes) rose from 16¢ during the post–World War II period prior to 1970 to 33¢ during the 1970s to an average of 56¢ during the 1980s. This increase in debt-service burden was accompanied by an increase in corporate bankruptcies and business failures throughout the 1980s. Although cyclical (more frequent in bad times than in good times), bankruptcies have been relatively high during the boom following the 1981–1982 recession. In addition, more large and prominent nonfinancial firms began defaulting on debt obligations (and failing) than at any other time since World War II. Noted economists and the U.S. Treasury Department have voiced concern that corporate restructurings during the 1980s exposed the economy to the risk of a "financial crisis."

As noted in the analysis of moral hazard, high levels of corporate debt confer both benefits and costs on the borrower. Most research suggests that financial structures emerge as ways of matching the needs of borrowers and lenders but that additional regulatory or tax biases can lead to overreliance on particular types of financing. The U.S. Treasury Department's 1992 study of corporate taxation suggested ways to remove tax biases favoring debt finance. If implemented, these would allow firms to make their financing decisions based on risk-sharing, liquidity, and information considerations, without interference from the tax code.

In the early 1990s, the realization that many firms borrowed too much during the 1980s led to another shift in financial structure. In 1991 and 1992, net new equity issues were again positive. Market participants, government officials, and academics began to consider mechanisms other than high levels of debt to reduce the costs of moral hazard in corporate finance. The mid- and late 1990s likely will be a time of more shareholder activism and reforms in the roles of managers and boards of directors in large firms.

CHAPTER 12

What Financial Institutions Do

The late 1980s and early 1990s were challenging times for financial institutions around the world. In the United States, taxpayers were reeling from the cost (estimated to be in the hundreds of billions of dollars) of bailing out failed savings institutions and banks. Economists and policymakers expressed concern that insurance companies and pension funds, essential participants in domestic financial markets, could be in trouble next. In 1992, the Securities and Exchange Commission announced sweeping changes in the mutual fund industry. At the same time, the Treasury Department and Congress worked on a comprehensive reform of the banking industry, blurring the distinctions among types of financial institutions. In Japan, financial deregulation had a similar effect. While the emerging market economies of Eastern Europe began developing private financial institutions, their Western European counterparts prepared for a unified financial market.

To understand these developments, we must focus on what financial institutions do. In the next five chapters, we analyze the activities and regulation of and innovation in financial institutions in the United States and abroad. In this chapter, we introduce the principal types of financial institutions and describe their roles in the saving-investment process and in providing key financial services.

One question guides our analysis in this chapter. **Q:** What services do the various types of financial institutions provide to savers and borrowers?

Types of Financial Institutions

Financial institutions fall into five broad groups: (1) *securities market institutions*, made up of investment banks, brokers and dealers, and organized exchanges; (2) *investment institutions*, consisting of mutual funds and finance companies; (3) *contractual saving institutions*, including insurance companies and pension funds; (4) *depository institutions*, made up of commercial banks, savings and loan associations, mutual savings banks, and credit unions; and (5) *government financial institutions*. Actually, securities market institutions aren't intermediaries but help financial markets function smoothly. The four remaining types of financial institutions *are* financial intermediaries. Table 12.1 shows that they have combined assets of $13.5 trillion, making them extremely important components of the financial system. In this chapter we examine the role played by each type of institution in the financial system. Depository institutions are the topic of the next four chapters, in which we analyze the business of banking, the banking industry, and banking regulation in more detail.

If all financial institutions are involved in matching savers and borrowers or in providing risk-sharing, liquidity, and information services, how do they differ? Mutual funds provide diversified portfolios of financial assets

TABLE 12.1	**FINANCIAL INTERMEDIARIES IN THE UNITED STATES[†]**
Class of institution	**Assets ($ billions)**
Mutual funds	
Money market mutual funds	548
Other mutual funds	1057
Finance companies	809
Insurance companies	
Life insurance companies	1625
Property and casualty companies	629
Pension funds	
Private pension funds	2347
State and local government retirement funds	988
Depository institutions	
Commercial banks	3629
Savings and loan associations	832
Mutual savings banks	245
Credit unions	266
Government financial institutions	550
Source: Board of Governors of the Federal Reserve System, *Flow of Funds Accounts: Flows and Outstandings,* March 10, 1993.	$13.5 trillion
[†]Data are as of December 31, 1992.	

to savers, which usually are more liquid than the underlying assets. Finance companies raise funds in financial markets to lend to households and firms. Insurance companies and pension funds provide important intermediary services by offering financial contracts for saving and risk pooling. Depository institutions raise money through liquid deposits issued to households and firms and make loans to households and firms. Government financial institutions use government subsidies and loan guarantees to encourage certain types of lending.

Securities Market Institutions

In Chapter 10, we pointed out that well-functioning markets for bonds, stocks, and other financial instruments enable the financial system to communicate information needed for saving, investment, and portfolio allocation decisions. **Securities market institutions**—in particular, investment banks, brokers and dealers, and organized exchanges—help securities markets to function smoothly. These institutions are not intermediaries because they don't acquire funds from savers in order to lend to borrowers. However, they do assist financial markets in channeling funds from savers to borrowers and in providing risk-sharing, liquidity, and information services to savers and borrowers.

We discuss securities market institutions in two steps. First, we consider the role that investment banks play in gathering information and helping borrowers raise funds in primary markets for debt and equity. Then, we analyze the contributions of brokers, dealers, and organized exchanges in providing liquidity in secondary markets. Liquid secondary markets provide information to savers and borrowers as well as risk-sharing services for savers.

Information: Investment Banking

Investment banks assist businesses in raising new capital in primary markets, and advise them on the best way to do so: issuing shares or structuring debt contracts. One way in which investment bankers earn income is by **underwriting** a firm's new capital. This entails guaranteeing a price to the issuing firm, selling the issue at a higher price, and keeping the profit, known as the *spread*. In exchange for this spread, the investment bank must assume the risk of not being able to resell the securities to investors.

For this reason, very risky new issues may not be sold in this manner. The risk of price fluctuations may cause investment banks to be wary of making a fixed commitment to the issuing firm. One alternative to guaranteeing the price is for the investment bank to sell the issue on an *all or none* basis. In this case, the company issuing the securities receives nothing unless the complete issue is sold at the offering price. Another alternative, called *best efforts*, allows the investment bank to make no guarantee, requiring it to sell to investors only as much of the issue as it can.

Relatively small issues may be handled by a single underwriter, whereas large issues are handled by groups of underwriters called **syndicates**. In a syndicated sale, the lead underwriter acts as manager and keeps part of the spread. The remainder of the spread goes to group members buying the issue and to firms selling the issue to the public. Investment bankers market new issues to institutional investors (such as pension funds or insurance companies) or to individual savers through advertisements in *The Wall Street Journal* (see the Using the news box). Leading underwriters include major securities firms, such as Merrill Lynch, Goldman Sachs, and First Boston.

Underwriting lowers information costs in the saving-investment process. Investment banks put their reputations behind the firms they underwrite, giving investors more confidence about a new issue (see Box 12.1). In addition, information disclosure and fraud prevention have been the focus of regulation. Public issues in the United States must be registered with the Securities and Exchange Commission (SEC), a federal government regulatory body authorized by the Securities and Exchange Acts of 1933 and 1934, in response to disreputable underwriting practices in the

---

Consider this...   ▼ BOX 12.1

Investment Banking: A Risky Business in the 1980s and 1990s

During the 1980s, risks associated with underwriting rose because of the higher volatility of interest rates. At the same time, underwriting fees dropped. This occurred in large part because of SEC Rule 415, which allows a firm to register a new issue with the SEC and then wait as long as two years before selling it. During the waiting period, issuers can sell securities when underwriting fees are expected to be low, thus fostering competition. An additional competitive feature of Rule 415 is that issuers may choose an underwriter after registration, permitting the firm greater flexibility in bargaining with investment bankers. In the mid-1980s, bargaining led to reductions in fee income for underwriters, encouraging them to hold larger positions in bonds than they could underwrite on their own account.

Investment banks during the 1980s also engineered corporate restructurings, mergers, and acquisitions in which substantial amounts of the firms' equity were bought with risky bonds. Investment banks helped financiers raise large amounts of risky debt through junk bonds, bonds with ratings of less than Baa (Moody's Investor Service) or BBB (Standard and Poor's). Michael Milken of Drexel Burnham Lambert helped develop a liquid secondary market in these securities. Drexel Burnham, along with other major underwriters such as Merrill Lynch, Goldman Sachs, First Boston, and Lehman Brothers, helped financiers raise large amounts of money through junk bonds. (Drexel Burnham filed for bankruptcy in 1990.) Also in the 1980s, investment banks engaged in *merchant banking;* that is, they placed their own funds at risk by investing in firms undergoing restructuring.

In the 1990s, investment banks have become masters of "deleveraging," helping firms raise equity in public markets to reduce their debt burdens. This illustrates how successful investment bankers develop innovative ways to meet the needs of savers and borrowers.

Using the news...

A Tombstone for Something New?

To learn about major financial offerings arranged by investment banks, you need only consult *The Wall Street Journal*. Advertisements for offerings—known as *tombstones*—state the size and price of the issue and the investment banks involved. In the tombstone shown here, Lehman Brothers, Alex Brown & Sons, and Salomon Brothers, respected U.S. investment banking firms, are managing the sale of 2,875,000 shares of stock in the BISYS Group, Inc.

The fact that some of the offering is being sold to foreign investors abroad through overseas affiliates of the investment banking firms underscores the importance of international borrowing and lending in today's financial system.

Courtesy of The BISYS Group, Inc.

1920s. Firms are required to file a prospectus with the SEC disclosing information on long-term issues of publicly traded securities.

▶ C H E C K P O I N T *Why do many issuers of bonds and stocks use underwriters?* The reason is that an important part of the underwriting process is information collection and communication. Investment bankers collect information on issuing firms and put their reputations on the line in issues they manage. This role is particularly valuable for issuers who are less well-known to small investors than to the major investment banking firms. ◀

Liquidity and Risk Sharing: Secondary Markets

For savers and borrowers, the need for liquidity motivates participation in secondary markets. Recall that the theory of portfolio allocation states that, holding other determinants of asset demand constant, the more liquid a financial claim, the lower is its required rate of return. In addition to being valued by savers, liquidity reduces costs for borrowers: The greater the liquidity of a financial claim, the lower are the transactions costs of buying or selling it.

Brokers and Dealers.   In secondary markets, brokers and dealers bring together buyers and sellers of securities for a fee. Because these traders intercede between buyers and sellers, the buyer-seller relationship is said to be at "arm's length." **Brokers** earn commissions by matching buyers and sellers in a particular market. **Dealers** hold inventories of securities and sell them for a price higher than they paid for them, earning the spread between the bid and asked price. The largest firms in securities markets, such as Merrill Lynch or Dean Witter, act as both brokers *and* dealers (and often as investment bankers as well). The fortunes of broker-dealers rise and fall with stock and bond prices and trading opportunities. Returns on U.S. broker-dealer equity were 40% in 1982, fell to zero by 1990, and rebounded to high levels in 1991 and 1992.

The SEC strictly regulates brokers and dealers to ensure disclosure of information, prevent fraud, and restrict trading based on **insider information.** Insider information is not known by the general public but only by those who possess it because of their status or positions within the firms involved in the transactions. From the 1930s until 1975, the SEC also regulated brokerage commissions. As a result of increased competition since 1975, investors pay significantly lower commissions—especially large institutional investors and individual investors using discount brokers. Discount brokers such as Charles Schwab offer lower commissions but fewer services (for example, no investment information libraries and minimal advice) than those offered by full-service firms such as Merrill Lynch. Trading volume expanded dramatically after commissions were lowered in 1975. Similarly, deregulation of commissions in England in 1986 (known as the "big bang") as well as in Canada (1983), Australia (1984), France (1988), and the Netherlands (1990) expanded trading volume. Japan began studying such a move in the early 1990s.

Exchanges.   Securities may be traded in one of two ways: through exchanges or in over-the-counter markets. An **exchange** is a physical location at which securities are traded. Essentially, an exchange acts as an auction market for securities: assets are bought from the offerer of the lowest price and sold to the bidder of the highest price. Exchanges don't set prices but provide a way for buyers and sellers of financial assets to trade anonymously, lowering information costs for savers.

The best-known U.S. exchanges are the New York Stock Exchange (NYSE) and the American Stock Exchange (AMEX) in New York. There are also various regional exchanges. The exchanges themselves, together with the SEC, regulate trading practices and enforce prohibition of inside trading. Around the world there are 142 exchanges. Among the oldest and best known (with their dates of formal establishment) are London (1773), Paris (1802), Tokyo (1818), and Sydney (1872).

Where a stock is listed for trading depends largely on the firm's size. The securities of the oldest and largest U.S. firms are listed on the NYSE; those of less well-known firms are listed on the AMEX; and those of the smallest and youngest business firms are traded in over-the-counter markets, which we discuss shortly.

In the New York Stock Exchange, buyers and sellers are matched on the floor of an exchange by a broker-dealer known as a **specialist,** who represents one or more stocks (see Box 12.2). For example, suppose that you place an order for 100 shares of General Motors stock. Your broker sends the order to a specialist in GM stock. As a broker, the specialist puts together buy and sell orders at the same price. Then as a dealer, the specialist uses inventory to match your buy order with someone else's sell order. The specialist system generally works well, but it can lead to a fragile market during a panic, as occurred during the stock market crash of October 19, 1987 (Chapter 10).

Over-the-Counter Markets. In **over-the-counter markets,** trading takes place over the telephone and by computer. This form of trading has grown dramatically owing to advances in computer technology. Traders keep track of the market by examining the activity in individual issues on their computer screens. Under the Securities Amendment Act of 1975, the SEC fostered development of a consolidated arrangement for trading securities: the National Market System. Member broker-dealers regulate themselves through the National Association of Securities Dealers. The National Market System provides computerized quotes through the National Association of Securities Dealers' Automated Quotation (NASDAQ) system, developed in 1971.

Trading Bonds. The market for U.S. Treasury bonds is the most liquid market in the world, with small bid-asked spreads. However, the market for most individual bonds is relatively illiquid, though some issues for prominent companies (such as GM or IBM) have liquid markets. These firms' bonds are usually traded on organized exchanges, such as the NYSE. The vast majority of secondary market trading of corporate bonds is done in over-the-counter markets. Owing to their relative illiquidity, the bid-asked spreads for corporate bonds are higher than those for U.S. government securities. For corporate bonds, the more highly rated bonds typically have lower bid-asked spreads than lower rated bonds do.

Consider this...

BOX 12.2

Will the NYSE See Its Next Centennial?

On May 17, 1992, the New York Stock Exchange celebrated its 200th birthday with great fanfare. Even as the oratory focused on the exchange's distinguished past, many analysts were concerned about its future because of increased competition.

Indeed, securities trading has become more computerized and efficient around the world, starting with the NASDAQ system in the United States. The Toronto Stock Exchange introduced CATS (Computer-Assisted Trading System) in 1977. The process of computerizing stock exchanges accelerated in the 1980s, with the introduction of a CATS-like system in the Paris Bourse and a NASDAQ-like system in the

London Stock Exchange. More recently, stock exchanges in Brussels, Madrid, and Sydney have introduced computerized trading systems. The Copenhagen Stock Exchange made perhaps the greatest strides by installing a fully computerized and integrated information, trading, clearing, and settlement system. In Switzerland, the Association Tripartite Bourse, which groups the Basel, Geneva, and Zurich exchanges, is devising a fully computerized order-matching, execution, and settle-ment system.

As a result of the revolution in computing technology, the NYSE now faces competition from many networks managed by financial services firms. In 1971, the NYSE

(an auction market) accounted for almost three-fourths of the shares traded on U.S. exchanges. In 1991 it accounted for only about half of such trades. Although auction markets can produce the best results for buyers and sellers, electronic auctions for large buyers and sellers in networks outside the NYSE can execute trades at lower cost. However, the NYSE remains important in finan-cial markets because it maintains a liquid central market for small and medium-sized investors. This suggests that, although the 1990s will certainly be a challenging period for the NYSE, it is likely to remain a useful institution well into the twenty-first century.

Investment Institutions

Investment institutions, which raise funds to invest in loans and securities, include mutual funds and finance companies.

Mutual Funds

Mutual funds are financial intermediaries that convert small indi-vidual claims into diversified portfolios of stocks, bonds, mortgages, and money market instruments by pooling the resources of many small savers.

Mutual funds obtain savers' money by selling shares in portfolios of financial assets and then using the funds of many savers to maintain and expand those portfolios. This approach benefits savers by reducing trans-actions costs. Rather than buying numerous stocks, bonds, or other finan-cial instruments individually—each with its own transactions costs—a saver can buy into all the shares in the fund with one transaction. Mutual funds provide risk-sharing benefits by offering a diversified portfolio of assets and liquidity benefits by guaranteeing to quickly buy back a savers' shares. Moreover, the fund manager specializes in gathering information about different investments.

The mutual fund industry in the United States dates back to the organization of the Massachusetts Investors Trust (managed by Massachusetts Financial Services, Inc.) in March 1924. The fund's marketing stressed the usefulness of mutual funds for achieving a diversified portfolio for retirement savings. Later in 1924, the State Street Investment Corporation was organized; in 1925, Putnam Management Company introduced its Incorporated Investment Fund. These three investment managers are still important in the mutual fund industry.

Types of Funds.   Mutual funds are operated as either closed-end or open-end funds. In **closed-end mutual funds**, a fixed number of nonredeemable shares are sold and then traded in over-the-counter markets like common stock. The price of these shares fluctuates with the value of the underlying assets. Owing to differences in the quality of fund management or the liquidity of the shares, fund shares may sell at a discount or a premium relative to the market value of the underlying assets. More common are **open-end mutual funds**, which issue redeemable shares at a price tied to the underlying value of the assets.

Most mutual funds are called **no-load funds** because they earn income only from management fees (typically about 0.5% of assets), not from sales commissions. The alternative, **load funds**, charge commissions for purchases and/or sales.

The largest category of mutual funds, with assets of $1057 billion at the end of 1992, consists of funds offering claims against portfolios of capital market instruments, such as stocks and bonds. Large mutual fund management companies, such as Fidelity, Vanguard, and Dreyfus, offer many alternative stock and bond funds.

The greatest growth in mutual funds has been in **money market mutual funds,** which hold high-quality, short-term assets, such as Treasury bills, negotiable certificates of deposit, and commercial paper. Representing only about 8% of the total mutual fund market in 1975, these funds (generally offered by the same fund management companies offering stock and bond funds) comprised more than 34% of the market by the end of 1992, with assets of $548 billion. The underlying instruments in these funds have short maturities, so their asset values do not fluctuate much. Hence the funds provide savers with a liquid account that pays market interest rates. Most money market mutual funds allow checks to be written against them (usually some minimum amount is specified).

Regulation of the Mutual Fund Industry.   Heavy losses during the stock market crash of 1929 led to calls for regulation of the mutual fund industry. With passage of the Securities Act of 1933, funds' shares had to be registered with the SEC prior to sale. The act also required disclosure to potential investors of information about portfolio holdings and investment policies and objectives. Mutual funds were prohibited from advertising anticipated returns, though they could state past returns. Although Congress and the SEC have amended the regulations governing mutual funds several times since 1933, concerns about information disclosure and fraud prevention still guide regulation. The Investment Company Act of 1940 assigned regulatory jurisdiction over mutual funds to the SEC. Subsequent regulation enhanced competition: amendments to the Investment Company Act in the 1970s reduced sales loads, and the Garn–St. Germain Act of 1982 allowed banks to offer money market deposit accounts.

In May 1992, the SEC unveiled regulatory proposals that, if adopted, would represent the most significant changes in mutual fund regulation in the United States since the 1940 Investment Company Act. One significant proposal is a requirement that the majority of the directors of any individual mutual fund be independent of the fund's sponsor, compared to 40% of the directors under existing law. (A company such as Fidelity or Vanguard offers several different funds and hence is the sponsor.) The idea is to limit the cost of administering the funds, particularly the increases in salaries that managers can vote for themselves when they sit on the board. The same proposal would amend the 1940 Act to set standards for maintaining liquidity of mutual funds and to require shareholder approval for any change in the fund's investment objectives. The SEC also proposed allowing foreign mutual funds to sell shares in the United States if the home-country regulation of those funds provides investor protection equivalent to that under U.S. law. If adopted, the SEC proposals would expand significantly the mutual funds' intermediary role in the saving-investment process.

Finance Companies

Finance companies are intermediaries that raise large amounts of money through the sale of commercial paper and securities in order to make small loans to households and businesses. These intermediaries had assets of about $800 billion at the end of 1992. Finance companies must invest in gathering and monitoring information about borrowers' default risks. Because finance companies do not issue deposits as banks do, however, federal and state governments generally have found little need for regulation beyond information disclosure and fraud prevention. However, some states regulate the terms of finance company loan contracts. The lower degree of regulation allows finance companies to provide loans more in line with the particular needs of borrowers than other, more regulated, institutions can provide.

The three main types of finance companies are consumer finance, business finance, and sales finance firms. Consumer finance companies make loans to enable consumers to buy cars, furniture, and appliances, to finance home improvements, and to refinance household debts. Finance company customers have higher default risk than good-quality bank customers do and so are charged higher interest rates.

Business finance companies are involved primarily in an activity called *factoring*, that is, purchasing accounts receivable of small firms at a discount and holding them until maturity for a profit. For example, Moneybags Finance Company might buy $100,000 of short-term accounts receivable of Axle Tire Company for $90,000—effectively lending Axle $90,000 and earning a $10,000 return when the accounts receivable are collected. Another activity of these finance companies is to purchase expensive equipment (airplanes, for example) and then lease it to businesses over a fixed length of time. Factoring loans generally are short-term, but leasing contracts can be for five years or more.

Sales finance companies are affiliated with companies that manufacture or sell goods. Their purpose is to promote the business of the underlying manufacturer or retailer. For example, General Motors Acceptance Corporation (GMAC) offers financing to customers when they buy new GM cars. Department stores issue credit cards with which customers finance purchases at those stores (Bloomingdale's or J.C. Penney, for example). This convenient credit is part of the selling effort of the manufacturer or retailer.

Contractual Saving: Insurance Companies

Some events impose significant financial hardship when they occur, such as a medical emergency, a car accident, or the death of a spouse. **Contractual saving institutions** allow individuals to pay money to transfer the risk of financial hardship to someone else (insurance) or to save in a disciplined manner for retirement (pension contributions). We discuss the first type here and the second type in the next section.

Insurance companies are financial intermediaries that specialize in writing contracts to protect their policyholders from the risk of financial loss associated with particular events. Insurers obtain funds by issuing promises to pay under certain conditions and then lend the money to borrowers. The prospect of financial hardship leads many people to pay insurance companies fees, called *premiums*, to assume risks.

In terms of premium income, U.S. insurance companies such as Allstate, Aetna, and Prudential are the largest insurers in the world. World premium volume is more than $1 trillion, with the U.S. accounting for more than one-third of the total. However, rapid growth in insurance coverage in the 1990s is likely to come from Europe, Asia, and the emerging market economies of Eastern Europe.

The insurance industry has two segments. Life insurance companies sell policies to protect households against a loss of earnings from disability, retirement, or death of the insured person. Property and casualty companies sell policies to protect households and firms from the risks of illness, theft, fire, accidents, or natural disasters. Before we analyze these two types of insurance companies, let's discuss some principles of insurance management and information collection that apply to both.

Principles of Insurance Management

At the end of 1992, the U.S. insurance industry controlled assets of more than $2.2 trillion. Insurance companies make profits from the excess of premiums over claims payments and from investments in businesses. These institutions have long been important participants in the financial system, investing policyholders' premiums in capital markets, usually in stocks, bonds, mortgages, and direct loans to firms known as *private placements*. Insurance companies have fueled U.S. industrial expansion for more than 150 years by holding capital market instruments as assets and issuing insurance policies as liabilities.

Risk Pooling.   Insurance companies can comfortably predict when and how much compensation savers will claim by taking advantage of the *law of large numbers*. This statistical concept states that, although the death, illness, or injury risks of an individual cannot be predicted, the average occurrences of any such event for large numbers of people can generally be predicted. Thus, by issuing a sufficient number of policies, insurance companies take advantage of risk pooling and diversification in order to estimate the size of reserves needed for potential claims. Statisticians known as *actuaries* compile probability tables to help predict event risk in the population.

Insurance Problems.   There is more to insurance management than simple risk pooling, however. An insurance company faces costs associated with asymmetric information because individuals or firms seeking insurance are likely to have information that it does not. Insurers also face both adverse selection and moral hazard problems. For an insurance company, adverse selection occurs when the buyers most eager to purchase insurance are individuals whose probability of experiencing the insured event over some period of time is highest. For example, if you learned that you had cancer, you probably would want to take out a generous health insurance policy. Moral hazard problems arise in insurance when individuals assume greater risk when covered by insurance than they would without it. With complete fire insurance on your business, for example, you might be tempted to save money by not buying fire extinguishers or flame-retardant office furniture. Insurance company procedures are aimed at reducing costs due to adverse selection and moral hazard.

Adverse Selection and Screening.   Because adverse selection stems from the policyholder's private information, insurance company managers develop information-gathering procedures in order to screen out poor insurance risks. If you apply for health insurance on your own (that is, not through a group plan offered by your employer), you have to provide information about your health history to the insurance company. Similarly, if you try to buy automobile insurance, you have to supply information about your driving record, including speeding tickets and accidents. When you buy life insurance—especially if you want to purchase a large policy—you have to answer detailed questions about your health history and personal habits (such as smoking and alcohol or drug use) and undergo urine and blood tests. These procedures may seem intrusive, but they are important tools for reducing problems of adverse selection. (Another approach to managing adverse selection problems is given in the Other times, other places box.)

Risk-Based Premiums.   A longstanding principle of insurance management to avoid adverse selection problems is that individuals should pay **risk-based premiums,** premiums based on the probability of their collecting claims. If Stanley Stolid applies for auto insurance with a record of no speeding tickets (he won't drive faster than 40 mph), and Gary Gunem applies to the same company with a record of 32 speeding tickets in the last 12 months, Gunem should pay a higher premium. Suppose that the Egalite Insurance Company offered both drivers the same premium, based on the average risk in the population. Stanley would say "no thanks" and buy insurance from Varyem Insurance Co. Gary would say "sure," leaving Egalite with a big potential loss. This version of the lemons problem (Chapter 11) explains why private insurance companies vary premiums according to differences in risk.

Moral hazard problems provide additional complications for managers of insurance companies. Recall that the financial system develops new financial arrangements to reduce information costs related to moral hazard.

Other times, other places...

Information: Key to the Kye?

Informal intermediaries have long been important in financing entrepreneurs in the developing and newly industrialized countries of Asia, West Africa, and the Caribbean. A good example is the Korean *kye*, or *keh*, translated traditionally as "solemn promise" or, more recently, as "cooperative."

As an intermediary, a kye works simply. An organizer invites friends and acquaintances to join and meet once a month, at which time each member contributes an agreed-upon sum of money. Each month, one group member receives the total sum, tax-free

and interest-free, to use as an investment. Liquidity is limited, but kye contributions are returned when the kye dissolves (say, in 12 months for a 12-member kye). Kye members share the risk involved in establishing a new business by investing in different types of businesses: If one member's business fails, each investor bears only a fraction of the total loss. The kye eliminates information costs related to adverse selection by restricting membership to "known" individuals. Moral hazard problems are reduced because individuals know that misusing kye funds

would bring shame on the individual and his or her family.

Kye arrangements have grown in South Korea during the past two decades because banks, under tight government regulations, lend only to large corporate borrowers. As these restrictions are lifted during the 1990s, banks will lack expertise in reducing information costs in lending. In fact, certain conventional Korean banking institutions failed in the early 1990s. Recent growth in conventional mortgage lending in Korea has been led by America's Citibank.

For insurance companies, these arrangements include such policy provisions as deductibles, coinsurance, and restrictive covenants.

Deductibles.   One way to ensure that the policyholder exercises some care to prevent the insured event is to place some of the policyholder's own money at risk. Insurance companies do so by requiring a **deductible**, that is, a specified amount to be deducted from the policyholder's loss when a claim is paid. A $500 deductible in your health insurance or automobile insurance policy, for example, holds you responsible for the first $500 of claimable expenses; the insurance company will pay the rest. The use of deductibles enables an insurance company to help align policyholders' interests with its own. Because deductibles reduce costs associated with moral hazard, insurance companies are able to lower the premiums that policyholders must pay.

Coinsurance.   Although the policyholder is at risk for the amount of a deductible, the insurance company is still responsible for 100% of all allowable claims above that amount. To give the policyholder further incentive to hold down costs, insurance companies may offer **coinsurance** as an option. This option requires the policyholder to pay a certain percentage of the costs of a claim in addition to the deductible amount. For example, when you choose among the health insurance options available through your employer, some may offer you a lower premium in exchange for agreeing to pay, say, 20% of insured expenses after you pay the deductible. Hence coinsurance helps align policyholders' interests with the company's.

Restrictive Covenants.   To cope with moral hazard problems, insurers also sometimes use **restrictive covenants,** which limit risky activities by the insured if a subsequent claim is to be paid. For example, a fire insurance company may refuse to pay your business's claim if you didn't install and maintain smoke alarms, fire extinguishers, or a sprinkler system in accordance with your contract. By forcing the policyholder to restrict risky activities in order to claim insured losses, restrictive covenants are a valuable management tool in helping insurance companies reduce moral hazard problems.

Other Insurance Policy Provisions.   Insurance companies use various methods to reduce the costs associated with moral hazard. First, most insurance involves a limit on individual claims paid, such as the lifetime claim limit imposed by health insurance companies. Second, insurance companies reserve the right to cancel policies if the policyholder engages in excessively risky behavior. Finally, insurance companies safeguard against fraud—as, for example, when policyholders seek reimbursement for theft or medical expenses that never took place—by hiring seasoned claims adjustors to investigate claims.

Life Insurance Companies

Life insurance companies provide insurance (and savings plans) to protect against financial hardship for the policyholder's survivors. In the United States in 1992, some 2300 life insurance firms had assets totaling more than $1.6 trillion. Two types of firms characterize this industry: (1) *mutual companies*, which are owned by the policyholders; and (2) *stock companies*, which are owned by the shareholders. The largest U.S. life insurance firms are mutual companies, which account for over half the industry's assets. However, these large companies represent only 10% of all life insurance companies; more than 90% are organized as stock companies.

Most policies issued are *whole life* or *term life*. For whole life insurance, the policyholder pays a constant premium over the life of the policy; cash value accrues in early periods and declines subsequently as the risk of death rises. Whole life insurance provides an investment vehicle for savers: Policyholders can borrow against the cash value, and individuals can either withdraw the total *cash value* at retirement or turn that value into annual payments, known as *annuities*. Saving through whole life insurance receives favorable tax treatment in the United States: Accumulated returns from investing the premiums are not taxed. This favorable treatment has particularly encouraged the growth of saving through annuities provided by most insurance companies. In addition, they allow the saver to withdraw accumulated savings in a lump sum at retirement, thereby deferring taxes on the accumulated investment income.

Term life insurance, by contrast, pays off only at the death of the policyholder; the policies have no cash value. Hence premiums reflect only the probability of the policyholder's dying during the insured interval, or term. During the past decade, investment opportunities with higher returns than those on whole life investments have become increasingly available for households. For this reason and because of investor concern about the financial condition of insurers, term life insurance has been growing in popularity relative to whole life insurance.

Property and Casualty Insurance Companies

Some 3800 **property and casualty insurance companies** in the United States, controlling assets of more than $600 billion at the end of 1992, provide insurance against events other than death. They also are organized as both stock and mutual companies. They sell insurance to cover such risks as theft, illness, fire, earthquakes, and car accidents. Premiums charged reflect the risk being insured. For example, high-risk drivers pay more than low-risk drivers for automobile insurance.

The asset portfolios of property and casualty insurance companies differ from those of life insurance companies. Because events such as fires or earthquakes are more difficult to predict statistically than death rates in the population, the portfolios of property and casualty insurers largely contain liquid assets, such as short-term credit market instruments. Another difference stems from federal income taxation. Unlike life insurance firms, property and casualty insurers pay U.S. income tax on their net income, but with allowances for tax-free reserves.[†]

Concern about a possible insurance crisis in this segment of the industry increased as claims and premiums rose dramatically during the 1980s. Proposals for reform address the ways in which certain lawsuits—particularly for negligence or malpractice—are settled. One troubling aspect of the situation is that insurance companies may turn to riskier assets or activities to increase their current returns, raising further concerns about their financial fragility. Figure 12.1 shows the financial investments of life insurance and property and casualty insurance companies.

▶   C H E C K P O I N T   *The earnings on savings through whole life insurance policies are not taxed. The policy provides both insurance (it pays a benefit when the policyholder dies) and savings (policyholders can cash in the policy prior to death). If the investment earnings on policy contributions were taxed, what would happen to the relative demand for term life and whole life policies? Savers would likely increase their demand for term life policies and decrease their demand for whole life policies because the savings component of the latter would no longer enjoy a tax advantage relative to other types of saving.* ◀

Regulation of Insurance Companies

State governments regulate insurance companies, usually through state insurance commissioners. Regulation focuses on portfolio disclosure rules (to resolve problems of information), examination against fraud, restriction of the amount of risky assets held by the company, and premium rates. Concern over financial solvency of insurance companies has prompted calls for federal regulation.

Contractual Saving: Pension Funds

For most people, saving for retirement is the most important form of saving. Retirement saving can be accomplished in two ways: through pension funds sponsored by employers or through personal savings accounts.

[†] Historically, these companies were allowed a deduction for funds set aside for future obligations, and much of their income was tax-exempt income in the form of interest on state and local government securities, for example. The U.S. Tax Reform Act of 1986 restricted these deductions, though property and casualty companies are still more lightly taxed than manufacturing companies are.

>FIGURE 12.1

Financial Assets of U.S. Insurance Companies†
The differing mix of assets held by life insurance companies and property and casualty insurance companies reflects the difference in risk-sharing services they provide.

† The data are as of December 31, 1992. Assets are listed by type and by percentage of total funds invested.

Source: Federal Reserve, Flow of Funds Accounts.

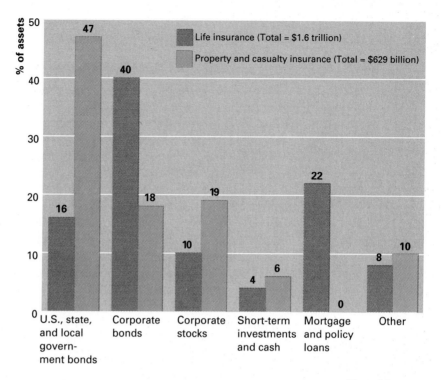

Financial assets

Pension funds invest contributions of workers and firms in stocks, bonds, and mortgages to provide for pension benefit payments during workers' retirement. Representing about $3.2 trillion in assets in the United States at the end of 1992, private and state and local government pension funds are the largest institutional participants in capital markets. With about one-fifth of all U.S. financial assets under their control, pension funds hold about 30% of the nation's publicly traded equities and about 25% of the value of corporate bonds.

Like insurance companies, pension funds are not deposit-taking intermediaries. An employee's right to pension benefits from employer contributions depends on whether the employee is vested. *Vesting* refers to the length of service required before an employee is entitled to future benefits, and the required amount of time varies among plans.

Employees may prefer to save through pension plans provided by employers rather than through savings accounts for three reasons. First, pension funds may be able to manage a financial portfolio more efficiently, with lower transactions costs, than employees can. Second, pension funds may be able to provide benefits such as life annuities, which are costly for individual savers to obtain. Third, the special tax treatment of pensions can make pension benefits more valuable than cash wages to employees.[†]

Ownership of Pension Funds Assets

A key distinction among pension plans is whether they are organized on the basis of *defined contributions* or *defined benefits*. In a **defined contribution plan**, contributions are invested for the employees, who own the value of the funds in the plan. If the pension plan's investments are profitable, pension income during retirement will be high, and vice versa. The pension fund for college professors is an example. It invests pension contributions in stocks, bonds, mortgages, and money market instruments. Pension assets in *Employee Stock Ownership Plans*, or ESOPs, are invested primarily in employer securities. The value of pension assets depends on the performance of the firm, as measured by the value of employer securities. Such plans are designed to do more than help employees accumulate savings for retirement; they also may increase productivity by providing employees with a stake in company profitability.

Other types of defined contribution plans in which employers or employees contribute an amount based on earnings are more diversified. In some plans, contributions are invested in a pool similar to a mutual fund. In others, participants may choose to allocate their assets among a limited number of investment funds. For example, a plan might offer three investment choices: one that purchases U.S. Treasury securities, a second that purchases private bonds, and a third that purchases a portfolio of common stocks.

In a **defined benefit plan**—the more common type for most employees, particularly those in unions—the employee is promised an assigned benefit based on earnings and years of service. The benefit payments may or may not be indexed for inflation. If the funds in the pension plan exceed the amount promised, the excess accrues to the issuing firm or institution. If the funds in the pension plan are insufficient to pay the promised benefit, the issuing firm is liable for the difference.

Funding of Pension Plans

The principal difference between defined contribution and defined benefit plans is the method of **plan funding** used to guarantee retirement benefits. For a defined contribution plan, funding is not an issue. By definition, these plans are *fully funded* by the employees who make the contributions and receive the returns on them. However, a defined benefit plan is fully

[†] Your contribution to a pension fund can be excluded from your current income for tax purposes; your employer's matching contribution is tax-deductible for your employer. In addition, you can't be taxed on the investment earnings of a pension fund. Your taxation is deferred until you receive your pension benefits. You also have the option of transferring certain pension benefit payments into an Individual Retirement Account (IRA) or other favorable distribution plan, which can reduce the tax you would otherwise owe on a lump-sum payment.

funded only when the contributions, together with the projected future earnings, are sufficient to pay the projected assigned benefits. If the plan lacks these resources, it is *underfunded*. For a private firm, an underfunded defined benefit plan represents a shareholder liability; an underfunded public plan represents a taxpayer liability. As the efficient market hypothesis would predict, the stock market lowers the value of the shares of firms with underfunded pension liabilities because those liabilities reduce the firms' value.

▶ C H E C K P O I N T *In the United States, direct ownership of equities supposedly is concentrated in the hands of the wealthiest individuals. One argument against this claim is that workers collectively own large amounts of stock through their companies' pension plans. Is this reasoning correct? Yes, for defined contribution plans, in which plan participants own the assets of the plan. However, more workers are covered by defined benefit plans. Because benefits are contractually specified, participants in these plans neither benefit from an increase in the market valuation of the pension plan's portfolio nor lose from a decrease in the market valuation. The shareholders of the firm benefit or lose, respectively. Hence participation in pension plans that own shares does not imply concentration of equity ownership in the hands of workers.* ◀

Regulation of Private Pension Plans

Because retirements are predictable, pension funds can invest in long-term capital market instruments. Indeed, private pension plans invest most of their assets in long-term bonds, mortgages, and stocks. Figure 12.2 summarizes the portfolios of pension funds. Disclosure of the composition of pension fund portfolios reduces information costs for both defined contribution and defined benefit plans. For defined contribution plans, regulations governing information provision and statutes for protection against fraud and mismanagement are sufficient. However, for defined benefit plans, the problem of underfunding raises additional regulatory concern. In response to difficulties in administering pension plans, Congress passed the Employee Retirement Income Security Act

▼ **FIGURE 12.2**

Assets of Pension Funds
Pension funds concentrate their investments in long-term capital market instruments.

† Data are as of December 31, 1992.

Source: Federal Reserve's Flow of Funds Accounts.

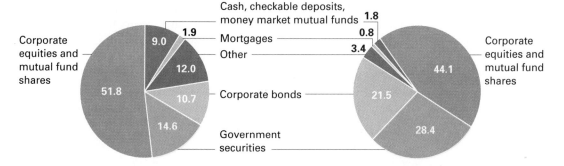

Private Pension Funds

State and Local Government Pension Funds

Cash, checkable deposits, money market mutual funds **1.8**
Mortgages **0.8**
Other **3.4**

Corporate equities and mutual fund shares

1.9
9.0
12.0
10.7
14.6
51.8

44.1
21.5
28.4

Corporate equities and mutual fund shares

Corporate bonds

Government securities

(ERISA) in 1974. This landmark legislation set national criteria for pension plan vesting and funding, restricted plans' ownership of certain types of risky investments, and enacted standards for information reporting and disclosure.

The act authorized creation of the Pension Benefit Guaranty Corporation (PBGC, or "Penny Benny") to insure pension benefits up to a limit if a company cannot meet its unfunded obligations (because of bankruptcy, for example). The PBGC charges companies a premium on pension liabilities and has an implicit line of credit from the U.S. Treasury.

Public Pension Plans

Like private companies, governments provide pension plans for their employees. At the federal level, these include civil service and military plans. (Social Security is a general retirement benefit plan.) State and local governments also provide plans, which closely resemble private plans, for their employees. In the late 1980s, underfunding became an important problem in many states, resulting in downgrading of bond ratings for some states.

Depository Institutions

Depository institutions are commercial banks, savings and loan associations, mutual savings banks, and credit unions. These institutions accept deposits and make loans, acting as intermediaries in the saving-investment process. They are introduced briefly here; their lines of business and regulation are explored in much greater detail in Chapters 13–16.

Commercial Banks

Commercial banks are financial intermediaries that offer risk-sharing, liquidity, and information services that benefit savers and borrowers. Savers obtain risk-sharing benefits from banks' diversified portfolios of loans; borrowers can obtain needed funds to finance the purchase of cars, inventories, or plants and equipment. Banks also provide liquidity services through checking accounts, which are available on demand.

Banks have stiff competition from other financial institutions in the provision of risk-sharing and liquidity services. Today, savers can deposit their cash in a money market fund that invests say, in Treasury bills, a transaction limited to large savers in the past. Savers can also purchase a diversified portfolio by buying shares in a mutual fund. However, many borrowers can't raise funds easily through bond or stock markets or other nonbank financial institutions. Commercial banks thus serve a special function in providing credit to particular types of borrowers by reducing the transactions and information costs of lending.

Transactions Costs. One reason that borrowers with small or medium-sized credit needs do not rely on stock or bond markets is the transactions costs associated with issuing such securities. A significant component of these costs is fixed (for example, payments for SEC registration and investment bankers' services), so the average cost per dollar of funds raised may be too high to justify the effort. Averaging about 4% of funds raised for large issues of stock or bonds (say, more than $50 million), these costs can range from 13% to 20% for small issues (say, $500,000 or less).

Information Costs. High information costs also restrict access to financial markets for households and small and medium-sized businesses. In fact, the most significant reason for the existence of commercial banks is their ability to reduce *information costs*. Recall that investors face high information costs in coping with adverse selection and moral hazard problems in financial markets. Banks, on the other hand, specialize in gathering information about borrowers' default risk, thereby reducing the severity of adverse selection problems. In the United States, bank loans are the dominant method of external finance for small and medium-sized firms but are much less important for large firms. This pattern holds for most industrialized countries. Banks reduce information costs associated with moral hazard by monitoring borrowers' activities. For the small saver to monitor borrowers' activities would be cumbersome and expensive. Banks act as *delegated monitors* for many individual savers and lenders who deposit their funds with the bank.

Savings Institutions

Q: What services do the various types of financial institutions provide to savers and borrowers?

A: Financial institutions are intermediaries in the saving-investment process and/or provide risk-sharing, liquidity, and information services to savers and borrowers.

In the United States, **savings institutions** (savings and loan associations and mutual savings banks) originated as building and loan societies, in which individuals pooled money to be loaned to members to build homes. The modern savings and loan industry emerged in the 1930s as the result of regulatory actions that favored the industry as part of a general federal government policy of subsidizing home ownership. Savings institutions reduce problems of asymmetric information and default risk by requiring a downpayment to make sure that the borrower maintains an economic interest in the value of the house. These savings institutions took on relatively short-term deposits to finance long-term home mortgages, thereby exposing themselves to risk in the event of market interest rate fluctuations. The mismatch of maturity assets and liabilities was a major factor in the deposit insurance crisis for U.S. savings institutions during the 1980s and early 1990s, which we address in Chapter 15.

Credit Unions

Consumer loans are subject to potentially severe private information problems and associated monitoring costs. **Credit unions** are another specialized intermediary in consumer lending, taking deposits from and making loans to individuals well-known to one another, who typically work at the same firm or in the same industry. Except for relatively small consumer loans, credit union assets are invested primarily in mortgage loans to members. The fact that the profits earned by credit unions are exempt from income taxes increases their attractiveness to savers in comparison with banks.

Table 12.2 presents a summary of the risk-sharing, liquidity, and information services offered by private financial intermediaries.

▶ C H E C K P O I N T *Why are mutual funds more likely to invest in stocks, bonds, or Treasury securities than in loans to households and small businesses, which is the business of banks?* Most mutual funds issue very liquid claims to savers, so they invest in assets that can be bought and sold with low transactions costs. Because converting loans to households and small businesses into marketable securities is costly, investors in mutual funds would face the risk of having assets sold at a discount to meet withdrawal demands. ◀

Government Financial Institutions

The U.S. government participates in financial intermediation both *directly*, through government-sponsored financial institutions, and *indirectly*, through guarantees of loans made by private financial intermediaries.

Direct Role: Federal Credit Agencies

Federal credit agencies are **government financial institutions** that engage in certain lending activities in the interest of public policy. At the end of 1992, they held more than $500 billion of assets. The three leading areas of involvement are agricultural finance, housing finance, and student loans.

Government lending to farmers is the oldest form of U.S. government involvement in financial intermediation. The Farm Credit System issues bonds and commercial paper in financial markets and uses the proceeds to make crop, equipment, and mortgage loans to farmers. Made up of a network of regional Banks for Cooperatives, Federal Land Banks, and Federal Intermediate Credit Banks, the Farm Credit System required a multibillion taxpayer bailout in 1987, as farm loan defaults soared.

Government involvement in intermediation for housing is the largest of the government lending activities. The Federal National Mortgage Association (FNMA, or "Fannie Mae"), the Federal Home Loan Mortgage Company (FHLMC, or "Freddie Mac"), and the Government National Mortgage Association (GNMA, or "Ginnie Mae") are government agencies that issue bonds in financial markets and use the proceeds to supply funds to the mortgage market. Only GNMA is a federal agency, but the others are federally sponsored agencies. Although their debt is not explicitly guaranteed by the federal government, most market participants believe that the Treasury would not permit FNMA or FHLMC to default on their obligations.

To encourage lending to students for educational expenses, the government created the Student Loan Market Association (SLMA, or "Sallie Mae") to purchase student loans made by private financial intermediaries

TABLE 12.2   SERVICES PROVIDED BY PRIVATE FINANCIAL INTERMEDIARIES

Financial institution	Risk sharing	Liquidity	Information
Commercial banks	Offer claims on diversified portfolios of assets, reducing transactions costs for individual savers	Offer liquid claims on portfolios of assets, as well as some less liquid saving methods	Offer lower transactions and information costs than financial markets for many savers and borrowers; specialize in resolution of adverse selection and moral hazard problems
Savings institutions	Similar to banks	Similar to banks	—
Credit Unions	Similar to banks	Similar to banks	Similar to banks
Investment banks	—	Participate in securities trading	Evaluate securities in the underwriting process and advise firms on corporate finance
Securities firms	Similar to banks, but with money market accounts	Participate in securities trading; offer liquid claims on portfolios of money and capital instruments	—
Mutual funds	Similar to banks, but with money market accounts	Offer liquid claims on portfolios of money and capital instruments	—
Finance companies	—	—	Collect information for credit analysis for borrowers (often similar to bank borrowers)
Insurance companies	Offer advantages of risk pooling against financial hardship from death or specified unforeseen events	— —	Gather and monitor information on policyholders and on some of the less well-known firms to which they lend
Pension funds	Offer claims on (typically) diversified portfolio of assets for retirement saving	—	—

under the auspices of the guaranteed Student Loan Program. In the late 1980s and early 1990s, SLMA experienced significant losses from loan defaults. In 1993, the Clinton administration proposed to replace the government's guaranteed-student-loan program (at the core of Sallie Mae's business) with a new direct-loan program.

In the early 1990s, many analysts questioned the advisability of maintaining or increasing the government's direct involvement in financial intermediation. Private financial institutions have complained about the inroads of federally sponsored credit agencies into mortgage and other lending activities.

MOVING FROM THEORY TO PRACTICE...

THE WALL STREET JOURNAL JUNE 19, 1992

Federal Credit Agencies: Is "Too Much" Lending Possible?

With assets of $147 billion, Fannie Mae is the nation's fourth largest financial institution. It has muscled into this position by zealously protecting government-backed privileges that enable it to borrow at low interest rates and underprice its private competition in the huge secondary market for mortgages.

Recently, those privileges have come under threat. Many in Congress want to tighten controls on Fannie Mae and its little brother, the Federal Home Loan Mortgage Corp. (Freddie Mac). The reason: The billions in mortgage securities the two companies have issued represent a potential liability to the U.S. taxpayer of more than $800 *billion,* according to estimates by the Office of Management and Budget. But the profits from the two companies go to private investors.

"They have a sweet deal" says Rep. J.J. Pickle, a Texas Democrat. "The risk is 99% public, and the profit is 100% private."

Fannie Mae and Freddie Mac pump money into housing markets in two ways. They either purchase mortgages and hold them in their portfolios, or they "securitize" mortgages by using them as collateral for mortgage-backed securities. These instruments, on which Fannie Mae and Freddie Mac guarantee payment of interest and principal, turn mortgages into securities that can be traded or held by pension funds, banks and other investors...

The special relationships the two institutions have with the Treasury and the Federal Reserve lead most investors to assume that the U.S. government would help them out of any problems, and Congress did bail out the Farm Credit System in 1987. This implied guarantee lowers borrowing costs an estimated third of a percentage point below what the most credit-worthy private corporations pay. (Some of that savings is passed on to the public through lower rates, while some helps ensure investors a profit.)

Fannie Mae and Freddie Mac—which are publicly held—don't have to pay state and local income taxes, and they don't have to register their securities with the Securities and Exchange Commission. The Treasury estimates these exemptions are worth $2 billion to $4 billion annually—benefits also shared by shareholders and by home buyers.

Their financial strength has enabled Fannie Mae and Freddie Mac to provide a steady stream of mortgage finance during a decade when thousands of banks and thrifts failed. Volatile interest rates and costly new regulations have made banks and thrifts less willing to hold mortgages and more eager to sell them. As a result, the residential mortgage markets are becoming increasingly federalized, with mortgage terms set by Fannie Mae and Freddie Mac...

Fannie Mae and Freddie Mac both had troubles in the 1980s. Fannie Mae showed heavy losses early in the decade amid surging interest rates, and Freddie Mac bungled a big multifamily housing program. But no bailout was needed, and since then, both have boosted the capital they hold to offset potential losses, tightened underwriting standards and taken other safety steps...

[A recent bill] would require them to hold capital equal to 2.5% of their assets and 0.45% of their guarantees to purchase mortgages and make payments on securities. That compares with a 5%-of-assets minimum for well-capitalized banks...

ANALYZING THE NEWS...

Federal credit agencies, known sometimes as government-sponsored enterprises, are increasingly important financial intermediaries. This situation is particularly true in housing finance. Fannie Mae and Freddie Mac purchase mortgages and sell packages of mortgages as securities, after guaranteeing payment of interest and principal.

(a) Private financial institutions develop to fill particular niches in matching savers and borrowers and to provide particular risk-sharing, liquidity, and information services to savers. Government financial institutions develop to fill important niches not filled by private intermediaries or to advance public policy objectives, such as promoting home ownership. The activities of Fannie Mae and Freddie Mac have lowered mortgage costs for home buyers and generated significant profits for their shareholders.

(b) The implicit government guarantees leave taxpayers exposed to the risk of losses when the value of federal credit agencies' mortgages fall (when market interest rates rise, for example). This taxpayer risk is compounded by the fact that private lenders have found it more difficult to compete with federal credit agencies.

(c) Is this expanding intervention a win-win situation, raising profits and implementing the public purpose? Not likely. As we showed in this chapter and Chapter 11, one purpose of financial arrangements is to make sure that borrowers or insured individuals have appropriate incentives to perform. If investors in mortgage securities packaged by Fannie Mae and Freddie Mac believe that they are insured, they have no incentive to monitor managers of the federal credit agencies. How can taxpayers' interests be safeguarded? One option is to require shareholders in government-sponsored enterprises to place more of their own capital at risk, giving them an incentive to monitor the managers.

For further thought...

If the federal government insured all mortgages, would the risk of fluctuating mortgage values be eliminated? Explain.

Source: Excerpted from Kenneth H. Bacon, "Privileged Position: Fannie Mae Expected to Escape Tighter Regulation," June 19, 1992, Reprinted by permission of *The Wall Street Journal,* ©1992 Dow Jones & Co., Inc. All Rights Reserved Worldwide.

The Bush administration required federally sponsored credit agencies to increase their capital as a cushion against future losses. Nonetheless, in the early 1990s proposals were being made for new agencies to administer such activities as municipal road-building loans, mortgage insurance for veterans, and insurance for pollution control bonds.

Indirect Role: Loan Guarantees

A second role for the federal government in intermediation is to guarantee loans made by private financial institutions. Such guarantees are analogous to insurance because the lender (a private financial institution) is held harmless if the borrower defaults. As with direct intermediation, loan guarantees are administered by many agencies: The Farmers Home Administration (FmHA) guarantees certain loans to farmers; the Federal Housing Administration (FHA) and the Department of Veterans Affairs (VA) guarantee certain mortgage loans; and the Department of Education guarantees student loans.

The tenfold growth in loan guarantees during the past two decades and recent increases in defaults trouble many analysts and policymakers. The reason is that overly generous loan guarantees encourage moral hazard problems that, in turn, cost taxpayers money. In the midst of the expensive bailout of federal deposit insurance in banking, the General Accounting Office (GAO) informed the Congress in 1990 that taxpayer losses from government loan guarantees may eventually exceed $100 billion.

Financial Institutions: Blurring the Lines

We have explained why various types of financial institutions—securities market institutions, investment institutions, contractual savings institutions, depository institutions, and government financial institutions—came into being and how they serve the needs of savers and borrowers. During the 1930s, laws and regulations built barriers that protected the services offered by each type of institution from competition. As deregulation of the financial services industry proceeded during the 1980s, more providers of various services emerged. As Table 12.3 shows, the services provided by different types of financial institutions now overlap greatly. For example, the equivalent of checkable deposits can be maintained not only at commercial banks, but also at savings institutions, brokerage firms, and mutual funds. Similarly, many different intermediaries offer numerous methods of money management and investment to the saver.

Common needs for the regulation of financial institutions and intermediaries emerge as distinctions among them blur. For example, transmitting information is an important activity for all financial intermediaries. When information costs are relatively unimportant, regulations guaranteeing disclosure of asset portfolios, investment management practices, and supervision and examination are likely to be sufficient. However, for financial institutions and

TABLE 12.3 WHAT FINANCIAL INSTITUTIONS DO[†]	Securities institutions		Investment institutions		Contractual savings institutions		Depository institutions		Government financial institutions
Services	Investment Banks	Securities Firms	Mutual Funds	Finance Companies	Insurance Companies	Pension Funds	Commercial Banks	Savings Institutions	
Transaction (checking) accounts		X	X				X	X	
Saving			X		X	X	X	X	
Consumer lending				X			X	X	X
Business lending				X			X		X
Mortgage lending				X			X	X	X
Security issuance	X	X							
Security trading	X	X							
Money management	X	X	X			X	X		
Insurance					X				

*Some types of banks and bank affiliates are permitted to offer these services (see Chapter 14). [†]Permissible activities as of January 1993.

intermediaries involved in reducing information costs in financial markets, such regulations alone may be insufficient. Additional regulatory interventions focusing on the lending activities of banks and insurance firms, as well as the market-making activities of securities firms and exchanges, may be necessary.

Key Terms and Concepts

Contractual saving institutions
    Coinsurance
    Deductible
    Defined benefit plan
    Defined contribution plan
    Insurance companies
    Life insurance companies
    Pension funds
    Plan funding
    Property and casualty insurance companies
    Restrictive covenants
    Risk-based premiums
Depository institutions
    Commercial banks
    Credit unions
    Savings institutions
Government financial institutions

Insider information
Investment institutions
    Closed-end mutual funds
    Finance companies
    Load funds
    Money market mutual funds
    Mutual funds
    No-load funds
    Open-end mutual funds
Securities market institutions
    Brokers
    Dealers
    Exchange
    Investment banks
    Over-the-counter market
    Specialist
    Syndicates
    Underwriting

Summary

1. Investment banks assist firms in raising funds in primary financial markets. Brokers and dealers match buyers and sellers in secondary financial markets. Financial instruments such as stocks and bonds are traded in organized exchanges and over-the-counter markets. The Securities and Exchange Commission is the primary regulator of securities market institutions.

2. Mutual funds convert small individual claims into diversified portfolios of money and capital market instruments. In addition to providing diversification, funds economize on costs associated with securities transactions.

3. Finance companies make loans to consumers and firms with funds they raise in money and capital markets. Some such firms—sales finance companies—are tied to companies that manufacture or sell goods.

4. Life insurance companies and property and casualty insurance companies provide risk-sharing services to savers and are large investors in financial markets. Insurance companies develop management procedures to reduce adverse selection and moral hazard problems by gathering and monitoring information about policyholders. The regulation of insurance companies centers on information disclosure and prevention of fraud.

5. Private and public pension funds invest contributions of employees and firms to provide retirement benefits. The two broad categories of pension plans are defined benefit and defined contribution plans. In a defined benefit plan, employees receive a specified schedule of benefits, irrespective of the market performance of pension fund assets. In a defined contribution plan, participants receive the returns on their contributions, accepting the residual claim on fund earnings and the associated risk.

6. Depository institutions (commercial banks, savings institutions, and credit unions) accept deposits and make loans and investments. Like mutual funds, they issue liquid deposit claims against a portfolio of loans and investments. However, as borrowers may have private information about their prospects or their plans for using the borrowed funds, lenders at arm's length face high information costs. Bank lending requires an investment in gathering and monitoring information about the borrower.

7. The U.S. government participates in financial intermediation directly, through government-sponsored financial institutions known as federal credit agencies. It is also involved indirectly, through guarantees of loans made by private financial intermediaries.

Review Questions

1. What are the five main groups of financial institutions? Which institutions belong in each group?

2. What role do underwriters play in bringing savers' funds to borrowers?

3. If you buy 100 shares of IBM stock on the New York Stock Exchange, does IBM get the money? Why or why not?

4. If you want to buy a $10,000 U.S. Treasury bond, and a securities firm sells you one from its own holdings, is it acting as a broker or as a dealer? If it arranges for you to buy one from someone else, is it acting as a broker or a dealer?

5. What are the different types of finance companies, and who uses them?

6. How do insurance companies know how high their premiums should be for life and accident insurance? What kinds of problems do they face in assessing risks?

7. Why do property and casualty insurance companies invest more heavily in short-term assets than life insurance companies do?

8. What is the advantage of saving for retirement through a pension plan at work as opposed to saving on your own?

9. How do banks address adverse selection problems?

10. What types of depository institutions specialize in loans to consumers and homeowners? How are they different from commercial banks?

11. Describe how mutual funds provide services related to risk sharing and liquidity. Distinguish a mutual fund from a bank. What do the differences you highlighted imply about the need for regulation of mutual funds as opposed to banks?

12. Why do sales finance companies exist? Why might the General Motors Acceptance Corporation at certain times offer a lower interest rate on loans to buy GM cars than commercial banks would?

Analytical Problems

13. Explain how life insurance companies and private pension funds provide risk-sharing services for savers. Why do individuals not choose to "self-insure," that is, insure their lives or retirement incomes on their own?

14. A country with restrictions on bank loan and deposit rates is more likely to develop significant markets in mutual funds for short-term claims. Would such mutual funds completely undo the interest rate regulations, that is, serve the same savers and borrowers equally well? Explain.

15. Is a compulsory government-sponsored Social Security retirement annuity system as subject to adverse selection as a private insurance company that offers individual annuity contracts? Explain.

16. What type of financial institution would each of the following people be most likely to do business with?

a. A person with $10,000 in savings who would like to earn a decent return at low risk and who does not know much about the stock and bond markets.

b. A person with $350 who needs a checking account.

c. A person who needs a $10,000 loan to open a pizza shop.

d. A person who is recently married, is starting a family, and wants to make sure that his children are well taken care of in the future.

e. The president of a small company who wants to list it on the stock exchange to obtain additional capital.

f. Someone who has just received a large inheritance and wants to invest it in the stock market.

g. A person with no credit history who is buying her first car.

h. A family needing a mortgage loan to buy a house.

i. A person who has declared bankruptcy in the past and is looking for a loan to pay off some past-due bills.

17. Suppose that you have a choice of one of three stock mutual funds. Fund One boasts an average return over the last five years of 8.33%, Fund Two has returned 8.10%, and Fund Three has earned 7.95%. You might think that Fund One is the best, but are there some reasons why Fund Two or even Fund Three might be better?

18. As an employee in a large firm, you are given the choice between a defined benefit pension plan and a defined contribution pension plan. What are the advantages and disadvantages of each?

Data Question

19. In *The Wall Street Journal* look at the listings of mutual funds. What types of funds are they, closed-end funds or open-end funds? How can you tell? Suppose that the price of a share in a mutual fund is less than the value of a share of the fund's portfolio. Should you buy into the fund?

CHAPTER 13

The Business of Banking

The managers of Russeco are awakening to the painful realities of the free marketplace after years of Soviet government support and regulation. They must address the firm's out-of-date technology, rising materials costs, and excess capacity. But Russeco is not a car maker or a steel manufacturer: It is a Russian bank. The issues that Russeco faces are little different from those that a U.S., German, or Japanese bank faces.

Banks and other financial institutions have been challenged in the 1980s and 1990s by deregulation, technological innovation, and globalization. In this chapter, we analyze the business of banking, and in the next three chapters, we discuss the banking industry's role in the financial system. The costs of using banks to channel funds from savers to investors are the transactions costs of matching borrowers and lenders and the costs of collecting and monitoring information. Despite these costs, savers and borrowers use banks as intermediaries because banks specialize in information collection and evaluation. Indeed, John Reed, a prominent banker, has referred to money in banks as "information on the move."

Commercial banks are an important segment of the U.S. economy. In early 1993, the U.S. banking industry held more than $3 trillion in assets and employed more people than the motor vehicles and equipment, steel, and petroleum industries combined. U.S. households had about one-fourth of all their financial wealth invested through banks.

In this chapter two questions are central to our exploration of banking. **Q:** What role do banks play as intermediaries in the saving-investment process? **Q:** How do banks manage the risks involved in their deposit and lending activities?

Banks as Financial Intermediaries

Banking is a business; that is, banks fill a market need for a service and earn a profit by charging customers for that service. As intermediaries, banks' primary profit-making activities entail acquiring funds at a cost from savers and lending those funds to borrowers, adding value by providing risk-sharing, liquidity, and information services. Like any business, banks try to maximize profits. The difference between the return earned from lending and the cost of obtaining the needed funds—the *spread*—represents profit. In this chapter, we describe how banks act as intermediaries.

In the United States and most developed economies, commercial banks are the leading financial intermediaries. Most payments in the U.S. economy are made by checks drawn on banks and then deposited in other banks. In this way, commercial banks play a key role in the economy's **payments system,** or the means of clearing and settling transactions. These transaction services are important for the efficient operation of the financial system and for a healthy economy.

A natural way to study the sources and uses of banks' funds, and hence banks' profit-making activities, is to look at their balance sheets. A **balance sheet** is simply a statement showing an individual's or firm's financial position at a particular time. It lists the uses of acquired funds, *assets*, the sources of funds, *liabilities*, and the difference between the two, *net worth*. Table 13.1 summarizes the consolidated balance sheet of all U.S. banks.

Bank Liabilities

Bank liabilities represent the funds acquired from savers in order to make investments or loans to borrowers. They include checkable deposits, nontransaction deposits, and borrowings.

Checkable Deposits. **Checkable deposits** are accounts that grant the depositor the right to write checks to individuals, businesses, or the government. These accounts include non–interest-bearing demand deposits, interest-bearing negotiable order of withdrawal (NOW) accounts, and super-NOW accounts. A NOW account is available to individuals and allows the owner to write checks while receiving interest; in super-NOW accounts, the owner's NOW and savings account at a bank are linked. Interest rates paid on NOW accounts are adjusted periodically. Taken together, checkable deposits account for about 25% of banks' funds, down from more than 60% in 1960. This decline reflects changes in banking regulations and the development of new financial instruments.

All checkable deposits are payable on demand. In other words, the bank must exchange a depositor's check for cash immediately, provided that the depositor has at least the amount of the check on deposit. Checkable accounts can be used easily to settle transactions involving buying goods and

TABLE 13.1	BALANCE SHEET OF U.S. COMMERCIAL BANKS, 1992[†]

Assets (uses of funds)		Liabilities (sources of funds) and net worth	
Reserves	2.1%	Checkable deposits	25.1%
Cash items in process of collection	3.5	Nontransaction deposits	
		Savings deposits	23.5
		Time deposits (CDs)	20.1
Deposits at other banks	1.1		
		Large, negotiable time deposits (CDs)	7.1
Securities	24.1		
U.S. government and agency	19.5	Borrowings (from the Federal	15.7
State and local government and other securities	4.6	Reserve, in the Federal funds market, from subsidiaries and affiliates, and through repurchase	
Loans	63.1	agreements)	
Commercial and industrial	14.0		
Mortgage	26.7	Equity capital (net worth)	8.5
Consumer	11.5		
Interbank	4.4		
Other loans	6.5		
Miscellaneous assets	6.1		

[†]Figures are expressed as a percentage of total assets for all domestically chartered commercial banking institutions in the United States as of December 30. 1992.

Source: Federal Reserve Bulletin April 1993, Table 1.25.

services. These deposits provide a liquid asset for savers; because savers value liquidity, they accept lower interest rates on checkable deposits than on less liquid instruments. Why would savers accept a zero interest rate on demand deposits when NOW accounts pay interest? One reason is that U.S. banking regulations do not permit businesses to hold NOW accounts. In addition, the interest on demand deposits is forgone by depositors because banks charge no explicit fees for checking services, whereas they often do charge fees for NOW account services.

Nontransaction Deposits. Not all bank deposits are intended to be used for day-to-day transactions. Depositors wanting to earn interest on their funds invest in **nontransaction deposits,** including savings accounts, money market deposit accounts (MMDAs), and time deposits (generally called certificates of deposit, or CDs). These liabilities accounted for about 44% of banks' funds in 1992 and were the largest source of their funds.

A generation ago, *savings accounts* (sometimes called *passbook accounts*) were the most important type of nontransaction deposit for banks. Technically, 30 days' notice may be required for a withdrawal, but this requirement is universally waived, making savings accounts, in practice, demandable. *Money market deposit accounts*, the second category of nontransaction deposits, are invested by banks. The interest rate paid to savers changes frequently with short-term yields in money markets.

Unlike savings deposits, *time deposits* have specified maturities that typically range from a few months to several years. The distinguishing feature of time deposits is a significant penalty for early withdrawal (the saver forfeits part of the accrued interest). Time deposits for less than $100,000, known as *small-denomination time deposits*, are not as liquid as savings accounts and thus pay a higher rate of interest. *Large-denomination time deposits* (for more than $100,000) are negotiable CDs and can be bought and sold in secondary markets prior to maturity. These instruments are held by financial institutions and nonfinancial corporations as alternatives to Treasury securities. Nonexistent in 1960, large-denomination CDs have become an important source of additional funds for banks.

In the United States, both transaction and nontransaction accounts at banks are covered by **federal deposit insurance,** which provides government guarantees for account balances of up to $100,000. Even though checkable and small-denomination time deposits together represent the largest single source of funds for banks, additional funds are raised by selling other instruments and securities, such as negotiable certificates of deposit, typically in large denominations. These deposits are not demandable and are riskier for savers because amounts over $100,000 are not covered by federal deposit insurance.

Borrowings.   Another important source of funds for banks is borrowings. **Borrowings,** or nondeposit liabilities, include short-term loans in the federal funds market, loans from a bank's foreign branches or other subsidiaries or affiliates, repurchase agreements, and loans from the Federal Reserve System (known as *discount loans*). Transactions in the federal funds market and through repurchase agreements have become especially important to banks. The *federal funds market* refers to the market for unsecured loans (often overnight) between banks. The interest rate on these interbank loans is called the *federal funds rate*. In *repurchase agreements* ("repos" or RPs), banks sell securities and agree to repurchase them, typically the next day. Banks use RPs to borrow funds from business firms or other banks, using the underlying securities as collateral. The corporation or other bank buying the securities earns interest, without any significant loss of liquidity. A negligible source of funds in 1960, borrowings accounted for about 16% of the funds raised by banks in 1992.

Bank Assets

Bank assets include cash items and funds used in securities investments, loans, and other holdings.

Cash Items.   The most liquid asset held by banks is **vault cash,** or cash on hand in the bank, in deposits at other banks, and in deposits with the Fed. **Reserves** consist of vault cash and banks' deposits with the Federal Reserve System. As part of its regulation of the banking system, the Fed requires that banks hold some of their deposits in non-interest-bearing accounts, known as *reserve accounts*, at a Federal Reserve bank. This reserve requirement is a tax on bank intermediation, as it bars banks from lending out all their deposits. Cash assets provide banks with the liquidity needed to meet normal outflows from demandable deposits.

A bank's claims on other banks for uncollected funds serve as assets. For example, suppose that your employer writes you a check drawn on another bank, which you deposit in your bank. Until the funds are collected, your bank holds the check as an asset, called a *cash item in process of collection*.

Small banks may hold deposits at other banks in order to obtain foreign-exchange transaction, check collection, or other services. This function, called *correspondent banking*, has diminished in importance during the past 30 years.

Cash items—reserves, cash items in process of collection, and deposits at other banks—account for about 7% of banks' assets (down from about 20% in 1960). Later in this chapter we describe how and why banks were able to make this change—and profit from it.

Securities.   **Marketable securities** are liquid assets that banks trade in securities markets. Banks are allowed to hold U.S. Treasury securities and limited amounts of municipal bonds, that is, obligations of state and local governments (see Box 13.1). Because of their liquidity, bank holdings of U.S.

Consider this...

BOX 13.1

Are Bank Holdings Sensitive to Tax Changes?

When banks decide how to allocate their funds among alternative assets, they compare expected rates of return, which are adjusted for risk, liquidity, and information characteristics. One reason for differences in expected rates of return involves differences in taxation. Commercial banks are taxed as ordinary business corporations, paying taxes on their profits and deducting interest payments and other allowed expenses.

Historically, banks could deduct interest payments to depositors even if they invested the proceeds in tax-exempt securities of state and local governments. This preferential treatment led banks to hold a significant proportion of their assets in state and local government securities. The Tax Reform Act of 1986 generally ended the deduction for such interest, beginning in 1987. The proportion of bank assets held in U.S. government securities remained steady during the 1980s at about 12%, but the proportion of bank assets devoted to state and local government securities declined significantly from 10% in 1980 to 3% by 1990. Like other investors, banks respond to changes in the tax treatment of alternative assets.

government securities are sometimes called *secondary reserves*. In the United States, commercial banks cannot invest checkable deposits in corporate bonds or common stock. Securities holdings totaled about 24% of bank assets in early 1993.

Loans.   The largest category of bank assets is **loans,** representing roughly 63% of the total in early 1993. Banks in the United States are not allowed to make a loan to a single borrower of more than 15% of the bank's capital. Loans are illiquid relative to government securities and entail greater default risk and information costs. As a result, the interest rates on loans are higher than those on marketable securities. In addition, banks make overnight loans to each other through the federal funds market.

For commercial banks, the most important types of loans are commercial, industrial, and real estate loans. Other commercial bank loans are made to consumers or overnight to other banks through the federal funds market. An important difference in the balance sheets of the principal types of depository institutions is evident in the *loans* category. Credit unions, for example, primarily make consumer loans, whereas mutual savings banks and savings and loan associations usually make home mortgage loans.

Other Assets.   This miscellaneous category covers banks' physical assets in equipment and buildings. It also includes collateral received from borrowers in default.

Bank Net Worth

Assets represent things of value that a bank owns, whereas liabilities are things of value that a bank owes to others. The difference between the two—assets minus liabilities—equals the bank's **net worth,** or equity capital. Net worth is the capital contributed by the bank's shareholders plus accumulated, retained profits. In other words, net worth (or equity capital) measures a bank's remaining value after all its liabilities have been met. Thus, as the values of a bank's assets or liabilities change in financial markets (say, because of new developments or information), a bank's net worth changes.

When savers deposit money in a bank, they expose themselves to the risk that, if the bank incurs losses from outside investments, they will lose some part of their deposits. Therefore a bank with a high net worth is appealing to investors because net worth provides a buffer against the risk of losses. This buffer is like that in other businesses, where the equity stakes of the owners are a cushion against potential losses.[†]

Bank net worth has been relatively stable during the past three decades at about 7% to 8% of total funds raised. The riskiness of bank assets

---

[†] Of course, some savers want to own equity stakes in a bank because the bank profits from intermediation. Depositors still get their promised return, and the residual accrues to the saver, a shareholder.

Other times, other places...
Banking in the 1960s and 1990s

The business of banking seems simple: A bank takes in deposits and makes loans. So long as the spread between interest rates on loans (adjusted for expected loan losses) and interest rates on deposits is positive, the banker makes a profit. However, the activities of banks have changed dramatically during the past three decades.

In 1960, banks obtained 61% of their funds from checkable deposits, with most of the remainder coming from passbook accounts. These funds were invested largely in loans for businesses, mortgages, consumer credit, and other purposes (46% of bank assets). Securities of federal, state, and local governments accounted for 31% of bank assets, with cash assets accounting for 20%.

What a difference a generation makes! In the 1990s, U.S. banks raise far less of their funds from checkable deposits, relying more on time deposits and negotiable certificates of deposit. Another dramatic change between the 1960s and the 1990s is the significant increase in borrowings from the federal funds market and through repurchase agreements.

Three changes account for these shifts in financing. First, interest rates increased, becoming volatile during the 1980s. Banks began to manage their asset and liability holdings to earn higher interest returns and reduce their exposure to risks of interest rate fluctuations. Second, in 1960, U.S. banking regulations prohibited the payment of interest on checkable deposits. As these regulations were relaxed, allowing interest payments, depositors shifted from demand deposits to interest-bearing accounts. Finally, by the 1990s, the interest rates that banks could pay depositors were fully deregulated, and banks were free to compete in the financial marketplace.

As a result, banks in the 1990s have increased the relative importance of loans in their asset portfolios. This step increased banks' exposure to credit risk as they obtained less liquid assets. The percentage of assets not held in marketable securities increased from 56% in 1960 to about 80% in the early 1990s, while bank equity capital fell from 15% of those assets in 1960 to about 8% in the early 1990s.

has increased substantially, however, with banks holding more loans relative to cash and government securities. As a result, the effective equity cushion for depositors has declined. Banks have an incentive to reduce their equity to increase their expected rate of return, whereas depositors prefer a more substantial equity cushion (see the Other times, other places box). Not surprisingly, then, bank regulation focuses on appropriate levels of bank net worth.

Bank Failure

Like other firms, banks can become financially distressed and fail. A **bank failure** occurs when a bank cannot pay its depositors in full, with enough reserves left to meet its reserve requirements. In practice, regulators can close a bank when they deem its net worth to be too low. The higher a bank's holdings of reserves, marketable securities, and/or equity capital, the less likely is the bank to fail. This reality underscores the trade-off between bank safety and returns. Being too conservative lowers bank profitability.

Q: What role do banks play as intermediaries in the savings-investment process?

A: Banks earn profits from their provision of transactions and intermediation services to savers and borrowers. Banks' balance sheets reflect their role as intermediaries. They raise funds from deposit and nondeposit sources and invest them in loans, securities, deposits at other banks, and cash assets and reserves.

How Banks Earn Profits

When a bank issues checkable deposits to finance business loans, it transforms a financial asset (a deposit) for a saver into a liability (a loan) for a borrower. Like other businesses, to profit and grow, banks take inputs, add value to them, and deliver outputs. Hence we can analyze changes in a bank's balance sheet as it enters into new contracts as we would the balance sheet of any business.

To do so, we use a simplified accounting tool known as a **T-account,** which lists changes in balance sheet items as they occur. Suppose, for example, that you decide to open a checking account at Megabank with $100 in cash. As a result, Megabank acquires $100 in vault cash, which it lists as an asset. Because you can go to the bank and withdraw your deposit at any time, Megabank must also list $100 of checkable deposits as a liability in the form of checkable deposits. The T-account looks like this:

MEGABANK

Assets		Liabilities	
Vault cash	+$100	Checkable deposits	+$100

Vault cash is part of Megabank's reserves, so the increase in deposits from your new checking account increases the bank's reserves by the same amount.

If you open your account with a $100 check from your uncle rather than with $100 in cash, the accounting process is similar. The check represents a promise from the issuing bank to pay you $100. The T-account for Megabank reflects new assets, not in the form of vault cash but in the form of cash items in the process of collection, and lists $100 in checkable deposits as a liability:

MEGABANK

Assets		Liabilities	
Cash items in the process of collection	+$100	Checkable deposits	+$100

To collect the $100, Megabank will go to your uncle's bank, Midasbank. Megabank and Midasbank have accounts with the Fed, which settles transactions among banks by adjusting their reserve account deposits. The Fed will transfer $100 of reserves to Megabank's account from Midasbank's account. The T-accounts of the two banks reflect this movement.

MEGABANK

Assets		Liabilities	
Reserves	+$100	Checkable deposits	+$100

MIDASBANK

Assets		Liabilities	
Reserves	−$100	Checkable deposits	−$100

Note the predictable link between deposits and reserves for a bank: An increase in deposits increases reserves by the same amount. A decrease in deposits decreases reserves by the same amount.

This connection between reserves and deposits helps explain how banks allocate assets and liabilities in their balance sheets to make a profit. In the preceding example, Megabank received an extra $100 in deposits. Suppose that banking regulations require Megabank to deposit 10% of its checkable deposits in a non–interest-bearing account with the Fed. These balances, known as **required reserves,** cannot be used by Megabank. However, banks may lend or invest **excess reserves,** or total reserves less required reserves. Hence, after Megabank receives the transfer of $100 from Midasbank, Megabank's T-account becomes:

MEGABANK

Assets		Liabilities	
Required reserves	+$10	Checkable deposits	+$100
Excess reserves	+$90		

Reserves kept in cash or in deposits at the Fed pay no interest. In addition, checkable deposits generate expenses for the bank: It must pay interest to depositors and pay the costs of maintaining checking accounts, including record keeping, check clearing, and so on. The bank therefore will want to use its excess reserves to generate operating income. One possibility is for the bank to lend its excess reserves. In doing so, it acquires claims on borrowers while providing savers with deposit claims.

The Relationship Between Savers and Banks

Why would savers look to banks to obtain financial assets? First, savers can hold claims against a diversified portfolio of loans through banks, thereby obtaining risk-sharing benefits. In addition, bank deposits (particularly checkable deposits) meet savers' demands for liquidity. Finally, banks are actively involved in gathering and monitoring information about borrowers. As delegated monitors, banks reduce information costs for individual savers. The role of banks in reducing information costs is particularly important, as savers could obtain risk-sharing and liquidity services from other financial intermediaries (such as mutual funds). Savers also can structure their relationships with banks to ensure that bankers do not exploit private information to savers' detriment. Figure 13.1 summarizes banks' role as financial intermediaries.

Two principal challenges are involved in the relationship between savers and banks: (1) managing moral hazard problems and (2) managing liquidity risk.

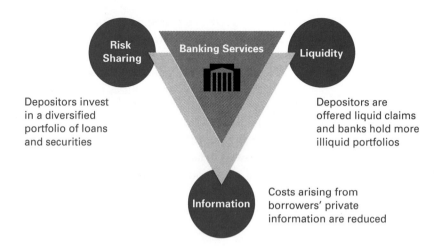

> FIGURE 13.1

Bank Intermediary Services
The risk-sharing, liquidity, and information services banks can provide give small savers and firms benefits that they could not otherwise afford.

Managing Moral Hazard Problems

Banks are important in reducing information costs for savers. Because the banker has private information about the quality and risk of the bank's loan portfolio, savers are concerned about the problem of moral hazard: Savers must ensure that bankers do not use their information in a manner detrimental to savers' interests. If the banker is a monitor, who monitors the monitor? Our analysis of solutions to moral hazard problems (Chapter 11) indicates that two important monitoring mechanisms are available: (1) investing in debt rather than equity, and (2) requiring bankers to put their own funds at risk.

Debt and Moral Hazard. Outside investors use a debt contract to exert discipline on bankers: If a bank fails to meet stipulated payments, forcing default, the banker will lose an equity stake in the bank. A short-term debt contract provides for both the liquidity needs of depositors and the discipline of bankers. Because an important component of bank liabilities are checkable deposits, the threat that savers will withdraw their funds on short notice ensures that bankers will not use their private information to their own advantage. Indeed, many economists have argued that this threat of fund withdrawal accounts for the longstanding importance of checkable deposits in financing bank lending.

Net Worth and Moral Hazard. A second way for savers to prevent problems of moral hazard is to mandate the amount of capital invested by bankers and bank shareholders. Bankers will act more responsibly when their own savings are at risk, so a rule requiring bankers and shareholders to invest their own funds increases incentives for performance. In general, the greater the banker's stake in the bank, the less severe the moral hazard problem will be. Government regulation and supervision have provided additional ways to reduce the cost of moral hazard to individual savers, as we relate in Chapters 14 and 15.

▶ **C H E C K P O I N T** *Banks economize on savers' costs of monitoring borrowers by acting as delegated monitors, but savers must guard against bankers' using their stock of private information to their own advantage. Suppose that the government guaranteed all bank deposits, without supervising banks' lending practices. What would you predict would happen to the riskiness of banks' loan portfolios?* With a full guarantee of deposits, individual savers no longer would have an incentive to monitor banks. As a result, bankers would have an incentive to take greater risks, unless large amounts of their own funds were at stake. Bankers would reap the profits from high interest rates charged to successful risky borrowers; the government would assume depositors' losses from risky loans to unsuccessful borrowers. ◀

Managing Liquidity Risk

In their dealings with savers, banks are faced with **liquidity risk**, or the possibility that depositors may collectively decide to withdraw more funds than the bank has on hand. Such withdrawals would force the bank to liquidate relatively illiquid loans and probably receive less than their full value.

The challenge to banks in managing liquidity risk in their dealings with savers is to reduce risk exposure without sacrificing too much profitability. For example, a bank can easily minimize liquidity risk exposure by holding substantial amounts of cash. However, such a strategy is not too profitable because the bank earns no interest on cash. As we noted earlier, U.S. banks are required to maintain reserves with the Federal Reserve System. Even in the absence of this regulation, exposure to liquidity risk would lead banks to hold reserves, although probably not in the form of non-interest-bearing deposits with the Fed. Hence banks utilize other strategies, which we classify as asset management and liability management approaches.

Asset Management by Banks. One way of addressing exposure to liquidity risk while earning interest is to lend money to other banks through the federal funds market, usually for one day at a time. Federal funds loans are liquid but have some, though small, default risk. A second option is to use repurchase agreements for government securities, lending securities to businesses and other banks overnight. However, these longer-maturity government securities involve some risk that interest rates will fluctuate. A combination of the two techniques are actually used by banks. This strategic mix reflects a trade-off between the lower expected return and default risk of the federal funds market and the higher expected return and risk of interest rate fluctuations in the government securities market.

Liability Management by Banks. Management of the liabilities side of a bank's balance sheet also is essential. Because bank liabilities usually are shorter-term than their assets, bankers must actively manage liquidity. They must keep on hand enough cash or assets that are easily convertible to cash to meet depositors' withdrawals. This must be done without sacrificing too much operating income by holding cash instead of loans or securities. Many large banks (for example, Citibank in New York) have more loan opportunities than they have deposits, so they must decide how to borrow additional funds to make loans. Options include certificates of deposit, Eurodollars, federal funds, RPs, and so on. These alternatives have different maturities and costs to the bank. However, banks must preserve their ability to borrow in order to use liability management, especially as most borrowing will be unsecured and not covered by federal deposit insurance. Relying *only* on overnight loans (though possibly at a lower current cost) is, in general, unwise. Hence banks also usually use longer-term borrowing with the attendant interest rate risk.

Asset and Liability Management Example. Suppose that Megabank's balance sheet initially looks like this:

MEGABANK

Assets		Liabilities	
Reserves	$50 million	Deposits	$200 million
Marketable securities	$10 million	Net worth	$20 million
Loans	$160 million		

If the bank is required to keep 10% of its deposits in the form of non-interest-bearing reserves with the Fed, its $50 million of reserves includes $20 million of required reserves and $30 million of excess reserves. If a group of Megabank's large depositors withdrew $15 million, Megabank would lose $15 million of reserves (and deposits) but would not have to alter other entries in its balance sheet. In other words, with enough excess reserves, a bank does not need to manage liquidity actively.

Holding excess reserves is costly to Megabank because it is forgoing interest earnings on loans and securities. At the other extreme, suppose that Megabank's initial balance sheets were such that it held no excess reserves, making more loans to increase its profitability. Its balance sheet shows:

MEGABANK

Assets		Liabilities	
Reserves	$20 million	Deposits	$200 million
Marketable securities	$10 million	Net worth	$20 million
Loans	$190 million		

Once again, suppose that Megabank faces withdrawals of $15 million. Its balance sheet becomes:

MEGABANK

Assets		Liabilities	
Reserves	$5 million	Deposits	$185 million
Marketable securities	$10 million	Net worth	$20 million
Loans	$190 million		

To meet the Fed's reserve requirement, Megabank should have $18.5 million, or (0.10)($185 million), of reserves; it is short $13.5 million, or $18.5 million – $5 million.

To meet this shortfall, the bank could sell its marketable securities and/or reduce loans. In the first case, the bank would sell off U.S. Treasury or other securities and deposit the proceeds with the Fed. Because government securities are traded in liquid markets, the bank's transactions costs will be low. Hence government securities are valuable as backup reserves. Alternatively, if Megabank has a large number of overlapping short-term loans, it could decide not to renew some of them. However, if the bank angered existing customers because it didn't renew their loans and lost those customers to another bank, it would have to pay information costs for new borrowers. In principle, Megabank could simply sell off some loans to other banks. Private information again complicates the transaction. Because other banks do not know the quality of Megabank's loans, they might not be willing to pay Megabank the full value of the loans.

In terms of liabilities, the bank can acquire reserves from other banks and corporations or from the Fed. Borrowing from other banks or corporations involves federal funds transactions and repurchase agreements. Borrowing from the Fed is accomplished through discount loans. If Megabank keeps its loan and securities holdings intact and meets its reserves shortage by borrowing equal amounts from these new sources, its balance sheet becomes:

MEGABANK

Assets		Liabilities	
Reserves	$18.5 million	Deposits	$185 million
Marketable securities	$10 million	Borrowings from other banks and corporations	$6.75 million
Loans	$190 million	Borrowings from the Fed	$6.75 million
		Net worth	$20 million

Megabank has managed its liquidity risk.

If Megabank is unable to manage its liquidity risk, it can fail. Suppose, for example, that rumors are circulating that $50 million of Megabank's loans were made to friends of J. P. Moregain, the bank's president, who have lost money in real estate speculation. Angry depositors withdraw $18.5 million immediately, leaving Megabank with $166.5 million in deposits, on which it should hold $16.65 million in reserves. But, as the balance sheet shows, its reserves are wiped out:

MEGABANK

Assets		Liabilities	
Reserves	$0 million	Deposits	$166.5 million
Marketable securities	$10 million	Borrowings	$13.5 million
Loans	$190 milllion	Net worth	$20 million

When the bank reduces the value of loans on its books to $140 million, it has a *net worth* of –$30 million, or $150 million in assets and $180 million in liabilities. Unless the bank can convince other banks or the Fed to lend it funds, it will have to close its doors. In this case, the Federal Deposit Insurance Corporation (FDIC) will take control of the bank and decide whether to liquidate it or merge it with another bank.

The Relationship Between Banks and Borrowers

Two principal challenges are involved in the relationship between banks and borrowers: (1) managing credit risk and (2) managing interest rate risk.

Managing Credit Risk

Banks make profits from the spread between the interest rate they charge to borrowers and the interest rate they pay to depositors. To ensure reasonable profits, banks attempt to make loans that will be fully repaid with interest. As with lending in financial markets, the bank is concerned about credit risk, that is, the risk that borrowers might default on their loans (see Box 13.2). If banks do not manage credit risk effectively, they won't be profitable for their shareholders and won't be in business very long. Banks can reduce their exposure to credit risk on individual loans by investing in information gathering and monitoring. One basic management principle for banks, as for other financial intermediaries, is that diversification can reduce the overall credit risk of the bank's portfolio. To manage credit risk of individual loans, banks use credit-risk analysis to examine borrowers and determine the appropriate interest rate to charge. In addition, bankers must cope with

Consider this...

How Do Banks Account for Loan Losses?

Bankers understand that their loans entail default risk, or the risk that the borrower will not repay the loan in full, with interest. When a loan is not repaid, the bank's net worth—its equity capital—suffers. During the term of the loan, if the bank decides that the borrower is likely to default, the bank must *write off* the loan. In other words, the value of the

loan is removed, entirely or in part, from the assets on the balance sheet. If an asset entry is reduced, a corresponding liability entry also must be reduced, so a loan loss reduces the bank's net worth.

In practice, a bank sets aside part of its net worth as a *loan loss reserve* to anticipate future loan losses. Using a loan loss reserve enables a bank to present a finan-

cially stable balance sheet. Each time the bank adds to its loan loss reserve, it reduces current profits. Hence, when a bad loan actually is written off, the bank's profits do not decline further. In a highly publicized example, Citibank added $4 billion in 1987 to its loan loss reserve in order to cover anticipated losses on its loans to some Latin American countries.

---

adverse selection and moral hazard problems in managing credit risks of individual loans.[†]

In loan markets, adverse selection problems occur because applicants with risky projects will be the most likely to apply for loans at a given interest rate: If their projects do well, they're big winners; but, if their projects fare poorly, the bank's the big loser (the lemons problem).

Moral hazard is a problem in bank loan markets because borrowers have an incentive, once they have obtained a loan, to use the proceeds for purposes detrimental to the bank. Banks use screening techniques, collateral requirements, credit rationing, monitoring, and restrictive covenants and develop long-term relationships with borrowers to help reduce costs associated with both adverse selection and moral hazard.

Diversification. The theory of portfolio allocation suggests that investors—individuals or financial institutions—can reduce exposure to the risk of price fluctuations by diversifying their holdings. If banks lend too much to one borrower, borrowers in one region, or borrowers in one industry, they are exposed to risks from those loans. Although banks' skills in information collection and evaluation focus on particular borrowers, most economists argue that banks should diversify within their chosen niche and manage the risk of their exposure if they do not diversify.

[†] The focus here is on banks' holdings of debt. Banks in the United States have been prohibited from investing deposits in significant equity holdings since passage of the National Banking Acts of 1863 and 1864. As a result, banks seldom hold equity stakes in firms.

Credit-Risk Analysis. In performing **credit-risk analysis,** the bank examines the borrower's likelihood of repayment and general business conditions that might influence the borrower's ability to repay the loan. Individuals and businesses apply for loans to a *loan officer*, who manages the bank's relationship with the borrower, gathers information about the borrower and the purpose of the loan, and assesses the credit risk. To reduce the likelihood of adverse selection, loan officers screen applicants to try to eliminate potentially bad risks and obtain a pool of creditworthy borrowers.

Individual borrowers usually must give the loan officer information about their employment, income, and net worth. Businesses supply information about their current and projected income and net worth. In addition, banks sometimes use *credit-scoring systems* to predict statistically whether an individual is likely to default. For example, individuals who change jobs often are more likely to default, statistically (all else being equal), than those who stay with the same employer. Some analysts have challenged the use of credit-scoring systems as discriminating against particular groups, but other analysts see these methods as a valuable tool for credit-risk analysis.

Loan officers not only collect information at the beginning of the loan, they also monitor the borrower during the term of the loan. Loan officers monitor large commercial loans by reviewing financial statements, meeting occasionally with the borrower's management, and studying the industry's prospects. For loans to individuals, the loan officer makes sure that scheduled loan payments are made and that the borrower's financial condition hasn't changed for the worse.

A bank bases the interest rate it charges for loans on (1) the bank's cost of funds, (2) the default risk of the loan, and (3) the rates of return available to the bank from alternative investments. A bank can't make a profit by lending at an interest rate lower than it pays for funds from deposit and nondeposit sources. In addition, to ensure that the bank is appropriately compensated for bearing risk, the spread between the interest rate charged by the bank for the loan and its cost of funds must reflect the default-risk premium. Finally, the determinants of asset demand (Chapter 6) indicate that the bank should not lend funds at an interest rate lower than it could earn on other assets. For example, a bank would not lend $10,000 to a risky borrower at 6% interest if it could invest the same funds in a default-risk-free U.S. Treasury security yielding 8%. However, competition from other lenders limits the interest rate that a bank can charge. That is, if a bank charges too much, borrowers will seek alternative sources of credit from other financial institutions.

Historically, loan rates to businesses were based on (pegged to) the **prime rate,** which is the interest rate charged on six-month loans to borrowers with the lowest expected default risk, called high-quality borrowers. Other loans carried rates greater than the prime rate, according to the credit risk. However, by the 1990s, most large and medium-sized businesses were receiving loan rates that reflected changing current market interest rates instead of the stated prime rate.

Collateral. To combat problems of adverse selection, banks also generally require that the borrower put up **collateral,** or assets pledged to the bank in the event that the borrower defaults. For example, if you wanted a loan from a bank to start a jewelry business, the bank likely would ask you to pledge some of your financial assets or your house as collateral. One form of collateral in commercial loans is a **compensating balance,** a required minimum amount that the business taking out the loan must maintain in a checking account with the lending bank. Collateral reduces the bank's losses in the event of default because it can sell the collateral.

Credit Rationing. In some circumstances, banks address costs of adverse selection and moral hazard through **credit rationing,** that is, by denying the borrower a loan at the going interest rate. In rationing credit, the bank either grants a borrower's loan application but limits the size of the loan or denies a borrower's loan application for any amount at the going interest rate.

The first type of credit rationing occurs in response to possible moral hazard problems. Limiting the size of bank loans reduces the risk of moral hazard by increasing the chance that the borrower will repay the loan to maintain a sound credit rating. Your MasterCard® or VISA® card has a credit limit for the same reason. With a loan limit of $2500, you are likely to repay the bank so that you can borrow again in the future. If the bank were willing to give you a $2.5 million line of credit, you might be tempted to spend more money than you can repay. Hence limiting the size of borrowers' loans to amounts less than borrowers demand at the going interest rate is both rational and profit-maximizing for banks.

The second type of credit rationing occurs in response to severe forms of adverse selection, when many borrowers have little or no collateral to offer to banks. What if a bank tries to raise the interest rate it charges in order to compensate itself for the presence of such high-risk borrowers? Low-risk borrowers then will tend to drop out, leaving the bank with even more potentially high-risk borrowers in its loan pool. Hence keeping its interest at the lower level and denying loans altogether to some borrowers can be in the bank's best interest. This type of adverse selection is costly for the economy because some low-risk borrowers also are denied credit.

Monitoring and Restrictive Covenants. To reduce the costs of moral hazard, banks monitor borrowers to make sure that a borrower doesn't use the funds borrowed from the bank to pursue unauthorized, risky activities. As with insurance arrangements (Chapter 12), much of banks' efforts center on determining whether the borrower is obeying *restrictive covenants*, or explicit provisions of the loan agreement that prohibit the borrower from engaging in certain activities.

Long-Term Relationships. One of the best ways for a bank to gather information about a borrower's prospects or to monitor a borrower's activities is for the bank to have a long-term relationship with the borrower. By observing the borrower over time—through checking account activity and loan repayments—the bank can significantly reduce problems of asymmetric information by reducing its information-gathering and monitoring costs. Borrowers also gain from long-term relationships with banks: The customer can obtain credit at a lower interest rate or with fewer restrictions because the bank avoids costly information-gathering tasks. Borrowers who value long-term relationships are less likely to default or violate restrictive covenants in loan agreements. Some analysts believe that the closer relationship between banks and nonfinancial businesses in other countries—notably Germany and Japan—improves the competitiveness of both. We explore the advantages and disadvantages of these financial ties in Chapter 14.

▶ **C H E C K P O I N T** *Suppose that government intervention restricts the types of loans that a bank can make or the communities in which it can lend. What likely will happen to the credit risk of the bank's portfolio?* Such government restrictions would reduce the bank's ability to diversify its loan portfolios. As a result, even if the bank analyzed the credit risks of individual borrowers, the aggregate credit risk of its portfolio would increase. ◀

Managing Interest Rate Risk

The profits that banks earn from lending to borrowers are exposed to risk due to changes in interest rates in financial markets, called **interest rate risk**. Recall that changes in interest rates affect the value of banks' financial assets and liabilities. That is, a rise in the market interest rate lowers the present value of the outstanding amount of a loan even if there is little risk that the loan will not be paid off under the terms of the loan agreement. Banks are particularly affected by interest rate risk when they raise funds primarily through short-term deposits (such as checkable deposits or short-term time deposits) in order to finance loans or the purchase of securities with longer maturities.

Banks must first be able to compare the interest sensitivity of the values of different assets and liabilities. For example, suppose that Mightybank has a balance sheet that shows:

MIGHTYBANK

Assets		Liabilities	
Fixed-rate assets	$350 million	Fixed-rate liabilities	$230 million
Reserves		Checkable deposits	
Long-term marketable		Savings deposits	
securities		Long-term CDs	
Long-term loans		Variable-rate liabilities	$230 million
Variable-rate assets	$150 million	Short-term CDs	
Floating-rate loans		Money market deposit accounts	
Short-term securities		Federal funds	
		Net worth	$40 million

Note that $150 million of Mightybank's $500 million in assets have variable interest rates that change at least once a year. Slightly less than half ($230 million out of $500 million) of Mightybank's total liabilities have variable interest rates. If interest rates go up, Mightybank will pay more for $230 million of its funds while increasing its interest earnings on only $150 million of its assets. Hence Mightybank is exposed to interest rate risk.

The significant increase in the volatility of market interest rates during the 1980s caused extensive interest rate risk for banks that had made fixed-rate loans using funds obtained from short-term, variable-rate deposits. An increase in market interest rates reduced the value of the banks' assets relative to their liabilities and contributed to the number of bank failures in the late 1980s.

To manage interest rate risk, banks must begin by evaluating the exposure of their portfolios to the risk of fluctuations in market interest rates. One measure is the **duration** of a bank asset or liability, which is the responsiveness (of the percentage change in) the asset's or liability's market value to a percentage change in the market interest rate.[†] Duration is an example of an *elasticity*, which you studied in your first economics course. (Because it is an elasticity, duration is scale-free and may be calculated for an asset or liability of any maturity.) On the liabilities side, checkable deposits have a short duration, whereas longer-term certificates of deposit have a long duration. On the assets side, loans to other banks in the federal funds market have a short duration, whereas commercial loans and marketable securities have a longer duration.

To assess the bank's exposure to interest rate risk, its managers calculate an average duration for bank assets and an average duration for bank liabilities. The difference between the two, known as the **duration gap,** mea-

[†] We present a more formal definition of *duration* in the Appendix to this chapter.

sures the bank's exposure to fluctuations in interest rates. Bank managers use the information contained in the duration gap to guide their strategy. Reducing the size of the duration gap helps banks to guard against interest rate risk. To anticipate a fall in interest rates, a bank should arrange the maturity structure of its assets and liabilities to have a positive duration gap. To anticipate a rise in interest rates, a bank should arrange to have a negative duration gap.

The actual uses of asset and liability management to affect the duration gap vary from bank to bank. For example, small and medium-sized banks usually have less control over the duration of liabilities than do large banks. As a result, they focus on manipulating the duration of their assets. Large banks actively manage both assets and liabilities. For example, if the Chase Manhattan Bank expected interest rates to go up, it might sell long-maturity instruments, such as negotiable certificates of deposit, and lend the money to other banks in overnight markets.

In addition to direct asset and liability management, banks cope with interest rate risk in other ways. One approach (discussed at length in Chapter 9) is for banks to use financial futures and options as hedges. Two additional ways in which banks deal with interest rate risk are to use floating-rate debt to reduce the duration gap and to use interest rate swaps.

Floating-Rate Debt.   One way to reduce risk arising from interest rate fluctuations is to utilize **floating-rate debt** by making the loan interest rate variable. With floating-rate debt, if market interest rates rise, the bank's interest income rises with its interest expense. Hence its profit margin from lending is less affected by interest rate movements than if the loan interest rate were fixed. Floating-rate loans became much more important in the United States in the early 1980s, as interest rate fluctuations became more pronounced. Most commercial loans have an interest rate equal to a benchmark rate plus some percentage set by the bank to reflect credit risk. The loan rate is adjusted as the benchmark rate changes. Typical benchmarks include commercial paper rates or the London Interbank Offering Rate (LIBOR), which measures rates that international banks charge on dollar-denominated loans. With adjustable-rate mortgages (ARMs), the mortgage interest rate rises and falls with market interest rates.

Floating-rate loans do not eliminate banks' exposure to risk, however. They reduce the bank's risk considerably, but the risk faced by the borrower goes up. If high rates occur during periods of low earnings and economic stress for firms (as they sometimes do), borrowers' default risk rises. The trade-off involves transferring interest rate risk to borrowers who may not be able or willing to bear it.

Swaps.   Introduced in 1981, swaps address banks' exposure to both interest rate and exchange rate risk. An **interest rate swap,** the most common form of swap, is an agreement to sell the expected future returns on one financial instrument for the expected future returns on another. The outstanding amount of these widely used arrangements rose to more than $5 trillion in 1992.

Suppose, for example, that Megabank is about to make a long-term, fixed-rate loan to Big Steel, Inc. Because Megabank's sources of funds are relatively short-term, it pays a floating rate on its liabilities. The bank can use interest rate swaps to reduce its exposure to interest rate risk by exchanging floating-rate payments for fixed-rate payments. The swap agreement gives Megabank a known interest rate on its debt, relieving it of the uncertainty of fluctuating interest rates. Conversely, the other bank or investor that has agreed to make the floating-rate payments in exchange for fixed-rate payments faces the possibility that a rise in interest rates would increase its payments. (It could use financial futures markets to reduce its exposure to risk.)

After making the loan to Big Steel, Megabank can sell swaps, eliminating its interest rate risk by transforming the fixed-rate payments from the loan into floating-rate payments. In addition to hedging, Megabank can use swaps to speculate on future interest rate movements. Suppose that Megabank bought more swaps than it sold. It promises to pay a floating rate in exchange for a fixed rate on the difference. If rates increase, Megabank takes a loss; if they fall, it earns a profit.

Figure 13.2 summarizes the risks to which banks are exposed in their relationships with savers and borrowers.

Q: How do banks manage the risks involved in their deposit and lending activities?

A: Banks' deposit and lending activities expose them to liquidity risk, credit risk, and interest rate risk. Banks have developed techniques including asset and liability management, credit-risk analysis, and the use of floating-rate debt, swaps, and futures to manage these risks while providing risk-sharing, liquidity, and information services to savers.

▶ **C H E C K P O I N T** *The efficient markets hypothesis states that stock market prices should be based on all available information. If banks are exposed to interest rate risk, what should investors expect with regard to the responsiveness of bank stock prices to changes in market interest rates?* An increase in market interest rates reduces the value of banks' assets and the price of banks' shares, whereas a decrease in market interest rates raises the value of banks' assets and the price of banks' shares. Indeed, banks' share prices generally are much more responsive to interest rate movements than are shares of industrial companies' stock. ◀

Expanding the Boundaries of Banking

Financial innovations by banks and financial markets from the 1960s through the early 1990s increased competition among financial institutions. To maintain profitability, banks had to find ways to capitalize on their greatest competitive advantage in relation to financial markets: their lower transactions and information costs in meeting the financial needs of many savers and borrowers. One category of new arrangements is off-balance-sheet lending, by which banks exploit these cost advantages without necessarily

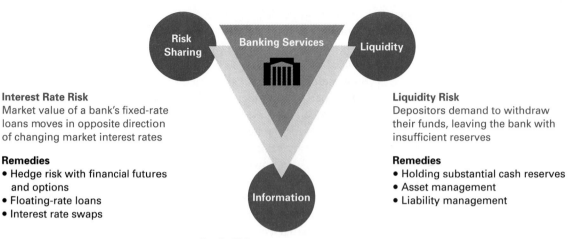

Interest Rate Risk
Market value of a bank's fixed-rate
loans moves in opposite direction
of changing market interest rates

Remedies
- Hedge risk with financial futures
  and options
- Floating-rate loans
- Interest rate swaps

Liquidity Risk
Depositors demand to withdraw
their funds, leaving the bank with
insufficient reserves

Remedies
- Holding substantial cash reserves
- Asset management
- Liability management

Credit Risk
Borrowers may default on their loans

Remedies
- Portfolio diversification
- Credit-risk analysis
- Monitoring and restrictive covenants
- Long-term relationships

FIGURE 13.2

Exposure to Risk in Banking Contracts
The services banks provide to savers and borrowers expose banks to liquidity risk, interest rate risk, and credit risk. Banks have developed remedies to manage those risks.

making traditional loans. A second category is credit card lending, by which banks take advantage of reduced costs of computerized credit transactions, as well as their skills in credit-risk analysis.

Off-Balance-Sheet Lending

Off-balance-sheet lending activities encompass bank lending in which the bank does not necessarily hold as assets the loans it makes. This category of arrangements includes three important innovations by financial institutions: (1) standby letters of credit, (2) loan commitments, and (3) loan sales.

Standby Letters of Credit. Changes in the competitive environment led banks to exploit their skills at information gathering and monitoring. By doing so, banks regained some of the lending business they had lost to the market for commercial paper (short-term debt of corporations traded in financial markets) during the 1970s through a contractual innovation. Because commercial paper is short-term and generally rolled over (refinanced), borrowers want to ensure steady access to their funds. Banks routinely sell to commercial paper borrowers a **standby letter of credit** (SLC), by which the bank promises to lend the borrower funds to pay off its maturing commercial paper if necessary. Historically, borrowers paid banks for this service by maintaining a compensating balance. In the 1990s, more often a fee (usually about 0.5%) is assessed.

The guarantee of creditworthiness symbolized by an SLC is particularly useful to less well-known borrowers. This approach splits credit provision into two parts: credit-risk analysis (information gathering) and actual funding. The SLC is a significant development because banks can provide credit-risk analysis efficiently, whereas a public market often can provide the actual funding more cheaply. Unlike conventional loans, SLCs do not appear on banks' balance sheets.

Growth in SLC issues has been phenomenal. The volume of bank SLCs expanded at a 26% annual rate through the 1980s, and growth continued in the early 1990s. The nation's biggest banks seized the largest share of this growth as part of their efforts to recapture their traditional corporate borrowers from the commercial paper market.

Loan Commitments.   In a **loan commitment,** a bank agrees to provide a borrower with a stated amount of funds during some specified period of time. Borrowers then have the option of deciding when or if they want to take the loan. Since the mid-1970s, the ratio of loan commitments (used and unused) to commercial and industrial (C&I) loans by banks rose from just over 1.5 in 1973 to almost 2.4 in 1981; by the end of the 1980s, it had fallen to about 1.9.

For a loan commitment, the participating bank earns a fee, which is usually split into two parts: an *upfront fee* when the commitment is written and a *nonusage fee* on the unused portion. For loans actually made, the interest rate charged in the usage fee is determined as a markup over a benchmark lending rate. Loan commitments fix the markup over the benchmark rate in advance, but not the interest rate. In addition, the bank's commitment to lend ceases if the borrower's financial condition deteriorates below some specified level.

Loan Sales.   During the 1980s, securitization in money and capital markets grew significantly, in which financial intermediaries sold loans or securities directly to investors through markets instead of holding them. Intermediaries currently sell many types of bank loans, including mortgage loans, automobile loans, credit card receivables, and business loans, through markets. The process of securitization helps lenders diversify and share risk because they can sell portions of the portfolio of loans that they originate. In addition, this process allows banks to focus on lowering information and transactions costs for many savers and borrowers without having to hold all their loans until maturity.

As part of the trend toward securitization during the 1980s, the market for bank loan sales in the United States grew from almost nothing to just under $250 billion. A **loan sale** is a financial contract by which a bank agrees to sell the expected future returns from an underlying bank loan to a third party. Formally, the loan contract is sold *without recourse*; that is, the bank provides no guarantee of the value of the loan sold and no insurance. Sales of C&I loans by banks surged from $27 billion in 1983 to $290 billion by the end of the 1980s, and the top-selling banks sold most of their C&I loan portfolios. The volume of loan sales declined in 1991, in part because banks had mispriced the loans of smaller firms with high debt levels. Many analysts predict that bank loan sales will begin to grow again.

Large banks sell loans primarily to domestic and foreign banks and nonbank financial institutions. Originally, they sold only short-term, high-quality loans with low information-gathering and monitoring costs. Increasingly, however, banks are selling lesser-quality and longer-term loans.

The existence of a flourishing loan sales market has implications for the role that banks play as intermediaries in the saving-investment process. For example, an active loan sales market effectively splits banking activities into deposit-taking and loan-making components, which raises a fundamental question: Does the growth of the market in loan sales imply that banks should disappear?

The answer is *no*. Loan sales represent an improvement in intermediation services. Such sales allow banks to achieve greater financial and geographic diversification by buying loans from and selling loans to other institutions (even in the face of bank branching restrictions) while economizing on their equity capital. Some economists believe that ensuring the performance of loan contracts no longer requires banks to risk their financial equity by holding loans until maturity. Thus banks can continue to provide their normal information-gathering and monitoring services while decreasing their exposure to credit risk and interest rate risk.

In selling loans, banks put their reputations on the line instead of their equity capital. A bank that performs poorly in its loan sales activities is unlikely to remain a successful player in that market. And the big banks (the largest loan sellers) are greatly concerned about their reputation. Prices of loans sold contain a risk premium representing both the default risk of the underlying borrowers and the default risk of the selling bank to pay for the bank's implicit promise to stand behind the loan. One way in which banks can ensure the quality of the loan is to hold part of the loan to convince buyers of its commitment to monitoring the original borrower's activities.

▶ **C H E C K P O I N T** *Suppose that changes in information-gathering methods significantly reduce the transactions and information costs of making small loans. What changes are likely to occur in bank lending activities?* If information costs are very low, banks can make the initial loans and sell them to investors in mutual funds, reducing the need to connect deposit taking and bank lending in bank intermediation. The growth in banks' off-balance-sheet lending reflects reductions in transactions and information costs of certain types of lending. ◀

Credit Card Lending

Credit card loans offer banks a way to profit from making small consumer and business loans through a preauthorized line of credit. In the past, banks found that small personal loans were unprofitable because of record keeping expenses; however, improvements in computerized data processing reduced such costs substantially and speeded development of this new form of bank lending.

The first credit cards to be widely accepted were introduced in the 1950s by Diners Club®, American Express®, and Hilton Credit Corporation. These nonbank *travel and entertainment cards* required payment of the balance in full each statement period. The Franklin National Bank of New York issued the first bank credit card in 1952. Like some nonbank cards, *bank credit cards* not only permit cardholders to purchase goods and services but also preauthorize their credit. If cardholders don't pay the balance in full, they pay a finance charge, or interest, on the unpaid balance. Credit card companies repay the merchant at a discount, typically from 2% to 5% of the amount charged. The two major credit card networks currently used are VISA® and MasterCard.® Some banks also use the cards' credit limits to offer *overdraft protection* to the consumer to avoid bouncing of checks in the event of insufficient funds in the consumer's checking account.

Credit cards are extremely profitable for banks. According to the Fed, the rate of return to banks from credit card lending is higher than that for other bank assets: about 12% *above* short-term, default-risk-free interest rates. That is, if the market rate is 4.5%, the rate charged for credit card lending is about 16.5%. At the same time, banks' losses on credit card lending averaged only about 3% during the 1980s and early 1990s.

On several occasions Congress has expressed concern that credit card margins are too high. In addition to charging high rates, banks have not in the past adjusted rates significantly in response to changes in the prime rate. For example, credit card interest rates generally did not change when the prime rate fell from 16% to 9% between 1982 and 1986. One possible explanation for this phenomenon is adverse selection, as the pool of borrowers who actually incur interest charges is likely to be riskier than the pool of those who don't. The Optima® card issued by American Express, for example, charges a lower rate of interest than does a VISA® or MasterCard® with similar features; the company is able to do so because the pool of American Express cardholders in all likelihood has a lower default risk, on average, than that of the bank cardholders. Banks' credit card business also may add to profitability by attracting consumers to other bank services, making it difficult to analyze how much of banks' costs apply to that line of business. Nonetheless, its high profitability and unresponsiveness to interest rate changes concern policymakers.

MOVING FROM THEORY TO PRACTICE...

THE NEW YORK TIMES   FEBRUARY 29, 1992

Will Russian Banking Be Russian Roulette?

The new system of commercial banks has emerged in Russia to feed loans to thousands of companies that are no longer financed by the state. But the free-wheeling lending practices of the new Russian banks could sink many of them in a flood of bad debt.

The transition to capitalism gave birth to the banks, although rules are still lacking to govern their behavior...

Loans are made without collateral, since the law does not yet give lenders the right to seize property if a borrower defaults. And the Central Bank of Russia, which is supposed to regulate the commercial banks, has few inspectors to evaluate loans and flag those unlikely to be repaid.

"We do not know how safe the loans are," said Nikolai Domonov, general director of bank supervision at the Central Bank. Nor does the Central Bank know the amount outstanding in bank loans. "We know that lending is growing, but we don't know yet by how much," Mr. Domonov said. Such data are to be compiled by April...

"Of course we have made mistakes; how do you analyze the profitability of someone in this country buying and selling shoes who comes to you for a loan?" said Kirill D. Legkobytov, until recently assistant to the chairman of Moscow's Inkombank, among the largest of the privately owned commercial banks that have blossomed since the late 1980s under perestroika. Initially, the private banks filled a niche: lending to cooperatives and other enterprises that the state banks shunned until recently. "When these entrepreneurs appeared, the state banks would say, 'You are not in our plan,'" Sergei Yegorov, president of the association, said.

So the rejected borrowers formed their own banks, putting up their own capital, in part to lend to themselves, although the Central Bank last summer put ceilings on such self-lending. Inkombank, among the first of these banks, is owned by 129 shareholders, who have contributed 500 million rubles in capital, or enough to pay off 5 percent of Inkombank's outstanding loans in case borrowers default. This capital-to-loan ratio is in line with Western standards.

The funds that Inkombank uses to make loans come from deposits—mostly those of companies, not individuals—and from heavy borrowing from other banks, in what has come to be known as Russia's interbank lending market...

Some shareholders at first received loans from Inkombank at two or three percentage points lower than other borrowers, Mr. Legkobytov said. "But our chairman convinced them that this was not a good idea."

ANALYZING THE NEWS...

Before the transition to market economies began, the central governments of the former Soviet Union and Eastern European countries allocated bank credit. A critical challenge for Russia and emerging market economies in Eastern Europe is the transition to a functioning private banking system that will serve as an intermediary in the saving-investment process and provide risk-sharing, liquidity, and information services to savers.

(a) If banks are to channel funds from savers to borrowers efficiently, they must be able to gather and monitor information on borrowers. Information costs will be high for Russian bank lending for two reasons. First, absence of the lender's right to seize the property of a defaulting borrower implies that all lending is unsecured, removing banks' ability to use collateral requirements and restrictive covenants in loan contracts. Second, as much of the value of banks' stock of information comes from experience in credit-risk analysis and long-term relationships with borrowers, new private banks in Russia must make significant initial investments in information gathering.

(b) In addition, prospective bankers are likely to have to raise substantial amounts of equity capital to be able to attract depositors. When equity capital levels are low, banks have an incentive to make risky loans with depositors' funds. The report of lending to insiders at subsidized rates suggests that moral hazard is as alive and well in Russia as in the United States.

For further thought...

Suppose that depositors in the new private Russian banks lose confidence in the banks and rush to withdraw their funds. How might the Russian central bank step in to prevent a wave of bank failures?

Source: "The Roulette of Russian Banking," by Louis Uchitelle, February 29, 1992. Copyright 1991/1992 by The New York Times Company. Reprinted by permission.

Key Terms and Concepts

Balance sheet

Bank assets
    Loans
    Marketable securities
    Reserves
    Vault cash

Bank failure

Bank liabilities
    Checkable deposits
    Nontransaction deposits
    Borrowings

Bank net worth

Credit card loans

Credit risk
    Credit rationing
    Credit-risk analysis
    Collateral
    Compensating balance

Excess reserves

Federal deposit insurance

Interest rate risk
    Duration
    Duration gap
    Floating-rate debt
    Interest rate swaps
    Prime rate

Liquidity risk

Off-balance-sheet lending
    Loan commitment
    Loan sale
    Standby letter of credit

Payments system

Required reserves

T-account

Summary

1. Banks earn profits by providing transactions and intermediation services. They invest in gathering and monitoring information about borrowers.

2. The sources of funds for banks (liabilities) include checkable deposits, time deposits, and nondeposit sources (borrowings from other banks and businesses, borrowings from the Federal Reserve System, and equity capital). The uses of funds for banks (assets) include cash and reserves, loans, securities, deposits at other banks, and other assets. Banks' net worth equals the difference between assets and liabilities.

3. The problem of moral hazard arises in banking because bankers have access to private information unknown to depositors and other investors. Bankers may be tempted to make a more risky investment with others' funds than they would with their own. Having bankers maintain a cushion of net worth, or

equity capital, aligns bankers' incentives with those of their suppliers of funds and reduces risk of moral hazard.

4. The relative reliance on alternative liabilities and assets has changed dramatically during the past 30 years. In terms of liabilities, checkable deposits are a less significant source of funds in the 1990s. There is greater reliance by banks on such sources as negotiable certificates of deposit and overnight borrowing. In terms of assets, loans have grown in importance relative to the holding of marketable securities by banks.

5. Typically, bank loans are less liquid than bank liabilities, posing a problem of liquidity risk. To avoid having to sell loans at a loss to pay unexpectedly heavy withdrawals by depositors, banks hold reserves in the form of cash and/or short-term mar-

ketable securities. While holding reserves is an easy strategy, it isn't profitable. Hence banks utilize various techniques of asset and liability management.

6. Banks face credit risk, or the risk that borrowers might not be able to repay the loan principal plus interest. When a borrower defaults, the bank suffers a loss. Banks deal with credit-risk problems by gathering information, monitoring borrowers, and diversifying their loan portfolios.

7. Interest rate risk is the risk of changes in banks' net worth arising from fluctuations in market interest rates. The concept of duration gives financial institutions a way to compare the interest sensitivity of the value of different types of assets and liabilities.

Strategies for reducing interest rate risk include using floating-rate debt, financial futures, options, and swaps.

8. In addition to their traditional activities of accepting deposits and making loans, banks have increasingly turned to off-balance-sheet activities. They generate fee income from trading financial instruments and from exploiting their transactions-cost and information-cost advantages on behalf of their customers. In addition, through credit card lending, banks have taken advantage of their skills in credit-risk analysis and the reduced costs of computerized credit transactions.

Review Questions

1. As financial intermediaries, what services do banks provide to savers and borrowers?

2. How does the federal funds market work? How does a loan in this market differ from a repurchase agreement?

3. Why would government regulators and taxpayers like to see banks have high net worth?

4. Describe the three types of risk that banks face.

5. How do banks try to reduce credit risk?

6. How do banks determine interest rates on loans?

7. What do banks do when some of their borrowers look like they may default? What do they do when the borrowers actually default?

8. What are the goals of asset management and liability management? What can a bank do to meet these goals?

9. What are floating-rate loans? How do they help to reduce interest rate risk for banks?

10. What are the main types of off-balance-sheet activities that banks engage in? Why have banks been involved in more of these activities recently and less in traditional banking?

Analytical Problems

11. Suppose that all borrowers could raise funds through securities markets—for example, through stocks or bonds. Would there be a special economic function for banks? Explain.

12. In developing countries without active markets for short-term financial instruments, savers tend to allocate more of their funds to bank deposits than in countries with more active financial markets. Explain.

13. Suppose that a bank uses checkable deposits to finance illiquid loans. If the bank has no private information about borrowers, can the bank fail because of *liquidity risk?* Why or why not? What if the bank has significant private information about the quality of its asset portfolio?

14. Suppose that banks collectively have not managed their exposure to interest rate risk well and that market interest rates increase and become more volatile. What do you predict will happen to the value of the equity capital in the banking industry? To the number of bank failures?

15. Why would banks usually welcome a reduction in reserve requirements? Would a reduction in reserve requirements matter to a bank that voluntarily held reserves for clearing purposes that were higher than required reserves?

16. Suppose that Bank A sells $10 million in securities to Bank B. Show what happens to the balance sheets of both banks.

17. Suppose that Ann, who has an account at First Bank, writes a check for $1000 to Bill, who has an account at Melon Bank. When the check clears, how have the balance sheets of First and Melon been affected?

18. Suppose that First Bank has $34 million in checkable deposits, Second Bank has $47 million in checkable deposits, and the reserve requirement for checkable deposits is 10%. If First Bank currently has $4 million in reserves and Second Bank has $5 million in reserves, how much excess reserves does each bank have? Now suppose that a customer of First Bank writes a check for $1 million to a real estate broker who deposits it at Second Bank. After the check clears, how much excess reserves does each bank have?

19. Suppose that you are considering investing (or making a large deposit) in a bank that is making

higher profits than other banks. You learn that profits are high because the bank has little equity capital and has nearly 100% of its assets in the form of loans and required reserves. Would you become an investor or depositor in such a bank?

20. In the early 1970s, savings institutions had mostly long-term mortgage loans as assets and many checkable deposits and time deposits with short maturities as liabilities. What do you think happened to the value of these institutions when interest rates rose dramatically in the mid- and late-1970s? In answering this question, use the concept that measures the interest sensitivity of assets and liabilities.

21. Prepare the balance sheet of a bank that has $20 million in reserves, $40 million in securities, $140 million in loans, $150 million in deposits, and $50 million in equity capital. What are the bank's excess reserves, if the reserve requirement is 10% of deposits? Suppose that checks drawn on the bank's accounts withdraw $10 million. Show what the revised balance sheet looks like. What are the bank's excess reserves? How much does the bank need to borrow? Suppose that the bank borrows one-half of its reserve deficiency in the federal funds market and the other half from the Fed. Now what does its balance sheet look like?

22. If you were a banker who believed that interest rates were about to rise, what would you try to do with your bank's portfolio?

Questions 23 and 24 relate to the Appendix:

23. Calculate the duration of an asset that makes nominal payments of $1100 one year from now, $1210 two years from now, and $1331 three years from now. The interest rate is 10%. About how much will the market value of the asset change if the interest rate rises from 10% to 12%?

24. Calculate the duration gap for a bank that has assets of $100 million with a duration of 13 and liabilities of $93 million with a duration of 7.

Data Questions

25. The *Federal Reserve Bulletin* contains a table called Bank Debits and Deposit Turnover that reports some interesting data about banks. Look at the data comparing the amount of money that flows through demand deposits and the turnover of demand deposits in major New York City banks and in other banks. What important conclusions about the U.S. payments system can you draw from this data? Why do you think that deposit turnover is so high in New York?

26. In the *Federal Reserve Bulletin*, find the table that reports Assets and Liabilities of Commercial Banks. What is the largest category of loans that banks make? What is the largest source of deposits? Add the total reserves of the banks (reserves with Federal Reserve Banks plus vault cash) and total investment securities. How does this amount compare to the total of funds in transaction accounts?

Appendix: Measuring the Duration of Bank Assets and Liabilities

To measure banks' exposure to interest rate risk, we must compare the interest sensitivity of the value of different assets and liabilities. Financial economists use a measure known as *duration* for this purpose. Duration measures the elasticity of the asset's (or liability's) market value with respect to a change in the interest rate.

Duration is the weighted sum of the maturities of the payments in the financial instrument, where the weights are equal to the present value of the payment divided by the present value of the asset or liability. If we denote the present value of a payment at time t by PV_t, then the market value MV of a T-period instrument is

$$MV = \sum_{t=1}^{T} PV_t,$$

and the duration d is

$$d = \sum_{t=1}^{T} t\left(\frac{PV_t}{MV}\right). \tag{13A.1}$$

One more step makes clear why the concept of duration is widely used to measure the responsiveness of the values of assets and liabilities to changes in market interest rates. The change in the market value of an asset or a liability is

$$\frac{\Delta MV}{MV} \cong -d\left(\frac{\Delta i}{1+i}\right), \tag{13A.2}$$

where i is the market interest rate, and the relationship between the interest rate and the market value is negative. The duration d indicates the magnitude of this effect. For instruments with a long duration—that is, with greater cash flows in the distant future relative to the present—the effect of interest rate changes on market value will be greater than for instruments with a shorter duration.

We can now determine the effects of interest rate changes on a bank's net worth. Because net worth NW is simply the difference between bank assets A and liabilities L, we have

$$\Delta NW = \Delta A - \Delta L$$

$$= \left(\frac{\Delta A}{A}\right)(A) - \left(\frac{\Delta L}{L}\right)(L).$$

If we substitute assets and liabilities for market value in Eq. (13A.2), we get

$$\frac{\Delta A}{A} \cong -d_A\left(\frac{\Delta i}{1+i}\right) \tag{13A.3}$$

and

$$\frac{\Delta L}{L} \cong -dL\left(\frac{\Delta i}{1+i}\right) \tag{13A.4}$$

where d_A and d_L represent duration measures for assets and liabilities, respectively. Hence

$$\Delta NW \cong -(d_A A - d_L L)\left(\frac{\Delta i}{1+i}\right). \tag{13A.5}$$

The terms in the first set of parentheses (scaled by assets A) represent the *duration gap* faced by the institution; that is,

$$\text{Gap} = d_A - d_L\left(\frac{L}{A}\right). \tag{13A.6}$$

Strategies for using the duration gap to guide bank management were discussed in this chapter.

CHAPTER 14

The Banking Industry

In the 1990s, many financial commentators argue that banking in the global marketplace is like sumo wrestlers: bigger is better. The aptness of the analogy is reflected by the prominence of Japanese banks. In the early 1980s, the two largest banks in the world (by assets) were American—Citibank and BankAmerica—and only one of the 10 largest banks was Japanese. By 1992, eight of the top 10 banks were Japanese; not one of the ten was a U.S. bank. Some bankers and policymakers argue that the U.S. banking industry cannot compete effectively with foreign banks in the 1990s, and many blame government regulation of the banking industry.

In Chapter 13, we described the role that banks play as intermediaries in the saving-investment process and how banks act on their advantages in reducing transactions and information costs in the financial system. Taken together, the approximately 12,000 commercial banks—as well as savings and loan associations, mutual savings banks, and credit unions—in the United States constitute the banking industry. In this chapter, we demonstrate that government regulation influences significantly the structure and operation of the banking industry. To do so, we examine the activities of federal and state banking regulators. Next, we explain why these regulatory authorities came into being and how they shaped the banking industry. Finally, we describe how banking industries have developed in other countries in response to differences in regulatory environments.

In this chapter we address two main questions. **Q:** Which regulatory authorities are responsible for monitoring the activities of U.S. depository institutions? **Q:** What aspects of banking explain why these regulatory authorities were introduced?

Development of the U.S. Banking Industry

Three characteristics make the U.S. banking industry unique in the world. First, although the United States has the world's largest economy, U.S. banks are not large by international banking standards. Only one of the top 30 banks in the world in 1993 (ranked by assets) is a U.S. bank: Citicorp, number 30. Large Japanese and European banks generally are much larger than the largest U.S. banks.

A second feature that distinguishes the U.S. banking industry from those in most other countries is the enormous number of firms involved. At the beginning of 1993, there were about 12,000 commercial banking firms in the United States (down from 15,145 in 1980). By contrast, Japan had fewer than 700 banks, and Canada had only eight major banks. Currently, the U.S. has about 50 banks per million people, versus slightly more than one per million in Japan and less than one per million in Canada.

Third, the U.S. banking industry isn't concentrated: The share of U.S. deposits held by the five largest banks is less than 20%; their counterparts in Japan, Canada, and Germany hold much higher percentages of their countries' deposits. However, these figures do not mean that U.S. households and businesses receive more banking services than their counterparts in other countries. The United States does not have more bank offices, including branches, per capita—only more separately owned banking firms per capita. To understand why, we need to consider historical developments.

Historical Influences

Cultural and historical influences in the United States greatly affected the development of the U.S. banking industry. These influences stemmed largely from the rural, populist fear of big-city banking interests, particularly those in New York City. In 1791, Treasury Secretary Alexander Hamilton tried to establish a nationwide banking system, with the Bank of the United States in Philadelphia as the central bank, in order to provide the nation with an efficient system of intermediation. Although the bank's 20-year charter was renewed (after a five-year hiatus) as the Second Bank of the United States in 1816, its survival was threatened by legislators from agricultural states. The election of President Andrew Jackson, a populist hero, doomed the Second Bank, and its charter was allowed to expire in 1836.

After 1836, states were given the right to control banks within their borders. This action ushered in the Free Banking Period during which banking was conducted with little government intervention. Some contemporary observers believe that the free banks were relatively successful intermediaries in the saving-investment process (see the Other times, other places box). The Free Banking Period lasted until passage of the National Banking Act during the Civil War.

Other times, other places...

Lessons from the Free Banking Period

Banking was not really "free" during the Free Banking Period. To obtain a state banking charter, banks typically had to agree to (1) pay gold to depositors on demand; (2) accept double liability for bank shareholders (that is, they would be responsible for twice the value of their contributed capital); and (3) deposit designated bonds (usually state bonds) with the state banking authority.

Historians often use the term "wildcat banking" to describe the Free Banking Period. They allege that banks frequently failed despite regulatory attempts to protect them, causing substantial losses to users of bank currency. Much of the subsequent concern

in the United States about the instability of free market banking came from the experience of this period.

Arthur Rolnick and Warren Weber, economists at the Federal Reserve Bank of Minneapolis, have vigorously challenged this view in their study of banking during that period in Indiana, Minnesota, New York, and Wisconsin.[†] They found that about half the free banks closed but that fewer than one-third of those ultimately failed to redeem bank notes at face value. In general, losses on notes were small—on average, about one cent per dollar. The wave of bank failures during that period can be attributed to

default on the bonds backing the bank notes, rather than to loss of consumer confidence in banks.

Two lessons emerge from that period. First, regulations are necessary to provide information to the public about the quality of the bank assets that back bank notes. Second, given public knowledge of what backs the notes of a bank, bank failures are rational and reflect large swings in the value of banks' assets. Government intervention in the banking industry is needed to help it adjust to such large variations in asset values.

[†] See Arthur J. Rolnick and Warren E. Weber, "The Free Banking Era: New Evidence on Laissez-Faire Banking," *American Economic Review,* 73:1080–1091, 1983.

The Dual Banking System

The National Banking Act of 1863 established the current **dual banking system** in the United States, in which banks are chartered by either the federal government or a state government. Federally chartered banks, known as **national banks,** are supervised by the Office of the Comptroller of the Currency (OCC) in the U.S. Treasury Department and originally were allowed to issue bank notes as currency. To eliminate the ability of state-chartered banks, known as **state banks,** to issue bank notes as currency, Congress imposed a prohibitive tax on state bank notes. Congress's intent was to eliminate competition for national banks by drying up state-chartered banks' source of funds. However, state banks came up with a close substitute for currency—a **demand deposit,** or an account against which checks convertible to currency can be written. National banks adopted this innovation, and as a result, the two types of banks coexist today.

Government Intervention

Three regulatory interventions after the National Banking Act shaped the U.S. banking industry. In 1913, Congress created the **Federal Reserve System** (the Fed) to promote stability in the banking industry. The

Fed was given a monopoly in issuing currency, now known as Federal Reserve Notes. All national banks were required to join the system and obey its regulations. State banks were allowed to choose whether they wanted to belong to the Federal Reserve System; most chose not to, owing to the costs of complying with the Fed's regulations.

The second major intervention came during the Great Depression in the form of **federal deposit insurance,** a federal government guarantee of certain types of bank deposits. Thousands of bank failures had destroyed the savings of many depositors and eroded their confidence in the banking system. In 1934, Congress responded by creating the Federal Deposit Insurance Corporation (FDIC) to guarantee deposits at commercial banks. [At the same time, Congress created the Federal Savings and Loan Insurance Corporation (FSLIC) to insure deposits at savings institutions.] The act required banks that were members of the Federal Reserve System to purchase deposit insurance. Nonmember banks were given a choice. Virtually all banks were covered eventually by deposit insurance. The purchase of deposit insurance subjected banks to additional regulation by the FDIC.

Another significant government intervention in the banking industry was restriction of bank competition. The first such measures imposed **branching restrictions,** geographic limitations on banks' ability to open more than one office, or branch. The National Banking Act of 1863 gave states the authority to restrict branch banking within their borders. Indeed, some states prohibited branch banking. By giving banks a monopoly over certain activities and limiting bank competition in local markets, the law sought to ensure a low cost of funds to banks and to stabilize the banking system. A second branching restriction, the McFadden Act of 1927, prohibited national banks from operating branches outside their home states. The act further required national banks to abide by state branching restrictions, thus placing them on an equal footing with state-chartered banks. These regulations led to a larger number of banking firms in the United States than would have existed otherwise. Anticompetitive restrictions also limited banks' ability to compete with investment banks, brokers, and dealers in the securities industry.

Chartering and Examination

How does someone go about establishing a bank? Individuals wanting to start a bank must file an application for a federal charter with the Office of the Comptroller of the Currency. For a state charter, an application must be filed with the appropriate state banking authority. When the federal or state regulatory agency evaluates the application, it considers whether the owners are supplying sufficient equity capital, the qualifications of the bank's proposed managers, and the bank's prospects for making profits. Prior to the late 1970s, the federal or state chartering authority also investigated whether the proposed bank's community "needed" a new bank. Often, an authority refused to grant the charter because it thought that the profits of existing banks would be harmed significantly, potentially causing them to fail. During the 1980s and early 1990s, chartering authorities generally have not turned down applications on anticompetitive grounds.

A chartered bank must file quarterly reports of its earnings, assets and liabilities, and operations; it also is subject to periodic examination of its financial condition by regulators. The FDIC examines banks at least every three years and generally more often. The Fed conducts examinations about every 18 months. Large national banks may be examined several times each year by the Office of the Comptroller of the Currency. These regulatory bodies often cooperate and accept each other's examination reports.

Examiners also make unexpected visits to banks to ensure that the banks are complying with all applicable laws and regulations. Examiners have fairly wide latitude to force a bank to sell risky investments or to write off the value of a worthless loan. An examiner who finds problems with excessive risk taking or low net worth may classify the bank as a "problem bank" and subject it to more frequent examinations. Although examiners help control risky or dishonest bank management practices, some analysts believe that allowing examiners too much discretion forces banks to be too conservative in their lending practices. Regulators generally try to strike a balance.

Overlapping Regulatory Authority

As a result of the dual banking system, bank regulation in the United States involves many regulators with overlapping authority for commercial banks, savings institutions, and credit unions.

Commercial Banks. As of 1993, the Office of the Comptroller of the Currency supervises the approximately 4000 national banks that are members of the Federal Reserve System. These banks account for more than half the assets in the U.S. commercial banking system. The approximately 1000 state banks that are members of the Federal Reserve System are jointly supervised by the Fed and state banking regulators. The Fed also has supervisory responsibility for **bank holding companies,** which are companies that own more than one bank. Most of the remaining 7000 banks are state banks that are not members of the Federal Reserve System but are covered by FDIC insurance: these are supervised by the FDIC. Approximately 500 very small state banks with no FDIC insurance are supervised solely by state banking regulators.

This network of commercial bank regulatory authority occasionally results in duplication of effort. Some analysts believe that regulation by more than one agency decreases the chance of lapses in supervision. They also believe that individual regulatory agencies may serve the banking industry better than they serve the interests of savers and borrowers. Nonetheless, in 1991 and 1992, the U.S. Treasury Department sought legislative approval to eliminate overlapping supervision. This proposal would retain the dual banking system, with state banks supervised by the Federal Reserve System and national banks supervised by a new regulatory authority called the Federal

Banking Agency. As of early 1993, Congress had not enacted the department's proposal and was waiting for a proposal from the Clinton administration.

Savings Institutions.   Savings institutions, comprising savings and loan associations and mutual savings banks, also are supervised by multiple regulatory agencies. Savings and loan associations (S&Ls) can be chartered by federal or state authorities. The majority of S&Ls are members of the Federal Home Loan Bank System (FHLBS), which was founded in 1932 as a "Federal Reserve" for S&Ls. The Office of Thrift Supervision, which is similar to the OCC, supervises the 12 district Federal Home Loan Banks of the FHLBS. It also charters and supervises federally chartered S&Ls. The FDIC provides federal deposit insurance to S&Ls through its Savings Association Insurance Fund (SAIF). [Prior to 1989, savings institutions were insured by the Federal Savings and Loan Insurance Corporation (FSLIC).]

About half the mutual savings banks are chartered by the states, and about half are chartered by the federal government. The primary regulators of mutual savings banks are state banking authorities. However, those with FDIC insurance must follow the FDIC's rules for state-chartered banks. The remainder of mutual savings banks generally have deposits insured by state deposit insurance funds.

Credit Unions.   Unlike commercial banks and savings institutions, both of which take deposits from any saver and make loans to any borrower, the 13,900 U.S. credit unions are cooperative lending associations for a particular group, usually employees of a particular firm or governmental unit. As a result, most credit unions are small, although shareholders of a credit union may live in many states (or even in many countries, as in the case of the U.S. Navy Credit Union). Both federal and state charters are available, but most credit unions are chartered and regulated by the federal government's National Credit Union Administration (NCUA). Federal deposit insurance is provided by the National Credit Union Share Insurance Fund (NCUSIF), a subsidiary of the NCUA.

Concluding Remarks.   Federal and state laws have created multiple regulatory authorities, which have shaped the U.S. banking industry in terms of the risks to which banks are exposed and their activities as financial intermediaries. Table 14.1 summarizes the chartering and supervisory responsibilities for U.S. depository institutions.

▶ C H E C K P O I N T   *Mutual funds with short-term money market assets don't require much ongoing supervision so long as the funds truthfully disclose to savers the contents of their portfolio of assets. By this reasoning, can we say that, if banks disclose the identity of loans in their asset portfolios, ongoing supervision won't be needed?* The answer is *no.* Ongoing supervision is necessary because bank

▼ TABLE 14.1	REGULATION AND SUPERVISION OF U.S. DEPOSITORY INSTITUTIONS[†]			
Type of institution...	Chartered by...	Supervised by...	Examined by...	Insured by...
Commercial Banks				
National banks	———————Comptroller of the Currency———————			FDIC
State-chartered banks (members of the Federal Reserve System)	State authorities	the Fed		FDIC
State-chartered banks (not members of the Federal Reserve System)	State authorities	————————FDIC————————		FDIC
State-chartered banks (not insured by FDIC)	————————————State authorities————————————			
Savings Institutions				
Federal associations (insured)	———————Office of Thrift Supervision (OTS)———————			FDIC
State savings associations (insured)	State authorities	OTS and state authorities		FDIC
State savings associations (not federally insured)	————————————State authorities————————————			
Credit Unions				
Federal credit unions (insured)	—— National Credit Union Administration (NCUA) ——			National Credit Union Share Insurance Fund (NCUSIF)
State credit unions (not federally insured)	————————State authorities————————			NCUSIF or state authorities

[†] Regulatory authority as of January 1993.

loans involve private information that cannot be evaluated well by outsiders, whereas mutual funds own more well-known assets. ◀

Why the Banking Industry Is Regulated

Now that we have identified *who* regulates banks, we are ready to explore *why* banks are regulated. Understanding that helps explain which types of regulation are most likely to benefit savers, borrowers, and the economy in the long run.

To begin, let's review the risks that banks assume in providing risk-sharing, liquidity, and information services. First, a difference in the maturities of banks' assets and liabilities can expose banks to interest rate risk, or the chance that banks' net worth will decline if interest rates rise. By itself, interest rate risk doesn't present much of a problem for banks. They can use instruments available in financial markets to reduce their exposure to it. And if deposit insurance didn't exist, banks could compensate depositors for the risk

Q: Which regulatory authorities are responsible for monitoring the activities of U.S. depository institutions?

A: Multiple regulatory authorities supervise depository institutions, including the Office of the Comptroller of the Currency, the Federal Reserve System, FDIC, the Office of Thrift Supervision, the National Credit Union Administration, and state banking authorities.

that the bank might fail because of interest rate risk by paying depositors a risk premium on their deposits.

Instead, concern for the health of banking institutions has focused on liquidity risk associated with unanticipated withdrawals of deposits and information problems. Banks hold reserves as a cushion against anticipated and unanticipated withdrawals by savers. Savers, however, cannot know the true health of the bank because it has private information about its loan portfolio. Because banks have private information, depositors may lose confidence in even financially healthy banks. When enough savers lose confidence in a bank's portfolio of assets, a bank run can occur.

The Nature of a Bank Run

Loss of confidence in a bank begins when depositors start to question the value of the bank's underlying assets. Often, the reason for a loss of confidence is bad news, whether true or false. Suppose that the major loans of Anytown Bank are likely to default. The assistant bank manager discovers the problem and tells two friends, who tell everyone they know. Fearing that the bank probably will not be able to repay them in full, many (if not all) of the depositors rush to the bank to get their money back. Because it must pay on demand, Anytown Bank will pay depositors in full on a first-come, first-serve basis until its liquid funds are exhausted. This sequence of events is known as a **bank run.** In this case the bad news is true, and a run forces the bank to close its doors.

Moreover, bad news about one bank can snowball and affect other banks. Suppose that State Bank of Anytown has no insolvency problem. Its loans are likely to be repaid in full and on time. However, as rumors spread that Anytown Bank will run out of funds and be unable to repay depositors, many of State Bank's depositors will not want to take any chances. They begin demanding *their* money back. If State Bank's assets are largely illiquid, it will be forced to liquidate its loans at deep discounts to raise money quickly as its reserves run out. As a result, it cannot repay its depositors in full and is forced to close its doors also. In this case, the bad news about State Bank is false, but the rumors made the news seem true and led to a second bank failure. The anatomy of a bank run is illustrated in Fig. 14.1.

The Cost of a Bank Run

This spreading of bad news about one bank to include other banks is known as **contagion.** Even if the rumors are unfounded, solvent banks such as State Bank of Anytown can fail during a bank run because of the costs associated with a forced liquidation of their assets. A bank run feeds on a self-fulfilling perception: If depositors *believe* the bank is in trouble, it *is* in trouble.

The underlying problem in bank runs and contagion lies in the private information about banks' loan portfolios. Lack of information leads to confusion about which banks are strong and which are weak. This situation is

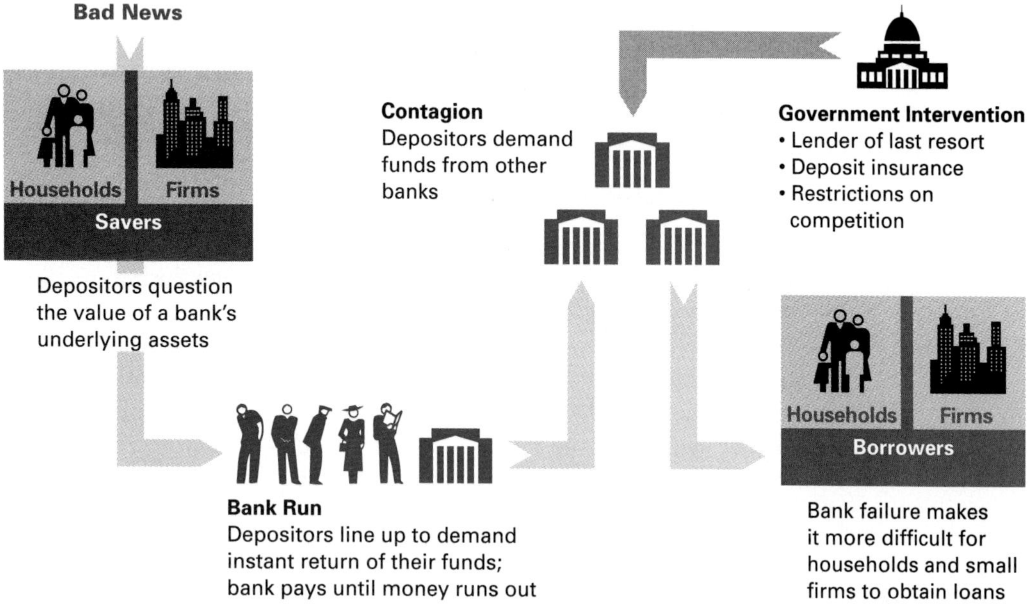

Bad News

Depositors question
the value of a bank's
underlying assets

Contagion
Depositors demand
funds from other
banks

Government Intervention
• Lender of last resort
• Deposit insurance
• Restrictions on
  competition

Bank Run
Depositors line up to demand
instant return of their funds;
bank pays until money runs out

Borrowers

Bank failure makes
it more difficult for
households and small
firms to obtain loans

▲ **FIGURE 14.1**

Bank Runs and Bank Failures
Bank runs can cause good banks
to fail as well as bad banks.
Bank failures are costly because
they reduce credit availability for
households and small firms.

similar to the adverse selection problem in financial markets, in which lenders cannot distinguish good from bad loan prospects. Because of the private information that banks obtain when acquiring assets, savers have little basis for assessing the quality of their banks' portfolios and distinguishing solvent from insolvent banks. Hence bad news about one bank can raise concerns about the financial health of others.

Policymakers are concerned about the health of the banking industry because of banks' importance in reducing information costs in the financial system. The failure of financially healthy banks hurts the ability of less well-known borrowers (households and small and medium-sized businesses) to obtain loans, thereby reducing the efficiency of the saving-investment process. In financial markets, government intervention focuses on reducing information costs through disclosure of information and prevention of fraud. For financial institutions—and banks in particular—government intervention focuses directly on maintaining the financial health of the lender. Concern over the financial stability of the banking industry prompted three types of government intervention: (1) the creation of a lender of last resort (the Federal Reserve System); (2) the introduction of federal deposit insurance; and (3) restrictions on competition in the banking industry.

▶ **C H E C K P O I N T** *Why is asymmetric information an important factor in the failure of solvent institutions during a bank run? Would runs be as likely to occur if banks held only marketable securities?* Banks acquire significant private information while collecting and monitoring information on borrowers.

As a result, uninformed depositors may be unable to distinguish between a strong bank and a weak bank, and their withdrawals could force the liquidation of the bank's loan portfolio at a loss. If banks held only marketable securities, the value of their assets would be known. Depositors would not make a run on an institution they knew to be solvent. ◄

Lender of Last Resort

Bank runs and collapses of commercial credit were unavoidable, often devastating features of the U.S. financial system during the nineteenth and early twentieth centuries. During the National Banking Period (from 1863 to 1913), at least five major **banking panics,** or waves of severe bank runs, caused credit availability to contract. The panics culminated in several deep business recessions. Simultaneously, stock and bond market prices fell, further spurring depositors' concerns about the net worth of business borrowers and their ability to repay bank loans. The onset of a banking panic was characterized by high information costs for uninformed savers, leading them to withdraw funds from banks to invest in gold or high-quality bonds.

What the banking industry was missing during this period was a "banker's bank," or **lender of last resort,** to serve as an ultimate source of credit to which banks could turn during a panic. The lender of last resort advances credit to solvent banks using a bank's good, but illiquid, loans as collateral. Insolvent banks are allowed to fail.

Prominent private bankers, such as J. P. Morgan and George F. Baker, understood the severity of the problems of bank runs and contagion and the need for a lender of last resort. In the late nineteenth century, they and several other New York City bankers used the New York Clearing House to attack the problem of contagion. Member banks agreed to lend funds to banks threatened with a run during a panic. To provide cash to satisfy the public's demand for currency instead of bank deposits, the clearing house issued *loan certificates* for use in transactions among member banks. To reduce the chance of a run on individual banks, the clearing house reported information about its balance sheet as a group, rather than for member banks separately. In theory, if the bad news hit all members of the clearing house at the same time, the members would have to break their promise of full convertibility of bank deposits into cash and issue certificates usable at other member banks to supplement their cash reserves.

Despite their significant advantages over individual banks in dealing with panics, private arrangements such as the New York Clearing House cannot easily cope in practice with *common shocks*, that is, shocks to the members as a whole. Hence the clearing house could not make a credible promise to lend during a common downturn. The severe panic of 1907 and associated business recession led President Woodrow Wilson and the Congress to create the Federal Reserve System. The Fed was designed to be a lender of last resort in order to prevent general banking panics. Member banks were compelled to keep reserve deposits at the Fed and could borrow from the Fed through *discount loans.* The Fed's resources, including gold, member bank reserves, and the statement of "full faith and credit of the U.S. government" enable it to deal with disturbances to the banking system better than private arrangements can. With the exception of its weak performance during the banking panics of the early 1930s, the Federal Reserve System's credible record as lender of last resort financially stabilized the banking industry. The Fed's role as lender of last resort has expanded over the years to include ensuring general financial stability. For example, the Fed's lending to banks during the stock market crash of October 1987 helped forestall the failure of securities firms.

Federal Deposit Insurance

The basic idea behind deposit insurance is to guarantee the value of savers' deposits—to promise that, if a bank fails, the insuring authority will reimburse the saver for funds lost. To be credible, the guarantee must be backed by sufficient funds to calm the fears of bank depositors during a panic.

Numerous bank failures during the 1920s and early 1930s led to the creation of the Federal Deposit Insurance Corporation (FDIC) in 1934. During the financial crisis from 1930 to 1933, more than one-third of all U.S. banks failed (about 2000 each year). These failures meant delays in receiving funds and, in many cases, outright losses for depositors. Following the establishment of the FDIC, calmer days resulted for the banking industry, with failure rates averaging fewer than 10 per year between 1934 and 1981.

The FDIC initially insured deposits up to $2500; it now insures deposits up to $100,000. Thus any depositor with less than $100,000 in a bank account is protected from loss in the event of failure of the bank. As a result, most depositors have little incentive to withdraw their money and cause the bank to fail if there are questions about the bank's strength. Although about 99% of all depositors are fully covered, the remaining 1% account for more than one-quarter of all deposits. Hence savers with more than $100,000 in deposits still have reason to question a bank's financial condition and demand their funds when in doubt about it. For example, if Cindy Croesus holds a $1 million negotiable CD at Doubtful Bank, $900,000 of her investment is at risk, and she will understandably withdraw her funds at a moment's notice if her bank's financial health is questioned.

Bank failures accelerated in the 1980s, climbing from 10 in 1981 to 79 in 1984, when the giant Continental Illinois National Bank, one of the 10 largest U.S. banks at the time, failed. The rate of failures increased later in the 1980s and in the early 1990s. The number of failures peaked in 1989 at 206, but the 124 failures in 1991 were still cause for concern.

How the FDIC Deals with Bank Failure

The FDIC generally uses one of two methods to handle bank failures. They are called the payoff method and the purchase and assumption method.

In the **payoff method,** the FDIC closes the bank and pays the insured depositors immediately. To recover its funds, the FDIC draws payments from the bank's remaining funds and net worth, including the sale of the bank's assets. If those funds are insufficient, the FDIC makes up the difference from its insurance reserves. After compensating insured depositors, any remaining funds are paid to uninsured depositors. Although the FDIC doesn't use this method often, it did so occasionally during the 1980s. For example, when the FDIC closed the Penn Square Bank of Oklahoma, uninsured depositors lost, on average, only about 20% of their deposits.

The FDIC prefers to use the **purchase and assumption method** to keep a failed bank running by finding a financial institution willing to take over the bank in order to gain entry into new geographic markets and access to the failed bank's *goodwill* (its network of customer relationships). Banks became especially interested in acquiring other banks after the Banking Act of 1982 permitted acquisition of failed banking institutions across state lines, providing a way around branching restrictions. The purchase and assumption method typically costs the FDIC money. Generally, it tries to find an acquiring bank to take on *all* of the failed bank's deposits. In that case, the FDIC subsidizes the assumption by providing loans at low rates of interest or buying problem loans in the failed bank's portfolio.

The FDIC must assess the relative costs of the two methods of dealing with a failed bank. The payoff method has the advantage of low cost to the deposit insurance fund because only insured depositors are compensated. So long as the perceived value of the insolvent bank's goodwill is less than the value of uninsured depositors' claims, the FDIC saves money using the payoff method. However, because banks have a special role in the saving-investment process, forcing all failed banks to close their doors may not be in the best interests of borrowers or the economy. Although keeping banks open under the purchase and assumption method may be costly, some economists argue that this method may actually be cheaper for the FDIC *in the short run.* Its reserves do not have to shrink, and regulators do not have to report operating losses. (We return to this point in Chapter 15 when we analyze the 1980s S&L crisis, in which insolvent institutions continued to operate, losing even more money, with regulators' approval.)

Stability of the Bank Insurance Fund

The FDIC earns income through the insurance premiums paid by insured banks (averaging $0.23 per $100 of deposits) and investment earnings. It receives no regular appropriation from Congress. The ability of the FDIC to make good on its guarantee of commercial bank deposits without significant regulatory reforms or a cash infusion from the Treasury was questionable at the end of the 1980s. In 1988, the FDIC's outflows exceeded inflows from bank insurance premiums for the first time in its history. The FDIC's Bank Insurance Fund held $13.2 billion at the end of 1990, or about 0.7% of total insured bank deposits. The FDIC paid out more than $9 billion in 1990, bringing reserves down to about 0.2% of insured deposits. It then paid out $11 billion in 1991, making its net worth a *negative* $7 billion at the end of 1991, or about −0.4% of total insured bank deposits. In November 1991, Congress approved the Treasury Department's emergency request for an infusion of $70 billion into the fund, including a $30 billion line of credit.

With this in mind, should you withdraw all your money from the bank? The answer is *no* because the size of the FDIC's insurance fund is not what maintains public confidence in it. The true deposit insurance is the implicit guarantee of the U.S. Treasury and the Federal Reserve System. In addition to the Treasury's recent rescue of the FDIC, the Fed on numerous occasions has lent large sums of money to troubled banks (including $5 billion in one transaction in the rescue of Continental Illinois).

Monitoring Banks

In Chapter 13 we noted that, because bankers have private information about the quality of their loan portfolios, savers have to monitor bankers. However, the introduction of federal deposit insurance weakens this incentive for savers with large deposits and eliminates it for savers with small deposits. As a result, legislation and regulations have had to provide ways to monitor banks, primarily addressing moral hazard problems (Chapter 11).

Insured banks have an incentive to make risky loans and investments. Therefore banking laws and regulations limit this behavior by restricting the types of assets that banks can hold. For example, banks are not allowed to invest deposits in common stocks. To ensure that bank examiners are doing their job, the Federal Deposit Insurance Corporation Improvement Act of 1991 (FDICIA) requires the FDIC, as insurer, to monitor the supervisory evaluation of the bank's federal or state examiner. In addition, the FDIC considers other information appropriate for evaluating risk, including results of statistical monitoring systems. Bank examiners may instruct bankers to sell risky assets from their portfolios.

Banking laws and regulations also require banks to maintain a minimum level of net worth, or equity capital. The bank's equity capital is its cushion against losses on loans and investments. Banks want to hold as little capital as necessary to attract depositors, in order to increase the return on their equity. For example, if a bank with $250 million in assets and $20 million in capital earns $2 million, it achieves a 10% return on equity. But with only $10 million in capital, it would earn a 20% return. In the absence of federal deposit insurance, to reduce the costs of moral hazard, savers would insist that bankers place their own net worth at risk. With deposit insurance, individual savers are less concerned about the value of a bank's assets, giving banks an incentive to hold less equity capital. FDICIA strengthened capital requirements for U.S. banks. However, even with a minimum level of capital requirement, capital-asset ratios for commercial banks are only about half their 1930 level (prior to the introduction of federal deposit insurance).

During most of the FDIC's existence, minimum capital requirements were stated as a fixed percentage of a bank's assets. However, as bank failures increased in the mid 1980s, regulators became concerned that the requirements did not reflect differences in banks' risk taking, especially the risk of their off-balance-sheet activities, such as trading in financial futures and options and interest rate swaps. In 1988, regulators from many countries worked under the auspices of the Bank for International Settlements in Basel, Switzerland, and agreed to design more stringent, risk-based capital requirements.[†]

Restrictions on Banking Industry Competition

The final category of government intervention that shaped the banking industry is restrictions on competition. These restrictions take two forms: (1) geographic branching restrictions, and (2) restrictions on permissible activities of banks.

Branching Restrictions

As we noted earlier, federal and state branching restrictions have figured prominently in banking regulation for decades. In order to promote competition among banks the McFadden Act prohibits national banks from establishing branches across state lines. In addition, it compels national banks to comply with the branching restrictions in the states in which they are located. State branching regulations take one of three forms: restricting banks to a single bank (*unit banking*), to branches within a narrow geographic area (*limited branching*), or to branches within a single state (*statewide branching*).

The combination of state branching restrictions and the McFadden Act protected small banks by limiting the ability of large banks to expand outside their regions or states. Branching restrictions for savings institutions and credit unions are less severe. Almost all states allow branching for savings and loan associations and mutual savings banks. Since 1980, federally chartered S&Ls have been permitted to establish branches statewide in all 50 states. Since 1981, mergers of financially troubled S&Ls have been allowed across state lines.

Geographic restrictions may push banks toward local lending, lowering the costs of providing risk-sharing, liquidity, and information services. However, geographic restrictions also reduce banks' ability to diversify assets, raising their exposure to credit risk. In addition, because the fixed costs of funding a bank (for example, computer systems, regulatory reporting, and so on) are high, branching restrictions may reduce banks' profitability. Indeed, in

---

[†] International coordination is important. Otherwise, banks in a country having a high capital requirement may be put at a short-term competitive disadvantage against banks in a country having a low capital requirement.

the debate over branching restrictions in the early 1990s, California-based Bank of America estimated that removal of branching restrictions alone would save it $50 million per year in duplicated overhead costs. Thus limited competition may lead to bank inefficiency and lower rates of return for investors, with significant costs to the economy.

Advocates of limited branching argue that the large number of U.S. banks benefits the banking system because it promotes competition. In fact, the opposite is true. When a bank's territory is protected by regulation, it may operate inefficiently yet still compete successfully against more efficient banks. Why has this anticompetitive inefficiency persisted so long? The answer lies in the politics of U.S. finance mentioned at the beginning of the chapter. Americans have long and continually distrusted large, big-city banks. Indeed, the states with the strongest populist, anti–big-bank sentiment in the nineteenth century—usually agricultural states in the Midwest or South— were more likely to have restrictive branching regulations after that time. The large number of relatively small commercial banks reflects in large part the legacy of those political struggles (see Box 14.1).

The Response to Branching Restrictions

Competitive forces in the banking industry are hard to restrain. Innovations by financial institutions, including bank holding companies, non-bank banks, and automatic teller machines, have steadily eroded restrictions on geographic competition.

Bank Holding Companies. As early as the 1950s, banks began to get around branching restrictions by forming bank holding companies (BHCs). A **bank holding company** is a large firm that holds many different banks as

---

Consider this...   BOX 14.1

What if the U.S. Banking Industry Were Like California's?

California presents a useful example of how the U.S. banking industry might be structured without branching restrictions. Since 1909, California banking authorities have allowed statewide branching throughout this geographically large and economically diverse state. California's 400 banks serve its population of more than 29 million people. If this ratio of banks to

people were applied nationwide, the United States would have about 3700 banks rather than the current 12,000. Although such a comparison doesn't take into account differences in state demographics, it does illustrate the potential for consolidation in the U.S. banking industry if branching restrictions were eliminated.

Would this consolidation be beneficial to bank customers?

Again, California's case is instructive. During the farm-debt crisis of the early and mid-1980s, California's regionally diversified banks withstood farm-loan losses better than the poorly diversified banks in the Midwest did. Thus the national economy likely would benefit from permitting greater regional diversification for banks, as in California.

subsidiaries. Congress relaxed branching restrictions in the Bank Holding Company Act of 1956, permitting bank holding companies to provide non-bank financial services on an interstate basis. The act directed the Fed to regulate the new activities of *multibank* holding companies, so a loophole existed for expansion into nonbanking activities by *one-bank* holding companies. Congress closed this loophole in the 1970 Amendment to the Bank Holding Company Act, but the period since 1970 has been one of significant expansion by bank holding companies. Citicorp, the holding company associated with Citibank in New York City, operates more than 1000 lending or other offices in the United States.

Nonbank Banks.   For many years, financial institutions circumvented branching restrictions through BHCs. The Bank Holding Company Act of 1956 defined a bank as a financial institution that accepts demand deposits and makes commercial loans. Financial institutions got around the regulation by splitting these two functions: They created **nonbank offices,** which did not take demand deposits but made loans, and **nonbank banks,** which took demand deposits but did not make loans. The regulatory response to this activity was the Competitive Equality Banking Act of 1987, which forbade opening additional nonbank banks, although it allowed additional nonbank offices to be opened.

Automated Teller Machines.   During the 1980s, banks further broke branching restrictions through the innovation of **automated teller machines** (ATMs). The development of ATMs was made possible by the combination of falling computer costs and regulatory opportunity. Because ATMs technically are not bank branches, they aren't subject to branching restrictions. These facilities can be located some distance from the main bank and actually function as bank branches, accepting deposits, processing withdrawals, making loans through credit cards, and conducting various other transactions.

Current Status.   Since the mid-1970s, limits imposed by branching restrictions have faded significantly. In 1975, Maine became the first state to allow complete interstate banking. In 1982, Massachusetts and other New England states entered into a regional compact to permit growth of larger banking organizations in New England. Such regional arrangements in New England and elsewhere spawned *superregional banks.* Indeed, some superregional banks approach *money center banks* (large, established national banks) in size and profitability. As of early 1993, 49 states and the District of Columbia were allowing some degree of interstate banking; 28 had legislated nationwide entry. Only one state, Hawaii, currently makes no provision for interstate banking.

However, these developments don't mean that full nationwide banking is near. Although virtually all the western states allow full interstate banking (some requiring reciprocity), many southern and midwestern states permit only regional interstate banking. As a result, nationwide banks, operating in every state, do not yet exist. Consolidation is slow because of regional restrictions and because, in the early 1990s, many large banks did not have sufficient capital to acquire networks of branches in other states.

Nonetheless, many analysts believe that the McFadden Act and state branching restrictions may be on their way out. That belief is supported by two recent developments: (1) the Treasury Department's proposal that all branching restrictions across state lines be abolished; and (2) Mexican and Canadian agreements (as part of the North American Free Trade Agreement), to allow U.S. banks to branch freely across their borders if the United States adopts interstate branch banking.

Restrictions on the Scope of Bank Activities

Before 1933, commercial banks were securities market financial institutions as well as depository institutions. In particular, banks were involved in investment banking activities. During the 1920s and early 1930s, some commercial banks underwrote corporate securities, selling good-quality issues to the public and placing poor-quality issues in trust accounts for individuals or pensions in its care. As a result, banks earned investment banking fees for risky activities, with the risk borne in part by their depositors.

The wave of bank failures during the 1930s and the public outcry over abusive banking practices led Congress to reduce conflicts of interest by limiting the scope of permissible activities for commercial banks. The Banking Act of 1933 (known as the Glass-Steagall Act) prohibited commercial banks from participating in underwriting corporate securities and broker-dealer activities, although banks were allowed to continue selling new issues of government securities (see Fig. 14.2). In addition, banks could hold only those debt securities approved by regulatory agencies. Thus the Glass-Steagall Act erected a wall between commercial banking and investment banking, forcing a wave of divestitures by financial institutions. For example, J. P. Morgan, a commercial bank, spun off Morgan Stanley, an investment bank and First National Bank of Boston spun off First Boston Corporation.

Another important aspect of the Glass-Steagall Act separated ownership of financial institutions and nonfinancial firms. The separation of finance from commerce reflected concern about the concentration of power; that is, financiers might be able to monopolize major industries and reward affiliates while starving their competitors' credit needs. Such fear was justified by the activities of J. P. Morgan and other financiers, who used their financial power to create monopolies in the late nineteenth and early twentieth centuries. However, such activities are much less likely today because of greater competition in finance and industry.

The Debate Over Retaining These Restrictions.   In today's regulatory environment, many analysts believe that the fears of the early 1930s about

► FIGURE 14.2

The Glass-Steagall Wall
The Glass-Steagall Act of 1933 sought to reduce conflicts of interest by creating a "wall" separating the permissible activities of commercial banking and investment banking.

Commercial Banking

Limited to the purchase of securities approved by regulatory agencies; permitted to continue selling new issues of government securities

Prohibited from underwriting corporate securities and broker/dealer activities

Investment Banking

Permitted to assist in sale of securities in the primary market

Prohibited from all deposit-taking activities: checking and savings accounts

**Glass-Steagall Act
(1933)**

abusive banking practices are unwarranted. They argue that the SEC and federal banking regulatory agencies—and banks' concern for their reputations—limit the potential for problems. In principle, the Glass-Steagall Act was designed to protect depositors of commercial banks from risky investment activities by the banks. In practice, however, it has protected the investment banking industry from competition, enabling it to earn higher profits than the commercial banking industry. As a result, borrowers pay more for issuing new securities than they would if competition from banks were allowed.

Opponents of breaking down the wall between commercial and investment banking point out that commercial banks have a cost advantage in obtaining funds because bank deposits are generally insured by the FDIC. Securities firms have no such insurance and pay a higher cost for funds, usually in the form of loans from banks themselves. Allowing commercial banks to participate in risky broker-dealer and investment banking activities exposes the FDIC—and, through it, taxpayers' funds—to additional risk. Some compromises are possible. They include charging risk-based premiums for bank deposit insurance or increasing net worth requirements for banks engaging in securities market activities.

Regulation still prohibits banking firms from entering the markets of nonfinancial firms. Allowing banks to be involved in nonfinancial activities is called **universal banking.** Although not permitted in the United States, universal banking is allowed in other countries (notably Germany). Advocates of universal banking argue that creating a role for commercial banks in corporate finance improves information gathering and monitoring, thereby reducing problems of adverse selection and moral hazard. If a bank holds shares in a nonfinancial firm and is represented on its board of directors, the information gap shrinks, and monitoring the firm's activities becomes easier and more efficient. One problem with integrating financial and commercial activities in the United States is the safety net afforded banks by deposit insurance. Further debate over expanding risk-taking by banks and whether U.S. banks are big enough to compete in the world banking market likely will await passage of comprehensive banking industry reform legislation, such as that proposed by the Treasury Department in 1991 and 1992 (see Box 14.2).

Current Status.   During the past two decades, commercial banks to a large degree have overcome the restrictions that kept them from offering investment services, as shown in Fig. 14.3. Because the role of banking in finance is to generate information, involvement in corporate finance is a logical extension of banking. Hence banks have been major players in underwriting commercial paper. Because the Glass-Steagall Act was passed before international banking networks became firmly established, it does not regulate the overseas activities of banks. Therefore Eurobonds can be and are under-

> **FIGURE 14.3**

Breaking Down the Glass-Steagall Wall
Beginning in the 1970s, commercial banks and investment banks introduced innovations which allowed them to offer competing services. These innovations continue to steadily erode the "wall" created by the Glass-Steagall Act. Over time, this financial innovation has been ratified by changes in regulation.

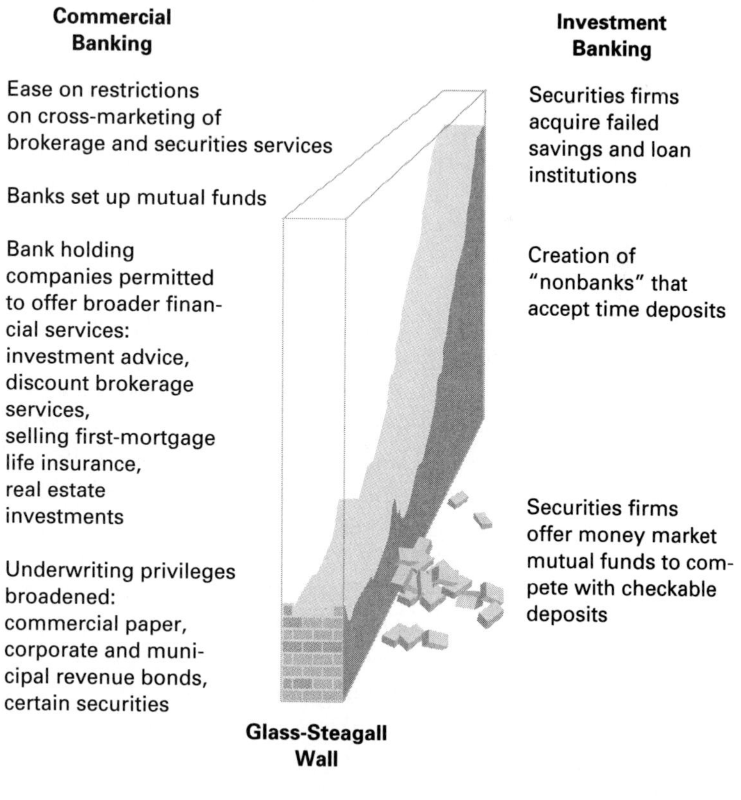

Commercial Banking

Ease on restrictions on cross-marketing of brokerage and securities services

Banks set up mutual funds

Bank holding companies permitted to offer broader financial services: investment advice, discount brokerage services, selling first-mortgage life insurance, real estate investments

Underwriting privileges broadened: commercial paper, corporate and municipal revenue bonds, certain securities

Investment Banking

Securities firms acquire failed savings and loan institutions

Creation of "nonbanks" that accept time deposits

Securities firms offer money market mutual funds to compete with checkable deposits

Glass-Steagall Wall

Consider this...

Are U.S. Banks Big Enough?

On average, commercial banks in the United States are relatively small. At the beginning of the 1990s, more than half of all U.S. banks had assets of less than $50 million and controlled only about 5% of total bank assets. At the other extreme, only about 3% of all banks had assets of more than $1 billion, yet those banks controlled more than 60% of total bank assets. Some banking analysts argue that the United States would be better off if the small banks merged to form larger, more efficient units. Many believe that large U.S. banks will have to get larger by acquiring smaller banks, in order to compete with giant Japanese and European banks in the global financial marketplace.

Studies of actual mergers are inconclusive. Some bank mergers have increased efficiency, but others have reduced it. Moreover, studies of cost efficiency generally find that economies of scale in banking are realized at levels well below the existing size of large U.S. banks. The strong competitive position of U.S. banks in international lending and off-balance-sheet activities bears out this finding. Very large banks in some other countries—notably Japan—are the result of regulatory policies restricting the number of banks, just as regulation promoted a large number of banks in the United States. Virtually all analysts support the erosion of branching and other anticompetitive restrictions, but there is no consensus about the need to make large U.S. banks even larger through mergers. During the 1990s and well into the twenty-first century, large and small banks are likely to continue to coexist, with the largest U.S. banks being competitive globally.

written by U.S. banks. In June 1988, the Supreme Court allowed the Federal Reserve System to authorize underwriting activities for commercial paper, municipal revenue bonds, and mortgage-backed and consumer-debt-backed securities by bank affiliates. Revenue from underwriting is restricted to 5% of the affiliate's gross revenue. In June 1989, the Fed gave some commercial banks limited power to underwrite corporate bonds, allowing them to compete with investment bankers. Initial participants included four New York City banks: Bankers Trust, Chase Manhattan, Citibank, and J. P. Morgan. These activities are to be conducted in separate subsidiaries within a bank holding company, with no access to insured bank deposits.

Banks also have become more involved in investment advice and brokerage services. In 1983, the Fed permitted bank holding companies to offer discount brokerage services. In 1987, the Office of the Comptroller of the Currency approved full-service brokerage powers for national banks. In 1987 and 1988, the Fed extended these powers to bank holding companies. Finally, in 1992, the Fed relaxed existing barriers between banks and their securities affiliates by lifting restrictions on the cross-marketing of banking and securities services. This action enables customers to deal with one institution whether discussing a bank loan or raising funds by selling commercial paper or issuing stock. Hence, from the banking side, the line between the banking and the securities industries is thin indeed.

By the early 1990s, banks had begun to compete with securities firms in setting up mutual funds. In 1992, bank mutual fund assets totaled only $54 billion compared to the $1.4 trillion mutual fund assets of securities firms. However, many economists and market analysts believe that a bank's reputation with its customers and its branch network make it a formidable competitor in the mutual fund market.

The clamor to eliminate Glass-Steagall restrictions has been heard from the other direction as well. Securities firms, such as Fidelity and Merrill Lynch, have long been active sellers of money market mutual funds, which provide a close substitute for bank deposits. Merrill Lynch and others have purchased banks and turned them into nonbanks. Regulators halted this activity in 1987, but securities firms have continued to establish nonbanks by acquiring failing savings institutions.

The separation of finance from commerce also is breaking down. Nonfinancial firms already engage in significant financial sector activities. General Motors, Ford, and Chrysler long have been involved in financial services by providing credit to customers to purchase automobiles, and each owns insurance companies. In addition, Ford is aggressively expanding its role as a holding company of savings institutions. Sears, a pioneer in the development of installment credit to finance purchases from its store, expanded into credit cards (Discover®). In late 1992, however, it sold some of its financial service businesses.

Q: What aspects of banking explain why these regulatory authorities were introduced?

A: The problem of liquidity risk and banks' role in reducing information costs in the saving-investment process led to concern over bank failures and to regulatory interventions, including creation of a lender of last resort, introduction of federal deposit insurance, and restrictions on banks' activities.

► **CHECKPOINT** *Suppose that commercial banks are allowed to enter all investment banking and securities activities. What do you predict would happen to profit margins in underwriting services and to the salaries and bonuses of investment bankers?* Full-scale entry by banks into investment banking and securities businesses likely would reduce the profitability of underwriting and related investment banking businesses, reducing investment bankers' compensation. ◄

The Banking Industry in Other Countries

The information role of banking suggests that several beneficial links can be developed between banking and industry: (1) financing growth opportunities in sectors in which information problems are important; (2) making sure that managers of large-scale enterprises are working to maximize the long-run value of those firms; and (3) reducing costs of financial distress for firms having difficulty meeting their current obligations to banks and other creditors. These roles relate to banks' basic function of lowering transactions and information costs.

The rapid growth of the Japanese and German economies since World War II can be traced in part to the role their banks played in lending to industry and commerce. After World War II, many new firms and industries in Japan and Germany entered new markets, creating problems of asymmetric information and a demand for bank finance. The banks in those countries took advantage of the opportunities presented for intermediation. We now evaluate how Japanese and German banks filled industry's needs following World War II and then briefly examine the prospects for the integration of banking in Europe.

Japanese Banking

Two features of the Japanese economy contributed significantly to the importance of bank finance in funding Japan's postwar industry: (1) regulation of activities of various capital markets and financial institutions; and (2) the cooperative nature of Japanese industry.

Regulation.   For much of the post–World War II period, government regulation kept Japanese firms from issuing securities internationally or issuing risky debt instruments in domestic financial markets. Hence firms turned to banks for finance, making Japanese nonfinancial corporations largely dependent on bank loans. Government authorities—in particular, the Ministry for Trade and Industry (MITI) and the Ministry of Finance (MOF)—greatly influenced the channeling of funds to industries by banks. Short-term banking was the province of city and regional banks. Long-term credit banks were the only institutions allowed to make long-term loans (usually three- to five-year unsecured loans), but they could not make short-term loans. Finally, small mutual banks, known as *sogos*, were created to ensure that local small firms had access to credit.

Structure.   The structure of Japanese industry differs significantly from that of U.S. industry. Many large Japanese firms are affiliated with industrial groups, or *keiretsu*. The six major keiretsu—Mitsubishi, Mitsui, Sumitomo, Fuyo, Daiichi Kangyo, and Sanwa—were established during the 1950s, but some trace their origins to the prewar period. These large groups are diversified and vertically integrated. In the early 1980s, such group firms accounted for about half of Japanese sales in the natural resources, primary metals, industrial machinery, chemicals, and cement industries. Moreover, group firms traded much more with other group members than with nongroup firms.

Two aspects of group finance are of interest. First, the extensive trading relationships are reinforced by cross-shareholding within the group; that is, firms with close ties often hold large equity stakes in each other. Second, each group has a **main bank** that (1) owns some equity in the member firms, (2) is a primary source of credit for group firms, (3) monitors the activities of member firms, in some instances even placing key bank personnel in managerial positions in the firms, and (4) helps member firms recover from financial distress, taking the lead in organizing financial restructurings (other banks defer to their leadership in this respect). In sum, the main banks' relationships with borrowers are structured to reduce adverse selection and moral hazard problems.

Benefits and Costs.   Economists have studied the value to savers and borrowers of this relationship between industry and banking. They found convincing evidence that group firms with access to main bank credit are able to invest more and grow faster than their often credit-rationed, nongroup counterparts. In addition, group firms in financial distress recover faster in terms of investment and sales growth than similarly situated nongroup firms. This success is attributed to the role of main banks, which provide supplementary credit and write down the value of their loans without a bankruptcy proceeding. Because the main banks actively monitor the firms, they have good information about their prospects for long-term recovery and growth.

However, these relationships also involve costs, including high interest rates on loans relative to those in bond markets and restrictions on firms' activities imposed by banks. Owing to these costs, Japanese firms pressed for and received relief from the government in the form of the Foreign Exchange Law Reform of 1980. It allowed firms to issue bonds abroad without government permission. Then, in January 1983, deregulation permitted firms to issue bonds without collateral. Many firms subsequently went outside their main bank relationships to obtain funds from securities markets in Japan and abroad. The share of external funds raised by bank borrowing fell from 80% in 1980 to about 50% in 1985, and has continued to decline.

Current Status.   Recent trends in Japanese banking resemble trends in the U.S. banking industry. As a consequence of financial deregulation, Japanese banks have lost many of their large-firm customers to financial markets. The large Japanese city banks—among the world's largest in terms of assets—earned low returns on assets relative to many large U.S. banks in the early 1990s. Japanese banks' strategy in the 1990s is to move into the securities business while remaining close enough to Japanese industry to lend money and provide advice. In a law patterned after the Glass-Steagall Act, Japan officially separated commercial and investment banking. Nonetheless, Japanese banks have expanded into foreign securities operations.

German Banking

Germany is one of only a few countries that allow universal banking (others are France, Luxembourg, The Netherlands, the United Kingdom, and, to some extent, Canada). Recall that universal banking allows banks to carry out banking and many nonbanking activities within a single firm and with no geographic restrictions. In Germany, for example, Deutsche Bank owns a 25% stake in Daimler-Benz, a large automobile manufacturer. German universal banking requires that bank participation in nonfinancial firms include direct voting rights for bank-owned shares. The significant reinforcement of proxy votes for shares held by the bank as custodian for its clients is also required.

Banking and industry developed together in Germany, with establishment of the first joint-stock bank in 1848. Initially, banks relied on their own capital to make long-term loans. Later, Deutsche Bank became the first major bank to seek deposits, although at that time it invested deposits only in safe and liquid short-term loans to merchants. Large national banks emerged in the late nineteenth century. Because of the strong role of banks for most of this century, securities markets are less well developed in Germany than in the United Kingdom or the United States.

Benefits and Costs.   Many observers have concluded that the close alliance between banking and industry helped accelerate industrialization and growth in post–World War II Germany. They contend that universal banking benefits German industry by extending to it the information-related strengths of commercial banking arrangements. However, many others have expressed concerns. One problem cited is the potential for conflicts of interest. (Recall that this concern prompted the separation of commercial and investment banking by the Glass-Steagall Act in the United States.) However, strict supervision, coupled with vigorous competition in financial and product markets, can counterbalance this problem. A second and more important concern regards the pricing of bank loans in Germany. Without aggressive competition from securities markets, banks may charge higher interest rates to firms than they could in the face of competition. A final significant concern is that the relationship between industry and banks under universal banking might require a wider role for the Bundesbank, the German central bank, in a financial crisis: If deposits in financial institutions are insured to protect depositors from losses when banks fail, commercial or industrial firms that own financial institutions also may need to be covered by insurance.

Current Status.   Complementing the three large banks in Germany—Deutsche Bank, Dresdner Bank, and Commerzbank—are numerous smaller banks. Current developments in German banking resemble those in the United States, Japan, and elsewhere. Increasing volatility of interest rates and exchange rates has generated a trend toward securitization. In addition, investment banking is emerging as an important activity within commercial banks.

Integration of European Banking

In the past, only very restricted bank branching across national borders has been allowed in Europe. The European Community (EC) has proposed removal of national barriers to trade in goods and financial markets beginning in 1992. It has also proposed a gradual shift to a banking industry that resembles interstate banking in the United States. The goal is a uniform EC-wide charter for banking operations. Hence, as with relaxed U.S. branching restrictions, substantial bank consolidation is likely to occur. Indeed, the Second Banking Directive (when effective) would have a long-run effect similar to that of repealing the McFadden Act, the Glass-Steagall Act, and the Bank Holding Company Act in the United States.

What predictions can we make as to the probable effect of European integration for the banking industry? First, integration should promote risk sharing and lead to greater diversification. In addition, activities of banks, securities firms, and insurance firms are likely to become more interconnected. In Europe, as in the United States, banks have successfully ventured into broader securities and investment activities. The information-gathering and monitoring skills of banks, as well as their branch networks, make them formidable competitors in Europe's increasingly important securities and insurance markets, for example.

Concluding Remarks

Banks throughout the world provide a variety of financial services, and all countries regulate their banking industries in various ways. Table 14.2 compares the effects of regulation on banking services in several industrialized countries.

▼ TABLE 14.2   LIMITS ON SERVICES PROVIDED BY COMMERCIAL BANKS

Are banks allowed to provide these services?	Canada	France	Germany	Italy	Japan	Switzerland	United Kingdom	United States
Insurance:								
Brokerage	N	Y	Y	N*	N	N	Y	N*
Underwriting	N	N*	Y*	N*	N	N	Y*	N
Equities:								
Brokerage	Y*	Y	Y	Y	N	Y	Y	Y
Underwriting	Y*	Y	Y	Y	N	Y	Y*	N*
Investment	Y	Y	Y	Y	Y	Y	Y*	N
Other underwriting:								
Government debt	Y	Y	Y	Y	N	Y	Y*	Y
Private debt	Y*	Y	Y	Y	N	Y	Y*	N*
Mutual funds:								
Brokerage	Y	Y	Y	Y	N	Y	Y	N*
Management	Y*	Y	Y	Y	N	Y	Y	N
Real estate:								
Brokerage	N	Y	Y	N	N	Y	Y	N*
Investment	Y	Y	Y	Y	N	Y	Y	N
Other brokerage:								
Government debt	Y	Y	Y	Y	Y	Y	Y	Y
Private debt	Y	Y	Y	Y	Y	Y	Y	Y
Branching restrictions	N	N	N	N	N	N	N	Y

Notes: N = No; N* = No, with exceptions; Y = Yes; Y* = Yes, but not directly by the bank.

Source: American Bankers Association, *International Banking Competitiveness*, March 1990, p. 82

MOVING FROM THEORY TO PRACTICE...

THE NEW YORK TIMES   AUGUST 16, 1992

A Safety Net for Money Funds?

At the same time that fund executives revel in the industry's prosperity, more and more of them worry about its Achilles' heel: money funds.

The public has basically been using money funds, with share prices fixed at $1, as substitutes for bank accounts. Prospectuses warn investors that share prices can fluctuate, but none has yet. Nevertheless, as the stakes grow higher if a money fund did fall below the $1 share price a crisis of confidence might reverberate through the entire industry...

The fragility of money funds' fixed $1 share price surfaces from time to time. In 1989, Integrated Resources defaulted on $23 million of commercial paper held by the Value Line Money Fund. The following year, the Mortgage and Realty Trust...defaulted on its commercial paper, leaving 10 money funds holding $75 million of sharply downgraded paper.

In these cases, the relatively small size of the bailouts allowed the funds to absorb the losses rather than reduce the share price.

That may change. Today the fund industry owns 36 percent of all commercial paper outstanding, a market that has doubled in size since 1984, according to Michael L. Goldstein, an analyst with Sanford C. Bernstein & Company. Commercial paper carries no guarantees and no insurance, and with "funds growing faster than the supply of low-risk commercial paper, eventually a financial accident could occur at a scale beyond that which can be covered by the liquid assets of management companies," he says...

James L. Pierce, an economics professor at the University of California at Berkeley, writes that money funds "present a real, though small, risk to their holders." Even so, he argues in his book "The Future of Banking," money funds are by nature better suited to handle the nation's cash flow than savings accounts, as the savings-and-loan crisis clearly shows.

That is because banks' deposit liabilities are largely backed by illiquid loans, making them vulnerable to runs and liquidity crises. By contrast, money funds back their deposits with highly liquid and relatively safe assets—a much better match.

He concludes that, with insurance, money funds "could be made safe with little need for additional regulation or supervision."...

In 1983, Vanguard introduced the Vanguard Money Market Reserves/Insured Portfolio, which bought either insured issues or private insurance for its paper. The insurance drove up the fund's costs; in 1988, its expenses were 79 percent of assets, more than double the expenses of Vanguard's Prime Money Market Reserves. That cut into yield, and investors, given the choice, opted for higher yield. In February 1989, Vanguard termed the experiment a failure and converted the $150 million fund into an all-Treasury money fund, which holds $2.2 billion today.

ANALYZING THE NEWS...

Money market mutual funds are important financial intermediaries for savers, and their assets have grown from virtually nothing in the late 1970s to about $600 billion in early 1993. These funds generally permit savers to write checks against their account balances, and savers consider their balances to be just like "money in the bank." Although yields may fluctuate with increases or decreases in market interest rates, the value of the shares (analogous to bank deposits) doesn't change.

ⓐ The credit-risk exposure of money market mutual funds is low because they invest primarily in short-term Treasury securities and high-quality commercial paper. Nonetheless, some analysts fear that continued rapid growth of money market funds could force them to invest in lower quality instruments. Our analysis of information costs indicates that, as long as investors are aware of this risk, the yield should increase to compensate them for bearing the risk. Note the contrast with banks: Bankers have substantial private information about their loan portfolios, and loans are less liquid than securities held by money market funds.

ⓑ Because of types of assets typically held by money market funds, savers are not likely to sacrifice much of their yield to buy shares in insured funds, as Vanguard found out the hard way. After all, savers can invest directly in liquid, default-risk-free Treasury instruments. Moreover, so long as mutual funds do not invest in assets for which high information costs require them to address adverse selection and moral hazard problems, minimum capital requirements are not as necessary as they are for banks. Such requirements give bankers an incentive not to exploit their private information to the detriment of savers.

For further thought...

Suppose that money market mutual funds began making short-term illiquid loans to less well-known borrowers. If the federal government established a Mutual Fund Insurance Corporation, funded by premiums paid by money market mutual funds, to maintain a $1 share price, should regulators set minimum capital requirements? Explain.

Source: Excerpted from "A Safety Net for Money Funds" by Carole Gould, August 16, 1992. Copyright 1991/1992 by The New York Times Company. Reprinted by permission.

Key Terms and Concepts

Automated teller machine

Bank holding company

Bank run

Banking panic

Branching restrictions

Contagion

Demand deposit

Dual banking system
   National banks
   State banks

Federal deposit insurance

Federal Reserve System

Lender of last resort

Main bank

Nonbank bank

Nonbank office

Payoff method

Purchase and assumption method

Universal banking

Summary

1. The U.S. banking industry comprises a dual banking system: Commercial banks are chartered and examined by both the federal government and by states. Regulatory agencies responsible for commercial bank regulation include the Federal Deposit Insurance Corporation (FDIC), the Office of the Comptroller of the Currency, the Federal Reserve System, and state banking authorities. Savings and loan associations generally are insured by the FDIC and regulated by the Office of Thrift Supervision. Mutual savings banks are also insured by the FDIC but regulated by state authorities. Credit unions generally are insured by the National Credit Union Share Insurance Fund and regulated by the National Credit Union Administration.

2. Loss of confidence by depositors in a bank can lead to a bank run, in which the bank is forced to liquidate its assets to pay depositors and close its doors. Because of private information in banking, bank runs can cause solvent banks as well as insolvent banks to fail. The cause for concern over the failure of sound banks in a run is the loss of bank intermediation, an important source of finance in the economy.

3. To promote stability, government has intervened in the banking industry by (a) creating a lender of last resort, (b) introducing federal deposit insurance, and (c) restricting permissible bank activities.

4. Federal deposit insurance was introduced in the United States in the 1930s to guarantee bank deposits and guard against bank runs. Until the early 1980s, it was very successful in reducing bank failures. In response to the greater number of bank failures in the 1980s and early 1990s, the FDIC and other regulatory agencies now require banks to hold greater minimum amounts of net worth, or equity capital, than before and to refrain from participation in risky activities.

5. Due to the McFadden Act, which prohibits branching across state lines, and state branching restrictions, the United States has a large number of relatively small commercial banks. In recent years, banks have circumvented branching restrictions by forming bank holding companies, creating nonbank offices and nonbank banks, and introducing automated teller machines. In addition, states are relaxing their branching restrictions, and federal legislation to permit nationwide banking is under consideration.

6. The Glass-Steagall Act separated commercial banking from investment banking and brokerage businesses. It has been circumvented by bank holding companies that can now underwrite many types of securities and engage in brokerage activities. Conversely, securities firms now compete with banks for deposits. Although some nonfinancial firms have entered the financial services industry, the separation of banking and commerce in the United States remains relatively strong.

7. The banking industry differs by country in response to differences in bank regulation. Banks in Japan and Germany are permitted to have closer relationships with borrowers than are U.S. banks; some analysts argue that these relationships contributed to the rapid growth of investment and output in these countries since World War II. Nonetheless, as domestic financial systems become more integrated internationally banking industries in various countries appear to be becoming more similar.

Review Questions

1. What is the dual banking system? Why does it persist?

2. What is the main function of federal deposit insurance?

3. Why does the United States have so many banks?

4. If bank runs closed only insolvent banks, should anyone care? Why might bank runs create a need for regulation?

5. How did the establishment of the Federal Reserve System reduce the chance of banking panics?

6. What are the advantages and disadvantages of the payoff method compared to the purchase and assumption method of dealing with failed banks?

7. How do risk-based capital requirements work?

8. Which government regulations restrict bank competition? How did they come about? Are they likely to continue into the future?

9. What are the costs to banks of geographic restrictions on bank competition? To savers? To borrowers? In a banking system with banks of different sizes, which banks stand to gain from geographic restrictions? To lose?

10. How have banks tried to get around restrictions on branching? What was the regulatory response to these attempts?

11. What is the difference between a nonbank office and a nonbank bank?

12. Which law forced the separation of commercial banking from investment banking in the United States? Why was it enacted? Is it still completely in force? Explain.

13. How does the U.S. experience of separating commerce from banking compare to that of countries having universal banking?

14. What can banks do to link banking and industry more beneficially?

15. How does universal banking work in Germany? What concerns might taxpayers have if universal banking were tried in the United States and banks were still covered by FDIC insurance?

Analytical Problems

16. *Evaluate:* The United States has more than 12,000 banks, whereas Canada has only a few, so the U.S. banking industry must be more competitive.

17. The ceiling on the size of an account covered by federal deposit insurance is $100,000. If you hear that your bank may be in trouble, what would you do if you had $10,000 in the bank? If you had $200,000 in the bank? Does deposit insurance fulfill its role in reducing failures if a bank has many large depositors? Why or why not?

18. Suppose that banks, preparing for increased international competition, are trying to improve their capital by making fewer loans, buying more securi-

ties, and holding more cash. Suddenly, bank funding for several large (and solvent) corporations is in jeopardy. What would you do if you were the Chairman of the Federal Reserve Board?

19. By the 1980s, the level of bank net worth (equity capital) relative to bank assets, had declined significantly from pre-1934 levels. All other things being equal, could the introduction of federal deposit insurance in 1934 account for this change? Explain.

20. *Evaluate:* A banking system with deposit insurance needs more supervision from third-party examiners than does a banking system without guarantees for depositors.

Data Question

21. Find the most recent issue of the *World Almanac* in your library and locate historical data on the number of U.S. bank failures each year. In the four decades following the introduction of federal deposit insurance (by the Banking Act of 1933), what happened to

the number of bank failures relative to the number in the decade prior to the introduction of deposit insurance? Based on this information, can you conclude that deposit insurance made financial intermediaries healthier? Explain.

CHAPTER 15

Banking Regulation: Crisis and Response

1992 was a sobering year for financial institutions. The Congressional Budget Office released a report on the high prospective cost of the taxpayer-financed bailout of federal deposit insurance. On the other side of the world, a worried Japanese Deposit Insurance Corporation made its first payments to depositors. Newspapers and magazines published stories about the financial condition of U.S. insurance companies and the potential failure of pension funds that could leave savers destitute.

In the past, managers of banks and savings and loan associations were said to follow a "3–6–3" rule: Borrow at 3%, lend at 6%, and be on the golf course at 3:00. This cozy world was maintained under the protection of regulation and by good luck. Today's marketplace for financial services has grown more competitive, driven by the process of financial crisis, regulation, financial innovation, and regulatory response.

In the preceding three chapters, we showed that financial institutions exist to fill specific market needs, and trends in regulation and deregulation cause them to adjust. In this chapter, we first consider regulation attempts to solve potential problems in banks' relationships with savers and borrowers. We then examine the successes and failures of banking regulation.

In this chapter we answer one main question. **Q:** How does regulation promote the effectiveness of banks as intermediaries in the saving-investment process?

The Cycle of Crisis and Response

To understand how banking regulations come about and how they affect the banking industry, its competitors, and savers and borrowers, we need to consider regulatory intervention as a *process*. In this process a financial crisis prompts the government to enact legislation and impose regulation. Financial institutions respond to the problems or opportunities created by innovating on the services offered. Government then responds with new or modified regulation. To understand how this cycle works, let's consider its four parts: financial crisis, regulation, financial innovation, and regulatory response.

The first part of the cycle is a crisis, such as a bank run caused by savers' loss of confidence in banks' ability to use their funds wisely. When savers lose confidence in them, banks are unable to fulfill their role as intermediaries for many borrowers. Adverse selection and moral hazard problems have the potential to create instability, which can lead to such crises in the financial system.

The second part of the cycle occurs when government steps in to end the crisis through regulation. The government generally intervenes when it perceives instability in financial institutions and when political pressures make intervention advisable. For example, government regulation in the United States and other countries has responded to banking panics by attempting to maintain banks' profitability and/or reducing monitoring costs for savers.

The third part of the cycle is response by the financial system. A major regulatory intervention—deposit insurance, for example—leads to changes and innovation in the activities of financial institutions (borrowing, lending, and provision of risk-sharing, liquidity, and information services). As in manufacturing companies or other service businesses, *innovation* (the development of new products or lines of business to serve consumers) is an important activity in financial institutions. The motivation for financial innovation is the same as that in other businesses: profit.

The fourth part of the cycle occurs as regulators observe the impact of regulation on changes in the way that financial institutions do business. In particular, when financial innovations circumvent regulatory restrictions, regulators must adapt their policies or seek new authority as a regulatory response.

This cycle of financial crisis, regulation, financial innovation, and regulatory response has been repeated many times. To illustrate the cycle, we focus on three specific interventions in the United States designed to promote stability of financial institutions: (1) the creation of a lender of last resort for banks; (2) the imposition of restrictions on bank competition in the form of limitations on interest rates paid to depositors; and (3) the introduction of federal deposit insurance.

Each of these interventions came after a financial crisis. Congress created the Federal Reserve System as the lender of last resort to provide liquidity to banks in response to banking panics. Congress limited interest payments on deposits following the banking panic of the early 1930s and attempted to reduce the chance of bank runs by bolstering bank profits. Congress introduced federal deposit insurance in response to the calamitous events of the early 1930s and tried to promote bank stability by reducing the default risk of holding bank deposits. These interventions created new government agencies having various regulatory powers and discretionary authority.

Each intervention led to innovation by financial institutions and further responses by regulators. Each intervention also illustrates important points about these actions and reactions. For a lender of last resort to be effective, its promise to lend to banks during a crisis must be credible and carried out swiftly. The evolution of the Fed's activities illustrates how regulation introduced in response to one crisis can be adapted in response to future crises. The protection that anticompetitive restrictions supposedly offers banks in reality encourages innovation and competition. Thus interest rate ceilings can lead to a further crisis, followed by financial innovation and regulatory response. Finally, the availability of deposit insurance highlights the problems for regulators, financial institutions, and savers and borrowers when regulation ignores the crucial adverse selection and moral hazard problems inherent in banking.

Taken together, these three instances demonstrate clearly the importance of considering the potential impacts of regulation on competitive incentives and information costs. The economic approach that we use in analyzing them should help you evaluate future developments in regulation and financial innovation.

Lender of Last Resort

Congress created the Federal Reserve System as the lender of last resort for the banking industry. Essentially, creation of the Fed was a regulatory response to waves of bank failures and contractions in bank lending during the late nineteenth and early twentieth centuries.

The Great Depression

The first crucial test for the Federal Reserve System's effectiveness in reducing the costs of financial instability followed the stock market crash of October 1929. In responding to the crash, the Fed performed its role as lender of last resort quickly and decisively by extending credit to the New York banks involved in lending to the securities business.

Despite this early intervention, the Fed faced a more serious problem: the banking panics that began in late 1930, as a wave of bank failures hit the U.S. economy. The loss of confidence in the banking system was obvious. Demand deposits shrank sharply as the public converted them to currency because of a perceived riskiness of bank deposits. Banks liquidated loans and raised their reserve holdings to 22% of deposits in 1932 (up from 15% of deposits in 1930), but bank intermediation had broken down. In March 1933, President Roosevelt declared a *bank holiday*, forcing all banks to close for a time.

The economic collapse during the early 1930s—the Great Depression—was the most severe financial setback in U.S. history. Many economists have identified the bank failures as an important factor in prolonging the depression. When banks failed, many borrowers, unable to find substitutes for bank loans (through sales of bonds or shares), couldn't obtain credit. Many small and medium-sized businesses and farms failed as a result. This pattern illustrates the role of the banking system in providing credit to those for whom information and its costs are important. The large number of small, poorly diversified banks—particularly those that held agricultural loans during a period of falling commodity prices—compounded the banking crisis.

During the banking panics, the Fed failed to act decisively as the lender of last resort; it did not lend aggressively enough to struggling banks. Moreover, the Fed actually *raised* the interest rate it charged on loans to member banks in 1931. Hindsight is 20–20, of course. At the time, the Fed shared the view of many economists that the depression would work itself out with no central bank intervention. In addition, the Fed's charter prohibited it from lending against all but good commercial loans, and adherence to its promise to maintain a fixed exchange rate under the gold standard limited its ability to act. England's suspension of convertibility of the pound into gold in 1931 caused concern in international financial markets that the United States might abandon its fixed exchange rate promise and gold convertibility. As a result, foreign investors rushed to convert dollars into gold. To maintain the exchange rate and protect its gold reserves, the Fed increased the interest rate it charged on loans to banks. This moved the foreign-exchange value of the dollar and restored the relative attractiveness of the United States as a place to keep funds.

Congressional action after 1932 attacked many of the problems that had prolonged the banking crisis. Congress amended the Fed's charter to limit convertibility of the U.S. dollar into gold and broadened the definition of permissible collateral for loans from the Fed. Decision making within the Fed was centralized to improve its ability to respond quickly during a crisis. (We examine these reforms in Chapter 19.) Nonetheless, considerable concern remained about whether the Fed could be an effective lender of last resort for the banking industry. The Fed's weakness during the calamitous early 1930s motivated introduction of federal deposit insurance in 1934.

▶ **C H E C K P O I N T** *Suppose that banks use checkable deposits to finance commercial loans that can be traded on secondary markets. Would there be a role for a lender of last resort?* If banks' loan portfolios were very liquid and sufficient information on their quality were available so that they could be traded, liquidity risk and information costs would be greatly reduced. As a result, there would be less need for a lender of last resort. However, if liquidity and information costs were extremely low, there also would be less need for traditional banking firms. ◀

Success in Recent Years

Despite its shaky start as a lender of last resort during the Great Depression, the Federal Reserve System has performed well since World War II. The following four episodes of Fed intervention are particularly important.

Penn Central Railroad Crisis. When the Penn Central Railroad, once one of the largest corporations in the United States, filed for bankruptcy in 1970, it defaulted on $200 million of commercial paper. Investors' concern over the quality of commercial paper issued by other large companies made them wary of supplying funds to that market. The Fed increased the availability of credit to commercial banks to encourage them to extend short-term credit to make up the difference. It also provided loans to these banks to make the extra lending possible. These actions averted a crisis in the banking system and financial markets.

Franklin National Bank Crisis. When the Franklin National Bank collapsed in 1974, it had issued a large amount of negotiable certificates of deposit. These time deposits could be bought and sold by individuals and institutions with a penalty for early withdrawal but weren't guaranteed by federal deposit insurance. As in the Penn Central situation, investors' concern about the quality of other banks' negotiable CDs led them to cut back their holdings of such deposits. This action worried bankers because negotiable CDs are a significant source of funds to banks. Discount lending to good banks by the Fed reduced information costs, thereby restoring order to the market and averting a banking panic.

Hunt Brothers' Silver Speculation Crisis. Herbert Hunt and Nelson Bunker Hunt, heirs of legendary oil baron H.L. Hunt, decided to commit their sizable fortunes and borrowed funds to attempt to corner the silver market in the 1980s. Their scheme worked for a while, but the price of silver ultimately tumbled. The collapse of this speculative scheme caused woes not just for the brothers but also for large brokerage houses to which they owed money, including industry giant Merrill Lynch. The amounts at stake were even large enough to threaten the financial stability of the exchange on which the futures contracts were traded. Such a failure also would have been costly to savers and borrowers who depended on the exchange to provide information services essential to trading in and liquidity of futures contracts. In this case, the Fed worked with a group of banks to provide loans to exchange members, thereby avoiding a rise in information costs and a market panic.

The Stock Market Crash of 1987. The stock market crash on October 19, 1987 raised fears of a repetition of the events that followed the 1929 crash. In particular, investors feared credit squeezes on broker-dealers in the securities industry. Before the stock market opened for trading the following day, Federal Reserve Chairman Alan Greenspan announced the Fed's readiness to provide liquidity in support of the economic and financial system. At the same time, the Fed, acting as lender of last resort, encouraged banks to lend to securities firms and extended discount credit to banks. This action by the Fed reduced information costs and allowed financial markets to provide risk-sharing and liquidity services to market participants. In addition, the action ensured the soundness of the payments system (see Box 15.1).

Concluding Remarks

A lender of last resort can help stabilize the banking system during a crisis. In the United States, the Federal Reserve System has generally per-

---

Consider this...   **BOX 15.1**

How Does a Lender of Last Resort Protect the Payments System?

Although Congress created it to act as the lender of last resort, the Fed today also is involved in a wide variety of lending activities to maintain the soundness of financial trading mechanisms. One important mechanism is the *payments system,* or the means for clearing transactions in the economy by check. The New York–based Clearing House for Interbank Payments and Settlements (CHIPS) settles dollar-denominated transfers among both domestic and foreign-owned banks. If a market participant in CHIPS fails during a business day,

all its payments are canceled. These cancellations in turn affect all other participants with which the failed bank was dealing. Hence the failure of a large bank could trigger failures of other institutions. The Fed must wrestle with difficult decisions about how to react, particularly when a crisis develops as the result of failure of a foreign-owned bank.

Another important mechanism is the *Fedwire* clearing system, which is used in clearing securities transactions. Positions are not closed during the day, so if a bank can't settle an overdraft by the

end of the day, the Fed effectively must convert it to a (possibly involuntary) discount loan. The role of lender of last resort in maintaining the health of the payments system gets murky when we consider the blurring of distinctions between commercial and investment banking and, in some instances, between finance and commerce. If commercial firms were allowed to conduct banking activities, a crisis in banking could force the Fed to make unsecured, interest-free loans to investment banking firms, or even to manufacturing firms.

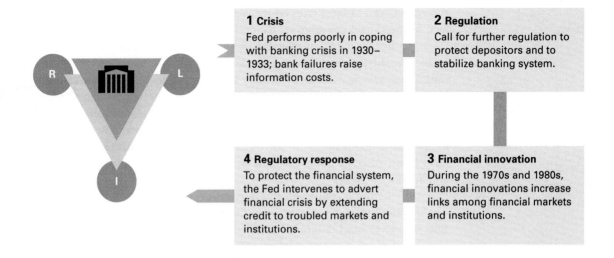

1 Crisis
Fed performs poorly in coping with banking crisis in 1930–1933; bank failures raise information costs.

2 Regulation
Call for further regulation to protect depositors and to stabilize banking system.

4 Regulatory response
To protect the financial system, the Fed intervenes to advert financial crisis by extending credit to troubled markets and institutions.

3 Financial innovation
During the 1970s and 1980s, financial innovations increase links among financial markets and institutions.

▲ **FIGURE 15.1**

Lender of Last Resort: Crisis, Regulation, Innovation, and Response
Instability in the banking system reduced the liquidity of bank deposits and raised information costs, leading to a collapse in bank lending and a call for a lender of last resort. After early failures by the Fed to act as a lender of last resort, its powers were broadened and additional bank regulation was developed.

formed this role successfully. Figure 15.1 summarizes the evolution of the Fed's role in the cycle of financial crisis, regulation, financial innovation, and regulatory response.

Anticompetitive Bank Regulation

A second way in which Congress sought to maintain banking stability was to limit competition among banks and between banks and other financial institutions. Such intervention was intended to (1) reduce the likelihood of bank runs, and (2) reduce the chance of moral hazard in banks' behavior. The argument for limiting competition is that it increases a bank's value, thereby reducing bankers' willingness to make excessively risky investments.

Unintended Results

Anticompetitive regulations do not promote banking stability in the long run. Instead, they create an incentive for unregulated financial institutions and markets to compete with banks by offering close substitutes for bank deposits and loans. A dramatic example of how anticompetitive regulation led to competition, financial innovation, and regulatory response occurred in the fight over limits on the interest that banks could pay depositors. The battle began with the Banking Act of 1933, which authorized **Regulation Q.** It placed ceilings on allowable interest rates for time and savings deposits and prohibited the payment of interest on demand deposits (then the only form of checkable deposits). The intent of Regulation Q was to maintain banks' profitability by limiting competition for funds and guaranteeing a reasonable spread between interest rates on loans and interest rates paid to depositors. In fact, it forced banks to innovate to survive.

Recall that the market for short-term credit is designed in large part to accommodate firms' demand for working capital (funds to pay for materials, labor, and inventories before the sale of products can generate revenue). Households and firms hold short-term liquid assets as a buffer against changes in income or spending. Historically, commercial banks dominated the short-term credit market. They specialize in reducing information costs by forming long-term relationships with borrowers and continually reauthorizing short-term loans. Also, by going through such banks, investors obtain risk-sharing and liquidity benefits.

Setting a ceiling on interest rates that banks could pay depositors was supposed to give banks a competitive advantage in the market for loans. But, whenever market interest rates rose above that ceiling, large and small savers seeking the highest rates of return had a strong incentive to search for alternatives in the marketplace. During the 1960s (and increasingly in the 1970s and 1980s), large corporations and wealthy households sought alternatives to short-term deposits at banks in order to earn higher returns. The alternatives included Treasury bills, commercial paper, and repurchase agreements. The benefits of greater rates of returns justify the transactions costs of hiring a cash management team or paying brokerage fees to find and manage these alternative investments when market interest rates are high.

Money market mutual funds were introduced in 1971 as an alternative to bank deposits. This innovation enabled depositors whose bank deposits were paying below-market interest rates (because of Regulation Q) to hold portfolios of government securities and commercial paper. This gave small and medium-sized depositors an opportunity to earn market rates of return with low transactions costs. Money market mutual funds ensured both liquidity and diversification, services formerly provided only by banks. These funds grew in popularity in 1978 when market interest rates climbed above the 5.25% ceiling on interest rates for savings accounts and time deposits. Their assets rose from $4 billion in 1977 to $230 billion in 1982 to more than $500 billion in 1993. The evolution of money market mutual funds in response to regulation is not unique to the United States (see the Other times, other places box).

Development of the mutual fund market also provided *borrowers* with a new source of funds. Large, well-established firms could raise funds in the commercial paper market where savers sought higher rates of return and low information costs. This alternative to bank borrowing created new competition between commercial and investment banks and significant loss of loan business for commercial banks. By the end of 1990, total lending in the commercial paper market accounted for 15% of short-term business finance, compared to 10% in 1980, 7% in 1970, and 2% in 1960. The loss of business that banks suffered was even more damaging than the statistics imply because, as

Other times, other places...

Money Market Mutual Funds: Japan and the United States

Interest rate regulation creates opportunities for financial innovation. In the United States, ceilings on interest payments by commercial banks contributed to the demand for money market mutual funds. Subsequently, banks were allowed to offer close substitutes in the form of money market accounts.

In Japan, the opposite occurred. Beginning in 1985, the Ministry of Finance relaxed interest rate regulation somewhat, permitting *money market certificates* (MMCs) that offered competitive interest rates. Although

the initial minimum denomination was large (¥30 million, or equivalent to just under $250,000 in 1993), the minimum denomination fell to much smaller levels by the end of the 1980s. In order to compete with the new MMCs, the Japanese securities industry developed a close substitute, known as *money market funds* (MMFs). These funds consist of portfolios of short-term credit instruments, and the interest rates offered float with those for comparable MMCs. Moreover, the maturities for the MMFs are chosen to mirror the MMCs. Hence Japanese

securities firms offer a short-term instrument paying market interest rates, which isn't, strictly speaking, a money market instrument. This innovation undermines the spirit of separation of banking and securities businesses outlined in Article 65 of Japan's postwar Securities and Exchange Act (modeled on the U.S. Glass-Steagall Act). As in the United States, however, the line between banking and securities firms in Japan is blurring rapidly as innovation after innovation occurs.

our analysis of the costs of adverse selection predicts, only high-quality borrowers had access to commercial paper, leaving banks with low-quality borrowers.

The exit of savers and borrowers from banks to financial markets is known as **disintermediation,** which costs banks lost revenue from not having savers' funds to loan. In some cases, it also costs borrowers and the economy: Although high-quality, established borrowers are able to raise funds in markets such as the commercial paper market, households and less well-established business firms aren't able to do so. As a result, banks aren't able to provide more efficient intermediation than financial markets even when the transactions and information costs of market alternatives are high. Let's look at how the costs of disintermediation can affect the economy.

The Credit Crunch of 1966

In 1966, deposits in commercial banks, savings banks, and S&Ls were subject to interest rate ceilings under Regulation Q. Rising market interest rates caused depositors to shift funds from commercial banks and S&Ls to financial markets. Large commercial banks redirected their investment strategies to raise funds through unregulated sources, such as Eurodollar deposits. Smaller banks and S&Ls had fewer alternative sources of funds and were forced to curtail lending. In the first half of 1966, primarily mutual savings banks and S&Ls were affected by disintermediation, because households' savings deposits were their primary source of funds and their mortgage lending fell dramatically. Commercial banks felt the pinch in the second half of the year when the Fed lowered the interest rate ceiling on bank time deposits, forcing them to cut back on interest paid to depositors.

The blow to mortgage lending and the housing industry caused a **credit crunch,** or a reduction in borrowers' ability to obtain credit at prevailing interest rates. A credit crunch affects small firms the most. In fact, smaller firms had to cut back disproportionately on investment because they normally depend on bank loans for external finance.

Innovation

Regulation of the interest rates that banks pay to depositors created opportunities for financial markets and nonbank institutions to innovate and lure savers and borrowers from banks. Banks actively countered with their own innovations. To reestablish their ties to borrowers, banks used their information cost and transactions cost advantages to enter the commercial paper market through the back door by offering standby letters of credit (Chapter 13). That innovation enabled banks to minimize the damage from anticompetitive regulation by earning fees that compensated them for their information services.

To circumvent the interest rate regulation, banks also developed new financial instruments for savers. Citibank introduced the **negotiable certificate of deposit** (or negotiable CD) as a time deposit with a fixed maturity of, say, six months, to compete with commercial paper. Negotiable CDs differ from demand deposits in that early withdrawal results in a penalty, making them relatively illiquid for the cash management needs of large firms. However, the instruments are *negotiable*; that is, they can be sold to someone else even though they can't be redeemed prior to maturity without penalty. This negotiability gave them greater liquidity. When Citibank created them, negotiable CDs of at least $100,000 were exempt from Regulation Q. Negotiable CDs are now an important source of funds for commercial banks, with a typical denomination of $1 million.

In addition, banks developed techniques to provide interest on depositors' funds. A break for small depositors came when a Massachusetts mutual savings bank created a substitute for checking accounts not governed by Regulation Q. Called a **negotiable order of withdrawal (NOW) account,** it required only the introduction of a "withdrawal slip" that the depositor could sign over to someone else. A NOW account is like a checking account. Technically, however, it isn't a demand deposit, so interest can be paid on it. Following a favorable Massachusetts court decision in 1972, NOW accounts spread throughout New England, New Jersey, and New York, effectively offering checking accounts paying 5.25% interest, as opposed to the 0% on traditional demand deposits. Small savers holding checking accounts and passbook savings accounts transferred their funds to NOW accounts. In an additional development in 1974, credit unions began issuing share drafts, or checkable deposits paying interest on minimum account balances.

For large depositors, banks used repurchase agreements (RPs), overnight Eurodollars, and automatic transfer system (ATS) accounts. Under a repurchase agreement, the bank regularly converts the balance of a demand deposit into overnight RPs. Recall that, in an RP, a corporation purchases Treasury bills from a bank, and the bank commits to repurchase them the next day for a slightly higher price, thereby paying interest to the depositor. In overnight Eurodollar transactions, a customer's demand deposit is automatically withdrawn and deposited in a foreign branch that pays interest. Finally, ATS accounts effectively pay interest on checking accounts by "sweeping" a customer's checking account balance at the end of the day into overnight RPs.

▶ **C H E C K P O I N T** *You are an intelligent banker, always looking for ways to increase your bank's profits. You notice that when someone moves money from a demand deposit into a savings account, interest is earned for that day as long as the transfer occurs before midnight. However, there is a law against paying interest on demand deposits. What can you think of to get around this law?* You could automatically transfer balances from demand deposits to savings accounts and back by computer each night at midnight. In this way, the demand deposits, in effect, would earn interest, even though technically you are allowed to pay interest only on savings accounts. ◀

Response to Innovation

The breakdown of interest rate regulation in banking came about because of pressure from small and medium-sized banks. These banks, like large banks, lost deposits to money market mutual funds. Unlike large banks, however, they had limited access to new market developments that circumvented the regulation. In response to financial innovation removing the burden of Regulation Q, Congress enacted two pieces of legislation: the Depository Institutions Deregulation and Monetary Control Act of 1980 (DIDMCA) and the Garn–St. Germain Act of 1982.

DIDMCA. With passage of the **Depository Institutions and Monetary Control Act of 1980,** Congress eased the anticompetitive burden on banks and helped provide fairness in the financial services industry. The act eliminated interest rate ceilings (known as *usury ceilings*) on mortgage loans and certain types of commercial loans. It also provided for uniform reserve requirements and access to Federal Reserve System services (such as discount loans and check clearing) for all depository institutions. In addition, DIDMCA permitted NOW and ATS accounts nationwide, thereby removing a stumbling block to banks' ability to compete with money market mutual funds. The effect of this change was dramatic: NOW and ATS deposits rose almost fourfold—from $27 billion to $101 billion—between 1980 and 1982. Also, DIDMCA phased out Regulation Q gradually from 1980 to 1986. As a result, DIDMCA was popular both with banks eager to compete and with depositors eager to earn interest on deposits.

Other depository institutions received benefits, too (in return for their political support of the legislation). The act allowed S&Ls and mutual savings banks to broaden their lending beyond mortgages. Savings and loan associations were allowed to invest as much as 20% of their assets in corporate bonds, commercial paper, and consumer loans; they also were allowed to expand into credit card lending and trust services. Mutual savings banks were permitted to compete with commercial banks by making commercial loans (for up to 5% of their assets) and accepting checkable deposits in connection with their loans.

However, DIDMCA was not a cure-all for financial institutions as interest rate ceilings were phased out. Because Regulation Q was eliminated only gradually, money market mutual funds continued to expand at the expense of S&Ls and mutual savings banks; by post–World War II standards, an unprecedented number of S&Ls and mutual savings banks failed (250 in 1982 alone). Regulatory change to address this problem soon followed.

Garn–St. Germain Act. Congress passed the **Garn–St. Germain Act of 1982,** to combat problems caused by the gradual demise of Regulation Q under DIDMCA. To give them a more potent weapon against money market mutual funds, the act permitted depository institutions to offer savers **money market deposit accounts** (MMDAs), which provide services analogous to money market mutual funds. These accounts were subject neither to reserve requirements nor Regulation Q ceilings. The combination of market interest rates and the safety and familiarity of banks made the new accounts an instant success, with balances in excess of $400 billion by 1983 and $500 billion today.

To address the special problems facing savings institutions, the Garn–St. Germain Act broadened the ability of federally chartered savings institutions to invest in areas other than mortgages (as much as 30% of their assets in consumer loans and 10% in commercial loans by 1984). Because these changes made savings institutions comparable to banks, the act required that (as of 1984) Regulation Q ceilings be applied uniformly to all depository institutions until they expired in 1986.

Concluding Remarks

The landmark DIDMCA and Garn–St. Germain legislation placed the banking industry on a more equal footing with its competitors. However, the Garn–St. Germain Act moved savings institutions from the usually calm

1 Crisis
During 1930–1933 crisis, public loses confidence in the banking system; savers convert deposits to currency and banks liquidate loans.

2 Regulation
Banking instability produces call for regulatory restrictions; to maintain bank profitability, Regulation Q imposes ceilings on deposit interest rates.

4 Regulatory response
Competitive pressures force legislation (DIDMCA and Garn-St. Germain) to dismantle interest rate ceilings; banks are allowed to compete more effectively.

3 Financial innovation
Securities firms push growth of money market mutual funds and commercial paper market; banks innovate to bypass ceilings in raising funds and use information-cost advantages in lending.

FIGURE 15.2

Interest Rate Ceilings: Crisis, Regulation, Innovation, and Response
Regulation Q imposed interest rate ceilings on bank deposits. Beginning in the late 1960s, non-bank financial firms created innovations that enabled savers to earn higher returns. These innovations allowed nonbanks to gain a competitive advantage in providing liquidity services and lending. Financial innovation by banks and regulatory changes allowed banks to compete more effectively against nonbanks.

waters of mortgage lending into the choppy waters of bank lending. Figure 15.2 summarizes the process of financial crisis, regulation, financial innovation, and regulatory response as it applies to interest rate ceilings.

The Deposit Insurance Crisis of the 1980s

Introduced as a response to the banking crises of the 1930s, federal deposit insurance functioned smoothly from its inception in 1934 until the early 1980s. Economists and politicians hoped that bank runs could be consigned to the history books and that the economic costs of a collapsing banking system could be avoided. However, unnoticed problems were building. The first of the depository institutions to exhibit signs of trouble were S&Ls; next were banks. The lessons of these episodes currently are shaping the activities and regulation of virtually all financial institutions, banks and nonbanks alike.

Worsening Conditions in S&Ls

The story unfolds in two parts. One relates to the outmoded structure of S&Ls (also called *thrifts*), and the other relates to the financial innovation and regulatory changes in the 1970s and early 1980s (discussed in the preceding section).

To promote mortgage lending, banking regulation created S&Ls in the 1930s from the remnants of building and loan societies (many of which had failed). These institutions held long-term, fixed-rate mortgages and financed them with short-term time deposits. So long as interest rates were stable and regulation limited interest payments to depositors (the situation from the 1930s through much of the 1960s), little went wrong. However, the mismatch between the maturities of S&Ls' assets and those of their liabilities created the potential for interest rate risk.

Some episodes of rising market interest rates worried S&Ls in the 1960s and 1970s. However, the real trouble began as U.S. interest rates rose dramatically in late 1979. As a result, the cost of funds for S&Ls escalated, the present value of their existing mortgage assets plummeted, and their net worth declined precipitously. At the same time, the 1981–1982 recession raised default rates on mortgages, particularly for S&Ls located in farm or energy-producing states (such as Texas), where conditions were especially bad. About half the S&Ls had a negative net worth by the end of 1982. Our analysis of moral hazard suggests that this condition should sound a warning for deposit insurance. Because savers' deposits (to a regulated amount) were guaranteed by the Federal Savings and Loan Insurance Corporation (FSLIC), managers of S&Ls were strongly tempted to engage in riskier investments.

Recall, however, that in the early 1980s Congress tried to help S&Ls by relaxing restrictions on their asset holdings. In making these regulatory changes, Congress intended to allow S&Ls to diversify and combat exposure to interest rate risk by making available new assets, including direct real estate investments, commercial mortgages, and junk bonds. Many S&Ls took advantage of these opportunities. By the early 1990s, S&Ls (originally created to bolster mortgage lending) accounted for less than half of U.S. mortgage loans.

In 1980, DIDMCA raised the federal deposit insurance ceiling from $40,000 per account to $100,000 per account, even as the phaseout of Regulation Q increased S&Ls' costs of funds. Now, insured CDs could be issued in larger amounts at high interest rates, with the proceeds invested in risky assets. Our analysis of the costs of adverse selection cautions the *uninsured* saver to be wary of the promise of higher yields (as it brings with it greater risks). Insured depositors flocked to the higher yields because the government guaranteed their deposits. To make matters worse, financial innovators effectively raised the deposit insurance limit many times over by creating **brokered deposits.** In a brokered deposit, a depositor with $1 million goes to a broker who buys ten $100,000 CDs in 10 different banks, giving the depositor ten different bank accounts with insurance on the entire $1 million. Federal authorities banned brokered deposits in 1984, but a federal court decision later reversed the ban. Moreover, many S&Ls did not use available techniques to reduce their exposure to interest rate risk (see Box 15.2).

Many analysts blame lax regulatory supervision during the 1980s for encouraging fraud and prolonging the crisis. Some S&L executives used savers' deposits to fund lavish lifestyles or simply embezzled funds. For example, the First Network Savings Bank, whose failure in 1990 cost federal deposit insurance agencies 25 cents on each dollar of deposits, used deposits to build the world's largest "museum of magic" at its headquarters. In another

Consider this....

BOX 15.2

Could S&Ls' Interest Rate Risk Have Been Avoided?

In principle, savings institutions could have lessened interest rate risk by using variable rate mortgages, known as *adjustable rate mortgages* (ARMs). The lender adjusts the mortgage interest rate when market interest rates rise or fall, thereby cushioning the effects of interest rate changes on the institution's net worth.

Although ARMs now are popular in mortgage lending, they haven't been a cure-all for at least two reasons. First, the indexes on which they are based are imperfect, and rate adjustment normally is subject to both annual and mortgage term caps. Second, an ARM increases credit risk. Significant increases in monthly payments may increase the risk of borrower default. That is, holding payments constant, the loan balance could balloon to more than the collateral value of the loan. During the 1980s, S&Ls also made little use of other risk-sharing devices available to them. This circumstance isn't really surprising: Moral hazard problems suggest that depository institutions with low net worth have an incentive to increase risky behavior rather than decrease exposure to interest rate risk.

notorious case, S&L entrepreneur Don Dixon was convicted of embezzling bank funds, which he spent on prostitutes, hot tubs, and designer shotguns. Dixon went to jail, but taxpayers paid for the 96% of his S&L's loans that had defaulted.

To avoid bankrupting its reserves, the Federal Home Loan Bank Board (FHLBB) and its deposit insurance subsidiary, the FSLIC, allowed insolvent S&Ls to continue to operate. The cost of closing insolvent S&Ls quickly escalated in the late 1980s and early 1990s. Economists have estimated that the costs to the FSLIC of closing the insolvent S&Ls in 1982 would have been about $20 billion. Although this number is small relative to the costs of the crisis by the 1990s (hundreds of billions of dollars), it was greater than the reserves the FSLIC had built up since 1934. Even so, the FSLIC could have made a credible deposit insurance guarantee based on the implicit backing of the Treasury and the Fed.

To understand the escalation of costs, we have to examine how insolvent institutions avoided closure. In the process of evaluating nonfinancial businesses, analysts gauge net worth. To avoid classifying S&Ls as insolvent and depleting deposit insurance funds to reimburse depositors, regulators changed the accounting rules. Instead of estimating economic net worth, they used regulatory accounting principles to allow S&Ls to carry on their books at face value many assets whose value actually had declined because of rising interest rates. In addition, regulators gave S&Ls an inflated value for goodwill, the intangible value of the institution as a going concern. In 1982, total industry net worth was reported at 3.7% of assets under regulatory accounting principles. Had market value corrections been made, the industry's net worth would have been −12%. As a result of such decisions, many insolvent or nearly insolvent S&Ls continued to operate, rather than being closed by the FSLIC.

Although deposit insurance reduces the need for individual depositors to do the monitoring, the principal-agent problem doesn't disappear. Bank regulators act as agents for the taxpayers who are the principals; taxpayers collectively bear the costs of deposit insurance bailouts. However, as studies by Edward Kane of Boston College have stressed, regulators' incentives differ from those of taxpayers. Regulators hold their positions for relatively short periods of time, so they have an incentive to loosen capital requirements and supervision at the first sign of trouble. They don't want troubled institutions to fail under their supervision. Regulators also have an incentive to pay more attention to elected lawmakers who can influence their careers than to taxpayers.

A good example of the principal-agent problem is the "Keating Five" scandal in 1990. Charles Keating, an S&L entrepreneur, contributed about $1.3 million to the campaigns of five U.S. senators in return for their assistance in getting FHLBB Chairman Edwin Gray to deal lightly with the problems of Keating's Lincoln Savings and Loan in 1987. Lincoln operated with severe financial problems until its failure in 1989, costing taxpayers about $2.5 billion. Keating and his son were convicted in 1992 on numerous counts of fraud and betrayal of fiduciary trust by both state and federal courts.

The S&L Bailout

By the end of 1986, losses in the S&L industry had wiped out the FSLIC's reserves. President Reagan requested $15 billion for FSLIC, an amount decried as inadequate by analysts. In the Competitive Equality Banking Act of 1987, Congress gave the administration even less than its request. Deprived of funds to resolve the situation, the FHLBB allowed insolvent institutions to continue operating, paying high interest rates to attract more funds guaranteed by deposit insurance.

Lack of decisive action brought disaster, with actual thrift losses approaching $20 billion by 1989. In January 1989, the FSLIC reported to Congress that 350 federally insured S&Ls were insolvent. Initial estimates of the costs of meeting obligations to insured depositors exceeded $90 billion. Because these estimates referred to costs net of recoveries from asset sales, the initial outlays needed to close insolvent institutions would be much greater. At the same time, William Seidman, then chairman of the FDIC, estimated that ultimately more than 700 FSLIC-insured S&Ls with combined assets of $400 billion would have to be reorganized or liquidated.

The incoming Bush administration and Congress mandated reform in the **Financial Institutions Reform, Recovery, and Enforcement Act of 1989** (FIRREA), the most comprehensive legislation for the S&L industry since the 1930s. The act eliminated the FSLIC, the separate deposit insurance authority for S&Ls, and formed the **Resolution Trust Corporation** (RTC) to handle thrift insolvencies and to sell off the more than $300 billion of real estate owned by failed S&Ls.[†]

The act also created the **Resolution Funding Corporation** and authorized it to borrow funds to cover insolvencies. The FDIC organized a new deposit insurance fund, the Savings Association Insurance Fund (SAIF), for the S&L industry. Finally, FIRREA mandated uniform capital requirements and accounting and disclosure standards for commercial banks and savings institutions. S&Ls now are supervised and examined by the Office of Thrift Supervision (OTS), an arm of the Treasury Department. Its responsibilities are similar to those the Treasury's Office of the Comptroller of the Currency has for national banks.

To restore SAIF reserves, the FDIC raised the deposit insurance premiums of S&Ls from 20.8 cents per $100 of deposits to 23 cents and then to 32.5 cents. It raised bank deposit insurance premiums from 8.3 cents to 15 cents per $100 of deposits, with an additional increase to 23 cents in 1991 and, depending upon bank riskiness, to as high as 31 cents (with an average of 25.4 cents) in 1993.

The 1989 legislation also reregulated investment activities of S&Ls, which had been deregulated under DIDMCA in 1980 and the Garn–St. Germain Act in 1982. It mandated that junk bond holdings be sold off by 1994 and tightened rules for other lending activities. It limited loans for commercial real estate to four times the institution's equity capital rather than to 40% of assets (which applied most severely to institutions with capital equal to less than 10% of assets). The act required that housing-related investments be at least 70% (instead of at least 60%) of total assets. Because low net worth was an important factor in the beginning of the S&L crisis, FIRREA raised capital requirements for S&Ls from 3% to 8% of assets, eventually conforming to risk-based capital standards mandated for commercial banks. Finally, it gave regulators broader authority to issue cease-and-desist orders, impose civil penalties, and fire managers. At the same time, it allocated an extra $75 million each year for three years to the Justice Department to aid regulators and law enforcement officials in investigating and prosecuting fraud.

On the one hand, FIRREA successfully dealt with the S&L crisis by providing substantial resources to close insolvent institutions. On the other hand, many analysts believe that the act imposed severe restrictions on depository institutions without satisfactorily addressing fundamental adverse selection and moral hazard problems arising from federal deposit insurance.

[†] The RTC Oversight Board, made up of the Secretary of the Treasury (as chairperson), the Chairman of the Board of Governors of the Federal Reserve System, the Secretary of Housing and Urban Development, and two other appointees, supervises the RTC. The FDIC manages the RTC.

The Congressional Budget Office has estimated that the present value of the cost of the S&L debacle through the year 2000 could be as much as $200 billion in 1992 dollars. The vast sums spent in resolving this crisis are transfers from taxpayers to depositors and not a loss of current output for the economy. However, they have caused inefficiency in the economy by diverting the nation's savings in the 1980s from productive investment financed from uninsured sources to less productive investment funded by insured deposits. This large-scale financial inefficiency raises the question: Can the same thing happen in the commercial banking industry?

The Widening Crisis: Commercial Banks

Like S&Ls, commercial banks in the United States prospered greatly between the Great Depression and the mid-1970s. Regulation protected bank profitability. Branching restrictions limited competition faced by local bankers. Regulation Q granted protection against competition by limiting payments to depositors and guaranteed a healthy margin between loan and deposit rates. Thus, owing to regulation, banks were earning above-normal profits, and their markets were protected from entry. The potential for interest rate risk was low.

As in the S&L industry, the pace of financial innovation in commercial banking accelerated in the 1960s and 1970s, owing in large part to the desire to circumvent protective regulation. Increased competition resulting from financial innovation reduced the value of a key part of banks' net worth: the market power associated with the value of bank charters.

As interest rates rose in the 1970s and early 1980s and the cost of funds to banks climbed, asset portfolios had to earn more income to maintain profitability. The quest for profitability forced banks to accept riskier loans in energy production, real estate, debt issued by developing countries, and agriculture. The two recessions of 1980–1982 caused a substantial number of defaults and business failures. Lack of diversification left many groups of banks particularly susceptible (lenders to energy producers in the Southwest and lenders to agriculture and import-sensitive manufacturing in the Midwest, for example). When oil and agricultural commodity prices fell in the 1980s, loans in these sectors declined in value.

Volatile interest rates and exchange rates also took their toll on banks' net worth. Because interest rate and exchange rate risks had been small in the past, banks had made few preparations for greater risk. Some bank failures in the 1970s reflected these risks, however. For example, the Franklin National Bank had tried to increase net worth by speculating in foreign currencies and lengthening the maturity of its assets. Collapse of the dollar and a significant increase in interest rates caused the bank's failure in 1974.

During the late 1980s and early 1990s, banks found themselves exposed to risk through their investment in *highly leveraged transactions* (HLTs), in which banks financed buyouts of firms by their managers or other investors. Some large banks lost heavily on HLT loans to financiers such as Robert Campeau and Donald Trump who ran into financial trouble. The fall in commercial real estate prices in New York, Boston, and other large cities bankrupted some prominent real estate developers, leaving banks with over-valued, empty office buildings and property in the midst of the recession.

During the 1980s, FDIC policy was not too successful in dealing with large-bank insolvencies. Tough with small banks, the FDIC relied primarily on the purchase and assumption method to make sure that no depositors and cred-itors lost money when large banks became insolvent.[†] Examples include the $1.7 billion bailout of Continental Illinois in 1984 and the $3 billion bailout of the First Republic Bank of Dallas in 1988. Many analysts expressed concern that FDIC protection of all deposits at large banks created a belief within large banks that the FDIC considered them *too big to fail*. This belief may have led to increased risk taking by large banks. We return to this problem later.

During the 1980s, branching restrictions limited diversification, which exposed banks to greater credit risk in their loan portfolios. For example, during the oil boom in the 1970s, Texas commercial banks grew sig-nificantly and were among the most profitable in the United States. Texas' branching restrictions limited banks to a single full-service location. With limited ability to diversify beyond local energy-related loans, Texas banks suf-fered greatly when the price of oil plummeted in the 1980s. By 1990, nine of the top ten banks in Texas at the beginning of the decade had gone out of business or had been aquired.

Bank failures remain a problem for the FDIC in the early 1990s as the FDIC, the Treasury Department, and Congress grapple for a solution. Although the number of bank failures fell from 206 in 1989 to 124 in 1991, the assets of failed banks in 1991 were $63.2 billion, or more than double the figure for 1989. As Box 15.3 shows, the United States isn't the only country facing deposit insurance problems.

Options for Reform

The principles of insurance management (Chapter 12) suggest sev-eral options for reform of the banking industry. They include changes in insurance coverage, insurance pricing, the scope of bank activities, regulatory supervision, and capital requirements.

Insurance Coverage. One option for reform is to reduce the level of deposit insurance coverage. The lower the amount of deposits covered, the greater is the incentive for depositors to monitor banks. However, the

---

[†] Since 1970, only about 25% of bank failures have been resolved using the payoff method. The banks involved have generally been small, the largest being Penn Square Bank in Oklahoma, which failed in 1982. Between 1985 and 1990—the period with the greatest number of bank fail-ures since the 1930s—full protection by deposit insurance was extended to more than 99% of *uninsured* deposits.

BOX 15.3

Consider this...
Will a Deposit Insurance Crisis Hit Japan?

From 1971, when its deposit insurance program was established, through the first half of 1992, Japan's Deposit Insurance Corporation accumulated $5.5 billion in insurance fees and made no disbursements to depositors. The Japanese deposit insurer is a quasi-governmental entity, with capital about equally provided by the government, the Bank of Japan (the Japanese central bank), and private financial institutions. In June 1992, the Japanese Deposit Insurance Corporation agreed to its first bailout grant: $156 million to help Sanwa Bank to assume the liabilities of the failed Toyo Shinkin Bank. The justification given was a concern about confidence in the Japanese financial system.

Japanese financial analysts were nervous in 1992 about the possibility of a crisis because of the weak condition of Japanese banks in the wake of falling stock market and real estate prices. In August 1992, the Japanese government announced a plan to bail out the banks by buying their bad loans. Some analysts believe that about 10% of bank loans are not paying interest. Whether the crisis in deposit insurance becomes as expensive in Japan as in the United States remains to be seen.

Source: Adapted from the discussion in "Japanese Deposit Insurer Makes First Bailout Grant," *American Banker,* June 2, 1992; and Clayton Jones, "Japan Will Support Debt-Ridden Banks Through U.S.-Style Bailout," *The Christian Science Monitor,* August 31, 1992.

economic rationale for deposit insurance is aimed as much at protecting the economy from the cost of banking panics as at protecting small or large depositors. Indeed, the speed with which uninsured depositors can now move their funds increases the likelihood of a bank run at the first hint of bad news.

This connection between insurance coverage and the likelihood of a run is particularly pronounced in the FDIC's handling of large-bank insolvencies. For example, when Continental Illinois became insolvent in 1984, the FDIC guaranteed all deposits—insured and uninsured—and even made sure that no Continental bondholder lost money. Afterward, the Comptroller of the Currency informed Congress that the FDIC maintained a list of banks that it deemed "too big to fail." In these cases, the FDIC would ensure that no depositor or creditor lost money.

This policy weakens the desire of large depositors to incur costs of monitoring a bank. For example, if large deposits were uninsured and large depositors thought that the FDIC would use the payoff method to deal with insolvent banks (closing the bank, paying off insured depositors, and using any remaining funds to pay uninsured depositors), they would monitor banks' lending practices closely. As a result, banks would be less likely to engage in very risky activities. Hence reducing insurance coverage provides a check on bank risk taking.

Moreover, the too-big-to-fail policy is unfair, because it treats small and large banks differently. For example, when the FDIC closed the minority-owned Harlem's Freedom National Bank in 1990 (with less than $100 million of deposits), its large depositors—including such charitable organizations as the United Negro College Fund and the Urban League—received only about

50 cents per dollar of uninsured deposits. Only a few months later in January 1991, the much larger Bank of New England failed as a result of a collapse in the value of its real estate portfolio. Its large depositors were fully protected by the FDIC, costing taxpayers about $2.3 billion.

These problems notwithstanding, bank regulators are not likely to allow a large bank to fail; to do so might lead to a banking panic. Regulatory authorities also have been cool to the use of *coinsurance*, in which depositors have only partial insurance coverage (Chapter 12). Although coinsurance (say, paying off depositors 85 cents per dollar) would give an incentive for depositors to monitor banks, the problem of bank runs remains. In the early 1990s, regulators instead stressed the need for better ongoing supervision of banks' activities, along with the authority to force banks to stop engaging in certain activities.

Narrow Banking.

Narrow Banking. In the late 1980s, some economists proposed **narrow banking,** that is, only insuring deposits in safe assets such as T-bills or high-quality commercial paper, as a method of deposit insurance reform. (Because of the low risk inherent in such assets, deposit insurance would be redundant but could promote public confidence.) Banks would make loans from bank equity and raise funds through risky securities. These funds would not be insured, and fewer limits would be placed on the scope of bank activities, sharply reducing moral hazard problems. However, these proposals would severely curtail the information-gathering and monitoring activities essential to bank lending. Because some borrowers have few alternatives to bank deposits, narrow banking could reduce these borrowers' access to the financial system. For a bank to make new loans, old loans would have to be sold or new funds attracted.

Private Deposit Insurance.

Private Deposit Insurance.   Several economists have suggested that deposit insurance be provided by private insurance companies, at least for deposits greater than the $100,000 ceiling covered by the FDIC. This option would provide an incentive for the private insurer to monitor the banks whose deposits are insured. However, a private insurer probably wouldn't be able to pay off depositors during a general banking crisis. As a result, the problems of bank runs and banking panics remain. Although private insurance alone cannot substitute for federal deposit insurance, economists and policymakers increasingly are offering suggestions that combine private insurance arrangements with a lender-of-last-resort role by the Fed to reduce the chance of a financial crisis.

Risk-Based Pricing of Deposit Insurance.

Risk-Based Pricing of Deposit Insurance.   Another option for reform is to make deposit insurance premiums reflect risk, as they do in automobile or fire insurance, so that banks would bear more of the risk associated with their lending decisions. A safe bank would pay a low premium, whereas a risky bank would pay a high premium. However, evaluating risk isn't easy. Assigning market values to some bank loans can be quite difficult. Moreover, risk can be assessed easily after the fact by examining operating income or losses, but risk-based pricing of deposit insurance must be forward-looking to be useful—a much more difficult task.

Risk-based pricing of deposit insurance was mandated in the **Federal Deposit Insurance Corporation Improvement Act of 1991** (FDICIA), which established three risk groups: "well capitalized," "adequately capitalized," and "less than adequately capitalized." These definitions are to be used for risk-based pricing of deposit insurance by 1994. In September 1992, the FDIC voted to implement risk-based premiums for the first time in the history of deposit insurance. These premiums became effective in January 1993, ranging from 23 cents per $100 for well-capitalized banks with no supervisory problems to 31 cents per $100 of deposits for less than adequately capitalized institutions with substantial supervisory problems. Most banks paid the lowest rate, although some large banks (including Citibank) initially paid higher premiums under the new system.

Supervision. Passage of FIRREA focused attention on giving the FDIC more supervisory responsibility. The act requires the FDIC as insurer to monitor the evaluation of a depository institution's federal or state supervisor. It broadens the authority of regulators to intervene in bank management, especially at poorly capitalized banks. New regulatory powers include the ability to set dividend payments and executive pay at poorly capitalized banks and to hire and fire managers in some cases. Proponents say that the new procedures will encourage better management because well-capitalized banks are exempt from the most severe restrictions. Opponents argue that the fear of regulatory intrusion will discourage banks from making commercial loans and encourage them to invest deposits in Treasury securities, thereby diminishing banks' role in the saving-investment process. How banks adjust to this regulatory response will shape the banking industry during the 1990s.

Capital Requirements. Problems of moral hazard occur when banks seek to use their equity capital in risky ways to grow and increase their return on equity. Setting higher minimum capital requirements reduces the potential for moral hazard problems and the cost to the FDIC of bank failures. As we noted earlier, FIRREA has moved toward accomplishing these purposes for S&Ls.

A bank's equity capital is its cushion for paying depositors if its assets decline in value. With deposit insurance, minimum capital requirements reduce the likelihood that banks will engage in risky activities. These requirements are based on *historical cost*, or *book-value* measures. In this case, changes in the market values of a bank's assets and liabilities (owing to changes in, say, default risk or market interest rates) don't affect the calculation by regulatory authorities of a bank's net worth. This flaw is significant because changes in market values of assets and liabilities are precisely what tell depositors and investors when shifts occur in the true value of banks' equity capital. They also set the incentives for bankers to create moral hazard.

Many economists support the use of *market-value accounting* in calculating minimum capital requirements. Periodically (say, once each quarter) regulators could determine the market value of a bank's assets and liabilities and whether its market value capital (the difference between the market values of its assets and its liabilities) meets minimum capital requirements. If not, the FDIC would be informed and the bank closed before its market value net worth became negative. This would prevent both a loss to the FDIC and excessive risk taking by the bank. Although only an approximation, market value assessments can be a valuable indicator to bank regulators—and shareholder and creditors—of a bank's financial condition. The push toward more market value accounting for measuring banks' equity capital will continue during the 1990s.

Another concern of experts is that bank capital requirements do not adequately reflect risk. The 1988 Basel capital standards (Chapter 14) classified bank assets and off-balance-sheet activities by credit risk. The bank's risk-weighted assets equal the sum of risk-weighted components. Banks' capital requirements are defined relative to risk-weighted assets. FDICIA authorized the FDIC to use capital-adequacy categories to limit banks' participation in certain activities.

These risk-based capital standards focus only on credit risk, and ignore interest rate risk. For example, if banks reduced their investments in short-term commercial and industrial loans and increased their investments in long-term Treasury securities, they would substitute interest rate risk for credit risk. As of early 1993, the Federal Reserve and the Office of Thrift Supervision are evaluating regulations to tie interest rate risk to capital requirements for banks and S&Ls, respectively. On April 30, 1993, banking supervisors from industrialized countries agreed in Basel to propose internationally coordinated capital requirements linked to interest rate risk and exchange rate risk. If accepted by the member countries, these rules would go into effect in 1997.

FDICIA implemented a "prompt closure" rule, which mandated that the FDIC and other regulators take action if a bank's capital falls below the required level. For example, closure or conservatorship is required within 90 days for "less than adequately capitalized" institutions. While this requirement reduces the likelihood of the long delays experienced in closing weak institutions in the S&L crisis, regulators must still confront the issue that book-value measures of bank capital do not accurately measure market-value net worth.

The Treasury Department's Reform Proposals

In February 1991, the U.S. Treasury Department suggested numerous regulatory reforms for the banking system. These proposals addressed many of the issues that we have discussed, including anticompetitive restrictions, deposit insurance coverage, and supervision. The department also suggested that banking regulation be more closely linked to bank capital, a proposal adopted in part in FDICIA.

Anticompetitive Restrictions.

The Treasury Department proposed that full nationwide branching be authorized by 1994 to take advantage of the benefits from diversification and consolidation of redundant operations. Its analysis of permissible bank activities concluded that banks should be allowed to participate in the securities and insurance businesses, but with separate capitalization of nonbank businesses within bank holding companies. Many analysts are concerned that these proposals would increase banks' ability to participate in risky new lines of business while leaving deposit insurance coverage virtually intact—a near duplication of the conditions that brought about the S&L disaster.

Insurance Coverage.

The Treasury Department also proposed reducing deposit insurance coverage to $100,000 per depositor per institution, with an additional $100,000 in coverage for an Individual Retirement Account (IRA). A goal is to eventually limit coverage to $100,000 per depositor regardless of the number of banks used by the depositor. Other recommendations included eliminating insurance coverage for brokered deposits and for nondeposit creditors. Such proposals are likely to be ineffective if depositors and banks perceive that the actual limits on insurance coverage are much greater.

Supervision by Regulatory Agencies.

Also proposed by the Treasury Department is the current overlapping federal regulation of depository institutions. The Federal Reserve System would regulate all state-chartered banks. A new Federal Banking Agency would regulate nationally chartered banks and savings institutions. The FDIC would act only as an insurer and manager of insolvent institutions.

This proposal would create some problems. Because the FDIC bears the costs of bank failures, it should be involved in bank supervision. In addition, in its supervisory role, the Fed currently gathers information about large national banks that is useful for its lender-of-last-resort activities. Thus removing the Fed as a supervisor of large national banks would make its lender-of-last-resort decisions more difficult.

Another concern about the Treasury's proposals for supervisory reform is that regulators would not be obliged to take corrective actions to close banks having low net worth. When supervisory regulators are committed to corrective action, incentives for banks to engage in greater risk taking are reduced. Such a commitment might tie the hands of bank regulators, because rules for corrective actions for individual depository institutions would dictate regulators' behavior. However, when many institutions are in trouble simultaneously, regulators and the Fed (acting as lender of last resort) could be allowed to be flexible in dealing with financially distressed banks.

Current Status. The Treasury Department's proposals addressed some of the major problems facing U.S. banking, but Congress did not enact this sweeping set of reforms. As of early 1993, the Treasury, congressional committees, and the banking and insurance industries were working toward compromise legislation to submit to Congress. The two most important elements relate to branching restrictions and banks' participation in insurance. Branching restrictions would be eliminated within three years of enactment, with an exception to protect small banks (entry into towns with fewer than 50,000 people would be through acquisition of existing banks). Each state would be allowed to regulate insurance sales within its borders, making difficult the establishment of uniform, national insurance businesses by banks.

Concluding Remarks

The deposit insurance crisis and its aftermath illustrate the cycle of financial crisis, regulation, financial innovation, and regulatory response, as depicted in Fig. 15.3. Recent reforms in deposit insurance and likely reforms in other areas of banking regulation generally allow banks to maintain their intermediary role in the saving-investment process. Regulatory intervention is to be used principally in the case of a systemwide crisis. Future comprehensive reform of U.S. banking regulation likely will increase the power of the Fed as the lender of last resort and of bank regulators as monitors.

Emphasis on the central bank as the manager of banking crises is not unique to the United States. Although most industrialized countries (and several developing countries) now have deposit insurance systems, deposit insurance authorities resolve bank failures differently. In the United States,

▼ FIGURE 15.3

Deposit Insurance: Crisis, Regulation, Innovation, and Response
Federal deposit insurance was introduced in response to bank runs in the early 1930s. Information problems led to a crisis in deposit insurance in the 1980s, which in turn led to regulatory reform.

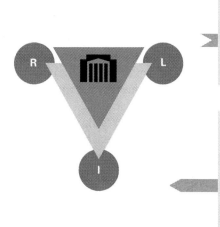

1 Crisis
In the 1960s and 1970s, rising interest rates threaten S&Ls with interest rate risk; the 1981–1982 recession causes high default rates on mortgages.

2 Regulation
Congress relaxes restrictions on the type of assets S&Ls can own, and it raises federal deposit insurance ceiling.

3 Financial innovation
S & Ls and banks increase risk-taking, including real estate investments, commercial mortgages, and junk bonds; savers use brokered deposits to ensure deposit protection.

4 Regulatory response
Lack of decisive action on failing thrifts increases the amount of money needed to pay insured depositors: Deposit insurance reform in FIRREA and FDICIA brought more stringent capital requirements, closer supervision, and reform of regulatory authorities.

the FDIC assumes the lead in handling financially distressed banks. In most other countries, private banks bear more of the costs of resolving failures but are backed by the central bank as the lender of last resort in the event of a general banking crisis. Some analysts believe that the relatively small number of banks in other countries allows private banks in those countries to monitor one another more closely in private insurance arrangements.

Lessons from Banking Regulation for Other Institutions

Our analysis of financial crisis, regulation, financial innovation, and regulatory response in the banking industry offers lessons for regulation of other financial institutions. Let's now consider current and likely future developments in the regulation of insurance companies and private pension funds.

Insurance Regulation

Q: How does regulation promote the effectiveness of banks as intermediaries in the saving-investment process?

A: On balance, a well-functioning lender of last resort contributes to financial stability. Anticompetitive restrictions on banking are undercut by market forces; and the failure of federal deposit insurance to address incentive problems has been recognized and is being corrected.

The distinction between banks and insurance companies for regulatory purposes may be outdated. Like banks, insurance companies are financial institutions that take in money and issue promises to repay. Just as banks are connected through interbank money markets and loan sales, insurers are linked through risk-sharing arrangements known as *reinsurance*. One important difference is that no federal program like deposit insurance is available to the insurance industry. And, whereas in a bank failure depositors can lose only what they have put in, in an insurance company failure policyholders can lose much more.

Developments in the insurance industry have paralleled those in the banking industry. Property and casualty companies experienced a crisis in the late 1800s by underpricing policies and then going broke after several major disasters occurred. Life insurance companies were protected from price competition by restrictions imposed by state regulation in New York (the headquarters of many large insurance companies). In the 1930s and after World War II, Congress attempted to provide stability in the insurance industry. Most notable was the McCarran-Ferguson Act of 1945, which explicitly protected insurers from prosecution under federal antitrust laws. Rapidly rising interest rates in the late 1970s made savers and investors more aware of nonbank opportunities, and financial deregulation broadened their options. Life insurance firms offered higher-yield investment options than banks, but the high yields paid to investors reduced profits significantly. Property and casualty firms competed for premium revenue to invest at record returns, only to discover that even those returns were not enough when record claims came flooding in.

Recently four trends in federal insurance regulation emerged. First, in 1990, Congress began to consider repeal of the McCarran-Ferguson exemption of insurers from federal antitrust laws. Second, some consumer groups want to make rules for supervision and liquidation more uniform among states, to increase the financial resources for supervision, and to institute federal regulation of insurance firms. Third, insurance companies and some regulators are pushing legislation to establish a self-regulatory organization for the insurance industry, using the securities industry as a model. Finally, the insurance industry and the federal government have discussed the consolidation of state "guarantee funds," which are similar to deposit insurance to protect policyholders. The funds do not cover all insurers or products. Nationwide, they would amount to only a few billion dollars per year, a small amount compared to the amount spent on the S&L bailout recently. In the aftermath of the multibillion dollar losses resulting from Hurricane Andrew during September 1992, some analysts questioned the industry's ability to withstand further crises. Many observers believe that any self-regulation should be augmented by a standing national guarantee fund financed by insurance companies or federal minimum standards for state insurance funds.

Life insurance companies and banks increasingly compete in providing financial services, although historically they have been treated separately by Congress, state legislatures, and regulators. Particularly in the area of deposit insurance, lessons from the banking industry's experience may be applicable to insurance regulation.

Pension Fund Regulation

Issues relating to deposit insurance protection also apply to pension funds. The Employee Retirement Income Security Act of 1974 (ERISA) created the Pension Benefit Guaranty Corporation (PBGC) to insure defined benefit pensions when companies go bankrupt. (No such need arises for defined contribution plans, which, by definition, are fully funded.) In 1992, pension liabilities guaranteed by the PBGC totaled about $800 billion. Private pension fund assets exceeded $1 trillion, but the value of those assets can fluctuate. In addition, the PBGC is concerned about the hundreds of large underfunded plans that loom as liabilities if the companies offering them fail. As of 1992, following the bankruptcies of Eastern Airlines and Pan American Airlines, the PBGC had a deficit of more than $2 billion. In addition, the PBGC estimated that unfunded, government-guaranteed liabilities amounted to between $20 billion and $30 billion.

As in the case of deposit insurance, pension fund managers have incentives to take risks if large profits from such risks accrue to the shareholders of the firm (the residual claimants of the plan) and any losses accrue to the PBGC. As the FDIC did in banking, the PBGC proposed reforms to make its insurance function more efficient. First, the PBGC increased premiums in 1990 and has proposed additional increases. Second, the PBGC suggested that underfunded plans pay much higher premiums relative to funded plans than under current law. Third, the PBGC argued that it should have a higher-priority claim in bankruptcy proceedings. Some economists even have questioned whether the government's PBGC is preferable to private insurance, which could simply adjust rates to reflect the cost of moral hazard concerns in companies' underfunding of pension liabilities.

MOVING FROM THEORY TO PRACTICE...

THE WALL STREET JOURNAL   MARCH 6, 1992

How High Should Bank Capital Requirements Be?

After a series of meetings **a** in the Swiss city of Basel in the late 1980s, the bank regulators of the major industrial countries agreed on a new common standard of capital requirements for commercial banks.... They require banks to have specific amounts of capital (primarily shareholder equity) for every dollar of their assets (loans, mortgages, bonds, and other moneys owed to the bank...).

The combination of significant capital requirements and careful regulatory supervision is important to prevent the kind of excessive risk taking that got so many banks and thrifts into trouble in the 1980s. When financial institutions were allowed to operate with little or no equity capital, taking big risks was a heads-I-win-tails-you-lose option. As long as the taxpayers continue to protect most depositors, there is good reason to require equity capital as an incentive for prudent behavior and a buffer between loan losses and government deposit insurance.

But excessive capital requirements also create problems for the economy. Current bank capital requirements limit the ability of healthy banks to expand their lending to businesses and households. This particularly hurts smaller businesses that cannot issue commercial paper or bonds and that are dependent on one or two banks for all of their borrowing needs. The inability of these businesses to borrow is a drag on the whole economy and a particularly serious problem in some regions and industries...

There is a widely shared concern in the government and private sectors that the bank capital regulations and overly tight supervision have created a credit crunch that is preventing a stronger economic recovery. But until now the government actions to alleviate regulator stringency have been concentrated on such technical things as the method of evaluating banks' real estate assets and the guidelines for bank lending to **b** borrowers in difficulty.

These actions have been rightly criticized as relatively ineffective.

A more fundamental reform would substantially increase the ability of banks to lend without any change in the Basel capital standards. It would change the extra domestically imposed "leverage capital requirement" to a uniform 3% standard. [This] change in the leverage capital requirement would more than double the amount of additional lending that New England banks **c** could currently do...

A decision to shift to a uniform 3% leverage standard can be made by America's three banking regulators—the Federal Reserve Board, the Federal Deposit Insurance Corporation and the Comptroller of the Currency—without legislation and without consulting authorities in other countries. Now that the Basel capital requirements are officially in effect, the time has come to make that revision. Doing so would help banks to provide the loans that will be needed for a healthy recovery.

ANALYZING THE NEWS...

High levels of bank equity capital reduce savers' exposure to moral hazard costs because bankers then have an incentive to monitor the behavior of borrowers. This in turn reduces the risk of bank failure in the event of unexpected defaults. Society as a whole also is concerned with the financial stability of banks because of their important role in the saving-investment process. During the early 1990s, significant debate occurred over whether stringent regulatory responses to the deposit insurance crisis of the 1980s impeded the ability of banks to channel funds from savers to borrowers. In the article, Martin Feldstein raises the possibility that higher capital requirements may harm the economy.

(a) How does raising capital requirements reduce banks' ability to lend? If banks are required to have a fixed amount of net worth per dollar of loans, many banks may not have sufficient net worth to increase lending even if the Fed increased reserves through open market purchases of securities. Banks with insufficient net worth likely would use increased reserves to purchase securities. Borrowers not able to obtain bank loans would be forced to turn to the commercial paper, bond, or equity markets for funds.

(b) Not all borrowers have easy access to financial markets. The combination of banks' role in reducing transactions and information costs in lending and regulators' desire to limit moral hazard problems in banking leads to a credit crunch: As a result of capital requirements, banks are less able to substitute loans for securities. As a result of high transactions and information costs, borrowers are less able to borrow through financial markets than from banks, and a cutback in bank loans requires them to reduce their spending. Many analysts argue that banks' unwillingness to lend deepened and prolonged the recession of the early 1990s.

(c) Lowering capital requirements increases banks' ability to lend. However, to reduce moral hazard problems, regulators have to invest more resources in examination and supervision. Without this additional investment, lower net worth requirements might encourage banks to assume too much risk.

For further thought...

Can you suggest explanations other than stringent bank capital standards for banks' reduction in business loans during the recession of the early 1990s? Can you suggest a way to distinguish between the alternatives you thought of and Feldstein's explanation?

Source: Martin Feldstein, "Revise Bank Capital Standards Now," March 6, 1992. Reprinted by permission of *The Wall Street Journal,* © 1992 Dow Jones & Co., Inc. All Rights Reserved Worldwide.

▶ **C H E C K P O I N T** *Suppose that a finan-cially distressed steel manufacturer with large underfunded pension liabilities is insured by the PBGC, which charges premiums that don't reflect differences in risk. The firm's CEO learns about a new steel-making technology that offers a 10% chance of huge profits and a 90% chance of failure. The investment has a negative present value and would bankrupt the firm if unsuccessful. Should the company undertake the project?* The prospect might be tempting. If the investment pays off, the CEO and other shareholders profit because they are residual claimants of the company's defined benefit plan. If the investment fails, the PBGC must fulfill the pension promises the company made to its workers. ◀

Key Terms and Concepts

Brokered deposit

Credit crunch

Depository Institutions Deregulation and
    Monetary Control Act of 1980

Disintermediation

Federal Deposit Insurance Corporation
    Improvement Act of 1991

Financial Institutions Reform, Recovery,
    and Enforcement Act of 1989

Garn–St. Germain Act of 1982

Money market deposit accounts

Narrow banking

Negotiable certificate of deposit

Negotiable order of withdrawal (NOW)
    account

Regulation Q

Resolution Funding Corporation

Resolution Trust Corporation

Summary

1. Bank regulation is best understood in terms of a cycle of financial crisis, regulation, financial innova-tion, and regulatory response. In response to a reduction in banks' ability to provide risk-sharing, liquidity, and information services during banking panics, government has intervened to promote bank stability. Major interventions in the United States include those to (a) create a lender of last resort, (b) restrict competition, and (c) reduce savers' risks through federal deposit insurance. In each case, both regulation and the banking industry were shaped by unintended consequences of intervention.

2. After its failures during the banking collapse in the early 1930s, the Fed emerged as a stabilizing lender of last resort. On many occasions it has provided emergency liquidity to temporarily weak institu-tions in the financial system.

3. Regulation Q placed restrictions on deposit interest rates, which created inefficiencies in bank interme-diation. To escape the interest rate ceilings, finan-cial institutions created alternatives to bank intermediation, including money market mutual funds and the commercial paper market. Two pieces of legislation, the Depository Institutions Deregulation and Monetary Control Act of 1980 and the Garn–St. Germain Act of 1982, effectively removed interest rate ceilings and reduced the like-lihood of disintermediation.

4. The deposit insurance crisis in the savings and loan industry began in the late 1970s and early 1980s. Deposit insurance provided a valuable source of financial stability, but moral hazard problems arose as insolvent S&Ls took on substantial risks and incurred large losses. Reforms center on changes in deposit insurance pricing and coverage, equity capital requirements, and regulatory supervision.

5. Problems faced by a lender of last resort or deposit insurance authority underscore the need for careful supervision of bank activities. The problems faced by banking regulatory authorities during the past decade likely will surface in the regulation of insurance companies and pension funds. Federal regulators continue to debate how to safeguard savers' funds without creating perverse incentives for intermediaries.

Review Questions

1. At the turn of the century, the New York Clearing House performed relatively well in coming to the rescue of individual member banks but did less well in paying off depositors when all its members were in trouble. Based on your understanding of that experience, can you suggest guidelines for creating a lender of last resort for banks?

2. What significant errors by the Fed worsened the Great Depression?

3. Some recent lender-of-last-resort actions by the Fed assisted *nonbank* segments of the financial system (in particular, the commercial paper market and securities exchanges). Suggest some potential information problems in those markets that might justify intervention by the lender of last resort.

4. What are the major costs of disintermediation?

5. What types of innovations did banks develop to get around ceilings on deposit interest rates?

6. How does deposit insurance encourage banks to take too much risk?

7. What initially caused the S&L crisis of the 1980s? What subsequent events caused S&Ls to lose even more money?

8. Why didn't regulators close all the insolvent S&Ls in the early 1980s?

9. Why did so many commercial banks fail in the 1980s?

10. What is narrow banking? How would the existence of narrow banks eliminate the need for deposit insurance?

11. How could a run on an insurance company occur? Is there a need for a government guarantee program similar to that in banking for the insurance industry? Why or why not?

12. What is the main problem with underfunded pension plans? Why is this potentially a serious political issue?

Analytical Problems

13. Describe what happened as interest rates rose above the fixed interest rate ceilings when Regulation Q was in effect.

14. Suppose that, as an innovative banker, you are thinking of ways to increase profits. You note that your bank is required to hold 10% in reserves on

deposits held in the United States but that there are no reserve requirements on deposits held outside the country. What innovation does this knowledge suggest?

15. As a smart banker, you are thinking of ways to increase profits. You recognize the time difference between the operating hours of your bank's branches in the United States and Europe. You also note that you can receive interest on loans made for a fraction of a day and that money left in U.S. accounts over a weekend earns nothing. What innovation does this knowledge suggest?

16. Suppose that you manage a small S&L having a net worth of −$50 million. You fear that within two years regulators will discover that your firm is insolvent and will shut you down. You have two possible investment strategies: (a) continue to operate as you have been, offering market interest rates on CDs to finance mortgage loans, or (b) offer higher than market interest rates on CDs and use the increased funds to speculate in junk bonds and real estate. Your analysis tells you that strategy (a) has a 10% chance of losing $10 million and a 90% chance of gaining $20 million, with an expected return of $17 million. Strategy (b) has an 80% chance of losing $50 million and a 20% chance of gaining $75 million, with an expected return of −$25 million.

What strategy should you follow? Why? What are the consequences of your choice? What should a regulator do in this situation?

17. Suppose that one of the largest banks in the United States defaults on its sales of securitized mortgages, throwing the market into shock. No one wants to buy securitized mortgage loans until they can reevaluate their riskiness, so banks all over the country stop making mortgage loans. As Chairperson of the Federal Reserve Board, what could you do?

18. Suppose that terrorists blew up the computers that run the CHIPS system, disrupting all payments nationwide. As a top official of the Federal Reserve System, what would you do?

19. Based on what you know about the history of the U.S. banking system, what deposit insurance program and set of regulations do you think would be ideal? What should be the limit on the size of accounts covered by deposit insurance? How can you minimize moral hazard problems? How can you encourage banks to diversify? Should different types of financial institutions exist, each with a different regulator, or should they all be the same? Should narrow banks exist? (*Hint*: There is no single correct answer.)

Data Question

20. In each issue of the *Federal Reserve Bulletin*, you can find consolidated balance sheet information for U.S. commercial banks. Using issues of the *Federal Reserve Bulletin*, calculate the fractions of banks' assets at the end of 1989, 1990, 1991, and 1992 held in the form of (a) U.S. government securities, and (b) commercial and industrial loans. Do relative changes in these holdings suggest that banks reduced their exposure to credit risk over this period? Explain. Do these changes indicate that banks may have increased their exposure to other types of risk? Explain. Does your analysis suggest any steps for improving the design of bank capital requirements?

CHAPTER 16

Financial Institutions in the International Economy

What would it take to throw the world into financial anarchy? Imagine... A Paris bank can no longer meet its swap payments to a larger bank in Zurich. As the Zurich bank stumbles, two large banks in New York fail. Deposit insurance authorities and central banks around the world try to sort out the mess—involving losses of tens of billions of dollars. Fiction? In this case, yes. But savers, borrowers, banks, and regulators are learning that globalization brings new complexities to the management of financial institutions.

Like many businesses in the 1990s, banking and other forms of financial intermediation have become international in scope. To survive and prosper, financial institutions must meet increased competition from abroad and deal with international capital market integration. By 1992, more than 100 U.S. banks had offices in other countries, with more than $500 billion in assets. Foreign banks have become active in the United States as well, accounting for a significant share of total U.S. banking activities. Sometimes unregulated by either U.S. or foreign authorities, these banks have deposits and loans in the *trillions* of dollars.

In this chapter we describe the activities of financial institutions in the global economy and address one primary question. **Q:** What are the principal activities of international banking?

International Banking

International banking comprises the risk-sharing, liquidity, and information services that banks provide to assist their customers in international trade and finance. For example, Sears may use a bank to provide credit for its purchase of shoes from an Italian firm. Royal Dutch Shell Oil Company may use a bank to help it manage daily fluctuations in the values of the currencies in which it deals. As they do for their customers domestically, U.S. banks operate internationally to gather information for credit-risk analysis and to help their customers with transactions. International banking activities performed by U.S. banks parallel those performed domestically. Similarly, foreign banks operate in the United States (and in other countries outside their domestic markets) for much the same reasons.

The activities of domestic and international banking have three important similarities. First, like domestic banking, the principal activities of international banking are accepting deposits from savers and lending to borrowers. Second, international banking lowers transactions costs for risk sharing and liquidity and lowers information costs for many individual borrowers and lenders. Finally, international financial regulation can lead to innovation in banking products and markets outside a country's borders, just as domestic regulations can stimulate innovation within those borders.

International banking hasn't always been important for U.S. banks, savers, and borrowers. Before World War II, the U.S. economy basically was a closed economy. Capital flows between the United States and other countries were restricted by regulation, and the volume of international trade was small relative to the level of domestic economic activity. In addition, prior to the development of computer-based information systems, cross-border communication costs were relatively high. The high cost of providing the risk-sharing, liquidity, and information services central to banking discouraged expansion of financial institutions across national boundaries.

The tremendous growth in international trade and capital mobility after World War II led to rapid expansion of international banking. By the 1960s, advances in data processing and telecommunications had decreased the costs of providing banking services. These developments led to significant expansion of international banking and competition among banks in deposit taking and lending. Growth in these activities was rapid in the 1980s: International bank lending in the United States, Western Europe, and Japan rose from $324 billion in 1980 to almost $8 trillion in 1992. At the beginning of the 1990s, deposits in U.S. banks from foreign savers and loans to foreign borrowers were valued at more than $500 billion.

International banking activities take place in many countries around the world, although they are concentrated in the United States, Japan, Europe, and the Caribbean. The concentration of international banking in the United States, Japan, and Europe reflects the commercial needs of businesses in those countries and the importance of the New York, Tokyo, and

London financial centers. About one-half of all foreign liabilities and assets are held (in order of size) by banks in the United Kingdom, Japan, the United States, and Switzerland. The United Kingdom and Switzerland have the longest history of international banking; involvement in international banking by U.S. banks reflects the growing importance of international trade to U.S. businesses.

The rapid growth of international banking activities by Japanese banks during the 1980s can be traced to financial liberalization in Japan. In particular, shifts in Japanese regulation allowed banks' industrial customers to obtain finance in capital markets. At the same time, deregulation of deposit rates (similar to the elimination of Regulation Q in the United States) reduced profits in domestic Japanese banking, giving Japanese banks an incentive to borrow and lend abroad: Although they held only 4% of international bank loans in 1980, Japanese banks held 40% by the end of the decade. Indeed, by the early 1990s, 10 of the 15 largest banks in the world (by assets) were Japanese, and Japanese banks surpassed U.S. banks as leaders in international banking. By 1992, the share of international bank loans held by Japanese banks had fallen to about 30%, as Japanese banks looked inward during a domestic banking crisis.

Some important international financial centers are located in unregulated **offshore markets** in the Caribbean (especially the Bahamas and the Cayman Islands), Hong Kong, and Singapore. In addition to having little or no regulation, these offshore markets tax bank profits at very low rates.

Overseas Activities of the U.S. Banking Industry

Some 100 U.S. banks have subsidiaries or branches abroad, with more than $500 billion of assets. To organize their foreign activities, U.S. banks can utilize (1) branches, (2) Edge Act corporations, (3) interests in foreign financial firms, or (4) international banking facilities.

Branches. Some U.S. banks operate wholly owned *branches* around the world to accept deposits and make loans. Branches in London control the most assets, owing to London's preeminence as a global financial center. However, U.S. bank branches in the Far East and Latin America have grown as U.S. trade with local firms in these regions has expanded. Finally, many U.S. banks operate branches in the tax-haven countries of the Caribbean. These branches largely act as "shell operations" that exist primarily to transfer funds around the world.

Edge Act Corporations. Special subsidiaries of U.S. banks, **Edge Act corporations,** conduct only international banking services. Created by the Edge Act of 1919, these subsidiaries serve customers that are active in international commerce. They also enjoy privileges not given to domestic banks, such as exemption from interstate branching restrictions.

Interests in Foreign Firms. A domestic bank holding company can own a controlling interest in foreign financial services companies such as banks or finance companies. Rules imposed by the Fed (which regulates the international banking activities of member banks, their bank holding companies, and their Edge Act corporations) require that U.S. banks' interest in foreign financial services firms be "closely related to banking." These activities are governed by Federal Reserve Regulation K.

International Banking Facilities. Created in 1981 by the Federal Reserve Board, **international banking facilities** (IBFs) are U.S. institutions that aren't allowed to conduct domestic banking business. IBFs accept time deposits from and make loans to foreign households and firms. They are exempt from reserve requirements, federal restrictions on interest payments to depositors, and (in some states) state and local taxation. Effectively, IBFs are regulated in the same manner as foreign branches of U.S. banks. The Fed has successfully encouraged both U.S. and non-U.S. banks to conduct a large share of their banking business in the United States through IBFs.

Activities of Foreign Banks in the United States

The same international forces that increased the presence of U.S. banks abroad led foreign banks to open offices in the United States. Foreign banks hold about $800 billion of assets in the United States, or more than 20% of total bank assets in this country (as of early 1993). Such extensive holdings have generated fears of foreign control of U.S. banking (particularly in regions such as California where foreign bank influence is strong). Some analysts worry that foreign bankers will lend their U.S. deposits abroad, denying credit to worthy domestic borrowers. However, experts studying the lending practices of Japanese and other foreign-owned banks in the United States found little evidence of this practice.

When operating in the United States, a foreign bank can organize its activities as (1) an agency office, (2) a branch of the foreign bank, or (3) a subsidiary of a U.S. bank. An **agency office** cannot take deposits from U.S. residents, although it can transfer funds and make loans in the United States. The prohibition on accepting deposits limits the activities of agency offices, but they benefit from not being subject to regulations for deposit-taking financial intermediaries (such as branching restrictions or requirements for FDIC insurance). A **foreign bank branch,** on the other hand, is a full-service institution, accepting deposits, making loans, and bearing the name of the foreign bank. A **subsidiary U.S. bank** is treated like a domestic bank; that is, it is subject to domestic bank regulations and may have any name. A subsidiary U.S. bank also may establish Edge Act corporations or international banking facilities.

Most foreign bank branches in the United States and other countries are primarily *wholesale* operations, meaning that they serve other banks that in turn serve the small *retail* accounts of individuals and firms. However, foreign banks are becoming increasingly involved with smaller accounts by buying interests in U.S. banks.

Before passage of the International Banking Act of 1978, foreign banks operating in the United States enjoyed cost advantages over U.S. banks because they were exempt from limits on branching across state lines and from reserve requirements. However, since 1978, foreign banks basically have been subject to the same rules as those governing U.S. banks. In particular, they may establish additional full-service branches only in a "home state" or in states permitting nationwide entry (although they may keep any full-service branches established before passage of the International Banking Act).

After scandals relating to the failure of the Bank of Credit and Commerce International (BCCI) in 1991 (see Box 16.1), Congress passed the Foreign Bank Supervision Enforcement Act of 1992 to strengthen oversight of foreign banks. Under the new law, foreign banks come under the scrutiny of the Federal Reserve System, in addition to the Office of the Comptroller of the Currency or state banking regulators. When approving establishment of a new U.S. branch of a foreign bank, the Fed must be satisfied that the foreign bank's worldwide activities are adequately supervised by regulators in its home country. The law's intent is to equalize operating standards for domestic and foreign banks. Early impressions indicate that the new scrutiny may help to avoid a repetition of the BCCI scandal.

Consider this...
Why Did Closing BCCI Take So Long?

BOX 16.1

International banking regulation is difficult for those who must scrutinize bank operations around the globe. The extent of this difficulty became apparent when the Bank of Credit and Commerce International (BCCI), incorporated in Luxembourg and the Cayman Islands, failed in July 1991. Founded by Agha Hassan Abedi, with the sheik of Abu Dhabi as a prominent investor, BCCI did business in 70 countries. Unfortunately, when it failed, supervisors in the United Kingdom, the United States, and other countries found

evidence of fraudulent behavior for several preceding years. In the United States, BCCI had hidden behind First American Bankshares and its well-connected leaders, Clark Clifford and Robert Altman. For Clifford, the scandal brought a sad end to a career as an attorney and presidential advisor that spanned four decades.

Although banking has become international, supervision has not. Central banks may agree about which country should take the lead in regulation and supervision, but cooperation is voluntary. The BCCI

scandal increased pressure for greater international coordination of bank regulation. However, important challenges include (1) lack of regulation in some developing countries, (2) confusion over the coverage of deposit insurance across national borders, and (3) disagreement over which authority should dispose of a bank's branch assets in an international bankruptcy. These key issues for international bank regulation will be debated for many years.

Services Provided by International Banks

Like domestic banking, international banking involves provision of risk-sharing, liquidity, and information services. And like domestic banks, international banks reduce transactions and information costs for savers and certain types of borrowers. They also develop new ways to manage interest rate risk in banking contracts. Let's explore some significant examples of each type of service.

Managing Exchange Rate Risk

Recall that banks involved in domestic transactions must develop ways to manage interest rate risk. Similarly, international banks are involved in managing **exchange rate risk,** which occurs when banks' net worth fluctuates with increases or decreases in exchange rates. Like interest rate risk, exchange rate risk can affect the value of bank assets and liabilities and hence net worth. For example, suppose that a U.S. bank makes a loan in German marks for DM150 million, but it has only DM100 million in deposits. The exchange rate at the time the loan is made is $1 = DM1.5$. Now suppose that the value of the mark falls against the dollar, say to $1 = DM2$. Hence the value of the bank's asset, the loan, in dollar terms falls from $100 million (DM150 million/1.5) to $75 million (DM150 million/2), a decline of $25 million. The value of the bank's liability, its deposits, measured in dollars also falls, from $67 million (DM100 million/1.5) to $50 million (DM100 million/2), a reduction of $17 million. Thus the bank's net worth, computed by subtracting the values of its liabilities from the values of its assets falls by $8 million, even though there is no change in the loan's repayment or default risk.

As in the case of interest rate risk, the bank can avoid exchange rate risk entirely by matching the currency denomination of assets and liabilities. However, banks may want to speculate deliberately against exchange rate movements. Because large banks can readily sell deposits in any major currency, currency mismatching problems are easy to manage.

One strategy that banks use to hedge against exchange rate fluctuations is financial futures or options (Chapter 9). For example, if a U.S. bank makes a loan abroad in yen when it holds yen deposits of less than the loan value, it can use futures contracts to hedge against the possibility that the value of the yen will fall relative to the dollar. Recall, however, that hedging involves costs and that no hedge is perfect (Chapter 9).

Another strategy is for two banks to arrange a **currency swap,** or an exchange of expected future returns on debt instruments denominated in different currencies. This form of hedge works much the same way as interest rate swaps do in domestic banking. Currency swaps provide risk sharing, and commercial banks are (as with interest rate swaps) instrumental in maintaining the market. For example, consider two multinational firms, Big Steel in the

United States and Le Taste in France. Big Steel wants to build a steelmaking plant in France, and Le Taste wants to manufacture men's suits in the United States. To make its investments, each firm needs local currency—French francs for Big Steel and U.S. dollars for Le Taste. Because a multinational corporation often is better known in its home country, borrowing in that country's currency in domestic capital markets often is cheaper for such firms.

Both Le Taste and Big Steel sell bonds, in France and the United States, respectively. They then swap the proceeds and pay off each other's obligations. For example, Le Taste's revenues and costs are both denominated in dollars after the swap. The swap matches currencies for financing needs while maintaining lower borrowing costs. The intermediary banks assisting the companies perform normal banking functions: assessing and sometimes bearing credit risk.

For banks, swaps provide a convenient way to take deposits and/or make loans in as many countries as they choose. Swaps can greatly reduce currency mismatch and the resulting exchange-rate risk. In this way, a U.S. bank can keep its balance sheet entirely in U.S. dollars, irrespective of the large number of non-U.S. transactions in which it participates. As the swap market has become more competitive, reducing the profitability of simple transactions to banks, banks have come up with more imaginative—and risky—swaps, requiring more elaborate hedging strategies in managing risk.

Reducing Transactions Costs

Bank trading contributes significantly to the liquidity of foreign-exchange markets and helps maintain efficient capital markets for international lending and borrowing.

International banks engage in foreign-exchange trading (buying and selling currencies on spot, forward, and futures markets) to reduce transactions costs for their customers and to assist in managing exchange rate risk. As a result, foreign-exchange trading is an important international banking activity, with daily volume in the hundreds of billions of dollars. Most of banks' foreign-exchange trading volume is with other banks to facilitate cross-border investments and financial transactions. Foreign-exchange trading by banks during the 1980s and early 1990s has grown more rapidly than the value of world trade in goods.

Providing Information Services

One of the difficulties of international transactions is changes in currency values. Suppose that Luxury Stores in Chicago wants to import men's suits from Le Taste in Lyons, France. Luxury Stores will have to pay Le Taste in francs. If Luxury Stores has agreed to pay Le Taste in French francs upon delivery, it has to worry about franc-dollar exchange rate movements in the meantime. International banks act as dealers in foreign exchange, helping firms move funds from country to country. A bank can assist by providing Luxury Stores with an interest-bearing account at its branch in Lyons, so that Luxury will have a local franc-denominated account to use in its dealings with Le Taste. Or the bank can help Luxury hedge its risk by using financial futures, options, or other strategies.

Credit risk also arises as a normal part of international commerce just as it does in domestic commerce. Exporters and importers enter into agreements in which the importer agrees to pay at some future date for goods delivered now. The credit risk inherent in such a transaction is magnified by the fact that the exporter often has limited information about the importer. These risks might deter the exporter from dealing with the importer, decreasing the volume of trade. However, international banks specialize in solving this type of information problem by substituting their own creditworthiness for that of the importer's.

One banking service aimed at reducing credit risk is the sale of bankers' acceptances. A **bankers' acceptance** is a time draft, that is, an order to pay a specified amount of money to the holder of the acceptance on a specified date. Acceptances are a form of the bills of exchange that have been used to finance international trade since the thirteenth century. The Federal Reserve Act of 1913 authorized U.S. banks to use these instruments for short-term financing of their customers' foreign and domestic trade. By the end of the 1920s, outstanding bankers' acceptances in the United States totaled $1.7 billion. Just after World War II, only $104 million were outstanding. By 1987, the amount had grown to $71 billion but, by 1992, had declined to $43 billion. The volume of bankers' acceptances mirrors the importance of international trade to the world economy.

How does a bankers' acceptance work? As shown in Fig. 16.1, a bank guarantees to pay the exporter for its goods by *accepting* an order to pay funds drawn on it by the exporter. The importer pays the bank a fee (averaging about 0.5% of the amount of the transaction) for this service, based on the importer's creditworthiness. The bank then either holds the acceptance in its own portfolio as an investment or sells it at a discount in a secondary market. Regardless of the bank's strategy, it pays the exporter immediately. The importer repays the bank when the acceptance matures; if the bank has sold the acceptance, the bank then repays the holder of the acceptance.

Let's return to the example of Luxury Stores' importing men's suits from Le Taste. To obtain the necessary financing, Luxury Stores asks its bank to issue a letter of credit for the amount of the sale. The bank does so and sends the letter of credit to Le Taste. When Le Taste ships the suits, it uses the letter of credit to draw a time draft on Luxury Stores' U.S. bank and presents the draft to its local bank in Lyons to obtain immediate payment. Next, Le Taste's French bank sends the time draft back to Luxury Stores' U.S. bank. When that bank accepts the draft, it pays Le Taste's bank. Finally, when the time draft matures, Luxury Stores is responsible for paying the accepting bank the face amount of the draft. Figure 16.1 summarizes this process, which works in reverse when a U.S. exporting firm wants to sell goods to a foreign importer. Bankers' acceptances generally have low default risk because both the importer and the bank sign it. (Note the similarity to U.S. banks' provision of standby letters of credit in the domestic commercial paper market.)

Like domestic banks, international banks are centers of information gathering. Banks need considerable specialized knowledge to create bankers' acceptances. As a result, bankers' acceptances are issued only by banks that have domestic and foreign departments staffed by personnel knowledgeable about the markets in which these instruments are used and traded.

▶ C H E C K P O I N T

Because bankers' acceptances allow banks to exploit their information role in financial markets, which banks would you predict are most involved in the bankers' acceptance market? In a bankers' acceptance transaction, the bank reduces information costs by substituting its creditworthiness for the borrower's. For a bankers' acceptance to be useful in international markets, the bank's creditworthiness must be easily ascertained. As a result, large, well-known banks dominate the bankers' acceptance market. ◀

▼ FIGURE 16.1

Information and the Bankers' Acceptance

To avoid the high information costs required for an exporter to assess the creditworthiness of an importer (for future repayment), the importer goes to a bank to obtain a letter of credit. With the bank's assurance of payment, the transaction can be completed. Bankers' acceptances are an example of the information services for international trade and finance that banks can provide.

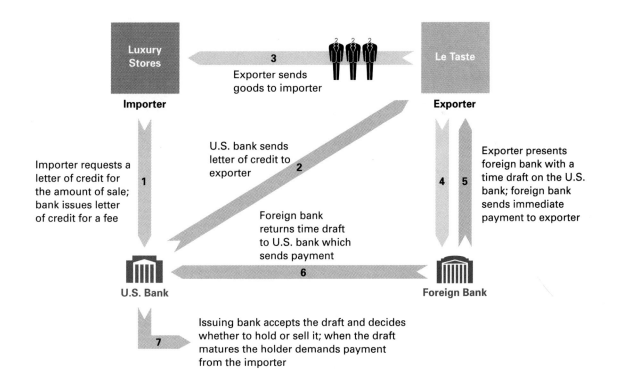

Luxury Stores — **Importer**

3 Exporter sends goods to importer

Le Taste — **Exporter**

1 Importer requests a letter of credit for the amount of sale; bank issues letter of credit for a fee

2 U.S. bank sends letter of credit to exporter

Foreign bank returns time draft to U.S. bank which sends payment

4 5 Exporter presents foreign bank with a time draft on the U.S. bank; foreign bank sends immediate payment to exporter

U.S. Bank

6

Foreign Bank

7 Issuing bank accepts the draft and decides whether to hold or sell it; when the draft matures the holder demands payment from the importer

International banks expand on domestic banks' provision of risk-sharing, liquidity, and information services as summarized in Fig. 16.2.

The Rise of Euromarkets

Before World War II, London was the leading global financial and commercial center. The British pound largely served as the **international transaction currency,** the currency of choice in settling international transactions. After World War II, the United States became the dominant financial and industrial nation. Thus the U.S. dollar became the international transaction currency, even when neither the buyer nor the seller was a U.S. firm. Certain markets, such as the world oil market, still operate almost entirely on dollars. During the years following World War II, the former Soviet Union and Eastern Bloc countries accumulated dollar reserves for international trade. For political reasons, they did not want to keep these reserves in banks inside the United States. Instead, they deposited their U.S. dollar reserves in European banks. Rather than converting them into European currencies, they kept them denominated in dollars, and these accounts became known as **Eurodollars.**

A new Eurodollar deposit is created each time a deposit in a U.S. bank account is transferred to a bank outside the United States while being kept in dollars. For example, if Royal Dutch Shell draws $10 million from an account in a U.S. bank and deposits the same amount in its London bank account in dollars, it has created $10 million Eurodollars. Royal Dutch Shell and other multi-

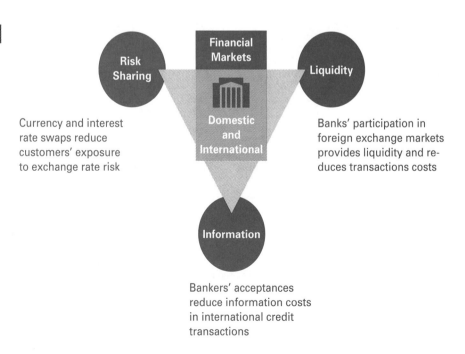

► FIGURE 16.2

International Banking Services
In international banking, banks specialize in providing risk-sharing, liquidity, and information services. They do so by acting as intermediaries in currency swaps, foreign-exchange trading, and credit transactions.

Risk Sharing

Financial Markets

Liquidity

Domestic and International

Information

Currency and interest rate swaps reduce customers' exposure to exchange rate risk

Banks' participation in foreign exchange markets provides liquidity and reduces transactions costs

Bankers' acceptances reduce information costs in international credit transactions

national corporations maintain dollar deposits outside the United States because of the dollar's wide use as a currency in international trade.

British banks, seeking to circumvent the Bank of England's restrictions on the use of British pounds in making loans outside the country, created a market for Eurodollars. By using Eurodollars, British banks could set competitive interest rates to attract deposits while making external loans in dollars. The emergence of Eurodollars illustrates how the shift in demand to U.S. dollars led to innovations in international financial institutions and markets.

Q: What are the principal activities of international banking?

A: The deposit-taking, lending, and currency trading activities of international banks reflect their roles as intermediaries and as providers of risk-sharing, liquidity, and information services in the global financial system.

Interestingly, domestic interest rate regulations and reserve requirements gave U.S. banks a further reason to participate in the growing Eurodollar market. When regulatory ceilings imposed by Regulation Q were binding and market interest rates were high, U.S. commercial banks were hard put to attract new domestic deposits. However, Eurodollar deposits at European branches of U.S. banks were not subject to interest rate ceilings and reserve requirements. Therefore U.S. banks began to acquire Eurodollar deposits in their European branches. The branch banks then transferred the deposits to the U.S. parent banks to buy securities or make loans. By 1970, when the rate ceilings on negotiable certificates of deposit under Regulation Q were dropped, U.S. banks already had a substantial interest in the Eurodollar market. This financial innovation in response to regulation is similar to development of negotiable CDs. Recall that negotiable CDs were created in response to disintermediation and the growth of money market mutual funds and the commercial paper market in the United States.

Since 1960, the Eurodollar market has grown from negligible size to about $3.1 trillion in gross assets and $1.4 trillion in net assets in 1990. From 1973 to the early 1990s, the market grew at a compound annual rate of about 20%.

Much of current international banking business is conducted in relatively unregulated banking centers known as **Euromarkets.** These are markets for **Eurocurrency deposits,** or time deposits denominated in a currency other than that of the issuing domestic financial center (for instance, dollar deposits at a French bank), as well as Euroloans, Eurobonds, and Euro-commercial paper (loans, bonds, and commercial paper denominated in a currency other than that of the issuing financial center). More than one-half of Eurocurrency deposits are in negotiable certificates of deposit with maturities of at least 30 days. Eurocurrency deposits account for the overwhelming majority of banks' foreign-owned deposits; within Eurocurrency deposits, the largest category are Eurodollars. (See also Box 16.2.)

The U.S. dollar remains the dominant currency in the Euromarkets. Before the mid-1980s, roughly 80% of Eurocurrency deposits were denominated in U.S. dollars. The U.S. dollar's share of the market fell during the late 1980s, reaching 66% in 1990, as the dollar depreciated against other currencies, particularly the Japanese yen and German mark.

As it is now used, the term *Eurodollar market* encompasses more than just Europe. It refers broadly to the international demand for dollar-denominated loans and deposits. The Eurodollar market is valued because of

Consider this...

Has Commercial Paper Gone Global?

In Chapter 15, we showed that banks responded to the rapid growth of securitized commercial paper lending in the United States during the 1970s and 1980s by issuing standby letters of credit. As of early 1993, outstanding issues in the U.S. commercial paper market totaled more than $500 billion.

Although the use of commercial paper began much later in Europe and Japan, today the largest commercial paper markets outside the United States are in Japan (established in 1987, with about $80 billion currently outstanding) and the Eurocommercial paper market based in London (established in the mid-1980s).

Two factors explain the later development of commercial paper markets outside the United States. First, regulatory and accounting rules in some countries had discouraged banks from pooling and selling assets. Second, since large European banks were well-capitalized in the 1980s, they were able to pursue traditional bank lending activities and did not need to find substitutes. The less well-capitalized U.S. banks faced pressure to engage in off-balance-sheet activities in order to reduce their need to maintain equity capital.

---

the usefulness of the dollar denomination and because international banking operations are less regulated than domestic banking operations. For example, by the mid-1980s, foreign branches of U.S. banks in low-tax countries (such as the Bahamas and the Cayman Islands) owned large amounts of Eurodollars because of fewer regulatory requirements.

Since 1981, international banking facilities have been authorized to provide Eurodollar banking in the United States. Called *booking sites*, these facilities, which may be within an office of a U.S. bank, weren't subject to interest rate ceilings when they existed. Booking sites don't have to meet reserve requirements and aren't covered by deposit insurance. However, they aren't allowed to conduct business in the United States.

Euromarket Customers

Euromarket customers have changed in response to shifts in international saving and investment. Through the early 1970s, loans were made primarily to governments or state-owned enterprises in industrial countries. Deposits were drawn from multinational corporations and U.S. banks. After the oil shocks of the 1970s, the huge dollar surpluses of the nations belonging to the Organization of Petroleum Exporting Countries (OPEC) were the largest source of deposits. Euroloans were made to developing nations, which needed the funds to pay higher import bills and for new investment. In the late 1980s, oil prices and OPEC deposits declined. Today, the countries with large trade surpluses to deposit in Eurodollar accounts are Japan and South Korea; borrowers include multinational corporations in the United States and abroad. In many cases, large Euroloans have been used to finance merger and acquisition activity in both Europe and the United States.

Loans in Euromarkets

The typical Euroloan is a floating-rate obligation of relatively long maturity, say, five to ten years. Banks charge interest rates based on a markup over the London Interbank Offered Rate (LIBOR). Analogous to the federal funds rate in the United States, LIBOR is the interest rate at which the Eurodollar banks lend to one another, reflecting the perceived credit risk of the loans.

Euroloans usually are quite large—often for billions of dollars—and therefore would result in lack of diversification for a single commercial bank lender. In a **loan syndication,** individual banks hold fractions of a loan. The loan is arranged and managed by a lead bank, which earns a fee for arranging the loan and its syndication. The primary motivation for syndication is risk sharing. Major money center banks as well as regional banks participate in loan syndication. These arrangements do not substitute for credit-risk management, however. Significant defaults on large syndicated loans to less developed countries during the 1970s and 1980s caused several medium-sized banks to stop participating, and the volume of newly syndicated loans declined. Since the mid-1980s, the growth in syndicated lending has resumed, as loans to private firms in industrialized countries have increased.

Eurobonds account for the vast majority of new issues in the international bond market. The value of new issues in the Eurobond market now exceeds that in the domestic corporate bond market in the United States. London has been the traditional center for Eurobond issues, but competition is emerging from other European financial centers and from Japan. Another development in the 1980s was the partial shift away from bank borrowing toward Eurocommercial paper and Eurobonds. The Glass-Steagall Act has never applied to overseas branches handling foreign accounts, so U.S. banks have eagerly entered these new markets.

▶ **C H E C K P O I N T** *Why might a regional bank in Nebraska be more likely to invest in syndicated Euroloans than to lend directly to European borrowers?* The bank obtains the benefit of diversification with low information costs, paying the lead bank a small fee for assessing borrowers' creditworthiness and arranging syndication. ◀

Financial Regulation in International Banking

Recall that government regulation of domestic financial institutions tends to set in motion a cycle in which banks respond by creating new services that are then subject to competition and government regulation. A similar cycle exists in international banking. As technology has lessened the cost of gathering and communicating information internationally, the cost of using overseas markets also has declined. These low costs allow domestic banks to conduct financial activities outside their domestically regulated jurisdictions, as the rise of Eurocurrency and Eurobond markets in the 1960s and 1970s demonstrated. Innovation by banks spurs regulatory response, but a country's domestic regulators must consider the effects of domestic regulation on banks' international competitiveness. For example, if one country restricts the ability of its banks to perform a financial activity, banks in countries with a more favorable regulatory climate will step in to perform the service. Thus, as financial systems become more globally integrated, the activities of financial institutions in various countries are becoming more similar.

In the 1980s, several governments in developing nations threatened to default on their Euroloans (see the Other times, other places box on pg. 412). Central banks in the United States, Europe, and Japan were forced to consider how to deal with the possibility of a global banking crisis. As in the domestic banking industry, three areas of regulation are the focus of greater international attention: (1) minimum levels of net worth (capital standards), (2) deposit insurance, and (3) central bank intervention.

Capital Standards

One way to reduce the chance that risky international banking activities will induce a global banking crisis is to increase the amount of money that banks can lose by raising capital requirements. Efforts to coordinate capital standards for commercial banks began in December 1987, when 12 countries, including the United States, met in Basel (Chapter 14). Implementing the Basel agreement has not been easy because of differences in regulation and accounting requirements, as well as difficulties in standardizing the definition of capital. The Basel agreement left loopholes in that definition and in how to account for off-balance-sheet items, such as interest rate swaps, in risk-weighting. In late 1992, the Bank for International Settlements and the International Organization of Securities Commissions issued common capital standards for banks and brokers engaging in swaps and the use of financial futures and options. Although some questions remain to be resolved, most observers believe that the international coordination of minimum capital requirements has reduced the exposure of central banks to the risk of an international banking crisis.

Deposit Insurance

In the 1990s, leaders of central banks and finance ministries are likely to push for coordination of and restrictions on deposit insurance programs. Table 16.1 highlights differences in coverage, funding, and administration of deposit insurance programs in the early 1990s. Deposit insurance programs outside the United States typically are less generous than U.S. programs and haven't experienced the large losses incurred recently by those in the United States.

Until international standards for insurance premiums are set and implemented, U.S. banks will continue to be charged higher premiums than banks in other countries. As of 1993, U.S. banks pay premiums significantly

▼ TABLE 16.1   DEPOSIT INSURANCE PROGRAMS AROUND THE WORLD

Country (date fund established)	How funded	Banks' annual contribution	Level of protection for depositors
United States (1933)	Participating institutions	0.23%-0.31% of deposits	$100,000 per account
Belgium (1985)	Participating institutions in event of loss	0.2% of Belgium franc liabilities	BFr 500,000 per depositor (but overall limited to assets available in fund)
France (1980)	Participating institutions in event of loss	Depends on losses; annual maximum for small banks is 1% of deposits	FF 400,000 per depositor
Germany (1966)	Participating institutions	0.03% of deposits	Maximum of 30% of bank's liable capital per depositor
Holland (1979)	Participating institutions in event of loss	Based on percentage of loss to be met; individual annual contributions not to exceed 10% of own funds	G35,000 per depositor
Ireland (1989)	Participating institutions	0.2% of deposits; minimum of IR£20,000 (no maximum)	80% of first IR£5,000 70% of next IR£5,000 50% of next IR£5,000
Italy (1987)	Participating institutions in event of loss; fund ceiling of L4 trillion	Total fund amount set at 1% of total deposits of participating banks	100% claims to L200 million 90% between L200 million and L1.0 billion 90% between L1.0 billion and L3.0 billion
Japan (1971)	Participating institutions and government	0.012% of savings deposits at year end annually	Up to ¥10 million per depositor
Spain (1977)	Participating institutions	0.2% of deposits; central bank contribution equivalent to half the banks' contributions	Pta1.5 million per depositor
United Kingdom (1982)	Participating institutions; fund ceiling of £6 million	Minimum initial contribution of £10,000; further calls when necessary up to £300,000; ceiling of 0.3% of bank's deposit base	75% of deposits up to £20,000 per depositor

Note: Most deposit insurance programs cover all deposits, irrespective of currency; countries in which deposit insurance programs cover only deposits denominated in the domestic currency are Belgium, Ireland, Japan, and the United States.

Source: Bank of England, U.S. Federal Deposit Insurance Corporation, Central Bank of Ireland, and the Japanese Ministry of Finance.

higher than those paid by German and Japanese banks. However, coordination could still mean higher costs for U.S. banks. Currently they pay premiums only on domestic and repatriated Eurodollar deposits; if coordinated international deposit insurance is included in an agreement, large U.S. international banks will face a significant increase in the cost of insurance. Also facing higher costs would be banks in countries such as France and Holland, because, under their current national regulations, they pay deposit insurance premiums only after payouts are made.

MOVING FROM THEORY TO PRACTICE...

THE WALL STREET JOURNAL   NOVEMBER 2, 1992

Swap 'Til You Drop?

Banks have worked to reduce the risk of complex hedging instruments known as derivatives, but significant gaps remain in efforts to limit potential shocks to the financial system, a study by central bankers concludes.

The report by the Bank for International Settlements in Basel, Switzerland, is the latest attempt by financial regulators to improve methods for assessing and controlling the risks posed by the multitrillion-dollar market in swaps, options, futures and other financial products used to hedge against changes in interest rates, commodity prices and foreign-exchange rates.

The exposure that banks and investment banks face from these derivatives is huge. As traders become adept at spreading risks across a range of markets at home and abroad, regulators worry that liquidity or credit problems encountered by one large participant could quickly infect other linked transactions.

In 1990, the report says, U.S. banks faced an exposure of $3.12 trillion from derivatives tied to interest-rate risk and an exposure of $3.33 trillion from foreign-exchange-related derivatives. In the same year, the exposure of Japanese banks was $1.58 trillion for interest-rate derivatives and $4.49 trillion in foreign-exchange derivatives.

The report concludes that market participants and regulators need more precise and current information about exposure from derivatives. Among other things, it recommends greater harmonization of international reporting and disclosure requirements, including more concerted efforts to disclose the market value of trading account portfolios.

On the positive side, the study, which was based on a survey of market participants, concludes that banks and securities firms are paying much more attention to evaluating and managing the risks of transactions in derivatives. One result is that transactions are increasingly concentrated among the strongest, best-capitalized banks and brokers.

But "a greater degree of concentration in the wholesale markets has meant that larger exposures are incurred vis-a-vis a smaller set of key players" deemed to face the lowest likelihood of default, the report says. It warns that "the perceived credit standing of a financial institution can deteriorate rapidly. Since the failure of one such key player would entail larger losses to other participants in the markets than if exposures were more dispersed, increased concentration implies that financial market stability could be affected more heavily than in the past by the sudden decline of any such firm."...

The report recommends that banks and brokers pay more attention to risk control. It also suggests that regulators and market participants work more diligently to improve the legal, accounting and institutional foundations of the evolving international derivatives markets.

Finally, the report says that central bank regulators and market participants must work more closely together to understand and contain risk. The BIS working group says that huge flows of derivative transactions could affect the "channels of transmission of monetary policy."

ANALYZING THE NEWS...

Interest rate swaps provide valuable risk-sharing and liquidity services for savers and borrowers. Simple interest rate swaps no longer provide healthy profits for financial institutions, however. Margins on such arrangements in the early 1990s were only about one-tenth their level in the mid-1980s. The result has been an increase in financial innovation and, in the minds of some analysts, risk.

(a) The concerns are the following: First, default by one party in a complicated swap could lead to a chain of defaults by other parties to the transaction. There is also concern over *contagion,* that is, well-publicized defaults in one transaction can reduce participation in swaps generally, depriving savers and borrowers of the risk-sharing services they provide. Perhaps the greatest question concerns who would play the role of lender of last resort in the event that major swap defaults affected banks in many countries.

(b) Swaps advocates sometimes ignore the possibility of default risk for the payments. Their argument also assumes that participating institutions have sufficient capital to withstand such defaults, a topic of ongoing review by international financial regulators.

(c) Concentration is not a reason to worry about recent developments in the swap market. However, the article's prediction of a domino effect caused by the failure of one key player raises two concerns. First, the full extent of default risk may not be known to all participants. Second, as the swaps frequently involve financial institutions from more than one country, issues of capital standards, lender-of-last-resort roles, and deposit insurance should be addressed. If the swap market becomes concerned about risks after the default of a prominent borrower, the possibility of contagion becomes more likely. In the event of a crisis, participants likely would turn to financial institutions with significant capital and solid reputations for gathering and monitoring information.

For further thought...

Can you suggest ways to use risk-based capital requirements to address the perceived exposure of lenders of last resort in a swap crisis?

Source: Kenneth H. Bacon, "Banks' Risks In Derivatives Found to Persist," November 2, 1992. Reprinted by permission of *The Wall Street Journal,* © 1992 Dow Jones & Co., Inc. All Rights Reserved Worldwide.

Other times, other places...

Do Sovereigns Default?

For banks, lending money to foreign governments involves more credit risk than private lending does. The banks have no way to prevent the borrower from defaulting on the loan, and incentives for foreign countries to maintain debt payments are weaker than for domestic units of government. Countries defaulting may lose access to foreign credit markets for a time, but a country's property within its own borders cannot be seized easily. During the 1980s, more than 40 developing countries restructured bank loans of about $300 billion.

From 1970 until the early 1980s, rising commodity prices and low real interest rates enhanced the creditworthiness of many developing nations. These conditions encouraged borrowing for investment and development and to finance government budget deficits. In the early 1980s, rising real interest rates and falling oil prices caused several Latin American countries to halt interest payments. In August 1982, Mexico was unable to roll over its obligations. Along with other countries, it began to renegotiate interest rates or repayment terms with private commercial banks in the United States, Europe, and Japan.

Default on loan obligations hit Citicorp, BankAmerica, Chase Manhattan, J. P. Morgan, Bankers Trust, Chemical, and First Chicago hard. At the onset of the crisis in 1982 and 1983, many analysts worried that the foreign-debt problems of these banks could create a

banking crisis. However, by adding funds to loan loss reserves to cover foreign-debt losses, the banking system managed to avoid a crisis. However, U.S. banks lost $10 billion in the second quarter of 1987, their worst performance since the Great Depression. Large banks' loan loss reserves now total more than half their exposure to developing-nation debt. In the late 1980s and early 1990s, large U.S. banks increased their equity capital from a low of about 4% of assets in 1981 to more than 7%. The foreign-debt problems didn't cause the international banking system to collapse, but it made international banks more conservative in their credit-risk analysis of foreign government as borrowers.

Central Bank Intervention

After the debt crisis in developing nations began in the early 1980s, central banks met on several occasions at the Bank for International Settlements to discuss their roles as lenders of last resort during a banking crisis. They concluded that each central bank would concentrate on ensuring the financial stability of its own domestic banks. However, the increasing international linkages among banks, especially in their off-balance-sheet activities, has led to continuing discussions among central banks about how to intervene in an international banking crisis.

In the 1980s and early 1990s, central banks also met to discuss the coordination of bank regulation and supervision. Regulatory differences are apt to diminish in the competitive global financial system of the 1990s. Regulation by function likely will emerge, and regulation by institutions likely will decline. Besides deposit insurance, regulation of commercial banks with respect to geographic extent and scope of permissible activities is likely to have two characteristics: First, in addition to owning banks, bank holding companies would be free to provide a broad range of financial services, including securities and insurance, with regulation and supervision of those lines of business. Second, the extent to which bank holding companies would be allowed to participate directly in nonfinancial business would depend on local legal tradition. Restrictions probably will be most stringent in the United States and less stringent in Europe and Japan.

International Coordination

Allocating supervisory responsibility and tasks in international banking is difficult. In particular, coordination of the activities of lenders of last resort and deposit insurance authorities, as well as restrictions on bank activities, is necessary. Economists and policymakers are debating various proposals, but some common themes have emerged. Branches and subsidiaries of foreign banks generally should be treated as the equivalent of domestic banks by the lender of last resort (if those banks abide by host-country supervisory rules and information-disclosure regulations). Cross-border transactions of domestic banks should be addressed by the home-country lender of last resort. Likewise, deposit insurance should follow host-country rules for branches and subsidiaries and home-country rules for cross-border transactions of domestic banks. Finally, restrictions on bank activities should be determined by home-country rules for cross-border transactions by domestic banks and by internationally coordinated rules for foreign branches and subsidiaries. How such coordination can be achieved is a subject of continuing debate in the 1990s.

Key Terms and Concepts

Agency office

Bankers' acceptance

Currency swap

Edge Act corporation

Euromarkets
  Eurocurrency deposit
  Eurodollars
  Loan syndication

Exchange rate risk

Foreign bank branch

International banking

International banking facility

International transaction currency

Offshore market

Subsidiary U.S. bank

Summary

1. The growth of international banking is a result of the explosion in international trade and the increasing integration of financial markets during the past 30 years. International banks primarily supply intermediation and transaction services.

2. International banks also produce risk-sharing, liquidity, and information services. For example, as with interest rate risk, international banks can manage their exposure to exchange rate risk by using financial futures, options, and swaps. Banks promote liquidity by reducing customers' transactions costs in buying and selling foreign exchange and deposits denominated in foreign currencies. Through bankers' acceptances, banks provide information services to customers involved in international trade.

3. The Eurodollar market developed after World War II as a market for dollar-denominated deposits and loans. In recent years, currencies other than the U.S. dollar have been included in the market. Deposits in the Eurodollar market are short-term time deposits. Loans are of longer maturity (typically, five to ten years) and are made with a floating interest rate, determined as a spread over the London Interbank Offer Rate. To share risk, many large Euroloans are syndicated, with participation by many banks.

Review Questions

1. Why does the international banking market exist?

2. Why has international banking grown so rapidly during the past two decades?

3. What are the most important international banking centers?

4. What are international banking facilities? What can they do that regular U.S. banks cannot do?

5. What is the major type of risk that international banks must manage? What techniques do they use?

6. What is a currency swap? What benefits have made it so popular?

7. Why has foreign-exchange trading by banks grown so much during the 1980s and early 1990s?

8. What is the fundamental problem that leads to credit risk in international trade? What financial instrument do banks use to avoid this problem?

9. What are Euromarkets? What brought them into existence? Who are their customers? What currencies do they use?

10. How did U.S. banks get involved in Euromarkets?

11. Relate the problem of exchange rate risk in international banking to interest rate risk in domestic banking. Based on your understanding of interest rate risk, suggest strategies for managing exchange rate risk in international banking.

12. Describe how domestic financial regulation in the United States and elsewhere contributed to the development of Euromarkets. How does the growth of such markets complicate the responsibilities of a lender of last resort?

Analytical Problems

13. Suppose that your bank made a loan of ¥1 billion but has no yen deposits. Describe a financial futures contract that would provide a hedge against exchange rate risk.

14. Would it surprise you to learn that a bankers' acceptance written on a U.S. firm and given to a firm in Japan ultimately is cashed by a firm in the United States? Why or why not?

15. Suppose that a U.S. firm, Big Ball, plans to sell 100,000 baseballs to a Japanese importer, Ichi-ball. Describe how Ichi-ball's bank in Japan could initiate a bankers' acceptance to finance the transaction.

16. *Evaluate:* Credit risk is less important in international banking than in domestic banking.

Data Question

17. Find the most recent edition of the *Statistical Abstract of the United States* (published by the Department of Commerce) in your library. In the section called "Banking, Finance, and Insurance," you should be able to find a table reporting summary statistics on the location of the 500 largest banks in the world. Has the relative importance of U.S. banks (measured in this way), increased or decreased since 1970? Based on our analysis of financial institutions in Part III, can you explain this trend? Does this trend tell you whether the profitability of U.S. banks is likely to rise or fall relative to that of banks in other countries? Explain.

part IV

The Money Supply Process and Monetary Policy

CHAPTER 17

The Money Supply Process

Once again, the Fed grabbed the headlines: It announced that the U.S. money supply was $3 billion lower than analysts had predicted. The announcement sent a ripple through financial markets. Commentators felt that the money supply decline would be bad news for the economy. Investors acknowledged the bad news by selling shares of stock, causing the stock market to fall. Business executives complained that interest rates would rise and that their businesses would have to cut back on spending for plants and equipment. However, some analysts predicted that the lower money supply might lead to lower inflation in the future.

At the root of such changes in financial markets is the money supply. The money supply process, which we discuss in this chapter, determines the level of the economy's medium of exchange. We identify the roles played by three participants: the central bank (the Federal Reserve System in the United States), banks, and the nonbank public. We then examine who controls the money supply. Understanding that helps policymakers, businesspeople, and investors know where to look for information about likely future changes in the money supply.

We proceed in two steps. First, we describe how the Fed controls the monetary base, that is, the total amount of currency in the hands of the nonbank public and in bank reserves. We then connect changes in the monetary base to changes in the money supply by developing a money multiplier. The money multiplier represents the amount by which the money supply changes in response to a change in the monetary base. The combined actions of banks, the nonbank public, and the Fed determine the money multiplier.

Four questions shape our analysis in this chapter. **Q:** How do the Fed's decisions affect the monetary base? **Q:** How are deposits created? **Q:** What factors determine the money multiplier? **Q:** How do the Fed, banks, and the nonbank public together influence the money supply process?

Overview

In Chapter 1 we noted that changes in the money supply influence many economic variables, including interest rates, exchange rates, inflation, and the economy's output of goods and services. These variables affect everyone's daily life. As a result, analysts known as *Fed watchers* closely follow the financial decisions of the Federal Reserve System, banks, and the nonbank public in order to predict changes in the money supply.

In this chapter, we develop tools to help you understand the **money supply process,** the actions that determine the quantity of money. First, we must define money. In Chapter 2 we stated that money functions as a medium of exchange, a unit of account, a store of value, and a means of deferred payment in the economy. Here, we define money as liquid assets used for the *medium of exchange* function. We use the Fed's narrowest measure of money, *M1*, to describe the money supply. *M1* consists of currency and checkable deposits in depository institutions. Broader measures of money include other liquid assets. In the Appendix, we describe the money supply process in terms of *M2*, the next broadest measure of money compiled by the Fed.

The process by which money is supplied in the economy has two essential parts. The first, the **monetary base,** comprises all reserves held by banks and all currency in circulation. The monetary base sometimes is called *high-powered money*, because a given amount of base allows creation of a multiple amount of money. Various factors affect how much monetary base is available, but by far the most important are the actions of the Fed.

The second part of the money supply process is the means by which the monetary base is transformed into money supply. It is called *multiple deposit expansion*, as it involves the depositing and redepositing of funds in banks. As the name implies, both banks and depositors play crucial roles here, although the decisions of the Fed are important, too. The degree to which the monetary base is ultimately magnified by deposit expansion is called the money multiplier. The end result is the money supply. In simple terms, the money supply process is

$$\text{Money supply} = (\text{Monetary base}) \times (\text{Money multiplier}).$$

To gain a deeper understanding of the money supply process, let's first look at how the Federal Reserve System affects the size of the monetary base. Then we can consider how the decisions of banks, the nonbank public, and the Fed convert the monetary base into the money supply and how their interactions influence the money supply process.

The Fed and the Monetary Base

The Federal Reserve System performs three general functions. The first two reflect the Fed's role as a banker's bank. The Fed operates a network to clear checks by settling claims among banks in commercial and financial transactions. It also regulates the operation of banks under federal law. The Fed's third general function is to guide monetary policy by managing the nation's money supply. The Fed does not directly control the money supply; rather, it influences the behavior of banks, which in turn affects the money supply.

The Fed affects the monetary base by manipulating its *balance sheet*. A detailed look at the Fed's balance sheet isn't necessary at this point. Instead, we focus on the four entries that matter most. The Fed's principal *liabilities* are currency in circulation and reserves (deposits by banks with the Fed and cash held by banks). The Fed's principal *assets* are U.S. government securities and discount loans (loans to banks).

BALANCE SHEET OF THE FEDERAL RESERVE SYSTEM

Assets	Liabilities
U.S. government securities	Currency in circulation
Discount loans to banks	Reserves

The Fed's Liabilities

The Fed's principal liabilities reflect its role in the money supply process. If we hold other elements of the money supply process constant, increases in either currency in circulation or reserves increase the money supply. The sum of these two liabilities, together with the monetary liabilities of the U.S. Treasury (primarily coins in circulation, called *Treasury currency in circulation*), equals the monetary base. Simply stated, the monetary base is the sum of the Fed's currency in circulation and reserves (because the monetary liabilities of the Treasury are so small), or

Monetary base = Currency in circulation + Reserves.

Currency in Circulation. The dollar bills in your wallet are *Federal Reserve Notes*. They are part of the Fed's currency outstanding, which includes currency in circulation and vault cash. Specifically, **currency in circulation** is the currency held by the nonbank public, and **vault cash** is the currency held by depository financial institutions (still a liability of the Fed but counted as reserves). Hence

Currency in circulation = Currency outstanding – Vault cash.

At the end of 1992, currency in circulation equaled $320.2 billion.

Reserves. The second largest liability of the Fed is **bank reserves,** or vault cash in banks and deposits by commercial banks and savings institutions with the Fed. Financial institutions record reserve deposits as assets on their balance sheets. The Fed records them as liabilities, because the Fed must redeem banks' requests for repayment on demand in Federal Reserve Notes. The total reserves of the banking system are the sum of banks' deposit accounts with the Fed ($25.5 billion at the end of 1992) and vault cash ($28.5 billion at the end of 1992). Thus,

Reserves = Deposits with the Fed by depository institutions + Vault cash.

Total reserves are made up of amounts that the Fed compels depository institutions to hold, called **required reserves,** and extra amounts that depository institutions elect to hold, called **excess reserves:**

Reserves = Required reserves + Excess reserves.

The Fed specifies a percentage of deposits that banks must hold as reserves, which is known as the **required reserve ratio.** For example, if the required reserve ratio is 10%, a bank would have to set aside 10% of its checkable deposits as reserves—vault cash and/or deposits with the Fed. At the end of 1992, of the $54 billion of bank reserves, less than $1 billion was excess reserves. Because the Fed doesn't pay interest on reserves, depository institutions prefer not to hold all their liquid balances as reserves. Instead, they hold some of their balances in marketable securities, on which they can earn interest.

The Fed's Assets

The two principal Fed assets are government securities and discount loans. These assets are significant because, by influencing them, the Fed can change the level of reserves and the money supply. These assets also are a source of income for the Fed because its portfolio of government securities and discount loans earns interest, and it does not pay interest on currency or reserves. In 1992, the Fed earned about $15 billion, most of which was returned to the Treasury.

Government Securities. The Fed's portfolio of government securities consists principally of holdings of U.S. Treasury obligations: Treasury bills, notes, and bonds. At the end of 1992, the Fed held about $280 billion in Treasury securities. An increase in the Fed's holdings of Treasury securities increases reserves and the money supply.

Discount Loans. By extending loans to depository institutions to help banks handle liquidity problems, the Fed can increase the level of reserves. It earns a market interest rate on the U.S. government securities that it holds as assets. However, when the Fed lends to depository institutions, the loans are called **discount loans.** In making such loans, the Fed specifies a rate known as the **discount rate.** An increase in the volume of discount loans made by the Fed increases reserves and the money supply.

▶ C H E C K P O I N T *Federal Reserve Notes essentially are IOUs of the Fed. Why do you accept them as money?* They serve as the official medium of exchange in the United States and are accepted for use in commercial and financial transactions. The IOUs that businesses or households might write are not so widely accepted in exchange. ◀

Effect of the Fed's Actions on the Monetary Base

The Fed affects the monetary base by buying and selling Treasury securities and by making discount loans to banks. The actual execution of these transactions involves some interesting institutional details, which we discuss in Chapter 20. For now, we focus on how these transactions affect the monetary base.

Open Market Operations

The most direct route by which the Fed can change the monetary base is through **open market operations**, that is, buying or selling securities, generally U.S. government securities. In an **open market purchase,** which raises the monetary base, the Fed buys government securities. To execute such a transaction (for example, to buy $1 million in government securities), the Fed draws checks totaling $1 million on the Federal Reserve Bank of New York and uses them to buy the securities through banks or from the nonbank public. Commercial banks can redeem these checks for currency, or, more likely, the banks can deposit the funds with the Fed as reserves. In either case, an open market purchase raises the monetary base, B, because the base is the sum of currency in circulation, C, and bank reserves, R. This relationship is expressed as

$$B = C + R. \tag{17.1}$$

Open Market Purchases from Depository Institutions. Suppose that the Fed buys $1 million in T-bills from Megabank and pays for them with a check for $1 million. Megabank can either deposit the funds in its account with the Fed or hold them in vault cash. Either action increases its reserves by $1 million. The banking system's T-account shows a decrease in security holdings of $1 million and an increase in reserves of the same amount:

BANKING SYSTEM

Assets		Liabilities
Securities	−$1 million	
Reserves	+$1 million	

The Fed's T-account reflects an increase in securities (an asset) and an increase in reserves (a liability) by $1 million:

FEDERAL RESERVE

Assets		Liabilities	
Securities	+$1 million	Reserves	+$1 million

The open market purchase from depository institutions increases reserves and thus the monetary base by $1 million.

Open Market Purchase from the Nonbank Public. If the Fed purchases government securities from the nonbank public, sellers have two options: (1) to hold the proceeds as checkable deposits, or (2) to hold the proceeds as currency. If the sellers deposit checks drawn on the Fed in the banking system, checkable deposits increase by $1 million. When banks deposit the Fed's checks in their account with the Fed, reserves also rise by $1 million:

NONBANK PUBLIC

Assets		Liabilities	
Securities	−$1 million		
Checkable deposits	+$1 million		

BANKING SYSTEM

Assets		Liabilities	
Reserves	+$1 million	Checkable deposits	+$1 million

As a result of the open market purchase, the Fed's portfolio of securities rises by $1 million, and bank reserves rise by the same amount:

FEDERAL RESERVE

Assets		Liabilities	
Securities	+$1 million	Reserves	+$1 million

As in the case of an open market purchase from depository institutions, this open market purchase from the nonbank public increases bank reserves by $1 million, thereby increasing the monetary base by $1 million.

If households and businesses decide to cash the Fed's checks and hold the proceeds as currency, the nonbank public decreases its holdings of securities by $1 million and increases its currency holdings by the same amount. The Fed increases currency in circulation by $1 million to acquire the $1 million of securities in the open market purchase:

NONBANK PUBLIC

Assets		Liabilities
Securities	−$1 million	
Currency	+$1 million	

FEDERAL RESERVE

Assets		Liabilities	
Securities	+$1 million	Currency in circulation	+$1 million

While the proceeds from the sale of securities to the Fed are held in currency, the monetary base (the sum of currency in circulation and bank reserves) increases by the amount of the open market purchase, or $1 million.

To summarize, an open market purchase increases the monetary base by the amount of the purchase in all cases. The effect of the open market purchase on bank reserves depends on whether the nonbank public chooses to hold some of the proceeds as currency.

Open Market Sale.   Similarly, the Fed can reduce the monetary base by an **open market sale** of government securities. Whether the securities are purchased with currency or with checkable deposits, an open market sale decreases the monetary base by the amount of the sale.

For example, suppose the Fed sells $1 million of securities to depository institutions or the nonbank public. If payments to the Fed are entirely in the form of checkable deposits, the Fed receives in payment $1 million in checks drawn on commercial banks. In this case, bank reserves with the Fed (a Fed liability) fall by $1 million, the Fed's securities holdings (an asset for the Fed) also fall by $1 million, and the monetary base falls by $1 million:

BANKING SYSTEM

Assets		Liabilities
Securities	+$1 million	
Reserves	−$1 million	

FEDERAL RESERVE

Assets		Liabilities	
Securities	−$1 million	Reserves	−$1 million

Q: How do the Fed's decisions affect the monetary base?

A: In an open market purchase, the Fed buys securities by issuing Federal Reserve Notes or increasing bank reserves. The result is an increase in the monetary base. In an open market sale, the Fed sells securities and receives Federal Reserve Notes or checks drawn on banks as payment. The result is a decrease in the monetary base. Like open market operations, discount loans (borrowing from the Fed) change the monetary base by the amount of the loans.

Thus, if payments to the Fed are entirely in the form of checkable deposits, reserves (and the monetary base) decline by the amount of the open market sale.

However, if payments to the Fed are entirely in the form of currency, the open market sale won't affect reserves:

NONBANK PUBLIC

Assets		Liabilities
Securities	+$1 million	
Currency	−$1 million	

FEDERAL RESERVE

Assets		Liabilities	
Securities	−$1 million	Currency in circulation	−$1 million

However, the monetary base (currency in circulation plus reserves) falls by $1 million.

The effects of open market operations on reserves and the monetary base are summarized in Fig. 17.1.

Discount Loans

Open market operations are the predominant means by which the Fed influences the monetary base. Recall that the Fed also can make discount loans to depository institutions, which increase bank reserves and hence the monetary base.

Let's examine the balance sheets for both the banks and the Fed to see what happens if banks obtain $1 million in discount loans from the Fed. For the Fed, assets rise by $1 million from the addition to discount loans, and liabilities rise by $1 million from the addition to bank reserves. Thus the discount loan affects both sides of the Fed's balance sheet:

FEDERAL RESERVE

Assets		Liabilities	
Discount loans	+$1 million	Reserves	+$1 million

Both sides of the banking system's balance sheet are also affected. Banks acquire $1 million of assets in the form of reserves and $1 million of liabilities in the form of discount loans payable to the Fed:

BANKING SYSTEM

Assets		Liabilities	
Reserves	+$1 million	Discount loans	+$1 million

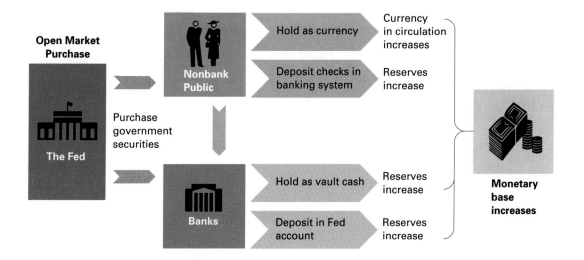

FIGURE 17.1

Effect of Open Market Operations on Reserves and the Monetary Base
One method that the Fed uses to increase the monetary base is open market purchases of securities from the nonbank public or banks. The nonbank public holds the proceeds of the sale as currency (increasing currency in circulation) or deposits the proceeds in banks. Banks may choose to hold the proceeds as vault cash or deposit the proceeds in a Fed account, increasing reserves in either case. Since increases in currency in circulation or in reserves raise the monetary base, open market purchases increase the monetary base. The process of reducing the monetary base (not shown here) works in reverse.

As a result of the Fed's making $1 million of discount loans, bank reserves and the monetary base increase by $1 million.

However, if banks repay $1 million in discount loans to the Fed, the preceding T-account transactions are reversed. Reserves fall by $1 million, as do the Fed's discount loans (assets) and the banking system's discount loans (liabilities):

FEDERAL RESERVE

Assets		Liabilities	
Discount loans	−$1 million	Reserves	−$1 million

BANKING SYSTEM

Assets		Liabilities	
Reserves	−$1 million	Discount loans	−$1 million

The effects of discount loans on reserves and the monetary base are summarized in Fig. 17.2.

Extent of Fed Control of the Monetary Base

Recall that the Fed has two ways of changing the monetary base: by open market operations and through discount loans. The Fed completely controls the volume of open market operations. It initiates purchases or sales of securities by placing orders with dealers in the government securities markets. Of course, if the Fed wants to sell a T-bill, someone must buy it, or there is no open market operation. The point is that the Fed can sell securities at whatever price it takes to accomplish its goal.

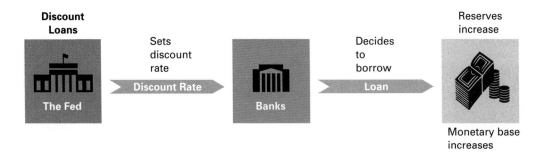

FIGURE 17.2

Effect of Discount Loans on Reserves and the Monetary Base
A second method for the Fed to increase the monetary base is through discount loans. The Fed does not control completely the volume of discount loans; it can reduce the discount rate, but banks must decide whether to borrow from the Fed. If banks choose to borrow from the Fed, reserves increase, increasing the monetary base. The process of reducing the monetary base using discount loans (not shown here) works in reverse.

However, the Fed's control over discount lending is much less complete because banks decide whether to borrow from the Fed. The Fed's limited control comes from its ability to set and change the discount rate. The fact that the Fed sets the discount rate distinguishes it from most interest rates, which are determined by market forces. An increase in the discount rate makes borrowing from the Fed more expensive for banks. If nothing else changes, banks then decrease their discount borrowing, which in turn reduces the monetary base. Hence decisions by both banks and the Fed determine the volume of discount loans.

The discount rate typically is less than other short-term market interest rates, such as the federal funds rate or the rate on three-month T-bills. (The federal funds rate is the rate that banks charge each other on overnight loans.) Thus banks have a profit opportunity in that they can borrow from the Fed at the discount rate and lend the funds at higher rates. However, the Fed discourages banks from borrowing from it too often. Instead, banks borrow more frequently in the federal funds market from other banks that have extra reserves; they are willing to pay a higher rate for doing so.

As a result of the difference in the Fed's control over open market operations and discount loans, we think of the monetary base as having two components: the *nonborrowed monetary base*, B_{non}, and *borrowed reserves*, BR, or discount loans. The monetary base B is

$$B = B_{non} + BR. \tag{17.2}$$

Although decisions by both the Fed and depository institutions determine the volume of discount loans, the Fed has greater control over the nonborrowed monetary base. We discuss the components of the monetary base and their controllability by the Fed in more detail in Chapter 18.

▶ C H E C K P O I N T   *Which has more impact on the monetary base: an open market purchase of $10 million or a discount loan of $10 million? What happens to bank reserves in the short run in each case? In each case, the mone-*

tary base rises by $10 million. The effect on bank reserves of an open market operation depends on how much currency the public chooses to hold. In the case of a discount loan, reserves rise by the amount of the loan. ◀

Multiple Deposit Expansion

Having shown how the Fed can change the monetary base, we now turn to the second step in the money supply process and examine how the monetary base supports a money supply many times its size. By varying the monetary base, the Fed changes the ability of banks to make loans. And the act of making a loan is what creates money.

How a Bank Responds to an Increase in Reserves

Suppose that the Fed purchases $100,000 in T-bills from Megabank, increasing Megabank's reserves by $100,000. Megabank's T-account reflects these transactions:

MEGABANK

Assets		Liabilities
Securities	−$100,000	
Reserves	+$100,000	

At this point, Megabank's increase in reserves represents an increase in excess reserves. The reason is that required reserves are determined as a percentage of the bank's checkable deposits. Thus this transaction doesn't change the amount of reserves that Megabank is required to hold. Megabank earns no interest on these additional reserves and will therefore try to use them to earn a return.

Suppose that Megabank loans $100,000 to Amalgamated Industries, thereby acquiring an asset on which it earns interest. Megabank extends the loan by creating a checking account for Amalgamated and depositing the loan proceeds in it. Both the asset and liability sides of Megabank's balance sheet increase by $100,000:

MEGABANK

Assets		Liabilities	
Securities	−$100,000	Checkable deposits	+$100,000
Reserves	+$100,000		
Loans	+$100,000		

By lending money to Amalgamated, Megabank creates checkable deposits, which in turn increase the money supply. Money is created because something that becomes money, namely, funds in the hands of the borrower, is exchanged for something that is not money, namely, a loan note in the hands of the lender.

Suppose that the required reserve ratio established by the Fed is 10%. That is, 10% of Megabank's checkable deposits must be held in cash reserves either at the Fed or as vault cash. Because Megabank increased its reserves by $100,000 and its deposits by $100,000, it must hold ($100,000)(0.10) = $10,000 as reserves. It now has additional excess reserves of $100,000 − (0.10)(100,000) = $90,000. However, the bank can't lend this amount because Amalgamated will be withdrawing its loan proceeds in order to buy goods and services supplied by other businesses and individuals. When Amalgamated has withdrawn the entire proceeds of the loan, Megabank will have lost $100,000 of reserves and checkable deposits:

MEGABANK

Assets		Liabilities
Securities	−$100,000	
Loans	+$100,000	

The recipients of Amalgamated's checks deposit the proceeds in other depository institutions, and they in turn make new loans. How much *can* banks lend from an increase in reserves? Because borrowers are likely to withdraw loan proceeds, banks cannot lend a greater amount than their total excess reserves before making a loan.

Effect of an Increase in Reserves

An increase in reserves leads to an even greater change in the volume of checkable deposits in the banking system. Banks serve as a link between the Fed and the nonbank public, taking increases in reserves from the central bank and funneling them to the nonbank public by making loans. This role of banks in the money supply process is referred to as **multiple deposit expansion.** (See Box 17.1 for a historical discussion.)

Suppose that Amalgamated uses the $100,000 it borrowed from Megabank to buy $100,000 of equipment from Toolco. Toolco deposits the $100,000 in its bank, Onebank. After this transaction, Onebank's T-account is:

ONEBANK

Assets		Liabilities	
Reserves	+$100,000	Checkable deposits	+$100,000

Onebank's reserves have increased by $100,000. If the required reserve ratio is 10%, Onebank now has additional excess reserves of $90,000. Because Onebank

BOX 17.1

Consider this....

What Are the Origins of Multiple Deposit Expansion?

Multiple deposit expansion influenced the money supply process long before the founding of the Federal Reserve System. Indeed, safekeeping of money (say, gold or silver) by means of a deposit contract can be traced to Greek or Roman times. However, the earliest banks served only as a warehouse for funds; that is, bankers did not make loans from deposits.

By the thirteenth and fourteenth centuries, deposit banking was well established in Italy and Spain, countries heavily involved in trade and commerce. Merchant

bankers there loaned money to businesses and maintained reserves to cover depositors' withdrawals. In Barcelona, for example, banks typically held reserves in gold of less than 30% of deposits. This system of banking, known as *fractional reserve banking,* was a significant step toward a more sophisticated financial system.

Although religious institutions objected to charging interest on loans financed by deposits, which they called *usury,* the importance of deposit banking for commerce

overcame those objections. Indeed, "a banker's social standing in thirteenth-century Florence was probably at least as good as in twentieth-century New York."[†] Deposit expansion, then and now, enables a greater volume of loans and deposits to be supported by a given level of bank reserves.

[†] Sidney Homer and Richard Sylla, *A History of Interest Rates.* New Brunswick, N.J.: Rutgers University Press, 1991, pp. 76–77.

can safely lend only this increase in excess reserves, it makes a $90,000 loan to Midtown Hardware to purchase new office equipment. Initially, Onebank's assets (loans) and liabilities (checkable deposits) rise by $90,000, but when Midtown spends the loan proceeds, Onebank's T-account becomes:

ONEBANK

Assets		Liabilities	
Reserves	+$10,000	Checkable deposits	+$100,000
Loans	+$90,000		

Midtown Hardware withdraws $90,000 to buy office equipment from Type-n-Serve. Type-n-Serve deposits the $90,000 in its bank, Twobank:

TWOBANK

Assets		Liabilities	
Reserves	+$90,000	Checkable deposits	+$90,000

Now, checkable deposits in the banking system have risen by another $90,000. In total, the volume of deposits has risen by $100,000 at Onebank and $90,000 at Twobank, for a total of $190,000.

Twobank faces the same decisions that confronted Megabank and Onebank. It wants to use the increase in reserves to expand its loans, but it can prudently lend only the increase in excess reserves. With a required reserve ratio of 10%, Twobank must add ($90,000)(0.10) = $9000 to its required reserves and can lend only $81,000. Twobank lends the $81,000 to Howard's Barber Shop for remodeling. Initially, Twobank's assets (loans) and liabilities (checkable deposits) rise by $81,000, but when Howard's spends the loan proceeds, Twobank's T-account becomes:

TWOBANK

Assets		Liabilities	
Reserves	+$9,000	Checkable deposits	+$90,000
Loans	+$81,000		

If the proceeds of the loan to Howard's Barber Shop are deposited in another bank, deposits in the banking system will have risen by another $81,000. In response to the $100,000 increase in reserves supplied by the Fed, the level of checkable deposits has increased by $100,000 + $90,000 + $81,000 = $271,000. The money supply is growing with each loan. The initial increase of the monetary base allows a multiple of that amount of money to be supplied.

The process still isn't complete. The recipient of the $81,000 check from Howard's Barber Shop will redeposit it, and checkable deposits at other banks will expand. The process continues to ripple through the system, as Table 17.1 shows. Note that new deposits continue to be created each time money is redeposited and loaned but that the increment gets smaller each time. The reason is that part of the money at each step cannot be lent; it must

TABLE 17.1 MULTIPLE DEPOSIT EXPANSION FOR THE FED'S PURCHASE OF $100,000 IN GOVERNMENT SECURITIES FROM MEGABANK AND A REQUIRED RESERVE RATIO OF 10%

Bank	Increase in deposits	Increase in loans	Increase in reserves
Onebank	$100,000	$90,000	$10,000
Twobank	90,000	81,000	9,000
Nextbank3	81,000	72,900	8,100
Nextbank4	72,900	65,610	7,290
Nextbank5	65,610	59,049	6,561
.	.	.	.
	$1,000,000	$900,000	$100,000

be held as reserves. So long as each bank lends the full amount of its excess reserves, we can calculate the amount of money created by the Fed's initial $100,000 purchase of securities. The change in deposits, ΔD, is related to the initial change in reserves, ΔR, as follows:

Change in deposits = Loan to Amalgamated + Loan to Midtown + Loan to Howard's + ···

or

$$\Delta D = \Delta R + \Delta R[1 - (\overline{R/D})] + \Delta R[1 - (\overline{R/D})]^2 + \cdots$$
$$= \$100,000 + \$100,000(1 - 0.10) + \$100,000(1 - 0.10)^2 + \cdots$$

where

D = deposits;

R = reserves; and

$\overline{R/D}$ = the required reserve ratio.

We can restate the relationship between the change in the level of checkable deposits and the change in the level of reserves by simplifying the preceding equation. The change in checkable deposits equals the change in reserves multiplied by the **simple deposit multiplier,** which is the reciprocal of the required reserve ratio:

$$\Delta D = \Delta R \left\{ \frac{1}{1 - \left[1 - \left(\overline{R/D}\right)\right]} \right\}$$
$$= \Delta R \left(\frac{1}{\overline{R/D}} \right), \tag{17.3}$$

or, in our example,

$$\Delta D = 100,000 \left(\frac{1}{0.10} \right) = \$1,000,000.$$

Eventually, the increase in reserves of $100,000 leads to a tenfold expansion of checkable deposits. Thus the volume of checkable deposits expands by a factor equal to the reciprocal of the required reserve ratio, in this case, $1/0.10 = 10$.

If a depository institution decides to invest all or some of its excess reserves in marketable securities, deposit expansion still results in the same relationship between the change in reserves and the change in deposits. Suppose that Onebank had decided to purchase $90,000 worth of Treasury bills instead of extending the $90,000 loan to Midtown. Onebank would write a check to the owner of the securities in the amount of $90,000, which the seller would deposit in the banking system, and so on. Thus the effect on multiple deposit expansion is the same whether banks use excess reserves to make loans or buy securities.

At first you may think that individual banks are creating money. However, an individual bank can lend only the amount of its reserves that exceeds the amount it wants (or is required) to maintain. Deposits are expanded or created when borrowers do not hold the proceeds of loans as currency. If funds are redeposited, money flows back into the banking system as reserves. If banks do not want to hold excess reserves, the multiple deposit expansion process ends only when all excess reserves have been eliminated. Multiple deposit expansion relates to the banking system as a whole, not to the action of an individual bank.

Q: How are deposits created?

A: Deposit expansion is the process by which a change in reserves leads to a greater change in the volume of checkable deposits in the banking system. When the proceeds of loans are not held as currency, money flows back into the banking system as reserves. If banks do not want to hold excess reserves, deposit expansion ends only when all excess reserves have been eliminated. Deposit expansion comes from actions in the banking system as a whole, not from the action of any individual bank.

▶ **C H E C K P O I N T** Let's consider an example of how the simple deposit multiplier works. *Suppose that in Nationia, bank reserves equal $10 million and the required reserve ratio is 10%. If citizens of Nationia do not hold currency, how large is the stock of checkable deposits (if banks hold no excess reserves)?*

$$D = \frac{R}{R/D}$$

$$= \frac{\$10 \text{ million}}{0.10} = \$100 \text{ million.}$$

What will happen to the level of checkable deposits if the central bank of Nationia increases the level of bank reserves by $500,000?

$$\Delta D = \Delta R \left(\frac{1}{R/D} \right)$$

$$= \frac{\$500,000}{0.10} = \$5 \text{ million.}$$

The level of checkable deposits rises by $5 million. ◀

Multiple Deposit Contraction

The Fed expands the volume of checkable deposits in the banking system by increasing reserves. Similarly, it can *contract* the volume of such deposits in the banking system by reducing reserves. The Fed does so by selling government securities in an open market operation. This action has a ripple effect similar to deposit expansion in the banking system, but in the opposite direction. The effect is known as **multiple deposit contraction.**

Suppose that the Fed sells $100,000 in Treasury securities to Megabank, thereby reducing Megabank's reserves by $100,000. If Megabank has not maintained any excess reserves, it cannot now meet its reserve requirement. Megabank continually makes loans, and loans continually come due. Megabank can, if it has to, *call* some loans, that is, not renew them. By doing so, Megabank replenishes its reserves and can thus meet withdrawals. To raise reserves, then, Megabank could demand repayment of $100,000 of loans, but could also sell $100,000 of securities. In either case, Megabank gains the needed $100,000 of reserves. In the process, however, another bank loses reserves and checkable deposits. For example, if a depositor at Onebank buys $100,000 of securities from Megabank, Onebank's reserves and checkable deposits fall by $100,000.

When it loses $100,000 in checkable deposits to Megabank (with a required reserve ratio of 10%), Onebank's required reserves decline by $10,000. Hence it must increase its reserves by $100,000 − $10,000 = $90,000. Onebank now faces the problem that Megabank experienced. If it has no excess reserves, it will have $90,000 less reserves than it needs to satisfy the reserve requirement. As a result, Onebank must sell securities or demand repayment of loans to raise its reserves by $90,000.

ONEBANK

Assets		Liabilities	
Reserves	−$10,000	Checkable deposits	−$100,000
Securities } Loans	−$90,000		

Onebank's contraction will ripple through the banking system to other banks. Suppose that the $90,000 that Onebank receives for its securities (or from loan repayments) is a check drawn on Twobank. Remember that Onebank faced a required reserves shortfall as a result of the loss of reserves to Megabank. The same problem now confronts Twobank. Twobank's required reserves are insufficient by $90,000 − (0.10)($90,000), or $81,000.

Our examination of multiple deposit expansion showed that an increase in reserves is multiplied in the banking system. Similarly, a decrease in reserves is multiplied in the banking system, resulting in multiple deposit contraction. If we assume that banks hold only required reserves, the reduction in deposits in the banking system because of the decrease in reserves is equal to the change in reserves multiplied by the reciprocal of the required reserve ratio:

$$\Delta D = \Delta R \left(\frac{1}{R / D} \right).$$

This is the same formula we developed for multiple deposit expansion.

Extending the Basic Process

So far we have stressed the Fed's influence on the money supply through the effects of open market operations and discount lending on the monetary base and the effects of reserve requirements on multiple deposit expansion. Indeed, sometimes you will see statements in the financial media suggesting that the Fed controls the money supply. However, the Fed does not completely control the money supply. In deriving the simple deposit multiplier, we assumed that all money was held as checkable deposits and that all excess reserves are loaned out. These assumptions aren't realistic: Everyone holds some money in cash. Moreover, banks do not always lend out all of their excess reserves.

Thus decisions by the nonbank public and by banks also affect the money supply. These decisions concern currency holdings by the nonbank public and reserve holdings by banks. We explore each, focusing on ways to predict these decisions to help explain changes in the money supply.

Currency Holdings by the Nonbank Public

The decisions made by the nonbank public about how to allocate liquid assets between currency, C, and checkable deposits, D, are an important part of the money supply process. Specifically, the nonbank public decides how much currency to hold in relation to checkable deposits. Such decisions collectively result in the **currency-deposit ratio,** (C/D). Figure 17.3 shows currency-deposit ratio trends during this century. The ratio generally declined from the late nineteenth century through the mid-1960s, except during World War I, the early 1930s, and World War II. Beginning in the late 1960s, C/D began to rise steadily. Because the decision about how much currency to hold is one of portfolio allocation, we can analyze how the decision is made by examining the determinants of asset demand that we introduced in Chapter 6: wealth, expected returns, and characteristics of risk, liquidity, and information.

Wealth.   One decision that the nonbank public makes is how much of its wealth to hold in the form of currency. Recall that currency is an example of a *necessity good*, which you studied in your first course in economics. The proportion of wealth held in cash doesn't increase as a person

▶ FIGURE 17.3

The Ratio of Currency to Checkable Deposits in the United States (1900–1992)
Movements in the currency-deposit ratio reflect portfolio decisions by the nonbank public.
Source: Federal Reserve Historical Chart Book, 1990, and *Federal Reserve Bulletin,* various issues.

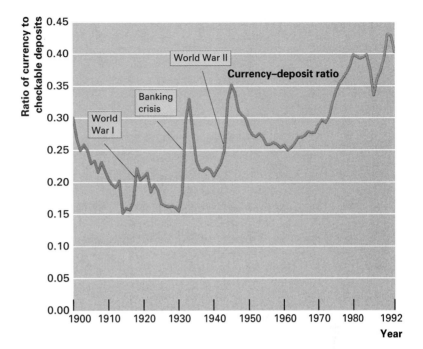

gets richer. In other words, a wealthy individual might hold more currency than a not-so-wealthy individual, but the wealthy person isn't likely to hold proportionately more. The reason is that checkable deposits are safer and more efficient than holding larger amounts of currency. Hence an individual's currency-deposit ratio declines with increases in income and wealth. Moreover, for the economy as a whole, as the economy grows and national wealth increases, the currency-deposit ratio, C/D, declines. This result explains the pattern in Fig. 17.1 of declining C/D before World War I, between the two world wars (except for the early 1930s), and after World War II until the early 1960s. These were periods of relatively steady economic growth, and therefore C/D decreased.

Expected Returns. A second factor that affects the nonbank public's decision regarding how much currency to hold in relation to checkable deposits is the expected returns on these assets. The demand for an asset (here currency or checkable deposits) depends on its expected return relative to expected returns on assets with similar risk, liquidity, and information characteristics. Two considerations affect the nonbank public's demand for currency. First, because holding currency yields no interest, an increase in the interest paid on checkable deposits decreases the demand for currency relative to checkable deposits, decreasing C/D. Second, a decrease in interest rates paid on checkable deposits increases C/D. Between 1933 and 1980, banking regulations prohibited banks from paying interest on checkable deposits; since 1980, regulations have allowed interest-bearing checkable deposits. As a result, the expected return has become a more significant influence in the nonbank public's decisions about how much currency to hold relative to checkable deposits.

Risk. Our discussion of asset demand in Chapter 6 showed that savers weigh three characteristics of an investment: risk, liquidity, and information. Those characteristics apply to the nonbank public's demand for currency relative to checkable deposits. Most of the time, there is little difference in the default risk associated with holding currency and checkable deposits. During a banking panic, however, the fact that currency's (0% nominal) return has no risk may lead to a significant increase in demand for currency, which increases the currency-deposit ratio. For example, as Fig. 17.1 illustrates, in the early 1930s, the loss of public confidence in the banking system led depositors to convert checkable deposits into currency, increasing C/D. Since the 1930s, most bank deposits have been covered (within limits) by federal deposit insurance. Reassured that their checkable deposits are safe, savers are less likely to take risk into consideration when deciding how much currency to hold relative to checkable deposits.

Liquidity. When making portfolio allocation decisions, savers also weigh the liquidity of an asset, that is, how easily it can be converted into money. Currency is the most liquid asset possible because Federal Reserve Notes are definitive money in the United States. Checkable deposits by definition are convertible upon demand into currency. Therefore the nonbank public doesn't generally consider liquidity differences when allocating how much currency to hold relative to checkable deposits.

Information. The final factor that influences the nonbank public's demand for currency is the amount of information required to assess the value of currency versus that of checkable deposits. At first, the cost of obtaining information about currency and checkable deposits might seem to be identical. After all, no information is required to assess the value of currency, and, with federal deposit insurance and bank supervision, individual depositors need little information to assess the value of checkable deposits. Nevertheless, there is an important difference between the two assets: Currency holdings are anonymous, whereas checkable deposits aren't. In other words, when you hold your money as checkable deposits you leave a trail of information, but how much currency you hold would be very difficult for someone to discover. Currency thus carries an *anonymity premium*, meaning that it is valued higher than checkable deposits for its usefulness in illegal activities, such as drug transactions, black-market sales, and tax avoidance. This feature can help explain two patterns in Fig. 17.1. First, the increase in C/D during wars, such as World Wars I and II, reflects the use of currency in black-market activities and high income tax rates during the war years. Second, from the late 1960s until the present, there has been a steady increase in C/D. Economists point to high marginal income tax rates during the 1960s and the apparent increase in illegal activity in the drug trade during the 1980s and early 1990s as reasons for this reversal. Analysts refer to economic activity that isn't measured in formal government statistics as the *underground economy.*

There is good reason to suspect the existence of a sizable underground economy in the United States because the amount of currency outstanding for every person in the country is more than $1000. Few individuals hold that much cash at any time, so the suggestion that large amounts of cash are circulating in the underground economy to finance illicit activities seems plausible. In fact, some experts estimate that the underground economy may account for more than 10% of total U.S. economic activity. In a $6 trillion U.S. economy, this amount would be more than $600 billion. Collecting tax revenue from underground economic activity would sharply reduce the federal budget deficit.

If the underground economy, by definition, isn't measured, how can we estimate its size? Using what we know about the determinants of currency holdings by the nonbank public, we can trace movements in C/D to the underground economy. For example, an increase in marginal tax rates or the imposition of rationing (as in wartime) would increase the anonymity value of currency and hence C/D. Conversely, legalization of drugs, prostitution, or gambling would decrease the need for currency for underground transactions, reducing C/D.

Concluding Remarks. Table 17.2 summarizes the principal determinants of the currency-deposit ratio. The currency-deposit ratio represents a portfolio allocation decision by the nonbank public. Currency holdings rela-

▼ TABLE 17.2   DETERMINANTS OF THE CURRENCY-DEPOSIT RATIO

An increase in...	Effect on *C/D*...	Because...
Wealth	Falls	In general, C/D decreases with rising income and wealth in the economy.
Expected returns on deposits	Falls	An increase in interest rates offered on checkable deposits increases the public's demand for those deposits relative to currency and decreases C/D.
Riskiness of deposits	Rises	Under normal circumstances, default risk does not affect C/D. During banking panics, an increase in the perceived riskiness of deposits increases C/D.
Liquidity of deposits	None	Under normal circumstances, there is little difference in the liquidity of currency and checkable deposits and thus little or no effect on C/D.
Information or anonymity value of cash	Rises	An increase in the demand for anonymity, owing to black-market, tax evasion, or other illegal activities, increases C/D.

tive to checkable deposits are influenced by the determinants of asset demand: wealth and expected returns adjusted for risk, liquidity, and information characteristics.

► **C H E C K P O I N T** *In each of the following cases, what would you expect to happen to the currency-deposit ratio?*

(a) Interest rates on checkable deposits rise.

(b) Higher tax rates prompt increased underground activity.

(c) A tremendous wave of counterfeit bills hits the United States.

Answers:

(a) Expected return on deposits rises, so C/D falls.

(b) Increased underground activity raises demand for currency, so C/D rises.

(c) Increased risk of currency reduces demand for currency, so C/D falls. ◄

Bank Behavior: Excess Reserves and Discount Loans

Banks influence the money supply process by their decisions about holding excess reserves and borrowing from the Fed. How do banks determine how much excess reserves to hold relative to deposits? Before we can develop ways to forecast such decisions, we need to analyze their determinants. Like those of the nonbank public, banks' portfolio allocation decisions are influenced by the determinants of asset demand.

Excess Reserves. As Fig. 17.4 shows, banks hold (generally small levels of) *excess reserves,* or reserves greater than those required by the Fed. The principal determinant of banks' decisions is the expected return from holding excess reserves. How do banks compare the expected return on holding excess reserves to the expected return on alternative uses of their funds? Because reserves deposited with the Fed pay no interest, the opportunity cost of holding excess reserves is the market interest rate—the rate that the bank could obtain by lending or investing its funds. For example, the high market interest rates of the early 1980s caused a significant decrease in excess reserves. An increase in the market interest rate, all else being equal, decreases excess reserves; a decrease in the market interest rate increases excess reserves. In other words holdings of excess reserves by banks are inversely related to the market interest rate.

The reason banks hold excess reserves despite the opportunity cost, has to do with Fed-bank relationships. The Fed stipulates certain reserve requirements, but it discourages banks from frequent borrowing at the discount rate to satisfy reserve requirements. When a bank's reserve holdings are insufficient, the Fed may impose penalties. Such penalties include a penalty rate on discount loans needed to satisfy the reserve requirement and a "stern discussion." To avoid relying on discount borrowing to satisfy reserve

Excess Reserves and Discount Loans
Banks hold some reserves in excess of their required reserves. Discount loans represent reserves borrowed by banks from the Fed.

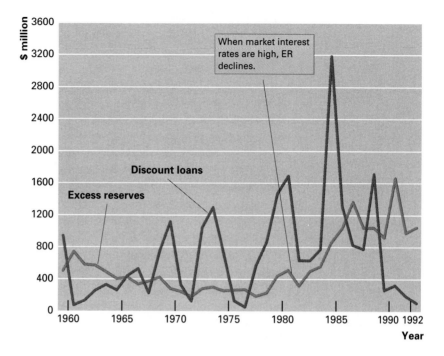

requirements, banks hold small amounts of excess reserves. In addition, when banks overestimate withdrawals expected from depositors, they end up with reserves in excess of those required.

An even more important reason for banks to hold excess reserves is that they serve as a cushion against high expected deposit outflows or significant variability in deposit outflows. Without this cushion, if deposit withdrawals exceeded reserves, a bank would be forced to bear the costs in one of three ways: (1) by selling securities, (2) by calling in loans, or (3) by borrowing from the Fed or in the open market. In extreme cases, the bank could fail. Hence the benefit of excess reserves as a cushion against deposit outflows can outweigh the opportunity cost of other uses of those funds. For example, the high excess reserve holdings during the early 1930s reflected concern over future deposit withdrawals. The theory of portfolio allocation predicts that an increase in the expected level or variability of deposit outflows increases excess reserves. Conversely, a decrease in the expected level or variability of deposit outflows decreases excess reserves. Thus the level of excess reserves in the banking system is positively related to the expected level or variability of deposit outflows.

Discount Loans. Although the Fed has discount loan criteria, it doesn't control the volume of discount loans; banks must initiate discount loan transactions. Banks are more inclined to borrow from the Fed when the market interest rate that can be obtained for lending or investment activities is greater than the discount rate. Banks are less likely to borrow from the Fed

TABLE 17.3	DETERMINANTS OF EXCESS RESERVES AND DISCOUNT LOANS	
An increase in...	**Causes...**	**Because...**
Market interest rates	Excess reserves to fall	Opportunity cost of holding excess reserves rises.
Average level or variability of deposit outflows	Excess reserves to rise	Banks require greater cushion against outflows.
Market interest rates relative to discount rate	Discount loans to rise	Banks' profits from discount borrowing increase.

when the spread between the market interest rate and the discount rate is small. Hence discount borrowing by banks is positively related to the market interest rate and negatively related to the discount rate.

Economists have documented that, when the spread between the rates on three-month T-bills and discount loans increases, so does the volume of discount lending. This factor is modified by the Fed's willingness to lend to banks. The Fed generally discourages routine discount borrowing, but on occasion it has strongly encouraged banks to borrow from it. For example, it did so during the October 1987 stock market crash.

Table 17.3 summarizes the determinants of banks' decisions regarding excess reserves and discount loans. Banks' portfolio allocation decisions about excess reserves and discount loans—decisions based on expected returns—influence the money supply.

Putting It All Together

The Fed influences the monetary base and the money multiplier. In addition, the nonbank public and banks make decisions that affect the monetary base and the money multiplier. We now put the pieces together to describe the complete money supply process.

Deriving the Money Multiplier

We build on our analysis of decisions by the Fed, the nonbank public, and banks to derive the money multiplier. In particular, we take into account (1) the effects of Fed decisions on the level of reserves; (2) the effects of portfolio allocation decisions by the nonbank public, assuming that the ratio of currency to checkable deposits, C/D, is constant; and (3) the effects of decisions by banks about excess reserves, ER, assuming that banks hold a constant proportion of deposits as excess reserves, ER/D.

Let's begin by considering how the Fed affects the money multiplier m by setting the required reserve ratio. Total reserves, R, equal the sum of required reserves, *RR*, and excess reserves, *ER*:

$$R = RR + ER. \tag{17.4}$$

The Fed sets the level of required reserves by requiring banks to hold a certain percentage of checkable deposits as reserves. Thus required reserves equal the required reserve ratio, $\overline{R/D}$, multiplied by the level of checkable deposits, *D*:

$$RR = \left(\overline{R/D}\right)(D). \tag{17.5}$$

Total reserves then are

$$R = \left(\overline{R/D}\right)(D) + ER. \tag{17.6}$$

Recall that we started our discussion of the money supply process by noting that the money supply can be thought of as the product of the monetary base and the money multiplier. Hence we need to move from reserves to the monetary base. The monetary base, *B*, equals the sum of currency, *C*, and reserves, *R*, so we use Eq. (17.6) to obtain

$$B = C + R$$
$$= C + \left(\overline{R/D}\right)(D) + ER. \tag{17.7}$$

Suppose, for example, that checkable deposits total $1 billion and that currency totals $300 million. Suppose also that the Fed requires banks to hold 10% of their checkable deposits as reserves and that banks hold no excess reserves. How large is the monetary base? It is the sum of currency ($300 million) and reserves (the required reserve ratio, 0.10, times the level of deposits, $1 billion):

$$B = \$300 \text{ million} + (0.10)\ (\$1 \text{ billion}) = \$400 \text{ million}.$$

We are now ready to incorporate the nonbank public's and banks' portfolio allocation decisions into the equation. If currency holdings by the nonbank public are a constant fraction of checkable deposits, then

$$C = \left(C/D\right)(D).$$

If banks' holdings of excess reserves are a constant fraction of checkable deposits, then

$$ER = \left(ER/D\right)(D).$$

Using these two expressions, we expand Eq. (17.7) to relate the monetary base to the level of checkable deposits. The monetary base is

$$B = (C/D)(D) + (\overline{R/D})(D) + (ER/D)(D)$$
$$= \left[(C/D) + (\overline{R/D}) + (ER/D)\right](D).$$
(17.8)

If we divide both sides of Eq. (17.8) by the term in the brackets and rearrange, we can express the relationship of checkable deposits to the monetary base as

$$D = \left[\frac{1}{(C/D) + (\overline{R/D}) + (ER/D)}\right](B).$$
(17.9)

Returning to our example, we can verify that checkable deposits are equal to $1 billion. The monetary base is $400 million; banks hold no excess reserves, so $ER/D = 0$; and the required reserve ratio is 0.10. The currency-deposit ratio is $300 million/$1 billion, or 0.30. Hence

$$D = \left(\frac{1}{0.30 + 0.10 + 0}\right)(\$400 \text{ million}) = \$1 \text{ billion.}$$

Finally, we are ready to complete the process by moving from deposits to the money supply, M, which is equal to currency, C, plus deposits, D. Then, because $C = (C/D)(D)$,

$$M = C + D = D\left[1 + (C/D)\right].$$

Substituting for D and using Eq. (17.9) gives an expression relating the money supply, M, to the monetary base, B:

Money supply = (Money multiplier) (Monetary base)

or

$$M = \left[\frac{1 + (C/D)}{(C/D) + (\overline{R/D}) + (ER/D)}\right](B).$$
(17.10)

The expression in brackets in Eq. (17.10) is equal to the money multiplier, m. The money supply equals the monetary base times the money multiplier. The money multiplier conveys by how much the money supply responds to a given change in the monetary base.

For example, suppose that Nationia's monetary base is $10 billion, the required reserve ratio is 0.15, the currency-deposit ratio is 0.35, and banks hold no excess reserves. How large is the stock of checkable deposits? The total money supply? The money multiplier in this case is

$$m = \frac{1 + (C/D)}{(C/D) + (R/D)} = \frac{1.35}{0.35 + 0.15} = 2.7.$$

Q: What factors determine the money multiplier?

The money supply is equal to the money multiplier times the monetary base, so

Money supply = 2.7($10 billion) = $27 billion.

A: The money multiplier is deter-mined by the required reserve ratio (set by the Fed), the currency-deposit ratio (deter-mined by the nonbank public), and the ratio of banks' excess reserves to deposits (deter-mined by banks). An increase in any of these factors reduces the poten-tial for deposit expansion and the size of the money multiplier.

Checkable deposits, D, are

$$D = M - C = M - (C/D)(D),$$

so

$$D = \frac{M}{1 + (C/D)} = \frac{\$27 \text{ billion}}{1.35} = \$20 \text{ billion}.$$

We now have a complete description of the money supply process:

1. The money supply equals the money multiplier times the monetary base.
2. The money multiplier depends on the required reserve ratio (determined by the Fed), the currency-deposit ratio (determined by the nonbank public), and excess reserves relative to deposits (determined by banks).
3. The monetary base comprises the nonborrowed base, determined primarily by the Fed through open market operations, and discount loans, determined jointly by the banks and the Fed.

Table 17.4 summarizes the determinants of the money supply. For an interesting historical example of the influence of all three participants in the process, see the Other times, other places box on pg. 450.

Using the Money Supply Process to Predict Money Growth

The money supply process provides a helpful way to forecast growth of the money supply. We analyze the determinants of changes in the money supply M (measured by $M1$), first by examining changes in the money multiplier, m, and then by examining changes in the monetary base, B. Recall that the monetary base, B, equals the sum of the nonborrowed base, B_{non}, and borrowed reserves, BR (discount loans). Thus we can express the money

Q: How do the Fed, banks, and the nonbank public together influence the money supply process?

A: The actions of all three partici- pants determine the money supply. Over long periods of time, the money multiplier is rela- tively stable, and changes in the money supply can be generally explained by changes in the monetary base. The most impor- tant factor under- lying changes in the base is the Fed's open market opera- tions to increase or decrease the non- borrowed base.

▼ TABLE 17.4	ELEMENTS OF THE MONEY SUPPLY PROCESS			
An increase in the...	Based on the actions of...	Causes the Money Supply to...	Because...	
nonborrowed base, B_{non}	the Fed (open market operations)	Rise	the monetary base rises, and more reserves are available for deposit expansion.	
reserve requirements, $\overline{R/D}$	the Fed (reserve requirements)	Fall	fewer reserves can be lent out, and the money multiplier falls.	
discount rate	the Fed (discount policy)	Fall	discount loans become more expensive, reducing borrowed reserves and the monetary base.	
currency-deposit ratio, C/D	the nonbank public (portfolio decisions)	Fall	the money multiplier falls, reducing deposit expansion.	
excess reserves relative to deposits, ER/D	banks (portfolio decisions)	Fall	the money multiplier falls, reducing deposit expansion.	
expected deposit outflows	the nonbank public (transactions considerations)	Fall	excess reserves rise relative to deposits, reducing the money multiplier and deposit expansion.	
variability of deposit outflows	the nonbank public (transactions and portfolio considerations)	Fall	excess reserves rise relative to deposits, reducing the money multiplier and deposit expansion.	

supply as

$$M = m\left(B_{non} + BR\right).$$

The money multiplier, m, depends on the required reserve ratio, the cur- rency-deposit ratio, and the ratio of excess reserves to checkable deposits.

To focus on growth rates of the money supply, we need an expres- sion for the percentage change in M: $\%\Delta M$. The percentage change in M is approximately equal to the sum of the percentage change in the money multi- plier, $\%\Delta m$, and the percentage change in the monetary base, $\%\Delta(B_{non} + BR)$:

$$\%\Delta M \cong \%\Delta m + \%\Delta\left(B_{non} + BR\right).$$

Let's begin with a simple example and assume that the money multi- plier is constant. Then, $\%\Delta m = 0$, and $\%\Delta M = \%\Delta(B_{non} + BR)$. In order to pre- dict the growth rate of the money supply, we need to predict the growth rate of the monetary base. To do so, we study Fed decisions about open market operations that affected the nonborrowed base, B_{non}, and bank and Fed decisions about discount loans, BR. As we noted earlier, BR is small relative to B_{non}, so, not surprisingly, most analysts studying the money supply process are Fed watchers, or careful observers of the Fed's actions and intentions. So long as the percentage change in the money multiplier is zero or very small, careful forecasting of changes in discount loans and especially in the nonborrowed base will produce a good prediction of the growth of the money supply.

Let's use some actual data to translate changes in the money supply into changes in the monetary base and the money multiplier. Figure 17.5 presents data on percentage changes in the money supply, the monetary base, and the money multiplier from 1979 through of 1992. During this period, the money supply grew at an average annual rate of 7.2%. Most of this growth reflected growth in the monetary base, which averaged 6.4% overall. The

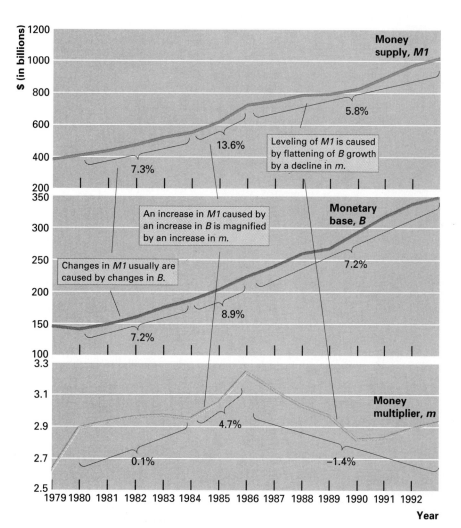

> **FIGURE 17.5**

Accounting for Changes in the Money Supply (M1)
Over long periods of time, fluctuations in the monetary base primarily determine changes in the money supply. Over short periods of time, fluctuations in the money multiplier magnify or dampen the effects of changes in the monetary base on the money supply.
Source: Federal Reserve Bulletin.

MOVING FROM THEORY TO PRACTICE...

THE WALL STREET JOURNAL   OCTOBER 23, 1992

The Fed, the Monetary Base, and Economic Recovery

The Federal Reserve has reduced the federal funds rate repeatedly from nearly 10% in 1989 to about 3% recently. According to conventional wisdom on Wall Street, that is evidence that monetary policy has been extremely easy, that the Fed has done all it can to stimulate the economy...

a For all practical purposes, the Fed directly controls one thing and one thing only: the volume of its own obligations—that is, high-powered money or the monetary base.

Control over the base enables it, if it chooses to do so, to control within narrow limits any one of a number of aggregates, such as *M1* or *M2* or *M3*. Its control over these is absolute: It could make the chosen aggregate rise or fall at the annual rate of 2% or 5% or 10%, or you name it, not day by day, or week by week, but certainly quarter by quarter...

The behavior of a broad monetary aggregate is clearly a better indicator of the stance of monetary policy than short-term interest rates. By that indicator monetary policy has been extremely tight, not easy, in the U.S. The Fed's own target range for growth of *M2* was 2.5% to 6.5% for both 1991 and 1992, or a midpoint of 4.5%. Actual monetary growth between the fourth quarter of 1990 and the third quarter of 1992 was 2.3% per year, and during the past four quarters even lower—1.8%—well below the bottom of the Fed's range... Could the Fed have produced a 4.5% rate of growth of *M2* over the past two years if it had taken that target seriously? Would its efforts not have been frustrated by banks' unwillingness to lend, or the shortage of demand for loans?

Absolutely not. The excess reserves of member banks have been small throughout the period and have shown no tendency to grow. Had the Fed created additional high-powered reserves, the banks would have used them to acquire assets. If, to take the extreme case, they had not been willing or able to make any additional commercial loans, they could have bought government securities, which, like loans, would have been matched by deposits on the liability side of the balance sheet. Non-banks would have bought fewer government securities, leaving them with additional funds to invest in other credit instruments.

b The bottom line is that the banks' unwillingness or inability to make loans does not hinder the Fed from increasing *M2*. (To give a historical example: *M2* rose by 26% from 1934 to 1936; loans by commercial banks fell a trifle.) In any event, increases in loans by banks are generally a result of increases in spending stimulated by higher monetary growth, rather than a cause of the greater spending.

It is hard to escape the conclusion that the restrictive monetary policy of the Federal Reserve deserves much of the blame for the slow, and interrupted, recovery from the 1990 recession.

ANALYZING THE NEWS...

Many analysts blamed the low rates of growth in the money supply in 1990, 1991, and 1992 for prolonging the U.S. recession and delaying the economic recovery from it. An obvious question is whether the Fed can control the money supply in the first place.

(a) Friedman notes that the Fed can control the monetary base through open market operations, as we explained in this chapter. The claim that the Fed can control monetary aggregates requires an additional assumption, however. In our analysis of the money supply process, we noted that the money supply is the product of the monetary base and the money multiplier. Hence Friedman's argument assumes that the money multiplier is constant. This is not an unreasonable assumption for long periods of time.

(b) If banks increased their holdings of excess reserves in response to open market purchases by the Fed, the money multiplier would fall, making it difficult for the Fed to increase the money supply. However, excess reserve holdings didn't increase during 1990–1992. Recall also from our analysis of the money supply process that, even if banks use additional reserves to buy Treasury securities, deposits and the money supply increase.

For further thought...

The author asserts that bank loans passively increase or decrease in response to changes in economic activity. If true, what does this response imply about concerns that stiff bank regulation can limit bank lending to many borrowers?

Source: Excerpted from Milton Friedman, "Too Tight for a Strong Recovery," October 23,1992. Reprinted by permission of *The Wall Street Journal,* © 1992 Dow Jones & Co., Inc. All Rights Reserved Worldwide.

Other times, other places...
The Money Multiplier and Money Supply during the Early 1930s

During the depths of the Great Depression in the United States (1930–1933), the money multiplier was extremely unstable. Why did this happen? What insights can we gain from that experience for predicting the multiplier in the future?

The most severe banking crisis in U.S. history occurred in the early 1930s. It actually began in the late 1920s, as falling farm prices caused farmers to default on agricultural bank loans. Other sources of the crisis were the failure of some prominent U.S. and European financial institutions in 1930 and 1931 and abandonment of the gold standard by Britain in September 1931. By 1933, more than one-third of the commercial banks in the United States had failed or had been taken over by other banks.

The banking crisis significantly changed the money multiplier by affecting the portfolio allocation decisions of the nonbank public and banks. First, because of the perceived increase in riskiness of bank loan portfolios, wary depositors converted (or tried to convert) deposits into currency. The currency-deposit ratio, C/D, increased steadily after 1931 and dramatically in early 1933, more than doubling. Currency holdings by the public represent a leakage from the deposit creation process, so the multiplier and money supply fell while the monetary base was relatively stable.

Because of the wave of bank runs, by 1932, banks had to anticipate greater deposit outflows and increased their holdings of excess reserves. As a result, the ratio of excess reserves to deposits ER/D

increased, further reducing the money multiplier.

The Fed did not aggressively increase its discount lending during the banking panic of 1931–1933, worsening the problems of the banking system and prompting the public to convert checkable deposits to currency and banks to convert loans to reserves. As a result of these portfolio allocation decisions by banks and the nonbank public, the money multiplier fell from 3.8 in March 1930 to 2.3 in March 1933. Although the monetary base *increased* by about 20% over the same period, the money supply actually *fell* by 28%.

Note: Figures are based on data from Milton Friedman and Anna J. Schwartz, *A Monetary History of the United States, 1867–1960.* Princeton, N.J.: Princeton University Press, 1963, pp. 299–419.

money multiplier increased at an average annual rate of only 0.8%. Figure 17.5 shows that virtually all the average annual rate of growth in the money supply (7.3%) from 1980 through 1984 can be explained by growth in the monetary base (7.2%); the money multiplier grew by only 0.1% per year. Virtually all the growth in the monetary base represented growth in the nonborrowed base from the Federal Reserve System's open market operations. The only significant exception during the 1980s and early 1990s came in 1984, when the Fed provided discount loans of about $5 billion to the distressed Continental Illinois Bank. Over periods of several years, the primary determinant of changes in the money supply is changes in the nonborrowed portion of the monetary base, B_{non}, which is controlled by the Federal Reserve System through open market operations.

Many forecasters in the financial community are concerned with predicting *short-term* movements in the money supply. Over short periods of time, however, the correlation between the Fed's actions to change the monetary base and actual changes in the money supply are much less precise. Short-run disturbances in the components of the money multiplier disrupt the relationship, as the second and third periods in Fig. 17.5 indicate.

Note that, over short periods of time, the money multiplier may change significantly. For example, in 1985 and 1986, the money multiplier grew at a rate of 4.7% per year. Over the same period, the monetary base grew by 8.9% per year, and the *M1* money supply grew by 4.7% + 8.9% = 13.6% per year. To account for the change in the money multiplier, we must analyze changes in its components. The culprit turned out to be the currency-deposit ratio, *C/D*. Not shown in Fig. 17.5, *C/D* declined by about 17% over these two years, increasing the money multiplier. This effect was reversed after 1986, and since then, the declining money multiplier has reflected a steady increase in the currency-deposit ratio.

Our analysis of changes in the money supply during the 1980s and early 1990s shows that changes in the money multiplier may lead to a significant change in the money supply in a short period of time. Nonetheless, over long periods of time, the majority of changes in the money supply can be explained by changes in the monetary base. By far the most important determinant of changes in the monetary base is the Fed's actions to change the nonborrowed base through open market operations.

Key Terms and Concepts

Bank reserves
    Excess reserves
    Required reserve ratio
    Required reserves
Currency-deposit ratio
Currency in circulation
Multiple deposit contraction
Multiple deposit expansion
    Simple deposit multiplier

Discount loans
Discount rate
Money supply process
    Monetary base
    Money multiplier
Open market operations
    Open market purchase
    Open market sale
Vault cash

Summary

1. The three participants in the money supply process are the Federal Reserve System, depository institutions (banks), and the nonbank public.

2. One measure of the money supply (*M1*) is the sum of currency in the hands of the nonbank public and checkable deposits at depository institutions. Checkable deposits account for about two-thirds of the money supply.

3. The complete money supply process involves two parts. First, actions by the Fed largely determine the monetary base. Then the money multiplier measures the amount by which the money supply changes in response to a change in the monetary base.

4. The Fed influences the monetary base primarily by buying and selling government securities (open market operations). Purchases of securities by the

Fed increase the monetary base. Sales of securities by the Fed decrease the monetary base. The Fed also can change the monetary base by making discount loans to banks. An increase in discount lending increases the monetary base; a decrease in discount lending decreases the monetary base.

5. The process by which an increase in bank reserves increases the level of checkable deposits is called multiple deposit expansion. The Fed can add to reserves in the banking system by buying government securities or making discount loans. The increase in reserves allows banks to make additional loans, which lead to additional deposits in banks. As a result, the money supply increases. In the simplest case—in which currency holdings do not change and banks do not hold excess reserves—multiple deposit expansion is limited only by the Fed's reserve requirements. An increase in the level of bank reserves raises the level of checkable deposits by a multiple of the change in the reserves. This multiple, the simple deposit multiplier, is equal to the reciprocal of the required reserve ratio.

6. The money multiplier represents the link between the monetary base and the money supply. If the multiplier is constant, the change in the money supply equals the multiplier times the change in the monetary base. An increase in currency or reserve holdings relative to checkable deposits reduces the money multiplier.

7. Despite the Fed's important role in the money supply process through open market operations, discount lending, and reserve requirements, the Fed doesn't completely control the money supply.

Portfolio allocation decisions by banks and the nonbank public also affect the monetary base and the money multiplier. The nonbank public decides how to allocate its holdings between checkable deposits and currency. An increase in the nonbank public's demand for currency relative to deposits increases the currency-deposit ratio, reducing the money multiplier. Banks must decide what proportion of checkable deposits to hold as reserves (above those required by regulation). Holdings of excess reserves raise the ratio of effective reserves to deposits and reduce the money multiplier. These portfolio allocation decisions by the nonbank public and banks are determined by the principal factors governing asset demand: wealth, expected returns, risk, liquidity, and information. Finally, the Fed doesn't control discount lending. The Fed sets the discount rate (the interest rate charged on discount loans), but the decision to borrow is made by banks.

8. Putting it all together, the money supply process involves important roles for the Fed, banks, and the nonbank public. We can express the money supply (represented by *M1*, the sum of currency and checkable deposits) as

Money supply = (Money multiplier)(Nonborrowed base + Discount loans).

Over long periods of time, the multiplier is relatively stable, and movements in the money supply are governed principally by changes in the nonborrowed base by the Fed. Over short periods of time, the multiplier may increase or decrease significantly and may even dominate movements in the nonborrowed base.

Review Questions

1. What are the major assets and liabilities of the Federal Reserve System? Describe each briefly.

2. What are the components of the monetary base? Why is the monetary base a useful concept?

3. What is the difference between currency in circulation and currency outstanding? Which is added to reserves to get the monetary base?

4. What are excess reserves and how are they calculated? What determines the amount of required reserves?

5. If the Fed wants to increase the money supply, should it make an open market purchase or sale? Should it make more discount loans or fewer? If the Fed wants to decrease the money supply, what should it do?

6. If a bank has $10,000 in excess reserves, what is the most new lending that it should do? Why shouldn't it do more than that amount?

7. If the discount rate is usually below the federal funds rate, why don't banks borrow from the Fed at the discount rate and lend the money out at the federal funds rate to profit from the difference in the interest rates?

8. Wealth in the United States has grown steadily. If wealth were the only factor affecting currency demand, what do you expect would have happened to the currency-deposit ratio over time?

9. What happens to the simple deposit multiplier when the Fed makes more discount loans?

10. Suppose that the Fed wanted to increase the money supply (*M1*) by 10% next year. It predicts that the money multiplier will increase by 2%. How much should it increase the monetary base?

Analytical Problems

11. Suppose that Bank Five lends $100,000 to the Monkey Wrench Company. Using T-accounts, show how this transaction is recorded on the bank's balance sheet. If Monkey Wrench spends the money to buy materials from Scrap Steel, Inc., which banks at Wonder Bank, show the effect on Bank Five's balance sheet. What is the total change in Bank Five's assets and liabilities?

12. Suppose that a bank currently has assets of $24,000 in reserves and $176,000 in loans and liabilities of $200,000 in deposits. If the required reserve ratio is 10%, what are the bank's required and excess reserves? What is the bank likely to do?

Questions 13 and 14 require use of the following bank balance sheet (amounts are in $ millions):

13. Calculate the bank's excess reserves when the required reserve ratio on checkable deposits is 14% and the required reserve ratio on time deposits is 3%. Now suppose that the required reserve ratios are changed to 16% on checkable deposits and 0% on time deposits. Again, calculate the bank's excess reserves.

14. Suppose that the bank sells $3 million in securities on the open market. Calculate the change in the bank's excess reserves when the required reserve ratio on checkable deposits is 14%.

15. In the following bank balance sheet, amounts are $ millions. The required reserve ratio is 3% on the first $30 million of checkable deposits and 12% on any checkable deposits over $30 million.

Assets		Liabilities	
Reserves	48	Checkable deposits	300
Loans	280	Time deposits	200
Securities	182	Net worth	10
	510		510

Assets		Liabilities	
Reserves	18.9	Checkable deposits	180.0
Loans	150.0		
Securities	31.1	Net worth	20.0
	200.0		200.0

a. Calculate the bank's excess reserves.

b. Suppose that the bank sells $5 million in securities to get new cash. Show the bank's balance sheet after this transaction. What are the bank's new excess reserves?

c. Suppose that the bank loans its excess reserves in (b) to a business. Show the bank's balance sheet after the loan has been made but before the business has spent the proceeds of the loan. Now what are the bank's excess reserves?

d. Suppose that the business spends the proceeds of the loan. Revise the bank's balance sheet and calculate its excess reserves.

16. If the required reserve ratio is 25%, banks hold no excess reserves, and the public holds currency equal to 25% of deposits, what is the value of the $M1$ money multiplier?

17. Suppose that the statistics for the economy as a whole (in $ billions) are as follows:

Currency held by the public	100
Reserves held by banks	200
Checkable deposits held at banks	800
Time deposits held at banks	1,200
Excess reserves held by banks	40

If the required reserve ratio on checkable deposits is 20%, what is the value of the $M1$ money multiplier?

18. What would the money multiplier be if banks held no excess reserves, the currency-deposit ratio was 1, and the reserve requirement for checkable deposits was 100%?

19. Analysts have noted that, at times, a substantial increase in demand for U.S. currency corresponds to a crisis in some foreign country. Is this a coincidence? Explain.

20. Suppose that First Bank discovered that its computer had been programmed incorrectly and that it suddenly was short of reserves by $100 million. What would you expect to happen to the federal funds rate, the number of discount loans made by the Fed, and the amount of excess reserves held by other banks?

21. Suppose that banks were so risk-averse that they would gladly sell securities in order to hold excess reserves. In other words, if the Fed engaged in open market purchases, banks would hold the entire amount of the increase in the monetary base in the form of excess reserves. What would be the money multiplier in such a case? Could the Fed increase the money supply if it wanted to?

Questions 22 and 23 pertain to the Appendix.

22. What would happen to $M1$ and $M2$ if the public decided to hold less currency and more time deposits, so that C/D fell by 1% and N/D rose by 1% (assuming that the ratio of reserves to deposits is less than 100%)?

23. Consider Bank A's balance sheet (all amounts are in $ millions):

Assets		Liabilities	
Reserves, R	48	Checkable deposits, D	300
Loans, L	280	Time deposits, N	200
Securities, S	182	Net worth, NW	10
	510		510

For the economy as a whole, the initial level of checkable deposits, D, is $2 trillion. Relevant ratios are

Currency-deposit ratio, C/D	0.2
Time deposit-checkable deposit ratio, N/D	1.5
Money market account-deposit ratio, MM/D	0.5
Excess reserve-deposit ratio, ER/D	0.06
Required reserve ratio, $\overline{R/D}$	0.14

a. Calculate the monetary base B, $M1$ (= $C + D$), and $M2$ (= $M1 + N + MM$). Does Bank A have any excess reserves? Are there any excess reserves in the economy as a whole?

b. Calculate the multipliers (the respective *m* values) for *M1* and *M2*.

c. Suppose that the Fed changes the required reserve ratio to 16%, or 0.16. In response, banks as a whole reduce their excess reserves to zero. What happens to Bank A's balance sheet? Calculate its required reserves. What are Bank A's excess reserves? Calculate the new *M1* and *M2* multipliers.

d. Suppose that, instead of taking the actions in (c), the Fed buys $88.888 billion in securities on the open market, including $1.5 million from Bank A. What happens to Bank A's balance sheet? Calculate its required and excess reserves. Calculate the new size of the monetary base.

Data Question

24. Look up the following data in the latest issue of the *Federal Reserve Bulletin* in your library: currency holdings, *C*, checkable deposits, *D*, required reserves, *RR*, excess reserves, *ER*, and the *M1* money supply. From these data, calculate the ratios *C/D*, *ER/D*, and $\overline{R/D}$. Calculate the *M1* money multiplier using the multiplier formula. Alternatively, calculate the *M1* money multiplier using the equation *M1* = (*m*)(*B*). Compare these multipliers. How do they compare with the simple deposit multiplier, $1/(\overline{R/D})$?

Appendix: The Money Supply Process for *M2*

In the aftermath of financial innovation during the 1980s (much of which we discussed in Chapter 15), many analysts and policymakers became concerned that *M1* no longer adequately covered assets functioning as the medium of exchange. As a result, they focused more attention on *M2*. It is a broader monetary aggregate than *M1*, including not only currency, *C*, and checkable deposits, *D*, but also the nontransaction accounts we introduced in Chapter 13. These accounts consist of savings and small time deposits, *N*, and certain money market accounts, *MM*. Money market items in *M2* include money market deposit accounts at commercial banks, general purpose and broker/dealer money market mutual funds, overnight repurchase agreements issued by banks, and overnight Eurodollars issued to U.S. residents by foreign branches of U.S. banks. As a sum of its components, *M2* is

$$M2 = C + D + N + MM. \tag{17A.1}$$

The *M2* measure of the money supply is less sensitive than *M1* to shifts in the nonbank public's portfolio preferences. Suppose that, because of financial innovation, the nonbank public wants to switch from checkable and nontransaction deposits to money market–type accounts. In that case, *D* and

N would fall, and MM would rise by the same amount, leaving $M2$ *unchanged*. However, $M1$, the sum of currency and checkable deposits, would *fall*.

If we make assumptions similar to those used in deriving the $M1$ multiplier, namely, that C/D, N/D, and MM/D are constant, we can express $M2$ as

Broader money supply = ($M2$ multiplier)(Base),

or

$$M2 = \left[\frac{1 + (C/D) + (N/D) + (MM/D)}{\left(C/D\right) + \left(\overline{R/D}\right) + \left(ER/D\right)} \right](B).$$ (17A.2)

The $M2$ multiplier is significantly larger than the $M1$ multiplier. The reason is that the terms N/D and MM/D are added to the numerator. Because the volume of both nontransaction accounts and money market–type accounts are greater than the volume of checkable deposits, N/D and MM/D are greater than 1. With no reserve requirements for these measures, $M2$ money expansion from a change in the monetary base is greater than that for $M1$. Indeed, the $M2$ multiplier has been more stable than the $M1$ multiplier during the 1980s and early 1990s.

Components of the $M2$ multiplier affect the size of the multiplier in a manner similar to that for $M1$. Increases in the required reserve ratio and the currency-deposit ratio reduce the extent of deposit expansion, thereby reducing the multiplier. However, an increase in the nonbank public's preference for nontransaction or money market–type accounts relative to checkable deposits increases the multiplier.

Fed watchers predict the growth of $M2$ in much the same way as they do for $M1$. They forecast changes in the monetary base—particularly in the nonborrowed base—and in the components of the $M2$ multiplier.

Changes in the Monetary Base

"The devil lies in the details," commented a frenzied trader at the government securities trading desk of the Federal Reserve Bank of New York. She was trying to implement the Fed's instructions for changing the monetary base. The trader and her colleagues had just finished a week of hectic buying and selling of securities on the Fed's behalf. None of the transactions was carried out to implement a planned change in the monetary base by the Fed. Instead, each of the trades was designed to offset some disturbance to the monetary base beyond the Fed's direct control. Each disturbance created the need for offsetting transactions by the Fed's traders—a vast amount of detailed work for them.

In Chapter 17, we noted that the principal factor influencing the money supply over the long run is change in the monetary base. We showed that the Fed's actions with regard to open market operations and discount loans are the major determinants of changes in the monetary base. In this chapter we examine other determinants of such changes. We also apply the study of determinants of the monetary base to examine connections between government budget deficits and changes in the monetary base, an important policy topic in the United States and other countries.

In this chapter our analysis focuses on a single question. **Q:** What are the determinants of changes in the monetary base?

Balance Sheet of the Federal Reserve System

Let's begin by extending the analysis of the Federal Reserve System's balance sheet that we began in Chapter 17. Doing so identifies additional factors that change the monetary base in the money supply process.

The Fed's Assets

Recall that the Fed's largest asset is its holdings of securities, which it acquires in open market operations. In addition, in its role as a banker's bank, the Fed holds discount loans (claims on banks that have borrowed funds from it) and other assets, including cash items in the process of collection, other Federal Reserve assets, gold and special drawing right (SDR) certificate accounts, and Treasury currency outstanding.

Securities. Most of the Fed's portfolio of securities consists of U.S. Treasury securities, with smaller amounts of U.S. government agency securities and bankers' acceptances. The Fed controls the amount of securities it holds through open market operations. An open market purchase increases the Fed's holdings of securities; an open market sale decreases the Fed's holdings of securities.

Discount Loans. The Fed makes discount loans to banks, generally to assist them in overcoming short-term liquidity problems. Although the Fed doesn't completely control the amount of discount loans, it influences the amount by setting the discount rate (the interest rate that it charges on loans to banks).

Cash Items in the Process of Collection. These assets are holdings from the Fed's check-clearing role in the payments system. They include funds not yet collected by the Fed from banks against which checks have been drawn and deposited in the banking system to be cleared. While the Fed holds a check before collecting funds from the bank on which it is written, the check is an asset for the Fed as a cash item in the process of collection.

Other Federal Reserve Assets. These assets include the Fed's foreign-exchange reserves—deposits and bonds denominated in foreign currencies—as well as buildings, equipment, and other physical goods owned by the Fed.

Gold and SDR Certificate Accounts. Gold used to be the official medium of exchange in international financial transactions. Currently, the International Monetary Fund provides special drawing rights (SDRs), for that purpose. When the U.S. Treasury acquires SDRs or gold in its international transactions, it issues SDR or gold certificates (claims on the SDRs or gold), to the Fed. The Fed then credits the Treasury with deposit balances. Hence the gold and SDR accounts consist of gold and SDR certificates issued to the Fed by the Treasury.

Treasury Currency Outstanding.   This small item in the Fed's balance sheet includes U.S. Treasury currency held by the Fed. Mostly it is in the form of coins.

The Fed's Liabilities

The Fed's principal liability is currency in circulation. Other Fed liabilities include Treasury cash holdings, U.S. Treasury deposits, foreign and other deposits, deferred availability cash items, other Federal Reserve liabilities and capital accounts, and deposits by depository institutions.

Currency in Circulation.   Currency issued by the Fed in the form of Federal Reserve Notes is a liability for the Fed.

Treasury Cash Holdings.   These holdings refer to the small amount of Federal Reserve Notes held by the Treasury.

U.S. Treasury Deposits.   The Treasury typically deposits receipts from taxes, fees, and sales of securities in accounts in commercial banks. When the Treasury needs the funds to pay for expenditures, it transfers the funds to its accounts at the Fed.[†]

Foreign and Other Deposits.   These deposits include those made at the Fed by international agencies (such as the United Nations), foreign central banks and governments, and U.S. government agencies (such as the FDIC).

Deferred Availability Cash Items.   These liabilities arise from the Fed's role in the check-clearing process. When a bank presents a check to the Fed to be cleared, the Fed promises to credit the bank within a certain period of time (never more than two days). Analogous to cash items in the process of collection on the assets side of the Fed's balance sheet, these promises to pay are liabilities of the Fed.

[†] We don't consider Treasury deposits with the Fed to be part of the monetary base because they aren't assets of either the nonbank public or banks, which along with the Fed, are the principal participants in the money supply process.

Other Federal Reserve Liabilities and Capital Accounts.   This catch-all account includes liabilities not contained in other categories of the balance sheet. It also includes shares of stock in the Federal Reserve System purchased by the Fed's member banks.

Deposits by Depository Institutions.   These deposits at the Fed are assets to banks and liabilities for the Fed. They are part of bank reserves, which also include vault cash held in banks.

Balance Sheet Summary

Table 18.1 summarizes the Fed's assets and liabilities in the order presented in the *Federal Reserve Bulletin*. This particular balance sheet is for October 31, 1992. Note the relative sizes of the various assets and liabilities.

Determining the Monetary Base

In Chapter 17 we examined changes in the monetary base arising from the Fed's open market operations and discount loans. We now turn to other determinants of change in the monetary base, which generally are less important than open market operations and discount loans.

We can use the components of the Fed's balance sheet to construct the monetary base. Recall that the monetary base equals currency in circulation, C, plus bank reserves, R. Currency in circulation is the total of Federal Reserve Notes and Treasury currency outstanding less Treasury cash holdings:[†]

$$B = C + R$$
$$= \text{Federal Reserve Notes } + \text{ Reserve deposits by depository institutions}$$
$$+ \text{ Treasury currency outstanding } - \text{ Treasury cash holdings.} \quad (18.1)$$

The terms on the right-hand side of Eq. (18.1) represent uses of the monetary base, that is, how the base is allocated among Federal Reserve currency held by the nonbank public, banks, bank reserves held by the Fed, and Treasury currency outstanding (less Treasury cash holdings). Equation (18.1) doesn't reveal the components of the monetary base. To identify them, we return to the Fed's balance sheet. Both Federal Reserve Notes and deposits by depository institutions are Fed liabilities. Because assets must equal liabilities, we use information from the balance sheet to equate the sum of Federal Reserve Notes and

---

[†] Federal Reserve Notes constitute about 90% of the nation's currency. The balance consists principally of coins issued by the U.S. Treasury, but some $300 million in U.S. Treasury Notes, called "greenbacks," dating back to Civil War issues, are still outstanding.

| TABLE 18.1 | THE FEDERAL RESERVE'S BALANCE SHEET ($ BILLIONS) |

Assets		Liabilities	
Securities (U.S. Treasury, government agency, and bankers' acceptances)	282.9	Currency in circulation	320.4
		Treasury cash holdings	0.5
		U.S. Treasury deposits	4.4
Discount loans	0.1	Foreign and other deposits	0.7
Cash items in the process of collection	4.8	Deferred availability cash items	4.2
Other Federal Reserve assets	31.1	Other Federal Reserve liabilities and capital accounts	8.0
Gold and SDR certificate accounts	21.1	Deposits by depository institutions	23.2
Treasury currency outstanding	21.4		
	$361.4		$361.4

Source: Data are for October 31, 1992, and are taken from Federal Reserve Bulletin, January 1993, p. A5.

deposits by depository institutions with the other entries. Specifically, the sum of Federal Reserve Notes and deposits by depository institutions equals the total of all Fed assets minus the total of the other liabilities:[†]

Federal Reserve Notes + Reserve deposits by depository institutions

    = Securities + Discount loans + Cash items in the process of collection

    + Other Federal Reserve assets + Gold and SDR certificates

    + Treasury currency outstanding – Treasury cash holdings

    – U.S. Treasury deposits – Foreign and other deposits

    – Deferred availability cash items

    – Other Federal Reserve liabilities and capital accounts.   (18.2)

We can simplify Eq. (18.2) by taking the difference between the two items relating to check clearing (cash items in the process of collection and deferred availability cash items) and calling it **Federal Reserve float.**[††] Simplifying in this way and substituting the elements on the right-hand side of Eq. (18.2) for the sum of currency in circulation and deposits by depository

[†] Not all bank deposits at the Fed are included in reserves because some are service-related deposits. Technically these deposits must be subtracted from the right side of Eq. (18.2) in order to define the monetary base precisely.

[††] When the Fed reports its balance sheet in the Federal Reserve Bulletin, the total of Federal Reserve float, securities, and bank borrowing is called "Federal Reserve credit."

institutions in Eq. (18.1) yield the complete expression for the monetary base, B:

B = Securities + Discount loans + Federal Reserve float

+ Other Federal Reserve assets + Gold and SDR certificates

+ Treasury currency outstanding – Treasury cash holdings

– U.S. Treasury deposits – Foreign and other deposits

– Other Federal Reserve liabilities and capital accounts.   (18.3)

Changes in the Monetary Base

Equation (18.3) contains the ten determinants of change in the monetary base. Increases in the six items added on the right-hand side of Eq. (18.3) increase the monetary base, and decreases in those items decrease the monetary base. Increases in the four items subtracted on the right-hand side of Eq. (18.3) decrease the monetary base, and decreases in those items increase the monetary base. Table 18.2 summarizes these relationships. In the Using the news box, we use the Federal Reserve Data section of *The Wall Street Journal* to show how these determinants affect the monetary base.

▼ TABLE 18.2	DETERMINANTS OF CHANGE IN THE MONETARY BASE	
An increase in...	**Causes the monetary base to...**	**Because...**
securities	rise	reserves rise
discount loans	rise	reserves rise
Federal Reserve float	rise	cash items in the process of collection rise relative to deferred availability cash items, increasing reserves
other Federal Reserve assets	rise	an increase is like an open market purchase, increasing reserves
Treasury currency outstanding	rise	bank vault cash or currency in circulation rises, increasing reserves
Gold and SDR certificate accounts	rise	an increase is like an open market purchase, increasing reserves
Treasury cash holdings	fall	currency in circulation falls
U.S. Treasury deposits at the Fed	fall	reserves and/or currency in circulation fall
foreign and other deposits at the Fed	fall	reserves fall
other Federal Reserve liabilities and capital accounts	fall	contributions to capital accounts reduce reserves

Using the news...

Federal Reserve Data and Change in the Monetary Base

Each week (on Friday or Monday), *The Wall Street Journal* publishes Federal Reserve data on bank reserve changes. The Member Bank Reserve Changes data provide information on sources of change in the monetary base. For example, for the week ending January 27, 1993, the predominant source of change in the monetary base came from the Fed's purchases of U.S. government securities. Other sources also are listed, including discount loans (adjustment, seasonal, and extended credit), which totaled $84 million. Note that the Fed's holdings of securities increased from the previous year (increasing the monetary base) but that discount loans fell (decreasing the monetary base). The predominant use of the monetary base was currency in circulation at $328 billion on this date.

The Reserve Aggregates data present information on various measures of reserves and the monetary base. For instance, the average value of the monetary base was $353.233 billion for the two weeks ending on January 20, 1993.

FEDERAL RESERVE DATA

MEMBER BANK RESERVE CHANGES

Changes in weekly averages of reserves and related items during the week and year ended January 27, 1993 were as follows (in millions of dollars)

	Jan. 27, 1993	Chg fm Jan. 20, 1993	wk end Jan. 29, 1992
Reserve bank credit:			
U.S. Gov't securities:			
Bought outright	296,880	− 1,751	+ 34,476
Held under repurch agreemt	....	− 2,290	....
Federal agency issues:			
Bought outright	5,331	− 72	− 637
Held under repurch agreemt	....	− 168	....
Acceptances			
Borrowing from Fed:			
Adjustment credit	71	− 270	− 6
Seasonal borrowings	10	− 5	− 9
Extended credit	3	+ 2	+ 1
Float	573	− 179	− 18
Other Federal Reserve Assets...	29,880	+ 107	− 4,584
Total Reserve Bank Credit	332,749	− 4,625	+ 29,223
Gold Stock	11,055	....	− 3
SDR certificates	8,018	....	− 2,000
Treasury currency			
outstanding	21,525	+ 14	+ 474
Total	373,347	− 4,611	+ 27,694
Currency in circulation	327,958	− 1,824	+ 27,395
Treasury cash holdings	502	....	− 176
Treasury dpts with F.R. Bnks	8,761	+ 1,773	− 92
Foreign dpts with F.R. Bnks	215	+ 4	− 68
Other dpts with F.R. Bnks	276	− 6	+ 68
Service related balances, adj	6,231	− 743	+ 1,590
Other F.R. liabilities			
& capital	8,739	+ 47	+ 224
Total	352,683	− 750	+ 28,941

RESERVE AGGREGATES

(daily average in millions)

	Two weeks ended: Jan. 20	Jan. 6
Total Reserves (sa)	54,373	54,604
Nonborrowed Reserves (sa)	54,171	54,336
Required Reserves (sa)	53,134	53,223
Excess Reserves (nsa)	1,238	1,381
Borrowings from Fed (nsa)-a	202	269
Free Reserves (nsa)	1,036	1,112
Monetary Base (sa)	353,233	352,727

a-Excluding extended credit. nsa-Not seasonally adjusted. sa-Seasonally adjusted.

Source: From *The Wall Street Journal*, January 28, 1993. Reprinted by permission of *The Wall Street Journal*, © 1993 Dow Jones & Co., Inc. All Rights Reserved Worldwide.

Determinants That Increase the Monetary Base

Securities and Discount Loans. In Chapter 17 we outlined the effects of the Fed's open market operations and discount loans on the monetary base. An increase in the Fed's holdings of securities acquired through open market purchases or an increase in the volume of discount loans increases the monetary base one-for-one.

Federal Reserve Float. Federal Reserve float occurs during the check-clearing process when the Fed doesn't credit a bank with payment at the same time it debits the bank on which the check is drawn. Suppose that Bigco receives a check for $1 million from Engulf, drawn on Engulf's bank, Megabank in New York. Bigco deposits the $1 million check in Onebank in Chicago. The clearing process works as follows: Onebank sends the check to the Federal Reserve Bank of Chicago, which sends it to the Federal Reserve Bank of New York, which presents it to Megabank. Float exists because the Fed doesn't credit Onebank at the same time it debits Megabank.

The Fed promises to credit the payee bank (Onebank) within two business days, even if the Fed takes longer to present the check to the payor bank (Megabank). Let's see how this affects the Fed's balance sheet. When the Federal Reserve Bank of Chicago gets the check, its assets rise by $1 million with an entry under cash items in the process of collection. The Fed's liabilities also rise by $1 million because there is an offsetting deferred availability cash items entry:

FEDERAL RESERVE

Assets		Liabilities	
Cash items in the process of collection	+$1 million	Deferred availability cash items	+$1 million

After two days, the Fed credits Onebank with $1 million, even if the check has not yet cleared. At this stage of the transaction, Onebank has gained $1 million of reserves, even though Megabank hasn't yet lost reserves. Total reserves in the banking system then have increased by $1 million.

FEDERAL RESERVE

Assets		Liabilities	
Cash items in the process of collection	+$1 million	Deferred availability cash items (Onebank)	+$1 million
		Deposits by Onebank	+$1 million
		Deferred availability cash items (Onebank)	−$1 million

When the check finally is presented to and accepted by Megabank, its account with the Fed is debited with $1 million:

FEDERAL RESERVE

Assets		Liabilities	
Cash items in the process of collection	0	Reserves	
		Deposits by Onebank	+$1 million
		Deposits by Megabank	−$1 million

After this transaction, the banking system's reserves return to the level that existed before the Bigco and Engulf transaction.

In reality, checks continually flow through the Fed's clearing system so that the amount of cash items in the process of collection exceeds the amount of deferred availability cash items. This Federal Reserve float is a source of increases in the monetary base. It fluctuates daily and is beyond the Fed's direct control. Over long periods of time, however, float is not a significant source of change in the monetary base. An increase in Federal Reserve float causes a one-for-one increase in the monetary base.

Gold and SDR Certificate Accounts. The acquisition of gold or SDRs by the Fed expands the monetary base just as an open market purchase of securities does. An increase in the Fed's gold or SDR certificate accounts leads to a one-for-one increase in the monetary base.

Other Federal Reserve Assets. An increase in the Fed's holdings of other assets—say, a deposit or bond denominated in a foreign currency—works like an open market purchase of securities, increasing reserves and the monetary base. Hence intervention by the Fed in the foreign-exchange market affects the other Federal Reserve assets balance. An increase in other Federal Reserve assets raises the monetary base one-for-one.

Treasury Currency Outstanding. Treasury currency outstanding is not an item on the Fed's balance sheet, but it does affect the monetary base. When the amount of Treasury currency held in bank vaults (where it becomes part of vault cash and reserves) or by the nonbank public (where it becomes currency in circulation) increases, the monetary base rises. An increase in Treasury currency outstanding leads to a one-for-one increase in the monetary base.[†]

Determinants That Decrease the Monetary Base

Increases in any of the remaining four determinants of change in the monetary base in Table 18.2 reduce the monetary base.

Treasury Cash Holdings. An increase in Treasury cash holdings reduces currency in the hands of the nonbank public and reduces the monetary base one-for-one.

U.S. Treasury Deposits at the Fed. Whenever the federal government makes a payment—for highway construction, the salary of a staff economist, or a retiree's Social Security benefits—the Treasury writes a check

[†] In practice, increases in Treasury currency generally are met with offsetting changes in other entries on the Fed's balance sheet. For example, if the Treasury mints more coins and sends them to the Fed, the Fed credits the Treasury's deposits. The monetary base is unaffected because coin (a Fed asset) and Treasury deposits (a Fed liability) rise by the same amount.

drawn on its account at the Fed. This Treasury account at the Fed is known as the **General Account.**

Suppose that the government buys $1000 worth of small tools from Toolco, which deposits the $1000 check in its bank, Megabank. Megabank then sends the check to the Fed, which credits Megabank and debits the Treasury's General Account. As a result of the purchase from Toolco, Megabank's reserves—and the banking system's reserves—rise by $1000, the amount of the payment:

FEDERAL RESERVE

Assets	Liabilities	
	Deposits	
	Megabank	+$1000
	U.S. Treasury	−$1000

Bank reserves and the monetary base rise whenever the federal government makes a payment. Likewise, bank reserves and the monetary base fall whenever the federal government receives a payment.

The flow of payments out of and into the General Account is extremely large. The U.S. government spends more than $1.5 trillion each year, or almost $6 billion each business day. Because government receipts and expenditures vary greatly from day to day, the Treasury's balance fluctuates significantly relative to the size of total bank deposits with the Fed.

To reduce the impact of its transactions on the monetary base, the Treasury first deposits most of its receipts (income tax withheld from your paycheck, for example) into **Treasury tax and loan accounts.** The Treasury keeps these accounts at most local banks. When the Treasury moves funds from its tax and loan accounts to the General Account, it times these transfers to match its payments from the General Account. In this way, the Treasury reduces the effects of its receipts and payments on bank reserves. An increase in U.S. Treasury deposits with the Fed reduces reserves and the monetary base one-for-one.

Before 1978, Treasury tax and loan accounts were an interest-free source of funds for banks. Since then, banks must pay interest on these deposits after one day at an interest rate equal to 0.25% below the average federal funds rate for the week.

Foreign and Other Deposits at the Fed. The Fed acts as the U.S. banker for foreign central banks and international agencies. Increases or decreases in the amount of these deposits affect bank reserves and the monetary base in a manner similar to the effect of fluctuations in the Treasury's General Account. However, these fluctuations are much smaller than those of Treasury deposits. An increase in foreign and other deposits at the Fed reduces reserves and the monetary base one-for-one.

Other Liabilities and Capital Accounts. If a bank joins the Federal Reserve System and purchases the required amount of stock in the Fed, the Fed's capital accounts increase. The bank's deposits with the Fed fall by the same amount. As a result, bank reserves and the monetary base fall. An increase in other liabilities and capital leads to a one-for-one reduction in the monetary base.

Concluding Remarks

The most important determinant of change in the monetary base is the Federal Reserve System's holdings of securities, which it controls through open market operations. Some determinants not under the Fed's control (such as U.S. Treasury deposits with the Fed and Federal Reserve float) can lead to significant fluctuations in the monetary base over a day or a week. However, these fluctuations usually are predictable, so they can be reversed by open market operations. Although some components of the monetary base fluctuate over short periods of time, those fluctuations do not significantly reduce the Fed's ability to control the monetary base.

▶ **C H E C K P O I N T** *What is the effect of each of the following events on the monetary base?*

(a) The Treasury withdraws $9 billion from its tax and loan account, and deposits the funds in the General Account.

(b) The Fed buys $1 billion of gold.

(c) The Fed sells $100 million worth of bonds denominated in German marks.

Answers:

(a) The increase in Treasury deposits with the Fed decreases the monetary base by $9 billion.

(b) The Fed's gold purchase, like an open market purchase, raises the monetary base by $1 billion.

(c) The sale reduces other Federal Reserve assets and the monetary base by $100 million. ◀

The Federal Budget Deficit and the Monetary Base

The federal budget deficit has been a frequent news item in the 1980s and early 1990s. Some businesspeople and policymakers complain about the deficit—the excess of government spending over tax revenue—because

---

Q: What are the determinants of changes in the monetary base?

A: Increases in the Fed's holdings of securities, discount loans, float, other Federal Reserve assets, gold and SDR certificates, and Treasury currency outstanding lead to increases in the monetary base. Increases in Treasury cash holdings, U.S. Treasury deposits with the Fed, foreign and other deposits with the Fed, and other Federal Reserve liabilities and capital accounts lead to decreases in the monetary base.

they are afraid that it will increase the monetary base. Behind this concern is the fear that persistent increases in the money supply lead to inflation (which we explore in Part V).

Is there a connection between the federal budget deficit and change in the monetary base? To answer this question, we need to begin with some simple government budget accounting. The government can finance a deficit by raising taxes, borrowing money (selling bonds), or creating money to finance part of its spending for goods and services and payments to individuals.

In the United States, the president and Congress determine federal government expenditures and tax rates, and they define the types of income and expenditures that are subject to taxation. A budget deficit results when government expenditures exceed tax revenue. To finance this deficit, the Treasury sells securities and uses the proceeds to pay the costs of government. This type of transaction (except possibly for short-term lags between receipts and expenditures) doesn't alter the monetary base. In terms of budget arithmetic,

$$\begin{aligned} \text{Government expenditures } - \text{ Tax revenue} \\ = \text{Federal budget deficit} \qquad\qquad\quad \\ = \text{Sales of securities by the Treasury.} \qquad (18.4) \end{aligned}$$

The president and Congress set spending and tax policies, but the Fed's actions most directly affect the monetary base. The Other times, other places box illustrates the potential for conflict in this arrangement. When the Treasury issues securities, the monetary base changes only to the extent that the Fed buys those securities.

Because the Fed, banks, and the nonbank public purchase Treasury securities in the market,

$$\begin{aligned} \text{Sales of securities} \qquad\qquad\qquad\qquad\qquad\qquad\qquad \\ \text{by the Treasury } = \text{ Change in Treasury securities} \qquad\qquad \\ \text{held by banks and the nonbank public} \\ +\text{Fed purchases of Treasury securities.} \quad (18.5) \end{aligned}$$

Recall that a purchase of securities by the Fed leads to an equivalent increase in reserves and expansion of the monetary base. Hence combining Eqs. (18.4) and (18.5) yields

$$\begin{aligned} \text{Federal budget deficit} = \text{Change in Treasury securities held by banks} \\ \text{and the nonbank public} + \text{Fed purchases of} \\ \text{Treasury securities} \qquad\qquad\qquad\quad \\ = \text{Change in Treasury securities held by banks} \\ \text{and the nonbank public} + \text{Increase in monetary} \\ \text{base.} \qquad\qquad\qquad\qquad\qquad (18.6) \end{aligned}$$

Other times, other places...

Dealing with the Debt: The Treasury–Federal Reserve Accord

Government budget deficits increase the monetary base only when the Fed purchases Treasury bonds issued to finance the deficit. The Fed is independent of the Treasury Department, and at times there have been conflicts between the Fed and the Treasury over the extent to which the Fed should finance the federal budget deficit.

One noteworthy conflict raged after World War II. In 1942, the Fed had agreed to peg the interest rate on short-term Treasury securities at 3/8% per year. In other words, to assist the Treasury's efforts to finance the war, the Fed agreed to buy quantities of securities sufficient to maintain that interest rate. Immediately fol-

lowing the war, no problem emerged because the federal government had budget surpluses in 1947–1949. The Fed didn't have to continue purchasing Treasury securities on the open market to maintain the agreed-upon yield. In fact, the Fed sold Treasury securities to maintain the interest rate at the pegged level.

The advent of the Korean War in 1950 significantly increased government spending and borrowing. To keep its promise, the Fed bought large quantities of Treasury securities, expanding the monetary base and fueling inflation. Fed officials publicly questioned the wisdom of effectively placing control of changes in the

monetary base in the hands of the Treasury. On March 3, 1951, the Treasury and the Fed reached a compromise: the Treasury–Federal Reserve Accord. The Fed stopped buying bonds and increasing the monetary base to keep yields on Treasury securities low. (The Treasury's delegate was William McChesney Martin, who later became Chairman of the Board of Governors.) President Truman nonetheless encouraged the Fed to buy bonds if interest rates rose sufficiently. It wasn't until President Eisenhower took office that the Fed finally ceased intervening to maintain the interest rate at or below a specified level.

Economists refer to Eq. (18.6) as the **government budget constraint** because it depicts the relationships among federal spending and tax decisions, sales of securities by the Treasury, and changes in the monetary base. Thus a federal budget deficit must be financed by a combination of an increase in Treasury securities held by banks and the nonbank public and an increase in the monetary base. The media sometimes refer to the latter strategy as "printing money." Although some countries allow their Treasury departments to determine the volume of currency, the United States does not. Here currency must be issued by the Federal Reserve System. In fact, the Fed is not literally printing money but purchasing Treasury securities in the market for its own account. When the Fed purchases Treasury securities to finance budget deficits, we say that it is **monetizing the debt.**

Alternative Strategies

We can use T-accounts to illustrate the effects on the monetary base of alternative strategies to finance government spending. Suppose that the president and Congress agree to embark on a new $2 billion program to repair interstate highways. This program could be paid for by raising taxes, selling bonds to the public, and selling bonds to the Fed.

Raising Taxes. Suppose that the president and Congress agree to raise the tax on gasoline to obtain the $2 billion. The nonbank public then collectively writes checks to the Treasury totaling $2 billion, which first are deposited in the Treasury's tax and loan accounts and then redeposited in the Treasury's General Account at the Fed. In the process, deposits in the banking system fall by $2 billion, reducing reserves by the same amount. The Treasury's deposits at the Fed rise by $2 billion. In the end, the T-accounts for the nonbank public, the Treasury, the banking system, and the Federal Reserve System show the following entries:

NONBANK PUBLIC

Assets		Liabilities	
Deposits	−$2 billion	Taxes due	−$2 billion

TREASURY

Assets		Liabilities	
Deposits at the Fed	+$2 billion		
Taxes due	−$2 billion		

BANKING SYSTEM

Assets		Liabilities	
Reserves	−$2 billion	Deposits	−$2 billion

FEDERAL RESERVE

Assets		Liabilities	
		Reserves	−$2 billion
		U.S. Treasury deposits	+$2 billion

When the Treasury pays contractors the $2 billion by check for the highway projects, the funds flow back into the banking system and have no net effect on reserves and monetary base.[†]

BANKING SYSTEM

Assets		Liabilities	
Reserves	0	Deposits	0

[†] If the transactions took place in currency (which is not very likely), the monetary base would also be unaffected.

FEDERAL RESERVE

Assets		Liabilities	
		Reserves	0
		U.S. Treasury deposits	0

Thus, in general, financing government spending by raising taxes doesn't affect the monetary base.

Selling Bonds to the Public. Suppose that to finance highway repair the Treasury sells $2 billion of bonds to the nonbank public, which pays by check. In this case, the Treasury's deposits increase by $2 billion, while the nonbank public loses $2 billion of deposits:

NONBANK PUBLIC

Assets		Liabilities	
Deposits	−$2 billion		
Securities	+$2 billion		

TREASURY

Assets		Liabilities	
Deposits	+$2 billion	Securities	+$2 billion

BANKING SYSTEM

Assets		Liabilities	
Reserves	−$2 billion	Deposits	−$2 billion

FEDERAL RESERVE

Assets		Liabilities	
		Reserves	−$2 billion
		U.S. Treasury deposits	+$2 billion

When the Treasury pays the highway contractors by check, the funds flow back into the banking system and have no effect on reserves and the monetary base:

BANKING SYSTEM

Assets		Liabilities	
Reserves	0	Deposits	0

MOVING FROM THEORY TO PRACTICE...

THE NEW YORK TIMES JULY 2, 1992

The Budget Deficit and the Monetary Base in Russia

As Russia's ruble began its precarious journey toward being a normal, convertible currency, acting Prime Minister Yegor T. Gaidar warned the Russian Parliament today that the Government budget deficit was running out of control.

"We have begun to allow ourselves to spend more than we can afford," Mr. Gaidar said, cautioning legislators that there could be no stability for the newly floated ruble if the deficit continued to grow, further fueling inflation.

Today was the beginning of a single exchange rate for the ruble, which will now have its value against the dollar determined by market forces, not Government decree. Previously, the Government set different rates of exchange for the ruble, most of them artificially overvalued.

Western economists and the International Monetary Fund, which is attempting to negotiate an economic program with the Government that will unlock up to $24 billion in Western aid and loans have been warn-ing for many weeks now that Russia's budget deficit has been slipping badly...

Mr. Gaidar said that Russia's budget deficit had increased sharply in May to more than 60 billion rubles, nearly half the cumulative deficit of 123 billion rubles over the first five months of the year...

But the parliamentary chairman, Ruslan I. Khasbulatov, a regular critic of the Government, told Mr. Gaidar, "On taxes you are absolutely wrong and we must resolutely lower them." Another deputy challenged Mr. Gaidar to a duel "for ruining the country's economy and humiliating the people." Aleksandr Pochinok, the chairman of the parliamentary commission on budget and finance, called the Government's budget "a provisional message by a provisional Government."

It is this sort of opposition from the Parliament, which was elected in March 1990 when the Communist Party still held power, that President Boris N. Yeltsin and Mr. Gaidar say has stymied their efforts to stabilize the economy, cut the deficit, reform large industry and strengthen the ruble.

But today also marked an important effort to discipline large state enterprises and force them to produce more efficiently.

These enterprises had avoided the effect of budget cuts by borrowing from one another and simply not paying each other for supplies and products. This inter-enterprise debt is now estimated to run about 2 trillion rubles.

As of today, under a decree by Mr. Yeltsin, enterprises must now pay their debts within three months or face bankruptcy, receivership and possibly sale at auction.

Western economists say the Government is likely to issue yet another 200 billion to 500 billion rubles in credits to tide over selected companies that seem viable. But to survive, companies will have to make products that people want to buy and lay off thousands of workers.

ANALYZING THE NEWS...

The government budget constraint tells us that a budget deficit can be financed by a combination of selling bonds to banks and the nonbank public and money creation (increases in the monetary base). Persistent rapid growth in the money supply leads to inflation. (We examine this process in Part V.) If the money multiplier is stable over the long run, persistent growth in the money supply can be traced to persistent growth in the monetary base from central bank decisions.

(a) The statement by Mr. Gaidar implies that the excess of Russian government spending over tax revenue will be financed by increases in the monetary base by the central bank, thereby "fueling inflation." The Russian central bank, which is not independent of the government, increases the monetary base through open market purchases of bonds issued by state-owned enterprises.

(b) Would you expect future budget deficits to increase inflation? This result seems likely because the Russian Parliament wants to cut taxes and delay spending reductions. Given the Russian public's unwillingness to hold government bonds, money creation will have to make up the difference.

(c) If the central bank monetizes the inter-enterprise debt of state-owned enterprises, the monetary base will grow even faster. Continued growth of the monetary base exerts upward pressure on the inflation rate.

For further thought...

Why would reducing the Russian budget deficit help to stabilize the ruble's exchange rate with the U.S. dollar?

Source: Excerpted from Steven Erlanger,"Ruble Floats While Russian Economy Still Sins" July 2, 1992. Copyright © 1991/1992 by The New York Times Company. Reprinted by permission.

FEDERAL RESERVE

Assets	Liabilities	
	Reserves	0
	U.S. Treasury deposits	0

As we noted earlier, financing government spending by selling bonds to the nonbank public doesn't affect the monetary base.

Selling Bonds to the Fed. Although the U.S. Treasury cannot directly finance government spending by creating money, selling bonds to the Fed has the same effect. Two steps are involved. First, as in the preceding case of bond financing, the Treasury sells $2 billion of bonds to the nonbank public to finance the highway repairs; as noted, this transaction doesn't change the monetary base. In the second step, however, the Fed buys the $2 billion of bonds from the nonbank public. This open market purchase increases the monetary base by the same amount. Financing government spending by selling bonds that the Fed ultimately acquires leads to a rise in the monetary base.

Impact of the Government Budget Constraint

Although useful for connecting the elements of government finance, the government budget constraint can be misinterpreted. In the United States, no one participant makes all of the government's budget and financing decisions: Authority is divided among the president, Congress, and the Federal Reserve. The Fed's decisions regarding changes in the monetary base reflect its own monetary policy objectives; the influence of federal budget deficits on those decisions is indirect (though the influence of interest rates on the economy concerns the Fed). The Fed has not monetized the large federal deficits of the 1980s and early 1990s to any great extent. During the 1980s, the monetary base increased by less than $15 billion per year, while the federal budget deficit averaged about $155 billion per year. In 1992, the federal budget deficit was $290 billion, and the monetary base rose by $34 billion. Hence, even in the presence of these large budget deficits, the Fed monetized only about 10% of the annual deficit. There is no direct relationship between government deficits and the monetary base. The monetary base rises when the government runs a deficit only when the Fed acquires government bonds used to finance the deficit.

The Treasury doesn't control the Fed and therefore can't force the central bank to monetize government deficits. In other countries the degree of central bank independence varies. Our analysis of the government budget constraint might lead you to suspect that the less independent the central bank is, the more likely it is to monetize government budget deficits and increase the money supply. In a study of monetary policy in 17 countries during the 1970s and 1980s, Alberto Alesina of Harvard University analyzed the independence of central banks.[†] The measure he used incorporated information on the formal relationships between the central bank and the government, including the presence of government officials on the bank's board and the existence of rules forcing the central bank to monetize portions of budget deficits. Countries in which the central bank had the least independence (such as Italy) experienced the most rapid growth of the money supply. Countries with relatively independent central banks (such as the United States and Japan) had slower rates of growth of the money supply.

[†] Alberto Alesina, "Politics and Business Cycles in Industrial Democracies," *Economic Policy*, no.8, April 1989.

Key Terms and Concepts

Federal Reserve float

General Account

Government budget constraint

Monetizing the debt

Treasury tax and loan accounts

Summary

1. Changes in the monetary base can be explained by ten determinants. Increases in the Fed's holdings of securities, discount loans, Federal Reserve float, other Federal Reserve assets, Treasury currency outstanding, and gold and SDR accounts lead to an equal increase in the monetary base. Increases in Treasury cash holdings, U.S. Treasury deposits with the Fed, foreign and other deposits with the Fed, and other Federal Reserve liabilities and capital accounts lead to an equal decrease in the monetary base.

2. The most important determinant of change in the monetary base is the Federal Reserve's holdings of securities. The Fed controls the amount of these holdings through open market operations. Some determinants not under the Fed's control (such as U.S. Treasury deposits with the Fed and Federal Reserve float) can lead to significant fluctuations in the monetary base over a day or week. However, these fluctuations are predictable and can be reversed by open market operations.

3. A given government budget deficit can be financed by selling government securities to banks and the nonbank public or to the Fed. Financing a deficit by selling bonds to banks and the nonbank public doesn't affect the monetary base. Financing a deficit by selling bonds to the Fed leads to an equivalent expansion of the monetary base.

Review Questions

1. What are the sources and uses of the monetary base?

2. What is the government budget constraint? Does it imply that budget deficits increase the monetary base? Explain.

3. State whether each of the following is an asset or a liability of the Fed:

   a. Holdings of securities

   b. U.S. Treasury deposits

   c. Cash items in the process of collection

   d. Deposits by depository institutions

   e. Coins

   f. Deferred availability cash items

   g. Foreign deposits

   h. Federal Reserve Notes outstanding

   i. Discount loans

   j. Gold and SDR certificate accounts

4. What is the Fed's biggest asset? What is its biggest liability?

5. Define Federal Reserve float. Do increases in float cause the monetary base to rise or fall?

6. Why does the relationship between a government's budget deficits and the inflation rate depend on how independent the central bank is from the government?

7. What is the Treasury's General Account? Does the Treasury keep all its money there?

8. *Evaluate*: Whether the Fed controls all determinants of change in the monetary base. Does the Fed therefore control the monetary base?

Analytical Problems

9. Suppose that the following changes take place in the Fed's balance sheet:

Securities	–	$1 billion
Discount loans	+	$250 million
SDR certificates	+	$500 million
Cash items in the process of collection	+	$2 billion
Deferred availability cash items	+	$1 billion
General Account	–	$2 billion
Deposits by depository institutions	+	$1 billion

   What are the changes in Federal Reserve float? The monetary base?

10. Suppose that the federal government's annual budget deficit is $250 billion and that the Fed's holdings of government securities increase by $10 billion over the year. How much of the deficit was monetized?

11. Suppose that the Treasury decides to move its principal checking account from the Fed to the Chase Manhattan Bank. Discuss the implications for the stability of the monetary base over time.

12. Suppose that the president and Congress sign a budget agreement that eliminates the federal budget deficit. Does this agreement mean that the monetary base will grow by less than it would otherwise? Explain.

13. Explain the effect on the monetary base of each of the following:

   a. $25 billion are withheld from payrolls as withholding taxes and paid to the U.S. Treasury through tax and loan accounts.

   b. A financial crisis erupts, and the Fed makes $2.5 billion of discount loans to the distressed Bigbank.

   c. The World Bank deposits $10 million in its account at the Fed.

   d. An electricity blackout knocks out banks' computers in New York for two days.

   e. The Treasury decides to buy $1 billion of earth-moving equipment for use in a new public highway construction program and puts the funds in the General Account.

f. The Fed buys $1 billion of U.S. Treasury securities.

g. The regional Federal Reserve banks decide to put expensive new marble shells around their buildings.

14. For cash items in the process of collection the Fed's balance sheet shows $10 billion, while deferred availability cash items are $8 billion. What is the size of the Federal Reserve float? Why do you think the Fed tries to keep the float as small as possible?

15. Suppose the Fed buys $150 million of Japanese yen with Federal Reserve Notes. What is the net effect on the monetary base? How has the Fed's balance sheet been affected?

16. Suppose the Fed buys $100 million of German marks with Federal Reserve Notes and, at the same time, sells $100 million of U.S. government securities for cash in a domestic open market operation. What is the net effect on the monetary base? How has the Fed's balance sheet been affected?

17. Suppose the Susan B. Anthony dollar coin suddenly becomes popular, and people stop using as many dollar bills as they used to. What happens to the monetary base?

18. Economic theory tells us that (under reasonable assumptions) a rise in the government budget deficit raises interest rates. Show how the debt is monetized if the Fed tries to maintain stable interest rates when the government budget deficit rises.

Data Questions

19. Obtain a copy of the latest *Economic Report of the President* from your library. Find the U.S. budget deficit for 1992 and the change in the monetary base in 1992. Do you think the Fed is actively monetizing Federal budget deficits? Why or why not?

20. Look at the assets and liabilities of the Fed over the past six months as listed in the latest *Federal Reserve Bulletin*. Which items seem to fluctuate greatly from month to month? Which items are fairly stable? Which seem to grow at a constant rate?

Organization of the Federal Reserve System

Will he or won't he? In the spring of

1991, analysts speculated about whether President Bush would nominate Alan Greenspan for a second term as Chairman of the Board of Governors of the Federal Reserve System, the "CEO" of the U.S. central bank. Some rumors suggested that the Fed chairman's reappointment was delayed to obtain a more expansionary monetary policy from the Fed. Financial markets were worried that the failure to reappoint Greenspan would deprive the central bank of the services of a well-respected leader. Greenspan was reappointed in July 1991, but internal and external pressure on the Fed led to a tug of war over the course of monetary policy in late 1991.

The Fed is a complex organization that plays many roles in the money supply process. In Chapters 17 and 18, we explored the money supply process: how decisions of the Fed, banks, and the nonbank public interact to determine the money supply. Although the actions of all three participants are important, the Fed exerts the most influence on the money supply through open market operations, reserve requirements, and discount lending. Before we look at how these interventions work in practice and how they fit into broad decisions about monetary policy, we need to understand *how* the Fed is organized. Doing so helps explain more clearly Fed interventions and *why* the Fed takes the actions it does.

In this chapter we analyze three questions that merit special attention. **Q:** How is power shared within the Federal Reserve System (in theory and in practice)? **Q:** Is the Fed an independent central bank? **Q:** Should the Fed be independent?

Power Sharing in the Federal Reserve System

Few countries have as complex a structure for their central bank as the United States has in its Federal Reserve System. The Fed's organization resulted largely from the same political consideration that gave the United States a fragmented banking system: fear of large, powerful economic interests. To understand why the Fed is organized as it is, we need to look back in history at the nation's earlier attempts to create a central bank.

Creation of the System

Early in the nation's history, Treasury Secretary Alexander Hamilton organized the Bank of the United States, which was meant to function as a central bank but had both government and private shareholders. Distrust of the Bank of the United States by southern and western agrarian and small-business interests resulted in the bank's demise in 1811. In 1816, the Second Bank of the United States was formed, but populist President Andrew Jackson didn't renew its national charter when it expired in 1836. (The bank survived for a time as a state-chartered bank in Pennsylvania.)

Abolition of the Second Bank of the United States left the nation without an official lender of last resort for banks. Private arrangements such as the New York Clearing House (Chapter 15) were tried, but severe nationwide financial panics in 1873, 1884, 1893, and 1907—and accompanying economic downturns—raised concerns in Congress. After the 1907 panic and economic recession, Congress was especially concerned that New York financier J. P. Morgan had served as a de facto lender of last resort. It appointed a National Monetary Commission to begin formal studies leading to the design of a new central bank. With the support of President Woodrow Wilson, the Federal Reserve Act became law in 1913. (We discussed banking regulation between 1836 and 1913 in Chapter 14.)

The Federal Reserve Act of 1913 created a central bank for the United States, the **Federal Reserve System.** The act provided for checks and balances designed to diffuse economic power in three ways: among bankers and business interests, among states and regions, and between government and the private sector. The act and subsequent legislation created three groups within the system, each empowered in theory to perform separate duties: the Federal Reserve Banks, the Board of Governors, and the Federal Open Market Committee (FOMC). The responsibilities assigned to each reflected the original intent of the 1913 act to give the central bank control over the amount of currency outstanding and the volume of discount loans to member banks (the lender-of-last-resort function). In theory, the president and Congress didn't envision that the Fed would control broad monetary policy. In practice, however, the Fed has assumed the lead role in making monetary policy. We discuss the roles of the principal groups within the Federal Reserve System in terms of open market operations, reserve requirements, and discount lending activities.

Roles in the System

Let's first consider the roles of the four principal groups in the Federal Reserve System: Federal Reserve Banks, member banks, the Board of Governors, and the Federal Open Market Committee.

Federal Reserve Banks. The Federal Reserve Act divided the United States into 12 Federal Reserve districts, each of which has a **Federal Reserve bank** in one city (and, in most cases, additional branches in other cities in the district) to conduct discount lending. Figure 19.1 shows the Federal Reserve districts and locations of the Federal Reserve banks. The map may appear strange at first glance: No state (not even California or New York) is a single Federal Reserve district. Some states are split by district boundaries, and economically dissimilar states are grouped. Most Federal Reserve districts represent a mixture of urban and rural areas, as well as manufacturing, agriculture, and service business interests. This organization is intentional, preventing any one interest group or one state from obtaining preferential treatment from the district Federal Reserve bank. Nor can a district easily have its way at the expense of other districts, owing to supervision by the Board of Governors and the Federal Open Market Committee. If one district is suffering from a recession, it cannot singlehandedly alter Fed money and credit policies to meet its needs. Some cities (New York, Chicago, and San Francisco) clearly were population centers in 1914 and thus were chosen as locations for Federal Reserve banks. Other cities were chosen because of

▶ FIGURE 19.1

Federal Reserve Districts and Banks

The division of the 50 states into 12 Federal Reserve districts was designed so that each district contained a mixture of urban and rural areas and manufacturing, agriculture, and service business interests.

Source: Federal Reserve Bulletin,
February 1993, p. A78.

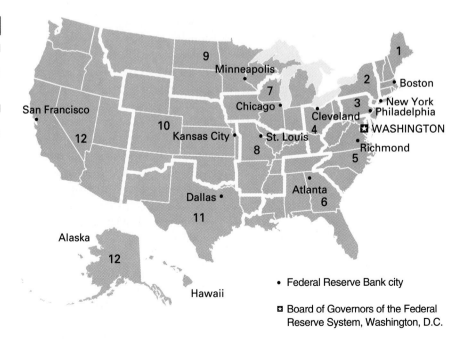

• Federal Reserve Bank city

◘ Board of Governors of the Federal Reserve System, Washington, D.C.

Source: Federal Reserve Bulletin, February 1993, p. A78.

political pressure during the debate over the Federal Reserve Act. (For example, Richmond, Virginia, was the home of Carter Glass, one of the legislative architects of the Federal Reserve System.)

Who owns the Federal Reserve banks? In principle, the private commercial banks in each district that are members of the Federal Reserve System own the district bank. In fact, each Federal Reserve bank is a private-government joint venture. Member banks receive dividends (limited to 6%) on the shares of stock they own in the district bank.

A guiding principle of the 1913 Federal Reserve Act was that one constituency (for example, finance, industry, commerce, or agriculture) would not be able to exploit the economic power of the central bank at the expense of another constituency. Thus Congress restricted the composition of the boards of directors of the Federal Reserve banks. The directors represent the interests of three groups: banks, businesses, and the general public. Member banks elect three bankers (*Class A directors*) and three leaders in industry, commerce, and agriculture (*Class B directors*). The Fed's Board of Governors appoints three public interest directors (*Class C directors*). Subject to the Board's approval, the nine directors of a Federal Reserve bank elect the president of that bank.

The 12 Federal Reserve banks carry out duties related to the Fed's roles in the payments system, monetary control, and financial regulation. Specifically, the district banks

- manage check-clearing in the payments system;
- manage currency in circulation by issuing new Federal Reserve Notes and withdrawing damaged notes from circulation;
- conduct discount lending by making and administering discount loans to banks within the district;
- perform supervisory and regulatory functions such as examining state member banks and evaluating merger applications; and
- provide services to businesses by collecting and making available data on district business activities and by publishing review articles on monetary and banking issues written by professional economists employed by the banks.

The district banks are involved in monetary policy both directly (through discount lending) and indirectly (through membership in Federal Reserve committees). In theory, Federal Reserve banks establish the discount rate and determine the amounts that individual (member and nonmember) banks are allowed to borrow.[†] The district banks indirectly influence policy through their representatives on the Federal Open Market Committee, (FOMC), which sets guidelines for open market operations (purchases and sales of securities by the Fed to affect the monetary base), and the Federal Advisory Council, a consultative body composed of district bankers.

[†] In practice, the discount rate is reviewed and approved for each Federal Reserve district by the Board of Governors in Washington.

Member Banks. The Federal Reserve Act required all national banks to become **member banks** of the Federal Reserve System. State banks may elect to become members, but currently only about one in seven state banks is a member. Some 40% of all banks in the United States now belong to the Federal Reserve System. These member banks hold about two-thirds of all bank deposits.

Historically, one reason for the low voluntary membership rate was the cost. The Fed's reserve requirements compel banks to keep part of their deposits as idle funds, effectively imposing a tax on bank intermediation. Most states mandated reserve requirements but allowed banks to hold reserves in the form of interest-bearing marketable securities. As nominal interest rates rose during the 1960s and 1970s, the opportunity cost of Fed membership increased, and fewer state banks elected to become or remain members.

During the 1970s, the Fed argued that the so-called reserve tax on member banks placed them at a competitive disadvantage relative to non-member banks. It claimed that declining bank membership eroded its ability to influence the money supply and urged Congress to compel all commercial banks to join the Federal Reserve System. Although Congress has not yet legislated such a requirement, the Depository Institutions Deregulation and Monetary Control Act (DIDMCA) of 1980 required that all banks (by 1987) maintain reserve deposits with the Fed on the same terms. This legislation gave member and nonmember banks equivalent access to discount loans and to payments system (check-clearing) services. It effectively blurred the distinction between member and nonmember banks and halted the decline in Fed membership. Today some 5000 banks are Federal Reserve System members.

▶ C H E C K P O I N T   *Suppose that City National Bank pays a 7% annual interest rate on checkable deposits, subject to a reserve requirement of 10%. What is City National's effective cost of funds?* Against $100 of deposits, City National must hold $10 in reserves (in vault cash or deposits with the Fed), leaving $90 to invest. The bank must pay depositors $(0.07)(\$100) = \$7$ to obtain $90 in funds to invest in loans or securities, so its effective cost of funds is not 7%, but $7/90 = 7.8\%$. Thus reserve requirements impose a tax on bank intermediation, raising City National's cost of funds from 7% to 7.8%. ◀

Board of Governors. Headquartered in Washington, D.C., the seven members of the **Board of Governors** are appointed by the president of the United States and confirmed by the U.S. Senate. To provide for central bank independence, the terms of board members were set so that one president generally cannot appoint a full Board of Governors. Governors serve a nonrenewable term of 14 years; their terms are staggered so that one term expires every other January.[†] Geographical restrictions ensure that no one Federal Reserve district is overrepresented.

Many board members are professional economists from business, government, or academia. Chairmen of the Board of Governors since World War II have come from a variety of backgrounds including Wall Street (William McChesney Martin), academia (Arthur Burns), business (G. William Miller), public service (Paul Volcker), and economic forecasting (Alan Greenspan). The chairman serves a four-year term and may be reappointed or serve out the balance of a 14-year member's term.

The Board of Governors administers monetary policy to influence the nation's money supply through open market operations, reserve requirements, and discount lending. Since 1935, it has had the authority to determine reserve requirements within limits set by Congress. The Board of Governors also effectively sets the discount rate (which is nominally established by the Federal Reserve banks) through its review and determination procedure. It holds seven of the 12 seats on the Federal Open Market Committee and therefore influences the setting of guidelines for open market operations. In addition to its formal responsibilities relating to monetary control, it informally influences national and international economic policy decisions. The chairman of the Board of Governors advises the president and testifies before Congress on economic matters.

The Board of Governors has certain responsibilities relating to financial regulation. Prior to elimination of Regulation Q in 1986, it administered interest rate regulations. It also sets *margin requirements*, or the proportion of the purchase price of securities that an investor must pay in cash as opposed to credit. In addition, it determines permissible activities for bank holding companies and approves bank mergers. Finally, it exercises certain administrative controls over individual Federal Reserve banks, reviewing their budgets and setting the salaries of their presidents and officers.

Federal Open Market Committee. The 12-member **Federal Open Market Committee** (FOMC) gives direction to the Fed's open market operations. Members of the FOMC are the chairman of the Board of Governors, the other Fed governors, the president of the Federal Reserve Bank of New York, and the presidents of four of the other eleven Federal Reserve Banks (who serve on a rotating basis). Only five Federal Reserve bank presidents are voting members of the FOMC, but all 12 attend meetings and participate in discussions. The committee meets eight times each year.

The Fed influences the monetary base primarily through open market operations. Thus, in practice, the FOMC is the centerpiece of Fed policymaking. The FOMC doesn't literally buy or sell securities for the Fed's

---

[†] Technically, a governor could resign before the term expired and then be reappointed, thereby lengthening the term. Since 1970, this practice has been rare.

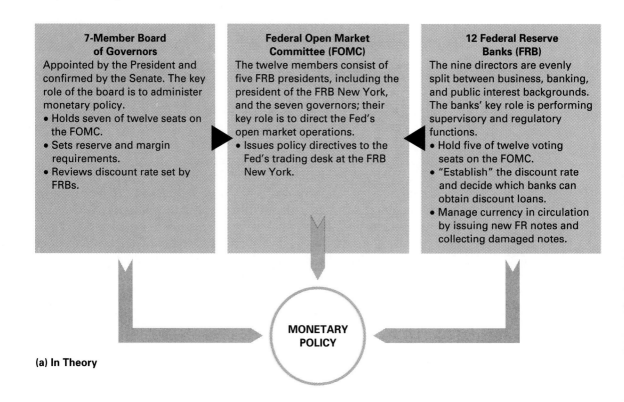

7-Member Board of Governors	Federal Open Market Committee (FOMC)	12 Federal Reserve Banks (FRB)
Appointed by the President and confirmed by the Senate. The key role of the board is to administer monetary policy. • Holds seven of twelve seats on the FOMC. • Sets reserve and margin requirements. • Reviews discount rate set by FRBs.	The twelve members consist of five FRB presidents, including the president of the FRB New York, and the seven governors; their key role is to direct the Fed's open market operations. • Issues policy directives to the Fed's trading desk at the FRB New York.	The nine directors are evenly split between business, banking, and public interest backgrounds. The banks' key role is performing supervisory and regulatory functions. • Hold five of twelve voting seats on the FOMC. • "Establish" the discount rate and decide which banks can obtain discount loans. • Manage currency in circulation by issuing new FR notes and collecting damaged notes.

MONETARY POLICY

(a) In Theory

▲ FIGURE 19.2

Organization and Authority of the Federal Reserve System
The Federal Reserve Act of 1913 established the Federal Reserve System but incorporated a series of checks and balances into the system. Part (a) shows that in theory, its economic power is diffuse. Part (b) shows that informal power within the Fed is more concentrated in the hands of the chairman of the Board of Governors than the formal structure suggests.

account. Instead, it summarizes its views in a *directive* issued to the Fed's trading desk at the Federal Reserve Bank of New York. There the manager for domestic open market operations communicates each day with members of the FOMC (and their staffs) about execution of the directive.

Power and Authority within the Fed

Because Congress configured the Federal Reserve System with many formal checks and balances to ensure that no one group could effectively control it, central (or national) control of the system was virtually nonexistent during the Fed's first 20 years. After the severe banking crisis of the early 1930s, many analysts concluded that the decentralized district bank system could not adequately deal with national economic and financial disturbances. The Banking Acts of 1933 and 1935 gave the Board of Governors authority to set reserve requirements and the FOMC the authority to direct open market operations. The Banking Act of 1935 also centralized the Fed's involvement in the money supply process, giving the Board of Governors a majority (seven of 12) of seats on the FOMC and thereby great influence in implementing monetary policy.

The Board of Governors and the FOMC exert most of the Fed's formal influence on monetary policy. However, many Fed watchers believe that the informal authority of the Chairman, the staff of the Board, and the

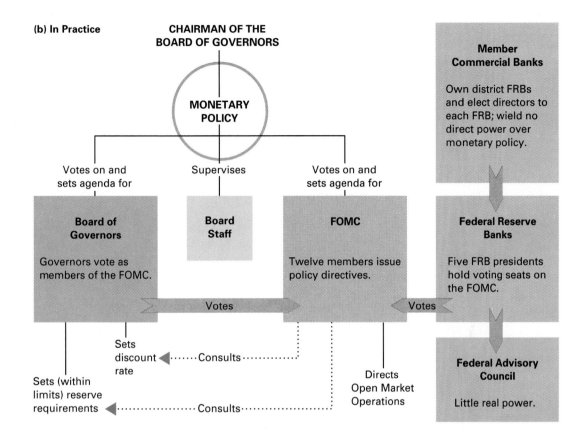

(b) In Practice

FOMC predominates. In other words, the informal power structure within the Fed may be more concentrated and influential than the formal power structure. Because the Federal Reserve Bank of New York always occupies a seat on the FOMC, the president of that bank also can be quite influential. Figure 19.2 shows the organizational and power-sharing arrangements within the Fed, both in theory and in practice.

Member banks, the nominal owners of Federal Reserve banks, have little actual influence within the system. The distinction between *ownership* and *control* within the Federal Reserve System is clear. Member banks own shares of stock in the Federal Reserve banks, but shareholding confers none of the rights typically granted to shareholders of private corporations. Member banks receive at most a 6% annual dividend, regardless of the Fed's earnings, and thus do not have the residual claim normally granted to equity. Moreover, member banks have virtually no control over how their stakes in the system are used because the Board of Governors in Washington formulates policy directives. Although member banks elect the six Class A and Class B directors, there is generally only one candidate per position, whom the Federal Reserve bank or Board of Governors suggests.

Although there is no direct evidence as to who actually holds power with the Fed, the impressions of experienced insiders are revealing. Based on his personal experience, economist Sherman Maisel estimated the relative influence of groups within the Fed in setting monetary policy: the chairman of the Board of Governors, 45%; the staff of the Board and the FOMC, 25%; and other governors and the Federal Reserve banks, not particularly powerful.[†] Those impressions were recorded in the 1970s, but current actions support them. Some board members and district bank presidents on the FOMC may challenge the chairman's agenda, but the chairman's influence still dominates.

How the Fed Operates

To understand the Fed's actions, we have to address three concerns about its operations: (1) whether its monetary policy decisions are free from political and other external pressures; (2) the factors that motivate it; and (3) whether it should be independent.

Handling External Pressure

Congress intended the Federal Reserve System generally to operate independently of external pressures (for example, from the president, Congress, the banking industry, or business groups). Board members are appointed for long, nonrenewable terms of office, reducing any one president's influence on the Board's composition and the temptation for governors to take actions merely to please the president and Congress.

An even more important factor in combatting external pressure is the Fed's financial situation. Generally, federal agencies are subject to the annual appropriations process, during which Congress scrutinizes budgetary requests, authorizes funds, and then appropriates the funds. Not only is the Fed exempt from this process, it is a profitable organization, contributing funds to the Treasury rather than receiving funds from it. Most of the Fed's earnings come from interest on the securities it holds; smaller amounts come from interest on discount loans and fees received from financial institutions for check-clearing and other services. In recent years, the Fed's net income has exceeded $15 billion annually—substantial profits when compared even to the largest U.S. corporations.

Despite the attempt to give the Fed independence, it isn't completely insulated from external pressure. First, the president can exercise considerable influence with respect to the membership of the Board of Governors. Often governors do not serve their full 14-year terms, because they can earn higher incomes in private business. Thus a president serving two terms of office may be able to appoint several governors. Additionally, the president may appoint a new chairman every four years (see Box 19.1). A chairman who is not reap-

---

[†] Sherman J. Maisel, *Managing the Dollar*. New York: W. W. Norton, 1973.

Consider this...

Importance of Selecting a Fed Chairman

In the summer of 1979, President Jimmy Carter perceived the failure of his economic policies to roll back inflation as a huge stumbling block in his quest for reelection. Inflation was accelerating, and the value of the dollar was declining sharply on foreign-exchange markets. To try to turn the economy around before the election, Carter sought to replace Federal Reserve Chairman G. William Miller (who was leaving to become Secretary of the Treasury) with a champion of price stability. On July 24, 1979, Carter offered the Fed chairman-

ship to Paul Volcker, the president of the Federal Reserve Bank of New York and former undersecretary of the Treasury for monetary affairs. Volcker's views on Fed policies were well-known. Earlier in 1979 he had argued for a contractionary monetary policy, with a significant increase in the federal funds rate, to fight inflation. The inflation challenge led Volcker to accept the new post (despite having to take a pay cut from $116,000 to $57,500).

In October 1979, the Volcker Fed began a restrictive policy of

significantly lower money supply growth that resulted in a dramatic increase in the federal funds rate. High interest rates and a sagging economy were major factors in President Carter's campaign woes. By 1982, the rate of inflation had declined significantly, but the decline was too late for Jimmy Carter. Carter had appointed Federal Reserve Chairman Volcker, but the short-term effects of his policies had helped hand the 1980 presidential election to Republican Ronald Reagan.

pointed may serve the remainder of his or her term as a governor but traditionally resigns, thereby giving the president another vacancy to fill.

Second, although the Fed's significant net income exempts it from the appropriations process (Congress's "power of the purse"), it remains a creation of Congress. The U.S. Constitution does not specifically mandate a central bank, so Congress can amend the Fed's charter and powers or even abolish it entirely. Members of Congress usually are not shy about reminding the Fed of this fact. Nor is Congressional oversight merely rhetoric. In the middle and late 1970s, Congress forced the Fed to explain its goals and procedures. Passed in 1975, House Concurrent Resolution 133 requires the Fed to announce targets for the growth of monetary aggregates. In addition, the Humphrey-Hawkins Act (officially the Full Employment and Balanced Growth Act of 1978) requires the Fed to explain how these targets are consistent with the president's economic objectives. Nevertheless, owing to the complex range of issues that Congress must address, its ability to challenge the Fed is limited.

A Case in Point: Treasury-Fed Conflict

The lack of formal control of monetary policy by elected officials in the United States at times has resulted in conflicts between the Fed and the president, who is often represented by the Secretary of the Treasury. During World War II the administration increased its control over the Fed. To help finance wartime budget deficits, the Fed agreed to hold interest rates on

Q: How is power shared within the Federal Reserve System (in theory and in practice)?

A: In theory, power within the Federal Reserve System is spread among the Board of Governors, the Federal Reserve banks, and the member banks. In practice, the chairman wields significant power by setting the agenda for the Board of Governors and the FOMC. The FOMC consults on changes in reserve requirements and the discount rate and directs open market operations. The board's staff influences the FOMC through its advisory role. The board effectively sets the discount rate.

Treasury securities at low levels. It could do so by buying bonds not purchased by private investors, thereby predetermining (pegging) the rates. After the war, the Treasury wanted to continue this policy, but the Fed didn't agree. The Fed's concern was inflation: Larger purchases of Treasury securities by the Fed increased the monetary base, potentially increasing the money supply growth rate and inflation. Price controls that had restrained inflation during the war were lifted after it ended.

Chairman of the Board of Governors Marriner Eccles particularly objected to the rate-fixing policy. His opposition to the desires of the Truman administration cost him the Fed chairmanship in 1948, although he continued to fight for Fed independence during the remainder of his term as a governor. On March 4, 1951, the wartime policy of fixing the interest rates on Treasury securities was formally abandoned with the *Treasury–Federal Reserve Accord*.

Conflicts between the Treasury and the Fed didn't end with that accord, however. For example, President Ronald Reagan and Federal Reserve Chairman Paul Volcker argued over who was at fault for the severe business recession of the early 1980s. Reagan blamed the Fed's contractionary monetary policy. Volcker held that the Fed could not expand money supply growth until the budget deficit was reduced.

Early in the Bush administration, the conflict was less severe, even though the Treasury typically argued for a more expansionary monetary policy than the Fed wanted. During the debate in 1991 over reforms of U.S. banking regulations, the Treasury and the Fed argued over which would have greater responsibility in overseeing the banking system. Finally, in late 1991 and early 1992, the Treasury pressured the Fed to reduce short-term interest rates. Although the Fed did reduce the discount rate, there is no way of knowing whether Treasury pressure was a factor. In early 1993, the Clinton Treasury argued that the Fed should not raise short-term interest rates in the face of the administration's budget package.

Factors That Motivate the Fed

We have shown that the Fed has considerable power over monetary policy. Let's now examine alternative explanations of how the Fed decides to use its power. We consider two views of Fed motivation: the public interest view and the principal-agent view.

The Public Interest View. The usual starting point for explaining the motivation of business managers is that they act in the interest of the constituency they serve, the shareholders. The **public interest view** of Fed motivation holds that the Fed also acts in the interest of its primary constituency (the general public) and that it seeks to achieve economic goals that are in the public interest. Examples of such goals are price and employment stability or economic growth.

Does the evidence support the public interest view? It doesn't appear to with regard to the price stability goal. The record of persistent

Q: Is the Fed an independent central bank?

A: The president and Congress exercise some constraints on the Fed, but it has considerable independence in making and implementing monetary policy.

inflation since World War II undercuts the claim that the Fed has emphasized price stability. Similarly, some economists dispute the Fed's contributions to the stability of other economic indicators.

The Principal-Agent View. The principal-agent problem suggests an alternative explanation of the Fed's motivation. Recall that when managers (agents) have little stake in their businesses, their incentives to maximize the value of shareholders' (principals') claims may be weak; in that situation the agents don't always act in the interest of the principals. Some influential economists, notably James Buchanan and Gordon Tullock, formulated a **principal-agent view** of motivation in bureaucratic organizations such as the Fed. They contend that bureaucrats' objective is to maximize their personal well-being—power, influence, and prestige—rather than the well-being of the general public. Hence the principal-agent view of Fed motivation predicts that the Fed acts in order to increase its power, influence, and prestige as an organization, subject to constraints placed on it by principals such as the president and Congress.

How can we determine whether the principal-agent view accurately explains the Fed's motivation? If it does, we might conclude that the Fed would fight to maintain its autonomy. Unquestionably it does so; the Fed has resisted congressional attempts to control its budget many times. In fact, the Fed is one of the most successful bureaucratic organizations in terms of its ability to mobilize constituents (such as bankers and business executives) in its defense.

The principal-agent view also implies that the Fed would avoid conflicts with groups that could limit its power, influence, and prestige. For example, the Fed could manage monetary policy to assist the reelection efforts of presidential incumbents. This concept of the **political business cycle** is an extension of the principal-agent problem. It suggests that the Fed would try to lower interest rates to stimulate credit demand and economic activity prior to an election. The facts don't completely support the concept, however. For example, expansion of money supply growth preceded President Nixon's reelection in 1972, but contraction of money supply growth preceded President Carter's and President Bush's unsuccessful bids for reelection in 1980 and 1992, respectively.

Nevertheless, the desires of the president may subtly influence Fed policy. One study of the influence of politics on changes in monetary policy from 1979 through 1984 measured the number of signals of desired policy from the administration in articles appearing in *The Wall Street Journal*. The author found a close correlation between changes in monetary policy and the number of administration signals.[†]

[†] Thomas Havrilesky, "Monetary Policy Signaling from the Administration to the Federal Reserve," *Journal of Money, Credit, and Banking,* vol. 20, February 1988, pp. 83–101.

One criticism of the principal-agent view addresses the need to separate the Fed's intentions from external pressure: The Fed itself might want to act in one way, whereas Congress and the president might try to get the Fed to pursue other goals. The principal-agent view also fails to explain why Congress allows the Fed to be relatively independent through self-financing. Some economists suggest that the Fed may provide Congress with long-run benefits through self-financing. If self-financing gives the Fed an incentive to conduct more open market purchases, thereby expanding the money supply, more residual revenue will accrue to the Treasury for appropriation by Congress.

▶ C H E C K P O I N T *Look for articles in* The Wall Street Journal *in which the president or the Treasury Department (or another arm of the administration) delivers strong policy suggestions to the Fed and then watch for the Fed's response.* ◀

The Issue of Fed Independence

Usually, the political issue of Fed independence arises not because of academic disagreement over monetary policy or even the role of the Fed in managing monetary policy, but because of the public's negative reaction to

Other times, other places...
Conflicts Between the Treasury and the Central Bank in Japan over Independence

The United States isn't the only country in which tensions between the Treasury and the central bank influence monetary policy. Japanese monetary policy during the late 1980s and early 1990s provides another good example. During the mid-1980s, Bank of Japan Governor Satoshi Sumita conducted expansionary monetary policy. Mr. Sumita, a former vice minister of finance (the Ministry of Finance is akin to the U.S. Treasury), favored low interest rates. Yasushi Mieno, appointed to head the Bank of Japan in 1989, pursued a more contractionary policy. *The Wall Street Journal* reported that "Mr. Mieno took away the *sake* bowl just as the

party started getting rambunctious."[†] That is, Japanese money growth would be reduced, leading to concerns that the runup in Japanese stock prices would end.

During 1990, increases in the Bank of Japan's discount rate sent Japanese stock market prices plunging and threatened some highly leveraged firms with financial distress. The surprise decision by the Bank of Japan to reduce its discount rate from 6% to 5.5% on July 1, 1991 caused Japanese central bank watchers to worry that Mieno was currying favor with Finance Minister Ryutaro Hashimoto. The finance minister was a strong candidate to be the Japanese prime minister. These

worries reflect a political business cycle interpretation of events.

Like Federal Reserve actions in the United States, the Bank of Japan's actions can be viewed as reflecting responsible, independent behavior: The bank may have tried to ease the likelihood of a financial crisis in Japan induced by high interest rates, even though it could attempt relatively contractionary policies over the medium term.

[†] Marcus W. Brauchli and Clay Chandler, "Financial Shift: In a Major Reversal, the Bank of Japan Cuts Its Key Interest Rate," *The Wall Street Journal,* July 2, 1991.

Fed policy. For example, legislation introduced in Congress in 1982 to decrease the Fed's autonomy stemmed from public reaction to high interest rates. Let's analyze the arguments for and against Fed independence (see also the Other times, other places box).

Arguments for Independence. The main argument for Fed independence is that monetary policy—which affects inflation, interest rates, exchange rates, and economic growth—is too important and technical to be determined in the political arena. Because of the frequency of elections, politicians may be *myopic,* or concerned with short-term benefits without regard to potential long-term costs. The most sensitive aspect of the economy over which short-term and long-term interests clash is inflation. Supporters argue that monetary policy tends to be too expansionary if left to policymakers with short horizons, provoking inflationary pressures. Thus the Fed cannot assume that politicians' objectives reflect public sentiment. The public may well prefer that the experts at the Fed, rather than politicians, make monetary policy decisions.

Another argument for Fed independence is that complete control of the Fed by elected officials increases the likelihood of political business cycle fluctuations in the money supply. For example, those officials might pressure the Fed to assist the Treasury's borrowing efforts by buying government bonds, increasing the money supply and fueling inflation.

Arguments against Independence. The main argument against central bank independence also is based on the importance of monetary policy for the economy. Supporters claim that in a democracy elected officials should make public policy. Because the public holds elected officials responsible for perceived monetary policy problems, some analysts advocate giving the president and Congress more control over monetary policy. The counterargument to the point that monetary policy is too technical for elected officials is that national security and foreign policy also require sophisticated analysis and a long-term view, and these functions are entrusted to elected officials. In addition, critics of Fed independence argue that placing the central bank under the control of elected officials could confer benefits by coordinating and integrating monetary policy with government taxing and spending policies.

Those who argue for greater control make the case that the Fed has not always used its independence well. For example, some critics note that the Fed, because of its deflationary bias, failed to assist the banking system during the economic contraction of the early 1930s. Another example cited by many economists is that Fed policies were too inflationary in the 1960s and 1970s. Finally, some analysts believe that the Fed acted too slowly in addressing credit problems during the recession of the early 1990s.

Concluding Remarks. Economists and politicians don't universally agree on the merits of Fed independence. Under the present system, however,

Q: Should the Fed be independent?

A: Some argue that the Fed should be independent because monetary policy is too technical for elected officials and requires a long-term view. Others argue that, as the public holds elected officials responsible for perceived monetary policy problems, the president and Congress should have more control over monetary policy. Debates generally center on proposals to limit Fed independence, not to eliminate it.

the Fed's independence is not absolute and thus sometimes satisfies one or the other group of critics. In practice, debates center on proposals to *limit* Fed independence in some respects, not to *eliminate* its formal independence. Some recent proposals include shortening the term of office of governors, making the chairman's term coincide more closely with that of the president, or placing the Secretary of the Treasury on the FOMC. Enacting any of these proposals would tend to make the Fed's economic policies more consistent with the president's.

Central Bank Independence in Other Countries

The degree of central bank independence varies greatly from country to country. When we compare the structure of the Fed with that of central banks in Europe and Japan, four patterns emerge. First, in countries where central bank board members serve fixed terms of office, none are as long as the 14-year term for Federal Reserve governors, implying nominally greater independence for the Fed. Second, in these countries the head of the central bank has a longer term of office than the four-year term of office for the chairman of the Board of Governors in the United States.

Third, of these countries only Germany has a federal structure for the central bank. The Central Bank Council of the Bundesbank consists of the president, deputy president, other members of the directorate, and the presidents of

---

Consider this...

BOX 19.2

Is a Fed for All of Europe Possible?

During the move toward economic integration in Europe, the European Community proposed a central bank—the European Central Bank (ECB)—to conduct monetary policy for all of Europe. Representatives of EC nations signed an important agreement in Maastricht, The Netherlands, in December 1991. The agreement detailed a gradual approach to monetary union to be completed between 1994 and 1999.

The proposed ECB would be structured along the lines of the Fed. The ECB Council would be composed of the six members of an ECB Executive Board (like the Fed's Board of Governors, appointed by a central authority, the European Council) and the central bank governors from the individual countries in the union (comparable to Federal Reserve bank presidents). Like the Fed, the ECB would be independent of member governments; Executive Board members would be appointed for nonrenewable eight-year terms to increase their political independence.

Some analysts believe that a future ECB is unlikely to be politically independent in practice. Countries likely will argue over the merits of expansionary or contractionary monetary policies. Also, concerns remain about how to accommodate domestic discretion in the lender-of-last-resort role in dealing with domestic financial crises. Finally, currency crises in Europe in 1992 and 1993 and political debates over ratification of the Maastricht treaty do not portend easy establishment of a Fed for all of Europe in the 1990s.

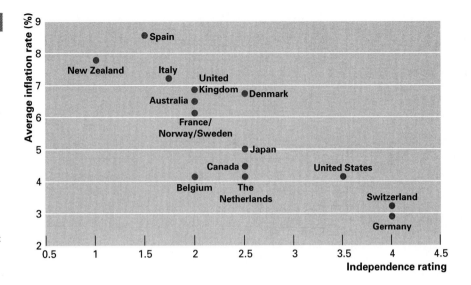

▶ FIGURE 19.3

Central Bank Independence and Inflation

Between 1955 and 1988, the greater the degree of central bank independence, the lower was the average rate of inflation. Independence is measured on a scale of 0.5 to 4.5, with 0.5 representing the greatest amount of government control.

Source: Alberto Alesina and Lawrence H. Summers, "Central Bank Independence and Macroeconomic Performance: Some Comparative Evidence," in Lawrence H. Summers, "How Should Long-Term Monetary Policy Be Determined?," *Journal of Money, Credit, and Banking,* vol 23, part 2 August 1991. Reprinted with permission of Ohio State University Press.

nine of the 16 Land Central (regional) banks, appointed by their respective state governments. The council meets biweekly to set monetary policy. The directorate makes day-to-day implementation decisions. Some analysts believed that the addition of five Land Central bank seats to accommodate former East German states would have put pressure on the Bundesbank to increase the money supply. However, the number of state seats was reduced from 11 to nine, requiring some eastern and western states to share representation. This result is similar to the Federal Reserve districts in the United States.

Finally, the overall degree of independence of the central bank varies. In Germany and Switzerland, the central bank is extremely independent, whereas the central banks of Japan, the United Kingdom, Italy, and France are much less independent.

What conclusions should be drawn from differences in central bank structure? Many analysts believe that an independent central bank improves the economy's performance by delivering a low rate of inflation with no increase in output or employment fluctuations. As Fig. 19.3 shows, the countries with the most independent central banks (Germany and Switzerland) had the lowest average rates of inflation during the 1970s and 1980s. Italy and France, with much less independent central banks, had higher rates of inflation.

Some European analysts are looking to the structure of the U.S. Federal Reserve System for guidance in designing a European central bank (see Box 19.2). However, designers of the European Monetary Union face a dilemma in attempting to balance individual national interests with decentralized administration. Dividing Europe into "EuroFed districts" across national boundaries might be one way to accomplish decentralized management without pitting European countries against one another.

MOVING FROM THEORY TO PRACTICE...

THE WALL STREET JOURNAL   AUGUST 5, 1992

Treasury Takes on the Fed

Treasury Secretary Nicholas Brady, frustrated by the Federal Reserve's failure to get the money supply growing, said he favors a review of congressional proposals to alter the Fed to make it more responsive to the economy.

In an interview with *The Wall Street Journal,* Mr. Brady said the Bush administration "could undertake some useful exploration" of proposals made by Rep. Lee Hamilton (D., Ind.), co-chairman of the Joint Economic Committee.

Mr. Hamilton has proposed, among other things, blocking presidents of the district Federal Reserve banks from voting on monetary policy, on grounds that they are appointed by private-sector bank directors without presidential or congressional review. He has also called for requiring regular meetings between administration economic officials and the entire Fed policy-making committee.

Mr. Brady said the Treasury hasn't begun studying on its own whether to restructure the Fed, but he said he is interested in "bringing Fed deliberations closer to the actual circumstances in the economy." He added, "I don't think we should change the basic theory of Fed independence. That's stood us well over the years."

His expression of interest in restructuring the Fed is a clear shot across the central bank's bow. Mr. Brady partly blames the Fed for the current sluggishness of the U.S. economy. "In my opinion, you cannot have satisfactory growth in the economy with a negative money supply," he said. The *M2* measure of the money supply—currency, checking accounts, money market funds and some certificates of deposit—has been shrinking since February.

Fed Chairman Alan Greenspan has argued that the traditional link between the money supply and the economy seems to be broken and that weak money growth doesn't necessarily presage a weakening economy. Mr. Greenspan argues that even though the Fed hasn't managed to increase the money supply as con-

ventionally measured, it has reduced short-term interest rates substantially.

Usually, Fed action to pump credit into the economy both increases the money supply and reduces short-term rates; Mr. Greenspan has said the Fed is still examining the reasons that isn't happening now...

Although Rep. Hamilton's bill isn't moving on Capitol Hill, Fed officials take it seriously because it is backed by respected members of Congress, it isn't as radical as some past proposals, and it comes at a time of anxiety about the economy. The legislation would also require the Open Market Committee to meet three times a year with the secretary of the Treasury, the White House budget director and the chairman of the Council of Economic Advisers. It also would give every president the right to pick a new Fed chairman one year after his inauguration; Fed chairmen now serve four-year terms that don't always coincide with the president's.

ANALYZING THE NEWS...

Although the Federal Reserve System has considerable independence from the executive branch, the president's leverage is greatest when a Fed chairman is to be appointed or reappointed. In 1991, shortly before President Bush renominated Alan Greenspan as chairman, Treasury Secretary Nicholas Brady urged Greenspan to adopt a "pro-growth" monetary policy.

(a) Brady's arguments reflect the belief that policymaking affecting the economy—including monetary policy—should be in the hands of elected officials. If the public interest view of the Fed's behavior is correct, the Fed's monetary policy was appropriate, even though Secretary Brady disagreed. In terms of the principal-agent view, the Greenspan Fed's constituency would have been anti-inflation bond markets, which normally favor slow rates of growth of the money supply. Analysts disagreed at the time over which view of the Fed's motivation was most believable.

(b) Does its failure to increase the money supply at the rate it publicly favored mean that the Fed was misleading the public about its objectives? Not necessarily. Remember that the money supply (here $M2$) equals the monetary base times the money multiplier. In the few months prior to Secretary Brady's remarks, the $M2$ multiplier fell, even though the monetary base was rising.

(c) Some analysts believe that Representative Hamilton's proposal increases the Fed's accountability for inflation. Others express concern that its enactment would lead to a political business cycle, in which money supply growth would rise prior to elections. Still others worry that higher rates of money growth, on average, would compound this effect, leading to higher inflation.

For further thought...

Suppose that the FOMC decides to increase the growth of the money supply and cut the discount rate. At the same time, senior administration officials argue publicly that more rapid money growth is needed to stimulate the economy. Under the public interest view, would the FOMC be more or less likely to proceed with its intentions? Why?

Source: Excerpted from David Wessel and Rick Wartzman, "Brady Backs Review of Plans to Alter Fed," August 5, 1992. Reprinted by permission of *The Wall Street Journal*, © 1992 Dow Jones & Co., Inc. All Rights Reserved Worldwide.

Key Terms and Concepts

Federal Reserve System
    Federal Reserve bank
    Member banks
    Board of Governors
    Federal Open Market Committee

Political business cycle
Principal-agent view
Public interest view

Summary

1. The Federal Reserve Act of 1913 created the U.S. Federal Reserve System (the Fed). Its three principal components are the Federal Reserve banks, Board of Governors, and Federal Open Market Committee (FOMC).

2. The Fed's formal activities are open market operations, reserve requirements, and discount policy. The FOMC issues guidelines for open market operations. The Board of Governors sets reserve requirements. Depository institutions obtain discount loans through district Federal Reserve banks, although the Board of Governors essentially determines the discount rate (the interest rate charged on discount loans).

3. In practice, power within the Federal Reserve System is more centralized than is apparent from the official structure. The Board of Governors, especially its chairman, typically dominates monetary policy decisions.

4. The Fed is relatively independent of the political process, owing to the long-term appointments of members of the Board of Governors and to the Fed's financial independence. However, because the Federal Reserve System was created by legislation, not by the Constitution, Congress could reduce its power (or even eliminate it) through the legislative process.

5. The public interest view of Fed motivation argues that the Fed pursues monetary policies and financial regulation in the broad national interest. Alternatively, the principal-agent view stresses that the Fed is more interested in enhancing its own well-being as an organization than it is in the national interest.

6. Should the Fed be independent? Some argue that it should because its longer time horizon (relative to those of elected officials) enables it to pursue monetary policies in the long-term interest of the nation. Critics of central bank independence note that monetary policy is an important part of the national policy agenda and hence should be controlled by elected officials.

7. The degree of independence from the political process and the general procedures for appointing governors vary for central banks of other industrialized countries. Countries having relatively independent central banks generally have lower inflation rates than do countries having less independent central banks.

Review Questions

1. What are the Board of Governors' duties and responsibilities with regard to monetary policy?

2. Who are the voting members of the Federal Open Market Committee?

3. Where does most of the Fed's income come from?

4. What features of the Fed help make it independent of political pressure? How does the U.S. Constitution protect the Fed?

5. How many district Federal Reserve banks are there? Where are they located?

6. Who guides the open market operations of the Fed?

7. Why do Federal Reserve districts cut across some state lines and why do the directors of the district banks represent business, banking, and the general public?

8. Is speculation in shares of stock of the Federal Reserve banks possible? Why or why not?

9. What are the duties of Federal Reserve banks?

10. *Evaluate:* The Federal Reserve System is independent of the political process in the United States.

11. *Evaluate:* In order to conduct monetary policy in the national interest, the Federal Reserve System should be independent of the political process in the United States.

12. *Evaluate:* The Fed's independence from the government's appropriations process necessarily rules out the principal-agent view of Fed motivation.

Analytical Problems

13. Suppose that you are the president of the country Moolah and that you are writing a new constitution for it. Would you give monetary policymakers complete independence from your government? Why or why not?

14. Research shows that nine to 18 months after the Fed eases monetary policy, the economy shows increased real growth. Suppose that you observe that, on average, monetary policy was more expansionary than normal 18 months before a presidential election. What would you conclude about the Fed's motivation?

15. Research shows that nine to 18 months after the Fed eases monetary policy, the economy shows increased real growth. Suppose that 18 months before a presidential election the Fed announces a reduction of the discount rate by 1 percentage point. What would you conclude about the Fed's motivation? Would your conclusion change if, six months earlier, real output growth had been forecast to be 3%, but the economy weakened and real output grew by only 1%?

16. Why might the president *not* want to appoint a tough-minded, independent chairman of the Federal Reserve Board of Governors but prefer someone with whom he or she had previous political ties?

17. Are the high rates of inflation that the United States experienced during the 1970s consistent with the public interest view of the Fed's motivation?

18. Is the principal-agent view of the Fed's motivation believable if Fed policymakers routinely turn down jobs on Wall Street that would double or triple their salaries?

19. A recent proposal would remove the presidents of the Federal Reserve banks from the FOMC and add the Secretary of the Treasury and the chair of the President's Council of Economic Advisers to the FOMC. What would such a proposal do to the Fed's independence? Would it make the Fed more accountable for its actions? How would regional concerns and information be communicated to the Fed?

20. Suppose that economic conditions worsen and that the Fed considers easing monetary policy. But before the Fed can act, the president's chief economic advisor holds a press conference and states that the Fed should ease its policy to stimulate the economy. Does this statement make easing the policy less or more difficult for the Fed? Why?

21. In Japan the central bank is not formally independent. Yet Japan's inflation rate is much lower than that of the United States. Does this condition suggest that low inflation doesn't really depend on central bank independence? Why or why not?

22. *Evaluate:* The Fed's occasional mobilization of banking interests to defend itself against legislative attacks is inconsistent with the public interest view of Fed motivation.

23. During the debate in 1991 over reform of U.S. banking regulations, the Treasury advocated removal of barriers between banking and commerce (for example, allowing nonfinancial firms to own depository institutions), but the Fed opposed such a move. Offer an explanation of the Fed's response in terms of (a) the public interest view of Fed motivation and (b) the principal-agent view of Fed motivation.

Data Questions

24. In the *Federal Reserve Bulletin*, the Federal Reserve Open Market Transactions table lists the changes in the Fed's holdings of U.S. government and other securities in the System Open Market Account. Determine how much its holdings have changed during the past three years. In which year has monetary policy been the "easiest"? In which year has it been the "tightest"?

25. In the latest *Annual Report of the Board of Governors of the Federal Reserve System*, look up the table that reports historical data on Income and Expenses of Federal Reserve banks. Find the column that lists payments to the U.S. Treasury—the Fed's profits that are returned to the government. What is the total amount of the Fed's profits for the past three years? Now determine the total amount of U.S. federal government revenue for the past three years from the *Economic Report of the President*. What proportion of the government's total revenue was the Fed's income?

CHAPTER 20

Monetary Policy Tools

It was the perfect holiday gift for financial markets and the economy. On Friday, December 20, 1991, the Fed announced a reduction in the discount rate of a full percentage point to 3.5%, the lowest level in 24 years. Chairman Greenspan suggested that the change in the discount rate signaled an attempt by the Fed to stimulate the U.S. economy as it recovered from the recession that began in 1990. Most analysts later agreed that the Fed's action helped the economy's recovery.

This episode illustrates one of the ways the Fed—like central banks in other countries—uses its monetary policy tools to aect the money supply and interest rates. But *how* does the Fed influence the money supply process with these tools? In this chapter, we analyze three monetary policy tools: open market operations, discount policy, and reserve requirements. Understanding how the Fed uses these tools will give you greater insight into how it actually influences the money supply process. We combine these tools to study the determination of the federal funds rate and the level of reserves. Using this analysis, you too can be a Fed watcher and predict actions that the Fed might take and their effects on the economy.

In this chapter we focus on two questions. **Q.:** How does the Fed use its three monetary policy tools to influence the money supply? **Q.:** What is a summary measure of the Fed's intentions?

Open Market Operations

Open market operations are purchases and sales of securities in financial markets by the Fed. They are the dominant means by which the Fed attempts to change the monetary base. Recall that an open market purchase increases the monetary base (generally by increasing bank reserves) and that an open market sale decreases the monetary base (Chapters 17 and 18). If the money multiplier is relatively stable, the Fed can use open market operations to regulate the money supply by changing the monetary base.

The Fed generally conducts open market operations in liquid Treasury securities markets. (Not all countries have liquid markets for government securities, as Box 20.1 shows.) These transactions affect interest rates in those markets. An open market purchase of Treasury securities increases their price, all else being equal, thereby decreasing their yield and expanding the money supply. Changes in yields on Treasury securities affect other interest rates as well. Recall that differences in the yields on various assets reflect differences in expected returns, adjusted for default risk, liquidity, and information characteristics (Chapter 7). An open market sale decreases the price of Treasury securities, thereby increasing their yield and contracting the money supply. Open market purchases tend to reduce interest rates and so are viewed as *expansionary;* open market sales tend to increase interest rates and so are viewed as *contractionary.*

To analyze the usefulness of open market operations as a monetary policy tool for the Fed, we examine how the Fed directs and conducts such operations and how Fed watchers can interpret its statements about them to understand its intentions for monetary policy.

Consider this...   BOX 20.1

How Open Market Operations Differ in the United States and Japan

The relative importance of different tools used by central banks to influence the money supply process varies among countries. The reason for this difference lies in the organization of domestic financial markets and institutions. For instance, in the United States, open market operations are an important policy tool for the Fed because of the existence of a liquid market for government securities. In contrast, the Bank of Japan historically hasn't relied on open market operations because, until recently, a market for government securities didn't exist. Japan issued its first six-month treasury bills in 1986 and its first three-month treasury bills in 1989. Until then the Japanese central bank had used interest rate controls and direct discount lending to banks to influence the money supply in the *Gensaki* market. That market conducts transactions by the Bank of Japan for repurchase agreements, is open to financial institutions and nonfinancial corporations, and has been free of interest rate regulations since its inception in 1949. Nevertheless, the government treasury bill market in Japan remains quite small. Economists studying the Japanese financial system predict that the market for short-term government securities will grow during the 1990s, providing a better environment for open market operations by the Bank of Japan.

Directing Open Market Operations

The original Federal Reserve Act didn't specifically mention open market operations because they weren't well understood in financial markets at that time. The Fed began to use open market purchases as a policy tool during the 1920s, when it acquired World War I Liberty Bonds from banks, enabling them to finance more business loans. Before 1935, district Federal Reserve banks conducted limited open market operations in securities markets with little coordination. The lack of concerted intervention by the Fed during the banking crisis of the early 1930s led Congress to establish the Federal Open Market Committee (FOMC) to guide open market operations. [Recall that the FOMC considers various monetary policy questions in addition to open market operations (Chapter 19).]

How does the FOMC guide open market operations? It meets eight times a year (or roughly every six weeks) and produces a **general directive** that states its overall objectives for monetary aggregates and/or interest rates. These directives are less precise than reserve requirement and discount rate policies because, lacking perfect foresight, the FOMC can't determine exactly the amount of open market purchases or sales that are necessary to achieve its objectives.

Implementing Open Market Operations

The Federal Reserve System's account manager (a vice president of the Federal Reserve Bank of New York) carries out the FOMC's instructions about open market operations. The **Open Market Trading Desk,** a group of traders at the Federal Reserve Bank of New York, trades government securities over the counter by electronic means with primary dealers, private dealers permitted to trade directly with the Fed. Before making transactions, the trading desk notifies all the dealers at the same time, asks them to submit offers, and gives them a deadline. The Fed's account manager goes over the list, accepts the best offers, and then has the trading desk buy or sell the securities until it reaches the Fed's desired goal. These securities are either added or subtracted from the portfolios of the various Federal Reserve banks according to their shares of total assets in the system.

How does the account manager know what to do? The manager interprets the FOMC's most recent directive, holds daily conferences with two members of the FOMC, and personally analyzes financial market conditions. Then the manager compares the level of reserves in the banking system with the desired level indicated by the directive. If the level suggested by the directive is greater than actual bank reserves, the account manager conducts open market purchases of securities to raise the level of bank reserves toward the desired level. If the level suggested by the directive is less than actual reserves, the account manager conducts open market sales of securities to lower reserves toward the desired level.

One way the account manager conducts open market operations is through **outright purchases and sales** of Treasury securities of various maturities by the trading desk, that is, by buying from or selling to dealers. More commonly, however, the manager uses **Federal Reserve repurchase agreements** (analogous to commercial bank repos discussed in Chapter 13). Through these agreements the Fed buys securities from a dealer in the government securities market, and the dealer agrees to buy them back at a given price at a specified future date, usually within one week. In effect, the government securities serve as collateral for a short-term loan. For open market sales, the trading desk often engages in **matched sale-purchase transactions** (sometimes called *reverse repos*) in which the Fed sells securities to dealers in the government securities market, and the dealers agree to sell them back to the Fed in the near future.

In conducting the Fed's open market operations, the trading desk makes both dynamic and defensive transactions. Open market operations aimed at achieving the changes in monetary policy desired by the FOMC are known as **dynamic transactions.** A much greater volume of open market transactions are **defensive transactions,** which the Fed uses to offset fluctuations in the monetary base arising from disturbances in portfolio allocation preferences of banks and the nonbank public, financial markets, and the economy. In other words, the Fed uses defensive transactions to offset the effects of disturbances to the monetary base, not to change monetary policy. Hence merely observing the Fed's trading activity doesn't necessarily provide reliable information regarding the Fed's *intentions* for monetary policy. For example, the Fed could acquire securities one day and dispose of securities the next day, while pursuing the same overall monetary policy.

Defensive open market operations may be used for either predictable or unexpected events. For example, the nonbank public predictably increases its demand for currency before Christmas and other holidays and in response to seasonal preferences for travel. Fluctuations in certain types of borrowing affect the monetary base and also may be predicted: Borrowing within the banking system occurs every other Wednesday to satisfy reserve requirements; and the U.S. Treasury, foreign governments, and large corporations often sell or buy blocks of securities at announced intervals. Other, less predictable, disturbances come from the Treasury or the Fed. Although the Treasury attempts to synchronize withdrawals from its bank accounts with its bill paying (in order to avoid large shifts in the currency or reserves), it doesn't always succeed. Disruptions in the Fed's own balance sheet caused by Federal Reserve float or changes in discount loans, the amount of Treasury coins outstanding, or the Treasury's holdings of Federal Reserve Notes also represent a significant source of short-term fluctuations in the monetary base. Fluctuations in Treasury deposits with the Fed and in Federal Reserve float are the most important of the unexpected disturbances to the monetary base.

However, not all defensive transactions are aimed at shifts in the monetary base. Even if the monetary base remains constant, movements of currency between the nonbank public and bank reserves affect the volume of bank deposits because of multiple deposit expansion or contraction. Economic disturbances (for example, major strikes or natural disasters) also cause fluctuations in the demand for currency and bank reserves. The Fed's account manager must try to anticipate unintended increases or decreases in the monetary base and sell or buy securities in order to maintain the monetary policy indicated by the FOMC's guidelines. Box 20.2 summarizes a typical day for the Fed's account manager.

Interpreting FOMC Directives

Fed watchers disagree over the Fed's practice of issuing vaguely worded directives expressing its objectives for monetary aggregates. Indeed, the Fed often is criticized for not being more precise in stating its policy objectives. One explanation for the vagueness of these policy statements and FOMC directives reflects the Fed's principal-agent motivation: To avoid

---

Consider this...

BOX 20.2

A Day's Work at the Open Market Trading Desk

9:00 A.M.
The account manager begins informal discussions with market participants to obtain a sense of conditions in the government securities market. These discussions, along with data supplied by the staff of the FOMC, provide a basis for estimating how the prices of government securities will change during the trading day.

10:00 A.M.
The account manager's staff compares forecasts on Treasury deposits and information on the timing of future Treasury sales of securities with the staff of the Office of Government Finance in the Treasury Department.

10:15 A.M.
The account manager reads staff reports on forecasted shifts in the monetary base arising as a result of temporary portfolio shifts, fluctuations in financial markets or the

economy, or weather-related disturbances (for example, affecting the speed with which checks are delivered).

11:15 A.M.
After reviewing the information from the various staffs, the account manager focuses on the FOMC's directive. This directive indicates the ranges for growth rates of the monetary aggregates and the level of the federal funds rate desired. The account manager must design *dynamic* open market operations to implement changes requested by the FOMC and *defensive* open market operations to offset temporary disturbances in the monetary base predicted by the staff. The account manager places the daily conference call to at least two members of the FOMC to discuss trading strategy.

11:30 A.M.
Upon approval of the trading

strategy, the traders at the Federal Reserve Bank of New York notify the primary dealers in the government securities market of the Fed's desired transactions. Quotations for selling prices are requested if open market purchases are planned. (Recall that government securities are traded over the counter.) The traders select the lowest prices offered when making purchases and accept the highest bids when making sales.

12:30 P.M.
Soliciting quotes and trading take about 45 minutes, so that by about 12:30 P.M. the trading room at the Federal Reserve Bank of New York is less hectic. No three-martini lunch for the account manager and staff, though: they spend the afternoon monitoring conditions in the federal funds market and the level of bank reserves to get ready for the next day of trading.

being accountable for errors, the Fed states monetary policy objectives in vague terms, so that virtually any outcome can be termed a success. Advocates of this view point to both the delay in the Fed's release of minutes of FOMC meetings and the practice of reporting targets only for several monetary aggregates (for example, $M1$, $M2$, and $M3$) whose growth corresponds most closely to the Fed's target ranges.

Other economists suggest that the Fed's vagueness may be its best means of communicating information without manipulating expectations. For example, suppose that the Fed wants to increase spending in the economy. It could say that it intends to push for much lower short-term interest rates, hoping to get households and businesses to increase their spending. If the announcement achieves its objective, the Fed would not have to follow through on its plan to reduce interest rates. Therefore households and businesses take the *cheap talk* view of Fed motivation and discount Fed announcements, rendering any precise announcement of its intentions useless.

Interestingly, because of the cheap talk view, the larger the change the Fed desires in monetary policy, the more vague it should be. Small changes provide less incentive for the Fed to manipulate expectations, so the Fed can state them more precisely. Therefore legislation to force the Fed to reveal more about its objectives would be self-defeating.

Both the principal-agent view and the cheap talk view of Fed vagueness are reasonable interpretations of the Fed's motivation. Skillful Fed watchers apply the logic of both views to try to "read between the lines." By interpreting the meaning of each word in the directive, Fed watchers try to discern the Fed's policy goals, as Box 20.3 shows.

Open Market Operations' Lead Role

We noted that open market operations are the Fed's primary policy tool for influencing the monetary base and money supply. Having examined how open market operations are decided and carried out, we turn briefly to the three reasons for their predominant role in conducting monetary policy: control, flexibility, and ease of implementation.

Control.   Because the Fed initiates open market purchases and sales, it controls completely their volume. If the Fed were to use discount loans to increase or decrease the monetary base, it would be able to influence but not completely control their volume.

Flexibility.   The Fed can make both large and small open market operations. Large purchases or sales sometimes are required to carry out dynamic transactions. Also, defensive transactions call for small purchases or sales, which can be easily carried out. Finally, reversing open market operations is simple for the Fed. For example, if it decides that its open market sales have made the money supply grow too slowly, it can quickly authorize open market purchases.

Consider this...

BOX 20.3

How Do You Decode FOMC Directives?

The essence of the FOMC's policy decisions is expressed in its Domestic Policy Directive, which it issues at the end of each meeting. Fed watchers who attempt to decode the meaning of each word in the directive have found that the opening sentence usually conveys the degree of immediate reserve pressure desired by the FOMC. The typical wording is "maintain the existing degree of reserve pressure," "increase reserve pressure," or "decrease reserve pressure." Fed watchers read each word for signals of policy shifts. Modifiers such as "slightly" or "somewhat" describe the degree of change desired. After the initial statement, the directive discusses the growth rates of monetary aggregates that are consistent with the FOMC's objectives. The directive also indicates an acceptable range of fluctuation in the federal funds rate.

The wording of desired changes also conveys the FOMC's concerns. If, for example, the committee is worried about inflationary pressures, the directive may say that "slightly" greater reserve restraint "would" be acceptable, whereas "somewhat" less reserve restraint "might" be acceptable. The last paragraph usually discloses the FOMC's operational intention. For example, the last paragraph of the directive issued at the end of the FOMC's meeting on June 30–July 1, 1992 reads as follows:

In the implementation of policy for the immediate future, the Committee seeks to maintain the existing degree of pressure on reserve positions. In the context of the Committee's long-run objectives for price stability and sustainable economic growth, and giving careful consideration to economic, financial, and monetary developments, slightly greater reserve restraint might or slightly lesser reserve restraint would be acceptable in the intermeeting period [emphasis added]. The contemplated reserve conditions are

expected to be consistent with growth of M2 and M3 over the period from June through September at annual rates of about 2 and 1/2 percent, respectively.

The italicized portion appears to indicate no direction. However, Fed watchers likely would interpret "slightly lesser reserve restraint would be acceptable" as indicating an expansionary intent. As a result, Fed watchers might predict more rapid growth in the money supply in the future and a lower federal funds rate. Indeed, at the June meeting some FOMC members felt that this directive, coming after the more strongly worded request for easing growth from the May meeting, would send a signal that the Fed would allow significant growth in the money supply. Fed watchers trying to decode directives often urge the Fed to make its directives public more quickly.

Ease of Implementation. The Fed can implement its securities transactions rapidly, with no administrative delays. All that is required is for the trading desk to place buy and sell orders with dealers in the government securities markets.

Discount Policy

Discount policy, which includes setting the discount rate and terms of discount lending, is the oldest of the Federal Reserve's principal tools for regulating the money supply. Discount policy affects the money supply by influencing the volume of discount loans, which are included in the monetary base. An increase in the volume of discount loans raises the monetary base and the money supply, whereas a decrease in the volume of discount loans reduces the monetary base and the money supply. The discount rate at which the Fed lends funds to depository institutions and its general attitude toward discount lending depend on the effects it wants to have on the money supply. The **discount window** is the means by which the Fed makes discount loans to banks, serving as a channel through which the liquidity needs of banks can be met.

Before 1980 (except for a brief period during 1966), the Fed made discount loans only to banks that were members of the Federal Reserve System. Indeed, banks perceived the ability to borrow from the Fed through the discount window as an advantage of membership, which partially offset the cost of the tax associated with reserve requirements. Since 1980, all depository institutions have had access to the discount window. Each Federal Reserve bank maintains its own discount window.

Using the Discount Window

The Fed influences the volume of discount loans in two ways: It sets the price of loans (the discount rate) and affects the quantity of loans by the terms it sets.

We can describe the *price effect* of a change in the discount rate as follows. Suppose that the Fed increases the discount rate. As the discount rate rises, banks reduce their borrowing at the discount window. Hence an increase in the discount rate decreases the volume of discount loans, reducing the monetary base and the money supply. In addition, the higher discount rate exerts upward pressure on other short-term interest rates when banks try to raise funds from other sources, such as by borrowing in the federal funds market or by issuing certificates of deposit. A decrease in the discount rate may lead to the opposite result: The volume of discount loans rises, increasing the monetary base and the money supply. However, there is no guarantee that banks will borrow from the discount window when the discount rate declines. If profitable lending and investment opportunities aren't available, banks may not increase their discount borrowing.

To analyze how the Fed influences the volume of discount loans, let's consider how it makes such loans. The Fed uses the discount window to make one of three types of loans: adjustment credit, seasonal credit, and extended credit. Temporary, short-term **adjustment credit** loans to depository institutions help them avoid more costly means of liquidity management. Temporary, short-term **seasonal credit** loans satisfy seasonal liquidity requirements of smaller depository institutions in geographical areas where agriculture or tourism are important. These loans reduce banks' costs of maintaining excess cash or seasonally liquidating loans and investments. Longer-term **extended credit** loans are made to a financial institution under exceptional circumstances to facilitate transition from severe liquidity problems to financial health. An example is the more than $5 billion in discount loans extended to Continental Illinois Bank in 1984 before its takeover by the FDIC.

Three discount policy issues have generated spirited discussion among economists and policymakers: (1) policing the discount window, (2) averting financial crises, and (3) forecasting the Fed's intentions for monetary policy. This last issue is particularly interesting, because, as we show, shifts in discount policy may signal Fed intentions about changes in interest rates and the money supply.

Policing the Discount Window

Figure 20.1 shows that the discount rate in the United States generally falls below short-term market interest rates, such as the federal funds rate. As a result, using the discount window heavily is a tempting option for banks. Recall that if banks could obtain discount loans freely through the discount window, they could earn a profit from the spread between the discount rate and market interest rates. Thus the Fed would be subsidizing banks' returns on lending. It would also increase its control over the money supply process because banks would have an incentive to borrow more, thus increasing the monetary base. For this reason, the Fed strongly discourages excessive discount borrowing by using public criticism, fines, and financial audits. Making discount borrowing public decreases requests for discount loans because banks fear that their investors and depositors will perceive their borrowing as a sign of poor financial health. What constitutes "too much borrowing"? The

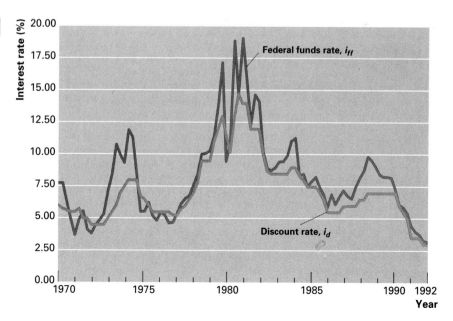

> **FIGURE 20.1**

The Discount Rate and the Federal Funds Rate
The discount rate set by the Fed generally is less than the market-determined federal funds rate. This gap gives banks an incentive to borrow from the Fed.

Source: Federal Reserve Bulletin.

answer isn't always precise, though sometimes the Fed's behavior suggests a rule of thumb (for example, the Fed may censure a bank that borrows in more than half the weeks during a certain period).

Over the years, many economists have suggested that the discount rate be set higher than short-term market rates, effectively making it a penalty rate. Borrowing would not offer profit opportunities, so banks would borrow only if they truly needed the liquidity. The Bank of England follows this strategy and sets its discount rate at one-half of a percentage point higher than the market interest rate on short-term government securities. Since the late 1970s the Fed sometimes has adjusted its discount rate in response to changes in short-term market rates. Thus, when market interest rates fall, the Fed decreases the discount rate to aid bank borrowing to meet liquidity needs; when market interest rates rise, the Fed increases the discount rate to limit profit opportunities from discount borrowing. Discount borrowing increases when market interest rates rise relative to the discount rate. Nonetheless, because the volume of discount loans is small even when the federal funds rate significantly exceeds the discount rate, the conclusion is that the Fed generally polices the discount window successfully.

Averting Financial Crises

The discount window provides the most direct way for the Fed to act as a lender of last resort to the banking system. Open market operations can change the level of bank reserves and affect short-term interest rates (such as the federal funds rate), but they can't address well the illiquidity problems of individual banks. Hence the Fed relies more on discount lending in its role as lender of last resort.

The Fed extends discount loans at its discretion, and economists continue to debate the merits of this practice. Some analysts believe that an overly generous discount policy during financial crises encourages too much risk taking by banks and the nonfinancial corporations that borrow from them. The reason is that banks, knowing that the Fed provides discount loans at favorable terms during business downturns, enforce credit standards less strictly, as happened during the 1980s (Chapter 15).

Other analysts praise the Fed's discount window interventions, such as those that took place during the Penn Central crisis of 1970, the Franklin National Bank crisis of 1974, the Hunt Brothers silver manipulation efforts in 1980, the Continental Illinois Bank collapse in 1984, and the stock market crash of October 1987. They conclude that these cases indicate the need for the Fed to continue its use of the discount window to extend credit on a case-by-case basis as a lender of last resort during financial crises.

Interpreting Fed Policy: The Announcement Effect

Because the Fed changes the discount rate infrequently relative to the continuous movement in market interest rates, Fed watchers pay close attention to announcements of such changes, which may indicate major policy changes. Changes in the volume of discount loans themselves do not significantly affect the money supply, so Fed watchers look to discount rate changes for signals of the Fed's *intentions*. For example, if market interest rates rise and the Fed doesn't then increase the discount rate, analysts might interpret the Fed's inaction either as a belief that the increase will be temporary or as an indication that it will make open market purchases to decrease short-term rates. Similarly, an increase in market rates followed by an increase in the discount rate might be interpreted as a commitment by the Fed to higher interest rates and more restrictive credit conditions. Fed watchers' guesses when market interest rates fall and the Fed does or doesn't decrease the discount rate also are easy to imagine. Fed watchers must look for *clues* of the Fed's intentions because the Fed makes its policy decisions known only after a six-week delay.

This interpretation of Fed intentions, called the **announcement effect,** illustrates the importance of new information for determining changes in security prices and returns. Recall that the *efficient markets hypothesis* (Chapter 10), implies that all available information is incorporated into market prices. Thus, when the announcement of a change in the discount rate communicates new information about future Fed policy, short-term market interest rates can change in an efficient market.

In late December 1991, for example, the Fed cut the discount rate by a full percentage point to 3.5% (and additional smaller cuts followed in 1992). Because the Fed had been reducing the discount rate gradually since the economy entered a recession in 1990, the big change signaled that the Fed was interested in expansion. The signals materialized in other interest rates. Within 90 minutes of the Fed's announcement, Morgan Guaranty Trust Company in New York cut its prime lending rate by a full percentage point, and many other major banks followed Morgan's lead. At the same time, long-term interest rates fell to levels not experienced for four years.

Using Discount Policy for Monetary Control

The main use of discount policy by the Fed is in its role of *lender of last resort* to financial institutions. Indeed, the Fed's successes in handling the Penn Central crisis in the commercial paper market in 1970 and the stock market crash of 1987 suggest that decisive discount policy can reduce the costs of financial disturbances to the economy.

Nonetheless, few economists advocate the use of discount policy as a tool of *monetary control.* Fluctuations in the spread between the federal funds rate and the discount rate set by the Fed can cause unintended increases or decreases in the monetary base and the money supply. Moreover, because of the announcement effect, analysts always try to anticipate the likely effects of a change in the discount rate on the money supply now and in the future. Finally, the Fed doesn't control discount policy as completely as it controls open market operations, and changing discount policy is much more difficult than changing open market operations. Hence, the Fed doesn't use discount policy as its principal tool for influencing the money supply.

▶ **C H E C K P O I N T** *As you are reading* The Wall Street Journal, *you notice that short-term market interest rates (such as the federal funds rate or the yields on three-month Treasury bills) have been declining but that the Fed hasn't reduced its discount rate. Are the Fed's intentions for monetary policy expansionary or contractionary?* The Fed may be trying to signal to financial markets that it wants short-term rates to rise. In that case, the Fed would be signaling a contractionary policy. ◀

Reserve Requirements

The Fed mandates that banks hold a certain fraction of their deposits in cash or deposits with the Fed. These **reserve requirements** are the last of the Fed's three principal monetary tools that we examine. In Chapter 17 we stated that the required reserve ratio is a determinant of the money multiplier in the money supply process. Recall that an increase in the required reserve ratio reduces the money multiplier and the money supply, whereas a reduction in the required reserve ratio increases the money multiplier and the money supply. Reserves can be stored as vault cash in banks or as deposits with the Federal Reserve. About 90% of banks meet their reserve requirements with vault cash. However, the other 10% comprise larger banks whose deposits at Federal Reserve banks account for more than 75% of all deposits. Hence most reserves are held as deposits with the Fed.

The Board of Governors sets reserve requirements within congressional limits, an authority granted by Congress in the Banking Act of 1935. Historically, reserve requirements varied geographically, with member banks in large cities required to hold more reserves relative to deposits than banks in smaller cities and towns. This difference dates back to 1864, following the passage of the National Banking Act of 1863, which reflected common political compromises between rural and urban interests. Representatives of agricultural states feared abuse by large eastern banks. To garner these representatives' support for the National Banking Act (1863) and later the Federal Reserve Act (1913), Congress authorized low reserve requirements for country banks. Between 1966 and 1972, the Fed altered reserve requirements to reflect the size as well as location of depository institutions. In 1980, the Depository Institutions Deregulation and Monetary Control Act established uniform reserve requirements for all depository institutions regardless of size or location.

Changes in Reserve Requirements

The Fed changes reserve requirements much more rarely than it conducts open market operations or changes the discount rate. Thus Fed watchers view the announcement of a change in reserve requirements as reflecting a major shift in monetary policy. Because changes in reserve requirements require significant alterations in banks' portfolios, frequent changes would be disruptive. As a result, in the 30 years between 1950 and

1980, the Fed adjusted required reserve ratios gradually (about once a year) and followed changes by open market operations or discount lending to help banks adjust.

During the 1980s, the only changes in reserve requirements were shifts mandated by the Depository Institutions Deregulation and Monetary Control Act. Examples were a reduction (from November 1980 through October 1983) in the maturity of nonpersonal time deposits subject to a 3% reserve requirement (from four years to 18 months) and the automatic adjustment of the level of checkable deposits subject to the 3% requirement. In 1990, the Fed lowered reserve requirements on certain other time deposits to zero. In 1992, it reduced the reserve requirement on checkable deposits to 3% on the first $46.8 million and 10% on those in excess of $46.8 million. Eurocurrency liabilities and nonpersonal time deposits currently have no reserve requirement.

Measurement and Compliance

Every two weeks the Fed monitors compliance with its reserve requirements by checking a bank's daily deposits, average daily balances, and liabilities. These two-week *maintenance periods* begin on a Thursday and end on a Wednesday. For each period, the Fed measures the bank's daily deposits with Federal Reserve banks. It calculates the average daily balances in the bank's transactions accounts over a two-week period ending the previous Monday. The Fed also checks the bank's vault cash over a two-week period ending the Monday three days before the maintenance period begins. These built-in accounting lags give the Fed time to analyze the reserve-deposit ratio and give the bank time to adjust its portfolio.

If a bank can't meet its reserve requirements, it can carry up to 4% or $50,000, whichever is greater, of its required reserves to the next two-week maintenance period. If this carryover proves inadequate and the bank still is deficient, the Fed charges interest on the deficit at a rate 2% above the discount rate. This higher rate gives banks an incentive to satisfy reserve requirements. (Similarly, a bank can carry forward up to 4% surplus of required reserves in anticipation of future deficits.) A bank with inadequate reserves also may borrow funds in the federal funds market or from the Fed through the discount window. The federal funds market can be very active on Wednesdays, when maintenance periods end, as banks try to meet their reserve requirements.

Effects of Reserve Requirements

Reserve requirements have an important cost: Reserves earn no interest, so the use of reserve requirements to control the money supply process effectively places a tax on bank intermediation. In other words, by not being able to lend reserves, banks face a higher cost on funds they obtain from depositors. For example, suppose that banks pay depositors 5% on deposits and that the required reserve ratio is 10%. On a deposit of $100, the bank must keep $10 in reserves and may loan the remaining $90. It must pay depositors $5 in interest, so its cost of funds to lend $90 is ($5/$90)(100) = 5.6%, rather than 5%.

As the Other times, other places box shows, large increases in reserve requirements can adversely affect the economy. Increasing the tax on bank intermediation reduces bank lending, which decreases credit availability and the money supply.

Because reserve requirements are a tax on bank deposits and because unwise changes in reserve requirements may have bad economic consequences, economists and policymakers often debate whether the Fed *should* set reserve requirements. Over the years, they have offered two arguments in support of reserve requirements: the liquidity argument and the monetary control argument. To analyze whether the Fed should set reserve requirements, we need to find out how well each argument stands up to close scrutiny.

Liquidity Argument. Recall that bank intermediation, by which liquid deposits are transformed into relatively illiquid loans, exposes banks to liquidity risk (Chapter 13). As a result, some analysts argue that reserve

Other times, other places...
An Early Mistake in Reserve Requirements

During the banking crisis of the early 1930s, commercial banks cut back on lending and accumulated excess reserves of about $800 million by the end of 1933. Excess reserves were greater than 40% of required reserves, compared to less than 1% today. By the end of 1935, the level of excess reserves reached more than $3 billion, or about 115% of required reserves. The newly created Federal Open Market Committee (FOMC) worried that significant levels of excess reserves would eliminate its ability to dominate the money supply process. For example, an economic upturn could lead banks to reduce their excess reserves, thereby expanding the money supply.

The Fed needed to find a way to reduce the level of reserves. Large-scale open market sales of securities weren't possible; at about $2.5 billion, the Fed's portfolio of government securities wasn't large enough to eliminate banks' excess reserves. As a result, after it obtained control over the setting of reserve requirements in 1935, the Fed's first significant change was a series of increases in required reserve ratios between August 1936 and May 1937. These effectively doubled the level of required reserves relative to deposits.

This strategy was unsuccessful because bank holdings of excess reserves reflected deliberate portfolio allocation decisions. Hence, when the Fed increased reserve requirements, banks maintained their high excess reserves by cutting back on loans. This decline in bank lending made credit unavailable for many borrowers. Many economists blame the large reduction in the growth of the money supply and in the supply of bank credit as important causes of the business recession in 1937 and 1938. As bank lending declined, the Fed was pressured to reduce reserve requirements, which it did.

requirements create a liquid pool of funds to assist illiquid, but solvent, banks during a banking panic. One problem with this argument is that, although reserve requirements do produce a pool of liquid funds for the banking system as a whole, they have a limited effect on the liquidity of an individual bank. The decision to hold liquid assets is a portfolio allocation decision made by a bank. Reserve requirements limit the funds available for a bank to invest in loans or securities, but they don't eliminate the need to maintain some portion of these funds in liquid assets. Individual banks still need to hold some of their portfolios in marketable securities as a cushion against unexpected deposit outflows.

Another problem with the liquidity argument is that the likelihood of a liquidity crisis depends not only on the volatility of withdrawals from banks, but also on the volatility of the value of bank assets and the availability to banks of nondeposit sources of funds. However, improvements in markets for loan sales and the growing number of nondeposit sources of funds make liquidity crises less likely, regardless of the volatility of depositors' withdrawals. Moreover, the Fed's ability to intervene directly in a liquidity crisis by making discount loans lessens the danger of such a crisis.

Monetary Control Argument. A second argument for reserve requirements is that they increase the central bank's control over the money supply process. Recall that the percentage of deposits held as reserves is one determinant of the money multiplier and hence of the responsiveness of the money supply to a change in the monetary base. Fed control of the reserve-deposit ratio through reserve requirements makes the money multiplier more stable and the money supply more controllable.

There are two problems with this argument. First, banks would hold reserves even if there were no reserve requirements. Hence reserve requirements need not greatly increase monetary control. Second, there is little evidence that reserve requirements actually improve the stability of the money multiplier.

Nobel laureate Milton Friedman proposed an extreme example of the monetary control argument: Banks should hold 100% reserves. Under such a system, bank reserves would equal deposits, and the monetary base (the sum of bank reserves and currency in the hands of the nonbank public) would equal the sum of currency and bank deposits, or the *M1* money supply. With 100% reserves, multiple deposit expansion would cease, giving the Fed complete control over currency plus deposits but not over the composition of deposits.

Would complete control of currency and bank deposits translate into control of the *effective* money supply? Probably not. Under a 100% reserve system, banks could not originate or hold loans. Alternative financial intermediaries would emerge to fill this lending vacuum. Because banks have special information advantages in certain types of lending, this shift in financial intermediation could be costly for the economy. Thus high reserve requirements are not likely to improve monetary control or promote financial intermediaries' role in matching savers and borrowers.

A Case in Point.   One of the initial incentives to form bank holding companies (BHCs) was the exemption of such companies' debt from reserve requirements. The Fed responded in 1970 to the growth in this alternative source of funds by imposing a 5% reserve requirement on commercial paper issued by BHCs. In October 1979, in an attempt to increase its control over the money supply, the Fed announced reserve requirements of 8% for several nondeposit sources of bank funds, including repurchase agreements, federal funds borrowing, and asset sales to foreign banks. Since passage of the Depository Institutions Deregulation and Monetary Control Act of 1980, the Fed has applied reserve requirements only to transaction accounts, Eurocurrency accounts, and nonpersonal time deposits with a maturity of less than 18 months. Hence, banks (particularly large banks) can effectively avoid the tax on intermediation as they acquire funds.

Q: How does the Fed use its three monetary policy tools to influence the money supply?

A: Reserve requirements are changed only gradually. Discount loans provide adjustment, seasonal, and extended credit to banks. Open market operations, the purchase and sale of U.S. government securities, are the primary means by which the Fed influences the money supply.

► **CHECKPOINT**   *In February 1992, the Fed reduced the reserve requirement on checkable deposits from 12% to 10%. How did your bank benefit? Did you and other depositors benefit?* In the short run your bank's profits increased; it could invest the freed funds and earn additional income from loans and investments (reserves pay no interest). In the long run, returns to depositors increased, as the bank became willing to pay more to attract deposits. ◄

Fed Watching: Analyzing the Policy Tools

All three of the Fed's principal monetary policy tools influence the monetary base primarily through changes in the demand for or supply of reserves. Hence to develop your skills as a Fed watcher (to predict what the Fed will do and how its actions will affect interest rates and the economy) you need to study carefully the market for reserves, also known as the federal funds market. Studying that market can help you predict the effect of changes in Fed policy on the level of bank reserves, R, and the federal funds rate, i_{ff}.

The Federal Funds Market

To analyze the determinants of the federal funds rate, we need to examine the banking system's demand for and the Fed's supply of reserves. We will use a graphical analysis of the demand for and supply of reserves to see how the Fed uses its policy tools to influence the federal funds rate and the money supply.

Demand.   Reserve demand reflects banks' demand for required and excess reserves. The demand function for federal funds, shown in Fig. 20.2, includes both required reserves, *RR*, and excess reserves, *ER*, for constant reserve requirements and market interest rates other than the federal funds rate. As the federal funds rate, i_{ff}, increases, banks prefer to hold a lower level of reserves; a higher federal funds rate increases the "reserve tax," so required reserves are negatively related to market interest rates. Banks' demand for excess reserves also is sensitive to interest rate changes; at a lower federal funds rate, the opportunity cost of holding excess reserves falls and the quantity of excess reserves demanded rises. Hence the total quantity demanded of reserves is negatively related to the federal funds rate.

Supply.   The supply function for reserves, also shown in Fig. 20.2, represents the supply by the Fed of borrowed reserves (discount loans) and nonborrowed reserves. Note that the supply curve is not a straight line: The vertical portion represents nonborrowed reserves, *NBR*, supplied by the Fed; that is, regardless of the federal funds rate, reserves equal to *NBR* are available. The change in slope of the supply curve occurs at the discount rate, i_d: As the federal funds rate falls below the discount rate, borrowing from the Fed is zero because banks can borrow more cheaply from other banks. Hence, in this case, reserves equal nonborrowed reserves. As the federal funds rate moves above the discount rate, borrowing increases. The slope of the supply curve indicates the sensitivity of borrowing to movements of the federal funds rate above the

►FIGURE 20.2

Equilibrium in the Federal Funds Market
Equilibrium in the market for reserves is at the intersection of the demand and supply curves. Given nonborrowed reserves *NBR* and the discount rate i_d, equilibrium reserves equal R^*, and the equilibrium federal funds rate is i_{ff}^*.

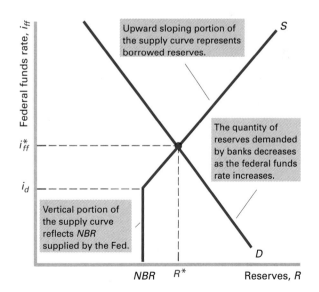

discount rate. A relatively flat slope tells you that even a small increase in the federal funds rate relative to the discount rate leads to substantial discount borrowing. A steep slope tells you that discount borrowing is less sensitive to the difference between the federal funds rate and the discount rate.

▼ FIGURE 20.3

Effects of Open Market Operations on the Federal Funds Market
As shown in (a):
1. An open market purchase of securities by the Fed increases nonborrowed reserves, shifting the supply curve to the right from S_0 to S_1.
2. Reserves increase from R_0^* to R_1^*, while the federal funds rate falls from i_{ff0}^* to i_{ff1}^*.

As shown in (b):
1. An open market sale of securities by the Fed reduces nonborrowed reserves, shifting the supply curve to the left from S_0 to S_1.
2. Reserves decrease from R_0^* to R_1^*, while the federal funds rate rises from i_{ff0}^* to i_{ff1}^*.

Equilibrium. The equilibrium federal funds rate and level of reserves occur at the intersection of the demand and supply curves in Fig. 20.2. Equilibrium reserves equal R^*, the equilibrium federal funds rate equals i_{ff}^*, and the discount rate is i_d.

Open Market Operations

Suppose that the Fed decides to purchase \$1 billion of Treasury securities. If nothing else changes, an open market purchase of securities by the Fed shifts the reserve supply curve to the right, as in Fig. 20.3(a), increasing bank reserves and decreasing the federal funds rate. As a result of the open market purchase, the volume of bank reserves increases from R_0^* to R_1^*, and the federal funds rate declines from i_{ff0}^* to i_{ff1}^*. Similarly, an open market sale of securities by the Fed shifts the reserve supply curve to the left in Fig. 20.3(b), decreasing the level of bank reserves from R_0^* to R_1^* and increasing the federal funds rate (from i_{ff0}^* to i_{ff1}^*). An open market purchase of securities by the Fed decreases the federal funds rate. An open market sale of securities increases the federal funds rate.

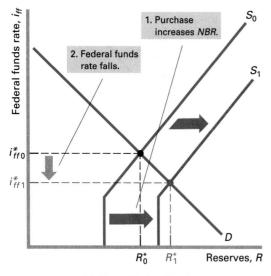

(a) Open Market Purchase

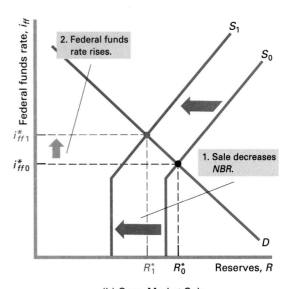

(b) Open Market Sale

Changes in Discount Rate

Now, let's examine the effects of a change in the discount rate on the level of reserves and the federal funds rate. Suppose that the Fed decides to raise the discount rate. An increase in the discount rate means that banks will find borrowing to be less attractive at any federal funds rate. Figure 20.4(a) shows that an increase in the discount rate from i_{d0} to i_{d1} lengthens the vertical part of the supply curve to the new, higher discount rate. The slope of the supply curve doesn't change, as a higher discount rate doesn't increase banks' sensitivity to changes in the federal funds rate. Less borrowing occurs at each federal funds rate because the spread between the federal funds rate and the (now higher) discount rate is smaller than before. The equilibrium level of reserves falls from R_0^* to R_1^*, and the federal funds rate rises from i_{ff0}^* to i_{ff1}^*.

Suppose that the Fed decides to cut the discount rate. In this case, banks now find borrowing more attractive at any federal funds rate. Figure 20.4(b) shows that a decrease in the discount rate shortens the vertical portion of the supply curve to the new, lower discount rate. More borrowing occurs at each federal funds rate because the spread between the federal funds rate and the (now lower) discount rate is greater than before. The equilibrium level of reserves rises from R_0^* to R_1^*, and the federal funds rate falls from i_{ff0}^* to i_{ff1}^*.

If nothing else changes, an increase in the discount rate by the Fed leads to an increase in the federal funds rate. A decrease in the discount rate leads to a decrease in the federal funds rate.

FIGURE 20.4

Effects of Changes in the Discount Rate on the Federal Funds Market
As shown in (a):
1. The Fed raises the discount rate from i_{d0} to i_{d1}.
2. The vertical portion of the supply curve lengthens; the new supply curve is S_1.
3. The level of reserves falls from R_0^* to R_1^*, and the federal funds rate rises from i_{ff0}^* to i_{ff1}^*.

As shown in (b):
1. The Fed cuts the discount rate from i_{d0} to i_{d1}.
2. The vertical portion of the supply curve shortens; the new supply curve is S_1.
3. The level of reserves rises from R_0^* to R_1^*, and the federal funds rate falls from i_{ff0}^* to i_{ff1}^*.

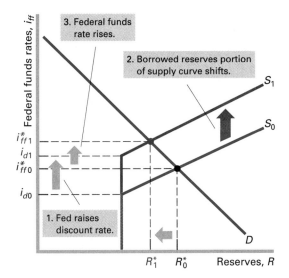

(a) Increase in the Discount Rate

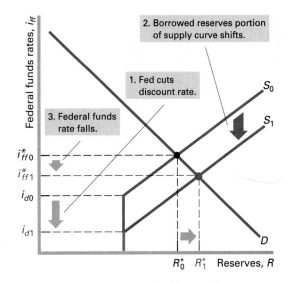

(b) Decrease in the Discount Rate

Changes in Reserve Requirements

Finally, suppose that the Fed decides to raise the required reserve ratio. Holding constant the other factors underlying the demand and supply curves for reserves, an increase in the required reserve ratio shifts the demand curve to the right (from D_0 to D_1) because banks have to hold more reserves, as in Fig. 20.5(a). As a result, the level of bank reserves increases (from R_0^* to R_1^*) and the federal funds rate increases (from i_{ff0}^* to i_{ff1}^*). However, a reduction in the required reserve ratio, as shown in Fig. 20.5(b), shifts the demand curve to the left because banks demand a smaller amount of reserves, decreasing bank reserves and the federal funds rate. If nothing else changes, an increase in reserve requirements increases the federal funds rate. A decrease in reserve requirements decreases the federal funds rate.

Other Disturbances of the Monetary Base

You can use the graphical approach to analyze other disturbances of the monetary base that might lead the Fed to conduct defensive open market operations. For example, recall that an increase in Federal Reserve float increases nonborrowed reserves (Chapter 18). Hence the supply curve for reserves shifts to the right, leading to higher reserves and a lower federal funds rate than otherwise would occur. As we noted in discussing defensive transactions earlier in this chapter, the Fed can shift the supply curve for reserves back to the left (by reducing nonborrowed reserves) with an open market sale of securities.

> ### ▼ FIGURE 20.5
>
> **Effects of Changes in Required Reserves on the Federal Funds Market**
> As shown in (a):
> 1. An increase in reserve requirements by the Fed increases required reserves, shifting the demand curve from D_0 to D_1 and raising reserves from R_0^* to R_1^*.
>
> 2. The federal funds rate rises from i_{ff0}^* to i_{ff1}^*.
>
> As shown in (b):
> 1. A decrease in reserve requirements by the Fed decreases required reserves, shifting the demand curve from D_0 to D_1 and reducing reserves from R_0^* to R_1^*.
>
> 2. The federal funds rate falls from i_{ff0}^* to i_{ff1}^*.

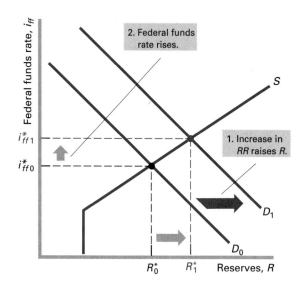

(a) Increase in Reserve Requirements

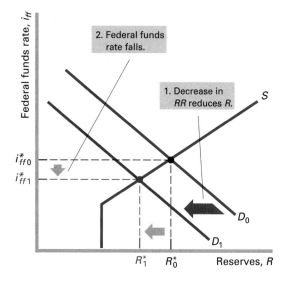

(b) Decrease in Reserve Requirements

As another example, a large increase in U.S. Treasury deposits with the Fed causes bank deposits to fall. As a result, reserves fall, the supply curve for reserves shifts to the left, and the federal funds rate rises. The Open Market Trading Desk, being in contact with the Treasury, knows about the Treasury action and therefore offsets it with another defensive open market purchase of securities. This action shifts the supply curve back to the right and restores the level of reserves and the federal funds rate to their initial levels.

The Federal Funds Rate and Monetary Policy

Many economists and financial market analysts focus on changes in the federal funds rate as a summary measure of the Fed's intentions for monetary policy. The reason is that the Fed's substantial control of the level of bank reserves gives it great influence over the level of the federal funds rate. An increase in the federal funds rate relative to other interest rates is interpreted as contractionary, signaling the Fed's intent to raise interest rates and discourage spending in the economy. Conversely, a decrease in the federal funds rate relative to other interest rates is interpreted as expansionary, signaling the Fed's intent to reduce interest rates and encourage spending.

Our graphical analysis confirms this view and shows how analysts can predict consequences of the Fed's actions for the level of reserves and the federal funds rate. Thus, if nothing else changes, an open market purchase of securities by the Fed reduces the federal funds rate. Purchases are expansionary because they increase the supply of reserves that banks use either to purchase securities or to make loans. As a result, the larger reserves in the banking system lead to lower short-term interest rates. Sales are contractionary because they reduce reserves and increase short-term interest rates. An increase in the discount rate is contractionary when it signals that the Fed wants to raise short-term interest rates. A reduction in the discount rate is expansionary when it signals that the Fed wants to reduce short-term interest rates. If nothing else changes, an increase in reserve requirements with no offsetting changes in the supply of reserves is contractionary and raises the federal funds rate. A decrease in reserve requirements is expansionary and lowers the federal funds rate.

Concluding Remarks

Fed watchers try to predict the Fed's actions regarding open market operations, discount policy, and reserve requirements in order to forecast changes in the federal funds rate. Predicting changes is the first step toward predicting the effects of monetary policy on other interest rates. However, the Fed's significant control over the federal funds rate does not imply that it can control other interest rates. Recall, for example, that the expectations theory of the term structure of interest rates states that longer-term interest rates reflect, in part, expectations of *future* short-term rates. Thus *expected future Fed actions*, not just current Fed policy, are important.

Q: What is a summary measure of the Fed's intentions?

A: The Federal Reserve System's substantial control of bank reserves gives it great influence over the level of the federal funds rate. A high federal funds rate relative to other interest rates indicates a contractionary monetary policy, whereas a low federal funds rate relative to other interest rates indicates an expansionary monetary policy.

MOVING FROM THEORY TO PRACTICE...

THE NEW YORK TIMES APRIL 10, 1992

Stepping in with the Policy Tools

Amid concern that the economic recovery remains dangerously weak, the Federal Reserve moved today to stimulate growth by pushing down an influential interest rate.

The Fed pumped more money into the nation's banking system to reduce the Federal funds rate—the rate at which banks lend each other money overnight—to 3.75 percent from 4 percent.

"The Fed has to be worried about keeping the little recovery that we have going," said Allen Sinai, economic adviser to the Boston Company...

Nervous that the sluggish economy could hurt their election chances this November, the White House and many Congressional Republicans and Democrats have in recent weeks asked the Federal Reserve to cut rates again. They repeatedly said that one reason the weak recovery that began last spring petered out last fall was that the Fed had moved too slowly to lower rates.

"This being a Presidential election year might explain why the Fed didn't want to run the risk of doing nothing, because that could abort the recovery," said Stuart Hoffman, chief economist, at the PNC Financial Corporation, a Pittsburgh-based bank holding company. "But at the same time, the Fed might have learned something from what happened last year."

The cuts in the funds rate could help bring down rates for consumer loans, adjustable-rate mortgages and loans to companies as banks pass on to consumers the lower rates they pay for money.

"Today's cut in the Federal funds rate implies a reduction in short-term interest rates across the board," said Hugh Johnson, chief economist for the First Albany Corporation, a New York-based brokerage...

Over the last two months, the Administration and many economists have voiced optimism that a recovery is taking hold based on a pickup in retail sales and housing starts. But analysts said today that the Fed had apparently become alarmed when it discovered that for the second straight week the money supply had fallen sharply. Economists say the Fed is concerned that the weak money supply numbers could push up interest rates and hamper the already fragile recovery.

Today, the Fed reported a sharp $7 billion drop last week in the most closely watched measure of the money supply, which followed an even steeper drop of more than $10 billion the previous week...

The Fed's most recent rate cuts came last Dec. 20, when it drastically lowered the Federal funds rate and the discount rate—the rate at which it lends money to banks. It lowered the discount rate a full percentage point, to 3 1/2 percent, from 4 1/2 percent, and the Fed funds rate by a half percentage point, to 4 percent from 4 1/2 percent.

ANALYZING THE NEWS...

Analysts first look for effects of the Fed's use of open market operations and discount policy in the federal funds market, the market through which banks lend to each other overnight. Actions by the Fed to push the federal funds rate down are interpreted as expansionary monetary policy, since interest rates charged to households and businesses fall, encouraging them to spend more.

a What does a reduction in the federal funds rate target from 4% to 3.75% mean? After all, the federal funds rate is a market-determined interest rate, not set by the Fed. We can illustrate what happens using the reserves market diagram. The Fed fulfills its intention to reduce the federal funds rate by increasing the supply of reserves. It conducts open market purchases to increase nonborrowed reserves. This action shifts the supply curve from S_0 to S_1, increasing reserves from R_0^* to R_1^* and reducing the federal funds rate from i_{ff0}^* to i_{ff1}^*.

b On December 20, 1991, the Fed reduced the discount rate from 4.5% to 3.5%, the largest one-day drop in more than 10 years. Policymakers and analysts praised the Fed for cutting the discount rate, believing that this step would stimulate economic recovery. They reasoned that the drop in the discount rate from i_{d0} (4.5%) to i_{d1} (3.5%) would shift the reserve supply curve from S_0 to S_1. As a result, reserves would increase from R_0^* to R_1^* and the federal funds rate would fall from i_{ff0}^* to i_{ff1}^*. To achieve a particular federal funds rate target, the Fed also can increase nonborrowed reserves, as in (a).

For further thought...

What would be the effect of a reduction in the discount rate on the yield on three-month Treasury bills? On 30-year Treasury bonds?

Source: Excerpted from Steven Greenhouse, "Fed Moves Again to Spur Growth and the Markets Respond Briskly," April 10, 1992. Copyright © 1991/1992 by The New York Times Company. Reprinted by permission.

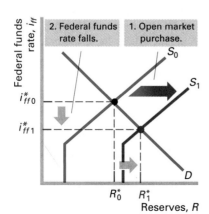

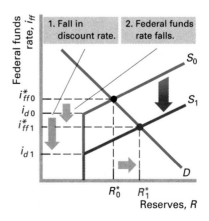

▶ C H E C K P O I N T *Suppose that you read in*
The Wall Street Journal *that the Fed raised its target for the federal funds rate by one-half*
of a percentage point. How would you expect the Fed to achieve its objective? Using the
graphical analysis of the federal funds market, you would expect the Fed to use open
market sales to reduce nonborrowed reserves, shifting the *NBR* curve to the left and raising
the federal funds rate. ◀

Key Terms and Concepts

Discount policy
  Adjustment credit
  Announcement effect
  Discount window
  Extended credit
  Seasonal credit

Open market operations
  Defensive transactions

Dynamic transactions
Federal reserve repurchase agreements
General directive
Matched sale-purchase transactions
Open market trading desk
Outright purchases and sales

Reserve requirements

Summary

1. Open market operations (purchases and sales of securities in financial markets) are the most widely used of the Fed's principal monetary policy tools. The Federal Open Market Committee issues guidelines for open market operations as general directives. Some transactions are dynamic, that is, designed to implement changes in the monetary base suggested by the FOMC. Most transactions are defensive, that is, designed to offset unintended disturbances in the monetary base.

2. The Fed's discount policy sets the discount rate and the terms of discount lending. The Fed fulfills its role as the lender of last resort by providing adjustment, seasonal, and extended credit.

3. Reserve requirements are a potent but drastic way to control the monetary base. Increases in reserve requirements decrease the money multiplier; decreases in reserve requirements increase the money multiplier. Because large changes in reserve requirements can cause costly reallocations of banks' portfolios, the Fed generally avoids them.

4. The federal funds rate is one indicator of monetary policy. A decrease in the federal funds rate relative to other market interest rates usually is associated with an expansionary monetary policy. An increase in the federal funds rate relative to other market interest rates usually is associated with a contractionary monetary policy.

Review Questions

1. Since the 1930s, what has been the Fed's most important tool for monetary policy? What part of the Federal Reserve System determines how this tool is used?

2. Why do borrowed reserves tend to rise when the federal funds rate rises?

3. What causes changes in the discount rate?

4. *Evaluate:* The Fed changes the reserve requirement frequently because it is such a powerful tool.

5. What is the maintenance period for bank reserves? How does the Fed calculate a bank's required reserves?

6. If a bank is required to hold reserves of $150 million but held only $149 million of reserves over the maintenance period, will the Fed penalize it? Why or why not?

7. What is wrong with the liquidity argument for reserve requirements?

8. Why must the Fed police the discount window? Would it need to do so if the discount rate was a penalty rate?

9. What type of credit (adjustment, seasonal, or extended) is each of the following discount loans:

   a. Bigbank borrows from the Fed because of liquidity problems when one of its major depositors suddenly switches its accounts to another bank.

   b. Fear that Megabank will fail prompts large depositors to withdraw their funds, forcing Megabank to borrow several billion dollars from the Fed for the next year.

   c. First Bank borrows $5 million so that it can make loans to farmers for planting, as it does every April.

10. What is a Fed watcher?

11. *Evaluate:* The efficient markets hypothesis implies that the market fully anticipates changes in the Fed's discount rate so that there is no announcement effect.

12. What are the two views as to why the Fed's policy statements are often vague? Could political pressure also explain the Fed's unwillingness to be precise? Why or why not?

13. In daily trading by the Open Market Trading Desk at the Federal Reserve Bank of New York, why does the account manager consult with market participants? With the Treasury department? With two or more members of the FOMC?

14. What are the differences between dynamic and defensive open market operations?

Analytical Problems

15. What interest rate is most directly affected by open market operations? What happens to this interest rate and the money supply when the Fed engages in open market purchases? When the Fed engages in open market sales?

16. If the money multiplier is 8, how large a change in the money supply will result from the sale of $1 billion of bonds by the Fed on the open market? Will the money supply increase or decrease?

17. How could the Fed use its three principal monetary policy tools to decrease the money supply by $100 million, if the money multiplier is 10 and the monetary base is $500 million?

18. What is the Fed likely to do near the Christmas holiday season, when the public uses more currency?

19. Which of the following open market operations are defensive and which are dynamic?

   a. The Treasury makes a large payment, which the Fed offsets with an open market purchase.

   b. The economy strengthens unexpectedly, to which the Fed responds with open market sales.

   c. Bad weather prevents checks from being cleared as quickly as usual, allowing float to increase in the banking system; the Fed responds with open market sales.

d. The dollar's foreign exchange value declines, prompting the Fed to respond with open market sales.

20. Suppose that, owing to an oil price shock, inflation in the economy is increasing, causing interest rates to rise. The Fed announces an increase in the discount rate. Does this signal a tightening of monetary policy? Why or why not?

21. The following list contains parts of five different directives to the trading desk from the FOMC. Rank them from most expansionary to most contractionary.

a. ...increase somewhat the existing degree of pressure on reserve positions...somewhat greater reserve restraint or somewhat lesser reserve restraint might be acceptable...

b. ...decrease somewhat the existing degree of pressure on reserve positions...somewhat greater reserve restraint or somewhat lesser reserve restraint might be acceptable...

c. ...maintain the existing degree of pressure on reserve positions...somewhat greater reserve restraint or somewhat lesser reserve restraint might be acceptable...

d. ...maintain the existing degree of pressure on reserve positions...somewhat greater reserve restraint would or slightly lesser reserve restraint might be acceptable...

e. ...maintain the existing degree of pressure on reserve positions...slightly greater reserve

restraint might or somewhat lesser reserve restraint would be acceptable...

22. On the reserves market diagram, show how the Fed can use open market operations to offset an increased demand for reserves by holding the federal funds rate constant.

23. On the reserves market diagram, show how the Fed can use discount policy to reduce the federal funds rate. First, show what would happen if the Fed reduces the discount rate (the point on the supply curve at which the slope changes moves lower). Second, show what would happen if the Fed allows more borrowing at a fixed discount rate (the sloping section of the supply curve becomes flatter).

24. For parts (a)–(d), use the graphical analysis of equilibrium in the reserves market to predict changes in nonborrowed reserves, borrowed reserves, and the federal funds rate.

a. The Fed conducts open market sales of securities.

b. The Fed discourages more strongly banks' use of the discount window.

c. Banks and the nonbank public become concerned that a banking crisis is imminent and that depositors will prefer to invest in securities in financial markets.

d. The Fed lowers the discount rate and conducts open market purchases of securities.

Data Question

25. Banks complain that reserve requirements hurt their profits because they pay interest to depositors but don't earn anything on their reserves. In the latest *Federal Reserve Bulletin*, find the table that lists reserve requirements. Suppose that a bank has $1 billion in transaction accounts. Calculate the bank's required reserves. In the same publication, look at the average federal funds rate for the past year. Multiply the federal funds rate times the amount of

required reserves to determine the cost to the bank of complying with reserve requirements. However, the bank would have held reserves for transaction purposes, even if no reserves were required. Suppose that the bank would hold 5% of its deposits in reserve, even if reserves were required. How much does this holding of nonrequired reserves reduce the bank's profits? What then is the *true* cost of reserve requirements?

21

The Conduct of Monetary Policy

In early October 1979, the Fed's Board of Governors met in an emergency session in Washington. Chairman Paul Volcker persuaded the other governors that the Fed should use its policy tools to "target" the money supply and let short-term interest rates fluctuate. Other events grabbed the newspaper headlines that weekend, but the shift in the way the Fed conducted monetary policy made headlines for years to come. During the 1980s, financial analysts devoted a great deal of time to Fed watching, trying to guess how the Fed would conduct monetary policy.

The Fed is only one of three participants in the money supply process, the other two being banks and the nonbank public. Yet, as we have shown, the Fed has more direct control over the money supply than over economic variables (such as GDP or employment or inflation). Based on an understanding of the tools of monetary policy, we now examine ways in which central banks conduct monetary policy.

In this chapter we address two questions. **Q:** How does the Fed conduct monetary policy to achieve goals related to economic variables? **Q:** Is the actual record of U.S. monetary policy consistent with the Fed's attempts to control the money supply?

Goals of Monetary Policy

Most economists and policymakers agree that the overall aim of monetary policy is to advance the economic well-being of the country's citizens. What is *economic well-being*? One definition encompasses the Fed's six **monetary policy goals:** (1) price stability, (2) high employment, (3) economic growth, (4) financial market and institution stability, (5) interest rate stability, and (6) foreign-exchange market stability.

Price Stability

Inflation, or persistently rising prices, erodes the value of money as a medium of exchange and a unit of account. Especially since inflation rose dramatically during the 1970s, U.S. economists, households, and businesses have become more concerned with its costs. As a result, policymakers have emphasized **price stability** as a policy goal. In a market economy, where prices contain important information about costs and demand, inflation makes prices less useful as signals for resource allocation. Overall price-level changes make decisions more difficult for households and firms. For example, families have trouble deciding how much to save for their children's education or for retirement; businesses hesitate to enter into long-term contracts with suppliers or customers because of uncertainty over future prices. Rates of inflation in the hundreds or thousands of percent per year—known as *hyperinflation*—can severely damage an economy's productive capacity and, in extreme cases, force citizens to take their cash in wheelbarrows to purchase groceries. For example, economic activity in Germany contracted sharply as the country experienced hyperinflation during the 1920s. The range of inflation's effects—from economic uncertainty to devastation—make price stability a desirable monetary policy goal.

High Employment

High employment, the maintenance of a low rate of unemployment, is an important monetary policy goal because a lack of jobs idles workers, underuses productive capacity (factories and machines) and lowers output (gross domestic product, GDP). Unemployment causes financial distress and decreases self-esteem for workers without jobs. The Employment Act of 1946 and the Full Employment and Balanced Growth Act of 1978 (or the Humphrey-Hawkins Act) codify the government's commitment to promote high employment consistent with price stability.

High employment doesn't necessarily imply a zero unemployment rate. Such a goal is neither practical nor in the economy's best interests. The reason is that some unemployment is *frictional unemployment*, that is, unemployment owing to workers moving in or out of the job market or being between jobs. For example, workers sometimes leave one job to pursue another and might be unemployed in the meantime. Individuals also leave the labor force to obtain more education and training or to raise a family, and reentry may take time. Hence a zero rate of unemployment would be inconsistent with a well-functioning economy in which individuals are searching for the best positions available to them.

Some unemployment always will exist, but how much coincides with the normal working of a healthy economy? Unfortunately, there is no hard and fast answer to that difficult question. In the 1960s, for example, economists and policymakers thought that the so-called natural rate of unemployment was about 4%. However, owing to structural changes in the economy, such as demographic shifts and technological advances, they now consider an unemployment rate of about 6% to represent full employment. As we point out in Chapter 28, variations in the high-employment goal and substantial uncertainty about what high employment means can lead to serious mistakes in monetary policy.

Economic Growth

Policymakers also seek steady **economic growth,** increases in the economy's output of goods and services, which raises household incomes and thereby increases government revenues. This goal partially depends on how well the goal of high employment is being met. With high employment, businesses are likely to grow by investing in new plants and equipment that raise profits, productivity, and workers' incomes. With high unemployment, businesses underutilize productive capacity and are much less likely to invest in capital improvements. Economic growth policies can provide incentives for saving to ensure a large pool of investment funds and direct incentives for business investment. For example, favorable tax treatment of business investment stimulates capital spending. In addition, *stability* of economic growth is important, as a stable business environment allows accurate planning and promotes long-term investment.

Financial Market and Institution Stability

A stable financial system makes possible efficient matching of savers and borrowers. We have already examined federal interventions aimed at increasing **financial market and institution stability,** that is, maintaining the viability of financial markets and institutions to channel funds from savers to borrowers. We noted that financial panics in the late 1800s and early 1900s led to the creation of the Federal Reserve System (Chapter 14). We also showed that, during the past two decades, the Fed's interventions in response to events in the commercial paper, stock, and commodity markets avoided financial panics. The policy goal of financial market and institution stability, of course, doesn't necessarily guarantee successful interventions. For example, federal deposit insurance reduced the severity of banking panics, but its existence might have been one cause of the crisis in financial institutions during the late 1980s and early 1990s.

Interest Rate Stability

Like fluctuations in price levels, fluctuations in interest rates make planning and investment decisions difficult for households and businesses. Because people often blame the Fed for increases in interest rates, the Fed's goal of **interest rate stability,** or limited fluctuations in interest rates on bonds, is motivated by political pressure as well as by a desire for a stable saving and investment environment.

Foreign-Exchange Market Stability

In the global economy, **foreign-exchange market stability,** or limited fluctuations in the foreign-exchange value of the dollar has become an important monetary policy goal of the Fed. Policymakers closely watch the value of the dollar relative to other currencies. A stable dollar makes planning for commercial and financial transactions simpler. In addition, fluctuations in the dollar's value affect the international competitiveness of American industry: A rising dollar makes U.S. goods more expensive abroad, reducing exports; a falling dollar makes foreign goods more expensive in the United States. Many economists urge monetary policymakers to intervene in order to offset extreme fluctuations in the foreign-exchange value of the dollar.

Possible Conflicts in Multiple Goals

Monetary policymakers may pursue more than one goal at the same time. For example, the goals of high employment and economic growth are likely to be consistent, as steady economic growth contributes to high employment. Similarly, attempts to foster stability in financial markets and institutions are likely to be consistent with interest rate stability; as stable interest rates promote stability in the net worth of financial institutions (Chapter 13). However, conflicts among goals often arise, for example, between Fed policies to promote high economic growth and those to encourage low inflation. Suppose that the Fed uses open market sales to reduce money supply growth in order to reduce inflation. Recall that open market sales likely will increase interest rates (Chapter 20), and higher interest rates likely will reduce consumer and business spending—and economic growth—in the short run. For its announced goals and actions to be believable, the Fed often has to state priorities for its goals.

Using Targets to Meet Goals

The Fed faces a basic paradox: Although it has broad goals of economic growth and price stability, it has no direct control over real output or the price level. Real output and price-level outcomes come from economic interactions of households and businesses. To influence the money supply, the

Fed has only the monetary policy tools discussed in Chapter 20: open market operations, reserve requirements, and discount policy. These tools aren't strong enough to help the Fed meet its goals directly.

Impediments to Achieving Goals

Specifically, the Fed faces two main obstacles in using its monetary policy tools to achieve its goals. The first is *information lags*, or the inability of the Fed to observe changes in GDP, inflation, or other economic variables instantaneously. Delays in receiving information about the state of the economy can lead to major policy errors. One famous instance occurred in June 1930, when President Hoover told a group of business leaders that their call for an economic stimulus package was unnecessary: "Gentlemen," he said, "you have come sixty days too late. The depression is over."[†] The economy's output continued to decline sharply until 1933. Hoover's astounding error reflected a lack of information about the economy: At that time, there were no GDP data and no regular employment data. Today the president and the Fed have much more data available, but output data are available only quarterly. Official real interest rate data are not issued by the government, and money supply data often are unreliable until checked and revised.

The second impediment facing the Fed is *impact lags*, or the time required for monetary policy changes to affect output, employment, or inflation. Changes in the monetary base translate into changes in the money supply, and changes in the money supply affect the economy over time, not immediately. Thus, if the Fed tries to focus directly on achieving full employment and price stability, its actions will affect the economy at the wrong times. Moreover, the Fed will not be able to recognize its mistakes soon enough to correct them.

Intermediate and Operating Targets

Information and impact lags make effective policymaking difficult, but the Fed cannot just throw up its hands in frustration. It needs some strategy to circumvent the lags. For much of the post–World War II period, that strategy has taken the form of intermediate targeting. **Intermediate targets** are objectives for financial variables (such as the money supply or short-term interest rates) that the Fed believes will directly help it achieve its goals.

To understand the logic of intermediate targets, imagine someone with a bow and arrow trying to hit a target that is out of sight on the other side of the hill. The archer would have to guess where the target is before shooting, then run to the top of the hill to see how close the arrow came to the target. After seeing where the arrow landed, the archer would go back

---

[†] Quoted in Arthur M. Schlesinger, Jr., *The Crisis of the Old Order*. Boston: Houghton Mifflin Company, 1957, p. 231.

down the hill and adjust the aim. Unfortunately, by the time she shoots again, wind conditions might shift, making the new aim incorrect.

The archer's life would be a lot simpler if a second target, an *intermediate target*, could be positioned at the top of the hill. This second target would be placed so that hitting it meant that the arrow would sail on and hit the bull's-eye at the bottom of the hill. The target at the top of the hill is in full view, so it will be much easier to hit than the one at the bottom of the hill. Moreover, the archer will get immediate feedback. If the new target is missed, it is obvious that the ultimate target is also being missed. No more trips up and down the hill!

The Fed is in a position similar to that of the archer. The Fed has a bow and arrow (its policy tools) which it uses to hit ultimate targets (such as price stability and full employment), which are obscured by information and impact lags. Like the archer, the Fed can do a better job of hitting its ultimate targets if it aims for an intermediate target that quickly guides its actions. Under this arrangement, the Fed would automatically adjust its tools whenever the target variable deviates from the desired level. Remember, though, that hitting an intermediate target has no intrinsic value. Rather, it only helps the Fed to reach its ultimate goals.

What constitutes a good intermediate target? First, the target should be *quickly measurable*, to overcome information lags. Second, the target should be *controllable*, to overcome impact lags. Finally, the target should be *predictably linked to one or more monetary policy goals*, to ensure relevance.

In the past the Fed used either interest rates or monetary aggregates, such as *M1* and *M2*, as intermediate targets. For example, the Fed might use statistical studies to calculate a rate of *M1* growth that is consistent with full employment and price stability. Suppose that it estimates the rate to be 3% per year but that the money supply actually grows 4% per year. The Fed then would automatically assume that it was stimulating the economy too much, setting the stage for future inflation. Its response would be to use its monetary policy tools (most likely open market operations) to slow *M1* growth to the target 3%. Hitting the *M1* growth target has no value in and by itself. It simply helps the Fed achieve its stated goals.

In fact, the Fed controls intermediate target variables, such as interest rates and monetary aggregates, only *indirectly* because private-sector decisions are dominant in the economy. Returning to the earlier example, the archer may be able to get early feedback on chances for success by observing the trajectory of the arrow as it leaves the bow. If the aim is too high to hit the target on top of the hill, the aim can be lowered for another attempt. That is, the archer can use as a second-level target this early positioning of the flying arrow; improper positioning can be corrected using "policy tools" (a new arrow).

To help improve monetary policy decisions, the Fed uses a second set of targets to help it achieve the first set. In the conduct of monetary policy, this second set of targets, called **operating targets,** are variables that the Fed can control more directly and that are closely related to the intermediate targets. Examples include the federal funds rate and nonborrowed reserves. The federal funds rate is a commonly used interest rate operating target, because the market for bank reserves, which the Fed heavily influences, determines the rate.

Thus the Fed's strategy involves two steps: (1) set an intermediate target (such as money supply growth) to help achieve goals; and (2) set an operating target (such as nonborrowed reserves growth) to help achieve the intermediate target. Typically, the type of variable chosen as an operating target coincides with that chosen as an intermediate target. In other words, both will be monetary aggregates, or both will be interest rates.

The primary advantage of this two-step targeting procedure is that the Fed can quickly monitor changes in operating targets and determine whether its intervention is having the desired effect. Operating targets provide checkpoints, enabling the Fed to gauge the effectiveness of its policies and to adjust them rather than waiting to evaluate the ultimate success or failure of efforts to achieve its goals. Obviously, the most crucial aspect of the targeting process is selecting the appropriate targets.

Monetary Aggregates and Interest Rates as Targets

In principle, the Fed has a range of intermediate targets from which to choose, including money and credit aggregates and interest rates. The Fed uses either money supply growth targets or interest rate targets—which should it choose? That is a complicated question which we will examine shortly. First, however, you need to understand that the Fed can use one or the other type of targets, but not both. Ultimately, then, the Fed *must* choose.

To understand why, let's turn to graphical analysis of the demand and supply of money (*M1*). We know that currency held pays no interest and that checkable deposits pay less than open market interest rates. Hence the opportunity cost of holding *M1* balances rises with the market interest rate. And, as Fig. 21.1 shows, in the money market the demand for *M1* and the market interest rate are negatively related.

Suppose that the Fed decides to use *M1* as an intermediate target, setting it equal to M^*, as in Fig. 21.1. For the money demand curve M_{d0}, the equilibrium market interest rate equals i_0^*. Any shifts in the nonbank public's demand for currency and bank deposits will be translated into interest rate movements. In other words, if the demand for money to use in transactions increases at any specific interest rate, the money demand curve shifts to the right from M_{d0} to M_{d1}. With the Fed holding the money supply constant at M^*, the equilibrium market interest rate rises from i_0^* to i_1^*. Suppose instead that the demand for money declines from M_{d0} to M_{d1} at any specific interest rate. In this case, if the money supply remains constant at M^*, the equilibrium

Q: How does the Fed conduct monetary policy to achieve goals related to economic variables?

A: After the Fed determines its goals, it selects intermediate targets consistent with achievement of the goals. Because the Fed doesn't control intermediate target variables, it selects as operating targets variables that it can directly influence and monitor and that relate to the intermediate targets.

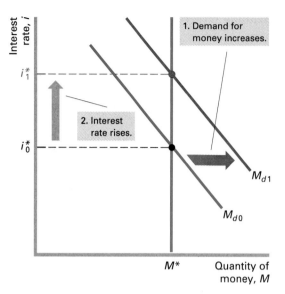

(a) Increase in Money Demand

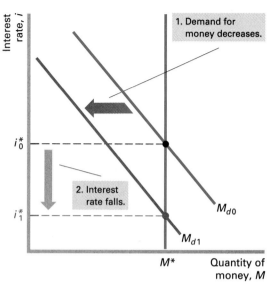

(b) Decrease in Money Demand

▲ **FIGURE 21.1**

Money Supply Targeting and Interest Rate Fluctuations
Setting an intermediate target in terms of a monetary aggregate causes interest rates to fluctuate.

As shown in (a):
1. An increase in money demand from M_{d0} to M_{d1} raises the interest rate from i_0^* to i_1^*.

As shown in (b):
1. A decrease in money demand from M_{d0} to M_{d1} lowers the interest rate from i_0^* to i_1^*.

market interest rate falls from i_0^* to i_1^*. Setting an intermediate target in terms of a monetary aggregate causes interest rates to fluctuate in response to changes in money demand.

Now let's see what happens if the Fed chooses an interest rate as the intermediate target. Let's assume, as in Fig. 21.2, that the initial money demand and supply curves are M_{d0} and M_0^*, respectively, and that the Fed sets an interest rate target at the equilibrium interest rate, i_0^*. In this case, when the demand for money increases from M_{d0} to M_{d1} at any specific interest rate, the interest rate rises from i_0^* to i_1^*. According to Fig. 21.2, if the Fed wants to maintain an interest rate of i_0^*, it will have to increase the money supply from M_0^* to M_1^*. Let's suppose instead that the demand for money declines from M_{d0} to M_{d2} at any specific interest rate. In this case, the interest rate falls from i_0^* to i_2^*. If the Fed wants to maintain an interest rate of i_0^*, it will have to reduce the money supply from M_0^* to M_2^*. Note that the money supply curve is, effectively, now horizontal at the targeted interest rate. Setting an intermediate target in terms of the interest rate causes the quantity of money to fluctuate in response to changes in money demand.

From this analysis of the money market, we conclude that the Fed cannot set intermediate targets in terms of both monetary aggregates and interest rates. How, then, does the Fed select targets?

▶ **C H E C K P O I N T** *Suppose that, owing to deregulation, the demand for checkable deposits (and, hence, M1) rises. Will using M1 as an intermediate target permit the Fed to accommodate this portfolio allocation shift*

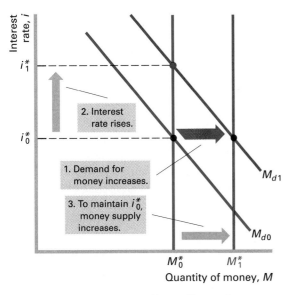

(a) Increase in Money Demand

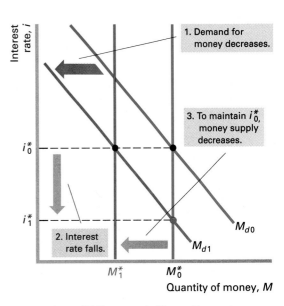

(b) Decrease in Money Demand

FIGURE 21.2

Interest Rate Targeting and Money Supply Fluctuations
Setting an intermediate target in terms of an interest rate causes the quantity of money to fluctuate in response to changes in money demand.

As shown in (a):
1. An increase in money demand from M_{d0} to M_{d1} requires the Fed to increase the money supply from M_0^* to M_1^* to maintain an interest rate of i_0^*.

As shown in (b):
1. A decrease in money demand from M_{d0}^* to M_{d1}^* requires the Fed to reduce the money supply from M_0^* to M_1^* in order to maintain an interest rate of i_0^*.

without affecting interest rates? If the Fed targets the money supply, an increase in the demand for money will, all else being equal, tend to increase short-term interest rates. If the Fed wanted to accommodate the portfolio allocation shift without affecting interest rates, it would conduct open market purchases to increase nonborrowed reserves and the money supply. ◄

Selecting Targets

A sensible approach for selecting targets is to evaluate whether one or the other better satisfies the three criteria of an effective intermediate target: measurability, controllability, and predictability.

Measurability

Suppose that the Fed identifies variables that have predictable impacts on its goals and can be controlled. It must be able to measure the variable over a short period of time in order to assess quickly whether its intermediate target is likely to be met. For example, the government compiles data on a goal variable such as nominal GDP quarterly and releases the data after a one-month delay. As potential intermediate targets, both interest rates and monetary aggregates are quickly observable and measurable. With computers, analysts can track interest rates continuously. Money measures are not quite as accessible, although they are reported with at most a two-week lag.

The instantaneous measurability of market interest rates doesn't necessarily make them better intermediate targets than monetary aggregates. The *nominal* interest rate can be measured easily, but assessing the *real* interest rate is more troublesome, owing to the difficulty of measuring market expectations of inflation. Hence, as with monetary aggregates, the Fed can't perfectly measure the relevant interest rates over a short period of time.

Controllability

After identifying the variables that are measurable, the Fed must determine whether it can control them. An effective intermediate target must be responsive to the Fed's attempts to shift course. For example, during the 1980s, many economists suggested that the Fed select a broader variable than conventional monetary aggregates, say, the stock of nonfinancial credit outstanding or even nominal GDP. However, the Fed cannot control such variables sufficiently with its policy tools. The Fed's influence over monetary aggregates and short-term interest rates is much greater, and thus it prefers to use them as intermediate targets.

By using its monetary policy tools (primarily open market operations), the Fed exerts significant control over the money supply. Absolute control is impossible, however, because the decisions of banks and the nonbank public also matter. The Fed can also affect interest rates because open market operations help determine the supply of bonds. Once again, however, absolute control is impossible, because the Fed cannot control inflation expectations and hence the real interest rate.

Predictability

Neither the criterion of measurability nor the criterion of controllability suggests a preferred alternative. What about the connection of interest rates and monetary aggregates to the Fed's goals? Here again, no clear answer emerges.

The case for interest rate targets rests on the observation that interest rates influence saving, investment, and portfolio allocation decisions (Chapters 5 and 6). Hence the Fed could increase economic activity by reducing real interest rates to stimulate consumer and business spending. If the Fed wanted to cool off the economy instead, it could discourage consumer and business spending by attempting to increase real interest rates.

This approach presents two problems. First, the Fed's influence over real interest rates is weaker than its influence over nominal interest rates. Second, a Fed policy to stabilize interest rates may be inconsistent with the Fed's goal of maintaining steady economic growth. Suppose that a wave of optimism about the future causes business and consumer spending to rise. The decline in desired current saving and the increase in desired investment cause interest rates to rise. If the Fed is trying to stabilize interest rates, it will make open market purchases to try to lower them. This fall in interest rates encourages consumers and businesses to spend even more. As a result, the policy of holding interest rates constant is like pouring gasoline on a fire.

The same problem occurs during an economic downturn. A loss of consumer and business optimism reduces spending and depresses interest rates. If the Fed didn't step in, lower interest rates eventually would encourage consumer and business spending, cushioning the downturn and putting the economy back on track. If the Fed were targeting interest rates, it would use open market sales to raise interest rates in the face of the downturn, worsening the economy's problems. Hence, in either case, if swings in consumer and business optimism are the major determinants of fluctuations in the economy's output of goods and services, a policy of stabilizing interest rates destabilizes the economy.

What if the Fed had targeted the money supply instead? In the case of economic expansion, the rising demand for money (to fund a higher level of transactions) increases interest rates, as shown earlier in Fig. 21.1. Higher interest rates help keep the economy from overheating by reducing consumer and business spending. In the case of economic downturn, the falling demand for money leads to lower interest rates, as shown in Fig. 21.1. The fall in interest rates cushions the downturn.

Do the problems encountered with interest rate targets when consumer and business spending fluctuate imply that the Fed should always target monetary aggregates? Not necessarily. As Fig. 21.1 shows, a money supply target means that shifts in the demand for money at any interest rate translate into interest rate changes. An increase in interest rates depresses the level of consumer and business spending, whereas a decrease in interest rates stimulates spending. Hence, if shifts in the money demand relationship occur frequently, money supply targets likely will produce interest rate fluctuations that destabilize the economy.

The foregoing discussion suggests that if the *real side* of the economy (consumer and business saving and investment decisions) is stable, interest rate targets offer the Fed a more predictable way to stabilize economic fluctuations (even though the Fed can't completely control the real interest rate, which is relevant to consumer and business decisions). However, if the *financial side* of the economy (demand for money and nonmoney assets) is stable, targeting monetary aggregates offers the Fed a more predictable connection with its goals. Actually the Fed doesn't have the luxury of complete real or financial stability and must cope with disturbances to both sides of the economy.

Selecting Operating Targets

Let's finish our analysis of target selection by examining criteria for selecting operating targets. After the Fed selects an appropriate intermediate target, it must decide on the operating target that will best influence the intermediate target. This important decision rests on the criteria that we analyzed for intermediate targets: The effect of the operating target should be measurable, controllable, and predictable. In addition, it should be consistent with the intermediate target. The Fed largely controls both reserve aggregates and the federal funds rate and accurately measures them quickly. Hence, if the Fed selects a monetary aggregate as the desired intermediate target, it will select a reserve aggregate (such as the monetary base or nonborrowed reserves) as the operating target, exploiting the predictable impacts on monetary aggregates. But, if it picks as the intermediate target a market interest rate, the Fed will select an interest rate (such as the federal funds rate) as an operating target to exploit relationships among market interest rates (Chapter 7). Whether the Fed selects a reserve aggregate or the federal funds rate, it uses its three monetary policy tools (principally open market operations) to influence that operating target.

The Monetary Policy Record

The record of U.S. monetary policy since the 1950s illustrates the need for suitable targets to help achieve economic goals. Reviewing the actual monetary policy record aids in understanding the pitfalls involved in using targets.

Early Interest in Targets: 1951–1970

The Fed's interest in targets emerged in the early 1950s from its struggle with the U.S. Treasury over the control of monetary policy. Recall that, during World War II, the Fed agreed to peg interest rates on government securities at their prewar levels (approximately 3/8% on Treasury bills and 2 1/2% on long-term Treasury bonds) to help the Treasury finance the war effort. The Fed did so by purchasing securities whenever their market prices fell below levels reflecting the pegged rates. However, with the onset of the Korean War in 1950, market interest rates rose, forcing the Fed to purchase even larger amounts of government securities. These open market purchases expanded the monetary base, eliminating the Fed's control of the money supply process and causing inflation to rise to 8% by early 1951. The Fed formally abandoned the policy under the Federal Reserve–Treasury Accord in March 1951.

That accord freed the Fed to pursue an independent monetary policy. Believing that fluctuations in consumer and business optimism were being managed by government tax and expenditure policy, the Fed promoted financial stability. Under the leadership of Chairman William McChesney Martin, the Fed began to implement a strategy targeted to respond to conditions in the money market. As we pointed out earlier, an emphasis on financial stability suggests using monetary aggregates as targets. In particular, Fed policy targeted short-term interest rates and the level of **free reserves,** or the difference between excess reserves, *ER*, and borrowed reserves, *BR* (discount loans), in the banking system.

The Fed believed that free reserves represented *slack* in the banking system, because banks could freely lend (nonborrowed) excess reserves, expanding the money supply through the deposit expansion process. Hence the Fed considered free reserves an indicator of money market conditions. An **indicator** is a financial variable whose movements reveal information about present or prospective conditions in financial markets or the economy. An increase in free reserves indicates an easing of money market conditions, whereas a decrease in free reserves indicates a tightening of money market conditions. However, during this period, the Fed used free reserves not just as an indicator, but also as an intermediate target, selling securities as free reserves rose and buying securities as free reserves fell.

Let's analyze whether such a procedure helps the Fed stabilize the economy. An increase in economic activity during a boom period causes market interest rates to rise. Higher rates increase the opportunity cost of holding excess reserves, so excess reserves decline. At the same time, higher market interest rates raise the incentive for banks to borrow at the discount window (assuming that the discount rate is unchanged), so borrowed reserves (discount loans) increase. These responses lead to a decline in free reserves. Because it is targeting free reserves, the Fed responds with open market purchases sufficient to reduce interest rates to a level consistent with previous positions in excess and borrowed reserves.

The process works in reverse during an economic downturn. A decline in national income reduces market interest rates. Hence excess reserves increase and borrowed reserves decrease; so free reserves increase. The Fed responds to the increase in free reserves with open market sales of securities in order to restore the existing level of free reserves.

When the demand for money rises, the Fed's actions expand the money supply; when the demand for money falls, the Fed's actions contract the money supply. Hence targeting free reserves gives the Fed little control over the money supply. In effect, the Fed passively responds to conditions in the economy. Financial economists refer to this approach as **procyclical monetary policy,** meaning that the Fed's policy *amplifies* rather than dampens economic fluctuations.

What about the argument that shifts in consumer and business spending could be ignored in favor of a focus on financial stability? In fact, government tax and spending policy did not completely stabilize the economy. Rather, the increases in government spending for the Vietnam War and the Great Society programs in the mid- and late 1960s overheated the economy. This example of procyclical monetary policy is inconsistent with economic stability. *Monetarists* (economists who believe that money supply targets are the best way to conduct monetary policy) were vocal critics of the Fed's targeting procedures.

Similar problems exist with the Fed's use of short-term interest rates as the primary operating target. In this situation, the Fed meets increases in market interest rates during an expansion by making open market purchases, expanding the monetary base and the money supply. During an economic downturn, a decline in market interest rates induces the Fed to sell securities, reducing the monetary base and the money supply. Hence interest rate targets promote neither monetary control nor economic stability. This strategy, too, results in procyclical monetary policy.

Because of the experience with procyclical monetary policy during the 1950s and 1960s, increased criticism of its targeting procedures by academic and business economists led the Fed to search for new targets in the late 1960s.

Experimenting with Monetary Targets: 1970–1979

Monetarist critics of the Fed's procyclical monetary policy during the 1950s and 1960s initially welcomed the appointment of Arthur Burns as chairman of the Board of Governors in 1970. Burns stated his belief that the Fed should commit itself to the use of monetary aggregates as targets. However, the Fed's monetary policy during Burns's tenure in the 1970s was as procyclical as during the previous two decades.

Why did the Fed's attempt at monetary targeting fail? Most critics attribute the failure to use of the federal funds rate as an operating target while using *M1* and *M2* as intermediate targets. The target range for the federal funds rate was narrow; ranges for the monetary aggregates were broad. The FOMC instructed the Open Market Trading Desk to implement policy that would achieve *both* targets. However, as we noted earlier, the Fed can't attain both targets simultaneously. The FOMC gave the federal funds rate top priority, countering departures from the narrow target range with open market purchases or sales, which significantly reduced monetary control. This priority for interest rate targeting made sense if, as the Fed believed, fluctuations in consumer and business spending had been stabilized.

However, such stability was lacking, and procyclical monetary policy reemerged. An increase in the federal funds rate led to open market purchases, causing faster growth of the monetary base and *M1* than the Fed intended. To address this problem, the FOMC attempted to put money growth back on course by widening the target range for the federal funds rate. When the economy expanded further, the federal funds rate increased, bringing open market purchases and faster money growth. As a result, both the federal funds rate and the money supply exceeded their target ranges, accompanied by significant inflationary pressures. From late 1972 to early 1973, the federal funds rate virtually doubled from 4 1/2% to 8 1/2%, and *M1* growth exceeded its target level by a wide margin.

The FOMC's procedure amounted to using the federal funds rate as an operating target for monetary policy. Just as this policy contributes to inflationary pressures during an economic expansion, it reinforces economic contraction. By the end of 1974, the U.S. economy had fallen into its most serious recession since the 1930s. As a result, decreasing credit demand led to a substantial decline in the federal funds rate. The rate was then at the bottom of the target range, so the trading desk used open market sales to keep it from falling further. As a result, money supply growth fell, and by early 1975, *M1* actually contracted, reinforcing the economic downturn.

The Fed's procyclical monetary policy continued through the 1970s. Burns and his successor, G. William Miller, publicly announced money

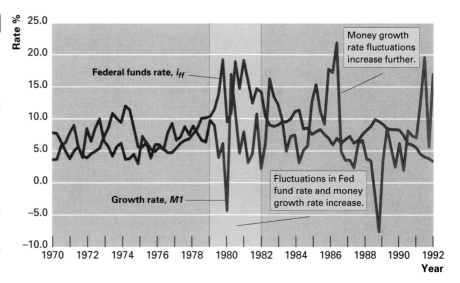

FIGURE 21.3

Federal Funds Rate and Money Supply Growth Rate, 1979–1992

The Fed's emphasis on controlling monetary aggregates from October 1979 to October 1982 led to large fluctuations in the federal funds rate, as our graphical analysis suggests. Note, though, that the *M1* growth rate was actually *less stable* during 1979–1982 than during 1975–1979. The Fed's targeting procedure focused on controlling nonborrowed reserves, but major shifts in the *demand* for money as a result of deregulation and financial innovation made money growth erratic. After October 1982, the Fed's renewed interest in stabilizing the federal funds rate further destabilized money supply growth.

Source: Federal Reserve Bulletin, various issues.

supply targets while privately targeting the federal funds rate. So long as economic activity fluctuated, the Fed's desire to control short-term interest rates simply was not consistent with controlling monetary aggregates.

Earlier we noted that Congress often puts pressure on the Fed to alter the conduct of monetary policy (Chapter 19). The procyclical monetary policy during Burns's tenure angered Congress, which moved to curb the Fed's powers. It passed a concurrent resolution calling for the Fed to be more accountable to Congress. It then passed the Humphrey-Hawkins Act in 1978, which codified those ideas, including the requirement that money and credit targets be set.

Deemphasizing Interest Rates: 1979–1982

In July 1979, President Jimmy Carter appointed Paul Volcker as chairman of the Board of Governors of the Federal Reserve System. Volcker was committed to crushing inflation and emphasized targets for monetary aggregates. Under Volcker, the Fed shifted its policy to emphasize nonborrowed reserves as an operating target. The FOMC reversed the practice of the previous decade by paying less attention to the federal funds rate, expanding its target range more than fivefold. As Fig. 21.3 illustrates, the federal funds rate became much more volatile. At the same time, the Fed didn't tighten its control over money growth. Note that fluctuations in the growth rate of *M1* in 1979–1982 were *greater* than fluctuations under Burns and Miller. The actual growth rate of *M1* exceeded the target range in 1980 and 1982 and fell below the range in 1981.

Why did the Fed's shift in targeting in October 1979 fail to produce greater monetary control? Many economists believe that the fluctuations in the economy and financial markets added too much uncertainty to make money growth targets attainable. Much of this instability resulted from deregulation of the banking industry. Financial innovation led to new substitutes for conventional demand deposits so that monetary aggregates had to be redefined. In addition, business recessions occurred in 1980 and again in 1981–1982. Finally, the Fed implemented credit controls from March until July 1980.[†]

Many economists believe that the Fed's intention in 1979 was not to gain control over monetary aggregates, but to reduce the high rate of inflation, which was widely viewed as unacceptable. These economists speculate that the Fed announced monetary targets to disguise its agenda of using high interest rates to combat inflation. As evidence, they point to the significant increase in the federal funds rate tolerated by the Fed in late 1979 and again in late 1980 and 1981, while inflation remained stubbornly high. Indeed, with the decline in inflation during the 1981–1982 recession, the FOMC permitted the federal funds rate to fall. As discussed in Box 21.1, the volatility of the federal funds rate and the growth rates of monetary aggregates from 1979 to 1982 say more about the Fed's concern with inflation than about monetary control.

Policy After 1982: Back to Interest Rates

In October 1982, the Fed began to pay more attention to the federal funds rate, emphasizing less the targets for monetary aggregates and ranges of acceptable fluctuations. Borrowed reserves became the stated operating target for monetary policy. Rising market interest rates during the boom following the 1981–1982 recession induced the use of borrowed reserves, putting upward pressure on the federal funds rate. To ease this pressure, the Fed purchased securities and increased nonborrowed reserves, which slowed the rise in interest rates and borrowed reserves. As a result, the monetary base increased, in effect returning the Fed to a procyclical monetary policy. Under this approach in an economic downturn, falling interest rates would slow discount borrowing, leading the Fed to sell securities to offset the drop in borrowed reserves. As a result, the monetary base and the money supply would decline.

Return to Fig. 21.3 and note the smaller fluctuations in the federal funds rate after 1982. Since February 1987, the Fed hasn't announced targets for *M1*. Fed officials justify this decision by reasoning that deregulation and financial innovation during the 1980s made *M1* less relevant as a measure of the medium of exchange.

In the early 1990s, the Fed became concerned that a *bank credit crunch*, or a severe contraction of the volume of bank lending, was reducing

---

[†] Reserve requirements added a further complication during this period. Until 1983, required reserves for a given week were based on the deposits made two weeks earlier, making the nonborrowed reserves target difficult to implement. Since 1984, the Fed has required contemporaneous reserve requirement accounting.

Consider this...

Does the Conduct of Monetary Policy Respond to Political Pressures?

Political factors sometimes exert strong influence on the Fed's practices. As the 1980 primary election season approached, politicians expressed beliefs that the high U.S. inflation rate and the low value of the dollar were unacceptable to voters. In part reflecting these concerns, the Fed adopted a strategy of targeting nonborrowed reserves to reduce the growth rate of the money supply and thereby stem inflation. Knowing that this anti-inflation strategy would increase interest rates and wanting to avoid being blamed for the resulting increase, the Fed did not publicly state its objective.

Instead, it stated in technical terms its intention to focus on monetary aggregates in order to deflect political criticism of high interest rates during its battle against inflation.

The intersection of economic and political considerations appeared again in 1982. Three years after the Fed announced its "policy" of targeting monetary aggregates, Congress criticized the Fed for the volatility of monetary aggregates and the economic downturn in 1981 and 1982. This criticism put the Fed in a bind: If it openly widened target ranges for monetary aggregates in order to

make interest rates less volatile, it would have to admit that it was to some extent using the federal funds rate as an operating target, which it had said before that it wouldn't do. Instead, the Fed chose to claim that it used borrowed reserves as the operating target. By this method of announcing one policy while following another, the Fed tried to balance its economic interest in fighting inflation with its political concern that it not be blamed for high interest rates.

---

economic growth. In addition to targeting the money supply, the Fed used its monetary policy tools to influence the level of bank lending, including reducing reserve requirements in December 1990 and February 1992.

Increasing International Concerns: The 1980s and 1990s

Just as the rising importance of international trade changed financial markets and banking, international financial concerns shaped Fed policy-making more during the 1980s and 1990s than ever before. Such concerns came to the forefront in 1985, when the foreign-exchange value of the dollar rose so high that U.S. businesses faced competitive losses in international markets. The FOMC indicated in its directives that bringing the dollar down would be appropriate. The Fed used an expansionary monetary policy to decrease the value of the dollar in foreign-exchange markets and to reduce short-term interest rates. To decrease the value of the dollar on foreign-exchange markets, the Fed tried to reduce the demand for dollars. By increasing money growth, the Fed tried to lower short-term rates, making investment in dollar-denominated assets less attractive than investment in assets outside the United States, which paid higher interest rates. As investors sold dollars to buy non-U.S. assets, the dollar's value against other currencies declined. Later in the 1980s, the Fed promoted an increase in short-term rates to raise the value of the dollar. The Fed's actions were joined by coordinated efforts of other central banks through the Plaza Accord (September 1985) and the Louvre Accord (February 1987).

Concluding Remarks

The Fed's approaches to targeting since World War II haven't been too successful in helping it smooth economic fluctuations or achieve its goal of price stability. Nor has targeting strengthened monetary control. Since 1982, the Fed basically has applied judgment to policymaking, giving no single variable the greatest weight consistently. The Fed's experience suggests that no single target is appropriate. The economy and the financial system experience many different types of disturbances, whose relative significance change over time. Hence the Fed's current strategy is a practical one, however imperfect.

Reevaluating Fed Targeting Policy

The underlying assumption of the intermediate targets approach is that financial variables that the Fed can directly measure and control may be useful in achieving objectives for variables that the Fed can't directly control but are affected by the financial variables in a predictable way. Our discussion of post–World War II monetary policy in the United States illustrates why many economists question the merits of financial variables as *targets* as opposed to *indicators*. Relationships between money and credit aggregates and economic activity appeared stable during the 1970s, when many economists and policymakers urged the Fed to use monetary aggregates as intermediate targets. However, the relationship between money and credit aggregates and nominal GDP weakened greatly during the 1980s. Critics conclude that, although no money or credit aggregate is a perfect intermediate target, owing to short-term instability (and even longer-term drift) in the relationship of the target to goals, other variables might be more useful as indicators.

Alternatives to Intermediate Targets

Indicator variables suggested to the Fed include nominal GDP, commodity prices, the yield curve, and the foreign-exchange value of the dollar. Let's consider them and then analyze the Fed's current strategy.

Nominal GDP. The collapse in the previously stable relationships between money and credit aggregates and nominal GDP caused some economists in the 1980s to suggest that the Fed focus on the rate of growth of nominal GDP. They reasoned that, if real economic activity is independent of monetary policy in the long run, the use of a nominal GDP target focuses attention on long-run price stability—and the unit of account function of money. Critics countered that the Fed's tools don't give it enough control over nominal GDP to achieve accurately any selected target. They proposed that the Fed adjust interest rate operating targets to influence nominal GDP. However, many Fed officials doubted that such a procedure could succeed.

Economists suggested three other variables to the Fed during the 1980s and early 1990s: commodity prices, the Treasury yield curve, and the foreign-exchange value of the dollar. They argued that the markets for these assets are *efficient*. In other words, their prices reflect available economic information, including information for the Fed about the current and expected future economic outlook.

Commodity Prices. The Fed could influence commodity prices through open market operations in commodity markets. Alternatively, if commodity prices provide advance information about future changes in inflation, the Fed could use price data as a signal of the need to adjust reserve aggregates or the federal funds rate. However, studies of this link show that commodity prices do not predict general inflation well. Hence commodity prices are not likely to be an effective indicator.

Yield Curve. Under the expectations theory of the term structure of interest rates, the nominal interest rate on long-term securities indicates the market's expectations of future short-term nominal interest rates (Chapter 7). If real interest rates were constant, the yield curve would indicate inflationary expectations, since expected inflation is the difference between the nominal and real interest rates. However, real interest rates aren't constant, so interpreting the slope of the yield curve requires guesses about the relative importance of expected shifts in real rates and inflation. Nevertheless, the slope of the yield curve contains statistically significant predictive power for both real output and inflation, and the Fed does examine the yield curve when evaluating changes in monetary policy.

Foreign-Exchange Value of the Dollar. Increasing sensitivity of the U.S. economy to international events prompted interest in the information content of changes in the foreign-exchange value of the dollar. Most economists don't advocate the usefulness of exchange rates as targets. However, some evidence suggests that exchange rate movements to a degree do predict future real output and inflation. In spite of this information benefit, analysts generally conclude that exchange rate movements are useful as indicators only in conjunction with such conventional indicators as domestic interest rates.

The Future of Targeting

Fed policymaking must strike a balance in its use of intermediate targets: Suitable intermediate targets can improve the chances of achieving goals; however, evidence from the 1980s and early 1990s suggests that suitable

Q: Is the actual record of U.S. monetary policy consistent with the Fed's attempts to control the money supply?

A: Most economists support the proposition that the Fed significantly influences the money supply. The Fed's lack of success in monetary control since World War II raises questions about why the Fed doesn't use operating targets that strengthen monetary control.

MOVING FROM THEORY TO PRACTICE...

THE WALL STREET JOURNAL JULY 23, 1992

The Fed's Semiannual Fireside Chat on Monetary Policy

Federal Reserve Chairman Alan Greenspan said officials of the central bank are leaning toward lowering their targets for money-supply growth but haven't yet made the move because they haven't finished studying its implications.

Mr. Greenspan, appearing before a House Banking subcommittee, said Fed policy makers recently discussed bringing the ranges down another notch "to conform to our long-term goal of price stability." He called the current ranges "still a fraction higher than they should be."

But the Fed elected to delay such a step, Mr. Greenspan said, until it has a better grasp of the connection between current money-supply figures and the overall economy. "What we did not want to convey to the Congress is that we have some insight...that we do not have," he said.

Asked by panel chairman Stephen Neal (D., N.C.) whether the Fed is "closing in on a better understanding," Mr. Greenspan answered, "Yes." Earlier, he said that the Fed's policy-setting committee would revisit the issue no later than its meeting next February.

In the past, setting the targets has been a source of tension within the Fed. Hardcore inflation fighters want to lower the targets to underscore the central bank's commitment to bringing down inflation. But other Fed officials, including those who are more concerned about fostering short-term economic growth than further reducing inflation, have resisted.

At their meeting this month, Fed policymakers left the target range for growth in the *M2* money-supply measure unchanged at 2 1/2% to 6 1/2%. But *M2* grew at an annual rate of only 2.1% in the first half of the year, and the measure has held steady for the past three months. *M2* includes currency, checking accounts, money-market funds and some certificates of deposit.

Lowering short-term interest rates, as the Fed has done 23 times since 1989, in the past would have been expected to spur *M2* growth, Mr. Greenspan said. He added that overall economic growth—even the slow growth being experienced now—also normally would coincide with an expansion of *M2*.

But Mr. Greenspan said that "a couple of years ago, both of those relationships broke down." A good part of that, he said, can be explained by people moving their money out of instruments that are included in *M2* and into more lucrative investments. But there are "lots of other secondary reasons" that still need to be explored, the Fed chairman said.

ANALYZING THE NEWS...

Since passage of the Humphrey-Hawkins Act in 1978, the chairman of the Board of Governors is required to testify before Congress twice each year on the Fed's conduct of monetary policy. This testimony covers the Fed's goals and the ways it intends to use its monetary policy tools to achieve those goals.

(a) Chairman Greenspan's comments seem to indicate that the Fed's primary goal is price stability and that the Fed is using the money supply as an intermediate target. Because the rate of inflation is closely related to the growth rate of the money supply over long periods of time, the discussion of "bringing ranges down another notch" implies that the Fed wants a lower rate of inflation for the economy and that it will reduce its target range for money supply growth to accomplish that goal.

(b) The Fed almost always faces conflicting goals. In the background of Greenspan's testimony was a struggle within the Fed over the goals of long-term price stability and the economy's recovery from the recession. A lower target range for the money supply might promote lower inflation but at the possible cost of higher interest rates, slowing down the U.S. recovery.

(c) The Fed hasn't used a strict intermediate target–operating target approach to achieve its goals. Instead, it has announced money supply targets consistent with the goal of low inflation while using information on a number of financial variables to monitor its progress on money supply growth and changes in economic activity. Chairman Greenspan's comments indicate the Fed's belief that using open market purchases and discount rate reductions to lower short-term interest rates should increase the public's demand for money holdings.

For further thought...

Some analysts believe that the Fed's inability to achieve its money growth targets reflects its private focus on reducing inflation. Chairman Greenspan indicated that relationships among the Fed's targets and goals have become less stable. How would you distinguish between these two explanations?

Source: Excerpted from Rick Wartzman, "Fed is Leaning Toward Cutting Money Target," July 23, 1992. Reprinted by permission of *The Wall Street Journal,* ©1992 Dow Jones & Co., Inc. All Rights Reserved Worldwide.

variables (those that the Fed can measure and control and that have a pre-dictable impact on goal achievement) are not easy to find. As we pointed out, the Fed deals with this tension by compromising. Although it specifies targets for money and credit aggregates, the Fed often defines them vaguely and as broad ranges in the FOMC directives. As a result, intermediate targets are less connected to day-to-day or month-to-month operating decisions than the theory of targeting suggests.

The Fed has done a substantial amount of research on the role for intermediate targets in the conduct of monetary policy, and ongoing analysis is likely. However, the practical importance of intermediate targets in the future conduct of monetary policy depends largely on whether controllability and predictability criteria for these targets can be satisfied.

The Fed's targeting efforts for monetary control since World War II haven't been as successful as those of other countries (see the Other times, other places box). Fed watchers believe that the most important reason for continuing to use targets for monetary policy is that a commitment to meeting those targets keeps the money supply process under control. Most economists support the idea that the Fed can significantly control the mone-tary base and, to the extent that money multipliers are stable over the long run, can influence the money supply greatly.

Other times, other places...
Money Growth Targets and Inflation in Germany

The German central bank, the *Bundesbank*, began experimenting with monetary targets in the late 1970s because of concerns about inflation. The aggregate selected, *central bank money*, is defined as a (weighted) sum of currency, checkable deposits, and time and savings deposits. The Bundesbank believed that movements in central bank money had a predictable impact on nominal GDP and that this monetary aggregate was sig-nificantly controllable using central bank tools. Target ranges were set each year during the late 1970s

and through the 1980s, during which the Bundesbank lowered its targets for money growth. For the first half of the 1980s, the central bank successfully achieved its tar-gets. Discretionary departures from its targets became more common from 1986 through 1988, as officials wanted to decrease the value of the (then) West German mark relative to the U.S. dollar. To do so, the Bundesbank increased money growth faster than its announced targets.

The reunification of Germany in 1991 posed problems for the

Bundesbank's commitment to its announced targets. Two pressures were particularly significant: First, the exchange of West German cur-rency for less valuable East German currency brought infla-tionary pressures. Second, political objectives for economic growth after reunification raised fears of a weakening of the resolve for low inflation. These pressures on the Bundesbank's operating proce-dures yielded a more flexible indi-cator approach similar to that used by the Fed.

Key Terms and Concepts

Free reserves

Indicator

Intermediate targets

Monetary policy goals
    Economic growth
    Financial market and institution stability

Foreign-exchange market stability

High employment

Interest rate stability

Price stability

Operating targets

Procyclical monetary policy

Summary

1. The Fed's broad monetary policy goals are price stability, high employment, economic growth, financial market and institution stability, interest rate stability, and foreign-exchange market stability. These goals are not generally attainable at the same time and in fact may conflict at times. Therefore trade-offs among them must be made.

2. The Fed cannot directly control its goals with its tools of monetary policy, so intermediate targets (financial variables that have a predictable impact on the goals) are selected. The Fed uses its monetary policy tools to influence operating targets (financial variables more directly under its control) that have a predictable impact on intermediate targets.

3. Because financial markets determine interest rates and money and credit aggregates together, the Fed must choose between them as intermediate targets.

To do so it uses the criteria of predictability, controllability, and measurability.

4. Since World War II, the Fed's use of targets in the conduct of U.S. monetary policy hasn't led to its control of the money supply. During the 1980s, deregulation and financial innovation made money supply targets more difficult to achieve. Since the mid-1980s, the Fed's policy has responded to direct information about changing conditions in the economy and financial markets.

5. Most economists believe that, as a technical matter, the Fed largely controls the money supply over the long run. Open market operations are a primary determinant of the monetary base. With an appropriately defined monetary aggregate (predictably affected by the monetary base through the money multiplier), monetary control should be possible.

Review Questions

1. What are the Fed's monetary policy goals?

2. What factors determine the variables selected as intermediate targets for monetary policy?

3. Why is price stability a goal of monetary policy?

4. Should a goal of monetary policy be to reduce the unemployment rate to zero? Why or why not?

5. Why should policymakers care about fluctuations in interest rates or exchange rates?

6. Why do policymakers use a two-step targeting procedure, with both operating and intermediate targets, instead of single-step targeting?

7. Why can't the Fed target both the money supply and interest rates?

8. Why was the Fed's pegging of interest rates before 1951 potentially inflationary?

9. Why was using free reserves as an intermediate target in the 1950s a procyclical monetary policy?

10. Why did the federal funds rate become more volatile in 1979? Did the Fed achieve greater monetary control? Why or why not?

11. If the Fed wants to decrease the value of the dollar on foreign-exchange markets, what should it do? What should it do if it wants to raise the foreign-exchange value of the dollar?

12. Why wouldn't commodity prices be useful intermediate targets for monetary policy?

13. How does political pressure influence the Fed's choice of targets? What did the Fed do in 1982 to accommodate these pressures somewhat?

14. Why is the choice of intermediate targets for monetary policy important for the selection of operating targets?

Analytical Problems

15. *Evaluate:* If the Fed uses the federal funds rate as an operating target, increases (decreases) in the demand for money increase (decrease) the money supply.

16. State whether each of the following variables is most likely to be a goal, an intermediate target, an operating target, or a monetary policy tool.

    a. *M2*

    b. monetary base

    c. unemployment rate

    d. open market purchases

    e. federal funds rate

    f. nonborrowed reserves

    g. *M1*

    h. real GDP growth

    i. discount rate

17. A recent proposal suggested that the Fed use the monetary base as its operating target to achieve a specified nominal GDP range as its intermediate target. What are the pros and cons of this suggestion?

18. How does using interest rates as operating or intermediate targets lead to procyclical monetary policy? How could policymakers use interest rates in the policy process and avoid procyclical policy?

19. Design a mechanism for monetary policy control of the economy, assuming that the Fed had a good model of the economy that provided accurate forecasts. Why would such a procedure be less useful with less accurate forecasts?

20. When would a simple rule for monetary policy, such as one that makes *M2* rise at a steady rate of 3% each year, be valid? When would problems with such a rule occur?

21. Outline a procedure for Fed control of the federal funds rate. Is this procedure consistent with control of the money supply process? Why or why not?

22. *Evaluate:* If the Fed uses nonborrowed reserves as its operating target, increases (decreases) in the demand for money increase (decrease) the money supply.

23. *Evaluate:* The money supply is inherently pro-cyclical, rising during (and amplifying) economic expansions and declining during (and amplifying) economic contractions.

Use graphical analysis of the money market to answer Questions 24 and 25.

24. Does using the federal funds rate as an operating target imply that the money supply curve is horizontal? Why or why not?

25. Do interest rate targets help the Fed soften the impact of economic downturns? Why or why not?

Data Question

26. Look through past issues of the *Federal Reserve Bulletin* to find when the chairman of the Fed's Board of Governors last testified before Congress as required by law under the Humphrey-Hawkins Act. The chairman testifies twice a year, in February and July. Read through the chairman's testimony and identify the variables being used by the Fed as operating targets and intermediate targets. What other variables does the chairman mention as important indicators for the economy? Can you identify the Fed's goals?

CHAPTER 22

The International Financial System and Monetary Policy

In 1985, Treasury Secretary James Baker and Federal Reserve Chairman Paul Volcker agreed that the U.S. economy faced a major problem. From 1981 through early 1985, the foreign-exchange value of the dollar had soared, making U.S. goods more expensive in foreign countries. Some in the Reagan administration believed that the rising dollar indicated market approval of U.S. policy. Baker and Volcker, however, worried about the calls for protectionist legislation in response to the decline in U.S. exports caused by the high exchange rate. As part of an international effort to lower the dollar's value, the Fed increased money supply growth, thereby reducing short-term interest rates in the United States. The dollar's value in foreign-exchange markets declined significantly in the second half of the 1980s.

So far we have presented the money supply process in the context of domestic policy. In the global economy of the 1990s, international concerns also figure prominently in the conduct and success of monetary policy. In particular, central banks—including the Federal Reserve System—sometimes must choose between domestic monetary policy goals and exchange rate objectives. In this chapter, we analyze the connections between monetary policy and transactions in the international financial system and discuss the implications of exchange rate policy for monetary policy.

In this chapter two questions shape our analysis. **Q:** How do a central bank's foreign-exchange market interventions affect the domestic money supply? **Q:** Why do central banks intervene in the foreign-exchange market?

Foreign-Exchange Intervention and the Money Supply

In our analysis of money supply determination, we noted the importance of three participants: the central bank, the banking system, and the non-bank public. However, because international financial markets are linked, actions of *foreign* central banks, banks, and savers and borrowers also can affect the domestic money supply. In particular, international financial transactions affect the money supply when central banks or governments try to influence the foreign-exchange values of their currencies.

As a result, such intervention may create tension between domestic and international monetary policy goals. To understand this connection, let's examine (1) how **foreign-exchange market interventions,** deliberate actions by a central bank to influence the exchange rate, affect a central bank's holdings of **international reserves,** or assets denominated in a foreign currency and used in international transactions, and (2) how changes in holdings of international reserves affect the domestic monetary base.

Suppose, for example, that the Fed buys $1 billion of foreign assets, say, short-term securities issued by foreign governments. This transaction increases the Fed's international reserves by $1 billion. Hence the Fed's assets rise by $1 billion, or the amount of foreign assets that it acquires. If the Fed pays for the foreign assets by writing a check for $1 billion, it adds $1 billion to banks' deposits at the Fed. And reserves of the banking system, a Fed liability, rise by $1 billion. The following T-account illustrates the effect of this transaction:

FEDERAL RESERVE

Assets		Liabilities	
Foreign assets (international reserves)	+$1 billion	Bank deposits at Fed (reserves)	+$1 billion

Alternatively, the Fed could pay for the foreign assets with $1 billion of currency. As currency in circulation also is a liability for the Fed, its liabilities still rise by $1 billion:

FEDERAL RESERVE

Assets		Liabilities	
Foreign assets (international reserves)	+$1 billion	Currency in circulation	+$1 billion

Recall that the monetary base equals the sum of currency in circulation and banking system reserves. Therefore the monetary base rises by the amount of the foreign assets (international reserves) acquired, regardless of how the Fed pays for them. In other words, a purchase of foreign assets by a central bank has the same effect on the monetary base as an open market purchase of government bonds. When a central bank buys foreign assets, its international reserves and monetary base increase by the amount of foreign assets acquired.

Similarly, if a central bank sells foreign assets to purchase its domestic currency, its holdings of international reserves and the monetary base fall. Suppose that the Fed sells $1 billion of foreign assets to buy $1 billion of domestic assets. The Fed loses international reserves, causing its assets to fall by $1 billion. At the same time, if the purchasers of the foreign assets sold by the Fed pay with checks drawn on domestic banks, banks' reserves at the Fed, a Fed liability, fall by $1 billion. The following T-account illustrates a sale of $1 billion of foreign assets:

FEDERAL RESERVE

Assets		Liabilities	
Foreign assets (international reserves)	−$1 billion	Bank deposits at Fed (reserves)	−$1 billion

If the Fed had instead purchased domestic currency with the proceeds of its sale of foreign assets, currency in circulation (another Fed liability) would have fallen by the amount of foreign assets sold. Because the monetary base is the sum of currency in circulation and reserves, it falls by the amount of foreign assets (international reserves) sold, regardless of whether the Fed buys domestic bank deposits or currency with the proceeds.

In other words, a sale of foreign assets by a central bank has the same effect on the monetary base as an open market sale of government bonds. Purchases of domestic currency by a central bank financed by sales of foreign assets reduce international reserves and the monetary base by the amount of foreign assets sold.

When a central bank allows the monetary base to respond to the sale or purchase of domestic currency, the transaction is called an **unsterilized foreign-exchange intervention.** Alternatively, the central bank could offset the effect of a foreign-exchange intervention on the monetary base by using domestic open market operations. Consider a Fed sale of $1 billion of foreign assets. In the absence of any offsetting interventions, the monetary base falls by $1 billion. At the same time, however, the Fed could conduct an open market purchase of $1 billion of government bonds to eliminate the decrease in the monetary base arising from the foreign-exchange intervention. In this case, the Fed's assets fall by $1 billion when it sells foreign assets. As we showed earlier, the monetary base falls by $1 billion if the Fed does nothing else. However, a Fed purchase of $1 billion of securities on the open market would restore the monetary base to its level prior to the foreign-exchange intervention. The following T-account illustrates these transactions:

FEDERAL RESERVE

Assets		Liabilities	
Foreign assets	−$1 billion	Monetary base (Currency	+$0 billion
(international reserves)		in circulation and reserves)	
Securities	+$1 billion		

A foreign-exchange intervention accompanied by offsetting domestic open market operations that leave the monetary base unchanged is called a **sterilized foreign-exchange intervention.**

▶ C H E C K P O I N T *What is the effect on the Japanese monetary base if the Bank of Japan purchases $5 billion in the foreign-exchange market?* The Bank of Japan's holdings of international reserves rise by $5 billion, and the Japanese monetary base increases by the yen equivalent of $5 billion. ◀

Foreign-Exchange Intervention and the Exchange Rate

To determine the effects of unsterilized and sterilized foreign-exchange market interventions on the exchange rate, we use the graphical analysis of exchange rate determination developed in Chapter 8. From that analysis recall that asset markets determine the exchange rate in the short run. The equilibrium exchange rate makes investors indifferent between holding domestic and foreign assets, at given domestic and foreign interest rates and expected future exchange rates.

Unsterilized Intervention

Let's begin with unsterilized intervention. Figure 22.1 depicts interventions to increase and decrease the exchange rate. The exchange rate EX is expressed in foreign currency per unit of domestic currency. The curve representing the expected rate of return on domestic deposits, R, is vertical (at the domestic interest rate, i). The curve representing the expected rate of return on foreign deposits, R_f, slopes upward to the right. Recall from Chapter 8 that $R_f = i_f - \Delta EX^e/EX$ where i_f is the foreign interest rate and ΔEX^e is the expected appreciation of the domestic currency. Thus if savers' expectations of the future exchange rate cause EX to rise, the foreign currency is expected to appreciate, which in turn increases R_f. When capital and foreign exchange markets are in equilibrium, the expected rate of return on domestic assets equals the expected rate of return on foreign assets ($R = R_f$); the equilibrium exchange rate is denoted EX_0^*.

Q: How do a central bank's foreign-exchange market interventions affect the domestic money supply?

A: If nothing else changes, when a central bank buys foreign assets, international reserves and the monetary base increase by the amount of foreign assets acquired. When the central bank sells foreign assets, international reserves and the monetary base fall by the amount of foreign assets sold. Sterilized foreign-exchange interventions do not affect the domestic monetary base.

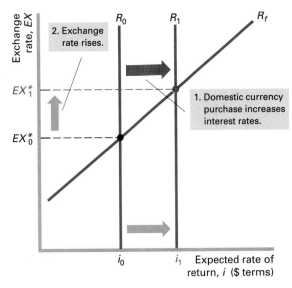

(a) Intervention to Raise the Exchange Rate

(b) Intervention to Lower the Exchange Rate

FIGURE 22.1

Unsterilized Foreign-Exchange Market Interventions and the Exchange Rate
As shown in (a):
1. To raise the exchange rate, the central bank must buy domestic currency, losing international reserves and decreasing the monetary base.

2. Domestic short-term interest rates increase from i_0 to i_1, so the expected rate of return on domestic assets rises from R_0 to R_1. That causes the exchange rate to rise from EX_0^* to EX_1^*.

As shown in (b):
1. To lower the exchange rate, the central bank must sell domestic currency, gaining international reserves and increasing the monetary base.

2. Domestic short-term interest rates decrease from i_0 to i_1, so the expected rate of return on domestic assets falls from R_0 to R_1. This causes the exchange rate to fall from EX_0^* to EX_1^*.

Suppose that the central bank wants to increase the exchange rate from EX_0^* to EX_1^*, as in Fig. 22.1(a). To raise the foreign-exchange value of its currency, the central bank must buy domestic currency (or domestic deposits) and sell foreign assets. The transaction resembles a domestic open market sale of securities because the foreign exchange intervention reduces the monetary base. If nothing else changes, the intervention increases the domestic short-term interest rate from i_0 to i_1. As a result, the domestic expected rate of return shifts to the right from R_0 to R_1. Because the expected rate of return on domestic assets has increased relative to the expected rate of return on foreign assets, savers will increase their demand for domestic assets and domestic currency. The exchange rate then rises from EX_0^* to EX_1^*.[†] Thus, if nothing else changes, an unsterilized intervention in which the central bank sells foreign assets to purchase domestic currency leads to a decrease in international reserves and the money supply and appreciation of the domestic currency.

Conversely, suppose that the central bank wants to lower the exchange rate by using an unsterilized foreign-exchange intervention, as represented in Fig. 22.1(b). The central bank buys foreign assets, increasing the monetary base and reducing the short-term interest rate from i_0 to i_1. The domestic expected rate of return shifts from R_0 to R_1. The expected rate of return on domestic assets has declined relative to the expected rate of return of foreign assets, so savers will lessen their demand for domestic assets and

[†] The decline in the domestic money supply may increase expected appreciation of the domestic currency, causing R_f to shift to the left, further raising the exchange rate. We ignore this effect here for simplicity.

domestic currency. The exchange rate falls from EX_0^* to EX_1^*. Thus, if nothing else changes, an unsterilized intervention in which the central bank buys foreign assets and sells domestic currency leads to an increase in international reserves and the money supply and depreciation of the domestic currency.

▶ C H E C K P O I N T *Suppose that the Fed pursues a contractionary monetary policy to increase the short-term interest rate in the United States. What would you predict the consequences for the exchange rate to be?* All else being equal, the higher expected rate of return on dollar assets increases the demand for U.S. assets relative to foreign assets, causing the dollar to appreciate. ◀

Sterilized Intervention

In analyzing the effects of an unsterilized foreign-exchange intervention, we assumed that domestic and foreign assets are perfect substitutes. This assumption means that the expected rates of return on domestic and foreign assets are equal in equilibrium. Because a sterilized foreign-exchange intervention doesn't affect the money supply, it will not affect domestic interest rates or expected appreciation of the domestic currency. Hence the domestic expected rate of return, R, and foreign expected rate of return, R_f, do not shift. Thus a sterilized intervention does not affect the exchange rate.

However, if domestic and foreign assets are not perfect substitutes—that is, don't have similar risk, liquidity, and information characteristics—a sterilized intervention can affect the exchange rate. Traditionally, an important liquidity difference stems from the imposition of **capital controls,** or government-imposed barriers to foreign savers investing in domestic assets or to domestic savers investing in foreign assets. (Explicit capital controls now are relatively rare in most industrialized countries.) Capital controls limit domestic investors' ability to diversify their portfolios internationally, leading those investors to require a higher expected return on domestic assets than on foreign assets. When domestic and foreign assets are imperfect substitutes, an increase in the supply of domestic assets implies greater exchange rate risk, raising the risk premium for the domestic expected rate of return and reducing the exchange rate.[†]

[†] In this case, the nominal interest rate parity condition in the foreign-exchange market reflects a currency risk premium $b_{f,d}$ (introduced in Chapter 8 Eq. 8.7):

$$i = i_f - \frac{\Delta EX^e}{EX} + b_{f,d}.$$

With the addition of a risk premium, a sterilized foreign-exchange market intervention can affect the exchange rate. That is, if a sterilized sale of the domestic currency increases, $b_{f,d}$, then, if nothing else changes, EX must fall in order to satisfy the interest rate parity condition.

In theory, with a currency risk premium, an increase in the domestic money supply from a sterilized intervention leads to depreciation of the domestic currency, as in the case of an unsterilized intervention. However, most studies by economists have concluded that a sterilized intervention has virtually no effect on the exchange rate. Hence effective interventions to affect the exchange rate are generally unsterilized.

The currency premium $h_{f,d}$ can be negative; domestic investors may require a higher expected return on foreign assets than domestic assets. Many economists believe that domestic and foreign assets are imperfect substitutes because of informational barriers to international diversification of portfolios, or because foreign assets may be exposed to risks of seizure by foreign governments.

Reasons for Central Bank Intervention

If foreign-exchange interventions affect the domestic money supply, why do central banks intervene? Central banks and governments often are concerned about the effects of exchange rate depreciation or appreciation on the economy. A depreciating domestic currency raises the cost of foreign goods and may lead to inflation. Central banks attempt to offset this effect by buying their own currencies in the foreign-exchange market. Conversely, an appreciating domestic currency can make a country's goods uncompetitive in world markets. Central banks attempt to offset this effect by selling their own currencies in the foreign-exchange market.

Q: Why do central banks intervene in the foreign-exchange market?

A: Central banks often are concerned about effects of exchange rate appreciation or depreciation on the economy and attempt to minimize these effects by buying or selling domestic currency in the foreign-exchange market.

The United States officially has followed a **flexible exchange rate system,** in which the foreign-exchange value of the dollar is determined in currency markets, since the early 1970s. Nonetheless, the Fed and the Treasury have intervened in the foreign-exchange market on several occasions to increase or decrease the exchange rate. Such intervention is accomplished through the Exchange Stabilization Fund at the Treasury. The Treasury is the senior authority in organizing foreign-exchange interventions, although it trades through the Federal Reserve Bank of New York. The FOMC has independent authority to conduct foreign-exchange interventions, but, in practice, the Treasury and the Fed coordinate their efforts.

During the 1980s, the Reagan administration and the Fed pursued interventions in both directions. In 1981, the incoming administration announced that it would not intervene in the foreign-exchange market, even though the dollar was appreciating because of high domestic real interest rates. After the dollar's value had almost doubled relative to other major currencies between early 1981 and September 1985, Treasury Secretary James Baker and Federal Reserve Chairman Paul Volcker met with their counterparts from France, Germany, Japan, and the United Kingdom in New York to achieve an agreement to "bring down" the dollar. These countries agreed, in the so-called Plaza Accord, to a concerted effort to reduce the dollar's value and stabilize the values of the other four currencies against the dollar. Another round of interventions followed in February 1987, the so-called Louvre

Accord, which established unofficial trading ranges for currencies. In January 1988, major central banks intervened to halt the dollar's slide and stabilize exchange rates for a time. In the late 1980s and early 1990s, the Fed continued to intervene in foreign-exchange markets. Most analysts believe that foreign-exchange interventions to affect the exchange rate have become increasingly difficult in today's vast foreign-exchange markets, in which more than $1 trillion changes hands daily.

Countries often seek to reduce exchange rate movements by agreements to stabilize or even fix exchange rates. After analyzing how countries account for international transactions and the effect of those transactions on central banks, we will examine how well historical and contemporary exchange rate agreements have achieved their goal of exchange rate stability.

Balance of Payments

The **balance of payments** measures the total flow of private and government funds between a country (say, the United States) and foreign countries. As the Using the news box shows, the balance of payments for the United States reflects a bookkeeping procedure similar to that which households or businesses would use to record receipts and payments. In the balance of payments, inflows of funds from foreigners to the United States are noted as *receipts*, with a plus sign. These receipts include inflows of funds to purchase U.S.-produced goods and services (exports), finance foreign acquisition of U.S. assets (capital inflows), and provide gifts to U.S. citizens (unilateral transfers).

Using the news...
The U.S. Balance of Payments

Information on the balance of payments is widely reported in newspapers. The trade balance receives special attention when it is reported near the end of each month. The U.S. Department of Commerce publishes the complete balance of payments accounts quarterly in the *Survey of Current Business*. Forecasters, traders, and financial institutions use them to predict changes in exchange rates and interest rates.

Source: Survey of Current Business, 72: December 1992, p. 38.

	Transactions, 1991	$ billion
Trade balance	1. Exports of goods, services, and income (2 + 3 + 4)	704.9
(2) + (6) =	2. Merchandise	416.0
–$73.4 billion	3. Services	163.6
	4. Income receipts on investments	125.3
Current account	5. Imports of goods, services, and income (6 + 7 + 8)	–716.6
balance	6. Merchandise	–489.4
(1) + (5) + (9) =	7. Services	–118.3
–$3.7 billion	8. Income payments on investments	–108.9
	9. Unilateral transfers	8.0
Official settlement	10. U.S. assets abroad, net [increase of capital	
balance	outflows (–)] (11 + 12 + 13)	–62.2
(11) + (15) =	11. U.S. official reserve assets	5.8
–$24.2 billion	12. U.S. government assets (other than ORA), net	3.4
	13. U.S. private assets, net	–71.4
Capital account	14. Foreign assets in the U.S., net [increase of capital	
balance	inflow (+)] (15 + 16)	67.0
(10) + (14) =	15. Foreign official assets, net	18.4
+$4.8 billion	16. Other foreign assets, net	48.6
	17. Allocations of Special Drawing Rights	0.0
	18. Statistical discrepancy	–1.1

Source: Survey of Current Business, 72: 38, December, 1992.

Outflows of funds from the United States to foreigners are noted as *payments*, with a minus sign. These payments include purchases of foreign goods and services (imports), money spent on purchases of foreign assets by U.S. households and businesses (capital outflows), and gifts to foreigners including foreign aid (unilateral transfers). The principal parts of the balance of payments summarize transactions for purchases and sales of goods and services (the current account balance, which includes the trade balance) and flows of funds for international lending or borrowing (the capital account balance, which includes the official settlements balance).

The Current Account

The **current account** summarizes transactions among countries for purchases and sales of currently produced goods and services. One component of the current account is the **trade balance,** the difference between merchandise exports and imports (line 2 plus line 6, since imports are entered with a minus sign). The U.S. trade balance in 1991 was a deficit of $73.4 billion, with imports of $489.4 billion exceeding exports of $416.0 billion. When exports exceed imports, the trade balance is a surplus.

The three other components of the current account are exports and imports of services (lines 3 and 7), net investment income (lines 4 and 8), and unilateral transfers (line 9). In 1991, the United States had a surplus in the sale of services, selling $45.3 billion more of services to foreigners than U.S. residents purchased abroad. Net investment income also was positive for the United States in 1991 by $16.4 billion. That is, U.S. residents paid out less investment income to foreign investors than they received from foreign investments. Finally, the United States received on balance $8.0 billion in unilateral transfers, with foreign governments' contributions for Operation Desert Storm more than offsetting U.S. foreign aid and other transfers. The **current account balance** equals the sum of the trade balance, services balance, net investment income, and unilateral transfers. There was a *deficit* of $3.7 billion in 1991.

Policymakers have been concerned about U.S. current account deficits in the 1980s and early 1990s because those deficits require the United States to borrow funds from foreign savers. As in the case of households and businesses, governments' current account surpluses or deficits require offsetting financial transactions. A current account surplus or deficit in the balance of payments must be balanced by international lending or borrowing or by changes in official reserve transactions. Hence the large U.S. current account deficits in the 1980s and 1990s imply that the United States is relying heavily on savings from abroad—international borrowing—to finance domestic consumption, investment, and the federal budget deficit. The current account balance also provides information about anticipated movements in exchange rates. The demands for imports and exports affect the exchange rate. Also international lending or borrowing to achieve a balance of payments of zero involves shifts in domestic and foreign asset demands that can affect the exchange rate.

Although the balance of payments is a set of accounting relationships, the saving-investment model introduced in Chapter 5 helps explain what is going on in the economy. For a large open economy such as that of the United States, factors that tend to increase desired national saving or international lending lead to a capital outflow and a current account surplus. Factors that tend to decrease desired national saving or increase desired international borrowing lead to a capital inflow and a current account deficit.

The Capital Account

The **capital account** measures trade in existing assets among countries. When someone in a country sells an asset (a skyscraper, a bond, or shares of stock, for example) to a foreign investor, the transaction is recorded in the balance of payments accounts as a **capital inflow** because funds flow into the country to buy the asset. When someone in a country buys an asset abroad, the transaction is recorded in the balance of payments accounts as a **capital outflow** because funds flow from the country to buy the asset. Thus, when a wealthy British investor buys the penthouse apartment in New York's Plaza Hotel, the transaction is recorded as a capital outflow for Britain and a capital inflow for the United States.

The **capital account balance** is the amount of capital inflows (line 14) minus capital outflows (line 10). The capital account balance is a surplus if those in the country sell more assets to foreigners than they buy from foreigners. The capital account balance is a deficit if those in the country buy more assets from foreigners than they sell to foreigners. In 1991, the United States had capital inflows of $67.0 billion and capital outflows of $62.2 billion, for a net capital account balance (an increase on U.S. assets) of $4.8 billion.

The Official Settlements Balance.   Not all capital flows among countries represent transactions by households and businesses; changes in asset holdings by governments and central banks supplement private capital flows. **Official reserve assets** are assets held by central banks that can be used in making international payments. Historically, gold was the leading official reserve asset. Official reserves now are primarily government securities of the United States and other industrialized countries, foreign bank deposits, and special assets called Special Drawing Rights created by the International Monetary Fund (an international agency, which we discuss later in this chapter).

The **official settlements balance** equals the net increase (domestic holdings minus foreign holdings) in a country's official reserve assets. Line 11 shows that the Fed decreased its holdings of official reserve assets by $5.8 billion. (Because an increase is represented by a minus sign in the accounts—as it is a capital outflow—the plus sign here indicates a decrease in holdings.) Line 15 shows that foreign central banks increased their holdings of U.S. dollar-denominated reserve assets by $18.4 billion. In 1991, then, the United States had an official settlements balance of –$5.8 (line 11) billion minus $18.4 billion (line 15), or –$24.2 billion.

The official settlements balance often is called the *balance of payments surplus or deficit*. In 1991, the United States had a balance of payments deficit of $24.2 billion. When a country has a balance of payments surplus, it gains international reserves because its receipts exceed its payments—foreign central banks provide the country's central bank with international reserves. When a country experiences an official settlements balance deficit, or a balance of payments deficit, it loses international reserves. Because U.S. dollars and dollar-denominated assets serve as the largest component of international reserves, a U.S. balance of payments deficit can be financed by a reduction in U.S. international reserves and an increase in dollar assets held by foreign central banks. Similarly, a combination of an increase in U.S. international reserves and a decrease in dollar assets held by foreign central banks can offset a U.S. balance of payments surplus.

Relationships among the Accounts

Each international transaction represents an exchange of goods, services, or assets among households, businesses, or governments. Therefore the two sides of the exchange must always balance. In other words, the payments and receipts of the balance of payments accounts must equal zero, or

$$\text{Current account balance } + \text{ Capital account balance} = 0. \quad (22.1)$$

In reality, measurement problems keep this relationship from holding exactly. An adjustment for measurement errors, the **statistical discrepancy** (line 18) is reported in the capital account portion of the balance of payments accounts. In 1991, it equaled –$1.1 billion (a capital outflow). Many analysts believe that large statistical discrepancies in countries' balance of payments accounts reflect hidden capital flows (relating to illegal activity, tax evasion, or capital flight because of political risk).

To summarize, international goods and financial transactions affect both the current account and the capital account in the balance of payments. To close out a country's international transactions, its central bank and foreign central banks engage in official reserve transactions, which can affect the monetary base.

▶ C H E C K P O I N T   *Using the balance of payments accounts, explain how the United States went from being a net creditor to being a net debtor during the 1980s.* Large U.S. trade deficits (a minus sign in the balance of payments) mean that the United States is borrowing from abroad. In the balance of payments, this shows up as an inflow of foreign capital (a plus sign in the balance of payments). Hence large trade deficits are associated with the country's becoming a net debtor to foreign savers. ◀

Exchange Rate Regimes and the International Financial System

To understand how the international monetary and financial system has evolved, you first need to understand **exchange rate regimes,** or systems of adjusting exchange rates and flows of goods and capital among countries. In the past, most exchange rate regimes were **fixed exchange rate systems,** in which exchange rates were set at levels determined and maintained by governments. Many analysts argue that fixed exchange rates promote international trade by lowering the transactions costs of buying and selling goods and assets and reducing uncertainty about prices of goods and assets caused by exchange rate fluctuations. In some cases, however, fixed exchange rate systems impose costs on the economy. We analyze exchange rate regimes in terms of (1) the promise that holds the system together; (2) how exchange rates adjust; and (3) how economies adjust to maintain equilibrium in the international monetary and financial system.

Fixed Exchange Rates and the Gold Standard

The classical gold standard that supported the international monetary and financial system before World War I is an excellent example illustrating the successes and failures of a fixed exchange rate system. Under a **gold standard,** currencies of participating countries are convertible into an agreed-upon amount of gold; exchange rate adjustment is ruled out. Based on this promise, the exchange rates between any two countries' currencies are fixed by their relative gold weights. For example, if $1 could be exchanged for 1/20 of an ounce of gold while FF1 (French franc) could be exchanged for 1/80 of an ounce of gold, $1 = FF4 and $0.25 = FF1. Let's consider an example of trade and capital flows between France and the United States to illustrate the effect of this system of fixed exchange rates.

Under a fixed exchange rate system based on a gold standard, a U.S. importer could buy goods from a French exporter by either (1) exchanging dollars for French francs in France and buying goods, or (2) exchanging dollars for gold in the United States and shipping gold to France to buy francs and French goods. Suppose that the demand for French goods rises relative to U.S. goods, leading to a rising demand for francs and a falling demand for dollars. Hence there is pressure for the exchange rate in francs per dollar to fall in the foreign-exchange market, say, from $1 = FF4 to $1 = FF3. In this situation, U.S. importers could make a profit from shipping gold to France to buy francs, so long as the United States and France continue to exchange currencies for gold at the agreed-upon rate.

Thus, if Sally Sharp, a cloth importer in Philadelphia, wants to buy FF5000 worth of cloth from Deluxe of Paris, she can use either of the two strategies described. First, if she tries to sell dollars for francs in the foreign-exchange market, she will find that she must pay 5000/3 = $1666.67 for the cloth. Alternatively, she can exchange $1250 for gold, ship the gold bars to France, and demand that the Bank of France exchange the gold for francs at the fixed exchange rate. At the official exchange rate of $1 = FF4, she will get FF5000 for her gold, enough to buy the cloth. The second strategy provides the cheaper solution for Sally. Sally's saving on this transaction, $416.67, makes it the best way to buy the cloth, so long as the cost of shipping the gold from Philadelphia to France does not exceed $416.67.

What happens in France as American importers like Sally Sharp ship their gold to Paris? Gold inflows into France expand that country's international reserves because gold is eventually exchanged for francs. The United States loses an equivalent amount of international reserves because dollars are given to the government in exchange for gold. An increase in a country's international reserves increases its monetary base, whereas a decrease in its international reserves lowers its monetary base. Hence the monetary base rises in France and falls in the United States, putting upward pressure on the price level in France and downward pressure on the price level in the United States. French goods become more expensive relative to American goods. Therefore the relative demand for French goods falls, restoring the trade balance and causing the exchange rate to rise toward the official rate of $1 = FF4.

However, if the relative demand for U.S. goods rises, market forces put upward pressure on the exchange rate. Gold then flows from France to the United States, reducing the French monetary base and increasing the U.S. monetary base. In this case, the accompanying increase in the U.S. price level relative to the French price level makes French goods more attractive, restoring the trade balance. The exchange rate moves back toward the fixed rate of $1 = FF4.

One problem with the economic adjustment process under the gold standard was that countries with trade deficits and gold outflows experienced declines in price levels, or deflation. Periods of unexpected and pronounced deflation caused recessions. During the 1870s, 1880s, and 1890s, several deflation-induced recessions occurred in the United States. A falling price level raised the real value of households' and firms' nominal debt burdens, leading to financial distress for many sectors of the economy.

Another consequence of fixed exchange rates under the gold standard was that countries had little control over their domestic monetary policies. The reason was that gold flows dominated changes in the monetary base. As a result, countries faced unexpected inflation or deflation caused by international trade or financial disturbances. Moreover, gold discoveries and production strongly influenced changes in the world money supply, making the situation worse. For example, in the 1870s and 1880s, few gold discoveries and rapid economic growth contributed to falling prices. In the 1890s, on the other hand, the gold rushes in Alaska and what is now South Africa increased price levels around the world.

In theory the gold standard required that all countries maintain their promise to convert currencies freely into gold at fixed exchange rates. In practice, England made the exchange rate regime's promise credible. The strength of the British economy, its frequent trade surpluses, and large gold reserves made it the anchor of the international monetary and financial system.

During World War I, the collapse of the international trading system led countries to abandon their promises to convert currency into gold. The gold standard had a brief revival during the period between the two world wars, but economists generally believe that it deepened the worldwide depression of the early 1930s. The Federal Reserve System's attempts to reduce gold outflows in 1930 and 1931, by increasing the discount rate, contributed to the U.S. financial crisis. Subsequently the United States suspended the general public's right to convert dollars into gold. Ben Bernanke and Harold James of Princeton University found that countries that tried to defend the gold standard in the early 1930s suffered more severe deflation and depression than countries that abandoned the gold standard.[†]

Adapting Fixed Exchange Rates: The Bretton Woods System

Despite the gold standard's demise, many countries remained interested in the concept of fixed exchange rates. As World War II drew to a close, representatives of the Allied governments gathered at Bretton Woods, New Hampshire, to design a new international monetary and financial system. The resulting agreement, known as the **Bretton Woods system,** lasted from 1945 until 1971. Its framers intended to reinstate a system of fixed exchange rates but to permit smoother short-term economic adjustment than was possible under the gold standard. The promise that was to hold the system together was that foreign central banks would be able to convert U.S. dollars into gold at a price of $35.00 per ounce. Hence agreed-upon exchange rates were defined foreign currencies in dollar terms, and dollars were convertible to gold by the United States at the official price of $35.00 per ounce. This special role given to the United States reflected its dominant position in the global economy at that time and the fact that it held much of the world's gold. Because central banks used dollar assets and gold as international reserves, the dollar was known as the *reserve currency*.

Under the Bretton Woods system, exchange rates were supposed to shift only when a country experienced fundamental disequilibrium, that is, persistent deficits or surpluses in its balance of payments at the fixed exchange

---

[†] Ben Bernanke and Harold James, "The Gold Standard, Deflation, and Financial Crisis in the Great Depression: An International Comparison," in R. Glenn Hubbard, ed., *Financial Markets and Financial Crises*, Chicago: University of Chicago Press, 1991.

rate. To help countries make short-run economic adjustment to a balance of payments deficit or surplus while maintaining a fixed exchange rate, the Bretton Woods agreement created the **International Monetary Fund** (IMF). Headquartered in Washington, D.C., this multinational organization grew from 30 member countries to more than 150 by 1993. In principle, the IMF was to be a lender of last resort to prevent the short-term economic dislocations that threatened the stability of the gold standard. In practice, the IMF also encourages domestic economic policies consistent with exchange rate stability and gathers and standardizes international economic and financial data to use in monitoring member countries.

Although not directly related to its focus on the international monetary system, the Bretton Woods agreement created the **World Bank,** or International Bank for Reconstruction and Development, to make long-term loans to developing countries. These loans were designed to build infrastructure (highways and bridges, power generation and distribution, and water supply, for example) to aid economic development. The World Bank raises funds to lend by selling bonds in the international capital market. As Box 22.1 indicates, continuation of the traditional roles of both the IMF and the World Bank is being debated.

The Fixed Exchange Rate System.   Central bank interventions in the foreign-exchange market to buy and sell dollar assets maintained the fixed exchange rates of the Bretton Woods system. Exchange rates could vary by 1% above or below the fixed rate before countries were required to intervene

---

Consider this...

Are the IMF and the World Bank Obsolete?

BOX 22.1

Some analysts argue for rethinking the purposes of the IMF and the World Bank. These multilateral lending institutions have outlived the Bretton Woods system that created them. In the 1940s and 1950s, the international capital market was small; in the 1990s, the international capital market is the conduit for billions of dollars each day. These analysts ask: Why not let the international market make loans to governments?

Proponents of continuing the present system give two arguments. First, the IMF and the World Bank play an important role in gathering and maintaining information and expertise on the economies of many nations, particularly those of developing countries. A loan from one of these institutions can be a better indicator to private lenders of creditworthiness than a privately rendered credit rating. Second, the IMF and the World Bank can subsidize lending by obtaining funds at a lower cost than the borrower. These reasons, they say, support

the conclusions that the IMF and the World Bank should not become obsolete.

During the early 1990s countries in Eastern Europe, the Commonwealth of Independent States, and Africa placed great demands on the IMF and the World Bank. Some critics propose a merger of the two institutions as an intermediate solution for an international monetary and financial system to meet existing demands.

to stabilize them. If a foreign currency appreciated relative to the dollar, the central bank of that country would sell its own currency for dollars, thereby driving the exchange rate back to the fixed rate. If a foreign currency depreciated relative to the dollar, the central bank would sell dollar assets from its international reserves and buy its own currency to push the exchange rate back toward the fixed rate.

A central bank can maintain the exchange rate within the acceptable level so long as it is able and willing to buy and sell the amounts of its own currency necessary for exchange rate stabilization. When a central bank buys its own currency, it sells dollars (international reserves); when it sells its own currency, it buys dollars. Hence there is an important asymmetry in central banks' adjustments in response to market pressures on the exchange rate. A country with a balance of payments surplus has no constraint on its ability to sell its own currency to buy dollars in order to maintain the exchange rate, although it may be unwilling to do so. However, the ability to buy its own currency (to raise its value relative to the dollar) is limited by the country's stock of international reserves.

As a result, reserve outflows associated with balance of payments deficits were cause for concern under the Bretton Woods system. When a country's stock of international reserves is exhausted, the central bank and the government would have to implement restrictive economic policies to reduce imports and the trade deficit or abandon the policy of stabilizing the exchange rate against the dollar.

Devaluations and Revaluations. As an alternative to defending the fixed exchange rate by buying or selling reserves or changing domestic economic policies, a country can change the exchange rate. When its currency is overvalued relative to the dollar, the country can implement a **devaluation,** lowering the official value of its currency relative to the dollar and thereby resetting the exchange rate. A country whose currency is undervalued relative to the dollar can implement a **revaluation,** raising the official value of its currency relative to the dollar.[†]

In practice, countries didn't often pursue devaluations or revaluations. Governments preferred to postpone devaluations because they were likely to face political charges that their monetary policies were flawed. Revaluations also were not a popular choice. Domestic producers and their workers complained vigorously when the currency was allowed to rise against the dollar because domestic goods became less competitive in world markets, reducing profits and employment. The political pressures against devaluations and revaluations usually limited government changes in the exchange rate to responses to foreign-exchange market pressures.

[†] Remember, in a flexible exchange rate system, a falling value of the exchange rate is known as *depreciation*, while a rising value of the exchange rate is known as *appreciation*.

Speculative Attacks on the Bretton Woods System: The British Pound, 1967

1. At A, the pound is overvalued at the official exchange rate, $\overline{EX}$. The Bank of England sells dollars to buy pounds, increasing short-term interest rates from i_0 to i_1. The domestic expected return shifts from R_0 to R_1, and the exchange rate returns to the fixed rate $\overline{EX}$ of £1 = $2.80 at B.

2. Market participants expect the Bank of England to run out of dollars, and the R_f curve shifts from R_{f0} to R_{f1}. A significant increase in i would be required to restore an equilibrium exchange rate of $\overline{EX}$ at C. The Bank of England was forced to devalue the pound.

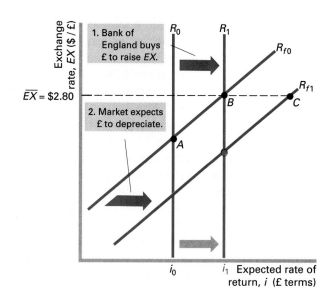

Speculative Attack. When market participants believe that the government is unable or unwilling to maintain the exchange rate, they may sell a weak currency or purchase a strong currency. These actions force a devaluation or revaluation of the currency known as a **speculative attack.** Speculative attacks sometimes produce international financial crises. That happened in 1967, when the British pound was overvalued relative to the dollar. To explain the situation, let's use the method of exchange rate determination shown in Fig. 22.2. The inter-section of the domestic expected rate of return, R, and the foreign expected rate of return, R_f, at point A gives an exchange rate (in $/£) lower than the fixed exchange rate $\overline{EX}$ of £1 = $2.80. To defend the overvalued exchange rate, the Bank of England had to sell dollars from its international reserves in order to buy pounds. The resulting decrease in the money supply increased short-term interest rates from i_0 to i_1, shifting the expected rate of return from R_0 to R_1 and momentarily restoring the exchange rate $\overline{EX}$ of £1 = $2.80, at point B.

   As the Bank of England's international reserves shrank, investors knew that at some point it would have to abandon its stabilization efforts. Speculators responded by selling pounds to the Bank of England (for $2.80/£1), expecting the pound to fall in value against the dollar. When the pound fell, the speculators used dollars to buy back even more pounds, thus earning a substantial profit. In terms of our graphical analysis, market participants expected the exchange rate (defined from the British perspective in $/£) to fall, thereby increasing the expected rate of return on non-British assets, R_f, relative to the British expected return R. Figure 22.2 shows the effect of this change in expectations in the shift from R_{f0} to R_{f1}. Note that the new intersection of R and R_f implies an even greater overvaluation of the pound. This weakness forced the Bank of England to buy even more pounds until it ran out of dollars. To defend the exchange rate $\overline{EX}$, the Bank of England would have had to increase short-term interest rates by an amount sufficient to maintain $\overline{EX}$ at point C. On November 17, 1967, the Bank of England lost more than $1 billion of international reserves (on top of earlier losses of several billion dollars). On November 18, it devalued the pound by 14%.

Devaluations are forced by speculative attacks when central banks are *unable* to defend the exchange rate, as in England's 1967 crisis. Revaluations, on the other hand, can be forced by speculative attacks when a central bank is *unwilling* to defend the exchange rate. A speculative attack on the undervalued German mark in 1971 forced a revaluation of the mark against the dollar and hastened the demise of the Bretton Woods system.

By 1970, the U.S. balance of payments deficit had grown significantly. By the first quarter of 1971, the large balance of payments surpluses outside the United States were causing concern in international financial markets because many currencies were undervalued relative to the dollar. This concern was greatest in Germany as the Bundesbank (the German central bank) focused on maintaining a low rate of inflation. The Bundesbank faced a dilemma. If it defended the fixed exchange rate, it would have to sell marks in the foreign-exchange market. By doing so, it would acquire international reserves, increasing the German money supply and putting upward pressure on German prices. If it revalued the mark, it would avoid inflationary pressures but would be breaking its promise under the Bretton Woods system.

This dilemma set the stage for a speculative attack on the mark. In this case, speculators bought marks with dollars, expecting the mark to rise in value against the dollar. When the mark did rise, the speculators used the marks to buy back even more dollars, thus earning a profit.

As Fig. 22.3 shows, the intersection of the R and R_f curves at point A in early 1971 yielded an exchange rate (from Germany's perspective in $/DM) that was higher than the fixed rate of $0.27/DM1. To defend the exchange rate, the Bundesbank had to sell marks. The resulting increase in the money supply lowered short-term interest rates in Germany, shifting the R curve from R_0 to R_1 and momentarily restoring the established exchange rate $\overline{EX}$ of DM1 = $0.27 at point B. Because foreign-exchange market participants expected the Bundesbank to revalue the mark to avoid inflationary pressures, they also expected the exchange rate to appreciate. These expectations decreased the expected rate of return on non-German assets relative to German assets, shifting the R_f curve to the left from R_{f0} to R_{f1}. This shift left the mark even more undervalued, and the Bundesbank had to increase its foreign-exchange intervention to maintain the fixed exchange rate. To defend the exchange rate $\overline{EX}$, the Bundesbank would have had to decrease short-term interest rates by an amount sufficient to maintain $\overline{EX}$ at point C.

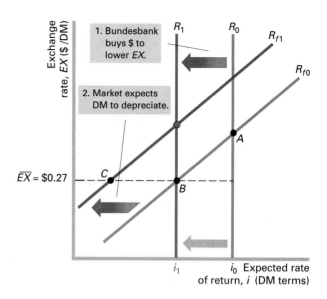

▶ **FIGURE 22.3**

Speculative Attack on the Bretton Woods System: The German Mark, 1971

1. At A, the mark is undervalued at the official exchange rate, $\overline{EX}$. The Bundesbank sells marks to buy dollars, and decreasing short-term interest rates from i_0 to i_1. The domestic expected return shifts from R_0 to R_1, so that the exchange rate returns the fixed rate $\overline{EX}$ of DM1 = $0.27 at B.

2. Market participants expect the Bundesbank to resist the money supply increases required to reduce the value of the mark. The expected appreciation shifts the R_f curve from R_{f0} to R_{f1}. A significant increase in the German money supply (to decrease i) would be required to restore an equilibrium with an exchange rate of $\overline{EX}$ at C. The Bundesbank revalued the mark.

Having purchased more than 1 billion U.S. dollars early on May 5, 1971 (and expanding its monetary base by the same amount), the Bundesbank halted its intervention later that day. The mark, along with the currencies tied to it, began to float against the dollar.

United States Abandons Bretton Woods. One problem with the Bretton Woods system was that, even though individual currencies could be devalued or revalued against the dollar, changing the *dollar's* value required a coordinated realignment of all other currencies. This requirement was difficult to achieve in practice. As U.S. inflationary pressures and balance of payments deficits mounted in the late 1960s, foreign central banks acquired large amounts of dollar assets. Recall that the promise holding the Bretton Woods system together essentially relied on the promise by the United States to exchange foreign central banks' dollars for gold at $35 per ounce. By 1971, however, the dollar assets owned by foreign central banks totaled more than three times the official U.S. gold holdings at the $35 per ounce of gold rate. Moreover, U.S. tax policies to encourage exports and discourage imports as a means of reducing the balance of payments deficit hadn't worked, and the Fed was unwilling to pursue a contractionary monetary policy. Nor would IMF intervention have worked; the IMF could not force countries such as Germany to pursue expansionary policies, and the United States as the linchpin of Bretton Woods could ignore the IMF.

On August 15, 1971, the Nixon administration attempted to force revaluations of other currencies against the dollar. The United States suspended convertibility of dollars into gold and imposed supplementary tariffs on imports that would be reduced only if a country revalued its exchange rate. This process of revaluations against the dollar was completed at the Smithsonian Conference in December 1971. Following the revised agreement, the Fed resumed control of its own domestic monetary policy rather than being guided by pressures under the Bretton Woods system.

The exchange rate conditions agreed to at the Smithsonian Conference were not stable in the face of world events. The oil price shocks of 1973 and 1974 had uneven effects on economies. For example, the inflationary effect of these price increases was greater for Japan than for the United States, creating market pressures for depreciation of the yen. Such pressures spread unevenly to other countries because of the global recession of 1974–1975. In practice, many currencies began to float, although central banks intervened to prevent large fluctuations in exchange rates. At its January 1976 conference in Jamaica, the IMF formally ratified the practice of allowing currencies to float. At that conference, IMF members also agreed to eliminate gold's official role in the international monetary system.

Even before formal abandonment of the Bretton Woods system, the IMF had begun issuing (in 1970) a paper substitute for gold. The IMF creates these international reserves, known as **Special Drawing Rights** (SDRs), in its role as lender of last resort. The price of gold is now determined by the forces of demand and supply in the market.

To summarize, the Bretton Woods system was a fixed exchange rate system with a lender of last resort to smooth out short-term economic adjustments in response to balance of payments deficits. The lack of commitment of the United States to price stability led to strong market pressures on fixed exchange rates, ultimately causing the market to collapse. Table 22.1 presents a comparison of the classical gold standard and the Bretton Woods system for fixing exchange rates.

Central Bank Intervention after Bretton Woods

Since 1976, many exchange rates have floated, being determined by demand and supply considerations. However, the Fed and central banks abroad haven't surrendered their right to intervene in the foreign-exchange market to encourage appreciation or depreciation of the domestic currency. Nonetheless, international considerations continue to affect domestic monetary policy.

Central banks generally lose some control over the domestic money supply when they intervene in the foreign-exchange market. To raise the exchange rate (if nothing else changes), a central bank must sell international reserves and buy the domestic currency, thereby reducing the domestic monetary base and money supply. To lower the exchange rate (if nothing else changes), a central bank must buy international reserves and sell the domestic currency, thereby increasing the domestic monetary base and money supply. Hence a central bank often must decide between actions to achieve its goal for the domestic money supply and actions to achieve its goal for the exchange rate.

▼ TABLE 22.1	COMPARISON OF EXCHANGE RATE REGIMES	
	Classical Gold Standard	**Bretton Woods System**
Promise anchoring the system	Currencies convertible into gold at fixed rates.	Currencies convertible into U.S. dollars at fixed rates; dollars convertible into gold at fixed rate.
Exchange rate adjustments	Not permitted.	Devaluation or revaluation permitted in response to fundamental disequilibrium.
Adjustment of economies	Money supply adjustments create inflation or deflation until the fixed exchange rate is restored.	IMF lending could smooth adjustment to short-term overvaluation of exchange rates.
Principal problems	Balance of payments deficits lead to deflation and recessions, with no gradual adjustment for short-term problems. Countries with balance of payments deficits have an incentive to abandon the promise of convertibility.	Difficult to devalue the U.S. dollar in response to U.S. balance of payments deficits.

Because of the traditional role of the dollar as a reserve currency, U.S. monetary policy hasn't been severely hampered by foreign-exchange market considerations. After the Bretton Woods system collapsed, the dollar retained its role as a reserve currency in the international monetary and financial system. However, during the 1980s, the Japanese yen and the German mark (as well as SDRs) became more important as additional reserve currencies. At the beginning of the 1990s, the U.S. dollar accounted for 60% of international reserves, with 9% and 19% accounted for by the Japanese yen and the German mark, respectively.[†] Most economists believe that the U.S. dollar isn't likely to lose its position as the dominant reserve currency in the 1990s.

The Fed experienced pressure during the 1980s and 1990s to abandon domestic monetary policy goals and either decrease or increase the value of the exchange rate. The soaring exchange rate in the early 1980s significantly hurt U.S. exports and raised criticism of the Fed for not pursuing a more expansionary monetary policy to cause the dollar to depreciate. The Fed responded by increasing money supply growth and agreed to intervene to reduce the dollar's value after the Plaza Accord in September 1985. By

[†] See Paul Volcker and Toyoo Ghoten, *Changing Fortunes*, New York: Times Books, 1992, p. 305.

February 1987, the dollar had fallen significantly from its 1985 high, and the United States and other industrialized countries met in Paris to consider interventions to halt the dollar's slide. In April and May 1991, the Fed intervened to halt the dollar's appreciation in response to political tensions in Eastern Europe and strains among the republics of the former Soviet Union. In April 1993 and August 1993, the Fed sold Japanese yen and bought dollars in an attempt to halt the dollar's plunge against the yen.

Fixed Exchange Rates in Europe

One benefit of fixed exchange rates is that they reduce the costs of uncertainty about exchange rates in international commercial and financial transactions. Because of the large volume of commercial and financial trading among European countries, interest in reducing costs associated with exchange rate fluctuations has been strong in Europe.

The Exchange Rate Mechanism

European Economic Community member countries formed the **European Monetary System** (EMS) in 1979. Eight European countries also agreed at that time to participate in an **exchange rate mechanism** (ERM) to limit fluctuations in the value of their currencies against each other. Specifically, the member countries promised to maintain the values of their currencies within a fixed range set in terms of the *ecu*, the composite European currency unit. They agreed to maintain exchange rates within these limits while allowing these rates to fluctuate jointly against the U.S. dollar and other currencies. The anchor of the ERM has been the German mark.

As part of the 1992 single European market initiative, EC countries drafted plans for **monetary union,** in which exchange rates would be fixed by using a common currency. These plans imply severe restrictions on domestic monetary policy for the participants. However, monetary union would have important economic benefits for member countries. With a single currency, for example, transactions costs of currency conversion and bearing or hedging exchange rate risks would be eliminated. In addition, the removal of high transactions costs in cross-border trades would increase production efficiency by offering the advantages of economies of scale.

Three conditions are necessary to ensure that monetary union will work in Europe, however. First, there must be either a single currency within the union or multiple currencies with immutable (absolutely unchanging) fixed exchange rates. Second, there must be a single exchange rate (and hence a single exchange rate policy) between the union's currency and other currencies. Third, central banks of member nations must surrender domestic autonomy in conducting open market operations, setting reserve requirements, making discount loans, enforcing capital controls, and intervening in foreign-exchange markets.

Will a European monetary union be successful? If it is, it must overcome several major concerns. Within Europe, there is no centralized mechanism for stabilizing adjustments to balance of payments fluctuations by individual countries. As a result, member countries of a monetary union would face greater impacts on income and employment from regional shocks to demand, because they wouldn't be able to adjust their exchange rates. Some economists believe that much of the political turmoil over monetary union in Europe indicates concern about the costs of being unable to conduct independent monetary policy under a flexible exchange rate regime.

Prospects for European Monetary Union in Practice

In 1989, a report issued by the EC addressed these concerns and focused on the need for a common central bank, the **European Central Bank** (ECB), to conduct monetary policy and, eventually, to control a single currency. The ECB is to be structured along the lines of the Federal Reserve System in the United States, with an Executive Board (similar to the Board of Governors), appointed by the European Council and governors from the individual countries in the union (comparable to Federal Reserve Bank presidents). Like the Fed, the ECB is to be independent of member governments; Executive Board members are to be appointed for nonrenewable eight-year terms to increase their political independence.

Some analysts believe that a future European Central Bank isn't likely to be politically independent. Countries may well argue the merits of expansionary or contractionary monetary policies. And there are concerns about how to accommodate domestic discretion in lender-of-last-resort roles in dealing with crises in domestic financial markets or institutions.

At Maastricht, Holland, in December 1991, member countries agreed on a gradual approach to monetary union, with a goal of convergent monetary policies by the mid 1990s and completion of monetary union in Europe by January 1, 1999. To have a single currency and monetary policy will require more convergence of domestic inflation rates and budget deficits than existed in the early 1990s. Four conditions are required for membership in the monetary union: (1) The country's inflation rate cannot be greater than 1.5 percentage points above the average rate for the three EC countries with the lowest inflation rates. (2) Its interest rate on long-term government bonds cannot be more than 2 percentage points greater than the rates in the three lowest-inflation countries. (3) Its government budget deficit can be no more than 3% of GDP. (4) Its outstanding government debt can be no greater than 60% of GDP. As of mid-1993, only four countries would have qualified: Germany, France, Denmark, and Luxembourg.

In the early 1990s, some analysts suggested that the foreign-exchange market might undermine fixed exchange rates in a speculative attack. The foreign-exchange market handles more than $1 trillion worth of dollar, yen, mark, and other currency transactions each day, as hedgers transfer risks to speculators betting on the direction of currency markets. Events of September 1992 showed that a market of this size can overwhelm the foreign-exchange market interventions of central banks and finance ministers, even when governments act in concert. During that month speculators launched attacks on several currencies as monetary unification was being debated in Europe (see the Other times, other places box). Following these speculative attacks, the United Kingdom and Italy withdrew from the ERM.

Under the exchange rate mechanism of the European Monetary System, the German mark serves as an anchor because few analysts expect it

Other times, other places...
Speculative Attack: 1990s Style

In 1991, the German government's budget deficit grew in order to finance the unification of East and West Germany. Concerned about inflationary pressures from the vast public expenditures required, the Bundesbank raised short-term interest rates. As German interest rates rose above those of England, Italy, France, and other European countries, speculators questioned whether those countries would be willing to raise their interest rates or instead would devalue their currencies against the mark. (Sweden, for example, briefly raised short-term interest rates to 500% to deter a speculative attack.)

England was the first test case. As shown in the figure, from point A, the Bank of England sold its foreign-exchange reserves of Deutchmarks to buy large quantities of pounds to support its exchange rate against the mark under the ERM. The purchase shrank the money supply and shifted short-term interest rates

from i_0 to i_1. The British domestic expected return shifted from R_0 to R_1, and the exchange rate returns to $\overline{EX}$ at point B. In this unstable situation, speculators used pounds to buy marks from the Bank of England, believing that the pound's imminent devaluation would enable them to use the marks to buy back more pounds. The R_f curve shifted from R_{f0} to R_{f1}.

To maintain the fixed exchange rate would require a significant increase in the British exchange rate to restore equilibrium at C. Because England was suffering a recession, few analysts believed

that it would be willing to tolerate high short-term interest rates to deflect a devaluation of the currency. They were right; after a week, the British government withdrew the pound from the ERM. After the British devaluation, Italy withdrew the lira and Spain devalued the peseta. As the accompanying graph shows, this episode is reminiscent of the British devaluation of the pound against the dollar in 1967. However, not all currencies were devalued; we analyze France's response in Moving from Theory to Practice.

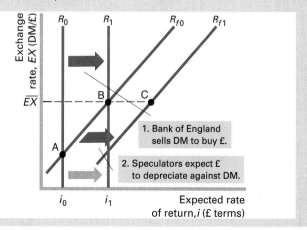

MOVING FROM THEORY TO PRACTICE...

THE NEW YORK TIMES   SEPTEMBER 28, 1992

Thwarting a Speculative Attack on the Currency

"I will fight, France and Germany will fight," vowed Michel Sapin, France's Finance Minister, as he declared war last week on speculators who were betting that a French franc would soon buy fewer German marks.

If Mr. Sapin seemed overwrought, it is understandable. The stability of the exchange rate between the franc and the mark had, for better or worse, come to symbolize the stability of the French–German alliance. And those who expected the franc to crack under pressure as easily as the British pound or the Italian lira did were clearly mistaken.

But for all the resolute words, there is still some reason to doubt the lock will hold. Defending a fixed exchange rate, even one that by all accounts reflects the relative values of the two currencies, can be very costly. And while France and Germany apparently have had the financial muscle to fend off the speculators so far, it is not clear even they would have the will to sacrifice jobs and output to

manage the feat for any prolonged period...

Governments have their own reason for preferring a currency lock: An obligation to sustain a fixed exchange rate justifies the sacrifices needed to hold down domestic inflation. That largely explains why Europe, led by France and Germany, has invested so much political capital in the European Monetary System.

But the work of a decade went up in smoke just days earlier as holders of Italian lira and British pounds rushed to profit—or to avoid losses—by exchanging tens of billions of dollars' worth of the two currencies for German marks. France and Germany have the means to resist a similar run on the franc, if it resumes. The issue, in the end, is whether they have the stomach.

France's first line of defense is to buy francs with foreign currency it holds in reserve, much the way Washington supports the price of wheat by purchasing the commodity from growers. France did indeed

buy francs this week. But there is a limit to its reserves, and after a week of heady outlays the cupboard is nearly bare.

The Bundesbank, keeper of the German currency, is under no such constraint. It can create as many marks as it wishes and use them to buy francs. Can—and has: The Bundesbank reportedly purchased more than $10 billion worth of francs in three days.

There is, however, a cost to this defense. Marks sold for francs end up as private deposits in German banks, swelling the amount of money circulating in Germany...

France and Germany plainly have the weapons at hand to defeat speculators. And if speculators were sure the weapons would be used, the speculation would end. But they can never know that until they have tested the franc to its limits. Neither, presumably, can the French and German governments, whose resolve must ultimately turn on the fortitude of the electorate.

ANALYZING THE NEWS...

In this chapter, we noted that turmoil rocked foreign-exchange markets in September 1992, as speculative attacks led Britain and Italy to withdraw their currencies from the exchange rate mechanism of the European Monetary System. France did not devalue the franc against the mark at the same time in response to a speculative attack. (Nor did France officially devalue the franc in the July 1993 crisis.) Let's see why.

a This looks like the classic beginning of a speculative attack. Let R represent the French expected return curve and R_G represent the German expected return curve. In the figure, we see that an increase in German interest rates shifts the R_G curve to the right from R_{G0} to R_{G1}, leading speculators to believe that the DM/FF exchange rate will fall from EX_0^* to EX_1^*. To defend the franc, the Bank of France uses its foreign-exchange reserves of German marks to buy francs in the foreign-exchange market, increasing short-term interest rates and shifting the R_{ff} schedule from R_{ff0} to R_{ff1}. The exchange rate was restored to EX_0^*. Indeed, the Bank of France used more than half its reserves in the early days of the speculative attack, leading many analysts and speculators to believe that it would run out of marks. That development would force the French government to devalue the franc against the mark.

b The German central bank cooperated with the French central bank, indicating its willingness to support the franc. If speculators believed that Germany valued the exchange rate mechanism—which would collapse if France pulled out—they would be hesitant to continue the attack on the franc. Whether the attack reappears depends on whether the Franco-German interest rate differential narrows and whether speculators believe that the inflation-conscious Bundesbank will be willing to let the German money supply expand to defend the franc.

For further thought...

Suppose that you are a currency trader and believe that domestic political concerns in France will lead the Bank of France to reduce French short-term interest rates significantly. How would you react?

Source: Excerpted from Peter Passell, "High Noon in Europe's Currency Standoff," September 28, 1992. Copyright © 1991/1992 by The New York Times Company. Reprinted by permission.

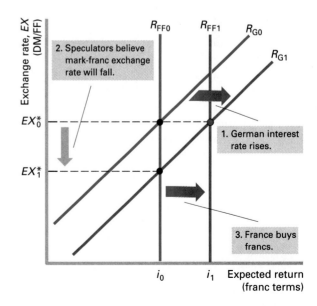

to be devalued. Therefore monetary unification is likely to give Germany, whose central bank has a strong anti-inflation reputation, the greatest power over unified monetary policy.

In the aftermath of the 1992 speculative attacks, the French ratified the Maastricht treaty in a close vote. The treaty had been rejected by popular vote in Denmark earlier in the year, though the Danes subsequently ratified the treaty in May 1993. As of August 1993, treaty ratification was virtually complete, though a speculative attack on the French franc in July 1993 and changes in the ERM raised concerns about the viability of monetary union. Most analysts believe that the Maastricht treaty's target date of 1999 for a single currency can't be achieved, owing to differences in inflation rates and budget deficits among countries. Some economists and policymakers suggest that a two-track approach to monetary unification is possible: Germany, France, Belgium, The Netherlands, and Luxembourg might bind their currencies together with fixed exchange rates, with England and Italy allowing more exchange rate flexibility against the German mark.

Key Terms and Concepts

Balance of payments
  Capital account
  Capital account balance
  Capital inflow
  Capital outflow
  Current account
  Current account balance
  Official reserve assets
  Official settlements balance
  Statistical discrepancy
  Trade balance

European Central Bank

Exchange rate regimes
  Bretton Woods system
  Devaluation
  European Monetary System
  Exchange rate mechanism

Fixed exchange rate systems
  Gold standard
  International Monetary Fund
  Revaluation
  Special Drawing Rights
  World Bank

Monetary union

Flexible exchange rate system

Foreign-exchange market interventions
  Capital controls
  Sterilized foreign-exchange intervention
  Unsterilized foreign-exchange intervention

International reserves

Speculative attack

Summary

1. A central bank's interventions in the foreign-exchange market affect its holdings of international reserves and the domestic monetary base. If nothing else changes, when a central bank buys foreign assets, its international reserves and monetary base increase by the amount of foreign assets acquired. When a central bank sells foreign assets, its international reserves and monetary base fall by the amount of foreign assets sold.

2. Central banks often are concerned about the effects of exchange rate depreciation or appreciation on the economy. A depreciating domestic currency raises the cost of foreign goods and may lead to inflation. Central banks hope to lessen this effect by buying their own countries' currencies. An appreciating currency may make domestic goods uncompetitive in world markets. Central banks attempt to lessen this effect by selling their own countries' currencies in the foreign-exchange market.

3. The balance of payments is an accounting system for keeping track of flows of private and government funds between a country and other countries.

The balance of payments accounts have two principal parts: the current account and the capital account. The official settlements balance in the capital account represents the net flows of international reserves that must move between countries to finance a balance of payments surplus or deficit.

4. Countries have entered into several international agreements to stabilize exchange rates. Prior to World War I, many countries agreed to convert their currencies into gold at fixed exchange rates. A second major effort came at the end of World War II with agreement on the Bretton Woods system, in which the U.S. dollar was convertible into gold and other currencies were convertible into dollars at fixed exchange rates. Because devaluing the dollar was difficult despite persistent U.S. balance of payments deficits, the Bretton Woods system collapsed in 1971. The present international financial system is best described as one in which exchange rates fluctuate with market forces but central banks intervene in the foreign-exchange market. In Europe, efforts to establish a fixed exchange rate system through monetary union are being debated.

Review Questions

1. If the Fed buys $3 billion worth of foreign assets with dollars, what happens to U.S. international reserves? What happens to the monetary base? Is this a *sterilized* or an *unsterilized* foreign-exchange intervention?

2. Suppose that the Fed sells $1 billion worth of foreign assets in exchange for dollars; at the same time, the Fed engages in a $1 billion open market purchase. What happens to the monetary base? Is this a *sterilized* or an *unsterilized* foreign-exchange intervention?

3. Using the exchange rate diagram, show how an unsterilized intervention by Japan can be used to

reduce the value of the yen relative to the dollar. Also show how an unsterilized intervention by the United States can be used to reduce the value of the yen relative to the dollar.

4. Under what key assumption does a sterilized intervention have no effect on the exchange rate? If this assumption isn't met, what is the effect on the dollar when the Fed buys foreign assets with dollars in a sterilized intervention? What do the data suggest about this assumption?

5. What are the problems with allowing a currency to appreciate relative to other currencies? What are the problems with allowing it to depreciate?

6. What is the difference between flexible and fixed exchange rate systems?

7. What is the purpose of the U.S. balance of payments system?

8. If Japan has a trade surplus, which is larger, its exports or its imports?

9. Why don't countries have control of their money supplies under a gold standard?

10. Why did the United States abandon the Bretton Woods system in 1971?

11. What are the purposes of the IMF and the World Bank?

12. Under a fixed exchange rate system, why do governments often put off devaluation or revaluation?

What do markets often do that forces them to devalue or revalue?

13. Why did Europe seek a monetary union in the early 1990s?

14. *Evaluate:* Because the U.S. dollar is the dominant reserve currency, the United States can experience large balance of payments deficits indefinitely.

15. *Evaluate:* If exchange rates are flexible, outcomes in the foreign-exchange market have no effect on domestic monetary policy.

16. Compare IMF assistance to halt a speculative attack on an overvalued currency in the Bretton Woods system to the Fed's lender-of-last-resort role for banks.

Analytical Problems

17. Suppose that new data show that the United Kingdom is about to head into a recession. Futures contracts on the pound indicate that it is expected to depreciate relative to the mark, yen, and dollar. What do you think financial markets expect the Bank of England to do in the future?

18. If you compared the sum of exports out of every country with the sum of imports into every country, what should be the world's current account balance?

19. If the U.S. current account surplus is $105 billion and the statistical discrepancy is –$25 billion, what is the capital account balance? Does this represent a capital outflow or inflow?

20. Under a gold standard, what happens to gold flows if a country runs persistent balance of payments deficits?

21. Suppose that the United Kingdom is attempting to maintain its exchange rate with Germany. But you

note that German real interest rates are higher than U.K. real interest rates and that inflation is lower in Germany than in the United Kingdom. What is your prediction about the future change in the DM/£ exchange rate? What actions might you take to try to profit from your knowledge? What would happen if many other people joined you, especially if the United Kingdom had few international reserve assets?

22. If the United States, Japan, and Germany agree to try to lower the value of the dollar relative to both the yen and the mark, while raising the value of the yen relative to the mark, what type of unsterilized interventions should take place?

23. Suppose that the United States has a trade deficit of $45 billion, but a current account balance of $20 billion. What is the balance of net services plus investment income plus unilateral transfers?

24. Suppose that a U.S. import company buys 10 Toyota autos from Japan at $10,000 each; the Japanese company uses the money to buy a $100,000 U.S. Treasury bond at the Treasury auction. How are these two transactions recorded in the balance of payments accounts for the United States?

25. Suppose that a Japanese firm donates $1 million of art to a U.S. art center; how is this transaction recorded in the balance of payments accounts for the United States? What is the change in the current account balance?

26. Suppose that the U.S. government sells old warships worth $300 million to Japan; Japan's government pays for them with its official holdings of dollar assets. How is this transaction recorded in the U.S. balance of payments accounts?

Data Questions

27. Look up exchange rate data in the latest *Economic Report of the President*. In 1991, the Fed increased money supply growth, reducing short-term interest rates. What happened to the value of the dollar compared to the German mark? Compared to the Japanese yen? Compared to the currencies of other countries? Are these results consistent with our theory about what happens to the exchange rate with expansionary monetary policy?

28. Describe, in general terms, the movements of the dollar against an index of the currencies of other industrial countries during the past 30 years.

part V

The Financial System and the Macro-economy

CHAPTER 23

The Demand for Money

By the end of the 1970s, inflation in the United States seemed to be spiraling out of control. Strong actions were needed, and the Fed, under the new leadership of Paul Volcker, responded. In October 1979, the Fed announced a new strategy: The Fed would use its policy tools to achieve predetermined targets for money growth. By the Fed's calculations, its money supply growth targets eventually would limit the economy's growth to a rate consistent with price stability and full employment.

Despite its bold statement, the Fed repeatedly overshot its own targets. Surprisingly, however, inflation fell markedly. What happened? Fed Chairman Volcker gave Congress the answer: The public's *demand for money* had become unstable and caused the Fed to rethink its targets. Above-target money supply growth wouldn't be inflationary, he explained, if people were demanding more money than usual each year to buy goods and services. Indeed, if extra money were not forthcoming to meet the higher demand, spending would fall, and the economy could lapse into recession.

This episode highlights the key roles that money demand plays in the economy. Money demand has an immediate impact in financial markets, helping to determine the amount of money available and the level of interest rates. It also serves as a link between financial markets and the real sector of the economy. For a specific supply of money, money demand helps determine the amount of goods and services bought and the overall price level. In this chapter we develop a simple model of money demand that includes both transactions and portfolio allocation considerations. We then evaluate how well the model explains actual money holdings.

In this chapter our analysis addresses two questions. **Q:** What factors determine the demand for money? **Q:** Can transactions and portfolio allocation motives explain actual money holdings?

Reasons for Holding Money

In Part IV we discussed determinants of the money supply process. In this chapter we analyze the demand for money: the decisions by people about how much of their wealth to hold in money balances. We already know that people hold money because of its usefulness as a medium of exchange, a store of value, a unit of account, and a means of deferred payment. How much money will households and businesses demand? The demand for money, as for other assets, reflects exchange and portfolio allocation decisions. People use money (currency, checkable deposits, and other close substitutes) in large part to carry out transactions. Hence the quantity of money demanded depends in part on the value of desired transactions. As we showed in Chapter 6, households and businesses allocate their resources among various money and nonmoney assets. In making these decisions, they take into account expected returns on alternative assets and the risk, liquidity, and information characteristics of those assets.

We describe transactions and portfolio allocation influences on the demand for money to help analyze links between financial markets and the economy. After we derive the determinants of money demand, we test how well our approach explains actual money holdings.

Transactions Motives

Let's begin the analysis of money demand by focusing on why households and businesses demand money for use in transactions. First, we show that households and firms think about their money holdings in real terms, that is, adjusted for changes in purchasing power. Then we demonstrate that the volume of transactions alone cannot completely explain the public's money holdings.

Real Money Balances

An important role of money is to help make transactions easy, suggesting that desired holdings of money should depend on the value of transactions. To understand why, let's consider two individuals who are deciding how to allocate their resources: Theodore Cleaver, an American, and Gundal Haskell, a German. Theodore and Gundal have identical real wealth holdings (that is, in terms of purchasing power) and preferences. They also face similar investment alternatives in terms of expected returns adjusted for asset risk, liquidity, and information characteristics. The theory of portfolio allocation (Chapter 6) suggests that these two individuals should hold the same proportion of their total resources as money balances.

What does this suggestion imply for their money holdings in nominal terms? Suppose that Gundal's wealth is measured in marks and that Theodore's is measured in dollars. Suppose also that it takes DM1.5 to equal $1 in purchasing power. That is, prices of goods measured in marks are higher (by 1.5 times) than prices of goods measured in dollars. If Theodore and Gundal have the same real wealth in money balances, the number of marks held by Gundal will be 1.5 times as large as the number of dollars held by Theodore. In other words, Gundal's nominal money balances are 1.5 times as large as Theodore's. Hence the demand for money for transactions is proportional to the price level.

We can apply this argument to money demand over time in an economy. In 1960, the price level in the United States was less than one-fourth of what it is today. No doubt your parents have told you how inexpensive eating out or going to the movies was before you were born. In fact, to conduct the same level of real transactions today as in 1960, you would need more than $4.00 for each 1960 dollar: Your nominal money balances would have to be more than four times as high. As was the case for Theodore and Gundal (if nothing else changes), a higher price level leads to a proportionately higher nominal demand for money.

Because changes in nominal money holdings are proportional to changes in the price level, we can focus on the demand for **real money balances,** or the value of money balances adjusted for changes in purchasing power. If we let M represent the money supply and P represent the price level in the economy (that is, the dollar price of a selected group of goods), real money balances are equal to the money supply divided by the price level, or

$$\text{Real money balances} = \frac{M}{P}.$$

The economy's real money balances represent the purchasing power of money holdings.

Velocity and the Demand for Real Balances

In the early 1900s, Irving Fisher of Yale University analyzed the relationship between money balances and transactions. He stressed the concept of **velocity of money,** which represents the average number of times a dollar is spent each year on a purchase of goods and services in the economy.[†] More precisely, velocity V is equal to total spending—the price level, P, times aggregate output, Y (representing the volume of real transactions)—divided by the quantity of money, M, or

$$V = \frac{PY}{M}. \tag{23.1}$$

[†] See Irving Fisher, *The Purchasing Power of Money*, New York: Macmillan, 1911. Fisher actually described velocity using transactions, rather than output. Output measures such as gross domestic product (GDP) are imperfect proxies for the volume of transactions. Purchases of assets, such as bonds, houses, or cars, require monetary transactions, but the purchases are not included in production or GDP. The annual volume of transactions is much higher than GDP, so transactions velocity is greater than velocity calculated by dividing GDP by the money stock.

For example, if the quantity of money is $2 trillion and nominal GDP is $6 trillion, velocity equals 3: On average, a dollar is spent three times each year to purchase goods and services in the economy.

If we multiply both sides of Eq. (23.1) by M, we get

$$MV = PY. \tag{23.2}$$

Equation (23.2), known as the **equation of exchange,** states that the quantity of money times the velocity of money equals nominal spending in the economy. Note that, because of the way we defined velocity in Eq. (23.1), the equation of exchange is an identity and therefore always holds.

To convert Eq. (23.2) into a *behavioral* theory of money demand, Fisher assumed that velocity, V, is a constant. Therefore we can rewrite Eq. (23.2) as

$$\frac{M}{P} = \left(\frac{1}{V}\right)Y. \tag{23.3}$$

Fisher reasoned that, if velocity were constant, the demand for real money balances M/P should be proportional to the level of real transactions.[†] Hence Fisher converted Eq. (23.2) into a **money demand function,** which relates the demand for real money balances to its underlying determinants. In Fisher's approach, the determinant of the demand for real balances is the real volume of transactions. Thus his approach is called the **quantity theory of money demand.**

Using the volume of transactions as a determinant of the demand for money makes sense. We stated earlier that, in order to conduct everyday transactions, households and businesses increase their nominal money holdings as prices rise. What about the demand for real money balances? As the real incomes of households and businesses increase, they typically conduct more real transactions. In other words, the value of high-income households' purchases will be greater than the value of low-income households' purchases. Similarly, a large department store with sales of $10 million per year will have a greater volume of transactions with suppliers, employers, and customers than the corner general store with annual sales of $100,000. We can generalize from this observation that the public's demand for money rises with the volume of transactions. The effect on real money balances is that (if nothing else changes) the quantity of real money balances rises with real incomes.

Not all economists at that time agreed with Fisher's assumption that velocity (or velocity growth) is constant. For example, others hypothesized that it could increase or decrease in response to changes in returns on money and nonmoney assets. We explore this possibility when we discuss portfolio allocation motives for holding money.

[†] Fisher actually allowed for a uniform rate of growth over time in velocity, reflecting changes in means of making payments. Changes in velocity must be *predictable* to ensure the usefulness of the money demand function in Eq. (23.3).

In Fisher's time, economic data were not measured as precisely as they are now, and thus his assumption about velocity wasn't testable; today it is. Economists generally use nominal income (GDP) to study the volume of transactions. We can obtain data on money holdings and nominal income from sources such as the *Federal Reserve Bulletin* and the Council of Economic Advisers' *Economic Report of the President* in order to calculate velocity. Figure 23.1 illustrates the year-to-year percentage change in the velocity of money (measured using *M1* and *M2*) for each year since the founding of the Federal Reserve System in 1914. Note that velocity isn't constant, even for short periods of time. Prior to the late 1940s, the velocity of both *M1* and *M2* fluctuated significantly, increasing in some periods and decreasing in others.

For example, velocity declined during economic downturns in the early 1920s and 1930s and during World War II. From the late 1940s to about 1980, the velocity of *M1* declined infrequently, but its growth wasn't always even. During the 1970s, some economists suggested that, so long as a trend in velocity was allowed for, the quantity theory could still accurately characterize the relationship between nominal GDP and money.

However, as Fig. 23.1 shows, the velocity of *M1* declined significantly during the 1980s. Economists point to two causative factors: financial innovation and movements in interest rates. The inclusion in *M1* of interest-bearing substitutes for conventional checkable deposits in the early 1980s increased the demand for *M1* at each level of nominal GDP, thereby decreasing velocity. The fall in interest rates on nonmoney assets in the early 1980s also likely increased the demand for money relative to other assets, implying a decline in velocity. The velocity of *M2* was generally more stable

> **FIGURE 23.1**

Changes in Velocity of *M1* and *M2* in the United States (Percentage Change from Previous Year)
The velocity of money measures depicted equal (1) nominal GDP divided by *M1*, and (2) nominal GDP divided by *M2*. Velocity is not constant, even over short periods of time.

Source: Federal Reserve Bulletin and Council of Economic Advisers, Economic Report of the President, various issues.

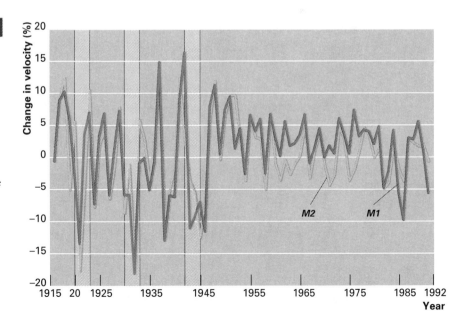

after the early 1950s, though, as Box 23.1 shows, the stable relationship between *M2* and nominal GDP deteriorated in the early 1990s.

Why are economists and policymakers so concerned about significant fluctuations in velocity? Recall that the Fed uses money supply and interest rate targets to influence its goals for inflation and real output growth (Chapter 21). Unpredictable changes in velocity make it more difficult for the Fed to use targets for the money supply to achieve its goals. The significant instability of *M1*'s velocity during the 1980s led the Fed to drop its targets for *M1* after 1987. Since that time, it has emphasized *M2* and indicators of inflation.

The fluctuations in velocity have a significant implication: Changes in the volume of transactions cannot completely explain changes in money holdings. What factors account for variations in velocity over time? Payments system factors, interest rate changes, and portfolio allocation decisions are the most important.

Payments System Factors.   Velocity is determined in part by the ways in which individuals conduct transactions, called **payments system factors.** In other words, if more substitutes for measured money, such as credit cards or automatic teller machines, become available to conduct transactions, the public needs less currency and checkable deposits to finance current spending. Hence *M1* velocity, *PY/M*, will increase. Alternatively, if money

Consider this...   BOX 23.1
The Money Growth Slowdown in 1992: Is Velocity the Culprit?

During the early 1990s, the Fed was unsuccessful in hitting its targets for *M2* growth. The Fed's 1992 annual target range for *M2* growth was 2.5–6.5%. However, the Fed achieved only about 1.5% growth. Thus 1992 was the third year in a row for which the Fed failed to achieve much above the lower end of its target growth rate range. Many analysts and policymakers blamed the Fed's failure to hit its money growth targets for the economy's slow recovery from recession.

The Fed focused on *M2* because of its predictable relationship to the level of nominal GDP. From 1959 to 1989, the *M2*

velocity—nominal GDP divided by *M2*—was stable. In the early 1990s, the relationship between *M2* and nominal GDP broke down. From 1989 through 1992, yields on Treasury bills and other short-term securities declined much faster than deposit rates on *M2* assets, thus lowering the opportunity cost of holding *M2*. This reduction in opportunity cost should have increased money demand and reduced velocity, but velocity stayed roughly constant.

What happened? Most of the collapse in *M2* growth can be explained by the drop in the amount of small time deposits, which resulted in part from the

closing of weak savings and loan institutions. In addition, time deposits at commercial banks fell because banks tend to adjust yields on small time deposits much more rapidly than they adjust yields on checking and saving accounts. As a result, a change in opportunity cost of holding checkable deposits (one component of *M2*) wasn't the same as a change in the opportunity cost of holding small time deposits (another component of *M2*), causing velocity to be unstable. The Fed is searching for ways to modify *M2* to improve its ability to achieve its money growth targets and policy goals.

becomes more convenient for carrying out transactions, the public will demand more money to finance current spending. For example, if credit card companies started imposing a $1 charge for processing each purchase, you probably would pay for fewer transactions with charge cards and carry more cash. Thus money balances would rise, and the velocity of money would fall. Payments system factors change in response to the same factors that determine financial innovation: shifts in the demand for, costs of providing, and regulation of financial services.

Interest Rate Changes. The early theories of money demand, such as the quantity theory, didn't include interest rates as a factor in the transactions demand for money. In separate contributions to the theory of money demand, William Baumol of Princeton University and James Tobin of Yale University developed models of the effects of interest rates on transactions demand.[†] To explore the logic of their approach, let's consider an example. Stanley Suffolk receives a paycheck of $2500 once each month and spends that amount at a constant rate during the month (the balances are held only for transactions purposes). One solution for him is to draw down his account evenly over the course of the month so that his average monthly balance is 2500/2 = $1250. At the end of the month, Stanley has $0 left. When he gets paid again, the process continues. The annual velocity of money for Stanley is his nominal income, $30,000, divided by his average monthly balance, $1250, or 24. Assuming that money pays a zero interest return, however, he foregoes earning interest on his money.

To earn interest instead of letting his funds lie idle, Stanley could invest part of his paycheck of $2500, say, $1250 in Treasury bonds, adding interest income to his spendable resources. If Stanley invests $1250, his money balance will be zero halfway through each month rather than at the end of the month. If the interest rate on Treasury bonds is 0.75% per month, he earns an additional $4.69 [(0.5)(0.0075)($1250)] per month, or $56.25 per year. Stanley cannot spend Treasury bonds directly, though he can convert them to money. This strategy does involve costs: the costs of converting other assets into money. Hence Stanley trades off the benefits of holding money with the opportunity cost measured by the market interest rate he could earn by holding bonds.

Baumol and Tobin noted that this trade-off indicates that the transactions demand for money does depend on interest rates. An increase in the

[†] The original Baumol and Tobin papers appeared in 1952 and 1956, respectively. Many years later, David Romer of the University of California, Berkeley expanded the Baumol-Tobin approach to address effects of shifts between money and nonmoney assets on the economy. William J. Baumol, "The Transactions Demand for Cash: An Inventory-Theoretic Approach," *Quarterly Journal of Economics*, 66: 545–556, 1952. James Tobin, "The Interest-Elasticity of the Transactions Demand for Cash," *Review of Economics and Statistics*, 38: 241–247, 1956. David Romer, "A Simple General Equilibrium Version of the Baumol-Tobin Model," *Quarterly Journal of Economics*, 101: 663–686, 1986.

market interest rate increases the opportunity cost of holding money balances for transactions purposes. As a result, individuals hold smaller money balances, and velocity increases. A decrease in money market interest rates reduces the cost of holding money; individuals will hold larger money balances, and velocity will decline. Hence transactions demand for money is negatively related to market interest rates, whereas the velocity of money balances held to conduct transactions is positively related to market interest rates. The Baumol-Tobin approach is yet another example of the economic concept of opportunity cost that you learned about in your principles of economics course and we referred to in discussing the theory of portfolio allocation (Chapter 6). Their approach shows clearly that interest rates do play a role in determining the transactions demand for money.

Portfolio Allocation Decisions.   Velocity also changes over time in response to portfolio allocation decisions. Because money is an asset as well as the medium of exchange, changes in expected returns on money or in risk, liquidity, or information costs associated with it will change households' and businesses' demand for cash balances.

▶   C H E C K P O I N T   *What are the effects of the following on the demand for real money balances and the velocity of* M1? *(a) Financial institutions offer cash-management services to firms. (b) Bank credit cards become less widely used.*

(a) Cash management allows more of investment portfolios to be in nonmoney assets, the demand for M/P falls, and V rises because people have less need to hold money.

(b) Because more cash is used in transactions, the demand for M/P rises and V falls. ◀

Portfolio Allocation Motives

As we have demonstrated, the volume of transactions cannot completely explain movements in money balances. The theory of portfolio allocation offers a clue to other influences on the demand for money. We can apply the theory of portfolio allocation to the demand for money by analyzing each determinant of asset demand.

Income and Wealth.   Real money balances held in currency and checkable deposits are an example of a necessity asset. Therefore households and businesses with greater income and wealth won't hold the same proportion of their assets in zero- or low-yielding money balances as households and firms with low incomes will. For example, individuals with high income may maintain higher-yielding accounts that they can easily transfer to checkable deposits; large firms may do the same. In addition, businesses may have a line of credit with banks, which permits them to conduct transactions with low cash or checkable deposit balances. Higher-income households can use bank credit cards (VISA® or MasterCard®) similarly. The demand for real balances increases with real income, but it does so less than proportionately.

Expected Returns. When assessing the return on money assets, households and businesses must take into account not only the interest paid on money balances, but also money's *convenience yield.* This is the amount of interest that they are willing to sacrifice in return for the low-risk, transactions, and information costs of holding money. If nothing else changes, an increase in the interest paid on money balances or in the convenience yield on money will lead households and businesses to increase their money balances and the quantity of money demanded. A decrease in the interest paid on money balances or in the convenience yield will lead households and businesses to decrease their money balances and the quantity of money demanded. Thus households and businesses compare the expected returns on nonmoney assets with the expected returns on money (from interest and convenience yield) in deciding how much money to hold.

Risk, Liquidity, and Information. When allocating how much of their assets to hold as money, individuals and firms also consider the risk, liquidity, and information benefits of holding money. If returns on alternative assets (such as commercial paper, bonds, or stocks) become more risky, savers may switch their holdings into money, increasing money demand. Innovations that allow easy movements of funds from less liquid forms to more liquid forms, such as from bonds or stocks to a checking account or from home equity to a line of credit, reduce the value placed on money's liquidity. The more liquid other assets become, the more savers focus on money's explicit interest return—the interest rate paid on money balances. Finally, some individuals place a high value on holding currency because it gives them anonymity. Those involved in the drug trade, tax evasion, and other illegal activities may value currency for that reason. Hence the demand for money may be affected by changes in the volume of illegal activity or the tax code.

▶ C H E C K P O I N T *Suppose that, of a total wealth of $25,000, Ms. Smart allocates $20,000 to Treasury bills yielding 8% and places $5000 in a checking account yielding 5%. What value does Ms. Smart place on her checkable deposits? What if the yield on T-bills rises to 10%?* Implicitly, Ms. Smart values the liquidity services of her checkable deposits at least as much as (0.03)($5000), or $150 per year, the interest foregone. If the yield on T-bills rises to 10%, however, Ms. Smart may decide that the liquidity benefits of checkable deposits is too expensive (with $250 per year of foregone interest) and reduce her money holdings to, say, $4000. ◀

Building Blocks for the Portfolio Approach

In the late nineteenth and early twentieth centuries, most analyses of money demand reflected only transactions considerations. The portfolio approach we develop in this chapter builds on the important contributions to money demand theory of John Maynard Keynes and Milton Friedman.

Keynes's Contribution. John Maynard Keynes offered an early analysis of portfolio allocation motives for money demand in his celebrated 1936 book, *The General Theory of Employment, Interest, and Money*. Although he believed that transactions demand was important, the key feature in his **liquidity preference theory** was his emphasis on the sensitivity of money demand to changes in interest rates.

Keynes viewed the role of nonmoney assets in the money demand relationship in terms of a simplified portfolio allocation problem, to which he referred as the *speculative motive* for holding money. Keynes supposed that wealth could be allocated between two assets: money and "bonds" (representing all other financial assets), assuming that the expected return on bonds is determined by the interest rate on bonds adjusted for expectations of capital gains or losses. For money, defined as the sum of currency and checkable deposits (*M1*), Keynes assumed that the return is zero. (At the time of his writing, the interest rate on currency was zero, and checkable deposits paid no interest.)

Suppose that you speculate that interest rates on bonds will fall, and therefore you expect a capital gain from holding bonds. Accordingly, you would want to hold less of your wealth in money and more of it in bonds. But, if you expect interest rates to rise (and hence expect a capital loss on bonds), the zero return on money may outweigh the potentially negative total return on bonds. Then you would hold more money and less wealth in bonds. Hence the demand for money balances is negatively related to the interest rate on nonmoney assets.[†]

Keynes identified two other reasons for holding money: (1) to carry out regular transactions (the *transactions motive*), and (2) to pay for unexpected transactions (which he called the *precautionary motive*). Based on these motives and the speculative motive, he theorized that money holdings depend on real income, as well as on the interest rate on nonmoney assets. Keynes's liquidity preference theory states that the demand for real money balances, *M/P*, is a function *L* (for liquidity preference) of aggregate output, *Y*, and the interest rate, *i*:

$$\frac{M}{P} = L(Y,i). \tag{23.4}$$

[†] Keynes recognized expectations by assuming that investors expect interest rates to return to some "normal" level. Thus if interest rates are above that normal value, individuals expect falling rates and capital gains on bonds (and the opposite if interest rates are less than the normal value). Evidence shows that the assumption of a normal value for nominal interest rates is much less plausible today than in the 1930s.

Because the quantity of real balances demanded rises with income and trans-actions, an increase in Y leads to an increase in M/P—a positive relationship. Because a higher interest rate raises the opportunity cost of holding money and reduces the quantity of money demanded, an increase in i leads to a decrease in M/P—a negative relationship.

The Keynesian liquidity preference approach also offers an explanation for changes in velocity that is based on the fact that the demand for money is negatively related to interest rates. Let's rewrite Keynes's expression for the demand for real balances in Eq. (23.4) as

$$\frac{P}{M} = \frac{1}{L(Y,i)}.$$

Multiplying both sides of this relation by Y yields an expression for velocity:

$$V = \frac{PY}{M} = \frac{Y}{M/P} = \frac{Y}{L(Y,i)}. \tag{23.5}$$

Suppose that the interest rate on bonds, i, rises but that aggregate income, Y, doesn't change. Because the opportunity cost of holding money has gone up, you would use some of your money holdings to buy bonds, reducing your demand for real money balances. Hence the denominator of the right-hand side of Eq. (23.5) would fall, raising velocity. More generally, the fact that interest rates fluctuate means that velocity fluctuates as well.

Friedman's Contribution. Milton Friedman proposed another approach to analyzing money demand in 1956.[†] He didn't attempt to separate money demand into components, or motives, as Keynes had done. Instead, he relied more generally on the determinants of asset demand.

In trying to explain the public's demand for money, Friedman examined *M2*, a broader measure of money than *M1*. Based on the determinants of asset demand, he reasoned, money holdings depend on the expected average income over a lifetime for an individual, Y^*. He called Y^* *permanent income* and assumed that it is proportional to wealth, one of the determinants of asset demand for money. To compare expected returns on money and non-money assets, Friedman theorized that the demand for money should depend negatively on two measures of the opportunity cost of holding money: (1) the difference between the expected return on financial assets, i, and the return on money, i_M, and (2) the difference between the expected return on durable goods measured by expected inflation, π^e, and the return on money. That is, Friedman's model for the demand for real money balances can be expressed as

$$\frac{M}{P} = L(Y^*, i - i_M, \pi^e - i_M). \tag{23.6}$$

[†] Milton Friedman, "The Quantity Theory of Money: A Restatement," in Milton Friedman, ed., *Studies in the Quantity Theory of Money*, Chicago: University of Chicago Press, 1956.

In Friedman's approach, the demand for real money balances increases with increases in permanent income, Y^*—a positive relationship—and falls with increases in the opportunity cost of holding money, $i - i_M$ and $\pi^e - i_M$—both negative relationships.

Comparing the Two Approaches. Both Keynes and Friedman used the theory of portfolio allocation in their analyses of money demand, but there are important differences in their approaches. In Friedman's theory, money demand depends on households' permanent income; hence money demand responds only slightly to short-run fluctuations in income or wealth. In addition, whereas Keynes considered only money and all other financial assets (lumped together as bonds), Friedman allowed for portfolio substitution among money, bonds, equities, and durable goods. His "expected inflation" term reflects the return on durable goods as their nominal values appreciate with inflation. Thus, according to Friedman, if households expect a high rate of inflation (and a low return on money as a result), they will invest more of their wealth in housing and consumer durable goods as inflation hedges. Finally, Keynes assumed the rate of return on money to be zero. In Friedman's model the return on money consists both of explicit interest payments on money and the services provided by financial institutions, such as check-clearing, bill-paying, and other deposit-related services. In Friedman's approach, the differences between the return on various nonmoney assets and the return on money influences the public's demand for real money balances. Friedman believed that such differences would be small, offering little hope that changes in interest rates would affect the demand for money.

Putting It All Together : Determinants of Money Demand

We can now synthesize our analyses of transactions and portfolio allocation motives for holding money to formulate a simple model of the public's demand for real money balances.

1. The demand for real money balances depends positively on the level of transactions, which we represent with real income, Y. For example, if you expect to make more purchases next year than this year, you will generally hold more money balances.
2. As we showed in the analysis of transactions demand, the demand for real balances depends negatively on payments system developments, S, that provide alternatives to money for making payments. For example, the widespread use of bank credit cards generally reduces money demand.
3. We need to consider portfolio allocation decisions. Because many alternatives to money as a financial asset are available, the expected return on each

Q: What factors determine the demand for money?

A: The demand for money depends on the price level, real output, availability of money substitutes as means of payment, interest rates on nonmoney assets, and the rate of return on money.

(adjusted for differences in risk, liquidity, and information costs) in principle influence the demand for money. Recall that returns on financial assets tend to move together (Chapter 7).

Hence we can summarize the role of expected returns on nonmoney assets through "the nominal interest rate," i. Consistent with the theory of portfolio allocation, if nothing else changes, the demand for real money balances depends negatively on the difference between the expected return on alternative assets, i, and the yield on money (including the convenience yield), i_M.[†] Thus, if Treasury bill yields rise relative to yields on money balances, savers will reduce their holdings of money to buy T-bills. The quantity of money demanded declines because wealth will be reallocated to the now higher-yielding alternatives.

The Money Demand Function

We combine these factors in a model that we can use to predict the demand for money in the United States and other countries. The demand for real money balances is the demand for nominal money balances, M_d, divided by the price level, P:

$$\frac{M_d}{P} = L(Y, \ S, \ i - i_M).\tag{23.7}$$

The liquidity function, represented by L in Eq. (23.7), describes the demand for real balances as a function of real income, Y, payments system factors, S, and expected returns on nonmoney assets and money, $i - i_M$. Thus:

- an increase in real income raises the real quantity of money demanded;
- an increase in the availability of money substitutes as means of payments reduces the real quantity of money demanded;
- increases in the opportunity cost of holding real money balances decrease the real quantity of money demanded (and the opportunity cost of holding money rises when market interest rates rise relative to the return on money); and
- an increase in expected inflation leads to an increase in the opportunity cost of holding money and hence to a decline in money demand, if market interest rates rise more than the interest paid on money balances as expected inflation rises.

The demand for money expressed by Eq. (23.7) provides potentially useful information about movements in real money balances over time in response to shifts in real income and expected returns on money and nonmoney assets. Table 23.1 summarizes these determinants of money demand.

[†] Note that we could have discussed *real* expected returns, subtracting expected inflation from i and i_M. The difference, $i - i_M$, would be unaffected, however.

TABLE 23.1	DETERMINANTS OF THE DEMAND FOR MONEY	
An Increase in...	Causes Money Demand to...	Because of...
price level P	increase proportionally	*transactions demand:* A doubling of the price level doubles the number of dollars needed for transactions.
real income Y	increase less than proportionally	*transactions demand:* Increases in income raise the amount of transactions and the demand for liquid assets.
availability of money substitutes, S, as means of payment	decrease	*transactions demand:* More money substitutes cause households and businesses to economize on money holdings.
interest rate on nonmoney assets, i	decrease	*transactions and portfolio allocation demand:* A greater return on alternative assets leads households and businesses to switch from holding money.
return on money i_M	increase	*portfolio allocation demand:* A greater return on money makes households and businesses more willing to hold money.

Measuring Money Demand

To connect the money demand expression, Eq. (23.7), to actual money holdings, we need to be able to measure money. Shifts in regulation and financial innovation affect the liquidity of certain financial assets. Recall that the Fed tries to solve this problem by grouping liquid financial assets into *monetary aggregates* (Chapter 2). The narrowest aggregate, *M1*, reflects the medium of exchange role for money and comprises currency and checkable deposits. Broader monetary aggregates, such as *M2* and *M3*, include the assets in *M1* plus other assets with less liquidity. Attempts to estimate money demand relationships, such as that expressed in Eq. (23.7), use alternative definitions of money drawn from the monetary aggregates.

The monetary aggregates approach is only a partial solution to the problem of measuring money. An aggregate is defined as the sum of the amounts of various assets outstanding, with each asset having the same weight. Recently, economists have developed *weighted aggregates*, sometimes called *Divisia aggregates*, which index assets by their liquidity. For example, a dollar held in currency or checkable deposits might be given more weight in a revised aggregate than a dollar held in time or savings deposits. This approach, used by many academic economists and the Fed, has led to money demand models that fit the data better.

Even if economists could measure money demand perfectly, a second problem remains: the closeness with which the demand for real balances can be related to its determinants in Eq. (23.7). Financial economists

Q: Can transactions and portfolio allocation motives explain actual money holdings?

A: Transactions and portfolio allocation determinants explain the demand for real money balances much of the time. The money demand function is unstable, however, owing to changes in payments system factors and financial innovation.

usually estimate money demand functions such as Eq. (23.7), using *M1* or *M2* and price level, real income, interest rate, and expected inflation data. In so doing, they can isolate the partial effect of individual determinants of money demand on real money balances, holding all other determinants constant. In 1973, Stephen Goldfeld of Princeton University showed that the simple money demand function fit the data at that time very well. (See the Appendix to this chapter for a discussion of Goldfeld's approaches.)

Problems with the validity of this simple model approach began to surface after 1973 (see the Other times, other places box). During the 1970s, high nominal interest rates created a demand for liquid alternatives to money. Financial innovation responded by producing liquid, interest-bearing substitutes for checkable deposits (which at the time paid no interest) for households, and overnight repurchase agreements for businesses. With such interest-bearing instruments in place, the demand for money, measured as *M1*, declined.

During the early 1980s, financial innovations *increased* money demand, thereby increasing velocity. As interest-bearing checkable deposits (such as negotiated order of withdrawal, NOW accounts and automatic transfer service, ATS accounts) were incorporated into the definition of *M1*, the demand for *M1* balances increased substantially.

Economists and policymakers have learned that, although explaining shifts in the simple money demand function is straightforward (at least after the fact), such factors often are hard to quantify. The finan-

Other times, other places...
The Case of the Missing Money

The theory of portfolio allocation identifies the most important determinants of asset demand, including the demand for money. In 1973, Stephen Goldfeld attempted to measure the strength of each variable in the model of the demand for *M1* in Eq. (23.7).

The trouble started soon after Goldfeld's 1973 paper[†] was published. Between late 1974 and the beginning of 1976, Goldfeld's money demand equation (based on Eq. 23.7) substantially overpredicted the actual demand for currency and checkable deposits in the United States. In other words,

for the changes in the price level, real income, and interest rates during that period—and the relationship Goldfeld had estimated prior to 1973—the actual demand for money was too low. Goldfeld referred to this episode as "the case of the missing money." After this episode, the money demand function performed much better for the rest of the 1970s. However, in the 1980s, the money demand function underpredicted money demand on several occasions (notably in 1982 and 1985).

How should we interpret this failure of the simple money

demand function? In theory, the model described by Eq. (23.7) captures the key factors affecting money demand. But in using the model, analysts had to make practical concessions. Specifically, variables representing changes in the payments system are hard to construct and hence were usually omitted. At times, however, such changes are important. And when they are, the simple money demand functions will yield inaccurate predictions.

[†] See Stephen Goldfeld, "The Case of the Missing Money," *Brookings Papers on Economic Activity*, 3:683–734, 1976.

MOVING FROM THEORY TO PRACTICE...

THE WALL STREET JOURNAL JANUARY 27, 1992

Restoring the Demand for Official "Money" in Russia

Top-notch monetary economists in the U.S. and Europe are focusing their considerable brainpower on how to stabilize the ruble, and who can blame them for wanting to tackle one of economic history's trickiest puzzles? People everywhere wish to help the Former Soviet Union (FSU) get back on its feet, as was evidenced by last week's 47-nation FSU aid conference in Washington... Dollars had long since become a black-market "parallel" currency in Russia, and the ruble was becoming quasi-money...

When price controls are removed after inflation, prices soar as the market tries to equilibrate the supply of currency with the supply of goods and services available. That is the trauma citizens of the FSU now are experiencing...

The lack of faith in the ruble is rational enough. The Russian government, it is widely believed, will have to continue printing rubles at a desperate rate just to finance the huge deficit it inherited from the old Soviet Union, a shortfall still eluding the accountants but estimated as high as 20% of gross national product. With prices rising and almost everyone still working for the government, there will continue to be heavy pressure for wage increases...

There is in fact only one way [to win confidence in money], by controlling its supply and convincing the broad public that a stable currency is the single goal of monetary policy. This feat was achieved by the West Germans in the postwar era by giving the Bundesbank a currency-stabilization mandate and a high degree of political independence. Russia and the other republics could do the same and will soon be aided politically in any such endeavor by a broad public abhorrence of inflation.

Just to be sure, they could go the "currency-board" route, fixing the value of the ruble and other national currencies to the dollar and not even establishing a central bank with discretionary money-creation authority. To draw hard currencies out of the black market and try to hasten development of a private banking system, governments could authorize private banks to issue bank notes, with strict requirements that they be backed with hard currency or gold.

The question is not really how, but whether. There will be those Westerners who will advise them that a hard currency would be foolhardy, that it would cause "deflation" and remove the government's principal tool, inflation, for getting out of budgetary jams. Both arguments are wrong. Deflation is not a risk when prices are soaring, and the junk heap of history is littered with governments that tried to inflate their way out of budget problems.

ANALYZING THE NEWS...

The demand for real money balances depends on real income, the opportunity cost of holding money (adjusted for differences in risk, liquidity, and information characteristics of money and nonmoney assets), and payments system factors. In our analysis of money demand in the United States, we noted that economists have to estimate how the public's demand for money responds to changes in these variables. The article notes that, prior to and in the wake of the collapse of the Soviet Union, the public's demand for rubles fell dramatically. Citizens lost confidence that the ruble would be accepted in ordinary commercial transactions and in the settlement of debts, that is, whether the ruble would satisfy the basic medium of exchange role of money.

ⓐ Why would citizens prefer to use dollars (or marks) in exchange rather than rubles? Rapid inflation reduces the real value of the ruble, which pays no interest. The values of foreign currencies, such as the dollar or the mark, are more stable in real terms. This relative stability increases their usefulness both as a medium of exchange and a unit of account.

ⓑ Why would rapid inflation following the removal of price controls reduce the demand for real ruble balances? Inflation increases the opportunity cost of holding currency and checkable deposits, encouraging the public to hold assets whose value does not fall with inflation (such as goods).

For further thought...

Evaluate the usefulness of the following proposals for increasing the demand for real money balances (currency and checkable deposits in financial institutions) in the Commonwealth of Independent States (Russia and the other new nations formed from the old Soviet Union): (1) pass a law stating that rubles must be used in transactions; (2) permit banks to pay market rates of interest on deposits; and (3) adopt the article's suggestion that private banks issue notes backed by U.S. dollars or gold.

Source: Excerpted from George Melloan, "How to Teach Russians to Trust Their Money," January 27, 1992. Reprinted by permission of *The Wall Street Journal*, ©1992 Dow Jones & Co., Inc. All Rights Reserved Worldwide.

cial system changes over time in response to shifts in the cost of providing, the demand for, and the regulation of financial services. Effects of these changes on the demand for money make forecasting it a difficult task. Similar challenges confront those making money demand forecasts in other countries.

Key Terms and Concepts

Equation of exchange

Liquidity preference theory

Money demand function

Payments system factors

Quantity theory of money demand

Real money balances

Velocity of money

Summary

1. Money assets held in the portfolios of households and firms represent the demand for money. The demand for money is a demand for real money balances; that is, the demand for nominal money balances is proportional to the price level.

2. The principal determinants of the demand for real money balances are real income and the opportunity cost of holding money. Higher levels of real income increase the volume of transactions and hence the demand for money as a medium of exchange. Increases in the returns on nonmoney assets relative to the return on money decrease the demand for money, holding constant risk, liquidity, and information characteristics of money and nonmoney assets.

3. The relationship among money demand, real income, and the opportunity cost of holding money

also depends on payments system factors: the means for making and receiving payments. Changes in these factors can cause the demand for real money balances to shift relative to its historical relationship to real income and the opportunity cost of holding money.

4. Financial economists have estimated the effects of real income, interest rates, and other variables on the demand for money using data from the United States and other economies. Such relationships were stable in the United States through the early 1970s. They shifted during the 1970s and 1980s, reflecting (among other things) changes in payments system factors, increases in the liquidity of nonmoney assets as a result of financial deregulation, and increases in the interest return on money assets. As money demand shifted, so did velocity— the ratio of nominal income to money.

Review Questions

1. How do *real* money balances differ from *nominal* money balances?

2. Who is likely to have greater money balances: someone with an income of $50,000 per year or

someone with an income of $25,000 per year? Explain.

3. Has velocity been constant over time in the United States? Explain.

4. Is it surprising that velocity varies greatly from one country to another? Why or why not?

5. Define *payments system factors*. Why are they important for money demand?

6. What happens to money demand if
   a. the risk of nonmoney assets rises?
   b. the liquidity of nonmoney assets rises?
   c. the information costs of nonmoney assets rises?

7. In the Baumol-Tobin approach, which opportunity cost affects money demand?

8. If your income doubles, is your demand for money balances likely to double? Explain.

9. According to Keynes's liquidity preference theory, what happens to money demand if interest rates are expected to fall?

10. According to the liquidity preference theory, what happens to money demand in a recession? In an expansion? What happens to velocity in a recession and an expansion?

11. What income concept is important in Friedman's approach to money demand? How is this income concept defined? Why does this concept make estimating money demand empirically more difficult?

12. Why does higher expected inflation reduce money demand if the yield on money does not change? If the yield on money rises, but expected inflation doesn't change, what happens to money demand?

13. What is a *weighted monetary aggregate*? Why might its use be superior to simple-sum aggregates such as *M1* and *M2*?

Analytical Problems

14. You have been asked to model the demand for *M1* and *M2* measures of money in the United States. Discuss effects on the demand for these monetary aggregates in response to
    a. a decrease in expected inflation;
    b. an increase in enforcement of laws against drug sales and tax evasion; and
    c. an expectation by investors that the stock market values will collapse in the near future.

15. Suppose real income in the economy is $6 trillion, the price level is 1.0, and velocity is constant at 3.0.
    a. What are the quantities demanded of nominal and real money balances?
    b. Suppose that the central bank sets the nominal money supply at $2.5 trillion. What happens to the price level? Why?

16. If nominal GDP is $6000 billion and the *M1* measure of the money supply is $1200 billion, what is velocity?

17. Between 1970 and 1980, the nominal demand for money doubled, but the real demand for money didn't change. What happened to the price level during this period?

18. If nominal money demand is proportional to nominal income, by how much will real money demand increase if real income rises 10%?

19. Suppose that on average a dollar is spent four times a year to purchase final goods and services. How big is the money supply if nominal GDP is $6 trillion?

20. If the Fed had based monetary policy in the 1980s on the assumption that velocity would be constant, would inflation have been higher or lower than it actually was? Why?

21. Suppose that you have a checking account that pays interest of 3%; you maintain at least $1000 in the account at all times so that you can avoid paying service charges. If you wanted to, you could put the

$1000 in a money market fund earning 8%. How much in service charges must you avoid for this deal to be profitable for you?

22. Why is money demand high in southern Florida and near the Mexican border?

23. Suppose that velocity rises but incomes haven't changed. What do you think happened to interest rates, according to the Keynesian liquidity preference theory? Why?

24. Suppose that expected inflation rises by 3%, the yield on money rises by 3%, and the yield on non-money assets rises by 3%. What is the effect on real money demand? What if expected inflation rose by only 2%? What if the yield on nonmoney assets rose by 4%?

25. Suppose that computer technology became so cheap that there was no need ever to use cash or to have money in a non–interest-bearing checking account. Computers make it possible to keep any money you have in the bank in an investment fund, to maximize your return. This system effectively makes bank deposits a nonmoney asset. What do

you think is likely to happen to the ability of money demand functions to track money demand when such an innovation occurs? How might the definition of money change if such an innovation occurs?

26. In Nationia, no explicit interest is paid on money balances, and households and businesses receive a constant convenience yield from holding money. The demand for real balances is

$$\frac{M_d}{P} = 1000 + 0.25Y - 1000i.$$

a. In Nationia, $Y = 2000$, $P = 100$, and $i = 0.10$. Solve for (i) nominal and real money balances, and (ii) velocity.

b. Using the values for Y, P, and i in part (a) as initial conditions, how is velocity affected by an increase in the interest rate? In real income?

27. Discuss at least one problem in estimating the demand for money using the approach derived in this chapter. Suggest an approach that would reduce the effect of this problem on forecasts of money demand.

Data Question

28. In the latest issue of the *Economic Report of the President*, find data on nominal GDP and the *M1* and *M2* measures of the money supply for the last three years. Calculate velocity for both *M1* and *M2* for each year. Do you see any trend in velocity? If so, what is it?

Appendix: Estimating the Demand for Money

Stephen Goldfeld of Princeton University was a pioneer in estimating money demand functions of the form we considered in this chapter. In his 1973 paper,[†] Goldfeld estimated the demand for real money balances as *M1* divided by the price deflator for the gross national product.

Our simple formulation in Eq. (23.7) suggests that income and short-term interest rates should be important determinants of money demand, because of transactions and portfolio allocation considerations. Goldfeld measured income as real GNP and measured interest rates using the rates on time deposits, i_{TD}, and commercial paper, i_{CP}. Time deposits are an alternative to *M1* for consumers; similarly firms can hold liquid assets in the form of commercial paper rather than checkable deposits. What about i_M, the return on holding money? At the time of Goldfeld's study, none of the components of *M1* were interest-bearing, and he implicitly assumed that the convenience yield on money was constant.

The money demand function in Eq. (23.7) is an *equilibrium* relationship, that is, a statement of long-run effects of changes in the determinants of money demand on money holdings. Goldfeld and others have used quarterly data, so empirical specifications allow for gradual adjustments in money holdings in response to changes in the various determinants of money demand. In his original study, Goldfeld found that households and businesses change money holdings gradually.

Relating Money Demand Determinants to Money Holdings

Using information from studies such as Goldfeld's, we can approximate the short-run and long-run effects of changes in real income and interest rates on real money balances. These effects differ because of the gradual adjustments that households and businesses make in their money holdings. We summarize these effects as elasticities, or the percentage response of real money balances to a 1% increase in real income or interest rates.

Response of Real Money Balances in the...	To a 1% Change In...		
	Y	i_{TD}	i_{CP}
Short run (first quarter)	0.193%	−0.045%	−0.019%
Long run	0.681	−0.067	−0.159

[†] Stephen Goldfeld, "The Demand for Money Revisited," *Brookings Papers on Economic Activity*, 3:577–638, 1973.

In Goldfeld's calculations, a 1% increase in real income raises the demand for real money balances by about 0.7% in the long run; a 1% increase in the commercial paper rate decreases real money balances by about 0.2% in the long run. The short-run effects of these changes are much smaller.

These findings are broadly consistent with our transactions and portfolio approaches for estimating money holdings. An increase in real income raises the demand for real balances, though less than proportionately even in the long run. Increases in the rate on time deposits or on commercial paper decrease the demand for money. Goldfeld's tests also confirmed that the demand for money in nominal terms is proportional to the price level. As our transactions and portfolio approaches suggest, the demand for money represents a demand for *real* money holdings. Most specifications of the sort used by Goldfeld and others also imply that expected inflation lowers the demand for real balances (all other factors held constant), suggesting that reductions in the real return on money accompanying higher rates of inflation make holdings of other assets (whose nominal returns increase with inflation) more attractive.

Shifts in Estimated Relationships

The conventional specification of the demand for real money balances is unstable, with shifts occurring on many occasions during the 1970s and 1980s. Recent research findings stress the potential relevance of more nonmoney assets and the need for sophisticated approaches to modeling expectations and gradual adjustment. One finding emerges as a consensus: Economists must continue to refine forecasting models of money demand in response to shifts in the demand for, cost of providing, and regulation of financial services. Some observers believe that a stable money demand relationship for *M2* may emerge in the early 1990s, as households and firms complete their adjustment to the wave of financial innovation and deregulation of the 1970s and 1980s.

Estimating the Demand for Money Abroad

If our theoretical approach to modeling the demand for money is correct, it should be useful also for estimating holdings of real money balances by households and businesses in other countries. Differences in institutions, regulation, and the availability of money substitutes can explain variations in the effects of real income, interest rates, and expected inflation on holdings of real money balances.

Ray Fair of Yale University estimated the demand for real money balances in a sample of 27 countries.[†] For purposes of comparison among countries, he defined money as real money balances per capita. Determinants

[†] Ray C. Fair, "International Evidence on the Demand for Money," *Review of Economics and Statistics*, 69:473–480, 1987.

of money demand included real income per capita, a short-term interest rate, and inflation. Like Goldfeld, Fair allowed for gradual adjustment of money holdings to changes in the determinants of money demand.

On average, the long-run responses of real money demand to changes in real income or interest rates are similar to those estimated for the United States. However, there are differences among countries. Fair concluded that the money demand functions were unstable over the sample period in most major countries (including Canada, France, Italy, Japan, and the United States), the only exception being the former West Germany. In his full sample, only four countries exhibited stable money demand functions.

Linking the Financial System and the Economy

Weary decision makers in the executive branch, Congress, Federal Reserve System, and the business community rubbed their eyes many times during the 1980s and early 1990s when reading the financial headlines. The federal government changed tax rates and spending, and its budget deficit increased dramatically. The Fed opened the decade of the 1980s with a contractionary monetary policy, only to reverse itself later. Many business executives were concerned that the rate of productivity growth in the United States was slowing down. Each of these headlined trends was documented in endless pages of statistics and charts and hours of briefings.

We have stressed the interrelationships between the financial system and the economy throughout this book. Even when economic events and interrelationships are complex, simple models can be useful in explaining them. Models characterize reality and help analysts assess the consequences (for output, interest rates, inflation, and so on) of economic events and public policy. In this chapter we develop a model that connects our previous analysis of saving and investment decisions in the economy with the operation of the financial system. In particular, two variables underscore the interdependence of the financial system and the economy: the real interest rate and current output of goods and services.

In this chapter our analysis focuses on four questions. **Q:** Which factors determine equilibrium in the *goods market* (the economy)? **Q:** Which factors determine equilibrium in *asset markets* (the financial system)? **Q:** Why are the economy and the financial system interdependent? **Q:** Do changes in the money supply affect the real interest rate and current output in the long run?

A Model for Goods and Asset Markets

The economy is complex. In a large market economy, such as that of the United States, hundreds of thousands of assets and goods and services are traded. Suppliers in each market make decisions about how much to produce, and buyers make decisions about how much to purchase based on the price of the good. In any specific market—for apples or autos or Treasury bills—the price adjusts to equate the quantities demanded and supplied by market participants. Taking into account the interactions among markets, economists refer to a **general equilibrium** as a situation in which all markets in the economy are in equilibrium at the same time. Such a situation is complex because the thousands of markets for goods and services and for financial and other assets are interrelated, and changes in prices in one market can affect quantities demanded and supplied in other markets. For our analysis, we need a simplified model that allows us to analyze the links between monetary policy and economic variables.

To illustrate the two way connection between markets for goods and services and markets for financial assets, we use a simplified model that analyzes three broad markets: (1) goods, (2) money, and (3) nonmoney assets. The **goods market** encompasses trade in all goods and services produced in a particular period of time. The **money market** includes trade of the assets used as the medium of exchange, that is, currency and measures of checkable deposits. The **nonmoney asset market** handles trade of the assets other than money that are stores of value, including stocks, bonds, houses, and so on. By grouping the economy's thousands of specific markets into three general market types, we can better describe and graphically analyze effects of changes in the economy or government policy on prices in markets for assets and goods and services.

In the graphical analysis, we use two variables to summarize equilibrium in goods markets and asset markets. The first, current output of goods and services, Y, is a measure of economic activity. The second, the expected real rate of interest, r, measures the return to savers and the cost of funds to borrowers. To describe the economy's equilibrium, we examine determinants of (1) aggregate demand for current output, (2) firms' willingness to supply current output, and (3) holdings of money and nonmoney assets. We then tie these determinants together and consider the economy's long-run equilibrium and factors that change it.

Aggregate Demand in the Goods Market

Equilibrium in the goods market occurs when quantities of goods demanded and supplied are equal. The model that we develop to study equilibrium in the goods market is based on the determinants of saving (sources of funds) and investment (uses of funds) presented in Chapter 5. For simplicity, we begin by analyzing goods market equilibrium in a closed economy (no international flows of saving and investment). Later, we extend the analysis to a more realistic open economy.

When current output supplied Y equals the quantity of goods demanded, the goods market is in equilibrium. In a closed economy, the total quantity of goods demanded, called *aggregate demand*, is the sum of the demand for:

Desired national consumption C: The quantity of goods and services that households want to consume;

Desired national investment I: The quantity of capital goods demanded by businesses for investment; and

Desired government purchases G: The quantity of goods and services purchased by the government.

The goods market is in equilibrium when current output supplied equals aggregate demand:

$$Y = C + I + G. \tag{24.1}$$

We return to the supply of current output later. Note that if we subtract C and G from both sides of Eq. (24.1), we get

$$Y - C - G = I.$$

The term on the left-hand side, $Y - C - G$, represents output not consumed in the current period by households or the government, that is, *national saving*, S. Therefore $Y - C - G = S$. Hence goods market equilibrium implies that national saving and investment are equal, or

$$S = I. \tag{24.2}$$

We now explore the most significant determinants of national saving and investment.

Determinants of National Saving

The determinants of national saving are current output, household consumption, and government purchases. Thus we need to consider both household and government spending and saving decisions. Let's begin with households.

Recall that households care not only about current consumption, but also about *future* consumption. For example, your saving decisions reflect your concerns for financing education, raising a family, buying a house, funding your retirement, and so on. Thus the three key factors determining household saving are current income, expected future income, and the expected real rate of interest (Chapter 5).

Current Income.   What would you do if your current income went up—say, you won $5000 in the lottery—but your future prospects didn't change? You would probably spend part of the income on consumption goods that you have been wanting, such as a stereo. Because you care about future consumption, too, you probably will save part of the extra income. Hence both your consumption and saving likely would increase when your current income increases. If your current income falls, the process works in reverse: Both current consumption and saving fall. This argument extended to the economy as a whole suggests that, when total output changes, current consumption also changes, but to a lesser degree than change in total output. Hence the level of national saving, $Y - C - G$, increases when current output rises and decreases when current output falls.

Expected Future Income.   Because of your meritorious service on the job, your boss tells you that you will receive a $5000 bonus next year. Because you anticipate receiving this extra income next year, you probably will begin to increase your spending today. Similarly, if you expect that your company will pay you less beginning next year, you may reduce your consumption today to build a cushion for the future. For the economy as a whole, an expected future increase in income raises consumption so that, if current output doesn't change, national saving, $Y - C - G$, falls. An expected future decrease in income lowers consumption so that, if current output doesn't change, national saving rises.

Expected Real Interest Rate.   The expected real interest rate represents the return that savers expect to earn from lending their funds to borrowers in the financial system. An increase in the real interest rate increases your reward for saving for future consumption while also allowing you to save less to pay for future consumption. A decline in the real interest rate decreases your reward for saving but requires that you save more to meet a given goal for future consumption. Available empirical evidence suggests that household saving increases with the interest rate, although the effect probably isn't large.

Government Purchases. Government purchases, G, include spending for goods and services such as military equipment, highways, education, public employees' salaries, and so on. If we hold current output constant, an increase in government purchases will reduce national saving so long as consumption falls less than dollar for dollar in response. Evidence suggests that consumers do not reduce their spending dollar for dollar in response to more government purchases. That is, if nothing else changes, an increase in government purchases lowers national saving.

Determinants of National Investment

Businesses invest to increase future profits. The two principal determinants of national investment are the expected future profitability of capital invested and the expected real interest rate.

Expected Future Profitability of Capital.   An increase in expected future profitability of capital (from, say, a new technology or discovery) enhances businesses' willingness to invest. Corporate taxes also influence expected future profitability. An increase in taxes on business income or a decrease in tax incentives for new investment will reduce businesses' willingness to invest at any level of expected future pretax profitability. Similarly, a decrease in business income taxes or an increase in tax incentives for new investment stimulates businesses' willingness to invest at any level of expected future pretax profitability.

Expected Real Interest Rate.   When businesses consider investment decisions, they must weigh other possible uses for their funds, including purchasing financial assets. The expected real interest rate represents the cost of funds for investment. Hence an increase in the expected real interest rate lowers the demand for investment, as businesses could hold funds more profitably in other assets. Conversely, a drop in the expected real interest rate raises investment demand.

▶ C H E C K P O I N T   *You and other investors have just formed Biopil, a pharmaceutical corporation. If* The Wall Street Journal *reports that the federal government has initiated a tax break for new investment, how does that news affect your investment decision?* If the expected future pretax profitability of your investment doesn't change, the tax break reduces your cost of funds. You should expand Biopil's capital investment. ◀

The *IS* Curve

We now combine our analysis of the determinants of national saving and investment to discuss equilibrium in the goods market. Figure 24.1(a) illustrates the saving–investment diagram introduced and analyzed in Chapter 5. The horizontal axis represents national saving and investment, and the vertical axis represents the real interest rate. (For simplicity, we assume that the expected and actual real interest rates are equal.) We hold the other determinants of saving and investment constant.

Figure 24.1(a) shows saving and investment curves for two values of current output Y: $5000 billion and $6000 billion. Recall that, when current output increases, desired saving also increases. Therefore each current output level is associated with a different saving curve. An increase in current output from $5000 billion to $6000 billion shifts the saving curve to the right from S_0 to S_1, thereby changing the equilibrium from E_0 to E_1 and reducing the real interest rate from 4% to 3%.

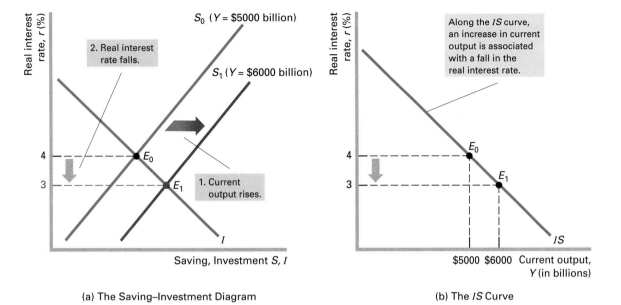

(a) The Saving–Investment Diagram

(b) The *IS* Curve

FIGURE 24.1

The *IS* Curve

As shown in (a):
1. An increase in current output from $5000 to $6000 billion, increases current saving, shifting the *S* curve to the right from S_0 to S_1.

2. The increase in saving reduces the real interest rate *R* from 4% to 3%.

As shown in (b):
The *IS* curve slopes downward, maintaining equality of saving and investment; higher levels of current output are associated with lower values of the real interest rate.

The two equilibrium points in Fig. 24.1(a) are plotted in Fig. 24.1(b) as two possible current output–real interest rate combinations that bring saving and investment into equilibrium. In Fig. 24.1(b) the **IS curve** depicts the general relationship between current output and the real interest rate. At each point on the *IS* curve, desired saving equals desired investment; that is, the *IS* curve presents combinations of current output and the real interest rate for which the quantities of goods demanded and supplied are equal. The slope of the *IS* curve is downward and to the right because, at higher levels of current output, current saving rises and the real interest rate falls to restore equilibrium in the goods market.

Points not on the *IS* curve represent unequal levels of desired saving and desired investment; the goods market is not in equilibrium for the corresponding real interest rates. Consider the example shown in Fig. 24.2(a). At a real interest rate of 5% and an output of $5000 billion, desired saving exceeds desired investment, creating an excess supply of goods, indicated at point 1. To restore equilibrium in the goods market, the real interest rate must fall to 4%, at point 3. At a real interest rate of 3% and output of $5000 billion, desired investment exceeds desired saving, creating an excess demand for goods, indicated at 2. To restore equilibrium in the goods market, the real interest rate must rise to 4%, at point 3.

The curve shown in Fig. 24.2(b) reflects this pattern. At point 3 the goods market is in equilibrium; therefore point 3 lies on the *IS* curve. Points such as 1 that lie above the *IS* curve represent an excess supply of goods. Point 1 represents the same level of current output supplied, as at point 3, but at a higher real interest rate. Recall that an increase in the real interest rate

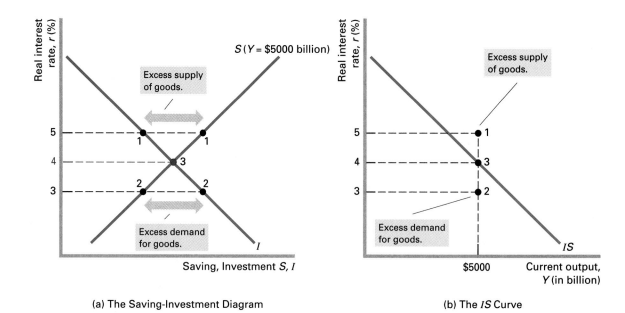

(a) The Saving-Investment Diagram   (b) The *IS* Curve

▲ FIGURE 24.2

Excess Demand and Supply in the Goods Market

As shown in (a):
When desired saving exceeds desired investment (as at 1), there is an excess supply of goods. When desired saving is less than desired investment (as at 2), there is an excess demand for goods. Desired saving equals desired investment at point 3.

As shown in (b):
When there is an excess supply of goods (as at 1), the real interest rate is above its equilibrium level. When there is an excess demand for goods (as at 2), the real interest rate is below its equilibrium level. Only points on the *IS* curve (as at 3) represent equilibrium combinations of the real interest rate and the quantity of output demanded.

reduces desired consumption, increasing desired saving and decreasing desired investment. The level of goods demanded at a real interest rate of 5% is less than the current output of goods; that is, there is an excess supply of goods at point 1.

Points such as 2 that lie below the *IS* curve represent an excess demand for goods. Point 2 represents the same level of current output as at point 3, but at a lower real rate of interest. Then desired consumption increases, decreasing desired saving and increasing desired investment. The quantity of goods demanded exceeds the current output of goods.

The *IS* Curve for an Open Economy

So far we have assumed that demand and supply in the goods market are limited to *domestic* saving and investment. When savings can be invested internationally in an open economy, the goods market is in equilibrium when desired international lending (or borrowing) by that country equals desired international borrowing (or lending) by other countries.

To understand how international capital mobility affects the *IS* curve in a *large open economy* such as that of the United States, Japan, or Germany, we must distinguish domestic saving (sources of funds from the economy) from domestic investment (demand for funds within the economy). As capital is mobile internationally in an open economy, an increase in desired domestic saving can finance either domestic or foreign investment.

Recall that an increase in desired domestic saving in a large open economy causes the domestic real interest rate to fall (Chapter 5). However, greater domestic saving finances investment at home and abroad, so the real interest rate doesn't have to fall by as much as it would in a closed economy in order to absorb the greater quantity of domestic saving. Likewise, an increase in a desired investment in the domestic economy can be financed by savings from abroad as well as from home. Hence the real interest rate won't have to rise by as much as it would in a closed economy to restore equilibrium in the goods market. In a large open economy, as opposed to a closed economy, any change in the demand for current output requires a smaller change in the domestic real interest rate. As a result, the *IS* curve for a large open economy is flatter than that for a large closed economy. (We analyze this difference graphically in the Appendix to this chapter.)

The flatter *IS* curve for the large open economy illustrates the important effects of financial market integration on the economy. Figure 24.2 showed that, when current output increases, desired saving increases and that the supply of goods exceeds demand at the initial real rate of interest. To restore equilibrium in the goods market, the domestic real interest rate must fall in order to raise the quantity of goods demanded to the quantity of goods supplied. The same events occur in an open economy, but the integration of the goods market and asset market modify them. As for the closed economy, the domestic real interest rate falls as desired domestic saving increases. However, the decline in the interest rate (which also is felt abroad in integrated capital markets) increases both the foreign and domestic demand for domestic goods. As a result, desired investment increases in the foreign country while desired foreign saving decreases. Foreigners increase their desired international borrowing so that some of the increased desired domestic saving flows abroad. Evidence of the extent of capital mobility for large open economies is discussed in Box 24.1.

The flow of goods matches exactly this movement of savings in an open economy. The domestic economy lends funds to foreigners, and its *current account balance*—the difference between exports and imports, or net exports—increases as foreigners increase their demand for domestically produced goods. The foreign economy borrows funds from the domestic economy, and its own current account balance decreases as foreigners demand more goods from the domestic economy. In a large open economy, the real interest rate doesn't have to fall by as much in order to restore equilibrium in the goods markets in response to an increase in current domestic output. Similarly, the real interest rate doesn't have to increase by as much to restore equilibrium in response to a decrease in current domestic output.

Our analysis of implications for the slope of the *IS* curve of international integration of goods and financial markets is relevant for the large open economies such as the United States, Germany, and Japan. Goods and financial markets in a *small open economy* are integrated with those of the rest of the world. However, flows of goods and capital to and from a small open economy are too small to affect the world interest rate. As a result, the *IS* curve for a small open economy simply is horizontal at the world real rate of

Consider this...

Are Savings Internationally Mobile?

Our discussion of the *IS* curve for a large open economy implies that, if saving were completely mobile among countries, domestic saving wouldn't have to equal domestic investment. Savings would flow to economies offering the highest expected return, and expected returns would equalize around the world (adjusting for differences in the risk, liquidity, and information characteristics of the financial instruments). As a result, if saving increased in a country, rather than reducing the domestic real interest rate below worldwide levels (thereby increasing investment at home), some of the additional funds would flow abroad.

Using data from the 1960s and 1970s, Martin Feldstein and Charles Horioka examined relationships between domestic saving and investment relative to aggregate output in the United States, Japan, and many European countries.[†] They estimated that a $1.00 change in domestic saving led to an approximately equal change in domestic investment, casting doubt on international capital mobility. However, Feldstein and Philippe Bacchetta later found that, during the 1980s, changes in domestic saving and investment were not so highly correlated.[††] Hence the most recent evidence suggests that the economies of

the United States, Japan, and many European nations are large open economies and that international borrowing and lending are significant in the financial markets.

[†] Martin Feldstein and Charles Horioka, "Domestic Saving and International Capital Flows," *Economic Journal*, 90:314–329, 1980.

[††] Martin Feldstein and Philippe Bacchetta, "National Saving and International Investment." In B. Douglas Bernheim and John B. Shoven (eds.), *National Saving and Economic Performance*, Chicago: University of Chicago Press, 1991.

interest r_w. A small open economy therefore can lend or borrow in international capital markets at that real rate of interest. Any value of output in the small open economy is consistent with the equilibrium real interest rate. In our graphic analysis of the economy's equilibrium, we use the *IS* curve for a large open economy.

▶ C H E C K P O I N T *Suppose that the real interest rate in Massachusetts is very low—say, 0.5%—but the real interest rate in California is very high—say, 10%. What would you do if you were a Massachusetts saver? You probably would invest part of your savings in California to take advantage of the higher expected return. As financial markets have become more global, saving can flow abroad in search of higher returns.* ◀

Shifts of the *IS* Curve

Increases or decreases in the demand for goods change the equilibrium real interest rate for each level of current output and cause shifts of the *IS* curve. These increases or decreases in the real interest rate may be the result of an increase or decrease in one of the determinants of desired saving and investment: government purchases, foreign demand for domestic goods, the expected future profitability of capital, or consumer or business confidence. An increase in one of these factors shifts the *IS* curve up and to the right by increasing the real interest rate required to reach equilibrium in the goods market for any given level of current output. For example, a military buildup, an increase in the overseas popularity of U.S. cars, a decline in households' willingness to save, or development of a major new technology leading to an environmentally safe substitute for plastics causes such a shift. A reduction in one of the determinants shifts the *IS* curve down and to the left by decreasing the real interest rate required to reach equilibrium in the goods market for any given level of current output. The Other times, other places box presents an example of a downward shift of the *IS* curve. Table 24.1 summarizes the factors accounting for shifts in the *IS* curve.

Other times, other places...
The Gulf War and "Confidence"

The determinants of household consumption and business investment are based on expectations of the future, which can be interpreted in part as a reflection of consumer confidence or optimism about the future. Iraq's invasion of Kuwait in August 1990 and the ensuing Gulf War in early 1991 adversely affected U.S. consumer and business confidence. Consumers worried about the effects of possible increases in oil prices on the purchasing power of their incomes. In fact, a University of Michigan survey measured consumer confidence dropping by 28% in the last half of 1990 and rebounding after the war's conclusion. Business confidence also dropped, and firms cut back on inventory investment and, to a lesser extent, on capital investment. At the same time, the U.S. government increased its expenditures to finance the war. How did these changes in spending affect aggregate demand?

Researchers at the Federal Reserve Bank of San Francisco found that reductions in consumption and investment from falling consumer confidence shifted the *IS* curve down to the left from IS_0 to IS_1. This effect dominated the higher U.S. government purchases which shifted the *IS* curve up to the right from IS_0 to IS_2, as shown in the accompanying diagram. Analysts believe that the net result of the two movements was a shift down to the left, because the military principally used its stock of existing weapons rather than spending money on new weapons.

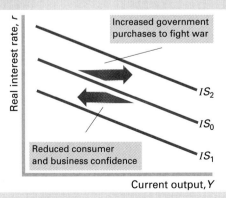

Source: "The Gulf War and the U.S. Economy," Federal Reserve Bank of San Francisco *Weekly Letter,* September 13, 1991.

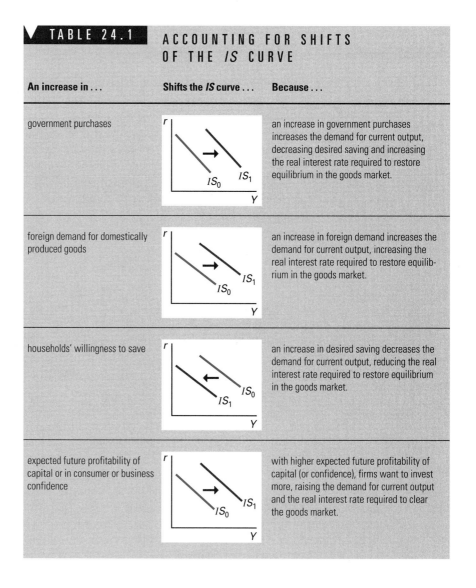

TABLE 24.1 ACCOUNTING FOR SHIFTS OF THE *IS* CURVE

An increase in ...	Shifts the *IS* curve ...	Because ...
government purchases		an increase in government purchases increases the demand for current output, decreasing desired saving and increasing the real interest rate required to restore equilibrium in the goods market.
foreign demand for domestically produced goods		an increase in foreign demand increases the demand for current output, increasing the real interest rate required to restore equilibrium in the goods market.
households' willingness to save		an increase in desired saving decreases the demand for current output, reducing the real interest rate required to restore equilibrium in the goods market.
expected future profitability of capital or in consumer or business confidence		with higher expected future profitability of capital (or confidence), firms want to invest more, raising the demand for current output and the real interest rate required to clear the goods market.

Determining Output: The Full Employment Line

The *IS* curve illustrates combinations of the level of current output and the real interest rate for which the goods market is in equilibrium. Each point on the *IS* curve represents equilibrium in the goods market, so what level of current output actually prevails? The answer depends on the level of output that firms are willing to supply in the goods market. The supply of **current output,** or the level of output that firms produce at any particular time is determined by two factors: the existing capital stock and the use of variable production factors, such as labor. The capital stock reflects the accumulated investment of previous years. We therefore assume that it is fixed, with new investment being incorporated as stock for use in the future. For simplicity, we also assume that the supply of variable factors is fixed. Hence **full employment output** in the economy in the current period is the production level achieved by the use of all available production factors, irrespective of the real rate of interest. Thus it is constant at Y^* in Fig. 24.3, and the resulting vertical line is called the **full employment (FE) line.**

The intersection of the *IS* curve and the full employment line represents goods market equilibrium. For example, suppose that (as shown in Fig. 24.3) the equilibrium in the goods market is described by the combination of current output of $5000 billion and a real interest rate of 4%. When aggregate supply equals $5000 billion, a real interest rate of 4% ensures that desired saving equals desired investment because the point ($Y = \$5000$ billion, $r = 4\%$) is on the *IS* curve.

Current output is influenced by the efficiency of existing production factors. An increase in the current productivity of either capital or labor shifts the *FE* line to the right. For example, if everyone decided to work harder each hour this year, current productivity would rise, shifting the *FE* line to the right. By contrast, an unexpected oil price increase reduces the productivity of energy-using machines, shifting the *FE* line to the left. Although changes in expected future productivity affect investment and the *IS* curve, they don't affect current output. Only the productivity of factors already in place affect current output. Table 24.2 summarizes those factors accounting for shifts in the *FE* line.

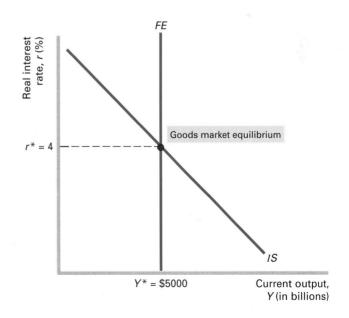

> **FIGURE 24.3**

Determining Current Output in the Goods Market
Equilibrium output in the goods market is Y^*, given by full utilization of all existing production factors. The equilibrium real interest rate, r^*, brings saving and investment into equilibrium at that level of output.

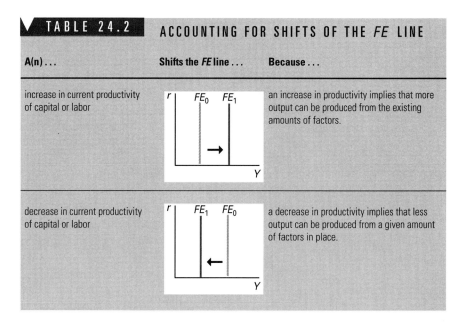

TABLE 24.2	ACCOUNTING FOR SHIFTS OF THE *FE* LINE	
A(n)...	Shifts the *FE* line ...	Because ...
increase in current productivity of capital or labor		an increase in productivity implies that more output can be produced from the existing amounts of factors.
decrease in current productivity of capital or labor		a decrease in productivity implies that less output can be produced from a given amount of factors in place.

▶ **C H E C K P O I N T** *Suppose that you manage a tool factory in northern Michigan. What would happen to your company's ability to use its plant and equipment if a series of snowstorms idled the factory for several weeks?* Because workers were unable to get to work, current output would fall, shifting your factory's *FE* line to the left. Weather fluctuations, strikes, and trade disruptions act as productivity shocks, shifting the economy's *FE* line. ◀

Q: Which factors determine equilibrium in the *goods market* (the economy)?

A: For the economy's available resources, the goods market equilibrium lies at the intersection of the *IS* curve and the *FE* line. Current output represents full utilization of existing factors of production, and the real interest rate balances saving and investment.

Asset Market Equilibrium

The interdependence of the goods and asset markets link the financial system and the economy. We have just shown that the *IS* curve represents combinations of the real interest rate and level of output that result in equilibrium in the goods market. Is the combination of output level and real interest rate also consistent with equilibrium in money and nonmoney asset markets? To answer this question, we need to determine the values of current output and the real interest rate for which the asset markets are in equilibrium. By grouping all asset markets into just two, we can focus on the money market. With just two asset markets, the money market will be in equilibrium only if the nonmoney asset market also is in equilibrium. As a first step we establish the link between equilibrium in the money market and equilibrium in the nonmoney asset market. We can then examine combinations of the real interest rate and the level of output for which the money market is in equilibrium.

Market Equilibrium: Money and Nonmoney Assets

Markets for money assets and for nonmoney assets (such as stocks and bonds) represent alternative ways of allocating wealth. For example, Jane Rich must decide how to allocate her nominal wealth, w, between money and nonmoney assets. Her demand for nominal money balances, m_d, added to her demand for nominal nonmoney assets, n_d, equals her total wealth, w, or

$$m_d + n_d = w.$$

Each household and business faces this portfolio allocation problem. The markets for money and nonmoney assets are in equilibrium when the total quantities demanded equal the total quantities supplied. Thus, for the economy as a whole, the total demand for nominal money balances M_d and nonmoney assets, N_d, equals total nominal wealth, W, or

$$M_d + N_d = W. \tag{24.3}$$

On the supply side, total nominal wealth W equals the sum of the total quantity of money supplied, M_s, and the total quantity of nonmoney assets supplied N_s, or

$$M_s + N_s = W. \tag{24.4}$$

Because the market mechanism ensures that, in equilibrium, the quantity of an asset supplied equals the quantity demanded, we can equate Eq. (24.3) and Eq. (24.4). Doing so gives us a relation between the equilibrium in the two asset markets:

$$(M_d - M_s) + (N_d - N_s) = 0,$$
$$M_d - M_s = N_s - N_d. \tag{24.5}$$

When the total quantity of money demanded exceeds the quantity supplied, that is, $M_d > M_n$, the expression on the left-hand side of Eq. (24.5) is positive, representing an excess demand for money. When $N_s > N_d$, the total quantity of nonmoney assets supplied exceeds the quantity demanded, creating an excess supply of nonmoney assets. Thus Eq. (24.5) states that the *excess demand* for one of the two assets (money or nonmoney) equals the *excess supply* of the other. In equilibrium, asset prices adjust so that there is no excess demand or supply in the money market; in other words, the left-hand side of Eq. (24.5) equals zero. Hence the right-hand side of Eq. (24.5) must then also equal zero. Therefore the money market is in equilibrium only if the nonmoney market is in equilibrium. Knowing that the equilibrium in one of the two asset markets is related to the equilibrium in the other, we can make an important simplification: Any combination of current output and the real interest rate for which the money market is in equilibrium will correspond to equilibrium in the nonmoney asset market, and vice versa. We use this simplification to confine our attention to determinants of equilibrium in the money market.

▶ **C H E C K P O I N T** *If Jane Rich is satisfied with the proportion of her wealth held in money, is she also satisfied with her nonmoney asset holdings of savings in bonds and stocks? Yes. Jane's demand for real money balances depends on the expected returns available on nonmoney assets. Her satisfaction with her wealth allocation implies that she has compared her returns from holding money with expected returns on other assets (adjusted for differences in risk, liquidity, and information costs).* ◀

Money Market Equilibrium: The *LM* Curve

We can now examine combinations of the real interest rate and current output for which the money market is in equilibrium. On the supply side, the quantity of real money balances supplied equals the aggregate money supply M_s divided by the general price level P, or $(M/P)_s$, which we simplify as *MS*. On the demand side, we saw in Chapter 23 that the demand for real money balances $(M/P)_d$, or *MD*, depends on real income (or output) Y, the interest rate on nonmoney assets i, the return on money i_M, and other factors. Equilibrium is reached when the quantity of real money supplied equals the quantity of real money demanded:

$$\left(\frac{M}{P}\right)_s = \left(\frac{M}{P}\right)_d = L(Y, i, i_M, \dots),$$

where L is the liquidity preference relation linking the demand for real money balances to its determinants.

Let's examine those determinants more closely. The variable i represents the nominal market interest rate on nonmoney assets and is the sum of the underlying real interest rate, r (assumed to be the expected real rate of interest) and expected inflation, π^e:

$$i = r + \pi^e.$$

Substituting this expression for the nominal interest rate i into the preceding expression, we get

$$\frac{M}{P} = L(Y, r + \pi^e, i_M, \dots). \tag{24.6}$$

Equation (24.6) contains too many variables for our analysis of r and Y. If we hold constant the other factors in Eq. (24.6)—the nominal money supply M, price level P, expected rate of inflation π^e, and nominal return on money i_M—we can describe combinations of current output Y and real interest rate r for which the money market (and hence the nonmoney asset market) generally is in equilibrium.

Suppose that households and businesses are satisfied with their real money balances M/P when output in the economy is $5000 billion and the real rate of interest is 4%, indicated by E_0 in Fig. 24.4(a); that is, the money market is in equilibrium at that point. If real output increases to $6000 billion, Eq. (24.6) indicates that the quantity of real money demanded $(M/P)_d$, increases; the money demand curve shifts from MD_0 to MD_1. With all the other factors held constant, the real interest rate r must increase from 4% to 5% to reduce the quantity of real money demanded, as shown by E_1 in Fig. 24.4(a).

Figure 24.4(b) illustrates the combinations of current output and the real interest rate for which the money market is in equilibrium, a set of points called the **LM curve**. It is a graph of the relationship in Eq. (24.6), in which the quantity of real money demanded (the liquidity preference relation L) equals the quantity of money supplied. Because a higher real interest rate is associated with a higher level of output in a money market equilibrium, the LM curve slopes upward to the right. The magnitude of the increase in the real interest rate required to restore equilibrium in the money market depends on how responsive money demand is to the interest rate. Therefore the slope of the LM curve depends on the sensitivity of the demand for real money balances to the nominal interest rate i.

▼ FIGURE 24.4

The *LM* Curve

As shown in (a):
1. When current output increases, real money demand increases.

2. Holding constant real money balances supplied, an increase in current output raises the real interest rate.

As shown in (b):
The *LM* curve slopes upward. To maintain equilibrium in the money market, higher levels of current output result in higher values of the real interest rate.

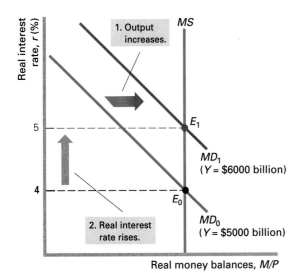

(a) The Money Market

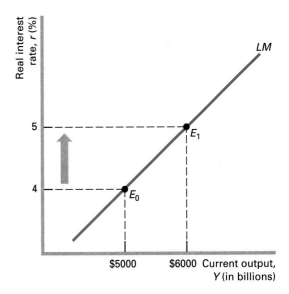

(b) The *LM* Curve

When the interest sensitivity of the demand for real money balances is low, interest rates must change a lot for the money market to remain in equilibrium if output changes. Since large interest rate changes are associated with a given output change, the *LM* schedule will be steeply sloped. If the demand for real balances were completely insensitive to the opportunity cost of holding money, the *LM* curve would be vertical. Conversely, if the demand for real money balances is sensitive to the interest rate, then whenever money demand changes in response to an increase in output, a much smaller increase in the real interest rate is required to restore equilibrium in the money market. In this case, the *LM* curve is relatively flat. If the demand for real balances were infinitely sensitive to the interest rate, the *LM* curve would be horizontal.

To summarize, the slope of the *LM* curve depends on the interest sensitivity of the demand for money. If the demand for money is sensitive to the interest rate, the *LM* curve is relatively flat; if the demand for money is insensitive to the interest rate, the *LM* curve is relatively steep.

At any point along the *LM* curve, the quantity of money demanded equals the quantity supplied. However, as was the case for the *IS* curve, only points on the *LM* curve represent an equilibrium in the asset markets. To understand why, consider Fig. 24.5(a). When current output is $5000 billion and the real interest rate is 5%, there is an excess supply of money, indicated by point 1. Households and businesses use some of this excess money to buy nonmoney assets, causing their prices to rise and the interest rate to fall until the real interest rate equals 4%, at point 3. Conversely, when output equals $5000 billion and the real interest rate is 3%, there is an excess demand for

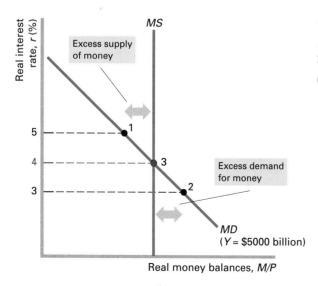

(a) The Money Market

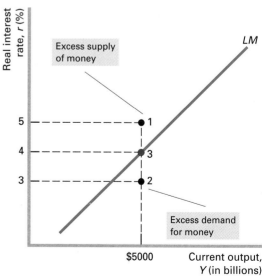

(b) The *LM* Curve

money, indicated by point 2. Households and firms sell nonmoney assets for money, causing their price to fall and the interest rate to rise until the real interest rate equals 4%, at point 3.

Figure 24.5(b) illustrates this process with the *LM* curve. Point 1 and others that are above the *LM* curve represent an excess supply of money and an excess demand for nonmoney assets. Point 2 and others that are below the *LM* curve represent an excess demand for money and an excess supply of non-money assets. Again money demand and supply are in equilibrium at point 3.

▶ **C H E C K P O I N T** *Suppose that the government wanted to induce you to hold $1000 of your assets in currency and non-interest-bearing checkable deposits. If you wanted to hold more than that because your income and volume of transactions are rising, how could the government convince you not to hold more currency in your wallet or checking account?* If the government could raise the real rate of return on other financial assets, you would want to increase your holdings of financial assets. How much the real rate would have to rise depends on how sensitive to interest rate changes your portfolio decisions are. Along your *LM* curve, then, an increase in *Y* is associated with an increase in *r*. ◀

Shifts of the *LM* Curve

When we analyzed the *IS* curve, we noted that changes in variables other than current output or the real interest rate could shift the curve. The same is true for the *LM* curve. The variables that explain shifts of the *LM* curve are those in Eq. (24.6): the nominal money supply *M*, the price level *P*, the nominal return on money i_M, and the expected rate of inflation π^e.

Changes in Real Money Balances Supplied. The level of real money balances—the nominal money supply divided by the price level—is taken as a given in the derivation of the *LM* curve. What happens to the money market equilibrium when the quantity supplied of real balances increases as, for example, when the Fed pursues an expansionary monetary policy? To restore equilibrium in asset markets, the quantity of money demanded must be increased in one of two ways. For a constant output level, a drop in the real interest rate makes the option of holding money more attractive and thus increases the quantity of money demanded. In other words, for constant expected inflation, the nominal interest rate falls to reduce the opportunity cost of holding money instead of nonmoney assets. Or, for a constant real interest rate, an increase in the equilibrium level of output increases the quantity of real balances demanded. In either case, the *LM* curve shifts down and to the right.

When the quantity supplied of real money balances declines, as in the case of a contractionary monetary policy, equilibrium is restored by reducing the quantity of money demanded. For a constant current output level, an increase in the real rate of interest restores equilibrium in the money market by lowering the quantity of real balances demanded. For a constant real interest rate, a decline in current output restores money market equilibrium. A decrease in the nominal money supply M, for a constant price level, shifts the LM curve up and to the left.

These possibilities illustrate shifts of the LM curve caused by changes in the nominal money supply (for a constant price level). Similarly, we can examine the effects on the LM curve of a change in the price level by holding the nominal money supply constant. For example, a decline in the price level because of a drop in energy prices increases real money balances causing the LM curve to shift down and to the right. An increase in the price level because of a rise in energy prices reduces real money balances so that the LM curve shifts up and to the left.

Changes in the Nominal Return on Money.

Increases or decreases in the nominal return from holding money affect the LM curve by their influences on the demand for money. Recall that households and businesses compare returns on money and nonmoney assets when making decisions about how much wealth to hold in the form of money balances. Although not all components of money (currency, for example) pay interest, some (such as interest-bearing checkable deposits) do. What is the effect on the LM curve of an increase in the nominal return on money, say, as the result of deregulation of the interest paid on checkable deposits?

If we assume that the other determinants of money demand do not change, an increase in i_M (the nominal return on money) makes money balances more attractive to investors relative to nonmoney assets. As a result, the quantity of real money balances demanded increases. A higher real interest rate, then, is required to restore equilibrium in the money market. As the real interest rate on nonmoney assets increases, the nominal interest rate on those assets rises relative to the nominal return on money, making them more attractive to investors than money, thereby reducing the quantity of money demanded. Asset market equilibrium is restored by increasing the real interest rate for any level of output. A decrease in the nominal return on real money balances makes nonmoney assets more attractive to investors than money. As a result, the quantity of money demanded declines. To restore equilibrium in the money market, the nominal interest rate must be lowered. Asset market equilibrium is restored by increasing the quantity of money demanded.

Therefore if nothing else changes, an increase in the nominal return on money shifts the LM curve up and to the left. A decrease in the nominal return on money shifts the LM curve down and to the right.

Changes in Expected Inflation.

Recall that the nominal rate of interest equals the sum of the expected real rate of interest r and the expected rate of inflation π^e. Increases or decreases in the expected rate of inflation affect asset market equilibrium by changing the nominal rate of interest associated with any real rate of interest.

What if expected inflation rises because of the public's expectation that the Fed is pursuing a policy that will spur inflation? If the *real* interest rate were to remain unchanged, the *nominal* interest rate would rise. For a constant nominal return on money, nonmoney assets would be relatively more attractive to savers, reducing the demand for real money balances. To restore equilibrium in the money market, the real interest rate must fall at any level of output to preserve asset market equilibrium.

An increase in expected inflation causes the *LM* curve to shift down by the amount by which the expected rate of inflation increases. Similarly, a drop in expected inflation causes the *LM* curve to shift up by the amount of decline in the expected rate of inflation. Table 24.3 summarizes the factors affecting the *LM* curve.

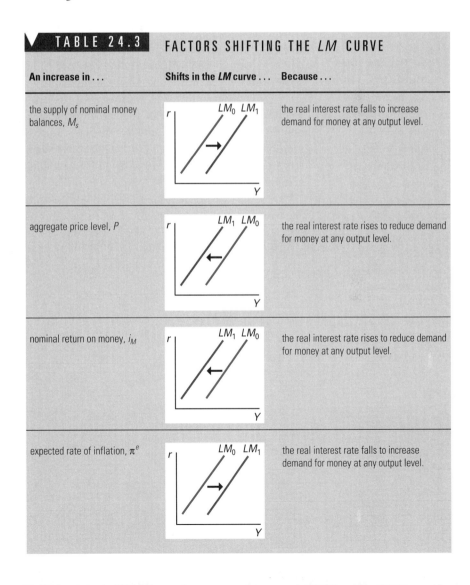

▼ TABLE 24.3	FACTORS SHIFTING THE *LM* CURVE	
An increase in . . .	**Shifts in the *LM* curve . . .**	**Because . . .**
the supply of nominal money balances, M_s	LM_0 LM_1 →	the real interest rate falls to increase demand for money at any output level.
aggregate price level, P	LM_1 LM_0 ←	the real interest rate rises to reduce demand for money at any output level.
nominal return on money, i_M	LM_1 LM_0 ←	the real interest rate rises to reduce demand for money at any output level.
expected rate of inflation, π^e	LM_0 LM_1 →	the real interest rate falls to increase demand for money at any output level.

Q: Which factors determine equilibrium in *asset markets* (the financial system)?

A: The asset markets are in equilibrium when households and businesses are satisfied with their relative holdings of money and nonmoney assets. When the money market is in equilibrium, the market for nonmoney assets also is in equilibrium. Combinations of the real interest rate and current output for which the money market is in equilibrium (and hence for which the nonmoney asset market is in equilibrium) are plotted as the *LM* curve.

▶   C H E C K P O I N T   *Suppose that widespread use of bank debit cards and credit cards reduces the demand for money at any particular level of income and interest rates. How does the* LM *curve respond if the money supply doesn't change?* Because the demand for money has fallen, the real interest rate at any particular income level would have to be lower to encourage the public to hold the quantity of money supplied. The *LM* curve shifts down and to the right. ◀

The Financial System and the Economy: Long-Run Equilibrium

We are now ready to use our model to show how the financial system and the economy interact. To do so, we focus on *general equilibrium*, in which all markets in the economy are in equilibrium at the same time. The *IS* curve represents points of equilibrium for aggregate demand in the goods market. The full employment *FE* line represents the amount of current output to be produced by full employment of existing production factors. The *LM* curve represents points of equilibrium for the asset markets. At the intersection of the *IS* and *LM* curves, the real interest rate equates saving and investment, leading households and businesses to accept the mix of money and nonmoney assets they hold. At the intersection of the *IS* curve and *FE* line, current output is consistent with full employment of existing production factors.

The financial system and the goods market both are in equilibrium when the *IS* curve, *FE* line, and *LM* curve all intersect at the same point, as Fig. 24.6 shows. This equilibrium point establishes the level of output and the

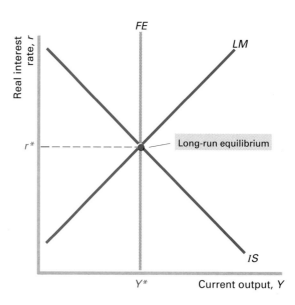

▶ FIGURE 24.6

The Economy and Financial System in Long-Run Equilibrium
Long-run equilibrium in the economy occurs when a combination of the real rate of interest, r^*, and the level of current output, Y^*, causes the *IS* curve, *LM* curve, and *FE* line to intersect.

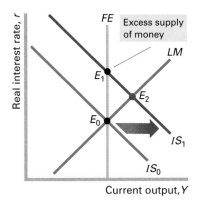

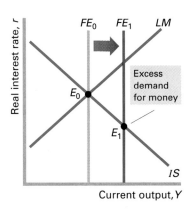

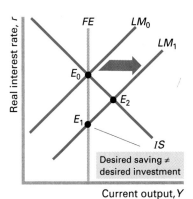

(a) Increase in
Government Purchases

(b) Temporary Increase in
Current Productivity

(c) Increase in the Nominal
Money Supply

▲ FIGURE 24.7

Changing the Equilibrium

As shown in (a):
At point E_0 the economy and the financial system are in equilibrium. The increase in government purchases shifts the *IS* curve from IS_0 to IS_1. The *IS* curve and *FE* line intersect at E_1, but the asset markets aren't in equilibrium. There is an excess supply of money.

As shown in (b):
At point E_0 the economy and the financial system are in equilibrium. The boost in current productivity shifts the *FE* line from FE_0 to FE_1. The new goods market equilibrium lies at point E_1, but the asset markets aren't in equilibrium. There is an excess demand for money.

As shown in (c):
At point E_0 the economy and the financial system are in equilibrium. When the Fed increases the nominal money supply, the *LM* curve shifts from LM_0 to LM_1. It intersects the *IS* curve at E_2, but that point isn't on the *FE* line. The *LM* curve and *FE* line intersect at E_1, but desired saving and investment are not equal.

real interest rate. Thus long-run equilibrium occurs at the real interest rate at which the current output supplied is equal to the current output demanded. We now analyze this equilibrium in the economy.

Changes in Equilibrium

Changes in the equilibrium of the financial system and the economy come from shifts in the *IS* curve, *FE* line, or *LM* curve. We consider some examples of each type of shift; we then examine how the financial system and the economy return to equilibrium.

Shifts in the IS Curve. Changes in government purchases of goods and services shift the *IS* curve. Suppose that the president and Congress decide that the United States should undertake a large-scale military buildup. Starting from equilibrium at E_0 in Fig. 24.7(a), an increase in government purchases shifts the *IS* curve up and to the right, from IS_0 to IS_1. Note that the IS_1 curve intersects the *FE* line at E_1, representing the same level of output as E_0, but at a higher real interest rate. However, if we hold expected inflation and the nominal return on money constant, the asset markets are no longer in equilibrium; the intersection of the *IS* curve and *FE* line is not on the *LM* curve, and there is an excess supply of money. Moreover, the intersection of the *IS* and *LM* curves at E_2 is not on the *FE* line, as the implied current output level is greater than the current output level indicated by the *FE* line. Hence, if we hold the determinants of the three curves constant, there is no combination of current output and real interest rate for which all markets in the economy and the financial system are in equilibrium.

Shifts in the FE line. Suppose that the economy is at equilibrium initially at E_0 in Fig. 24.7(b) and that a decline in energy prices leads to a temporary increase in productivity. The increase in productivity shifts the *FE* line

Q: Why are the economy and the financial system interdependent?

A: The asset markets and the goods market are jointly in equilibrium at the intersection of the *IS* curve, *FE* line, and *LM* curve.

to the right from FE_0 to FE_1 while the positions of the *IS* and *LM* curves remain unchanged. As a result, the *IS* curve and FE_1 now intersect at E_1, at which the asset markets are no longer in equilibrium. At E_1, the real rate of interest is too low to maintain asset market equilibrium at current levels of output, prices, expected inflation, and nominal return on money. The excess demand for real money balances throws the asset markets out of equilibrium. At the intersection of the *IS* and *LM* curves at E_0, the output level is less than that at FE_1.

Shifts in the LM Curve. What happens to the equilibrium of the financial system and the economy if the Fed increases the money supply by 10%? Suppose that the goods market and asset markets are in equilibrium at E_0 in Fig. 24.7(c). An increase in the nominal money supply shifts the *LM* curve down to the right from LM_0 to LM_1.

As a result, E_0—where the *IS* curve and *FE* line intersect—no longer denotes an asset market equilibrium. Because E_0 lies above the *LM* curve, it represents an excess supply of money. At E_1, the *LM* curve intersects the *FE* line, but the goods market is no longer in equilibrium. As E_1 lies below the *IS* curve, there is an excess demand for goods at that point. Note that at E_2—where the *IS* and *LM* curves intersect—desired saving and investment are not equal, and implied current output is greater than actual current output (represented by the *FE* line). Hence, if we hold the determinants of the three curves constant, there is no combination of current output and real interest rate for which all markets in the economy and the financial system are in equilibrium.

Restoring Equilibrium: Price-Level Adjustment

How can the economy and financial system achieve equilibrium when one of the three curves shifts? Some variable will have to change in response to the changes we analyzed. Let's assume that the price level P is flexible and can adjust freely in response to such changes. Is this assumption realistic? The answer depends on the definition of the period over which prices adjust. If the period is a week, the assumption of flexible prices may not be realistic. If the period is three years, the assumption may be more accurate. In Chapter 25, we examine reasons why prices may not be flexible in the short run. Those reasons have important implications for short-run equilibrium. For now, however, let's assume that prices are flexible in the long run and return to the shifts in the *IS* curve, *FE* line, and *LM* curve that we analyzed earlier.

Shifts in the IS Curve. Recall that the shift in the *IS* curve resulting from a military buildup left the asset markets out of equilibrium, with a higher real interest rate than at initial equilibrium. With the increased opportunity cost of money, households and businesses try to use their higher than desired real money balances to buy goods, putting upward pressure on prices.

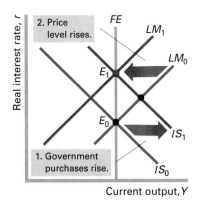

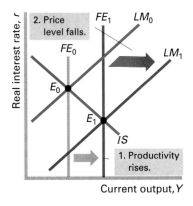

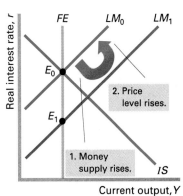

(a) Increase in
Government Purchases

(b) Temporary Increase
in Productivity

(c) Increase in the Nominal
Money Supply

FIGURE 24.8

**Price Level Adjustment to
Restore the Economy's
Equilibrium**

As shown in (a):
1. From an initial equilibrium at E_0, higher government purchases shift the IS curve from IS_0 to IS_1.

2. The price level rises, shifting the LM curve from LM_0 to LM_1 to restore equilibrium at E_1.

As shown in (b):
1. From an initial equilibrium at E_0, increased productivity shifts the full employment line from FE_0 to FE_1.

2. A fall in the price level shifts the LM curve from LM_0 to LM_1 and restores equilibrium at E_1.

As shown in (c):
1. From an initial equilibrium at E_0, an increase in the nominal money supply by 10% shifts the LM curve from LM_0 to LM_1.

2. The price level increases by 10%, shifting the LM curve back from LM_1 to LM_0 and restoring equilibrium at E_0.

As Fig. 24.8(a) shows, the higher price level reduces the supply of real money balances, causing the LM curve to shift from LM_0 to LM_1, where it intersects the IS curve and the FE line at E_1.

Hence, if nothing else changes, an increase in government purchases has no effect on output in the long run when prices are flexible. However, both the real rate of interest and the price level increase so that the quantity of real money balances demanded equals the quantity supplied. For any expected rate of inflation, the higher real rate of interest implies a higher nominal rate of interest and a decline in the quantity of real money balances demanded.

The higher real rate of interest in the economy increases private saving and decreases current consumption and investment. The reduction in private consumption and investment accompanying an increase in government purchases in a closed economy is known as *crowding out*.[†]

Shifts in the FE Line. In Fig. 24.8(b), starting from equilibrium at E_0, an increase in the full employment level of current output generates an excess demand for real money balances. At levels of the real interest rate and current output that lead to equilibrium in the goods market, households prefer to hold larger money balances. The excess supply of goods pushes prices down. Lower prices, in turn, increase the demand for goods and increase households' real money balances. The LM curve shifts from LM_0 to LM_1 to intersect the IS curve and FE line at E_1, and the asset markets return to equilibrium, but at a lower level of the real interest rate and a higher level of current output.

[†] In a large open economy, such as the U.S. economy, an increase in the real rate of interest increases desired international lending by foreign investors, resulting in capital flows from abroad into the domestic economy. Consequently, the current account balance of the domestic economy deteriorates. In other words, an increase in government purchases results in a decrease in net exports.

MOVING FROM THEORY TO PRACTICE...

THE WALL STREET JOURNAL OCTOBER 1, 1991

Are High Real Interest Rates an Answer to or Cause for Prayer?

The markets are expecting the Federal Reserve to cut the discount rate once again—close on the heels of its last cut... But don't expect the stock market to go up. After the [last] drop in the discount rate, the U.S. stock market went down, not up. Analysts said that the market fell because the decline in the discount rate signaled that the Fed thought that the prospects for the economy were worse than people had believed...

Shifts to the expected profitability of investment, and hence investment demand, mean that real interest rates are high in good times, such as the mid-1980s, and low in bad times, such as the middle and late 1970s. It is not that high real interest rates are good, per se, for economic activity, but rather that high real rates are typically symptomatic of other events that make investment attractive...

While domestic monetary and fiscal policies can change real interest rates by altering desired saving and perhaps also by changing investment demand, these effects tend to be secondary. Because of the integration of capital and goods markets among the developed countries, the real interest rates in the United States depend mainly on international forces, such as *world-wide* monetary and fiscal policies and *world-wide* stock-market fluctuations. Domestic monetary and fiscal policy affect domestic real interest rates only to the extent that the local government can affect the world aggregates of monetary and fiscal policies.

Of course, real interest rates in individual countries do vary from what might be called the world real interest rate. These departures are sometimes substantial, but they turn out not to relate systematically to the individual country's stock return, investment spending, monetary and fiscal policies or any of the other variables that I have examined...

What matters above all is the shifting perception of the profitability of investment, which shows up as fluctuations of stock-market prices... The relationship between stock prices and interest rates would be the other way around—high rates in bad times, low rates in goods times—if it were the supply of credit, rather than the demand, that moved markets. And sometimes this relationship does hold: The world monetary contraction in 1979–1980 contributed to the rise in real interest rates in 1980–1981 and the world monetary expansion in 1986 induced a decline in real interest rates in 1987.

But normally it is the demand for capital, and not its supply, that is the determining factor.

ANALYZING THE NEWS...

The real interest rate adjusts to maintain equilibrium in the goods market and the asset markets. Hence, to analyze whether a change in the economy's real interest rate is cause for joy or gloom, we need to examine its underlying determinants in terms of saving–investment and portfolio allocation decisions.

(a) In the case of a single country, the United States, an increase in expected future profitability of capital (signaled, say, by an increase in stock prices) shifts the IS curve up to the right from IS_0 to IS_1, as shown in Fig. (a). At any real interest rate, firms are willing to invest more. Both the real interest rate and demand for current output increase. If the economy is in equilibrium at E_0 initially, current output can rise to E_1 only if the economy's resources can "work harder," that is, if the FE line shifts to the right. If it doesn't, the price level increases, shifting the LM curve up to the left and equilibrium to E_2. Hence, a stock market boom is associated with a higher real interest rate. As investment increases production in the future, the FE line *does* shift to the right, signaling good economic times.

(b) The ability of savings to flow abroad implies that the IS curve for open economies, such as the U.S. economy, is flatter than it would be for a closed economy. In response to the worldwide investment boom, the world IS curve shifts upward, and the world real interest rate rises. The article argues that the IS curve in the United States is roughly horizontal at the world interest rate. In response to the investment boom around the world, the U.S. IS curve shifts upward from IS_{US0} to IS_{US1}, as Fig. (b) shows. The U.S. price level rises, shifting the LM curve from LM_{US0} to LM_{US1} to restore equilibrium at E_1.

For further thought...

The article claims that *domestic* monetary policy (for example, a decrease in the nominal money supply by the Fed) has no effect on the U.S. real interest rate. In the context of our IS–LM–FE diagram approach, what assumptions is he making? Suggest a method of testing the author's conjecture.

Source: Excerpted from Robert Barro, "Pray for High Interest Rates," October 1, 1991. Reprinted by permission of *The Wall Street Journal,* © 1991 Dow Jones & Co., Inc. All Rights Reserved Worldwide.

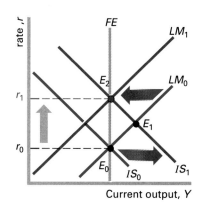

(a) United States

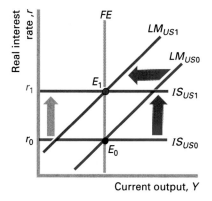

(b) United States

Hence, if nothing else changes, an increase in productivity in the current period raises output while decreasing the price level and the real interest rate. For expected inflation, the lower real interest rate increases the quantity of real money balances demanded. The lower price level raises the real value of money balances.[†]

Q: Do changes in the money supply affect the real interest rate and current output in the long run?

A: Over time, the price level adjusts to restore equilibrium at the intersection of the *IS* and *LM* curves and the *FE* line. In the long run, money is neutral. An increase in the nominal money supply leads to an increase in the price level, leaving the real interest rate and output unaffected; a decrease in the nominal money supply leads to a decrease in the price level, with no effect on the real interest rate or output.

Shifts in the LM Curve. Finally, recall the situation in which the Fed increased the nominal money supply 10%, shifting the *LM* curve down and to the right. In that case, at E_0 in Fig. 24.8(c), households and businesses have more real money balances than they desire. What would happen if households and businesses try to spend their excess real money balances to purchase additional goods and services in the goods market? If the aggregate output of goods is fixed in the current period (represented by the *FE* line), higher spending by households and businesses will not raise current output but will raise the price level.

As the price level rises, real money balances fall because they equal nominal money balances divided by the price level. The reduction in real money balances causes the *LM* curve to shift up and to the left (from LM_1 back to LM_0). To restore equilibrium in all markets, the price level must rise by 10%, or the amount by which the nominal money supply initially increased. The economy and the financial system return to equilibrium at E_0.

Money, Output, and Prices in the Long Run

Our findings on the effects of changes in the money supply on equilibrium strongly suggest that any percentage increase in the nominal money supply leads to an equal percentage increase in the price level, leaving real money balances unchanged. This feature of money's effect on the economy in the long run is known as the **neutrality of money.** Monetary neutrality implies that a one-time change in the nominal money supply affects only nominal variables, such as nominal output or the price level. Real output and the real interest rate remain unaffected by a one-time increase or decrease in the nominal money supply.

The concept of monetary neutrality depends on the assumption that prices are flexible. Recall that the way in which neutrality is achieved in response to an increase in the money supply is for the price level to rise. Over short periods of time, the assumption of price flexibility isn't realistic. Many economists believe that changes in the money supply do affect the real economy *in the short run* (as we will demonstrate in Chapter 26). However, economists generally accept the *long-run* neutrality of money.

[†] In a large open economy, such as the U.S. economy, a drop in the real interest rate reduces desired international lending from abroad to the domestic economy, and the current account balance increases.

Key Terms and Concepts

Current output
    Full employment (*FE*) line
    Full employment output
General equilibrium
Goods market
IS curve

LM curve
Money market
Neutrality of money
Nonmoney asset market

Summary

1. Combinations of current output and the real rate of interest for which the goods market is in equilibrium make up the *IS* curve. The *IS* curve slopes downward: Higher current output requires a lower real interest rate to equate desired saving and investment and achieve equilibrium.

2. The *IS* curve shifts in response to changes in variables that change the equilibrium real interest rate associated with a specific level of current output. These variables include government purchases, foreign demand for domestic goods, consumer and business confidence, and an increase in expected future productivity.

3. The full employment (*FE*) line represents current output supplied by full employment of existing factors of production. It is assumed to be independent of the real rate of interest. Equilibrium current output equates aggregate demand with current output and occurs at the intersection of the *IS* curve and the *FE* line.

4. Asset market equilibrium refers to equilibrium in the markets for money and nonmoney assets. When one of the two asset markets is in equilibrium, the other also is in equilibrium. Plotting combinations of the real interest rate and current output for which the money market is in equilibrium yields the *LM* curve.

5. The *LM* curve slopes upward because money demand depends positively on current output and

negatively on the real interest rate. The more sensitive the demand for money is to the real interest rate, the flatter the *LM* curve is.

6. Factors that change the supply of or demand for real money balances shift the *LM* curve. They include the nominal money supply, price level, nominal interest rate on money, and expected rate of inflation.

7. When the financial system and the economy are in long-run equilibrium, the *IS* curve, *LM* curve, and *FE* line intersect at the same real interest rate and level of current output. When the curves do not intersect simultaneously, the price level adjusts, causing the *LM* curve to shift to maintain equilibrium.

8. The financial system and the economy are in general equilibrium when the goods and asset markets are in equilibrium simultaneously. Interactions among these markets determine asset returns, output, and the price level.

9. In long-run equilibrium, one-time changes in the nominal money supply affect only the price level, not real output or the real interest rate. Hence, so long as the price level in the economy is flexible, money is neutral.

Review Questions

1. How does an increase in the nominal money supply affect the *IS* and *LM* curves and *FE* line?

2. Suppose that the quantity of money balances supplied equals the quantity of money balances demanded. Can the demand for nonmoney assets exceed the supply of nonmoney assets? Why or why not?

3. Of the *IS* curve, *LM* curve, or *FE* line, which is shifted directly by a change in fiscal policy in a closed economy? In which direction does it shift if government expenditures increase?

4. The *LM* curve shows points of equilibrium in the money market for what two variables?

5. What is general equilibrium? In the *IS–LM–FE* model, what happens to the *IS* and *LM* curves and *FE* line at general equilibrium?

6. What are the three components of aggregate demand in a closed economy? What is the relationship of national saving and investment in a closed economy at equilibrium?

7. What are the two principal determinants of desired investment?

8. Why does the *IS* curve slope downward?

9. Suppose that data showed no relationship between the levels of saving and investment in various countries. What would that suggest about whether the countries have closed or open economies? Suppose that, instead, the data showed saving and investment to be highly correlated. What would that imply?

10. Why does the *LM* curve slope upward?

11. Why is the *FE* line vertical? What determines the location of the *FE* line?

12. What does *money is neutral* mean? If money is neutral, what effect does a 10% increase in the nominal money supply have on current output? On the real interest rate? On real money demand? On the price level?

Analytical Problems

13. Suppose that firms become nervous about the future because of increased uncertainty; as a result, they reduce their investment spending. Of the *IS* curve, *LM* curve, or *FE* line, which would be shifted by this reduction? In what direction would it shift?

14. What effect do each of the following events have on national saving, and what happens to the *IS* curve as a result?

   a. The government cuts defense spending by 10%.

   b. The size of the Alaskan oil fields actually are much smaller than earlier believed, cutting expected future income by 3%.

   c. Barriers to international trade are lowered, allowing gains from specialization and increasing expected future income by 5%.

   d. The government expands its health-care coverage, increasing government purchases by 15%.

15. Suppose that a large open economy is initially at equilibrium with domestic saving equal to domestic

investment so that the current account balance is zero. Now suppose that current domestic output decreases. What happens to the real interest rate, domestic saving, domestic investment, and the current account balance?

16. Suppose that a country having a small open economy passes a law taxing investment heavily. What effect would the tax have on desired investment? What happens to the real interest rate? What happens to the country's current account balance?

17. What effect do each of the following events have on real money demand and real money supply? What happens to the *LM* curve as a result?

    a. Expected inflation rises because of an oil price increase.

    b. Increased bank regulation forces banks to reduce the nominal interest rate they pay on checking accounts.

    c. A drop in the exchange rate causes an increase in the price level.

    d. The Fed makes open market purchases.

18. Consider a small open economy that is in general equilibrium. What effect on the real interest rate and output level do each of the following events have after equilibrium is restored?

    a. An increase in expected future productivity of investment.

    b. A decrease in government purchases.

    c. An increase in expected inflation.

    d. A decrease in foreign demand for domestically produced goods.

    e. An increase in the nominal interest rate on money assets.

    f. An increase in households' willingness to save.

    g. A decrease in nominal money balances.

    h. A decrease in the price level.

19. Suppose that a closed economy is in general equilibrium when new antipollution laws go into effect, reducing current productivity. What happens to the real interest rate, current output, the price level, saving, investment, and real money demand?

20. What happens to the price level to restore equilibrium in each of the following cases for a closed economy?

    a. *IS* curve shifts up and to the right.

    b. *IS* curve shifts down and to the left.

    c. *FE* line shifts to the right.

    d. *FE* line shifts to the left.

    e. *LM* curve shifts down to the right.

21. What happens if Europeans reduce their demand for U.S.-made automobiles? Which curve or line shifts in response? Does the price level rise or fall to restore equilibrium? What happens to the real interest rate and the level of current output? What happens to saving, investment, real money demand, nominal money supply, and the current account, assuming that the United States has a large open economy?

22. In the *IS–LM–FE* model, what happens when expected inflation declines? Which curve or line shifts initially? What happens to restore equilibrium? What are the ultimate effects on the real interest rate and current output?

23. In a small open economy, what happens to the price level if the world real interest rate falls?

24. What happens to the *IS* curve of a large open economy in which capital controls are enforced to prevent international borrowing or lending?

25. Suppose that new computer technology greatly enhances the ability of doctors to diagnose and treat diseases, sharply reducing the amount of time that workers spend on sick leave. What effect does this have initially on the *IS–LM–FE* model? How

does the price level change to restore equilibrium? What is the ultimate effect on the real interest rate and the level of current output?

26. Suppose that widespread use of bank debit cards and credit cards reduces the demand for money at any particular level of income and interest rates. What would be the effect on long-run equilibrium in the *IS–LM–FE* model? (In long-run equilibrium, prices are flexible.)

27. In the early 1980s, the U.S. government cut income taxes without reducing spending, significantly increasing the government's budget deficit (the difference between government purchases and taxes, net of transfers). Suppose that private saving didn't increase to offset the decrease in government saving.

    a. What are the effects on the price level and real interest rate, assuming that nothing else changes and that the United States has a closed economy?

    b. Now suppose that the United States and its principal trading partners (such as Germany) have large open economies. What is the effect of the U.S. tax cut on the real interest rate and price level in Germany?

    c. What could Germany or the United States do to offset the effects of U.S. budget deficits on the price levels in the two countries?

The following question pertains to the discussion in the Appendix.

28. A closed economy has the following characteristics.

    Consumption: $C = 0.75(Y - T) - 120r + 450$.

Investment: $I = 600 - 180r$.

Government purchases: $G = 300$.

Taxes, net of transfers: $T = 225$.

Demand for real money balances:
    $L = 0.15Y - 120i + 87.75$.

Nominal money supply: $M_s = 600$.

Expected rate of inflation: $\pi^e = 0.05$.

The goods market equilibrium is represented by the *IS* curve.

    a. What is the equation of the *IS* curve?

    b. Plot the *IS* curve.

Asset market equilibrium is described by the *LM* curve.

    c. Suppose that the price level is 3. What is the equation of the *LM* curve?

    d. For the assumption in (c), draw the *LM* curve.

Current output supplied is represented by the *FE* line.

    e. Suppose that full employment current output $Y^* = 4665$. What are the equilibrium values of the price level and the real interest rate in the economy?

Suppose that the nominal money supply increases from 600 to 660.

    f. What happens to the price level, the real interest rate, and output in the new long-run equilibrium?

Data Question

29. Olivier Blanchard of M.I.T. and Lawrence Summers of Harvard University calculated the annual real interest rate on medium-term U.S. Treasury bonds for each year from 1980 through the first quarter of 1984 to be 1.0%, 2.2%, 6.9%, 4.3%, and 6.5%. Find a recent issue of the *Economic* *Report of the President* in your library and calculate the percentage change in aggregate output in each year (from Table B-2). Using the *IS–LM–FE* diagram, offer an explanation for the observed pattern in real interest rates and output growth during this period.

Appendix: Derivation of the *IS* Curve

By making simple assumptions about the relationship between national saving and investment, we can derive the *IS* curve algebraically. We do so here for a closed economy, a large open economy, and a small open economy.

Closed Economy

As discussed in the chapter, we determine equilibrium in the goods market by equating national saving, S, and investment, I, or

$$S = I. \tag{24A.1}$$

In a closed economy the financial system matches domestic saving and investment, so national saving consists of domestic private saving, S_P, and government saving, S_G.

Private saving equals income, Y, minus taxes, net of transfers, T, less current consumption, C.[†] Government saving equals taxes, net of transfers, T, minus government purchases, G. Substituting these variables into Eq. (24A.1) we have

$$\underbrace{(Y - T - C)}_{S_P} + \underbrace{(T - G)}_{S_G} = I. \tag{24A.2}$$

$$\underbrace{}_{S}$$

Note that equating saving and investment in Eq. (24A.2) yields an expression for *aggregate demand* for current output in the closed economy:

$$Y = C + I + G. \tag{24A.3}$$

Total output is the sum of current consumption, investment, and government spending on goods and services.

Equation (24A.3) is an accounting identity, not a model of economic decisions. *Current consumption C depends positively on current disposable income* (total current income Y minus taxes, net of transfers, T) and negatively on the real interest rate r (which measures the opportunity cost of trading current for future consumption). Hence

$$C = c_1(Y - T) - c_2 r + C_0, \tag{24A.4}$$

where C_0 represents other potential determinants of consumption (for example, wealth, consumer confidence, or households' preference for current consumption relative to expected future consumption). The coefficient on

---

[†] We do not consider business saving separately here. In the economy, households own businesses and business savings.

income after taxes, net of transfers, c_1, represents the *marginal propensity to consume:* Holding constant the real interest rate and other determinants of consumption, an increase in $(Y - T)$ by \$1.00 raises C by c_1, which has a value between 0 and 1.

Investment I, depends positively on the profitability of investment opportunities I_0 and negatively on the real interest rate, r, or

$$I = -ar + I_0. \tag{24A.5}$$

An increase in the profitability of investment opportunities increases I_0. John Maynard Keynes, whose work in the 1930s led to development of the *IS–LM* model, thought that shifts in the investment schedule were driven by businesses' confidence about the future, which he called *animal spirits.*

For simplicity, let's take government spending on goods and services and taxes, net of transfers, as a given at levels G and T, respectively. We can now equate domestic saving and investment in the economy:

$$\underbrace{\underbrace{[Y - T - (c_1(Y - T) - c_2r + C_0)]}_{S_P} + \underbrace{(T - G)}_{S_G}}_{S} = \underbrace{-ar + I_0}_{I}. \tag{24A.6}$$

Collecting terms, we express Eq. (24A.6) as a relationship between aggregate demand for current output and the real interest rate:

$$Y = \frac{C_0 + I_0 + G - c_1T}{1 - c_1} - \left(\frac{c_2 + a}{1 - c_1}\right)r. \tag{24A.7}$$

Current output increases in response to an increase in C_0, I_0, and G. Increases in T and r decrease current output. The first term in Eq. (24A.7) consists of variables whose values are *exogenous,* that is, given outside the model. We know that r and Y are *endogenous* variables, the equilibrium values of which we are trying to determine.

By how much does aggregate demand increase in response to an increase in these variables? From Eq. (24A.7) and for a constant r, a \$1.00 increase in C_0, I_0, or G raises the demand for current output by \$1/(1 - c_1)$. If the marginal propensity to consume c_1 were 0.8, a \$1.00 increase in C_0, I_0, or G would raise demand by \$1.00/(1 - 0.8)$, or \$5.00.[†]

[†] Note that the coefficient of G in Eq. (24A.7) is $1/(1 - c_1)$, whereas the coefficient of T is $-c_1/(1 - c_1)$. Hence raising both G and T by \$1.00 (a "balanced budget" change) raises aggregate demand by

$$\frac{1}{1 - c_1} - \frac{c_1}{1 - c_1} = 1.$$

An equal increase in government purchases and taxes, net of transfers, raises aggregate demand by the amount of the increase in G and T in this approach.

Large Open Economy

We derive the *IS* curve for a large open economy by extending our closed economy model to include net saving supplied by foreigners S_F. The equality of saving and investment then becomes

$$S_P + S_G + S_F = I. \tag{24A.8}$$

When $S_F > 0$, foreign saving flows into the domestic economy. This capital inflow finances greater domestic consumption and investment. As a result, the current account balance CA, the difference between exports and imports, falls. Hence, as we showed in Chapter 22,

$$S_F = -CA.$$

The national income accounting identity for an open economy is

$$Y = C + I + G + CA. \tag{24A.9}$$

To specify the *IS* curve, we let

$$CA = CA_0 - dr.$$

The CA_0 term allows for shifts in demand for domestic versus foreign goods. An increase in the domestic real interest rate r increases the flow of foreign savings into the domestic economy, thereby decreasing the current account balance. Substituting for the elements of the right-hand side of Eq. (24.9) gives us the equation for the *IS* curve:

$$Y = \underbrace{[C_0 + c_1(Y - T) - c_2 r]}_{C} + \underbrace{(I_0 - ar)}_{I} + \underbrace{G}_{G} + \underbrace{(CA_0 - dr)}_{CA}.$$

Rearranging terms, we get

$$Y = \frac{(C_0 + I_0 + G + CA_0) - c_1 T - (c_2 + a + d)r}{1 - c_1},$$

or

$$r = -\left(\frac{1 - c_1}{c_2 + a + d}\right)Y + \left(\frac{1}{c_2 + a + d}\right)(C_0 + I_0 + G - c_1 T + CA_0). \tag{24A.10}$$

The *IS* curve is flatter (that is, $\Delta r/\Delta Y$ is smaller in absolute value) than the closed economy *IS* curve derived in the text.

We can illustrate this result graphically. Figure 24A.1(a) and (b) show saving and investment curves for a domestic economy D and a foreign economy F obtained by plotting current output against the real interest rate. Note in Fig. 24A.1(a) that the saving functions S_D and S_F slope upward, indi-

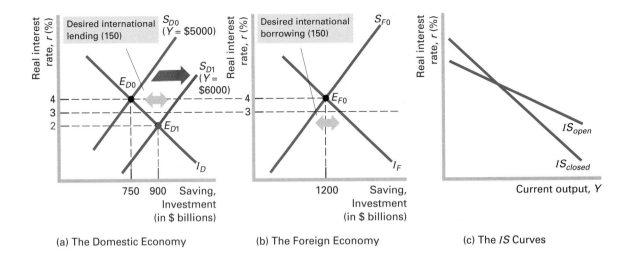

(a) The Domestic Economy   (b) The Foreign Economy   (c) The *IS* Curves

▲ FIGURE 24A.1

International Borrowing and Lending and the *IS* Curve

As shown in (a):
An increase in saving in the domestic economy puts downward pressure on the domestic real interest rate. To the extent that some of domestic saving flows abroad, the real interest rate doesn't fall by as much as it would in a closed economy.

As shown in (b):
The domestic economy's current account balance increases while the current account balance of the foreign economy decreases.

As shown in (c):
An increase in domestic current output leads to a smaller decline in the domestic real interest rate than occurs in a closed economy. Hence the *IS* curve for the large open economy is flatter than for the closed economy, all else being equal.

cating that the quantity of funds supplied rises with the interest rate. The investment functions I_D and I_F slope downward, indicating that the quantity of funds demanded falls with the real interest rate.

At an output level of $5000 billion in the domestic economy, domestic saving and investment are equal (at $750 billion) at a real interest rate of 4% (at E_{D0}). For simplicity, let's assume initially that, at a real interest rate of 4%, saving and investment in the foreign economy (Fig. 24A.1b) are equal at $1200 billion (at E_{F0}). Therefore domestic saving and investment match in both economies; no trade in goods or assets occurs between them, which is analogous to the earlier discussion of the *IS* curve for a closed economy.

Domestic saving depends in part on domestic current output. Suppose that domestic current output increases to $6000 billion. As a result, desired domestic saving shifts to the right from S_{D0} to S_{D1}. Derivation of the *IS* curve for a closed economy showed that saving and investment would be equal at point E_{D1} at a real rate of interest of 2%, with national saving and investment of $900 billion.

However, that real rate of interest is too low for an open economy if domestically saved funds can be used to finance investment abroad (in the foreign economy). In fact, as Fig. 24A.1(a) and (b) show, the equilibrium real interest rate with international capital flows is 3%, *not* 2%. At a world real interest rate of 3%, the desired lending of the domestic economy is the excess of domestic saving over investment of $150 billion. This amount matches exactly the desired international borrowing of the foreign economy, or the excess of investment in the foreign economy over foreign saving of $150 billion. In this case, goods flow from the domestic economy to the foreign economy, which is investing more than it is saving. At a real interest rate of 3%, the domestic economy wants to lend exactly the amount that the foreign economy wants to borrow at that rate.

Fortunately, as we noted in the chapter, a large open economy and a closed economy are quite similar. For both, an increase in current output lowers the real rate of interest, and a decrease in current output raises the real rate of interest. However, the magnitude of the response of the real interest rate to a shift in current output differs: The *IS* curve for the large open domestic economy is flatter than for the closed domestic economy, as Fig. 24A.1(c) shows. A shift in current domestic output has a smaller effect on the world interest rate in an open economy than in a closed economy. Because capital is mobile internationally, an increase in desired domestic saving can finance either domestic or foreign investment. Thus, as the quantity of both domestic and foreign desired investment rise, the real interest rate doesn't have to fall by as much to absorb the greater quantity of savings.

Small Open Economy

In a small open economy, the rate of interest for the *IS* curve is the world real rate of interest, or $r = r_w$. Unlike a large open economy, a small open economy cannot affect the world real rate of interest by increasing or decreasing its desired national saving or investment.

CHAPTER 25

Aggregate Demand and Aggregate Supply

The economic "stagflation" of 1973–1975 was unsettling for economists and policymakers alike. As the economy's output fell, prices increased. This was a double blow to the economy because, as workers lost jobs, the prices of the goods they bought rose. These events transformed the way economists, businesspeople, and policymakers thought about the interaction of the financial system and the economy and about how the price level and current output are determined in the economy.

In this chapter, we consider the determinants of output and the price level in both the short and long run. We use our analysis of saving and investment and portfolio allocation decisions to emphasize aggregate demand and aggregate supply. Aggregate demand is the level of output that households and businesses are willing to demand and purchase at any price level. Aggregate supply is the level of output that producers in the economy are willing to supply and produce at any price level. We use graphical analysis to show how current output and the price level are determined and to explain changes in them. It will help you understand the implications of current economic events and what you should expect in making future financial decisions.

In this chapter three questions guide us. **Q:** How are output and the price level related in determining aggregate demand? **Q:** How are output and the price level related in determining aggregate supply? **Q:** How are the equilibrium price level and output level determined in both the short and long run?

Interactions of the Financial System and the Economy

We are now ready to consider the interactions of the financial system and the economy and to identify the ways in which monetary policy affects economic outcomes. To begin, let's return to our simple description of the financial system.

Recall that the public's demand for real money balances $(M/P)_d$ is a portfolio allocation decision. It depends on current output Y (as a measure of the volume of transactions), the real interest rate[†] on nonmoney assets r, and other factors (including expected inflation, the interest paid on money holdings, and payments system technologies). In other words,

$$(M/P)_d = L(Y, r, \ldots),$$

where L is the liquidity preference relation linking the demand for real money balances to its determinants. If we hold other determinants of money demand constant, current output Y is positively related to the demand for real money balances. Hence an increase in Y increases $(M/P)_d$, and a decrease in Y reduces $(M/P)_d$. The real interest rate on nonmoney assets, r, is negatively related to the opportunity cost of holding real money balances. Hence a rise in r reduces the quantity of real money balances demanded, and a drop in r increases that quantity. For simplicity, we leave aside for now the other determinants of money demand examined in Chapter 23: the interest paid on money, expected inflation, and payments system factors.

As Fig. 25.1(a) shows, if we take the price level, expected inflation, and the level of current output as givens, we can determine the real interest rate in the market for money and nonmoney assets. The money demand curve, given by MD, slopes downward because an increase in the real interest rate causes the public to increase holdings of nonmoney assets, thereby reducing the quantity of real money balances demanded. The MS curve indicates the economy's real money supply, $(M/P)_s$. If we assume that the Fed[††] supplies nominal money balances, M_s, and that the price level P is given, MS is vertical at $(M/P)_s$. The equilibrium real interest rate on nonmoney assets lies at the intersection of the money demand and money supply curves.

Changes in the price level or current output in the economy affect the real interest rate in the financial system. As Fig. 25.1(b) shows, an increase in the price level from P_0 to P_1 shifts the money supply curve to the left from MS_0 to MS_1, reducing real money balances and increasing the real interest rate from r_0 to r_1. Figure 25.1(c) illustrates the effect of an increase in current output on the real interest rate. An increase in current output increases the demand for real money balances, shifting the money demand curve to the right from MD_0 to MD_1 and increasing the real interest rate from r_0 to r_1.

[†] We use the term *real interest rate* as shorthand for the expected real interest rate.

[††] This assumption simplifies the discussion. Recall that, actually, the Fed, banks, and the nonbank public jointly determine the money supply.

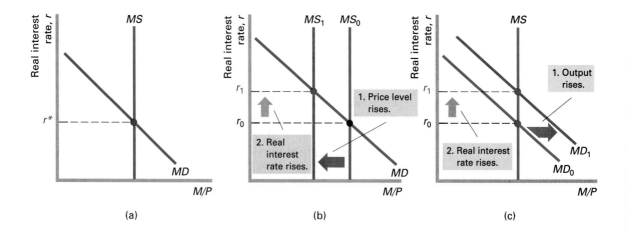

(a)   (b)   (c)

FIGURE 25.1

Interest Rate Determination in the Market for Money and Nonmoney Assets

As shown in (a):
The equilibrium interest rate, r^*, is at the intersection of the real money demand (MD) and real money supply (MS) curves.

As shown in (b):
1. An increase in the price level from P_0 to P_1 shifts the money supply curve from MS_0 to MS_1.

2. The real interest rate rises from r_0 to r_1.

As shown in (c):
1. An increase in current output shifts the money demand curve from MD_0 to MD_1.

2. The real interest rate rises from r_0 to r_1.

Money market equilibrium—for a given price level, current output, and expected rate of inflation—determines the real interest rate in the financial system.

To establish the interactions between the financial system and the economy, however, we cannot assume that either the price level or current output is fixed. How then do we determine the equilibrium price level and current output? How do changes in the equilibrium real interest rate and portfolio allocation in the financial system affect the price level and current output? To answer these questions, we need to develop an aggregate demand–aggregate supply model.

The Aggregate Demand Curve

Aggregate demand for the economy's output equals the sum of demands for (1) goods and services for desired consumption, C; (2) desired investment in business plant and equipment, inventories, and housing, I; (3) government purchases of goods and services (not including transfer payments to individuals), G; and (4) net exports (domestic sales of goods and services to foreigners minus domestic purchases of goods and services from foreigners), CA. Hence aggregate demand for current output, Y_d, is

$$Y_d = C + I + G + CA. \tag{25.1}$$

Deriving the Aggregate Demand Curve

The **aggregate demand (AD) curve** illustrates the relationship between the aggregate demand for goods and services (the goods market) and the aggregate price level. The aggregate demand curve slopes downward. Hence an increase in the price level reduces the aggregate demand for goods and services, if nothing else changes. The aggregate demand curve is a different type of demand curve from the demand curve for, say, wheat that you studied in your microeconomics course. The quantity of wheat demanded also depends negatively on the price of wheat, but the demand curve for wheat relates the demand for wheat to the price of wheat relative to the prices of other goods. However, the aggregate demand curve relates the aggregate quantity of output demanded Y_d to the aggregate price level P. Thus, if prices of all goods rise by 5%, the aggregate price level P rises by 5%, but relative prices do not change. Nonetheless the increase in the price level P reduces the aggregate quantity of output demanded, Y_d.

To see how this relationship results from interaction of the financial system and the economy, let's return to the markets for money and nonmoney assets that we introduced in the analysis of money demand in Chapter 23. For any nominal money supply M, an increase in the price level reduces real money balances (M/P). For the public to be willing to hold a smaller quantity of real money balances and a larger quantity of nonmoney assets, the real interest rate must rise. A higher real interest rate on nonmoney assets, increases the opportunity cost of holding money, so that the public is willing to hold the lower level of real money balances.

We now return to our analysis of saving, investment, and interest rate determination in Chapter 5. Recall that an increase in the real interest rate raises desired saving, lowers desired consumption, and reduces desired investment in consumer durables, housing, and business plant and equipment. As a result, because the values of C and I in Eq. (25.1) fall, the aggregate quantity of output demanded falls. An increase in the real interest rate also lowers aggregate demand for current output, owing to international trade and capital flows. A higher domestic real interest rate makes returns on domestic financial assets more attractive relative to those on foreign assets, raising the exchange rate. The rise in the exchange rate increases imports and reduces exports, causing a reduction in NX in Eq. (25.1). This means that the quantity demanded of domestic output falls. Thus an increase in the price level reduces consumption, investment, and net exports, resulting in a decline in the aggregate quantity of output demanded.

Conversely, a decrease in the price level increases real money balances, leading to a drop in the real interest rate in the markets for money and nonmoney assets. The lower real interest rate reduces desired saving and raises desired investment and net exports. Hence, from Eq. (25.1), the quantity of aggregate output demanded rises. As Fig. 25.2 shows, the aggregate demand curve AD slopes downward to the right. Points along the aggregate demand curve represent combinations of the price level and current output for which the goods market (the economy) and the asset markets (the financial system) are in equilibrium at the same time. The money market is in equilibrium because the quantity of real money balances equals the available supply. The nonmoney asset market is in equilibrium because households and businesses are satisfied with their holdings of nonmoney assets. The goods market (the economy) is in equilibrium because desired saving equals desired investment. The simultaneous equilibrium of all three markets comprising the financial system and the economy is called *general equilibrium*.

FIGURE 25.2

The Aggregate Demand Curve
The aggregate demand curve *AD* illustrates the negative relationship between the price level and the aggregate quantity of output demanded. The aggregate demand curve slopes downward. Increases in the price level reduce real money balances, raising the real interest rate and reducing the quantity of output demanded.

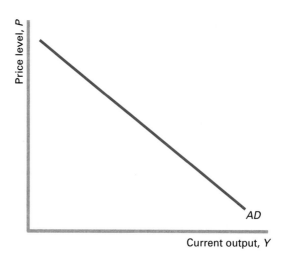

Shifts of the Aggregate Demand Curve

Shifts of the aggregate demand curve reflect increases or decreases in the aggregate demand for the economy's current output at a particular price level. A shift of the aggregate demand curve to the right is *expansionary* because the price level is associated with a higher level of aggregate demand for current output. Expansionary shifts in aggregate demand can be traced to the asset markets or the goods market. A shift of the aggregate demand curve to the left is *contractionary* because the price level is associated with a lower level of aggregate demand for current output. Like expansionary shifts, contractionary shifts in aggregate demand can originate either in the asset markets or in the goods market.

Shifts Originating in the Asset Markets. In the markets for money and nonmoney assets, if the Fed increases the nominal money supply, real money balances rise. The real interest rate then falls in the asset markets. For that lower real interest rate to be consistent with equilibrium in the goods market, desired saving must fall (raising desired consumption, *C*), and desired investment, *I*, must rise. As a result, aggregate demand rises, shifting the aggregate demand curve to the right.

Another cause of expansionary shifts originating in the asset markets is a decline in money demand. It can be the result of a drop in the interest paid on money relative to that on other assets or to a change in the payments system that makes money less desirable for use in transactions. At any level of real money supply, the decline in money demand reduces the real interest rate. As in the case of an increase in the nominal money supply, the drop in the real interest rate raises aggregate demand in the goods market and shifts the *AD* curve to the right.

In the asset markets, contractionary shifts are attributable to a decline in the nominal money supply or a rise in money demand at each level of output. If the Fed restricts the nominal money supply, real money balances fall; the real interest rate rises to restore equilibrium in the asset markets. For the higher real interest rate to be consistent with equilibrium in the goods market, desired saving must rise (reducing desired consumption, C), and desired investment, I, must fall. As a result, aggregate demand falls. A rise in money demand means that, at any level of money supply, the real interest rate must rise to restore equilibrium in the money market. The increase in the real interest rate reduces aggregate demand.

Shifts Originating in the Goods Market. Expansionary shifts also can originate in the goods market owing to changes in desired saving and investment, in government purchases, or in net exports. A decline in desired saving or a rise in desired investment at any real interest rate raises aggregate demand. Such a drop reflects an increase in expected future income or consumer confidence (raising consumption, C). Many, though not all, economists also believe that increases in current income from tax cuts reduce desired saving and increase consumption. Box 25.1 discusses this controversy. An increase in desired investment, I, reflects an increase in the expected future

---

Consider this...

BOX 25.1

Do Tax Cuts Stimulate Aggregate Demand?

Economists and policymakers have debated vigorously whether reductions in current taxes—holding government spending constant—increase aggregate demand. Those who believe that tax cuts increase aggregate demand reason that consumers spend some of the additional income from the tax cut. This raises desired consumption and lowers desired saving, thereby increasing output. Those who believe that tax cuts don't increase aggregate demand argue that a tax cut today increases the deficit and that the public understands that the government's borrowing eventually must be repaid (with interest). In this view—known as the *Ricardian equivalence*

proposition[†]—the reduction in taxes doesn't improve consumers well-being: The increase in current income from a tax cut is offset by higher taxes in the future to pay off the debt.

Economists who hold the view that tax cuts raise aggregate demand make two arguments. The first is that a tax cut gives consumers who may face restrictions on the amount they can borrow the opportunity to increase their consumption, thereby raising aggregate demand. The second is that consumers may not understand that government borrowing must be repaid by themselves as taxpayers. Thus they will then try to increase current consumption—and aggregate demand—

even though they are no better off.

Which school of thought is right? Indirect evidence indicates that part of the population faces borrowing constraints on consumption. More directly, consumption rose in the United States following the large deficit-financed tax cuts legislated in 1981. In other cases, however, tax cuts have not significantly increased consumption.

[†] The Ricardian equivalence proposition traces its origin to David Ricardo, an eighteenth-century economist. Robert Barro has recently argued the proposition most persuasively: see "The Ricardian Approach to Budget Deficits," *Journal of Economic Perspectives*, 2: 37–54, 1989.

profitability of capital or a decrease in business taxes. An increase in government purchases, G, directly adds to aggregate demand. An increase in foreign demand for U.S.-produced goods raises the demand for current output. Each of these shifts in desired saving or investment increases aggregate demand in the goods market and shifts the AD curve to the right.

In the goods market, contractionary shifts reflect a decline in desired consumption or investment, in government purchases, or in net exports. A decline in desired consumption reflects a decrease in expected future income or consumer confidence. A reduction in desired investment reflects a decline in the expected future profitability of capital or an increase in business taxes. A drop in government purchases directly reduces aggregate demand, as does a decline in foreign demand for U.S.-produced goods. Table 25.1 summarizes factors that shift the aggregate demand curve.

▶   C H E C K P O I N T   *Many businesspeople and policymakers argue that an investment tax credit—giving firms the right to subtract part of the purchase price of new plants and equipment from their income tax bill—is an effective way to stimulate aggregate demand. Why? An investment tax credit reduces the cost of investing, raising the after-tax profitability of building a new plant and/or installing new equipment. As a result, desired investment rises, shifting the AD curve to the right.* ◀

The Aggregate Supply Curve

The **aggregate supply (AS) curve** illustrates the relationship between the aggregate output that firms in the economy are willing to supply and the aggregate price level. The aggregate supply curve is a different type of supply curve from those you studied in your microeconomics course. The quantity of output that an individual firm is willing to supply depends on the price of its output relative to the prices of other goods and services. In contrast, the aggregate supply curve relates aggregate output supplied to the price level.

We identify the determinants of the aggregate supply curve in both the short and long run. As we did for aggregate demand, we begin by considering the relationship between aggregate output supplied and the price level. We examine two approaches to **aggregate supply,** the output businesses are willing to produce: the new classical approach and the new Keynesian approach. Both suggest that the aggregate quantity of output supplied in the short run increases as the price level rises and that, in the long run, changes in the price level have no effect on the aggregate quantity of output supplied.

Short-Run Aggregate Supply Curve

Most economists believe that short-run aggregate supply is positively related to the general price level and the production level. Therefore the **short-run aggregate supply (SRAS) curve** slopes upward.

Q: How are output and the price level related in determining aggregate demand?

A: An increase in the price level reduces the quantity of output demanded; the *AD* curve slopes downward. Shifts in aggregate demand at any price level reflect changes in the nominal money supply, money demand, desired saving, or desired investment.

TABLE 25.1 — DETERMINANTS OF SHIFTS IN THE AGGREGATE DEMAND CURVE

An increase in ...	Shifts the *AD* curve ...	Because...
nominal money supply	P, $AD_0 \rightarrow AD_1$, Y (rightward shift)	real money balances rise and the real interest rate falls.
interest rate on money balances	P, $AD_1 \leftarrow AD_0$, Y (leftward shift)	money demand rises and the real interest rate rises.
expected future output	P, $AD_0 \rightarrow AD_1$, Y (rightward shift)	desired consumption rises.
government purchases	P, $AD_0 \rightarrow AD_1$, Y (rightward shift)	aggregate demand increases directly.
expected future profitability of capital	P, $AD_0 \rightarrow AD_1$, Y (rightward shift)	desired investment rises.
business taxes	P, $AD_1 \leftarrow AD_0$, Y (leftward shift)	desired investment declines.

New Classical Approach. The **new classical approach** to this short-run relationship builds on research by Robert E. Lucas, Jr., of the University of Chicago. He studied the effects on aggregate supply of the imperfect nature of information that firms possess. Because Lucas' explanation centers on firms' misperceptions, this approach is also known as the **misperception theory.** To understand how it works, let's begin with an example.

Consider the supply decisions of Bigplay, a toy manufacturer. Bigplay maximizes profits by increasing the volume of toys it produces when the relative price of toys is high and decreasing production when the relative price of toys is low. Bigplay's managers face an information problem: They care about *relative* prices, so they need to know the price of toys *and* the general price level. Although they know a lot about toy prices, their knowledge of the general price level is not complete because they lack continuous information on all prices outside the toy market.

Suppose that the price of toys increases by 15%. If the general price level doesn't change at the same time, the relative price of toys has increased, and Bigplay should supply more toys. But, if all prices in the economy are 15% higher, the relative price of toys is unchanged, and Bigplay would have no incentive to manufacture more toys. The observed change in the price of toys can be separated into a change in the general price level and a change in the relative price of toys. Lacking complete information about the general price level, Bigplay guesses that a 15% increase in the price of toys reflects an increase in the general price level of 10% and an increase in the relative price of toys of 5%. Because of the increase in the relative price, Bigplay will increase the quantity of toys it produces.

Bigplay is only one producer. Generalizing to encompass all producers in the economy, we discover why the misperception theory suggests a relationship between aggregate output and the price level. Suppose that all prices in the economy rise by 15% but that relative prices don't change. If individual producers fail to recognize the situation, aggregate output increases. This occurs because producers think that some of the increase in prices represents increases in their products' relative prices and they raise their output.

How do producers sort out general and relative price increases? Suppose that, before any prices are observed, some producers forecast that the general price level will rise by 10%. If those producers observe an increase of 15% in the prices of their goods, they will assume that the relative prices of their products have increased by 5% and increase the quantities supplied of their goods.

The misperception theory addresses this case: An increase in the price of toys should affect the quantity of toys supplied *only* if that increase differs from the expected increase in the general price level in the economy. If all producers expect the price level to increase by 10%, and Bigplay sees the price of toys increase by only 5%, the toy manufacturer will *cut* toy production. If all prices actually increase by only 5%, producers (having expected a 10% increase in the price level) collectively cut production.

Hence the misperception theory suggests a positive relationship between the aggregate supply of goods and the difference between the actual and expected price level. If P is the actual price level and P^e is the expected price level, the relationship between aggregate output and the price level, according to the misperception theory is

$$Y = Y^* + a(P - P^e), \tag{25.2}$$

where Y is aggregate output, Y^* is **full employment output,** or the output produced by full employment of existing factors of production, and a is a positive number that indicates by how much output responds when the actual price level is greater than the expected price level.

Equation (25.2) states that output supplied, Y, equals full employment output, Y^*, when the actual price level and the expected price level are equal. When the actual price level is greater than the expected price level, firms increase output. When the actual price level is less than the expected price level, output falls. As a result, output can be higher or lower than the full employment level in the short term until firms can distinguish changes in relative prices from changes in the general price level. Thus, in the short run, for an expected price level, an increase in the actual price level raises the aggregate quantity of output supplied.

▶ **C H E C K P O I N T** *Chair Lair—your custom-made furniture store—is experiencing its best year ever. Sales are up 25%, and you raise the prices on your popular models. How can you determine whether to increase production or just raise prices?* If the increased sales are the result of increased customer demand increasing their demand for your chairs relative to other goods, you should increase your production. If the higher sales are the result of rising prices generally, you should increase prices without changing production. You can check aggregate economic statistics on inflation and sales of goods generally. You can gather information on your prices and sales (and those of other businesses in the furniture industry) based on your own experience faster than reliable data for the economy are published. This information allows you to estimate on average how much of a given price change reflects general price movements and how much reflects changes in relative prices. ◀

New Keynesian Approach. Keynesian economists maintain that the short-run aggregate supply curve is horizontal at any price level. They argue that prices are "sticky," or slow to adjust to changes in demand. Traditionally, Keynesian economists *assumed* that prices change slowly in the short run. Over the past two decades, however, the **new Keynesian approach** has furnished economic explanations for short-run price stickiness.

These explanations are based on features of many real-world markets: the rigidity of long-term contracts and imperfect competition among sellers in the goods market.

One form of rigidity arises from the use of long-term nominal contracts for wages (between firms and workers) or prices (between firms and their suppliers or customers). Under a long-term nominal contract, a wage rate or price is set in advance for several to many periods in nominal terms.[†] Suppose, for example, that *all* workers agreed to a fixed wage for the next three years. Then, based on this labor cost and other components of expected total costs, all firms set prices that would remain fixed for the next three years. In this case, firms would not be able to change prices easily in response to changes in demand.

Although many such long-term arrangements exist in the economy, not all contracts come up for renewal during a particular period; that is, contracts are overlapping or staggered. Hence, only some wages and prices can be adjusted in the current period. Contracts ultimately will be adjusted to changes in expected money growth, but they can't all be adjusted immediately. For example, businesses that expect high current money growth to lead to a rise in the aggregate price level in the future can negotiate price changes for the future, but not for the period under contract. Proponents of this view reject the notion that all prices are flexible in the short run; they believe that the price level adjusts slowly to changes in the nominal money supply.

Another explanation of nominal rigidity emphasizes price-setting decisions in markets. In markets for wheat or stocks or Treasury bills, the product is standardized, many traders interact, and prices adjust freely and quickly to shifts in demand and supply. In such markets the purchases and sales of individual traders are small relative to the total market volume. For example, a few wheat farmers can't raise their prices above those of other wheat farmers; in the competitive wheat market no one would buy their wheat. Individual traders are *price takers;* that is, they take the market price (as reported on the floor of an exchange or in the newspaper) as a given. The arguments of the new classical approach are based on perfectly competitive markets in which participants are price takers.

However, many markets in the economy—such as the markets for high-fashion clothing, art, and medical care—don't resemble the continuously adjusting price-taking markets of exchanges because their products are not standardized. In these markets, *monopolistic competition* results, meaning that products have individual characteristics and there are few sellers of each product. A seller raising prices might see the quantity demanded fall, but not to zero. In monopolistically competitive markets, sellers do not take prices as

---

[†] If wages or prices in a long-term contract were fully indexed to, say, changes in the general price level, wages or prices could still adjust to aggregate nominal disturbances. An example is *cost of living adjustments* (COLAs) in many wage contracts. Evidence for the United States suggests that such contracts generally are only partially indexed.

a given because they are *price setters*. New Keynesian economists argue that prices will adjust only gradually in monopolistically competitive markets.

To understand why, let's return to the market for high-fashion clothing. A competitive organization in this market might have a central meeting place where buyers submit bids and sellers quote asking prices (much as buying and selling in the market for Treasury securities is conducted). If a designer gets favorable reviews, the product becomes more expensive, whereas unfavorable reviews by critics reduce the product's price. Individual high-fashion clothing stores do not continuously adjust prices. Instead, they set the price of clothes in nominal terms for periods of time and meet the demand at that price. They may, however, change prices from time to time in response to major changes in demand or costs of production.

New Keynesian economists contend that this pricing behavior can be in firms' interests so long as markets are monopolistically competitive and costs of changing prices must be incurred. The costs of changing prices—informing current and potential customers, remarking prices, and so on—may not seem that large. Why then are they so important in the new Keynesian approach?

To return to our example of a perfectly competitive market, when a seller of goods or assets traded on exchanges charges a price that is just a bit off, that seller will sell nothing at all. However, a monopolistically competitive firm (such as a clothing boutique) won't lose many of its customers if its prices deviate slightly from the "right" price. If potential profits are small relative to the cost of changing prices, the firm won't change its price.

Why is a firm willing to meet demand at the posted price? For a monopolistically competitive firm, the product price is higher than the marginal cost, that is, the cost of producing an extra unit. Hence the firm is happy to sell extra output. As a result of satisfying the level of demand, the firm's output will rise and fall, depending on aggregate demand.

Let's examine the consequences of the sticky prices stressed by new Keynesian economists for aggregate supply. We can relate the price charged by an individual firm, p, to two macroeconomic variables: the price level, P, and the level of aggregate output, Y, relative to full employment output, Y^*. An increase in the price level means that the firm's costs are higher and that the firm would like to charge more for its output. An increase in aggregate output implies that higher incomes in the economy are likely to raise the demand for the firm's product. As the marginal cost of producing output tends to rise at higher levels of production (because of, for example, the need to pay overtime wages to workers), the firm's desired price rises with the level of demand. That is,

$$p = P + b(Y - Y^*), \tag{25.3}$$

where b is a parameter with a value greater than zero. Equation (25.3) reveals that a price-setting firm's desired price depends on the price level, P, and the level of aggregate output relative to full employment output $(Y - Y^*)$.

Actually there are two kinds of firms in the new Keynesian view. Firms with flexible prices can change their prices freely and continually set their prices according to Eq. (25.3). Firms with sticky prices set their prices in advance based on their expectation of economic conditions. If we let the superscript e denote expectation, we can rewrite Eq. (25.3) for price-setting firms as

$$p = P^e + b(Y^e - Y^{*e}).$$

To keep the analysis simple, let's further assume that firms expect output to be at the full employment level. In this case, $b(Y^e - Y^{*e})$ is zero, and

$$p = P^e.$$

Price-setting firms base their prices on their expectations of other firms' prices.

We combine our analysis of pricing decisions by the two types of firms to develop the new Keynesian aggregate supply curve. The aggregate price level, P, is the weighted average of the prices charged by the flexible-price and sticky-price firms. If c represents the fraction of firms with sticky prices and $(1 - c)$ represents the fraction of firms with flexible prices, the aggregate price level is

$$P = cP^e + (1 - c)[P + b(Y - Y^*)].$$

Subtracting $(1 - c)P$ from both sides of the equation and dividing both sides by c gives the general price level:

$$P = P^e + b\left(\frac{1 - c}{c}\right)(Y - Y^*). \qquad (25.4)$$

This expression for the aggregate price level is a reminder that (1) an increase in the expected price level raises expected costs and leads firms to raise prices; and (2) an increase in current output raises demand for an individual firm's products, so flexible-price firms raise their prices.[†]

The short-run aggregate supply curve implied by the new Keynesian approach slopes upward: An increase in current output leads to an increase in the price level in the short run. The larger the proportion of firms in the economy with sticky prices, the flatter the $SRAS$ curve will be. Indeed, if all firms had sticky prices in the short run, the $SRAS$ curve would be horizontal.

[†] Note that we can rearrange terms in (25.4) to yield an expression similar to (25.2):

$$Y = Y^* + \left[\frac{c}{b(1 - c)}\right](P - P^e).$$

► **C H E C K P O I N T** *Amalgamated Industries has two major divisions: one grows fruit in California, and the other manufactures and sells designer sweaters in New York. If aggregate demand rises, which price should rise first?* Agricultural products largely are sold in competitive markets with flexible prices. An increase in aggregate demand will raise the price of Amalgamated Industries' fruit because the quantity supplied can't increase in the short run. In the designer sweater market, markups of price over cost are much higher, and Amalgamated's stores are less likely to change the price tags in the short run. Its sweater stores will meet the greater demand at the unchanged price in the short run. ◄

Long-Run Aggregate Supply Curve

The short-run aggregate supply curve, *SRAS*, slopes upward in both the new classical and new Keynesian approaches to aggregate supply, but this relationship doesn't hold in the long run. In the new classical approach, firms learn in the long run that the price level is changing in response to a change in current output. They adjust their estimates of the expected price level until the actual and expected price level are equal; that is, when $P = P^e$. This relationship implies that current output Y equals full employment output Y^*, so the **long-run aggregate supply (*LRAS*) curve** is vertical at Y^*. In the new Keynesian approach, both firms with flexible prices and firms with sticky prices adjust their prices in response to a change in demand in the long run. As with the new classical approach, the *LRAS* curve is vertical at the full employment level of output $Y = Y^*$.

Figure 25.3 summarizes the short-run and long-run aggregate supply relationships between price level and current output.

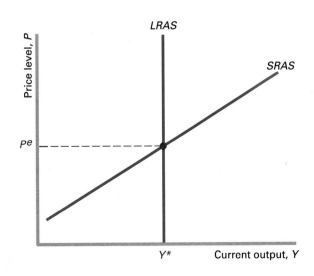

▶ **FIGURE 25.3**

The Short-Run and Long-Run Aggregate Supply Curves
The *SRAS* curve slopes upward: When the price level *P* exceeds the expected price level P^e, the quantity of output supplied rises. In the long run, the actual and expected price levels come together: The *LRAS* curve is vertical at the full employment level of output, Y^*.

Shifts in the Short-Run Aggregate Supply Curve

Changes in aggregate supply can explain changes in output in the short run. In both the new classical and new Keynesian approaches, the factors that shift the short-run aggregate supply curve also affect the costs of producing output. These factors are (1) changes in labor costs, (2) changes in other input costs, and (3) changes in the expected price level.

Q: How are output and the price level related in determining aggregate supply?

A: In both the new classical and new Keynesian approaches, output supplied rises as the price level rises in the short run; the *SRAS* curve slopes upward. In the long run in both approaches, output supplied equals full employment output; the *LRAS* curve is vertical. Shifts in the aggregate supply curve at any price level reflect changes in input costs, the expected price level, the level of inputs, and productivity.

Changes in Labor Costs. Labor accounts for most of the costs of producing output. When output Y exceeds the full employment level Y^*, the high volume of output produced raises the demand for labor. The higher labor demand, in turn, bids up wages, increasing firms' labor costs. As a result, the short-run aggregate supply curve shifts up. When output falls below the full employment level, workers' wages decline. The resulting drop in production costs shifts the short-run aggregate supply curve down.

Changes in Other Input Costs. Shifts in the price or availability of raw materials or in production technologies affect production costs and the aggregate supply curve. Such changes are commonly referred to as **supply shocks.** Supply shocks include changes in technology, weather, or the prices of oil and other inputs of energy and materials. Positive supply shocks, such as the development of labor-saving technologies or lower food prices owing to good growing seasons, shift the aggregate supply curve down and to the right. Negative supply shocks, such as an increase in the price of oil, shift the aggregate supply curve up and to the left.

Changes in the Expected Price Level. When workers bargain for wages, they compare their wages to the costs of goods and services they buy. When the expected price level rises, workers will demand higher nominal wages to preserve their real wages. Similarly, firms make decisions about how much output to supply by comparing the price of their output to the expected prices of other goods and services. When the expected price level rises, firms raise prices to cover higher labor and other costs. An increase in the expected price level shifts the short-run aggregate supply curve up and to the left. A decline in the expected price level shifts the short-run aggregate supply curve down and to the right. This occurs because firms reduce prices as nominal wages and other costs fall.

Shifts in the Long-Run Aggregate Supply Curve

The long-run aggregate supply curve, *LRAS,* indicates the full employment level of output in the economy at a specific time. The *LRAS* curve shifts over time to reflect growth in the full employment level of output. Sources of output growth include (1) increases in capital and labor inputs, and (2) increases in productivity growth (output produced per unit of input).

Increases in inputs raise the economy's productive capacity. An increase in the capital stock may result from increases in investment in plant and equipment (excluding replacement of old plant and equipment). An increase in labor inputs may result from population growth or an increase in the number of people participating in the labor force. Studies of output growth in the United States and other countries show that, over long periods of time, the pace of output growth also is influenced significantly by productivity growth. Productivity growth consists of improvements in the efficiency with which capital and labor inputs produce output.

The principal sources of change in productivity growth are energy prices, technological advances, worker training and education, and regulation of production. The huge increases in oil prices in 1973 reduced productivity in heavy energy-using industries and (in the view of many analysts) led to a worldwide slowdown in productivity growth. Technological advances, as in communications technology and computers, raise productivity. Many economists believe that environmental, health, and safety regulations reduce productivity growth, because capital and labor inputs are devoted to these activities instead of to producing goods and services. However, such consequences of regulation do not necessarily mean that they are not in society's interest. For example, society must weigh the benefits of cleaner air or increased workplace safety against the potential costs of reduced productivity.

Table 25.2 summarizes factors that shift the short-run and long-run aggregate supply curves. For an interesting application, see the Other times, other places box.

Equilibrium in Aggregate Demand and Aggregate Supply

Having examined the determinants of aggregate demand and aggregate supply, we are now ready to put the two concepts together. This will allow us to analyze how the economy's price level and current output are determined. The economy's equilibrium occurs at the intersection of the aggregate demand curve and aggregate supply curve.

Short-Run Equilibrium

To examine the economy's equilibrium in the short run, we combine analysis of the aggregate demand curve, AD, and the short-run aggregate supply curve $SRAS$. Figure 25.4 shows these two curves.

In both the new classical and new Keynesian approaches, the economy's short-run equilibrium occurs at the intersection, E_0, of the AD and $SRAS$ curves. No other point represents equilibrium. For example, E_1 is consistent with an equilibrium level of aggregate demand, but at price level P_1 firms would supply more output than households and businesses would demand. The price level would fall to restore equilibrium at E_0. Point E_2 lies

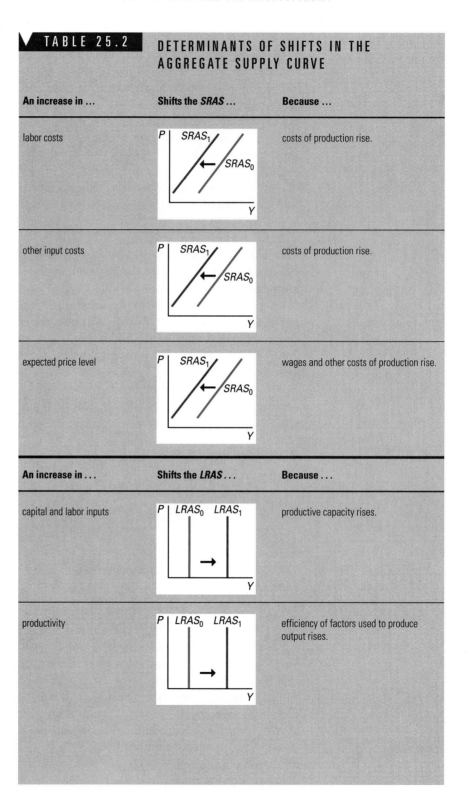

TABLE 25.2   DETERMINANTS OF SHIFTS IN THE AGGREGATE SUPPLY CURVE

An increase in ...	Shifts the *SRAS* ...	Because ...
labor costs		costs of production rise.
other input costs		costs of production rise.
expected price level		wages and other costs of production rise.

An increase in ...	Shifts the *LRAS* ...	Because ...
capital and labor inputs		productive capacity rises.
productivity		efficiency of factors used to produce output rises.

> FIGURE 25.4

Short-Run Equilibrium
The economy's short-run equilibrium is represented by the intersection of the *AD* and *SRAS*
curves at E_0. The equilibrium
price level is P_0. Higher price
levels are associated with an
excess supply of output (at 1, for
example), and lower price levels
are associated with excess
demand for output (at 2, for
example).

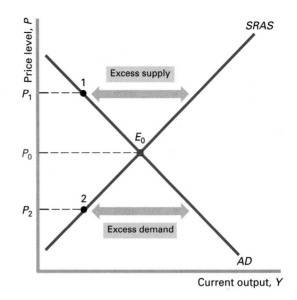

on the *SRAS* curve. However, at price level P_2, households and businesses
would demand more output than firms would be willing to produce. The
price level would rise to equate the quantity of output demanded and the
quantity of output supplied.

> ### C H E C K P O I N T   *Does a rising price level*
indicate good news or bad news about the economy? It depends. If the price level rises
because of a shift in the *AD* curve, output rises in the short run. For example, a tax cut to
spur business investment increases aggregate demand for current output and the price
level. However, if the price level rises because of a shift in the *SRAS* curve, output falls in
the short run. For example, a harsh winter during which workers often can't get to their
jobs reduces the quantity of output supplied and increases the price level. ◀

Long-Run Equilibrium

Our analysis of the economy's equilibrium in the short run suggests
many possible combinations of output and the price level, depending on
where the aggregate demand curve and the short-run aggregate supply curve
intersect. However, in the long run the price level adjusts to bring markets for
goods and assets into equilibrium at full employment output. In Fig. 25.5, the
aggregate demand curve AD_0 and the short-run aggregate supply curve
$SRAS_0$ intersect at this level of output, with a price level of P_0. Now suppose
that aggregate demand expands unexpectedly, shifting the aggregate demand
curve to the right from AD_0 to AD_1.

In both the new classical and new Keynesian approaches, output
and the price level increase in the short run. The new short-run equilibrium,

Other times, other places...

Shock Therapy and Aggregate Supply in Poland

The close of 1992 brought holiday cheers to the beleaguered Polish economy after three years of "shock therapy" prescribed by Western economic advisers. Although factory output dropped by nearly 40% in 1990 and 1991, output was growing and inflation was beginning to decline.

Like other former communist countries in Eastern Europe, Poland had tried to transform its centrally planned economy and remove price controls by pursuing radical economic reforms—but much more rapidly than most of the others. Lifting price controls (which had fixed the price level) increased the expected price level, shifting the SRAS curve up. Because reductions in the growth rate of the nominal money supply and elimination of many subsidies decreased aggregate demand, the shift in the SRAS

curve led to a severe decline in output in the short run.

The immediate result of the shock therapy was a rise in the price level (a result of the shift in the SRAS curve) as well as a decline in output. By 1992, falling economic activity in Poland placed downward pressure on inflation.

The primary focus on events in Poland was not so much on the short-run effects of policy changes, but on their long-run consequences for developments in the economy. Long periods of price control and government allocation had reduced the efficiency with which the Polish economy produced and distributed goods and services. Hence the big question was whether the reforms would improve the outlook for long-run aggregate supply.

While experts maintained that

the end of price controls and government allocation would lead to more efficient and competitive firms, it was clear that many individuals would be worse off in the short run. The gamble in Poland was that these short-term costs would be rewarded handsomely in long-term gains in production and consumption possibilities for Polish citizens.

Many economists, notably Jeffrey Sachs, argued that the rebound of the Polish economy in 1992 was the beginning of favorable shifts in long-run aggregate supply in Poland. The removal of central planning and improvements in factory productivity shifts the LRAS curve to the right, increasing output and dampening inflationary pressures. These long-run developments hold the key to the future growth of Poland's economy.

$E_{1'}$, lies at the intersection of the AD_1 and $SRAS_0$ curves. Over time, as firms learn that the general price level has risen, the SRAS curve shifts to the left from $SRAS_0$ to $SRAS_1$ because at the new price level, firms are willing to supply less output. In the long run, the SRAS curve will have to shift far enough to intersect AD_1 at Y^*. The long-run equilibrium is at point E_1, with a price level P_1 and full employment output Y^*. If aggregate demand contracted unexpectedly so that the AD curve shifted to the left, the process would be reversed. Initially, output and the price level decline. Over time, as firms learn that the price level has fallen, the SRAS curve will shift to the right. This process of adjustment is more gradual (owing to sticky prices for many firms) in the new Keynesian approach than in the new classical approach. At the new long-run equilibrium, output equals Y^*, and the price level is lower than P_0.

In the long run, the LRAS curve is vertical at Y^*, the full employment output level. The economy will produce Y^*, and the price level will

> FIGURE 25.5

Adjustment to Long-Run Equilibrium

1. From initial equilibrium at E_0, an increase in aggregate demand shifts the AD curve from AD_0 to AD_1, increasing output from Y^* to Y_1.

2. Because $Y_1 > Y^*$, prices rise, shifting the SRAS curve from $SRAS_0$ to $SRAS_1$. The economy's new equilibrium is at E_1. Output has returned to Y^*, but the price level has risen to P_1.

The LRAS curve is vertical at Y^*, the full employment level of output. Shifts in the AD curve affect the level of output only in the short run. This outcome holds in both the new classical and new Keynesian approaches, although price adjustment is more rapid in the new classical approach.

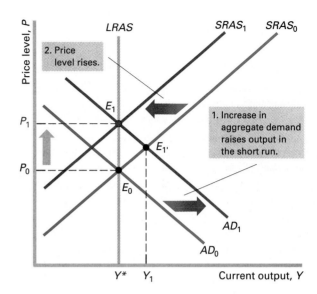

Q: How are the equilibrium price level and output level determined in both the short and long run?

A: In the short run, the price level and output are described by the intersection of the AD and SRAS curves. In the long run, output is determined by the LRAS curve; shifts in the AD curve affect only the price level.

adjust to shifts in aggregate demand to ensure that all markets for goods and assets are in equilibrium.

Because the LRAS curve is vertical, economists generally agree that changes in aggregate demand affect the price level but not the output level in the long run. (An area of controversy is discussed in Box 25.2.) An application of this general proposition, referred to as **monetary neutrality,** is that money has no effect on output in the long run, because an increase in the nominal money supply raises the price level in the long run but doesn't change equilibrium output. Conversely, a decline in the nominal money supply lowers the price level in the long run but has no effect on output.

The Real Business Cycle Model

In the new classical and new Keynesian approaches, changes in aggregate demand can affect output in the short run. A third approach holds that changes in aggregate demand have no effect on output, even in the short run. In other words, not only is the long-run aggregate supply curve vertical, but the short-run aggregate supply curve also is vertical. Unlike the new classical approach, the alternative **real business cycle model** assumes perfect information. Unlike the new Keynesian approach, it assumes perfectly flexible prices. Based on these assumptions, this alternative approach explains short-term changes in output primarily as temporary shocks to productivity. These shocks include changes in the availability of raw materials (food, energy, and minerals, for example), regulatory restrictions on production or markets, and innovations that make the economy more productive.

Shocks to productivity result in increases or decreases in current productivity, which in turn affect the SRAS curve, as Fig. 25.6 shows. During the Gulf War, for example, the crisis in the Middle East reduced the supply of

Consider this...   ▼ BOX 25.2

Can Shifts in Aggregate Demand Affect Output in the Long Run?

In general, increases or decreases in aggregate demand have no effect on the full employment level of output. That is, the *LRAS* curve does not shift in response to a shift in the *AD* curve. Some economists believe that large negative shifts in aggregate demand actually reduce the full employment level of output. In that situation, known as *hysteresis*, unemployment rates can be higher than those associated with the full employment level of output for extended periods of time.

Advocates of the hysteresis view argue that persistent unemployment can lead both to an actual (or perceived) loss of skills, making difficult the rehiring of

unemployed individuals, and to the withdrawal of discouraged workers from the labor force. These effects inhibit the job search process and reduce the full employment level of output. Some economists argue that the persistently high unemployment rates in many European countries (particularly in the United Kingdom) in the early 1980s reflected hysteresis. The government of Prime Minister Margaret Thatcher pursued a contractionary monetary policy in the early 1980s, but effects on output and unemployment lasted for several years. In the hysteresis view, expansionary monetary or fiscal policies were needed to restore the economy's initial level of

output and employment.

Not all economists accept the proposition that expansionary shifts in aggregate demand are necessary to restore higher output and employment. They note for example that generous unemployment insurance systems (that pay workers benefits when they are unemployed) in many European countries might account for persistent unemployment. Evidence for hysteresis is inconclusive. The phenomenon remains a topic of ongoing research because it suggests that economic downturns caused by a decline in aggregate demand can impose costs on the economy for long periods of time.

oil on world markets, increasing somewhat the price of oil. In this case, starting from an initial equilibrium at E_0 in Fig. 25.6, the productivity of energy-using producers decreases, and the *SRAS* curve shifts to the left from $SRAS_0$ to $SRAS_1$. If the productivity shock is expected to be temporary, that is, to last only for the current period, future productivity is unaffected and the *AD* curve doesn't shift. Because the *AD* curve doesn't shift, the new short-run equilibrium lies at the intersection of the *AD* curve and the $SRAS_1$ curve—at E_1 in Fig. 25.6. At that point, output is lower and the price level is higher than at the economy's initial equilibrium, E_0.

Ongoing research on the real business cycle model focuses on the significance of temporary disturbances to productivity in explaining output fluctuations. As we discuss next (and in Chapter 26), however, evidence from many episodes suggests that increases or decreases in aggregate demand affect output in the short run.

Economic Fluctuations in the United States

Fluctuations in current output can be explained by shifts in the aggregate demand curve or aggregate supply curve. We now use *AD–AS* analysis to help explain three episodes of economic fluctuations in the United

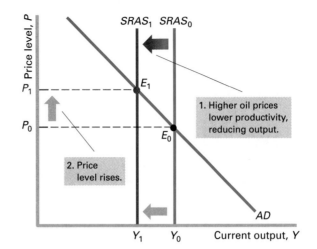

> **FIGURE 25.6**
>
> **Productivity and Short-Run Fluctuations in the Real Business Cycle Model**
> In the real business cycle model, short-run movements in output are explained by shocks to productivity.
>
> 1. From an initial equilibrium at E_0, an increase in the price of oil reduces productivity, shifting the *SRAS* curve from $SRAS_0$ to $SRAS_1$. Output falls from Y_0 to Y_1.
>
> 2. The price level rises from P_0 to P_1.

States: (1) shocks to aggregate demand, 1964–1969; (2) a supply shock, 1973–1975; and (3) a credit crunch shock to aggregate demand, 1990–1991. We examine the effects of monetary policy on economic fluctuations in detail in Chapter 26.

Shocks to Aggregate Demand, 1964–1969

By 1964, U.S. participation in the conflict in Vietnam had grown to a major war effort, and real government purchases—principally for military equipment and personnel—had expanded by about 9% since 1960. Those expenditures would expand by another 21% from 1964 through 1969. The Fed was alarmed by the prospect of rising interest rates. (Recall from Fig. 25.1 that, if nothing else changes, the rise in aggregate demand from government purchases would increase money demand and the interest rate.) As a result, the Fed pursued an expansionary monetary policy: The annual growth rate of *M1* rose from 3.7% in 1963 to 7.7% in 1964.

The combination of fiscal and monetary expansions led to a series of shifts to the right of the aggregate demand curve. Rising aggregate demand caused output to exceed the full employment level in the mid-1960s, putting upward pressure on costs and the expected price level. As we demonstrated in the analysis of short-run and long-run equilibrium with the *AD–AS* diagram, the *SRAS* curve shifts up and to the left, restoring the economy's full employment equilibrium at a higher price level. Because fiscal and monetary expansion continued for several years, the *AD–AS* analysis indicates that output growth and inflation (the rate of change in the price level) should have risen from 1964 through 1969. As Fig. 25.7 on pg. 666 shows, that is what happened.

Supply Shock, 1973–1975

By the early 1970s, many economists and policymakers believed that output growth and inflation went hand in hand—a sensible conclusion when

MOVING FROM THEORY TO PRACTICE...

THE WALL STREET JOURNAL   DECEMBER 7, 1992

How Will Japan Deal with a Decline in Aggregate Demand?

"Business is bad, it's all messed up," Mr. Watanabe explains, shaking his head...

These days, leaders of Japan's most powerful corporations are echoing Mr. Watanabe's lament. With the country's economy mired in recession, many feel they have been raking in nothing but trouble... And last week, Japan said its gross domestic product contracted for the second consecutive quarter, something that hasn't happened since the aftermath of the 1973 oil crisis.

But it isn't just the severity of this slump that has business leaders entreating the gods of commerce. A growing number of executives, government leaders and economists here harbor a deeper concern that this recession marks the beginning of a new and worrisome era in Japan's industrial evolution. They fear their economy—the world's second-largest—is downshifting into an era of considerably slower growth...

This recession is largely home-grown. Japan is now experiencing the brutal aftermath of the sudden surge in asset prices in the late 1980s—the "bubble" years—when loose monetary policy let cheap capital flood into the stock and property markets. It is now evident that that response simply delayed the inevitable day of reckoning, when Japan would have to deal with its maturing economy.

That speculative asset bubble has long since burst. Falling land and stock prices have wiped out vast wealth over the past couple of years. Businesses that once were rolling in profits, and were thus able to afford inefficiencies such as excess labor, now see bloated cost structures as a major problem.

What's more, Japan may not be able to export its way out of this recession as easily as it has others: It has already severely tested the patience of its trading partners...

"In my time, our job was simple," says Naohiro Amaya, a former MITI official and an architect of Japan's postwar economic miracle. "We had only to solve a single equation"— how to promote exports...

Labor costs are also rising for Japanese companies. Still, most Japanese firms aren't able to trim the fat from payrolls quickly. Big companies are dismissing part-time workers, and many... have announced plans to reduce their full-time work force over the next several years, mostly through attrition. But these cautious adjustments may not be enough. Break-even points for Japanese companies have risen to their highest levels in 20 years, according to a recent survey by Daiwa Institute of Research.

ANALYZING THE NEWS...

For most of the post–World War II period, the Japanese economy has been a growth miracle. By the early 1990s, slowing growth of aggregate demand and rising production costs worried many analysts and policy-makers in Japan. We can use AD–AS analysis to explain the developments discussed in the article.

(a) During the 1980s, Japanese financial markets experienced an unprecedented boom in the values of stocks and land. The collapse of asset prices in the early 1990s reduced consumer wealth and reflected a decline in consumer and business optimism about future growth. As shown in the figure (a), the aggregate demand curve shifts to the left from AD_0 to AD_1, reducing output from an initial full employment level, Y^*, to Y_1.

(b) Traditionally, Japan relied on export promotional policies when domestic demand for investment or consumption declined. Such policies increased foreign demand for Japanese goods, shifting the aggregate demand curve in figure (b) to the right from AD_0 to AD_1. The large Japanese trade surplus at the time the article was written dimmed prospects of continued success for this strategy.

(c) Many Japanese business-people and economists acknowledge that costs are too high. The initial recession shifted the AD curve from AD_0 to AD_1. Reductions in labor costs and efforts to improve the efficiency of production and distribution amount to a favorable development for aggregate supply. The result is to shift the SRAS curve down from $SRAS_0$ to $SRAS_1$ in figure (c), thereby increasing output from Y_1 to $Y_{1'}$.

For further thought...

Suppose that the Japanese government's policies are unsuccessful in raising aggregate demand and that efforts to reduce production costs and raise productivity fail. Discuss the implications for short-run equilibrium output in the United States.

Source: Excerpted from Clay Chandler, Jacob M. Schlesinger, and John Bussey, "Gearing Down: Japan Economy, Built on Rapid Expansion, Faces Wrenching Shift," December 7, 1992. Reprinted by permission of *The Wall Street Journal*, © 1992 Dow Jones & Co., Inc. All Rights Reserved Worldwide.

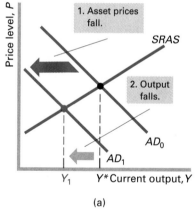

(a)

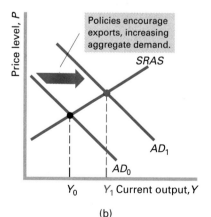

(b)

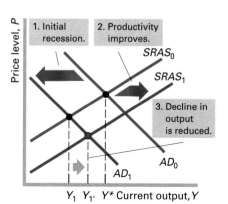

(c)

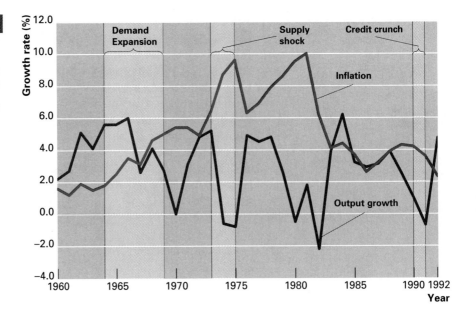

▶ **FIGURE 25.7**

Output Growth and Inflation, 1960–1992

The short-run changes in output growth and inflation observable between 1964 and 1969 can be explained by shifts in aggregate demand that caused output to exceed the full employment level.

Source: Economic Report of the President.

changes in the economy's equilibrium output and price level are driven by changes in aggregate demand. The United States (and other industrialized countries) experienced negative supply shocks in 1973 and 1974. In 1973, the Organization of Petroleum Exporting Countries (OPEC) sharply reduced the supply of oil in the world oil market in an attempt to punish the United States and other countries for supporting Israel in the 1973 Arab-Israeli conflict. Along with the quadrupling of world oil prices, poor crop harvests around the world caused food prices to rise significantly. In the United States, these two negative supply shocks were reinforced by the lifting of wage and price controls that had been in effect since 1971, which caused a round of catch-up wage and price increases.

In *AD–AS* analysis, this set of negative supply shocks shifts the short-run aggregate supply curve up to the left, raising the price level and reducing output. As Fig. 25.7 shows, output growth fell in 1974 and 1975 while inflation rose. This type of inflation causes the economy to stagnate, a result that is known as *stagflation*. The falling output and rising prices indicated that aggregate supply shocks, as well as aggregate demand shocks, could change the economy's short-run equilibrium.

Credit Crunch and Aggregate Demand, 1990–1991

Many analysts believe that a reduction in banks' ability or willingness to lend, called a *credit crunch*, deepened the 1990–1991 recession. The Gulf War provided a negative supply shock early in the recession. Recall that financial institutions such as banks are likely to be important suppliers of funds to borrowers having few alternative sources of finance from nonmoney markets. Two events may have led to a credit crunch during this recession. First, more stringent bank regulation (Chapters 14 and 15) reduced banks' ability to lend. Second, declines in real estate values and the large debt burdens of many corporations reduced banks' willingness to lend to borrowers at any expected real interest rate. Because households and small and medium-sized businesses weren't able to replace bank credit with funds from other sources, spending for consumer durable goods and business plants and equipment fell.

In *AD–AS* analysis, the decline in spending translates into a reduction in aggregate demand, shifting the *AD* curve to the left. Over time, the drop in aggregate demand puts downward pressure on prices, shifting the *SRAS* curve down. Figure 25.7 shows that output growth fell during the 1990–1991 recession and that inflation fell from 4.3% in 1989 to 2.9% in 1992.

Key Terms and Concepts

Aggregate demand

Aggregate demand (AD) curve

Aggregate supply

Aggregate supply (AS) curve
    Long-run aggregate supply (*LRAS*) curve
    Short-run aggregate supply (*SRAS*) curve

Full employment output

Misperception theory

Real business cycle model

Monetary neutrality

New classical approach

New Keynesian approach

Supply shocks

Summary

1. Aggregate demand represents the level of current output that households and firms are willing to purchase at a particular price level. Aggregate supply represents the amount of output that producers in the economy are willing to sell at a particular price level.

2. The aggregate demand curve, *AD*, illustrates the quantity of current output demanded at each price level. The price level and the aggregate quantity of output demanded are negatively related. Each point along the *AD* curve represents a combination of price level and aggregate output for which the

goods and asset markets are in equilibrium. Factors that shift the *AD* curve include increases or decreases in the nominal money supply, money demand, determinants of desired saving, and determinants of desired investment.

3. The aggregate supply curve, *AS*, represents the quantity of output supplied at each price level. The long-run supply curve *LRAS* is vertical at the full employment level of output. Increases or decreases in the current productivity of factors of production shift the *LRAS* curve. The short-run aggregate

supply curve, *SRAS*, slopes upward. In the new classical approach, an unexpected increase in the aggregate price level increases the quantity of output firms are willing to supply in the short run. In the new Keynesian approach, the *SRAS* curve slopes upward because many firms have sticky prices and are willing to meet the demand for their output over a range from an initially stated price. In both new classical and new Keynesian approaches, shifts in the *SRAS* curve reflect shifts in the expected price level or costs of production.

4. The economy's short-run equilibrium output and price level occur at the intersection of the *AD* curve and the *SRAS* curve. The economy's long-run equilibrium occurs at the intersection of the *AD* curve and the *LRAS* curve.

5. Changes in the equilibrium price level and output can be explained by shifts in the aggregate demand curve, aggregate supply curve, or both.

Review Questions

1. Why is there a negative relationship between the price level and aggregate output along the *AD* curve?

2. Why does a rise in the price level increase aggregate output supplied in the short run, according to the new classical approach?

3. What is meant by the term *price stickiness* in the new Keynesian approach? What elements of the economy lead to price stickiness?

4. What is the slope of the long-run aggregate supply curve? Why does it have this slope?

5. What predictions do the new classical and new Keynesian approaches yield about monetary neutrality in the long run?

6. According to the new Keynesian approach, what is the effect on output in the short run of an increase in government defense purchases?

7. What is a real business cycle? If a winter storm temporarily reduces agricultural output, which curves shift in the *AD–AS* diagram?

Analytical Problems

8. Using the new classical approach and the *AD–AS* diagram, describe the effects on the price level and current output of an increase in the price of oil. How would your answer differ if the Fed increases the money supply to stimulate aggregate demand?

9. Suppose that the economy is initially in equilibrium at full employment. Then the government unexpectedly increases income taxes. What are the

effects on output and the price level in the short run and the long run, according to the new Keynesian approach?

10. In the mid-1970s and again in the late 1970s, OPEC raised oil prices sharply. The higher cost of oil reduced the productivity of energy-using industries. Show what would happen to output and the price level in the short run according to the new Keynesian approach.

11. One way in which misperception of the aggregate price level is thought to affect the economy is through the labor market. Suppose that the unemployment rate u is related to the rate of inflation π and the expected rate of inflation π^e, as follows:

$$\pi = 0.08 - 2u + \pi^e.$$

   a. If there is no misperception of inflation (so that $\pi = \pi^e$, what is the unemployment rate (in percent)?

   b. If expected inflation is 8% and actual inflation is 4%, what is the unemployment rate?

   c. If expected inflation is 4% and actual inflation is 8%, what is the unemployment rate?

12. John Maynard Keynes stressed the role played by *animal spirits*—changes in the confidence or optimism of entrepreneurs and managers—in economic fluctuations. Suppose that a wave of optimism hits the U.S. business community. Describe the effects of aggregate demand and the price level in terms of the new Keynesian approach.

13. Suppose that, as a result of a vigorous "thrift campaign" by U.S. policymakers, the public increases its saving rate. In other words, at any particular combination of income and real interest rate, the public saves more income. Describe the short-run and long-run effects on output in terms of the new Keynesian approach.

14. Because of an increase in the expected future productivity of capital, the stock market rises. Describe the effects on investment, current output, and future output in terms of the new classical approach.

15. Many economists and policymakers worry that increased government purchases are not expan-

sionary because they crowd out private investment spending. Using the derivation of the AD curve, explain the logic of this argument.

16. Suppose that Congress passes a law allowing all taxpayers to subtract $500 from their tax bill while government spending remains unchanged. Assuming that the Ricardian equivalence proposition holds, describe the effect of this policy on aggregate demand.

17. Suppose that the president and Congress agree on an infrastructure program to raise federal spending on highways, bridges, and airports. Proponents of the program argue that it will increase productivity in the long run. Opponents of the program argue that it will reduce private investment in the short run. Using the AD–AS diagram, illustrate these positions.

18. The Fed can use expansionary or contractionary policy to shift the AD curve. Using the AD–AS diagram, illustrate how monetary policy should be used to return output to its full employment level when

   a. the AD curve intersects the $SRAS$ curve to the left of the full employment level of output; and

   b. the AD curve intersects the $SRAS$ curve to the right of the full employment level of output.

19. Throughout the 1980s, the interest rate that banks' customers received on their deposits increased, owing in large part to improvements in computer and communications technologies. What effect did this development have on the AD curve? If not offset by other factors, what effect did this development have on the price level, assuming a vertical $LRAS$ curve?

Data Questions

20. Find the latest volume of the *Economic Report of the President* in your library and calculate the annual

percentage change in the gross domestic product (in constant dollars) and in the price deflator for the gross domestic product. Using these two series, identify episodes in which shifts in aggregate demand are more important in explaining changes in output as well as episodes in which shifts in aggregate supply are more important.

21. Using data in the *Economic Report of the President*, calculate the growth rate of output per worker in

the nonfarm business sector for three time periods: 1960–1969, 1973–1979, and 1985–1990. Evaluate the implications of the patterns of growth in output per worker for shifts in the *LRAS* curve during the three periods.

Appendix: Deriving the *AD* and *AS* Curves from the *IS–LM–FE* Model

To describe how the economy works, we grouped the thousands of markets in the economy into three broad markets for goods, money assets, and non-money assets (Chapter 24). This simplification enabled us to focus on the ways in which the financial system and the economy are connected and to study ways in which changes in monetary policy, fiscal policy, and productivity affect interest rates and output. We can also use the concepts of aggregate demand and aggregate supply to describe a relationship between current output and the price level.

Deriving the Aggregate Demand Curve

In the *IS–LM–FE* model, the intersection of the *IS* and *LM* curves represents the combination of the real interest rate and the level of current output that yields an equilibrium aggregate demand for the economy's output.

What does the *IS–LM–FE* model predict about the relationship between the price level and aggregate demand for current output? Let's go back to our description of equilibrium in the goods market and the asset markets and examine effects of an increase in the price level in the *IS–LM–FE* model. As Fig. 25A.1(a) shows, if nothing else changes, an increase in the price level lowers real money balances, shifting the *LM* curve to the left from LM_0 to LM_1. The resulting higher interest rate reduces the demand for interest-sensitive spending on consumer durables, housing, and business investment. As a result, the intersection of the *IS* and *LM* curves represents a lower level of aggregate demand. Conversely, a decline in the price level increases real money balances, as Fig. 25A.1(b) shows, shifting the *LM* curve to the right from LM_0 to LM_1 and reducing aggregate demand.

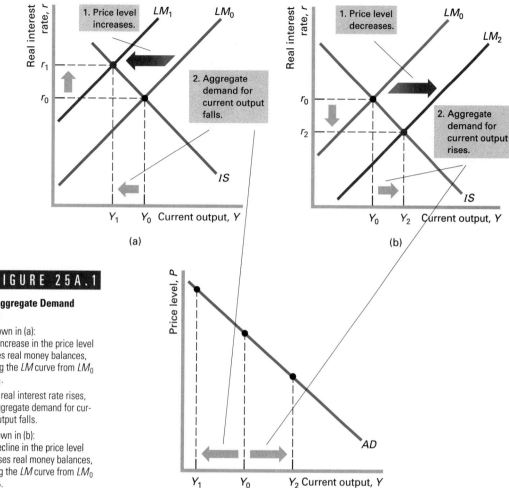

The Aggregate Demand Curve

As shown in (a):
1. An increase in the price level reduces real money balances, shifting the *LM* curve from LM_0 to LM_1.

2. The real interest rate rises, and aggregate demand for current output falls.

As shown in (b):
1. A decline in the price level increases real money balances, shifting the *LM* curve from LM_0 to LM_2.

2. The real interest rate falls, and aggregate demand for current output rises.

As shown in (c):
Along the aggregate demand curve, the relationship between the price level and aggregate demand for current output is negative.

Then, as Fig. 25A.1(c) shows, the relationship between the price level and aggregate demand for current output in the economy is negative. This downward-sloping *AD* curve resembles downward-sloping demand curves that you studied in your first economics course. There is an important difference, however: The *AD* curve slopes downward to the right because of the relationship between the goods and asset markets. Each point along the *AD* curve represents a possible combination of the price level and current output.

Points along the *AD* curve represent potential combinations of the price level and current output for which the goods and asset markets are in equilibrium. The *AD* curve can be shifted by factors that shift either the *IS* curve or the *LM* curve. A shift of the *AD* curve to the right is *expansionary*, whereby any price level is associated with a higher level of demand for current output. Expansionary shifts are attributed either to factors that shift the *IS* curve to the right or to factors that shift the *LM* curve to the right. Expansionary shifts of the *IS* curve result from declines in desired saving or increases in desired investment. The principal cause of an expansionary shift of the *LM* curve is an increase in the nominal money supply. Shifts of the *AD* curve to the left are *contractionary* and reflect shifts of the *IS* or *LM* curves to the left.

The Aggregate Supply Curve

In the basic *IS–LM–FE* model of the connections between the financial systems and the economy, the *IS* and *LM* curves represent the demand side of the economy, that is, aggregate demand. The *FE* line represents the level of output consistent with full employment of the existing factors of production (in other words, the *supply* side of the economy). The *FE* line shows the simultaneous determination of output and the price level. By now focusing more directly on determinants of the price level, we can provide a better description of aggregate supply in the short run. The *AS* curve represents the aggregate quantity of output supplied at each potential price level.

In the new classical approach, an unexpected increase in the price level leads to an increase in aggregate supply in the short run. Because firms misperceive part of the price level increase as an increase in the *relative price* of their own products, they perceive higher profits and are willing to supply more output. Hence the *AS* curve slopes upward in the short run. The new Keynesian approach views many firms' prices as sticky in the short run: firms with sticky prices are willing to meet the demand for their output over a range from an initially stated price.

Money and Economic Activity in the Short Run

CHAPTER 26

A group of business executives gathered for a dinner at New York's Waldorf-Astoria Hotel to hear a speech entitled "Monetary Policy and the New World Order" by a respected member of the Fed's Board of Governors. The question and answer period was lively: "You can talk about long-run adjustments," an angry CEO whose firm suffered losses and layoffs in the recession said to the group's dinner speaker, "but answer this: Why does a fall in the money supply put people out of work?"

Changes in the structure of financial markets and institutions can affect the efficiency of the economy. In Chapter 25, we developed a framework that allows us to examine how monetary policy affects the economy in the long run. However, the short-run effects of Fed policy on the economy often cause greater public concern. In this chapter, we focus on the short run to examine the effects of monetary policy on output, using the aggregate demand–aggregate supply model. We begin by studying the short run in the real business cycle model, in which prices can adjust freely in response to economic disturbances. We also apply the new classical and new Keynesian approaches to the analysis.

In this chapter we focus on two questions. **Q:** Can changes in the money supply lead to changes in output in the economy in the short run? **Q:** If its actions can affect the economy's short-run equilibrium, should the Fed try to smooth out upturns and downturns in the economy?

Money and Output Movements in the Short Run

When we examined the impact of changes in the nominal money supply on the level of economic activity in the long run, we stated that money is *neutral*; that is, the level of output is independent of the nominal money supply. However, households, businesses, and policymakers also are concerned about the effects of monetary policy on economic activity in the short run. Understanding the long run is important, but understanding how the economy behaves in the short run is even more important in shaping economic and financial decisions.

Many economists believe that contractionary monetary policy by the Fed has been responsible for many of the economic downturns in the United States since World War II. These downturns bring unemployment and idle factories. Similarly, many economists believe that expansionary monetary policy by the Fed has contributed to economic recoveries. For example, monetary policy has been blamed for the 1981–1982 recession and praised for the recovery that followed. In the chapter preview, a CEO was quoted who asked, "Why does a fall in the money supply put people out of work?" Whereas the CEO was concerned about the short-term effects of monetary policy, we are interested in the broader question of whether changes in the money supply actually *cause* changes in output and the real interest rate. These are the measures that summarize equilibrium in the financial system and the economy. To understand the connection between monetary policy and economic activity, we need to consider ways in which changes in the money supply might affect the economy in the short run. This understanding will help you interpret politicians' speeches and financial news reports.

First, let's describe what we mean by the short run. The relationship between money and output changes during the **business cycle,** which lasts from several months to several years and consists of an expansion of current output (a *boom*) to a *peak* (high point) followed by a contraction in current output (a *recession*) to a *trough* (low point), is our focus. Booms and recessions vary in intensity. Business cycles have been a feature of modern economies since the Industrial Revolution and have been reported and analyzed by economists since the nineteenth century. Figure 26.1 shows U.S. business cycles since 1950.

Figure 26.1 also depicts the nominal money supply growth rate. Note that movements in the growth rate of the money supply are *procyclical*; that is, the growth rate generally increases during booms and decreases during recessions. Moreover, economists have found that changes in the nominal money supply often precede a business cycle; that is, monetary expansions precede business cycle peaks and monetary contractions precede business cycle troughs. However, the relationship between changes in the money supply and changes in output in the short run is controversial. Some economists contend that changes in the money supply actually are *responsible for* sub-

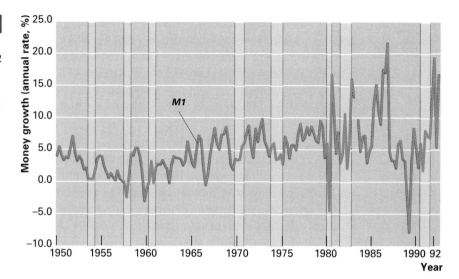

FIGURE 26.1

Money Supply Growth and the Business Cycle, 1950–1992 Data are for *M1* growth at an annual percentage rate. The shaded areas represent recessions designated by the National Bureau of Economic Research, a private economic research organization responsible for dating U.S. business cycles.

Source: Federal Reserve Bulletin.

sequent changes in output. Others believe that changes in the money supply reflect, rather than cause, changes in output. A particular issue of concern is whether reductions in the nominal money supply growth rate lead to subsequent recessions. If true, this outcome would imply that money isn't neutral in the short run. It would also raise the question (which we analyze later in this chapter) of whether the Fed should try to stabilize output fluctuations.

To establish whether changes in the money supply could be responsible for changes in output and real interest rates in the short run, we need to demonstrate that changes in the money supply *independent of changes in output* lead to output or interest rate movements. We can then examine how money supply changes might affect output and real interest rates in the short run. We use the aggregate demand–aggregate supply (*AD–AS*) framework developed in Chapter 25 to examine three approaches linking short-run money and output movements: the real business cycle model, the new classical approach, and the new Keynesian approach. We examine whether each can explain actual patterns in the data.

Money, Output, and Real Business Cycles

Recall that, in the long-run, prices are flexible; that is, they can adjust to changes in cost or demand. Price flexibility implies that over a long period of time, money is neutral. One-time increases or decreases in the nominal money supply affect the price level but not real output or the real interest rate.

The real business cycle model holds that prices are flexible even in the short run and that output is at the full employment level in the economy's short-run equilibrium. Hence the economy's short-run aggregate supply curve, *SRAS*, is vertical. But actual output fluctuates over time. The real business cycle model says that the observed fluctuations in output in the short run primarily are caused by temporary shocks to productivity. These shocks include shifts in the availability of key raw materials (food, energy, and minerals, for example), regulatory restrictions on production or markets, and innovations that make the economy more productive.

Reverse Causation

The real business cycle model also holds that increases or decreases in the money supply have no effect on economic activity, even in the short run. However, the data graphed in Fig. 26.1 show that the money supply grows more rapidly before and during expansions than it does during contractions. Does this fact necessarily contradict the assumption that money is neutral? Proponents of the real business cycle model answer *no*, arguing that, simply because money and output move together, changes in the money supply don't necessarily *cause* changes in output. The correlation between money supply and output movements also could be explained by (1) shifts in some variable that affects both money and output, or (2) reasoning that changes in output in fact cause changes in the money supply, a form of reasoning known as *reverse causation*.

The second explanation is used more often by proponents of the real business cycle model, who argue that current and anticipated future changes in output affect the *demand for money*. For example, suppose that the economy experiences a boom brought on by a favorable productivity shock, such as a temporary decline in oil prices. Anticipating a future increase in output, households and businesses demand more currency and checkable deposits because of greater transactions demand for money. The increase in demand for money resulting from the rise in output and the boom causes the Fed passively to increase the money supply. Thus real business cycle advocates argue that changes in output increase the money supply, rather than that a change in the money supply affects output—a classic example of reverse causation.

▶ **C H E C K P O I N T** *During the fourth quarter of each year and especially the month of December, measures of money and retail sales are higher than during the rest of the year. Does this condition imply that the increase in the money supply caused the change in output?* Real business cycle economists note that a more likely explanation is that the demand for goods rises for the holiday season, increasing the public's demand for currency and checkable deposits. The Fed smooths the surge in money demand by increasing the money supply to satisfy demands of households and businesses. ◀

Evidence against Reverse Causation

Historical episodes offer an opportunity to isolate changes in the money supply that are "independent" of changes in current output. In the early 1960s, in a classic study of the links between the money supply and economic activity, Milton Friedman (then of the University of Chicago, now at Stanford University) and Anna Schwartz (of the National Bureau of Economic Research) found that the money supply growth rate falls before output declines.[†] This pattern held for every business cycle for the period studied, almost one hundred years. Friedman and Schwartz documented that the peak in the nominal money supply growth rate precedes the peak in output on average by sixteen months. This time period was not constant for all business cycles; it ranged from a few months to more than two years. Based on their examination of many business cycles in the period between the Civil War and 1960, Friedman and Schwartz concluded that *changes in money growth cause output fluctuations.* They also concluded, however, that money's effects on output appeared only after long and variable lags.

The test of Friedman and Schwartz's assertion is whether the changes in the money supply they identified were "independent," that is, not influenced by a change in output or by some third factor that influenced both money and output. They studied specific historical episodes that fit the description of independent events: the banking panics prior to the founding of the Federal Reserve System, the wave of bank failures during the early 1930s, and the increase in reserve requirements in 1936 and 1937. They associated the decline in the money supply during banking panics, such as the panic of 1907, when the public converted bank deposits into currency, with the subsequent decline in economic activity caused by deposit contraction and reduction of money growth. The wave of bank failures during the early 1930s significantly reduced the money supply, and Friedman and Schwartz blamed the loss of output during the early 1930s on this "Great Contraction." They also traced the pronounced recession of 1937–1938 to the monetary contraction resulting from the increase in the required reserve ratio, which reduced the money supply. The change in reserve requirements was independent because it was associated with the Fed's desire to increase its control over monetary policy, not with a concern over the current level of economic activity. All these episodes show linkage from a change in money supply growth to a change in the level of output.

More recently, Christina Romer and David Romer of the University of California, Berkeley identified six independent monetary policy shifts after 1960 in which the FOMC announced a contractionary monetary policy to fight inflation.[††] Each episode was followed by a decline in output. They maintain that, as the monetary contractions were intended to reduce inflation, they are independent of current output conditions.

[†] Milton Friedman and Anna J. Schwartz, *A Monetary History of the United States*, Princeton: Princeton University Press, 1963.

[††] Christina Romer and David Romer, "Does Monetary Policy Matter?: A New Test in the Spirit of Friedman and Schwartz," in O.J. Blanchard and S. Fischer, eds., *NBER Macroeconomics Annual*, Cambridge: MIT Press, 1989, pp. 121–170.

Another way to explore whether changes in money growth cause changes in output is to study more continuous measures of the extent to which monetary policy is expansionary or contractionary. By means of statistical tests, Ben Bernanke and Alan Blinder of Princeton University documented that increases in the federal funds rate cause output to fall.[†] They argue that changes in the federal funds rate are independent, as they are determined largely by actions of the Fed (as shown in our analysis of the reserves market in Chapter 20). These findings confirm that the money supply declines almost immediately in response to a contractionary policy by the Fed and that output declines with a lag of between six months and one year. Thus the evidence on money and output movements doesn't support the classical model; in the short run, money appears not to be neutral.

The real business cycle model offers a simple, conceptually consistent description of the economy's long-run equilibrium. However, it isn't consistent with historical evidence on the effects of money supply changes on output. Traditionally, many economists explained the evident short-run nonneutrality of money by *assuming* that prices are necessarily fixed for a period of time. That assumption doesn't explain *why* individuals and firms fail to change prices of services and goods if doing so would raise the level of output. After all, as you learned in your first course in economics, households and businesses optimize when they make economic decisions. Two recent schools of thought—the new classical and new Keynesian approaches—offer explanations of the short-run nonneutrality of money in a setting where households and businesses are optimizing.

Money and Output: The New Classical Approach

New classical economists believe that the lack of monetary neutrality in the short run arises from imperfect information and misperceptions on the part of firms. Recall that, in the misperception theory, output increases when the price level is higher than expected. Households and businesses incorporate expectations of changes in the money supply into their forecasts of the aggregate price level. In this approach, whether changes in the nominal money supply affect output in the short run depends on whether those changes are expected or unexpected.

Expected Changes in the Money Supply.   To understand the distinction between expected and unexpected changes in the nominal money supply, suppose that the economy is in equilibrium and that the Fed announces a 10% increase in the nominal money supply. This announcement becomes part of the information that households and businesses use in forecasting the aggregate price level. We illustrate this process using the *AD–AS* diagram. Starting

---

[†] Ben S. Bernanke and Alan S. Blinder, "The Federal Funds Rate and the Channels of Monetary Transmission," *American Economic Review*, 82: 901-921, 1992.

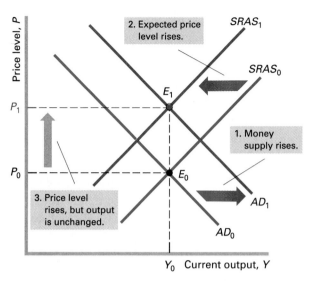

(a) Expected Increase in the Money Supply

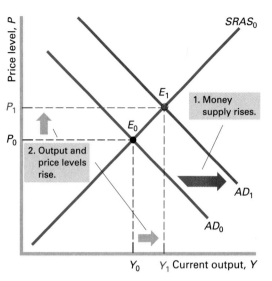

(b) Unexpected Increase in the Money Supply

FIGURE 26.2

Money and Output Changes in the New Classical Model

As shown in (a):

1. From an initial equilibrium at E_0, an expected increase in the nominal money supply shifts the AD curve from AD_0 to AD_1.

2. The expected price level increases, shifting the $SRAS$ curve from $SRAS_0$ to $SRAS_1$.

3. At the new equilibrium, E_1, the price level rises to P_1, and output remains unchanged at Y_0.

As shown in (b):

1. From an initial equilibrium at E_0, an unexpected increase in the nominal money supply shifts the AD curve from AD_0 to AD_1.

2. At the new equilibrium, E_1, the price level rises to P_1, and output rises to Y_1.

In the new classical approach, only unexpected changes in the money supply affect output in the short run.

from the economy's equilibrium at E_0 in Fig. 26.2(a), a one-time increase in the nominal money supply shifts the aggregate demand curve from AD_0 to AD_1 and increases the expected price level, thereby shifting the short-run aggregate supply curve up from $SRAS_0$ to $SRAS_1$. The economy's new short-run equilibrium has a higher price level, P_1, but output doesn't change. In this case, households and businesses expect the price level to increase. Hence they are not surprised when the price level does increase, and so real output is not affected. Therefore a perfectly anticipated change in the money supply has no effect on real output in the new classical approach.

Unexpected Changes in the Money Supply. What if an increase in the money supply were *unexpected?* For example, suppose that the Fed surprises households and businesses by suddenly increasing the money supply by 10%. In Fig. 26.2(b), from an initial equilibrium at E_0, the monetary expansion shifts the aggregate demand curve to the right from AD_0 to AD_1. The expected price level doesn't change, so the short-run aggregate supply curve remains at $SRAS_0$. At the new equilibrium, E_1, output has risen from Y_0 to Y_1, and the actual price level has risen from P_0 to P_1. Because the actual price level exceeds the expected price level, firms are fooled into thinking that the relative prices of their products have increased. They thus increase their output. An unanticipated change in the money supply is not neutral because output increases in response to an unexpected increase in the nominal money supply and decreases in response to an unexpected decrease.

New classical economists have examined whether unexpected and expected changes in the money supply have different effects on output or prices. They haven't arrived at a consensus, but the available evidence suggests that *both* expected and unexpected changes in the nominal money supply affect current output (see the Appendix to this chapter). This evidence is inconsistent with the pure new classical view. New Keynesian economists have tried to explain this evidence while retaining the sensible assumption in the new classical approach that households and businesses use available information in forming their expectation of money growth or the price level.

▶ **C H E C K P O I N T** *Suppose that you knew that the aggregate price level was closely correlated to the size of the money supply and that you could observe the size of the money supply continuously. Would the misperception theory be useful in explaining the business cycle? Why or why not?* No. Because you can observe the money supply continuously, there would be no misperception. ◀

Money and Output: The New Keynesian Approach

New Keynesian economists link output movements to changes in the money supply by arguing that prices are not completely flexible. As we noted earlier, many economists once *assumed* that prices are not flexible in the short run and, as a result, that money is not neutral in the short run. Recall that the new Keynesian approach gives two reasons for price stickiness in the short run: long-term contracts, and imperfect competition among sellers in the goods market.

The new classical approach stresses that expected changes in the money supply are neutral in the short run, whereas unexpected changes in the money supply are not. The new Keynesian approach holds that neither expected nor unexpected changes in the nominal money supply are neutral in the short run. Figure 26.3(a) illustrates this case for an unexpected decline in the money supply. Suppose that the Fed announces a reduction of the money supply not anticipated by Fed watchers. From an initial equilibrium at E_0, the monetary contraction shifts the AD curve to the left from AD_0 to AD_1. The contraction was unexpected, so expected prices do not adjust downward, and the $SRAS$ curve remains at $SRAS_0$. The new equilibrium lies at E_1, the intersection of the AD_1 and $SRAS_0$ curves. Because the expected price level doesn't adjust in the short run, output falls from Y_0 to Y_1. This pattern closely resembles that suggested by the new classical approach.

Now let's consider the case of an expected monetary contraction. In the new Keynesian approach, households and businesses use all available information to forecast demand and the price level. Hence, when the money supply is expected to fall, the expected price level also should fall. Firms with flexible prices—those that can be changed in the current period—lower their prices, as in the new classical approach. However, many prices do not adjust in the current period, so the aggregate price level falls slowly in response to the expected decline in the nominal money supply. Similarly, if firms are monop-

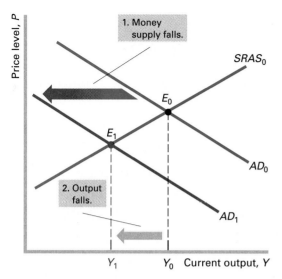

(a) Unexpected Decrease in the Money Supply

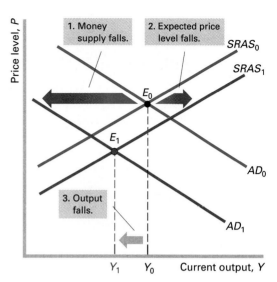

(b) Expected Decrease in the Money Supply

▲ FIGURE 26.3

Money and Output in the New Keynesian Approach

Money is not neutral in the short run in the new Keynesian approach.

As shown in (a):

1. From an initial equilibrium E_0, a monetary contraction shifts the AD curve from AD_0 to AD_1.

2. Because the decline in the money supply is unexpected, the $SRAS$ curve remains at $SRAS_0$. At the new equilibrium E_1, output has fallen from Y_0 to Y_1.

As shown in (b):

1. From an initial equilibrium E_0, a monetary contraction shifts the AD curve from AD_0 to AD_1.

2. Because the decline in the money supply is expected, the expected price level falls and some but not all prices fall. The $SRAS$ curve shifts from $SRAS_0$ to $SRAS_1$.

3. At the new equilibrium, E_1, output has fallen from Y_0 to Y_1, which is greater than Y_1 in (a).

olistically competitive and prices are costly to adjust, prices will adjust only gradually in response to an anticipated change in the money supply and only if its predicted effect on the price level is relatively small.

Figure 26.3(b) illustrates the effect on output of an expected decrease in the money supply. Starting from the economy's equilibrium at E_0, the drop in the money supply shifts the aggregate demand curve to the left from AD_0 to AD_1. In this case some prices can and do adjust by falling in the short run. The short-run aggregate supply curve shifts downward from $SRAS_0$ to $SRAS_1$. At the new equilibrium E_1, however, output is lower than at E_0, so the price level hasn't completely adjusted. This drop in output isn't as large as that in the case of an unexpected decrease in the money supply, depicted in Fig. 26.3(a). In the new Keynesian approach, even expected changes in the nominal money supply can have real effects in the short run, although those effects are smaller than for an unexpected change.

To explain better how changes in the money supply affect output, we focus on specific ways in which monetary policy affects the economy. In the new Keynesian approach, it does so principally by influencing the determinants of aggregate demand through changes in interest rates. Because the price level adjusts gradually to a change in the money supply, an increase in the nominal money supply raises real money balances in the short run. In order to induce households and firms to hold greater real money balances, the real interest rate must fall. A drop in the nominal money supply reduces real money balances in the short run. To restore equilibrium, the real interest rate must rise. These interest rate movements affect aggregate demand by influencing consumption, investment, and net exports (see Box 26.1).

Consider this...

How Does Money Affect the Economy in the New Keynesian Approach?

Suppose that the Fed increases the nominal money supply and that the price level adjusts gradually as in the new Keynesian approach. The real interest rate falls in the short run, affecting the cost of funds for investment, stock prices, and exchange rates.

Interest Rates and Investment

A lower real interest rate reduces the opportunity cost of investing in new plants and equipment. Investment rises, increasing aggregate demand. Lower real interest rates also reduce the cost to firms of carrying additional inventories and therefore increase inventory investment. Thus, in the new Keynesian approach, lower real interest rates lead to higher levels of current output by lowering the cost of funds for business investment. Lower interest rates also reduce borrowing costs and the opportunity cost of housing and consumer durable goods relative to financial assets, leading to greater household investment in durable goods.

Stock Prices

Changes in the money supply cause portfolio shifts, leading to higher stock values in two ways. First, higher money balances lead households and businesses to spend money balances on goods and other assets including stocks, thereby increasing stock prices. Second, when an increase in the money supply lowers interest rates, stocks become a more attractive investment relative to bonds, increasing the demand for shares and raising stock prices. In either case, higher stock prices raise the market value of firms. Changes in stock prices affect both consumer and business spending. An increase in stock prices raises financial wealth (part of lifetime resources) and thus consumer spending. For business, higher stock prices signal improved profitability prospects. Firms often issue new shares, using the proceeds to buy new plants and equipment and thereby increase investment. When stock market valuation of firms is low, firms reduce investment in new plants and equipment.

Exchange Rates

If the price level adjusts gradually in response to a monetary expansion, the real interest rate available on domestic assets falls relative to rates on foreign assets. As a result, global investors rebalance their portfolios to allocate more of their holdings to foreign assets and less to domestic assets. The demand for U.S. dollars declines, so the value of the dollar relative to other currencies—the exchange rate—declines. The less valuable dollar makes U.S.-produced goods cheaper relative to foreign goods, stimulating exports from the United States and reducing imports to the United States. This results in improving net exports and increasing aggregate demand.

▶ C H E C K P O I N T   *You are a new Keynesian and chairman of the Federal Reserve Board. The staff tells you that a decline in business optimism has reduced desired investment and aggregate demand. How could you use monetary policy to restore the level of aggregate demand?* The decline in business optimism shifts the *AD* curve to the left. If you did not want to wait for the process of gradual price adjustment to restore the economy's equilibrium, you could use open market purchases to increase the nominal money supply. Because the price level adjusts gradually, this change would increase real money balances supplied, reducing the real interest rate and raising aggregate demand (shifting the *AD* curve to the right). ◀

Can Public Policy Stabilize Economic Fluctuations?

Q: Can changes in the money supply lead to changes in output in the economy in the short run?

A: Evidence suggests that changes in the money supply can affect output in the short run. Proponents of the new classical approach argue that only unexpected changes in the nominal money supply can affect output. Supporters of the new Keynesian approach maintain that both expected and unexpected changes in the nominal money supply can alter the economy's short-run equilibrium, although effects of unexpected changes are greater.

Both the new classical and new Keynesian approaches suggest that changes in the nominal money supply can affect the economy in the short run. Therefore we must ask whether policymakers should try to smooth fluctuations in the economy. Public policies designed to smooth short-run fluctuations in output, known as **stabilization policies** (or activist policies) involve shifts of the *AD* curve by changes in government purchases or taxes or by changes in the nominal money supply. Two issues arise regarding the effectiveness of monetary policy as stabilization policy. At one level is the matter that we've been discussing: the effect on output and interest rates of an increase or decrease in the nominal money supply. At a deeper level is another issue: whether monetary policy *should* be used to stabilize economic fluctuations. We consider these issues, using the three approaches that we've analyzed.

The Real Business Cycle and New Classical Responses

The real business cycle model places no value on policies intended to stabilize economic fluctuations because of the assumption that productivity disturbances cause fluctuations. Prices adjust quickly to these disturbances, so changes in the nominal money supply have no effect on current output or the real interest rate. Thus economists who favor the real business cycle model see no reason to consider stabilization policy.

Economists who advocate the new classical approach also are critical of stabilization policy. They stress that only unexpected changes in policy have real effects. Their view is that the only way public policy could smooth economic fluctuations is by confronting households and businesses with surprise moves. In practice, they argue, such surprises are likely to introduce substantial uncertainty in households' and businesses' decisions, leading to random output fluctuations.

The reason is the assumption that the public uses **rational expectations.** That is, the public bases its estimates of economic variables such as the price level or change in the money supply on all available information.[†] The rational expectations concept does not imply, however, that households and businesses can tell the future, only that errors in forecasts are unpredictable. If households and businesses form rational expectations about the price level, the actual price level will be close to the expected price level on average. On average, the actual and expected price levels are close, so the Fed gains little

---

[†] In Chapter 10 we stated that the efficient markets hypothesis holds that asset prices increase or decrease in response to the arrival of new information. For example, when analysts predict an increase in the price of a share of Bigco, that information is incorporated into the share price because of rational expectations. When the firm's earnings are greater than is predicted by analysts, the price of the stock rises. Hence only deviations from expectations change the price. This utilization of information and the reaction of prices to new information are features of an efficient market.

by using unexpected changes in the money supply to stabilize output fluctuations. As a result, new classical economists recommend against stabilization policy.

The New Keynesian Response

In the new Keynesian approach, upturns and downturns in economic activity may represent times when the economy is not at its long-run equilibrium. These departures are particularly serious when output is below the full employment level because recessions bring unemployment. The new Keynesian approach stresses the importance of shifts in aggregate demand for explaining movements in current output. Therefore we need to consider whether that approach favors stabilization policy to reduce output fluctuations and especially recessions.

In the new Keynesian approach, both expected and unexpected changes in monetary policy affect current output and the real interest rate in the short run.[†] Because of sticky prices, this outcome is true even when the public uses rational expectations to estimate the expected price level. Hence using monetary policy to smooth output fluctuations is a possibility. Let's see how it might be done. Suppose that, from an initial full employment equilibrium at E_0 in Fig. 26.4(a), a decline in business confidence shifts the AD curve to the left from AD_0 to AD_1. As a result, at E_1, the economy is in a recession. With no policy intervention, the economy will eventually correct itself. In other words, with output less than full employment at E_1, prices will fall over time, shifting the $SRAS$ curve down from $SRAS_0$ to $SRAS_1$, restoring the initial level of output at the economy's equilibrium at E_2. Economic activity eventually rebounds, so the possibly long period of gradual price adjustment brings lost output and unemployment.

Alternatively, as Fig. 26.4(b) shows, the Fed could try to speed recovery by increasing the nominal money supply, shifting the AD curve back to the right from AD_1 to AD_0. Because prices adjust only gradually, the expansionary policy moves the economy from recession at E_1 to its initial full employment equilibrium at E_0 more quickly than the "do nothing" alternative. Stabilization policy, however, has a side effect: It also leads to a higher price level than if no action were taken.

During the 1960s, many economists encouraged the use of monetary and fiscal policies to smooth fluctuations in the economy. However, others warned that there may be realistic lags in the policy process and uncertainty about the length of time between a policy action and changes in the economy. These factors could limit the effectiveness of stabilization policy.

The concern is this: Even if activist policy can affect the economy, there may still be long and variable **lags in the policymaking and implementation process** that make it difficult to "fine-tune" the

---

[†] Fiscal policy (changes in taxes or government purchases) also affects output in the short run in the new Keynesian approach. Here we analyze only monetary policy.

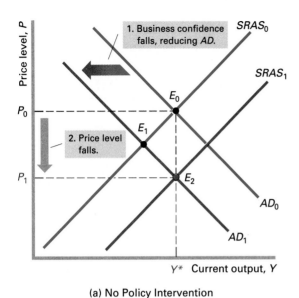

(a) No Policy Intervention

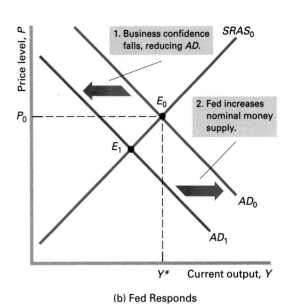

(b) Fed Responds

⋀ FIGURE 26.4

Effects of Activist Policy in the New Keynesian Approach

As shown in (a):
1. From an initial full employment equilibrium at E_0, a decline in business confidence shifts the AD curve from AD_0 to AD_1. At E_1, the economy is in a recession.

2. Over time, the price level adjusts downward, restoring the economy's full employment equilibrium at E_2.

As shown in (b):
1. From an initial full employment equilibrium at E_0, a decline in business confidence shifts the AD curve from AD_0 to AD_1. At E_1, the economy is in a recession.

2. The Fed speeds recovery by increasing the nominal money supply, which shifts the AD curve back from AD_1 to AD_0. Relative to the nonintervention case, the economy recovers more quickly (to E_0) but with a higher long-run price level.

economy. One such lag is that caused by the time needed to gather data on economic variables, called a *data lag*. Gross domestic product (GDP) data for a quarter are not published until several months later, although data on related variables (say, retail sales) are available sooner. Second, even with data in hand, policymakers often need a substantial amount of time to analyze the trends suggested by the economic variables, which results in a *recognition lag*. In addition, although policy interventions such as open market purchases can be initiated by the Fed outside the legislative process, fiscal policy interventions (such as tax or spending changes) require legislative action. This is often a time-consuming process, resulting in a *legislative lag*. Putting tax and expenditure policy into effect typically requires even more time, called an *implementation lag*. Even after a policy is finally implemented, its effect on the economy isn't immediate, creating an *impact lag*. Because of these lags, policy interventions can't begin to counterbalance every economic fluctuation. Therefore economists generally advocate a long-term focus (absent extreme events) in enacting policy changes designed to affect the economy.

Lags in the policymaking and implementation process haven't convinced most new Keynesian economists that stabilization policy lacks value. However, many concur that policymakers shouldn't attempt to fine-tune the economy, trying to smooth every minor disturbance in aggregate demand. Instead, they argue that policymakers should restrict the use of activist policy to fighting major downturns in the economy. For an application of the new Keynesian view to events in Japan in the early 1990s, see the Other times, other places box on pg. 692.

▼ TABLE 26.1	SUMMARY OF MONETARY POLICY AND OUTPUT: THREE ALTERNATIVES		
	Is current output affected by an ...		
Alternative	Unexpected change in the money supply?	Expected change in the money supply?	Is activist policy desirable?
Real business cycle approach	No	No	No
	Prices are perfectly flexible, so monetary policy cannot affect real money balances or output in the short run.		
New classical approach	Yes	No	No
	Only unexpectecd changes in the money supply affect output.		Monetary policy affects output and the real interest rate only by "fooling" households and firms.
New Keynesian approach	Yes	Yes	Rarely
	Both unexpected and expected changes in the money supply affect output, although effects of unexpected changes are greater.		Frequent changes in monetary policy can reduce credibility of monetary authority.

Table 26.1 presents a summary of the money-output relationship and the desirability of stabilization policy in the real business cycle model and the new classical, and new Keynesian approaches.

Explaining Events of the 1980s and 1990s

Both the new classical and new Keynesian approaches offer explanations for the short-run nonneutrality of money, and both are consistent with rational decisions by households and businesses in saving and investment and portfolio allocation. But are they consistent with actual economic events? We can find out by using these approaches to interpret macroeconomic effects of policy shifts in the early 1980s and the early 1990s. Although the different approaches may produce varying predictions about the responses of output and the real interest rate to policy, they share an emphasis on the importance of policy credibility for shaping those responses.

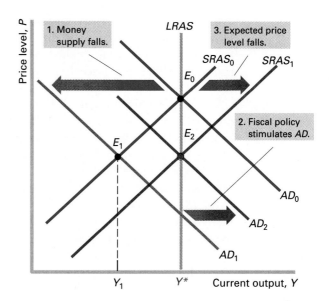

> **FIGURE 26.5**
>
> **Policy Mix in the Early 1980s**
> The economy's adjustment to aggregate demand shock in the early 1980s is consistent with the new Keynesian approach.
>
> 1. From an initial equilibrium at E_0, a monetary contraction shifts the AD curve from AD_0 to AD_1, and output falls from Y^* to Y_1. At E_1, the economy is in a recession.
>
> 2. The fiscal stimulus from tax cuts and increases in government purchases shifts the AD curve from AD_1 to AD_2.
>
> 3. Over time, the net contraction in output places downward pressure on inflation, shifting the $SRAS$ curve down from $SRAS_0$ to $SRAS_1$, restoring full employment output at E_2.

That is, announced changes in policy will influence households' and businesses' decisions only to the extent that announcements are *believed*.

Effects of Policy Shifts in the Early 1980s

The early 1980s witnessed major shifts in both monetary and fiscal policies. Changes in monetary policy had already begun in October 1979 when the Fed, under Chairman Paul Volcker, announced that it would target monetary aggregates (instead of the federal funds rate) and that it would reduce the rate of money supply growth. Monetary restraint continued more or less through 1981. In 1981, Congress and President Reagan agreed to the Economic Recovery Tax Act, which cut income tax rates significantly. At the same time, government purchases of military equipment rose. Thus the monetary policy was contractionary, but the fiscal policy was expansionary.

We can use the *AD–AS* diagram for the new Keynesian approach to analyze the effects of these policy changes. In 1979, the economy was essentially at full employment, at E_0 in Fig. 26.5. The monetary contraction shifted the aggregate demand curve to the left from AD_0 to AD_1. In response to the tax cut and the military buildup, the AD curve shifted to the right from AD_1 to AD_2.

According to the new Keynesian approach, the effect on output of the policies of the early 1980s is ambiguous because the two shifts in aggregate demand were in opposite directions. As the monetary contraction preceded the fiscal expansion by more than a year, output should have fallen first—from Y^* to Y_1—which the actual drop in output in two recessions during 1980–1982 confirmed. Inflation fell from double-digit levels to about 4% by

1983, shifting the short-run aggregate supply curve from $SRAS_0$ to $SRAS_1$. However, this occurred only after the economy endured the recession, a process consistent with gradual price adjustment in the new Keynesian approach. When the price level adjustment was completed, the economy returned to a long-run equilibrium at E_2.

What about the predictions of the new classical approach? The Fed implied on many occasions that its shifts in monetary policy were intended to combat inflation. In the new classical approach, an announced policy to reduce inflation could lead to a combination of falling prices and lower expected inflation, which would soften the shift of the AD curve. This process of adjustment—the shift of the short-run aggregate supply curve from $SRAS_0$ to $SRAS_1$—would be quicker than in the new Keynesian approach. Hence, at first glance, the new classical prediction is inconsistent with the experience of the economy during that period.

However, both the new Keynesian and new classical approaches stress the importance of policy announcement *credibility*. Although Federal Reserve Chairmen Arthur Burns and G. William Miller expressed concern about inflation in the 1970s, actual Fed policy was inflationary. In both the new classical and new Keynesian approaches, a lack of credibility about the Fed's anti-inflation stance would fail to lower prices or expectations of future inflation. Long-term interest rates *increased* from late 1979 through late 1981 (with the exception of the second quarter of 1980). Under the expectations theory of the term structure of interest rates, the long-term rate is an average of expected future rates, so financial market participants probably didn't expect inflation to abate.

In the new classical approach, the Fed should try to reduce inflation in a major one-shot policy shift, *so long as that shift is announced and is credible*. With the gradual adjustment of prices in the new Keynesian approach, gradual reduction in money growth could reduce inflation with smaller costs from reduced output, again so long as the reductions are announced and are credible.

Effects of Policy Shifts in the Early 1990s

At the beginning of the 1990s, the U.S. economy was at full employment equilibrium at E_0 in Fig. 26.6. Monetary and fiscal policy shifts in the early 1990s moved in opposite directions from the policy shifts of the early 1980s. After substantial negotiation, President Bush and the Congress compromised on a deficit-reduction bill in October 1990 that increased taxes and reduced federal government spending, shifting the AD curve to the left from AD_0 to AD_1. Fed Chairman Alan Greenspan, who had often expressed concern about the federal budget deficit, indicated to Congress that the Fed would ease monetary policy if a deficit-reduction measure were adopted. The Fed followed through (but not fast enough in the minds of some economists and policymakers), increasing the money supply growth rate. This shifted the aggregate demand curve to the right from AD_1 to AD_2.

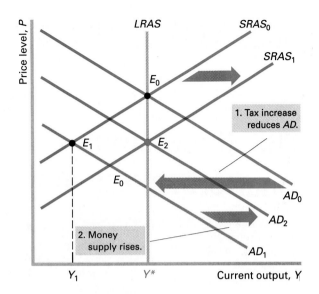

▶ FIGURE 26.6

Policy Mix in the Early 1990s
The economy's adjustment to aggregate demand shock, in the early 1990s is consistent with the new Keynesian approach.

1. From an initial equilibrium at E_0, a fiscal contraction shifts the AD curve from AD_0 to AD_1. Output falls from Y^* to Y_1. The economy's equilibrium shifts to E_1.

2. Monetary stimulus shifts the AD curve from AD_1 to AD_2.

3. Over time, the contraction in output places downward pressure on inflation, shifting the SRAS curve from $SRAS_0$ to $SRAS_1$ and restoring full employment output at E_2.

The economy suffered a recession, reducing output from Y^* to Y_1 in 1990 and 1991 and suggesting that the monetary stimulus may not have been sufficiently strong at the time.[†] Over time, the weak economy put downward pressure on inflation, shifting the SRAS curve down from $SRAS_0$ to $SRAS_1$. The short-term real interest rate fell, consistent with the new Keynesian approach. The recession and gradual price adjustment don't support the new classical approach prediction that expected policy changes should have no effect on unemployment. The move toward a new equilibrium at E_2 in 1993 reflects full employment output, with a lower inflation than at E_0.

Although the credibility of U.S. monetary policy announcements may well be higher in the early 1990s than in the early 1980s, long-term interest rates did not decline by as much as short-term rates during 1990–1992. This resistance suggests that the public didn't believe that inflation would be low in the long run (recall that the long-term rate is the sum of the real rate and expected inflation). Both the new Keynesian and new classical approaches suggest that a lack of credibility could weaken the ability of monetary or fiscal policies to stimulate the economy.

Concluding Remarks

Evidence of effects on output of monetary and fiscal policies during the early 1980s and early 1990s supports the new Keynesian approach. In particular, even expected changes in monetary policy can affect

---

[†] In addition, during the early 1980s and early 1990s, there were adverse supply shocks from significant increases in oil prices.

MOVING FROM THEORY TO PRACTICE...

THE NEW YORK TIMES   DECEMBER 17, 1991

The Recession: Monday Morning Quarterbacking at the Fed?

A new pessimism, evident in Alan Greenspan's latest speeches and in other recent comments, suggests that the chairman of the Federal Reserve now believes that new efforts by the Federal Reserve to lower interest rates will not necessarily revive the economy, as lower rates have in the past. So additional measures might have to be tried, among them Federal spending or tax cuts.

For months, the Federal Reserve confidently suggested that an economic upturn was just around the corner. Now, for the first time, Mr. Greenspan is suggesting that he has no clear idea when the economy's current stagnation might end: by spring, by Election Day, by early 1993 or perhaps not until later in the decade.

Mr. Greenspan's statements appeared to be in part an answer to critics, both in the Bush Administration and in the economics profession, who say that the economy would bounce back if the Federal Reserve would cut short-term interest rates more than the 3.75 percentage points already cut by the Federal Reserve since the recession started 18 months ago. The chairman, who until recently had thought that lower rates would do the job, is now in effect asking for help, and in doing so, he is putting pressure on the White House and Congress to play a role in ending the recession, said David Jones, chief economist at Aubrey G. Lanston, a Wall Street investment house.

"Mr. Greenspan appears to have undergone a major conversion," Mr. Jones said. "What he has been saying recently is that the economy is in more difficulty than he thought it was a few months ago, and recovery requires more than just cutting interest rates...

The essence of Mr. Greenspan's alarm about the economy—the reason he seems willing to debate fiscal policy—lies in what he calls "a heavy overhang of debt" and "the unusual degree of caution" that it has engendered among businesses, consumers and lenders...

The problem, in sum, is more a psychological one than a process that can be measured with statistics, Mr. Greenspan suggests. Economists must rely more on anecdotal evidence than on such things as income-to-debt ratios or the level of mortgage rates to gauge progress toward a healthy economy. That is an unusual acknowledgement for Mr. Greenspan, whose forte is statistics. It means that the economic profession lacks the tools to forecast just when this recession might end.

Americans, in fact, might be so shaken by their experiences of the last two years—stagnant wages, insecure jobs, falling real estate prices, the reluctance of banks to renew loans, incomes inadequate to make debt payments—that they might not regain their confidence until they work down debt to 1950's or 1960's levels, Mr. Greenspan suggests. Car loans in the 1950's, for example, normally ran two years; today the norm is four years to five years.

ANALYZING THE NEWS...

During part of 1990 and 1991, the U.S. economy suffered a recession, depicted in the accompanying diagram as a shift in the AD curve from AD_0 to AD_1. Most economists didn't blame the Fed exclusively for the recession, but many believed that the Fed took too little action to counter the economy's decline and improve its prospects for recovery.

a   The Fed pursued a gradualist policy, reducing short-term interest rates in small steps. As shown in Fig. (a), it fostered slow expansion, shifting the AD curve initially from AD_1 to AD_2, and recovering part of the short-run loss in output. Why didn't it attempt to go all the way back to AD_0, thereby returning the economy to full employment at E_0? The chairman's decisions were conditioned by the difficulty the Fed had during the 1980s in identifying the factors that accounted for short-term movements in the money supply.

b   The Fed also may have misunderstood at the outset the likely severity of the recession. Suppose that the AD curve shifted from AD_0 to AD_1, in Fig. (b), but that the Fed perceived the new AD curve to be at $AD_{1'}$. It used expansionary monetary policy to restore what it perceived to be full employment, leading to a short-run equilibrium at $E_{1'}$. With the benefit of hindsight, the expansion wasn't enough. Output was still lower than its full employment level. Why might the Fed be unable to predict the precise shift in the AD curve? Chairman Greenspan believed that falling consumer confidence combined with high household and business debt burdens added a hard-to-quantify factor.

For further thought...

The article suggests that "the reluctance of banks to renew loans" might be part of the economy's problem. How might such a "reluctance" affect the AD curve?

Source: by Louis Uchitelle, "Pessimism at the Fed", December 17, 1991. Copyright © 1991/1992 by The New York Times Company. Reprinted by permission.

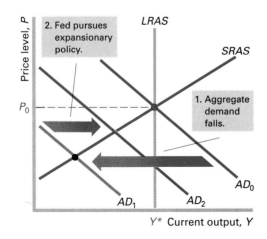

(a)

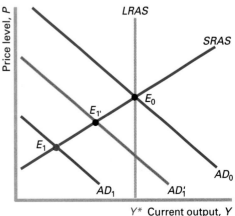

(b)

Other times, other places...
Yasushi Mieno and the Stabilization Policy Debate in Japan

In early 1992, Yasushi Mieno, the Governor of the Bank of Japan, was feeling pressure. The Japanese stock market had declined significantly, and the economy was heading into its worst slowdown in almost twenty years. The Bank of Japan had reduced the discount rate from 6% in the summer of 1991 to 4.5% six months later, but business leaders lobbied Mieno to pursue a more expansionary policy. Some leading politicians even advised Prime Minister Miyazawa to fire the governor of the central bank.

Mieno essentially faced pressure to conduct stabilization policy. Why did he resist? Mieno and the Bank of Japan believed that the Japanese economy had overheated in the late 1980s and early 1990s and that the stock market decline was just reversing an inflationary bubble. Using the AD–AS diagram, we can trace this reasoning. Mieno believed that the Japanese economy was proceeding from a short-run equilibrium at E_0, at which output Y_0 is

greater than long-run full employment output Y^*, toward E_1. The declining stock market and falling business confidence shifted the AD curve to the left from AD_0 to AD_1.

If the Bank of Japan pursued an expansionary policy in an attempt to maintain output at Y_0, in the short run, the AD curve would shift to the right from AD_1 to AD_0. However, to achieve the economy's long-run equilibrium—

the intersection of the AD_0 and $LRAS$ curves at E_3—the price level must rise. Mieno's strategy was to await downward adjustment of the price level as the $SRAS$ curve shifted from $SRAS_0$ to $SRAS_1$. With that strategy, the long-run equilibrium at E_2 has full employment output but a lower price level than at E_3. Mieno believed that the $SRAS$ adjustment would be rapid, so he sought to avoid implementing a stabilization policy.

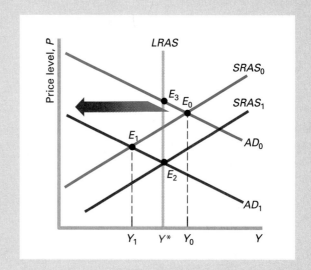

output and the real interest rate, with prices and inflation adjusting only gradually. Also important is the implication of both the new Keynesian and the new classical approaches that policy credibility is an important determinant of the effect of policy shifts on the economy.

Key Terms and Concepts

Business cycle
    Lags in the policymaking and
        implementation process
    Data lag
    Impact lag
    Implementation lag

Legislative lag
Recognition lag
Rational expectations
Stabilization policies

Summary

1. Economists generally agree that money is neutral in the long run, but many disagree about whether changes in the nominal money supply lead to changes in output in the short run. Determining whether changes in the money supply cause changes in output requires looking at independent increases or decreases in the money supply. Historical evidence suggests that independent reductions in the rate of growth of the nominal money supply have preceded declines in output. To interpret whether this relationship is causal, economists describe the way(s) in which money affects the economy.

2. The long-run neutrality of money reflects the fact that prices are flexible in the long run. In the real business cycle model, prices are flexible even in the short run. The intersection of the *AD* curve and the *SRAS* curve, which is vertical at the full employment level of output, represents the economy's equilibrium. Fluctuations in output (real business cycles) are the result of changes in productivity factors. Changes in the nominal money supply have no effect on output, even in the short run. Instead, movements of money and output together in the short run represent reverse causation: the effect of output on money demand, not the effect of the money supply on output.

3. Historical evidence for the United States is not consistent with the view that money is neutral in the short run. New Keynesian economists offer a simple explanation of short-run nonneutrality of money: Prices are not flexible in the short run. As a result, changes in aggregate demand can affect output in the short run.

4. New classical economists advance a different explanation of the relation of money and output. The misperception theory suggests a positive relationship between output and unexpected changes in the price level, based on the assumption that people have rational expectations. Expected changes in the nominal money supply are neutral. Unexpected increases in the nominal money supply increase real output. Evidence suggests that both expected and unexpected changes in the nominal money supply affect real output in the short run, implying that the new classical approach may be incomplete.

5. New Keynesian economists explain short-run nonneutrality of money by referring to sticky prices. In other words, prices are slow to adjust, either because of long-term nominal contracts or the combination of monopolistic competition and costs of adjusting prices. Both expected and unexpected changes in the nominal money supply affect output in the short run, but unexpected changes have a greater effect.

6. Efforts to smooth short-run fluctuations in output are known as stabilization policies. Stabilization policy is completely ineffective in the real business cycle approach. Unexpected policy changes can

affect output in the new classical approach, but they do so only by fooling households and firms; policy credibility is enhanced by not fine-tuning short-run economic fluctuations. Similarly, although new Keynesian economists argue that monetary policy can affect output and real interest rates in the short run, they believe that long-run policy goals are likely to be inconsistent with numerous short-term interventions.

Review Questions

1. Define *business cycle*. Why do economists care about business cycles?

2. *Evaluate*: Price flexibility necessarily implies that money is neutral.

3. Why might money be nonneutral when prices are set by monopolistically competitive firms? Why might money be nonneutral when long-term nominal contracts are important?

4. Why is it important to identify whether changes in the money supply are independent of changes in output?

5. Why is money neutral in the short run in the real business cycle model? If money is neutral, what causes business cycles in the real business cycle model?

6. How can money be neutral in the long run, but not in the short run, in the new Keynesian approach? What is the primary difference between the real business cycle model and the new Keynesian approach?

7. What are the major differences between the new classical and new Keynesian approaches? What role does the idea of rational expectations play in these two approaches?

8. What is meant by stabilization policy? In theory, how can stabilization policy be used during the business cycle?

9. Define these lags in the policymaking and implementation process:

    a. data lag;

    b. recognition lag;

    c. legislative lag;

    d. implementation lag; and

    e. impact lag.

10. Why does a monetary contraction put people out of work? Use the *AD–AS* diagram for the new Keynesian approach to explain your answer.

11. If money is neutral, why is money growth correlated with output growth in the real business cycle model?

Analytical Problems

12. Suppose that you observed a substantial decline in the money growth rate six months before the start of every recession. Would that be enough to convince you that money affects output? Why or why not?

13. You are the Chairman of the Board of Governors of the Federal Reserve System and have just learned that the federal government is going to reduce expenditures sharply. This shock shifts the *AD*

curve to the left. How would you respond in order to keep the economy at full employment equilibrium if

a. you use the new classical approach?

b. you use the new Keynesian approach?

In each case, show the *AD–AS* diagram associated with your answer.

14. After years of spending more than their incomes, people decide to reduce their debt, thus increasing saving. What effect does this action have on the *AD* curve? If you are a new Keynesian economist in charge of monetary policy, what should you do?

15. Suppose that for a long period of time the Fed maintained that it would not change monetary policy in response to recessions but, in fact, expanded the money supply each time the economy was in a recession. How would this pattern affect the Fed's credibility? Suggest implications for the responses of interest rates on Treasury bills and 30-year Treasury bonds to the Fed's interventions.

16. Suppose that the federal government seriously tried to balance its budget by raising business taxes. According to the new classical approach, what effect would this action have on output and the price level? How could monetary policy be used to offset this effect?

17. Fed officials, who can use expansionary or contractionary monetary policy to shift the *AD* curve, sometimes say that they "can't do everything." Using *AD–AS* diagrams, illustrate how monetary policy can be used to offset the effects of both *AD* and *AS* shocks on output. How does the equilibrium price level change in the two cases? Suppose that monetary policy were used to stabilize the price level instead. Draw *AD–AS* diagrams to show the effects of both aggregate demand and aggregate supply shocks on output. How does the equilibrium output level differ in the two cases?

18. The increasing power of personal computers has greatly increased the economy's expected future productivity, increasing expected future output. What is the likely effect of this development on aggregate demand today? How might monetary policy be used to offset this effect?

19. According to the new classical approach, how should the Fed use monetary policy to stabilize output in the short run if the expected price level increases, shifting the *SRAS* curve up? What would the Fed need to do in the long run to restore the initial price level? How would your answer differ if you applied the new Keynesian approach?

20. (Difficult problem) Suppose that the economy is in either a *good* state or a *bad* state and that monetary policy is either *contractionary* or *expansionary*. Suppose further that the state of the economy and the condition of monetary policy tell you all you need to know to determine the unemployment rate and the inflation rate. Finally, suppose that people care most about the sum of the unemployment rate, *u*, and the inflation rate, π, which is called the *misery index*, or $m = u + \pi$. The respective factors and their values are

Monetary Policy	Factor	Economy	
		Good	Bad
Contractionary	u	5%	10%
	π	5	3
	m	10	13
Expansionary	u	4	8
	π	10	4
	m	14	12

If the economy is in a good state, a contractionary monetary policy to prevent inflation is best. But if the economy is in a bad state, an expansionary monetary policy to help the economy recover is best. For example, with a contractionary monetary policy in a bad state, the unemployment rate rises to 10% with only 3% inflation; with an expansionary monetary policy, the unemployment rate is lower at 8%, with inflation only slightly higher at 4%.

a. If the Fed knows exactly when the state of the economy changes and it changes policy to minimize the misery index, what is its monetary policy and the misery index when the economy is good? When the economy is bad?

b. Now suppose that there are some lags in the process. Suppose further that the Fed doesn't know the current state of the economy, but only knows what it was six months earlier (that is, there may be both recognition and data lags). Then suppose that, if the economy was in a good state six months ago, the probability is 90% that it is still in a good state today and 10% that it is now in a bad state; if the economy was in a bad state six months ago, the probability is 75% that it is now in a good state and 25% that it is now in a bad state. If the Fed wants to minimize the misery index on average,

what should its policy be if the economy was in a good state six months ago? If it was in a bad state six months ago?

c. Suppose that, in addition to the data and recognition lags, there is also an effectiveness lag of six months. What should policy be today if the economy was in a good state six months ago? If it was in a bad state six months ago?

d. What do your answers to (a)–(c) suggest about the ability of policymakers to use stabilization policies?

Data Questions

21. Find monthly or quarterly data on the (civilian) unemployment rate from 1946 to the present in a source such as *Business Statistics* or *Employment and Earnings* (for more recent data, see the *Survey of Current Business* or the *Economic Report of the President*). Looking just at the unemployment rate data, try to guess when all the recessions since 1946 began and when they ended. Compare your answers to the information in Fig. 26.1.

22. Find some measure of the inflation rate (consumer price index, producer price index, GDP deflator) in a major data source, such as the *Economic Report of*

the President, for each year since 1946. Cover the inflation rates shown for 1960 to the present with a piece of paper. Now, based on the historical inflation rates for 1946 to 1959, estimate the inflation rate for 1960. Then, looking only at the data for 1946 to 1964, estimate the inflation rate for 1965. Repeat for 1970, 1975, 1980, 1985, and 1990. Now compare your estimates to the actual inflation rates. How close were you? Were your estimates of inflation based on rational expectations? What other information besides past inflation rates would you find useful when forecasting inflation?

Appendix: The Money-Output Relationship

Data Interpretation Issues

To understand relationships between the money supply and the financial system and the economy, researchers use one of two methods to analyze data: (1) a *reduced-form approach*, or (2) a *structural model*. Reduced-form approaches focus on correlations among variables, or how levels of or changes in the variables are related. Structural models emphasize behavioral relationships, or how changes in one variable affect the behavior of another.

Examples from scientific disciplines help to illustrate differences between the two approaches. Suppose that you were researching whether smoking during pregnancy leads to a low infant birth weight. The reduced-form approach would be to look for a simple correlation: Are low-birth-weight infants born more often to smoking than to nonsmoking mothers? Alternatively, a structural model would relate the effects of smoking on the mother's respiratory and circulatory systems to how changes in these functions affect prenatal development.

Short-Run Money and Output Movements

Economists have used reduced-form and structural models to evaluate relationships that connect a change in output or the real interest rate to a change in the money supply. We examine the different types of evidence considered in the new classical and new Keynesian approaches. (Recall that, in the real business cycle model, changes in the nominal money supply have no effect on output or the real interest rate, even in the short run.)

The New Classical Approach: Reduced-Form Evidence.

The new classical approach—combining the misperception theory with the assumption of rational expectations—clearly predicts the nonneutrality of money: Changes in the money supply affect real output only to the extent that they are unexpected. The new classical approach has a different explanation from that of the new Keynesian approach: Changes in the money supply affect output through firms' supply decisions based on imperfect information. Modeling this mechanism is difficult, however. The actual change in the money supply ΔM is the sum of the expected change ΔM^e and the unexpected portion of the change ΔM^u, or $\Delta M = \Delta M^e + \Delta M^u$. Even though the Fed publishes data on actual changes in the money supply, how do we know how much of this change was expected by households and businesses?

Robert Barro of Harvard University applied the notion of rational expectations to construct an alternative for ΔM^e. Using statistical techniques, he estimated the change in the money supply expected by the public each year from 1941 through 1976.[†] With a proxy for ΔM^e, Barro constructed a measure of unexpected changes in the money supply ΔM^u by subtracting ΔM^e from the actual change ΔM. Using a reduced-form approach, he found that real GNP was positively related to current and lagged ΔM^u (by up to three years). By contrast, ΔM^e had no effect on the level of real GNP. The new classical approach—combining the misperception theory with rational expectations—predicts that only changes in the money supply that are unexpected

[†] Robert J. Barro, "Unanticipated Money, Output, and the Price Level in the United States," *Journal of Political Economy*, 86:549–580, 1978.

will have real effects, Barro's results provided important evidence supporting this approach.

Not all researchers have agreed with Barro's findings. Frederic Mishkin of Columbia University examined effects of changes in the money supply on real GNP within five years. (Barro had studied effects only over three years.) In his analysis of Barro's model, Mishkin found that expected and unexpected changes in the money supply had roughly equivalent effects on real GNP over a five-year period. Mishkin's evidence is not consistent with the new classical view.[†]

Robert Gordon of Northwestern University provided another criticism of Barro's findings. Whereas Mishkin extended Barro's model, Gordon focused on another prediction of the new Classical approach: that the price level should increase in proportion to an expected increase in the nominal money supply and decrease in proportion to an expected decrease in the nominal money supply. Gordon's work rejected this prediction, providing additional evidence against the view that expected changes in the nominal money supply are neutral.[††]

Mishkin's and Gordon's findings raise both statistical and conceptual issues. On a statistical level, we are left with the problem of measuring expected and unexpected changes in the money supply, which are unobservable economic variables. Also important is the issue of reverse causation that we discussed earlier: A change in the money supply could occur in response to current or expected future changes in output. On a conceptual level, the statistical findings do not identify a particular underlying source of monetary nonneutrality, a task undertaken by new Keynesian economists.

Money and Output in the New Keynesian Approach.   New Keynesian economists focus on analyzing structural models of the ways in which monetary policy affects the economy. During the 1960s and 1970s, economists began building large-scale econometric models of components of aggregate demand (and, to a lesser extent, of aggregate supply). These models used equations based on historical data to describe (statistically) saving and investment decisions, money and financial markets, and wages and prices. Prominent early models include the M.I.T.–Pennsylvania–Social Science Research Council (MPS) model (pioneered by Franco Modigliani of M.I.T. and Albert Ando of the University of Pennsylvania), the Wharton Econometric model (developed by Lawrence Klein of the University of Pennsylvania), and the Data Resources, Incorporated (DRI) model (developed by the late Otto Eckstein of Harvard University).

[†] Frederic S. Mishkin, "Does Anticipated Monetary Policy Matter? An Econometric Evaluation," *Journal of Political Economy*, 90:22–51, 1982.

[††] Robert J. Gordon, "Price Inertia and Policy Ineffectiveness in the United States, 1890–1980," *Journal of Political Economy*, 90:1087–1117, 1982.

Analysts currently use revised versions of these models for forecasting purposes. Indeed, the Fed uses a descendant of the MPS model for forecasting. In that model, a drop in the nominal money supply is neutral in the long run. However it decreases real interest rates and increases consumption, investment, and net exports, thereby raising aggregate demand in the short run. This pattern is consistent with the evidence gathered from the U.S. data that we discussed in this chapter.

The Debate over Validity. New classical economists argue that large-scale econometric models are not useful for evaluating effects of (even independent) future changes in the money supply on economic activity. In other words, these models could misinform businesses and government agencies about the effects of monetary policy on output and interest rates. According to the new classical economists, households and businesses are likely to react to announced changes in monetary policy in ways potentially different from the past behavior on which the models are based.

In a celebrated critique of the applicability of econometric models to analysis of the ways in which monetary policy affects the economy, Robert E. Lucas, Jr., of the University of Chicago, restated an implication of rational expectations and the efficient markets hypothesis: When monetary policy changes are expected, the behavior of forecasted variables changes. New classical economists argue that, as a result, conventional econometric models that use historical data are not useful for examining the short-run relationship between money supply and output.

Many new Keynesian economists counter that forecasting models may nonetheless be useful for predicting effects of unexpected policy changes and for providing some guidance in assessing effects of expected policy changes so long as prices adjust gradually to policy changes. Econometric forecasting models no longer enjoy the popularity they had in the 1960s and 1970s, but many businesses and government agencies still use them as an analytic tool. Recent versions of these models encompass more determinants of aggregate supply.

CHAPTER 27

Financial Institutions and the Macroeconomy

In the fall of 1991, the president's economic advisors were worried. The Gulf War had gone well earlier in the year, and the President's prospects for reelection were excellent. Nevertheless, the weak economy was a nagging concern. The president's pollsters warned that failure to recover from the recession that began in 1990 could adversely affect the 1992 election.

In September 1991, President Bush, Treasury Secretary Nicholas Brady, and Council of Economic Advisers Chairman Michael Boskin issued a statement that the economy was suffering from a *credit crunch,* or an inadequate supply of bank loans. The supply of loans was believed to be "too low" because banks were nervous about the economy and regulators were anxious to avoid a repeat of the savings and loan industry debacle. In addition, President Bush and his principal economic advisors argued that Fed policy was "too tight." These same arguments later were heard during the early days of President Clinton's administration.

The idea of a credit crunch seems to contradict our assumption in the two preceding chapters that the actions of banks and the Federal Reserve System can be analyzed in terms of the money market. In other words, if banks cut back on their lending, some other financing mechanism should take up the slack, making a credit crunch impossible. In this chapter, we reexamine the role of financial institutions in the economy, concentrating particularly on the information services that they provide to ultimate savers and borrowers.

In this chapter, we focus on two questions: **Q:** How do changes in the ability or willingness of financial institutions to lend affect economic activity? **Q:** What is the role of financial institutions in the effects of monetary policy on the macroeconomy?

Macroeconomic Costs of Information Problems

We begin by considering the possibility that breakdowns in lending by financial institutions affect the volume of funds in the financial system channeled from savers to borrowers. For some forms of finance to be special in this sense, alternative sources of funds to borrowers must be imperfect substitutes. The reason is that information problems in financial markets make alternative forms of finance imperfect substitutes. For example, if a firm is denied a bank loan, it may decide to forego its investment projects because its only other options may be to issue bonds or shares of stock.

Information Problems in the Saving-Investment Process

We based the analysis of interactions of the financial system and the economy in the aggregate demand–aggregate supply model on the assumption that alternative forms of finance are perfect substitutes. Thus we were able to collapse the financial system into a single market: the market for money. In assessing links between the financial system and the economy, we assumed that the real interest rate in financial markets represents the return to savers and the cost of funds to borrowers. As a result, adjustments in the real interest rate bring into balance the quantity of funds supplied by savers and the quantity of funds demanded by borrowers. That rationale builds on the analysis in Chapter 5, in which we examined demand and supply factors in the market for finance much as we would in the market for wheat.

However, important differences exist between the two markets. In the market for wheat a farmer receiving competing bids will sell to the buyer offering the highest price. As we showed in examining financial institutions in Part III, markets for finance do more than allocate funds at a market-clearing price (the real interest rate): The financial system provides risk-sharing, liquidity, and information services to savers and borrowers. In our analysis of adverse selection and moral hazard problems, we demonstrated that savers would be unwise to supply funds to borrowers willing to pay a high interest rate because those borrowers may not be able (or want) to repay. Because of asymmetric information in real-world financing arrangements, savers must spend resources to learn about the characteristics of borrowers.

Because banks specialize in gathering information about the creditworthiness of borrowers (borrowers' prospects and likelihood of repayment) and in monitoring borrowers' activities, banks can offer funds more cheaply than can financial markets to many borrowers. For this reason, a majority of lending from savers to borrowers occurs through financial intermediaries, such as commercial banks, savings and loan associations, mutual savings banks, and credit unions, rather than through the stock and bond markets. As a result, the ability and willingness of banks to make loans can significantly affect economic activity.

Consequences for Large Firms

Because banks reduce costs of asymmetric information in lending, bank credit is an important source of funds for small firms. Large businesses also may borrow from banks, but such firms alternatively may turn to the stock and bond markets for investment funds. Nevertheless, problems of asymmetric information can affect investment decisions, even in large companies.

When discussing banking in Part III, we noted that alternative sources of financing investment by small firms are not perfect substitutes. For large firms, economists have found that internal funds (available to a firm from its current and past profits) are a cheaper source of finance than external funds (obtained from outside investors), owing to asymmetric information problems. Outside investors have less information about firms' investment plans and opportunities than do inside managers or large shareholders. Thus they require a premium in the cost of funds to compensate them for having to obtain information about firms. These problems of asymmetric information for large firms suggest that, all else being equal, increases in firms' internal funds will increase investment.

Suppose, for example, that a temporary adverse shock to the oil supply plunges the economy into a recession. Because of the recession, firms earn smaller profits, reducing their internal funds, and investment spending falls (even if true future investment opportunities do not change). The drop in output is magnified, worsening the recession. Conversely, a favorable current productivity disturbance may raise investment and output by increasing firms' internal funds. Thus problems of asymmetric information may magnify short-run fluctuations in output. Recent evidence shows that shifts in internal funds have important effects on investment for young, rapidly growing firms and smaller effects on more mature firms. These differential effects reflect the greater severity of asymmetric information problems facing outside investors in young firms.

▶ **C H E C K P O I N T** *The managers of Toolco want to expand their small chain of four hardware stores. They believe that the economy is about to turn around and that spending on home improvement will rise. Mainbank, Toolco's banker for 10 years, acknowledges Toolco's reputation but won't grant the loan. What are Toolco's financing alternatives? Unless the managers have personal resources to invest, Toolco has few alternatives. It could attempt to borrow from its suppliers, who have good information about its prospects. The transactions costs of a commercial paper or bond offering are too great to justify the expense. For businesses like Toolco, current and past profits and bank loans provide most of the finance for growth.* ◀

Consequences of a Drop in Bank Lending

We use the AD–AS model to explore the importance of bank lending for the economy as a whole. Suppose, for example, that the federal government issued a regulation restricting bank lending. Such a restriction isn't likely to affect all borrowers equally. Some borrowers—particularly households and small and medium-sized businesses—probably can't replace bank credit with other forms of finance. As a result, spending on consumer durables or business plant and equipment by these bank-dependent borrowers falls. Figure 27.1(a) shows that the initial short-run equilibrium lies at E_0, with a price level P_0 and output Y_0. The decline in bank lending reduces the availability of credit to bank-dependent borrowers, shifting the AD curve to the left from AD_0 to AD_1; output falls in the short run from Y_0 to Y_1.

Figure 27.1(b) depicts the market for money. Recall that the public's demand for real money balances depends positively on the level of output (Chapter 23). Hence, as output falls in response to the decline in bank lending, the money demand curve in Fig. 27.1(b) shifts to the left from MD_0 to MD_1, and the equilibrium real interest rate in the money market (the open market interest rate) falls from r_0 to r_1. (The decline in the price level from P_0 to P_1 increases real money balances from MS_0 to MS_1.)

The effect of less lending on output and the real interest rate is different from the effect of the Fed's reducing the nominal money supply which we analyzed in Chapter 26. In the case of a restriction on lending, banks can't lend to households and businesses as easily, so they prefer instead to hold Treasury bills. The nominal money supply doesn't change, because securities dealers will deposit the proceeds of the sale of T-bills in bank accounts. The

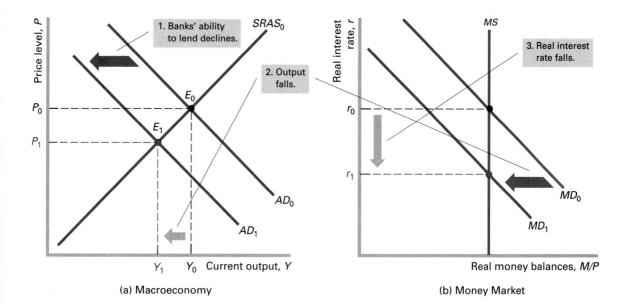

(a) Macroeconomy   (b) Money Market

drop in the open market real interest rate from r_0 to r_1 reflects a feedback effect (the decline in money demand) from the decline in aggregate demand resulting from the regulation.

We can generalize the responses illustrated in Fig. 27.1. So long as bank loans are imperfect substitutes for other sources of funds for many borrowers, a decline in banks' ability or willingness to lend reduces output and the real interest rate in the short run.

Costs of Lending Restrictions

As we have demonstrated, shifts in lending practices by financial institutions affect output and interest rates in the economy. Let's now consider two important examples of such shifts: (1) financial panics and (2) credit controls and credit crunches.

Financial Panics

During the late nineteenth and early twentieth centuries, the United States experienced several episodes known as **financial panics,** or periods characterized by violent fluctuations in financial markets, bank runs, and bankruptcies of many firms. In the financial panics, "bad news" associated with a particular firm or bank sent interest rates up and stock prices down in financial markets. In addition, concerned depositors withdrew funds that had been available for bank lending, decreasing the money supply. The crisis atmosphere in financial markets and institutions intensified costs imposed by asymmetric information. Because of the decline in the money supply (of which bank deposits are an important component) and its effects on bank-dependent borrowers, the decline in bank lending magnified reductions in economic activity. In some of the financial panics, an unanticipated drop in the price level raised the real value of firms' debt obligations, reducing firms' net worth. The collapse in internal funds raised information costs in lending and led to declining investment and output. Hence a financial panic causes the AD curve to shift to the left (as depicted in Fig. 27.1a), which results in less output.

Ben Bernanke of Princeton University has stressed that the wave of bank failures in the early 1930s led to a financial panic and increased the severity of the Great Depression. Depositors converted significant quantities of bank deposits to currency or default-risk-free U.S. government securities. Banks sharply reduced their willingness to lend to risky borrowers, preferring to hold only marketable securities of the highest quality. The increase in the demand for safe securities decreased yields significantly. The spread in interest rates on so-called safe and risky securities widened to levels not seen again since that time. Spending by households, farms, and small and medium-sized businesses (all heavily dependent on bank finance)

Other times, other places...

The Global Banking Crisis and the Great Depression

The banking crisis in the United States during the early 1930s spurred the decline in economic activity by reducing credit to many types of borrowers. The Great Depression of the 1930s was not confined to the United States. Major banking panics occurred in 1931 in Austria, Germany, and many Eastern European, South American, and Middle Eastern countries, where the banking systems were fragile. Some countries, notably Canada and the United Kingdom, had stable systems with a few large, well-diversified national banks. These countries were less vulnerable to banking panics than were countries with small, undiversified local banks, such as France and

the United States.

Ben Bernanke and Harold James examined data from 24 countries and grouped them according to whether they experienced a banking crisis:

Banking Crisis	No Banking Crisis
Austria	Australia
Belgium	Canada
Estonia	Czechoslovakia
France	Denmark
Germany	Finland
Hungary	Greece
Italy	Japan
Latvia	Netherlands
Poland	Norway
Romania	New Zealand
United States	Spain
	Sweden
	United Kingdom

Bernanke and James found that the countries that suffered a banking crisis experienced greater subsequent declines in output and employment than countries that did not experience a banking crisis. The divergence was greatest in 1932, the year following the main banking crises, when declines in industrial production averaged 16% and 2%, respectively, in the two groups of countries.

Source: Ben Bernanke and Harold James, "The Gold Standard, Deflation, and Financial Crisis in the Great Depression: An International Comparison." In R. Glenn Hubbard (ed.), *Financial Markets and Financial Crises,* Chicago: University of Chicago Press, 1991.

declined substantially. The Other times, other places box shows that the banking crises of the Great Depression also affected many countries.

Credit Controls and Credit Crunches

Full-scale financial panics are rare nowadays in the United States because of legislation that created a lender of last resort (the Fed) and federal deposit insurance. A more recent example illustrating the effects of a drop in bank lending on the economy is the imposition of **credit controls,** or regulatory restrictions on bank lending. Because of the importance of bank lending to many borrowers, an independent reduction in the supply of bank credit should contract the spending of bank-dependent borrowers and reduce open market interest rates.

In March 1980, President Carter attempted to reduce aggregate demand and inflation by authorizing the Fed to implement direct credit controls on consumer lending by banks, department stores, and certain other firms. The Fed implemented a voluntary Special Credit Restraint Program for the banking system, which requested that banks reduce their acquisition of funds from nondeposit sources. The Fed also imposed a surcharge of 3% on some discount borrowing by large banks, a special reserve requirement of 15% on new money market mutual fund assets, and increased reserve requirements on certain large-denomination certificates of deposit. Borrowing by households and many small businesses fell dramatically. As in Fig. 27.1, the reduction in bank credit availability shifted the *AD* curve to the left, reducing output. Indeed, real GDP and industrial production declined in the spring and summer to produce a short but relatively sharp recession. The reduction in output led to a drop in money demand, causing the real open market interest rate to fall. At the same time, the yield on three-month T-bills dropped from 15% to about 7% (the drop in the federal funds rate was still more dramatic); long-term rates also declined. Spending by households contracted significantly, and there was a smaller, though still important, reduction in business spending. The effect of the credit controls on the economy was so severe that the controls were removed by July 1980. As soon as the controls were lifted, interest rates and economic activity increased. This episode shows the strong impact that credit control can have on the macroeconomy.

Economists also point to credit crunch episodes to support the view that reductions in bank lending can have macroeconomic consequences. A **credit crunch** is a decline in either the ability or the willingness of banks to lend at any particular interest rate. An example of a credit crunch caused by regulation of banks' *ability* to lend occurred prior to the early 1980s, with Regulation Q's limitation on the interest rates that banks could pay on deposits. When open market interest rates on T-bills and other financial instruments rose above the Regulation Q ceiling, depositors shifted funds from bank deposits to those alternatives, a process called *disintermediation*. As a result, banks were not able to lend as much. Spending in sectors dependent on bank finance (particularly housing and small business investment) declined significantly, contributing to downturns in economic activity.

A credit crunch also may occur because of a decline in banks' *willingness* to lend. The reason is weakness on the part of either banks (because of low levels of bank capital, for example) or borrowers (because evaluating and monitoring financially distressed borrowers entails greater transactions and information costs for banks). In a credit crunch, banks decide to hold much smaller portions of their portfolios in loans, thereby decreasing the volume of bank loans and increasing the effective bank loan rate. For borrowers, the transactions and information costs of nonbank finance are high, so a reduction in bank lending decreases spending.

At the beginning of the 1990–1991 recession, the U.S. economy experienced a credit crunch. The decline in bank lending in large part reflected banks' concern about the strength of borrowers' balance sheets (that is, about the ability of borrowers to carry out long-term projects). The investment activities most severely affected were real estate development and the activities of highly leveraged firms. The volume of lending declined dramati-

Q: How do changes in the ability or willingness of financial institutions to lend affect economic activity?

A: Banks specialize in reducing costs asssociated with asymmetric information in the saving-investment process. For many borrowers, nonbank financing is an imperfect substitute for bank loans so that shifts in the ability or willingness of banks to make loans affect aggregate output and the real interest rate.

cally in the fall of 1990, and surveys of small businesses revealed that credit had become more difficult to obtain, even for firms with a good credit history.

Financial Institutions and Monetary Policy

In our discussion of monetary policy and economic activity in Chapter 26, we assumed that borrowers are indifferent to how or from whom they raise funds and regard alternative sources of credit as close substitutes. This assumption allows us to focus on the market for money. In the market for money, the supply of money (influenced strongly by actions of the Fed) and the public's demand for money determine open market interest rates, which affect spending decisions by households and businesses.

The Money View

In the **money view** of how changes in the money supply affect output and the real interest rate in the short run, the public's portfolio decisions determine the allocation of wealth between money and nonmoney assets. Financial institutions (banks) are passive intermediaries, meeting the public's demand for money by supplying deposits.

Recall that banks can change the level of deposits either by purchasing securities on the open market or by making loans to households and businesses (Chapter 17). Banks pay for securities in financial markets by channeling deposits to securities sellers. When a bank makes loans, it makes borrowers' deposits available in exchange for a promise to repay with interest. Banks earn profits on these activities, as interest rates on marketable securities or loans are higher than those on banks' more liquid deposit liabilities. When banks want to increase the level of deposits at current interest rates, they can buy securities in financial markets. The resulting price increases of securities reduce yields on those securities and encourage households and firms to allocate more of their portfolios to bank deposits than to securities. If loans and securities are close substitutes in the eyes of the public, interest rates in general will fall. Banks can also increase the level of deposits by reducing interest rates on loans. The lower rates encourage households and firms to borrow additional funds, thereby increasing deposits. Banks can reduce the level of deposits desired at current interest rates either by selling securities in their portfolios (to encourage the public to accept them instead of deposits) or by decreasing the demand for deposits by raising interest rates on loans. Either method changes deposits by affecting interest rates.

Because financial institutions play a passive role in the money supply process in the money view, Fed policy can be used to stimulate economic activity. If the Fed wants to encourage additional economic activity, it can increase the level of bank reserves, causing banks either to increase deposits by buying securities or to make more loans at lower interest rates. Either way, the public accepts the increase in money because of lower interest rates. The lower interest rates that result from the increase in the money supply expand the economy by increasing business investment and consumer spending on durable goods and housing.

The Credit View

The money view provides a simple framework for analyzing the effects of monetary policy on economic activity resulting from changes in interest rates. However, its assumption of financial intermediaries' passive role ignores their importance in reducing information costs of borrowing and lending. An alternative view, the **credit view,** is that *bank loans* differ from other assets because the public regards them as money. The credit view holds that banks play an active role in the macroeconomy; that is, as we saw earlier, bank lending affects output and interest rates. The credit view's focus on bank loans suggests a modified view of how monetary policy affects the economy.

Money View and Credit View Predictions

In the money view, changes in the nominal money supply affect output by influencing the open market interest rate in the money market. Figure 27.2 illustrates this process graphically with the *AD–AS* model. For simplicity, let's assume that all firms have sticky prices in the short run, so the *SRAS* curve is horizontal. Consider an unexpected monetary expansion, in which the Fed increases the level of bank reserves through open market operations, raising the nominal money supply from M_0 to M_1. The real money supply curve in Fig. 27.2(a) shifts to the right from MS_0 to MS_1. With the

▼ FIGURE 27.2

Money View of Monetary Expansion Effects

In the money view, monetary expansion reduces the real interest rate and raises output in the short run.

As shown in (a):
1. The Fed increases the nominal money supply from M_0 to M_1, raising the real money supply in the short run from MS_0 to MS_1.

2. The real open market interest rate falls from r_0 to r_1, bringing the money market back into equilibrium.

As shown in (b):
3. The drop in the real interest rate causes the aggregate demand curve to shift from AD_0 to AD_1, increasing output from Y_0 to Y_1. Money demand rises from MD_0 to MD_1, so the interest rate rises to $r_{1'}$. On balance, the real interest rate declines, from r_0 to $r_{1'}$ as a result of the monetary expansion.

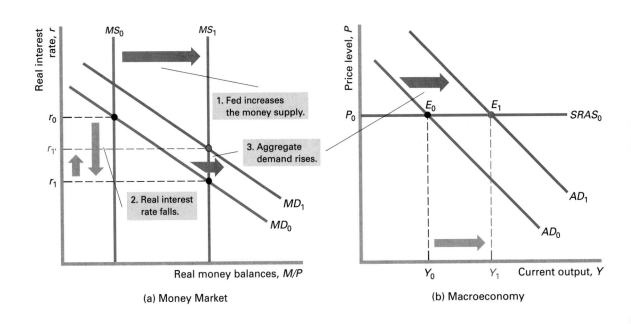

(a) Money Market

(b) Macroeconomy

FIGURE 27.3

Credit View of Monetary Expansion Effects
In the credit view, monetary expansion raises output in the short run, but the effect on the real interest rate is ambiguous.

As shown in (a):
1. The Fed increases the money supply from M_0 to M_1, raising the real money supply in the short run from MS_0 to MS_1.

2. The real open market interest rate falls initially from r_0 to r_1.

As shown in (b):
3. Aggregate demand rises because of an increase in interest-sensitive spending and in spending by bank-dependent borrowers. These effects raise money demand from MD_0 to MD_1.

In part (a) we see that:
4. In the new equilibrium, the real interest rate actually rises from r_0 to $r_{1'}$; that is, the larger feedback effect in the credit view can cause the real interest rate to rise during monetary expansion.

higher level of reserves, banks try to increase deposits by buying securities in financial markets, making loans, or both. When they buy securities, security prices rise and yields fall. Interest rates on bank loans decline. The increase in the nominal money supply leads to a decline in the real interest rate from r_0 to r_1 in the short run. In Fig. 27.2(b), the increase in the money supply shifts the AD curve to the right from AD_0 to AD_1. At the new equilibrium, E_1, output rises to Y_1. The higher level of current output raises money demand from MD_0 to MD_1 in Fig. 27.2(a). Thus the real interest rate rises from r_1 to $r_{1'}$. When the feedback between the financial system and the economy is complete, output rises and the real interest rate falls in the short run in response to monetary expansion.

Hence, in the money view, an increase in the nominal money supply decreases the real interest rate and increases output in the short run. This expansion occurs because, if nothing else changes, open market interest rates fall in the short run to induce households and firms to hold a greater quantity of money.

In both the money and credit views, when banks expand deposits by making loans, the increase in bank reserves leads to lower loan interest rates. Many borrowers can choose between bank or nonbank loans, so lower bank loan rates lead to lower interest rates in financial markets. The credit view also holds that monetary policy affects the economy through the volume of bank lending to and spending by bank-dependent borrowers.

Let's examine these outcomes by returning to a Fed expansionary monetary policy. In the credit view, the initial effect in the money market is the same as in the money view: As Fig. 27.3(a) shows, the increase in the

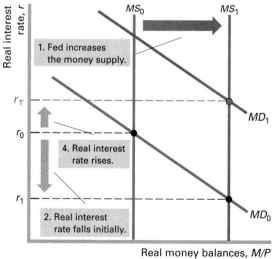

(a) Money Market

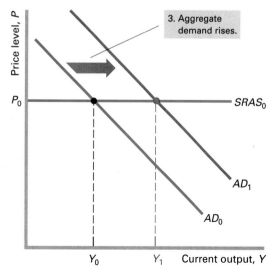

(b) Macroeconomy

money supply from MS_0 to MS_1 reduces the open market real interest rate from r_0 to r_1. In the credit view, the AD curve shifts to the right for two reasons: (1) the response of households' and firms' spending to the drop in the interest rate, and (2) the increased availability of bank loans. In other words, if banks expand deposits by lowering interest rates on loans, the amounts that bank-dependent borrowers can borrow and spend increases at any real interest rate in financial markets. The shift of the AD curve from AD_0 to AD_1 in Fig. 27.3(b) is greater than in the money view, as is the increase in output (from Y_0 to Y_1).

Because of the greater spending at any particular interest rate, the money demand curve in Fig. 27.3(a) shifts to the right from MD_0 to MD_1. As a result, the short-run effect of the monetary expansion on the open market real interest rate is ambiguous. The case depicted in Fig. 27.3(a), with the new equilibrium real interest rate at $r_{1'}$, is one in which the effect on the interest rate of the increase in money demand is greater than the effect of the increase in money supply.

In both views, expansionary monetary policy by the Fed generally decreases the level of interest rates, increasing spending and economic activity in the short run. Similarly, contractionary monetary policy increases interest rates, decreasing spending and economic activity in the short run. The credit view recognizes an aspect of monetary policy not considered by the money view: Banks' portfolio decisions about lending cause bank-dependent sectors of the economy to change their spending. As many borrowers are bank-dependent and have few substitutes for bank loans, changes in banks' ability or willingness to lend may significantly affect the volume of credit and economic activity.

Monetary Policy and Balance Sheets in the Credit View

The analysis of effects of monetary expansion in the money and credit views focused on the ways that monetary policy affects economic activity. Recall that most of the short-run effects of changes in the money supply have an impact on the real interest rate and, through the real interest rate, on output. The credit view stresses the importance of changes in financial institutions' willingness to supply or borrowers' willingness to demand funds for investment at any real interest rate. Analysts have attempted to model this method statistically using the **liquidity of balance sheet positions**—that is, the quantity of liquid assets that households and firms hold relative to their liabilities. These analysts emphasize balance sheet liquidity as a determinant of spending on business investment, housing, and consumer durable goods.

In the credit view, holdings of liquid assets reduce the likelihood of **financial distress,** which arises when households or businesses have to sell illiquid assets, possibly at a loss, to meet current obligations. As a result of financial distress, household and business spending would fall for any particular level of market interest rates.

For both households and businesses, the likelihood of experiencing financial distress decreases when they have substantial liquid financial assets (and/or access to credit from financial institutions) relative to their liabilities. When households have high levels of liquid assets relative to their liabilities, they are more willing to invest in consumer durable goods or housing because they estimate the likelihood of financial distress to be low. Similarly, when firms' liquid asset holdings are high relative to their liabilities, they are more willing to invest in new plants and equipment, all else being equal.

During some significant episodes, declining liquidity of household and business balance sheets reduced spending on consumer durable goods, housing, and business plants and equipment. After the stock market crash of 1929, the number of households and businesses experiencing financial distress grew. This situation was caused by the reduction in the value of financial assets combined with the increase in the real value of outstanding debt obligations (because of the decline in the price level). From 1929 to 1933, expenditures on business fixed investment (in constant dollars) fell by 73%, and expenditures on consumer durable goods and housing declined by 50% and 80%, respectively. Many economists suggest that deteriorating balance sheet positions also were important in the recessions of 1974–1975, 1981–1982, and 1990–1991.

Monetary policy can affect the likelihood of financial distress. Recall that independent increases in the money supply lower interest rates and raise stock prices, thereby raising the value of liquid financial assets. When the value of financial assets is relatively greater than financial liabilities, the probability of financial distress diminishes. This increases spending on consumer durable goods and investment. In addition, short-term declines in interest rates can reduce the cost of servicing outstanding debt obligations, thereby increasing liquidity for households and firms.

Validity of the Credit View

To consider whether the credit view aids in understanding the effects of monetary policy, let's examine its predictions for (1) impacts of monetary policy on bank-dependent and non-bank-dependent borrowers, and (2) the existence of shifts in bank loan supply independent of shifts in bank loan demand.

Effects of Monetary Policy on Borrowers. Unlike the money view, the credit view acknowledges differences among borrowers in the financial system. Transactions costs of bank and nonbank finance, particularly those related to information, are higher for households and small and medium-sized firms than for large, well-known firms. If the credit view is correct, a credit crunch in bank lending should be felt disproportionately by borrowers for which transactions and information costs of nonbank finance are the highest. We noted earlier the significant effect on households during the Carter credit controls episode. Moreover, economists have documented the importance of credit supply effects on small firms relative to large firms. For example, a study of manufacturing firms since World War II by Mark Gertler of New York University and Simon Gilchrist of the Federal Reserve Board examined the effect of contractionary monetary policies on the output of manufacturing firms.[†] They found that changes in the *M2* money supply and in the federal funds rate were much more important in explaining changes in bank loans and output for small firms than for large firms. These pronounced differences in the output responses of manufacturing firms to monetary policy suggests the relevance of the credit view for the current U.S. economy.

Distinguishing Changes in Supply and Demand for Credit.   When analyzing real-world data, we need to distinguish whether shifts in *bank loan supply* are independent of shifts in *bank loan demand*. For example, a decline in bank lending during a recession doesn't necessarily indicate a credit crunch. Rather, it might be explained by a reduction in the demand by households and firms for credit of all types.

Some episodes clearly support a role for independent shifts in bank loan supply. The decline in output and interest rates during the monetary contraction associated with the Carter credit controls are inconsistent with the money view. Moreover, as the credit controls were unexpected and imposed by the government, the decline in economic activity as a result of the controls clearly caused the decline in money demand, and the fall in interest rates.

An additional example comes from the banking collapse of the 1930s. In their explanation of monetary factors as causing the Great Depression, Milton Friedman and Anna Schwartz blamed the drop in the money supply accompanying the contraction of the banking system. Credit view advocates see two problems with this conclusion as a complete explanation for the severe economic decline from 1930 to 1933. First, it doesn't explain why the decline was so protracted. Second, the decline in the *real money supply* (which affects the *AD* curve) wasn't nearly so great as the drop in the nominal money supply because the aggregate price level declined significantly as well.

More generally, one way to learn whether less bank lending reflects an independent shift in banks' ability or willingness to lend is to examine the behavior of borrowers having some access to nonbank sources of finance. Do these borrowers seek funds elsewhere, such as the commercial paper market? Anil Kashyap of the University of Chicago, Jeremy Stein of M.I.T., and David Wilcox of the Federal Reserve Board studied bank lending and the issuing of commercial paper to learn what happens to the mix of borrowing from banks and the commercial paper market when the Fed contracts the level of bank

---

[†] Mark Gertler and Simon Gilchrist, "Monetary Policy, Business Cycles, and the Behavior of Small Manufacturing Firms," Working Paper No. 3892, Cambridge: National Bureau of Economic Research, November 1992.

Q: What is the role of financial institutions in the effects of monetary policy on the macroeconomy?

A: In the money view, banks are passive intermediaries, and monetary policy primarily affects the macroeconomy through changes in open market interest rates.
      In the credit view monetary policy also affects bank lending, which can independently shift the *AD* curve. Thus, monetary policy affects the macroeconomy through changes in interest rates, lending to bank-dependent borrowers, and borrowers' balance sheet positions.

reserves.[†] They found that commercial paper issues increased significantly but that bank lending remained flat or declined. The fact that commercial and bank loans did not move together in those episodes strongly suggests that changes in overall credit demand are not responsible for the pattern. Kashyap, Stein, and Wilcox found that changes in the mix of short-term finance (away from bank loans and toward commercial paper) accompanying contractionary monetary policy reduced business inventories (for which bank credit is an important source of finance). It also had a smaller effect on business equipment investment.

The evidence broadly supports the idea that lending by financial intermediaries plays an important role in determining output and interest rates. Indeed, some analysts and policymakers blamed a credit crunch for worsening the 1990-1991 recession (see Box 27.1).

The credit view suggests that financial institution strength is necessary for the financial system and the economy to function smoothly. Adverse shocks to banks' ability or willingness to lend (as in a credit crunch) may have severe economic effects. Monetary policy can work by affecting the public's portfolio allocation decisions regarding money and nonmoney assets or by affecting banks' portfolio allocation decisions regarding loans and securities. A general unwillingness of banks to lend does not imply that monetary policy is ineffectual, even in the credit view. An increase in bank reserves through open market purchases will still raise the volume of bank deposits as a result of banks' greater holdings of marketable securities. Accepting the credit view, then, does not require rejecting the money view's implication that monetary policy works through interest rates. Instead, the credit view offers additional methods by which the financial system and monetary policy can affect the economy.

▶ **C H E C K P O I N T**   *Bigmart, a major discount retailer, wants to expand the number of its stores but is concerned about the implications of a recent decline in bank lending in the economy. The CEO of Bigmart believes that the drop in bank lending is the result of a credit crunch, which will be reversed soon by policy actions to loosen regulations on bank lending. Bigmart's treasurer warns against expansion, saying that the decline in bank lending is the result of weak loan demand and reflects a sluggish economy. To support one of the two positions, what information should you assemble? A credit crunch implies greater declines in lending to and investment by bank-dependent borrowers. Thus you could compare data on borrowing by households and small-businesses with data on borrowing by large businesses. In addition, you could compare recent trends in bank lending with other short-term finance, say, in commercial paper markets. If bank lending and commercial paper issues are both declining, the credit crunch explanation is less convincing.* ◀

[†] Anil Kashyap, Jeremy Stein, and David Wilcox, "Monetary Policy and Credit Conditions: Evidence from the Composition of External Finance," **American Economic Review**, 83: 78-98, 1993.

MOVING FROM THEORY TO PRACTICE...

THE WALL STREET JOURNAL OCTOBER 9, 1991

Henry Kaufman on Credit Crunches

Stabilization of the economy through monetary policy works through credit crunches. It does not work through the seamless, incremental fine-tuning that is possible only in textbook economic models. Monetary restraint operates not so much by restraining everyone in an economy a little bit, but by restraining some individuals, firms or institutions a great deal—by strictly limiting or even eliminating access to credit altogether for marginal borrowers.

Those involved in formulating monetary policy are aware of this vulnerability but can do little about it. The reason is that the waves of financial innovation have effectively brought to an end the rigid segmentation of the financial markets that was the primary characteristic of the U.S. system in the early years of the post-World War II period. Innovation has altered market conditions so thoroughly that each successive credit crunch has taken on unique features that defy standard analytic methods. The central bank is never going to know before the event exactly where credit restraint is going to hit, when it is going to hit, how hard it is going to be felt, and when the crunch will pass...

The latest credit crunch, which began in 1990 and which is now [in 1991] subsiding, centered entirely on credit quality deterioration. While high-grade corporate bond yields have stayed well below previous cyclical peaks, and creditworthy companies and households have found credit amply available, junk bond yields have soared and marginal credits have found it difficult to borrow from banks or in the open market on almost any terms.

As this history shows, credit crunches and crises did not vanish with the removal of interest rate ceilings, the dismantling of financial market segmentation, the globalization of credit markets or the extension of broader lending and investing powers to financial institutions. I think that this has come as something of a disappointment to academic economists, who have generally supported financial innovation on the grounds that more open and flexible credit markets would react more smoothly to modest changes in credit conditions and would thereby improve monetary policy control. And it's fair to say that the continuing potential for credit crunches has usually been underestimated by the financial authorities.

ANALYZING THE NEWS...

(a) Henry Kaufman, a highly respected business economist, disagrees with analyses of monetary policy that focus only on its effects on interest-sensitive spending. In those analyses, a reduction in the nominal money supply shifts the AD curve to the left from AD_0 to AD_1, as diagram (a) shows. This leads to a short-run decline in output by raising real interest rates and reducing interest-sensitive spending. In Kaufman's view, bank-dependent borrowers find credit more difficult to obtain. That is, at any open market interest rate, they can obtain less financing for consumption or investment, shifting the AD curve farther to the left, from AD_1 to $AD_{1'}$, in diagram (a). Though not shown, the feedback effects cause money demand to fall from MD_0 to MD_1. Feedback is larger in the credit view than in the money view: The increase in the open market real interest rate is lessened, and the fall in output is magnified.

(b) Kaufman points out that, for a constant monetary policy, a deterioration in firms' net worth reduces their ability to obtain financing at any open market interest rate. As diagram (b) shows, the deteriorating balance sheet positions of many borrowers shift the AD curve to the left from AD_0 to AD_1, shrinking output from Y_0 to Y_1. Though not shown, as a result of falling money demand, the open market real interest rate (on obligations of the Treasury and other high-quality borrowers) falls. Real interest rates charged to risky borrowers increase significantly.

For further thought...

In the approach outlined in Kaufman's article, does a low real interest rate on Treasury securities necessarily imply that the Fed is pursuing an expansionary monetary policy? Why or why not?

Source: Henry Kaufman, "Credit Crunches: The Deregulators Were Wrong," October 9, 1991. Reprinted by permission of *The Wall Street Journal,* ©1991 Dow Jones & Co., Inc. All Rights Reserved Worldwide.

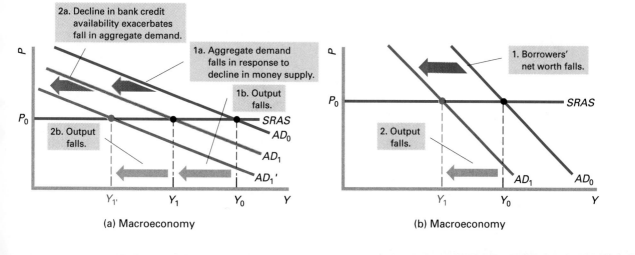

2a. Decline in bank credit availability exacerbates fall in aggregate demand.

1a. Aggregate demand falls in response to decline in money supply.

1b. Output falls.

2b. Output falls.

(a) Macroeconomy

1. Borrowers' net worth falls.

2. Output falls.

(b) Macroeconomy

BOX 27.1

Consider this...

Was There a Credit Crunch during the 1990–1991 Recession?

The National Bureau of Economic Research determined that the economy entered a recession in July 1990. In the spring of 1990, the media reported that banks were cutting back on lending, with adverse consequences. Commerce Secretary Robert Mosbacher argued in June that the credit crunch would harm the economy unless the Federal Reserve intervened.

Some economists claim that a credit crunch deepened the recession. The banking system was under close scrutiny by regulatory authorities because of large losses and the ongoing deposit insurance crisis, which may have contributed to the decline in bank lending in 1990. New bank lending declined significantly more than already existing commitments. As the accompanying chart shows, bank loans to businesses *declined* in the fall of 1990 while commercial paper issues *increased*, a pattern often indicative of a credit crunch under the credit view. In addition, small

manufacturing firms grew more slowly than large ones in 1990. Later in the recession, the demand for credit from all forms of finance fell, suggesting the

weakening of a credit crunch (strictly interpreted).

Source: The Federal Reserve Bank of St. Louis, *U.S. Financial Data,* October 31, 1991.

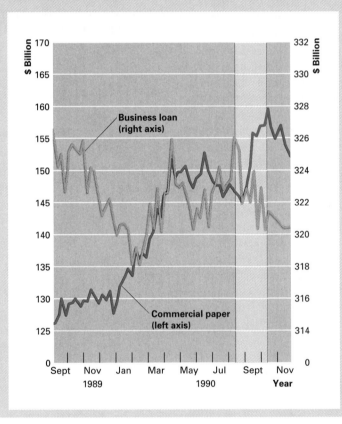

Implications for Public Policy

For a mature economy, such as that of the United States, efficient bank intermediation is essential to economic performance. During the debate over the reform of federal deposit insurance, most commentators agreed that some form of government intervention—a lender-of-last-resort role for the Fed or a modified form of deposit insurance—has to be retained to avoid negative effects on the economy due to troubles in the banking system. There are other implications for regulatory policy. In the past, for example, financial regulation influenced credit crunches in the United States. In particular, binding ceilings on interest rates paid to depositors formerly caused contractions in mortgage lending, consumer finance, and small-business loans. In addition, as bank lending often is localized, credit crunches often have regional or industry dimensions. For example, bank troubles in farming regions reduced the agricultural credit supply in the early 1980s, and bank credit scarcity and output declines hit in New England in the early 1990s. Removing regulatory restrictions on diversification of bank portfolios would reduce the likelihood of such credit crunches.

In the credit view, long-term policy directions for developing economies and emerging market economies center on the need for strong private financial institutions and strong financial markets. The growth of healthy banking institutions specializing in reducing transactions and information costs for small savers and borrowers can help reduce the effective cost of finance for households and young, growing enterprises. As a result, fostering a sound banking system in an economy that previously relied on incomplete, informal, or nonmarket mechanisms for allocating funds can stimulate economic activity toward the full employment level.

Key Terms and Concepts

Credit controls

Credit crunch

Credit view

Financial distress

Financial panics

Liquidity of balance sheet positions

Money view

Summary

1. Transactions costs related to asymmetric information may be high for some borrowers (households and small and medium-sized businesses). As a result, obtaining finance from lenders other than banks is expensive for such borrowers. Nonbank financing is an imperfect substitute for bank loans for many borrowers. Thus shifts in the ability or willingness of banks to make loans can have a significant impact on economic activity. An increase in the ability or willingness of banks to lend shifts the *AD* curve to the right. An independent decrease in bank lending shifts the *AD* curve to the left.

2. Studies of financial panics, credit crunches, and credit controls have documented the link between economic activity and financial institutions' ability or willingness to extend credit. In these episodes,

reductions in bank lending lead to lower output and a lower real interest rate.

3. Economists have documented differential effects of monetary policy on small and large firms. The spending of households and small firms (largely bank-dependent borrowers) is more sensitive to changes in monetary policy than is the spending of large firms.

4. Monetary policy can be analyzed in terms of either the money view or the credit view. In the money view, an expansionary policy by the Fed to increase the nominal money supply shifts the *AD* curve to the right, increasing current output and decreasing the real interest rate. In the credit view, monetary

policy can also shift the *AD* curve in another way. If banks increase deposits in a monetary expansion by increasing their willingness to make loans, the amount that bank-dependent borrowers can borrow and spend increases at any level of the open market real interest rate. The result is a shift of the *AD* curve to the right.

5. Because asymmetric information problems are important, policies that promote efficient financial intermediation should improve economic performance. Healthy financial institutions can reduce transactions and information costs for small savers and borrowers. This lowers the effective cost of finance for households and young, growing enterprises.

Review Questions

1. Why are internal funds a cheaper source of finance for many firms than external funds?

2. Suppose that your research shows that the rate at which firms generate internal funds is closely related to the amount of their new investment spending if they are growing rapidly, but not if they are growing slowly. What economic theory does this result support?

3. What is a financial panic? What happens to bank lending in such a situation?

4. In a financial panic, what would you expect to happen to the difference in interest rates on commercial paper and T-bills? Why?

5. How effective were the Carter administration's credit controls in reducing credit expansion?

6. How did Regulation Q lead to credit crunches before 1980? In answering this question, define *disintermediation*.

7. Compare and contrast the money view and the credit view.

8. What is financial distress?

9. How does the liquidity of balance sheet positions affect the likelihood of financial distress?

10. How does expansionary monetary policy help reduce financial distress?

11. Which view is supported by actual economic data: the money view or the credit view? What are the main pieces of evidence?

12. How did the Carter credit controls cause a recession?

13. You have been assigned to determine whether the economy is experiencing a credit crunch. What patterns in movements in the federal funds rate, the volume of bank lending, and the volume of short-term lending in financial markets would you look for? Why?

14. *Evaluate:* The money and credit views of how monetary policy affects the economy are necessarily inconsistent.

15. *Evaluate:* The money view stresses portfolio allocation decisions of the public, whereas the credit view stresses portfolio allocation decisions of banks.

Analytical Problems

16. Suppose that new tax laws increase the tax rate on retained earnings, that is, the profits of firms that are not distributed to shareholders. How is this change likely to affect the economy?

17. Why is a credit crunch more likely to occur in a recession?

18. If Congress were to tax banks 100% on any "excess profits" (that is, profits above some level), what effect would this tax have?

19. *Evaluate:* Low real interest rates represent expansionary monetary policy, whereas high real interest rates represent contractionary monetary policy.

20. Suppose that new developments in information technology reduce significantly the information-gathering advantage of banks. Discuss the implications for the credit view.

21. In the early 1990s, the banking system in the United States went through a period of restructuring in which banks moved their portfolios into safer assets (T-bills), and bank regulations became more restrictive. According to the credit view, what effect should these changes have had on the macroeconomy?

22. Suppose that the economy goes through a recession in which many people are unable to repay their credit card debt. Banks lose a lot of money and decide to curtail credit card issuance sharply. Is this action likely to be expansionary or contractionary? Why?

23. Suppose that the Fed reduces the nominal money supply. Will the open market real interest rate rise more under the money view or the credit view? Illustrate your answer by using the *AD–AS* diagram for the new Keynesian approach. (For simplicity, you can assume that the *SRAS* curve is horizontal.)

24. Does a reduction in bank lending during a recession necessarily imply that the economy is experiencing a credit crunch? Why or why not? What data would you examine to determine whether there is a credit crunch?

Data Question

25. Look in the *Federal Reserve Bulletin* for data on the amount of bank loans and the amount of commercial paper for the latest six months for which data are available. Is the amount of bank lending rising, falling, or steady? Is the amount of commercial paper issued rising, falling, or steady? Is the economy in a credit crunch? Why or why not?

Appendix: Using the *IS–LM–FE* Model

The *IS–LM–FE* model provides a useful tool for analyzing effects of shifts in bank lending on output and interest rates. We apply it to consider (1) how bank lending affects economic activity and (2) the money view and credit view of how monetary policy affects the economy.

Bank Lending and the *IS* Curve

Let's begin with the saving-investment diagram, as shown in Fig. 27A.1(a). A decline in banks' ability or willingness to lend shifts the investment curve to the left from I_0 to I_1. The saving curve doesn't shift because savers don't change the volume of saving at any real interest rate. As a result, the real interest rate falls from r_0 to r_1 to clear the goods market. Figure 27A.1(b) depicts the accompanying shift in the *IS* curve. A decline in banks' ability or willingness to lend reduces the real interest rate at any level of output in a goods market equilibrium, shifting the *IS* curve to the left from IS_0 to IS_1.

We incorporate this effect into the *IS-LM-FE* diagram, as shown in Fig. 27A.2. The shift in the *IS* curve shifts the economy's equilibrium from E_0 to E_1, reducing the real interest rate and output in the short run.

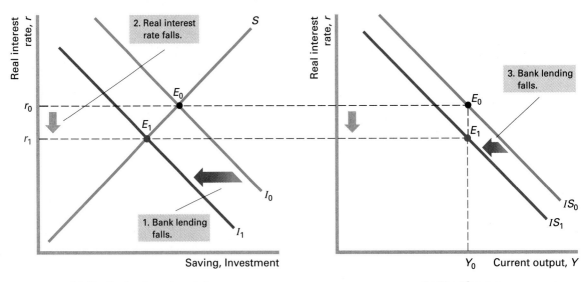

(a) The Saving-Investment diagram   (b) The *IS* curve

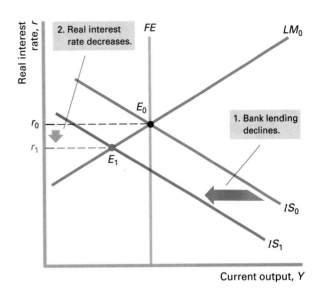

Effects of a Decline in Bank Lending on Output

1. A decline in banks' willingness to lend at given open market interest rates reduces credit supply to bank-dependent borrowers (who face high transactions and information costs of borrowing in financial markets).

2. As a result, spending declines at any open market real interest rate, shifting the *IS* curve to the left from IS_0 to IS_1. Unlike what occurs with a standard monetary contraction by the Fed, a lower real interest rate accompanies the decline in output in the short run.

The Money View and the Credit View

In the money view, changes in the nominal money supply shift the *LM* curve. The *IS* and *LM* curves can intersect at a point to the left of the full employment line in the short run. Let's consider an unexpected monetary expansion, in which the Fed increases the level of bank reserves through open market operations. With a higher level of reserves, banks try to increase deposits by buying securities in financial markets, making loans, or both. When they buy securities, security prices increase, yields fall, and loan rates decline. An increase in the nominal money supply shifts the *LM* curve to the right in the money view. This decreases the real interest rate and increases current output. This expansion occurs because, if nothing else changes, open market interest rates fall to induce households and firms to hold a greater quantity of money in the short run, as Fig. 27A.3(a) shows.

The credit view offers an additional method by which monetary policy affects the economy. In both the money and credit views, when banks expand deposits by making loans, the increase in bank reserves reduces the effective loan interest rate. Because many borrowers can choose between bank or nonbank arrangements, lower bank loan rates tend to cause interest rates in financial markets to fall. An important effect will be to increase the volume of bank lending to and spending by households and small and medium-sized businesses, which depend primarily on banks for finance.

However, unlike the money view, expansionary and contractionary monetary policy also can shift the *IS* curve in the credit view. If banks increase deposits by lowering interest rates on loans, the amounts that bank-dependent borrowers can borrow and spend increase for any real interest rate in financial

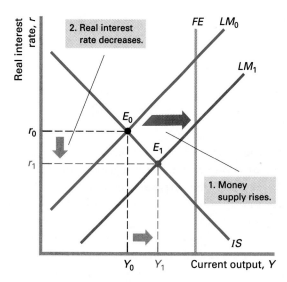

(a) Monetary Expansion in the Money View

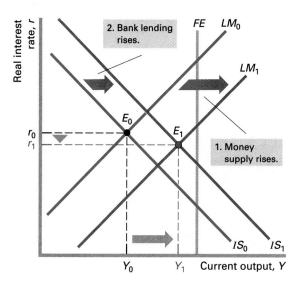

(b) Monetary Expansion in the Credit View

FIGURE 27A.3

Monetary Expansions in the Money and Credit Views

As shown in (a):
1. An increase in the nominal money supply shifts the *LM* curve from LM_0 to LM_1.

2. The real rate of interest decreases from r_0 to r_1 in the short-run equilibrium. The lower rate of interest stimulates spending and increases output from Y_0 to Y_1.

As shown in (b):
1. An increase in the nominal money supply shifts the *LM* curve from LM_0 to LM_1.

2. At the same time, banks' ability to lend affects some bank-dependent borrowers directly, increasing their spending and shifting the *IS* curve from IS_0 to IS_1. The effect on the real open market interest rate is smaller than in the money view.

markets. (Lower interest rates also improve the liquidity of borrowers' balance sheets.) The *IS* curve shifts to the right, as Fig. 27A.3(b) shows. The shifts in both the *LM* and *IS* curves increase output in the short run; the effects on the open market real interest rate are ambiguous and depend on the amounts by which the *IS* and *LM* curves shift. If the *LM* curve shifts more than the *IS* curve, the open market real interest rate will decrease. If the *IS* curve shifts more, the real rate of interest will increase. Figure 27A.3(b) depicts a greater shift in the *LM* curve than in the *IS* curve.

CHAPTER 28

Inflation: Causes and Consequences

Inflation is the rate of change in the general level of prices. It is the topic of stern lectures ("Young man, I remember when the price of a hamburger and a movie was..."). It makes newspaper headlines ("Surprise Increase in Consumer Price Worries the Fed"). President Nixon tried to regulate it. President Ford passed out "Whip Inflation Now" (WIN) buttons. Political analysts say that inflation helped to oust President Carter from the White House. Presidents Reagan, Bush, and Clinton lived with its ups and downs.

So far, we have illustrated the linkage of the financial system and the economy by using simple models. We also have used those models to study how shocks to either the financial system or the economy affect the other sector, and how monetary policy affects the level of economic activity. To examine inflation, we need to focus more explicitly on connections between output and price changes. When we explored the effects of money on economic activity, we considered both the new classical and new Keynesian approaches. Although they frequently offer different predictions about effects of monetary policy on output and real interest rates, both approaches offer similar views on the causes of inflation. Here we extend our model of the financial system and the macroeconomy to an analysis of inflation. This analysis can also help in forecasting inflation for making economic decisions.

In this chapter we address three questions: **Q:** What causes inflation? **Q:** Why are households, businesses, and governments so concerned about inflation? **Q:** How can policymakers reduce the rate of inflation?

Explaining Inflation

Inflation is the rate of change in the price level. For example, when the federal government reports that inflation is 5%, it means that a measure of the general price level has risen by 5%. Three commonly used measures of the price level are the consumer price index (CPI), the producer price index (PPI), and the implicit price deflator for the gross domestic product. To get the most up-to-date information on them, consult U.S. government publications such as the Bureau of Labor Statistics's *Monthly Labor Review* or the Council of Economic Advisers' *Economic Indicators*.

Figure 28.1 shows that consumer prices rose by 950% from 1939 through 1992. In other words, at the end of 1992, you would have needed $1.00 to make a purchase that would have cost less than $0.10 in 1939. Since World War II, inflation has been ever present but uneven. It rose in the 1960s and 1970s and fell in the 1980s and early 1990s. Earlier history reveals that inflation isn't normal. Indeed, throughout U.S. history, prices have fallen in more years than they have risen. In this chapter, we extend the aggregate demand–aggregate supply model of the financial system and the economy developed in Chapter 25 to study the causes and consequences of inflation.

Causes of Inflation

To understand the causes of inflation, we need to begin with the equation of exchange [see Eq. (23.2) in Chapter 23], which connects move-

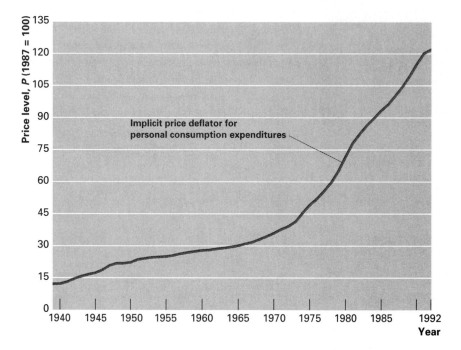

> **FIGURE 28.1**
>
> **Consumer Prices in the United States, 1939–1992**
> Throughout U.S. history, the price level has increased and decreased at various times. During the past several decades, the price level has increased, although at an uneven rate. The data graphed represent the implicit price deflator for personal consumption expenditures.
>
> *Source: Council of Economic Advisers, Economic Report of the President, various issues.*

ments in the nominal money supply M, the price level P, and output Y:

$$MV = PY,$$

where V is the velocity of money. Recall that V is defined as PY/M and that the equation of exchange is an identity.

Because inflation represents the rate of change in prices, we can express the equation of exchange in percentage change form. We link the percentage change in the nominal money supply, $\dot{m}$, the percentage change in velocity, $\dot{v}$, inflation, π, and the percentage change in output, $\dot{y}$, as

$$\dot{m} + \dot{v} = \pi + \dot{y}.$$

Rearranging terms to focus on the determinants of inflation gives

$$\pi = \dot{m} + \dot{v} - \dot{y}. \tag{28.1}$$

Equation (28.1) states that inflation, π, equals the rate of growth of the nominal money supply, $\dot{m}$, plus the rate of growth of velocity, $\dot{v}$, less the rate of growth of real output, $\dot{y}$. In terms of the AD–AS model, if the growth rate of aggregate supply (or the growth rate of output, $\dot{y}$) is less than the growth rate of nominal aggregate demand (or the sum of the growth rate of the nominal money supply, $\dot{m}$, and velocity, $\dot{v}$), inflation must occur.

Short-Term Inflation

To assess potential causes of short-term inflation, we must determine whether the growth rate of nominal aggregate demand can exceed the growth rate of aggregate supply over short periods of time. Equation (28.1) presents three explanations of short-term inflation: (1) Nominal aggregate demand could rise in response to an increase in the nominal money supply. (2) Nominal aggregate demand could rise because of short-run increases in velocity owing to increases in government spending, consumer spending, or investment spending. (3) Even if nominal aggregate demand does not change, the growth rate of aggregate supply could fall.

Response to Monetary Policy. In both the new classical and new Keynesian approaches, the aggregate supply curve slopes upward in the short run, as Fig. 28.2 shows. In the new classical approach, unexpected changes in the price level may cause producers to change their output. Hence the actual level of output can be less than or greater than the level consistent with long-run full employment. In the long run, the aggregate supply curve is vertical at the full employment level of output.

What is the effect of an *unexpected* increase in the money supply on the price level? An unexpected increase in the money supply shifts the AD curve to the right, from AD_0 to AD_1 in Fig. 28.2. As a result, the economy moves from initial equilibrium at E_0 to a new short-run equilibrium at $E_{1'}$, representing both a higher price level and increased output. In other words,

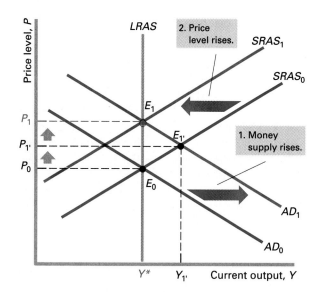

> FIGURE 28.2

Short-Term Inflation Resulting from a Money Supply Change

1. In both the new classical and new Keynesian approaches, an unexpected increase in the nominal money supply shifts the AD curve from AD_0 to AD_1, moving the equilibrium from E_0 to $E_{1'}$.

2. In the short run, actual output, $Y_{1'}$, exceeds full employment output Y^*. As a result, upward pressure on prices pushes the $SRAS$ curve from $SRAS_0$ to $SRAS_1$ to intersect the AD_1 curve at E_1. A one-time increase in the money supply produces inflation in the short run; the price level rises from P_0 to $P_{1'}$. In the long run, only the price level is affected, rising to P_1.

the short-run reaction to an unexpected increase in aggregate demand in the new classical approach is an increase in both output and inflation.

During the process of adjustment, however, the gap between the full employment and actual levels of output puts upward pressure on the price level, shifting the $SRAS$ curve to the left from $SRAS_0$ to $SRAS_1$. Because firms recognize the true price level over time, the economy's long-run equilibrium lies at the intersection of the AD_1 and $LRAS$ curves at E_1. Money is neutral in the long run; only the price level, not the level of output, is affected.

Although some prices are sticky in the short run in the new Keynesian approach, the process of price adjustment to an output change is similar to that in the new classical model. However, the adjustment is slower. From a full employment equilibrium at E_0, an unexpected increase in the nominal money supply shifts the AD curve to the right, from AD_0 to AD_1. In the short run, output increases to $Y_{1'}$ at $E_{1'}$. However, the higher aggregate demand puts upward pressure on wages and prices, shifting the $SRAS$ curve gradually upward from $SRAS_0$ to $SRAS_1$. The economy returns to full employment equilibrium at E_1, with output Y^* and a higher price level $P_1 > P_0$. Hence in the new Keynesian approach, as in the new classical approach, an unexpected increase in aggregate demand causes output to increase and prices to rise in the short run.

Response to Other Changes in Aggregate Demand. The aggregate demand curve describes the combinations of the price and output levels at which the goods and asset markets are in equilibrium. Recall that changes in the nominal money supply can shift the aggregate demand curve and affect the price level. What about factors that affect desired saving and investment, such as a change in government spending, consumer spending, or investment spending?

Let's consider a one-time unexpected increase in government spending on roads and bridges, for example. (Shifts in consumer or investment spending have similar effects.) As was the case for a one-time increase in the money supply, in the short run, the AD curve shifts to the right, as it did in Fig. 28.2. This shift increases both output and the price level. In both approaches, inflation results in the short run, and the excess of actual output over full employment output puts upward pressure only on prices in the long run. Hence increases in government spending (and consumer spending or investment spending) raise output and the price level in the short run. Such changes increase only the price level in the long run, leaving output unchanged.

Response to Supply Shocks. Shifts in the short-run aggregate supply curve due to supply shocks, such as changes in raw materials' prices or workers' wage demands, can cause short-term inflation in both approaches, as Fig. 28.3 shows. Therefore an adverse supply shock, such as a one-time increase in the price of oil, raises input prices and shifts the short-run aggregate supply curve from $SRAS_0$ to $SRAS_1$. If the money supply and government taxes and spending don't change, the aggregate demand curve remains at AD_0. As a result, the economy's equilibrium shifts from E_0 to E_1. The price level has risen from P_0 to P_1, resulting in inflation in the short run.

At E_1, however, output Y_1 is below the full employment level of output, Y^*. Over time, prices fall, and the $SRAS$ curve shifts back down from

> ## FIGURE 28.3

Short-Run Inflation from an Oil Price Increase

1. An increase in the price of oil shifts the short-run aggregate supply curve from $SRAS_0$ to $SRAS_1$.

2. The price level rises from P_0 to P_1, causing inflation in the short run.

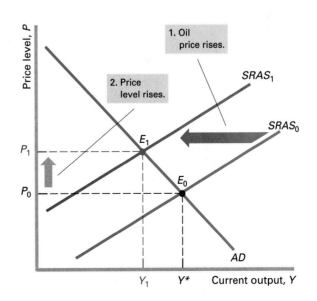

$SRAS_1$ to $SRAS_0$. The economy eventually returns to equilibrium at E_0. Thus supply shocks can affect the price level in the short run, leading to short-term inflation, but they do not cause long-term inflation.

Long-Term Inflation

One-time increases in the money supply, short-run increases in nominal aggregate demand, or supply shocks can increase the price level in the short run, causing inflation. However, of greater concern are repeated increases in the price level over a long period of time. We can use Eq. (28.1) to determine sources of long-term inflation. Long-term inflation arises whenever the growth rate of nominal aggregate demand exceeds the growth rate of aggregate supply over sustained periods of time.

One-time changes in government spending or taxes cannot by themselves produce long-term inflation. Such inflation would have to result from persistent increases in government spending or decreases in taxes. Government spending and the size of government are limited by both the obvious consideration that government spending cannot exceed the economy's total production (GDP) and practical limitations on spending imposed by the political process. These same constraints apply to tax changes. If the money supply is unchanged, expansionary fiscal policy alone cannot produce inflation for a long period of time. Similarly, whereas one-time adverse supply shocks can increase the price level in the short run, a one-time supply shock alone can't lead to prolonged inflation.

In both the new classical and new Keynesian views of the macroeconomy, the cause of sustained inflation is sustained growth in the nominal money supply at a rate faster than the growth rate of velocity and the growth rate of output. Figure 28.4 illustrates the process. Suppose that households and businesses expect the growth rates of velocity and output to be 0% and the money supply to increase steadily by 5% each year.

Let's begin with the new classical approach. From initial equilibrium at E_0, the AD curve shifts to the right as the nominal money supply increases. The expected money supply growth leads to upward revisions of the expected price level from P_0 to P_1. (Recall that anticipated changes in the money supply lead households and businesses to expect a higher price level.) The $SRAS$ curve shifts upward to E_1 (quickly, in the new classical approach). As the nominal money supply increases again, the AD curve shifts to the right from AD_1 to AD_2. The process then repeats, as the $SRAS$ curve shifts upward from $SRAS_1$ to $SRAS_2$ to reflect the rise in the expected price level. At the economy's new equilibrium, E_2, the price level has risen to P_2. Thus sustained increases in the price level over the long run can be traced to persistent increases in the nominal money supply.

In the new Keynesian approach, sustained increases in the nominal money supply also shift the aggregate demand curve to the right, from AD_0 to AD_1. The $SRAS$ shifts upward gradually from $SRAS_0$ to $SRAS_1$. Output initially rises from Y^* to Y' until the $SRAS$ curve is at $SRAS_1$, as households and

> FIGURE 28.4

Persistent Money Supply Growth and Inflation
Money is neutral in the long run. Persistent growth of the money supply leads to inflation with no long-term increase in real output.

1. Increases in the nominal money supply shift the aggregate demand curve from AD_0 to AD_1 and then from AD_1 to AD_2.

2. Increases in the expected price level as a result of the increase in the money supply shift the $SRAS$ curve upward. In both the new classical and new Keynesian approaches, the shift is from $SRAS_0$ to $SRAS_1$ (as the expected price level increases from P_0 to P_1) and then from $SRAS_1$ to $SRAS_2$ (as the expected price level increases from P_1 to P_2).

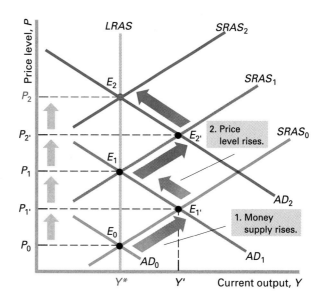

businesses change their expectations of the price level. At the new equilibrium E_1, the price level has risen to P_1, but output remains at its initial level, Y^*. As the money supply increases again, the AD curve shifts farther to the right, from AD_1 to AD_2. Before prices adjust, output rises from Y^* to Y'. As the expected price level rises from P_1 to P_2, the $SRAS$ curve shifts upward from $SRAS_1$ to $SRAS_2$. At the new equilibrium E_2, output is Y^* and the price level is P_2.

Hence in both the new classical and new Keynesian approaches, money is neutral in the long run. In other words, sustained growth in the money supply doesn't affect real output in the long run but does lead to sustained growth in the price level, or inflation. As Fig. 28.1 shows, the U.S. economy has experienced long-term inflation since World War II. The reason is that, as our analysis of long-term inflation reveals, the rate of growth of the nominal money supply has been "too fast" relative to the rates of growth of velocity and output. The statement that long-term inflation is principally a monetary phenomenon also is consistent with evidence from other countries. During the 1980s, countries with high average rates of inflation (such as Argentina and Israel) experienced rapid average rates of growth of the nominal money supply. Countries with low average rates of inflation experienced slow average rates of growth of the nominal money supply.

▶ C H E C K P O I N T *Do government budget deficits cause inflation?* In the short run, government budget deficits can raise aggregate demand and thus [according to Eq. (28.1)] lead to short-term inflation. For government budget deficits to be inflationary in the long run, the Fed must be expanding the monetary base to acquire government bonds. More rapid growth of the monetary base raises the growth rate of nominal money supply, leading to inflation if nothing else changes. ◀

Costs of Inflation

Widely voiced concerns by households, businesses, and policy-makers about inflation suggest that there must be some costs to the economy from inflation. To identify these costs, let's examine two situations: (1) *expected inflation*, which households and businesses take into account when conducting financial transactions; and (2) *unexpected inflation*, which can cause households and businesses to redistribute funds.

Expected Inflation

Expected inflation can affect the allocation of the economy's resources in three ways. First, inflation places a tax on money balances when those balances pay less than the market rate of interest. This tax is a loss in purchasing power. For example, if you held $100 in currency in 1992 when the rate of inflation was about 3%, you lost $3 of purchasing power over the year. By imposing a tax on money balances, inflation reduces the public's demand for real money balances. One cost of this tax, known as **shoe leather costs,** is the cost to consumers and businesses of making more trips to the bank to avoid holding significant amounts of currency or of shifting funds from interest-bearing assets into money. When the public's shoe leather costs exceed the government's revenue gain from the inflation tax, inflation generates an "excess burden," or social loss. Stanley Fischer of M.I.T. has estimated that the annual excess burden in the United States of a modest inflation rate of 5% is approximately 0.3% of GDP, or about $18 billion in 1992 dollars.[†]

A second cost of expected inflation arises because the U.S. tax system is defined in nominal terms. This definition means that the individual income tax is progressive and not fully indexed against inflation. As a result, higher nominal incomes (for constant real incomes) can lead to a higher tax burden relative to income. This problem, called *bracket creep*, was particularly severe in the 1970s, when the individual income tax was more progressive than it is in the early 1990s. The failure of the tax code to adjust values of inventories and the value of depreciation allowances for inflation also raises corporate tax burdens.

Expected inflation also can distort financial decisions because lenders pay taxes on nominal rather than real returns. Suppose that expected inflation is 4% and that an individual faces a marginal tax rate of 30%. A nominal interest rate of 8% yields the individual a real after-tax return of (1 − 0.30)(8%) − 4% = 1.6%. Suppose that the expected inflation rate rises to 8% and that the nominal interest rate rises by the same amount to 12%. The real

---

[†] See Stanley Fischer, "Towards an Understanding of the Costs of Inflation: II," in K. Brunner and A. Meltzer, eds., *Carnegie Rochester Conference Series on Public Policy*, 15, 1981.

after-tax return falls to $(1 - 0.30)(12\%) - 8\% = 0.4\%$. Hence nominal interest rates would have to increase by more than the change in inflation $(8\% - 4\%)$ to maintain the real return of 1.6%. Conversely, borrowers such as corporations and individual home buyers benefit from expected inflation, because borrowers deduct nominal interest payments (*not* real interest payments) in calculating their income tax liabilities. Changes in expected inflation can change the real after-tax cost of borrowing. For example, with high expected inflation, corporations find debt financing more attractive, because nominal interest payments are deductible. Households find housing investment more attractive relative to stocks, because home mortgage interest is deductible for tax purposes.

A third cost of expected inflation in the new Keynesian approach arises from so-called **menu costs,** or costs to firms of changing prices (reprinting price lists, informing customers, and so on). Faced with different menu costs, not all firms change prices at the same time; that is, price changes brought on by inflation are not synchronized throughout the economy. Even so, expected inflation can change relative prices in the short run and affect the allocation of the economy's resources.

Unexpected Inflation

Many contracts in labor, goods, and financial markets are written in nominal terms, cover a substantial period of time, and take expected inflation into account. However, unexpected inflation, or the difference between actual and expected inflation, redistributes wealth. For example, suppose that a borrower and lender expect no inflation and agree to a one-year, $1000 loan at 4% interest. Regardless of the inflation rate for the year, the lender receives $(\$1000)(1.04) = \$1040$ from the borrower at the end of the year. If the actual rate of inflation is 7%, the lender's real return (the return in terms of purchasing power) is −3%. Conversely, the borrower's real interest rate is −3%. The unexpected inflation of 7% $(7\% - 0\%)$ effectively transferred $70 of real purchasing power from the lender to the borrower. Another example of this redistribution occurs when unexpected inflation reduces real wages for employees with nominal wage contracts.

The implications of unexpected inflation are more difficult to gauge than those of expected inflation for the macroeconomy. *Losses* to some parties are matched by *gains* to others. Nonetheless, for individuals that are risk-averse, the possibility of redistribution can distort behavior. For example, amounts that businesses or households spend on forecasting inflation in order to protect themselves against unfavorable redistributions represent a cost of unexpected inflation.

▶ C H E C K P O I N T *Consider four people: Ms. A borrowed money at a fixed nominal interest rate; Mr. B lent money at a fixed nominal interest rate; Ms. C borrowed money at a variable interest rate (indexed for inflation);*

and Mr. D lent money at a variable interest rate. If inflation rises, who loses the most? Who gains the most? Lenders and borrowers incorporate expected inflation into the agreed-upon interest rate. When the interest rate is fixed, additional (unexpected) inflation redistributes purchasing power from lenders to borrowers: Mr. B loses the most, and Ms. A gains the most. ◄

Inflation Uncertainty

Uncertainty about the rate of inflation can introduce the most serious costs of inflation. In a market economy, households and businesses look to prices of goods and assets as signals for resource allocation. For example, an increase in the price of beef relative to chicken encourages farmers to produce more beef and individuals to consume more chicken. An increase in stock market prices relative to the general level of prices is a signal that businesses' prospects are good and that there are opportunities for profitable investment. *Relative prices*, not individual prices, provide these signals. When inflation fluctuates significantly, relative prices may change in response to general price-level changes, distorting the valuable signals provided by markets. Variations of relative prices because of uncertain inflation cause households and businesses to waste resources investigating price differences.

An extreme case of uncertain inflation occurs in a **hyperinflation,** in which the rate of inflation is hundreds or thousands or more percentage points per year for a significant period of time. The costs of hyperinflation are extremely high. Households and businesses must minimize currency holdings, and firms must pay employees frequently. Employees must spend money quickly or convert it to more stable foreign currencies before prices increase further.

A classic example of hyperinflation occurred in Germany after World War I. A burst of money creation by the government ignited inflation, increasing the price level by a factor of more than 10 billion between August 1922 and November 1923. For example, if a candy bar cost the equivalent of 5 cents in August 1922, this increase in the price level would have raised its cost to more than $500,000,000 by November 1923. Our analysis of money demand tells us that, in such an extreme case, the demand for real money balances should plummet. In Germany that proved to be the case: By October 1923, real money balances had shrunk to only about 3% of their August 1922 value. The German hyperinflation ended suddenly in late 1923, with a strong government commitment to stop the printing presses. With a significant decline in growth of the money supply, hyperinflation ended.

Confusing signals from prices are particularly problematic during hyperinflation. With overall prices rising very rapidly, merchants change prices as often as possible. Prices therefore quickly fail to indicate value or direct resource allocation. The government's tax-collecting ability diminishes significantly during hyperinflation. Because tax bills typically are fixed in nominal terms, households and businesses have a major incentive to delay payment of taxes in order to reduce their real tax burdens.

Why Policymakers Allow Inflation to Occur

Despite the fact that inflation can generate tremendous costs for the economy, in order to achieve other goals (such as full employment of the economy's resources), governments sometimes pursue inflationary monetary policies. In particular, measures related to current output (such as the levels of GDP, household incomes, and the unemployment rate) capture the attention of voters and public officials alike. Indeed, movements in current output can greatly influence presidential elections, creating a temptation to increase aggregate demand in the short run. Ray Fair of Yale University has noted that significant GDP growth and a falling unemployment rate increased the reelection chances of the incumbent president and other candidates of the same party.

Full Employment Targets and Inflationary Bias

Q: Why are households, businesses, and governments so concerned about inflation?

A: Both expected and unexpected inflation have economic costs. Costs of expected inflation include shoe leather costs and distortions because the tax system is defined in nominal terms. Costs of unexpected inflation include unanticipated redistributions of economic resources, wasted resources for protection against inflation, and reductions in the value of prices as signals for resource allocation in the economy.

Low inflation may be desirable, but it also brings significant social costs, in terms of lost output and jobs when the economy isn't operating at or near full capacity. Angry voters pressure elected officials to do something when recessions idle factories and swell unemployment lines.

The Full Employment Act of 1946 and the Humphrey-Hawkins Act of 1978 committed the federal government to promoting full employment and a stable price level. Particularly during the 1960s and 1970s, U.S. policymakers often pressed for full employment even at the expense of inflation. Two types of inflationary pressures resulted: **cost-push inflation,** which results from workers' pressure for higher wages; and **demand-pull inflation,** which results from policymakers' attempts to increase aggregate demand for current output above the full employment level.

Cost-Push Inflation. Cost-push inflationary pressures begin when workers push for higher wages either to raise their real wages (wages adjusted for changes in purchasing power) or to "catch up" to current or expected future inflation. As Fig. 28.5 shows, when the economy starts at full employment at E_0, an increase in wages raises production costs and the expected price level, shifting the $SRAS$ curve upward from $SRAS_0$ to $SRAS_1$. With no change in monetary policy, short-run equilibrium occurs at the intersection of the AD_0 and $SRAS_1$ curves, at $E_{1'}$, with a drop in output from Y^* to Y' (and more unemployment) and a rise in the price level from P_0 to $P_{1'}$. Without any other government action over time, wages and prices would fall in response to the slack economy, and the economy's equilibrium would return to E_0.

However, if policymakers were committed to maintaining the full employment level of output even in the short run, expansionary policy would follow wage increases. This effect would be to push the aggregate demand curve to the right from AD_0 to AD_1, with the short-run equilibrium at E_1 and a higher price level at P_1 rather than at $P_{1'}$. If this process continues (that is, if workers again push for higher wages and policymakers increase the money

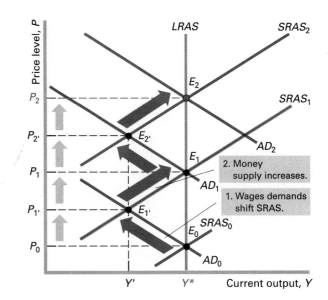

> **FIGURE 28.5**

Cost-Push Inflation
If policymakers expand the money supply to accommodate workers' demands for higher wages for a significant period of time, cost-push inflation will result.

1. Cost-push inflation can occur in the short run if workers push for higher wages so that the SRAS curve shifts from $SRAS_0$ to $SRAS_1$. In the short run, output falls from Y^* to Y'.

2. In the long run, cost-push inflation can occur only if the Fed pursues an inflationary policy (shifting the aggregate demand curve to the right from AD_0 to AD_1) to avoid output and job losses. These effects occur in both the new classical and new Keynesian approaches.

supply), sustained inflation can occur. Hence, if a second wage push shifts the *SRAS* curve to the left from $SRAS_1$ to $SRAS_2$ and policymakers' actions shift the *AD* curve from AD_1 to AD_2, the price level eventually rises from P_1 to P_2, although output remains at Y^*. At each point, higher wages lead to lost output and jobs; policymakers then pursue an *accommodating policy*, stimulating aggregate demand to restore output and jobs but at the cost of greater inflation. A sustained cost-push inflation is a monetary phenomenon. Without inflationary responses in terms of monetary policy actions, cost-push inflation could not persist in the long run.

> ***Demand-Pull Inflation.*** Another source of inflationary pressure stems directly from policymakers' attempts to keep the economy operating at a level greater than its long-run full employment level.[†] Full unemployment doesn't necessarily mean a 0% rate of unemployment. The **natural rate of unemployment** is the rate of unemployment that exists when the economy produces the full employment level of output. Even at the full employment level of output, unemployment exists because of (1) *structural unemployment* (a mismatch between the skills or location of workers and job requirements) or (2) *frictional unemployment* (searches by workers and firms for suitable matches of workers to jobs).

Let's see what happens if policymakers try to keep the rate of unemployment below the natural rate of unemployment for a sustained period of

---

[†] The Appendix extends the analysis to consider a possible policy trade-off between inflation and the unemployment rate.

> FIGURE 28.6

Demand-Pull Inflation
If policymakers attempt to increase current output above the full employment level Y^* for a significant period of time, demand-pull inflation will result.

1. When expansionary monetary policy shifts the aggregate demand curve from AD_0 to AD_1, output is temporarily above the full employment level at Y'.

2. The higher expected price level shifts the $SRAS$ curve upward so that, in the long run, only the price level and not the output level is affected. The longer policymakers attempt to increase output above the full employment level (or, equivalently, to reduce the unemployment rate below the natural rate), the greater the cumulative inflation.

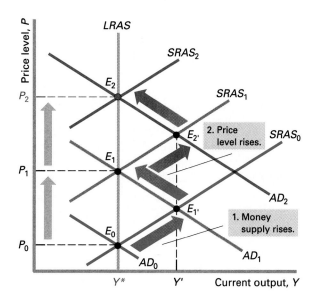

time. Suppose, as in Fig. 28.6, that the economy starts at full employment equilibrium E_0. To increase output above the full employment level to Y', policymakers unexpectedly expand the money supply to shift the aggregate demand curve to the right, from AD_0 to AD_1. As a result, output rises in the short run in both the new classical and new Keynesian approaches, and the economy's equilibrium shifts from E_0 to $E_{1'}$. As prices adjust, however, the $SRAS$ curve shifts upward from $SRAS_0$ to $SRAS_1$, and output returns to the full-employment level, Y^*, with the price level increasing from P_0 to P_1. The new equilibrium occurs at the intersection of the AD_1 and $SRAS_1$ curves, at E_1. (The expansion of output above the full employment level lasts longer in the new Keynesian approach than in the new classical approach because the price adjustment is gradual.)

  If the process continues, the AD curve shifts to the right, from AD_1 to AD_2, raising output to Y' in the short run (at $E_{2'}$). Over time, the $SRAS$ curve shifts upward from $SRAS_1$ to $SRAS_2$, placing the economy at full employment equilibrium E_2, with a higher price level at P_2. Because the long-run aggregate supply curve is vertical, policymakers cannot permanently maintain the unemployment rate below the natural rate or, equivalently, permanently maintain a level of output greater than the full employment level.

  Both cost-push and demand-pull inflation are associated with sustained increases in the price level. Cost-push inflation is associated with periodic episodes of unemployment higher than the natural rate (caused by attempts to keep real wages "too high"). Demand-pull inflation is associated with attempts to keep the unemployment rate below the natural rate. Recognizing these differences in the real world can be difficult, however.

Economists do not agree on how to measure the natural rate of unemployment. In addition, cost-push inflation can occur as a "catch up" response to demand-pull inflation.

Costs of Reducing Inflation

When policymakers are more concerned with maintaining high levels of output and employment growth than with maintaining a low inflation rate, they may exert an inflationary bias on monetary policy. (Another possibility—not considered here—is that the Fed may incorrectly estimate the growth rate of velocity over long periods of time, allowing an inflationary money supply growth.) Suppose that, whatever the cause, policymakers decide at some point that the economy's sustained inflation rate is too high. How to achieve **disinflation** (a decline in the long-run rate of inflation) and whether there are costs to the economy from reducing inflation are viewed differently in the new classical and new Keynesian approaches.

New Classical Approach: Reducing Inflation Cold Turkey

A hallmark of the new classical approach is that wages and prices adjust quickly to changes in expectations. Hence the new classical suggestion, illustrated in Fig. 28.7, for reducing the rate of inflation is to lower expectations about future money growth and inflation **cold turkey,** that is, all at once.

For example, suppose that, because of ongoing inflation, the public expects Fed actions to shift the AD curve from AD_0 to AD_1. As the expected price level increases, the short-run aggregate supply curve shifts from $SRAS_0$ to $SRAS_1$. Hence, with a built-in expected rate of inflation, the economy's equilibrium moves from E_0 to E_1.

Figure 28.7 shows that, in the cold turkey approach, when the Fed announces that it will reduce the rate of money supply growth to eliminate inflation, the $SRAS$ curve shifts back to $SRAS_0$. Because money supply growth doesn't continue, the AD curve shifts back to AD_0. Hence, because the policy shift is expected, the economy's equilibrium lies at E_0. Wages and prices adjust rapidly in the new classical approach, so inflation falls with little or no loss in output. Accordingly, the costs of cold turkey disinflation in terms of lost output and jobs are small.

Thomas Sargent of Stanford University has stressed the importance of changing expectations in order to reduce inflation while keeping costs low in terms of lost output and jobs.[†] He focused on hyperinflation in four European countries during the period between World War I and World War II, including Germany, which we discussed earlier. Financing rising govern-

---

[†] Thomas J. Sargent, "The Ends of Four Big Inflations," in R.E. Hall, ed., *Inflation: Causes and Effects*, Chicago: University of Chicago Press, 1991.

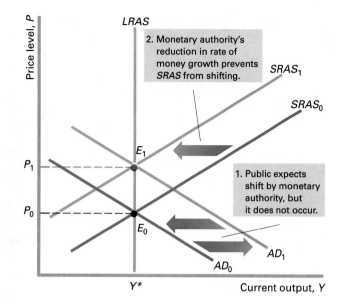

> FIGURE 28.7

**New Classical Suggestion:
Cold Turkey Disinflation**
When the public expects inflation, the economy's equilibrium
moves from E_0 to E_1.

1. In cold turkey disinflation, the
Fed announces that it will
reduce the rate of money growth
to eliminate inflation; the *AD*
curve does not shift from AD_0 to
AD_1.

2. The price level adjusts rapidly
to this policy change, shifting
the *SRAS* curve from $SRAS_1$ to
$SRAS_0$. Equilibrium remains at
E_0, and disinflation occurs with
no loss in output.

ment budget deficits with money creation ignited rapid inflation. In each case
announcements of budget reforms and cessation of inflationary increases in
the domestic money supply reduced inflation dramatically. In those cases
output losses were small, lending support to the new classical view that the
costs of disinflation will be significantly less for expected reductions in money
growth than for unexpected reductions.

New Keynesian Approach: Reducing Inflation Gradually

The new classical approach concludes that costs of the cold turkey
approach are small, owing to the rapid adjustment of wages and prices to
changes in expectations. Ironically, this adjustment is potentially the greatest
in hyperinflationary situations, such as those studied by Sargent. During
hyperinflation, contracts tend to be indexed to changes in the price level, and
households and businesses pay great attention to inflation and changes in
inflation. Can the gains of the cold turkey approach be realized in reducing
moderate rates of inflation, such as those now being experienced in the
United States, Japan, and European countries? In countries with relatively
low rates of inflation, there is some nominal price stickiness. New Keynesian
economists argue that long-term nominal contracts and the costs of changing
prices slow the adjustment of the price level to changes in expectations. Even
when households and businesses have rational expectations, not all prices
adjust immediately to changes in expectations about future inflation.

Let's reconsider cold turkey disinflation in terms of the new
Keynesian approach. Suppose that the economy is at full employment with
the inflation rate and growth rate of the nominal money supply at 10%. In

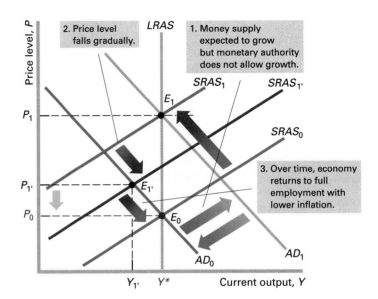

> FIGURE 28.8

New Keynesian Suggestion: Gradual Disinflation
With a built-in expected rate of inflation, the economy's equilibrium will shift from E_0 to E_1.

1. In cold turkey disinflation, the Fed announces that the growth rate of the nominal money supply will be reduced to lower inflation; the AD curve does not shift from AD_0 to AD_1.

2. The price level falls gradually in the short run from $SRAS_1$ to $SRAS_{1'}$.

3. Instead of shifting to E_1, the economy shifts to $E_{1'}$, with a significant output loss. Only gradually will the economy return to full employment E_0 with a lower rate of inflation.

Labels within figure:
- Price level, P
- 2. Price level falls gradually.
- LRAS
- 1. Money supply expected to grow but monetary authority does not allow growth.
- $SRAS_1$
- $SRAS_{1'}$
- E_1
- P_1
- $SRAS_0$
- $P_{1'}$ $E_{1'}$
- 3. Over time, economy returns to full employment with lower inflation.
- P_0 E_0
- AD_0
- AD_1
- $Y_{1'}$ Y^* Current output, Y

Fig. 28.8, from initial equilibrium at E_0, the aggregate demand curve is expected to shift from AD_0 to AD_1, with the $SRAS$ curve shifting from $SRAS_0$ to $SRAS_1$. Hence the public expects the new equilibrium to lie at E_1, with output Y^* and a higher price level P_1. Now, suppose that the Fed decides that the rate of inflation is too high and announces that it will reduce money growth to zero to reduce the long-run inflation rate to zero. (For simplicity, we assume that long-run rates of output and velocity growth are zero.) As a result, instead of the aggregate demand curve shifting to AD_1, consistent with expected money growth of 10% per year, it remains at AD_0. In the short run, the $SRAS$ curve shifts to $SRAS_{1'}$ because in the new Keynesian view not all prices can change instantly. As a result, output falls. Disinflation (the price level is $P_{1'}$, lower than P_1) is accompanied by a loss of current output and jobs. Only over time does the economy return to full employment equilibrium at E_0.

Because of these costs, new Keynesian economists support a policy of **gradualism,** or slowly and steadily reducing the rate of growth of the money supply so that the inflation rate can adjust slowly, with smaller losses of output and jobs. These economists concede that such a process of disinflation is slower than the cold turkey approach but maintain that overall costs to the economy are smaller.

Central Bank Credibility

We have shown that, in order to achieve disinflation at a low cost, the public's expectation of the inflation rate must be reduced. This will shift the $SRAS$ curve down so that lower inflation is not "paid for" by lost output and jobs. However, merely announcing a disinflationary policy may not be enough to change the public's expectations. An additional, crucial factor is the **central bank credibility:** For households and businesses to respond to an announced "commitment" to reducing inflation, the public must believe that the central bank will in fact carry out its disinflationary promises. The public might not believe the central bank because disinflation entails economic costs—lost output and jobs—which are likely to be politically unpopular. If the public believes that policymakers will back off, inflationary expectations will change very slowly until the central bank convinces the public of its credibility. The Other times, other places box illustrates the role of credibility in reducing inflation in the United States and Japan.

Strategies for Building Credibility

We can illustrate the importance of central bank credibility by considering the strategies pursued by the Fed and the public. Let's assume that both groups pursue the strategies that they perceive will give them the greatest possible benefits. Consider how the Fed and the public respond to each other's actions.

Other times, other places...
Central Bank Credibility in the United States and Japan

Since World War II, the U.S. Federal Reserve System frequently stated an anti-inflation policy. During the second half of the 1970s, when inflation rose steadily, the credibility of the Fed's promise to fight inflation eroded. In October 1979, the Fed announced that it would focus on targets for the growth rates of monetary aggregates and that target ranges would be reduced significantly to reduce inflation.

The Fed experienced difficulty in achieving its targets, owing in part to deregulation and the wave of financial innovation in the early 1980s. The Fed's announced intention to combat inflation indeed succeeded over time. Inflation fell from double-digit levels in 1979 to about 4% per year by 1982 and has remained relatively low since

then. In part because of the Fed's lack of credibility at that time, disinflation was not without cost, however. In response to the contractionary monetary policy initiated in late 1979, output and employment declined and real interest rates increased. The economy experienced a severe recession in 1981 and 1982.

Because Japan relied wholly on imported oil, the oil shocks of 1973 and 1974 led to wholesale price inflation of more than 30% by 1974. In 1975, the Bank of Japan (the Japanese central bank) announced that it would target the growth rate of the Japanese $M2$ in order to reduce inflation. The consistency with which the Bank of Japan fulfilled its promises quickly bolstered its credibility. The central bank did indeed succeed in

reducing inflation in the 1980s and did so without large losses in output and employment.

What do these episodes tell us? The experiences of the United States and Japan illustrate that a prolonged effort by the central bank to reduce the rate of growth of the nominal money supply will reduce inflation. The importance of credibility in determining the costs of disinflation is striking. On the one hand, the U.S. Federal Reserve System, with low initial credibility and a poor performance in hitting its announced money growth targets, achieved disinflation only after a recession and significant unemployment. On the other hand, the highly credible Bank of Japan managed to reduce inflation with little direct output loss.

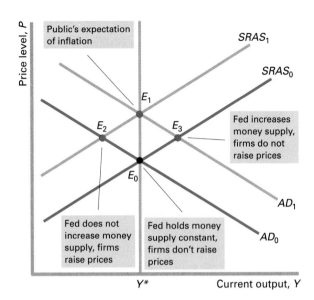

►FIGURE 28.9

Strategies for Changing the Economy's Equilibrium
From initial full employment equilibrium at E_0, the public expects that money supply growth and the resulting increase in inflation will lead to a new equilibrium at E_1. If the Fed agrees to hold the nominal money supply constant and firms agree not to raise prices, the economy can remain at E_0, with full employment and no additional inflation. If the Fed doesn't increase the money supply, but firms raise prices, output falls, as at E_2. If the Fed unexpectedly increases the nominal money supply and firms do not raise prices, output rises, as at E_3.

We use Fig. 28.9 and assume that the economy is at full employment equilibrium E_0, that the growth rate of real output is 0%, and that the nominal money supply and the price level are both growing at 5% each year. Accordingly, next year the public expects the economy's equilibrium to be at E_1.

The Federal Reserve Board chairman wants a 0% inflation rate but doesn't want output to fall. Accordingly, the chairman offers a bargain to firms in an interview with *The Wall Street Journal*, the gist of which is "You businessmen don't like inflation, and the Fed doesn't either. If you don't raise prices this year, the Fed won't increase the money supply." This proposition offers some attractive benefits: If neither the nominal money supply, M, nor the price level, P, shifts, the aggregate demand curve won't shift. By announcing the agreement in *The Wall Street Journal*, the Fed hopes that the short-run aggregate supply curve will not shift either. The economy will remain in equilibrium at E_0, and the Fed and businesses will avoid inflation with no loss of output.

To obtain cooperation from firms, the Fed chairman adds a threat to the offer: "If your firms increase prices anyway, the Fed will stick by its promise of no money supply growth." That would be unattractive to the public. If the nominal money supply didn't increase, but prices did, the economy would come to equilibrium at E_2, making everyone worse off. Inflation would result, firms would lose output and profits, and workers would lose jobs. The public doesn't like inflation, and firms don't like output losses. Although the Fed's anti-inflation stance is clear, political pressures may be exerted on the Fed if its actions are perceived to have caused a recession.

(a) Payoffs for the Economy

		Firms	
		Raise prices	Don't raise prices
Fed	Increase the money supply	$Y = Y^*$ (E_1) Inflation = 5%	$Y > Y^*$ (E_3) Inflation < 5%
	Don't increase the money supply	$Y < Y^*$ (E_2) Inflation < 5%	$Y = Y^*$ (E_0) Inflation = 0%

(b) Payoffs to Players

		Firms	
		Raise prices	Don't raise prices
Fed	Increase the money supply	E_1 Fed | Firms Status | Status quo | quo	E_3 Fed | Firms Better than | Worse than status quo | status quo
	Don't increase the money supply	E_2 Fed | Firms Worse than | Worse than status quo | status quo	E_0 Fed | Firms Better than | Better than status quo | status quo

Payoffs from Alternative Actions

a. The Fed and firms would like the economy to achieve equilibrium at E_0.

b. Payoffs for the economy are the greatest at E_0. Economic equilibrium can remain at E_0 (the status quo) if firms believe that the Fed's concern with unemployment is much greater than its concern with inflation.

Let's examine the payoffs for the economy from alternative actions of the Fed and firms. For simplicity, each side has two strategies: Firms can raise prices or not raise prices; the Fed can increase the nominal money supply or not increase the nominal money supply. Figure 28.10(a) represents the payoffs for the economy in each case. The top left square represents the initial situation, with the economy at full employment and the nominal money supply and the price level expected to grow at a rate of 5% per year. If the Fed and firms accept the bargain not to raise the money supply and prices (bottom right square), the economy remains at full employment and inflation falls to zero. If firms increase prices and the Fed follows through on its threat to leave the nominal money supply unchanged (bottom left square), inflation (though less than 5%) results, but the economy enters a recession. If firms keep their promise not to raise prices but the Fed increases the money supply anyway (top right square), short-term expansion results.

These four outcomes are the potential payoffs for the economy, but recall our assumption that the Fed and firms pursue the strategy that will give each the greatest payoff. Therefore we must consider the payoffs presented in Fig. 28.10(b). The top left square represents the status quo at which current output is at full employment.

Let's first consider the Fed's view, as indicated in the left-hand portion of each square. Because the Fed dislikes inflation, it wants firms to keep their promise not to raise prices; the Don't raise prices squares at the top and bottom right represent an improvement over the status quo from the Fed's perspective. Both result in full or greater than full employment and inflation lower than 5%. If political pressures associated with rising unemployment prevail, the top right-hand square (short-term expansion) is a good outcome from the Fed's point of view; the bottom left-hand square (a recession) is a situation to be avoided.

Now let's consider firms' decisions. Suppose that they believe that the Fed is more likely to favor a strategy to minimize the chance of a recession (even though it says that it is firmly committed to reducing inflation). In this case firms believe that the Fed will increase the money supply. Firms then will raise prices (their best move for the Fed's expected action). As Fig. 28.10(a) shows, the result is an inflationary equilibrium.

To achieve the disinflation without costs depicted in the lower right-hand corner, the Fed's promise must be credible. If firms believe that the Fed will not increase the money supply, they will not raise prices. Central bank credibility is essential to achieving disinflation at low cost to the economy.

In the new classical view, cold turkey disinflation not only works, but it enhances the central bank's credibility. When the public observes that money growth has been sharply reduced, inflationary expectations fall quickly. However, new Keynesian economists question the credibility of the cold turkey approach in the real world. Whereas a cold turkey reduction in money growth will make headlines, it also will reduce output and employment substantially in the short run. As a result, political objections could force the central bank to back off. New Keynesian economists stress that a gradualist policy, by being more feasible politically, may be a more credible way to reduce inflation than the cold turkey approach.

Rules versus Discretion

Many economists and policymakers believe that the key to central bank credibility is the adoption of and adherence to rules. A **rules strategy** for monetary policy suggests that the central bank follow specific and publicly announced guidelines for policy. One example of such a rule is a commitment by the Fed to expand the monetary base by 5% each year, regardless of disturbances in money and financial markets or the economy. The main criterion for formulating rules, advocates suggest, is that rules should apply to variables significantly controllable by the Fed. An instruction to "maintain the growth rate of real GDP at 4%" is not a useful rule because the Fed has no direct control over GDP. When the central bank chooses a rule, this strategy requires that it follow the rule, whatever the state of the economy.

Economists and policymakers who oppose the rules approach support a **discretion strategy** for monetary policy, which suggests that the central bank should adjust monetary policy as it sees fit to achieve goals for economic growth, inflation, and other economic and financial variables. This approach differs from the rules strategy in that it allows the Fed to change its policy to adjust to changes in the economy.

Proponents of the rules strategy argue that the central bank must commit to rules that limit its ability to adjust monetary policy to achieve

---

Q: How can policymakers reduce the rate of inflation?

A: Disinflation represents a decrease in long-term inflation. In a cold turkey strategy, the central bank announces that money supply growth will be cut immediately and drastically. In a gradualist strategy, money supply growth is reduced slowly and steadily. The costs of disinflation in terms of lost output depend on the speed with which prices adjust to changes in money growth and on the credibility of the central bank.

short-term objectives. However, inflexible rules may be needlessly rigid and have unforeseen consequences. For example, if a rule specifying a constant rate of growth of *M1* had been in effect in the early 1980s (when deregulation and financial innovation increased the demand for money), monetary policy would have led to more contraction than the Fed intended.

Many economists believe that a middle course is desirable. They argue that rules can allow policymakers to make adjustments in policy so long as those adjustments are stated as part of the rules. For example, the Fed could decide to maintain the growth of *M2*, not at a constant rate but at a rate adjusted in a predetermined manner for movements in inflation. The problem with this approach is one of limiting a central bank's discretion over monetary policy. If rules are not binding and central banks can modify their policies, the rules will not be successful. The central bank will be tempted to abandon the announced policy in favor of short-term objectives. Hence establishing a credible commitment to a rule is more important than stating a precise form of the rule (such as a specified growth rate for *M2*).

Even a modified rule isn't foolproof. The same lack of flexibility that can make a rule credible can limit the central bank's ability to respond during a financial crisis. Both the new classical and new Keynesian economists agree that, if the central bank avoids the temptation to intervene regularly to fine-tune the economy, its ability to respond effectively during a crisis will be enhanced (see Box 28.1). Most economists believe that the best way to achieve commitment to rules is to remove political pressures on the central bank (Chapter 19).

Consider this...   BOX 28.1

Can Credibility Enhance Central Bank Flexibility?

Achieving credibility in the conduct of monetary policy brings benefits in terms of future flexibility. Once a central bank establishes a credible reputation for carrying out its promises, inflexible rules may no longer be required. The successful track record of the German central bank in fighting inflation has convinced participants in international financial markets to believe that price stability will be the Bundesbank's dominant concern. This credibility has given the bank some flexibility in responding to short-term changes such as those raised by German reunification in the early 1990s.

A case in which a central bank's lack of credibility led to economic problems is the Reserve Bank of New Zealand's announcement in 1989 of a policy to reduce inflation nearly to zero by 1993. The salary of the governor of the central bank was actually tied to the central bank's success in reducing inflation. However, the Reserve Bank of New Zealand lacked credibility because of its past behavior. Although the central bank exceeded its targets in 1991 and 1992 in bringing down inflation, the early lack of credibility gave the central bank little room to react to the decline in economic activity that began in 1990. In fact, the Reserve Bank had to pursue a contractionary monetary policy (worsening the recession) to convince the public of its commitment to lower inflation.

MOVING FROM THEORY TO PRACTICE...

THE NEW YORK TIMES   MARCH 30, 1992

Low Inflation and Economic Growth

"Largely due to actions which took place before I joined the Fed, we have a good chance to achieve effective price stability in America by mid-decade," Lawrence B. Lindsey, a newly appointed Fed governor, told members of the Government Bond Club of New England in a speech two weeks ago.

If Mr. Lindsey is right, some of the consequences for individuals and the economy could be quite unexpected. Most startling, lower inflation would have the same impact on the economy as a supply-side tax cut aimed at raising savings and investment...

A permanent drop in inflation raises the after-tax returns of savings and investment. The reason: When Congress revised the tax code in the mid-1980's to eliminate "bracket creep," which forced taxpayers to pay higher income taxes merely because inflation had swelled nominal incomes, the tax-writing body did not do the same for most kinds of investment income. Owners of bonds or real estate, for example, must pay taxes on nominal gains, which merely reflect inflation...

"The net effect of our tax system, coupled with current levels of inflation, is to make the effective tax rate on real capital gains well over 50 percent," Mr. Lindsey said.

For businesses that buy new equipment, lower inflation amounts to an investment tax credit, Mr. Lindsey argued. A two-percentage-point decline in inflation is roughly equivalent to a 2 percent investment tax credit, he figured.

The reason is that businesses are allowed to deduct capital outlays from their incomes over a period of years. Income—or in this case, a depreciation allowance—a few years off is worth more or less depending on how much it must be discounted to account for the level of interest rates. Lower inflation makes depreciation more valuable because interest rates typically come down with inflation.

Lower inflation would also bolster the payoff to savers, just as a cut in the top income tax rate would...

To be sure, skeptics would say that higher returns alone would not necessarily produce more savings and investment. Real returns rose sharply when inflation fell from double digits to less than 5 percent in the early 1980's, but personal saving actually declined and business investment was about average. But most economists agree with Mr. Lindsey that higher real returns can only help.

ANALYZING THE NEWS...

Federal Reserve Governor Lindsey argues that disinflationary monetary policy could actually provide a stimulus to the economy. Because the U.S. tax code is defined in nominal terms, higher inflation taxes returns on saving and investment. For example, in an inflationary environment, savers pay taxes on nominal capital gains: Suppose an investor buys a share of stock for $100 and sells it 20 years later for $500—while the price level has risen fivefold. Tax is paid on the $400 "gain" even though the real value of the stock hasn't increased at all. Similarly, firms deduct depreciation expenses in calculating tax liability, and investment decisions depend on the present value of those deductions. A drop in the expected inflation rate reduces nominal interest rates. As a result, the present value of firms' depreciation deductions increases, to the benefit of the firms.

(a) Suppose that the economy is at full employment at E_0, with output Y^*, as the accompanying diagram shows, and the Fed pursues a disinflationary monetary policy. The contraction in money growth shifts the AD curve to the left from AD_0 to AD_1. Over time, the lower price level shifts the $SRAS$ curve down from $SRAS_0$ to $SRAS_1$, so that the economy's new equilibrium lies at E_1.

(b) The tax cuts for returns on saving and investment made possible by lower inflation shift the AD curve to the right from AD_1 to AD_2. (Though not explicitly stated in Lindsey's approach, other determinants of the $SRAS$ and AD curves are held constant.) For the new short-run equilibrium at E_2 to become a long-run equilibrium, Y^* must rise. Lindsey's argument suggests that the $LRAS$ curve shifts as well. The economy becomes permanently more productive as a result of reducing distortions from inflation. Although possible, such a productivity increase probably would reflect gains from improved resource allocation.

For further thought...

The author suggests that an increase in saving and investment didn't accompany the drop in inflation in the early 1980s. Does this result imply that Lindsey's analysis is incorrect? Why or why not?

Source: Excerpted from Sylvia Nasar, "Some Predict Era of Low Inflation," March 30, 1992. Copyright © 1991/1992 by The New York Times Company. Reprinted by permission.

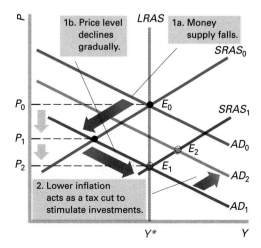

1b. Price level declines gradually.

LRAS

1a. Money supply falls.

2. Lower inflation acts as a tax cut to stimulate investments.

Price Controls and Credibility

Political constraints may limit the central bank's willingness to follow a disinflationary policy, raising an interesting question: Wouldn't **price controls,** or official government restrictions on price changes, stop inflation?

Binding and enforced price controls can reduce increases in the price level, but may not stop inflation, for two reasons. First, the mechanics of demand and supply tell us that, if the price of a product is prevented from rising to equate the quantity demanded and quantity supplied, shortages and long lines will develop. Second, and more important, if the public expects the price controls to be removed sometime in the future, inflation is suppressed, only to burst forth when controls are lifted. Price controls combined with a credible disinflationary monetary policy are more likely to reduce inflationary expectations than are price controls alone.

The U.S. experience with price controls in the early 1970s during the Nixon administration (August 1971–April 1974) bears out this conclusion. The Nixon administration and the Fed (under Chairman Arthur Burns) pursued expansionary policies during the period in which price controls were in effect. As a result, the controls reduced inflation only during that period. Robert J. Gordon of Northwestern University found that the burst of inflation between April 1974 and mid-1975 was so great that the price level was even higher than it probably would have been without the controls.[†]

[†] See Robert J. Gordon, "The Impact of Aggregate Demand on Prices," *Brookings Papers on Economic Activity*, 3: 613-685, 1975.

Key Terms and Concepts

Cost-push inflation

Demand-pull inflation

Discretion strategy

Disinflation
  Central bank credibility
  Cold turkey
  Gradualism
  Price controls

Hyperinflation

Inflation

Menu costs

Natural rate of unemployment

Rules strategy

Shoe leather costs

Appendix

Natural rate of unemployment

Okun's law

Phillips curve
  Expectations-augmented Phillips curve
  Simple Phillips curve

Summary

1. Inflation is the rate of change in the price level. Price level and output changes result from the interaction of shifts in aggregate demand and aggregate supply. Increases in the price level over the short run (short-term inflation) can be explained by factors that shift the *AD* curve or the *SRAS* curve. In particular, increases in the money supply, other increases in nominal aggregate demand, or supply shocks may lead to short-term inflation.

2. Long-term inflation is primarily a monetary phenomenon. In both the new classical and new Keynesian approaches, sustained increases in the nominal money supply cause sustained inflation.

3. Both expected and unexpected inflation have economic costs. By imposing a tax on money holdings, expected inflation reduces the public's demand for real money balances. Costs of expected inflation include shoe leather costs and distortions to saving and investment that arise because the U.S. tax system is defined in nominal terms. Unexpected inflation redistributes economic resources, forcing households and businesses to spend resources on forecasting inflation. It also distorts the relative price signals for resource allocation provided by markets.

4. Monetary policy can have an inflationary bias (despite the costs of inflation) if policymakers perceive that growth in output and jobs can be achieved with higher inflation. In the long run, policymakers cannot maintain output above the full employment level without high and rising inflation.

5. Disinflation represents a decrease in the economy's long-run rate of inflation. In the new classical approach, disinflation can be achieved with only small losses in output if money growth is cut drastically and immediately: the cold turkey approach. New Keynesian economists argue that prices adjust only gradually in response even to expected changes in money growth. Accordingly, they suggest a strategy of gradualism for disinflation: By reducing the rate of growth of the money supply gradually, the price level can adjust slowly, with smaller losses of output and jobs.

6. Another factor influencing the costs of disinflation is the credibility of the central bank. If the public believes that policymakers will not carry through on their disinflationary promises, inflationary expectations will change very slowly—until the central bank convinces the public of its credibility. New classical economists believe that cold turkey disinflation enhances the central bank's credibility. New Keynesian economists believe that a gradualist policy is a more credible way than the cold turkey approach to reduce inflation.

Review Questions

1. How does inflation hurt people? Who gets hurt?

2. The president proposes spending an additional $100 billion on a large telescope to look for life in other galaxies. Opponents of the plan argue that this spending would be inflationary. As a presidential advisor, what would you tell the president about this argument?

3. What is the principal cause of long-term inflation?

4. According to the new classical approach, what will be the effect on the economy of an increase in the money supply that people fully anticipate?

5. What does "inflation is a tax on money balances" mean?

6. According to the new classical approach, what is different about each short-run aggregate supply curve?

7. Why would you never expect the unemployment rate to be zero?

8. What are people likely to do (financially) in a hyperinflation?

9. How does the tax system distort financial decisions in its interaction with inflation?

10. According to the new classical approach, what actions should policymakers take to reduce inflation?

11. How might menu costs affect the allocation of resources in the economy when there is inflation? For what types of firms might menu costs be important?

12. Why don't new Keynesians believe in cold turkey disinflation? What do they suggest instead?

13. Why don't economists find price controls an attractive way to reduce inflation?

14. *Evaluate:* Inflation isn't necessarily a monetary phenomenon. Workers can push up wages in cost-push inflation. Increases in government spending can lead to demand-pull inflation.

15. *Evaluate:* An announced monetary contraction can reduce inflation with no loss in output in the new classical approach.

16. Why is it important to policymakers that people believe them when they say they are going to reduce the inflation rate?

Analytical Problems

17. Describe what happens in both the short and long run in the new Keynesian approach when the Fed reduces the money supply unexpectedly.

18. If the Fed wanted to reduce the inflation rate, why might a coordinated fiscal policy move to reduce the federal budget deficit help reduce the costs of disinflation? How would the credibility of such a move be aided by such coordination between fiscal and monetary policies?

19. Suppose that the economy initially is in equilibrium at full employment. Then the government unexpectedly increases income taxes. What are the effects on output and the price level in the short and long run, according to the new classical approach?

20. Suppose that the economy initially is at a point at which output exceeds the full employment level of output. In the new Keynesian approach, what could the Fed do to restore equilibrium at the full employment level of output? (Use the aggregate demand–aggregate supply diagram.) What would happen in the long run if the Fed didn't do anything?

21. Suppose that Ms. A is in the 50% tax bracket. When inflation is zero, she earns a nominal return (before taxes) of 4%. Suppose that inflation rises to 10% and that the nominal return (before taxes) rises to 14%. What is Ms. A's after-tax real return when inflation is zero? When inflation is 10%?

22. In the new classical approach, can optimism among consumers be self-fulfilling? Use the aggregate demand–aggregate supply model to show why or why not.

23. Suppose that monetary policymakers take actions that shift the *AD* curve so that it intersects both the *SRAS* curve and the *LRAS* curve, to maintain full employment. What would happen to the economy if the true *LRAS* curve were to the left of where the policymakers perceived it to be?

24. What should money growth be if real output grows 3% per year, velocity grows 2% per year, and the Fed wants inflation to be 4% per year? What should it be if the Fed targets zero inflation?

25. Would it be a good idea to pass a law that requires the Fed to keep money supply growth below 5% each year? Why or why not?

26. Suppose that the nominal interest rate is 8% and that expected inflation is 5%. What is the expected real rate of return? Calculate the actual real rate of return for each of the following cases and state whether lenders or borrowers are better off than they expected to be.

   a. Actual inflation is 10%.

   b. Actual inflation is 0%.

   c. Actual inflation is 5%.

27. The Federal Reserve Board chairman announces a policy of keeping short-term interest rates low. The financial press criticizes the policy as inflationary. Why?

28. Is it possible for policymakers to trade off more inflation for higher output in the short run? In the long run? In your answer, explain the differences in the new classical and new Keynesian approaches.

29. At a meeting with his cabinet, the president decides that the country's inflation rate of 15% is too high. The central bank is independent of the administration and announces that it will maintain the rate of money growth at current levels. The president imposes price controls, outlawing all increases in wages or prices.

   a. Using the new Keynesian approach, illustrate the effects of the price controls on output and the price level. (Assume that firms have a maximum capacity for production; that is, output can't exceed production capacity.)

   b. Having kept inflation at bay for two years, the president hands out "Inflation: Rest in Peace" buttons and removes the controls. Use the aggregate demand–aggregate supply analysis to illustrate the effects on the economy. Do these effects necessarily accompany the removal of price controls? Why or why not?

30. Suppose that the Fed gets new information suggesting that the aggregate demand curve has shifted to the left but that the public doesn't have this information. Using the new classical approach, what will happen to output and inflation if the Fed does nothing? What will happen to the price level if it uses expansionary policy to offset the shock and stabilize output?

31. Milton Friedman argued in 1968 that there was no permanent trade-off between unemployment and inflation. Demonstrate what would happen in both the new classical and new Keynesian approaches if the Fed continuously attempted to keep output above its full employment level.

32. Suppose that the Fed believes that the new classical approach is correct and tries cold turkey disinflation to reduce inflation from 10% to 0%. What happens to the economy (output, unemployment rate, and inflation rate) if in fact the new Keynesian approach is the correct one?

Data Questions

33. In the latest *Economic Report of the President*, look up data on the consumer price index for the past 11 years. Calculate the inflation rate for the last 10 years from the index levels. Has the inflation rate been declining or rising? What do you think have been the major factors causing this movement in the inflation rate?

34. Look in the latest *Economic Report of the President* for data on the percentage change in the consumer price index and producer price index from December of any one year to December of the following year and compare these two measures of the inflation rate. Could you use one to predict the other? Why or why not?

Appendix: Inflation versus Unemployment: The Phillips Curve

If there are costs to inflation, why is it tolerated? Virtually everyone feels the pinch of rising prices, so policymakers have reason to worry about inflation: It is a real economic problem and it angers voters. However, another issue concerns voters: unemployment. The fear of losing a job and the income it represents is a major worry. News stories often point to the *misery index*, the sum of the inflation rate and the unemployment rate, as a measure of economic problems.

Inflation and Unemployment

Why should we think about inflation and unemployment *together?* In an influential article, A.W. Phillips analyzed data on British inflation and unemployment rates from 1861 to 1957 and reported a statistical regularity which quickly was dubbed the **Phillips curve.** The unemployment rate tended to be high when the inflation rate was low, and vice versa.[†] This finding raised a tantalizing possibility: Could a policymaker choose between inflation and unemployment (depending on the relative social concern over the two problems), tolerating a higher value of one to obtain a lower value of another? Exploiting this trade-off, U.S. economic policy in the 1960s favored a steadily declining unemployment rate accompanied by a gradually

---

[†] A.W. Phillips, "The Relationship Between Unemployment and the Rate of Change of Money Wage Rates in the United Kingdom, 1861–1957," *Economica*, 283–299, 1958. Phillips's study focused specifically on *wage* inflation.

increasing inflation rate. Events of the 1970s and since fundamentally changed this relationship.

To analyze whether there is a trade-off between inflation and unemployment, we need to examine the relationships between (1) output changes and the unemployment rate and (2) price adjustment and output changes. As we consider these relationships, note that analysis of an inflation-unemployment trade-off follows closely the development of the aggregate demand–aggregate supply model.

Output Changes and the Unemployment Rate

How responsive is the unemployment rate to changes in output? **Okun's law**, a statistical relationship between changes in output, Y, and the unemployment rate, u, provides a widely cited answer.

We begin our explanation of Okun's law by defining the **natural rate of unemployment,** u^*, as the rate of unemployment that exists when the economy produces the full employment level of output, Y^*. This unemployment rate is not zero. (Recall that even at the full employment output level, unemployment exists because of structural or frictional unemployment.) The late Arthur Okun, chairman of the Council of Economic Advisers under President Lyndon Johnson, found that the unemployment rate increased whenever actual output is less than full employment output, or

$$\frac{Y - Y^*}{Y^*} = 2.5\left(u - u^*\right).$$

In other words, the gap between actual and full employment output rises by 2.5 percentage points for each percentage-point increase in the unemployment rate. Okun's law enables us to discuss changes in the unemployment rate in terms of particular changes in actual output.[†]

We can now trace the potential relationship between unemployment and inflation depicted in Fig. 28A.1. When the unemployment rate equals the natural rate, actual output and full employment output are equal. When the unemployment rate is above the natural rate, actual current output is below full employment output, and when the unemployment rate is below the natural rate (the portion of the Phillips curve above the line for 0% inflation), actual current output exceeds the full employment level.

In this chapter we showed that output changes and inflation are connected by the process of price adjustment in both the new classical and new Keynesian approaches. When actual and full employment output are equal, there is no pressure for inflation to change. When actual output

---

[†] Okun actually estimated that each percentage-point increase in the unemployment rate raised the output gap by 3.0 percentage points, but more recent research suggests that the coefficient is closer to 2.5. See Arthur M. Okun, "Potential GNP: Its Measurement and Significance," reprinted in Arthur M. Okun, *The Political Economy of Prosperity*, Washington D.C.: The Brookings Institution, 1970, pp. 132–145.

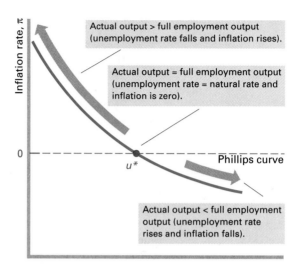

►FIGURE 28A.1

The Simple Phillips Curve
The simple Phillips curve shows the relationship between unemployment and inflation, for a constant natural rate of unemployment. When the unemployment rate equals the natural rate, u^*, the rate of inflation π equals zero.

exceeds full employment output, the inflation rate increases, and when actual output is less than the full employment level, the inflation rate declines.

Linking Okun's law and the process of price adjustment yields a negative relationship between inflation, π, and the unemployment rate, u:

$$\pi \equiv -h(u - u^*), \qquad\qquad (28A.1)$$

where $h > 0$ indicates the extent to which the inflation rate is associated with the deviation of the actual unemployment rate from the natural rate of unemployment. The relationship in Eq. (28A.1) is known as the **simple Phillips curve,** where inflation is positive when $u < u^*$ and negative when $u > u^*$, as plotted in Fig. 28A.1.

The well-defined, negatively sloped Phillips curve disappeared in the 1970s. This result had been anticipated in the late 1960s when various economists stressed the importance of distinguishing between expected and unexpected inflation in assessing a trade-off between output and inflation. Whether monetary policy can exploit such a trade-off between inflation and unemployment rates as suggested by the simple Phillips curve depends on whether money supply changes are expected or unexpected. Milton Friedman of the University of Chicago (now of the Hoover Institution) and Edmund Phelps of Columbia University argued that only the portion of inflation that is *unexpected* (and not the total rate of inflation) could affect output. The thrust of the Friedman-Phelps argument is that there is no long-run trade-off between output and inflation.

We use the new classical approach to determine whether there is a trade-off between output and expected inflation. (Results from the new Keynesian approach are qualitatively similar.) Suppose that the economy is at full employment (with no real growth) but with an ongoing expected rate of inflation and money growth of 5% each year; that is, the aggregate demand curve shifts upward each year, as Fig. 28A.2 shows.

The long-run aggregate supply curve for any year is represented by the full employment level of output. What about the short-run aggregate supply curve? Because households and businesses expect the money supply growth, they expect the price level to increase each year. Hence the short-run aggregate supply curve shifts to the left and the economy's full employment equilibrium shifts from E_0 to E_1 in any year. Output doesn't change, but the price level increases in response to the expected increase in the money supply.

Now suppose that the rate of expected inflation changes. Instead of growing at 5% per year, the money supply unexpectedly grows by 10%. Because a 5% rate of money growth and inflation had been expected, the aggregate demand and short-run aggregate supply curves had shifted from AD_0 and $SRAS_0$ to AD_1 and $SRAS_1$. However, as money growth was higher than expected, the economy's equilibrium lies at the intersection of $SRAS_1$ (conditional on an expected rate of inflation of 5%) and AD_2 (representing an increase in money growth of 10%), at point $E_{1'}$. Output is higher than the full employment level, and the price level rises by more than 5% but by less than 10% in the short run. In the long run, as producers realize that the equilibrium aggregate price level is higher, prices rise and the economy's equilibrium is characterized by full employment output and a higher price level (reflecting inflation of 10%), at E_2.

Therefore output increases in response only to *unexpected* inflation. If we connect output and the unemployment rate through the relationships of Okun's law, we obtain a revised relationship between the inflation and unemployment rates:

$$\pi = \pi^e - h(u - u^*), \tag{28A.2}$$

where π^e is the expected rate of inflation. The fundamental contribution of Friedman and Phelps yields an **expectations-augmented Phillips curve,** in which the simple Phillips curve is combined with expected inflation. If the expected rate of inflation were zero, the expectations-augmented Phillips curve and the simple Phillips curve would be identical.

For any expected rate of inflation, a Phillips curve (a relationship between inflation and unemployment rates) exists. However, if expected inflation changes over time, as it did in the 1970s and 1980s, the Phillips curve relationship isn't stable.

The expectations-augmented Phillips curve suggests an important difference between short-term and long-term trade-offs between inflation and unemployment rates. The *short-run Phillips curve* describes the relationship between the inflation and unemployment rates, as Fig. 28A.3 shows. The short-run Phillips curve suggests a trade-off only between the unemployment rate and *unexpected* inflation.

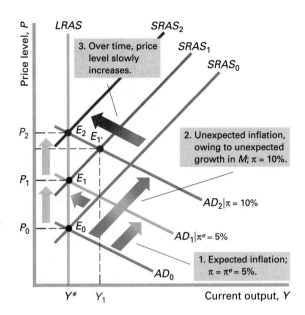

If expected inflation changes, the short-run Phillips curve shifts. An increase in expected inflation from π_1 to π_2 shifts the short-run Phillips curve upward. A decrease in expected inflation from π_1 to π_3 shifts the short-run Phillips curve downward. Hence the point raised by Friedman and Phelps is that any observed relationship between the unemployment rate and the actual inflation rate will change over time as the expected inflation rate changes. As a result, actual inflation can be high even when the unemployment rate is higher than the natural rate.

The Long-Run Phillips Curve

Both new classical and new Keynesian economists agree that policy-makers cannot maintain an unemployment rate below the natural rate without permanently maintaining a high rate of inflation. Over time, rational expectations of the inflation rate will equal the actual rate, on average. That is, expected inflation π^e equals actual inflation π. Hence, for the expressions represented by the expectations-augmented Phillips curve, u must equal u^* in the long run. Then, as Fig. 28A.3 shows, the *long-run Phillips curve* is vertical.

With a vertical long-run Phillips curve, changes in the nominal money supply cannot affect output or the unemployment rate in the long run. In other words, money is neutral in the long run, as we demonstrated in the aggregate demand–aggregate supply analysis. This proposition is common to both the new classical and new Keynesian approaches.

Trade-off Exploitation in the Short Run

Both new classical and new Keynesian economists stress that the long-run Phillips curve is vertical: There is no trade-off between inflation and

► FIGURE 28A.3

**Output, Unemployment, and
Inflation in the Expectations-
Augmented Phillips Curve**
For any expected inflation rate,
the short-run expectations-
augmented Phillips curve slopes
downward. An increase in
expected inflation shifts the
short-run Phillips curve upward.
A decrease in expected inflation
shifts the short-run Phillips curve
downward.

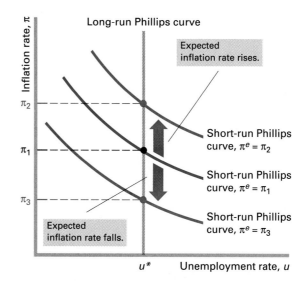

unemployment rates in the long run. New classical economists also question whether policymakers can exploit a trade-off between inflation and unemployment rates even in the short run. In the new classical approach, households and businesses have rational expectations. They learn over time about the behavior of the Fed, the president, and Congress—and they will anticipate changes in policy in reaction to economic events. So long as the public expects changes in policy, those changes will have no real effects (on output or the unemployment rate). Expectations of policy shifts will be correct on average, so unexpected inflation will be zero on average. Because unexpected inflation cannot be created repeatedly, the Phillips curve doesn't offer a short-run trade-off for policymakers in the new classical approach.

New Keynesian economists agree that rational expectations on the part of the public limits the short-run trade-off offered by the Phillips curve. However, in the new Keynesian approach, the expected inflation is the forecast made at the time sticky prices are set. If actual inflation exceeds expected inflation, inflationary expectations adjust gradually in the aggregate. As a result, the unemployment rate can exceed the natural rate for a period of time. Nevertheless, many new Keynesian economists believe that policymakers should limit their attempts to exploit a short-run trade-off between inflation and unemployment rates in order to enhance the long-run credibility of policy.

If the new classical and new Keynesian approaches do not suggest important reductions in unemployment from unexpected inflation, why might policymakers be tempted to allow inflation? One possibility in the new Keynesian view is that exploiting a short-run trade-off can have political pay-offs for policymakers, as we discussed in the chapter.

Glossary

Accommodating policy Actions to stimulate aggregate demand to restore output and jobs, but at the cost of greater inflation. (28)

Adverse selection The problem of distinguishing the good-risk applicants from the bad-risk applicants before making a loan or providing insurance. (11, 12)

Aggregate demand The sum of demands for an economy's goods and services for consumption, investment, government purchases (not including transfer payments), and net exports. (25)

Aggregate demand (*AD*) curve The graph of the relationship between the aggregate demand for goods and services and the aggregate price level. (25)

Aggregate supply The total amount of output that producers in the economy are willing to supply and sell at a given price level. (25)

Aggregate supply (*AS*) curve The graph of the relationship between the aggregate output that firms in the economy are willing to supply and the aggregate price level. (25)

Appreciation An increase in the value of a currency against another currency. (8, 22)

Asset A thing of value that can be owned; a use of funds and a claim on a borrower's income. (2, 3)

Asymmetric information A condition that occurs when borrowers have some information about their opportunities or activities that they do not disclose to lenders, creditors, or insurers. (3, 11)

Auction market Secondary financial market in which prices are set by competitive bidding by a large number of traders acting on behalf of individual buyers and sellers. (3)

Balance of payments An accounting device for measuring private and government flows of funds between a country and foreign countries. (22)

Balance sheet A statement showing an individual's or firm's financial position at a point in time. It lists assets, liabilities, and net worth. (13)

Bank failure A situation in which a bank cannot pay its depositors in full and still have enough reserves to meet its reserve requirements. (13)

Bank holding companies Large firms that hold many different banks as subsidiaries. They were originally used by banks to get around branching restrictions. (14)

Bank run A sequence of events in which depositors lose confidence in a bank, for real or imagined reasons, and make withdrawals, exhausting the bank's liquid funds. (14)

Bankers' acceptances Time drafts that establish credit between parties who do not know each other, facilitating international trade. (3, 16)

Banking panics Waves of severe bank runs that cause contractions in credit availability, often culminating in business recessions. (14)

Basis risk The imperfect correlation of changes in the price of a hedged instrument and changes in the price of the instrument actually traded in the futures market. (9)

Board of Governors Board of the Federal Reserve System, made up of seven members, appointed by the President, who administer monetary policy and set the discount rate. (19)

Bond rating A single statistic summarizing the assessment of a firm's net worth, cash flow, and prospects — in short, its likely ability to meet its debt obligations. (7)

Borrowed reserves (*BR*, discount loans) A component of the monetary base consisting of reserves borrowed from the central bank. (17)

Branching restrictions Geographical limitations on banking firms' ability to open more than one office, or branch. (14)

Bretton Woods system A fixed exchange rate system that permitted smoother short-term economic adjustments than were possible under the gold standard, based on the convertibility of U.S. dollars into gold at a price of $35.00 per ounce. (22)

Brokered deposits A financial innovation in which a depositor with an amount to invest over the deposit insurance limit goes to a broker who buys certificates of deposit in different banks, giving the depositor insurance on the entire amount. (15)

Brokers Individuals who earn commissions by matching buyers and sellers in a particular market. (12)

Bubble A situation in which the price of an asset is more than its fundamental value. (10)

Budget deficit The excess of government spending over tax revenue. (5, 18)

Business cycle The periodic fluctuations in aggregate output, consisting of expansion (a boom) followed by contraction (a recession). (1, 26)

Call option The right to buy an underlying asset, which is obtained by the buyer of the call option. Sellers have an obligation to sell. (10)

Capital account Balance of payments account that measures trade in existing assets among countries. (22)

Capital controls Government-imposed barriers to foreign savers' investing in domestic assets or to domestic savers' investing in foreign assets. (22)

Capital markets Financial markets for trading debt instruments with a maturity greater than one year and equity instruments. (3)

Central bank Special governmental or quasi-governmental institution, within the financial system, that regulates the medium of exchange. (2)

Certificate of deposit (CD) A fixed-maturity instrument, sold by a bank to depositors, that pays principal and interest at maturity, with a penalty for early withdrawal. (3)

Checkable deposits Accounts that grant a depositor the right to write checks to individuals, firms, or the government. (13)

Circuit breakers Interventions that are designed to restore orderly securities markets. (10)

Closed economy An economy of a country that neither borrows from nor lends to foreign countries. (5)

Closed-end mutual fund A fund that sells a fixed number of nonredeemable shares, which are then traded over-the-counter like common stock. The price fluctuates with the value of the underlying assets. (12)

Coinsurance An insurance option that requires the policyholder to pay a certain fraction of the costs of a claim, in addition to the deductible. (12)

Collateral Assets that are pledged to pay for a loan in the event of default on the loan. (11, 13)

Commercial bank(s) The largest group of depository institutions, which offer risk sharing, liquidity (checking accounts), and information services that benefit savers and borrowers. (3, 12, 13)

Commercial bank loan A loan to businesses or consumers that is made by banks and financial companies. (3)

Commercial paper A liquid, short-term investment for savers that is used by high-quality, well-known firms and financial institutions to raise funds. (3, 13)

Compensating balance A required minimum amount in a checking account that is used as a form of collateral in commercial loans. (13)

Consol A (perpetual) coupon bond with an infinite maturity; its price is based on the present value of the coupon payments. (4)

Consumer price index (CPI) An index of prices of the marketbasket of goods purchased by urban consumers. It is a commonly used measure of inflation. (2, 28)

Contagion The spreading of bad news about one bank to other banks. (14)

Corporate bonds Intermediate and long-term obligations issued by large, high-quality corporations in order to finance plant and equipment spending. (3, 7)

Corporate control A contest for ownership and control of a firm that pits shareholders against managers in an effort to direct the firm's resources to their highest valued use. (11)

Cost-push inflation Price increases resulting from workers' pressure for higher wages. (28)

Coupon bond A credit market instrument that requires multiple payments of interest on a regular basis, such as semiannually or annually, and a payment of the face value at maturity. (4)

Coupon rate An interest rate equal to the yearly coupon payment divided by the face value. (4)

Credit controls Regulatory restrictions on bank lending. (27)

Credit crunch A decline in either the ability or the willingness of banks to lend at any given interest rate. (14, 26, 27)

Credit market instruments Methods of financing debt, including simple loans, discount bonds, coupon bonds, and fixed payment loans. (4)

Credit rationing The restricting of credit by lenders, so that borrowers cannot obtain the funds they desire at the given interest rate. (11, 13)

Credit-risk analysis The examination of a borrower's likelihood of repayment and general business conditions that might influence the borrower's ability to repay the loan. (13)

Crowding out Reduction in private consumption and investment that accompanies an increase in government purchases in a closed economy. (24)

Currency A type of money, such as dollar bills and coins. (2)

Currency-deposit ratio The relationship of currency, C, held by the nonbank public to checkable deposits, D. (17)

Currency in circulation Federal Reserve Notes held by the nonbank public. (17)

Currency premium A number that indicates investors' collective preference for financial instruments denominated in one currency relative to those denominated in another. (8, 22)

Currency swap An exchange of expected future returns on debt instruments denominated in different currencies. (16)

Current account Balance of payment account that summarizes transactions among countries for purchases and sales of currently produced goods and services. (22)

Current yield The coupon payment divided by the current price of a bond. (4)

Dealers Individuals who hold inventories of securities and sell them for a price higher than they paid for them, earning the spread between the bid and the asked price. (12)

Debt Claim that requires a borrower to repay the amount borrowed (the principal) plus a rental fee (interest). (3)

Debt-deflation A decrease in prices that raises the real value of households' and firms' outstanding debt, reducing their net worth and their ability to finance desired spending. (11, 27)

Deductible A specified amount to be subtracted from a policyholder's loss when a claim is paid by the insurance company. (12)

Default The inability to repay all or part of an obligation. (3)

Default risk (credit risk) The probability that a borrower will not pay in full promised interest, principal, or both. This characteristic of a credit market instrument influences its interest rate. (7)

Default-risk-free instruments Securities that guarantee that principal and interest will be repaid in nominal terms. For example, U.S. Treasury securities are default-risk-free. (7)

Defensive transactions Open market transactions used by the Fed to offset fluctuations in the monetary base arising from disturbances in portfolio preferences of banks and the nonbank public, financial markets, and the economy. (20)

Defined benefit pension plan Common pension plan in which the employee is promised an assigned benefit based on earnings and years of service, and payments may or may not be indexed for inflation. (12)

Defined contribution pension plan Pension plan in which contributions are invested for employees, who own the value of the funds in the plan. (12)

Definitive money Money that does not have to be converted into a more basic medium of exchange, such as gold or silver. (2)

Deflation A condition in which falling prices cause a given amount of money to purchase more goods and services. (2)

Demand deposit Account against which checks convertible to currency can be written. (13)

Demand for money A decision by the public concerning how much of its wealth to hold in money balances, which is affected by current and anticipated future changes in output. (23, 26)

Demand-pull inflation Price increases resulting from policymakers' attempts to increase aggregate demand for current output above the full employment level. (28)

Depository institutions Commercial banks, savings and loan institutions, mutual savings banks, and credit unions that accept deposits and make loans, acting as intermediaries in the saving-investment process. (3, 12)

Depreciation A decrease in a currency's value against another currency. (8, 22)

Derivative instrument An asset, such as a futures or option contract, that derives its economic value from an underlying asset such as a stock or bond. (9)

Determinants of asset demand The key factors affecting a saver's portfolio allocation of assets. They are a saver's wealth, expectations of return on assets, degree of risk of assets, liquidity of assets, and the cost of acquiring information about assets. (6)

Devaluation The lowering of the official value of a country's currency relative to other currencies, thereby resetting the exchange rate. (22)

Discount bond A credit market instrument in which the borrower repays the amount of the loan in a single payment at maturity, but receives less than the face value initially. (4)

Discount loan A loan made by the Federal Reserve System to a member bank. (14, 17)

Discount policy The oldest of the Federal Reserve's principal tools for regulating the money supply. It includes setting the discount rate and terms of discount lending. (20)

Discount rate The interest rate specified by the Fed for loans to depository institutions. (17)

Discount window The means by which the Fed makes discount loans to banks, serving as a channel for meeting the liquidity needs of banks. (20)

Disintermediation An exit of savers and borrowers from banks to financial markets. (15)

Diversification Splitting wealth among many different assets to reduce risk. (3, 6)

Dividends Periodic payments (usually once each quarter) that owners of equities generally receive from the firm. (3)

Dual banking system System in the United States

in which banks are chartered by either the federal government or a state government. (14)

Duration For an asset or liability, the responsiveness of the percentage change in the asset's or liability's market value to a percentage change in the market interest rate. (13)

Duration gap A bank's exposure to fluctuations in interest rates, measured as the difference between the average duration for bank assets and the average duration for bank liabilities. (13)

Dynamic transactions Open market operations aimed at achieving desired changes in monetary policy indicated by the Federal Open Market Committee. (20)

Economies of scale A fall in the transactions costs per dollar of investment as the size of the transactions increases. (11)

Edge Act corporations Special subsidiaries of U.S. banks that conduct only international banking services, as provided in the Edge Act of 1919. (16)

Efficient financial market A market in which all information available to market participants is reflected in market prices. (10)

Efficient markets hypothesis Proposition that applies rational expectations to the pricing of assets. It says that when traders and investors use all available information in forming expectations of future rates of return and the cost of trading is low, the equilibrium price of the security is equal to the optimal forecast of fundamental value based on the available information. (10)

Electronic funds transfer systems Computerized payment clearing devices, such as debit cards and automated teller machines. (2)

Equation of exchange Equation stating that the quantity of money times the velocity of money equals nominal spending in the economy. (23)

Equilibrium real interest rate The interest rate at which desired saving and desired investment are equal. It is determined by the intersection of the saving curve and the investment curve in a closed economy. (5)

Equity A claim to a share in the profits and assets of a firm. (3)

Eurobonds Obligations that are denominated in a currency other than that of the country where they are sold, usually in U.S. dollars. (3)

Eurocurrency deposits Time deposits denominated in a currency other than that of the issuing domestic financial center (for instance, dollar deposits at a French bank). (16)

Eurodollars A deposit denominated in dollars in a bank or bank branch outside the United States. (3, 16)

Excess reserves Reserves that depository institutions elect to hold that are greater than the reserves required by the Fed. (13, 17)

Exchange rate The price of one country's currency in terms of another, such as yen per dollar or francs per pound. (1, 8)

Exchange rate risk The potential fluctuations in an asset's value because of increases or decreases in exchange rates. (16)

Exchanges Auction markets at which buyers and sellers of securities trade, such as the New York and American Stock Exchanges. (3, 12)

Expectations theory of the term structure of interest rates Proposition that investors view assets of all maturities as perfect substitutes, given the same levels of default risk, liquidity, information costs, and taxation. (7)

Expected real interest rate The nominal interest rate minus the expected rate of inflation. (4)

Fads Overreaction to good or bad news about an issue or a class of assets. (10)

Federal deposit insurance A federal government guarantee of certain types of bank deposits for account balances of up to $100,000. (13, 14)

Federal funds instruments ("Fed funds") Overnight loans between banks of their deposits with the Fed. (3)

Federal funds rate The interest rate charged on the overnight loans among banks. (3, 13, 20)

Federal Open Market Committee (FOMC) Federal Reserve System committee, with twelve members, which gives directions for open market operations. Members include the Board of Governors, the president of the Federal Reserve Bank in New York, and the presidents of four other Federal Reserve banks. (19)

Federal Reserve bank A district bank of the Federal Reserve System that, among other things, conducts discount lending. (19)

Federal Reserve System (the Fed) The central bank in the United States, which promotes stability in the banking industry and issues currency. (1, 14, 17, 19, 20, 21)

Fiat money Money authorized by central banks as the definitive money, which does not have to be exchanged by the central bank for gold or some other commodity money. (2)

Financial distress A situation in which households or firms must sell illiquid assets, possibly at a loss, to meet current obligations. (27)

Financial futures (contracts) Claims that imply settlement of a purchase of a financial instrument at a specified future date, though price is determined at the outset. (3, 9)

Financial innovation Alterations in the operation of financial markets and institutions caused by changes in costs of providing risk-sharing, liquidity, or information services, or changes in demand for these services. (3, 15)

Financial institutions Go-betweens for savers and borrowers, such as banks or insurance companies. (1, 3, 12)

Financial instruments IOU notes created by financial institutions, which are assets for savers and liabilities for (claims on) borrowers. (1, 3)

Financial intermediaries Institutions such as commercial banks, credit unions, savings and loan associations, mutual savings banks, mutual funds, finance companies, insurance companies, and pension funds, that borrow funds from savers and lend them to borrowers. (1, 3)

Financial markets Places or channels for buying and selling newly issued or existing bonds, stocks, foreign exchange contracts, and other financial instruments. (1, 3)

Financial panics Periods characterized by violent fluctuations in financial markets, bank runs, and bankruptcies of many firms. (14, 27)

Financial structure   The mix of finance between equity and debt, as well as the source of funds (direct finance through financial markets or indirect finance through financial intermediaries). (11)

Financial system   A network of markets and institutions to transfer funds from individuals and groups who have saved money to individuals and groups who want to borrow money. (1, 3)

Fisher hypothesis   Proposition stating that the nominal interest rate rises or falls point-for-point with expected inflation. (4)

Fixed exchange rate system   System in which exchange rates are set at levels determined and maintained by governments. (22)

Fixed payment loan   Credit market instrument that requires the borrower to make a regular periodic payment (monthly, quarterly, or annually) of principal and interest to the lender. (4)

Forward transactions   Agreements to exchange currencies, bank deposits, or securities at a set date in the future. They provide savers and borrowers the ability to conduct a transaction now and settle it in the future. (8, 9)

Free cash flow   Funds that represent the difference between the firm's cash receipts and cash disbursements, including payments to equityholders and debtholders. (11)

Free reserves   The difference between excess reserves and borrowed reserves (discount loans) in the banking system. (21)

Free-rider problem   A situation in which individuals obtain and use information paid for by others. (11)

Frictional unemployment   Unemployment caused by searches by workers and firms for suitable matches of workers to jobs. (28)

Full employment output   The production level achieved by using all available factors of production in place in the economy in the current period, irrespective of the real rate of interest. (24, 25, 28)

Fully funded pension plan   Pension plan in which the contributions, together with the projected future earnings, are sufficient to pay the projected assigned benefits. (12)

Fundamental value   The present value of an asset's expected future returns, which equals the market price of the asset in an efficient financial market. (10)

Futures contract   An agreement that specifies the delivery of a specific underlying commodity or financial instrument at a given future date at a currently agreed upon price. (10)

GDP deflator   An index of prices of all goods and services included in the gross domestic product, which is the final value of all goods and services produced in the economy. (2)

General directive   A summary of the Federal Open Market Committee's overall objectives for monetary aggregates and/or interest rates. (20)

Gold standard   A fixed exchange rate system in which the currencies of participating countries are convertible into an agreed-upon amount of gold. (22)

Government budget constraint   An equation depicting the relationships among federal spending and tax decisions, sales of securities by the Treasury, and changes in the monetary base. (18)

Gradualism   A policy, recommended by new Keynesian economists, in which the rate of growth of the money supply is slowly reduced so that the inflation rate can adjust slowly, with smaller losses of output and jobs. (28)

Hedging   Reducing one's exposure to risk by receiving the right to sell or buy an asset at a known price on a specified future date. (9)

Hyperinflation   Rapid inflation in excess of hundreds or thousands of percentage points per year for a significant period of time. (2, 28)

Hysteresis   A situation in which unemployment rates can be higher than those associated with full employment for extended periods of time. (25)

Idiosyncratic risk (unsystematic risk)   Unique risk which assets carry that does not affect the market as a whole. For example, the price of an individual stock is influenced by factors affecting the company's profitability, such as a strike or the discovery of a new product. (6)

Income   The flow of earnings over a period of time. (2)

Indicator A financial variable whose movements reveal information to the central bank about present or prospective conditions in financial markets or the economy. (21)

Inflation A condition in the economy in which rising prices cause a given amount of money to purchase fewer goods and services, thus decreasing the purchasing power of money. (2, 28)

Information costs The costs savers incur in finding out the creditworthiness of borrowers and monitoring how borrowers use the funds acquired. (3, 11)

Information lag A condition that makes it impossible for the Fed to observe instantaneously movements in GDP, inflation, or other goal variables. (21)

Interest rate The cost of borrowing funds, usually expressed as a percentage of the amount borrowed. (1, 4)

Interest rate risk The risk that the value of financial assets and liabilities will fluctuate in response to changes in market interest rates. (13)

Interest rate swap An agreement to sell the expected future returns on one financial instrument for the expected future returns on another. (13)

Intermediate targets Objectives for financial variables — such as the money supply or short-term interest rates — that the Fed believes will directly help it achieve its ultimate goals. (21)

Intermediate-term debt A debt instrument that has a maturity of between 1 and 10 years. (3)

International banking The risk-sharing, liquidity, and information services that banks provide to assist their customers in international trade and finance. (16)

International banking facilities (IBFs) Institutions within the United States that cannot conduct domestic banking business, but can take time deposits from and make loans to foreign households and firms. They are exempt from reserve requirements, federal restrictions on interest payments to depositors, and, in some states, state and local taxation. (16)

International capital market The market for lending and borrowing across national boundaries. (1, 5)

International capital mobility The ability of investors to move funds among international markets. (8)

International Monetary Fund (IMF) Multinational lender of last resort, created by the Bretton Woods agreement to help countries make short-run economic adjustments to a balance of payments deficit or surplus while maintaining a fixed exchange rate. (22)

International reserves A central bank's assets that are denominated in a foreign currency and used in international transactions. (22)

Investment banks Securities market institutions that assist businesses in raising new capital and advise them on the best means of doing it (issuing shares or structuring debt instruments). (12)

IS curve The negative relationship between the real interest rate and the level of income, all else equal, that arises in the market for goods and services. (24)

Junk bonds Corporate bonds issued by lower-quality and thus riskier firms. (3, 7)

L Broadest monetary aggregate, that includes *M3* short-term Treasury securities, commercial paper, savings bonds, and bankers' acceptances. (2)

Large open economy The economy of a country whose domestic saving and investment shifts are large enough to affect the real interest rate in the international capital market. The United States, Japan, and Germany are examples of countries with large open economies. (5)

Law of one price Theory stating that if two countries produce an identical good, profit opportunities should ensure that the price of the good is the same around the world, no matter which country produces the good. This law assumes the goods are tradeable and allows differences that reflect transportation costs. (8)

Lemons problem An adverse selection problem in which individuals do not know the quality of asset choices (for example, of used cars), so they average quality, overvaluing some assets and undervaluing others. At the average price, owners of the undervalued assets are less likely to sell, but owners of the overvalued assets are more likely to sell. (11)

Lender of last resort The ultimate source of credit to which banks can turn during a panic. (14)

Leveraged buyout (LBO) A type of restructuring in which external equity is replaced by debt. (11)

Liabilities Sources of funds and claims on future income of borrowers. (3)

Life-cycle model of consumption and saving A theory of consumption that emphasizes the role of saving and borrowing as transferring resources from those times in life when income is high to those times in life when income is low (such as from working years to retirement). (5)

Liquidity The ease with which one can exchange assets for cash, other assets, or goods and services. (1, 3, 7)

Liquidity of balance sheet positions The quantity of liquid assets that households and firms hold relative to their liabilities, which is a determinant of spending on business investment, housing, and consumer durables. (27)

Liquidity preference theory Proposition, developed by John Maynard Keynes, that emphasizes the sensitivity of money demand to changes in interest rates. (23)

Liquidity risk The possibility that depositors may collectively decide to withdraw more funds than the bank has on hand. (13)

LM curve The positive relationship between the real interest rate and the level of income, all else equal, that arises in the market for real money balances. (24)

Load fund A mutual fund that charges commissions for purchases and/or sales. (12)

Loan commitment An agreement by a bank to provide a borrower with a stated amount of funds during some specified period of time. (13)

Loan sale A financial contract in which a bank agrees to sell the expected future returns from an underlying bank loan to a third party. (13)

Long-run aggregate supply curve (LRAS) The graph of the relationship of firms' output to price level in the long run. It is vertical at the full employment output. (25)

Long-term debt A debt instrument that has a maturity of 10 years or more. (3)

Luxury asset An asset for which the wealth elasticity of demand exceeds unity. (6)

M1 The narrowest monetary aggregate, which measures money as the traditional medium of exchange, including currency, traveler's checks, and checkable deposits. (2)

M2 A monetary aggregate that includes the components of *M1* plus short-term investment accounts that could be converted to definitive money, but not as easily as the components of *M1*. *M2* now includes money market deposit accounts, noninstitutional money market mutual fund shares, and other very liquid assets of firms such as overnight repurchase agreements and overnight Eurodollars. (2)

M3 A monetary aggregate that includes *M2* plus some less liquid assets, including large-denomination time deposits, institutional money market mutual fund balances, term repurchase agreements, and term Eurodollars. (2)

Main bank In Japan, a large bank within a finance group that owns some equity in member firms, is a big source of credit for group firms, and monitors activities of member firms. (14)

Management buyout (MBO) A form of restructuring in which a firm's managers acquire a greater stake in the firm by buying back shares from other shareholders. (11)

Market risk (systematic risk) Risk common to all assets of a certain type, such as potential general fluctuations in economic conditions that can increase or decrease returns on stocks collectively. (6)

Matched sale-purchase transactions (reverse repos) Agreements often used by the Fed Trading Desk for open market sales, where the Fed sells securities to dealers in the government securities market and the dealers agree to sell them back to the Fed in the very near future. (20)

Maturity The length of time before a debt instrument expires. The maturity can be a very short period of time (30 days or even overnight) or a long period of time (30 years or more). (3)

Medium of exchange A term used by economists to describe money. (2)

Menu costs Costs to firms caused by changing

prices because of inflation (reprinting price lists, informing customers, and so on). (28)

Misperception theory Propositions about the effects of imperfect information on the part of firms on aggregate supply. *See also* new classical approach. (25)

Monetary aggregates Measures of the quantity of money that are broader than currency. They include *M1*, *M2*, *M3*, and *L*. (2)

Monetary base All reserves held by banks as well as all currency in circulation. (17)

Monetary neutrality Proposition that money has no effect on output in the long run because an increase (decrease) in the nominal money supply raises (lowers) the price level in the long run but does not change equilibrium output. (25)

Monetary policy The management of the money supply and its links to prices, interest rates, and other economic variables. (1, 21, 26)

Monetary theory Area of study concerning the relationships linking changes in the money supply to changes in economic activity and prices in the economy. (1)

Monetary Union (European) Plan drafted as part of the "1992" single European market initiative, in which exchange rates would be fixed by using a common currency. (22)

Monetizing the debt The Fed's purchasing of Treasury securities to finance budget deficits. (18)

Money Anything that is generally accepted as payment for goods and services or in the settlement of debts. Money acts as a medium of exchange, is a unit of account and a store of value, and offers a standard of deferred payment. (1, 2)

Money center banks Large, established national banks. (14)

Money demand function Function relating the demand for real money balances to its underlying determinants. (23)

Money markets Financial markets that trade assets used as the medium of exchange, such as currency or shorter-term instruments with a maturity of less than one year. (3, 12)

Money multiplier The number indicating how much the money supply changes in response to a given change in the monetary base. (17)

Moral hazard Lender's difficulty in monitoring borrowers' activities once the loan is made. (11)

Mortgages Loans, usually long-term, to households or firms to purchase buildings or land. The underlying asset — house or factory or piece of land — serves as collateral. (3)

Multiple deposit expansion Part of the money supply process in which funds are deposited and redeposited in banks. Banks serve as a link between the central bank and the nonbank public, taking increases in reserves from the central bank and funneling them to the nonbank public by making loans. (17)

Municipal bonds Obligations of state and local governments that are exempt from federal, state, and local income taxes. (7)

Mutual funds Financial intermediaries that raise funds by selling shares to individual savers and investing them in diversified portfolios of stocks, bonds, mortgages, and money market instruments. (3, 12)

National banks Federally chartered banks supervised by a department of the U.S. Treasury, the Office of the Comptroller of the Currency. Originally, national banks were allowed to issue bank notes as currency. (14)

Natural rate of unemployment The rate of unemployment that exists when the economy produces the full employment level of output. (28)

Net worth (equity capital) The difference between a firm's current and expected future holdings (assets) and its debts (liabilities). (11, 13)

New classical approach Theory stating that, for short-run aggregate supply, there is a positive relation between aggregate supply and the difference between the actual and the expected price level. (25)

New Keynesian approach Economic explanations for price stickiness in the short run, based on features of many real-world markets: the rigidity of long-term contracts and imperfect competition among sellers in the goods market. (25)

No-load funds Funds that earn income only from management fees (typically about 0.5% of assets), not from sales commissions. (12)

Noise traders Relatively uninformed traders who pursue trading strategies with no superior information and who may overreact. (10)

Nominal exchange rate The value of one currency in terms of another currency. (8)

Nominal interest rate An interest rate that is unadjusted for changes in purchasing power. (4)

Nominal interest rate parity condition The market equilibrium condition in which domestic and foreign assets have identical risk, liquidity, and information characteristics, so their nominal returns — measured in the same currency — also must be identical. (8)

Nonbank banks Financial institutions that take demand deposits, but do not make loans. (14)

Nonmoney asset market A market that handles trading in assets that are stores of value, including stocks, bonds, and houses. (24)

Off-balance-sheet lending Bank lending activities in which the bank does not necessarily hold as assets the loans it makes, including standby letters of credit, loan commitments, and loan sales. (13)

Offshore markets International financial centers that are located in unregulated areas with low tax rates on banks — for example, in the Caribbean (Bahamas and Cayman Islands) and in Hong Kong and Singapore. (16)

Open economy An economy in which borrowing and lending take place in the international capital market. (5)

Open-end mutual funds Funds that issue redeemable shares at a price tied to the underlying value of the assets. (12)

Open market operations The purchase and sale of securities in financial markets by the Federal Reserve System. Open market operations are its most direct route for changing the monetary base. (17, 20)

Open market purchase The buying of government securities by the Fed, with the intent of raising the monetary base. (17)

Open market sale The sale of government securities by the Fed, with the intent of reducing the monetary base. (17)

Operating targets Variables directly under the Fed's control that are closely related to the intermediate targets of monetary policy. Operating targets include the federal funds rate and nonborrowed reserves. (21)

Options contract A right (option), conferred upon a trader, to buy or sell a particular asset (shares of stock, a bond, or unit of foreign currency, for example) within a predetermined time and at a predetermined price. (3, 9)

Over-the-counter (OTC) markets Secondary financial markets for brokers-dealers organized via telephone and computer, with no centralized place for auction trading. (3, 12)

Payments system Mechanism for conducting transactions in the economy. Commercial banks play a key role in this system by clearing and settling transactions in the economy. (2, 13)

Phillips curve Relationship, found by A. W. Phillips, in which high unemployment was associated with a low rate of wage inflation, and vice versa. (28)

Political business cycle model Theory that the policymakers will urge the Fed to try to lower interest rates to stimulate credit demand and economic activity prior to an election. (19)

Portfolio A collection of assets. (3, 6)

Preferred habitat theory of the term structure of interest rates Proposition that investors care about both expected returns and maturity, viewing instruments with different maturities as substitutes, but not perfect ones. (7)

Present value (PV, present discounted value) A concept used to evaluate credit marked instruments by placing all payments in terms of today's dollars so that they can be added together. (4)

Price index A summary statistic that incorporates changes in the price of a set of goods relative to the price in some base year. (2)

Price level The average price of a market basket of goods and services in the economy. (1)

Primary markets Financial markets in which newly issued debt or equity claims are sold to initial buyers by private borrowers to raise funds for durable-goods purchases or new ventures and by governments to finance budget deficits. (3)

Principal-agent problem Type of moral hazard that may arise when managers (agents) who control a firm's assets do not own very much of the firm's equity, and thus do not have the same incentive to maximize the firm's value as the owners (principals) do. (11)

Producer price index: (PPI) An index of the prices that firms pay in wholesale markets for crude materials, intermediate goods, and finished goods. It is a commonly used measure to calculate inflation. (2, 28)

Productivity growth Measure of the growth of output in a country relative to the growth of inputs. (8)

Program trading Using computer-generated orders to buy or sell many stocks at the same time, causing rapid adjustments of institutional portfolios. (10)

Purchasing power The ability of money to be used to acquire goods and services. (2)

Purchasing power parity (PPP) theory of exchange rate determination Proposition that changes in the nominal exchange rate between two currencies are accounted for by differences in inflation rates in the two countries. This theory assumes that real exchange rates are constant. (8)

Put option The right to sell an underlying asset, which is obtained by buying the put option. Sellers of put options have an obligation to buy the asset. (10)

Quantity theory of money demand Theory, developed by Irving Fisher and others, which states that the determinant of the demand for real balances is the real volume of transactions. (23)

Quota A common trade barrier that limits the volume of foreign goods that can be brought into the country. (8)

Rate of capital gains The percentage change in the price of a financial asset. (4)

Rational expectations Assumption in the model of an efficient market that participants will use all available information in estimating the expected price level or change in the money supply so that the market price equals the present value of expected future returns. (10, 26)

Real business cycle model Theory that changes in aggregate demand have no effect on output, even in the short run, assuming perfect information and perfectly flexible prices. Short-term changes to output are primarily temporary shocks to productivity, such as changes in the availability of raw materials. (25)

Real exchange rate The purchasing power of a currency relative to the purchasing power of other currencies. (8)

Real interest rate An interest rate that is adjusted for changes in purchasing power caused by inflation. (4)

Real money balances The value of money balances adjusted for changes in purchasing power. (23)

Recession A contraction in current output in the business cycle. (26)

Regulation Q Regulation, authorized by the Banking Act of 1933, that placed ceilings on allowable interest rates on time and savings deposits and prohibited the payment of interest on demand deposits (then the only form of checkable deposits). (15)

Repurchase agreements (repos or RPs) Very short-term loans that are used for cash management by large corporations. Maturities are typically less than two weeks and often the next day. (3, 13)

Required reserve ratio The percentage of deposits that banks must hold as reserves, as specified by the Fed. (17)

Required reserves The minimum amount that depository institutions are compelled to hold as reserves by the Federal Reserve System. (13, 17)

Reserves Bank asset consisting of vault cash (cash on hand in the bank), plus deposits with the Federal Reserve. (13)

Restrictive covenants Limits on the actions of a borrower or insured person made by a lender or insurer. For example, a lender may restrict risk-taking activities of the borrower, require the borrower to maintain a certain level of net worth, or require the borrower to maintain the value of collateral offered to the lender. (11, 12)

Restructuring Rearranging the financial structure of a firm to shift control over the resources of the firm and to provide incentives for managers to maximize the firm's value. (11)

Revaluation Raising the official value of a country's currency relative to other currencies, thereby resetting the exchange rate. (22)

Risk The degree of uncertainty of an asset's return. (1)

Risk-averse Desiring to minimize variability in return on savings. (6)

Risk-based premiums Fee for insurance that is based on the probability of the insured individual's collecting a claim. (12)

Risk premium The difference between the yield on a financial instrument and the yield on a default-risk-free instrument of comparable maturity. It measures the additional yield a saver requires in order to be willing to hold a risky instrument. (7)

Risk structure of interest rates The differences in risk, liquidity, information costs, and taxation that result in differences in interest rates and yields across credit market instruments of the same maturity. (7)

Saving curve A graph that illustrates the relationship between aggregate saving and the expected real rate of interest. (5)

Saving-investment diagram A graph that shows the relationship between the saving and investment curves. It is used to determine the equilibrium real interest rate. (5)

Secondary markets Financial markets in which claims that have already been issued are sold by one investor to another. (3)

Segmented markets theory Proposition that yields on each financial instrument are determined in a separate market, with separate market-specific demand and supply considerations. (7)

Short-term debt A debt instrument that has a maturity of less than one year. (3)

Simple deposit multiplier The reciprocal of the required reserve ratio. (17)

Simple loan A credit transaction in which the borrower receives from the lender an amount of funds called principal and agrees to repay the lender principal plus an additional amount called interest (as a fee for using the funds) on a given date (maturity). (4)

Small open economy An economy in which total saving is too small to affect the world real interest rate, so the economy takes the world interest rate as a given. (5)

Special Drawing Rights (SDRs) Paper substitute for gold, issued as international reserves by the International Monetary Fund in its role as lender of last resort. (22)

Specialist A broker-dealer on the floor of the exchange who makes a market in one or more stocks and matches buyers and sellers. (12)

Speculation The attempt to profit from disagreements among traders about future prices of a commodity or financial instrument by anticipating changes in prices. (10)

Speculative attack The sale of weak currencies or purchase of strong currencies by market participants who believe a government will be unable or unwilling to maintain the exchange rate, in an attempt to force a devaluation or revaluation of the currency. (22)

Spot transactions Transactions in which trade and settlement occur at the same time. (9)

Stabilization policies (activist policies) Public policies designed to smooth short-run fluctuations in output involving shifts of the AD curve by changes in government purchases or taxes or by changes in the nominal money supply. (26)

Standby letter of credit (SLC) A promise that a bank will lend the borrower funds to pay off its maturing commercial paper if necessary. (13)

State and local government bonds (municipal bonds) Intermediate and long-term bonds issued by municipalities and state governments that are exempt from federal income taxation and allow governmental units to borrow the funds to build schools, roads, and other large capital projects. (3)

State banks Banks that are chartered by a state government. (14)

Sterilized foreign-exchange intervention A transaction in which a foreign-exchange intervention is accompanied by offsetting domestic open market operations to leave the monetary base unchanged. (22)

Stock market A market where owners of firms buy and sell their claims. (1)

Stocks Equity claims issued by corporations. They represent the largest single category of capital-market assets. (3)

Store of value A function of money; the accumulation of value by holding dollars or other assets that can be used to buy goods and services in the future. (2)

Supply shocks Shifts in the price or availability of raw materials or in production technologies that affect production costs and the aggregate supply curve. (25)

T-account A simplified accounting tool that lists changes in balance sheet items as they occur. (13)

Takeover A struggle for corporate control in which a group of current or new shareholders buys a controlling interest in a firm, reshapes the board of directors, and even replaces managers. (11)

Tariff A common trade barrier consisting of a tax on goods purchased from other countries. (8)

Term premium The additional yield that investors require for investing in a less preferred maturity. (7)

Term structure of interest rates The variation in yields for related instruments differing in maturity. (7)

Theory of portfolio allocation Statement that predicts how savers allocate their assets based on their consideration of their wealth, expected return on the assets, degree of risk, liquidity of the assets, and the cost of acquiring information about assets. (6)

Time deposits Accounts with a specified maturity, which could range from a few months to several years. (13)

Total rate of return The sum of the current yield of a credit instrument and the actual capital gain or loss on it. (4)

Trade balance Component of the current account equal to the difference between merchandise exports and imports. (22)

Transactions costs The cost of trade or exchange; for example, the brokerage commission charged for buying or selling a financial claim like a bond or a share of stock. (3, 11)

Underfunded A term used to describe a defined benefit plan when contributions, together with the projected future earnings, are not sufficient to pay off projected defined benefits. (12)

Underground economy Economic activity that is not measured in formal government statistics. (17)

Underwriting A way in which investment banks earn income: in the simplest form, they guarantee a price to an issuing firm that needs capital, sell the issue at a higher price, and keep the profit, known as the "spread." (12)

Unit of account A function of money; the provision of a way of measuring the value of goods and services in the economy in terms of money. (2)

United States government agency securities Intermediate or long-term bonds issued by the federal government or government-sponsored agencies. (3)

United States Treasury bills (T-bills) Debt obligations of the U.S. government that have a maturity of less than one year. (3)

United States Treasury bonds Securities issued by the federal government to finance budget deficits. (3)

United States Treasury securities Debt obligations issued by the federal government to finance budget deficits. (3)

Universal banking Allowing banks to be involved in many nonbanking activities with no geographic restrictions. (14)

Unsterilized foreign-exchange intervention A transaction in which the central bank allows the monetary base to respond to the sale or purchase of domestic currency. (22)

Vault cash The cash on hand in the bank. (13, 17)

Velocity of money The average number of times a dollar is spent each year on a purchase of goods and services in the economy. (23)

Venture capital firm A firm that raises equity capital from investors to invest in emerging or growing entrepreneurial business ventures. (11)

Wealth The sum of the value of assets. (2)

Wealth elasticity of demand The relationship of the percentage change in quantity demanded of an asset to the percentage change in wealth. (6)

World Bank (International Bank for Reconstruction and Development) Bank created by the Bretton Woods agreement to grant long-term loans to developing countries for their economic development. (22)

World real interest rate The real interest rate determined in the international capital market. (5)

Yield curve A graph showing yields to maturity on different default-risk-free instruments as a function of maturity. (7)

Yield to maturity The interest rate measure at which the present value of an asset's returns is equal to its value today. (4)

Selected Answers to Questions and Problems

Chapter 1

REVIEW QUESTIONS

1. No, the funds would not generally be allocated to most valued uses; financial markets and institutions work better.
3. The money supply is determined jointly by actions of the Federal Reserve, banks, and the nonbank public. Decisions about monetary policy are made by the Federal Reserve.

ANALYTICAL PROBLEMS

5. The local bank provides you risk-sharing, liquidity, and information services.
7. In a global economy, their exports to the United States would decline, possibly lending to an economic downturn.

Chapter 2

REVIEW QUESTIONS

1. To serve as money, they must generally be accepted as means of payment. Your acceptance of dollar bills and checks as money is based on your belief that others will accept them.
3. In a barter system, there are too many prices, and nonstandard goods complicate pricing. Trade requires a double coincidence of wants.
5. Commodity money has real uses (e.g., gold, silver); fiat money has no intrinsic value.
7. A payments system is a mechanism for conducting transactions. If the payments system became less efficient, the costs to the economy would be fewer and more costly transactions, i.e., losing gains from specialization.
9. No. Houses, bonds, and stocks are also stores of value. There is an advantage to money's

being a store of value, since after trading for it, it can be held; otherwise, something else is likely to become money that is also a store of value.

ANALYTICAL PROBLEMS

11. The reason is convenience; one avoids transactions costs of running to the bank all the time.
13. Not necessarily; if prices rose more than 10%, your real income has fallen.
15. In Friedmania, bad money drives out the good; people will spend the new crowns and hoard the old crowns.
17. Liquidity indicates the ease with which asset can be converted to definitive money. Ranking from most to least liquid: dollar bill, checking account, money market mutual fund, passbook savings account, corporate stock, gold, house.
19. Solve the equation $311.1/100 = 100/x$; x = new CPI for 1967 = 32.1.

DATA QUESTIONS

21. In *ERP* 1992:
    a. 1980: $2708.0 billion; 1990: $5513.8 billion.
    b. 1980: $71.7; 1990: $112.9.
    c. 1980; $3776.8 billion; 1990; $4883.8 billion
    d. legal GDP rose by 29%.
23. GDP deflator values: 1950 unknown as of early 1993, 1960 = 26.0, 1970 = 35.1, 1980 = 71.7, 1990 = 112.9; Inflation: 1960s = 35%, 1970s = 104%, 1980s = 57%. PPI values: 1950 = 28.2, 1960 = 33.4, 1970 = 39.3, 1980 = 88.0, 1990 = 119.2; Inflation: 1950s = 18%, 1960s = 18%, 1970s = 124%, 1980s = 35%.

Chapter 3

REVIEW QUESTIONS

1. Savers have more resources than they want to spend currently; borrowers have fewer

resources than they currently want to spend. Risk sharing allows diversification and transfer of risk; liquidity allows flexibility in asset holdings; and information is efficiently gathered by financial intermediaries who specialize in doing so. Taken together, the three services reduce the costs of financial transactions.

3. "Integration" represents the extent to which financial markets are tied together geographically. Increased integration tends to equalize yields same returns across geographic boundaries (raising costs and returns for some, and lowering them for others), likely reducing borrowing costs by allowing for geographical diversification.

5. The transaction: a. takes place through a financial intermediary; b. is in a primary market; and c. is in a capital market.

7. The transaction: a. takes place in a financial market; b. is in a primary market; and c. is in a capital market.

9. The transaction: a. takes place through a financial intermediary; b. is in a primary market; and c. is in a money market.

ANALYTICAL PROBLEMS

11. Asset 1 yields 6% after taxes; asset 2 yields 6%; asset 3 offers the highest return, yielding 6.5%.

13. Investors want to eliminate unnecessary risk in their returns; they may trade off additional risk for additional return.

15. Leading candidates include government regulation and economic and financial stability; it is unlikely that financial technology varies greatly across industrialized countries.

Chapter 4

REVIEW QUESTIONS

1. In a discount loan, the borrower repays face value at maturity, while in a simple loan the borrower repays the stated principal plus interest at maturity.

3. The yield to maturity is the interest rate that equates value of asset today with present value of future payments. It can be derived from present-value formulas.

5. The total return includes current interest payment plus capital gain; it equals current yield plus percentage change in price.

7. According to the Fisher hypothesis, the nominal interest rate moves one-for-one with expected inflation. While there is broad support for the proposition that nominal interest rates move in response to changes in expected inflation, the Fisher effect narrowly defined is not supported exactly by U.S. data.

ANALYTICAL PROBLEMS

9. The present value is $5000.

11. Option b. has the highest present value.

13. At an initial interest rate of 7%, the bond's value is: $700/1.07 + 700/(1.07)^2 + 700/(1.07)^3 + 700/(1.07)^4 + 10,000/(1.07)^4 = 654.21 + 611.41 + 571.41 + 549.43 + 7849.02 = $10,235.48$. At an interest rate of 5%, the bond's value is: $700/1.05 + 700/1.05^2 + 700/1.05^3 + 700/1.05^4 + 10,000/1.05^4 = 666.67 + 634.92 + 604.69 + 575.89 + 8227.02 = $10,709.19$. Hence the bond's value rises as the yield falls.

15. You would be willing to pay $100/.05 = 2000$ pounds. At a 10% interest rate, you would be willing to pay $100/.10 = 1000$ pounds.

17. a. Value = $10,000; current yield = $600/10,000 = 6\%$.

   b. Value = $600/1.05 + 600/1.05^2 + 600/1.05^3 + 10,600/1.05^4 = $10,354.60$; current yield = $600/10,354.60 = 5.79\%$.

   c. Value = $600/1.05 + 600/1.05^2 + 10,600/1.05^3 = $10,272.33$; $(600 + 272.33)/10,000 = 8.72\%$; total rate of return a year ago = $[600 + (10,272.33 - 10,354.60)]/10,354.60 = 5\%$.

   d. Value = $600/1.10 + 10,600/1.10^2 = $9,305.78$; current yield over the next year = $600/9305.78 = 6.45\%$; total return given price calculated in c. = $[600 + (9305.78 - 10,272.33)]/10,272.33 = -3.57\%$.

19. The expected real interest rate equals 7% - 3%, or 4%. The actual real interest rate equals 7% - 5%, or 2%.

21. In the first institution's case, there should be little effect due to short maturities of the assets. In the second institution's case, however, there will be a major loss of net worth on account of capital loss on long maturities.

Chapter 5

REVIEW QUESTIONS

1. a. The saving curve shifts to the right in response to a fall in current income, a rise in expected future income, or a fall in precautionary or bequest saving.
   b. The saving curve shifts to the right in response to a rise in current income, a fall in expected future income, or a rise in precautionary or bequest saving.
   c. The investment curve shifts to the left in response to a fall in expected future profitability or a rise in corporate taxes.
   d. The investment curve shifts to the right in response to a rise in expected future profitability or a fall in corporate taxes.

3. In a small open economy and a large open economy, domestic desired saving and investment need not be equal. The difference between saving and investment is international lending — if desired saving exceeds desired investment — or international borrowing — if desired investment exceeds desired saving.

5. Shifts in domestic desired saving and investment in a small open economy have no effect on the world real interest rate, while such shifts in a large open economy can affect the world real interest rate.

ANALYTICAL QUESTIONS

7. The shift in the investment curve is greater than the shift in the saving curve, so the real interest rate rises. In a small open economy, there is no such affect, as the world real interest rate is given.

9. In a small open economy, the real interest rate is unaffected in each case.
   a. Domestic investment rises.
   b. Domestic investment falls.
   c. Domestic investment does not change.
   d. Domestic investment does not change.

11. The saving curve shifts to the right; aggregate saving falls on account of the decline in precautionary saving. The equilibrium real interest rate rises.

13. a. Net expected profitability falls, so aggregate investment falls.
    b. Expected profitability rises, so aggregate investment rises.
    c. The increase in the expected after-tax real interest rate reduces aggregate investment.

15. The increase in business taxes shifts the investment curve to the left. The real interest rate falls to a new equilibrium level at which desired international lending by the country equals desired international borrowing by the rest of the world. Domestic desired saving and investment both fall; desired investment falls by more, so the country now lends internationally.

17. If private saving does not rise one-for-one, the saving curve shifts to the left, increasing the real interest rate and reducing the quantity of investment. If private saving exactly offsets the change in government saving, the saving curve does not shift, and the real interest rate and the quantity of investment do not change.

19. If savings were not mobile internationally, the real interest rate would be lower in the mature economy. Once savings flow across borders, the real rate rises in the mature economy and falls in the growing economy. Global efficiency in investment is improved, and the quantity of investment rises in the growing economy and falls in the mature economy.

DATA QUESTIONS

21. The United States experienced large current account deficits. One possibility: Large gov-

ernment budget deficits reduced national saving, increasing international borrowing. Another possibility: Increased profitability of investing in the United States encouraged foreign financing of domestic investment.

Chapter 6

REVIEW QUESTIONS

1. The five key determinants of asset demand are wealth, relative return, relative risk, relative liquidity, and relative cost of acquiring information.
3. The difference lies in the attitude toward risk relative to return. A risk-loving individual is more likely to hold stocks and options. A risk-averse individual is more likely to hold bonds and cash.
5. The saying states the benefit of diversification. It means that one can reduce portfolio risk by owning many different assets.
7. Transactions costs limit the desirability of diversification.

ANALYTICAL PROBLEMS

9. Your increase in holdings will be 2 x 10% = 20%. You will buy 0.2 x 1000 = 200 shares.
11. Yes, asset 1 offers the highest return, with a 6.6% yield after taxes.
13. They offer greater liquidity: Some people (who wanted to invest for the long term) did not like having to reinvest coupon payments with unknown interest rates; they preferred the second part. Others preferred the steady income stream, but did not want to have to reinvest the principal; they preferred the first part.
15. a. Your rates of return are, respectively, 20%, -10%, 35%, -15%, 27.5%, and -12.5%.
    b. Your rates of return are now, respectively, 15%, -15%, 30%, -20%, 22.5%, and -17.5%. You are now less likely to hold both stocks and may be more likely to hold riskier Lowrunner stock.
17. a. You are more willing (higher wealth). b. You are less willing (higher risk). c. You are more willing (higher return). d. You are less willing (alternative asset has increased liquidity).

Chapter 7

REVIEW QUESTIONS

1. The bonds have different times to maturity.
3. Long-term yields fall below current short-term yields.
5. In the preferred habitat theory, term premiums account for the upward bias in the slope.
7. U.S. Treasury bonds have no default risk.
9. The taxable bond pays a higher before-tax interest rate.
11. A recession raises default risk. The phenomenon is known as a flight to quality.
13. Factors include default risk, liquidity, and taxability. In the latter case, information cost is an additional factor.
15. Markets are not very liquid, and may consist only of specialists with a lot of information.

ANALYTICAL PROBLEMS

17. Option a. pays 26/3 = 8 2/3 %; option b. pays 9%; option c. pays 8.5%; you should choose option b.
19. a. ($1000 - $10) x 1.06^4 = $1249.85; b. ($1000 - $10) x 1.055^3) – $10) x 1.09 = $1256.22; c. ($1000 - $10) x 1.05^2) - $10) x 1.07) – $10) x 1.09 = $1250.42; d. ($1000 – $10) x 1.04) - $10) x 1.065) – $10) x 1.07) – $10) x 1.09 = $1243.89. You should choose option b.
21. The yield curve should slope: a. downward, b. flat, c. upward, and d. flat.
23. Federal income tax rates were lower in the 1980s than in the 1970s.
25. Liquidity is an important consideration; as a young firm, Fred's may have only a thin market for its assets.
27. According to expectations theory it should not; but it should according to preferred habitat theory or segmented markets theory, because the Fed is unlikely to have any reason to prefer a particular maturity (at least for its long-run portfolio).

29. The expected future short-term rate is higher, so the borrower gets the same rate over the 2-year period.

Chapter 8

REVIEW QUESTIONS

1. This idea is the nominal interest rate parity condition.
3. a. The franc/dollar exchange rate rises. b. The dollar/pound exchange rate falls. c. The yen/dollar exchange rate falls. d. The dollar/mark exchange rate rises.
5. $\Delta EX/EX = \Delta EX_r/EX_r + \pi_f - \pi$. Mark: $\Delta EX/EX = 2\% + 3\% - 5\% = 0\%$. Yen: $\Delta EX/EX = -3\% + 1\% - 5\% = -7\%$.
7. There will be no change in the exchange rate. The theory assumes that real exchange rates are unchanged.
9. The franc should appreciate due to productivity improvement.
11. The difference should become smaller as currency premium shrinks.

ANALYTICAL PROBLEMS

13. Both appreciate relative to the dollar.
15. You should invest at home.
17. The United States should benefit from greater investment flow from Japan.
19. a. $EX_r = (EX \times P)P_f = (200 \text{ yen}/\$) \times (\$16/CD)/(3{,}500 \text{ yen}/CD) = 0.91$.
    b. $EX_r = (EX \times P)P_f = (\text{ pound}/\$) \times (\$16/CD)/(6 \text{ pounds}/CD) = 1.33$.
21. $\Delta EX^e/EX = -1\%$, so $EX^e = 247.5$ yen/dollar.
23. In this case, the difference is maturity (preferred habitat) versus country (currency premium) for assets that are otherwise perfect substitutes. The preference arises because of differences in risk, liquidity, or information across countries versus across maturities. A "segmented markets" analogue is inconsistent with large observed capital flows.
25. Portfolio investors would prefer to invest in German bonds if inflation were lower in Germany (so that the total return is higher) or if the pound were expected to depreciate.

Chapter 9

REVIEW QUESTIONS

1. The difference is trade today (spot transaction) versus trade in future (forward transaction). A futures contract offers greater liquidity and lower information costs.
3. A hedge transaction reduces risk for the hedger; in speculation a trader accepts increased risk to try to profit.
5. Options work like life insurance; by paying a small premium, you can hedge against changes in your asset's value.
7. The exchanges guarantee all contracts, so that information and search costs are reduced, thereby permitting anonymous trading.
9. At a price of 60, the put is in the money; at a price of 70, neither is in the money; at a price of 80, the call is on the money.
11. You might well disagree, as these markets provide useful risk-sharing benefits, promoting liquidity and the transmission of information.

ANALYTICAL PROBLEMS

13. Buy both put and call options, so if the price swing is large enough you can profit no matter which way the court ruling goes. There is a potential problem: The market price on the options contract may reflect this information, so your opportunity to profit may be lost.
15. You could buy put options; if interest rates rise, your Treasury bonds lose value, but you make money on the put option; if interest rates fall, your Treasury bonds rise in value, and your puts are worthless.
17. You could buy Treasury put options.

Chapter 10

REVIEW QUESTIONS

1. Yes; prices in liquid markets reflect information better.
3. There is a bubble. In the future, the bubble is likely to burst. Yes, bubbles have burst many

times; the latest prominent examples occurred in 1987 in the United States and in 1991-1992 in Japan.

5. Not always. Usually, an informed trader can profit from noise traders, but only if they do not make the equilibrium price deviate from fundamental value.

7. Fads are characterized by overreaction to good or bad news, so that prices do not reflect fundamental value. Someone could profit by investing when there is bad news and selling when there is good news.

ANALYTICAL PROBLEMS

9. No; this seasonality in returns is not consistent with efficient markets. An investor could profit by buying at end of December, and selling at end of January.

11. Darts are cheaper (but don't balance risk).

13. At a 4% discount rate, you would be willing to pay $(1 + i)D/(i - g) = 1.04 \times \$7/(.04 - .02) = \$364$. At a 3% discount rate, you would be willing to pay $1.03 \times \$7/(.03 - .02) = \$721$. If Bigbuck's dividends grow at only 1% per year you would be willing to pay $1.04 \times \$7/(.04 - .01) = \$242.67$.

15. In this case, you could adopt a contrarian strategy — buy after bad news, sell after good news.

REVIEW QUESTIONS

1. Symmetric information is known to both borrowers and lenders; asymmetric information occurs when borrowers have private information — something the borrowers know that the lenders do not know. The information asymmetry makes it more difficult to channel funds efficiently from lenders to borrowers.

3. The answer is *adverse selection:* Good borrowers' projects will not be viable at the higher interest rate, so the bank has a higher percentage of bad borrowers. The bank could, alternatively, use credit rationing and not raise interest rates to match the quantity demanded and supplied of loans.

5. This is the *principal-agent problem:* Managers maximize own benefits and achieve personal goals, and do not maximize firm's value. Remedies include giving managers a larger equity stake, limiting the firms free cash flow, monitoring the firm closely, or threatening a takeover.

7. To reduce adverse selection, banks can ration credit. To reduce moral hazard, banks custom-tailor loans with covenants, lenders require high internal net worth, stockholders insist that free cash flow go into dividends, and that inefficient firms be restructured. To reduce both moral hazard and adverse selection, banks specialize in gathering information and serve as delegated monitors, and venture capitalists take equity stake and positions on boards of directors.

9. In a takeover, a group buys a controlling interest in a firm. A restructuring rearranges the financial structure of a firm, usually by increasing debt.

11. Excessive debt levels can lead to cutbacks in employment and investment, greater vulnerability to recession, and a rise in bankruptcies and defaults.

Chapter 11

ANALYTICAL PROBLEMS

13. The problems are moral hazard (once insured, you won't work as hard) and adverse selection (people who are more likely to be fired or get low raises would be more likely to buy such insurance).

15. Make sure the owner's own funds are at risk, by making her take out a mortgage loan and pledging stocks and bonds as collateral. You would like to get her to pledge her first-born child as well (great collateral value), but that's not legally enforceable.

17. Yes. Insiders may buy good firms first, leaving lemons to the general public.

19. You could encourage the firm to pay out cash flow as dividends, rather than wasteful investment. You could accomplish this by organizing other shareholders, or by getting the firm to take on more debt.

21. No, because business cycles are less pronounced in Japan than in the United States.

Chapter 12

REVIEW QUESTIONS

1. The five main groups of financial institutions are securities market institutions (investment banks, brokers and dealers, and organized exchanges); investment institutions (mutual funds, and finance companies); contractual savings institutions (insurance companies and pension funds); government financial institutions; and depository institutions (commercial banks, savings institutions, and credit unions).

3. No, the NYSE is a secondary market. You are buying the shares of stock from someone else, not from IBM.

5. Finance companies' business includes consumer finance (loans to high-risk borrowers who cannot always borrow from banks), business finance (loans to small firms or firms who need to lease large capital items), and sales finance (loans to people who buy consumer or business goods on credit).

7. It is more difficult to predict property and casualty losses than it is to predict deaths.

9. Banks address adverse selection problems by specializing in gathering information about the credit risk of borrowers and by custom-tailoring loans (though, e.g., including collateral and covenants).

11. Mutual funds pool resources in order to invest in a diversified portfolio (allowing risk sharing). They also lower transactions costs of investing — increasing liquidity. Mutual funds do not make commercial loans; they pass funds through to existing direct instruments. There is less need for regulation because they just pass funds through, so long as information is made available to investors.

ANALYTICAL PROBLEMS

13. These institutions pool risk of death and investment risk that individuals may not be able to do. Self-insurance would be more costly for individuals.

15. It is not, since participation is compulsory you get all risks, not just selective ones, thus avoiding adverse selection problems.

17. Yes: Past performance is not necessarily a guide to future returns; risk levels may be different; transactions costs may be different; sales loads may be different; liquidity may be different; and taxability may be different.

DATA QUESTIONS

19. They are closed-end funds, since these are the only kind that sell shares on a secondary market. Buying closed-end funds at a discount is usually a good deal, unless the reason for the discount is that the management of the fund is weak and is likely to make bad future investments.

Chapter 13

REVIEW QUESTIONS

1. Banks provide risk-sharing, liquidity, and information services to savers and borrowers.

3. In that case, if a bank fails, only its stockholders lose, and not depositors or the government insurance fund (taxpayers).

5. Banks reduce credit-risk exposure by developing long-term relationships with customers, gathering information on their prospects, as well as general business conditions, and monitoring borrowers' behavior with the loan proceeds.

7. To provide for future defaults, banks create loan-loss reserves; when borrowers default, banks write off the loans.

9. In a floating-rate loan, the loan interest rate changes with market interest rates. Interest-rate risk is reduced for the bank, since the bank's interest income rises with its cost of funds.

ANALYTICAL PROBLEMS

11. Yes, there would still need to be transactions services and a payments system, even if there

were no need for commercial lending by banks.

13. If depositors had full information on borrowers, there would not be a bank run started by the unfounded fear that bad loans had been made; this would be possible if bankers had private information. However, a run could start for other reasons, like bad economic times.

15. Banks welcome it because the action reduces the implicit tax on reserves (because reserves pay no interest); banks can then lend the freed reserves at a positive interest rate. In the second case, no, since they would not reduce their level of reserves.

17. First: assets: -$1000 in reserves, liabilities: -$1000 in checkable deposits; Melon: assets +$1000 in reserves, liabilities: +$1000 in checkable deposits.

19. No, because with such a large proportion of assets in the form of loans —and no securities — it has no defense against a liquidity crisis; also, with no equity cushion, a small bad event could cause the bank to fail.

21. $5 million excess reserves; reserves $10 million, securities $40 million, loans $140 million, deposits $140 million, capital $50 million; -$4 million excess reserves, so borrow $4 million; same as before but reserves $14 million, borrowings from banks $2 million, borrowings from Fed $2 million.

23. $MV = \Sigma PV_t = \$1100/1.1 + \$1210/1.1^2 + \$1331/1.1^3 = \$3000$. Duration $= d = \Sigma t(PV_t/MV) = 1(\$1000/\$3000) + 2(\$1000/\$3000) + 3(\$1000/\$3000) = 1/3 + 2/3 + 3/3 = 2$. $\Delta MV/MV \approx -d\ [\Delta i/(1+i)] = -2(.02/1.1) = -0.036$, so market value falls 3.6%.

Chapter 14

REVIEW QUESTIONS

1. Under the dual banking system, some banks have national charters, while others have state charters. There are different sets of regulations for national versus state banks that allow specialization by different types of banks.

3. Historically, political concerns over large banks have been fueled by fear by the public of large banks. These concerns led to the creation of the Federal Reserve System, federal deposit insurance, and branching restrictions.

5. The creation of the Federal Reserve provided a lender of last resort with a lot of liquidity.

7. Risk-based capital requirements categorize assets in broad risk categories; they require less capital against less risky assets, more capital against riskier assets.

9. Costs include undiversified portfolios and unrealized scale economies. Savers and borrowers suffer if banks fail as a result. Small banks gain, while large banks lose due to unrealized scale economies.

11. A nonbank office makes loans, but does not accept demand deposits; a nonbank bank accepts demand deposits, but does not make loans.

13. In the United States there has been a fear of concentration of power, especially through industrial monopolies. Universal banking countries such as Germany do not seem to have fallen prey to monopolization, however.

15. Universal banks can own direct stakes in industrial and other firms; there is no separation of banking and commerce. This setup helps to reduce information costs. U.S. taxpayers might fear, however, that deposit insurance would be extended to cover losses from nonfinancial firms that are owned by banks.

ANALYTICAL PROBLEMS

17. You do not care, since you are fully insured. You pull at least $100,000 out of the bank. No, because runs can occur, as they did at Continental Illinois Bank in 1984.

19. Possibly. Prior to the introduction of federal deposit insurance, depositor discipline forced banks to have a lot of capital; with deposit insurance, depositors are no longer concerned about the banks' level of capital.

Chapter 15

REVIEW QUESTIONS

1. A lender of last resort should: a. lend to solvent banks that are threatened by a run; and b. have a large source of funds to handle large, common shocks.

3. a. The Penn Central default caused a temporary shock to the supply of funds to commercial paper issuers, as lenders questioned the default risk on commercial paper. This could have disrupted the supply of funds to firms (and thus caused reduced output) if the Fed had not stepped in to accelerate bank lending to firms. b. The stock market crash of 1987 could have caused markets to shut down due to illiquidity of market makers. This would have reduced the flow of information about firms that had issued stock, making it difficult for them to raise funds for investment. The Fed's action prevented a loss of information and allowed smooth working of the system.

5. Innovations to circumvent deposit-rate ceilings included the use of negotiable CDs, repos or overnight Eurodollars, and ATS and NOW accounts.

7. The sudden rise in interest rates in late 1970s and early 1980s led to big capital losses at S&Ls, which had loaned long-term and borrowed short-term. The problems were magnified owing to the interaction of deregulation, undiscovered fraud, lax supervision, and failure to close insolvent institutions (which assumed additional risks) made losses greater.

9. Reasons include: increased competition due to regulation, leading to increased risk-taking, poor diversification, making many banks subject to sector- or area-specific shocks; volatile interest rates and exchange rates, increasing risk to banks, exposure to highly leveraged transactions, the fall in commercial real estate values in early 1980s, and use of brokered deposits; failure of FDIC to deal adequately with moral hazard problems in deposit insurance arrangements.

11. A run on an insurance company can occur: People who fear that a company is weak may cash in their policies, causing the company to fail; a failure could lead to contagion affecting other insurance companies. There may be a need for a government guarantee program to deal with systemic risk, as private systems are small and unable to handle a major crisis.

ANALYTICAL PROBLEMS

13. As interest rates rose, bank deposits were not competitive investments, so disintermediation occurred — people put their money elsewhere. This curtailed the supply of funds to firms and households that must borrow from banks, slowing down the economy.

15. You could move money to Europe after closing on Friday in the United States, so that you can earn interest on Monday morning in Europe, then move the money back to the United States later on Monday. Similarly, you could do this every day, earning morning interest in Europe, and all-day interest in the United States.

17. Here is one possibility: If it is solvent, you could lend to the big bank to get it to cover its securitized mortgages and end the crisis; if it is not solvent, the bank must be shut down, however. In this case, you could organize other banks together to convince them to cover the large banks' losses, paving the way for this by offering discount loans at below-market interest rates.

Chapter 16

REVIEW QUESTIONS

1. The international banking market exists to satisfy the demand banking services (risk sharing, liquidity, and information) with lower transactions costs than could be provided by domestic banks, especially with regard to international trade.

3. The leading financial centers are located in

United Kingdom, Japan, United States, and Switzerland.

5. The leading risk managed by international banks is exchange rate risk. Techniques to manage this risk include the use of financial futures, options, or currency swaps.

7. Foreign-exchange grew on account of increased world trade and the growth in cross-border financial transactions.

9. Euromarkets are offshore banking centers that deal extensively in foreign exchange. They emerged on account of U.S. regulation and the demand for dollars overseas. Up to early 1970s, the leading customers were governments and state-owned enterprises. By the late 1970s, the leading customers were oil-producing countries. By the late 1980s, the leading customers were countries with large trade surpluses. The principal Eurocurrencies are the U.S. dollar, German mark, and Japanese yen.

11. The problem of interest rate risk is reflected in a mismatch of the duration of assets and liabilities. The problem of exchange rate risk is reflected in the mismatch in the value of currencies of assets and liabilities. Possible risk management strategies include hedging with futures or options or using currency swaps.

ANALYTICAL PROBLEMS

13. You could enter a contract to sell one billion yen when the loan is due; such a transaction effectively locks in a known exchange rate today.

15. Ichi-ball's bank writes a letter of credit and sends it to Big Ball to pay for the balls. When Big Ball ships the baseballs from the United States to Japan, it presents the letter of credit to its own bank in the United States, which pays it in dollars. Big Ball's bank issues a time draft and sends it to Ichi-ball's bank. Ichi-ball's bank pays Big Ball's bank. All that remains is for Ichi-ball to pay off its bank at some point in the future; in the meantime, the "banker's acceptance," which is a liability of Ichi-ball's bank, exists and can be traded in the market.

Chapter 17

REVIEW QUESTIONS

1. Principal assets include (1) U.S. government securities, held to earn interest; and (2) discount loans to banks, usually due to banks' short-run financing needs. Principal liabilities include (1) currency, held by the nonbank public for transactions purposes; and (2) reserves, held by banks as vault cash or as deposits with the Fed.

3. Currency in circulation = Currency outstanding – Vault cash. Currency in circulation is part of the monetary base.

5. To increase the money supply, the Fed can conduct open market purchase or increase the volume of discount loans. To decrease the money supply, the Fed can conduct open market sales or reduce the volume of discount loans.

7. The Fed discourages borrowing and imposes other costs.

9. The simple deposit multiplier is unchanged.

ANALYTICAL PROBLEMS

11. Assets: ΔLoans = +\$100,000; Liabilities: ΔDeposits = +\$100,000; Assets: ΔReserves = -\$100,000; Liabilities: ΔDeposits = -\$100,000; ΔAssets = 0: ΔLoans = +\$100,000; ΔReserves = -\$100,000; ΔLiabilities = 0.

13. Required reserves: (0.14 x 300) + 0.03 x 200) = 42 + 6 = 48; 0.16 x 300 = 48. Excess reserves are 0 in both cases.

15. a. RR = (0.03 x 30) + (0.12 x 150) = 18.9. ER = 0.

   b. Assets: Reserves = 23.9, Securities = 26.1; everything else the same. Total reserves are now 23.9; since RR still equal 18.9, ER = 5.

   c. Assets: Loans = 155; Liabilities: Checkable deposits = 185; everything else the same as in part b. RR = 19.5, R = 23.9, ER = 4.4.

   d. Assets: Reserves = 18.9; Liabilities: Checkable deposits = 180; everything else the same as in part c. RR = 18.9 = R, so ER = 0.

17. $(1 + 100/800)/(100/800 + 0.20 + 40/800) = 3$.

19. No, the demand for U.S. dollars rises, as the United States is a safe haven for wealth.

21. The money multiplier is one; the Fed cannot affect the money supply beyond the change in the monetary base.

23. a. $B = C + R = [(0.06 + 0.14) \times 2000] + (0.2 \times 2000) = 400 + 400 = 800$; $M1 = C + D = 2400$; $M2 = M1 + N + MM = 2400 + (1.5 \times 2000) + (0.5 \times 2000) = 6400$. Bank A required reserves are $300 million x 0.14 = $42 million; total reserves are $48 million; excess reserves are $6 million. Economy required reserves are $2000 billion x 0.14 = $280 billion; total reserves are $400 billion; excess reserves are $120 billion.

   b. Using multiplier formulas: M1 multiplier = $(1 + (C/D)/[(C/D) + (R/D) + (ER/D)] = 1.2/(.2 + .14 + .06) = 3$; M2 multiplier = $[(1 + (C/D) + (N/D) + (MM/D)]/[(C/D) + (R/D) + (ER/D)] = (1 + .2 + 1.5 + .5)/(.2 + .14 + .06) = 3.2/.4 = 8$.

   c. Bank A's balance sheet is unchanged; required reserves = $300 million, so excess reserves = 0. M1 multiplier = $(1 + C/D)/[(C/D + (R/D) + ER/D)] = 1.2/(.2 + .16) = 3\ 1/3$; M2 multiplier = $[1 + (C/D) + (N/D) + (MM/D)]/[(C/D) + (R/D) + (ER/D)] = 3.2/.36 = 8\ 8/9$. [Notice that other variables can be calculated, given the same ratios defined above: Since $B = 800$, and given the multipliers, we can derive $M1 = \$2666\ 2/3$ billion, $M2 = \$7111\ 1/9$ billion; $N + MM = M2 - M1 = \$4444\ 4/9$; billion; $N/D + MM/D = 2$ implies $D = \$2222 = 2/9$ billion; $C/D = 0.2$ implies $C = \$444\ 4/9$ billion; $B = R + C$ implies $R = \$355\ 5/9$ billion, since B is unchanged at $800 billion.]

   d. Bank A loses $1.5 million in securities and gains $1.5 million in reserves. Required reserves are $42 million, as in part a.. Total reserves are $49.5 million, so Bank A has $7.5 million in excess reserves. The new monetary base is $888 8/9 billion. [*Additional effects:* Multipliers

for $M1$ and $M2$ are 3 and 6, as in part b., so with $B = \$888\ 8/9$ billion, $M1 = \$2666\ 2/3$ billion, $M2 = \$7111\ 1/9$ billion; so $M1$, $M2$, N, MM, D, and C are all the same as in part c., but now reserves are higher (888-8/9) - 444 4/9 = $444 4/9 billion) than in part c.]

Chapter 18

REVIEW QUESTIONS

1. Sources of the monetary base are enumerated in equation (18.3). Uses of the monetary base are enumerated in equation (18.1).

3. Items a., c., e., i., and j. are assets of the Fed. Items b., d., f., g., and h. are liabilities of the Fed.

5. Federal Reserve float equals cash items in the process of collection minus deferred availability cash items. It represents the amount of money the Fed has paid out for checks on which the Fed has not yet collected. Increases in float cause the monetary base to rise.

7. The General Account is an account at the Fed from which Treasury disbursements are made. No, the Treasury maintains tax and loan accounts at banks as well, as in the General Accounts it keeps funds in tax and loan accounts until they are due to be spent.

ANALYTICAL PROBLEMS

9. Federal Reserve float rises $1 billion; the monetary base rises $1.75 billion (just add up sources of the base and subtract uses of the base in equation (18.3)).

11. The monetary base would be more stable in this case, because the Treasury would stop moving funds into and out of the monetary base whenever it wanted to spend money.

13. The monetary base...
    a. Does not change.
    b. Rises by $2.5 billion.
    c. Falls by $10 million due to foreign deposit at the Fed.
    d. Both float and the monetary base would

rise, as the Fed would allow extra liquidity to prevent a disruption of the payments system.

e. Falls by $1 billion.

f. Rises by $1 billion.

g. Rises as other Federal Reserve assets rise.

15. The monetary base rises by $150 million: The Fed has $150 million more of foreign exchange reserves and $150 million more of Federal Reserve Notes outstanding.

17. Although just from equation (18.3) it appears that the increase in Treasury currency outstanding would increase the monetary base, in reality the Fed issues coins by purchasing them from the Treasury. Thus the increase in coins (Treasury currency outstanding) is matched by an increase in the Treasury's General Account, and there is no change in the monetary base.

Chapter 19

REVIEW QUESTIONS

1. The members of the Board of Governors serve on the FOMC, set reserve requirements, and establish the discount rate.

3. Most of the Fed's interest income is derived from its holdings of government securities.

5. Regional Federal Reserve Banks are located in Boston, New York, Philadelphia, Cleveland, Richmond, Atlanta, Chicago, St. Louis, Minneapolis, Kansas City, Dallas, and San Francisco.

7. This pattern was designed to diffuse power and influence within the system, and to ensure that no special interest group monopolizes power.

9. The principal activities of the Federal Reserve Banks are to manage the payments system (clearing checks), manage currency, conduct discount lending, supervise and regulate banks, and provide other services.

11. This is not necessarily true; monetary policy is a type of public policy, so should be the responsibility of elected officials. Also, independence of the Fed may make it more diffi-

cult to coordinate monetary and fiscal policy.

ANALYTICAL PROBLEMS

13. Limited independence may be best: Some independence reduces short-run political interference, while some accountability prevents major errors from going uncorrected.

15. The Fed is operating a political business cycle to get incumbents reelected. The conclusion would change, as the weakening economy justifies the monetary easing; doubts remain, however, that the Fed would have eased as much if there were not an election coming up.

17. It might appear that this contradicts the public-interest view, but it could be that Fed policymakers really were pursuing what they believed were correct policies. As we discuss in later chapters, in the early 1970s, policymakers and staff at the Fed (like most macroeconomists at that time) did not understand the difference between short-run and long-run tradeoffs between inflation and unemployment. Having never before faced large supply shocks, such as those caused by OPEC in the 1970s, the Fed's response did not place enough weight on reducing inflation. In other words, the Fed tried to pursue socially beneficial policies, but lacked the knowledge to do so successfully.

19. Reduce independence: The President of the United States would have much more control over the FOMC; it would be more accountable, as all members of the FOMC would be political appointees, whereas the Federal Reserve Bank presidents are not; would lose information about regional concerns, except as they are communicated through political channels (currently at each FOMC meeting there is a "go around" at which each Federal Reserve Bank President discusses conditions in each district).

21. Yes, to some extent. But generally, worldwide, higher inflation is associated with less independence of the central bank. Japan may just be a unique case in that the government itself takes a long-run view and understands

(partly due to its bad experience in the mid 1970s) that monetary policy should keep inflation low.

23. a.   The Fed believes this is bad for the economy due to too much additional financial risk.
    b.   The Fed's turf gets invaded as it gets less to regulate.

Chapter 20

REVIEW QUESTIONS

1.   The Fed's most important policy tool is open market operations. Guidance for open market operations is given by the Federal Open Market Committee.
3.   The discount rate is set by the Fed, depending on what effect it wants to have on the money supply and its attitude toward discount lending.
5.   The maintenance period is the average level of reserves at the Fed for a two-week period beginning on a Thursday and ending on a Wednesday; checkable deposits are averaged over a two-week period ending the preceding Monday; vault cash and other reservable liabilities are averaged over a two-week period ending on Monday, four weeks earlier.
7.   Banks can hold *securities* as a source of liquidity; they do not need cash for this purpose. Moreover, the liquidity rationale would suggest that reserve requirements should be higher for banks that are more likely to suffer a liquidity crisis.
9.   a. adjustment credit; b. extended credit; c. seasonal credit.
11.   False. The announcement effect occurs because the announcement of a change in the discount rate communicates new information about future Fed policy.
13.   The Trading Desk consults with market participants in order to understand market conditions. Consultations with the Treasury are useful for learning what the Treasury balance will be. Consultations with members of the FOMC ensure that the planned daily action is consistent with the directive from the FOMC.

ANALYTICAL PROBLEMS

15.   The interest rate most directly affected by open market operations is the federal funds rate. It falls in response to open market purchases, and it rises in response to open market sales.
17.   The Fed could conduct open market sales of bonds of $100 million; it could increase discount rate to reduce borrowed reserves by $100 million; or increase reserve requirements, in order to reduce the money multiplier.
19.   Defensive: a., c.. Dynamic: b., d..
21.   Easiest to tightest: b (immediate easing), e (no change in policy, asymmetric directive towards easing), c (no change in policy, symmetric directive), d (no change in policy, asymmetric directive towards tightening, a (immediate tightening).
23.   The answer is given away by the question. Just do the exercise to write out the supply and demand schedules to determine the equilibrium.

Chapter 21

REVIEW QUESTIONS

1.   The principal goals of monetary policy are to stabilize the price level, promote high employment, promote economic growth, stability in financial markets and institutions, promote interest rate stability, and promote stability in foreign-exchange markets.
3.   The Fed is interested in price stability because inflation erodes money's value as a medium of exchange and unit of account. Inflation makes prices less useful as signals for resource allocation.
5.   Interest rates affect saving and investment decisions, so fluctuations in interest rates might reduce saving and investment due to uncertainty. Similarly, exchange rate fluctuations might discourage businesses from expanding their trade with other countries.
7.   If targeting money, interest rates become more volatile; if targeting interest rates,

money supply becomes more volatile. It is impossible to target both simultaneously.

9. In an economic boom, interest rates rise, so excess reserve holdings fall and borrowed reserves increase — so free reserves fall. This is not a sign of tighter policy, but of higher economic growth, so the proper response of policy actually would be to tighten. Instead, the Fed took it as a sign that policy was tight and eased to increase free reserves, so the economy grew even faster.

11. To decrease the foreign-exchange value of the dollar, it should use expansionary policy. To increase the foreign-exchange value of the dollar, it should use contractionary policy.

13. If the Fed wants to tighten policy but is using interest rate targets, people blame the Fed for raising interest rates. If, instead, the Fed targets something else, like nonborrowed reserves and monetary aggregates, it can avoid direct blame for changing interest rates. In 1982, the Fed switched from targeting nonborrowed reserves to borrowed reserves as an operating target to smooth changes in interest rates.

15. True. If an interest rate target is selected, monetary aggregates will fluctuate.

ANALYTICAL PROBLEMS

17. This is a proposal by Bennett McCallum of Carnegie-Mellon University. On the plus side, it is a simple rule and the monetary base is a reasonable operating target. On the minus side, nominal GDP may not be a good intermediate target because it is not measurable as frequently as things like money growth, and it may not be closely related to the main goal variables of real GDP and inflation, since a fixed nominal GDP could lead to high inflation and low growth.

19. Use the model to simulate how the economy would behave with different monetary actions; choose the monetary policy that is best (by some criterion, such as minimizing unemployment with stable inflation). If the forecasts are inaccurate, the policy advice given by such a model may be much worse

than using other methods.

21. Use open market operations to stabilize the funds rate — open market purchases when the funds rate is above target, and open market sales when the funds rate is below target. This strategy may lend to procyclical monetary supply growth if the target is not moved appropriately.

23. False. This depends on the type of monetary policy pursued by the Fed; it is only true if monetary policy is procyclical.

25. Interest rate targets are not useful for this purpose if the targets do not adjust frequently. If, for example, interest rate targets are fixed, then in a recession demand for money falls, reducing interest rates, and the Fed tightens to raise interest rates, further reducing money supply and worsening the economy further.

Chapter 22

REVIEW QUESTIONS

1. U.S. international reserves and the monetary base both increase by $3 billion. This is an unsterilized intervention.

3. The Japanese central bank sells yen and buys dollars; the Fed sells yen and buys dollars.

5. The appreciation makes exports more expensive, while depreciation raises the cost of imports.

7. It is an accounting device for keeping track of private and government flows of funds between the United States and foreign countries.

9. Maintaining fixed exchange rates to gold means that gold flows adjust in response to international trade or financial disturbances, affecting the money supply.

11. The IMF is a lender of last resort to avoid the short-term economic dislocations that threaten exchange-rate stability. The World Bank makes long-term loans to developing countries to build infrastructure for economic development.

13. European countries sought a monetary union in order to reduce transactions costs of cur-

rency conversion and hedging exchange-rate risks.

15. This is true only if central banks do not intervene or care about the exchange rate.

ANALYTICAL PROBLEMS

17. Financial market participants expect expansionary monetary policy on the part of the Bank of England, reducing short-term interest rates, and causing depreciation of the pound.

19. The capital account balance is -$80 billion. This represents a capital outflow of $80 billion.

21. You would expect pound to depreciate. To profit from this knowledge, you would sell pound assets, and buy mark assets. Such a collective effort would constitute a speculative attack on the pound.

23. The net balance is $45 billion + $20 billion, or $65 billion.

25. Merchandise imports equal -$1 million. Net unilateral transfers equal +$1 million. There is no change in the current account balance.

DATA QUESTIONS

27. The value of the dollar compared to the mark was: stable in the 1960s; it fell in the 1970s, and rose in the 1980s until 1985, declining from 1985 through the early 1990s.

Chapter 23

REVIEW QUESTIONS

1. Real money balances equal nominal money balances divided by the price level.

3. No; see Figure 23.1 in the text.

5. Payments system factors represent the means through which people conduct transactions. If non-money substitutes are used, money demand drops; depends on financial innovation and regulation.

7. The interest rate, which is the opportunity cost of holding money, affects money demand in the Baumol-Tobin approach.

9. Individuals expect capital gain on bonds, so they reduce their demand for money.

11. The relevant income concept in Friedman's approach is permanent income —expected present value of future income. Permanent income is not directly measurable, so proxies must be developed.

13. A weighted monetary aggregate sums monetary assets using weights according to how liquid the assets are, in order to approximate the "moneyness" of different assets. Such aggregates have closer relationships with other economic variables than the simple-sum aggregates.

ANALYTICAL PROBLEMS

15. a. $MV = PY$ so $M = PY/V = \$2$ trillion. $P = 1$, so $M/P = \$2$ trillion.

   b. Assume that V is constant, and assume no change in Y. Hence $P = MV/Y = \$2.5$ trillion x 3/$6 trillion = 7.5/6 = 1 1/4; so the price level rises 25%.

17. The price level doubled during this period.

19. $M = (1/V) \times PY = 1/4 \times \$6$ trillion = $1.5 trillion.

21. To represent a good deal, you must be avoiding service charges of at least $1000 x (8% - 3%), or $50.

23. According to the liquidity preference theory, the interest rate rises, reducing money demand and increasing velocity.

25. Money demand functions would break down completely. There is no longer any transactions demand for money, so you would have to redefine money as a collection of assets. At the same time, all financial assets would become very liquid, so you could call them all money.

27. Financial innovation is difficult to quantify. You could reduce the effect of this problem on forecasts of money demand by trying to guess at some quantitative measure for S.

Chapter 24

REVIEW QUESTIONS

1. The LM curve shifts down to the right; the IS curve and FE line are unaffected.

3. The *IS* curve is directly shifted by a change in fiscal policy in a closed economy. An increase in government spending shifts the *IS* curve up to the right.

5. In a general equilibrium, all markets in the economy are in equilibrium at the same time; *IS*, *LM*, and *FE* all intersect at the same point.

7. The two principal determinants of desired investment are the expected future profitability of capital and expected real interest rate.

9. If data show that there is no relationship across countries between their levels of saving and investment, the economies must be open, since domestic saving does not equal investment. If domestic saving and investment are highly correlated, the economies are closed.

11. The *FE* line shows output produced by fully employed resources in the economy; it is vertical because output produced today depends on current factors in place, which are not affected by the current real interest rate.

ANALYTICAL PROBLEMS

13. The fall in desired investment shifts the *IS* curve down to the left.

15. The decrease in current domestic output reduces domestic saving. To equate desired international borrowing by the domestic economy to desired lending by the foreign economy, the real interest rate must rise, reducing investment. At equilibrium, saving and investment are both lower than before (but saving is less than investment, so the domestic economy borrows from abroad), the real interest rate is higher, and there is a current account deficit.

17. a. In response to an increase in expected inflation, money demand falls, shifting the *LM* curve down to the right.
    b. In response to the fall in the return on money, money demand falls, shifting the *LM* curve down to the right.
    c. In response to an increase in the price level, the money supply falls, shifting the *LM* curve up to the left.
    d. In response to the open market purchas-

es, the money supply rises, shifting the *LM* curve down to the right.

19. The reduction in current productivity shifts the *FE* line to the left. To restore equilibrium, the price level rises so that the *LM* curve shifts left. As a result, the economy has is a higher real interest rate and lower output with a higher price level. Since the real interest rate is higher, investment is lower. Since desired saving must equal investment, saving is lower. Since the real interest rate is higher, real money demand is lower.

21. As a result of the fall in foreign demand for U.S. goods, the *IS* curve shifts down to the left. To restore equilibrium, the price level falls. In the new equilibrium, the real interest rate is lower, and current output is unchanged. Since the real interest rate falls, saving falls and investment rises, reducing the current account balance. The nominal money supply is unchanged, so real money demand rises (since the price level falls, raising real money balances supplied).

23. In a small open economy, if the world interest rate declines, the *LM* curve must shift down to the right to restore equilibrium. Hence, the price level must fall.

25. The new development increases current productivity, so the *FE* line shifts right. The price level falls to restore equilibrium. In the new equilibrium real interest rate is lower, and current output is higher.

27. a. As a result of the fall in government saving, the *IS* curve shifts up to the right, so the price level rises (in order to shift the LM curve up to the left to restore equilibrium at higher real interest rate).
    b. Because Germany and the United States are both large open economies, Germany also experiences a higher real interest rate and higher price level.
    c. To mitigate the increase in the price level, the U.S. Fed or the German Bundesbank could reduce money supply. Such an action shifts the *LM* curve up to the left, reducing upward pressure on the price level.

Chapter 25

REVIEW QUESTIONS

1. Along the *AD* curve, there is a negative relationship between the price level and aggregate output. A higher price level reduces real money balances. If nothing else changes, the real interest rate rises, reducing consumption and investment, so aggregate demand declines.

3. In the new Keynesian approach, prices are sticky; that is, prices adjust slowly to restore equilibrium. Underlying explanations for price stickiness include long-term contracts and imperfect competition.

5. The *LRAS* curve is vertical in both the new classical and new Keynesian models. Hence, expansionary or contractionary shifts in the *AD* curve from a change in the nominal money supply have no effect on output in the long run: Money is neutral.

7. In the real business cycle approach, short-term changes in output are explained by temporary shocks to productivity. If a winter storm temporarily reduces agricultural output, the *SRAS* curve shifts to the left.

ANALYTICAL PROBLEMS

9. In the short run (in the new Keynesian approach), the rise in income taxes reduces desired consumption, shifting the *AD* curve to the left and reducing output and the price level. In the long run, the *SRAS* curve shifts to the right, reducing the price level further and restoring full employment output.

11. a. With no perception of inflation, $\pi = \pi^e$, and $u = 4\%$.
    b. If $\pi = 4\%$ and $\pi^e = 8\%$, $2u = 12\%$, or $u = 6\%$.
    c. If $\pi = 8\%$ and $\pi^e = 4\%$, $2u = 4\%$, or $u = 2\%$.

13. A thrift campaign reduces desired consumption, shifting the *AD* curve to the left. In the short run, output falls. In the long run, the price level falls to restore equilibrium at the full employment level of output.

15. Recall that aggregate demand equals $C + I + G$. An increase in government purchases reduces desired saving, shifting the saving curve to the left in the saving-investment diagram. If desired investment is very sensitive to changes in the real interest rate, private investment may fall sufficiently to offset much of the fiscal stimulus. That is, the fall in *I* may offset the stimulative effect on aggregate demand of an increase in *G*.

17. The *proponents'* claim focuses on aggregate supply: If the infrastructure program makes private labor and capital inputs more productive, the *LRAS* curve shifts to the right. The *opponents'* claim focuses on aggregate demand: In the short run, the increase in government purchases reduces desired saving and raises the real interest rate, possibly crowding out private investment.

19. All else being equal, the increase in the interest rate paid on bank deposits raises money demand and shifts the *AD* curve to the left. In the long run, the price level falls.

Chapter 26

REVIEW PROBLEMS

1. A business cycle is an episode in which an expansion of current output toward a peak is followed by a contraction in current output toward a trough; they affect people's economic well-being, and it may be possible to design policies to reduce their severity.

3. Money is non-neutral because of the cost of changing prices by firms with price greater than marginal cost, so prices are sticky, money is non-neutral because wages and prices are set in advance, so prices are sticky.

5. Money is neutral in the short run in the real business cycle model because prices are flexible. Business cycle movements reflect shocks to productivity.

7. In the new classical model, money is nonneutral due to misperceptions. In the new

Keynesian model, money is nonneutral due to price stickiness. Both models assume rational expectations about the price level or inflation, so unexpected changes in the money supply affect output. In the new Keynesian model, even expected changes in the money supply affect output in the short run.

9. a. *Data lag*: data are not available quickly; b. *Recognition lag*: It may take some time to recognize trends in the data; c. *Legislation lag*: legislative action is a time-consuming process; d. *Implementation lag*: Carrying out policy changes takes time; e. *Impact lag*: it takes time for a policy change to affect the economy.

11. The correlation of money growth and output growth in the real business cycle model is an example of reverse causation: Output growth causes money to grow.

ANALYTICAL PROBLEMS

13. a. Do nothing, if the *AD* shift were anticipated.
    b. You could stabilize output by increasing the money supply, shifting the *AD* curve to the right, but you would probably not do so in order to preserve your long-run credibility.

15. There would be less belief that the Fed would do what it says it will in the future. The real interest rate may decline faster in recessions as people come to expect Fed intervention, but inflation would not decline as much. You would expect that a monetary expansion by the Fed would reduce short-term rates such as Treasury bill rates, but would not reduce (and could possible increase) long-term interest rates.

17. In the case of an *AD* shock, monetary policy can be used to restore both output and the price level to their original level. In the case of an *AS* shock, if the Fed tries to stabilize output, the price level differs from its original level; if the Fed tries to stabilize the price level, output differs from its initial level.

19. In the new classical approach, the Fed could stabilize output by increasing aggregate demand unexpectedly. To restore the econo-

my's initial price level, the Fed would have to decrease aggregate demand. In the new Keynesian approach, either an expected or unexpected increase in aggregate demand could be used to stabilize output.

Chapter 27

REVIEW QUESTIONS

1. Internal funds are a cheaper source of finance than external funds for many firms due to asymmetric information (insiders know more than outsiders about the firm's prospects).

3. A financial panic period characterized by violent fluctuations in financial markets, bank runs, and bankruptcies of many firms. During a financial panic, bank lending falls as depositors withdraw funds from the banking system, thus magnifying the decline in economic activity.

5. The Carter credit controls were "too effective" in reducing credit availability as they led to a recession.

7. In the money view, the credit market *per se* is not important, since banks are just passive intermediaries. Monetary policy affects the economy through effects on the real interest rate determined in a money market. In a credit view, banks are specialized providers of financial services. Bank loans are special; and monetary policy affects the economy both through the money market and the credit market.

9. The more liquid assets a household or business has, the less likely it is to have to sell illiquid assets to meet current obligations.

11. Both views are important. Evidence of a role for the credit view is provided by Gertler and Gilchrist, who find that small firms are more affected by monetary policy than large firms; and Kashyap, Stein, and Wilcox find commercial paper issuance rises when bank loans decline with contractionary monetary policy.

13. In a credit crunch, the federal funds rate should decline as there is less demand for reserves. The volume of bank lending

declines as banks reduce loans to many borrowers; the volume of non-bank lending rises as businesses turn elsewhere for funds. If the volume of non-bank lending declines, this suggests that there is a recession, not a credit crunch.
15. The statement is true to the extent that banks are passive intermediaries in the money view and that bank loans are special in the credit view. However, in the credit view, the public's decisions matter, also.

ANALYTICAL PROBLEMS

17. The financial weakness of borrowers is greater in recession.
19. False. Under the credit view, contractionary monetary policy could lead to a credit crunch that reduces the real interest rate.
21. The credit restrictions shift the *AD* curve to the left, resulting in a lower level output and a lower price level than would have prevailed otherwise.
23. The real interest rate will fall more under the money view. The credit view has an offsetting effect on account of the fall in money demand.

Chapter 28

REVIEW QUESTIONS

1. Costs of expected inflation arise because expected inflation: (1) taxes money holdings and leads to shoe leather costs; (2) distorts saving and investment decisions because of the interaction of inflation and the tax code; and; (3) leads to menu costs of changing prices. Costs of unexpected inflation arise because unexpected inflation: (1) leads to redistribution of wealth; and (2) distorts price signals.
3. Over the long run, the principal cause of inflation is sustained growth of the nominal money supply.
5. People holding money lose purchasing power because of inflation, just as if they were taxed on their money balances.

7. Because of structural and frictional unemployment, we would never expect the unemployment rate to be zero.
9. Taxes are based on nominal rather than real returns.
11. With menu costs, firms may not adjust prices simultaneously in response to inflation; as a result, relative prices will change, thus affecting the allocation of resources. Menu costs are most important for firms that print prices on catalogues, or those who must fix prices for a long time, such as magazine companies or video-game companies.
13. Price controls lead to shortages, since prices do not change to equate supply and demand. Price controls simply repress inflation; they do not cure it.
15. The statement is true in the new classical view only if the announcement is credible.

ANALYTICAL PROBLEMS

17. In the short run, the *AD* curve shifts left, reducing output and the price level. In the long run, the *SRAS* curve shifts downward to reduce price level farther and restore full-employment output.
19. In the short run, the *AD* curve shifts to the left, reducing output and the price level. In the long run, the *SRAS* curve shifts downward, reducing the price level further and restoring full-employment output.
21. When inflation is zero, Mr. Feldstein's after-tax real rate of return is 2% {[4% nominal return x (1 - 0.50 tax rate)] - 0% inflation}. When inflation is 10%, Mr. Feldstein's after-tax real rate of return is -3% {[14% nominal return x (1 - 0.50 tax rate)] - 10% inflation}.
23. The policy would be too expansionary, and the price level would rise continuously as policymakers tried to hit an unreachable target.
25. If velocity and output growth are both stable, this might be a good way to restrain inflation. If velocity is not stable, however, the restriction might force the Fed to pursue a procyclical monetary policy. Moreover, the move might limit the use of monetary policy in combatting recession.

27. The low interest rate means fast money growth with the *AD* curve shifting to right, causing inflation in the long run.

29. a. With the price controls, there is excess demand, but the economy's output and price level are as before. b. The *SRAS* curve shifts up immediately, leading to a large increase in the price level. The effect is not necessary, the Fed could use contractionary monetary policy to shift the *AD* curve back to the left and return to the original state.

31. Both models would predict ever-accelerating inflation as a consequence.

Index

long-run, 754-755
simple, 752
Pickens, T. Boone, 254
Pierce, James L., 358
Plaza Accord, 542, 556, 570
Pochinok, Aleksandr, 472
Poland, aggregate supply in, 660
Political business cycle, 489, 491
Pollution rights, futures contracts on, 214-215
Portfolio, 40
Portfolio allocation. *See also* Theory of
     determinants of, 127-132
     and efficient markets, 229
     and money demand, 590-594
Precautionary motive, 592
Precautionary saving, 102, 105
Preferences, and real exchange rate, 180
Preferred habitat theory, 162-163, 165
Premiums
     of insurance companies, 281
     risk-based, 283
Present value, 73-76
Price
     bid versus asked, 88
     bond, 82-86
     exercise, 205
     futures, 205-206
     law of one, 178, 179
     market, 222-225
     spot, 206
     strike, 205
Price controls, 746
Price-earnings ratio, among countries, 132
Price index, 21, 36, 176
Price level
     and aggregate demand, 644-645
     anomalies in, 231-232
     changes in, 628-629, 632, 643
     costs of fluctuations in, 236-237
     expected, and short-run aggregate supply, 655
     and misperception theory, 651
     and rational expectations, 683-684
     in real business cycle model, 675-676
     and unexpected changes in money supply,
          725-726
     and velocity of money, 585
Price setters, 653, 654

Price stability, 526
Price stickiness, 651-654, 672, 680
Price takers, 652
Primary markets, 43-44
Prime rate, 316-317
Principal, 43, 255
Principal-agent problem, 255
     and deposit insurance, 378
     and moral hazard, 254-257
     predicting, 265-270
Principal-agent view, 489-490
Privatization, in Eastern Europe, 260-261
Procyclical monetary policy, 537, 538
Producer price index (PPI), 36, 724
Productivity, 180, 657
Program trading, 236
Property and casualty insurance companies,
     285-286
Public interest view, 488
Purchase and assumption method, 344
Purchasing power, 20
Purchasing power parity (PPP) theory, 178-180
Put option, 205
Putnam Management Company, 279

Quantity theory of money demand, 586
Quotas, 180

Random walk, 224
Rate of capital gains, 87
Rate of return
     expected, 128-129, 437-438, 591
     total, 86-87
Rational expectations, 223, 683, 697
Reagan, Ronald, 235, 378, 488, 556, 687
Real business cycle model, 661
     and equilibrium, 661-662
     and money supply, 675-678
     and stabilization policies, 683
Real exchange rate, 174-176
     factors in changes in, 179-180
Real interest rate, 90
     and aggregate demand, 645
     determining, 109-119
     effects of increases in, 630-631
     in equilibrium, 110-112
     and exchange rate, 189-190, 192

State Street Investment Corporation, 279
Statistical discrepancy, 560
Stein, Jeremy, 712
Sterilized foreign-exchange intervention, 553, 555-556
Stock(s)
    as financial instrument, 64-65
    prices of, in new Keynesian approach, 682
Stock market. *See also* Financial market(s)
    and adverse selection, 253
    efficiency of, 231-233
    price fluctuations in, 227-228
Stock market crash of 1987, 213, 233-236, 368
Store of value, 19
Strike price, 205
STRIPS, 73
Structural models, 696, 698-699
Structural unemployment, 734
Student Loan Market Association, 292-293
Subsidiary U.S. bank, 398
Sumita, Satoshi, 490
Superregional banks, 348
Supply. *See* Aggregate supply
Supply shocks, 655
    and inflation, 727-728
    and short-run aggregate supply, 655
    in United States, 663, 666
Survey of Current Business, 557
Syndicates, 273-274
Systematic risk, 134-135

T-account, 308
T-bills, 61-62, 80
Taiwan, financial regulation in, 56-57
Takeover, 267, 269
Targets. See Monetary targets
Tariffs, 180
Tax(es)
    and banks, 305
    and federal budget deficit, 470-471
    and inflation, 728, 730
    and interest rates, 151-153
    loss of, with underground economy, 439
    and shifts in aggregate demand, 647, 648
    transaction, 237
Tax-exempt bonds, 129
Tax Reform Act of 1986, 305

Term premium, 162
Term structure of interest rates, 155-156
    and expectations theory, 158-162
    and forecasting, 166-167
    and preferred habitat theory, 162-163
    and segmented markets theory, 157-158
Thatcher, Margaret, 662
Theory of portfolio allocation, 127-132
    and credit risk, 315
    and exchange rates, 181
    and liquidity, 149
    and risk, 147
Time deposits, 304
Tobin, James, 133, 589
Tombstones, 275
Total rate of return, 86-87
Trade
    barriers to, 180
    by barter, 17-18
    and need for money, 16-21
Trade balance, 558
Trading mechanisms, 235-236
Transaction taxes, 237
Transactions cost, 17, 246
    and commercial banks, 290-291
    and financial structure, 246-247
Transactions motives for money, 584-590, 592
Treasury bills (T-bills), 61-62, 89
Treasury bonds
    information on, 88-89
    sale of, and budget deficit, 471, 474
    30-year, 164-165
Treasury-Federal Reserve Accord, 469, 488, 494-495, 536
Treasury Investment Growth Receipt (TIGR), 73
Treasury securities
    as Fed asset, 422, 458
    as financial instrument, 64
    future contracts on, 210-211
    yield curves for, 156
Treasury tax and loan accounts, 466
Trough, 674
Truman, Harry, 469, 488
Trump, Donald, 154, 381
Tulipmania, 234
Tullock, Gordon, 489